THE INTERRELATIONS OF THE GOSPELS
A SYMPOSIUM

BIBLIOTHECA EPHEMERIDUM THEOLOGICARUM LOVANIENSIUM

XCV

THE INTERRELATIONS OF THE GOSPELS

A SYMPOSIUM LED BY

M.-É. BOISMARD – W.R. FARMER – F. NEIRYNCK

JERUSALEM 1984

EDITED BY

DAVID L. DUNGAN

1425

LEUVEN
UNIVERSITY PRESS

UITGEVERIJ PEETERS
LEUVEN

1990

CIP KONINKLIJKE BIBLIOTHEEK ALBERT I, BRUSSEL

ISBN 90-6186-396-1 (Leuven University Press)
D/1990/1869/46

ISBN 90-6831-261-8 (Uitgeverij Peeters)
D. 1990/0602/77

Leuven University Press/Presses Universitaires de Louvain
Universitaire Pers Leuven
Krakenstraat 3, B-3000 Leuven-Louvain (Belgium)

© Uitgeverij Peeters, Bondgenotenlaan 153, B-3000 Leuven (Belgium)

TABLE OF CONTENTS

INTRODUCTION

D.L. DUNGAN, The Jerusalem Symposium 1984 . . . . IX-XXX
Acknowledgements XXXI

PART ONE
THE THREE MAJOR POSITION PAPERS

THE TWO-SOURCE HYPOTHESIS

F. NEIRYNCK, Introduction : The Two-Source Hypothesis . . 3-22
F. NEIRYNCK, Matthew 4:23-5:2 and the Matthean Composition
of 4:23-11:1 23-46
C.M. TUCKETT, Response to the Two-Gospel Hypothesis:
I. The Position Paper 47-62
II. The Eschatological Discourse 63-76
— Note on the Eschatological Discourse, by F. NEIRYNCK 77-80
F. NEIRYNCK, Response to the Multiple-Stage Hypothesis:
I. The Introduction to the Feeding Story 81-93
II. The Healing of the Leper 94-107
III. The Eschatological Discourse 108-124

THE TWO-GOSPEL HYPOTHESIS

W.R. FARMER, The Statement of the Hypothesis 125-156
A.J. McNICOL, The Composition of the Synoptic Eschatological
Discourse 157-200
D.L. DUNGAN, Response to the Two-Source Hypothesis . . 201-216
D.B. PEABODY, Response to the Multi-Stage Hypothesis . . 217-230

THE MULTIPLE-STAGE HYPOTHESIS

M.-É. BOISMARD, Théorie des niveaux multiples 231-243
M.-É. BOISMARD, Introduction au premier récit de la multiplication des pains 244-253
— La guérison du lépreux 254-258
M.-É. BOISMARD, Réponse aux deux autres hypothèses:
1. La théorie des deux sources : Mc 3:7:12 et parallèles . 259-265
2. La «Two-Gospel Hypothesis»: Le discours eschatologique 265-288

PART TWO
INVITED PAPERS ON RELATED ISSUES

B. REICKE, The History of the Synoptic Discussion 291-316

D.L. DUNGAN, Synopses of the Future 317-347

J.K. ELLIOTT, The Relevance of Textual Criticism to the
Synoptic Problem 348-359

D. DAUBE, Zukunftsmusik. Some Desirable Lines of Exploration
in the New Testament Field 360-380

S.O. ABOGUNRIN, The Synoptic Gospel Debate. A Reexamination from an African Point of View 381-407

P. BORGEN, John and the Synoptics 408-437

F. NEIRYNCK, John and the Synoptics: Response to P. Borgen 438-450

— Reply, by P. BORGEN 451-458

P.L. SHULER, The Genre(s) of the Gospels 459-483

P. STUHLMACHER, The Genre(s) of the Gospels: Response to
P.L. Shuler 484-494

— Reply, by P.L. SHULER 495-496

B. GERHARDSSON, The Gospel Tradition 497-545

B.F. MEYER, Objectivity and Subjectivity in Historical Criticism
of the Gospels 546-560

R.H. FULLER, Response to B.F. Meyer 561-564

— Afterword, by B.F. MEYER 564-565

H. MERKEL, Die Überlieferungen der Alten Kirche über das
Verhältnis der Evangelien 566-590

B. ORCHARD, Response to H. Merkel 591-604

— Note on Patristic Testimonies, by F. NEIRYNCK 605-606

PART THREE
CONCLUSION

AGENDA FOR FUTURE RESEARCH 609-610

B. REICKE, Sermon 611-613

APPENDIX: Synopsis. The Eschatological Discourse 615-628

INDEXES

BIBLICAL REFERENCES 631-659

INDEX OF ANCIENT WRITERS 660-662

INDEX OF AUTHORS 663-668

LIST OF CONTRIBUTORS 668-669

CONTENT ANALYSIS 670-672

INTRODUCTION

THE JERUSALEM SYMPOSIUM 1984

A. THE ROAD TO THE SYMPOSIUM IN JERUSALEM

The Jerusalem Symposium on the Interrelations among the Gospels was the capstone and climax of an extraordinary series of conferences focused on questions associated with a better understanding of the interrelations among the Gospels. No less than six, one-week international conferences had been held prior to it, from 1970 until 1984, on both sides of the Atlantic. In addition, seminars were organized both in the Society for New Testament Studies in Europe and the Society for Biblical Literature in America, to carry on advanced research and facilitate the pooling of results. This widespread scholarly collaboration, concentrating on a single problem area and stimulated at regular intervals by six major conferences, was quite unprecedented in contemporary biblical study. On the other hand, it all took place in a curiously muted fashion. The momentous discoveries of the Dead Sea Scrolls and the Nag Hammadi Library resulted in much more public interest and discussion, but it is my impression that neither of those discoveries succeeded in causing as much systematic scholarly collaboration.

The initiating spark occurred when more than 200 biblical scholars from around the world gathered at Pittsburgh Theological Seminary in April, 1970, to commemorate that institution's bicentennial anniversary. Called the "Pittsburgh Festival of the Gospels," this conference was designed to assess all aspects of Gospel research. Papers were commissioned to summarize the currently accepted "established results" for a whole series of major topics, while others were commissioned to criticize the same.[1] Although unusually large, the Festival was beautifully planned and carried out. All week, scholarly debates could be heard emanating from seminary classrooms. It soon developed, however, that the sharpest disagreements were occurring in the Seminar on Mark, particularly over the question of the priority of Mark. The Festival

---

[1] The papers commissioned for this conference were subsequently published under the title *Jesus and Man's Hope*, 2 vols., edited by Donald G. Miller. For the names of the Planning Committee and those who contributed papers, see *New Synoptic Studies*, ed. William R. Farmer (Macon, Mercer Univ. Press), p. viii note 1.

planners thereupon scheduled an *ad hoc* evening session to discuss the
issue before a wider audience. However, that meeting proved less than
satisfactory. Clearly, the question needed further discussion. But where
and when?

In the years that followed the Pittsburgh Festival of the Gospels,
William R. Farmer and Dom Bernard Orchard visited a number of
leading European scholars to sound them out as to the most effective
way to reopen the discussion concerning the order of composition of the
Gospels. A key meeting took place near Basel in 1973, with Bo Reicke
acting as host. Other scholars were also consulted, including E. Lohse,
E. Grässer, H. Greeven, K. Rengstorf and K. Aland, and out of these
consultations emerged the Griesbach Bicentenary Colloquium at Münster,
July 1976. It was sponsored by the Rector of the University, the local
Roman Catholic Diocesan Office and the Evangelical Church of West-
phalia. Prof. Dr. K. H. Rengstorf served as our esteemed host during
the conference. [2]

This Colloquium examined all three aspects of Griesbach's scholarly
activity: text criticism, synopsis editing, and source criticism. As anticipated, the papers dealing with the issue of Griesbach's source theory
generated the most discussion. The attacks on the Two-Document
Hypothesis by the neo-Griesbachians present seemed devastating to
some and totally unconvincing to others. By the same token, attacks on
Griesbach's source theory were equally impressive and/or implausible.
This pattern continued to increase to the point that, by the end of the
Colloquium, there was a great sense of frustration among the participants. The statement by H. Riesenfeld in the closing session of the
Colloquium came the closest to expressing the consensus: "we seem to
be entering a pluralistic situation where no source theory may be taken
for granted." [3]

Meanwhile, American scholars were planning another week-long
conference on the Synoptic Problem. It was held the following year at
Trinity University, San Antonio, Texas, in May of 1977. This conference was unique, however, in that it explicitly went outside the
boundaries of biblical scholarship to learn what light, if any, could be

---

[2] Thirty-five participants took part in the Griesbach Bicentenary Colloquium from
fourteen countries. The papers given at the Colloquium were subsequently edited by Dom
Bernard Orchard and T. R. W. Longstaff under the title, *J. J. Griesbach: Synoptic and
Text-critical Studies 1776-1976* ([SNTS Monogr. ser. 34], Cambridge Univ. Press 1978). A
list of the participants is given on p. ix; see also W. R. Farmer, ed., *New Synoptic Studies*
p. xi.

[3] See Longstaff's observation in W. R. Farmer, *New Synoptic Studies*, p. xii.

shed on the Synoptic Problem from scholars' experience of similar problems in other fields. Leading scholars in Greek and Roman rhetoric, Hellenistic Judaism, oral tradition of central Europe, Shakespeare studies, Old Testament text criticism, and the social world of early Christianity, were invited to address the Synoptic Problem from the perspective of their own specialties. They transformed this conference into a rare and exciting feast in "cross pollination."

Nevertheless, as far as the basic issue was concerned, namely, the question of which theory most adequately explained the composition of the Gospels, the Colloquy seemed to be unable to reach any definite conclusion. Rather, they issued two warnings: scholars should pay much more attention to the actual characteristics of the behavior of sacred traditions in oral cultures (such as first century Palestinian Judaism is alleged to have been); secondly, the literary-historical facts of the synoptic problem are far more complex than is usually realized.[4] Thus, although no particular source theory emerged victorious, there were clear indications of some elements of an agenda for future research.[5]

Contrary to all expectations, these conferences were making matters more confusing, not the reverse. With each successive assembly of biblical scholars, the list of new questions grew longer and longer, while the list of answered questions grew very slowly or not at all. This "negative progress" was frustrating to all concerned. In hindsight, it is perhaps accurate to say that much of the lack of progress was due, not to stubborn resistance but to the fact that as major questions were raised, new and complex scholarly tools were called for, taking years to complete, and meanwhile everyone just had to be patient.[6] Part of the

---

[4] The major papers, responses and group discussions were subsequently edited by William O. Walker, Jr., in what undoubtedly is one of the most gracefully arranged and complete records published so far. See *The Relationships Among the Gospels. An Inderdisciplinary Dialogue* ([Trinity University Monograph Series in Religion 5], San Antonio, Trinity Univ. Press, 1978).

[5] See the concluding remarks by Albert Outler, ibid., pp. 17-29.

[6] For example, there were numerous requests for more accurate data regarding the phenomena of order. J. B. Tyson, "Sequential Parallelism in the Synoptic Gospels," *New Testament Studies* 22 (1976) 276-308, was the first attempt to document in an objective manner the phenomenon of order of pericopes; more elaborate statistics were published in J. B. Tyson and T. R. W. Longstaff, eds., *The Computer Bible* Synoptic Abstract 15 (Wooster, Ohio 1978); Frans Neirynck (working with F. van Segbroeck and T. Hansen) responded to the call for a more comprehensive list of the "minor agreements" of Matthew and Luke against Mark; see *The Minor Agreements of Matthew and Luke Against Mark* (Leuven, University Press 1974). Again, the Griesbachians had complained from the beginning that they could not use the existing synopses because they were too

problem seemed to be that, even though the neo-Griesbachians could mount a very powerful critique of the Two-Document Hypothesis, when they were asked in turn to elaborate their own understanding of the Griesbachian alternative, they seemed surprisingly ill-prepared and unconvincing. This curious fact led to the next conference: a test run of the Griesbach Hypothesis all by itself. Could the adherents of the Griesbach Theory give a convincing explanation of the synoptic phenomena *sine ira et studio?* The test was set for two years later, and, eventually, in August of 1979, at Pembroke College, Cambridge University, another week-long conference came to pass.

As before, the planning committee had put a great deal of time and effort into making this convocation of biblical scholars as fruitful as possible. They consulted with colleagues in Europe, Great Britain and America. They asked: who should be invited to read papers? On what topics? Who should respond to these papers? What kind of format would produce the kind of careful dissection of the issues that was needed? How many should be invited? In August of 1979, the Owen-Griesbach Conference, as it was officially known,[7] came to pass with

---

biased toward the Two-Document Hypothesis, and set to work compiling new ones. W.R. Farmer, *Synopticon.The Verbal Agreement Between the Greek Texts of Matthew, Mark and Luke Contextually Exhibited* (London and New York, Cambridge Univ. Press 1969), was the first to come from this group. It was followed by J. Bernard Orchard, *A Synopsis of the Four Gospels in Greek Arranged According to the Two Gospel Hypothesis* (Edinburgh, T & T Clark 1983), and an English translation published by Mercer Univ. Press in 1982. In 1984 F. Neirynck and F. van Segbroeck published a massive collection of relevant linguistic and philological data: *New Testament Vocabulary*, BETL 65 (Leuven, University Press/Peeters 1984). Also from very early on, in view of the fact that all existing analyses had relied on the Two-Document Hypothesis and were therefore fundamentally biased, queries had been raised as to the possibility of identifying the stylistic characteristics of the authors of Matthew, Mark, and Luke, *without using any source theory in the process.* After years of fundamental research led by W. R. Farmer, the first of the new generation of unbiased analyses was finally published for the Gospel of Mark by David Peabody; see *Mark as Composer*, New Gospel Studies 1 (Macon, Mercer University Press/Leuven, Peeters 1987). Similar analyses for Luke by Frank Collison and for Matthew by Dennis Tevis will appear soon in the same series (published by Mercer/Peeters). Of course, many had called for a comprehensive bibliographical survey of all relevant publications. As with the other tasks, this proved to be much more difficult than anticipated. However, it, too, finally appeared, containing 1747 items and a number of very helpful indices; see *The Synoptic Problem. A Bibliography, 1716-1988*, New Gospel Studies 4; compiled and edited by T. R. W. Longstaff and P. A. Thomas (Macon, Mercer/Leuven, Peeters 1988).

[7] The conference received this title from the names of Johann Jakob Griesbach and a little-known English contemporary, Henry Owen who, nineteen years before Griesbach's first published statements on the matter appeared, had promulgated the identical theory in England, namely that Luke had used Matthew and Mark had used both. See *Observations on the Four Gospels* (London 1764).

some thirty scholars, mostly from the West, but also including representatives from India and Australia, in attendance. Clearly there was considerable curiosity as to what the neo-Griesbachians had to offer.

When it finally opened, the Cambridge Owen-Griesbach Conference addressed many major issues related to the source criticism of the Gospels: analyses of neglected patristic evidence supporting the priority of Matthew, form-critical analyses of passages giving evidence of the posteriority of Mark, new methodological approaches to the Synoptic Problem, redactional studies assuming the Two-Gospel Hypothesis, more general reports indicating the impact on Gospel studies if there were to be a shift in this major source-critical paradigm, and finally a response to J. Fitzmyer's defense of the Two-Document Hypothesis.[8] By the time the Conference had drawn to a close after five days of exhausting work, a number of general resolutions were voted on and passed unanimously:

1. No longer should the Two-Document Hypothesis be regarded as an "assured result" of biblical scholarship. Indeed, recent criticism of it has been so devastating that it now requires new critical foundations.
2. The Owen-Griesbach Theory has shown that, in general, it is as viable as any other theory currently in use. That is, we are in a time of pluralism with respect to the use of *any* source theory. Henceforth, scholars should be open to different approaches toward the same synoptic phenomena.
3. Dom Bernard Orchard's new synoptic arrangement presupposing the Two-Gospel Hypothesis should be published as soon as possible for comparative study with existing synopses. Likewise, Christopher Tuckett's critical review of recent neo-Griesbachian research should be published.[9]
4. The major papers from the Cambridge Griesbach Conference, together with additional papers required to fill in certain gaps to which the Conference has drawn attention, should be published so that scholars will be able to have a full selection of Gospel studies employing the Griesbachian hypothesis.
5. A further international conference is required which will permit the three main research paradigms to be exhaustively scrutinized and compared *simultaneously*. The Cambridge Conference planning committee was encouraged to begin informally sounding out colleagues for names of those who should be on the planning committee for this next major conference.

[8] See W. R. Farmer, ed., *New Synoptic Studies, The Cambridge Gospel Conference and Beyond* (Mercer Univ. Press 1983). The conference volume includes a number of additional reports not given at Cambridge but which serve to round out important features of the Two Gospel Hypothesis.

[9] Dom Bernard Orchard's new synopsis was soon available in both Greek and English. T & T Clark published the *Greek Synopsis Arranged According to the Two Gospel Hypothesis* (Edinburgh 1983). Mercer University Press published the English version: *A Synopsis of the Four Gospels Arranged According to the Two Gospel Hypothesis* (Macon, 1982). Tuckett's monograph was also speedily published: *The Revival of the Griesbach Hypothesis. An Analysis and Appraisal* ([SNTS Monogr. Ser. 44], Cambridge Univ. Press 1983).

Looking back from our vantage point a decade later, it seems as if the Cambridge Conference achieved two things: first, it recognized the emergence of a fundamental breach in the international scholarly consensus, not only with respect to the most basic assumptions underlying Gospel research as a whole, but also, and this was far more serious, regarding the very tools to be used in that study. This breach was signaled most clearly by the unanimous call for the publication of Orchard's radically different synoptic arrangement so that scholars could compare it with existing synopses in greater detail. His synopsis illustrated one of the basic problems we had begun to encounter in our discussions of the Synoptic Problem. On the one hand we found ourselves in profound disagreement with other groups over a number of basic issues, and yet on the other hand, there were no shared scholarly instruments available to resolve the differences. We were actually looking at *different evidence*. Secondly, it called for a complete reexamination of all aspects of the Synoptic Problem, and authorized the Cambridge planning committee to canvas members of the biblical scholar's guild as to who should be on the planning committee for the next comprehensive conference.

Once again, the scholars who had been responsible for planning the Cambridge Gospel Conference went out and canvassed their colleagues for names of those who should form the next planning committee. The criteria for membership on this committee were exacting. To carry out the mandate assigned to it by the Cambridge Gospel Conference participants, this next planning committee had to be international, ecumenical, balanced (with respect to the several major source theories), able to work together, and number no more than eight or nine persons. In addition, prospective committee members had to be generally recognized as leaders in their particular area of research. Numerous suggestions as to potential candidates for this planning committee were received from colleagues in North America, Great Britain, Europe, Africa, India, Japan, Korea, and Latin America.

While this process was going on, a few preparatory conferences were held in England and in Germany, to continue the process of identifying potentially central topics and desirable participants for the Jerusalem Symposium. The first of these took place in April, 1982, at Ampleforth Abbey, Yorkshire. Dom Henry Wansbrough was our host.[10] The topics

---

[10] It is appropriate to acknowledge here the gracious hospitality of Dom Henry during two successive Easter vacations. Both Ampleforth Gospel Conferences were models of scholarly disputation and debate. As with all of us in one way or another, the Synoptic

of this week-long conference were: Luke's relation to Matthew (the question of Q), the relationships between the midrashim and the Gospels, the parables, and the value of Eusebius' testimony regarding Papias.

The second Ampleforth Gospel Conference occurred a year later in 1983, also during the Easter vacation. Composed of a different set of scholars with some returnees, it focused on rabbinic biographies, contemporary analogies to the Gospels, Luke's relation to Matthew, the argument from order in the Griesbach and the Two-Document Hypotheses, questions of methodology, and the patristic testimony pertaining to order of composition of the Gospels. The papers from both conferences have subsequently been edited by Christopher Tuckett and published.[11]

In September of 1983, another preparatory conference was held at the University of Tübingen. Bringing together sixteen scholars from England, Scandinavia, America and Europe, it was entitled: *Internationales Symposium 'Das Evangelium und die Evangelien'*. The Symposium was sponsored by the Deutsche Forschungsgemeinschaft, das Ministerium für Wissenschaft und Kunst (Baden-Württemberg) as well as the Evangelische Landeskirche in Württemberg. Prof. Peter Stuhlmacher was the host. This conference was undoubtedly the most ambitious so far in its authoritative evaluation of all major aspects of contemporary Gospel research. Taking up four full days, invited papers dealt with the following topics: strengths and weaknesses in current source-criticism; the meaning of 'Gospel' in Jesus' preaching; new insights regarding the transmission of the Gospel tradition; the theological center of Q; the earliest form of the Gospel tradition; the contents of Paul's 'gospel;' the origin of the Gospel of Mark; Matthew as a creative interpreter of Jesus' sayings; Luke as a redactor of the Gospel tradition; the Christology of the Gospel of John; the sayings of Jesus in Justin Martyr; the *agrapha* of Jesus; the debate over the genre of the Gospels; and the Gospels compared with ancient biographies. The uniformly impressive quality of each of these reports made this conference a landmark in the history of the discussion of the Synoptic Problem.[12]

Problem was of considerable immediate importance for Dom Henry also, since he was just then preparing the notes and New Testament translation for the next edition of the *Jerusalem Bible*, of which he was General Editor; see *The New Jerusalem Bible* (Garden City, Doubleday & Co. 1985) p.v.

[11] See *Synoptic Studies. The Ampleforth Conferences of 1982 and 1983*, edited and given an Introduction (with lists of participants) by C. M. Tuckett, Journ. for the Study of the N.T. suppl. ser. 7 (Sheffield, JSOT Press 1984).

[12] The papers were edited and given a valuable introduction by Peter Stuhlmacher; see

As anyone who participated in these conferences will testify, a powerful current of scholarly excitement was manifesting itself in the years after the Pittsburgh Festival of the Gospels, not only in the Synoptic Problem *per se,* but in many of the related issues that depend on it for their own solution. Once the stone had been cast into the quiet pond of total confidence in the priority of Mark, the widening ripples reached to the farthest shores of Gospel research. Nor was this an entirely pleasant experience for those involved; years of established patterns of thought were being called into question, oftentimes with no idea as to how the uncertainties thus aroused might be resolved. At times, the way forward had to wait until we had literally constructed the road ahead by means of comprehensive, new research instruments. Indeed, this process still continues as confidence in our older research tools continues to erode as our "assured results" become less and less certain.[13] In any case, the period between 1970 to 1984 was a time of great creativity in fundamental Gospel research.

B. Steps in the Planning Process of the 1984 Jerusalem Symposium

While these conferences and seminars were laying the foundations for the Jerusalem Symposium, a planning committee was formed by the previous committee to channel and formalize the powerful trends and impulses that were emerging. Two years after the Cambridge Owen-Griesbach Colloquium in 1979, a new Planning Committee had been formed, one that was a balance of many different points of view and scholarly expertise, a committee that could inspire the respect of our colleagues in the Society of Biblical Literature, the Societas Novi Testamenti Studiorum, as well as New Testament colleagues in Africa, India, Korea and Japan.

By the summer of 1981, the members of the new Planning Committee had been identified and were ready to begin their historic task. The inaugural meeting took place in the weekend prior to the SNTS meeting at Domus Pacis, Rome. The new Planning Committee members were:

Das Evangelium und die Evangelien. Vorträge vom Tübinger Symposium 1982; Wissensch. Untersuch. z. N.T. 28 (Tübingen, J.C.B.Mohr /Paul Siebeck 1983).

[13] Two areas of major new "revisionist" activity are (a) creation of a totally new *type* of critical Gospel text, one that is completely free of any source theory bias or any other bias, and (b) a re-examination of role that liberal German Lutheran biblical research played in the 19th century's *Kulturkampf*, specifically how the Markan Hypothesis fit into (and still fits into) this political/ecclesiastical struggle.

M.-É. Boismard, École Biblique et Archéologique française de Jérusalem
†F. Collison, United Theological College, Bangalore
D.L. Dungan, University of Tennessee, Knoxville
W. Dalton, Pontificio Istituto Biblico, Roma
W. Farmer, Perkins School of Theology, Dallas
B. Gerhardsson, Lunds Universitet
U. Luz, Universität Bern
J. Mejía, Secretariatus ad christianorum unitatem fovendam, Vatican
F. Neirynck, Katholieke Universiteit Leuven
B. Orchard, O.S.B., Ealing Abbey, London
†B. Reicke, Theologische Fakultät, Universität Basel
P. Stuhlmacher, Evangelische Fakultät, Universität Tübingen
H. Wansbrough, O.S.B., Ampleforth Abbey, York

Some of these men either had extensive experience in planning and leading conferences on the Synoptic Problem, or they were leading exponents of one of the major theories currently in use,[14] or they were "bridge persons" who could bring us into contact with New Testament scholars in Africa, Latin America and Asia. This third category represented another decision of fundamental importance that will hopefully have long-term consequences for the future discussion of the Synoptic Problem. That is, despite the considerable increase in expenses as well as additional logistical problems, it was decided immediately after the Cambridge Colloquium in 1979 that the Planning Committee for the Jerusalem Symposium should have ample representation from Third World biblical scholars. This decision was made for two major reasons: (a) it would definitely help the Symposium's objectivity if we had representatives from a whole spectrum of cultural contexts take part in our discussions. (b) The SNTS meetings had demonstrated that there

---

[14] A fundamental decision was made by the Planning Committee at the very outset that only those hypotheses would be given consideration in this conference that had been or were now widely adopted by Gospel scholars. This decision led to the narrowing of the conference agenda to the three "classic" hypotheses: (a) multiple stage, (b) priority of Matthew, and (c) priority of Mark. The committee made this decision in the full realization that there were many qualified scholars, some with a vast erudition in the Synoptic Problem, who could make important contributions to the discussion in Jerusalem, yet who espoused such unique or hybrid theories that we would soon lose sight of what we were discussing. Indeed, there even was a procedural issue involved. For the examination of the Synoptic Problem to succeed on the scale envisioned, only theories that were already supported by a considerable international scholarly literature would be able to repay the kind of intense analysis of root problems hoped for. In this respect, the partisans of the Two-Gospel Hypothesis often found themselves overwhelmed by those advocating the Two-Document Hypothesis or the Multiple Stage Hypothesis who could draw upon a wealth of scholarship to support their points, while the neo-Griesbachians had relatively little. The situation would have been·impossible with any of the "one-man hypotheses."

were numerous, learned New Testament scholars in Africa, Asia and Latin America who were all too rarely heard from. For these reasons, it was decided that a few qualified biblical scholars from these countries should help plan and take part in this conference as well as western scholars.

Given the years of careful preparation, the agenda for the first meeting of the new Planning Committee was understandably very full.

1. The meeting opened with prayers and a hymn.
2. The committee agreed to a revolving chairmanship for all of our planning sessions. B. Reicke was elected chairman of the first session, U. Luz chaired the second, F. Neirynck was third. D. Dungan was elected secretary.
3. Reports of up-coming conferences were given by Stuhlmacher and Wansbrough.
4. It was decided that the conference should take place in Jerusalem rather than Europe. M.-É. Boismard reported on various alternatives.
5. Conference participants. The committee decided to divide conference participants into two types; Research Teams — who would have the responsibility of explaining and defending one of the three major hypotheses, and Other Participants, representing various areas of expertise in New Testament research, who would act like a kind of "jury." Furthermore, it was decided that since a small conference would get more work done than a large one, each of the Research Teams should be limited to five persons, giving a total of fifteen. The committee thereupon decided to limit the Other Participants to fifteen also. M.-É. Boismard was asked to head the "Multiple-Stage Hypothesis" Team, W. Farmer the "Two-Gospel Hypothesis" Team, and F. Neirynck the "Two-Source Hypothesis" Team. They agreed, and were invited to choose four other persons to work with them, with instructions to find the best scholars available. The Planning Committee firmly believed that the Synoptic Problem was so important and ramified into so many fundamental areas of New Testament research, that each of the "classic" hypotheses had to be given as full and comprehensive a presentation as was humanly possible. The goal was to give the international scholarly community a comprehensive review of all three simultaneously so that all could draw their own conclusions. This had never been done before.
6. Conference schedule. The committee decided to divide up the conference into three "stages." The first stage would be devoted to rhetorically powerful presentations of the essence of each theory, by each major protagonist, followed by questions from the whole group.

This would then be followed by a second stage consisting of textual analyses of a passage chosen by each Team. The third stage would then be devoted to discussions of a series of closely related issues. The committee estimated that these three stages would require two weeks to complete, an unprecedented length of time for a scholarly conference. It was therefore decided to adopt a very leisurely pace during the conference, so that participants could last until the end. It was also voted that each participant had to agree in advance to attend all meetings of the Symposium. Finally, the committee chose the Easter season, 1984, in Jerusalem, as the most appropriate time and place for the conference.

7. Conference participants. Discussion of possible conference participants occupied the rest of our time together. Each committee member agreed to canvass potential candidates from different parts of the world before the next meeting.

8. Guidelines for the three Position Papers. The Committee voted unanimously that each Research Team should prepare a Position Paper that would eventually contain three elements: (a) a statement of essentials of the Hypothesis ("Overview"), (b) a textual discussion, and (c) a critique of the other two Hypotheses. They asked the three main protagonists to have the rough draft of (a) ready by the following year. To aid them, the Committee adopted a Guideline list of questions bearing on the Synoptic Problem to guide the Research Teams as they prepared their summary Overviews. This Guideline represented the result of several years' work, being based on questions and issues put forward at the the six previous conferences, as well as numerous comments and questions raised by scholars in Europe and America.

C. GUIDELINES ADOPTED FOR WRITING THE POSITION PAPERS,
CONTAINING A SUMMARY LIST OF ALL MAJOR QUESTIONS PERTAINING TO
THE SYNOPTIC PROBLEM

I. *Presuppositions (External Considerations)*

A. What text of the Gospels do you use and why?
B. What synopsis do you use and why?
C. Should primary importance be ascribed to Hebrew, Aramaic or Greek in the words of Jesus?
D. Does your theory assume primarily written or oral form of the Gospel tradition? What is the evidence for your assumption?

E. What role(s) did individuals (e.g., "Christian prophets") or the "Christian community" play in the formation and preservation of the Jesus tradition?

F. How were the Gospels composed? Identify the closest analogies (if any) in Greco-Roman or Jewish literature.

G. What was the nature and extent of the influence of the Holy Spirit on the Gospel writers?

II. *Overview of the theory proper (Internal Considerations)*

A. What are the facts regarding the relations among the *four* Gospels (i.e., briefly state your theory).

B. How do you distinguish "original" from "secondary" Jesus tradition? How do you determine early or source material as compared to late or redactional material? What role do such commonly used criteria as: "semitisms," amplitude vs. brevity, and whole vs. broken form, play in your theory? State your view of the general tendencies of the successive Gospel redactions regarding not only the *ipsissima verba* but also the *ipsissima gesta Jesu*.

C. How does your theory explain the phenomenon of the order of pericopes in the Synoptic Gospels?

D. How does your theory explain the phenomena of the order of words and phrases within pericopes in the Synoptic Gospels?

E. How does your theory deal with the following alleged problems: doublets, "Q material," "minor agreements against Mark," and the complex phenomena associated with the Old Testament quotations in the Gospels?

F. Does your theory rest on any non-reversible stylistic arguments? Is there any conceivable evidence that could prove your theory false? If so, what would it look like?

III. *Role of evidence closely related to the Gospels.*

A. What role does evidence from Tannaitic Judaism play in your theory?

B. What role does evidence from Hellenistic culture play in your theory?

C. What role does evidence from the Patristic period play in your theory?

   i. direct statements regarding the order of composition of the Gospels

   ii. quotations from the Gospels

iii. manuscript evidence

D. What role do the non-canonical Gospels play in your theory?

IV. *Value for theology/preaching*

A. How does your theory assist in a better understanding of the
    incarnation of the Word of God in its three key "moments:"
    i. Jesus as the incarnate Word of God.
    ii. The Gospels as incarnations of the Word of God.
    iii. The situation of the theologian/preacher as incarnator of the
    Word of God.

The committee recognized that most of these questions had already
been under active debate in scholarly circles for a considerable period of
time. For this reason, they agreed that it would be presumptuous for
this conference to set out to "solve" these disputes. Rather it was hoped
that this conference would make a unique contribution to the on-going
debate by *treating the Synoptic Problem as holistically as possible*. In the
opinion of the Planning Committee, this was something that had never
been carefully and systematically attempted before. Therefore, the
summary list of questions was recommended to each of the Research
Teams as a guideline to follow when they wrote their Position Papers, as
an *ideal picture* of the way in which all major issues pertaining to the
central question of the relationships among the Gospels fit together. By
adopting the same "paradigm" of closely related questions for all three
Position Papers, it was believed that the relative strengths and weaknesses of the three hypotheses might reveal themselves more clearly. In this
sense, the Committee expected that the Position Papers which emerged
from this rigorous exercise would present to the scholarly world, for the
first time, a complete, more or less similar "portrait" of each of the three
major hypotheses. With these in hand, the scholarly community could
perhaps discern those *deeply buried root disagreements* (or undetected
systematic errors, such as was identified by B. C. Butler) that are the real
reasons why the different points of view have so far not attained
resolution in this fundamental area. It is clear that they are arguing from
different starting points and make different basic assumptions, but no
one has been able to see what they are. Hopefully, this exercise in triple
parallel theoretical elaboration should help "smoke out" these buried
disagreements.

With all these things accomplished, the Committee disbanded until
the following year.

The second meeting of the Planning Committee took place in Leuven,
prior to the 1982 SNTS meeting. At this time, the Research Group

leaders announced the texts they would be willing to present as well as the names of the individuals they had asked to be in their Groups. Preliminary drafts of each of the three main Position Papers were presented and commented upon at this time. The committee made particular suggestions regarding each one in view of the guideline set of questions listed above. Scholars were chosen to give the invited papers. Boismard reported on conditions at the proposed conference location, the Notre Dame de Jerusalem Pilgrimage Center. A final list of Other Participants was drawn up, and the secretary instructed to contact them. It was announced that funding for the conference had been secured through a German philanthropic institution.

The third and final meeting of the Planning Committee took place at Ealing Abbey, London, prior to the 1983 SNTS meeting at Canterbury. D. Dungan reported on a visit to the Notre Dame Pilgrimage Center where he had made final arrangements. Penultimate drafts of each of the Position Papers were examined and final suggestions regarding each were made to bring it more into line with the others as well as with the guideline list of questions. As might be imagined, it proved difficult to attain to the ideal we had set for ourselves. A conference Steering Committee was established to take over management of the events during the conference itself. P. Stuhlmacher was elected chair of this committee. A Resolutions Committee was also set up to collect and organize suggestions and ideas arising in the course of the conference into an "Agenda for Future Research." B. Reicke was elected head of this committee. Dungan reported on those who had responded to invitations, and a final list of 30 participants was drawn up. The Two-Source Hypothesis Team, led by Frans Neirynck, was to include J.K. Elliott, H. Merkel, C.M. Tuckett and F. Van Segbroeck. The Two-Gospel Hypothesis Team, led by William R. Farmer, was to include D. Dungan, A. McNicol, J.B. Orchard and D. Peabody. The Multiple-Stage Hypothesis Team, led by M.-É. Boismard, was to include R. Riesner and P. Rolland.

Finally, the committee decided that, in view of the extremely ambitious agenda set before it, none of the reports would be read at the Symposium itself. Instead, the secretary was instructed to xerox and mail out to every participant copies of everything to be discussed at the Symposium three months prior to the Symposium. In addition, the reports read at the Ampleforth and Tübingen Conferences were about to be published and the secretary was instructed to buy copies of each and mail them to every participant. In these ways, every participant, especially those who had not attended any of the preliminary conferences, would, it was hoped, arrive at Jerusalem fully prepared to discuss the issues.

D. The 1984 Jerusalem Symposium
on the Interrelations of the Gospels

Members of the Planning Committee began arriving as much as ten days prior to the actual starting day of the Symposium in order to make final preparations. We were greeted by Msgr. Richard Mathes, Chargé to the Holy See and Director of the Notre Dame Center, who spared no efforts to help bring everything into readiness for the Symposium. Indeed, he and the entire staff of the Center were doubly excited and interested since Notre Dame had never hosted a scholarly conference before, although superb facilities had been built for just this eventuality when the great building had been renovated after the 1967 war. Our meeting room was a model of modern planning, including glass-fronted, sound-proof booths and state-of-art equipment for simultaneous translation. Of course, we planned to use the same languages as was customary at the SNTS meetings: German, French and English. However, since not all Participants could easily understand these languages, we were immensely fortunate to have in our number Msgr. Jorge Mejía, who combined a thorough knowledge of the technical terminology, superb fluency in the requisite languages, and an indefatigable constitution, to do the simultaneous translations for us.

Moreover, the Secretary leased a computer and printer in order to produce an immediate record of the discussions each day.[15] Xeroxing services had to be arranged for, final room arrangements made, and special dietary instructions given to the kitchen. We even made, and this literally turned out to be a life-saver for one of us, arrangements for the services of the Notre Dame resident nurse to watch over our group, in view of the extreme old age of some of the Participants and the great

---

[15] The Planning Committee decided, after three previous unsatisfactory attempts, to avoid using any recording devices. In addition to mechanical difficulties, we found that it led to rather stilted and formal interchanges, as everyone was very conscious of having every brilliant thought and/or slip of the tongue recorded for posterity. In addition it was expensive and cumbersome to use. For these reasons, the Planning Committee instructed the secretary David Dungan and Dom Henry Wansbrough (who had been secretary at the Cambridge Conference) to take notes on all discussions and prepare a transcript at the end of each day. Using the conference computer, they combined their notes and printed out a rough draft of the discussions which was checked for accuracy and completeness the next afternoon. These "Protocols" then became part of the permanent record of the Symposium. It was also voted by the Participants to keep these Protocols private and not to publish them. Everyone was agreed that we did not want anything to hamper our discussion, such as the possible fear that what one said might eventually be published. This is why this Symposium Volume contains no record of the actual deliberations which took place during the Symposium.

pressure which was expected to develop over the two week course of the Symposium.

Finally, the Participants themselves began to arrive. In alphabetical order, they were:

Samuel O. Abogunrin, University of Ibadan, Nigeria
Marie-Émile Boismard, École biblique, Jerusalem
Peder Borgen, University of Trondheim, Norway
Adam Civu, Notre Dame Center Staff and University of Nairobi, Kenya
David Daube, University of California at Berkeley
David Dungan, University of Tennessee at Knoxville
J. Keith Elliott, University of Leeds
William R. Farmer, Perkins School of Theology, Dallas
Reginald H. Fuller, Protestant Episcopal Seminary, Alexandria
Birger Gerhardsson, Lund University
Robert Guelich, Northern Baptist Seminary, Chicago
Shigeo Hashimoto, School of Theology, Doshisha University
Lee Jong Yun, Asian Center for Theological Study, Seoul
Allan J. McNicol, Institute for Christian Studies, Austin
Jorge Mejía, Secretariat for Relations between Christians and Jews, Vatican
Ben Meyer, McMaster University, Hamilton, Ontario, Canada
Helmut Merkel, Institute for New Testament Study, Friedrich Alexander
    University in Erlangen
Frans Neirynck, Catholic University, Leuven
Bernard Orchard, Ealing Abbey, London
David Peabody, Department of Religion, Nebraska Wesleyan University
Bo Reicke, Theological Faculty, University of Basel
Rainer Riesner, Evangelical Faculty, Tübingen
Philippe Rolland, Séminaire de Saint-Sulpice, Issy-les-Moulineaux
Philip Shuler, Department of Religion, McMurry College, Abilene
Peter Stuhlmacher, Evangelical Faculty, Tübingen
Christopher M. Tuckett, Faculty of Theology, University of Manchester
Frans Van Segbroeck, Catholic University, Leuven
Henry Wansbrough, Ampleforth Abbey, York [16].

Old friends greeted each other warmly, and there were many intro-ductions to the new faces present. At first, everyone was somewhat inclined to be rather stiff and formal, but our host quickly saw to that. To everyone's surprise and delight, Msgr. Mathes greeted and welcomed us with champagne at our opening session! Soon we were feeling much better as the participants unanimously agreed that all scholarly confer-ences should begin in this way.

Perhaps it would be appropriate at this time to indicate what transpired for each day of the Symposium.

---

[16] Two members of the Planning Committee did not attend the Symposium: Ulrich Luz and William Dalton.

E. Symposium — Daily Schedule

April 8 Sunday

8 p.m. Formal welcome to the symposium for participants and guests.

Mons. Dr. Richard Mathes, Chargé to the Holy See: "Welcome to Notre Dame"

Prof. Dr. Pierre Benoit, École biblique française: "Welcome to Jerusalem"

Prof. Dr. David Dungan, Secretary, Planning Committee: "The Planning Process"

General Discussion: Participants' expectations of the Symposium

Discussion of program and Symposium committees

Champagne reception, courtesy of Msgr. Mathes.

April 9 Monday

Summary Overview of Each Hypothesis; P. Benoit, presiding.

 8:50 — 9:00 Morning Prayers — Orchard
 9:00 — 10:00 Two Source Hypothesis — Frans Neirynck
10:00 — 11:00 Two Gospel Hypothesis — William Farmer
11:00 — 11:30 Coffee
11:30 — 12:30 Multiple Stage Hypothesis — Marie-Émile Boismard
12:30 — 12:40 Midday Prayers — Bo Reicke
13:00   Lunch
15:30 — 16:00 Tea
16:00 — 16:30 Adoption of Conference Schedule and Committees
16:30 — 18:15 "History of the Synoptic Discussion" — Bo Reicke
18:15 — 18:40 Evening Prayers (Chapel); Presiding — S. Hashimoto
19:15   Dinner. Evening (open)

April 10 Tuesday

Textual Discussion: Group Neirynck. Matt. 4,23 - 5,2 and Parallels in Mark; B. Gerhardsson, presiding.

 8:50 — 9:00 Morning Prayers (Chapel)
 9:00 — 10:00 Presentation by Group Neirynck
10:00 — 10:30 Response by Group Farmer
10:30 — 11:00 Coffee
11:00 — 11:30 Response by Group Boismard
11:30 — 12:00 Concluding response by Group Neirynck
12:00 — 12:30 Open Discussion
12:30 — 12:40 Midday Prayers — S. Abogunrin
13:00   Lunch
15:30 — 16:00 Tea
16:00 — 16:30 Approval of protocol for previous day
16:30 — 18:15 General discussion of Two Source Theory
18:15 — 18:40 Evening Prayers (Chapel)
19:15   Dinner. Evening (open)

April 11 Wednesday

Textual Discussion: Group Farmer. The Synoptic Apocalypse; H. Wansbrough, presiding.

 8:50 — 9:00 Morning Prayers — J.Y. Lee
 9:00 — 10:00 Presentation by Group Farmer

10:00 — 10:30 Response by Group Boismard
10:30 — 11:00 Coffee
11:00 — 11:30 Response by Group Neirynck
11:30 — 12:00 Concluding response by Group Farmer
12:00 — 12:30 Open discussion
12:30 — 12:40 Midday Prayers — P. Borgen
13:00   Lunch Visit to the École Biblique and the Garden Tomb.
15:30 — 16:00 Tea
16:00 — 16:30 Approval of Protocol for previous day
16:30 — 18:15 General Discussion of Two Gospel Theory
18:15 — 18:40 Evening Prayers (Chapel)
19:15   Dinner. Evening (open)

April 12 Thursday

Textual Discussion: Group Boismard. Mc 6, 30-34 and Parallels; P. Benoit, presiding.
8:50 — 9:00 Morning Prayers — D. Dungan
9:00 — 10:00 Presentation by Group Boismard
10:00 — 10:30 Response by Group Neirynck
10:30 — 11:00 Coffee
11:00 — 11:30 Response by Group Farmer
11:30 — 12:00 Concluding response by Group Boismard
12:00 — 12:30 Open discussion
12:30 — 12:40 Midday Prayers — R. Riesner
13:00   Lunch Excursion to Tunnel of Hezekiah and Pool of Siloam.
15:30 — 16:00 Tea
16:00 — 16:30 Approval of Protocol for previous day
16:30 — 18:15 General discussion of Multiple-Stage Theory
18:15 — 18:40 Evening Prayers (Chapel)
19:15   Dinner. Evening: *ad hoc* session on the Argument from Order.

April 13 Friday

Open. Tour — "Archeology of Jerusalem" led by Prof. Benoit
18:30 — 18:40 Evening Prayers (Chapel). After dinner: *ad hoc* discussion of Group Neirynck's synoptic passage by Group Farmer.

April 14 Saturday

Reflection Day. Scheduled papers and *ad hoc* discussions of important issues raised in previous meetings; F. Van Segbroeck, presiding. (Agenda prepared by Steering Committee; P. Stuhlmacher, chairman.)
8:50 — 9:00 Morning prayers
9:00 — 10:15 D. Peabody, "Chapters in the History of the Linguistic Argument for Solving the Synoptic Problem: the 19th Century in Context"
10:15 — 10:45 Coffee
10:45 — 11:45 D. Dungan, "Synopses of the Future"
12:00 — 12:30 K. Elliott, "The Relevance of Textual Criticism for the Synoptic Problem"
12:30 — 12:40 Midday Prayers — B. Gerhardsson

13:00   Lunch
15:15 — 15:45 Tea/Coffee
15:45 — 16:15 Approval of Protocol for Thursday
16:15 — 17:15 D. Daube, "Zukunftsmusik"
17:30 — 18:30 S. Abogunrin, "The Synoptic Problem in African Perspec-
                tive"
18:30 — 18:40 Evening Prayers (Chapel)
19:00   Dinner. Evening (open)

April 15 Palm Sunday

Morning — attend various churches and celebrations.
Afternoon — ecumenical procession from Bethany to St. Anne's through
    Stephen's Gate.
Alternative: excursion to Samaritan Passover, Mt. Gerizim.

April 16 Monday

Theme: the Four Gospels; J. Mejía, presiding.
 8:50 — 9:00 Morning Prayers — J. Mejía.
 9:00 — 9:45 P. Borgen, "John and the Synoptic Gospels"
 9:45 — 10:00 Response by F. Neirynck
10:00 — 10:30 Concluding comment by P. Borgen
10:30 — 11:00 Coffee
11:00 — 12:30 Open discussion on "John and the Synoptics"
12:30 — 12:40 Midday prayers — C. Tuckett
13:00   Lunch
Excursion to Essene Gate, and Church of the Redeemer ("Golgotha"
    excavations underneath).
15:30 — 16:00 Tea
16:00 — 16:30 Approval of Protocol for previous days
16:30 — 17:00 P. Shuler, "The Genre(s) of the Gospels"
17:00 — 17:30 Response by P. Stuhlmacher
17:30 — 18:30 Open discussion on Genre(s) of the Gospels
18:30 — 18:40 Evening Prayers (Chapel)
19:15   Passover Seder — D. Daube, host

April 17 Tuesday

Theme: The Gospel Tradition; J. Y. Lee, presiding.
 8:50 — 9:00 Morning Prayers — F. Van Segbroeck
 9:00 — 9:30 B. Gerhardsson, "The Gospel Tradition"
 9:30 — 10:30 General discussion of Gospel Tradition
10:30 — 11:00 Coffee
11:00 — 11:30 B. Meyer, "Criteria for Determining Historicity in the Jesus
                Tradition"
11:30 — 11:40 Response by R. Fuller
11:40 — 12:30 General discussion of Criteria...
12:30 — 12:40 Midday Prayers — S. Hashimoto
13:00   Lunch Excursion to "Burnt House" (Jerusalem A.D. 70).
15:30 — 16:00 Tea
16:00 — 16:30 Approval of Protocol for previous day
16:30 — 18:30 General discussion of Gospel Tradition and Criteria...
18:30 — 18:40 Evening prayers (Chapel)

19:15   Dinner. Evening (open)

April 18 Wednesday

Theme: The Patristic Testimony; B. Meyer, presiding.

8:50 — 9:00 Morning Prayers — H. Wansbrough
9:00 — 9:30 H. Merkel, "Patristic Testimony on the Order of Composition of the Gospels"
9:30 — 10:00 Response by B. Orchard
10:00 — 10:30 Concluding response by H. Merkel
10:30 — 11:00 Coffee
11:00 — 12:30 General discussion of patristic evidence
12:30 — 12:40 Midday Prayers — R. Guelich
13:00   Lunch

Excursion to Franciscan Museum (relics from "Peter's House" Capharnaum).

15:30 — 16:00 Tea
16:00 — 16:30 Approval of Protocol for previous day
16:30 — 18:30 Brief Summation by each of the Team Leaders
              General Discussion: Appraisal of Symposium as a whole
18:30 — 18:40 Evening Prayers (Chapel)
19:15   Dinner Evening: Joint meeting Agenda/Steering Committee
              — prepare Agenda for Future Research.

April 19 Thursday

Adoption of Agenda for Future Research; K. Elliott, presiding.

8:50 — 9:00 Morning Prayers — P. Stuhlmacher
9:00 — 10:30 Presentation of Agenda for Future Research (Stuhlmacher/Reicke)
10:30 — 11:00 Coffee
11:00 — 12:30 Discussion and adoption of Agenda
12:30 — 12:40 Midday Prayers — W. Farmer
13:00   Lunch

Afternoon — excursion to Herodion, Bethlehem.
Maundy Thursday Services.

April 20 Good Friday

6:30   Departure for tour to Masada, Qumran, Dead Sea.
Evening — Good Friday Services.

April 21 Holy Saturday

Group Tour to Franciscan Archeological Site in Capharnaum (Peter's House), Bethsaida, "Springs of Capharnaum — traditional site of Jesus' preaching (Tabgha), Mount of Beatitudes (where we read the Sermon on the Mount together in the native languages of the Participants), followed by a picnic on the hill overlooking the Sea of Galilee, then a visit to Nazareth, a stop at Beth Shean (Roman amphitheatre) and back to Jerusalem.
Evening: Easter vigil.

April 22 Easter

Morning: sunrise service, Mount of Olives. Participants attended various services.

18:30   Symposium Eucharist (Chapel); Bo Reicke, homilist.
19:00   Concluding Banquet

F. Symposium Committees

Steering Committee A "process" committee that monitored day to day activities, received suggestions, complaints and proposals for further discussion. It had full authority to rearrange the schedule so as to permit immediate response to developments during Symposium. Chairman: P. Stuhlmacher, with K. Elliott, A. McNicol, P. Rolland, R. Guelich, and B. Meyer.

Agenda Committee A writing committee that considered each day's discussions in order eventually to formulate an Agenda for Future Research, which it presented to the Symposium Participants on the last day for their ratification. The Agenda was to contain (a) a Statement of Consensus that would define areas of general agreement, followed by (b) the Agenda itself, listing subjects needing further research, concluding with a proposal for the general theme of the next Gospel Conference. It was agreed that this Agenda should be published at the end of the volume of the Symposium Proceedings without comment.
Chairman: B. Reicke, with D. Peabody, C. Tuckett, and R. Riesner

Symposium Secretariate Was responsible for making sure all Participants had copies of all papers, xeroxed materials, books from the École Biblique, etc., etc. This committee typed and duplicated the Symposium Protocols each evening and distributed them the next morning.
A. Civu, D. Dungan, H. Wansbrough,

Recreation Committee Planned outings and excursions to places of interest chosen by the Participants, to give everyone opportunities to sightsee, do some shopping, get exercise, etc. etc. Chairman: R. Guelich, with Anne Dungan, and A. Civu.

Worship Committee A pastoral committee that acted as the Symposium Chaplaincy. It planned all worship services, from daily prayers to the final Eucharist. Co-chairmen were F. Collison and P. Borgen, with B. Orchard and Msgr. R. Mathes, ex-officio.

G. Conclusion

Looking back, in addition to the many exciting scholarly events that transpired during the Symposium, there were many memorable moments as well, such as the rare privilege of being conducted around Jerusalem by Père Benoit himself, or being led by David Daube in an unforgettable Passover Seder. Of course, the events of Holy Week in Jerusalem provided an awesome conclusion to an already momentous conference. For me the high point was sitting under the trees on the Mount of Beatitudes overlooking the Sea of Galilee as different Symposium Participants read the Beatitudes in his or her own native language: French, Yoruba, Japanese, Norwegian, German, English, Korean, Dutch... It was pure music. When we left Jerusalem on the Monday after Easter, we were in a kind of daze as we rode up to Ben Gurion and mechanically went through security checkout. Already the days together were mingling into a blurred mist of countless impressions and feelings. It would take months if not years for them to settle out into a few, shining memories.

David L. Dungan

ACKNOWLEDGEMENTS

On behalf of all of the Participants at the *Symposium de inter-relatione evangeliorum*, I take this opportunity to thank the C&A Foundation for the funding that made it a truly extraordinary and productive experience for all of us. Secondly, for the many hours of preparations, including remodeling and special dietary requirements, I wish to thank here, on behalf of all of the Participants, Msgr. Richard Mathes, Fr. Adam Civu and all of the staff of Notre Dame Center for their outstanding service, attention to details, and patience. Conferences like this have many additional costs for which we were not billed. Once again, we express our deep appreciation to Msgr. Mathes for quietly and generously absorbing these without a word to us.

As for the publication of this volume, I would like to thank the C&A Foundation and the Dallas Governors of the Institute for Renewal of Gospel Studies for providing the necessary subventions. In addition, I am sure all will join me in expressing our appreciation to Prof. F. Neirynck for including this volume in the series *Bibliotheca Epheme-ridum Theologicarum Lovaniensium*.

A special word of thanks must be directed to our departmental secretaries, Debbie Myers and Joan Riedl, for retyping these manu-scripts so skillfully and well. Their assistance has made an enormous contribution toward completing this difficult task.

Above all, on behalf of the Participants and the Institute, I would like to express our deep gratitude and appreciation to Mr. E. Peeters for his willingness to see these many reports through to publication.

The Editor

PART ONE

THE THREE MAJOR POSITION PAPERS

THE TWO-SOURCE HYPOTHESIS

INTRODUCTION [1]

The Two-Source Theory can be summarized in a few sentences: the Gospel of Mark was written first and it has been used by the other Synoptics as a written source for the so-called triple-tradition material. The Q document is the second common source of Matthew and Luke: it includes the double-tradition sayings material and it has been employed independently by both evangelists. In confrontation with the two other theories which are promoted to competing theories in this Symposium, the Two-Source Hypothesis is in a middle position. It combines inter-dependence of the Gospels and the use of one hypothetical source: "La théorie du juste milieu".

Our discussion on the relations of the Synoptic Gospels is the continuation of a long-standing debate. It began in the 18th century with a confrontation of the traditional view of Matthean priority with the (modern) theory of the priority of Mark. For some time the Griesbach theory took the relief of the "Augustinian" hypothesis (Mt-Mk-Lk) as the leading synoptic theory. The Gospel of Luke now received the rank of an earlier gospel. Much more than Luke, the Gospel of Mark was at the center of the discussion. To the priority of Mark, the Griesbachians opposed its secondary character as an abbreviation, combination and conflation of Matthew and Luke. The decisive debate engaged in the middle of the 19th century, from the thirties to the sixties. As a result, the Markan hypothesis became the predominant scholarly opinion. The Griesbach theory tended to disappear or at least to fossilize. [2]

---

[1] This Introduction was delivered at the opening session of the Symposium, April 9, 1984. The footnotes were added to the text for this edition. The abbreviation *Evangelica* is used for F. NEIRYNCK, *Evangelica. Gospel Studies - Études d'évangile. Collected Essays*, ed. F. VAN SEGBROECK (BETL, 60), Leuven, 1982.

[2] Cf. F. NEIRYNCK and F. VAN SEGBROECK, "The Griesbach Hypothesis: A Bibliography," in B. ORCHARD and T.R.W. LONGSTAFF (eds.), *J.J. Griesbach: Synoptic and Text-critical Studies 1776-1976* (SNTS MS, 34), Cambridge, 1978, 176-181. Cf. B. Reicke's note, *ibid.*, 200 (n. 56). As can be seen from this Bibliography, the Griesbach hypothesis continued to be defended in the years after Strauss and Baur, also by Roman Catholics, who tended to correct the hypothesis by the assumption of Mark's contact with an original Petrine tradition. H. Pasquier (1911) was a late representative of this approach.

In the midst of our century a new development took place in some quarters of New Testament scholarship, repeating over a much shorter period of time the same successive stages of gospel criticism. First, objections were raised against the two-source theory, mainly by Catholic scholars pleading for the priority of Matthew in the form of a Proto-Matthew (L. Cerfaux, L. Vaganay) or, in the pure Augustinian tradition, of the canonical Matthew (J. Chapman, B.C. Butler). None of them gave serious attention to the Griesbach theory.[3] Nevertheless, Butler's book (1951) is at the origin of an anti-Streeter reaction in British and American gospel study and it has contributed much to W.R. Farmer's new defence of the Griesbach hypothesis as an alternative to Markan priority (1964). Once more, the Augustinian hypothesis found its successor in Griesbach (redivivus).[4] An active cell of new Griesbachians is now definitely present in the field of gospel criticism. But, at the same time, the proliferation of redaction-critical studies in the last decades gave reassurance to the two-source theory. If we look at the scholarly production and the university teaching of our days, it appears that the theory still holds its position. It is even fair to say that through redaction criticism the theory has received a new development and an expansion it never had before.

It should be added, however, that within this fundamental solution, adopted by so many scholars, a considerable amount of variety can be observed. The assumption that Mark is the first Gospel does not close the debate about its composition and its sources (the pre-Markan passion narrative, pre-Markan collections or individual pericopes and sayings), about the unity of its style and its theology. Mutatis mutandis, such questions are raised also concerning the Q source. The Q hypothesis is in some sense a subsidiary hypothesis – subsidiary to Markan priority – and there is a great diversity with regard to the unity of the source, its nature and its extent.

All agree that there are some overlappings of Mark and Q, but Mark's knowledge of Q is a point of dispute. In the more common view the sayings in Mark and Q rely on parallel traditions, probably with a common *Vorlage*, but the precise reconstruction of this *Vorlage* will often remain a most delicate performance.

---

[3] Cf. B.C. BUTLER, *The Originality of St Matthew. A Critique of the Two-Document Hypothesis*, Cambridge, 1951, 5: "Every serious scholar recognizes that to explain Mark as a conflation of Matthew and Luke is a surrender of critical principles"; L. VAGANAY, *Le problème synoptique. Une hypothèse de travail*, Tournai, 1954, 6: "l'école de Tubingue tourna le dos à la critique littéraire ... en soutenant le système de J.J. Griesbach."

[4] Cf. C.M. TUCKETT, *The Revival of the Griesbach Hypothesis. An Analysis and an Appraisal* (SNTS MS, 44), Cambridge, 1983.

The special material of Matthew and Luke gives rise to new divergences. Some *Sondergut* sayings are included in the common source, or are combined with Q in a pre-Matthean or pre-Lukan redaction, or, more radically, the Q source is combined with Lukan *Sondergut* in one Proto-Lukan Gospel. This, of course, affects the evangelist's redaction of Q and, in this last instance, it even has a considerable effect upon Luke's use of Mark.

The more central thesis of Matthew's and Luke's independent use of Mark is sometimes mitigated by the acceptance of tradition variants or by a combination of Luke's dependence upon Mark with a subsidiary acquaintance with Matthew. And, of course, there is an almost constant temptation to find a solution for the problem of the Matthew-Luke agreements against Mark by changing the text of Mark (Urmarkus, textual corruption, text recension, Deuteromarkus). With all that, the two-source theory becomes a very large house with many dwelling-places, or a big family with many family quarrels. A great deal of the discussion that is going on with other theories is taking place also within the two-source theory.

Such a comprehensive two-source theory is certainly not what I am pleading for. It is at least not my opinion that there is an urgent need for important modifications or mitigations of our hypothesis. The basic conviction of the Markan hypothesis can be seen in the fact that the Gospel of Mark has so much in common with Matthew and Luke that a literary relationship, not only of individual pericopes but of the gospel as such, is undeniable and that the most adequate solution resulting from a comparative study of the language, the style and the content of the Synoptic Gospels is the use of Mark as a common source by Matthew and Luke. The theory has its antecedents in the 18th century, but when it took its more definite form in the middle of the 19th century, it was proposed as an alternative to the more commonly accepted Griesbach hypothesis, arising from a dissatisfaction with the treatment of Mark as a secondary gospel on the basis of the phenomena of order and conflation. In the discussion of the last twenty years we are now again confronted with the theory of Markan "zig-zag" (as some new Griesbachians continue to call Mark's alternation between Matthew and Luke) and with the interpretation of Mark's duplicate expressions as combinations of Matthew and Luke, or, as recently suggested, of Proto-Matthew and Proto-Luke. The argument from order and the dual expressions in Mark are inevitably among the items to be discussed at our Conference.

A third item of discussion, equally unavoidable, and as old as the

Markan hypothesis itself, is that of the minor agreements of Matthew
and Luke against Mark. Within the hypothesis of Markan priority
almost all modifications of the basic theory had their starting point
more or less with the Matthew-Luke agreements in the triple tradition.
With Vaganay (1954), Farmer (1964) and, in the line of Vaganay, M.-É.
Boismard (1972), a new prestige has been given to these "minor
agreements". Not so much because of the difficulty of some individual
cases, but much more because of their high number, their concentration
in particular passages, and the conjunction of negative and positive
agreements, they are cited now as objection number one against the
priority of Mark. The advocates of the two-gospel hypothesis add to
that: "if these 'minor agreements' demonstrate that Mt and Lk were not
independent of one another, then the need for 'Q' is also obviated". But
this last conclusion is valid only for those who exclude other possibilities, such as indirect dependence or the combination of Lukan dependence on the leading source (Mk) with a subsidiary dependence on
Matthew. [5]

In our hypothesis Matthew and Luke depend on a second source. The
usually cited indications for the Q source are the very existence of the
double-tradition material in Matthew and Luke, the high degree of
verbal agreement in some of these passages, the presence of primitive
elements in both versions, the more or less common order of pericopes
which, with a few exceptions, are found in different Markan contexts,
and, more specifically, the so-called source doublets in Matthew and
Luke. In the history of the Q hypothesis since Weisse much consideration
has been given to the phenomenon of the doublets and, as it can be seen
from the papers submitted to this Conference, the doublets in Matthew
and Luke are still now cited as an important piece of evidence. In order
to avoid misunderstanding, let me recall once more that the Q source is
a second source and, in some sense, a secondary hypothesis: for those
who hold the priority of Mark the "proof from doublets" can become a
real proof for the existence of a second source. Never in the history of
the Q hypothesis has the argument from the doublets been separated
from the assumption of the priority of Mark (or some Proto-Mark): one
form of the doublet is recognized as Markan and the other is non-
Markan.

The phenomenon of order, duality in Mark, minor agreements of
Matthew and Luke against Mark, and the source doublets in Matthew

---

[5] Cf. F. NEIRYNCK, "Recent Developments in the Study of Q," in J. DELOBEL (ed.),
Logia (BETL, 59), Leuven, 1982, 29-75, 31-35: "Q and the Synoptic Problem."

and Luke: those are the four aspects of the synoptic problem which we have to discuss and about which at least some clarification can be expected from this Conference.

1. *The Phenomenon of Order*

With regard to the phenomenon of order, I would like to make only some introductory remarks.

1. The Markan material appears to a large extent in the same order in the three synoptic Gospels. This is, I think, a common statement in our three theories, although the multiple-stage hypothesis sometimes tends to become a multiple-source hypothesis in which each section of the gospel and each pericope can get its own synoptic theory. Such a fragmentizing approach is, to say the least, not recommended by the common order in the triple tradition.

2. Concerning the differences in order the main literary-critical solutions to the synoptic problem (Markan priority, Augustinian hypothesis, Griesbach hypothesis) agree about one statement: the absence of Matthew-Luke agreement against Mark. On the assumption of Markan priority, the absence of agreement between Matthew and Luke against Mark becomes an indication for the independence of Matthew and Luke in their use of Mark. However, by itself, this statement allows for no other conclusion than the medial position of the Gospel of Mark. This had been emphasized long before Butler by 19th century defenders of Griesbach (Maier, Schwarz), and the participants of the SNTS Seminar on the Synoptic Problem at the Southampton meeting in 1973 will remember that the leading neo-Griesbachians then solemnly declared that this was also their own position.[6]

3. The argument from order for Markan priority is nothing more, and nothing less, than the demonstration that the differences of the order in Matthew and Luke receive a plausible explanation as changes of Mark which are consistent with the general redactional tendencies and the compositional purposes of each gospel. It is clear that in this area, as in any other area of the synoptic problem, our method should be a

---

[6] Cf. F. NEIRYNCK, "The Argument from Order and St. Luke's Transpositions," *ETL* 49 (1973) 784-815 (790-799: "The Absence of Agreement and its Significance"); reprinted in *The Minor Agreements* (n. 13), 291-322; = *Evangelica*, 1982, 737-768 (743-752). See also, "The Griesbach Hypothesis: The Phenomenon of Order," *ETL* 58 (1982) 111-122; and C.M. TUCKETT, *The Revival*, 26-40; "The Argument from Order and the Synoptic Problem," *TZ* 36 (1980) 338-354; "Arguments from Order: Definition and Evaluation," in ID. (ed.), *Synoptic Studies. The Ampleforth Conferences of 1982 and 1983* (JSNT SS, 7), Sheffield, 1984, 197-219.

joint effort of source criticism and redaction criticism (or composition criticism).

2. *Duality in Mark*

The duplicate expressions in Mark are much more than a mechanical combination of two single expressions.

1. Even on the two-gospel hypothesis only a portion of Mark's dual expressions can be explained as combinations of Matthew and Luke, and our conclusion that duality is a feature of Markan style is an acceptable view also in other hypotheses.

2. The instances which, in the Griesbach hypothesis, can be seen as combinations (A in Mt, B in Lk, and AB in Mk) become, on the assumption of Markan priority, indications of Matthew's and Luke's independent use of Mark. It has been said that "selon la Théorie des Deux Sources, Matthieu et Luc auraient simplifié le texte de Marc, choisissant, comme par hasard, chacun ce que l'autre rejetait". According to the two-source theory, it is not a selection made at random, by chance, but in many instances the choice of each evangelist can be explained in light of the redactional context and in accordance with the more general tendencies of the gospel.

The most famous example is Mk 1:32a, ὀψίας δὲ γενομένης, ὅτε ἔδυ ὁ ἥλιος. It continues to be cited, with the use of the particle δέ in the first element, as a clear sign of its Matthean origin. However, it should be observed, that the use of δέ (instead of καί) in Mk 1:32 is less un-Markan than it is supposed to be. It is rightly noted that καί is used at the opening of the Markan pericopes in 1:21-39, but it is less correct to split the unit of verses 29-34 into two pericopes. The locale of the story is provided in v. 29 (the entry into the house: εἰς τὴν οἰκίαν Σίμωνος...) and it is maintained in v. 33 (πρὸς τὴν θύραν: at the door of the house); the new section will begin with v. 35 (ἐξῆλθεν καὶ ἀπῆλθεν εἰς ἔρημον τόπον). Within the unit of verses 29-34, the healing story starts with ἡ δὲ πενθερὰ Σίμωνος (v. 30) and a new sub-section begins in v. 32: ὀψίας δὲ γενομένης. The formula-like character of Matthew's ὀψίας δὲ γενομένης has been overemphasized. A substitution of δέ for καί in Mt 14:15 (Mk καὶ ἤδη ὥρας πολλῆς γενομένης); 14:23 (Mk καί); 26:20 (Mk καί); 27:57 (Mk καὶ ἤδη) (see also Mt 20:8; but see Mt [16:2] ὀψίας γενομένης, at the opening of direct discourse) is a far too general Matthean characteristic to be significant. In the context of Mt 8:16, the specific reason for the motif of the sunset (the sabbath day of Mk 1:21-34) has disappeared and ὅτε ἔδυ ὁ ἥλιος could be omitted. In the composition of Matthew, the link with the scene in the house of Simon (8:14-15) has not been retained, *and* there is an overlapping of the evening time of Mk 1:32 (the day of Capernaum) and Mk 4:35 (the day of the parables, with another example of Mark's double-step expressions: ἐν ἐκείνῃ τῇ ἡμέρᾳ ὀψίας γενομένης, before the crossing of the lake: cf. Mt 8:18). – In Luke the sunset at the end of the day in Capernaum retains its full meaning. Luke has never adopted Mark's ὀψίας γενομένης (diff. Mk 1:32; 4:35; 14:17; 15:42; om. Mk 6:47). It is omitted here also, although it may have influenced Luke's use of the genitive absolute in 4:40 (δύνοντος δὲ τοῦ ἡλίου) and again in 4:42 (γενομένης δὲ ἡμέρας, diff. Mk 1:35 πρωΐ: compare Lk 22:66 καὶ ὡς ἐγένετο ἡμέρα, diff. Mk 15:1 πρωΐ; genitive absolute in Acts 12:18; 16:35; 23:12; cf. 27:33,39 ὅτε).

Boismard has made the objection that in some instances one expression in Mark is typically Matthean, and therefore borrowed from Matthew, and the other expression is typically Lukan, and therefore borrowed from Luke. But what is meant, in this connection, by Matthean style? Boismard's treatment of Mk 3:7ff. is most typical. He quotes the verb ἀναχωρέω in v. 7: only here in Mark and 9 times elsewhere in Matthew. No consideration is given to the possibility of Matthean redaction in some or in all these instances nor to the possible influence of Mark's significant use of ἀνεχώρησεν for Jesus' retirement (Mk 3:7, cf. v. 6).[7] In his study of double-tradition passages in Matthew, such as Mt 3:7-10, Boismard has noted quite correctly that "Matthieu avait tendance à systématiser certaines expressions qu'il lisait dans ses sources".[8] To accept Matthean systematization with regard to double-tradition texts and to refuse this possibility with regard to the Markan text is, it seems to me, an unjustifiable dichotomy in the study of Matthew.

3. P. Rolland's list of "expressions doubles" (or minor doublets) is not a list of duplicate expressions in the strict sense.[9] It includes a considerable number of so-called "conflations" of a Matthean and a Lukan element which do not necessarily form a unit in the text of Mark. What I call a Markan double-step expression is a much more specific stylistic phenomenon, *one* double expression and something more than the sum of two single phrases.[10] Therefore, the designation by the name of "minor doublets" ("doublets mineurs") is quite inadequate and even misleading. The Markan expression is not a mechanical combination of two parts but a stylistic unit with a progression to greater precision in

---

[7] Cf. F. NEIRYNCK, "Urmarcus redivivus? Examen critique de l'hypothèse des insertions matthéennes dans Marc," M. SABBE (ed.), *L'évangile selon Marc* (BETL, 44), Leuven, 1977,²1988, 103-145 (132-134); reprinted in *Jean et les Synoptiques. Examen critique de l'exégèse de M.-É. Boismard* (BETL, 49), Leuven, 1979, 319-361 (348-350).

[8] In this volume, 273.

[9] P. ROLLAND, "Marc, première harmonie évangélique," *RB* 90 (1983) 23-79 (35-79: "Expressions doubles chez Marc"); *Les premiers évangiles* (Lectio Divina, 116), Paris, 1984, esp. 109-128. See also *infra*, n. 21. Cf. F. NEIRYNCK, "Les expressions doubles chez Marc et le problème synoptique," *ETL* 59 (1983) 303-330; cf. *infra*, n. 10.

[10] F. NEIRYNCK, *Duality in Mark. Contribution to the Study of the Markan Redaction* (BETL, 31), Leuven, 1972,²1988 (with a Supplement on "Duplicate Expressions and Synoptic Problem," 227-235).

the second half of the expression, and, in my view, is pointing to the originality of Mark.

3. *The Minor Agreements of Matthew and Luke against Mark*

On many occasions it has been argued that numerous minor agreements are in fact not so striking and that for most of the so-called significant agreements a satisfactory redactional explanation can be given. Nevertheless the objection is raised again and again: you can be right with your explanation of the individual agreements but, as a whole, the phenomenon of the minor agreements remains unexplained. If this is something more than a polite way of avoiding the "textual discussion", such a reaction reveals that the minor agreements are taken as *one* phenomenon; and I have no objection, at least in this sense: the minor agreements share one common characteristic, they are all post-Markan. That is the truth in A. Fuchs's *Deuteromarkus* hypothesis.[11]

1. The minor agreements are first of all agreements against Mark and the first cause of the common change in Matthew and Luke is the text of Mark. Mark's Greek style has not always been rightly evaluated, and Matthew and Luke are not alone in their feeling that there is an overuse of καί, of historic presents, pleonasms, etc. Jesus who asks questions, the disciples who remain unintelligent, and many other motifs in Mark are "corrected" in Matthew and Luke. A priori it is not unlikely that two independent redactions on the basis of Mark will show some coincidences. Someone has written that "if Matthew omits something it is unattractive to him for some reason and what is unattractive to one Christian author has by that very fact an *increased* chance of being unattractive to another".[12] In any case it is not enough to list the Matthew-Luke agreements, and certainly not simply to count them. The parallel text in Mark and the possibilities of understanding and misunderstanding should be studied more than is usually done in the literature on the minor agreements.

2. In the volume *The Minor Agreements* I have added, in Part III, "A classification of stylistic agreements with comparative material from the triple tradition".[13] Reviewers and users of the book are usually more interested in the cumulative list of the agreements (Part II) than in the comparison with other triple tradition material. In my view, however,

---

[11] Cf. F. NEIRYNCK, "Deuteromarcus et les accords Matthieu-Luc," *ETL* 56 (1980) 397-408; = *Evangelica*, 769-780.
[12] S. MCLOUGHLIN, in *The Downside Review* 90 (1972) 201-206, 202. Cf. "Les accords mineurs Mt-Lc contre Mc et le problème synoptique," *ETL* 43 (1967) 17-40; = I. DE LA POTTERIE (ed.), *De Jésus aux évangiles* (BETL, 25), Gembloux-Paris, 1967, 17-40.

the description of the minor agreements is only one part of the evidence. The word "atomization" has been used with reference to the various explanations of the agreements, but there is also the atomization of the evidence by concentrating on one passage and collecting all sorts of agreements without studying each type of agreement together with all other similar changes of Mark elsewhere in the Gospel. Many times the minor agreement works like a signal: it draws our attention to Matthean or Lukan non-coincidental parallels, and I have the impression that without those cases of coincidence some aspects of Matthean and Lukan usage would have remained partially unexplored. The minor agreements force us again and again to study each passage in the light of the whole Gospel. Without undertaking such a full-scale examination of the gospel redaction, the use of the minor agreements as an objection against Markan priority will remain quite inoffensive.

3. It is, of course, not a reasonable expectation that in every instance a redactional explanation can be made acceptable for all Markan priorists. Some will be inclined to ascribe one or another agreement to the influence of Q. Others will reckon here and there with oral tradition and the possibility of tradition variants. Others will give more importance to the textual factor, textual corruption and harmonization. But these various explanations given to residual "difficult cases" do not at all modify our general synoptic hypothesis. M.D. Goulder's contention that some agreements are Matthean in style but characteristically un-Lukan has been answered by C.M. Tuckett.[14] Boismard has made a similar observation with regard to Lk 9:10-11, and I have attempted to give a response in the paper submitted to this Conference. I quote here one sentence from the conclusion: "The examination of the minor agreements of Matthew and Luke in the light of their context in each gospel leads us to the conclusion that these agreements imply a certain amount of disagreement." This conclusion can be applied to many other instances. Similar phrases can become very dissimilar in their respective contexts and such a dissimilarity in the agreements is in fact an argument for Matthew's and Luke's independence.

[13] F. NEIRYNCK (with T. HANSEN and F. VAN SEGBROECK), *The Minor Agreements of Matthew and Luke against Mark, with a Cumulative List* (BETL, 37), Leuven, 1974, 198-288 (11-48: "The Study of the Minor Agreements"; 49-195: "A Cumulative List"). See now also T.A. FRIEDRICHSEN, "The Matthew-Luke Agreements against Mark. A Survey of Recent Studies: 1974-1989," in F. NEIRYNCK (ed.), *L'Évangile de Luc – The Gospel of Luke* (BETL, 32), Leuven, 1989, 335-391.

[14] M.D. GOULDER, "On Putting Q to the Test," *NTS* 24 (1977-78) 218-234; C.M. TUCKETT, "On the Relationship between Matthew and Luke," *NTS* 30 (1984) 130-142. See now also F. NEIRYNCK, "ΤΙΣ ΕΣΤΙΝ Ο ΠΑΙΣΑΣ ΣΕ. Mt 26,68 / Lk 22,64 diff. Mk 14,65," *ETL* 63 (1987) 5-47.

4. *The Source Doublets in Matthew and Luke*

I can quote here the team advocating the two-gospel hypothesis: "The question of 'doublets' within the Synoptic gospels clearly requires further research and that research needs to begin with a definition of the term"; and "When all of the evidence from 'doublets' is taken into consideration there is almost twice as much evidence (20/12) in support of some other hypothesis as there is in support of the Two-Document Hypothesis, assuming, of course, that here is a valid argument for Markan priority from the appearance of Doublets." [15] The assumption is, of course, not that there is an argument for Markan priority but rather that the doublets offer "the decisive evidence for a common, written source for Mt and Lk" (W.G. Kümmel). As to the requirement that we should begin with a definition of the term, J.C. Hawkins (and others before him) has given at least some definition of doublets: "repetitions of the same or closely similar sentences in the same gospel" (1898). He has added a footnote in [2]1909: "I have thought it best to restrict the name 'doublet' to such important cases as are collected here, and not to include under it smaller similarities as some other writers would do." In a later Additional Note he refers to T. Stephenson (1918): "He distinguishes between the doublets which are 'due to the editors,' and those which are doublets in the sources themselves". [16] Taken together, these three utterances give a workable definition of the term doublet. Editorial repetitions or "redactional doublets" (Vaganay: "doublets-répétition") have no direct source-critical relevance. The notion of "source doublets" (Vaganay: "doublets-source") applies when the saying appears twice, e.g., once in the form and the context of Mk and once in a different form and context. It can be extended here to include also the "conflations" of sources in one passage (Vaganay: "doublets condensés").

The probative force of the doublets is contested by the advocates of the two-gospel hypothesis (not by the defenders of the multiple-stage hypothesis). But is it not so that, in the hypothesis of Matthean priority, similar questions must arise about the repetitions in Matthew? As long as the use of sources and traditions in Matthew is not completely ignored, critical analysis will have to make the distinction between merely editorial repetitions, editorial repetitions of a saying borrowed from a source, and repetitions resulting from the use of more than one

---

[15] Quoted from the 1984 paper; in this volume, 226 and 227.

[16] J.C. HAWKINS, *Horae Synopticae*, Oxford, 1898, 64;[2]1909, 80, n. 1; Note, cf. "Hawkins's Additional Notes," *ETL* 46 (1970) 78-111, 91.

source. At least in this description of the phenomenon there is a lot of similarity with our approach.

The proof from the doublets is accepted as a valid argument by the advocates of the multiple-stage hypothesis. Within this Conference such an agreement among two groups is certainly not a minor one. Of course, the reconstruction of the source will not be the same, but the existence of a hypothetical sayings source is a common assumption. For Rolland the distinction between the triple tradition and the double tradition is an essential part of his theory. A new suggestion is offered by Boismard who now ascribes the double-tradition passages to Proto-Luke. In my view, however, it is more than doubtful whether the presence of some words and phrases which are attested as "Lukanisms" elsewhere in Luke and Acts can prove the case! A more or less isolated use of the same word in the source is not necessarily Lukan usage.

In connection with Proto-Luke, we should mention here also the problem of the Lukan omission of Mk 6:45−8:26. It has been cited as one of the principal weaknesses of the two-source theory. But I find it a curious way of arguing to present first as a difficulty the common omission in Matthew and Luke of Mk 7:31-37 and 8:22-26 and then also the omission of the whole section in Luke.[17] In the same way the common omission of Mk 4:26-29 (the seed growing secretly) is cited, although in Luke the entire section of Mk 4:26-34 has no parallel in chapter 8. And can we say that there is no acceptable explanation for the Lukan omission of Mk 6:45−8:26? When it is agreed that Luke could have omitted the second feeding story, the consequence of this omission cannot be overlooked. We can do our guess-work about Luke's possible intentions in omitting this section, but in this stage of the discussion it is more important to study the reminiscences of Mk 6:45−8:26 in Luke, in the immediate context of the omission (9:10 Bethsaida; 9:18 Jesus praying κατὰ μόνας), and elsewhere in Luke (e.g., 11:16; 11:38) and in Acts (e.g., 5:15-16). From these reminiscences we conclude that Luke knew that section of Mark and there is no need for a Proto-Luke or an Urmarkus without Mk 6:45−8:26.

In the course of the preparation of this Conference it has been decided that preference should be given to the Textual Discussion, with a concentration on triple-tradition texts. It is indeed in the study of the text that our different approaches can be tested and that agreements and disagreements will become manifest, much better than in an abstract

---

[17] In this volume, 234-235.

statement and in the elaboration of a sort of grammar of source-critical criteria.

The phenomenon of order, and particularly the relative order of Mt 4:23–13:58 / Mk 1:21–6:13, is a major issue in the discussion of the synoptic problem. For that reason, our analysis will concentrate on the crucial passage of Mt 4:23–5:2 and the problem of dislocations in Mt 4:23–11:1.

We add here, to conclude this Introduction, two more preliminaries: a brief survey of the assumptions of the two-source theory compared with the other hypotheses and a short presentation of the argument from order.

I. THE ASSUMPTIONS OF THE TWO-SOURCE THEORY COMPARED WITH THE OTHER HYPOTHESES

1. It is a common assumption in our three solutions to the synoptic problem that the important similarities between the Synoptic Gospels imply a literary relationship, direct or indirect. A pure oral tradition hypothesis and the fragment hypothesis are rejected as inadequate.

2. If not all adherents of the three solutions, at least Boismard, Farmer and Neirynck agree that the Fourth Gospel is later than the Synoptic Gospels and that the fourth evangelist (for Boismard: Jn II-B) knew and used the Synoptics. However, John's use of the Synoptics is a special problem and should be treated separately.[18]

3. The Markan hypothesis holds the priority of Mark, i.e., the literary dependence of Matthew and Luke upon Mark with regard to the triple-tradition material. The double-tradition material and the Matthean and Lukan Sondergut are not directly concerned.

   a. Although the priority of Mark is quite the opposite to the assumption of Griesbach, both theories place Mark in a medial position: "Er ist also das Bindeglied, und zwar bestimmter entweder die Quell- oder die Schlußeinheit seiner Mitreferenten".[19]

---

[18] Cf. *infra*, 438-450: "John and the Synoptics. A Response to P. Borgen."
[19] F.J. Schwarz (1844), quoted in "The Argument from Order" (*supra*, n. 6), 793 (=' 746), n. 29.

The two theories can concur, for instance, in the description of duplicate expressions in Mark of which one element is found in Matthew and the other in Luke. This same phenomenon can be interpreted either as conflation of two sources or as an original feature of Markan style. A similar observation can be made concerning the relative order of pericopes.

One of the new developments in the neo-Griesbachian two-gospel hypothesis is the emphasis given to Luke's dependence upon Matthew:

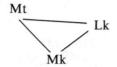

With regard to the triple tradition, Luke's use of Matthew can be compared with the use of Mark in the Markan hypothesis. In passages with a similar text in Matthew and Mark, the definition of distinctive Lukan redaction will be more or less the same in both theories.[20]

b. The Griesbach solution appears in an adapted form ("un Griesbach déguisé") in the multiple-stage hypotheses represented at this Conference. This is clearly the case with P. Rolland: Mark is a conflation of Proto-Matthew and Proto-Luke.[21]

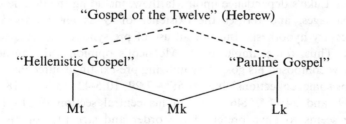

[20] Cf. 77-80: "Note on the Eschatological Discourse." See also C.M. TUCKETT, *The Revival*, 167-185 ("The Apocalyptic Discourses"), esp. 167: "Matthew and Mark are very close here. Hence, many of Farmer's explanations of Luke's procedure have the implicit agreement of many other scholars. For example, the differences in Lk xxi.20-24 can be (and are) explained as due to Luke's writing after the fall of Jerusalem, and this accounts for the differences between Luke and Mark just as well as those between Luke and Matthew."

21 Cf. *supra*, n. 9. See now also P. ROLLAND, "La question synoptique demande-t-elle une réponse compliquée?" *Biblica* 70 (1989) 217-223 (on Boismard's interpretation of Mk 6:14-16). For a reply, see F. NEIRYNCK, "Marc 6,14-16 et par.," *ETL* 65 (1989) 105-109.

This theory shows only a weak analogy with the priority of Mark in the suggestion of one primitive Gospel at the origin of the triple-tradition material.

Boismard's theory is much more a combination of the two-gospel hypothesis with the Markan hypothesis. The "Mark" Matthew and Luke are using as a source is not our Gospel of Mark but a Proto-Mark ("Mc-intermédiaire"). The final Mark is a later redaction ("l'ultime Rédacteur marcien") on the basis of Proto-Mark but also influenced by Proto-Matthew ("les insertions matthéennes dans Marc") and Proto-Luke.

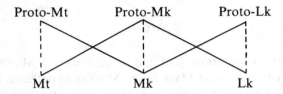

In some sections and in particular sentences, the Proto-Mark used by Matthew and Luke is almost identical with the text of our Mark and in these cases Boismard's solution scarcely differs from Markan priority.

4. The Q hypothesis can be accepted without difficulty by Rolland and, at least in principle, by Boismard.[22] The two-gospel theory, however, assumes Luke's dependence upon Matthew, including the double-tradition passages, and refuses the existence of Q as an unproven and unnecessary hypothesis. But not all use of pre-synoptic sources can be denied. Thus, for example, in A. McNicol's opinion, "the author of Matthew composed his gospel by utilizing pre-existing source materials; perhaps some 'collections' like Mt 5:7 – 7:29; 10:5-42; 13:3-50; 18:1-35; 23:1-39, and 24:1 – 25:46", and in his central section (9:51 – 18:14) "Luke seems to have preferred the order and structure of his non-Matthean source".[23] With these presuppositions, if not a common source, at least some overlapping of sources seems to be unavoidable. W.R. Farmer has made a significant observation regarding Lk 17:23-37: "That section of Luke constitutes a special problem. In all probability Luke had access to a special source which contained apocalyptic material parallel to material in Matthew 24. Luke 17:26-30 ... is probably in a more original form than its parallel in Matthew 24:37-39" (1964: 272). In "A Fresh Approach to Q" (1975), he is even more

---

[22] Cf. *infra*, "A New Debate: Q or Proto-Luke," 108-114.
[23] "The Composition" (in this volume, 160).

explicit: "it seems to me that the Lucan form of that material is more original than the form of the material in Matthew 24. Therefore, I cannot derive that apocalyptic material in Luke 17 from Mt 24. At that point it is necessary for me to hypothecate ... another source, an apocalyptic source, that Luke has copied".[24] The recognition of non-Markan, common material in Matthew and Luke, more original in Luke than in Matthew, and not derived from Matthew: is this not the basis for the acceptance of Q?

5. The two-source theory is sometimes modified or supplemented with subsidiary hypotheses to explain literary phenomena such as,

(1) the minor agreements of Matthew and Luke against Mark in the triple tradition (Luke's subsidiary dependence on Matthew, Proto-Mark, Deutero-Mark):

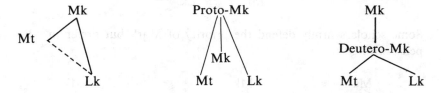

(2) the existence of extensive special material in Matthew and Luke (Four-document hypothesis):

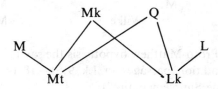

(3) the combination of Q and L (Proto-Luke):[25]

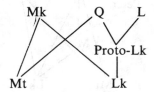

[24] J. NEUSNER (ed.), *Christianity, Judaism and Other Greco-Roman Cults*. FS M. Smith, vol. I (Studies in Judaism in Late Antiquity, 12), Leiden, 1975, 39-50, esp. note 4 (46-48).
[25] It should be noted that Boismard's Proto-Luke differs from this classic notion of Proto-Luke (L + Q).

(4) the differences in the double tradition material of Matthew and Luke (Q^{Mt}, Q^{Lk}):

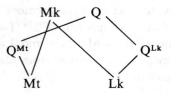

(5) the overlappings of Mark and Q (Mark's use of Q):

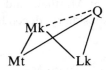

Some scholars firmly defend the priority of Mark but prefer to "dispense with Q":

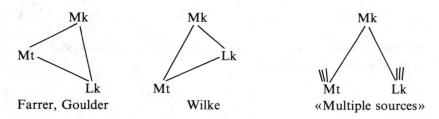

Farrer, Goulder   Wilke   «Multiple sources»

In L. Vaganay's Proto-Matthew hypothesis the sayings source is restricted to double-tradition passages in Lk 9:51 – 18:14 (S = "Seconde Source Synoptique Supplémentaire"):

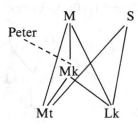

II. The Phenomenon of Order

1. *The Absence of Matthew-Luke Agreements*

Much has been written on the relative order of pericopes in the triple tradition, starting from two statements. "Marcus ... ordinem a Matthaeo observatum ita retinuit, ut, sicuti ab eo recederet, Lucae vestigiis insisteret et hunc ordinemque narrationis eius κατα ποδα sequeretur" (Griesbach). "Sed narrationum evangelicarum ordinis non tanta est quanta plerisque videtur diversitas; maxima sane si aut hos scriptores eadem conplexione omnes aut Lucan cum Matthaeo conposueris, exigua si Marcum cum utroque seorsum" (Lachmann). The same phenomenon can be described more formally as Mark's alternating support or as absence of Matthew-Luke agreements wherever Matthew or Luke departs from Mark's order. This absence of agreement has been acknowledged repeatedly by Markan priorists,

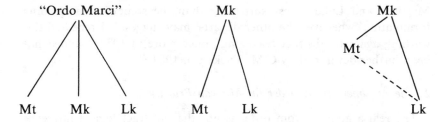

as well as by adherents of the Griesbachian and the Augustinian hypothesis (Matthean originality),

Logically, any synoptic diagram with Mark (or the order of Mark) as the linking middle term can provide a valid explanation.

Occasionally, one or another pericope has been noted as a possible exception to the rule, but none of these coincidences between Matthew and Luke is really convincing,[26] and the "exception" is unable to modify the general statement. In the case of the cleansing of the temple,[27] Luke omits the fig tree episode, Mk 11:12-14, 20-25, but there is no real change of Mark's order.

Much more significant is the undoing of Butler's correction of logical error by opposing, again, "authorial intent" (in the two-gospel hypothesis) to "literary accident due to random chance" (in the two-source hypothesis). Do we really need either the deliberate intention of a writer (Mark) or a "concerted action" (of Matthew and Luke) to explain this absence of agreement? As I wrote already in 1973: "The significance of the phenomenon of order may become questionable with a more concrete approach. ... In Luke the alterations of the Markan order are limited in number and the transpositions in Matthew are confined to Mt 4:23 – 11:1. Emphasis on alternating support seems to imply that agreements and disagreements with the relative order of Mark are treated as comparable quantities. In fact, the disagreement against Mark is the exception and the absence of concurrence between Matthew and Luke is less surprising than the somewhat misleading formulation 'whenever the other departs' may suggest". I repeated this warning against "abstract reasoning" once more in 1982[28] and it has been further developed by C.M. Tuckett in 1984.[29]

2. The Argument from Order for Markan Priority

The real argument from order is not that abstract logical inference based upon the absence of Matthew-Luke agreements. The phenomenon of order cannot be taken in isolation from the general comparative study of the Gospels.

[26] See my critique of Sanders' list of Mt-Lk agreements, in "The Argument from Order" (1973). With regard to Mk 3:13-19 (Mt 10:2-4; Lk 6:12-16), I can repeat my observation that in Lk 6:*12-16*,17-19 there is merely an inversion of order within the same section of Mk 3:7-12,*13-19* (ctr. TUCKETT, 1984, 204, 215 n. 27).

[27] W.R. FARMER, The Synoptic Problem, 1964, 212 (in this volume, 142). Cf. L. VAGANAY, Le problème synoptique, 1954, 59.

[28] "The Argument from Order" (1973), 791-792 (= The Minor Agreements, 298-299; Evangelica, 744-745); "The Griesbach Hypothesis" (1982), 114. – The paper on the argument from order has been presented at the Southampton meeting in 1973 (cf. "Introduction", 7).

[29] "If one restricts attention to strict changes in order of the same material, then the number of changes made by Matthew and Luke, assuming Markan priority, is relatively small." In his counting, "Luke changes the order of 4 Markan pericopes, Matthew changes the order of 6;" and: "There is no reason for thinking that the phenomenon of order poses a positive problem for Markan priority, as Farmer and Dungan have suggested" (204-205).

Can it be "methodologically incorrect ... to focus initially upon Matthew and Mark on the one hand, and then Luke and Mark on the other" (134)? And what does it mean that the three synoptic Gospels "be perceived together"? Of course, it would be incorrect to exclude a priori any possible relationship, but is it not a normal and unavoidable procedure to compare the agreements and disagreements of the individual Gospels one by one?[30] Lachmann's statement may seem uncomfortable for a Griesbachian: "exigua [diversitas], si Marcum cum utroque seorsum [conposueris]", but a true Griesbachian arrives at the same conclusion: "Noch grössere und anhaltendere Übereinstimmungen in der Aufeinanderfolge und Verknüpfung einzelner Begebenheiten finden wir, wenn wir zwei dieser Evangelisten mit einander vergleichen, besonders den Marcus im Verhältniss sowohl zum Matthäus als zum Lucas."[31]

The changes of Mark's order in the Gospel of Luke are found more particularly in the passion narrative (Lk 22:15-18, 21-23, 24-27, 33-34, 56-62, 63-65, 66-71; 23:26-49 passim). There are also some transferences of pericopes, within the same context:

Mk	Lk	Mk	Lk	Mk	Lk
1:16-20		3:7-12		3:31-35	(8:1-3)
1:21-39	4:31-44	3:13-19	6:12-16	4:1-25	8:4-18
	5:1-11		6:17-19		8:19-21

or into a more distant context:

Lk		
	4:16-30	←————————Mk 6:1-6a
	7:36-50	←————————Mk 14:3-9
	10:25-28	←————————Mk 12:28-31.

Lachmann and many after him have shown that there is an acceptable redactional explanation for these *traiectiones* in Luke.[32]

In Matthew, the alterations of the Markan order are restricted to the section of Mk 1:21 – 6:13. All dislocations are anticipations: Mt 4:23 – 5:2 (summary); 8:2-4; 8:18-34; 9:18-26 (miracles); 9:35; 10:1-14 (disciples). As indicated below, they find a quite satisfactory explanation

---

[30] See below, 77, my response to "The Composition".
[31] F. BLEEK, 1862, quoted in *ETL* 58 (1982), 115, n. 19.
[32] Cf. "The Transpositions in Luke" (1973), 804-814 (= *The Minor Agreements*, 311-321; *Evangelica*, 757-767).

in the analysis of Matthew's unique editorial composition of Mt
4:23 – 11:1.[33]

Lachmann rightly concentrated his study on the variations in order
between Matthew and Mk 1:21 – 6:13. And before him, Griesbach
correctly indicated the problem of order for Markan priorists: "si
statuas, Marcum consultum fuisse a Matthaeo et Luca, obscurum
manet, cur v.c. Matthaeus ea, quae habentur Marc. 1,21 – 3,6. partim
omiserit, partim in alium ordinem redegerit." In this case, Griesbach's
own solution is far too simple: "omnia a Matth. 4,23 ad cap. 12,14
Marcus transsilierat."[34]

Note: The Markan Order in the Proto-Gospel

Boismard does not treat explicitly the problem of the relative order of
pericopes. In *Synopse* II he seems to suppose that Proto-Mark had the
order of Mark. The Matthean redactor followed this order, especially
from ch. 13 on. The Matthean redaction is also responsible for the
separation of Mt 9:1-17 and 12:1-14 (cf. Mk 2:1 – 3:6) and for the
composition of Mt 8 – 9.[35]

In Vaganay's hypothesis the Markan order of the triple-tradition
material in M is explicitly acknowledged: his "Proto-Matthew" has the
order of Mark![36]

Frans NEIRYNCK

ADDITIONAL NOTE:
See now also F. NEIRYNCK, art. "Synoptic Problem," in *The New Jerome Biblical
Commentary* (1990), 587-595. — On synopsis construction, cf. F. NEIRYNCK, "The Order
of the Gospels and the Making of a Synopsis," *ETL* 61 (1985) 161-166; "Once More: The
Making of a Synopsis," *ETL* 62 (1986) 141-154.

[33] Cf. "La rédaction matthéenne et la structure du premier évangile," *ETL* 43 (1967)
41-73, 63-72; = I. DE LA POTTERIE (ed.), *De Jésus aux évangiles* (BETL, 25), Gembloux-
Paris, 1967, 41-73, 63-72 (*Evangelica*, 1982, 3-35, 25-34).

[34] *Commentatio* (ed. J.B. Gabler, 1825), 398, 373.

[35] *Synopse* II, 35, 36, 37 (cf. 106).

[36] *Le problème synoptique*, 59: "A considérer l'ordonnance particulière des péricopes
dans les livrets, on peut justifier les différences entre Mt. - Mc. - Lc. en partant de l'ordre
de Mc. – La plupart des arrangements propres à Mt. et à Lc. (additions, omissions,
transpositions) trouvent une raison valable dans l'hypothèse où leurs auteurs ont connu un
ordre à peu près semblable à celui de Mc. ... Inversement, en manière de contre-épreuve,
on ne saurait justifier l'ordre de Mc., si l'on suppose qu'il a travaillé d'après Mt. ou Lc." –
This aspect of Vaganay's theory seems to be neglected in B. REICKE, *The Roots of the
Synoptic Gospels*, Philadelphia, 1986, 19 (in this volume, 312).

MATTHEW 4:23 – 5:2
AND THE MATTHEAN COMPOSITION OF 4:23 – 11:1

Mt 4:23 – 5:2 is one of the key passages in the study of the synoptic problem. There is an obvious parallelism between Matthew and Mark in the preceding pericopes:

    Mt 3:1-12   3:13-17   4:1-11   4:12-17   4:18-22
    Mk 1:1-9   1:10-11   1:12-13   1:14-15   1:16-20.

The interruption of this parallelism at Mt 4:23ff./Mk 1:21ff. plays an essential role in Griesbach's theory of Mark's alternating use of Matthew and Luke and his avoidance of the Sermon on the Mount.[1] The passage of Mt 4:23 – 5:2 is equally important in the hypothesis of Markan priority. Mt 4:23 – 5:2 is Matthew's preparation for the insertion of the Sermon (from his second source) in the framework of Mark, and this introduction to the Sermon should be studied in connection with the Matthean editorial composition of Mt 4:23 – 11:1. The study of this section in Matthew and its parallels in Mark inevitably implies a confrontation with the thesis of Matthean originality and with the hypothesis of a traditional pre-Matthean summary underlying the synoptic Gospels.[2]

The usual arrangement of the Synopses places Mt 4:23 in parallel to Mk 1:39, separated from the Sermon on the Mount either by a single paragraph, Lk 5:1-11 (Huck: in between Mt 4:23-25 and 5:1-2) or by the some nine paragraphs of Lk 5:1-11; 5:12 – 6:16, par. Mk (Aland and, with some variation, B-B[2] and B-L).

Aland	B-B	B-L	
§ 40 Mt 4:23	§ 37 Mt 4:23-25	§§ 43, 44, 45	Mt 4:23, 24a, 24b
§ 50 Mt 4:24-5,2	§ 48 Mt 5:1-2	§§ 55, 56	Mt 4:25; 5:1
		§ 58	Mt 5:2(-12)

---

[1] Griesbach's note at Mt 4:22: "Marcus, ad Matth. 4,21. [= 22] progressus, seponit Matthaeum et transit ad Lucam, quoniam orationem ... praeterire decreverat." At Lk 6:16: "Marcus hic abrumpit filum, propter orationem montanam h. l. apud Lucam sequentem, et transit ad Matthaeum."

[2] "Les textes de Mt 4:25 – 5:1, 12:15 et 15:21a, 29b, 30 ne formaient, dans le Mt-intermédiaire, qu'un seul et même récit" (M.-É. BOISMARD, *Synopse* II, 120; see also 121, on the expressions in Mk 3:7-8 "en provenance du Mt-intermédiaire").

Synopsis: Mt 4:23 — 5:2 and Parallels in Mark

Mt 4:12-17,18-22		Mk 1: 14-15,16-20	
4:23a	καὶ περιῆγεν	1:39	καὶ ἦλθεν 6:6b καὶ περιῆγεν
	ἐν ὅλῃ τῇ Γαλιλαίᾳ		τὰς κώμας κύκλῳ
b	διδάσκων	(1:21)	κηρύσσων διδάσκων.
	ἐν ταῖς συναγωγαῖς αὐτῶν	(1:21)	εἰς τὰς συναγωγὰς αὐτῶν
			εἰς ὅλην τὴν Γαλιλαίαν
c	καὶ κηρύσσων		1:14 (ἦλθεν) ... κηρύσσων
	τὸ εὐαγγέλιον		τὸ εὐαγγέλιον τοῦ θεοῦ
	τῆς βασιλείας		1:15 ... ἤγγικεν ἡ βασιλεία τοῦ θεοῦ
d	καὶ θεραπεύων	(1:23-27)	καὶ τὰ δαιμόνια ἐκβάλλων.
	πᾶσαν νόσον καὶ πᾶσαν μαλακίαν		
	ἐν τῷ λαῷ.		
24a	καὶ ἀπῆλθεν ἡ ἀκοὴ αὐτοῦ	1:28	καὶ ἐξῆλθεν ἡ ἀκοὴ αὐτοῦ
			εὐθὺς πανταχοῦ
	εἰς ὅλην τὴν Συρίαν·		εἰς ὅλην τὴν περίχωρον τῆς Γαλιλαίας.
			Mt 8:16/Mk 1:32-34
24b	καὶ προσήνεγκαν αὐτῷ	1:32	... ἔφερον πρὸς αὐτὸν
	πάντας τοὺς κακῶς ἔχοντας		πάντας τοὺς κακῶς ἔχοντας
			(34 ... κακῶς ἔχοντας
	ποικίλαις νόσοις		ποικίλαις νόσοις)
	καὶ βασάνοις συνεχομένους		
	καὶ δαιμονιζομένους		
	καὶ σεληνιαζομένους		καὶ τοὺς δαιμονιζομένους·
	καὶ παραλυτικούς,		
	καὶ ἐθεράπευσεν αὐτούς.		Mt 12:15-16 / Mk 3:7-12
		1:34	καὶ ἐθεράπευσεν πολλοὺς ...
25	καὶ ἠκολούθησαν αὐτῷ	3:10	πολλοὺς γὰρ ἐθεράπευσεν, ...
	ὄχλοι πολλοὶ		
	ἀπὸ τῆς Γαλιλαίας	3:7	... καὶ πολὺ πλῆθος
	καὶ Δεκαπόλεως		ἀπὸ τῆς Γαλιλαίας
	καὶ Ἱεροσολύμων		ἠκολούθησεν,
	καὶ Ἰουδαίας		
			καὶ ἀπὸ τῆς Ἰουδαίας
		3:8	καὶ ἀπὸ Ἱεροσολύμων ...
	καὶ πέραν τοῦ Ἰορδάνου.		καὶ πέραν τοῦ Ἰορδάνου ...
5:1	ἰδὼν δὲ τοὺς ὄχλους	3:9	... διὰ τὸν ὄχλον ...
	ἀνέβη εἰς τὸ ὄρος	3:13	καὶ ἀναβαίνει εἰς τὸ ὄρος
	καὶ καθίσαντος αὐτοῦ		καὶ
			προσκαλεῖται οὓς ἤθελεν αὐτός,
	προσῆλθαν αὐτῷ		καὶ ἀπῆλθον πρὸς αὐτόν.
	οἱ μαθηταὶ αὐτοῦ·		
5:2	καὶ ἀνοίξας τὸ στόμα αὐτοῦ	1:21	καὶ ... εἰσελθὼν εἰς τὴν συναγωγὴν
	ἐδίδασκεν αὐτοὺς λέγων·		ἐδίδασκεν.
7:28	... ἐξεπλήσσοντο οἱ ὄχλοι	1:22	καὶ ἐξεπλήσσοντο
	ἐπὶ τῇ διδαχῇ αὐτοῦ·		ἐπὶ τῇ διδαχῇ αὐτοῦ·
29	ἦν γὰρ διδάσκων αὐτοὺς		ἦν γὰρ διδάσκων αὐτοὺς
	ὡς ἐξουσίαν ἔχων		ὡς ἐξουσίαν ἔχων
	καὶ οὐχ ὡς οἱ γραμματεῖς		καὶ οὐχ ὡς οἱ γραμματεῖς.
	αὐτῶν.		

9:35a	καὶ περιῆγεν ὁ Ἰησοῦς	6:6b	καὶ περιῆγεν
	τὰς πόλεις πάσας καὶ τὰς κώμας		τὰς κώμας κύκλῳ
b	διδάσκων ἐν ταῖς συναγωγαῖς αὐτῶν		διδάσκων.
c	καὶ κηρύσσων τὸ εὐαγγέλιον τῆς βασιλείας		
d	καὶ θεραπεύων πᾶσαν νόσον καὶ πᾶσαν μαλακίαν.		

It is unique to B-L (Boismard-Lamouille, 1986) that Mt 4:25/Mk 3:7-12 (§ 55) and Mt 5:1/Mk 3:13 (§ 56) are printed as primary parallels (cf. B-B[1]). The newly published VBS Synopsis (Denaux-Vervenne, 1986)[3] now presents for the first time Mt 4:23 – 5:2 as one paragraph (§ 24: par. Mk 1:21), directly followed by Mt 5:3-12 (§ 25).

The Greek text of the parallels in Mark is printed in our Synopsis of Mt 4:23 – 5:2. Our purpose in this section is to show that Matthew's dependence on these parallel passages in Mark provides a satisfactory explanation and that no Proto-Matthean or other non-Markan source is needed.

A first presentation of this analysis of Mt 4:23 – 5:2 was published in my contribution on the structure of the Gospel of Matthew (1967) and, a few years later, in a study of the summaries in Matthew (1971).[4] More or less similar descriptions of this conflation of Markan passages are found for instance in a monograph on Matthew by J. Lange (1973)[5] and, more recently, in R.H. Gundry's commentary (1982),[6] in a special study by G. Lohfink (1983)[7] and in the commentary on Matthew by U. Luz (1985)[8]. J. Gnilka's reaction is more reserved. He accepts contacts ("Anknüpfungspunkte") with Mark in Mt 4:24a (Mk 1:28); "möglicherweise" Mt 4:24bc (Mk 1:32, 34); Mt 4:25 (Mk 3:7b, 8), but: "Weitere mk Einwirkungen sind abzulehnen"; and he raises a critical question: "wie soll man sich dann die Arbeitsweise von E[vangelist] vorstellen?". Of course, Gnilka is right when he observes that the contacts with Mark "nicht als Waffe gegen seine Gestaltungskraft angewendet werden sollten."[9] The originality of Matthew's composition can first of all be demonstrated in his use of Mark.

---

[3] Cf. *ETL* 62 (1986) 145-154.

[4] "La rédaction matthéenne" (1967), 66-68 (= *Evangelica*, 28-30); "The Gospel of Matthew" (1971), 56-67, esp. 63-67: "The First Day of Jesus' Ministry in Mt" (= *Evangelica*, 717-721).

[5] J. LANGE, *Das Erscheinen des Auferstandenen im Evangelium nach Mattäus. Eine traditions- und redaktionsgeschichtliche Untersuchung zu Mt 28,16-20* (Forschung zur Bibel, 11), Würzburg, 1973, 393-404 (see also 25-28, 41: Mt 7:29; 364-365: Galilee).

[6] *Matthew*, 63-67.

[7] "Wem gilt die Bergpredigt? Eine redaktionskritische Untersuchung von Mt 4,23 – 5,2 und 7,28f," *Theologische Quartalschrift* 163 (1983) 264-284 (esp. 272: "Die Literargeschichte der Rahmung"); and, only slightly revised, in *Wem gilt die Bergpredigt? Beiträge zu einer christlichen Ethik*, Freiburg-Basel-Wien, 1988, 15-38 ("Teil I: Wem gilt die Bergpredigt?"), 210-213, notes (esp. 24-25). See also the appendix: "Das Publikum der Bergpredigt," 199-209; in reply to: K.-S. KRIEGER, "Das Publikum der Bergpredigt (Mt 4,23-25)," *Kairos* 28 (1986) 98-119 (a critique of Lohfink's 1983 article).

[8] *Matthäus*, 178-179. Cf. n. 2: "Eigentlich müßte man 4,23 – 5,2 als *eine* Perikope fassen" (with reference to Neirynck and Lohfink).

[9] *Das Matthäusevangelium*, I, 1986, 106 (and note 3).

1. *Analysis of Mt 4:23—5:2*

Mt 4:23-24a

Mk 1:39 is usually presented as the primary Markan parallel to Mt 4:23:

καὶ ἦλθεν κηρύσσων εἰς τὰς συναγωγὰς αὐτῶν
εἰς ὅλην τὴν Γαλιλαίαν
καὶ τὰ δαιμόνια ἐκβάλλων.

Matthew changed the preposition εἰς + accusative to ἐν + dative (compare κηρύσσειν with εἰς in Mk 14:9 and with ἐν in Mt 26:13): ἐν ὅλῃ τῇ Γαλιλαίᾳ is directly connected with the initial *verbum eundi* περιῆγεν (instead of ἦλθεν), and ἐν ταῖς συναγωγαῖς αὐτῶν is preceded by διδάσκων (instead of κηρύσσων). It is followed by καὶ κηρύσσων, to which the object is added: τὸ εὐαγγέλιον τῆς βασιλείας. Mark's second participial phrase, καὶ τὰ δαιμόνια ἐκβάλλων, is replaced by Matthew's third participle: καὶ θεραπεύων πᾶσαν νόσον καὶ πᾶσαν μαλακίαν ἐν τῷ λαῷ.

Mk 1:39 is certainly not the unique parallel in Mark. Mt 4:23 is repeated in 9:35, with only some minor changes. Repetition is here a better word than inclusio. Mt 9:35 opens a new section in Matthew: compare 9:35 with 11:1, at the conclusion of the sermon, μετέβη ἐκεῖθεν τοῦ διδάσκειν καὶ κηρύσσειν ἐν ταῖς πόλεσιν αὐτῶν (cf. 9:35 περιῆγεν ... τὰς πόλεις ... διδάσκων ... καὶ κηρύσσων ...) and with 10:1, the commissioning of the twelve before the sermon: καὶ θερα-πεύειν πᾶσαν νόσον καὶ πᾶσαν μαλακίαν (cf. 9:35 καὶ θεραπεύων...). Mt 9:35 precedes 10:1,5a like Mk 6:6b precedes 6:7, and two differences between Mt 4:23 and Mk 1:39 are probably due to the influence of this Markan parallel to Mt 9:35:

Mt 9:35	Mk 6:6b
καὶ **περιῆγεν** ()	καὶ **περιῆγεν**
τὰς πόλεις πάσας καὶ τὰς κώμας	τὰς κώμας κύκλῳ
διδάσκων...	**διδάσκων**.

Mark's κύκλῳ is omitted in Mt 9:35. The word κύκλῳ is used three times in Mark (compare περιῆγεν τὰς κώμας κύκλῳ in 6:6 with 3:34 περιβλεψάμενος τοὺς **περὶ** αὐτὸν **κύκλῳ** καθημένους and with 6:36 τοὺς **κύκλῳ** ἀγροὺς καὶ **κώμας**) and three times omitted in the parallel text of Matthew (9:35; 12:49; 14:15). Mt 9:35 retains the *accusativus loci* and renders the idea of completeness (περιῆγεν ... κύκλῳ) by τὰς πόλεις **πάσας** καὶ τὰς κώμας. Compare the combination πόλιν ἢ κώμην

in Mt 10:11 (cf. Lk 10:8,10 πόλιν).[10] Besides Mt 4:23 and 9:35 there is
one more use of περιάγειν in Matthew, again with the accusative (23:15
περιάγετε τὴν θάλασσαν καὶ τὴν ξηράν). The construction with ἐν ...
in 4:23 looks like a conflation of Mk 1:39 and 6:6b:

Mt 4:23	Mk 1:39	Mk 6:6
καὶ **περιῆγεν**	καὶ ἦλθεν	καὶ **περιῆγεν**
ἐν ὅλῃ τῇ Γαλιλαίᾳ		τὰς κώμας κύκλῳ
διδάσκων...	**κηρύσσων**...	**διδάσκων**.
	εἰς ὅλην τὴν Γαλιλαίαν	

Two minor differences between Mt 4:23 and 9:35 should still be
mentioned: the insertion of ὁ Ἰησοῦς and the omission of ἐν τῷ λαῷ in
9:35. The addition of the subject ὁ Ἰησοῦς (diff. Mk 6:6b) is quite
natural after the preceding pericope of Mt 9:32-34: αὐτῶν, προσήνεγκαν, τοῦ δαιμονίου, ὁ κωφός, οἱ ὄχλοι, οἱ Φαρισαῖοι (the pronoun
αὐτῷ in v. 32 is the only reference to Jesus). The omission of ἐν τῷ λαῷ is
also understandable in light of the preceding context: the phrase would
be repetitious after ἐν τῷ Ἰσραήλ in v. 33.

The Markan parallel in Mk 1:39 deserves further consideration. It
contains the participle κηρύσσων but not (κηρύσσων) τὸ εὐαγγέλιον
τῆς βασιλείας. Yet, Mark's καὶ ἦλθεν κηρύσσων ... εἰς ὅλην τὴν
Γαλιλαίαν in 1:39, after the Day of Capernaum (1:21-38), appears as an
echo of the first summary in 1:14-15, ἦλθεν ὁ Ἰησοῦς εἰς τὴν Γαλιλαίαν κηρύσσων τὸ εὐαγγέλιον τοῦ θεοῦ, followed by the direct
discourse: ... ἤγγικεν ἡ βασιλεία τοῦ θεοῦ· ... πιστεύετε ἐν τῷ
εὐαγγελίῳ. The complement which is added to κηρύσσων in Mt 4:23,
τὸ εὐαγγέλιον τῆς βασιλείας, conveniently summarizes Mk 1:14b-15.
Compare Mt 24:14 τοῦτο τὸ εὐαγγέλιον τῆς βασιλείας, diff. Mk 13:10
τὸ εὐαγγέλιον (see also Mt 13:19 τὸν λόγον τῆς βασιλείας, Mk ὁ
λόγος).

There is still another aspect in Mk 1:39. This summary is a generalizing statement in which what happened in the synagogue of Capernaum
is extended over the whole of Galilee. Compare κηρύσσων ἐν ταῖς
συναγωγαῖς αὐτῶν with 1:21-22 εἰσελθὼν εἰς τὴν συναγωγὴν ἐδίδασκεν ..., and τὰ δαιμόνια ἐκβάλλων (cf. 1:34) with Jesus casting out the
unclean spirit ἐν τῇ συναγωγῇ αὐτῶν (1:23-27). The Markan parallel
which would be expected in Mt 4:23 after Mt 4:18-22 / Mk 1:16-20 is
that story of Jesus' action in the synagogue of Capernaum. But the

---

[10] The parallel in Lk 8:1, διώδευεν κατὰ πόλιν καὶ κώμην, is too distant and too
different from Mt 9:35 for supposing here a Q text (Lk 8:1 is a typical Lukan editorial
verse).

arrival at Capernaum (Mk 1:21a) is anticipated in Mt 4:13 (ἐλθὼν κατῴκησεν εἰς Καφαρναούμ, emphasized by the fulfillment quotation in 4:14-16), and Matthew apparently has no parallel to the individual story of Mk 1:23-27. Or should we say that, by anticipating here the generalization of Mk 1:39, he created a substitute for that story? There is a firm indication in that sense. After 4:23 Matthew continues with the conclusion of that story:

Mt 4:24a	Mk 1:28
καὶ ἀπῆλθεν ἡ ἀκοὴ αὐτοῦ	καὶ ἐξῆλθεν ἡ ἀκοὴ αὐτοῦ εὐθὺς πανταχοῦ
εἰς ὅλην τὴν Συρίαν.	εἰς ὅλην τὴν περίχωρον τῆς Γαλιλαίας.

The use of ἀπῆλθεν for ἐξῆλθεν, the omission of Mark's εὐθύς (both ἐξῆλθεν and εὐθύς are less fitting after a summary than in the conclusion of a particular healing story), the avoidance of the pleonastic πανταχοῦ (before εἰς ὅλην...) as well as the substitution of τὴν Συρίαν[11] for τὴν περίχωρον τῆς Γαλιλαίας (understood as the region around Galilee) can be attributed to Matthean editorial intervention.

A last feature in Mt 4:23 should be examined: καὶ θεραπεύων πᾶσαν νόσον καὶ πᾶσαν μαλακίαν ἐν τῷ λαῷ (diff. Mk 1:39 καὶ τὰ δαιμόνια ἐκβάλλων). The replacement of (τὰ δαιμόνια) ἐκβάλλων with θεραπεύων[12] is not unique in Matthew. At the conclusion of the healing of the epileptic boy the disciples ask Jesus, διὰ τί ἡμεῖς οὐκ ἠδυνήθημεν ἐκβαλεῖν αὐτό, i.e., τὸ πνεῦμα (Mt 17:19, par. Mk), but in the story itself ἐκβάλλειν is replaced with θεραπεύειν: Mt 17:16 οὐκ ἠδυνήθησαν αὐτὸν θεραπεῦσαι (Mk 9:18 ... ἵνα αὐτὸ ἐκβάλωσιν καὶ οὐκ ἴσχυσαν) and 17:18 ἐθεραπεύθη (diff. Mk 9:27). The healing of the dumb man in Lk 11:14 (ἦν ἐκβάλλων δαιμόνιον, τοῦ δαιμονίου ἐξελθόντος) is probably a Q text, which is used by Matthew in 9:32-33 (δαιμονιζόμενον, ἐκβληθέντος τοῦ δαιμονίου) and again in 12:22: δαιμονιζόμενος, καὶ ἐθεράπευσεν αὐτόν. In the story of the Syro-phoenician woman Matthew has changed Mark's τὸ δαιμόνιον ἐξεληλυθός (7:30, cf. 29)

---

[11] "Die Bemerkung ist nur sinnvoll, wenn Syrien als nichtjüdisches Land aufgefaßt wird, die an Galiläa nach Norden angrenzende Provinz. Interpretiert man Syrien im weiteren, Palästina miteinschließenden Sinn, im Sinn der Παλαιστίνη Συρίη, oder denkt man an die in Syrien ansässige jüdische Minderheit, die allein die Kunde erreicht habe, geht man in die Irre" (J. GNILKA, ad loc., 108).

[12] Some commentators tend to neglect this correspondence to Mark's τὰ δαιμόνια ἐκβάλλων. Cf. J. LANGE, Das Erscheinen, 400: "ganz dem Mattäus zu zu schreiben"; "in den markinischen Summarien zwischen Mk 1,14 und 3,13 (und auch sonst) keine Entsprechung."

to ἰάθη (Mt 15:28, see v. 22 δαιμονίζεται; compare ἰάθη in Mt 8:13 and θεραπεύσω αὐτόν in v. 7).

Matthew's emphasis on the healing ministry of Jesus is most obvious in passages where he substitutes θεραπεύειν for Mark's διδάσκειν: Mt 14:14; 19:2; 21:14 (compare Mk 6:34; 10:1; 11:17). No less significant is his reaction to Mark's combination of θεραπεύειν and (τὰ δαιμόνια) ἐκβάλλειν in Mk 1:32-34. Matthew's version in Mt 8:16 is much shorter. Verse 1:33 is omitted and the verses 32 and 34 are brought together; the injunction to silence (v. 34c) is cancelled, ἐξέβαλεν and ἐθεράπευσεν are inverted and the final phrase πάντας τοὺς κακῶς ἔχοντας ἐθεράπευσεν is emphasized by the following fulfillment quotation. In the parallel to Mk 3:7-12, where again ἐθεράπευσεν (v. 10a) is followed by a reference to "the unclean spirits" and, at the end, an injunction to silence (3:11-12), Matthew connected καὶ ἐπετίμησεν αὐτοῖς... directly with ἐθεράπευσεν αὐτοὺς πάντας, without referring to the πνεύματα (12:15-16, followed by the fulfillment quotation in vv. 17-21). Both summaries of Mk 1:32-34 and 3:7-12 are precisely the Markan background of Mt 4:24-25.

The phrase of Mt 4:23 and 9:35 is repeated in 10:1, καὶ θεραπεύειν πᾶσαν νόσον καὶ πᾶσαν μαλακίαν, where it is added to ἐκβάλλειν αὐτά, i.e., πνεύματα ἀκάθαρτα (cf. Mk 6:7 and 3:15).[13] Matthew's phraseology πᾶσαν νόσον and πᾶσαν μαλακίαν has been compared with Deut 7:15 (πᾶσαν μαλακίαν· καὶ πάσας νόσους; cf. 28:61 πᾶσαν μαλακίαν καὶ πᾶσαν πληγήν). The word μαλακία is used only here in Matthew and never elsewhere in the New Testament. The word νόσος appears five times in Matthew,[14] and only once in Mark: in the phrase κακῶς ἔχοντας ποικίλαις νόσοις (Mk 1:34), which is borrowed by Matthew in 4:24 (cf. infra). Ποικίλαις νόσοις is omitted in Mt 8:16 but may have influenced Matthew's translation of Isa 53:4 in 8:17, diff. LXX (αὐτὸς τὰς ἀσθενείας ἡμῶν ἔλαβεν καὶ τὰς νόσους ἐβάστασεν).[15]

Our final observation concerns the "parallel" in Lk 4:14-15:[16]

[13] Luke has a similar addition to Mk 6:7. He changes ἐξουσίαν τῶν πνευμάτων τῶν ἀκαθάρτων to δύναμιν καὶ ἐξουσίαν ἐπὶ πάντα τὰ δαιμόνια and adds καὶ νόσους θεραπεύειν. In Lk 9:1 this detail has probably been brought forward from Mk 6:13.

[14] Mt 4:23; 9:35; 10:1 (πᾶσαν νόσον καὶ πᾶσαν μαλακίαν); 4:24 (cf. Mk 1:34); 8:17 (Isa). – Νόσος in Luke: 4:40 (= Mk); 6:18; 7:21; 9:1; Acts 19:12.

[15] Cf. W. ROTHFUCHS, Die Erfüllungszitate des Matthäus-Evangeliums (BWANT, 88), Stuttgart, 1969, 71-72: "Am wahrscheinlichsten wird die Autorschaft des Mt für die Form dieses Zitats in der Übersetzung von מכאבינו durch καὶ τὰς νόσους. ... Mt übersetzt die Stelle ... sozusagen kontextgemäß."

[16] For a critique of the hypothesis of its non-Markan origin, cf. J. DELOBEL, "La rédaction de Lc., IV,14-16a et le 'Bericht vom Anfang'," F. NEIRYNCK (ed.), L'évangile de Luc (BETL, 19), 1973, 203-223; Leuven, ²1989, 113-133 (with additional note).

14b καὶ φήμη ἐξῆλθεν καθ' ὅλης τῆς περιχώρου περὶ αὐτοῦ
   (cf. Mt 4:24a)
15a καὶ αὐτὸς ἐδίδασκεν ἐν ταῖς συναγωγαῖς αὐτῶν
   (cf. Mt 4:23b).

Compare φήμη ... περὶ αὐτοῦ with Mk 1:28 ἡ ἀκοὴ αὐτοῦ, par. Lk 4:37 ἦχος περὶ αὐτοῦ (cf. 7:17 ὁ λόγος οὗτος ... περὶ αὐτοῦ) and Mk 1:45 διαφημίζειν τὸν λόγον, par. Lk 5:15 διήρχετο ... ὁ λόγος περὶ αὐτοῦ. The phrase καθ' ὅλης for εἰς ὅλην in Mk 1:28 is Lukan style (Lk 23:5; Acts 9:31,42; 10:37) and the omission of τῆς Γαλιλαίας is quite natural after εἰς τὴν Γαλιλαίαν in v. 14a. Lk 4:14b has some similarity with Mt 9:26 καὶ ἐξῆλθεν ἡ φήμη αὕτη εἰς ὅλην τὴν γῆν ἐκείνην (diff. Mk 5:43, before the Nazareth episode in Mk 6:1-6a), but this verse is itself due to Matthean redaction on the basis of Mark.

The Nazareth pericope in the Gospel of Luke (4:16-30), though it is placed before the day in Capernaum (4:31-44, par. Mk 1:21-39), refers back to the γενόμενα εἰς τὴν Καφαρναούμ (4:23) and it is said that Jesus went to the synagogue on the sabbath day κατὰ τὸ εἰωθὸς αὐτῷ (4:16). This seems to suggest that we can interpret the preceding summary of Lk 4:14b-15 in the light of the Capernaum episode: the φήμη ... περὶ αὐτοῦ has to do with Jesus' reputation as a miracle-worker (Mk 1:28) and ἐδίδασκεν ἐν ταῖς συναγωγαῖς αὐτῶν is a generalization of Mk 1:21-22 (cf. v. 23 ἐν τῇ συναγωγῇ αὐτῶν), probably under the influence of Mk 1:39.

To conclude: the phrase of Mt 4:23 is more directly inspired by Mk 1:39, but, as it is placed just before Mt 4:24a (= Mk 1:28) and in continuation of Mt 4:18-22 / Mk 1:16-20, Mt 4:23b can be seen as the Matthean parallel to Mk 1:21, and Mt 4:23d θεραπεύων ... can be considered the Matthean substitute for the (exorcism-)healing in the synagogue (Mk 1:23-27).

Mt 4:24b-25

In Mark's Day of Capernaum Mk 1:(21-)28 is followed first by the private scene of an individual healing in the house of Simon (1:29-31) and then by the more public healing of many sick at the evening (1:32-34). By omitting its temporal connection (32a ὀψίας δὲ γενομένης, ὅτε ἔδυ ὁ ἥλιος) and its local setting (33 καὶ ἦν ὅλη ἡ πόλις ἐπισυνηγμένη πρὸς τὴν θύραν), this little story of Mk 1:32,34 can be used by Matthew in the summary before the Sermon on the Mount, in keeping with the Markan order (after v. 24a = Mk 1:28).

Mt 4:24b   Mk 1:32,34
καὶ προσήνεγκαν αὐτῷ   32 ... ἔφερον πρὸς αὐτὸν

πάντας τοὺς κακῶς ἔχοντας   πάντας τοὺς κακῶς ἔχοντας
  ποικίλαις νόσοις ...   34
καὶ δαιμονιζομένους ...   καὶ τοὺς δαιμονιζομένους·
καὶ ἐθεράπευσεν   34 καὶ ἐθεράπευσεν
αὐτούς.   πολλοὺς κακῶς ἔχοντας
                                              ποικίλαις νόσοις...

The two expressions of Mk 1:32,34 are united into πάντας τοὺς (κακῶς ἔχοντας) ποικίλαις νόσοις, and ἐθεράπευσεν αὐτούς includes the healing of the δαιμονιζόμενοι (cf. *supra*). The addition of καὶ βασάνοις συνεχομένους can be understood in three different ways:
(1) π. τ. κ. ἐχ. ποικίλαις νόσοις | καὶ βασάνοις συνεχομένους
sufferers from every kind of illness, racked with pain (NEB),
(2) π. τ. κ. ἐχ. | ποικίλαις νόσοις καὶ βασάνοις συνεχομένους
all the sick, those afflicted with various diseases and pains (RSV),
(3) π. τ. κ. ἐχ. ποικίλαις νόσοις καὶ βασάνοις συνεχομένους |
all sick people that were taken with divers diseases and torments (KJV).
In the most commonly accepted interpretation ποικίλαις νόσοις is linked with συνεχομένους (compare νόσοι καὶ βάσανοι with μαλακία καὶ νόσος in 4:23), though some doubts remain because of the absence of τούς and because of the parallel in Mk 1:34. Anyhow Matthew has expanded πάντας of Mk 1:32 (*all* the sick = "all kinds") with ποικίλαις νόσοις (from Mk 1:34) and καὶ βασάνοις συνεχομένους (Mt). Mark's καὶ τοὺς δαιμονιζομένους becomes one of the three specific kinds of illness: [καὶ] δαιμονιζομένους καὶ σεληνιαζομένους καὶ παραλυτικούς. In contrast to Luke, Matthew ·has no restraint in using the word δαιμονιζόμενος: 4:24; 8:16 (= Mk 1:32); 8:28 (diff. Mk 5:2); 8:33 (cf. Mk 5:15); 9:32; 12:22 (diff. Lk 11:14); 15:22 δαιμονίζεται (diff. Mk 7:25). Matthew adds here καὶ σεληνιαζομένους: compare 17:15 (diff. Mk) σεληνιάζεται καὶ κακῶς πάσχει, *v. l.* ἔχει (the verb does not appear elsewhere in the Bible). The term παραλυτικός is used by Matthew in 9:2a,b par. Mk (Luke avoids the word) and, more significantly, in 8:6 (diff. Lk): βέβληται ... παραλυτικός, δεινῶς βασανιζόμενος (compare 4:24 βασάνοις συνεχομένους ... καὶ παραλυτικούς). The term βάσανος/βασανίζω (torture) is not used elsewhere in the New Testament for disease.

Mark's ἔφερον πρὸς αὐτόν is replaced with προσήνεγκαν αὐτῷ in Mt 4:24 and 8:16. Compare the "bringing" of the sick in Matthew:
9:2 προσέφερον αὐτῷ (Mk 2:3 φέροντες πρὸς αὐτόν, cf. v. 4 προσενέγκαι αὐτῷ)
9:33 προσήνεγκαν αὐτῷ, cf. 12:22
12:22 προσηνέχθη αὐτῷ (diff. Lk 11:14)

14:35 προσήνεγκαν αὐτῷ πάντας τοὺς κακῶς ἔχοντας (Mk 6:55 τ. κ.
    ἐχ. περιφέρειν)
17:16 προσήνεγκα + dative (diff. Mk 9:18, cf. v. 17 ἤνεγκα τὸν υἱόν
    μου πρὸς σέ).[17]

The Gospel of Mark shows a deliberate analogy between 1:34c and
3:11-12. Whereas Luke has combined both passages in Lk 4:41, Matthew has consistently cancelled the motif of the demons' knowledge in
8:16 and 12:16. In Mt 4:24b,25 he has his own way of combining Mk
1:32-34 and 3:7-12:

    καὶ προσήνεγκαν αὐτῷ... cf. Mk 1:32
    καὶ ἐθεράπευσεν αὐτοὺς ... 1:34; 3:10
    καὶ ἠκολούθησαν αὐτῷ... 3:7-8.

In the summary of Mk 3:7-12, πολλοὺς γὰρ ἐθεράπευσεν (v. 10)
explains why the crowd pressed upon Jesus, and likewise ἀκούοντες ὅσα
ἐποίει (v. 8) indicates why they came to him. In a logical order of events
Matthew can write ἐθεράπευσεν αὐτούς and then continue with καὶ
ἠκολούθησαν αὐτῷ...

Mt 4:25	Mk 3:7-8
καὶ ἠκολούθησαν αὐτῷ	
ὄχλοι πολλοὶ	7 ... καὶ πολὺ πλῆθος
ἀπὸ τῆς Γαλιλαίας	ἀπὸ τῆς Γαλιλαίας
	ἠκολούθησεν
... καὶ Ἱεροσολύμων	8 καὶ ἀπὸ Ἰουδαίας
καὶ Ἰουδαίας	καὶ ἀπὸ Ἱεροσολύμων
καὶ πέραν τοῦ Ἰορδάνου.	καὶ πέραν τοῦ Ἰορδάνου...
	πλῆθος πολὺ...
	ἦλθον πρὸς αὐτόν.

The addition of καὶ Δεκαπόλεως after the mention of Galilee may be
editorial. The word is used twice in Mark, 5:20 (the verse is omitted in
Mt) and 7:31 (Matthew has simplified the complex geographical indication: ἐκ τῶν ὁρίων Τύρου ... διὰ Σιδῶνος ... ἀνὰ μέσον τῶν ὁρίων
Δεκαπόλεως are omitted in Mt 15:29). The omission of καὶ περὶ Τύρου
καὶ Σιδῶνα[18] (Mk 3:8) can be seen in connection with the mention of

---

[17] See also 18:24 (ὀφειλέτης) and 19:13 (παιδία, cf. Mk). Other instances of προσφέρειν in Mt: 2:11; 5:23,24; 8:4 (Mk); 22:19 (Mk ἤνεγκαν); 25:20. Cf. infra, 104.
[18] The distinction, correctly made by Lohfink (271 = 23), between Mt 4:23-24a
("Reines Summarium") and 4:24b-25 ("Neu ansetzende Überleitung zur Erzählung") does
not allow for a complete isolation of this omission (of Mark's Tyre and Sidon) from the
mention of Syria in verse 24a. Contrast, e.g., R.H. GUNDRY, Matthew, 64. For an
exaggeration in the opposite sense, see G. THEISSEN, Lokalkolorit und Zeitgeschichte in den

τὴν Συρίαν already in v. 24a. By cancelling the phrase καὶ ἀπὸ τῆς Ἰδουμαίας (after the mention of Jerusalem), and by inverting Judea and Jerusalem, Matthew obtains a formulation which is quite parallel to his description of the audience of John the Baptist:

3:5 Ἱεροσόλυμα	4:25 ... καὶ Ἱεροσολύμων
καὶ πᾶσα ἡ Ἰουδαία	καὶ Ἰουδαίας
καὶ πᾶσα ἡ περίχωρος τοῦ	καὶ πέραν τοῦ Ἰορδάνου.
Ἰορδάνου	

Mark's double expression in 3:7,8, καὶ πολὺ πλῆθος ... ἠκολούθησεν / πλῆθος πολὺ ... ἦλθον πρὸς αὐτόν, is simplified by Matthew in 4:25 and in 12:15 with a typically Matthean phrase: καὶ ἠκολούθησαν αὐτῷ ὄχλοι πολλοί. Compare:

8:1 ... ἠκολούθησαν αὐτῷ ὄχλοι πολλοί
14:13 οἱ ὄχλοι ἠκολούθησαν αὐτῷ
    (Mk 6:33 πολλοὶ ... συνέδραμον ἐκεῖ)
19:2 καὶ ἠκολούθησαν αὐτῷ ὄχλοι πολλοί
    (Mk 10:1 καὶ συμπορεύονται πάλιν ὄχλοι πρὸς αὐτόν).
Cf. 20:29 ἠκολούθησεν αὐτῷ ὄχλος πολύς (diff. Mk 10:46 ὄχλου ἱκανοῦ).[19]

Mt 5:1-2

The phrase καὶ ἠκολούθησαν αὐτῷ ὄχλοι πολλοί, as it appears for the first time in Mt 4:25, with the complement ἀπὸ τῆς Γαλιλαίας κτλ., is a Matthean reworking of Mk 3:7-8. With the exception of ἐθεράπευσεν (Mk 3:10a; in Mt 4:24b from Mk 1:34), no other use of Mk 3:7-12 has been made in Mt 4:25. Compare the parallel in Mt 12:15-16, where Mark's opening phrase (the transitional formula of Mk 3:7a) and Mark's conclusion (the injunction to silence in Mk 3:12) are used by Matthew:

15a ὁ δὲ Ἰησοῦς ἀνεχώρησεν ἐκεῖθεν (cf. Mk 3:7a)
  b καὶ ἠκολούθησαν αὐτῷ ὄχλοι πολλοί (cf. Mk 3:7b) / Mt 4:25
  c καὶ ἐθεράπευσεν αὐτοὺς πάντας (cf. Mk 3:10a) / Mt 4:24b
16 καὶ ἐπετίμησεν αὐτοῖς, ἵνα μὴ φανερὸν αὐτὸν ποιήσωσιν (cf. Mk 3:12).

Evangelien (NTOA, 8), Freiburg-Göttingen, 1989, 59: "Aus 'ganz Syrien' ... strömen Menschen zu Jesus."

[19] See also 15:30 καὶ προσῆλθον αὐτῷ ὄχλοι πολλοὶ ἔχοντες μεθ' ἑαυτῶν (diff. Mk 7:32 φέρουσιν αὐτῷ): compare Mt 5:1 προσῆλθον αὐτῷ οἱ μαθηταὶ αὐτοῦ.

Mark changes the locale in 3:13a: καὶ ἀναβαίνει εἰς τὸ ὄρος. The change is rather abrupt and unexpected after the instruction to the disciples in Mk 3:9 (cf. 3:7 πρὸς τὴν θάλασσαν, om. Mt). In Mt 5:1, after the parallel to Mk 3:(10a)7-8 in the preceding verse 4:25, Matthew continues with Mk 3:13, but not without adding a connecting formula:

1a ἰδὼν δὲ τοὺς ὄχλους (cf. 4:25 ὄχλοι πολλοί)
1b ἀνέβη εἰς τὸ ὄρος (Mk 3:13 καὶ ἀναβαίνει εἰς τὸ ὄρος).

The crowds are still there at the end of the Sermon: ἐξεπλήσσοντο **οἱ ὄχλοι** ἐπὶ τῇ διδαχῇ αὐτοῦ... (Mt 7:28; the subject οἱ ὄχλοι is added to the text of Mk 1:22), and one has the impression that the crowds form the audience of Jesus' sermon. In 8:1b the phrase of 4:25 will be repeated: when Jesus came down from the mountain, ἠκολούθησαν αὐτῷ ὄχλοι πολλοί.

However, Matthew's combination of Mk 3:7-8 (the crowds) and 3:13 (the disciples) creates a more complex situation.

Mt 5:1	Mk 3:13
ἰδὼν δὲ τοὺς ὄχλους	καὶ
ἀνέβη εἰς τὸ ὄρος	ἀναβαίνει εἰς τὸ ὄρος
καὶ καθίσαντος αὐτοῦ	
	καὶ προσκαλεῖται οὓς ἤθελεν αὐτός,
προσῆλθαν αὐτῷ	καὶ ἀπῆλθον πρὸς αὐτόν.
οἱ μαθηταὶ αὐτοῦ.	

This is the first mention of "his disciples" in Matthew and the only reference to them in Mt 4:23 – 8:17. Since in Matthew "his disciples" are the twelve disciples (cf. 10:1), this precision added to the text of Mark may be inspired by the context of Mk 3:13 (v. 14 καὶ ἐποίησεν δώδεκα). For the substitution of προσῆλθαν αὐτῷ for ἀπῆλθον πρὸς αὐτόν, compare Matthew's use of προσέρχομαι (in the Gospels: 51/5/ 10/1), more particularly 8:2 (Mk ἔρχεται πρός); 15:1 (Mk συνάγονται πρός); 21:23 (Mk ἔρχεται πρός); 22:23 (Mk ἔρχονται πρός); 27:58 (Mk εἰσῆλθεν πρός). The verb is used twelve times in Matthew for the disciples who come to Jesus: 5:1; 8:25; 13:10,36; 14:15 (= Mk); 15:12,23; 17:19; 18:1; (18:21); 24:1,3; 26:17. It implies an association of the disciples with Jesus and some separation from the crowd, which is sometimes expressly indicated: in the house (13:36; 18:1, cf. 17:25), or κατ' ἰδίαν (17:19; 24:3). The transitional formula, ἰδὼν δὲ τοὺς ὄχλους, may suggest a similar situation in Mt 5:1. The formula appears in two other passages:

8:18 ἰδὼν δὲ ὁ Ἰησοῦς ὄχλον περὶ αὐτόν (v. l. ὄχλους S, πολλοὺς ὄχλους ς T V B G): cf. Mk 4:36 καὶ ἀφέντες τὸν ὄχλον; only the disciples will follow Jesus in the boat (Mt 8:23).

9:36 ἰδὼν δὲ τοὺς ὄχλους: cf. Mk 6:34 καὶ ἐξελθὼν εἶδεν πολὺν ὄχλον (= Mt 14:14); the verse is placed before Jesus commissioning the twelve.

In the light of these parallels Mt 5:1 seems to indicate that Jesus went away to avoid the crowds and that the Sermon on the Mount is addressed to the disciples (T.W. Manson). However, other commentators tend to reduce the tension between the double audience: Jesus who saw the crowds went up to the mountain and sat down ... to teach them. The audience can be a composite one, as it is in Mt 23:1 (ἐλάλησεν τοῖς ὄχλοις καὶ τοῖς μαθηταῖς αὐτοῦ), the wider audience of the crowds and the inner circle of his disciples.

Καθίσαντος αὐτοῦ in 5:1 prepares for the teaching theme in 5:2. Jewish teachers sat to teach (cf. Mt 23:2) and so did Jesus in Matthew: 26:55 ἐκαθεζόμην διδάσκων (Mk ἤμην ...), the teaching in the Temple; cf. 13:1,2 καθῆσθαι (par. Mk), the parable teaching to the crowds; 24:3 καθημένου αὐτοῦ (par. Mk), the last discourse to the disciples, on the Mount of Olives.

Ἀνοίξας τὸ στόμα αὐτοῦ in 5:2 is a biblical phrase (cf. Acts 8:35; 10:34; 18:14), which is found in Matthew's quotation of Ps 77:2 LXX: ἀνοίξω ἐν παραβολαῖς τὸ στόμα μου (Mt 13:35). In 5:2 it is probably a redactional expansion of ἐδίδασκεν.

Since the phrase διδάσκων ἐν ταῖς συναγωγαῖς αὐτῶν in Mt 4:23b (before 4:24a = Mk 1:28) has drawn our attention to Mk 1:21, it is to this first mention of ἐδίδασκεν in Mark that we turn now at the end of Matthew's introduction to the Sermon. The text of Mk 1:22 is used by Matthew, in combination with Mt 7:28a, as the conclusion of the Sermon on the Mount:

... ἐξεπλήσσοντο **οἱ ὄχλοι** ἐπὶ τῇ διδαχῇ αὐτοῦ·

ἦν γὰρ διδάσκων αὐτοὺς ὡς ἐξουσίαν ἔχων,

καὶ οὐχ ὡς οἱ γραμματεῖς **αὐτῶν**.

The rather strict correspondence between Mt 4:25—5:2 and 7:28—8:1 indicates that the parallel of Mt 7:28-29 / Mk 1:22 can be extended to Mt 5:2 / Mk 1:21b (ἐδίδασκεν).

Together with Mt 8:1, it forms an inclusio with the introduction to the Sermon:

4:25   καὶ **ἠκολούθησαν** αὐτῷ ὄχλοι πολλοὶ ...
5:1a   ἰδὼν δὲ τοὺς ὄχλους
5:1b   **ἀνέβη** εἰς τὸ ὄρος ...
5:2   καὶ ... **ἐδίδασκεν** αὐτοὺς λέγων·
5:3 – 7:27
7:28-29   ... ἐξεπλήσσοντο οἱ ὄχλοι ...· **ἦν γὰρ διδάσκων** αὐτοὺς ...
8:1a   **καταβάντος** δὲ αὐτοῦ ἀπὸ τοῦ ὄρους
8:1b   **ἠκολούθησαν** αὐτῷ ὄχλοι πολλοί.

2. The Setting of the Sermon in Q

Before drawing further conclusions regarding the composition of Matthew, the problem of the setting of the Sermon in the Q source should be considered here. The transitional formula at the conclusion of the Sermon in Mt 7:28a shows striking agreements, if not in wording, at least in content, with Lk 7:1a:

Mt καὶ ἐγένετο
     ὅτε ἐτέλεσεν ὁ Ἰησοῦς τοὺς λόγους τούτους.
Lk ἐπειδὴ ἐπλήρωσεν πάντα τὰ ῥήματα αὐτοῦ
     εἰς τὰς ἀκοὰς τοῦ λαοῦ.

Most critics admit that Mt 7:28a and Lk 7:1a had a common origin in Q. Both A. Polag and W. Schenk accept the concluding formula in their reconstructions of the Q text, Polag in the Matthean version and Schenk in the Lukan form (without εἰς τὰς ἀκοὰς τοῦ λαοῦ). Harnack was more reserved: "Aber die Form der Aussage haben beide geändert... Also muß man leider darauf verzichten, hier den ursprünglichen Wortlaut ... herzustellen" (in his translation: "Nachdem er diese Worte gesprochen hatte").[20] Compare now also J.S. Kloppenborg: "both evangelists have thoroughly reworked Q at this point."[21] The debate is not closed.[22] It is important for us to observe that οἱ ὄχλοι in Mt 7:28 (insertion in the text of Mk 1:22) and εἰς τὰς ἀκοὰς τοῦ λαοῦ in Lk 7:1 (Lukan phrase) are usually supposed to be redactional.

In our proposal, the mention of "the crowds" is also Matthean in Mt 4:25; 5:1. Many will agree with G.D. Kilpatrick: "The Q sermon must

[20] A. POLAG, *Fragmenta Q*, 38; W. SCHENK, *Synopse*, 37; A. HARNACK, *Sprüche und Reden Jesu*, 54 (cf. 91, 180).

[21] *Q Parallels*, Sonoma, CA, 1987, 50 (Harnack 74, 54).

[22] Cf. U. WEGNER, *Der Hauptmann von Kafarnaum* (WUNT, 2/14), Tübingen, 1985, 102-126: "Der urspr Q-Wortlaut wird mit großer Wahrscheinlichkeit von Mt wiedergegeben" (126). Cf. U. LUZ, *Matthäus*, 415: "Ist er relativ treu dem Q-Text gefolgt? [n. 5] Eine merkwürdigerweise kaum je erwogene Möglichkeit!". On the parallel in Lk 7:1a: "ganz lukanisch"; but n. 4: "Vorlk könnte πληρόω sein." See also J. GNILKA, *ad* Mt 7,28: "Lk 7,1 lk geprägt, vielleicht mit Ausnahme des ἐπλήρωσεν... Auch Mt 7,28 ist durch E gestaltet."

have had some kind of introduction, perhaps one very like that preserved in Luke vi.20."[23] In Schenk's reconstruction: καὶ ἐπάρας τοὺς ὀφθαλμοὺς αὐτοῦ εἰς τοὺς μαθητὰς αὐτοῦ ἔλεγεν (6:20a, αὐτός redactional). Polag also adopts τοὺς μαθητὰς αὐτοῦ ἔλεγεν from Luke (cf. Mt 5:1-2 οἱ μαθηταὶ αὐτοῦ, λέγων), in a conjectural combination with elements from Mt 5:1: καὶ ὁ ᾿Ιησοῦς ἀνέβη εἰς τὸ ὄρος. καὶ ἰδὼν τοὺς ὄχλους καὶ ... (cf. Lk 6:12 εἰς τὸ ὄρος, 17 ὄχλος). If Matthew used such a Q text, including the location on the mountain and the mention of "the crowds", associated with the disciples, then there is much less originality in his composition. In H. Schürmann's opinion, the Q text not only included Lk 6:12-13a.(17).20a (cf. Polag) but also 6:13b-16 (the appointment of the Twelve).[24] In a more recent study, T.L. Donaldson now proposes that "the source for the mountain setting of Matthew's Sermon is to be found solely in Mk 3.13a" (ctr. Schürmann) but agrees with the other part of Schürmann's hypothesis assuming "that in Q the Sermon was preceded by a list of the Twelve, and that it was addressed to the disciples in the hearing of the crowds."[25] For Donaldson, "Matthew and Luke have brought their accounts of the Sermon into relationship with Mk 3.7-19, though in different ways. ... Such a coincidence ... calls for an explanation." The agreements between Lk 6:13-16 and Mt 10:2-4 "supply some evidence that Matthew and Luke had access to a list other than that of Mark." The presence of the crowds (Mt 5:1-2; 7:28-29; Lk 6:17-20; 7:1) is another coincidence which "may well be due to a similar description of the audience in Q."[26] This "evidence" of Matthew-Luke agreements is not new and has been discussed in my study of "The Transpositions in Luke" (1973).[27] R.A. Guelich is less impressed by the fact that "Matthew and Luke have the crowd(s) in the larger context": "Matthew's Q tradition specified the disciples as the actual audience," and: "In Luke the crowds are deliberately introduced into the setting from Mark 3:7-12. They interrupt the Q tradition between the call of disciples (6:12-16) and the giving of the Sermon (6:20-49)."[28] On the contrary, for K. Syreeni the

[23] For references to Kilpatrick, Polag, Schenk, see J.S. KLOPPENBORG, *Q Parallels*, 22.

[24] *Lukasevangelium*, 319, 323.

[25] T.L. DONALDSON, *Jesus on the Mountain. A Study in Matthean Theology* (JSNT SS, 8), Sheffield, 1985, 105-121, 110. Donaldson agrees about the placing of the Sermon in the Markan outline at Mk 1:21-22 (251, n. 8).

[26] *Ibid.*, 109, 110, 111.

[27] *ETL* 49 (1973), esp. 808-811 (= *Evangelica*, 761-764).

[28] R.A. GUELICH, *The Sermon on the Mount*, Waco, TX, 1982, 59-60. For the two separate traditions at work in Lk 6:12-20a, Guelich refers to Schürmann (*Lukasevangelium*, 318-319), without mentioning Schürmann's position on the influence of Q in Lk 6:17 (323: "eine Notiz über zusammenströmende Volksscharen" in Q). Compare

assumption that Q contained the call of the disciples is unprovable, and
Mk 3:13 suffices to explain the mountain setting. He proposes that the
Sermon in Q was preceded by a transitional link introducing the crowds
"in a brief summary passage with the healing of the crowds – i.e.,
something like ... Mt 4:24b/Lk 6:18."[29]

These contrasting views on the traditional setting of the Sermon in Q
have one common purpose: to explain the coincidence between Luke's
placing of the Sermon after Mk 3:7-19 on the one hand and Matthew's
use of Mk 3:7-8,13 in Mt 4:25; 5:1 on the other. But the Q origin of the
mountain setting is rejected by Donaldson, the mention of the crowds is
refused by Guelich and the call of the Twelve is unprovable for
Syreeni... All we can possibly retain from this discussion is the assumption that the Q introduction had the disciples as the audience of the
Sermon.

3. The Composition of Mt 4:23 – 8:17

The study of Mt 4:23 – 5:2 and its parallels in Mark has to face the
problem of the dismantling of Mark's Day of Capernaum and the
apparent disorder of the Matthean parallels to Mk 1:21-45. The doublet
to Mt 4:24b in 8:16 is part of the Markan context, Mk 1:29-31,32-34 /
Mt 8:14-15,16(-17). The evening in Mk 1:32-34 is the end of Jesus' day
in Capernaum. In Matthew, too, Mt 8:16 forms the conclusion of a stay
in Capernaum (cf. 8:5), but Matthew's first day of Jesus' ministry is a
much larger complex. It starts in 4:24b, after the summary statements of
4:23,24a,[30] with a first parallel to Mk 1:32,34, and the story-line
continues until 8:16, the second parallel to Mk 1:32-34. The quotation
in 8:17 marks a pause:

4:24b   καὶ προσήνεγκαν αὐτῷ ... καὶ ἐθεράπευσεν αὐτούς.
8:16   ... προσήνεγκαν αὐτῷ ... καὶ ... ἐθεράπευσεν,
17   ὅπως πληρωθῇ ...

Almost all commentators consider 8:1-17 a special section within Mt
8 – 9. The study of Matthew's sources does corroborate this position.

Guelich's observations on "the crowds" (redactional) in Mt 4:25; 5:1; 7:28: The Sermon,
49, 50-51, 417.
    [29] K. SYREENI, The Making of the Sermon on the Mount, Part I (AASF, 44), Helsinki,
1987, 121-122. In Syreeni's view "the Q passage of Mt 11,4-6/Lk 7,22-23 suggests that
Jesus' healings were reported in Q previously, just as the πτωχοι ευαγγελιζονται was
realized in Jesus' inaugural speech" (121).
    [30] Compare Lohfink's distinction between Mt 4:23-24a and 24b-25. Cf. supra, n. 18.

From 8,18 on, the Markan material comes predominantly from Mk 4:35 – 5:20,21-43, anticipated before and after Mt 9:1-17 = Mk 2:1-22. The second-source material in 8:19-22; 9:37ff. is anticipated from Lk 9:57ff. (in Q: following on Lk 7:18-35). In Mt 8:5-13, however, the Q passages are connected with a double sequence of Q in Mt 5 – 7:

Mt	5 – 7	Lk	6:20-49
	(7:13-14,22-23)		13:23-27
	8:5-10,13		7:1-10
	(8:11-12)		13:28-29.

The Markan material in Mt 8:2-4,14-16 is derived from Mk 1, in continuation of the parallels to Mk 1 before and after the Sermon. Source-critically, the material of 8:1-17 holds together with Mt 5 – 7 and the doublets of 4:24b and 8:16 form an inclusio around this larger section.

'Οψίας δὲ γενομένης in Mk 1:32 denotes the evening of the day in Capernaum, and the expression is used again in 4:35 with reference to the day of Jesus' teaching in parables. In Matthew the parallel to Mk 1:32-34 (Mt 8:16, at the conclusion of 4:24b – 8:17) is followed by the parallel to Mk 4:35ff. and there is no need to repeat ὀψίας γενομένης in 8:18.

The inverted order of Mt 8:2-4 (Mk 1:40-45) and 8:14-16 (Mk 1:29-34) can be seen in relation to the composition of Mt 8-9. The insertion of the story of the leper in between two Q texts has probably been facilitated by some analogy with the Markan context. Mk 1:40-45 is followed by Jesus' entry into Capernaum (2:1) and the healing of the paralytic (2:1-12). Matthew presents a similar sequence (8:5 = Lk 7:1 Q εἰσῆλθεν εἰς Καφαρναούμ) and in Mt 8:6 the centurion's servant (or son) is said to be παραλυτικός. A further observation can be added. Mk 2:1, Jesus' second coming to Capernaum (πάλιν), refers back to 1:21, followed by 1:29 (Jesus in the house of Peter). In Matthew, this last episode is at 8:14 (καὶ ἐλθὼν ὁ Ἰησοῦς εἰς τὴν οἰκίαν Πέτρου) and the preceding entry into Capernaum (cf. Mk 1:21) is that of Mt 8:5. Thus, the context before and after Mt 8:5-13 seems to suggest that the Q motif of Jesus' entry into Capernaum has been associated with both Mk 1:21 and 2:1:

Mk	Mt	Mk
	8:2-4—————————	1:40-45
(1:21)	8:5(-13) Q	(2:1)
1:29-34 —————	8:14-16	

4. *Mt 4:23 — 11:1 and the Relative Order of Mark*

1. First observation: the modifications of the Markan order in Matthew
are restricted to the sections of Mk 1:21 — 6:13. From Mt 14:1 / Mk
6:14 on there are no more transpositions of pericopes and only a few
changes of order within the pericopes:[31]

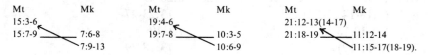

Mt	Mk	Mt	Mk	Mt	Mk
15:3-6		19:4-6		21:12-13(14-17)	
15:7-9	7:6-8	19:7-8	10:3-5	21:18-19	11:12-14
	7:9-13		10:6-9		11:15-17(18-19).

In doublets such as Mt 9:27-31; 20:29-34 (Mk 10:46-52) the original
location is preserved in Matthew and the editorial duplication is found
in the first half of the Gospel. Compare also:[32]

Mt	Mt		Mk
5:29-30	18:8-9	/	9:43, 45, 47
10:17-22	24:9-14	/	13:9-13.

2. The relative order of Mark can be observed in Mt 8:18 — 13:58, on the
one hand, in a series of transpositions (B) and, on the other, in the list of
the remaining Markan pericopes (A):[33]

---

[31] "La rédaction matthéenne (1967), 59-60 (= *Evangelica*, 21-22): "Si l'on constate
l'une ou l'autre transposition, elle se place à l'intérieur d'une péricope (ou unité littéraire)
et s'explique par un procédé de composition matthéenne qui nous servira aussi à
comprendre l'ordonnance de Mt 4:12 — 13:58. Dans la discussion sur la pureté de Mt 15,
les vv. 3-6 (Mc 7:9-13) sont avancés de manière à ce que, dans les vv. 7-9, la citation d'Is
29:13 fait presque figure de *Reflexionszitat*, comparable à Mt 13:14-15, dont on ne devrait
d'ailleurs pas mettre en doute l'authenticité. Dans la péricope sur le divorce (Mt 19:3-9),
plusieurs indices plaident en faveur de la priorité de Mc 10:2-9,10-12. Ici, les vv. 4-6 sont
anticipés, avec la répétition de ἀπ' ἀρχῆς (par manière d'inclusion) et le rapprochement
antithétique Moïse - Jésus qui nous rappelle le contexte de Mt 5:31-32. Le troisième cas se
présente au chap. 21. Matthieu organise à sa manière ce qui chez Marc est réparti sur trois
jours (Mc 11:11,12-19,20-25): la purification est rapprochée de la première visite au temple
(21:12-13), la conversation sur le figuier se trouvant ainsi immédiatement liée au récit de la
malédiction (21:18-22). Dans les trois cas, Matthieu a donc avancé quelques versets (15:3-
6; 19:4-6; 21:12-13), et c'est ce même mouvement d'anticipation que nous retrouverons
dans les transpositions de Mt 4-13."

[32] On Mt 5:29-30, cf. R.H. GUNDRY, *Matthew*, 1982, 88: "In giving us a preview of
these sayings, which he will later record in their original context, Matthew makes some
changes..."; J. GNILKA, *Das Matthäusevangelium*, I, 1986, 160: "Die Veränderungen in
5:29f gegenüber 19,8f / Mk 9,43ff lassen sich gut als MtR erklären." Contrast U. LUZ,
Matthäus, I, 1985, 261: "vermutlich nicht aus Mk, sondern anderswoher, vielleicht aus
Q"; but this is scarcely "die verbreitete Ansicht" (sic Gnilka, n. 2). – On Mt 10:17-22, cf.
infra, 123-124.

[33] Cf. "The Gospel of Matthew and Literary Criticism. A Critical Analysis of A.
Gaboury's Hypothesis" (1971), *Evangelica*, 691-723, 705-707.

Mt	Mk (A)	Mk (B)
8:18,23-34		4:35 – 5:20
9:1-17	2:1-22	
9:18-26		5:21-43
9:35		6:6b
10:1-14		6:7-11 (+ 3:16-19)
12:1-16	2:23 – 3:12	
12:24-32	3:22-30	
12:46-50	3:31-35	
13:1-35	4:1-34	
13:53-58	6:1-6a	

3. None of the transpositions in Matthew (B) corresponds to a similar alteration of the Markan order in Luke. In our hypothesis, the transpositions of individual pericopes in Luke are explicable by Lukan redaction on the basis of Mark:[34]

Mk	Lk	
1:14-15	4:14-15	4:16-30 (d)
1:16-20 (a)	——	
1:21-39	4:31-44	→ 5:1-11 (a)
1:40 – 3:6	5:12 – 6:11	
3:7-12 (b)	——	
3:13-19	6:12-16	→ 6:17-19 (b)
3:20-30		
3:31-35 (c)	——	
4:1-34	8:4-18	→ 8:19-21 (c)
4:35 – 5:43	8:22-56	
6:1-6 (d)	——	
6:7-13	9:1-6	

4. The anticipation of Markan material in Mt 8:18,23-34; 9:18-26; 9:35; 10:1-14 can be compared with a similar movement in the double-tradition material:

Mt	Lk	
5 – 7	6:20-49	
8:5-10,13	7:1-10	
8:19-22		9:57-60
9:37-38; 10:7-14		10:1-12
11:2-19	7:18-35	
11:20-24	10:13-15	

[34] Cf. *supra*, 21 (n. 32).

If we accept Lk 7:1-10,18-35 as the original sequence in Q, then Matthew returns to the order of his second source at Mt 11:2. He resumes the order of Mark at Mt 12:1 and adheres to the (remaining) Markan material in Mt 12 and 13 (and not only from 14:1 on, as is sometimes suggested).

5. The Sermon on the Mount is placed in the Markan order at Mk 1:21,[35] with a solemn summary-introduction utilizing several passages from Mk 1 and Mk 3:7-8,13; 6:6b. Mt 4:23 is repeated in 9:35 and further echoed in 11:1.

5. The Doublets of Mt 4:25 and 12:15(-16)

The doublets of Mt 4:25; 12:15 have been studied in Boismard's paper.[36] With regard to Mt 12:16 he accepts Matthew's dependence upon Mk 3:12. He compares the use of φανερόν (only here in Mt) with Mk 6:14 (φανερόν); 4:22 (φανεροῦν, φανερόν); 1:45 (φανερῶς). The injunction to silence has a more convenient context in Mark, after the confession of the unclean spirits in v. 11. It can be added that, in our hypothesis, Matthew's omission of Mk 3:11 can be compared with the omission of Mk 1:34c in Mt 8:16.

The case of Mt 12:15 is different. Mt 12:15 and 4:25 are perfectly Matthean in style and may be two occurrences of the Matthean formula rather than the reduplication of a single text. In Luke 6:17-19 the vocabulary and style are characteristically Lukan. Mk 3:7-8 is a combination of these two texts, the multitude that followed or came to him: πολὺ πλῆθος ... ἠκολούθησεν (cf. Mt) and πλῆθος πολὺ ... ἦλθον πρὸς αὐτόν (cf. Lk),[37] and the names of the regions, ἀπὸ τῆς Γαλιλαίας ... καὶ πέραν τοῦ Ἰορδάνου (Mt 4:25) and καὶ περὶ Τύρον καὶ Σιδῶνα (cf. Lk 6:17).

The alternative hypothesis is to take Mk 3:7-8 at the origin of both parallel texts. First, καὶ πολὺ πλῆθος ... ἠκολούθησεν (cf. 5:24 καὶ ἠκολούθει αὐτῷ ὄχλος πολύς) is at the origin of καὶ ἠκολούθησαν αὐτῷ ὄχλοι πολλοί in Mt 4:25 = 12:15, and ἀκούοντες ... ἦλθον πρὸς αὐτόν (following on the mention of Tyre and Sidon and the resuming πλῆθος πολύ) underlying οἳ ἦλθον ἀκοῦσαι αὐτοῦ in Lk 6:18. Boismard now raises a new objection: in Mark verbs describing the movements of the

[35] "The Sermon on the Mount in the Gospel Synopsis" (1976), Evangelica, 729-736.
[36] In this volume, 259-265: "Mc 3:7-12 et parallèles."
[37] Boismard seems to have abandoned his hypothetical reconstruction of Proto-Mark including ὄχλος πολύς from Lk 6:17 and καὶ πᾶς ὁ ὄχλος ἐζήτουν ἅπτεσθαι αὐτοῦ (Lk 6:19a). Cf. Synopse II, 122.

crowd or of a group of persons are usually not in the aorist and therefore the verbs in Mk 3:7 and 8 betray Mark's dependence on Matthew (ἠκολούθησεν) and on Luke (ἦλθον). He refers to the use of the imperfect or the present in phrases with ἀκολουθέω, ὄχλος, and ἔρχομαι: Mk 1:45; 2:13,15; 3:20; 4:1; 5:24; 6:1; 9:25; 10:1; 15:41. However, the phrase with ὄχλος cannot be isolated from its context. One of the examples is Mk 10:1b (συμπορεύονται, present) in parallel to Mt 19:2 (ἠκολούθησαν, aorist). The preceding verse 1a should be included in the comparison:

Mt 19:1-2	Mk 10:1
μετῆρεν ἀπὸ τ. Γ.	ἐκεῖθεν ἀναστὰς
καὶ ἦλθεν εἰς...	ἔρχεται εἰς...
καὶ ἠκολούθησαν...	καὶ συμπορεύονται...
καὶ ἐθεράπευσεν αὐτούς	καὶ ... ἐδίδασκεν αὐτούς.

Compare also 3:20 (συνέρχεται) and 6:1 (ἀκολουθοῦσιν), both preceded by ἔρχεται. The use of the present is not at all a specific characteristic for descriptions of the movement of the crowd. In other passages Mark uses the aorist. Boismard quotes 5:21 συνήχθη (cf. v. 24 ἠκολούθει). See also 2:2 καὶ συνήχθησαν πολλοί and 6:33 πολλοὶ ... συνέδραμον ἐκεῖ. Boismard gives special attention to the imperfect in Mk 15:41 and the aorist in the parallel text of Matthew. Again, the context should not be neglected: Mt 27:55b αἵτινες ἠκολούθησαν τῷ Ἰησοῦ ἀπὸ τῆς Γαλιλαίας διακονοῦσαι αὐτῷ (ἐν αἷς...) combines αἳ ὅτε ἦν ἐν τῇ Γαλιλαίᾳ ἠκολούθουν αὐτῷ καὶ διηκονοῦν αὐτῷ and καὶ ἄλλαι πολλαὶ *συναναβᾶσαι* αὐτῷ εἰς Ἱεροσόλυμα (Mk 15:41). In Mt 3:7-12, W. Egger notes the distinction between the use of the aorist in vv. 9-10 ("ein einmaliges Geschehen") and the imperfect in vv. 11-12 ("andauernd").[38] More correctly, the distinction can be observed between vv. 7-10a (ἀνεχώρησεν, ἠκολούθησεν, ἦλθον, εἶπεν, πολλοὺς γὰρ ἐθεράπευσεν) and vv. 10b-12 (ὥστε ἐπιπίπτειν, προσέπιπτον, ἔκραζον, ἐπετίμα). The "complexity" of the two movements in Mk 3:7-8 is in fact the artful use of an inclusio, with a double step to greater precision, from "followed" to "came to him":

> πολὺ πλῆθος ... ἠκολούθησεν
> πλῆθος πολὺ ... ἦλθον πρὸς αὐτόν.

Second, Transjordan (Mk 3:8 = Mt 4:25 καὶ πέραν τοῦ Ἰορδάνου), omitted in Lk 6:17, is never mentioned in Luke and Acts, but is it not so

---

[38] W. EGGER, *Frohbotschaft und Lehre. Die Sammelberichte des Wirkens Jesu im Markusevangelium* (FTS, 19), Frankfurt, 1976, 93.

that Luke's ἀπὸ πασῆς τῆς Ἰουδαίας here includes Galilee, Judaea as well as Transjordan? The mention of Tyre and Sidon can be retained by Luke in preparation of Lk 10:13-14 (Q), where the cities are mentioned in contrast to the Jewish cities of Chorazin and Bethsaida. The omission of Tyre and Sidon in Mt 4:25 is almost inevitable after the reference to Syria in the preceding verse (Mt 4:24a εἰς ὅλην τὴν Συρίαν, cf. Mk 1:28 εἰς ὅλην τὴν περίχωρον τῆς Γαλιλαίας).[39] Matthew also changed the order of Jerusalem and Judaea (before Transjordan) as he did in Mt 3:5 before πᾶσα ἡ περίχωρος τοῦ Ἰορδάνου (diff. Mk 1:5), and in accordance with the sequence of Judaea and Transjordan in Mk 10:1 = Mt 19:1.

Matthew's dependence on Mark, which is accepted by Boismard in Mt 12:16 (par. Mk 3:12), remains the most plausible solution also in Mt 12:15 (par. Mk 3:7-8). The vocabulary statistics, if applied to really parallel texts, seem to confirm this solution. Out of the 23 words in Mt 12:15-16, only eight do not occur in the parallel text of Mark: δέ (Mk καί), γνούς, ἐκεῖθεν (add.), αὐτῷ (add., but v. 8 πρὸς αὐτόν), ὄχλοι (Mk πλῆθος), καί (Mk γάρ), αὐτοὺς πάντας (Mk πολλούς), all distinctively "Matthean" (i.e., MtR).

Mt 12:15 reads ἠκολούθησαν - ἐθεράπευσεν, in the same order as ἠκολούθησαν and ἐθεράπευσεν in Mk 3:7-10 but with an obvious distortion of the logical order of the passage in Mark: πολλοὺς γὰρ ἐθεράπευσεν, "for he had healed many" (cf. Mt 4:24b,25: ἐθεράπευσεν - ἠκολούθησαν).

For Boismard, Mark depends upon "un texte matthéen" in Mk 3:7-8, and also in the verse preceding the summary (3:6), as can be seen in the use of the phrase with συμβούλιον and ὅπως. With regard to συμβούλιον, the reader can find in *Synopse* II the following observations, at Mt 22:15 συμβούλιον ἔλαβον (diff. Mk): "L'ultime Rédacteur matthéen ... remanie le début (vv. 15-16) de façon à introduire le thème des Pharisiens qui 'tiennent conseil' contre Jésus;" at Mt 27:7: "on peut attribuer également ce dernier récit [27:3-10] à l'ultime Rédacteur matthéen. L'analyse du vocabulaire le confirme. ... Au v. 7, 'tenir conseil' (*symboulion lambanein*) est propre à Mt"; at Mt 28:12: "Ce récit [28:11-15] est tout entier de la main de l'ultime Rédacteur matthéen. Au v. 12, il reprend la formule très matthéenne 'tenir conseil' (*symboulion lambanein*)."[40] This "Matthean" formula in 22:15; 27:7; 28:12 is from the Matthean redactor. The two other occurrences of

[39] Cf. *supra*, n. 18.
[40] *Synopse* II, 346, 411, 447.

συμβούλιον λαμβάνειν are Mt 27:1 συμβούλιον ἔλαβον (Mk 15:1 συμβούλιον ποιήσαντες, var. ἑτοιμάσαντες T h S M N) and Mt 12:14 συμβούλιον ἔλαβον (Mk 3:6 συμβούλιον ἐδίδουν, var. ἐποίησαν, ἐποίουν). Matthean usage, indeed, but redactional usage! We can add the use of συνεβουλεύσαντο in Mt 26:4: although the verb is unique in Matthew, there is no reason to deny its Matthean (redactional) character.[41] The conjunction ὅπως is used 17 times in Matthew. Five occurrences are found in the same context of Mt 6:2,4,5,16,18 (peculiar to Matthew); compare 5:16 (redactional?).[42] See also 2:8. Three instances are found in double-tradition passages: once, in 9:38, with parallel in Luke, but probably redactional in 5:45 (Lk καί) and 23:35 (Lk ἵνα). The formula ὅπως πληρωθῇ in 2:23; 8:17; 13:35 "est certainement de l'ultime Rédacteur matthéen". Besides Mt 12:14 (= Mk 3:6) there are three occurrences in Markan material and in all three the use of ὅπως can be editorial: Mt 8:34 (Mk infinitive); 22:15 (συμβούλιον ἔλαβον ὅπως, cf. Mk 12:13 ἵνα); 26:59 (Mk εἰς τό + infinitive). It is only by using "Matthean" indiscriminately for Matthean tradition and Matthean redaction[43] that can be argued for Proto-Matthew in Mt 12:14 / Mk 3:6.

Boismard proposes a similar argument with reference to ἀνεχώρησεν (Mt 12:15 / Mk 3:7): ten occurrences of the verb ἀναχωρεῖν in Matthew and unique in Mark. But *Synopse* II assigns six instances to the "ultime Rédacteur matthéen" (2:12,13,14,22; 4:12; 27:5) and only four to "Mt-intermédiaire," including the less characteristic use of the imperative ἀναχωρεῖτε in 9:24 (diff. Mk). In Mt 14:13, after the death of John the Baptist, ἀκούσας δὲ ὁ Ἰησοῦς ἀνεχώρησεν ἐκεῖθεν (diff. Mk 6:32 καὶ ἀπῆλθον) corresponds to 4:12 ἀκούσας δέ (ὅτι Ἰωάννης παρεδόθη) ἀνεχώρησεν (diff. Mk 1:14; cf. Mt 2:22).[44] The two remaining instances, Mt 12:15 and 15:21a, are supposed to be reduplications of a unique Proto-Matthean summary:[45]

καὶ ἐξελθὼν ἐκεῖθεν	15:21a
ὁ Ἰησοῦς ἀνεχώρησεν	21a
παρὰ τὴν θάλασσαν τῆς Γαλιλαίας	29b

---

[41] Ctr. *Synopse* II, 370; *Synopse* III, 296.

[42] According to Boismard (*Synopse* II, 132; cf. *infra*, *112*), a more original version of Mt 5:16 is preserved in Justin and 1 Pet 2:12: both read ἵνα for Matthew's ὅπως! On the "Mattheanisms" in Mt 6:1-18, cf. *ETL* 63 (1987), 412.

[43] Cf. *supra*, 9 (n. 7), on Matthew's use of ἀναχωρεῖν.

[44] Cf. *infra*, 91, n. 19.

[45] The first element of the summary (= Mt 15:21a, 29b) is redactionally omitted before Mt 4:25 – 5:2. Compare Matthew's use of Mk 3:7b-8, without v. 7a, in our hypothesis.

If in Mt 12,15, as suggested in *Synopse* II, both the addition of γνούς (cf. ἀκούσας in 4:12; 14:13) and the omission of παρὰ τὴν θάλασσαν... (cf. Mk 3:7 πρὸς τὴν θάλασσαν) are redactional, I see no reason why the text of Mk 3:7 should be refused as the source of Mt 12:15.[46]

6. Conclusion

It appears from our analysis that Mt 4:23-24a.24b-25; 5:1-2 forms a compositional unit and can be placed in the Markan order at Mk 1:21. The Markan parallels at Mk 1:39 and 3:7b-8, which are noted in all Synopses, can be explained as "anticipations" together with other summary-like elements from Mark:

Mt	4:23	Mk	(1:21) 1:39	6:6b	(1:15)
	4:24a		1:28		
	4:24b		1:32,34		
	4:25		1:7b-8		
	5:1		3:13		
	5:2		1:21		
	7:28-29		1:22		

One could call Mt 4:23 – 5:2 a collection of all summaries found in Mk 1:14 through 3:13-19,[47] but this is not an adequate description of Matthew's deliberate composition. The parallel in Mk 6:6b should not be neglected. The repetition of Mt 4:23 in 9:35 (cf. 10:1; 11:1) clearly indicates that Mt 4:23ff. is not simply the introduction to the Sermon on the Mount, or the beginning of 4:23 – 9:34. The story-line shows a division from 4:24b to 8:16(-17). The theme of discipleship is undeniably present in 8:18-27 (8:19-22 / Lk 9:57-60 Q) and prepares for the Sermon in chapter 10. Mt 9:35 – 11:1 should be included in the larger compositional unit, Mt 4:23 – 11:1.[48]

F. NEIRYNCK

---

[46] Cf. *supra*, "Introduction," p. 9, n. 7.

[47] Cf. J. LANGE, *Das Erscheinen*, 402: "So findet sich von Mk 1,14 bis Mk 3,8 kein Summarium oder etwas vergleichbares, das Mattäus nicht herangezogen und verwendet hätte bei der Formung seines Großsummariums Mt 4,23-25."

[48] Cf. F. NEIRYNCK, "ΑΠΟ ΤΟΤΕ ΗΡΞΑΤΟ and the Structure of Matthew," *ETL* 64 (1988) 21-59, esp. 59: "all dislocations of Markan pericopes in Mt are found in 4:23 – 11:1 and nowhere else. Mt 4,23 – 11,1 is a unique editorial construct in the Gospel, a typical Matthean composition."

RESPONSE TO THE TWO-GOSPEL HYPOTHESIS

I

THE POSITION PAPER*

The *Position Paper* prepared by the team defending the Two-Gospel Hypothesis (2GH) puts forward a number of general arguments in favour of the hypothesis. This Response attempts to reply to some of the general points raised here from the side of the Two-Document Hypothesis (2DH).

1. *External Evidence*

The importance of patristic testimony as evidence favouring the 2GH is strongly asserted in the *Position Paper* (cf. pp. 125-130, 145-146), and elsewhere advocates of the 2GH claim that this testimony constitutes one of the two "foundational pillars" on which the hypothesis rests (see the discussion of the Eschatological Discourse, in this volume on p. 200). It may therefore be appropriate to devote some space in this Response to a consideration of that testimony.

One of the most important pieces of evidence is seen by the advocates of the 2GH in the statement by Clement of Alexandria (recorded by Eusebius in *E.H.* VI.14.5-7) about the "order" (τάξις) of the gospels, to the effect that the gospels with genealogies were written first. This implies that Matthew and Luke were written before Mark. Further, the antiquity of this tradition is attested by the fact that Clement is not simply voicing his own opinion here but claims to be reproducing the testimony of the "primitive elders". Such a view about the relative order of the gospels remained current, being supported by the Monarchian Prologue to Mark and the 9th century writer Sedulius Scotus.

* *Position Paper by the Team Defending the Two-Gospel Hypothesis* by W.R. Farmer (ed.), with D.L. Dungan, A. McNicol, B. Orchard, D. Peabody. This Response was originally prepared for discussion at the Symposium in Jerusalem and has been only slightly modified to take account of small changes made in the *Position Paper* itself. Cf. in this volume, pp. 125-156: "The Statement of the Hypothesis."

It was also probably the view of Augustine.[1] Much of this evidence is however of rather uncertain value.

1. *Clement*. The witness of Clement is not unambiguous. As we have it, the relevant sentence is a claim of the "primitive elders" reported by Clement who in turn is being reported by Eusebius. There are thus at least two stages in the alleged chain of reporting and at neither stage can we be sure that we have a direct citation of the earlier person(s) involved. Certainly Eusebius records Clement's statement only in indirect speech. G. Kennedy points out that this may have obscured Clement's meaning: the δέ in the following sentence about Mark's origins may not be adversative at all, and the temporal contrast intended by Clement may not have been between Matthew-Luke and Mark-John but between Matthew-Mark-Luke and John.[2] This view has received further support from H. Merkel[3] who argues persuasively that the long statement by Clement about Mark may be of separate origin: it is quite unrelated to the other statements in the context (the statement about gospels with genealogies which precedes it, and the statement about John writing a spiritual gospel which follows), both of which involve contrasts between different gospels. Hence the long statement about Mark's origins is probably a secondary insertion into a single statement which involved the claim that (a) gospels with genealogies came first, (b) John came last writing a spiritual gospel in contrast to the earlier ones. As such, this claim is then simply contrasting John and the Synoptics and it says nothing about intra-synoptic relationships.[4]

Other interpretations have been suggested. F. Neirynck points out that Th. Zahn took Clement's statement as possibly implying that

---

[1] See *Position Paper*, p. 130. The *Position Paper* is to large extent summarising the more detailed essays in W.R. Farmer (ed.), *New Synoptic Studies* (Macon: Mercer University, 1983) by W.R. Farmer, "The Patristic Evidence Reexamined: A Response to George Kennedy" (pp. 3-15); G. Gamba, "A Further Reexamination of Evidence from the Early Tradition" (pp. 17-35); D. Peabody, "Augustine and the Augustinian Hypothesis: A Reexamination of Augustine's Thought in *De Consensu Evangelistarum*" (pp. 37-64).

[2] G. Kennedy, "Classical and Christian Source Criticism", in W.O. Walker (ed.), *The Relationships among the Gospels* (San Antonio: Trinity University, 1978), p. 150.

[3] H. Merkel, "Clemens Alexandrinus über die Reihenfolge der Evangelien," *ETL* 60 (1984) 382-5.

[4] The separate origin of Clement's statement about Mark is also supported by Farmer ("Patristic Evidence", p. 8), though Farmer claims that the first statement by Clement here, i.e. the assertion that gospels with genealogies were written first, is independent of the statement about John and hence does refer to intra-synoptic relationships.

Matthew came before Mark, and Luke before John.[5] One may also note possible ambiguity in the phrase "the gospels with genealogies". No doubt Eusebius, in recording Clement's statement, thought that Clement was referring to Matthew and Luke. But in view of Clement's readiness to use other gospels we cannot be so confident that this was Clement's own meaning.[6] In any case Clement's witness is preserved for us only as a fragment of a lost longer work, and we thus have no means of discovering the wider context. Moreover, the value of this work, the *Hypotyposeis*, is rather dubious. The only person in antiquity to write about the whole work from first hand knowledge of it was Photius; but Photius said that it contained such an extraordinary mixture of myths and fables that he regarded it as inauthentic.[7]

It is thus probably highly precarious to build too much on an isolated sentence whose meaning is so uncertain.

2. *The Monarchian Prologues and Sedulius Scotus.* Although the Monarchian Prologue to Mark is often thought to support the 2GH, one must again exercize critical caution. The key phrase is the claim in the Prologue that Mark omitted the story of Jesus' birth "quam in prioribus viderat"; possibly too the reference earlier in the prologue to the "word" "quod in consonantibus perdiderat" is also relevant. In his later commentary on the prologue, Sedulius Scotus interpreted both "in prioribus" and "in consonantibus" as referring to the two gospels of Matthew and Luke.[8]

The Latin text of these prologues is notoriously obscure, but it is almost certain that Scotus' interpretation of "in consonantibus" is wrong. Chapman calls it a "brilliant conjecture" but "quite impossible". Rather, the reference is to the consonants of the alphabet as opposed to the vowels: the latter represent the Word, present in men but now hidden under the flesh, represented by the consonants.[9] The phrase "in prioribus viderat" presents more problems. Some have taken "in prioribus" as referring to the gospels of Matthew and Luke. There is however a well-attested variant reading of "vicerat" for "viderat"

---

[5] See p. 605 in this volume; cf. Th. Zahn, *Einleitung in das Neue Testament* 2. Band (Leipzig, 1907³), p. 156.

[6] Cf. H. von Campenhausen, *The Formation of the Christian Bible* (Philadelphia: Fortress, 1972), p. 294: Clement "has no misgivings about employing other, 'apocryphal' Gospels (though he does not call them that) to supplement them [i.e. the four canonical gospels]".

[7] Cited in J. Quasten, *Patrology* II (Westminster, Maryland: Newman, 1962), p. 17.

[8] Migne, *P.L.* 103, col. 283.

[9] J. Chapman, *Notes on the Early History of the Vulgate Gospels* (Oxford: Clarendon, 1908), p. 234; see also J. Regul, *Die antimarcionitischen Evangelienprologe* (Freiburg: Herder, 1969), p. 246.

and Chapman argues that viderat is "an obvious correction for the difficult vicerat".[10] However, it is not easy to make much sense of the phrase "in prioribus vicerat" if the "prioribus" are Matthew and Luke. More convincing is the interpretation of Chapman, who takes "in prioribus" as a reference to the opening verses of Mark's gospel itself. He paraphrases the argument of the prologue thus:

> Mark ... did not trouble to recount the birth of the flesh which *in prioribus* — "in his opening paragraphs" — he has conquered, viz., by declaring that the beginning of the Gospel was (not the flesh, the consonants, but) the voice, the divine soul.[11]

This interpretation has the merit of giving more sense to the phrase within its wider context. It also implies that the crucial phrase is quite unrelated to the question of the relative order of the gospels. Thus the Monarchian prologue gives only doubtful support to the 2GH. Any support may only arise from a textual variant in the later tradition.

With this in mind, the value of the witness of Sedulius Scotus also becomes rather questionable. Scotus is commenting on the Monarchian prologues and struggling (on his own admission) to make sense of the text. Certainly Scotus' evidence may show that Clement's testimony (if that indeed is what Scotus is referring to when he says "ut ecclesiastica dicit historia") was remembered. Whether it was actually believed is another matter. There is no justification for saying that this evidence shows that "Scottus makes this view (i.e. that Mark wrote after Matthew and Luke) his own" (*Position Paper*, p. 126). For in his commentary on the prologue to Luke, Scotus accepts without demur the assertion that Luke's gospel was written after Matthew and Mark.[12] It is more likely, bearing in mind Scotus' other writings, that Scotus himself accepted the standard view that the gospels were written in the order Matthew-Mark-Luke.[13] Scotus' allusion to Clement's statement may thus simply be an attempt to make some sort of sense of his, possibly corrupted, text of the prologue to Mark.[14]

3. *Augustine.* The evidence of Augustine is also ambiguous. The *Position Paper* cites the text at the end of Augustine's *De Consensu Evangelistarum* (4.10.11) where Augustine, having mentioned the view

---

[10] Chapman, *op.cit.*, p. 234; cf. too Regul, *op.cit.*, p. 48. The argument in the *Position Paper* appears to assume the reading *viderat* without any question.

[11] *Op.cit.*, p. 234.

[12] *P.L.* 103, col. 287. Cf. Gamba, "Early Tradition", p. 24.

[13] Gamba also refers to Scotus' other writings (*P.L.* 103, cols. 331 ff.) where Scotus does not record any difficulty about accepting the view that the order of the gospels was Matthew-Mark-Luke.

[14] Scotus assumes the reading *viderat*, not *vicerat*.

that Mark came second and abbreviated Matthew, regards it as "more probable" that Mark "holds a course in conjunction with both (i.e. Matthew and Luke)" "cum ambobus incedit". The interpretation of this single clause does not however clearly support the 2GH. In fact, by this stage in his argument, Augustine seems to be no longer considering the personal relationships between the evangelists. Rather he is considering the thematic and symbolic relationships between the gospels. Mark is represented by the figure of a man, Matthew by a lion and Luke by a calf, the latter two representing the royal and priestly natures of Christ respectively. Mark's combining Matthew and Luke means that Christ's manhood combines his royal and priestly natures. It is this last claim which Augustine is really interested in at this point in his argument and he is unconcerned about the personal relationships involved.[15] Further, Augustine regards it as preferable, theologically, to view Mark as uniting Matthew and Luke. (This is more likely to be the force of the phrase "quod probabilius intelligentur": it is a judgement about the symbolic relationships, not about personal details of the evangelists.) Augustine's own views of the personal relationships between the evangelists had already been given in the earlier part of the work (1.2.4). There is nothing in the later context to compel the belief that Augustine held any other view than that traditionally associated with his name., that the gospels were written in the order Matthew-Mark-Luke.

4. *Other Factors.* Further appeal is made by the *Position Paper* to explain why the original order of Matthew-Luke-Mark was altered to Matthew-Mark-Luke, referring in particular to the reaction against Marcion (see p. 127).

This is not easy to substantiate. The order Matthew-Mark-Luke-John is said to be the order "in which the Anti-Marcionite bishops wanted the Gospels to be read" (p. 127) with the "apostolic" gospels (Matthew and John) enclosing the other two. There is, however, little if any evidence that the Gospels were required to be read in their entirety in their canonical order. It is also hard to see how such a "sand-

---

[15] Pace Peabody (as in n. 1). Peabody provides a detailed analysis of the logic of Augustine's argument, and claims that Augustine is giving two closely parallel arguments involving the personal, symbolic and thematic relationships between the gospels and the evangelists: hence the claim that Mark "cum ambobus incedit" is precisely parallel to the earlier view about the personal relationship that Mark was Matthew's "comes". However, the arguments are not precisely parallel. Earlier Augustine deduced the personal relationship on the basis of textual and thematic considerations. In his later argument, Augustine makes the thematic claim as a consequence of the assertion that Mark "cum ambobus incedit". Thus, pace Peabody, it is unlikely that we can take this latter claim as precisely parallel to the earlier assertion (that Mark was Matthew's *comes*) and deduce that both are statements at the same level.

wiching" really effects anything. Further, it has no relevance to the question of whether the order should be Mark-Luke or Luke-Mark. How much of this is anti-Marcionite is also uncertain. It should be noted that the present canonical order of the gospels was not universally held, even by the "orthodox", especially in the West where many old latin MSS have the order Matthew-John-Luke-Mark.[16] Tertullian too can refer to the gospels in this order. For Tertullian, writing explicitly against Marcion, there may be a distinction between gospels written by apostles and those written by disciples of apostles. But the order within the latter group seems to be less important and Tertullian can use both orders Mark-Luke and Luke-Mark happily.[17] It is easy to see how the status of Luke in relation to Matthew and John might have been an issue in the anti-Marcionite reaction (cf. *Adv.Marc.* IV.2.2,4). But it is difficult to see how the relative order of Mark and Luke would have been an issue.

The *Position Paper* also appeals to the "'Salvation History' consciousness of the Anti-Marcionite Catholic Church" (p. 127), whereby the Petrine gospel of Mark precedes the Pauline gospel of Luke, since Peter preceded, and had precedence over, Paul. This is, however, difficult to document. At one point, in arguing against Marcion Tertullian does refer to the fact that Paul was the last apostle to be converted (*Adv.Marc.* IV.2.4f.). But it is unlikely that this is seriously meant to downgrade Paul or Luke,[18] or to give any preference for Mark over against Luke. In fact this is the context where Tertullian uses the order John-Matthew-Luke-Mark (*Adv.Marc.* IV.2.1.). Only in a later context (IV.5.3) does he reverse the order of the last two gospels. The point about Paul is simply a debating point and is in no way related by Tertullian to the relative merits of Luke and Mark.

5. *Other Evidence.* Other patristic testimony almost unanimously supports the view that the gospels are written in the order Matthew-Mark-Luke-John. As is well known, Irenaeus can enumerate the gospels in varying orders, but in his discussion in *A.H.* III.1.1, the order Matthew-Mark-Luke-John is "obviously intended as a chronological order".[19] Origen's statement about the gospels in his *Commentary on Matthew* (in *E.H.* VI.25.3-6) speaks of the gospels in terms of πρῶτον

---

[16] Cf. Regul, *op.cit.*, p. 214.

[17] *Adv.Marc.* IV.2.1-5; IV.5.3.

[18] Cf. von Campenhausen, *op. cit.*, p. 282: "all this is so much polemical swordplay. It is not Tertullian's custom elsewhere to pay less attention to Luke than to Matthew, or to demote Paul to a status below that of the first apostles."

[19] Pace Farmer, "Patristic Evidence", p. 13f.

Matthew, δεύτερον Mark, τρίτον Luke and then finally John. The clear sequence implied means that this is almost certainly meant to be a statement about the relative dates of the gospels.[20] Similarly Eusebius accepts without demur the order Matthew-Mark-Luke-John in his discussion of the gospels (*E.H.* III.23). This view of the order of the gospels is also that of Jerome (*Prol.Quatt.Evang.*), the Monarchian prologues (or at least the prologue to Luke: cf. above) and Epiphanius (*Haer.* VI.10ff.).

Practically all the patristic evidence favouring the 2GH derives from the single sentence of Clement. Clement's other remarks about Mark in the same context (that Mark was written during Peter's lifetime) scarcely inspire confidence. There does not seem sufficient evidence to warrant altering the conclusion drawn recently:

> Clement's statement is very much out on a limb as far as the patristic evidence is concerned. Farmer's own earlier judgment on this evidence seems much more justifiable, when he refers to the "almost unanimous tradition of the early church fathers, that the gospels were written in the order Matthew, Mark, Luke and John".[21]

A final observation about the value of this patristic evidence may be in order. Two quite separate problems should be carefully distinguished. There is first the problem of determining just what the patristic evidence is: did Augustine, or Sedulius Scotus, believe that Mark used Matthew and Luke? Such questions involve the exegesis of the patristic texts themselves. But there is then a quite different problem of how one should evaluate the views of the church fathers. Some patristic writers may have been Griesbachians before Griesbach, but how are we to determine whether they were right? The answer to the last question can only be determined by critical study of the gospel texts themselves. Patristic evidence may have confirmatory value when coupled with arguments based on an analysis of the gospel material, but it can do no more than that. Patristic statements about the gospels do not in general inspire confidence with regard to their accuracy in the light of critical scholarship. We should therefore perhaps give more weight to study of the gospel texts themselves in seeking to determine the interrelationships between the gospels.

---

[20] Again this is denied by Farmer, "Patristic Evidence", p. 13f; but it is difficult to deny the chronological meaning of the initial πρῶτον which then determines the meaning of the subsequent δεύτερον and τρίτον as temporal.

[21] C.M. Tuckett, *The Revival of the Griesbach Hypothesis* (Cambridge: University Press, 1983), p. 60, citing W.R. Farmer, "A 'Skeleton in the Closet' of Gospel Research", *Biblical Research* 6 (1961), p. 28.

2. *Order*

The second of the "foundational pillars" on which the 2GH rests is said to be "the internal evidence of the order of pericopes" (see the discussion of the Eschatological Discourse, p. 213 in this volume), and arguments based on order are referred to at a number of points in the *Position Paper* (pp. 142-143). The issue has however been fully debated in recent scholarly literature,[22] and is also discussed in F. Neirynck's article in this volume (pp. 7, 19-22). The arguments concerned therefore do not need repeating in full here. The basis for the argument from order to support the 2GH is the phenomenon of the lack of agreement between Matthew and Luke against Mark in order. (The question of the extent and significance of possible exceptions to this general rule need not be discussed here.[23]) It is claimed that this phenomenon is best explained by the theory that Mark follows the order of his two (presumed) sources alternately. This evidence is clearly regarded as extremely important by advocates of the 2GH.[24]

It is, however, doubtful if this phenomenon can prove very much either way. The phenomenon in question, the absence of Matthew-Luke agreements against Mark, is in fact the basis of the famous "Lachmann fallacy" to support the 2DH.[25] Certainly since Butler's analysis of this "fallacy", the inconclusive nature of the argument to support Markan

---

[22] From the side of the 2GH, see W.R. Farmer, *The Synoptic Problem* (New York: Macmillan, 1964); "The Two-Document Hypothesis as a Methodological Criterion in Synoptic Research", *ATR* 48 (1966) 380-396, esp. 387-9; "The Lachmann Fallacy", *NTS* 14 (1968) 441-443; "Modern Developments of Griesbach's Hypothesis", *NTS* 23 (1977) 275-295, esp. 293-5; H.H. Stoldt, *Geschichte und Kritik der Markushypothese* (Göttingen: Vandenhoeck & Ruprecht, 1977), pp. 125-144; D.L. Dungan, "A Griesbachian Perspective on the Argument from Order", in C.M. Tuckett (ed.), *Synoptic Studies* (Sheffield: JSOT, 1984), pp. 67-74. From the side of the 2DH, see F. Neirynck, "The Argument from Order and St. Luke's Transpositions", *ETL* 49 (1973) 784-815; "The Griesbach Hypothesis: The Phenomenon of Order", *ETL* 58 (1982) 111-122; C.M. Tuckett, "The Argument from Order and the Synoptic Problem", *TZ* 36 (1980) 338-354; *Revival*, pp. 26-31; "Arguments from Order: Definition and Evaluation", *Synoptic Studies*, pp. 197-219.

[23] Cf. E.P. Sanders, "The Argument from Order and the Relationship between Matthew and Luke", *NTS* 15 (1969) 249-261, and the reply in Neirynck, "Argument from Order", 786ff. See too Neirynck's observations in this volume, esp. pp. 19-20.

[24] The *Position Paper* calls it a "prime reason" for regarding Mark as third (p. 134); the Eschatological Discourse paper here describes it as one of the two "foundational pillars" on which the hypothesis rests (cf. above). See also earlier Farmer, "Modern Developments", 280: the phenomenon of order is the 2GH's "central and essential strength"; also 293: the failure of Matthew and Luke to agree against Mark can "only" be explained by Mark being third. "There seems to be no other satisfactory solution."

[25] See Neirynck, "Phenomenon of Order", 121; also Tuckett, "Arguments from Order", 205f.

priority has been recognized: the evidence is ambiguous and allows a variety of hypotheses, i.e. any hypothesis which places Mark in a "medial" position.[26] Such a possibility includes the 2DH, the 2GH and the Augustinian hypothesis. But Butler's analysis was essentially unrelated to the 2DH itself: he simply showed that the facts in question can be explained by a number of hypotheses and it is logically fallacious to assume that one and only one hypothesis can adequately explain them. Thus any claim that the facts are explicable by one and only one hypothesis is a logical fallacy, whatever that hypothesis is. The assertion in the *Position Paper* that the argument from order for the 2GH is one "which would be very difficult to explain equally well in reverse order" (p. 144) is effectively making such a claim; it is thus open to the criticism that it represents a revival of the Lachmann fallacy in a slightly different form.[27]

At another point in the *Position Paper* it is implicitly conceded that the 2DH can also explain the facts in question, but in a less satisfactory way: unlike the 2GH which can explain the phenomenon of order by "authorial intent" (i.e. by Mark's editorial decision to follow the order of Matthew and Luke in turn), the 2DH has to "resort to the less satisfactory appeal to a literary accident due to random chance" to explain the absence of Matthew-Luke agreements against Mark in order (*Position Paper*, p. 142). The claim that such an appeal to random chance is less satisfactory is not easy to sustain. The probability that the number of changes in order between Matthew and Mark and between Luke and Mark could have occurred by "random chance" and never coincided is in fact relatively high. One estimate is a probability of over 0.7.[28] *If* the changes in order were due to random chance, the absence of Matthew-Luke agreements against Mark would thus be entirely as expected. There is therefore no difficulty for the 2DH in explaining this phenomenon in relation to the order of events in the gospels. The

[26] B.C. Butler, *The Originality of St. Matthew* (Cambridge: University Press, 1951), pp. 62-71.

[27] Neirynck, "Phenomenon of Order", 113; Tuckett, "Arguments from Order", 206.

[28] For details, see Tuckett, "Arguments from Order", 204f. According to one way of describing the parallels between the gospels (and hence of describing the differences in order), Matthew and Mark differ in the ordering of 6 pericopes, Luke and Mark in 4 pericopes. On the 2DH, the probability that these will not coincide, assuming that the changes are due to random chance, is about 0.7. The mathematical model is of course absurdly simplistic: one can scarcely assume that the reordering of material by a later evangelist is due to "random chance". However, without such an assumption the model would become almost impossibly complex mathematically. The figures are simply produced to counter the claim that the failure of Matthew and Luke to agree in changing the order of Mark, on the 2DH, is too coincidental to be credible.

appeal to order is thus entirely reversible and in no way supports the 2GH as against other competing hypotheses.

One other point about arguments from order should also be noted here. The *Position Paper* argues that only the 2GH adequately explains the *whole* pattern of arrgements in order between *all three gospels together*.[29] The 2DH splits the evidence up by comparing at most two of the gospels with each other and explaining their agreements and disagreements, but the three-fold pattern of agreements remain unexplained. Such an argument is however scarcely compelling, since it assumes, almost a priori, what is to be proved, i.e. that there really is a *three*-fold literary relationship between the gospels. It is this which is asserted by the 2GH and denied by the 2DH. It is true that a modern synopsis displays a three-fold pattern of agreements, but there is no firm evidence that such a pattern corresponds directly to historical realities. It may well be that such a pattern is the result of the work of modern synopsis makers. The *Position Paper*'s defence of its theory rests on the claim that the agreements between the gospels should be explained, if possible, without appealing to hypothetical sources, and this demands that the evangelist who wrote third must have had both his predecessors' works available to him. However, the propriety of refusing to appeal to hypothetical sources is somewhat dubious when examined critically. This whole issue will be discussed further below (see Section 6). As will be seen there, the 2GH implicitly makes just as extensive appeal to other sources to explain the gospel material as the 2DH. It is thus doubtful if this criticism by advocates of the 2GH of explanations of the order in the gospels from the side of the 2DH can be sustained.

3. *The Gospels in Their Historical Context*

The final section of the *Positon Paper* presents an account of each gospel, assuming the order Matthew-Luke-Mark, setting each gospel in a proposed Sitz im Leben. The argument is given in very general terms and, as an analysis of the Sitz im Leben of each gospel, could be questioned at a number of points.[30] However, the proposed settings of the three gospels are not tied to any particular period within first-

---

[29] Cf. the *Position Paper*, p. 142 (in this volume, pp. 133-134); also Dungan (as in n. 22).

[30] For example, the section on Matthew suggests that Matthew's gospel is intended to appease hostile Jews; but it is doubtful how far Mt 23 could easily function as appeasing non-Christian Jews.

century Christianity, and hence do not really affect the issue of the relative datings of the gospels. Jewish persecution of Christians (the proposed setting of Matthew's community) continued from the very earliest period (cf. Paul's pre-Christian persecutions of the church) to at least as late as the second Jewish revolt under Bar Cochba (cf. Justin, *1 Apol.* 31). Roman persecution (faced by Mark's community) was an intermittent feature of the earliest period (cf. 2 Cor 11:23) as well as later. The proposed settings for the gospels could thus be placed quite easily relatively early, or relatively late, in the first century. They therefore probably do not have much bearing on the more limited question of the interrelationships between the gospels and their relative datings.

4. *Criteria*

As part of its "overview" of the 2GH, the *Position Paper* proposes a number of criteria for distinguishing primary and secondary traditions (see section B, pp. 139-141). The criteria are not new. They were enunciated by Farmer in his book of 1964 and, as such, they have been discussed elsewhere.[31]

The first criterion states that traditions which reflect a Jewish or Palestinian milieu are more original. This seems to assume a unilinear development by which Christianity spread out from Palestine into the Hellenistic world (almost, one might conclude, never to return), so that a geographical milieu is taken as an indication of relative temporal priority. Such a criterion appears to ignore the continued existence of Jewish, Palestinian Christianity over the whole period of the writing of the gospels; also the possibility of a tradition being rejudaised is not considered. The second criterion refers to the presence of redactional glosses as indicative of a secondary text. But whether such a text is secondary to, and dependent on, a parallel text lacking such glosses is by no means certain. The presence of glosses in a gospel may indicate something of the geographical and sociological milieu for which that gospel was written; but, as before, one cannot necessarily make a precise correlation between geographical and temporal differences. "Explanatory glosses may thus say more about the different intended audiences of the gospel writers that about their relative dates."[32]

---

[31] Farmer, *Synoptic Problem*, p. 227f.; cf. Tuckett, *Revival*, pp. 10ff.
[32] Tuckett, *Revival*, p. 10.

The section on the application of these criteria is couched in very wide-ranging terms, with some rather general claims being made. For example, the *Position Paper* claims that

> There is a general tendency for the Matthean form of sayings of Jesus to be free from words or phrases clearly attributable to the final redactor, and [for the Matthean form of these sayings] to be completely conformable to a Palestinian and Jewish cultural milieu.... The Jesus tradition in Matthew is seldom glossed or modified by the Evangelist. (p. 140)

However, many would regard the fact that the Matthean form of some of the sayings of Jesus fits into a Jewish milieu better as due to Matthew's rejudaising of the tradition. Moreover, many would dispute whether Matthew's gospel is as free from redactional glosses as the above statement implies. There will obviously be debate about what can be "clearly" seen as MattR, but what of the reference to δικαιοσύνη in Mt 5:6, or the fact that the Prophets and the Law "prophesy" in Mt 11:13, or all the formula quotations? (The latter are not strictly part of "sayings" of Jesus, but such limitation of the synoptic evidence seems rather arbitrary; texts like Mt 8:17; 12:17-21; 21:4f are all "glosses", probably due to MattR, and occurring in triple tradition passages.) What too of Mt 12:11, where the assumption of Matthew's version of the saying (i.e. that drawing an animal out of a pit was a justifiable breach of the Sabbath law) does not fit very easily into a Palestinian milieu?[33] What too of the fact that Matthew seems generally unaware of the differences between the various groupings within Judaism at the time of Jesus?[34] The consideration of Matthew's text probably needs a more detailed analysis to be useful in the present context.

It may also be worth noting that one assumption, implicitly built in to the criteria proposed, is that the original tradition of Jesus' sayings was entirely conformable with Judaism. Other critics would argue that precisely where a form of the tradition shows Jesus not conforming with Jewish presuppositions, then just for that reason is it likely to be original.[35] Forms of the tradition which make Jesus' sayings more "Jewish" would be seen by many as secondary attempts to modify the radicalness of the more original form of the tradition.

---

[33] See Tuckett, *Revival*, p.97f., for more details; also G. Strecker, *Der Weg der Gerechtigkeit* (Göttingen: Vandenhoeck & Ruprecht, 1962), p. 19.

[34] Cf. R. Walker, *Die Heilsgeschichte im ersten Evangelium* (Göttingen: Vandenhoeck & Ruprecht, 1967).

[35] I.e. the so-called "criterion of dissimilarity".

5. Q

At a number of points in the *Position Paper*, and also in the paper discussing the Eschatological Discourse, reference is made to the implications of the relevant discussion for the so-called "double tradition", usually called "Q" on the 2DH.

According to the 2GH, "Q" had no real existence: "Q" is simply that body of material which Luke took from Matthew and which Mark (for whatever reason) did not subsequently re-use. Some other points are made about this material, and its possibly characteristic features, in the *Position Paper*. These characteristics are said to arise from "the fact that Luke selected from Matthew only material which was useful for his Gentile readers". Q "is generally free of Jewish *Tendenz* which would be offensive to Gentile readers". Q is thus basically Luke's choice of material, and so Q's alleged theology is really Lukan theology: "'Q' is more representative of Luke's version of the Jesus tradition than it is of Jesus himself." (See below, p. 143.)

All this would be more convincing if recent studies of the theology of Q had produced a theology that was basically Lukan. But this is scarcely the case. Parts of Q show a markedly strong Jewish *Tendenz* particularly in its attitude to the Jewish Law (cf. Mt 5:18/Lk 16:17; Mt 23:23d/Lk 11:42d).[36] So too the "Wisdom Christology", often thought to be one of the most distinctive feature of the Q material, can hardly be said to be very characteristic of Luke since it does not recur outside the Q passages concerned (Mt 11:19/Lk 7:35; Mt 23:34/Lk 11:49).

In the detailed discussion of the Eschatological Discourse by advocates of the 2GH, the Q hypothesis is questioned at a number of points on the grounds that advocates of the 2DH have to posit an overlap between Mark an Q which then makes Q effectively one of Mark's sources:

> If a hypothetical document is reconstructed by concentrating on material which is not in Mark, then that hypothetical document cannot at the same time, be one of Mark's sources. (p. 167)
> "Q", by definition, is material common to Matthew and Luke. Logically "Q" cannot be defined expressly as non-Markan material and, at the same time, be the source of Mark. (p. 192)

> If Mark is thought to have drawn upon "a pure 'Q' source", the question remains, "How can a hypothetical source ('Q'), which is defined expressly

---

[36] See C.M. Tuckett, "Q, the Law and Judaism", in B. Lindars (ed.), *Law and Religion* (Cambridge: James Clarke, 1988), p. 90-101, for more details.

as non-Markan material, at the same time, be the source of Mark?"
(p. 212)

This represents a possible misunderstanding of the 2DH. No theory
about "Q" has ever suggested that Q be "defined" tout court as
material which never appears in any form in Mark. One of the oldest
arguments used to promote the 2DH has been based on the existence of
doublets in Matthew and Luke, one half of the doublet having a
parallel in Mark and the other not. On the 2DH this is explained by the
existence of the tradition in question in Mark and Q. The implicit
assumption has therefore always been that Mark and Q overlapped at
times. Whatever source theory one adopts, the existence of doublets in
Matthew and Luke is undeniable. On the 2GH, these can no doubt be
explained by the existence of overlapping traditions lying behind Matthew. The difference between the 2DH and the 2GH is simply that,
where for the 2GH the overlapping traditions both remain unknown,
the 2DH claims to be able to identify one of the traditions more
precisely as the Gospel of Mark. The other tradition is simply one of
the traditions which was also available to Matthew and Luke. (Whether
such traditions ever constituted as single "document" is a further issue
and need not be considered here.)

It is however usually assumed by advocates of the 2DH that there is
no direct literary relationship between Mark and Q.[37] This then
explains the difficulty raised against the 2DH with regard to the
relationship between the gospels in a typical overlap passage such as Mt
24:42-51/Mk 13:33-37/Lk 12:39-46. The authors of the paper on the
Eschatological Discourse ask:

> If Luke and Matthew independently utilized a stage of a source which was
> also used by Mark at some other stage of the tradition, why is Mark so
> different from both Matthew and Luke? And why are Matthew and Luke
> so similar? (p. 167)

The answer is already implied in the word "independently". Precisely
because Matthew's and Luke's use of the tradition in question is via the
use of a "Q" tradition which is independent of Mark, Matthew and
Luke both differ considerably from Mark; but precisely because there is
an indirect literary relationship between Matthew and Luke (with both
using a common tradition), these two gospels are very similar to each
other. Such a situation (Matthew and Luke very similar, and Mark
rather different) is easily explained by the 2DH, provided Mark and Q

---

[37] For a survey of this issue, see F. Neirynck, "Recent Developments in the Study of
Q", in J. Delobel (ed.), *LOGIA. Les Paroles de Jésus – The Sayings of Jesus* (BETL 59;
Leuven: University Press, 1982), esp. pp. 41-53.

are regarded as independent. Yet precisely this situation (which, whatever one makes of it, is there in the texts) causes problems for the 2GH. A close similarity between Matthew and Luke is easy to explain, but Mark's text becomes highly problematic: Mark, who is supposed to be taking care to reproduce the common testimony of his two sources, suddenly decides to produce a text form which is very different from that of his sources. One would have to argue, on the 2GH, that *all* the differences in Mark are due to MkR, as well as finding reasons why Mark should suddenly have adopted such a different redactional procedure from elsewhere in the tradition.[38] The so-called "overlap" passages turn out on analysis to be far more problematic for the 2GH than for the 2DH.

6. The "Economy" of the 2GH

One of the arguments put forward by the *Position Paper* in favour of the 2GH is that this hypothesis does not have to appeal to the existence of hypothetical sources to explain the synoptic data. Such an appeal to "simplicity", or "economy", makes an implicit assumption that a "simpler" solution to the Synoptic problem is preferable to a less simple one. Further, this assumption plays a key role in the argument of the *Position Paper* where solutions to the Synoptic problem which posit additional sources (cf. Q on the 2DH) are excluded a priori, at least initially.

Such an argument is of doubtful value in the present discussion. Advocates of the 2GH have never denied the existence of other traditions available to the later evangelists. The *Position Paper* itself asserts that "The Two Gospel Hypothesis does not require the critic to deny the existence of earlier sources used by the evangelists" and that Luke made "extensive use of other source material" besides Matthew (cf. p. 132). Similarly the discussion of the Eschatological Discourse suggests that, in Luke's great Central section, the evangelist "had access to another ordered source in addition to Matthew" (p. 161). If this is the case, it becomes highly questionable how "simple" the 2GH really is. Whilst berating the 2DH's appeal to the existence of a "hypothetical" source (Q), the 2GH postulates other "material", or "traditions", available to Luke but not Matthew, and at times these can

---

[38] For the difficulties faced by the 2GH in many of the texts often regarded as Mark-Q overlaps, see Tuckett, *Revival*, ch. 8, pp. 76ff.

be referred to as "sources". A truly "economic" solution to the Synoptic problem along Griesbachian lines might be to ascribe all non-Matthean material in Luke to LkR, and all non-Matthean and non-Lukan material in Mark to MkR.[39] But such a step is not one which has (so far as I am aware) been taken by contemporary advocates of the 2GH.

The 2GH appeals potentially to a multiplicity of sources to explain the origin of the non-Matthean material in Luke (and to a certain extent in Mark). One could argue that the 2DH is rather "simpler" in this respect. If one were to regard the Q material as constituting a unitary source in the tradition,[40] then an enormous amount of material in the gospels can be ascribed to just two major sources, Mark and Q. By appealing to a number of "earlier traditions" to which Luke had access, the 2GH potentially multiplies the number of prior sources behind the gospels to a greater extent than does the 2DH. An appeal to "economy", or "simplicity", to support the 2GH is thus unpersuasive. An appeal to such a criterion would appear to work against, rather than for, the hypothesis.

The *Position Paper* by the team advocating the 2GH has presented a concise statement of the main arguments in favour of that hypothesis. Limitations of space have meant that not every argument in the *Position Paper* has been considered here. Nevertheless it is hoped that the counter-arguments proposed in this Response will further the debate by way of critical and friendly dialogue, and enable progress to be made in archieving a better understanding of the gospel texts.

Christopher M. Tuckett

---

[39] Cf. the theories of M.D. Goulder, who would see Matthew as a "midrashic" expansion of Mark, with virtually all the extra material in Matthew as due to MattR; similarly Luke's only source would be Mark, Matthew and his own redactional activity. See his *Midrash and Lection in Matthew* (London: SPCK, 1974), and *Luke - A New Paradigm* (Sheffield: Sheffield Academic Press, 1989).

[40] This is assumed by many, but by no means all, advocates of the 2DH.

II

THE ESCHATOLOGICAL DISCOURSE*

The paper on the Eschatological Discourse (henceforth *ED*) constitutes one of the most detailed and sustained textual analyses of an individual section of the gospels undertaken by contemporary advocates of the 2GH. Some of this material was discussed earlier from the side of the 2GH by W.R. Farmer, as well as being the subject of part of the debate between Talbert-McKnight and Buchanan.[1] These discussions have been considered elsewhere.[2] Hence, to avoid undue repetition, reference can be made to these earlier discussions for more detailed considerations of individual points (and for fuller bibliographical references).

Some more general comments may be made initially. First, Matthew's gospel is never analysed by itself in any detail. This is entirely appropriate at one level since the development of the tradition prior to Matthew is not necessarily relevant in a discussion of the 2GH where the main aim is to account for the development of the tradition after Matthew, through Luke to Mark. Nevertheless, an analysis of Matthew's account is not without significance, as will be seen. Second, most of the detailed arguments function at the level of describing what must have happened according to the 2GH. The claim is frequently made that the resulting Lukan version is in Lukan terms (and similarly for Mark). This is a welcome procedure, clarifying the detailed development of the tradition which the 2GH implies, but it does not show that other source hypotheses are excluded. The fact that Luke's version is LkR cannot distinguish between the possibilities of its being LkR of Matthew or LkR of Mark. There are very few concrete applications of the third criterion proposed in the *Position Paper* of the 2GH (cf.

---

* Cf. below, pp. 157-200: "The Composition of the Synoptic Eschatological Discourse", by A.McNicol. This Response was prepared for discussion at the Symposium and is reproduced here with only minor variations. For further discussion, see also F. Neirynck in this volume, pp. 77-80.

[1] See W.R. Farmer, *The Synoptic Problem* (New York: Macmillan, 1964), pp. 271-278; G.W. Buchanan, "Has the Griesbach Hypothesis been Falsified?", *JBL* 93 (1974) 550-572 (esp. pp. 570ff.), replying to C.H. Talbert & E.V. McKnight, "Can the Griesbach Hypothesis be Falsified?", *JBL* 91 (1972) 338-368.

[2] See C.M. Tuckett, *The Revival of the Griesbach Hypothesis* (Cambridge: University Press, 1983), ch. 17 "The Apocalyptic Discourses", pp. 167-185.

p. 140): a small number of instances of possible MattR reappearing in Luke are noted, but none of MattR or LkR reappearing in Mark. (Instances of the opposite phenomenon, i.e. elements of possible MkR appearing in Matthew or Luke, are not noted.) Third, attention has been confined very strictly to the passages which are actually parallel in the gospels. Implications of the argument for a slightly wider context are ignored. For example, although the whole paper is concerned with all the texts in Mt 24:1-51 and parallels, discussion of the Markan text is mostly restricted to the Matthean and Lukan parallels to Mk 13:1-37 itself, i.e. Mt 24:1-36 and Lk 21:5-36. Little attention is given to the problem of Mark's omissions from Lk 12 and 17 and from Mt 24:43ff. In fact the whole question of the choice and arrangement of material by the secondary authors causes some problems for the 2GH, and it is at this level that the present Response focusses most attention. As in the paper under discussion, Luke and Mark will be treated separately.

1. *Luke*

I start with the question of Luke's choice and arrangement of material. On p. 162 it is stated that Luke "noted ... the large 'blocks' of Matthean material he wished to use in his composition. One of these 'blocks' was Matt 24:1-51." There is however the further question why Luke decided to split this material into three separate blocks in chs. 12, 17 and 21. The argument given is that in ch. 12, after an item of *Sondergut* material in vv. 35-38, Luke appends material from Mt 24 on the "watching" theme. This explains things at one level: Luke is attracted by the word ἐγρηγόρησεν in Mt 24:42 and thus uses Mt 24:43-51a (v. 42 being considered redundant after Lk 12:35-38). But why does Luke not place all the thematically related material, including what he will use later in chs. 17 and 21, in a single block? The material in Lk 12 is said to be concerned with the theme of "watching" (cf. p. 163), that in Lk 17 with the theme of "observation" (p. 168). It is difficult to distinguish these two themes in terms of substance. Further, at the end of the section in Lk 21, the *ED* paper claims that Lk 21:29-31 takes up a section from Matthew (Mt 24:32f.) on the theme of "watchfulness" (p. 180). Why then was this not included by Luke in Lk 12 when the latter was supposedly constructed with all the material from Mt 24-25 on "watching"? Luke's placing of the material he takes from Matthew in three separate blocks still seems problematic for the 2GH.

Why too does Luke stop at Mt 24:51a? It is said that "Luke will use Mt 24:51b ... in his 13:28a"; he has similar material to Mt 25:1-13 in 12:35-38, and he "will use Mt 25:14-30a ... in Lk 19:11-27" (p. 165). This certainly states what must have happened, but it does not explain *why* Luke has held back Mt 24:51b and 25:14-30a for a later context. One answer might be that this material is not quite so closely related thematically to the other material in the Matthean context. This might indicate that these sections in Matthew come from different sources. This in turn would mean that Luke is succeeding in sorting out Matthew's version into its constituent parts very cleverly. A simpler alternative is to say that Luke only knows the material in unconnected form, i.e. before it has been put together in its present Matthean form.

A similar situation arises in the case of the material in Lk 17. The *ED* paper argues that Luke takes up various sayings from Matthew on the "observation" theme, focussing especially on the sayings which speak of the parousia of the Son of Man (p. 169) and following *Stichworte* such as παρουσία (cf. p. 170 for Mt 24:27 to 24:37) and ἐν τῷ ἀγρῷ (p. 172 for Mt 24:10 to 24:18). (The latter suggestion, about the influence of *Stichworte*, is not so easily reconcilable with the theory that Luke's choice of material is governed primarily by thematic considerations: παρουσία might be taken as a prominent theme, rather than just a *Stichwort* (though Luke himself does *not* use the word itself!), but ἐν τῷ ἀγρῷ can only be so regarded with some difficulty.)

It is noticeable, however, that the parousia sayings in Matthew can be separated from their present Matthean context on internal grounds. Vv. 26-28, referring to the parousia, come too early prior to v. 29; also vv. 26-28, which speak of the coming of the Son of Man, have quite different presuppositions from vv. 23-25, which seem to refer to expectations associated with the coming of messianic figures. Further, vv. 37-41 change the tone after vv. 29-36 from an exhortation to perseverance to a threat of unexpected catastrophe. [3] One could easily argue, on the 2GH, that these sayings come to Matthew from one of his sources, and Luke has subsequently separated this material from the rest of Mt 24, perhaps on the basis of thematic considerations. This would mean that Luke has again succeeded in separating Mt 24 into its constituent parts. As before, it may be simpler to assume that Luke only knows the material in its pre-Matthean form.

As far as the detailed linguistic arguments are concerned, not all the

---

[3] See Tuckett, *Revival*, pp. 170f., 175, with further references.

points discussed in the *ED* paper need be considered since advocates of the 2DH and of the 2GH will often have to find reasons for almost identical changes of the tradition by Luke. In triple tradition passages, where Luke's wording differs from Matthew/Mark, and where Matthew and Mark are very close to each other, Luke's redactional activity as postulated by either hypothesis will be the same. Thus although one might wish to question some details of the arguments put forward in the *ED* paper to explain Luke's redaction, advocates of the 2DH must still explain virtually the same activity by Luke.

This does not however apply in the case of double tradition passages. Here, the 2GH posits dependence by Luke on Matthew and so must explain the differences in wording as LkR (unless appeal is made to Luke's use of *Sondergut* material which overlapped with Matthew). In the case of the parables in Lk 12:39-46/Mt 24:43-51, the *ED* paper does not appeal to the existence of any Lukan *Sondergut* and seeks to explain Luke's text as LkR of Matthew alone. It notes that others try to explain the same texts as due to dependence by both evangelists on a common tradition (Q) by appealing to certain words in Luke and omissions in Matthew. "However, an examination of these words or phrases reveals that none of these are 'characteristic' of Matthew or of Luke. The evidence is neutral." (p. 166 with n. 21). This however rather misses the force of the evidence concerned. Whether a word or phrase is positively characteristic of Matthew or Luke is not so much the point here. Rather, what is significant is a possible change being *un*characteristic. For example, n. 21 here refers to Mt 24:44/Lk 12:40, where Luke omits διὰ τοῦτο. The note refers to Tevis' claim that διὰ τοῦτο λέγω ὑμῖν is a Matthean characteristic. Since λέγω ὑμῖν does not occur in Mt 24:44 this is irrelevant here. Further, the issue is not whether διὰ τοῦτο in Matthew can be adequately explained: rather it is whether the omission of the phrase by Luke can be explained as LkR. This issue is not addressed in the *ED* paper. In fact there is little evidence to suggest that Luke dislikes the phrase. On the 2GH, Luke takes the phrase over from Matthew quite happily in Lk 11:19, 49; 12:22; 14:20 is a case of Luke using the phrase redactionally or adopting it from his special source material. There is no other instance on the 2GH of Luke's simply omitting a διὰ τοῦτο from Matthew: in all other cases of διὰ τοῦτο in Matthew, Luke's failure to use the phrase is part of a much more extensive omission and can scarcely be explained as due to dislike of the phrase alone. Thus whilst the presence of διὰ τοῦτο in Matthew causes no difficulty on any hypothesis, the omission of the phrase by Luke on the 2GH is less easy to envisage.

Similar difficulties arise in the explanation of the difference ὑποκρι-τῶν (Mt 24:51) / ἀπίστων (Lk 12:46). It is admitted that ἄπιστος "is not a Lukan linguistic characteristic", but since Luke "rarely uses" ὑποκριτής "it is more likely that ἀπίστων was a Lukan alteration of Matthew at Lk 12:46" (n. 21). But given two unusual words it is difficult to see why it is "more likely" to assume that one is due to a redactional alteration by Luke even though it is "not a Lukan linguistic characteristic". It is noteworthy too that, although Luke allegedly "rarely uses" ὑποκριτής, he does use it three times in his gospel. On the 2GH, one of these may be from his special source material (Lk 13:15), one is repeated without change from Matthew (Lk 6:42), and one may be added redactionally to Matthew (Lk 12:56: however, the textual status of the Matthean parallel in Mt 16:2f. is doubtful). It would obviously be precarious to place too much weight on a single word, especially in view of Luke's wide range of vocabulary. Nevertheless this verbal difference between Matthew and Luke constitutes an anomaly for the 2GH.

The discussion in the *ED* paper is confined to a consideration of linguistic and stylistic features but, as already noted, possible strata in Matthew's text are not generally considered. One example where this might be relevant concerns the word ἐγρηγόρησεν in Mt 24:43. The idea of "watching" fits well in the parable of the waiting servants in Lk 12:37, but rather poorly in the parable of the thief: "watching" implies readiness for an event at an unknown time, whereas the conditional clause in Mt 24:43 states the case of what would happen if the householder does not know the time when the thief is coming. On the 2DH, Matthew's wording can be explained as a secondary reminiscence of the "watching" theme (perhaps from Mt 24:42, perhaps from Lk 12:37 if that verse stood in Q).[4] On the 2GH, Luke may have recognised the secondary nature of the word in Matthew and cut it out.[5] (However, it is slightly odd that Luke, who is allegedly constructing a section on the theme of "watching" and is attracted by the word ἐγρηγόρησεν to just this section in Matthew, should omit the one key word in his source.) In making this omission, Luke may have again

---

[4] Tuckett, *Revival*, p. 182, with further references.

[5] There is some doubt about the Lukan text here, with some MSS including the words ἐγρηγόρησεν ἂν καί. Despite attestation in representatives of all the major textual groupings (as noted in the *ED* paper, p. 164), the variant is probably due to assimilation to the text of Matthew, and secondary addition of the words to the Lukan text is easier to envisage than the reverse process. See B.M. Metzger, *A Textual Commentary on the Greek New Testament* (London: United Bible Societies, 1971), p. 159f.

succeeded in reconstructing Matthew's source. It is perhaps easier to assume that Luke knows the source itself, rather than Matthew.

In the discussion of the material in Lk 17, difficulties also arise. Few would dispute that Lk 17:22 is substantially LkR, but what of vv. 23-24? Luke must have omitted the references here to the "desert" and the "inner chamber". This, it is said, is part of Luke's tendency to "omit considerable vivid imagery often very closely associated with Jewish apocalypses ... Luke and his more urbanized readers are not interested in any further speculations about eschatological events in the Palestinian wilderness" (pp. 169-170). This is certainly possible. However, the Matthean text itself is rather problematic here and does not fit very easily with "imagery associated with Jewish apocalypses". As is well known, the references to the "desert" and "inner chamber" refer to various expectations about the coming of a Messianic figure, rather than a Son of Man figure. This has led many to assume that the saying must be a formulation of the post-Easter community which identified Jesus as both Messiah and Son of Man.[6] But this applies only to the Matthean version: the Lukan version, which makes no such confusion of Messianic and Son of Man expectations, is free from such difficulty. Luke may have managed to remove the difficulties of Matthew's text secondarily; alternatively, and more simply, the shorter Lukan version may represent one of Matthew's sources.

Lk 17:26-29 also raises some problems. In explaining the extra material in v. 28f. about Lot, the *ED* paper appeals to the traditional link between Noah and Lot in Jewish writings, so that "Luke inserts the Lot material into his narrative here because it is in his source material" (p. 171). However, if v. 28f. come from Luke's source material, there is the further question of the extent of that material here. The traditional link appealed to here to explain the conjunction of Noah and Lot[7] suggests that the Lot reference was always linked with a similar warning based on the example of Noah. This would suggest that Lk 17:28f. was linked in Luke's tradition with some kind of substantive

---

[6] Ph. Vielhauer, "Gottesreich und Menschensohn in der Verkündigung Jesu", *Aufsätze zum Neuen Testament* (München: Kaiser, 1965), p. 75, is often referred to in this context.

[7] For the traditional link, cf. D. Lührmann, *Die Redaktion der Logienquelle* (Neukirchen: Neukirchener, 1969), pp. 71-83, and his "Noah und Lot (Lk 17:26-29) — Ein Nachtrag", *ZNW* 63 (1972) 130-132. For this as pre-Lukan (and Q), see D.R. Catchpole, "The Law and the Prophets in 'Q'", in G.F. Hawthorne & O. Betz (eds.), *Tradition and Interpretation in the New Testament* (FS for E.E. Ellis; Tübingen: Mohr, 1987), pp. 95-109, on p. 102.

parallel to Lk 17:26f. It is very difficult to envisage Lk 17:28f. existing as an isolated saying. But then the question arises of whether Lk 17:26f. itself may not be the missing half of the double warning in Luke's tradition. Previous discussions of these verses by advocates of the 2GH conceded that Lk 17:26f. and 17:28f. belonged together in Luke's tradition, and that Luke's version here represented a tradition which was independent of, and more primitive than, Matthew's parallel.[8] This seems a more plausible hypothesis, but it is one which creates a rather anomalous situation for the 2GH since it effectively reduces to a form of the Q hypothesis (Matthew and Luke both dependent on common tradition).

In Lk 17:30-31 Luke is said to have switched back to Mt 24:17f. due to the presence of the *Stichworte* ἐν τῷ ἀγρῷ. This is possible, though it seems a somewhat arbitrary move by Luke who is supposed to be collecting material on a thematic basic. However, the 2DH, which would explain the verse as an anticipation of material in Mk 13, must postulate a similar change. In v. 33 Luke is said to bring in a saying on saving/losing life, but he has redacted it to avoid a doublet with 9:24 (p. 172). This seems scarcely sufficient to explain the presence of a clear doublet in Luke despite the alleged redactional tendency of Luke to avoid redundancy and doublets elsewhere (cf. Luke's omission of Mt 24:42 to avoid redundancy). If Luke really wanted to avoid creating a doublet with 9:24, he could simply have not included the verse here. There is no compulsion from his major alleged source in Mt 24 to force him to put the verse in at this point. The creation of the doublet is due entirely to LkR on the 2GH.

The detailed discussion of the material in Mt 24/Lk 21 may be treated more cursorily here, since the 2DH and the 2GH have to find explanations for similar changes: Luke's redaction of Matthew on the 2GH is frequently the same as Luke's redaction of Mark on the 2DH. Certainly the similarity of the redaction presupposed means that one cannot easily distinguish between the claims of competing hypotheses.

This applies even in the case of Mt 24:9-14/Lk 21:12-19. This will be discussed in more detail in the section on Mark below, but one may note at this point that the explanation of the Lukan text here by advocates of the 2GH seems rather forced (see p. 178). In addition to the changes in wording which both the 2GH and the 2DH must

---

[8] Farmer, *Synoptic Problem*, p. 272; Buchanan, "Griesbach Hypothesis", p. 571, appealing to the parallelism in Luke's version. This factor is not mentioned in the *ED* paper.

explain, the 2GH has to account for a switch by Luke from following Mt 24 to using parallel material in Mt 10. (On the 2DH, Luke follows Mk 13 all the time.) Luke apparently recognised a Matthean doublet in Mt 24:9-13 and 10:17-22, having already used Mt 10:19f. in Lk 12:11f.; he may also have been influenced by the fact that Mt 10:17 has a milder "hated by all" instead of Mt 24:9 "hated by all the Gentiles". So Luke followed Mt 10:17ff. here, but then paraphrased Mt 10:19f. in order to avoid a doublet. This seems a rather clumsy redactional procedure. If Luke objected to Christians being hated by "all the Gentiles", he could simply have omitted τῶν ἐθνῶν without making this elaborate switch. The procedure with regard to the doublet is also odd: Luke, aware of the doublet here but generally anxious to avoid doublets, deliberately switches contexts in Matthew to bring a doublet into view but then has to paraphrase when the doublet actually threatens to materialise. Such a procedure seems somewhat irrational.

2. Mark

As in the case of Luke, the problem of Mark's choice of material seems to cause most difficulties for the 2GH. The *ED* paper offers a number of explanations for Mark's procedure in choosing what to include and what to omit. Thus, for example:

> Mark overwhelmingly limits himself to source material common to Matthew 24 and Luke 21. Indeed, whenever Mark finds material unique to Matthew 24, he usually omits it. Similarly, whenever Mark finds material unique to Luke 21 he always omits it. (p. 183)

> Marks tends to follow the wording of his Matthean source closely ... On several occasions Mark will copy material from Matthew which is not in Luke. (p. 183)

Already contradictory tendencies arise: Mark "tends to omit" material unique to Matthew (and Luke) but his respect for his Matthean source leads him to copy material in Matthew alone "on several occasions". This ambiguity emerges in the detailed analysis which follows, as will be seen.

For the most part, attention is restricted to the parallels to Mk 13 in Mt 24 and Lk 21. What though of Mark's attitude to the material which appears in Luke in Lk 12 and 17? To explain Mark's omissions from Matthew (Mt 24:10-12, 14, 26-28, 30a), the *ED* paper says that "none of these has a Lukan parallel" (p. 184), this apparently being the prime reason for Mark's omission. As already noted, however, Mark does include material from Matthew where there is no Lukan parallel "on several occasions". Further, the statement is not strictly true, There is "no Lukan parallel" only if attention is confined to Lk 21: Mt 24:26-28 has a parallel in Lk 17:23f.; moreover, Mark has omitted large parts of Mt 24:43-51 where there are substantial parallels in Lk 12 and 17. Why then does Mark appear to ignore nearly all the Lukan parallels to Mt 24 which occur in other contexts in Luke?

One could argue that this is due to Mark's lack of familiarity with his sources (in using Lk 21 Mark is unaware of the existence of Lukan parallels elsewhere); or it could be due to Mark's conscious decision to limit his choice of material to the present context in his sources and not use out-of-order parallels. But both these solutions are implicitly rejected by the *ED* paper. Elsewhere it is argued that Mark was aware of both Matthean and Lukan parallels to Mt 24/Lk 21 in Mt 10:17-22 and Lk 12:11f. (see p. 187), so that one cannot appeal to Mark's lack of familiarity with either of his sources. It is also argued that Mark may have used Lk 12:35-38 in Mk 13:35-37 (p. 198). Further, the reference to the "holy" spirit in Mk 13:11 must presumably be explained by the 2GH as deriving from Lk 12:12 (unless it is due to MkR of Matthew, thus creating a "minor agreement" between Luke and Mark[9]). Thus the 2GH asserts that Mark has made some use of the material in Lk 12. Some of this overlaps with Matthew (Lk 12:11f.); some has no parallel in Matthew (Lk 12:35-38). But this then raises a further question of why Mark uses Lk 12:35-38 at all since elsewhere Mark is said to have omitted material from Lk 21 precisely because it has no parallel in Matthew (p. 184). Further, if Lk 12:35-38 is in Mark's mind, why does Mark not include the further material in Mt 24:43-51 which has such a close parallel in Lk 12:39-46? No very satisfactory explanation seems to be implied here.

As well as the problems of omissions, Mark's principle of inclusion is also unclear. In explaining the omissions from Matthew, it is said that "when he [= Mark] does not follow Matthew it is because there is no text shared by Matthew and Luke. He, therefore, omits" (p. 184). This explains omissions such as Mt 24:26-28, 30a (though only if one limit attention to Lk 21 in Luke). However, Mark retains vv. 18, 23-25, 31, 36 from Mt 24 even though there is no Lukan parallel. V. 23 may well be retained because of Mark's special concerns (cf. p. 195),[10] but no

---

[9] This is not discussed in the *ED* paper. For the phenomenon of "Luke-Mark minor agreements" on the 2GH, see F. Neirynck in this volume, p. 78.

[10] Though the reason given here, that Mark is concerned with persecution, would

such explanation is offered for the other verses retained from Matthew. Is this then simply due to Mark's greater respect for his Matthean source?

On other occasions, Luke does have a parallel to Matthew but it is a very distant one (cf. Mt 24:8, 15f., 17f.) Here Mark seems to follow his alternative principle of following Matthew alone. At times it is claimed that Mark recognised the secondary nature of the Lukan text (p. 193 on Mt 24:17f); at other points, Mark's procedure is said to be due to the fact that his source were so different that he found it impossible to conflate them (cf. p. 187 on Mt 24:8). But it is difficult to see how this fits with Mark's alleged aim of uniting and reconciling his conflicting sources. Elsewhere, the fact that the sources differed widely is taken as a reason for a Markan omission. [11] In any case it is difficult to see how Mark's procedure here would in any way solve problems raised by the differing accounts in Matthew and Luke. A detailed conflation might solve such problems; but a decision simply to omit one of the sources completely solves nothing.

The *ED* paper thus seems to present rather contradictory reasons for Mark's choice of material on the 2GH. Mark ignores some, but not all, of the Lukan parallels to Mt 24 outside Lk 21. Mark omits some parts of Mt 24 because there is no Lukan parallel, yet includes other parts which also have no Lukan parallel. Is it Mark's aim to conflate the common features of Matthew and Luke, or to give what is basically another version of Matthew's text with some Lukan supplementation? The two aims are not the same, and the explanations of Mark's choice of material, which seem to combine these two aims, seem correspondingly slightly contradictory at times.

The detailed analysis of the wording of the Markan text is in many respects unexceptional, describing what must have happened on the presuppositions of the 2GH. The claim is however made that "most of the words and phrases in Mark which differ from Matthew and Luke can be explained as Markan linguistic characteristics", and that this constitutes (with other considerations) "literary evidence" for the 2GH (p. 185). This may overstate the value of the evidence. The fact that Mark's text is Markan simply shows that Mark has stamped his own

---

apply only to v. 23, and not to vv. 23-25 as suggested. Vv. 24-25 are about the dangers associated with coming messianic pretenders, not persecution.

[11] Cf. the *Position Paper* of the 2GH's team, in this volume, p. 155, explaining Mark's omission of the birth narratives and the temptation story (though how Matthew and Luke differ so drastically in the temptation story is not easy to see).

style on his tradition. It says nothing about the origin of his tradition. More interesting would be instances of MattR or LkR appearing in Mark, but none is noted. In fact there are a number of places where Mark's text is seen as characteristic of Mark and where one of the parallel versions has the same text. E.g., βλέπετε in Mk 13:5/Mt 24:4 (p. 187);[12] the repetition of πλανᾶν in Mk 13:6/Mt 24:4f. (p. 187 and of παρελεύσονται in Mk 13:31/Lk 21:33 (p. 197). In each case it is argued that Mark is so fond of the feature involved (e.g. duality) that he picks it out of his sources to use. But one could perhaps argue that these features may be MkR, and that their presence in the parallel text of Matthew/Luke constitutes literary evidence in favour of the dependence of Matthew/Luke upon Mark.

Mk 13:9-13 and Parallels

A lot of space is devoted to explaining this part of the Discourse in the three gospels. In particular, it is claimed that the 2GH has a decided advantage in being able to explain the synoptic parallels much more easily than the 2DH. The redactional activity which must be presupposed by the 2DH is described as being far too complex and devious to be credible: Matthew's activity (in allegedly redacting Mark) would involve "an extremely clumsy redactional procedure with a trail of doublets left behind in his wake"; Luke's activity would involve "an amazing redactional amalgamation of paraphrasing, copying, omitting, and providing additional unique material, all within seven verses" (p. 192).[13]

The answers to the problem faced by the 2DH are however provided by the *ED* paper itself elsewhere. As far as Matthew's text is concerned, there is a "trail of doublets" here on any hypothesis. Explaining this from the point of view of the 2GH, the paper refers to "a Matthean doublet" (cf. pp. 176, 188), which is presumably to be accounted for by some kind of development in the pre-Matthean tradition. The 2DH is simply slightly more specific in identifying the origin of this doublet as

[12] The *ED* paper stresses the redactional nature of βλέπετε in Mk 13, but it regards the main uses of the word to be in vv. 9, 23, these verses forming an *inclusio* to highlight the persecution motif. However, vv. 21-23 are concerned with the problem of messianic pretenders, not persecution (cf. n. 10 above); vv. 21-23 thus repeat the concerns of vv. 5-7. This suggests that the *inclusio* should be seen in vv. 5-23, not vv. 9-23, and the major uses of βλέπετε are in vv. 5, 23. This reinforces the conclusion that βλέπετε in v. 5 is MkR; but then the presence of the word in Matthew and in Luke is perhaps better explained on the 2DH, being a feature of MkR reappearing in the parallel texts (cf. above).

[13] For the references in the *ED* paper here to the Q hypothesis, see my Response to the 2GH's *Position Paper*, in this volume p. 59, and also F. Neirynck here p. 79.

due to Mark and (probably) MattR. With regard to the Lukan text, all
the stages of Luke's redaction described on p. 191 which allegedly
constitute a "very awkward and clumsy redactional procedure" are
related to Luke's redaction of Mk 13:9-13. But Mk 13:9-13 is verbally
extremely close to Matt 10:17-22 (however this is to be explained).
Thus any explanation of how Luke could have redacted Mt 10:17-22 to
produce Lk 21:12-19 will serve equally well as an explanation of how
Luke might have redacted Mk 13:9-13 to produce the same result.
However, the 2GH has to explain a further complexity in accounting
for Luke's decision to switch from Mt 24 to Mt 10 at this point. As we
have seen there may be a slight problem here (cf. above); but in any
case the Lukan redaction implied by the 2GH here is one stage even
more complex than that presupposed by the 2DH. On the 2DH Lk 21
involves no change in context: Luke is dependent on Mk 13. The 2DH
has to explain the change in context in Matthew's gospel, but this is not
impossible: for Matthew, persecution is not a sign of the End-time but
is a matter of present, if not past, experience.[14] The *ED* paper itself
provides a detailed series of reasons explaining how Luke redacted Mt
10 to produce his present version (pp. 177-178). All these can be transferred
to explain LkR on the 2DH and to account for the allegedly "awkward
and clumsy redactional procedure". If this procedure is indeed "very
awkward and clumsy", then it is equally so whether Luke is regarded as
redacting Mark or Matthew. The discussion thus gives no justification
at all for regarding the 2GH as preferable to the 2DH.

In analysing the wording of Mark here, it is said that Mark noted the
doublet in Mt 10 and 24 as well as the presence of the material in Lk 21
and Lk 12. It is then claimed that Mark decided to follow two sources
whenever possible, "following the principle of accepting the text of the
majority of witnesses" and hence following "the text of the two closest
parallels" (p. 188) (even to the extent of then conflating the two halves
of Matthew's doublet with each other — such a procedure seems
unparalleled elsewhere in Mark on the 2GH and somewhat at variance
with the claims made elsewhere that Mark was seeking to reconcile
Matthew *and Luke*). This is then offered as the explanation for Mark's
omission of Mt 24:10-12 and Lk 21:18. On the other hand, one may
again note the possible relevance of an analysis of Matthew's text
alone. Mt 24:10-12 is full of Mattheanisms and may well be due
entirely to MattR.[15] Similarly, Lk 21:18 is probably due to LkR (cf.

---

[14] Cf. D.R.A. Hare, *The Theme of Jewish Persecutions of Christians in the Gospel
according to St Matthew* (Cambridge: University Press, 1967), p. 100.

[15] See Tuckett, *Revival*, p. 178.

p. 178, on how this verse serves Luke's redactional aims here in stressing the sustenance theme). Mark on the 2GH has thus managed to excise just the redactional material from his sources, and has produced a version which must be very similar to the source lying behind Matthew. It is perhaps rather simpler to identify Mark as that source.

In the rest of the section in Mk 13:14-32, some aspects of the analysis have already been discussed. One small anomaly for the 2GH arises in Mk 13:30, where Mark must have changed a ἕως ἄν in both his sources to μέχρις οὗ. The *ED* paper says that "this difference is not substantial", appealing to Dan 11:36 LXX and Θ (p. 196). But the important issue in the present discussion is not whether the change is "substantial"; rather, it is whether this insubstantial change can be attributed to MkR. Since μέχρις occurs only here in Mark, this is difficult to do.[16] On the other hand, a change of the rarer μέχρις to the more usual ἕως is easier to envisage.

Mk 13:33-37 and Parallels

The *ED* paper argues that these verses in Mark represent a summary by Mark of Lk 21:34-36 and Mt 24:37-25:30 (p. 197). Problems are again raised implicitly by this explanation at the level of Mark's choice of material. Mk 13:33a is said to be a summary of Lk 21:34-36, where there is no Matthean parallel, although elsewhere the lack of a Matthean parallel is taken as a necessary and sufficient condition for Mark's omission of a section from Luke (cf. p. 183: "Whenever Mark finds material unique to Luke he always omits it"). Further, Mark's procedure on the 2GH up to this point in his gospel has not generally involved drastic summarising of his sources in this way. Mk 13:33b is said to be a conflation of Mt 25:13 with Lk 21:36; but why should Mark have tried to conflate Lk 21:36 on the Lukan side when Lk 19:12 provides a much closer parallel to Mt 25:13? (Elsewhere the differences between Matthew and Luke were said to have put Mark off trying to conflate at all: cf. above on Mk 13:8). Mk 13:34 is then said to be a condensation of Mt 25:14f. (apparently without reference to the substantive parallel in Lk 19). Once again this has not been Mark's normal procedure on the 2GH in his gospel.

---

[16] In a footnote, reference is made to a "thorough analysis of μέχρις οὗ in D. Peabody, "A Pre-Markan Prophetic Sayings Tradition and the Synoptic Problem", *JBL* 97 (1978) 391-409. However, Peabody gives no analysis at all: he simple notes the singularity of μέχρις in Mark (pp. 393, 407). The difficulty of ascribing this to MkR on the 2GH is not discussed.

For verses 35-37 Mark switches to Mt 24:42 via the *Stichwort* γρηγορεῖν with Lk 12:35-37 in mind as well. As already noted, this raises problems not only why Mark has chosen to include material which appears in Luke alone, but also why Mark decides not to include the further material in Mt 24:43ff. which has such a close parallel in Lk 12 and which would have been ripe for conflation. The alleged use of Lk 12:35-38 is also noteworthy, for Mark must have redacted the Lukan text by reducing the number of people who are to "watch" to a single doorkeeper in the parable. This is accepted as MkR in the *ED* paper and explained as probably intended to highlight the demand to watch (p. 198). However, this scarcely fits Mark's redactional aim here which is to encourage *all* to watch (cf. Mk 13:37, which owes a great deal to MkR on any hypothesis). The "watching" theme is undoubtedly of importance to Mark here, but it is not clear how the reduction of the number of the people in the parable who are to "watch" to a single doorkeeper affects this at all. Mark's change also succeeds in reproducing a form of the parable which many have postulated as lying behind the Lukan text. It seems easier to assume that Mark's form of the text is independent of the Lukan one, that Mark adopts his version from his tradition, and that Luke has access to a similar tradition which overlaps with, but is not identical with, the Markan tradition.[17]

Advocates of the 2GH and the 2DH can agree about a large number of individual points in the redactional activity of the evangelists in the Eschatological Discourse(s). The fact that Matthew and Mark are so close to each other means that Luke's activity in using Matthew on the 2GH is very similar to Luke's use of Mark on the 2DH. This Response has however tried to show that the 2GH still faces some problems, above all in accounting for the choice and arrangement of the material concerned by the two secondary evangelists. In seeking to identify the problems here, it is hoped that the relative merits of each hypothesis can be clarified and scholars be thus placed in a better position to be able to judge between the competing claims of the two hypotheses and to come a more informed decision about the interrelationships between the gospels.

C.M. TUCKETT

---

[17] See Tuckett, *Revival*, pp. 180ff. for futher details.

An analysis of the composition of the eschatological discourse "on the presupposition of the Two-Gospel Hypothesis"[1] can be a neutral project to show the implications of the neo-Griesbachian position. Such a study, however, is no longer an innocent exercise when it is supposed to indicate that "the Two-Gospel Hypothesis more adequately explains the literary history of parallel synoptic pericopae than do other hypotheses held by critical scholars," and in particular, that "the Two-Source Theory cannot explain them without extraordinary difficulty." In accordance with the original planning of the Conference to concentrate on triple-tradition sections, let us consider here Mk 13 and parallels.

Luke 21:5-36

I begin by recalling a formal statement made by the team defending the two-gospel hypothesis: "we reject as methodologically incorrect any attempt to divide the three Gospels and focus attention first ... upon the agreements and disagreements in content and order between any two of them, such as, for example, ... Matthew and Luke" (134). If therefore the Lachmann approach is "methodologically incorrect" (*ibid.*), what should we say of the analysis presented by the same group examining in its first part the text of Lk 21:5-36 in relation to Mt 24:1-42 without any consideration of Mk 13?

Some of M.'s observations on Lukan compositional changes are quite acceptable in the hypothesis of Markan priority. The parallel pericopae in Mt 24 and Mk 13 have the same relative order and, at least in some verses, an almost identical wording. Thus, for instance, Mt 24:19 and Mk 13:17 (par. Lk 21:23a om. δέ) are strictly identical, and it may surprise the reader that this verse provides "strong evidence in favor of (the) thesis that Luke was literarily dependent upon Matthew as a source" (p. 179). The "Matthean linguistic characteristic" (sic) in this case is ἐν γαστρὶ ἔχω (Tevis, no. 248), used here in the three Synoptics (ταῖς ἐν γαστρὶ ἐχούσαις) and in Mt 1:18,23, where ἐν γαστρὶ ἔχουσα in v. 18 is clearly formulated under the influence of Isa 7:14 LXX, quoted in v. 23 (ἐν γαστρὶ ἕξει). Another "Matthean linguistic feature",

---

[1] Cf. "The Composition of the Synoptic Eschatological Discourse" by Allan J. McNicol, Fort Worth, TX. The abbreviation M. is used here for the author's name.

λέγω ὑμῖν + οὐ μή subjunctive verb + ἕως subjunctive verb (Mt 5:26; 16:28; 23:39; 24:34; 26:29; not in Tevis' list) occurs in Lk 21:32 and "again (as in Lk 21:23) this evidence is consistent with the view that Luke was dependent upon Matthew" (p. 181). At a closer examination it appears that each of the five occurrences has a synoptic parallel: Mt 5:26 (Lk 12:59 Q); 16:28 (Mk 9:1; Lk 9:27); 23:39 (Lk 13:35 Q); 24:34 (Mk 13:30 μέχρις οὗ; Lk 21:32 ἕως ἄν; cf. p. 196: the two readings are "interchangeable"); 26:29 (Mk 14:25; cf. Lk 22:16,18).

For at least three reasons dependence on Mark is a better solution than dependence on Matthew. First, a number of differences in the parallel sections of Matthew and Luke can be cited as minor agreements of Luke and Mark against Matthew:[2] Lk 21:5 om. προσῆλθον, λίθοις/ λίθοι, om. ἀποκριθείς, 6 om. πάντα, om. ἀμὴν λέγω ὑμῖν, 7 om. προσῆλθον, ἐπηρώτησαν/ἐπηρώτα, διδάσκαλε (Mk 13:1), ὅταν μέλλῃ ταῦτα (γίν)εσθαι, om. τῆς σῆς παρουσίας, 8 δέ, om. ἀποκριθείς, om. ὁ χριστός, 9 ὅταν (ἀκού)σητε, om. ὅρατε, om. ἐστιν, 11 σεισμοί - λιμοί (order), 12-19: par. Mk 13:9-13 (cf. Mt 10:17-22), 12 εἰς (τ. σ.), 14 προ(μ.) 20 δέ, om. τὸ ῥηθὲν διὰ Δανιὴλ τοῦ προφήτου, 21 εἰσερχέσθ- ωσαν/εἰσελθάτω, 25 ἔσονται, 26 ἐν (νεφ.), 27 om. φανήσεται ... τῆς γῆς καί (Mt 24:30a), om. τοῦ οὐρανοῦ, 30 ἐστίν, 31 om. πάντα, γινόμενα. Second, there is no problem of Lukan omission of Mt 24:26-28, 43-44, 45-51 (without parallel in Mk 13). Third, the dependence of Lk 21:12-19 on the parallel section in Mk 13:9-13 is a simpler solution[3] than the more complex theory of Luke departing here from his source in Mt 24 for Mt 10:17-22. There is no need to explain "Luke's first major omission from Matthew" (Mt 24:10-12). Following on Mk 13:12 (= Lk 21:16) Luke reads μισούμενοι ὑπὸ πάντων in Mk 13:13a (= Lk 21:17) and there is no need to suggest Lukan avoidance of Matthew's τῶν ἐθνῶν (24:9b). Mk 13:10, omitted here, will be used by Luke in 24:47.

In Part II, M. qualifies the explanation of Lk 21:12-19 on the basis of Markan priority as very difficult: "an amazing redactional amalga- mation of paraphrasing, copying, omitting, and providing additional unique material all within seven verses" (p. 192). If we presume that Luke is using only Mk 13:9-13 as a source, he will have anticipated Mk 13:11 in Lk 12:11-12 and will offer a paraphrase when he comes to Mk

[2] Compare, throughout "The Composition", Part II (esp. p. 188, on Mk 13:1-8), the emphasis given to Matthew-Luke agreements, "these so-called 'minor agreements' (which) constitute strong evidence in favor of the Two-Gospel Hypothesis." – For the Mt-Lk agreements against Mk 13, see *The Minor Agreements*, 160-167.

[3] "We believe that the simplest solution to a literary problem should be preferred unless there is compelling evidence against it" (p. 167; cf. 199: "a simpler explanation").

13:11 (Lk 21:14-15).[4] That is precisely what happened elsewhere according to M.: "Lk 21:21b-22 paraphrases in lieu of copying Mt 24:17-18. Since Luke had already used Mt 24:17-18 in his 17:31, perhaps he felt the need to paraphrase at 21:21 to avoid creating a doublet" (p. 178).[5] Why should what is described here as a normal compositional procedure be "awkward and clumsy" in the case of Lk 21:14-15 (par. Mk 13:11)?

It is more usual among Markan priorists to consider the saying in Lk 12:11-12 (cf. Mt 10:19-20) a Q-doublet, i.e., another traditional form of the saying preserved in Mark (13:11).[6] "But to derive Mt 10:17-23 and Lk 12:11-12 from the so-called Logienquelle leads to an intolerable contradiction since it means that Mk 13:9-13 should also be derived from this hypothetical document which is defined as non-Markan" (B. Reicke). M. agrees: "Logically, 'Q' cannot be defined expressly as non-Markan material and, at the same time, be the source of Mark" (p. 192). This "logical fallacy" is, it seems to me, no more than a misunderstanding. There is no good reason for arguing against the possibility of some overlapping in two gospel sources of the size of Mark and Q.[7] By assigning a doublet to Q, it is not suggested, as M. seems to suppose, that Mark was literarily dependent upon the Q source.[8]

Mark 13:1-37

The purpose of Part II is to show how the literary evidence supports

[4] Cf. A. Fuchs, *Sprachliche Untersuchungen*, 1971, 171-191. Because of the minor agreements between Lk 12:11-12 and Mt 10:19, he accepts "eine Mt und Lk vorliegende Bearbeitung des Mk-Textes" (174). But are the agreements significant enough to justify a *Deuteromarkus*?

[5] Cf. *infra*, 267, 269 (Boismard, on Lk 17:31).

[6] See, e.g., J. Dupont, "La persécution comme situation missionnaire (Mc 13,9-11)," [1977], *Études sur les évangiles synoptiques*, 1985, 456-473.

[7] In M.'s opinion Luke uses special source material in 12:37-38; then, "Luke decided to copy Mt 24:42-51 ... Luke considered the essence of Mt 24:42 already to be contained in his Lk 12:37-38. In order to avoid redundancy, Luke commences copying Matthew 24 at verse 43" (p. 164). If not in M.'s view, at least in the view of Luke according to M., an overlap of sources is accepted in this case.

[8] Compare M.'s thesis of Matthean originality with Boismard's two-stage theory: Mk 13:9-11,13a has its source in Mt 10:17-20,22a (Proto-Matthean mission discourse), but Mt 10:21,22b depends on Mk 13:12,13b (eschatological discourse). Cf. *infra*, 000. D. Wenham defends a similar theory: Mk 13:9,11 has its original position in the pre-synoptic mission discourse (Mt 10:17-20). The pre-synoptic tradition in the eschatological discourse comprises:

Mt 24: 9a,	–	9b,	13,	14
Mt 10: –	21,	22a,	22b,	–
Mk 13: –	12,	13a,	13b,	10.

The Rediscovery of Jesus' Eschatological Discourse (Gospel Perspectives, 4), Sheffield, 1984, 219-285. Cf. *ETL* 61 (1985) 192-193.

the thesis that "Mark utilized two major sources in composing Mk 13, namely, Mt 24 and Lk 21." The demonstration will hardly convince readers who, with good reason, decline this thesis, but the paper is not without value because of its description of the evidence. Extensive use is made of tools such as *Duality in Mark*, *The Minor Agreements*, and D. Peabody's *Mark as Composer*. A few synoptic parallels that are normally not found in a Synopsis are noted here. Mt 10:17-22 / Mk 13:9-13 are printed in all Synopses, but M. rightly adds a parallel which is not insignificant for the interpretation of Mt 10:23, ὅταν δὲ ... / Mk 13:14. See also, for instance, ἐξαίφνης in Mk 13:16: cf. αἰφνίδιος in Lk 21:34. The paper indicates the minor agreements, apparently without adding new examples. Special attention is given to conflation of Matthew and Luke. Some examples correspond to P. Rolland's dual expressions:[9] 13:1 (no. 134); 13:8 (no. 135); 13:15 (no. 137); 13:25 (no. 139); 13:33 (no. 140). See also the conflation of the doublets in Mt 10 and 24 at Mk 13:9. Conflation is a more elastic notion than Rolland's "expression double". It includes, for instance, Mk 13:4 συντελεῖσθαι (Mt συντελείας, Lk γίνεσθαι), but also 13:3 ἐπηρώτα κατ᾽ ἰδίαν (Mt κατ᾽ ἰδίαν, Lk ἐπηρώτησαν); 13:26 ἐν νεφέλαις (Mt ἐπὶ τῶν νεφελῶν, Lk ἐν νεφέλῃ); and 13:28,29 γένηται (Mt), γινόμενα (Lk). That means that the evidence of the Mark-Luke agreements against Matthew, missing in his study of Lk 21 (Part I), appears here in the form of conflations in Mark.

The description of the evidence is one thing. To give it probative force against the priority of Mark is quite another task. The main point in M.'s analysis is perhaps the emphasis he gives to "Markan linguistic characteristics". But is it Mark who, copying and conflating his two sources, "utilizes a favorite literary device", or was this Markan expression already present in the common source of Matthew and Luke? The last alternative cannot be denied without serious examination.

In M.'s opinion, the conclusion of the discourse in Lk 21:34-36 comes from Luke's own store of source material and Mark condenses Lk 21:34-36 to form his 13:33a. In the alternative hypothesis, Lk 21:34-36 can be explained as a Lukan expansion of Mk 13:33:

Mk 13	Lk 21
33 βλέπετε,	34 προσέχετε δὲ ἑαυτοῖς ...
ἀγρυπνεῖτε	36 ἀγρυπνεῖτε δὲ
[καὶ προσεύχεσθε·]	ἐν παντὶ καιρῷ δεόμενοι ...
οὐκ οἴδατε γὰρ πότε ὁ καιρός ἐστιν.	

F. NEIRYNCK

---

[9] See "Supplementary Note" in *Duality in Mark*,[2]1988, 232-235.

RESPONSE TO THE MULTIPLE-STAGE HYPOTHESIS

I

The Introduction to the Feeding Story*

Mt 14:13-14; Mk 6:30-34; Lk 9:10-11

M.-É. Boismard has chosen this section to illustrate his multiple-stage hypothesis. Already in 1979 he had published an article in *NTS* under the promising(?) title: "The Two-Source Theory at an Impasse,"[1] which in fact was a study of the same section, with a reformulation of the theory he presented for the first time in his *Synopse II*. His fundamental solution is a two-stage composition of Matthew and this has not changed through the years 1972, 1979, 1984. It is less clear whether he still holds the two-stage composition in Luke.[2] He now concludes that Luke depends on Proto-Matthew in 9:10b-11 without mentioning Proto-Luke. In 1972 he made a distinction between Proto-Luke (dependent on Proto-Matthew) and the final Redactor, "l'ultime Rédacteur lucanien," who depends on Proto-Mark in v. 11a (γνόντες) and v. 11b (the theme of Jesus' teaching). These similarities with Mark no longer have source-critical relevance. At least three stages can be observed in Boismard's interpretation of Lk 9:10a. In 1972 both Mk 6:30 and Lk 9:10a are redactional additions; in 1979 Luke depends on Mark; in 1984 Luke and Mark depend on a common source (Proto-Mark?).

1. *Matthew 14:13-14*

We can start our discussion with a common assumption regarding Mt 14:13-14. In Boismard's theory the words ἐν πλοίῳ (v. 13a), πεζῇ ἀπὸ τῶν πόλεων (v. 13b), καὶ ἐξελθὼν εἶδον πολὺν ὄχλον καὶ ἐσπλαγχ-

---

* Cf. in this volume, 244-253.

[1] *NTS* 26 (1971-72) 1-17. Cf. *Synopse* II, 1972, 221-223 (§ 151, IA). See my response, "The Matthew-Luke Agreements in Mt 14,13-14 / Lk 9,10-11 (par. Mk 6,30-34). The Two-Source Theory beyond the Impasse,,' *ETL* 60 (1984) 5-24.

[2] On the regression of Proto-Luke in Boismard's commentary on John (1977), see my *Jean et les Synoptiques*, 1979, 19-20.

νίσθη ἐπ' αὐτοῖς (v. 14a) are taken from Mark. We can also agree with Boismard's other observation: "les vv. 13 et 14 du récit de Mt ont une tonalité typiquement matthéenne;" Matthew's text is "parfaitement matthéen" and *can* be explained as a reworking of Mk 6:30-34, "un remaniement du texte de Mc."

The somewhat curious way of arguing that οἱ ὄχλοι is not usual in Mt as the subject of a verb of movement and that therefore "the chances are very slight... that in regard to this particular point, Matthew's text could be explained as transformation of that of Mark" (1979:8) is now rightly left out.[3] On the contrary, I miss his note on Mk 6:31: "Matthew who has neither the theme of the missionary activity of the disciples nor their return, could not retain this address of Jesus to his disciples, since the disciples do not appear in his account" (1979:9).

We can conclude that, for Boismard, the real problem of the Matthew/Luke agreements in this section is on the side of Luke. With regard to Matthew, however, we should fustigate once more the ambiguity in his use of "Matthean" and "typical of Matthew". In the course of the argument, Matthean characteristics are transferred, without correction, to the level of an earlier redaction.[4]

2. *Luke 9:9-10*

a) Besides the positive agreements Matthew-Luke (10b ὑπεχώρησεν, 11a οἱ ὄχλοι ἠκολούθησαν αὐτῷ, 11b the healing motif) the negative agreement in omitting Mk 6:31 plays an important role in Boismard's hypothesis (25 words!). But is it really so that Luke has nothing parallel to Mk 6:31? The expression εἰς ἔρημον τόπον, which is replaced in Luke by εἰς πόλιν καλουμένην Βηθσαϊδά, is preceded by ἐν (τῷ) πλοίῳ and followed by κατ' ἰδίαν in Mt 14:13/Mk 6:32. The order of the words in Lk 9:10b is much closer to that of Mk 6:31:

δεῦτε ...   κατ' ἰδίαν   εἰς ἔρημον τόπον
ὑπεχώρησεν   κατ' ἰδίαν   εἰς πόλιν κ. Β.

In the Synopses the words καὶ παραλαβὼν αὐτούς are generally placed in parallel to Mk 6:32 (Lk 9:10b is even separated from Mk 6:31 by the division of the text: §§ 145 and 146 in Aland's Synopsis; §§155 and 156 in Boismard-Lamouille). Greeven's Synopsis presents a better arrangement:

---

[3] Cf. *ETL* 60 (1984), 29-31.

[4] Cf. "Urmarcus redivivus? Examen critique de l'hypothèse des insertions matthéennes dans Marc" [1974], in *Jean et les Synoptiques*, 319-361, esp. 346-361. See also *ETL* 60 (1984), 32.

Mk   Lk
6:30   9:10a
31 καὶ λέγει αὐτοῖς· δεῦτε ...   10b καὶ παραλαβὼν αὐτοὺς
32 καὶ ἀπῆλθον ...   ὑπεχώρησεν ...

The expression παραλαβὼν αὐτούς is used elsewhere in Luke. Jesus takes the twelve disciples apart for the prediction of passion (18:31 παραλαβὼν δὲ τοὺς δώδεκα, par. Mk 10:32; Matthew adds κατ' ἰδίαν) and he separates the three disciples from the others and takes them along with him for the transfiguration on the mountain (9:28 παραλαβὼν Πέτρον καὶ Ἰάκωβον, par. Mk 9:2 παραλαμβάνει ...).[5] In Lk 9:10b καὶ παραλαβὼν αὐτούς, after Lk 9:10a and preceding ὑπεχώρησεν ... (Mk 6:32 ἀπῆλθον ...), is Luke's parallel to Mk 6:31. The return of the disciples in Mk 6:30 is followed by a reaction of Jesus: καὶ λέγει αὐτοῖς ..., and in the Lukan parallel the return of the disciples (9:10a) is followed by καὶ παραλαβὼν αὐτούς: he took them with him, in his company, apart from the crowd.

b) The recognition of this parallel to Mk 6:31 (καὶ λέγει αὐτοῖς ...) sheds some light on Luke's change from Mark's plural (ἀπῆλθον) to the singular ὑπεχώρησεν in Lk 9:10b. The shift from the disciples to Jesus is somewhat analogous to Luke's concentration on Jesus in the introduction to the transfiguration:

Lk 9:10   Lk 9:28   Mk 9:2
παραλαβὼν αὐτοὺς   παραλαβὼν ...   παραλαμβάνει ...
ὑπεχώρησεν   ἀνέβη εἰς ...   ἀναφέρει αὐτοὺς εἰς ...
                     ... προσεύξασθαι.   ... κατ' ἰδίαν μόνους.
                                          ... ἔμπροσθεν αὐτῶς.

Obviously the plural ἀπῆλθον in Mk 6:32 (and αὐτοὺς ὑπάγοντας and αὐτούς in v. 33), followed by the singular in v. 34, denotes the movement of the group of Jesus and his disciples. The retention of such a plural, frequent in Mark, is extremely rare in Luke (cf. Lk 8:26, par. Mk 5:1). In the following instances Luke replaces the plural by a singular:[6]

---

[5] Compare also Mk 14:33 (om. Lk) and 5:40 (diff. Lk 8:51). In Mk 4:36 (diff. Lk) the disciples are taking Jesus. The verb παραλαμβάνειν is used six times in Acts, always in the form παραλαβών with the accusative of the person(s).

[6] Contrast Boismard: "le changement du pluriel en singulier... si peu normal pour lui." See also Mk 5:38 ἔρχονται, transferred before v. 37 in Lk 8:51 (ἐλθών). In other instances Luke has no parallel (Mk 6:53-54; 8:22; 11:12,19-20) or omits the whole clause (and the plural); 9:14,30,33; 10:32; 11:15,27; 14:22. Cf. C.H. TURNER, in JTS 26 (1925), 228-231 (with some corrections). — Matthew has the singular diff. Mk 1:29; 5:38; 6:32; 14:18,32 (see also Mk 9:33; 10:32; 11:12). Besides Mk 6:32 only Mk 5:38 is mentioned in Boismard's commentary as a Mt/Lk agreement relying on Proto-Mt (1972, 209b).

Mk		Lk	
1:21	εἰσπορεύονται	4:31	κατῆλθεν
1:29	ἐξελθόντες ἦλθον	4:38	ἀναστὰς ... εἰσῆλθεν
6:32	ἀπῆλθον	9:10	ὑπεχώρησεν
10:46	ἔρχονται	18:35	ἐγγίζειν αὐτόν
11:1	ἐγγίζουσιν	19:29	ἤγγισεν
14:18	ἀνακειμένων αὐτῶν	22:14	ἀνέπεσεν
	καὶ ἐσθιόντων		καὶ οἱ ἀπόστολοι σὺν αὐτῷ
14:26	ὑμνήσαντες ἐξῆλθον	22:39	ἐξελθὼν ἐπορεύθη
14:32	ἔρχονται	22:40	γενόμενος

c) Lk 9:10b ὑπεχώρησεν, diff. Mk 6:32 ἀπῆλθον (εἰς ἔρημον τόπον). The only other occurrence of the verb ὑποχωρεῖν in the New Testament is found in the gospel of Luke, in connection with the desert theme: Lk 5:16 ἦν ὑποχωρῶν ἐν ταῖς ἐρήμοις (Mk 1:45 ἔξω ἐπ᾽ ἐρήμοις τόποις ἦν).

Boismard (1979:4) opposes another parallel: Mk 1:35 ἀπῆλθεν εἰς ἔρημον τόπον and Lk 4:42 ἐπορεύθη εἰς ἔρημον τόπον. "In fact, in the eleven cases where Luke is faced with the verb ἀπέρχεσθαι in Mark, in five he retains this same verb (Lk 5:13; 8:37,38; 19:32; 22:4), while in two instances he changes it to πορεύεσθαι (Lk 4:42; 9:12)." Two more changes of ἀπέρχεσθαι to πορεύεσθαι can be added: Lk 9:13 (Mk 6:37) and 22:8 (Mk 14:12). The verb πορεύεσθαι is very common in Luke. In the case of Mk 1:35 the avoidance of two compounds of ἔρχεσθαι can be one reason for Luke's change of ἀπέρχεσθαι to πορεύεσθαι: Mk 1:35 ἀναστὰς ἐξῆλθεν καὶ ἀπῆλθεν, par. Lk 4:42 ἐξελθὼν ἐπορεύθη. However, it should be noted that κἀκεῖ προσηύχετο (Mk 1:35b) is.omitted in Lk 4:42. The theme appears in Lk 5:16 which looks like a delayed parallel to Mk 1:35b: αὐτὸς δὲ ἦν ὑποχωρῶν ἐν ταῖς ἐρήμοις καὶ προσευχόμενος. At the conclusion of the section, and before the solemn introduction of the larger unit of 5:17-39, Lk 5:16 combines Mk 1:35 and 1:45c into a generalizing summary statement: "But Jesus himself would often retire to deserted places to pray."[7]

But in Lk 9:10b "Luke specifically omits Mark's mention of the desert"! A partial answer to this objection is given by Boismard himself: κατ᾽ ἰδίαν, more than the desert, could have urged Luke to use a verb derived from χωρεῖν (cf. Ac 23:19 ἀναχωρήσας κατ᾽ ἰδίαν). Some analogy with the use of ἀναχωρεῖν in Acts (23:19; 26:31: to retire from

---

[7] Fitzmyer's translation. On the iterative sense see *Luke*, p. 575.

an assembly) should not be denied. In ὑπεχώρησεν κατ᾽ ἰδίαν[8] the emphasis is on the separation from the crowd (cf. Mk 6:31). Yet, the theme of the desert did not disappear in Luke. In the feeding story itself Mark's ὅτι (rec.) ἔρημός ἐστιν ὁ τόπος (6:35) is preserved in Lk 9:12: ὅτι (causal) ὧδε ἐν ἐρήμῳ τόπῳ ἐσμέν.

d) The study of Luke's οἱ ὄχλοι, parallel to πολλοί in Mk 6:33, should not be restricted to an examination of his reaction to the substantive adjective πολλοί. Due consideration should be given to the context in Mark:

Mk		Lk	
6:33	καὶ ἐπέγνωσαν πολλοί	9:11a	οἱ δὲ ὄχλοι γνόντες
34	πολὺν ὄχλον	11b	αὐτούς
36	ἀπόλυσον αὐτούς	12	ἀπόλυσον τὸν ὄχλον
	(45 ἀπολύει τὸν ὄχλον)		
41	ἵνα παρατιθῶσιν αὐτοῖς	16	παραθεῖναι τῷ ὄχλῳ
	(cf. 8,6 παρέθηκαν τῷ ὄχλῳ)		

The preceding context, before the mission of the disciples (Lk 9:1-10), is Lk 8:40-56 (par. Mk 5:21-43):

Mk		Lk	
5:21	ὄχλος πολύς	8:40	ὁ ὄχλος
24	ὄχλος πολύς (ἠκολούθει)	42	οἱ ὄχλοι (!)
27	ἐν τῷ ὄχλῳ	44	om.
30	ἐν τῷ ὄχλῳ	46	om.
31	τὸν ὄχλον	45	οἱ ὄχλοι

After Lk 9:10-17 Luke omits Mk 6:45-8:26 and continues with Mk 8:27 and the question of Jesus: τίνα με λέγουσιν οἱ ἄνθρωποι εἶναι; in Luke: οἱ ὄχλοι (9:18).

If Luke "decided ... to change Mark's text, he could certainly have used οἱ ὄχλοι (4,42)" (p. 8). Is Boismard still correct when he adds: "but he could as well have used ὄχλοι πολλοί, as in 5.15 (opposed to Mark 1.45), or again ὄχλος πολύς (7.11; 9.37)" (ibid.)? Luke used ὄχλος πολύς five times in his gospel:

---

[8] Besides Lk 9:10 (= Mk) and Ac 23:19, Luke used κατ᾽ ἰδίαν only in Lk 10:23: καὶ στραφεὶς πρὸς μαθητὰς κατ᾽ ἰδίαν εἶπεν. Compare Mk 4:34 κατ᾽ ἰδίαν ... τοῖς ἰδίοις μαθηταῖς; 9:28 οἱ μαθηταὶ αὐτοῦ κατ᾽ ἰδίαν (in the house: cf. 7:17 ἀπὸ τοῦ ὄχλου; see also 7:33); without parallel in Lk. Luke omits κατ᾽ ἰδίαν in Mk 9:2 (diff. Lk 9:28; but see 9:18 προσευχόμενον κατὰ μόνας) and 13:3 (Lk 21:7). Ac 23:19 can be compared with Mk 7:13:

Mk	7:33	ἀπολαβόμενος αὐτὸν ἀπὸ τοῦ ὄχλου κατ᾽ ἰδίαν
	8:23	ἐπιλαβόμενος τῆς χειρὸς τ. τ. ἐξήνεγκεν ...
Ac	23:19	ἐπιλαβόμενος δὲ τῆς χειρὸς αὐτοῦ ...
	23:19	καὶ ἀναχωρήσας κατ᾽ ἰδίαν ἐπυνθάνετο ...

5:29   ὄχλος πολὺς τελωνῶν καὶ ἄλλων ... (Mk 2:15 πολλοί τ. κ. ἄμ.)
6:17   ὄχλος πολὺς μαθητῶν αὐτοῦ (Mk 3:7 μετά τ. μ. αὐ.)
7:11   ὄχλος πολύς, cf. 12 ὄχλος τῆς πόλεως ἱκανός
8:4   ὄχλου πολλοῦ καὶ τῶν ... (Mk 4:1 ὄχλος πλεῖστος)
9:37   ὄχλος πολύς (Mk 9:14 ὄχλον πολύν).

In 5:29 and 6:17 ὄχλος πολύς is followed by a genitive and in 8:4 the καί is probably epexegetic: "the multitude consisted wholly of those who were following from different town" (Plummer). In 7:11 ὄχλος πολύς is contrasted to ὄχλος τῆς πόλεως ἱκανός in v. 12, again with a genitive. Thus, the use of ὄχλος πολύς in 9:37 is in some sense unique in Luke; it depends clearly on Mk 9:14. Compare ὄχλος πολύς in Mk 5:21 (Lk ὁ ὄχλος); 5:24 (Lk οἱ ὄχλοι); 6:34; 8:1 (no parallel); 12:37 [ὁ] πολὺς ὄχλος (Lk παντὸς τοῦ λαοῦ). See also Mk 4:1 ὄχλος πλεῖστος, πᾶς ὁ ὄχλος (cf. Lk 5:1 τὸν ὄχλον, 3 τοὺς ὄχλους); 10:46 ὄχλου ἱκανοῦ (cf. Lk 18:36 ὄχλου). The plural ὄχλοι πολλοί is used by Luke in 5:15 and in one other instance: 14:25 (cf. Mk 10:1 ὄχλοι). Lk 5:15 is parallel to Mk 1:45 and seems to combine Mk 1:45d and 2:2 (par. Lk 5:17). The subject ὄχλοι πολλοί is probably added under the influence of Mark's πολλοί:

Mk 1:45d καὶ   ἤρχοντο πρὸς αὐτὸν πάντοθεν.
   2:2   καὶ συνήχθσαν   πολλοί, ... καὶ ἐλάλει αὐ. τ. λ.
Lk 5:15b καὶ συνήρχοντο ὄχλοι πολλοὶ   ἀκούειν
                               καὶ θεραπεύεσθαι... (Lk 5:17 ἰᾶσθαι).

The substantive πολλοί occurs in Lk 1:1 (the prologue!) and in 14:16 (in the parable: from the source?). Boismard adds two instances in the gospel narrative: 7:21 and 4:41 (diff. Mk 1:34 δαιμόνια πολλά), but seems to neglect the parallel in Mk 3:10. Lk 7:21 is an addition in Lukan style (θεραπεύειν ἀπό, πνεύματα πονηρά, χαρίζεσθαι: cf. p. 165b) but it depends on Mk 3:10: ἐθεράπευσεν πολλούς (Mk 3:10 πολλοὺς γὰρ ἐθεράπευσεν) ἀπὸ νόσων (cf. Lk 6:18a) καὶ μαστίγων (Mk 3:10) καὶ πνευμάτων πονηρῶν (cf. Mk 3:11; Lk 6:18b). In Lk 4:41, too, the style is Lukan: ἐξήρχετο ἀπό instead of ἐξέβαλεν and the change of δαιμόνια πολλά (acc.) to δαιμόνια (nom.) ἀπὸ πολλῶν is not quite significant. Yet, Lk 4:41 has a double parallel in Mark (κραυγάζοντα ... ἐπιτιμῶν: cf. Mk 3:11-12) and the substantive πολλούς in Mk 3:10 is part of the parallel (in Mk 1:34 ἐθεράπευσεν πολλοὺς ... = adj.).

In parallel to Mk 10:48, πολλοί is replaced by ὁ ὄχλος in Matthew and by οἱ προάγοντες in Luke (18:39); in parallel to Mk 11:8, Matthew has ὁ πλεῖστος ὄχλος and in Luke the verb is left without subject (19:36, but see v. 36 ἅπαν τὸ πλῆθος τῶν μαθητῶν). To replace πολλοί in Mk 6:33 by οἱ ὄχλοι is, of course, not "necessary to Luke" but it is a perfectly understandable Lukan redaction. The association of πολλοί and (πολὺν) ὄχλον in Mk 6:33 and 34 is a well known feature of his Markan source: 2:2 πολλοί, cf. 4 διὰ τὸν ὄχλον (compare also 2:2 and 3:20 ὁ ὄχλος; cf. 6:31b); 3:10 πολλούς, cf. v. 9 διὰ τόν ὄχλον; 9:26 τοὺς πολλούς, cf. v. 25 ὄχλος; 10:48 πολλοί, cf. v. 46 ὄχλου ἱκανοῦ.

e) "Si Lc avait remanié ici le texte de Mc, il aurait eu relativement peu de chances d'utiliser la formule οἱ ὄχλοι; il aurait eu peu de chances d'utiliser le verbe ἀκολουθεῖν; et enfin, il aurait certainement mis le verbe à l'imparfait, et non à l'aoriste" (Boismard, 1984).
"When Luke describes a crowd that follows Jesus, he prefers to use the verb συνπορεύεσθαι. When he wishes to describe a crowd gathering around Jesus, as here, he more often uses the verb συνέρχεσθαι" (1979:8).
A few remarks on Luke's use of συμπορεύεσθαι, συνέρχεσθαι and ἀκολουθεῖν may be useful.

συμπορεύεσθαι is used three times in Luke and in each instance it responds to a preceding πορεύεσθαι. This is clear in 24:15 συνεπορεύετο αὐτοῖς (v. 13 ἦσαν πορευόμενοι; cf. v. 28) and also in 7:11: ἐπορεύθη... καὶ συνεπορεύοντο αὐτῷ οἱ μαθηταὶ αὐτοῦ καὶ ὄχλος πολύς. It is not enough to say that Luke describes here "a crowd that follows Jesus". Jesus, the disciples and a great crowd form one group and the ὄχλος τῆς πόλεως ἱκανός with the widow (σὺν αὐτῇ) is another group. The third instance is 14:25 συνεπορεύοντο δὲ αὐτῷ ὄχλοι πολλοί, in the context of the journey to Jerusalem: τοῦ πορεύεσθαι εἰς Ἰερουσαλήμ (9:51, cf. v. 53); διεπορεύετο... καὶ πορείαν ποιούμενος εἰς Ἰεροσόλυμα (13:22); ἐν τῷ πορεύεσθαι εἰς Ἰερουσαλήμ (17:11): great crowds went with him, accompanied him. The Lukan journey to Jerusalem and probably also the motif of 14:25 are inspired by Mk 10:1. The verb συμπορεύεσθαι by which Mark resumes the theme of the crowd coming to Jesus,[9] takes a different meaning in Luke's usage: to go along with, to travel with (Jesus).

συνέρχεσθαι can have a similar meaning. Thus, the Galilean women in Lk 23:55: ἦσαν συνεληλυθυῖαι ἐκ τῆς Γαλιλαίας αὐτῷ (cf. Mk 15:41 αἱ συναναβᾶσαι αὐτῷ εἰς Ἰεροσόλυμα). But in 5:15 Luke uses the verb to

---

[9] Mk 10:1b καὶ συμπορεύονται πάλιν ὄχλοι πρὸς αὐτόν. Cf. Mk 1:45; 2:2,13; 3:8,20; 4:1; 5:21. See esp. Mk 4:1 συνάγεται πρὸς αὐτὸν ὄχλος πλεῖστος (cf. 6:30; 7:1: συν- πρός), par. Lk 8:4 συνιόντος δὲ ὄχλου πολλοῦ καὶ κατὰ πόλιν ἐπιπορευομένων πρὸς αὐτόν.

describe "a crowd gathering around Jesus": καὶ συνήρχοντο ὄχλοι πολλοὶ ἀκούειν καὶ θεραπεύεσθαι (Mk 1:45 ἤρχοντο πρὸς αὐτὸν πάντοθεν; cf. 3:20 συνέρχεται ὁ ὄχλος). But is it "very close to 9:10"?

ἀκολουθεῖν in Lk 9:10 has, I think, a different connotation. The verb ἀκολουθεῖν is used in Lk 7:9 τῷ ἀκολουθοῦντι αὐτῷ ὄχλῳ, where its association with ὄχλος is probably redactional (Mt τοῖς ἀκολουθοῦσιν Q). Another redactional usage (Boismard agrees: cf. p. 422b) is found in Lk 23:27: ἠκολούθει δὲ αὐτῷ πλῆθος τοῦ λαοῦ καὶ γυναικῶν αἳ ἐκόπτοντο καὶ ἐθρήνουν αὐτόν. In this case there is clearly a separation between those who led him away and the multitude of those who followed him. Neither the verb συμπορεύεσθαι (together in one group) nor the verb συνέρχεσθαι (to come to the place where Jesus stays) would be appropriate here. Compare also Acts 21:36 ἠκολούθει γὰρ τὸ πλῆθος τοῦ λαοῦ κράζοντες· αἶρε αὐτόν. In Lk 9:10, too, Luke presents two distinct groups, Jesus and the disciples who withdrew κατ᾽ ἰδίαν and the crowds who followed. In Mark Jesus and the disciples went by boat and the crowds went by land and arrived before him. This contrast between ἐν τῷ πλοίῳ and πεζῇ is retained in Matthew but not in Luke. In parallel to Mk 6:34a Luke omits ἐξελθών ("when he came ashore") and he replaces εἶδεν πολὺν ὄχλον καὶ ἐσπλαγχνίσθη ἐπ᾽ αὐτούς by ἀποδεξάμενος αὐτούς. Jesus received them, he welcomed them (Meyer: "er wies sie nicht zurück, obgleich er die Einsamkeit suchte"). To denote the crowds who, before their "reception", followed at a distance (cf. Lk 22:54: μακρόθεν),[10] Luke has used the right verb: ἠκολούθησαν αὐτῷ. In contrast to Lk 23:27 and Acts 21:36 (ἠκολούθει), Luke has here the aorist, in parallel with Mark (ὑπεχώρησεν, ἠκολούθησαν, cf. Mk 6:32-33 ἀπῆλθον... συνέδραμον, προῆλθον), and aptly uses the imperfect for the description of Jesus' action in 9:11b (ἐλάλει, ἰᾶτο).

f) Lk 9:11b καὶ ... ἐλάλει αὐτοῖς περὶ τῆς βασιλείας τοῦ θεοῦ, par. Mk 6,34b καὶ ἤρξατο διδάσκειν αὐτοὺς πολλά. "Thème commun de la prédication aux foules ... exprimé chez Mc et Lc en termes totalement différents, si bien qu'il est difficile de parler d'un emprunt de l'un à l'autre" (Boismard); "literary influence between them in either direction cannot be assumed" (1979:13). It may suffice here to show that literary influence can be assumed in one direction. The use of ἤρξατο with

[10] Cf. W. SCHMITHALS, Lukas, 1980, 110: "wegen V. 12 spielt sich die Speisung anscheinend noch auf dem Weg nach Bethsaida ab". Cf. H.A.W. MEYER, Lukas, ⁴1857, 360: εἰς in 9,10 "von der Richtung wohin (versus) zu fassen". Compare Lk 7:11 ἐπορεύθη εἰς πόλιν καλουμένην Ναΐν (followed by ὡς δὲ ἤγγισεν ... in v. 12). Cf. the mention of Bethsaida in Mk 6:46 and 8:22 (after the feeding miracle).

infinitive in Mk 11:15; 12:1; 14:19 is retained by Luke (19:45; 20:9; 22:23) but not in Mk 1:45*; 2:23*; 4:1 (cf. Lk 5:1); 5:17,20; 6:7,34*; 8:31; 10:28, 32, 41, 47; 13:5; 14:33, 65*, 69, 71; and in four instances(*) it is replaced by an imperfect (5:15; 6:1; 9:11; 22:63; compare also Mk 8:11 and Lk 11:16).[11]

The phrase πολλὰ παθεῖν in 8,31 is retained by Luke (9:22; cf. 17:25) but the adverbial πολλά in Mk 1:45; 3:12; 4:2; 5:10, 23, 26, 38, 43; 6:34; 15:3 is omitted.[12] Mark's διδάσκειν αὐτοὺς πολλά has a parallel in Mk 4:2 ἐδίδασκεν αὐτοὺς ἐν παραβολαῖς, cf. 4:33 τοιαύταις παραβολαῖς πολλαῖς ἐλάλει αὐτοῖς τὸν λόγον (inclusion). Mk 4:1-2 has influenced Lk 5:1-3: v. 3 (end) ἐδίδασκεν τοὺς ὄχλους, followed by ὡς δὲ ἐπαύσατο λαλῶν. (On the other hand, in parallel to Mk 2:2b καὶ ἐλάλει αὐτοῖς τὸν λόγον, Luke writes καὶ αὐτὸς ἦν διδάσκων.)

In contrast to Mk 6:34b, Luke indicates the content of Jesus' teaching: he spoke to them about the kingdom of God. Cf. Lk 4:43 εὐαγγελίσασθαί με δεῖ τὴν βασιλείαν τοῦ θεοῦ (and 8:1 εὐαγγελιζόμενος τὴν βασιλείαν τοῦ θεοῦ). The verb λαλεῖν (Lk 31, Ac 59)[13] is used with περί in Lk 2:17,33,38; Ac 22:10 (cf. Ac 1:3 λέγων τὰ περὶ τῆς βασιλείας τοῦ θεοῦ; 8:12 Philippus εὐαγγελιζομένῳ περὶ τῆς βασιλείας τοῦ θεοῦ καὶ τοῦ ὀνόματος Ἰησοῦ Χριστοῦ; 19:8 Paul διαλεγόμενος καὶ πείθων [τὰ] περὶ τῆς βασιλείας τοῦ θεοῦ).

g) Lk 9:11c καὶ τοὺς χρείαν ἔχοντας θεραπείας ἰᾶτο. Luke's vocabulary is... in part related to that of Matthew: the article τούς and θεραπείας/ἐθεράπευσεν. These verbal agreements are noted since Rushbrooke, but what is their source-critical relevance? The healing theme, substitute for or addition to Jesus' teaching, implies a specific object: not the whole crowd but the sick among them are cured, in Matthew: τοὺς ἀρρώστους αὐτῶν, in Luke: τοὺς χρείαν ἔχοντας θεραπείας. And each evangelist uses his most characteristic verb for healing: ἐθεράπευσεν (Matthew), ἰᾶτο (Luke). "The same idea is present, the wording is entirely different".[14]

"Luke, who loves to juxtapose the two themes, could have completed Mark's text by adding the healing theme" (1979:9). Boismard reverses the argument: "Luke could have supplemented the theme of healings

---

[11] *The Minor Agreements*: 242-244 (no. 13).

[12] *Ibid.*, 278 (no. 28). See note 189: διδάσκειν πολλά (4:2; 6:34), adverbial or accusative.

[13] Cf. H. JASCHKE "λαλεῖν bei Lukas. Ein Beitrag zur lukanischen Theologie," *BZ* 15 (1971) 109-114, 112: in 9:11; 24:6,44, "Jesu Wort als verpflichtendes ... Evangelium der Kirche seiner Zeit".

[14] J.A. FITZMYER, *Luke*, p. 766.

with that of teaching" independently from Mark (13). He refers to Lk 5:15; 5:17; 6:6; 6:18. In Lk 6:6 the words καὶ διδάσκειν are added by Luke but is it not a normal addition to εἰσελθεῖν εἰς τὴν συναγωγήν in the light of Mk 1:21 and 6:2? Cf. Lk 14:15, (16), 31; 13:10. In Lk 5:17 ἦν διδάσκων corresponds to ἐλάλει αὐτοῖς τὸν λόγον (Mk 2:2) and the added element is: καὶ δύναμις κυρίου ἦν εἰς τὸ ἰᾶσθαι αὐτόν. In 5:15 ἀκούειν καὶ θεραπεύεσθαι ἀπὸ τῶν ἀσθενειῶν αὐτῶν is probably an anticipation of Mk 2:2 (ἐλάλει) and then the added element is θεραπεύεσθαι ... Or does it anticipate Lk 6:18 ἦλθον ἀκοῦσαι αὐτοῦ καὶ ἰαθῆναι ἀπὸ τῶν νόσων αὐτῶν, which is an adaptation of Mk 3:8 ἀκούοντες ὅσα ἐποίει ἦλθον πρὸς αὐτόν? I quote a recent commentary: "To the listening to Jesus that Luke has added to his source, the mention of the cures in now appended. ... The emphasis in the Lucan form of the summary is on listening to him ... If Luke mentions the healings and exorcisms, this is because they were in the Marcan source."[15] It should be noted, however, that the healing theme is much more than an appendage in this Lukan summary. The phrase ἰαθῆναι ἀπὸ τῶν νόσων αὐτῶν (before ἐθεραπεύοντο in v. 18b) is an addition as well. Luke has transferred Mk 3:11b-12 to Lk 4:41, and the summary ends in 6:19b with a new addition: ὅτι δύναμις παρ' αὐτοῦ ἐξήρχετο καὶ ἰᾶτο πάντας (cf. Lk 8:46, par. Mk 5:30). The summary of Lk 6:17-19 prepares for the sermon in 6:20-49. The Q sequence of the sermon and the healing of the centurion's servant (7:1-10) is followed by another miracle story, the raising of the widow's son at Nain (7:11-17; cf. Boismard, 164a: "Lc rédige lui-même ce récit"), and then Jesus' answer to John the Baptist in 7:18-23 will be preceded by a redactional notice on Jesus' healing activity (7:21; cf. Lk 6:18).

The double theme of Lk 9:11, preaching (the Kingdom of God) and healing, appears also in Luke's description of the disciples' mission: εὐαγγελιζόμενοι καὶ θεραπεύοντες (9:6; cf. Mk 6:12-13 ἐκήρυξαν ... ἐθεράπευον), in response to 9:2:[16]

Lk 9:2	Mk 3:14b-15
ἀπέστειλεν αὐτοὺς	ἵνα ἀποστέλλῃ αὐτοὺς
κηρύσσειν τὴν βασιλείαν τοῦ θεοῦ	κηρύσσειν
καὶ ἰᾶσθαι [τοὺς ἀσθενεῖς]	καὶ ἔχειν ἐξουσίαν ἐκβάλλειν τὰ δαιμόνια.

The association of the verb ἰᾶσθαι in 9:2 with θεραπεύειν in 9:1,6 (compare 9:11 θεραπείας/ἰᾶτο) is found also in 6:18-19; 8:43, 47; 14:3-4

[15] J.A. FITZMYER, Luke, p. 624, 622, 623.
[16] In his complex text of 9:1-2 Luke combines Mk 6:7 with Mk 3:14b-15. In v. 1 he adds healing to exorcism: δύναμιν καὶ and καὶ νόσους θεραπεύειν added to ἐξουσίαν ἐπὶ πάντα τὰ δαιμόνια (cf. Mk 6:7c), and in v. 2 he replaces exorcism by healing (in the text). Compare the omission of Mk 6:13a in Lk 9:6.

(see also 5:15 and 5:17; 5:15 and 6:18).[17] The expression τοὺς χρείαν ἔχοντας θεραπείας in Lk 9:11 is a reminiscence of Mk 2:17a οὐ χρείαν ἔχουσιν οἱ ἰσχύοντες ἰατροῦ ἀλλ᾽ οἱ κακῶς ἔχοντες (Lk 5:31 οἱ ὑγιαίνοντες).[18] The word θεραπεία is used in Lk 12:42 (diff. Mt 24:45 οἰκετεία, household).

The examination of the minor agreements of Matthew and Luke in the light of their context in each gospel leads to the conclusion that these agreements imply a certain amount of disagreement. Following on the death of John the Baptist, Matthew's ἀνεχώρησεν reminds us of Mt 4:12 ἀκούσας δὲ ὅτι Ἰωάννης παρεδόθη ἀνεχώρησεν εἰς τ. Γ. "The connotation of 'taking refuge' from some peril"[19] is less suitable in the case of Luke's ὑπεχώρησεν: Jesus takes with him the disciples after their return and retires from the crowd. In Matthew οἱ ὄχλοι ἠκολούθησαν is very much a stereotyped formula which is used here not quite fittingly after the preceding ἐν πλοίῳ.[20] In Luke there is no such a confusing distinction between ἐν τῷ πλοίῳ and πεζῇ and the crowds are described as a distinct "following" group. The third agreement, the healing theme, is in Matthew a substitute for teaching, and in Luke teaching and healing are juxtaposed.

From his presentation of the Matthew/Luke agreements, Boismard draws the following conclusion: "When Matthew parallels Mark and Luke, his text is closer to Luke than to Mark. ... When Matthew parallels Mark alone, the texts are nearly identical. ... The Two-Source theory is unable to account for this fact". "The Two-Source theory is incapable of explaining why, after this almost *ad litteram* adherence to Mark [Lk 9:10a], Luke offers a text quite close to that of Matthew, at the precise point where Matthew enters upon the scene" (1979:11, 13). We have seen above that Luke's expression παραλαβὼν αὐτούς in 9:10b summarizes Mk 6:31 and that ἀποδεξάμενος αὐτούς in 9:11b is Luke's

---

[17] Cf. 4:23; 8:43: ἰατρός and θεραπεύειν.

[18] The use of θεραπεία instead of the personal ἰατρός can be compared with Lk 22:71 μαρτυρίας χρείαν (diff. Mk 14:63 χρείαν ἔχομεν μαρτύρων) and Lk 15:7 οὐ χρείαν ἔχουσιν μετανοίας (cf. Lk 5:32 εἰς μετανοίαν and δικαίους - ἁμαρτωλούς, in parallel with 5:31).

[19] Cf. MOULTON-MILLIGAN, *s.v.* I would add: and in Mt, after some warning. Cf. 2:12 (χρηματισθέντες κατ᾽ ὄναρ); 2:14 (v. 13 ἄγγελος ... κατ᾽ ὄναρ); 2:22 (ἀκούσας ... χρηματισθεὶς κατ᾽ ὄναρ); 4:12 (ἀκούσας); 12:15 (γνούς); 14:13 (ἀκούσας). See also ἀνεχώρησεν in 15:21 (Mk ἀπῆλθεν): "bei ihm scheint die Reise Jesu eine Flucht vor seinen Widersachern su sein" (J. SCHMID, *Matthäus*, ad loc.).

[20] For that reason L. Vaganay defends the short reading in Mt 14:13 (om. ἐν πλοίῳ, "le texte 'occidental' représenté par Sy^{sc}"): "la suite: 'les foules le *suivirent* à pied' suffit à montrer ..." (*Le problème synoptique*, 72).

parallel to Mk 6:34a. If the text of Mt 14:13a "parallels Mark and Luke", is it then closer to Luke than to Mark? Compare:

... ἀνεχώρησεν ἐκεῖθεν	ἀπῆλθον	ὑπεχώρησεν
ἐν πλοίῳ	ἐν τῷ πλοίῳ	
εἰς ἔρημον τόπον κατ' ἰδίαν	εἰς ἔρ. τ. κατ' ἰδίαν	κατ' ἰδίαν
		εἰς πόλιν καλ. Β.

3. *Mark 6:31-34*

The "Matthean" structure in Mt 12:15 and 19:1-2 is cited as a parallel and confirmation of Proto-Matthew in 14:13-14. We can refer here to the study of these Matthean summaries in our investigation of Mt 12:15, par. Mk 3:7-10.[21]

A further confirmation of Proto-Matthew is found in the analysis of the text of Mark: the Proto-Matthean summary has its parallel in one of the two sources of Mk 6:31-34. Unfortunately, the Matthew/Mark equivalences reappear on the level of the sources: ἀναχωρεῖν/ἀπέρχεσ-θαι, οἱ ὄχλοι/πολλοί, ἀκολουθεῖν/συντρέχειν, θεραπεύειν/διδάσκειν. Boismard agrees that Matthew's rewriting of Mark can present a reasonable explanation for these differences. When they are transferred to the level of a pre-Proto-Matthean source, they are no longer under control and become an insoluble problem.[22]

The combination of two different sources in Mk 6:31-34 is based on the observation that the account mentions two different 'crowds', the people of v. 31 (ἦσαν ... πολλοί): εἶδον ... προῆλθον, and the πολλοί of v. 33: ἐπέγνωσαν ... συνέδραμον. Of course, in Mk 6:33 there is a widening of the horizon as to include those who come "from all the towns", but in Mark those who "arrived first" and those who "ran there on foot" are the same people, and, in any event, before taking refuge in a "two-source" hypothesis, the possibility of Markan redaction[23] should be considered. Not all duality in Mark is a duality of sources.[24]

---

[21] Cf. *supra*, 42-46.

[22] "Il serait vain, ici, de se demander si c'est le proto-Matthieu qui dépend de la tradition marcienne ou au contraire le (proto-)Marc qui dépendrait de la tradition matthéenne" (Boismard 1984).

[23] One of the indications of Markan redaction is the contact with the summary of Mk 6:53-56: 54 καὶ ἐξελθόντων αὐτῶν ἐκ τοῦ πλοίου εὐθὺς ἐπιγνόντες αὐτὸν 55a περιέδαμον ὅλην τὴν χώραν ἐκείνην, cf. 6:33 ἐπέγνωσαν, ἀπὸ πασῶν τῶν πόλεων συνέδραμον, 34 καὶ ἐξελθών (32 ἐν τῷ πλοίῳ). Cf. *Synopse* II, 229: "Ce 'sommaire' ... est probable-ment une composition-marcienne" (Mc-interm.; 6:55d-56a red.). "Ce sont les deux seuls textes de Mc (et des évangiles) où le verbe *epiginôskein* et l'action de 'courir' soient dits des foules" (229a). But see Mk 9:25 ἐπισυντρέχει ὄχλος!

[24] Boismard's suggestion that Mark incorporated here the introduction to the second feeding story has no real basis. The summary in Mt 15:29-31 is a redactional composition. On the negative agreement of Matthew/Luke against Mk 6:37-38 (cf. 8:5), see *ETL* 60 (1984), 31.

Mt 14	Mk 6:30-34	Lk 9
12b καὶ ἐλθόντες ἀπήγγειλαν τῷ Ἰησοῦ.	30 καὶ συνάγονται οἱ ἀπόστολοι πρὸς τὸν Ἰησοῦν καὶ ἀπήγγειλαν αὐτῷ πάντα ὅσα ἐποίησαν καὶ ὅσα ἐδίδαξαν.	10 καὶ ὑποστρέψαντες οἱ ἀπόστολοι διηγήσαντο αὐτῷ ὅσα ἐποίησαν.
13 ἀκούσας δὲ ὁ Ἰησοῦς	31 καὶ λέγει αὐτοῖς· δεῦτε ὑμεῖς αὐτοὶ κατ' ἰδίαν εἰς ἔρημον τόπον καὶ ἀναπαύσασθε ὀλίγον. ἦσαν γὰρ οἱ ἐρχόμενοι καὶ οἱ ὑπάγοντες πολλοί, καὶ οὐδὲ φαγεῖν εὐκαίρουν.	καὶ παραλαβὼν αὐτοὺς
ἀνεχώρησεν ἐκεῖθεν ἐν πλοίῳ εἰς ἔρημον τόπον κατ' ἰδίαν·	32 καὶ ἀπῆλθον ἐν τῷ πλοίῳ εἰς ἔρημον τόπον κατ' ἰδίαν.	ὑπεχώρησεν κατ' ἰδίαν εἰς πόλιν καλουμένην Βηθσαϊδά.
καὶ ἀκούσαντες οἱ ὄχλοι ἠκολούθησαν αὐτῷ πεζῇ ἀπὸ τῶν πόλεων.	33 καὶ εἶδον αὐτοὺς ὑπάγοντας καὶ ἐπέγνωσαν πολλοί καὶ πεζῇ ἀπὸ πασῶν τῶν πόλεων συνέδραμον ἐκεῖ καὶ προῆλθον αὐτούς.	11 οἱ δὲ ὄχλοι γνόντες ἠκολούθησαν αὐτῷ· καὶ ἀποδεξάμενος αὐτοὺς
14 καὶ ἐξελθὼν εἶδεν πολὺν ὄχλον καὶ ἐσπλαγχνίσθη ἐπ' αὐτοῖς καὶ ἐθεράπευσεν τοὺς ἀρρώστους αὐτῶν.	34 καὶ ἐξελθὼν εἶδεν πολὺν ὄχλον καὶ ἐσπλαγχνίσθη ἐπ' αὐτοὺς ὅτι ἦσαν ὡς πρόβατα μὴ ἔχοντα ποιμένα καὶ ἤρξατο διδάσκειν αὐτοὺς πολλά.	ἐλάλει αὐτοῖς περὶ τῆς βασιλείας τοῦ θεοῦ, καὶ τοὺς χρείαν ἔχοντας θεραπείας ἰᾶτο.

II

THE HEALING OF THE LEPER*

Mt 8:2-4; Mk 1:40-44; Lk 5:12-14

Boismard's position regarding Mk 1:40-44 and parallels is threefold. First, the story in the three Synoptic Gospels is characteristically "Matthean". Second, the text in P. Egerton 2, apart from a later expansion (the account of the disease), shows a shorter, more archaic, Proto-Lukan version. Third, Mk 1:42 receives a special treatment: the phrase ἐκαθαρίσθη αὐτοῦ ἡ λέπρα is a more primitive element in Mt 8:3 ("certainement plus primitive") and Mk 1:42 is a combination of "Matthew" and Proto-Luke (cf. Griesbach).[1]

1. P. Egerton 2

The text in P. Egerton 2 ends with τοῖ[ς ἱερεῦσιν ... and allows for conjectural reconstruction. Boismard's proposal is to read τοῖς ἱερεῦσιν εἰς μαρτύριον αὐτοῖς and to take the phrase on offering the gift that Moses commanded (Mt 8:4 and par.) for a "Matthean" addition to the original story. However, since the publication of P. Köln 255 the missing words can be added:

πορε[υθεὶς σεαυ]τὸν ἐπίδειξον τοῖ[ς ἱερεῦσιν]
καὶ ἀνένεγκον [περὶ τοῦ καθ]αρισμοῦ ὡς προ[σ]έ[ταξεν Μω(ϋσῆς)
καὶ μ]ηκέτι ἁ[μά]ρτανε ...[2]

P. Egerton 2 can no longer be used as a witness for a shorter version in which τοῖς ἱερεῦσιν was immediately followed by the final phrase εἰς μαρτύριον αὐτοῖς.[3] On the contrary, the text of Egerton 2 continues with καὶ μηκέτι ἁμάρτανε (cf. Jn 5,14) and the omitted words are εἰς

---

* Cf. in this volume, 254-258.

[1] Boismard's interpretation of the Healing of the Leper has developed in three stages (1972, 1981, 1984): *Synopse II*, 1972, 101-105 (§ 39); "La guérison du lépreux (Mc 1,40-45 et par.)," in R. AGUIRRE - F. GARCIA LOPEZ (eds.), *Escritos de Biblia y Oriente* (Bibliotheca Salmanticensis. Estudios, 38), Salamanca-Jerusalem, 1981, 283-291; in this volume (= 1984). Cf. F. NEIRYNCK, "Papyrus Egerton 2 and the Healing of the Leper," *ETL* 61 (1985) 153-160.

[2] Ed. M. GRONEWALD, 1987. Cf. F. NEIRYNCK, "The Apocryphal Gospels and the Gospel of Mark," in J.-M. SEVRIN (ed.), *The New Testament in Early Christianity* (BETL, 86), Leuven, 1989, 123-175, esp. 162-164: "Papyrus Köln 255 (Inv. 608)."

[3] On the witness of Clement of Alexandria and Tatian (*Synopse II*, 102), cf. *ETL* 61 (1985), 156.

μαρτύριον αὐτοῖς. Moreover, Egerton 2 reads περὶ τοῦ καθαρισμοῦ (= Mk/Lk), which is not in Matthew.⁴

The new evidence confirms Bell & Skeat's restoration (on the basis of πορε[   ]γτοι) and the contact with Lk 17:14: πορε[υθεὶς ἐπίδειξον σεαυτὸ]ν τοῖ[ς ἱερεῦσι ...], with one correction: σεαυ]τὸν ἐπίδειξον, in the inverted order of Mt/Mk (σεαυτὸν δεῖξον, diff. Lk). The double vocative διδάσκαλε Ἰησοῦ (line 33) is another possible contact with Lk 17:11-19 (v. 13 Ἰησοῦ ἐπιστάτα). It should be noted, however, that it appears again in line 45, in parallel to διδάσκαλε in Mk 12:14 and/or ραββί in Jn 3:2.⁵

The verb ἀφιστάναι (line 39 ἀπέστη) is one of the "Lukan" words in Egerton 2; as Boismard observes, it is used in a similar phrase in Acts 12:10.

The words of the leper: λεπροῖς συνοδεύων καὶ συνεσθίων αὐτοῖς ἐν τῷ πανδοχείῳ ἐλέπρησα καὶ αὐτὸς ἐγώ (lines 33-36) are taken for "des notes secondaires" ("ces détails ... ajoutés à un récit archaïque"). But can one prove this distinction between the original story and the later addition if both are written in the same "Lukan" style? The verb συνεσθίειν (Acts 10:41; 11:3; never in the other Gospels) is used in Lk 15:2: ἁμαρτωλοὺς προσδέχεται καὶ συνεσθίει αὐτοῖς, a (redactional) passage which looks like the model of Egerton 2. The verb συνοδεύειν is used once in the New Testament: οἱ συνοδεύοντες αὐτῷ (participle!) in Acts 9:7, and the simple verb ὁδεύειν occurs once in the New Testament, and most significantly in the parable of the good Samaritan: Σαμαρίτης δέ τις ὁδεύων (Lk 10:33). The word πανδοχεῖον (another hapaxlegomenon in the New Testament) occurs in the next verse (Lk 10:34; cf. v. 35 πανδοχεύς). The writer of Egerton 2 seems to associate the good Samaritan of the parable and the thankful Samaritan of the healing story.

The common Lukan vocabulary is not the only link between the "insertion" and its context in Egerton 2. Boismard has drawn our attention on the difference between δύνασαί με καθαρίσαι (Syn.) and καθαρίζομαι ("la formule de Egert. 2 est plus primitive que celle de Mt"). However, two factors may have contributed to a secondary simplification of the Synoptic formula. First, the words of Jesus (θέλω, καθαρίσθητι) are left unchanged in Egerton and the writer may have assimilated the words of the leper to those of Jesus (θέλῃς, καθαρίζομαι).

---

⁴ If, as suggested by Boismard, P. Egerton 2 has the more original version, Matthew's formulation in 8:4 will be secondary (ctr. *Synopse* II, 103-104).

⁵ Cf. "The Apocryphal Gospels," 167.

Second, the phrase καθαρίζομαι, without δύνασαι, concentrates on the person of the speaker and this corresponds with the *Individualismus* of the account of his disease (in the first person). By adding οὖν after ἐάν the leper's request becomes the conclusion of his account, and this connection is emphasized by the contrast between (καὶ αὐτὸς) ἐγώ and the added word σύ.[6]

The Synoptic formula δύνασαί ... is not the only omission in Egerton 2. Once it is agreed that the writer of Egerton 2 has been influenced by the story of the healing of the ten lepers, the absence of the worshipping (Mt 8:2 προσεκύνει αὐτῷ), of the stretching out of Jesus' hand and the touching of the leper (Mt 8:3 ἐκτείνας τὴν χεῖρα ἥψατο αὐτοῦ) and of the injunction to silence (Mt 8:4 ὅρα μηδενὶ εἴπῃς) can be understood as secondary omissions in Egerton 2.

2. How "Matthean" Are the Three Synoptic Stories?

"Tous les trois sont marqués par la façon d'écrire de Mt." Is this "Matthew" the source of the Gospel of Mark or is it post-Markan redaction?

a) ἐκτείνας τὴν χεῖρα (Mt 8:3/Mk 1:41)

The formula ἐκτείνας τὴν χεῖρα (Mt 8:3; Mk 1:41; Lk 5:13) is found only in Mt 12:49; 14:31 (said of Jesus) and 26:51: "Elle est donc matthéenne."

Mt 26:51   Mk 14:47
ἐκτείνας τὴν χεῖρα
ἀπέσπασεν τὴν μάχαιραν αὐτοῦ   σπασάμενος τὴν μάχαιραν

"Matthew chooses to color the description provided by Mark with some biblical imagery. The expression ἐκτείνας τὴν χεῖρα is generally recognized as a biblical expression denoting a gesture of strength or threat. The phrase occurs over 75 times throughout the Old Testament. ... The expression is found in almost all sections of the Old Testament literature. In several contexts it is associated with the use of a sword: Jdg 3:21; 15:15 (the jawbone of an ass used as a weapon); Ex 25:13; 30:25; particularly noteworthy is the text in Gen 22:10: καὶ ἐξέτεινεν Αβρααμ *τὴν χεῖρα αὐτοῦ λαβεῖν τὴν μάχαιραν* σφάξαι τὸν υἱὸν αὐτοῦ. ... The motivation for this change [ἀπέσπασεν for Mark's σπασάμενος]

---

[6] Of course, [σύ] is part of the hypothetical reconstruction. Compare the phrase καὶ αὐτὸς (ἐγώ) with καὶ αὐτός in Lk 5:14 (said of Jesus) and Luke's use of καὶ αὐτός elsewhere. The verb λεπρᾶν (in ἐλ[έπρησα) is not used in the New Testament; it occurs in the LXX (Lev 22:4 B; Nu 12:10 bis; cf. λεπροῦσθαι in 4 Kgs 5:1,27; 15:5: λελεπρωμένος).

might be found in the strong probibition Matthew has added in the next verse: ἀπόστρεψον τὴν μάχαιράν σου εἰς τὸν τόπον αὐτῆς. The addition of the biblical expression ἐκτείνας τὴν χεῖρα in 26:51 and the logion in 26:52 put much more attention on the complete action of 'drawing' the sword and 'replacing' the sword than in Mark. The added pronoun (μάχαιραν) αὐτοῦ, compensating in part for the change from Mark's middle to the active voice, also aligns itself with the (μάχαιράν) σου in the saying that follows."[7]

Mt 12:49	Mk 3:34
ἐκτείνας τὴν χεῖρα αὐτοῦ	περιβλεψάμενος
ἐπὶ τοὺς μαθητὰς αὐτοῦ	τοὺς περὶ αὐτὸν κύκλῳ καθημένους

"Dans le texte de Marc iii.34-5, il n'est pas clair si le regard de Jésus sur 'ceux qui étaient assis en cercle autour de lui' désigne ceux qu'il considère comme sa mère et ses frères. La parole de Jésus peut être comprise d'après le parallèle de Luc qui a omis le motif du regard: 'Voici ma mère et mes frères: celui qui fait la volonté de Dieu ...'. En Matthieu, par contre, le regard est remplacé par un geste qui n'a plus rien d'équivoque ...."[8] According to Boismard, the text of Matthew's source is almost identical with Mk 3:34: "il désigne, *soit* de la main (Mt), *soit* du regard (Mc), ceux qui sont assis autour de lui (Mc, *tandis que Mt a banalisé en mettant 'ses disciples'*) en affirmant: 'Voici ma mère et mes frères'" (*Synopse* II, 178a).

Mt 14:31 ἐκτείνας τὴν χεῖρα ἐπελάβετο αὐτοῦ

The Peter episode of Mt 14:28-31 is a Matthean insertion in the story of Jesus walking on the sea (at Mk 6:50/51). Boismard agrees: it has been added to Mark (Mc-interm.) by *l'ultime Rédacteur matthéen* (*Synopse* II, 228b; cf. 227a).

We should mention also Mt 12:13 ἔκτεινόν (σου) τὴν χεῖρα· καὶ ἐξέτεινεν, strictly parallel to Mk 3:5 (cf. Lk 6:10).

To conclude: the three instances of Matthew's use of ἐκτείνας τὴν χεῖρα can be attributed to post-Markan redaction and provide no indication of Matthean tradition. The methodological principle that Boismard has formulated elsewhere can be applied here: "Les textes cités ... sont tous de l'ultime niveau rédactionnel matthéen, ce qui ne permet pas de faire

---

[7] D.P. SENIOR, *The Passion Narrative according to Matthew. A Redactional Study* (BETL, 39), Leuven, 1975, ²1982, 129-130.

[8] *Evangelica*, pp. 288-289 (= "Les femmes au tombeau," 1969, pp. 182-183).

remonter l'expression au Document A [Matthew's source]" (*Synopse* II, 178b).

b) ἥψατο αὐτοῦ (Mt 8:3/Mk 1:41)

"Par l'importance essentielle donnée au fait de 'toucher' le malade pour le guérir, le récit ... est de tonalité matthéenne." The evidence is found in Mt 8:15 (diff. Mk 1,31) and Mt 20:34; 9:29 (diff. Mk 10:52).

Mt 9:29 ἥψατο τῶν ὀφθαλμῶν αὐτῶν
20:34 ἥψατο τῶν ὀμμάτων αὐτῶν

The healing of two blind men in Mt 9:27-31 is a doublet of the healing story of Mt 20:29-34 (two blind men), in parallel to Mk 10:46-52 (the healing of the blind Bartimaeus). Mark has only the word of Jesus: ὕπαγε, ἡ πίστις σου σέσωκέν σε (10:52), and no touching of the eyes. In the hypothesis that Matthew knew the Gospel of Mark he could be influenced by Mark's first story of the healing of a blind man in Mk 8:22-26:

22 ... ἵνα αὐτοῦ ἅψηται
23b καὶ πτύσας εἰς τὰ ὄμματα αὐτοῦ
ἐπιθεὶς τὰς χεῖρας αὐτῷ
25a εἶτα πάλιν ἐπέθηκεν τὰς χεῖρας ἐπὶ τοὺς ὀφθαλμοὺς αὐτοῦ.

Compare the healing of the deaf and dumb man in 7:31-37:

32b ... ἵνα ἐπιθῇ αὐτῷ τὴν χεῖρα.
33 καὶ ... ἔβαλεν τοὺς δακτύλους αὐτοῦ εἰς τὰ ὦτα αὐτοῦ
καὶ πτύσας ἥψατο τῆς γλώσσης αὐτοῦ.

Boismard's comment on Mk 7:33 is hardly correct. The use of ἥψατο in 7:33 is not unique and I do not see how its "valeur curative" can be denied in 8:22.

The word ὄμματα is used in Mk 8:23 and Mt 20:34, and not elsewhere in the New Testament, and the variation ὄμματα - ὀφθαλμοί (Mk 8:23, 25) has its echo in Mt 9:29 and 20:34. While in Mt 20:34 ἥψατο τῶν ὀμμάτων αὐτῶν replaces the word of Jesus (Mk 10:52), Mt 9:29 combines ἥψατο τῶν ὀφθαλμῶν αὐτῶν with the word of Jesus: λέγων· κατὰ τὴν πίστιν ὑμῶν γενηθήτω ὑμῖν. Is it the combination of Mk 10:52 (ἡ πίστις σου!) with its parallel in Mt 20:34 (ἥψατο)? Compare:

Mt 20:33-34 | Mk 10:51-52
33b ... ἵνα ἀνοιγῶσιν οἱ ὀφθαλμοὶ ἡμῶν. | 51b ... ἵνα ἀναβλέψω
34 σπλαγχνισθεὶς δὲ ὁ Ἰησοῦς | 52 καὶ ὁ Ἰησοῦς
ἥψατο τῶν ὀμμάτων αὐτῶν, | εἶπεν αὐτῷ· ὕπαγε, ἡ πίστις σου σ. σε.
καὶ εὐθέως ἀνέβλεψαν | καὶ εὐθὺς ἀνέβλεψεν.

Mt 9:29-30
29a τότε ἥψατο τῶν ὀφθαλμῶν αὐτῶν | 29b λέγων· κατὰ τὴν πίστιν ὑμῶν γ. ὑμῖν.
30 καὶ ἀνεῴχθησαν αὐτῶν οἱ ὀφθαλμοί.

It can be seen more correctly, I think, as the combination of Mk 10:52 with Mk 1:41 (ἥψατο καὶ λέγει ...). This is certainly not the only reminiscence of Mk 1:40-45 in Mt 9:27-31:

Mt 9:27-31	Mk 1:40-45
28 προσῆλθον αὐτῷ ...	40 καὶ ἔρχεται πρὸς αὐτὸν ...
πιστεύετε	ἐὰν θέλῃς
ὅτι *δύναμαι* τοῦτο ποιῆσαι;	*δύνασαί* με καθαρίσαι
	41* καὶ σπλαγχνισθεὶς
29 τότε *ἥψατο* τῶν ὀφθαλμῶν αὐτῶν	ἐκτείνας τὴν χεῖρα αὐτοῦ *ἥψατο*
λέγων· ... γενηθήτω ὑμῖν.	*καὶ λέγει αὐτῷ·* θέλω, καθαρίσθητι.
30 καὶ ἀνεῴχθησαν αὐτῶν οἱ ὀφθαλμοί.	42 ... καὶ ἐκαθαρίσθη.
καὶ *ἐνεβριμήθη αὐτοῖς* ὁ Ἰησοῦς	43 καὶ *ἐμβριμησάμενος αὐτῷ* ...
λέγων·	44 καὶ λέγει αὐτῷ·
ὅρατε, μηδεὶς γινωσκέτω.	ὅρα μηδενὶ μηδὲν εἴπῃς, ...
31 οἱ δὲ ἐξελθόντες	45 ὁ δὲ ἐξελθὼν
διεφήμισαν αὐτόν.	ἤρξατο ... διαφημίζειν τὸν λόγον.

*Mt 8:3 καὶ | ἐκτείνας τὴν χεῖρα | ἥψατο αὐτοῦ
λέγων· ...

Mt 8:15	Mk 1:31
καὶ	καὶ προσελθὼν
ἥψατο τῆς χειρὸς αὐτῆς,	*ἤγειρεν αὐτὴν κρατήσας τῆς χειρός·*
καὶ ἀφῆκεν αὐτὴν ὁ πυρετός·	καὶ ἀφῆκεν αὐτὴν ὁ πυρετός.
καὶ ἠγέρθη,	
καὶ διηκόνει αὐτῷ.	καὶ διηκόνει αὐτοῖς.

"C'est le fait de 'toucher' la main de la malade qui effectue la guérison: il a bien une vertu curative par lui-même." This is apparently a good description of Matthew's version. But is it a correct statement that in Mark "le fait de prendre la main de la malade a simplement pour but de l'aider à se lever"? To take her (or him) by the hand is at least part of the curative action (ἐγείρειν). Compare:

5:41 κρατήσας τῆς χειρὸς τοῦ παιδίου λέγει αὐτῇ· ... ἔγειρε.
   42 καὶ εὐθὺς ἀνέστη τὸ κοράσιον.
9:27 κρατήσας τῆς χειρὸς αὐτοῦ   ἤγειρεν αὐτόν,
   καὶ ἀνέστη.

In Mk 1:31 the healing action is the same: he took her by the hand and lifted her up. In this case ἤγειρεν is not followed by ἀνέστη but by καὶ ἀφῆκεν αὐτὴν ὁ πυρετός, in response to v. 30: κατέκειτο πυρέσσουσα. Matthew has separated the verb ἐγείρειν from κρατήσας ... (Mt ἥψατο). It is used as καὶ ἠγέρθη after καὶ ἀφῆκεν αὐτὴν ὁ πυρετός, either as an indication that the healing took place (ἥψατο ... καὶ ἠγέρθη: cf. 9:25) or as a transition from the healing to the service: καὶ ἠγέρθη καὶ διηκόνει αὐτῷ (compare Luke's ἀναστᾶσα).

In Mt 9:25 Matthew has retained Mark's κρατήσας ... in a simplified and slightly modified form:

Mt 9:25	Mk 5:41-42
ἐκράτησεν τῆς χειρὸς αὐτῆς	41 καὶ *κρατήσας* τῆς χειρὸς τοῦ παιδίου λέγει αὐτῇ· ... *ἔγειρε*.
καὶ *ἠγέρθη* τὸ κοράσιον	42 καὶ εὐθὺς ἀνέστη τὸ κοράσιον καὶ περιεπάτει.

Compare also Mt 12:11 κρατήσει αὐτὸ καὶ ἐγερεῖ (diff. Lk 14:5). A Lukan substitute for κρατήσας is found in Acts 3:7 καὶ πιάσας αὐτὸν τῆς δεξιᾶς χειρὸς *ἤγειρεν* αὐτόν. Matthew's substitute (ἥψατο in 8:15) has a parallel in Mt 17:7:

Mt 17,7	Cf. Dan 10:10 (Theod.):[9]
καὶ προσῆλθεν ὁ Ἰησοῦς	καὶ ἰδοὺ
καὶ *ἁψάμενος* αὐτῶν	χεὶρ ἁπτομένη μου
εἶπεν· *ἐγέρθητε*	καὶ *ἤγειρέν* με ἐπὶ τὰ γόνατά μου.
καὶ μὴ φοβεῖσθε.	

Of course, the context of Mt 17:6-7 (an editorial insertion in the transfiguration story; cf. Boismard: "l'ultime Rédacteur matthéen") is different from the healing story in parallel to Mk 1:29-31. Yet, there is a curious coincidence: προσελθών,[10] ἤγειρεν, κρατήσας (Mt ἥψατο).

Our conclusion: 1. the use of ἅπτεσθαι in Mt 8:15 can be assigned to the Matthean redaction; 2. ἥψατο in Mt 8:15 probably has a more specific connotation than mere "touching" (cf. ἐγείρειν). There is no basis for the suggestion that ἥψατο αὐτοῦ in Mt 8:3 (par. Mk. 1:41) depends on Matthean tradition. Some influence of Mk 1:41 on Mt 9:29 is not unlikely. And in Mt 8:15, because of the similarity of the phrase, "he *touched* her *hand*" (8:15) and "he stretched out (his) *hand* and *touched* him" (8:3), and because of the related context,[11] some reminiscence of the leper story cannot be excluded.

c) **καὶ λέγει αὐτῷ ὁ Ἰησοῦς** (Mt 8:4a/Mk 1:44a)

"Tonalité matthéenne: une consigne de silence formulée en style direct, introduit par le verbe 'dire'."

First remark: I do not see the reason why Mk 1:25 (cf. 4:39) should be

---

[9] Compare Dan 8:18 ἥψατό μου καὶ ἔστησέν με ἐπὶ πόδας (Theod.), ἁψάμενός μου ἤγειρέ με ἐπὶ τοῦ τόπου (LXX). Cf. 9:21; 10:16,18 (ἥψατό μου).
[10] Cf. *Evangelica*, pp. 11-12 (= «La rédaction matthéenne», 1967, pp. 49-50) and p. 285 ("Les femmes au tombeau," 1969, p. 180). The verb προσέρχεσθαι is used five times in Mark and 51 times in Matthew; Mk 1:31 and Mt 17:7; 28:18 are the only instances where προσελθών/προσῆλθεν is said of Jesus.
[11] In Matthew's arrangement: Mk 1:40-45 *before*, and Mk 1:29-31 *after* the Q passage, Mt 8:2-4 ( ) 14-15. On the order in Matthew, cf. *supra*, 39.

excluded in a list of the injunctions to silence that includes Mk 3:12 (v. 11 τὰ πνεύματα τὰ ἀκάθαρτα; cf. 1:34).

Mk 1:41 καὶ λέγει αὐτῷ· ὅρα... can be compared with:

Mk			Mt	
1:25	ἐπετίμησεν	λέγων·	—	
3:12	ἐπετίμα	ἵνα	12:16 ἐπετίμησεν	ἵνα
(4:39)	ἐπετίμησεν	καὶ εἶπεν	8:26 ἐπετίμησεν	
5:43	διεστείλατο	ἵνα	9:26 diff.	
7:36	διεστείλατο	ἵνα	—	
8:30	ἐπετίμησεν	ἵνα	16:20 διεστείλατο	ἵνα
9:9	διεστείλατο	ἵνα	17:9 ἐνετείλατο	λέγων

In this list Mt 17:9 is the only instance of direct discourse in Matthew. It forms the conclusion of the transfiguration story:[12]

Mt 17:9	Mk 9:9
καὶ καταβαινόντων αὐτῶν	καὶ καταβαινόντων αὐτῶν
ἐκ τοῦ ὄρου	ἐκ τοῦ ὄρου
ἐνετείλατο αὐτοῖς ὁ Ἰησοῦς	διεστείλατο αὐτοῖς
λέγων· μηδενὶ	ἵνα μηδενὶ
εἴπητε	ἃ εἶδον
τὸ ὅραμα	διηγήσωνται
ἕως οὗ ὁ υἱὸς τοῦ ἀνθρώπου	εἰ μὴ ὅταν ὁ υἱὸς τοῦ ἀνθρώπου
ἐκ νεκρῶν ἐγερθῇ	ἐκ νεκρῶν ἀναστῇ.

E.P. Sanders's list of direct discourse in Matthew where Mark has indirect speech[13] includes Mt 3:2*; 8:32; 10:9-10; 12:10*; 13:10; 15:15, 22*, 25*; (16:7*); 17:9*; 18:1*; (19:3*); 21:33; 26:1-2, 15, 27*, 66 (I added 16:7 and 19:3; the asterisk denotes the use of λέγων/λέγοντες).[14]

---

[12] Cf. *Synopse* II, 254a: "La consigne de silence (Mt 12:16; 16:20: cf. p. 120b, 244a) ... doit remonter au Mc-intermédiaire et fut reprise par l'ultime Rédacteur matthéen. Mais chaque évangéliste garde son style propre: le verbe 'donner l'ordre' est *diastellomai* chez Mc (1/5/0/0/1/1) et *entellomai* chez Mt (5/2/3/2/2); il est suivi du style indirect chez Mc, mais du style direct chez Mt qui le préfère; Mt emploie le mot 'vision' (*horama*), probablement sous l'influence de Dn 10,1 (LXX); enfin, la conjonction 'jusqu'à ce que' (*heôs hou*) est conforme au style de Mt (7/0/7/2/5)."

Compare also ἐγερθῆναι (Mk ἀναστῆναι) in Mt 16,21; 17,23; 20,19 (and 9,25). For μη(δενὶ)... ἕως οὗ, see K. BEYER, *Semitische Syntax im Neuen Testament* I/1 (SUNT, 1), Göttingen, 1962, 134: "Mt 17,9 verbessert εἰ μὴ ὅταν in ἕως οὗ, wie es LXX in Jes 55,10.11; 65,6; Rt 3,18 getan hat" לֹא־כִּי אִם LXX ἕως ἄν). Cf. Mt 5:26; 23:39: οὐ μὴ ... ἕως ἄν (Lk om. ἄν); 24,39 οὐκ ... ἕως (diff. Lk); 1:25 οὐκ ... ἕως οὗ. The phrase ἕως οὗ (1:25; 17:9) is used without preceding negative in Mt 13:33 (Lk); 14:22; 26:36 (Mk ἕως); 18:34; ἕως ὅτου; 5:25 (diff. Lk).

[13] *The Tendencies*, 260. Cf. *Evangelica*, 134-136 (*Duality in Mark*, 64-66).

[14] Cf. *The Minor Agreements*, 246-248: λέγων/λέγοντες in Matthew (no. 15), for καὶ λέγει in Mark (Mk 1:41; 2:18; 4:2,38,41; 6:50; 10:47; 11:2,28; 12:14; 14:24,65,67; cf. 7:5,26: ἐρωτᾶν); for a finite verb of saying in Mark (Mk 4:26,31; 5:7; 6:35; 9:17; 11:21; 12:14,18,35,36,38; 13:3; 14:12,63; 15:39; cf. 7:6); added to introduce Mark's direct speech:

Although "pure transformation from *oratio obliqua* to *oratio recta*, such as in Mt 17:9, is rather exceptional"[15] (but see 12:10; 16:7; 19:3), redactional substitution of ἐνετείλατο λέγων for διεστείλατο ἵνα[16] is most likely in Mt 17:9. Assimilation of Mk 9:9 to Mk 8:30 can explain on the one hand the use of εἴπητε and on the other the transference of διεστείλατο unto Mt 16:20,

Mk 8:30 ἐπετίμησεν ... ἵνα μηδενὶ λέγωσιν
Mt 16:20 διεστείλατο ... ἵνα μηδενὶ εἴπωσιν.

The addition of the subject ὁ Ἰησοῦς in Mt 17:9 and in 8:4, is a characteristic feature of Matthean redaction.[17]

Mt 17:9, where διεστείλατο has been replaced by ἐνετείλατο (... λέγων), remains very close to Markan formulation (cf. 1:25 ἐπετίμησεν ... λέγων). Mt 8:4 has the simple introduction καὶ λέγει αὐτῷ ὁ Ἰησοῦς, in parallel to Mk 1:44a καὶ λέγει αὐτῷ.[18] Yet, Mk 1:44a should not be isolated from the preceding verse, καὶ ἐμβριμησάμενος αὐτῷ εὐθὺς ἐξέβαλεν αὐτόν (om. Mt[19]): "ἐμβριμάομαι entspricht hier ἐπιτιμάω in 3,12; 8,30; 10,48" (Pesch).

d) ὅρα μηδενὶ εἴπῃς (Mt 8:4/Mk 1:44)

"Tonalité matthéenne: l'impératif ὅρα suivi de la négation μή (Mt 9:30; 18:10; 24:6)."

Once more, we should ask the question: Matthean tradition or Matthean redaction? Mt 24:6 and its context are attributed to the Matthean redaction by Boismard himself: "on peut l'attribuer tout entier à l'ultime Rédacteur matthéen qui a repris le texte du Mc-intermédiaire" (1972: 361b). Thus, ὁρᾶτε, before Mark's μὴ θροεῖσθε, is supposed to be a Matthean addition. Mt 18:10 is peculiar to Matthew and probably editorial.[20] Verse 10a resumes and concludes the theme of

Mk 1:11; 9:7 (φωνή); 10:48; 11:9; 15:14 (κράζειν); 3:2; 14:4; 15:2,18,34 (misc.); added to Mark and change to *oratio recta*: Mk 3:2; 6:52; 8:16,32; 9:9,34; 10:2 (Mt 12:10; 14:33; 16:7,22; 17:9; 18:1; 19:3).
[15] Cf. *Evangelica*, 136 (*Duality*, 66).
[16] Cf. *The Minor Agreements*, 217-219: ἵνα in Mark and not in Matthew and Luke (no. 7).
[17] Cf. *The Minor Agreements*, 261-262 (no. 22: Matthew defining the subject): Mt 3:16; 4:1; 8:4,14,18; 9:9,19,23,35; 10:5; 12:1; 13:1,34; 14:13,16,27; 15:21,28,29,32,34; 16:6,8,21,24; 17:9,17,18,22; 19:1; 21:1,12; 22:18; 23:1; 24:1; 26:6,19,26,36,63; 27:11.
[18] For Boismard, this is a "Matthean" introduction: "Dans Mc, une consigne de silence ... est toujours introduite par un verbe signifiant 'commander'."
[19] But see Mt 9:30 ἐνεβριμήθη ... λέγων.
[20] Cf. *Evangelica*, 819. Boismard's commentary is less clear (266b). Note, however, that the related verse Mt 18:6 depends on Mark (265b).

"one of these little ones" (v. 6) and the second part of the verse anticipates the conclusion of the parable (v. 14).

In both cases ὁρᾶτε is followed by μή. In Mt 16:6 we read ὁρᾶτε καὶ προσέχετε ἀπό, in parallel to Mk 8:15 ὁρᾶτε, βλέπετε ἀπό. Because of the introductory phrase, καὶ διεστέλλετο αὐτοῖς λέγων, this ὁρᾶτε in Mark is a close parallel to the injunctions to silence. In Matthew the typical διαστέλλεσθαι (cf. Mk 5:43; 7:36 bis; 9:9) is omitted (ὁ δὲ Ἰησοῦς εἶπεν αὐτοῖς).

In parallel to Mt 8:4, the text of Mark has a double negative ὅρα μηδενὶ *μηδὲν* εἴπῃς (compare 16:8 οὐδενὶ οὐδὲν εἶπαν)[21] and it is followed by ἀλλὰ ὕπαγε... The double negative and the οὐκ ... ἀλλά construction are not infrequent in Mark.[22]

For both the direct discourse with λέγων and the phrase ὅρα μηδενὶ ... Boismard cites Mt 9,30 as a "Matthean" parallel. As indicated above this is not an independent parallel, and in 1972 Boismard has given a good description of the dependence of Mt 9:27-31 (*l'ultime Rédaction matthéenne*) on the story of the leper (*Mt-intermédiaire*) (102b-103a). That means, his reconstruction of *Mt-intermédiaire* includes the "Markan" elements; ἐμβριμᾶσθαι (Mk 1:43) and διαφημίζειν (Mk 1:45). Is it then a Proto-Matthew or a Proto-Mark?

Besides the double dependence of Mt 9:27-31 on Mk 10:46-52 (par. Mt 20:29-34) and on Mk 1:40-45 (par. Mt 8:2-4), there is a third dependence to be mentioned. In the order of Matthew, the healing of the two blind men is preceded by the healing of Jairus' daughter (Mt 9:18-26). The correspondence in the conclusions is obvious:

Mt 9:26 καὶ ἐξῆλθεν   ἡ *φήμη* αὕτη   εἰς ὅλην τὴν γῆν ἐκείνην
   9:31 οἱ δὲ ἐξελθόντες διεφήμισαν αὐτὸν ἐν ὅλῃ τῇ γῇ ἐκείνῃ.

Compare:

Mk 1:28 καὶ ἐξῆλθεν   ἡ ἀκοὴ αὐτοῦ ... εἰς ὅλην τὴν περίχωρον ...
   1:45 ὁ δὲ ἐξελθὼν ... διαφημίζειν τὸν λόγον

The conclusion of Mt 9:26 replaces Mark's injunction to silence (Mk 5:43) which has been omitted by Matthew or, more correctly, transferred unto the following story of the two blind men:

Mt 9:30b	Mk 5:43a	Mk 1:43-44
καὶ ἐνεβριμήθη αὐτοῖς	καὶ διεστείλατο αὐτοῖς	καὶ ἐμβριμησάμενος αὐτῷ ...
ὁ Ἰησοῦς λέγων·	πολλὰ ἵνα	44 καὶ λέγει αὐτῷ· (dir.)
ὁρᾶτε,		ὅρα
μηδεὶς γινωσκέτω.	μηδεὶς γνοῖ τοῦτο	μηδενὶ μηδὲν εἴπῃς.

[21] Cf. *Evangelica*, 263.
[22] Cf. *Duality in Mark*, 84-85: "Double negative" (no. 6); 90-94: "οὐκ ... ἀλλά and allied constructions" (no. 9B).

Mt 9:27-31 is a secondary Matthean composition, and it is on the level of the Matthean redaction that Mt 9:28 (δύναμαι τοῦτο ποιῆσαι) shows some contact with δύνασαί με καθαρίσαι in Mk 1:40.

e) **προσένεγκον τὸ δῶρον** (Mt 8:4/cf. Mk 1:44)

"Le verbe προσφέρειν: Contrairement à Mc, Mt l'emploie volontiers à propos de 'choses' que l'on offre (2:11; 5:23,24; 22:19; 25:20)."

Mk 1:44b refers to "the law of the leper" (cf. Lev 14:1,32) and there is nothing strange in the fact that its vocabulary shows echoes of Lev 13-14:

Mk 1:44	Lev 13-14
σεαυτὸν δεῖξον τῷ ἱερεῖ	13:49 δείξει τῷ ἱερεῖ
	(passim ὄψεται ὁ ἱερεύς)
καὶ προσένεγκε	14:23 προσοίσει αὐτὰ ...
	εἰς τὸ καθαρίσαι αὐτὸν πρὸς τ. ἱερέα
περὶ τοῦ καθαρισμοῦ σου	14:32 εἰς τὸν καθαρισμὸν αὐτοῦ
ἃ προσέταξεν	14:4,5,36,40 προσέταξεν ὁ ἱερεύς
Μωϋσῆς	13:1; 14:1 (ἐλάλησεν κύριος πρὸς) Μωϋσῆν

It depends on the subject matter that the words καθαρισμός, προστάσσειν and προσφέρειν (said of "things") are used here and not elsewhere in Mark.

Matthew omits περὶ τοῦ καθαρισμοῦ σου and changes προσένεγκε ἃ to προσένεγκον τὸ δῶρον ὅ.[23] The phrase προσφέρειν δῶρον, which is found 23 times in Lev (but not in Lev 13-14), is used by Matthew also in 2:11 (δῶρα); 5:23,24 (τὸ δῶρόν σου) and it has a Matthean flavor. Compare also Mt 22:19 προσήνεγκαν αὐτῷ δηνάριον (par. Mk 12:16 ἤνεγκαν, cf. v. 15 φέρετέ μοι δηνάριον) and Mt 25:20 προσήνεγκαν ... τάλαντα (diff. Lk).[24] But again, this Matthean usage is post-Markan. And we can conclude: no trace of Matthean *tradition* can be found in the so-called indications of Matthean "tonalité" in Mk 1:40-44.

3. *Mark 1:42*

For Boismard the combination hypothesis presents a satisfactory explanation of the duplicate expression in Mk 1:42:
καὶ εὐθὺς ἀπῆλθεν ἀπ' αὐτοῦ ἡ λέπρα
καὶ ἐκαθαρίσθη.

[23] P. Egerton 2: καὶ ἀνένεγκον περὶ τοῦ καθαρισμοῦ ὡς προσέταξεν Μωϋσῆς. Compare -ένεγκον in Mt. The synonym ἀναφέρειν is frequently used in the LXX, e.g., in the chapter on the leper. Lev 14,20 καὶ ἀνοίσει ὁ ἱερεὺς ... καὶ καθαρισθήσεται.

[24] On προσφέρειν in Mt, see *Jean et les Synoptiques*, 355-356 (= "Urmarcus redivivus," 139-140); *The Minor Agreements*, 279 (no. 29).

Mt 8:3b is accepted as the original formulation and Egerton 2 as the Proto-Lukan substitute:[25]

Mt 8:3b　　καὶ εὐθέως ἐκαθαρίσθη αὐτοῦ ἡ λέπρα

Egerton 2　καὶ εὐθέως ἀπέστη ἀπ' αὐτοῦ ἡ λέπρα

Cf. Lk 5:13b　καὶ εὐθέως ἡ λέπρα ἀπῆλθεν ἀπ' αὐτοῦ

Mk 1:42a　καὶ εὐθέως ἀπῆλθεν ἀπ' αὐτοῦ ἡ λέπρα.

Boismard observes that the word order in Mk 1:42 is more "Lukan" than in Lk 5:13: compare Lk 1:38; 2:15; and Egerton 2! However, the Lukan character of Egerton 2 should not be exaggerated. There is no stereotyped Lukan order.[26] Compare:

Egerton 2　καὶ εὐθέως ἀπέστη ἀπ' αὐτοῦ / ἡ λέπρα

Acts 12:10　καὶ εὐθέως ἀπέστη ὁ ἄγγελος / ἀπ' αὐτοῦ

Lk 4:13　καὶ ... ὁ διάβολος / ἀπέστη　ἀπ' αὐτοῦ.

The "Proto-Lukan" ἀπέστη can be no more than a post-Lukan substitution for ἀπῆλθεν, like the D-reading in Lk 1:38 ἀπῆλθεν (D ἀπέστη) ἀπ' αὐτῆς ὁ ἄγγελος. The word order of Egerton 2 is the same as in Mk 1:42. We can add the curious phenomenon that the phrase ἐκτείνας τὴν χεῖρα (Mk 1:41), which is not used in the story of the leper, appears in Egerton 2, lines 67-68: καὶ ἐκτείνας τὴν χεῖρα αὐτοῦ τὴν δεξιάν, and that ἐμβριμησάμενος (Mk 1:43) appears in line 51. The possibility remains that the writer had some knowledge of Mk 1:40-45.

The contact with Mt 8:2a is obvious in the first words of the story: καὶ ἰδοὺ λέπρος προσελθὼν αὐτῷ (line 32). Therefore we cannot exclude the possibility that the writer of Egerton 2 had some knowledge of the Matthean text, but the formula he uses, in a slight adaptation, is that of Lk 5:13b.

The original formula of the Synoptic story can hardly be preserved in Mt 8:3b.

Mt	Mk
καὶ εὐθέως	καὶ εὐθὺς
ἐκαθαρίσθη	ἀπῆλθεν ἀπ' αὐτοῦ
αὐτοῦ ἡ λέπρα.	ἡ λέπρα
	καὶ ἐκαθαρίσθη

---

[25] On Boismard's more complex theory in *Synopse* II (1972), cf. *ETL* 61 (1985), 157.

[26] Pesch rightly observes that in Luke "die Gebrauchsverwendungen des Verbs sehr verschieden sind" and he refers to a more significant parallel in Lev 13:58: ἀποστήσεται ἀπ' αὐτοῦ ἡ ἀφή. Cf. *Jesu ureigene Taten? Ein Beitrag zur Wunderfrage* (Quaestiones Disputatae, 52), Freiburg, 1970, 110 (n. 207). Cf. U. Busse, *Die Wunder des Propheten Jesus* (Forschung zur Bibel, 24), Stuttgart, 1977, 110: "Lukas personifiziert den Aussatz"; n. 2: "Lk unterscheidet schon in V 12 zwischen dem Kranken und seiner Krankheit. Mit der Umstellung des Subjekts in V 13 hebt Lk die Befreiung von der Krankheit ausdrücklich hervor."

The implied subject in Mk 1:42 is ὁ λεπρός: δύνασαί με καθαρίσαι —
καθαρίσθητι — ἐκαθαρίσθη (1:40,41,42). Compare Lk 17:14,17 ἐκαθα-
ρίσθησαν (δέκα λεπροὶ ἄνδρες); Mt 11:5/Lk 7:22 λεπροὶ καθαρίζονται;
Mt 10:8 λεπροὺς καθαρίζετε; Lk 4:27 ἐκαθαρίσθη, i.e. Naaman; in the
LXX: 4 Kgs 5:10,12,13,14. The verb καθαρίζειν is used passim in Lev
13-14 for the priest who declares a person clean and for a man who is
declared clean. Matthew's use of ἐκαθαρίσθη with the leprosy as subject
(αὐτοῦ ἡ λέπρα) is a biblical rarity,[27] almost certainly due to Matthew's
editorial reworking of Mk 1:42 (avoidance of Mark's duplicate expression and concentration on the *Stichwort* καθαρίζειν).[28]

The double phrase in Mk 1:42 is not without a parallel. In the unique
Old Testament parallel, the healing of Naaman, we read:

4 Kgs 5:14   καὶ ἐπέστρεψεν ἡ σὰρξ αὐτοῦ ὡς σὰρξ παιδαρίου μικροῦ,
             καὶ ἐκαθαρίσθη (cf. v. 13 καθαρίσθητι).
Mk 1:42   καὶ εὐθὺς ἀπῆλθεν ἀπ' αὐτοῦ ἡ λέπρα,
             καὶ ἐκαθαρίσθη (cf. v. 41 καθαρίσθητι).

Similar double phrases are found at the conclusion of other healing
stories in Mark. In some cases the interpreters speak of *Konstatierung*
and *Demonstration*, but such a sharp distinction will not be possible in
every case:

1:31b   καὶ ἀφῆκεν αὐτὴν ὁ πυρετός,
             καὶ διηκόνει αὐτοῖς.
2:12a   καὶ ἠγέρθη
             καὶ εὐθὺς ἄρας τὸν κράβαττον ἐξῆλθεν ...

---

[27] "Er bildete die merkwürdige Aussage, daß der Aussatz rein wurde" (H.J. HELD,
Matthäus als Interpret der Wundergeschichten, 203). Boismard seems to neglect this
exceptional usage when he now writes: "La formule de Mt 'et fut purifiée sa lèpre' est
certainement plus primitive (cf. Lv 14)" (1984:3c). Contrast the reconstruction of the
original story and of proto-Matthew in *Synopse* II: "et il [le lépreux] fut purifié", καὶ
ἐκαθαρίσθη (= Mk 1:42b). But Matthew's supposedly redactional addition of αὐτοῦ ἡ
λέπρα (cf. Mk 1:42a) is not even mentioned in § 39.
   W. Wojciechowski has recently argued that Mt 8:3 could represent an older tradition
but, in contrast to Boismard, he emphasizes the "clumsy and unique" character of the
sentence. Quite unconvincingly, he supposes a Semitic original with the root *brr* =
"separated" rather than "cleansed". Cf. "The Touching of the Leper (Mark 1,40-45) as a
Historic and Symbolic Act of Jesus," *BZ* 33 (1989) 114-119, 115.
[28] "Mt. combines two clauses in Mk." (ALLEN); "ἐκαθαρίσθη αὐτοῦ ἡ λέπρα (vgl.
νόσον θεραπεύειν 4:23): scheint aus ἀπῆλθεν ἀπ' αὐτοῦ ἡ λέπρα καὶ ἐκαθαρίσθη
zusammengezogen" (KLOSTERMANN).
   B. Weiss refers to "den feierlich-monotonen Fortschritt der wortkargen Erzählung in
dem καθαρίσαι – καθαρίσθητι - ἐκαθαρίσθη" in the original gospel source (*Das
Matthäusevangelium*, 1876, 227), but is such a correspondence "wobei letzteres die Heilung
nicht von dem Kranken, sondern von der Krankheit selbst prädicirt" (*ibid.*) likely to be
original?

3:5b   καὶ ἐξέτεινεν
        καὶ ἀπεκατεστάθη ἡ χεὶρ αὐτοῦ.
4:39b   καὶ ἐκόπασεν ὁ ἄνεμος
        καὶ ἐγένετο γαλήνη μεγάλη.
5:29   καὶ εὐθὺς ἐξηράνθη ἡ πηγὴ τοῦ αἵματος αὐτῆς
        καὶ ἔγνω τῷ σώματι ὅτι ἴαται ἀπὸ τῆς μάστιγος.
5:42a   καὶ εὐθὺς ἀνέστη τὸ κοράσιον
        καὶ περιεπάτει.
6:42   καὶ ἔφαγον πάντες
        καὶ ἐχορτάσθησαν.
7:35   καὶ εὐθέως … καὶ ἐλύθη ὁ δεσμὸς τῆς γλώσσης αὐτοῦ
        καὶ ἐλάλει ὀρθῶς.
8:25b   καὶ διέβλεψεν καὶ ἀπεκατέστη
        καὶ ἐνέβλεψεν τηλαυγῶς ἅπαντα.
10:52b καὶ εὐθὺς ἀνέβλεψεν
        καὶ ἠκολούθει αὐτῷ ἐν τῇ ὁδῷ.

Mk 1:42 is one of Mark's duplicate expressions of which Matthew has one half and Luke has the other half.[29] On the Griesbach hypothesis it is a passage where "die Darstellung des Marcus … unverkennbar die sekundäre ist".[30] The old answer is still valid: "der Schein entsteht, als combinirte Marcus den Matthäus und Lucas, während derselbe doch auch 7,35. 8,25 ohne solchen Anlass ganz analoge doppelte Ausdrücke hat."[31]

---

[29] Cf. F. NEIRYNCK, The Minor Agreements, 287: no. 34 "Duplicate Expressions in Mark and Simple Phrases in Matthew and Luke." See also "Les expressions doubles chez Marc et le problème synoptique," ETL 59 (1983) 303-330. Cf. supra, 9.

[30] F. BLEEK, Einleitung in das Neue Testament, Berlin, ⁴1886, 187-189. His list of the most significant passages includes Mk 1:32,34,42; 4:15; 11:1; 12:14 (with reference to a more complete list in de Wette's Einleitung).

[31] B. WEISS, Das Marcusevangelium, 1872, 75.

III

THE ESCHATOLOGICAL DISCOURSE

A. *Luke 17 and 21: Two Proto-Lukan Discourses?*

In Boismard's hypothesis Proto-Luke has a discourse on the Coming
of the Son of Man, Lk 17:23-24, 26-27, 28-30, 34-35; (21:34-36), and a
discourse on the Fall of Jerusalem, Lk (19:41-44); 21:20, 21b-22, 23b-24,
25-26a, 28.

1. *A New Debate: Q or Proto-Luke*

By accepting a common source for the double-tradition material in
Lk 17 and Mt 24 (i.e., 24:26-27, 37-41), Boismard in this section adopts
the solution of the Two-Source hypothesis. In 1972 he attributed to
Proto-Luke the insertion of Lk 17:25 in the Q Document (43a, 303b),
but now he defends the more radical thesis of the (proto-)Lukan origin
of the Q material. His argument is based on an analysis of the common
vocabulary in the double-tradition sections. He notes two Lukan
phrases in Lk 17:27, ἤσθιον, ἔπινον (eat/drink) and ἄχρι ἧς ἡμέρας,
and then turns to Lk 7:18-35 and 3:7b-9.

What is the force of the argument? Can we declare a source used by
Luke "proto-Lukan" because of the presence of some words and
phrases which are attested as "Lukanisms" elsewhere in Luke (diff. Mk)
and in Acts? Is it not rather the relative frequency in Luke (editorial)
and in Acts which allows us to speak of a word or phrase characteristic
of Luke? A more or less isolated use of the same word in another gospel
or in a source of Luke is not necessarily Lukan usage. Let us take some
examples from Hawkins's list that are generally accepted as "Lukanisms". Some of them are found occasionally in the Markan material, in
Luke and in the parallel text of Mark. In those cases we can safely
conclude that the word has not been avoided by Luke (it is not a
Meidewort), but we cannot extend the Lukan characteristic to the use of
this word in Mark. In a diachronic view, a word used once in Luke's
source (= Mark or Q) can become a characteristic word in the Lukan
redaction.

ἀναστάς Mk 2:14 = Lk 5:28	γίνομαι ἐπί + acc. Mk 15:33 = Lk 23:44
ἀπόστολος Mk 6:30* = Lk 9:10	δοξάζω τὸν θεόν Mk 2:12* = Lk 5:26
τὸ γεγονός Mk 5:14* = Lk 8:34	ἐγένετο + finite verb Mk 2:23 = Lk 6:1

εἶπεν παραβολήν Mk 12:12 = Lk 20:19
εἰρήνη Mk 5:34* = Lk 8:48
ἐν τῷ + infinitive Mk 4:4* = Lk 8:5
ἰάομαι Mk 5:29* = Lk 8:47 (∽)
καθ᾽ ἡμέραν Mk 14:49* = Lk 22:53
λαός Mk 14:2 = Lk 22:2
παραγίνομαι Mk 14:43 = Lk 22:52 (∽)

πλῆθος Mk 3:7,8* = Lk 6:17
προσδέχομαι Mk 15:43* = Lk 23:51
ῥῆμα Mk 9:32; 14:72 = Lk 9:45; 22:61
τις, with noun Mk 15:21 = Lk 23:26
ὕψιστος Mk 5:7* = Lk 8:28
χαίρω Mk 14:11* = Lk 22:5

Some of these words are explicitly noted in Boismard's commentary (1972) as "Lukan" words in Mark (marked here with an asterisk) and are therefore attributed to the *Rédacteur marco-lucanien*. Is it not the same misinterpretation of "Lukan" words which is at the origin of both theories, the Lukan redaction of Mark and the (proto-)Lukan origin of Q?

Luke 7:18-35

A few observations can be made on the examples found in Lk 7:18-35.

ναὶ λέγω ὑμῖν Lk 7:26/Mt 11:9 ("c'est le cas le plus significatif"). In the phrase ἀμὴν λέγω ὑμῖν of his source Luke substituted ἀληθῶς for ἀμήν in Lk 9:27; 21:3 (Mk); 12:44 (Q), but is it correct to say: "il remplace ἀμὴν ... par ναί (Lc 11:51; 12:5)"? In Lk 12:5c the phrase ναὶ λέγω ὑμῖν, τοῦτον φοβήθητε has no parallel in Mt 10:28, and for those who assign it to the source this is another instance of ναὶ λέγω ὑμῖν in Q (Marshall, Polag). Others reconstruct a Q text with λέγω ὑμῖν ... and consider the word ναί as added by Luke (Schenk). In the more common opinion (Harnack, Schmid, Schulz, *et al.*)[1] there are three Lukan additions in 12:4-5:

4a λέγω δὲ ὑμῖν τοῖς φίλοις μου
5a ὑποδείξω δὲ ὑμῖν τίνα φοβηθῆτε
5c ναὶ λέγω ὑμῖν, τοῦτον φοβήθητε.

This was in 1972 also the opinion of Boismard, who then emphasized "le caractère lucanien de ces ajouts" (279a). The imitation of the Q model, more than Lukan style, may be at stake here. Compare, at the conclusion of the preceding discourse in Luke:

Lk 11:51b ναὶ λέγω ὑμῖν, ἐκζητηθήσεται ἀπὸ τῆς γενεᾶς ταύτης
Mt 23:36 ἀμὴν λέγω ὑμῖν, ἥξει ταῦτα πάντα ἐπὶ τὴν γενεὰν ταύτην.

Harnack's view that in Lk 11:51 ἀμήν is altered by Luke to ναί tends to become a minority opinion (Marshall; *ctr.* Steck, Schulz, Polag, Schenk, Légasse).[2] J. Jeremias, who maintained an original ἀμήν,

[1] Cf. "Recent Developments in the Study of Q," 56-59: "Excursus: The λέγω ὑμῖν Formula" (esp. 62).
[2] *Ibid.*, 66.

emphasized that this and all other uses of ναί in Lk (7:26 par. Mt; 11:51; 12:5; and 10:21 ναί par. Mt) are pre-Lukan (and different from ναί in Acts 5:8; 22:27, where it is used in answer to a question asked by another person).[3]

τίνι ὁμοιώσω ... ὁμοία ἐστίν Lk 7:31/Mt 11:16 (cf. Lk 13:18; 13:20). This is a most curious argument for Lukan origin of the Q passage. The only parallel is the introduction to a pair of parables in Q (Lk 13:18-21/ Mt 13:31-33), with a similar rhetorical question in Lk 13:18,20, which is generally assigned to Q precisely because it is un-Lukan: "da Lukas sonst rhetorische Fragen gern umwandelt" (Harnack); "das Verb ὁμοιοῦν ... ist für Lk in keiner Weise typisch" (Schulz).[4]

ἐσθίειν/πίνειν Lk 7:33,34/Mt 11:18,19; Lk 12:29/Mt 6:31; Lk 12:45/ Mt 24:49; Lk 17:27,(28)/Mt 24:38. There can be no doubt about Luke's preference for the dual form: Lk 5:30 + πίνετε (diff. Mk 2:16); 5:33 (diff. Mk 2:18); 10:7; 12:19; 13:26; 13:26; 17:8 bis; 22:30; Acts 9:9; 13:12,21. However, its use in the four Q passages is not Lukan but Biblical usage: cf. Gen 24:54; 25:34; 26:30; 27:25; 31:46,54; Ex 24:10; 32:6; 34:28; etc.

ἤρξατο λέγειν (3/6/9/0/0). The instances in Matthew (3) and Mark (7, instead of 6: 10:28,32,47; 13:5; 14:19,65,69) are all narrative introductions to sayings (ἤρξατο λέγειν). Three instances in Luke are taken from sayings material, with ἄρχομαι but not the form ἤρξατο: 3:8 (ἄρξησθε); 13:26 (ἄρξεσθε); 23:30 (ἄρξονται). In two of the 6 instances of ἤρξατο λέγειν the use of ἤρξατο depends on Mark: 4:21 (cf. Mk 6:2 ἤρξατο διδάσκειν); 20:9 (cf. Mk 12:1 ἤρξατο λαλεῖν), and, in our hypothesis, Lk 7:24/Mt 11:7 is a Q text. Lk 7:49 καὶ ἤρξατο ... λέγειν ἐν ἑαυτοῖς ... is a variation of 5:21 καὶ ἤρξαντο διαλογίζεσθαι ... λέγοντες (diff. Mk 2:6). The two remaining Lukan introductions with ἤρξατο λέγειν are 11:29 and 12:1. The evidence is less overwhelming than the numbers 3/9 may suggest.

ἐξέρχεσθαι ἰδεῖν Lk 7:24-26 / Mt 11:7-9 (Lk 8:35; 14:18). The first text is a Markan passage:

Mk 5:14b καὶ ἦλθον ἰδεῖν τί ἐστιν τὸ γεγονός. 15 καὶ ἔρχονται...
Lk 8:35 ἐξῆλθον δὲ ἰδεῖν τὸ γεγονός, καὶ ἦλθον ...

The other is from the parable of the great supper: ἔχω ἀνάγκην ἐξελθὼν

---

[3] J. JEREMIAS, Die Sprache des Lukasevangeliums (KEK), Göttingen, 1980, 210: "ναί dient an allen vier Stellen, an denen es im LkEv vorkommt, nicht als Antwort auf die Frage eines anderen, sondern zur Verstärkung der vorangegangenen eigenen Aussage, Mahnung bzw. Frage."

[4] Luke has in 7:31 (diff. Mt) and 13:18 (diff. Mt, but see Mk 4:30) a double question, of which the attribution to Q is less certain. Cf. "Recent Developments in the Study of Q," 52.

ἰδεῖν αὐτόν (i.e., ἀγρόν). In both cases we have a combination of ἐξέρχεσθαι with ἰδεῖν, but is it really comparable with the composition of Lk 7:24-26 / Mt 11:7-9 (τί ἐξήλθατε ... θεάσασθαι; ... ἀλλὰ τί ἐξήλθατε ἰδεῖν; ... ἀλλὰ τί ἐξήλθατε ἰδεῖν;)?

φίλος (1/0/15/6/3). "Auch wenn Lukas die Vokabel in der Apg 3 mal verwendet, so sind zum mindesten einige Fälle profilierten Gebrauchs wie Lk 7:34 (par. Mt 11:19) oder 16:9 typisch für die vorlukanische Tradition".[5]

ἀκούετε καὶ βλέπετε (Mt 11:4): the inversion in Lk 7:22 (εἴδετε καὶ ἠκούσατε) is probably due to Luke, but the association of ἀκούειν and ἰδεῖν / βλέπειν can be compared with another Q passage: ἰδεῖν ἃ ὑμεῖς βλέπετε καὶ οὐκ εἶδαν, καὶ ἀκοῦσαι ἃ ἀκούετε καὶ οὐκ ἤκουσαν (Lk 10:24 / Mt 13:17). In the first part of the saying Luke has probably lost the parallelism of seeing and hearing. Matthew has preserved (or added?) καὶ τὰ ὦτα ὑμῶν ὅτι ἀκούουσιν (13:16; cf. Mk 8:18) and has connected the saying with Mt 13:13 = Mk 4:12 (βλέποντες – ἀκούοντες). The association of seeing and hearing may be Lukan (because of its occurrences in Acts), but it is not a Lukan exclusivity.

προσδοκᾶν and προσφωνεῖν are rightly cited as characteristics of Luke, but a pre-Lukan occurrence of these words is not necessarily proto-Lukan.

Boismard concludes: "une origine matthéenne de ces textes est impossible (contre la *Two-Gospel Hypothesis*)". And, indeed, most of the words and phrases he examines have no parallels in Matthew. But he adds a second conclusion: "L'analyse du vocabulaire ... a prouvé que l'origine de ces textes était lucanienne". As we have seen, his description of the evidence needs emendation and the presence of some true "Lukanisms" in Lk 7:18ff. / Mt 11:2ff. hardly proves the (proto-)Lukan origin of the text.

Luke 3:7b-9

The examination of the parallel text in Mt 3:7b-10 contains an important corrective of the statistical argument: "Matthieu a systématisé l'expression γεννήματα ἐχιδνῶν qu'il lisait dans sa source (3:7b; cf. 12:34; 23:33). De même, en 7:19, il reprendra *ad litteram* le texte de 3:10b". This acceptance of Matthean "systematization" is clearly a correction of *Synopse* II, where he attributes Mt 3:7b,10 / Lk 3:7b,9 to Proto-Matthew because of "les thèmes ... spécifiquement matthéens" (74a; but see 157a: 7:19 and 12:34a Matthean redaction!). But is it not a

---

[5] J. JEREMIAS, *Die Sprache*, 153.

similar mistake to suggest now a Proto-Lukan origin of Mt 3:7b-10 / Lk 3:7b-9 because of its "tonalité lucanienne"?

τίς ὑπέδειξεν ὑμῖν + infinitive (Lk 3:7b): compare Lk 6:47 ὑποδείξω ὑμῖν τίνι ἐστὶν ὅμοιος (add. Mt 7:24) and 12:5 ὑποδείξω δὲ ὑμῖν τίνα φοβηθῆτε (add. Mt 10:28). Although both phrases are accepted as Q text in some reconstructions of the source (Polag), they are more probably due to Luke (cf. also Acts 9:16; 20:35). However, the case of Lk 3:7b is somewhat different because of the rhetorical question: "Who has shown you how to flee from the wrath to come?", indicating the impossibility of escaping the judgment, and not: "Who warned you ..." (RSV, NEB). Luke avoids questions in parallel to Mk 2:18; 4:13,21,38; 5:35b,39; 6:37-38; 11:17; 12:15,24,26; 13:2; 15:12; 16:3; Mt 5:46b,47b; 6:25,26,30; 7:16; 18:21.

ποιήσατε οὖν καρποὺς ἀξίους τῆς μετανοίας (Lk 3:8a). The use of the plural instead of the singular (Mt καρπὸν ἄξιον) is probably a conscious Lukan intervention in the text of the source. By using the plural Luke transforms John's eschatological preaching to ethical instruction (cf. 3:10-14). The phrase in Acts 26:20 looks like a reminiscence: ἄξια τῆς μετανοίας ἔργα πράσσοντας.

μὴ δόξητε λέγειν (Mt 3:9). Here the Proto-Lukan phrase, δοκεῖν + infinitive, is supposed to be preserved in Matthew. The phrase ἤρξατο λέγειν (Lk) is equally Lukan ... and Proto-Lukan in Lk 7:24.[6]

Luke 17:27

In Lk 17:23-24,26-30,34-35 only two indications of Proto-Luke are noted, both in v. 27: ἤσθιον – ἔπινον (repeated in v. 28) and ἄχρι ἧς ἡμέρας. On the "Lukanism" of eating and drinking in Lk 7:33,34, see above. To eating and drinking as a description of human activity, other pairs are added here: marrying and being married (v. 27), buying and selling, planting and building (v. 28). Lk 17:28 has no parallel in Matthew. In v. 27 ἐσθίειν for the less common τρώγειν and γαμίζεσθαι for γαμίζειν (be given in marriage in contrast to give in marriage) are probably Luke's improvements of the source.

The phrase ἄχρι ἧς ἡμέρας (Mt 24:38 / Lk 17:27) is found in Lk 1:20; Acts 1:2, and ἄχρι τῆς ἡμέρας ταύτης in Acts 2:29; 23:1; 26:22 (diff. 20:6 ἄχρι ἡμερῶν πέντε; 27:33 ἄχρι οὗ: cf. Lk 21:24; Acts 7:18); compare also ἄχρι καιροῦ (Lk 4:13; Acts 13:11). The use of ἄχρι is a

---

[6] *Synopse* II attributes Mt 3:8-9 and Lk 3:8 to the Mattheo-Lukan and Lukan redactors (!) because of the Lukanisms (75a). See also 166a: Mt 11:7a and Lk 7:24a (ἤρξατο λέγειν).

true Lukanism, but, as noted by Boismard, "pas assez fort pour emporter la conviction".

A new development has been given to the Proto-Luke hypothesis in Boismard's 1984 paper. Lk 21:34-36, which in *Synopse* II (1972) and in a preliminary paper (1983) was supposed to be the conclusion of the other Proto-Lukan discourse in Lc 21, is now taken as the original conclusion of the discourse in Lk 17 (cf. below, 286). The new suggestion avoids the difficulties of the earlier hypothesis: the reference to the Son of man (v. 36) and the double warning in verses 34a and 36a are more appropriate to a discourse on the coming of the Son of man than to a discourse on the destruction of Jerusalem. But this discussion is ir-relevant as long as Lk 21:34-36 can be understood on the level of the Lukan redaction as the conclusion of the discourse including Lk 21:27. In 1983 at least one step was taken in that direction by accepting a redactional addition in v. 36b (the mention of the Son of man). The link with Lk 17 on the basis of the allusion to Gen 7:23 is far from convincing. The LXX phrase ἐπὶ πρόσωπον πάσης τῆς γῆς in Lk 21:35 can scarcely be interpreted as a specific reference to Gen 7:23.

There is no unanimity among the defenders of the Q hypothesis concerning Lk 17:28-29, the example of what took place in the days of Lot: is it a Lukan (or pre-Lukan) addition to the common source (Schulz, *et al.*) or has it been omitted by Matthew (Polag, Schürmann, Boismard 1972, *et al.*)? The problem of Lk 17:28-29 becomes a crucial question in a confrontation of Proto-Luke with Matthean priority (Two-Gospel Hypothesis). For Boismard the repetition of the formula of comparison in Mt 24:37,38a (ὥσπερ γὰρ ... ὡς γὰρ ...) demonstrates the originality of Lk 17:28-29 (the example of Sodom).

Mt 24	Lk 17
37 ὥσπερ γὰρ	26 καὶ καθὼς ἐγένετο (Noah)
οὕτως ἔσται	οὕτως ἔσται
38a ὡς γὰρ	—
38b-39a (ἦσαν) τρώγοντες...	27 ἤσθιον...
—	28 ὁμοίως καθὼς ἐγένετο (Lot)
—	29 ἤσθιον ...
39b οὕτως ἔσται	30 κατὰ τὰ αὐτὰ ἔσται

The "preuve irréfutable" is in fact a tacit correction of the earlier 1983 paper: "Mt a dédoublé les expressions afin d'introduire celle de 'Parousie': sa structure complexe s'oppose à la structure simple que l'on trouve aux vv. 26 de Lc et 37 de Mt". This remains, it seems to me, an acceptable explanation of the repetition in Mt 24:37,38, with a variation of ὥσπερ γάρ (cf. 24:27 = Lk 17:24) in ὡς γάρ and of "(the days of) Noah" in "(those days) before the flood":

37 αἱ ἡμέραι τοῦ Νῶε   26 ἐν ταῖς ἡμέραις Νῶε
   ἡ παρουσία   ἐν ταῖς ἡμέραις τ. υἱοῦ τ. ἀ.
38 ἐν ταῖς ἡμέραις ἐκείναις
   ταῖς πρὸ τοῦ κατακλυσμοῦ

The explanation of Mt 24:38a,39b as a transposition of the ὥσπερ – οὕτως formula of the second example (cf. Lk 17:28a,30) is not the only possibility. In the source, Mt 24:39b / Lk 17:30 may have been the original conclusion of the description of the days of Noah: οὕτως ἔσται (καὶ) ἐν τῇ ἡμέρᾳ τοῦ υἱοῦ τοῦ ἀνθρώπου.[7]

In Mt 24:40-41 / Lk 17:34-35 (παραλαμβάνεται – ἀφίεται) the allusion to Gen 19:17 μήποτε συμπαραλημφθῇς (and not to Gen 7:23 κατελείφθη μόνος Νῶε) will remain problematic. "The two verbs mean only that the two meet different fates; it is not clear which is the better destiny—to be 'taken' or to be 'left'. In any case, the theme of an all-encompassing destruction, as in the flood, is not sustained."[8]

2. Proto-Luke in Lk 21

Boismard gives a list of verses peculiar to Luke: 20:21b-22, 23b-24, 25-26a, 28[9] and repeats the traditional arguments for Proto-Luke: the pronouns αὐτῆς, αὐτήν in v. 21b (after v. 21a, par. Mk 13:14b) and ἐγγίζει in v. 28 (after v. 27, par. Mk 13:26). The introduction to this Proto-Lukan discourse on the Fall of Jerusalem is found in 19:41-44.

This Proto-Luke (anno 1984) can be compared with the reconstruction of Document B in Synopse II (1972): 19:41-44; 21:(10-11), 20, 21b-22, 23b-24, 25-26a, 28, (29-30), (34-36). The conclusion, vv. 34-36, is now assigned to the discourse on the Son of Man (Lk 17). The other supplementary verses, 10-11 and 29-30, are not mentioned in the 1984 paper: the discourse now ends with v. 28.

According to Synopse II, the Proto-Lukan redaction inserted vv. 12a, 14-15, 18 in the text of Document B and, under the influence of Proto-Matthew ("Mt-intermédiaire"), substituted the introduction of Document A (21:5-7) to that of Document B (19:41-44). Such a Proto-Lukan redaction, intermediate stage between the Document B and the Gospel of Luke, is no longer mentioned in 1984.

[7] Cf. J. ZMIJEWSKI, Die Eschatologiereden des Lukasevangeliums (BBB, 40), Bonn, 1972, 450.

[8] F.W. BEARE, The Gospel according to Matthew, Oxford, 1981, 474-475.

[9] Verse 26a, which is not included in the list (1984, but see 1972) should be added: compare Boismard's study of the vocabulary.

Boismard's personal emphasis is now clearly placed on the Lukan vocabulary.

1. *Lukan Vocabulary*. The following Lukan words are noted in the special material of Lk 21:20 κυκλοῦν, Ἰερουσαλήμ, 21 ἐκχωρεῖν, χώρα, 22 ἐκδίκησις, πιμπλάναι, πλησθῆναι πάντα τὰ γεγραμμένα, 24 Ἰερουσαλήμ, 25 ἦχος, 26 προσδοκία, ἐπέρχεσθαι, οἰκουμένη, 28 ἀνακύπτειν, ἐπαίρειν.

We should recall here one of the basic principles of Boismard's interpretation of Luke: "il est à peu près impossible de distinguer le vocabulaire et le style du proto-Luc de ceux de l'ultime rédaction lucanienne, l'un et l'autre s'apparentant étroitement au vocabulaire et au style des Actes" (*Synopse* II, 46a). In these conditions the vocabulary argument can be of no direct utility in the discussion on the alternatives, Lukan rewriting of Mark or Proto-Lukan source. One of the examples is πλησθῆναι πάντα τὰ γεγραμμένα in 21:22. Compare Boismard's comment on 24:44: "le 'discours de mission' [24:44-49] est une création littéraire de l'ultime Rédacteur lucanien [!]: ... Jésus est venu 'accomplir' les Écritures (v. 44; cf. Lc 18:31; 21:22; 22:37; Ac 13:29 et les citations scripturaires dans les discours des Actes)" (1972, 449-450; see also 316b). The verb πίμπλημι is "Lukan", but note the use of τελέω in Lk 18:31; 22:37; Acts 13:29 and πληρόω in Lk 24:44. Another example: οἰκουμένη (2:1; 4:5; 21:26). Cf. 4:5 "Lc change 'monde' en 'univers' (1/0/3/0/5). ... Dans tous ces cas, il est impossible de préciser si les modifications viennent du proto-Lc ou de l'ultime Rédacteur lucanien" (87a). More particularly, a Lukan word or phrase of which the "Lukanism" is shown in its redactional use in parallel to Mark (diff. Mk) can hardly become an argument against Lukan rewriting of Mark in Lk 21. Thus, Luke's preference for the form Ἰερουσαλήμ (cf. Boismard's statistics) is apparent in the Markan material: Lk 5:17 (add. Mk 2:2: cf. Mk 3:8,22); 6:17 (diff. Mk 3:8); 18:31 (diff. Mk 10:33); 19:11 (cf. Mk 11:1). For the verb ἐκχωρεῖν (a hapaxlegomenon in the New Testament) Boismard refers to the compound ὑποχωρεῖν: 5:16 (diff. Mk 1:45); 9:10 (diff. Mk 6:32).[10] The word ἦχος is used in Lk 4:37 (diff. Mk 1:28).

The following characteristics of Lukan style in 19:41-44 are listed by Boismard: 41 ὡς ἤγγισεν, ἔκλαυσεν ἐπ᾽ αὐτήν, 42 τὰ πρὸς εἰρήνην, νῦν δέ, 43 ἤξουσιν ἡμέραι, συνέξουσίν σε, 44c ἀνθ᾽ ὧν. The same Lukanisms can be listed for instance by J. Dupont who attributes 19:41-42, 44c to Luke and combines the acceptance of a source in 19:43-44b

---

[10] Cf. above, 84-85.

with some redactional intervention of the evangelist.[11] Here, no more than in Lk 21, "Lukanisms" can prove a Proto-Lukan origin.

2. *Lk 21:20,21bc and Proto-Luke*. Boismard's first argument for Proto-Luke in Lk 21 is taken from verse 21. The pronouns αὐτῆς and αὐτήν in v. 21bc refer back to Jerusalem in v. 20 and not to the nearest feminine noun, Judaea in v. 21a: this suggests that v. 21a (= Mk 13:14b) has been inserted in a non-Markan source (21:20,21bc).[12]

My first observation concerns the sharp distinction between the Markan verse 21a and the non-Markan verses 20,21bc. In Lk 21:20 some contact with Mk 13:14 is undeniable: ὅταν δὲ ἴδητε ..., τότε ..., and ἡ ἐρήμωσις. The saying in Lk 21:21bc about those who are inside the city and those who are out looks like an adaptation of Mark's "on the housetop" and "in the field" (Mk 13:15-16; cf. Lk 17:31)[13] in parallel with v. 21a (= Mk 13:14b):

21a τότε *οἱ ἐν τῇ* Ἰουδαίᾳ
        φευγέτωσαν εἰς τὰ ὄρη,
   b *καὶ ὁ ἐν* μέσῳ αὐτῆς
        ἐκχωρείτωσαν
   c *καὶ οἱ ἐν* ταῖς χώραις
        μὴ εἰσερχέσθωσαν εἰς αὐτήν.

Compare ἐν ταῖς χώραις with Mk 13:16 εἰς τὸν ἀγρόν (Lk 17:31 ἐν ἀγρῷ) and ἐκχωρείτωσαν / μὴ εἰσερχέσθωσαν with Mk 13:15 μὴ ... εἰσελθάτω.

With regard to the use of αὐτῆς and αὐτήν, a combination of two sources is not the only possible explanation.[14] It can be a "tension" between the Lukan source (the unaltered text of Mark in v. 21a) and Luke's own application to Jerusalem in vv. 20,21bc.[15]

[11] J. DUPONT, "Il n'en sera pas laissé pierre sur pierre (Marc 13,2; Luc 19,44)," *Biblica* 52 (1971) 301-320, esp. 311 (notes 1-4), 315 (note 4); = *Études sur les évangiles synoptiques* (BETL, 70), Leuven, 1985, 444, 448. His arguments for tradition in Lk 19:43-44b are questionable, particularly the parallel in Lk 23:29-31: cf. F.G. UNTERGASSMAIR, *Kreuzweg und Kreuzigung Jesu*, Paderborn, 1980, 125-145.

[12] Compare, e.g., I.H.MARSHALL, *Luke*, 772: "the pronoun must refer back grammatically to Ἰουδαίᾳ, but the sense demands a reference back to Jerusalem; this suggests that Luke has incorporated the saying from Mk. in the middle of another source."

[13] Boismard rightly observes that Lk 17:31 "provient de Mt 24:17-18 ou de Mc 13:15-16" (in our view, from Mk 13:15-16).

[14] Almost all recent commentators note (correctly, I think) that the pronouns refer to Jerusalem. But see A. Schlatter's interpretation: "Verlaßt Judäa und wandert nicht in Judäa ein" (*Lukas*, 415), and J. ZMIJEWSKI, *Die Eschatologiereden*, 211: "Flucht aus Judäa = "Absetzung vom Judentum".

[15] Cf. A. LOISY, *Luc*, p. 497: "l'idée de Jérusalem domine tout le développement, et l'équivoque existe à peine; l'évangéliste ne l'a pas sentie en retouchant à mesure le texte de Marc"; and J. SCHMID, *Lukas*, 310: on the origin of the grammatical irregularity "durch

3. *Lk 19:41-44, the Introduction?* A Proto-Lukan sequence of Lk 19:41-44;[16] 21:20,21b etc. is hardly provable. On the level of the Lukan redaction, however, the thematic connection of Lk 19:41-44; 20:20-24; 23:27-31 is most significant.[17] These three Lukan elaborations are grafted into the framework of Mark. The shift from (the profanation of) the Temple in Mark to (the fall of) Jerusalem in Luke is obvious in Lk 21:20, par. Mk 13:14. It is also apparent in Lk 19:41-44, not only in the saying of 19:44 compared with Mk 13:2, but also in the location in parallel to the cursing of the fig tree,[18] before the cleansing of the temple:

Mk	Lk
11:1-10 ————————	19:29-40
11	(41a)
12-14	41-44!
15-17 ————————	45-46

diese Verbindung des alten und des neuen Textes." See now also H. BAARLINK, "Ein gnädiges Jahr des Herrn — und Tage der Vergeltung," *ZNW* 73 (1982) 204-220, 215-216: "Zwar bin ich nicht der Meinung, αὐτῆς beziehe sich grammatisch oder gar dem Sinne nach auf Judäa. Man muß 21b+c schon parallel neben 21a stellen. Alle drei Aussagen beziehen sich zurück auf die in v. 20 angekündigte Katastrophe. Dabei übernimmt Lk den v. 21a von Markus. Danach präzisiert er das Gesagte durch zwei parallele Sätze, wobei die auf Haus und Acker weisenden Aussagen von Mk 13:15 deutlich umgebogen werden zu Aussagen über ungleich größere Bereiche:

v. 21b: Wer in Jerusalem ist, möge ausweichen;
v. 21c: Wer auf dem Lande ist, der gehe nicht erst in die Stadt (Jerusalem) hinein (sondern fliehe sogleich ins Gebirge außerhalb Judäas)."

Judaea (cf. Lk 4:44; 6:17; 23:5): "das jüdische Land." He concludes that "Lukas aus der Aufforderung zur Flucht zugleich einen Hinweis heraushört, daß die junge Kirche sich von dem unter dem Gericht stehenden Judentum trennen soll" (215: cf. Zmijewski),

[16] On the so-called "Proto-Lukan" vocabulary in this paragraph, cf. *supra*, 115.

[17] Cf. J. ZMIJEWSKI, *Die Eschatologiereden*, esp. 206.

[18] In the Synopses Lk 19:41-44 is normally placed before Mk 11:11,12-14 (after Mk 11:1-10). Huck-Greeven should be corrected by separating at Lk 19:39-40/41ff. The arrangement in Benoit-Boismard is based on Matthew: § 275 Mt 21:10-17 / Mk 11:11 / Lk 19:45-48(!); §276 Mk 11:12-14; § 277 Mk 11:15-19.

Compare the correction in Boismard-Lamouille (1986): § 295 Mk 11:11; §296 Mk 11:12-14; §297 Mt 21:10-14 / Mk 11:15-17 / Lk 19:45-46; §298 Mt 21:17 / Mk 11:18-19 / Lk 19:47-48.

On the hypothesis of Proto-Luke in Lk 21, see now also J. VERHEYDEN, "The Source(s) of Luke 21," in *L'Évangile de Luc – The Gospel of Luke* (cf. above, 11 n. 13), 1989, 491-516.

B. *Mark 13 and Proto-Matthew*

In *Synopse* II (1972) Boismard's hypothesis regarding Mk 13 and parallels is a slightly modified two-source theory. His Proto-Mark (*Mc-intermédiaire*) scarcely differs from our Mark (13:11 and 33-37 are added by the redactor). It has been combined with Q sections in Mt 24, and Mt 10:17-22 is an anticipation of Mk 13:9-10,12-13. Luke used a Proto-Lukan source and added insertions from "Mark". The source of Proto-Mark is Document A and the source of Proto-Luke is Document B, a more Hellenistic adaptation of Document A. The most striking aspect of this theory is the disappearance of Proto-Matthew: "Il est curieux que l'on ne trouve dans tout ce discours aucune trace du Mt-inter-médiaire, ni dans le Mt actuel qui dépend tout entier du Mc-intermé-diaire, ni dans le proto-Lc qui dépend tout entier du Document B; force nous est de conclure que le Mt-intermédiaire avait cru bon de l'omettre" (363b).

In the Preliminary paper (1983) there is an important change in Boismard's position regarding Mark 13. Proto-Mark, which in 1972 was the main source of Mk 13 and Mt 24, is now drastically reduced: Mk 13:7,9-11,13b,19-20,21-23,24-27(!) are later additions. The Markan influence on Mt 24 is restricted to Mk 13:5b-6 (Mt 24:4b-5) and Mk 13:8 (Mt 24:7). The emergence of Proto-Matthew is certainly the most radical new development. Mt 10:17-20 and 24:13,21-22,23-25,29-31 are all Matthean, "ce qui suppose un emprunt de Mc au proto-Matthieu". More particularly, the coming of the Son of man in Mt 24:29-31 is typically Matthean: "Le discours de Jésus dans le proto-Marc ne parlait que de la ruine du Temple; le thème de l'Avènement du Fils de l'homme et de la 'fin du monde' n'y fut introduit qu'au niveau de l'ultime rédaction marcienne" (28).

In the Final paper (1984) the Proto-Matthew hypothesis has been reinforced by defending the Matthean origin of the sayings in Mk 13:30,32 (Mt 24:34,36) and, in a significant contrast to 1983, by denying the post-Markan redaction of the Introduction (Mt 24:1-3).

He still now accepts dependence on Mark in Mt 24:4b-5 (Mk 13:5b-6); Mt 24:7,21 (Mk 13:9,12); Mt 24:9-14 ("une composition du Rédacteur matthéen"; cf. Mk 13:9-10,13). But, in partial agreement with the Two-Gospel Hypothesis, he defends the dependence of Mark on Proto-Matthew in Mk 13:21-23 (Mt 24:23-25); Mk 13:9-11,13 (Mt 10:17-20,22); Mk 13:24-27 (Mt 24:29-31).

Let us see which are his objections against Matthew's dependence on Mark.

1. The Introduction (Mt 24:1-3)

The difficulties he cites in this paragraph are Matthew-Luke agreements against Mark (κατέναντι τοῦ ἱεροῦ, ἐπηρώτα, Πέτρος καὶ Ἰάκωβος καὶ Ἰωάννης καὶ Ἀνδρέας in Mk 13:3 and the double phrase λίθοι – οἰκοδομαί in 13:1).

It is instructive to note the dissimilarities in these Matthew-Luke agreements:

Mt 24:3	Mk 13:3	Lk 21:7
καθημένου αὐτοῦ	καθημένου αὐτοῦ	om.
ἐπὶ τοῦ ὄρους τῶν ἐλαιῶν	εἰς τὸ ὄρος τῶν ἐλαιῶν	om.
om.	κατέναντι τοῦ ἱεροῦ	om.
προσῆλθον αὐτῷ	ἐπηρώτα αὐτόν (impf.)	ἐπηρώτησαν αὐτὸν
οἱ μαθηταὶ / κατ᾽ ἰδίαν	κατ᾽ ἰδίαν / Π.κ.Ἰ.κ.Ἰκ.Ἀ.	om.
λέγοντες		λέγοντες

The independence of their reactions to Mark is manifest in parallel to Mk 13:1. In Luke the scene is still inside the temple (om. Mk 13:1a) and the comment is made on the internal decoration ("adorned with noble *stones* and offerings"). In Matthew Jesus left the temple (par. Mk) and "was going away" (Mt) when the disciples pointed to the temple *buildings*. A suggestion for the "omission" of λίθοι in Mt 24:1 can be found in Mk 13:2 βλέπεις ταύτας τὰς μεγάλας οἰκοδομάς; (Mt 24:2 οὐ βλέπετε ταῦτα πάντα; cf. v. 1 τὰς οἰκοδομὰς τοῦ ἱεροῦ).

In Mark the saying of Jesus in 13:2 is a reply to the intervention of "one of his disciples" (βλέπεις) and the discourse is Jesus' answer to the question asked by the four (κατ᾽ ἰδίαν). Matthew maintains the κατ᾽ ἰδίαν but replaces the separation between the four and the disciples (cf. 13:37 ὃ δὲ ὑμῖν λέγω, πᾶσιν λέγω) by a separation between the disciples and the people: 24:1,3 "his disciples", "the disciples", in contrast with the audience of the preceding woes (23:1 τοῖς ὄχλοις καὶ τοῖς μαθηταῖς αὐτοῦ).

The omission of the (almost superfluous) phrase (καθημένου) κατέναντι τοῦ ἱεροῦ may be connected with the omission of Mk 12:41-44, with the corresponding formula καθίσας κατέναντι τοῦ γαζοφυλακίου (v. 41). The expression προσῆλθον αὐτῷ ... λέγοντες (for ἐπηρώτα αὐτόν)[19] is, of course, typically Matthean. Together with

---

[19] On the aorist for Mark's imperfect in Lk 21:7 (see also diff. Mk 5:9; 8:27; 10:17; 12:18), cf. *The Minor Agreements*, 229-239 (no. 11: "Imperfect in Mark"). Note that only in 7 instances of Mark's 15 occurrences of the imperfect ἠρώτα the sentence has a parallel in Luke (cf. diff. Mk 8:29; 14:61; add the secondary parallel of Mk 15:4 in Lk 23:9).

παρουσία and συντέλεια τοῦ αἰῶνος, it gives a special Matthean coloration to Mt 24:3. "Le vocabulaire de Mt 24:3 est typiquement matthéen. ... L'hypothèse la plus vraisemblable est qu'il fut introduit par Mt" (1983, 27).

2. The False Prophets (Mt 24:23-25)

In both sections on false christs and false prophets the parallel texts of Matthew (24:4b-5,23-25) and Mark (13:5b-6,21-23) are almost identical, but Mt 24:23-25 / Mk 13:21-23 is attributed to Proto-Matthew because of the "Matthean" theme of the ψευδοπροφῆται and the "more primitive" phrase δώσουσιν (σημεῖα) in Mt 24:24 (Mk 13:22 ποιήσουσιν).

The theme of the false prophets appears in Mt 7:15 and 24:11, and both passages are redactional (cf. Synopse II, 156b, 362a; see also below, 280: Mt 24:9-14!).

In Mk 13:22 Boismard reads ποιήσουσιν. Nestle-Aland[26] has δώσουσιν (= Mt); cf. Textus Receptus H S V M (Taylor, Pesch, Gnilka, et al.). However, δώσουσιν is not necessarily the most primitive text. It could be a Matthean "correction", under the influence of Deut 13:2, of ποιήσουσιν in Mark (D Θ f[13] 28 565 pc; printed text in T N B Greeven).

3. The Coming of the Son of Man (Mt 24:29-31)

The arguments for Matthean origin of Mt 24:29-31 / Mk 13:24-27 ("la fin du monde et la venue du Fils de l'homme") are the theme of the question in Mt 24:3b (contrast Mk 13:4; Lk 21:7: "ne parlent que de la ruine du Temple") and the parallels in Mt 13:24-30, 36-43,47-50, peculiar to Matthew.

In 1972 all these Matthean parallels were recognized as clearly secondary Matthean redaction:
24:3b: "l'ultime Rédacteur matthéen ... introduit le thème de l'avènement de Jésus (parousia), comme aux vv. 27.37.39, et change le verbe 'finir' de Mc en 'fin du monde'" (365a).
13:30 τὸν δὲ σῖτον συναγάγετε εἰς τὴν ἀποθήκην μου: "Il est probable que la phrase ... est une insertion de l'ultime Rédacteur matthéen, inspirée de Mt 3,12" (191b).
13:40b οὕτως ἔσται ἐν τῇ συντελείᾳ τοῦ αἰῶνος. 41 ἀποστελεῖ ὁ υἱὸς τοῦ ἀνθρώπου τοὺς ἀγγέλους αὐτοῦ καὶ συλλέξουσιν ...: "L'ultime Rédacteur matthéen aurait remanié cette grille (d'interprétation) en introduisant des termes nouveaux, et surtout en ajoutant le discours

apocalyptique des vv. 40-43, comme il le fera pour la parabole du filet" (195; Mt 13:49-50, "une addition de l'ultime Rédacteur matthéen").

When it is said now about συντέλεια τοῦ αἰῶνος: "Matthieu l'a probablement formée en s'inspirant des chapitres 11 et 12 de Daniel" (275), what is meant by this Matthean "formation"? And the Matthean "systematization" and "reutilization" in Mt 13:40 (270, 274: ὥσπερ – οὕτως), is it not Matthean redaction? If Boismard's opinion is now that all these passages are Proto-Matthean, it should be said plainly. If not, how can they prove the Proto-Matthean origin of Mt 24:29-31?

In Mk 13:4 the second member of the double question is not a mere repetition of the first:[20]

4a πότε 4b τί τὸ σημεῖον ὅταν
  ταῦτα ταῦτα ... πάντα
  ἔσται μέλλῃ ... συντελεῖσθαι.

"Die erste Frage kann nur nach der in 2 genannten Tempelzerstörung fragen, die zweite Frage geht auf das Ende der alten Welt" (W. Schmithals, 571). "Die Doppelfrage insinuiert eine enge Verbindung von Tempelzerstörung und Weltende. ... Diese enge Verbindung wird dann in der Antwort Jesu aufgelöst" (R. Pesch, 276).[21]

4. The Sayings in Mt 24:34,36

Mt 24:34 / Mk 13:30 and Mt 24:36 / Mk 13:32 are cited as a confirmation of the Matthean origin of Mt 24:29-31. The first saying is identical in Matthew and Mark, with the exception of the "Matthean" ἕως ἄν (Mk μέχρις οὗ). The formulation of Mt 5:18, ἕως ἄν (παρέλθῃ), ἕως ἄν πάντα γένηται (diff. Lk 16:17) is probably influenced by Mt 24:34 / Mk 13:30. The other uses of ἕως ἄν are in Mt 2:13 (Red.?); 5:26 (Lk ἕως); 10:11 (= Mk); 12:20 (LXX); 16:28 (= Mk); 22:44 (= Mk, LXX); 23:39 (Lk ἕως): there is no one instance of Matthean "tradition". In Mt 16:28 the change of (ἕως ἄν ἴδωσιν) τὴν βασιλείαν τοῦ θεοῦ ἐληλυθυῖαν ἐν δυνάμει to τὸν υἱὸν τοῦ ἀνθρώπου ἐρχόμενον ἐν τῇ βασιλείᾳ αὐτοῦ can be influenced by the preceding verse (om. καὶ ἔλεγεν αὐτοῖς) and by Mk 13:26 ὄψονται ... (cf. Mk 14:62).

A few minor differences can be noted in Mt 24:36: om. τῆς before ὥρας; τῶν οὐρανῶν for ἐν οὐρανῷ (compare the plural in Mt 19:21; 24:31: diff. Mk; 5:12; 7:11; 18:14: diff. Lk); the addition of μόνος after εἰ μή ... (compare εἰ μή in Mk 2:26, add. μόνοις Mt 12:4, and in Mk

---

[20] Cf. *Evangelica*, 124, 517, 590; *Duality in Mark*, 54.

[21] See also E. BRANDENBURGER, *Markus 13 und die Apokalyptik* (FRLANT, 134), Göttingen, 1984, 96.

11:13, add. μόνον Mt 21:19). See also the addition of μόνον in Mt 10:42 (Mk 9:41); 5:47 (Lk 6:33); 8:8 (Lk 7:7); 9:21 and 14:36 (Mk 5:28 and 6:56 κἄν. — Mt 25:13 clearly depends on Mk 13:32 (and 35). The reference to Mt 24:50; 24:44 and 11:27 can be expected in a Two-Gospel argumentation but is less understandable in Boismard's hypothesis (Q = Proto-Luke).

5. Mk 13:9-13 and the Doublet in Mt 10:17-22; 24:9-14

The explanation of Mk 13:11 by Mark's dependence on Proto-Matthew (1972) is now extended to Mk 13:9-11 but not, as in the Two-Gospel Hypothesis, to the entire section of Mk 13:9-13.

Mt 24:9-14

The acceptance of Mt 24:9-14 as "une composition du Rédacteur matthéen" (280) implies Matthean dependence on Mk 13:9-13, and not on Mt 10:17-22.

Mt 24		Mk 13	
9a παραδώσουσιν ὑμᾶς εἰς		9b	παραδώσουσιν ὑμᾶς εἰς
b ἀποκτενοῦσιν ὑμᾶς		12b	θανατώσουσιν αὐτούς
c ἔσεσθε μισούμενοι ...	= 13a		
10b ἀλλήλους παραδώσουσιν			cf. 12a παραδώσει ...
c μισήσουσιν ἀλλήλους			cf. 13a μισούμενοι
11a πολλοὶ ψευδοπροφῆται ἐγ.			6a πολλοί, 22a ἐγερθήσονται ...
b πλανήσουσιν πολλούς			6b πολλοὺς πλανήσουσιν, cf. 22b
13 ὁ δὲ ὑπομείνας ...	= 13b		
14a καὶ κηρυχθήσεται ...		10	
εἰς μαρτύριον ...		9c	
b καὶ τότε ἥξει τὸ τέλος		10	πρῶτον, cf. 7b.

In Mt 24:10-12 the contacts with the context in Mk 13:6,9-13,22 (par. Mt 24:5; 10:17-22; 24:24) are undeniable. This can be a first indication of dependence on the same context of Mk 13 rather than combination of Mt 10 with Mt 24:5,24. Decisive evidence is provided by the parallel to Mt 24:14 in Mk 13:10[22] and the absence of such a parallel in Mt 10.

Mt 10:17-20

Three indications of Matthean priority are cited: 1. the preaching of the gospel and the persecution of the missionaries is a typical theme of

[22] On the influence of Mk 13:10, cf. J. LANGE, Das Erscheinen des Auferstandenen im Evangelium nach Mattäus (FzB, 11), Würzburg, 1973, 301: "Die Wendung πάντα τὰ ἔθνη findet sich bei Mattäus — von 28,19 abgesehen — an drei Stellen: Mt 24,9; 24,14; 25,32. Alle drei Stellen erklären sich aus der — sehr umsichtigen — Rezeption des Verses Mk 13,10 durch Mattäus. Nicht anders aber steht es dann wohl letztlich um die Herkunft des πάντα τὰ ἔθνη in 28,19."

the mission discourse; 2. the common vocabulary is Matthean; 3. there is an original connection between the verses 8 and 12 in Mk 13.

1. The exclusion of Mk 13 as a more original context for Mt 10:17-20 depends to a large extent on a certain conception of the pre-Markan discourse. There is no place for Mk 13:9-11 in a Jewish apocalyptic *Flugblatt*, and no one would expect Mk 13:9-11 in a Proto-Markan discourse if it is merely "un discours sur la ruine du Temple". It is less unexpected that the sufferings of the christians be seen in connection with the eschatological tribulations and the universal preaching of the gospel put in relation to the End. But "essayons de nous laisser guider par les textes, sans idée préconçue" (278).

2. The "Matthean" vocabulary in Mk 13:9-11:

εἰς συναγωγὰς δαρήσεσθε Mk 13:9 / ἐν ταῖς συναγωγαῖς αὐτῶν μαστιγώσουσιν ὑμᾶς Mt 10:17. Cf 23:34 ἐξ αὐτῶν μαστιγώσετε ἐν ταῖς συναγωγαῖς ὑμῶν. "Les retouches de l'ultime Rédacteur matthéen sont nombreuses. Au v. 34, il ajoute les mots suivants: 'et crucifierez' (cf. Mt 20:18; 26:2), 'et vous en flagellerez dans vos synagogues' (cf. Mt 10:17b), 'de ville en ville' (cf. Mt 10,23)" (1972, 358a).

ἡγεμών Mk 13:9 / Mt 10:18. Ten(!) occurrences in Mt: 2:6 in a quotation; the eight occurrences in 27:2ff. represent one specific application: "L'ultime Rédacteur matthéen [27,2] a ajouté le titre de 'gouverneur' (*egemôn*) après le nom de Pilate (cf. vv. 11.14.15.21.27 et 28:14)" (409; add 27:11a).

ἕνεκεν ἐμοῦ Mk 13:9 / Mt 10:18. Cf. Mt 5:11; 10:39; 16:25. The formulation in Mk 13:(9-)10 can be compared with the "more complete" formula in Mk 8:35 and 10:29, and the omission of Mk 13:10 in Mt 10:18 can be compared with the omission of καὶ τοῦ εὐαγγελίου in Mt 16:25 and 19:29.

13:9	par. Mt 10:18
ἕνεκεν ἐμοῦ	ἕνεκεν ἐμοῦ
εἰς μαρτύριον αὐτοῖς.	εἰς μαρτύριον αὐτοῖς ...
10 καὶ ... τὸ εὐαγγέλιον.	
8:35	par. Mt 16:25 (doublet in 10:39)
ἕνεκεν ἐμοῦ	ἕνεκεν ἐμοῦ
καὶ τοῦ εὐαγγελίου[23]	

[23] Compare also 8:38 με καὶ τοὺς ἐμοὺς λόγους.

10:29   par. Mt 19:29
ἕνεκεν ἐμοῦ   ἕνεκεν τοῦ ὀνόματός μου
καὶ ἕνεκεν τοῦ εὐαγγελίου

In Mt 5:11 ἕνεκεν ἐμοῦ (diff. Lk 6:22 ἕνεκα τοῦ υἱοῦ τοῦ ἀνθρώπου) is probably Matthean redaction: compare Mt 10:32 (diff. Lk 12:8); Mt 16:21 (diff. Mk 8:31).

ἐν ἐκείνῃ τῇ ὥρᾳ Mt 13:11 / Mk 10:19. Cf. Mt 8:13; 18:1; 26:55; cf. ἀπὸ τῆς ὥρας ἐκείνης Mt 9:22; 15:28; 17:18.
In Mt 18:1 (diff. Mk 9:33) and 26:55 (diff. Mk 14:48) ἐν ἐκείνῃ τῇ ὥρᾳ is a Matthean transition formula. In both instances it resumes the Markan narrative after a Matthean expansion (compare Mt 17:24a,25b with Mk 9:33a; Mt 26:52a with Mk 14:48a.) A more typically Matthean formula is the conclusion of healing stories with ἐν τῇ ὥρᾳ ἐκείνῃ in Mt 8:13 (diff. Lk 7:10) and ἀπὸ τῆς ὥρας ἐκείνης in Mt 9:22 (diff. Mk 5:34); Mt 15:28 (diff. Mk 7:30); Mt 17:18 (diff. Mk 9:27);[24] "c'est l'ultime Rédacteur matthéen qui a ajouté l'expression" (1972, 159b, 210a, 235b, 256b).

3. Mk 13:9-11, in the second person, in contrast to v. 12, in the third person and originally connected with v. 8? Such a connection between Mk 13:8 and 12 has been suggested by L. Hartman (1966), R. Pesch (1968), et al., but see now Pesch's commentary: "Gegen eine unmittelbare Zusammengehörigkeit der VV 8.12 in einer nicht paränetischen, bloß weissagenden Vorlage spricht nicht nur der Stilunterschied (Asyndese in V 8, καί-Reihung in V 12), sondern auch die anders gerichtete Intention von V 12 sowie der traditionskritische Befund, der die Zusammengehörigkeit von VV 12-13a erweist" (1977, 283).

Boismard separates Mk 13:13a (in the second person: mission discourse) and Mk 13:12,13b (in the third person: eschatological discourse). If he can accept that Mt 10:21,22b (= Mk 13:12,13b) were secondarily added to the mission discourse (279-280: harmonization), why not Mt 10:21-22 (= Mk 13:12-13), and why not the entire section of Mt 10:17-22 (= Mk 13:9-13)? And finally how can Mk 13:13b (= Mt 10:22b; 24:13) be "Matthean" because of its contact with Dan 12:13 when Mk 13:4, too, depends on Dan 12 (275: "selon toute vraisemblance la formule de Marc reprend celle de Dan 12:7, sans dépendre ni de Matthieu ni de Luc")?

F. NEIRYNCK

---

[24] Cf. *Evangelica*, 485-7.

THE TWO-GOSPEL HYPOTHESIS

THE STATEMENT OF THE HYPOTHESIS

I. THE TRADITION OF THE CHURCH

The historical evidence indicates that Matthew and Luke
were composed before Mark and John.

The Two-Gospel Hypothesis is given this name, in the first instance, because it consists of a hypothesis that the two Gospels Matthew and Luke were written before Mark and John.

First: this hypothesis is supported by the testimony of Clement of Alexandria who, according to Eusebius, wrote in his *Hypotyposeis* that the Gospels with genealogies were written first. Subsequent interpreters in the Church have understood this to mean that the Gospels according to Matthew and Luke, each of which has a genealogy, were written before the Gospels according to Mark and John, neither of which has a genealogy.

Eusebius certainly accepted Clement's testimony in this sense. He states that Clement is handing on a tradition from the primitive elders "concerning the order (τάξις) of the gospels." After mentioning the sequential priority of the Gospels with genealogies, Clement next mentions Mark and then John. This suggests that as far as Clement was concerned Mark and John were Gospels which came in order of composition after Matthew and Luke.

All scholars familiar with the nature and value of tradition will be interested in Clement's Testimonium which may be found in Eusebius, *Hist. eccl.* 6.14.5-7.

> "And, again in the same books [*Hypotyposeis* 6], Clement has inserted a tradition from the primitive elders with regard to the order of the gospels as follows: he said that those gospels were written first which include the genealogies, and that the gospel according to Mark came into being in this manner:..."

Eusebuius' report of Clement's Testimonium is quite clear, as Lawlor and Oulton recognize. It tells us plainly that: concerning the order of the Gospels (περὶ τῆς τάξεως τῶν εὐαγγελίων) Matthew and Luke were earlier than Mark. The use of τάξις in this context is decisive. It indicates that Matthew and Luke were written first, and that Mark and John came after Matthew and Luke.

Moreover, this tradition is not to be understood as tradition which has originated with Clement's immediate teachers, whom he also calls "elders", but from the primitive elders, i.e. "the elders who lived in the first days." It is not unreasonable to suppose that some of these primitive elders themselves had living contact with the Gospel writers or at least with their disciples. Much depends, of course, on when the Gospels were written. The point is that the burden of proof in this matter, in any case, rests upon the critic who would discount this tradition as having no historical value. This Testimonium from the primitive elders, which has come to us through Clement and Eusebius, was accepted in the Church according to the plain sense of the text as Eusebius understood it, all the way down into the ninth century. This is made certain by the learned ninth century Irish monk Sedulius Scottus. He explains that Mark omitted the birth narratives because he knew that they had already been recorded "in the first two evangelists." Scottus makes this comment while explaining a passage from the "Monarchian" prologue of Mark. This fourth or fifth century prologue also shares the view that the Gospel of Mark was composed after Matthew and Luke and that Mark had seen both of these earlier Gospels.

In commenting on this Scottus writes: "... Matthew and Luke, who, according to some, as the *Ecclesiastical History* relates, wrote their gospels before Mark..." The reference to "*The Ecclesiastical History*" clearly refers to Eusebius' *E.H.* 6.14.5. While all writers known to Scottus might not have agreed with the view that Matthew and Luke were written before Mark, this is the view which is represented by the learned Eusebius in his *Ecclesiastical History*, i.e. according to the understanding of Scottus. That Scottus makes this view his own is clear from what he says about the Gospels in the section cited above (Migne, *Patrologia Latina,* vol. 103, col. 279-86).

There is, however, an alternative tradition in the Church that the Gospels were composed in the order Matthew, Mark, Luke, John. One finds support for this tradition in various places including the "Monarchian" prologue of Luke. According to this prologue, Luke was written in Achaia after Matthew had been written in Judea and after Mark had been written in Italy. But the wording of this relatively late prologue to Luke is so close to the wording of the earlier "Anti-Marcionite" Prologue of Luke, that it seems probable that the agreement between the two prologues is due to literary dependence. In any case we have two differing traditions; Luke before Mark, and Mark before Luke. How can this apparent discrepancy in Church tradition be resolved?

We should bear in mind that in the second century, when the "Anti-Marcionite" Prologues were written, the current order of the Four-fold Gospel canon probably represented the order in which the Anti-Marcionite bishops wanted the Gospels to be read. The particular order Matthew, Mark, Luke, John places the two genuine works from the circle of the Twelve Apostles at beginning and end, enclosing those by "apostolic men" in between. In this way, the genuine version of Luke (associated with the Apostle Paul, the darling of the Marcionites), is placed after Mark (penned in the name of the Apostle Peter), between two bulwarks of orthodox tradition: Matthew and John.

Assuming for the sake of discussion that this was the way in which the fourfold Gospel canon was originally arranged in the Greek manu-script tradition, how can we explain the fact that this order does not follow the chronological order of composition reflected in the tradition from the primitive elders accepted by Clement in the famous and influential school of Alexandria?

One answer suggests itself immediately: in the orthodox tradition, it was more important to have a "theological order" than a merely chronological or historical order. From a theological point of view there were powerful reasons for placing Luke after Mark in between Matthew and John. Marcion had given preference to the gospel tradi-tion preserved in Luke in reconstructing his gospel text. In the process he had rejected the authority of all the apostles except Paul. In reply, the Anti-Marcionite bishops placed Luke, the Pauline Gospel, next to and after Mark, Peter's Gospel, reinforcing the Irenaean "Salvation History" (first Peter, then Paul) consciousness of the Anti-Marcionite Catholic Church which formed the fourfold Gospel canon. There is no reason to think that this "theological order" was regarded in the school of Alexandria as contradicting the tradition regarding the order of composition from the "primitive elders" accepted by Clement. Euse-bius, who is aware of this "theological order," gives not the slightest hint of any implied contradition. The two traditions were on different planes of tradition.

There are of course certain practical pedagogical advantages in placing Mark before Luke in the Canon. For example this sequence serves the principle of "incremental gain." If Matthew is read first, then by also reading Mark one can learn more, and after reading Matthew and Mark, one can learn still more by reading Luke, and finally still more by reading John. Whereas if one waits to read Mark until after having read Matthew and Luke, one learns very little that has not already been covered by Matthew and Luke. Again, when read in the canonical order Mark carries the reader forward from the very Jewish account of Matthew to the more universal account of Luke. Moreover, one notes that in the process Mark's account remains essentially faithful to that of Matthew while it fittingly prepares the reader to take up Luke's quite different account. These practical advantages may not have contributed to the origin of the canonical order, but they would have commended this order once adopted.

One major requirement of contemporary New Testament and patristic study is to reassess in an impartial manner the early tradition of the Church concerning the provenance, authorship, and date of composition of the Gospels. Proponents of the Two-Document Hypothesis generally disregard their responsibility to understand or explain the Church's traditions on these matters.

Any adequate treatment of early Church tradition must do justice to the fact that the tradition which places the composition of Luke after Mark cannot with confidence be traced back any earlier than an anonymous anti-Marcionite prologue from the late second century. There it hangs in mid-air in a text whose author cannot be connected with any known person in the Church. Compare this considerable uncertainty with the tradition that places the composition of Matthew and Luke first. This tradition can be connected with known historical figures like Eusebius and Clement. These scholars were well acquainted with all relevant traditions, written and oral. Consider that Clement had this particular tradition (it appears to have been oral) about the priority of Matthew and Luke from "primitive" (ἀνέκαθεν) elders who lived even earlier than Clement's teachers, i.e. elders who were active during the generation of Papias and Ignatius. One of those "blessed and truly notable men" whom Clement tells us he was privileged to hear was an Ionian whom he met in Greece. This sage could have been acquainted with Ionian Greeks who had known disciples of the bishops Polycarp and Papias. And when Clement tells us of another of those early Christian sages who lived in Coele-Syria, we may be sure that this mentor would have known some persons who could remember having heard the Antiochian bishop Ignatius preach and teach.

If this prolonged discussion of the reasons for giving due weight to Clement of Alexandria's Testimonium appears somewhat tedious in the light of the plain sense of the text, the reader must bear in mind the full impact of this piece of external evidence on the question of Marcan priority. Defenders of Marcan priority cannot accept this evidence and hold to their theory. If they hold to their theory they must ignore, explain away or deny the value of this tradition.

One purpose of this discussion is to prepare the reader to weigh carefully any attempt to discount Clement's testimony. For example, in answer to the possible objection that the tradition that Luke was written after Mark may also go back to the time of the primitive elders, and if so would serve to cancel out the value of Clement's testimony, it may be asked: If Papias' five volume *Exposition of the Lord's Oracles,* or if any other writing from that era of scholarship had contained a tradition from an earlier time which in any way contradicted the tradition which Clement passed on from the "primitive elders" in his *Hypotyposeis,* could Clement have overlooked it? Our answer is that, while such an oversight could have been made, it would have been corrected, certainly by Eusebius if not long before, by, for example, Origen. Scholarly texts then available were gathered together in the libraries of Alexandria and/or Caesarea, to which scholars like Clement, Origen, Pamphilius and Eusebius, and their several assistants and disciples, had ready access. An essential function of these schools or centers of Christian learning was to note and correct such errors. Otherwise, the teachings of these schools would be held up to public ridicule as inconsistent.

In sum, it is a distinct advantage of the Two-Gospel Hypothesis that it enjoys the support of the historical evidence critically evaluated. The Gospel of Matthew and the Gospel of Luke were, as far as this external evidence is concerned, clearly believed to have been composed before the other Gospels — certainly by Clement and presumably by all scholars who accepted Clement's Testimonium, including Eusebius, clear down to the ninth century.

Second: it was Augustine of Hippo who, building on the work of Ammonius in the form of the canons of Eusebius, first laid out in detail the results of a prolonged and exhaustive comparative study of all four Gospels (*De consensu evangelistarum*). From his painstaking study of the texts of the Gospels Augustine came to the conclusion that each succeeding evangelist made use of the work of his predecessor(s).

The Clementine view that Mark was sequentially composed after Matthew and Luke would have meant for Augustine that Mark had made use of both Matthew and Luke. Indeed, the view which Augustine preferred comports with, though it does not strictly require, the conclusion that Mark did know both Matthew and Luke.

After mentioning his earlier view set forth in Book I, that Mark was second and has abbreviated Matthew, Augustine himself in Book IV turns to another view that he says is more probable:

"...in accordance with the more probable account of the matter [*vel quod probabilius intelligitur*] he [Mark] holds a course in conjunction with both [Matthew and Luke] [*cum ambobus incedit*]. For although he is at one with Matthew in the larger number of passages he is nevertheless at one rather with Luke in some others [*Nam quamvis Matthaeo in pluribus, tamen in aliis nonnullis Lucae magis congruit*];..." [*De cons. evang.* 4.10.11].

If we consider this excerpt within its larger context and in relation to all other relevant passages in *De consensu*, we must draw the conclusion that it was Augustine's final opinion that "Mark is literarily dependent upon both Matthew and ... Luke."

Augustine's literary analysis is paralleled by a recognition of the theological themes that characterize both Matthew and Luke. In the human face of Mark's Gospel, says Augustine, one can discern the figure of one who fulfills both the kingly office of Christ lifted up by Matthew and the priestly image of Christ emphasized by Luke.

Although Augustine makes no reference to the Testimonium of Clement, his preferred view is certainly consonant with that tradition.

II. THE PURPOSE OF MARK ON THE TWO-GOSPEL HYPOTHESIS

*Mark created a more encompassing theological future
for his church by unifying Matthew and Luke.*

The unanimous consensus of early tradition locates the composition of the Gospel of Mark with the church in Rome. Further, it is associated with the oral proclamation of the Apostle Peter while he was in Rome. Beyond this, the early traditions are silent, and scholarly conjecture must fill the gap. In particular, all that the earliest tradition says about Mark is that Mark took pains to record carefully what Peter had said. For us to understand this Gospel more fully, however, we must first observe the two Gospels on either side of it. The Gospel of Matthew represented the continuing vital interests of those who stood in the apostolic tradition of the Jerusalem Apostles. Luke, in its own way, represented the vital interests of the Gentile oriented churches which had been founded by Paul. Mark, by blending these two traditions together, made it possible for local churches to retain and cherish at one and the same time both Matthew and Luke and to do that within the theological context of a profound Pauline-Petrine orientation to the faith. In bringing this about, Peter/Mark underlined the need for more than one perspective on the tradition. In this "more-than-one-

Gospel canon" no single written account of the Church's Gospel was or ever will be an adequate textual basis for Christian doctrine or practice. At the same time, Mark, under the auspices of the Pauline εὐαγγέλιον unified within the collective consciousness of the Church the diverse and sometimes diverging accounts of Matthew and Luke. "Whoever loses his life for my sake *and for the sake of the Gospel will save it."* (Mark 8:35. Only Mark adds: καὶ τοῦ εὐαγγελίου. This fourfold Gospel canon, expecially under Mark's influence, was to steel Christians under persecution and unite then in their apostolic *martyria* to leave all for the sake of Christ and for the sake of the Gospel; "Truly, I say to you, there is no one who has left house or brothers or sisters or mother or father or children or lands, for my sake *and for the sake of the Gospel,* who will not receive a hundredfold now in this time, houses and brothers and sisters and mothers and children and lands with persecutions, and in the age to come eternal life." (Mark 10:29-30. Only Mark adds: καὶ ἕνεκεν τοῦ εὐαγγελίου).

Outside of Mark in the New Testament, it is only the Apostle Paul who uses εὐαγγέλιον absolutely in this same way. It is striking evidence of Mark's close relationship to Paul that he begins his Gospel with the dramatic statement: ἀρχὴ τοῦ εὐαγγελίου Ἰησοῦ Χριστοῦ. Mark is the first Evangelist, therefore, to identify his written text with "the Gospel." It would have been Mark's Gospel, perceived as a written account of "the Gospel of Jesus Christ," that first would have been seen as: "The Gospel according to [a particular author]." From this viewpoint the fourfold Gospel canon can be seen as a deutero-Pauline construction, where these four narrative texts were each perceived as separate but authentic written expressions of the one true εὐαγγέλιον for which Christians were to leave all [Mk 10:29-30], and, if necessary, suffer persecution and even death [Mk 8:35]. Once one recognizes the preeminent importance the Church gave to this deutero-Pauline construction, and sees how, through these uniform ascriptions, this theological construction gives shape and impetus to the collective influence of the fourfold Gospel canon, then it becomes possible, on the Two-Gospel Hypothesis, to see that Mark not only unites Matthew and Luke, but also unifies the narrative corpus of the Gospels with the Pauline theology of the Cross. Moreover, Mark, by making a Pauline εὐαγγέλιον available to those who composed the fourfold Gospel canon, has pioneered the way for the Church to prevail against Marcion and the Gnostics in its determination to hold together the Pauline epistles with the fourfold Gospel canon, and thus Paul with the Twelve. Briefly put, Mark is a bridge not only between Matthew and Luke, but also

between the Gospels (with Acts) and the Pauline corpus. Mark's
εὐαγγέλιον provided the Church with the unifying principles of its
canon.

III. LITERARY EVIDENCE

The internal evidence considered as a whole confirms that Mark used both Matthew and Luke.

First: the Two-Gospel Hypothesis does not require the critic to deny
the existence of earlier sources used by the evangelists, written and/or
oral. In fact, advocates of the Two-Gospel Hypothesis give full recognition to the importance of oral tradition in the development of the Jesus
traditions utilized by the evangelists. Moreover, oral tradition continued alongside the compositional activity of the evangelists, no doubt
exercising its influence upon each evangelist even as he was making use
of the written compositions of his predecessors. But the Two-Gospel
Hypothesis makes it quite unnecessary to appeal to hypothetical documents like Q in order to explain close verbatim agreement among the
Gospels which can be more readily explained by a recognition that, as
Augustine saw, no one of the evangelists did his work in ignorance of
that of his predecessor. Thus, according to the Two-Gospel Hypothesis,
Matthew wrote first, making extensive use of existing sources (oral and
written), Luke wrote second, making extensive use of Matthew and
extensive use of other source material (oral and written), Mark composed
his Gospel making extensive use of both Matthew and Luke with a
limited use of other source material (oral and written). All three
evangelists exercized their authorial freedom in different ways, and all
three made distinctive contributions to their compositions.

Second: It was not until the 18th century that scholars in general
began to take note of the internal evidence that demonstrates that
Mark had artfully combined the texts of Matthew and Luke. By this
time Augustine's earlier view that Mark was the epitomizer of Matthew
had mistakenly become fixed as the traditional view of the Church.
Since this putative tradition of the Church conflicted with the newly
discovered internal evidence that Mark had united Matthew and Luke,
it soon appeared to represent a view of Mark that was very much out
of date. As such it only served to justify scholars under the influence of
the Enlightenment in their low estimate of Church tradition as a whole.
If the great Augustine could be mistaken, whom could you trust? This

may explain in part why these 18th century scholars appeared to have placed no weight on Clement's Testimonium. In any case an increasing number of scholars became convinced that Mark, quite apart from the Clement Testimonium, had indeed combined his texts of Matthew and Luke. The evidence for this seems first to have been publicly pointed out by the Rev. Dr. Henry Owen, Rector of St. Olave in Hart-Street, London, and Fellow of the Royal Society. In his book, *Observations on the Four Gospels; Tending Chiefly to Ascertain the Time of their Publication; and to Illustrate the Form and Manner of their Composition,* published in London in 1764, Owen wrote:

> In compiling this narrative [i.e. the Gospel of Mark], he had little more to do, it seems, than to abridge the Gospels which lay before him — varying some expressions, and inserting additions, as occasion required. That St. Mark followed this plan, no one can doubt, who compares his Gospel with those of the two former Evangelists. He copies largely from both; and takes either the one or the other almost perpetually for his guide. The order indeed is his own, and is very close and well connected. In his account of facts he is also clear, exact, and critical; and the more so perhaps, as he wrote it for the perusal of a learned and critical people. For he seems to proceed with great caution, and to be solicitous that his Gospel should stand clear of all objections. [pp. 51-2]

Later on Owen writes:

> It is apparent that St. Mark makes quick and frequent transitions from one Evangelist to the other; and blends their accounts, I mean their words, in such a manner as is utterly inexplicable upon any other footing, than by supposing he had both these Gospels before him. [p. 74]

Owen offers as a specimen set of parallel passages, Mark 12:13-27 // Matt. 22:16-32 // Luke 20:20-38, and suggests that here the reader will find "as ample a proof of such a commixture of phrases and sentences, as can well be desired" [p. 74].

This understanding of Mark was subsequently made famous by Johann Jacob Griesbach of Jena University, whose name became associated with this hypothesis. It was widely held by many competent New Testament critics, representing widely diverse approaches, including Friedrich Bleek and Friedrich Schleiermacher in Berlin, and F.C. Baur, Eduard Zeller and David Friedrich Strauss in Tübingen. It was brought to its most critically defensible form in the highly esteemed work of W.M.L. De Wette of Basel. This is hardly a mean list of scholars!

Third: The first step in proposing any solution to the Synoptic Problem is the recognition of the literary fact that Matthew, Mark and Luke all three agree significantly with one another to varying degrees in

content and order of episodes. It is fundamental to any valid solution
to the Synoptic Problem that the respective content and order of the
three Synoptic Gospels be perceived together. It cannot be emphasized
too strongly that the fundamental fact of the Synoptic Problem is
precisely this complex set of agreements and disagreements in content
and order between Matthew, Mark and Luke. The only way to begin to
solve the Synoptic Problem is by attending to this fact. Negatively
stated, we reject as methodologically incorrect any attempt to divide
these three Gospels and focus attention first either upon some part or
section of them, or upon the agreements and disagreements in content
and order between any two of them, such as, for example, Matthew and
Mark, or Matthew and Luke, or Mark and Luke. It follows that
it is methodologically incorrect for Karl Lachmann (followed by
W.G. Kümmel and F. Neirynck), to focus initially upon Matthew and
Mark on the one hand, and then Luke and Mark on the other.

To discuss the content and order of Mark and Luke without reference
to the content and order of Matthew (as advocated by Lachmann,
Kümmel and Neirynck) requires the critic to leave out of view the
whole network of evidence tying these two to Matthew, and the same
thing is true of their treatment of Mark and Matthew, leaving Luke out
of view. It is the interlocking web of agreement among all three that
convinced Owen, Griesbach and their successors that Mark had used
Matthew and Luke. Specifically, one can see clearly that it is the
evidence from Matthew which explains much of the content and almost
all of the order of Mark when it differs from the content and order of
Luke, and so it is with Luke when Mark disagrees with Matthew. The
fact that one can thus explain the order and content of Mark, and at
the same time do this without needing to appeal to the use of
a hypothetical source like "Q," or even better, without appealing
to hypothetical sources like "Q" and "Ur-Markus" or "Deutero-
Markus," is a consideration which clearly constitutes a prime reason
for regarding Mark as third.

Fourth: It is a fact that there exists a positive correlation between
agreement in order and agreement in wording among the Synoptic
Gospels which is most readily explicable on the hypothesis that Mark
was written after Matthew and Luke and is the result of a compositional
procedure where Mark made use of both Matthew and Luke. If Mark
were third, it would not have been unnatural for him to have given
some preference to the text of Matthew when he had deliberately
chosen to follow Matthew's order instead of that of Luke, and,
conversely, it would not have been unnatural for him to have given

some preference to the text of Luke when he had deliberately chosen to follow Luke's order in preference to that of Matthew. One would not expect Mark to follow such a procedure inflexibly. Indeed, he does not.

Fifth: In 1843 Eduard Zeller, classicist, published in the *Theologische Jahrbücher* (pp. 443-543), the results of an important study of certain linguistic phenomena within the synoptic gospels. The title of the article is "Vergleichende Übersicht über den Wortervorrath der neutestamentlichen Schriftsteller."

In this article, Zeller compiled lists of words and phrases which were shared by any two Evangelists. He then refined these lists by limiting his attention to shared expressions which appeared in the text of one Evangelist *only* in literary contexts parallel to another Evangelist while those same expressions appeared in the text of that other Evangelist *not only* in parallel literary contexts but also elsewhere in his Gospel.

Zeller reasoned that an Evangelist who used an expression *only* in parallel literary contexts was most likely literarily dependent upon that Evangelist who used the same expression not only in parallel literary contexts but also elsewhere. He probably reasoned that every occurrence of a particular expression which *only* appeared in parallel literary contexts could be explained by copying while the same could not be claimed for every occurrence at the same expression in another gospel where it appears both in parallel literary contexts and also elsewhere.

Neither Holtzmann nor his contemporary defender, C.M. Tuckett, has recognized the fine point in Zeller's method of argumentation represented by the words "only" and "not only" emphasized above. Therefore, their responses to Zeller are inadequate. To date, then, Zeller's linguistic argument in favor of the Griesbach Hypothesis stands in the literature as the most adequate linguistic argument for solving the Synoptic Problem. Zeller concluded that his results on balance support the view that Luke used Matthew, and Mark used both Matthew and Luke.

Sixth: Basically Mark retells the story of the flesh and blood martyrdom of the Son of God in terms remarkably faithful to the common language and story line of Matthew and Luke. It was because Luke had made extensive use of Matthew that the possibility of this literary achievement existed for Mark. Had Luke not made extensive use of Matthew, Mark could not have been written.

Mark was a very creative and skillful author, whose Gospel serves to re-present the popular encomiastic biography of Jesus familiar to readers of either Matthew or Luke, in terms that conflict with neither. As such, Mark supplements Matthew, with material from Luke, and

Luke, with material from Matthew. Readers of Matthew, through reading Mark, could be encouraged to read Luke. And readers of Luke, through reading Mark, could be encouraged to read Matthew.

IV. Answers to Planning Committee's Questions

1. Presuppositions

A. We do not restrict ourselves to any particular text of the Gospels. We find Nestle-Aland and the United Bible Societies' texts useful. We realize that textual criticism is influenced by the solution to the Synoptic Problem. Since all recent critical editions of the Gospel texts have been made by text critics who assume Marcan priority, there is no way that we, denying Marcan priority, can, with confidence, choose between the current critical texts. To construct a critical edition of the text of the Gospels based on the Two-Gospel Hypothesis is a task that lies out ahead of us. We also recognize the usefulness of a critical text constructed without dependence upon any source theory during an interim period while the Synoptic Problem is under critical review and there is no secure critical consensus on the matter.

B. We recommend the use of the new T. & T. Clark edition of *A Synopsis of the Four Gospels in Greek, arranged according to the Two-Gospel Hypothesis*; edited by John Bernard Orchard, O.S.B. (Edinburgh, 1983). But we do not use it exclusively. We use this synopsis because it applies the text of Luke directly to the text of Matthew and makes it easier for the eye to move from the text of Matthew and see immediately how Luke has modified the text of Matthew. Then it is not too difficult for the eye to move further to the right, where one can see how, at the hands of the Evangelist Mark, the texts of Matthew and Luke were modified to meet the needs of those churches for which Mark wrote his Gospel.

Orchard's synopsis, however, is not well-suited to study Mark as a whole in relationship to the texts of Matthew and Luke if one wants to understand how Mark combined the episodes and chronology of Matthew and Luke. For that purpose a new and differently constructed synopsis is needed. Such a synopsis would place Mark in the middle between Matthew and Luke, but would set forth the parallels so that one could readily see how Mark has combined Matthew and Luke. Such a synopsis would differ significantly from standard synopses which have no such purpose, even though they also place Mark in the middle.

C. The Two-Gospel Hypothesis assumes the written form of the Gospel traditions as the primary data for study. However, it is clear that this written form of the Gospel tradition, especially when it is logia material, preserves the oral forms of the Aramaic or Hebrew Vorlagen. The evidence in support of this assumption resides chiefly in the fact of parallelism in much of the logia material. Also important is the fact that the Greek texts of the Gospels often exhibit detailed linguistic features of translation from the Aramaic and Hebrew original.

D. The Gospels belong to the general category of Hellenistic biography. As such, they display the literary intentions and purposes normally associated with redactors/editors/authors of the period. Analyses of topoi, literary techniques, and authorial intent place them in the genre of encomium biography, examples of which concentrate on praise accounts designed to defend someone's reputation, to commend someone on public occasions, and/or to offer someone as an object of emulation. The Evangelists drew both from the "model formative texts" (e.g. Isaiah) and from the topoi (such as the Elisha miracle cycles in II Kings 4:1-8:6) of Judaism to compose the cycles of material within their Gospels. But within the total literature of the Greco-Roman world the closest literary analogies to the Gospels themselves as a literary genre would be such works as Tacitus's *Agricola,* Philo's *Life of Moses*, several of Plutarch's *Lives of Famous Men,* and Philostratus's *Life of Apollonius of Tyana.* This dual "Jewish-Hellenistic" character of the Gospel narratives served the early Church effectively within the Greco-Roman environment both in the preservation of traditions about Jesus and in the proclamation of Jesus as Messiah, to the Jew and to the Gentile.

E. Paul, as head of the mission to the Gentiles, is the silent partner of each of the Evangelists. They portray in vivid images the redemptive story of the flesh and blood martyrdom (obedience unto death) of the Son of God. Paul's own martyrdom in Rome, together with that of Peter, is the unexpressed premise of the apostolic Christianity represented by these four Gospels. Paul's collected letters were received in the Church as the letters of a martyred Apostle. These letters, along with the four Gospels, are the *sine qua non* of life and faith within this new humanity which I Peter portrays as a new race — one brotherhood throughout the world, established on Christ and the Apostles (I Peter 2:17; 5:9). That explains why, once these Gospels were formed into a fourfold Gospel canon, it was necessary for the Church to place alongside them the letters of Paul, along with those of Peter and the other Apostles who, according to Paul's own testimony, had given Christ's Apostle to the Gentiles the right hand of fellowship (Gal. 2:9).

2. Overview of the Theory

A. The facts regarding the relations among the four Gospels may be described as follows:

1. The similarity among Matthew, Mark, Luke and John is such as to justify the assertion that they stand in some kind of literary relationship to one another. The verbal agreement among Matthew, Mark, and Luke indicates some kind of direct literary relationship among these three. The agreement in the sequence of episodes among all four Gospels can best be explained by some kind of literary relationship among all four.

2. There are agreements between Matthew and Mark against Luke, between Matthew and Luke against Mark, and between Mark and Luke against Matthew. Since there are agreements among all three sets of two of these Gospels against the third, it follows that, barring an unnecessary appeal to hypothetical documents, no hypothesis is valid that does not allow for a direct literary relationship among all three.

3. Thus, whichever Evangelist wrote third must have made use of both his predecessors, one of which had previously made use of the other. There are certain definite redactional limitations and possibilities within which a writer under such circumstances is able to function, and this fact will suggest which of the three wrote last.

A writer in the position of being third can (1) follow the text to which both earlier Gospels bear concurrent testimony; (2) deviate from one, but follow the other, when his sources disagree; (3) attempt to combine them when they disagree; (4) deviate by omission or alteration from both when they disagree; (5) deviate by omission or alteration from both even when they agree.

4. In philosophical (i.e., ethical-religious) schools of antiquity it was necessary for each school to take care to produce teaching documents that made clear that what the school taught was defensible. To prove that the teachings of a school were inconsistent or self-contradictory was clear proof that the school did not teach the truth. Since the Gospels eventually came to be used as the chief teaching documents of the Church, it follows that for the Church to be free from the charge of inconsistency and/or self-contradiction, it would have been necessary to be able to show that essential doctrines were not contradicted by the Church's chief teaching documents.

5. Luke and Matthew, at many points, differ from one another in such a manner as to appear to contradict each other. This is clear proof that they were not originally intended for the same Church audience. Or, at least it suggests that the Christian audience for which the second was written did not accept the first as altogether suitable for use as a public teaching document.

6. The fact that Mark is both internally self-consistent and free from contradictions with Matthew and Luke at every point where they appear to contradict one another, strongly suggests that this Gospel was written after Matthew and Luke, and for a Church which valued both earlier Gospels as teaching documents. In spite of many differences and occasional apparent contradictions between Matthew and Luke, Mark's narrative can be used to demonstrate that these two Evangelists tell essentially the same story. This suggests that Mark was written after these two earlier Gospels and for the purpose of establishing the true doctrine of the community of which the Evangelist was a member. That this community was partial to the Pauline school is strongly suggested by the close parallels (especially in *theologia crucis*) between Paul and Mark. That this community may have had a Roman provenance is consistent with the fact that it is the irenic Paul of Romans that has influenced Mark most of all, not, if would it have to be admitted, the polemical Paul of Galatians.

7. All other categories of evidence such as the phenomenon of order, the historical evidence, compositional and genre considerations, minor agreements of Matthew and Luke against Mark, etc., are fully commensurate with, if not better explained by, Mark coming after Matthew and Luke, rather than coming first or second.

8. That Luke is dependent on Matthew and not Matthew on Luke, is clear primarily on form-critical grounds. But it is also supported by redaction-critical considerations, as well as by external evidence.

9. The question of whether Mark was written before or after John has never been settled on the grounds of internal evidence. Both Bleek and De Wette concluded that, on balance, Mark appears to have been written after John. But the external evidence consistently favors the view that John was written last of the four. This problem awaits further study.

B. The critical criteria utilized to differentiate primary from secondary tradition (i.e., "original" from "secondary" Jesus traditions) are as follows:

1. Assuming (A) that the original events in the history of the

Christian movement took place in Palestine, within predominantly Jewish (however Hellenized) circles, and (B) that by the time the Gospels were written, Christianity had expanded outside of Palestine, and outside of circles which were predominantly Jewish in culture, whenever there is a particular tradition which exists in parallel texts in different Gospels, with agreement so close as to indicate copying: *That form of the tradition which reflects an extra-Palestinian, or non-Jewish provenance is to be adjudged secondary to a form of the same tradition which reflects a Palestinian or Jewish provenance.*

2. Assuming the redactional tendency to add explanatory glosses, and otherwise to expand tradition to make it applicable to new situations in the churches: *That form of a tradition which exhibits explanatory redactional glosses, and expansions aimed to make the tradition more applicable to the needs of the Church, is to be adjudged secondary to a form of the tradition which is free of such redactional glosses and expansions.*

3. Assuming the tendency of all writers to use some words and phrases more frequently than is true for writers in general when dealing with the same subject: Whenever there is a particular tradition which exists in parallel texts in different Gospels, and the degree of verbatim agreement indicates copying: *that form of a tradition which exhibits words or phrases characteristic of a redactor whose hand is clearly traceable elsewhere in the same Gospel is to be adjudged secondary to the parallel form of the same tradition in the other Gospel providing it is free of such words and phrases.*

By applying this criterion it is clear that when we confine our attention to Jesus tradition preserved in parallel texts of the Synoptic Gospels, there is a general tendency for the Matthean form of sayings of Jesus to be free from words or phrases clearly attributable to the final redactor, and completely conformable to a Palestinian and Jewish cultural and religious milieu. On the other hand, the parallel texts in Luke frequently exhibit the hand of the Evangelist, and frequently reflect changes which make the tradition more understandable for extra-Palestinian and Gentile readers.

The Jesus tradition in Matthew is seldom glossed or modified by the Evangelist. The same is true of much of the Jesus tradition in Luke not paralleled in Matthew. On our hypothesis it is clear that the need to accommodate the form and content of the Jesus tradition Luke drew from Matthew was greater than the need to accommodate the rest of the Jesus tradition available to the Evangelist. This suggests that Luke was writing for churches which were less familiar with the Jesus tradition he drew from Matthew than with the rest of the Jesus tradition he incorporated into his Gospel. Moreover, the fact that Luke often destroys the parallelism of the oral form of the Jesus tradition he takes over from the text of Matthew, whereas he tends to preserve the oral form of much of the rest of the Jesus tradition he incorporates into his text, strongly suggests that much of the Jesus tradition in Luke which Luke had not taken from Matthew had already achieved a certain fixed form within the churches for which Luke was writing.

Mark tends to add words and phrases to the Jesus tradition he takes over from Matthew and Luke. Frequently, these are words and phrases that are characteristic of Mark. Seldom, if ever, does Mark preserve a form of the Jesus tradition which, by applying the above criterion, can be shown to be original in comparison to Matthew or Luke. There may be one class of exceptions. Mark may sometimes appear to be more Jewish and more original than Luke. In these cases the text of Mark is always close to the text of Matthew. Thus, one can always explain the text of Mark on the assumption of Mark being third, and very often there is confirmatory evidence of this from the hand of the Evangelist himself. This is well illustrated and amply documented in the exegesis of Mark 13 and parallels that follow this position paper.

C. Our theory explains the phenomena of the order of pericopes in the Synoptic Gospels as follows:

1. Matthew has organized the narrative framework of his Gospel in accordance with a fulfillment of prophecy motif from Isaiah 9:1-2. First, those sitting in darkness in Galilee proper are to see the great light of God's salvific work. Then those across the Jordan shall see this light. After this fulfillment of prophecy, Jesus and his disciples will go to Jerusalem where he will be delivered up in accordance with a thrice-repeated prediction of his own passion and resurrection. Into this narrative framework the Evangelist has introduced several lengthy discourses, most of which are homogeneous collections of Jesus tradition, like the Sermon on the Mount (Matt. 5-7) and the Woes against the Scribes and Pharisees (Matt 23).

2. Luke has in general followed the basic narrative outline of Matthew's Gospel; first, a ministry in Galilee and then, the Passion Narrative in Jerusalem. But Luke has considerably rearranged the narrative framework. All of the lengthy Matthean discourses are represented in Luke, and except for one reversal, Luke's parallels to Matthew's discourses are all in the same relative sequence, a clear sign of a close compositional relationship between Luke and Matthew. Moreover, when in following

Matthew's narrative framework, Luke comes to one of Matthew's lengthy discourses, he generally takes only a few sayings, yet he always makes his selection from the opening sayings in Matthew's respective discourses. This is another clear sign of a close literary relationship between Matthew and Luke. In between the ministry in Galilee and the passion narrative in Jerusalem Luke includes a great central section of sayings material. This section includes a great deal of sayings material Luke has taken from other sources. However, Luke has also introduced into this central section many sayings which he has taken from the Matthean discourses. Luke follows understandable literary procedures in his use of material taken from Matthew. In this compositional process Luke generally works forward through Matthew, often returning to material from the earlier part of Matthew after completing a forward sweep. This is certainly consonant with Luke's compositional dependence on Matthew. In some instances Luke, after moving forward in Matthew in order to bring into his text material pertinent to his own composition, will copy into his text the pericope immediately preceding the pericope he has just copied. This is further evidence that Luke is compositionally dependent on the sequential arrangement of the Matthean pericopes.

3. Mark, writing third, has a power, denied the other two, of controlling how the text of his Gospel will be related to the text of both his predecessors. Matthew, writing before the other two Gospels were in existence, had no control over how his Gospel was to be related to either Luke or Mark. Luke could control how his Gospel was to be related to Matthew, but not to Mark. Mark alone could control the relationship of his text to that of both the other Synoptists. It is a distinct merit of the Two-Gospel Hypothesis that it can attribute the unique Synoptic phenomenon of order of episodes (Matthew and Luke almost never agree against Mark or Mark almost always maintains the common order of Matthew and Luke) to authorial intent and does not need to resort to the less satisfactory appeal to a literary accident due to random chance. (Random chance is how, on the Two-Document Hypothesis, one must explain the fact that whenever Matthew departs from the order of episodes in Mark, Luke supports Mark's order and vice versa.)

Mark had before him two works concerning Jesus. Often they agreed in the sequence they gave to particular episodes in Jesus' ministry. Often they disagreed. In accordance with his authorial intent to produce a version of the Gospel that was free from open contradictions with the other great teaching instruments of the Christian community of which he was a member, Mark, in general, followed the common order of his sources. Where they depart from one another in order, he even-handedly follows now the order of one and now the order of the other. Mark always supports the order of the pericopes of one of his predecessors, and wherever possible, the order of both. The one major exception to this, the order of the episode of the Cleansing of the Temple, is the exception that proves the rule. Mark places this episode after the first day Jesus was in Jerusalem, whereas both Luke and Matthew place it during the first day.

D. The so-called "Q" material is simply material Luke copied from Matthew which, in turn, was not taken over by Mark. This explains why it is so difficult to identify the extent or purpose of "Q". That "Q" could have produced an "intelligible" theology is explained by the fact that Luke selected from Matthew only material that was useful for his Gentile readers. This explains the appeal of "Q" to modern theologians. It is generally free of Jewish *Tendenz* which would be offensive to Gentile readers. But in omitting Matthean Jesus tradition which was particularly Jewish, Luke's selection becomes historically unrepresentative, and in important respects quite unbalanced. Any reconstruction of the so-called "theology of the 'Q' community" will thus be correspondingly unrepresentative of the Jesus tradition and historically skewed. This is a point of the greatest importance for contemporary theology. "Q" is more representative of Luke's version of the Jesus tradition than it is of Jesus himself. This is especially true in the case of critics like Harnack who, after showing on linguistic grounds that the Lucan form of the "Q" material was generally secondary to the Matthean, nonetheless preferred the Lucan form of "Q" as more historical, appealing quite unconvincingly to an argument from Luke's order and arrangement. Harnack has been widely followed. Like the idea of Marcan priority, the view that the Lucan form of "Q" is a particularly trustworthy avenue to Jesus is a theologoumenon of liberal Protestant theology.

E. The minor agreements of Matthew and Luke against Mark are to be explained as follows: (a) In composing his Gospel, Luke frequently copied the text of Matthew verbatim. (b) In composing his Gospel, Mark frequently copied the text of Matthew or Luke where Luke had copied Matthew closely. In these instances Mark could be said to have followed the text to which Matthew and Luke bore concurrent testimony. In any case, whether by copying Matthew or Luke, Mark often copied into his text a text which was nearly identical in both his sources. Even if Mark compared the texts of both his sources at all times, he could hardly have succeeded in incorporating every instance of verbatim agreement between Matthew and Luke without becoming quite pedantic. It is clear that Mark was not that kind of author. Thus, where a small stylistic change can be made without affecting the sense of the text, Mark will frequently introduce it into his version of the Gospel. It is not likely that this was done consciously. In all probability, for example, Mark simply preferred the use of the historic present and since its use did not alter the sense of the scripture, he was quite prepared to use the historic present even when both of his sources used the aorist tense. In this way a so-called "minor agreement between Matthew and Luke against Mark" would materialize. A "so-called" minor agreement in omission would occur whenever Mark has added a word or phrase to a text from Matthew and/or Luke where Luke had copied Matthew closely.

F. The "Two-Gospel Hypothesis" is scientifically testable.

1. The "Two-Gospel Hypothesis" rests on evidence and arguments at a number of points which, in our view, it would be very difficult to explain equally well in reverse order. These are: (1) The argument from patristic evidence; (2) The argument from order; (3) The argument from Jewish and Christian history; (4) The argument from compositional considerations; (5) The argument from form-critical considerations; (6) The argument from text-criticism based on literary characteristics.

2. There are categories of evidence which if examples could be found would tend to falsify the Two-Gospel Hypothesis; (a) Patristic evidence at variance with the hypothesis: e.g. any explicit statement by Clement of Alexandria or Irenaeus that he had it from the primitive elders that the Gospels with genealogies were written after those without genealogies would constitute evidence that would serve to falsify the Two-Gospel Hypothesis; (b) Any of the three critical criteria listed under II B above could be used to prove that the Two-Gospel Hypothesis is false if applicable evidence were available: e.g., (1) evidence that a parallel passage in Mark (where the verbatim agreement is so close as to indicate some direct literary dependence) is more Jewish or Palestinian than the same material in the parallel text of Matthew; (2) explanatory glosses in the text of Matthew but absent from the parallel text in Mark; (3) literary characteristics of Matthew showing up more frequently in common sayings material than do those of Mark and/or Luke.

G. Evidence from Tannaitic Judaism serves to prove that Matthew is more Jewish and Palestinian than Mark.

H. Evidence from Hellenistic culture serves to prove on form-critical grounds that Mark is secondary to Matthew and Luke. For example: Two of Mark's miracles represent Jesus using spittle in his healing. The use of spittle in healing is characteristic of Hellenistic miracle stories. There is no case of spittle being used in any of the miracle stories in Matthew or Luke.

I. Evidence from the patristic testimony strongly supports the "Two-Gospel Hypothesis."

1. Direct statements regarding the Gospels. The earliest and by far the most important direct Patristic statement bearing on the question of the sequence in which the Gospels were written is cited by Eusebius from the *Hypotyposeis* of Clement of Alexandria. Clement testifies that he had received from the primitive elders the tradition that the Gospels with genealogies (Matthew and Luke) were written before those without genealogies (Mark and John). Clement was widely-traveled and one of the teachers he contacted in Achaea was from Asia Minor who may have known Christian teachers from the earlier circle of Polycarp. It is reasonable to conclude that one of the 'primitive elders' from whom Clement's tradition came was Polycarp. This one direct statement by Clement, the most highly respected Christian scholar of his day, is of more historical value than all of the theories that have ever been propounded about the sequence in which the Gospels were written, including the theories of Augustine.

It is well known that Irenaeus knows the canonical order. But von Campenhausen has noted that when Irenaeus argues against the heretics he takes up the Gospels in the order Matthew, Luke, Mark and John. This, says von Campenhausen, is probably "the order most familiar to Irenaeus himself." Was this the tradition in which Irenaeus was schooled? If so, we can trace this tradition from the city of Lyons back to Asia Minor and Irenaeus' teacher, the primitive elder, Polycarp. In this way, from the Rhone Valley north and west of Rome to the city of Alexandria in Egypt on the southeastern shores of the Mediterranean, we would have a united testimony supporting the tradition of an order older than that of the fourfold Gospel canon, and, as Clement clearly says, this tradition is a witness to the sequence in which the Gospels were composed. This tradition need by no means be attributed to Polycarp of Smyrna in the sense of his having originated it, even if he would appear to be the best point of contact for this tradition common to Irenaeus and Clement. For Clement tells us that this tradition had been received from the primitive elders — plural. And Clement had had contact with Christian teachers in Italy, Syria, Palestine and other places, as well as Achaea. It is ironic that it is Polycarp and Irenaeus who are the most likely to have had a hand in forming the fourfold Gospel canon, and thus to have originated the order: Matthew, Mark, Luke, John. Perhaps this is why the Church of Irenaeus, Clement, Origen and Eusebius appears to have sensed no conflict between these two diverging orders.

2. Quotations of the Gospels. We have already noted that Irenaeus, when refuting the heretics, begins with Matthew, then goes to Luke and then, to Mark and John, in that order. Actually the Patristic sources seldom cite Mark. The magisterial work of E. Massaux shows that Matthew was the foundational Gospel of the Church. This is the Gospel cited more often than all the others. That this Gospel, which is clearly more Jewish than the others, should be the foundational Gospel in the Gentile church, is powerful evidence in favor of its having achieved a place of primacy before Mark was written. For, since Mark so well adapted his Gospel to meet the needs of Gentiles, were his Gospel to have preceded the others, his Gospel, plus that of Luke, would have made Matthew unnecessary in those very Gentile Christian circles where we know that Matthew was in fact foundational. The sequence presupposed in the Two-Gospel Hypothesis explains the way in which the Gospels are quoted in the early Church far more satisfactorily than does the Two-Document Hypothesis.

J. The non-canonical Gospels exhibit characteristics and theological tendencies that are closer to those of Mark and John than to Matthew and Luke. With reference to Mark, this fact was first noticed by Schleiermacher and confirmed by Wilhelm Wrede in 1901. In circles which follow the lead of Wrede in recognizing the non-historical character of Mark's Gospel, this view of the Gospels, when combined with the Two-Document Hypothesis, has led to a reconstruction like that of Helmut Koester where the non-canonical Gospels of Thomas and Peter share with Mark and John direct access to the earliest documents, whereas Matthew and Luke have only indirect access to the earliest collection of sayings of Jesus lying behind "Q", and only indirect access to the primitive Passion Narrative of Ur-Marcus lying behind Mark. Against this reconstruction there is on balance the combined weight of both the direct statements about the Gospels and the quotations of them by the Patristic sources.

On the view of the "Two-Gospel Hypothesis," Matthew and Luke come before Mark and John, and Mark and John come before most if not all non-canonical Gospels. Mark and John are characterized by tendencies to omit some very important topics and motifs treated by the earlier Gospels, and to expand on others. These same tendencies of Mark and John are even more developed in the second century apocryphal Gospels. So long as one realizes that once Matthew and Luke had been produced, the need for further Gospels would have been best served when each supplemented and/or complemented in some way the Gospel literature already available, then the actual state of affairs as pictured by the Two-Gospel Hypothesis is very reasonable. There would also be room by the second century for norming attempts like Tatian's *Diatessaron*, Marcion's *Evangelion*, and the Church's Four-fold Gospel Canon, to help Christians sort out the earlier "Apostolic" witness from the later Gospel literature.

3. The value of the Two-Gospel Hypothesis for theology/preaching

1. The main value of the Two-Gospel Hypothesis is that it is (most likely) true. That is sufficient reason, theological and practical, for adopting it for theology and preaching.

2. A secondary value is that it restores to the critically trained preacher the same text of the Gospels that the Church has delivered to its members. To base theology and preaching on "Q," as one is constrained to do if one holds to the Two-Document Hypothesis, is to introduce an additional note of uncertainty into theology and preaching since there is no scholarly consensus on what the text of "Q" is. To be sure, all advocates of the Two-Gospel Hypothesis who hold to the historical critical method distinguish layers of tradition in the Gospels just as much as advocates of the Two-Document Hypothesis. But advocates of the Two-Gospel Hypothesis are prepared to argue that this hypothesis affords theologians and preachers a more adequate avenue to the earliest layer of the synoptic tradition, a more adequate avenue to New Testament christology, and a more adequate avenue to Church history.

V. An Historical Account
of the Composition of the Gospels on the Hypothesis
they were written in the sequence Matthew, Luke, Mark

1. The Gospel of Matthew

The gospel of Matthew clearly reflects the history of the primitive Palestinian Jewish Christian communities which suffered persecution at the hands of the authorities. The Jewish Christian orientation of much of the text of Matthew is unmistakable. The Evangelist begins with the genealogy of Christ from Abraham, refers to Jewish customs, relates many sayings of Jesus against Jewish errors and religious hypocrisy, quotes the greatest number of passages from Jewish scriptures among the Gospels, answers Jewish objections against the Christian believers, and frequently makes use of the terms and phrases of Jewish theology.

In composing this Gospel, Matthew had a constant regard for the circumstances of those for whom he intended his narrative. This affected his choice of material and his treatment of it. This gave his Gospel its peculiar character. Since the Gospel of Matthew was accommodated to the stage, temper and disposition of the times in which it was written, it is clear that it was composed when the Church was or recently had been laboring under persecution. Clearly it contains many obvious references to such a situation.

The Evangelist informs the injured and persecuted Christians that their afflications were no more than they had been taught to expect and what they had promised to bear when they embraced the Gospel (10:21, 22, 34-36; 16:24). No matter how unreasonable their sufferings might be, considered as the effects of the malice of their enemies, they were nevertheless useful and profitable to themselves as trials of their faith and fidelity (5:11; 24:9-13). Though grievous to bear at present, these trials operated powerfully to their future joy (5:4, 10-12). Desertion of the Faith would not improve that state and condition. On the contrary, they would be exposed to greater calamities by separating themselves from any hope of life to come after judgment (10:28, 32, 33, 39). They were not, however, forbidden to use the lawful means of preservation; but even enjoined to put them in practice, whenever they could do it with innocence (10:16; 17:23). The due observance of the Christian percepts was an excellent method to appease the wrath and fury of their enemies, as well as what they were obliged for reasons of prudence and duty to consider and do (5:29-30; 7:12, 24-27; 5:13-20). If their inevitable fate should be suffering martyrdom for their faith, it was infinitely better to continue faithful to their important trust, than by any base compliance to incur displeasure of God in whose hands are the issues not only of this life but also of that which is to come (16:25-27; 10:28; 25:31-46).

On the other hand, there is much in Matthew that serves to calm the passions of enraged Jews (like the former persecutor Paul), and win them over to the profession of the Gospel. Matthew labors to soften and abate Jewish prejudices, and to engage them in the practice of meekness and charity (9:13; 12:7). To this end the Evangelist lays before them the dignity and amiableness of a compassionate, benevolent disposition; the natural good consequences that flow from it here; and the distinguished regard, which God himself will pay to it hereafter (5:5,7,21-26, 43-48; 10:40-42; 18:23-35; 25:31-46).

Matthew reminds Jewish readers of the repeated punishments, which God had inflicted on their forefathers for their cruel and barbarous treatment of his Prophets, and assures them that a still greater vengeance is reserved for themselves, if they obstinately persist in the ways of cruelty (23:27-39; 10:14, 15): For God, though patient and long-suffering, was certain at the end to vindicate his elect, and to punish their oppressors (unless they repented, believed, and reformed), with the dreadful ordeal of a general destruction. (13:36-43; 24:2, 19-22, 48-51; 25:30, 46).

For those who recognize Jesus according to his various messianic titles, Son of God, Son of David, Son of Man, Immanuel, Lord, etc., there is a call to carry forward an apostolic mission to all nations. With divine assurance the Lord will abide with those who take up this salvific mission (28:17-20).

With such arguments as these, Matthew comforted, exhorted, and inspired afflicted Christian readers, while he put on notice all who oppressed and injured them.

Clearly these arguments relate to or closely reflect a situation of distress and persecution. Now the greatest persecution ever raised against the Church, while it was still a predominantly Jewish Christian community of believers, was first begun by the Jerusalem authorities and afterwards continued and conducted by agents, like Paul, with implacable rage and fury. The danger of such persecution from zealous Jews was a continuous threat to believers who were linked from the earliest days with a mission to Gentiles. The Jewish populace would be agitated by the question whether the non-observance of the law by Christians was provoking a jealous God. The oppression of the Christian minority by Jews zealous for the law would rise in direct proportion to the tension between Jerusalem and Rome.

Caligula's threat in A.D. 40 to erect a graven image of himself in the temple at Jerusalem occasioned great distress within the Jewish populace (Josephus, *War* 2.184-7, 192-203; *Antiquities* 18.261-309). Every effort would have been made to achieve compliance with the law within Jewish circles including the churches in Judea mentioned by Paul (Gal. 1:22) and those in other areas which were under the jurisdiction of recognized Jewish authorities.

Certainly the reference to the abomination of desolation spoken of by Daniel (in Matt. 24:15; cf. Dan. 12:11; 8:13; 9:27; I Macc. 1:54) points us to the importance of this particular crisis in the history of the Jewish nation and in the history of those Christian communities which continued to look to the Temple in Jerusalem as a locus of the divine presence.

After this particular crisis, there followed in the next decade, renewed tension between Jerusalem and Rome during the rule of Nero, especially upon Festus' coming into Judea (Josephus, *Antiquities* 20.182-196, Cf. *War* 2.271). Finally in 67 a full scale revolt broke out against Rome. This revolt was not settled until the early 70's, and it appears that tensions continued for some time thereafter. Sometime during this era of turmoil in Palestine Matthew took in hand the task of composing a powerful statement of faith aimed to support, comfort, and assist Christians in an uncertain and hostile environment. But what comfort could they possibly receive, in their stressful situation, comparable to that which resulted from the example of their suffering Master, and the promises he had made to his faithful followers? This example therefore, and these promises, Matthew appropriately laid before his readers, for their imitation and encouragement. In this stressful situation Matthew most likely wrote his Gospel. He then delivered it to his fellow Christians as the anchor of their hope to keep them steadfast in the face of persecution, while pointing them forward to their apostolic mission to all the nations. The task of composition was not accomplished all at once.

Since Matthew had no close model to follow he carefully prepared himself to write his Gospel. Regardless of the need for care in composing, certainly the need to complete his task as soon as possible was ever more pressing. Persecution came not only from zealous Jews but also from Roman authorities and their Jewish advisors. These authorities responsible for maintaining order would understandably find it difficult to distinguish carefully among the various sectarian groups in Jewish society. The authorities could not always be expected to be certain just who was responsible for the unrest in the land. Or how could they assess the destabilizing effect of eschatologically oriented preaching, regardless of whether that were Jewish or Christian? The end result was great peril for Christians, especially for those who were genuinely committed to a Gospel of the Kingdom which required that it be preached publicly throughout the whole world as a testimony (*martyrion*) to all the nations (Matt. 24:14).

It is not necessary for our argument to pinpoint the exact year or even the exact decade of Matthew's composition in order to see its original readers taking on flesh and blood within the history of the Church under threat from persecuting authorities, including Jewish persecutors, whether from synagogues, or the Sanhedrin in Jerusalem or both.

2. The Gospel of Luke

The composition of Luke-Acts follows naturally the composition of Matthew. Matthew compressed everything he had to say into the "dramatic" story of the flesh and blood martyrdom of the Son of God. Anything decisive in the history of the Church that had taken place following the death and resurrection of Jesus was cast into some form appropriate to be presented as a part of that story. But this use of dramatic license by Matthew was ill suited to the needs of the Gentile oriented Hellenistic Christian communities addressed by Luke.

Luke wrote for readers sensitive to the standards of Hellenistic historiography. His first decision, vis-a-vis his model Matthew, was to make his a two volume work — one for the "historical" account of the flesh and blood martyrdom of the Son of God, and the other, for the story of the spirit of the Risen Christ operating through the apostolic mission featuring the exploits and sufferings of the Apostles.

Luke-Acts tells the story of the westward expansion of the Church, its growth from Jerusalem to Rome. It is far better suited than is Matthew to meet the needs of predominantly Gentile churches.

The purpose of Luke is clearly stated in his preface. He wrote that his readers might see and be convinced as to how well founded are those things in which they had been instructed by their teachers (1:3, 4).

Writing mainly to Gentiles, removed, as many think, from the scene of action and consequently ignorant of Jewish affairs, and to accomplish what he had in view, he was compelled to trace the subject right up to its source, and then proceed through Jesus' ministry in a circumstantial and methodical order. This explains the fact that his "history" begins with the birth of John the Baptist (1:5ff), as introductory to that of Christ, and this careful specification of the times and places [e.g. 2:1-7; 3:1, 23]. Such detailed information was demanded in the urbane, Greco-Roman world, but hardly had to be recited to the Jews, who could easily supply it from their own knowledge.

Although Luke wrote his Gospel primarily for the use of Gentile churches, these churches often had been founded by Jews like Paul and had many members of Jewish extraction. Luke was writing for a mixed Church. For the sake of the Jewish heritage still very alive in the Gentile churches, Luke retains the Gospel's essentially Jewish character in his narrative.

In its general construction, Luke's Gospel seems to follow Matthew's, differing mainly in the way he handles the discourses of Jesus. Matthew arranges most of Jesus' teaching into several lengthy discourses. Luke takes over some opening units from each of Matthew's discourses, keeping them in the same relative order in his account except for the discourse on the parables and the discourse on the apostolic mission, the order of which he reverses. Other sayings from these several discourses which Luke takes over into his account from Matthew are either given appropriate settings in his narrative or are worked together thematically with sayings material from other sources in his great Central Section (9:52-18:14). In reading Luke's account one can skip from 9:1 to 18:31. If one skips over this section his narrative moves along much more efficiently over essentially the same ground covered by Matthew. There is Jesus with John in the Jordan valley. Then there is the ministry in Galilee. Finally there is the climactic account of Jesus' passion in Jerusalem.

If now it appears that Luke's account follows that of Matthew more closely, it is because his essential purpose is not all that different. The state and condition of the Gentile converts was similar to that of the Jewish.

Of course, it was necessary that Luke should adjust the points of his history, as Matthew had done before, to the circumstances of the persons to whom he wrote and so modify his materials as to make them applicable to those particular times. Luke directs his arguments with great propriety both to the support of the persecuted Christians (6:20-23; 12:4-12,31; 18:28-30; 21:12-19), and to the conversion of their obstinate and malicious adversaries (6:24-26; 10:12; 13:1-5; 19:41-44) — the chief of whom were still some of the Jews residing in the diaspora. This explains why the scope and shape of Luke's arguments are in so many places so very similar to those of Matthew. Both Evangelists had similar designs.

There are, however, some essential differences between Matthew and Luke on the issue of persecution. The sociological ground for the Jewish persecution of Christians in Matthew is religious. Jews zealous for the law perceive that some measure of transgression of the law seems to be inherent in the Christian Gospel — at least as it is preached to the Gentiles. Matthew wants to reassure the Jews at this point. Though Jesus may have broken the Sabbath law, he had legal precedent to do so. Jesus was by no stretch of the imagination an antinomian. Matthew's teaching on the point is unambiguous. The disciples are instructed by the risen Christ in the Great Commission to "make disciples of all the Gentiles... teaching them to observe all that I have commanded." Included with this Gentile mission was an admonition to keep the law even down to its smallest detail (5:17-20).

It is quite otherwise in Luke's account. There is no such dominical command to keep the law in Luke's Gospel. The sociological ground for persecution of Christians is more political than religious. In the diaspora, Christians had no legal standing apart from their being perceived as Jews. But in the eyes of diaspora Jews the Christians' claim to be heirs of the promises contained in the Law and the Prophets was groundless. Most Gentile Christians were not circumcised as a sign of the covenant. The rage and envy of the Jews sprang now from a different cause. They were moved by indignation at Gentile Christian claims to be sons of Abraham with all the privileges appertaining thereunto — above all the privileges of being accounted persons adhering to a legal religion in the eyes of the Roman authorities. Ironically, the Gentile Christian's claim to Jewishness was often his best defense against harassment and persecution from his own countrymen.

It was necessary for Luke to prove that Christian claims to the promises of the Law and the Prophets were just and valid ones. To support the Christian claim to Jewishness, Luke reminds the unbelieving Jews — and any Roman authorities who wanted to read his account — that, though they were formerly God's chosen nation, and consequently entitled to his peculiar favour, God had often directed his Prophets to confer on persons of other nations those blessings which they had rendered themselves unworthy to receive by their ingratitude (4:25-27; Acts 13:45-51). This was again the case with regard to the Gospel. It was ungratefully rejected by unrepentant Israel and it was therefore proper to preach it to the more obedient Gentiles (20:9-16). The resentment and hatred which unrepentant Israel expressed on that account was both unreasonable and inhuman (15:11-32). God, when he came to vindicate his elect, would severely punish them for the injurious attempts they made on his elect, and for the aggravated provocation they had offered to himself (18:7, 8). Therefore unrepentant Israel had better look at the consequences and strive to avert by faith and penitence the grievous judgments coming upon them (13:1-5; 21:5-6).

But so strong was animosity from some Jews toward the Gentile Christians that they endeavored to degrade the character of those who asserted the full acceptance of the Gentiles without their being bound by the tradition of Moses.

Jewish Christians, susceptible to the arguments of their still unconverted countrymen and supported by certain traditions that have been preserved in the Gospel of Matthew, argued that Jesus chose no more than twelve Apostles to whom he committed the care of his Church. Anyone other than the Twelve who undertook to preach to the Gentiles were consequently only deputies, the truth of whose doctrine entirely depended on its agreement with the teaching of the original Apostles. Therefore, the grand fundamental teaching of Paul and his associates must needs be false, since it lacked the seal of apostolic authority. (This appears to be the anti-Pauline case which Paul's autobiographical statements in Galatians 1-2 are aimed to counter. Matthew's Gospel could be used to strengthen this anti-Pauline case).

To obviate these objections, Luke informs his readers that the Lord appointed Seventy others (10:1-16), besides the Twelve, who were particularly called Apostles, to convey the knowledge of his teaching to the world; and not only so, but invested them with the same authority — charged them with the same instructions — and endowed them with like power of working miracles in proof of their mission, as he had done to the brethren before; and consequently that the Twelve Apostles were not the sole commissioned Preachers of the Gospel, though they were indeed the first and principal.

It can be seen, therefore, that while the Gospels of Matthew and Luke are very similar in fundamentals, they diverge from one another in significant ways which were potentially divisive for the Church. If the ecumenical tendencies integral to both Matthew and Luke-Acts, when taken separately, were to continue to bear fruit for the Church, it was necessary for their common witnesses to be unified in some way. This was especially the case with a Church facing persecution.

3. The Gospel of Mark

The Gospel of Matthew opens with an account of an Herodian persecution which forced Joseph and Mary with the infant Jesus to take refuge in Egypt. Thus Christians who are being persecuted by the Roman government know that they are in solidarity with the infant Jesus and his threatened parents.

The Gospel of Luke, by way of contrast, opens with a series of peaceful and orderly scenes featuring the stable role of the Temple cultus within the Roman Empire.

The Gospel of Mark bypasses the conflicting infancy narratives of Matthew and Luke and begins with the fulfillment of the prophecy of Isaiah [Mark 1:1-3]. After an account of Jesus' baptism, Mark again bypasses the conflicting Matthean and Lucan accounts of Jesus' temptations and has Jesus thrown by the Spirit out into the wilderness where he was with the wild beasts — and where the angels ministered to him. Like Daniel thrown into the lions' den, Roman Christians had been thrown out onto barren arenas to face the wild beasts. Facing those wild beasts, these Roman Christians had been able to identify with the Master Martyr. He too had been tested by Satan. As he had endured to the end, so had they [cf. Mark 13:13]. They drank the cup that he drank, and they had been baptized with the baptism with which he had been baptized [Mark 10:38-39].

In Luke's Gospel, Peter had asked Jesus whether his warning about the end was for the disciples "or for all" [Luke 12:41]. In Mark's Gospel Jesus answers: "What I say to you, I say to all: Watch!" [Mark 13:37].

Mark's Gospel is fundamentally a restatement of the Gospels of Matthew and Luke for Roman Christians facing persecution. It was written for a Church which had known persecution first hand. Like Luke, Mark's Church had also known peaceful times — probably the rule of the Flavians. In combining and reconciling Matthew and Luke, Mark gave the Roman Church the "bedrock message of the new Faith" which they wanted to know. Using Peter's public speeches as his guide and model Mark sought to produce the kind of vivid narrative message that the Apostle Peter had consistently proclaimed. But the memory of the persecution of Christians in Rome has left its indelible stamp on Mark's Gospel. And the Church was to be ever on guard [Mark 13:32-37]. Mark's Gospel story could serve admirably as a drama filled liturgical guide for such a Church.

Mark's repeated emphasis upon "the Gospel" used in its Pauline sense (1:1, 15; 8:35; 10:29; 13:10; 14:9 [16:15?]) made it possible for this Evangelist to omit Luke's apostolic mission of the Seventy without diminishing his Gospel's Gentile tendency. Mark's retention of the mission of the Twelve, attested by both Matthew and Luke, is thus balanced with a strong Pauline concern which emphasizes an important intention of Luke without repeating a major Lucan discrepancy with Matthew, i.e., an additional mission of the Seventy. After 70 A.D., for

the Church in Rome, there was only one apostolic mission and that was
to preach the Gospel to all the nations (Mark 13:10).*

William R. FARMER

* [What is written in this historical account, especially about the Gospels of Matthew
and Luke, has been largely taken over with some editing from Henry Owen's *Observations
on the Four Gospels*, London, 1764. While some parts of Owen's history have been
omitted, and while much has been added in this account, and while the whole of this
historical account has undergone more than one revision, indebtedness to the text of
Owen's work will be unmistakable to its readers, and its use is gratefully acknowledged.]

THE COMPOSITION OF THE SYNOPTIC
ESCHATOLOGICAL DISCOURSE

PREFACE

This paper is a linguistic and stylistic explanation of the composition of the synoptic eschatological discourse (Mt 24:1-51; Mk 13:1-37; Lk 21:5-36).[1] The paper is based on the hypothesis that the Synoptics were composed in the order, Matthew, Luke, and Mark; that Luke utilized Matthew as a source for his composition; and that Mark utilized both Matthew and Luke. Since Mark is believed to have used the two extant gospels of Matthew and Luke, this synoptic source theory is called the Two-Gospel Hypothesis.

The paper develops along the following lines. After brief descriptions of the compositional methods of Matthew and Luke, we will demonstrate, with the aid of an original synopsis, how Luke drew material from Mt 24:1-51 in order to compose three separate units of his gospel (Lk 12:35-48; 17:20-37; 21:5-36). Based on this synopsis, our analysis will indicate that, after Luke composed the eschatological discourses in 12:35-48 and 17:20-37, he followed the same order as Matthew in composing Luke 21:5-36. In Luke's three eschatological accounts, we will see that Luke omits from Matthew 24 only 24:10-12, 14, 20-22, 24-25, 30a, 31, and 36. Our discussion will provide possible reasons for these omissions by Luke and for other significant stylistic and linguistic changes made by Luke when he drew from Matthew.

This analysis is necessary in order to understand the compositional procedure of the Gospel of Mark; especially the Markan omissions. When Mark constructs his eschatological discourse, as the second section of the paper will indicate, he has before him two similar

---

[1] It will be necessary to refer to Mt 25:1-30 from time to time in the course of the paper because it will be shown, on the presupposition of the Two-Gospel Hypothesis, that both Luke and Mark consider Mt 24:1-25:30 to be a literary unit. Nevertheless our intention is to discuss Mt 25:1-30 only when it has some effect on the composition of Mk 13 and Lk 21.

sources.[2] We will attempt to show by linguistic and stylistic analysis that Mark followed the *common* testimony of Matthew and Luke to compose his eschatological discourse.[3] We believe that Mark omits material from Matthew and Luke because Mark was attempting to use material in his eschatological discourse which was common to his two sources.

We will also produce examples of Mark's use of conflation, glosses, various rhetorical devices, vivid pictorial imagery, and redactional techniques that will enable us to show with precision how Mark artfully composed Mark 13:1-37.

In the course of our discussion, two units in Mark will emerge which will warrant special attention; first, Mk 13:9-13, because it has four parallels rather than the usual one or two (Mt 10:17-22/24:9-13/Lk 12:11-12/21:12-19); second, Mk 13:33-37, which seemingly diverges widely from both Matthew and Luke. Our analysis will indicate that the compositional structure of these passages in Mark can be explained most adequately by the Two-Gospel Hypothesis whereas the Two-Source Theory cannot explain them without extraordinary difficulty.

Throughout this paper the focus is limited to addressing compositional problems in Jesus' eschatological discourses based on the Two-Gospel Hypothesis.[4] The discussion of text-critical issues, redaction-critical issues, points of interpretation, etc., are only addressed when they directly affect the special compositional argument here under discussion.[5] In no way is this paper meant to include the whole panorama of exegetical issues or the history of the critical discussion of the synoptic eschatological discourse that would be discussed in a traditional commentary.

The thrust of this exercise is to show how the versions of the

---

[2] (Mt 24:1-51; Lk 21:5-36). On the presupposition of the Two-Gospel Hypothesis, Mark does not regularly use material from the Central Section of Luke (9:51-18:14) as a source, although our analysis will indicate that he was aware of its existence.

[3] Whenever the text of Luke 21 paralleled Matthew, Mark copied very closely. When Luke does not parallel Matthew there is no longer a common source and Mark showed very little interest in Luke at these points. Mark 13 follows Matthew 24 where Luke 21 does not at Mk 13:10, 21-23, 27, 36, for what will be shown to be special compositional reasons.

[4] For our working purposes we presuppose that Luke and Acts were composed by the same author. From time to time in the commentary, observations will be made on the basis of that presupposition.

[5] Our Greek text is based on Nestle-Aland, *Novum Testamentum Graece*, 26. Auflage (Stuttgart: Deutsche Bibelstiftung, 1981). Where we differ with Nestle, an indication is made by the use of brackets in the synopses and a brief discussion in the analysis. The relevance of these synopses and analyses for a fresh historical reconstruction of early Christianity are discussed in the position paper of our team.

eschatological discourses in Lk 12:35-48, 17:20-37, 21:5-36 and Mk 13:1-37 were composed, *given the presupposition of the Two-Gospel Hypothesis*. We believe our analysis of these units will confirm the Two-Gospel Hypothesis as the best explanation of the Synoptic Problem because it adequately explains the existence of all the literary evidence without postulating the existence of unnecessary hypothetical sources. Throughout the paper we provide various reasons why the Two-Gospel Hypothesis more adequately explains the literary history of parallel synoptic pericopae than do other hypotheses held by critical scholars. A detailed literary history of the Synoptic eschatological discourses based on various alternative source theories will be left to those who critique this paper. We will debate alternative explanations of these literary units only occasionally in the course of this paper.

Following the suggestion of David Dungan that no synopsis is without bias, our synoptic displays have been constructed on the presupposition of the Two-Gospel Hypothesis.[6] We show how Luke utilized material from his basic source, Mt 24:1-51; then, how Mark made use of both Matthew and Luke. Pericope divisions in the Matthew-Luke sections of the synopsis are made on the basis of our view of Luke's composition. (Note how Lk 21:21-28 emerges as a distinct literary unit in Luke which is not apparent in most synopses.) When Mark is brought into the picture, pericope divisions are made on the basis of our view of Mark's composition. Cf. below, 615-628.

I. Luke's Use of Matthew 24 as a Major Source in the Composition of his Eschatological Discourses

The Compositional Methods of Matthew and Luke

1. Matthew

On the Two-Gospel Hypothesis Matthew is presupposed as the basic source for Luke and one of the two basic sources for Mark. Since Luke and Mark come after Matthew, the compositional method of Matthew cannot be determined by an examination of Matthean redaction of any known source.[7] Thus, the literary critic must analyze the text of

---

[6] David L. Dungan, "Theory of Synopsis Construction," *Biblica* 61 (1980) 305-329; "Synopses of the Future," *Biblica* 66 (1985) 457-497.

[7] The recent commentary of R. H. Gundry [*Matthew: A Commentary on His Literary and Theological Art* (Grand Rapids: William B. Eerdmans 1982) 11], after a summary of twentieth century redaction critical discussion of the structure of Matthew, which overwhelmingly presupposes the Two-Source Theory, states, "We conclude that the Gospel of Matthew is structurally mixed."

Matthew itself in order to determine the compositional method of the author.

It appears that the author of Matthew composed his gospel by utilizing pre-existing source materials; perhaps some "collections" like Mt 5:1-7:29; 10:5-42; 13:3-50; 18:1-35; 23:1-39, and 24:1-25:46.[8]

An important recent step toward determining Matthew's compositional method has been taken by Dr. Dennis Tevis who has isolated, analyzed and compiled a list of characteristic words and phrases of Matthew.[9] Tevis' list of characteristic phrases constitutes primary data for isolating Matthew's sources.[10] Where discussion of Matthew's compositional method will arise in this paper, the evidence derived from linguistic characteristics will guide us in our attempt to ascertain what is likely to be Matthean compositional material. In addition, an indicator for determining literary dependence among the Synoptic gospels will be provided. When the linguistic characteristics of Matthew appear in the texts of Luke and/or Mark *only* in passages paralleled in Matthew where there is evidence of copying, a strong probability exists that Luke and/or Mark are literarily dependent upon Matthew. Likewise, when the linguistic characteristics of Matthew and/or Luke appear in the text of Mark *only* in passages paralleled in the other two gospels where there is evidence of copying, then a strong probability exists that Mark is literarily dependent upon either Matthew or Luke or both.

2. Luke

On the Two-Gospel Hypothesis it is essential to understand that Matthew is a major source for Luke. On this hypothesis the major

---

[8] William R. Farmer, "A Fresh Approach to Q," *Christianity, Judaism, and Greco-Roman Cults:* Studies for Morton Smith at Sixty (3 vols; ed. J. Neusner; Leiden: E.J. Brill, 1975) 1.45.

[9] Dennis Gordon Tevis, *An Analysis of Words and Phrases Characteristic of the Gospel of Matthew* (Ann Arbor, Michigan: University Microfilms, 1983). William Thompson, "Reflections on the Composition of Mt 8:1-9:34," *CBQ* 33 (1971) 365-388, has some helpful comments on Matthean compositional methods; cf. Jack Dean Kingsbury, *Matthew: Structure, Christology, Kingdom* (Philadelphia: Fortress Press, 1975) 1-39. cf. William O. Walker, "A Method for Identifying Redactional Passages in Matthew on Functional and Linguistic Grounds," *CBQ* 39 (1977) 76-93.

[10] Tevis, *Analysis of Words*, relies on John C. Hawkins [*Horae Synopticae*, 2nd ed. (Oxford: Clarendon Press, 1909) 168] which is still valuable for his definition of a characteristic phrase as "one that appears to be a writer's favorite or habitual way of expressing himself." Tevis [p. l] has developed a method whereby he can claim that each phrase in his list of Matthean phrases "... is sufficiently distinctive that it seems likely that each occurrence of that phrase in the Gospel of Matthew comes from the same writer."

literary "blocks" of the entire Gospel of Matthew are incorporated into Lk 1:5-9:51 and 18:15-24:53. Moreover, a considerable number of pericopae in these "blocks" appear in the same relative sequence in Matthew and Luke.[11] The sequence of pericopae (order) provides evidence for the claim that Luke follows the valid literary procedure of moving forward through his main source repeatedly. Therefore, his gospel has a literary structure which, in some ways, is remarkably similar to, and in other ways, remarkably different from Matthew.[12]

The major differences between the structure of Matthew and the structure of Luke can be noted readily on the Two-Gospel Hypothesis. The major differences are (1) the Central Section of Lk 9:52-18:14, which has no analogue in Matthew; and (2) the sometimes vastly different material on certain similar topics in Luke and Matthew; for example, the birth and resurrection stories.

The Central Section of Lk 9:52-18:14 is a unique Lukan creation. On the Two-Gospel Hypothesis, in this section, Luke incorporates both material from Matthew and source material he found elsewhere into his own literary composition. It has been observed that Luke composes by arranging his material following the literary principle of thematic association.[13] Apparently, Luke systematically works forward through Matthew and arranges the material from Matthew with his other source material following that principle. If one assumes that Luke follows this method in the composition of the Central Section, it is not necessary to resort to the hypothetical source, "Q", to understand Luke's compositional procedure. Perhaps Luke's change from following the Matthean order to following an order based on topics, as in Luke 9:52-18:14, indicates that Luke had access to another ordered source in addition to Matthew.

Perhaps, Luke preferred the order of topics he found in his special source material, followed it, and used thematic association to incorporate Matthean material into that order in his gospel.

The other major compositional difference betweeen Matthew and Luke on the Two-Gospel Hypothesis is the vastly different wording in some places when the general subject matter is similar. It is suggested that these variations, in principle, can be explained on the basis of one or more of the following observable Lukan compositional strategies.

---

[11] Bernard Orchard, *Matthew, Luke & Mark: The Griesbach Solution to the Synoptic Problem* Vol. 1 (Manchester: Koinonia, 1976) 39-42.

[12] Farmer, "A Fresh Approach," 48.

[13] Orchard, *Matthew, Luke, & Mark,* 60-68.

(1) A dominant desire of Luke to incorporate non-Matthean material into the basic structure of Matthew.

As was stated above, the exception which proves this rule is Luke's Central Section where Luke seems to have preferred the order and structure of his non-Matthean source.

There Luke seems to incorporate Matthean material into the basic structure of his non-Matthean source.

(2) A Lukan preference, in many instances, for content or wording found in his non-Matthean source(s) when the non-Matthean material overlaps topically with Luke's main source, Matthew (e. g. in the nativity stories).

(3) A Lukan preference for his own phrasing, particularly in his own redactional passages.

(4) A freedom on Luke's part to add, freely omit, or rearrange material from Matthew because, for him, Matthew was a valued and respected account of, but not the final word on, the sayings and deeds of Jesus.

This understanding of Luke's compositional method, in principle, accounts for the major compositional similarities and differences between Matthew and Luke on the presupposition that Luke used Matthew as his major source.

Before Luke began to compose his gospel he perhaps noted the doublets in Matthew and the large "blocks" of Matthean material he wished to use in his composition. One of these "blocks" was Matt 24:1-51. Luke utilized material in Mt 24:1-51 and moved some of it to two other literary contexts within the Central Section of his gospel to supplement source material he utilized there on themes similar to what he took from Matthew 24 (Lk 12:35-48 and 17:22-37). After he completed this process, Luke utilized what remained of Matthew 24 in his account of Jesus' last eschatological discourse (Lk 21:5-36), always following the order of Matthew.

We now turn to the analysis of the composition of Lk 12:35-48, 17:22-37, and 21:5-36 on the presupposition of the Two-Gospel Hypothesis.

A. Luke 12:35-48 / Matthew 24:42-51

Luke 12:35-48 is the first of three major units in Luke that focus on Jesus' teachings about eschatological matters. The unit opens with a warning to servants to be prepared for the return of the Lord of the house (12:35-38). This is followed by a warning that the householder should be ready for the coming of a thief; otherwise, dire consequences will follow (12:39-40). A question by Peter opens the concluding section of this three-part literary unit, emphasizing preparation for the coming of the Son of Man (12:41-48).[14] As a whole the unit stresses the need for readiness on the part of the believing community for the end of history.

At Luke 12:34, Luke had utilized the logion from Matthew's Sermon on the Mount (Mt 5:1-7:28), "Where your treasure is, there will your heart be also (Mt 6:21/Lk 12:34)." Immediately following this logion in Matthew are two verses dealing with "the eye as the lamp (λύχνος) of the body (Mt 6:22-23)."

Matthew 25:1-13 records "The Parable of the Wise and Foolish Virgins" with their lamps (λαμπάδες). The theme of lamps may have united these two sections of Matthew (6:19-23 and 25:1-13) together in Luke's mind.

The next verse in Luke, Lk 12:35, begins with "Let your loins be girded and your lamps burning," unlike those Foolish Virgins whose lamps went out for lack of oil (Mt 25:1-13).

The common themes of a marriage feast (γάμοι, Mt 25:10/ Lk 12:36), a coming master/bridegroom (Mt 25:10/Lk 12:36) and opening (ἀνοίγειν, Mt 25:11/Lk 12:36) also serve to unite Mt 25:10-13 with Lk 12:35-38.

The Matthean literary unit (Mt 24:36-25:13[46]) with which Luke is working is concerned with "the day and the hour of the coming Son of Man (Mt 24:36, 37, 39, 42, 44, 50; 25:13)." The emphasis in Matthew is stressed by the repeated phrase in Mt 24:42 and 25:13, "Watch, therefore, for you know not the day (nor the hour)." This Matthean linguistic characteristic has been preserved in a fragmentary form in the Lukan parallel (Mt 24:42/Lk 12:37). The verb, γρηγορεῖν, appears 6 times in Matthew (Mt 24:42/Lk 12:37; Mt 24:43/[Lk 12:39]; Mt 25:13; 26:38, 40, 41) and once or twice in Luke, always in passages paralleled in Matthew where there is evidence of copying. The appearance of the verb, γρηγορεῖν, in Matthew and Luke suppports the theory of Luke's direct literary dependence upon Matthew.

---

[14] I.H. Marshall, *Commentary on Luke* NIGTC (Grand Rapids: Wm. B. Eerdmans, 1978) 533.

Apparently Luke found in his special source material a parable on "slaves waiting for the coming of the master" (Lk 12:36-37a). Luke uses this parable for thematic purposes. Luke either adds logia both before and after the parable (Lk 12:35a, 37b-38), or, more probably, he received Lk 12:35-38 as a single unit from special source material on "girding the loins."[15] (See Lk 12:35a and 37b-38.) After Luke incorporated Lk 12:35-38 into his gospel, he reviews his main source, Matthew, for any parallels on the "watching" theme. Apparently by the use of the *Stichwort*, γρηγορεῖν, Luke arrives at Mt 24:42-51.

Luke decided to copy Mt 24:42-51 as an addition to the special material he utilized in Lk 12:35-38. Luke considered the essence of Mt 24:42 already to be contained in his Lk 12:37-38. In order to avoid redundancy, Luke commences copying Matthew 24 at verse 43 where he picks up the "coming master" aspect of his theme, (οἰκοδεσπότης, Mt 24:43/Lk 12:39).

The appearance of ἐγρηγόρησεν ἄν καί at Lk 12:39 is suspect, being omitted by 𝔓⁴⁵, ℵ*, (D), and some versions. Yet it does have strong textual support including ℵ¹, (A), B, W, (Θ) 𝔐 and many other uncials and minuscules. Since this clause has attestation from all of the major text types it has been included in our synoptic display but enclosed in brackets because it is not accepted by Nestle 26.

Peter's question in Lk 12:41 represents Lukan composition. εἶπεν δέ occurs at the beginning of a sentence in Luke over 50 times and only once in Matthew. It is introduced by Luke 19 times into material paralleled in Matthew. It is certainly a linguistic usage of Luke.[16] Luke may have adopted εἶπεν δέ from his source material (since it is found a number of times in material peculiar to Luke), but the view that the verse is Lukan redaction is supported by the fact that the construction, verb of saying + παραβολή, appears in Luke thirteen times. The construction, verb of saying + πρός + accusative, has been identified as a Lukan Septuagintism.[17] We, therefore, conclude that Lk 12:41 is probably Lukan redaction.

Now, it is clear that Luke copied Matthew very closely in the Parable of the Thief in the Night (Mt 24:43-44/Lk 12:39-40) and the parable

---

[15] Cf. William R. Farmer, *The Synoptic Problem: A Critical Analysis* (New York: Macmillan, 1964) 273.

[16] Franklyn J. G. Collison, *Linguistic Usages in the Gospel of Luke* (Ann Arbor, Michigan: University Microfilms, 1977) 47-48.

[17] Collison, *Usages in Luke*, 223, cf. 204, τὴν παραβολὴν ταύτην. Also, the construction, πρός + accusative + verb of saying, has been identified as a Lukan Septuagintism. Cf. Joseph A. Fitzmyer, *The Gospel According to Luke I-IX: Introduction, Translation and Notes*, AB 28, (Garden City, NY: Doubleday, 1981) 116.

of the Chief Servant and Slaves (Mt 24:45-51/Lk 12:42-46). With respect to the latter parable, Lukan linguistic characteristics account for his few small changes of the Matthean text. For example, οἰκόνομος appears in Lk 12:42 and in Luke 6:1, 3, 8 but in no other canonical gospel. A similar thing could be said of θεραπεία at Lk 12:42. It appears elsewhere in Luke (9:11) but in no other canonical gospel. Luke also prefers the introductory formula ἀληθῶς λέγω ὑμῖν (Lk 9:27; 12:44; 21:3).[18] Luke's change of Matthew's συνδούλος (Mt 24:49) to παῖδας καὶ τὰς παιδίσκας (Lk 12:45) can be explained on the basis of Luke's generally recognized interest in women.

At the end of Lk 12:46 (cf. Mt 24:51a) Luke has finished copying material on the "coming master" from Matthew. Later, Luke will use Mt 24:51b (or the doublet thereof, Mt 25:30) in his 13:28a.

Luke's one use of the Matthean linguistic characteristic, ἐκεῖ ἔσται ὁ κλαυθμὸς καὶ ὁ βρυγμὸς τῶν ὀδόντων, in a passage paralleled in Matthew constitutes hard evidence for Luke's literary dependence upon Mattthew at this point (See Mt 8:12, 13:42, 13:50, 22:13, 24:51/ Mt 25:30/Lk 13:28a).

Luke has something similar to the Parable of the Ten Virgins (Mt 25:1-13) in Lk 12:35-38 so he doesn't use that parable in his gospel. Luke will use Mt 25:14-30a, which concludes with the *Stichwort* δοῦλος, in Lk 19:11-27. Δοῦλος appears in Luke's source both in Mt 24:50 and at Mt 25:30. Therefore, at this stage, Luke looks to his *Sondergut* for material on the theme of the faithful δοῦλος. He finds some and so he gives us Lk 12:47-48. With this move, Luke leaves his source of eschatological material in Mt 24:1-51 for a time. Of course, he will come back to this source later but he will never again use the material he has utilized here from Matthew 24:43-51 anywhere else in his Gospel.

We have demonstrated compositionally how Luke arrived at Mt 24:1-51, copied Mt 24:43-51 as his main source for Lk 12:39-46, and left Mt 24 again to continue his account.

The Two-Gospel Hypothesis presumes that Mt 24:43-51 is the source of Lk 12:39-40, 42-46. But is this argument totally reversible? Can Mt 24:43-51 be dependent on Luke? Or, perhaps more likely, could Matthew be dependent upon a Lukan-type source ("Q") or on proto-Luke?

Linguistic and compositional arguments, which might be taken to favor the priority of Proto-Luke or "Q" to Matthew, are worth

---

[18] Collison, *Usages in Luke*, 225.

examination.[19] Some scholars claim that Luke 12:39-40, 42-46 represents a more original form of this tradition than the parallel tradition preserved in Mt 24:43-51.[20] This judgment is based, in part, upon the presence of certain words or phrases in Luke and the absence of others found in Matthew. However, an examination of these words or phrases reveals that none of these are "characteristic" of Matthew or of Luke. The evidence is neutral.[21]

The argument for the priority of Lk 12:39-40, 42-46 or for the priority of a proto-Luke/"Q" similar to Luke to the parallel tradition found in Mt 24:43-51, based on compositional considerations, is also problematic. A very detailed argument for this position has recently been made by C.M. Tuckett.[22] Briefly stated, Tuckett believes that there is a "Q"-type source behind both Lk 12:39-40, 42-46 and Mt 24:43-51. After noting some parallels between this "Q"-type source and Mk 13:33-37, Tuckett concludes that Mk 13:33-37 is derived from the same tradition as Mt (24:43-51) and Lk (12:39-46) who independently utilized another stage of this same hypothetical source.

This argument fails for two reasons. First, it contains a fundamental methodological flaw. As Tuckett admits, he must appeal to a "Q"-type source to explain the difficulties in Mk 13:33-37.[23] But such reasoning is circular. If a hypothetical document is reconstructed by concentrating on material which is not in Mark, then that hypothetical document

---

[19] C. M. Tuckett, *The Revival of the Griesbach Hypothesis, An Analysis and Appraisal* SNTSMS 44 (Cambridge: Cambridge University Press, 1983) 180-184.

[20] *Ibid.*

[21] The major verbal differences between Mt 24:43-51 and Lk 12:39-46 are as follows:

1) Mt 24:43, ἐκεῖνο; Lk 12:39, τοῦτο. Neither ἐκεῖνο for Matthew or τοῦτο for Luke has been identifeid as a characteristic usage of Matthew or Luke. Luke and Matthew (Mt 24:46/Lk 12:43 and Mt 12:48/Lk 12:45) both use ἐκεῖνος in the same pericope.

2) Mt 24:44, διὰ τοῦτο; Lk 12:40, omits . This phrase appears in Matthew three times as διὰ τοῦτο λέγω ὑμῖν (Mt 6:25; 12:31; 21:43). Tevis, *Words and Phrases*, Table 218, counts it as a characteristic phrase of Matthew. Therefore, there is precedent for διὰ τοῦτο in Matthew. It is not a characteristic phrase in Luke.

3) Mt 24:48, κακός; Lk 12:46, omits. This appears to be Lukan redaction. κακός appears three times in Matthew (21:41; 24:48; 27:33) and in Luke twice (16:25; 23:22).

4) Mt 24:51, ὑποκριτῶν; Lk 21:46, ἀπίστων. Tuckett, *Revival of Griesbach*, 180-181, claims on the basis of this one word change that Lk 12:39-40 and 42-46 could not have come from Matthew but from a source common to Matthew and Luke. This is a case of building a very large structure on a small foundation. ἀπίστος appears three times in Luke/Acts (Lk 9:41; 12:46; Acts 26:8) and once in Matthew (17:17). ἀπίστος is not a Lukan linguistic characteristic. Luke rarely uses ὑποκριτής from Matthew (Mt = 13 uses; Mk = 1 usage; Lk = 3 usages) Therefore, it is more likely that ἀπίστων was a Lukan alteration of Matthew at Lk 12:46 than that some hypothetical source lies behind both Matthew and Luke on the basis of this limited evidence.

[22] Tuckett, *Revival of Griesbach*, 180-185.

[23] *Ibid.*

cannot, at the same time, be one of Mark's sources. Second, if Luke (Lk 12:39-40, 42-46), and Matthew (Mt 24:43-51) *independently* utilized a stage of a source which was also used by Mark (Mk 13:33-37) at some other stage of the tradtion, why is Mark so different from *both* Matthew and Luke?[24] And why are Matthew and Luke so similar?

We believe, in balance, that the simplest solution to a literary problem should be preferred unless there is compelling evidence against it. The simpler solution (i. e. one that does not need to postulate unnecessary hypothetical source[s]) is to be preferred to a solution which requires such a postulation. The simplest solution is that Lk 12:39-40, 42-46 is derived from Mt 24:43-51. This is the position of the Two-Gospel Hypothesis.

[24] Discussion of the origin of Mk 13:33-37 will come later in the paper.

B. Luke 17:20-37 / Matthew 24:1-51

We are now in a position to take a look at the second complex of eschatological sayings which Luke has compiled. This is Lk 17:20-37. In structure and content this unit of Luke may be divided into two sections (Lk 17:20-21 and Lk 17:22-37). Lk 17:20-21 is Jesus' response to a question from the Pharisees about the Kingdom of God. Lk 17:22-37 has Jesus teaching his disciples about the coming of the Son of Man.

These two sections of this unit seem to be connected by the common theme of "observation." In Lk 17:20-21 the kingdom does not come with "observation" (παρατηρήσεως). In Lk 17:22-37 men will long to observe (ἐπιθυμήσετε... ἰδεῖν) the days of the Son of Man (i.e. see fool-proof signs of the end) but will not see them (οὐκ ὄψεσθε) (cf. Lk 17:22). Finally, when the Son of Man does come (Lk 17:24), all will know or observe the time! It will be as apparent as lightning.

Linguistically the two sections are united by similarities in language and these similarities are chiastically related to one another. This appears to be a good sign of Lukan composition.

Lk 17:21　　　　　　　ἰδοὺ ὧδε ἢ ἐκεῖ
Lk 17:23 ἰδοὺ ἐκεῖ [ἢ] ἰδοὺ ὧδε

Lk 17:20 has no Matthean parallel. Lk 17:21 has a rough parallel with Mt 24:23. Bultmann regards Lk 17:20-21 as an independent dominical saying which has been provided with a setting.[25] But what is actually present in the text of Luke is a *chreia*. Luke may have known the saying in his source material in just this form. With a version of Lk 17:20-21 before him, Luke seems to have checked Matthew for other material about "beholding" (ἰδού). He would have found Mt 24:23. Luke may have conflated Mt 24:23e with his other source material in order to create Lk 17:21a (cf. Mt 24:23/Lk17:21a). This would explain Luke's somewhat awkward restatement of the negative logion of the *chreia*. Luke omits ὁ χριστός from Mt 24:23 because his subject is the Kingdom of God.

ἐκεῖ in Lk 17:21a is a 'likely' linguistic usage of Luke since it is introduced six times into a passage paralleled in Matthew.[26] Lk 17:21b

---

[25] Rudolf Bultmann, *The History of the Synoptic Tradition*, ET by John Marsh (New York: Harper & Row, 1963) 54.

[26] Collison, *Usages in Luke*, 151, concedes that this usage may not be valid for those

constitutes Luke's famous positive statement of Jesus' dominical saying on the kingdom. Perhaps its form came from Luke's *Sondergut*.

At the beginning of Lk 17:23 the Two-Gospel Hypothesis enables us to see a fascinating compositional move made by Luke. Since Luke already had Mt 24:23 before him, Luke lets his eye go down the text of Matthew to Mt 24:26, another source of his obervation sayings in Matthew (ἰδοὺ ἐν τῇ ἐρήμῳ). What he sees are several formulaic Son of Man sayings in Mt 24:26-27, 37, 39 which are key points in the structural arrangement of the whole unit in Mt 24:26-40 about the parousia of the Son of Man. Luke decides to add to his unit on "observations" about the coming of the kingdom (Lk 17:20-21) from this Matthean material.

He developed the following compositional procedure. First, he constructed an introduction to this unit of Matthean material (Lk 17:22). Lk 17:22a is definitely Lukan redaction. εἶπεν πρός + the accusative is one of Luke's famous Septuagintisms.[27] Perhaps Luke 17:22b is *Sondergut*. The use of μίαν + the partitive genitive is said by Fitzmyer to be characteristic of Luke.[28] The use of εἷς as an indefinite pronoun may be characteristic of Luke's source material.[29] We may well agree with Bultmann when he says that this verse is "a formulation by Luke (or some earlier editor), meant to serve as an introduction to the following eschatological discourse."[30]

Then Luke follows Mt 24:26-27 to form his 17:23-24. These verses in Luke conform to what one would expect if Luke copied Matthew. Mt 24:26 and Lk 17:23 share a similar grammatical structure; namely, an unexpressed subject followed by a verb of saying is present in both verses. Luke's use of ἐροῦσιν shows his preference for a 3rd person plural active verb as a substitute for the passive.[31] The parallel phrases, ἐν τῇ ἐρήμῳ and ἐν τοῖς ταμείοις, in Mt 24:26 are dropped by Luke. It is noticeable, on the Two-Gospel Hypothesis, that throughout the eschatological discourses Luke omits considerable vivid imagery often very closely associated with Jewish apocalypses (cf. Mt 24:15b/ Lk 21:20; Mt 24:20-21/Lk 21:23; Mt 24:21b, 22, 29/Lk 21:24; Mt

---

working under the Two-Source Hypothesis. See Collison's explanation of the "*" in this context (p. 151) on his p. 25.

[27] J. Fitzmyer, *Luke*, 116, contains a more detailed analysis of this construction. Also see Collison, *Usages in Luke*, 9-10, 47-48.

[28] Fitzmyer, *Luke*, 121-122.

[29] Collison, *Usages in Luke*, 213. cf. 218-219, 230.

[30] Bultmann, *History*, 130.

[31] Collison, *Usages in Luke*, 76-77.

24:31/Lk 21:27). Hence, Luke's omission of the Matthean material here which is associated in Jewish literature with the appearance of eschatological figures in the wilderness is not surprising.

After Jesus' ministry, Luke and his more urbanized readers are not interested in any further speculations about eschatological events in the Palestinian wilderness. παρουσία is a Matthean linguistic characteristic, and is omitted consistently by Luke (Mt 24:27 cf. Lk 17:24, Mt 24:37 cf. Lk 17:26; Mt 24:39 cf. Lk 17:30). The most important linguistic evidence which suggests that Luke used Matthew in this unit is the shared usage of the word, ὥσπερ. Although Luke does not usually use ὥσπερ he adopts it here presumably because it is in his Matthean source.

The use of ἀστράπτειν, at Lk 17:24, is a Lukan change of Matthew's wording.[32] The ἐν τῇ ἡμέρᾳ αὐτοῦ of Lk 17:24 may not belong to the original text of Luke.[33]

At this point Luke looked at Mt 24:28, the next verse in sequence in his major source. Apparently, Luke concluded that this verse would be a suitable ending for this material on "observations" on the coming of the Son of Man. Between the beginning (Lk 17:23/Mt 24:26) and the ending of Luke's literary unit (Lk 17:37/Mt 24:28) he arranges further material on the coming of the Son of Man, some of which he found in Matthew (mostly from chapter 24) and some of which came from other source material on the same theme.

Following the *Stichwort*, παρουσία, (from Mt 24:27 to Mt 24:37 to Mt 24:39) Luke has before him three Son of Man sayings. He combines these sayings with *Sondergut* to compose Luke 17:25-37. Similar to his procedure in 17:22, Luke introduces the unit with a comment on the fact that the Son of Man must suffer. Luke makes absolutely sure his readers connect the Son of Man with Jesus. This verse functions to introduce a two-fold parallel statement about the times of Noah, Lot, and Jesus. Lk 17:25-32 seems to be a coherent literary unit. Lukan redaction may be seen in Lk 17:25 (cf. Lk 9:22).[34]

Lk 17:25 δεῖ αὐτὸν   πολλὰ παθεῖν
Lk 9:22 δεῖ τὸν υἱὸν τοῦ ἀνθρώπου πολλὰ παθεῖν

---

[32] The two NT uses of this word are both in Luke (24:4; 17:24). See also ἐξαστράπτειν in Lk 9:29. The compound does not appear elsewhere in the NT.

[33] Bruce M. Metzger, *A Textual Commentary on the Greek New Testament: A Companion Volume to the United Bible Societies' Greek New Testament* third edition (London/New York: United Bible Societies, 1975 corrected edition) 167. These words are set in brackets in the 26th edition of Nestle.

[34] Collison, *Usages in Luke*, 217.

καὶ ἀποδοκιμασθῆναι ἀπό...
καὶ ἀποδοκιμασθῆναι ἀπό...

The use of ἡ γενεὰ αὕτη in Luke 17:25 is also an expression which Luke prefers.[35]

In Lk 17:26-27 Luke integrates Mt 24:37-38 into his final composition. Luke skips from Mt 24:27 to Mt 24:37 for his source material because of the similarity of the two verses in Matthew. Luke's use of καθώς is a certain Lukan expression which appears 17 times in Luke and only 3 times in Matthew.[36] Luke's literary sensibilities prevent him from continuing to repeat the Matthean ὥσπερ (Mt 24:37). Luke writes a more literary Greek and conforms the passage to his own literary style. The phrase, καθώς + ἐγένετο, combines two expressions which Luke prefers, καθώς, and the well-known Lukan usage, ἐγένετο ἐν ταῖς ἡμέραις.[37] Luke follows his customary procedure and omits the Matthean παρουσία.[38] Luke also omits Matthew 24:38a because it is redundant. In Lk 17:27, ἐσθίειν + πίνειν is probably a linguistic usage of Luke. This explains his different wording from Matthew here. Luke uses this expression 14 times.[39] In 17:28-29 Luke follows the pattern of a well-known connection between the experiences of Lot and Noah which is used in Jewish materials. It is probable that Luke inserts the Lot material into his narrative here because it is in his source material. The construction ὁμοίως καθὼς ἐγένετο does not appear elsewhere in Luke. This indicates Luke's probable dependence upon his own special source material.

This brings us to the composition of Lk 17:30-31. Still on the theme of "observations" at the time of the coming of the Son of Man, Luke either follows the Stichwort, ἡμέρα, (Lk 17:29, 30) to Sondergut on the same theme (17:31), or, in the next verse of his main source (Mt 24:40), he noticed the Stichwörter, ἐν τῷ ἀγρῷ. With Matthew 24 in front of him, Luke notices the same phrase, ἐν τῷ ἀγρῷ, in Mt 24:18, another eschatological saying. Luke considers Mt 24:17-18 to be an eschatological saying about conditions at the final time of salvation. Luke apparently decides to join this saying and the saying of Mt 24:39b, thereby adding another eschatological saying on the coming of the Son of Man to his composition. This accounts for Lk 17:30-31. At

---

[35] Collison, Usages in Luke, 204.
[36] Collison, Usages in Luke, 155-56.
[37] Collison, Usages in Luke, 155-56, 132-33.
[38] See Mt 24:3/Lk 21:7; Mt 24:27/Lk 17:24; Mt 24:37/Lk 17:26; Mt 24:39/Lk 17:36.
[39] Collison, Usages in Luke, 50.

the point where Luke joins these two sayings, certain Lukan linguistic preferences stand out. For example, the attraction of a relative pronoun to the case of its antecedent, ᾗ ἡμέρᾳ rather than Matthew's παρουσία; ἀποκαλύπτεται (cf. Lk 17:22), ἐν ἐκείνῃ τῇ ἡμέρᾳ (7 times in Luke), and ὅς in place of a demonstrative pronoun are established Lukan usages.[40]

The two logia on the loss of the life of Lot's wife and the call for the disciple to lose his life rounds out Luke 17:25-34. It is not possible to say whether this is Lukan redaction or whether these further reflections were already linked together in the Lukan *Sondergut*. Luke attached the additional logia on saving life (cf. Mt 10:39, 16:25, Lk 9:24) as a common piece of hortatory material to form Lk 17:32-33. περιποιήσασ-θαι and ζῳογονεῖν are *hapax legomena* in Luke's gospel.[41] Perhaps, Luke has redacted this material in such a way that he is able to avoid making a doublet with Lk 9:24.

In his 17:34-35 Luke continues to follow his main source, Mt 24:40-41. First Luke supplies an introduction to this material with the words, λέγω ὑμῖν ταύτῃ τῇ νυκτί. This wording is used by Luke to reflect back to Lk 17:24 (the lightning scene) which he apparently perceives as taking place at night. Luke may use the dative without ἐν (Lk 12:20; Acts 12:6) although this is not usual for him. Having understood that the appearance of the Son of Man comes at night Luke copies Mt 24:40b-41, making minimal compositional changes. Luke has already made reference to a man in the field (Lk 17:31/Mt 24:18 ἐν τῷ ἀγρῷ) so, in order to prevent a doublet with Mt 24:40 (ἐν τῷ ἀγρῷ), and since the coming is at night, Luke has the two in one bed (ἐπὶ κλίνης μιᾶς). The use of ἕτερος instead of εἷς by Luke (Mt 24:40/Lk 17:34) is a Lukan linguistic characteristic. It is certain that ἕτερος is a linguistic usage of Luke (32 times in Luke; 10, in Matthew).[42] In Lk 17:35 the use of ἐπὶ τὸ αὐτό by Luke is a Lukan Septuagintism.[43] Again, he changes the second Matthean μίαν (Mt 24:41) to his preferred ἑτέρα (Lk 17:35c; see also ἡ μία in Lk 17:35). Lk 17:36 is probably not part of the original text.

Finally, with his 17:35 Luke has come to the end of his source material on this theme in Matthew. It should be remembered that Luke has used Mt 24:42-51 in Lk 12:39-46. In Lk 17:37a, Luke simply

---

[40] Collison, *Usages in Luke*, 205-206, 133-134.

[41] περιποιέομαι occurs once at Acts 20:28 and ζῳογονέω occurs once in Acts 7:19.

[42] Collison, *Usages in Luke*, 184-85. See also 213.

[43] S. Schulz, *Q: Die Spruchquelle der Evangelisten* (Zurich, 1972) 277-287.

reverts to his redactional structure of a conversation between Jesus and the disciples (Lk 17:22).

In Lk 17:20-37, Luke made use of Mt 24:26-28, 37-41 and 17-18. Luke used the last verse of this first unit from Matthew 24 (Mt 24:28) to conclude his eschatological section, Lk 17:20-37. After Luke placed Mt 24:28 into place in his 17:37b this unit of eschatological sayings was complete.

A major alternative to our position is the view that a common source, which was used both by Matthew and by Luke, stands behind Lk 17:23f., 26f, 30, 34f, 37/Mt 24:26-28 and 37-41.[44] It is not the purpose of this paper to enter into a detailed argument with those who hold opposing views on the Synoptic Problem. However, a methodological point needs to be stressed. The Two-Gospel Hypothesis, like other hypotheses about the origins of the Synoptic gospels, assumes that Luke utilized *Sondergut* in the composition of Lk 17:20-37 in addition to the materials from Matthew 24. This assumption, however, does not, of itself, warrant the claim that this source material was the so-called "Q" or a proto-Luke. We believe that one should follow the critical principle of presuming the existence of a hypothetical source only when it is clear that the literary evidence cannot be explained without such a source. Our analysis of Lukan compositional activity in this unit, in keeping with the Two-Gospel Theory, is, in our view, an adequate explanation of the evidence. We do not need to bring "Q" or Proto-Luke into the picture.

---

[44] Boismard, *Symposium de interrelatione evangeliorum, Jerusalem: Pâques 1984, Texte V: Le discours eschatologique* (Preliminary unpublished paper) 24-25.

C. Luke 21:5-36 / Matthew 24:1-42/10:17-22/5:18

When Luke arrived at the stage of his composition where his account
paralleled Matthew 24, even though he had used some of this material
earlier, Luke decided that he would weld what was left of the Matthean
version of Jesus' eschatological discourse into his gospel. If subject
matter is any clue to Luke's intention here, Luke apparently is very
interested in reminding his readers that Jesus predicted both the end of
the Temple and of Jerusalem (Lk 13:35a, 19:42-44, 21:5-6, 20-24).
Previously, Luke had not raised that issue directly in the eschatological
material in Lk 12:35-48 and 17:20-37. Now he addresses the issue of
the destruction of Jerusalem and its connection with other eschatological events, especially the coming of the Son of Man.[45]

Our division of the pericopae (on the presupposition of the Two-
Gospel Hypothesis) enables us to see Luke's intention and purpose in
constructing his 21:5-36. The pericopae divisions are as follows: 21:5-7,
8-11; 12-19; 20-27(28); 29-33; 34-36.

In 21:5-7 the announcement of the end is made. This is followed by
accounts of three different kinds of eschatological signs (false teachers,
8-11; persecutions, 12-19; and the destruction of Jerusalem, 20-28) —
these culminate in the coming of the Son of Man (21:27, cf. 21:36). The
purpose is clear. Luke's readers will observe the three groups of signs.
They constitute the warning to prepare for the coming of Jesus as the
Son of Man. When the Son of Man comes, no sign will be given.

Lk 21:29-33 and 34-36 conclude the discourse with further exhortations to be ready for the coming of the Son. In contrast to the false
teachers who claim "the time has come" (ὁ καιρὸς ἤγγικεν; Lk 21:8),
Luke argues that the signs indicate that the redemption of the faithful is
near (ἐγγίζει, Lk 21:28), but not yet present. In this expectant situation
his readers are to await the coming of the Son of Man.

We will now proceed to show that Luke utilized one major source
(Matthew 24) and *Sondergut* in the composition of Lk 21:5-36. We will
utilize the common sequence of the material, the pattern of omissions in
Luke when compared to Matthew, the appearance of several Matthean
linguistic characteristics within the text of Luke in parallel passages,

---

[45] Marshall, *Luke*, 753.

and the pattern of Luke's own compositional changes as evidence in favor of the Two-Gospel Hypothesis.

We begin with Lk 21:5. The opening remarks of the discourse as given in Matthew are shortened by Luke. Since Jesus is already in the temple precincts for Luke (Lk 19:47, 21:2) Matthew's statement about Jesus coming out of the temple is omitted. Luke has changed Matthew's οἱ μαθηταὶ αὐτοῦ to an indefinite τινων λεγόντων. This is understandable since the indefinite τις is introduced over 20 times by Luke into parallel passages in Matthew.[46] This is a Lukan linguistic usage. The genitive absolute is also a Lukan linguistic preference.[47]

In Lk 21:6, Luke follows his frequent custom of omitting the Matthean ἀμήν (31 times in Matthew and only 6 in Luke).[48]

In his 21:7a Luke omits καθημένου... τῶν ἐλαιῶν from Mt 24:3 because, for him, Jesus is within the temple precincts. The construction καὶ ἐπηρώτησέν τις αὐτὸν ἄρχων λέγων διδάσκαλε is found at Lk 18:18. This is similar to Lk 21:7 and reflects a common style. The collocation of καί/δέ + ἐπερωτάω + 3rd person personal pronoun + a participle of λέγω + the vocative, διδάσκαλε, occurs at Lk 18:18; 20:21 and here at Lk 21:7. It never appears within the text of Matthew. This indicates a strong probability that this construction is Lukan redaction.[49]

Luke retains the Matthean two-fold response of the disciples and follows it almost word for word (Lk 21:7/Mt 24:3). The second question in Luke is difficult to understand. Luke has omitted Matthew's παρουσίας and συντελείας τοῦ αἰῶνος. It is clear that Matthew means his second statement to refer to the end of the age. But Luke may have read this text in Matthew differently.

Only a thorough exegetical analysis could possibly reveal what Luke meant by ὅταν μέλλῃ ταῦτα γίνεσθαι. Perhaps he meant his second question merely as a reposing of the first question, πότε οὖν ταῦτα ἔσται; ("When will the temple be destroyed?") More likely, however, since, in Luke's view, the earliest Christian community was living in the last days, and this era was marked by eschatological signs in the heavens and on earth (cf. the use of Joel 2:28-32 in Acts 2:17-21), ταῦτα γίνεσθαι in Luke 21:7 may refer to the whole *sequence* of eschatological events in the last days. These would include the destruction of the temple which, in turn, would lead to the final climax in the

---

[46] Collison, *Usages in Luke*, 210.
[47] Collison, *Usages in Luke*, 77-78.
[48] Collison, *Usages in Luke*, 149.
[49] Collison, *Usages in Luke*, 216.

coming of the Son of Man. The precise time is unclear and is thus left ambiguous (cf. Lk 21:28a).

In Lk 21:8 Luke starts out by following Mt 24:4-5 in this statement of awareness about the appearance of deceivers. The only significant change Luke makes in Matthew is the addition of ὁ καιρὸς ἤγγικεν. καιρός is a word which Luke sometimes uses for eschatological time (cf. Lk 19:44; Acts 1:7, 3:20). ἐγγίζειν is used over 20 times in Luke-Acts (including Lk 21:8, 20, 28).[50] It is prominently used in eschatological contexts. The evidence would indicate this is Lukan redaction and he is simply bringing out for his audience what is implicit in Mt 24:4-5, namely, not to listen to the eschatological timetables of various "other" teachers (cf. Lk 17:20-23). Also, this passage in Luke could explain why Luke omits Mt 24:24-25 which has content similar to Luke 17:8.

Luke continues to follow Matthew closely in the account of Jesus' teaching about eschatological concerns in Lk 21:9-10/Mt 24:6-7. ταῦτα and πρῶτον may have been added by Luke to reinforce the idea that τὸ τέλος (the eschatological climax?) has not yet come (cf. Lk 21:12a.)

With his 21:10 Luke continues to follow Matthew (Mt 24:7). Luke apparently believes he needs a further connecting statement in Jesus' discourse. So he introduces this logion with τότε ἔλεγεν αὐτοῖς. ἔλεγεν is a certain linguistic usage of Luke. [51]

The disastrous heavenly signs of Lk 21:11b, φόβητρα... ἔσται are an enigma. It is noteworthy that the textual tradition for this line has many variants and is almost impossible to reconstruct.[52]

Lk 21:11b perhaps represents an isolated logion known by Luke and is inserted here to give balance to the idea that as well as on earth there are σημεῖα in heaven.

Luke's second sign of the last days is carefully crafted with one paramount idea in mind. From the outset persecution was a way of life for believers but, paradoxically, the difficult times provide the opportunity for the work of the divine sustaining power in the community.

Lk 21:12 has πρὸ τούτων which is Lukan in style (cf. Acts 5:36, 21:38). Luke uses traditional terminology as an introduction to his pericope on persecution. Apparently Luke was aware of a Matthean doublet (Mt 10:17-22 and 24:9-14). Luke (24:12b) decides to use Mt 10:17-22 rather than 24:9-14 as his source for Lk 21:12-19. And this is the basis for Luke's first major omission from Matthew 24 (Mt 24:10-

---

[50] Collison, *Usages in Luke*, 46.
[51] Collison, *Usages in Luke*, 55.
[52] Metzger, *Texual Commentary*, 172.

12). Probably there were several reasons why Luke did this. First, there is the reference to being hated by the Gentiles in Mt 24:9. For a diaspora audience Luke probably preferred the milder μισούμενοι ὑπὸ πάντων. Also, Luke appears to be very interested in saying that the church is sustained in persecution (Acts 4:1-4, 5:14-6:1, 6:7-15, etc.). Mt 24:9-13 is a grim recitation of persecutions without any encouragement from the sustenance theme. Given the fact that Luke has already used Mt 10:19-20 (see Lk 12:11-12) Luke prefers to follow Mt 10:17-22. This gives Luke the advantage of being able to paraphrase Mt 10:19-20, thus highlighting a sustenance theme. At the same time this gives Luke an opportunity to remove the appearance of a doublet.[53]

In Lk 21:12b-13 Luke follows Mt 10:17-18. For his diaspora audience Luke substitutes the more understandable φυλακάς for the technical Palestinian συνέδρια. Luke's substitution of the awkward ἀπαγομένους for Matthew's μαστιγώσουσιν is an indication that Luke is interested in finding some worth in the persecutions. These persecutions lead ultimately to a μαρτύριον ("testimony" or "evidence") for the faith in even the highest circles of Hellenistic kings and emperors (cf. Acts 24:1-17; 25:13-26:32; 28:19). Having said this, Luke can now dispense with Mt 24:14 which would be redundant for him. The same may be said of καὶ τοῖς ἔθνεσιν in Mt 10:18.

At this point Luke arrives at Mt 10:19-20. For Lk 21:14-15 Luke paraphrases Mt 10:19-20 because he had already used it in Lk 12:11-12. Here, he takes the opportunity to stress the theme of sustenance in persecution. Stylistically, Lk 21:14-15 shows evidence of Luke's compositional interests. τίθημι occurs 15 times in Luke as opposed to only 5 times in Matthew. It appears to be a Lukan linguistic usage.[54]

At his 21:16 Luke omits εἰς θάνατον from Mt 10:21 because persecution "unto death" does not go with the sustenance theme and is by no means a blanket description of the first generation of Christianity. συγγενῶν and φίλων are perhaps from Lukan source material.[55] The first word appears 4 times in Luke and in John 18:26. The second word appears 15 times in Luke and only once in Matthew. Neither word is in Mark. Even when Luke copies θανατώσουσιν from Mt 10:21 he adds the qualifying genitive "some of you." The theme of sustenance is maintained.

Having covered this material on persecution, Luke is able to omit entirely the parallel to Mt 10:17-22 in Mt 24:9-12. The fact that Luke

[53] Farmer, *Synoptic Problem*, 271.
[54] Collison, *Usages in Luke*, 66.
[55] Collison, *Usages in Luke*, 187, 177.

does not use ἐθνῶν further indicates that Luke is following Mt 10:22 and not Mt 24:9b in Lk 21:12-19. We presume further that Lk 21:19 parallels Mt 10:22b rather than Mt 24:13 which are doublets in Matthew. In Lk 21:18, Luke continues to stress the sustenance theme and so he inserts a logion on protection (cf. Acts 27:34) and maintains the same theme in his paraphrase of Mt 10:22b in his Lk 21:19. Luke drops τέλος because he has already used the word in his 21:9 and probably considers it to be redundant here. With the omission of Mt 24:14 Luke finished his utilization of Mt 10:17-22.

We have shown how Luke chose Mt 10:17-22 as his source for Lk 21:12-19 rather than Mt 24:9-14, which he omitted as an unnecessary doublet. This explains Luke's omission of Mt 24:10-12, 14 in Lk 21. Luke now reverts back to following his major source for this unit at Matthew 24 and, as he always does in Lk 21, he follows the Matthean order.

The central theme of Lk 21:20-28 is very clear. There is a further sure sign of the eschatological era, the destruction of Jerusalem and its temple. Luke connects these events with earlier prophetic utterances by Jesus against Jerusalem in 13:33-35; 19:42-44; and 21:6.

The language of Lk 21:20-24 follows the source of Mt 24:15-20. However, the following should be noted. (1) Luke has already used Mt 24:17-18 in his 17:31. (2) Luke seems to intend (perhaps from *Sondergut*) to give particularly graphic descriptions of the destruction of Jerusalem (cf. 21:20, 21b-22, and 23b-24), thereby reminding his readers of the importance of Jesus' prophecy. (3) The pericope provides an excellent opportunity for Luke to use his well-known pattern of prophecy and fulfillment reinforcing his Matthean source with numerous allusions to the OT. (4) Luke apparently shifts the focal point of Mt 24:15-22 from the "desolating sacrilege" to the destruction of Jerusalem.

In Lk 21:20 Luke "fills out" Mt 24:15a with his own material on the destruction of Jerusalem. Luke omits Mt 24:15b because he is not interested in "the desolating sacrilege." In his 21:21 Luke has three successive uses of a substantivised prepositional phrase with ἐν, οἱ ἐν τῇ 'Ιουδαίᾳ, οἱ ἐν μέσῳ, and οἱ ἐν ταῖς χώραις. This constructuion is an established Lukan usage.[56]

Lk 21:21b-22 paraphrases in lieu of copying Mt 24:17-18. Since Luke had already used Mt 24:17-18 in his 17:31, perhaps he felt the need to paraphrase at 21:21 to avoid creating a doublet. He may have also seen

---

[56] Collison, *Usages in Luke*, 227.

this as an opportunity to develop his prophecy-fulfillment theme. Lk 21:22 reflects Lukan style. Luke uses πίμπλημι 13 times, 10 times in material peculiar to him. It seems to be a Lukan linguistic characteristic although it is possible that it may derive from Luke's other source material.[57]

The conclusion of Lk 21:22 seems to be a formulation of traditional biblical language about the eschaton by Luke in order to highlight the judgment theme against Jerusalem which was already prophesied in Scripture and which was now being, or had been, fulfilled (πίμπλημι) (cf. Lk 1:20, 18:31 and 24:44). Luke probably has in mind Daniel 9:26 here. If this is the case, this is the reason why he has no interest in the "desolating sacrilege" of Mt 24:15b. For Luke, the true ἐρήμωσις (21:20) is the destruction of both the temple and the holy city and this in fact is what Daniel 9:26 says.

Luke gives a word for word repetition of the woe saying (Mt 24:19/Lk 21:19/Lk 21:23a). In doing so he utilizes a Matthean linguistic characteristic (ἐν γαστρὶ ἔχω ; Mt 1:18, 23; 24:19 [cf. Mk 13:17; Lk 21:23]. This is strong evidence in favor of our thesis that Luke was literarily dependent upon Matthew as a source. Luke omits from Matthew material which is irrelevant for non-Palestinians (Mt 24:20), such as the flight on the Sabbath; and gives further details about the destruction of Jerusalem.

Luke also has no parallel for Mt 24:21b-22. Presumably Mt 24:21b-22 is omitted by Luke because he has already completed to his satisfaction the descriptive account pertinent to the destruction of Jerusalem at Lk 21:23b-24. This second major omission from Matthew is also understandable. It is called for by Luke's compositional purpose which is different from Matthew's.

At this stage Luke makes another compositional move that can be seen easily if one presupposes the Two-Gospel Hypothesis. Since Luke has already used Mt 24:23, 26-28 in Lk 17:20-37 and since Mt 24:24-25 (the warning against "false Christs") has been dealt with in Lk 21:8, following the Matthean order, Luke omits Mt 24:24-25 and skips down to Mt 24:29 where he begins to copy again (Lk 21:25).[58] He notices that Mt 24:29 talks about the tribulation τῶν ἡμερῶν ἐκείνων ("of those days"). Since Luke has identified ἐν ἐκείναις ταῖς ἡμέραις as the times of the Gentiles (καιροὶ ἐθνῶν) (Lk 21:24), Luke omits Mt 24:29a

[57] Collison, *Usages in Luke*, 60.

[58] It is possible that the omission of Mt 24:24-25 came about not only to prevent duplication but also because of the *Stichwörter*, θλῖψις + ἐκεῖναι + ἡμέραι in Mt 24:21-22, 29 which encourages Luke to skip from Mt 24:22 to Mt 24:29.

and immediately proceeds with his further discussion of heavenly signs which will climax in the coming of the Son of Man. It is possible on the Two-Gospel Hypothesis that the heavenly signs of Lk 21:25-26 refer to the destruction of Jerusalem and not to the coming of the Son of Man as they do in Matthew. Thus, unlike other synopses, we do not interrupt the pericope at this point.

Luke omits Mt 24:30a-b. Luke conflates τότε from Mt 24:30a with Mt 24:30b to form his transition (Lk 21:27a) into the description of the coming of the Son of Man. The omission here is for purposes of structural clarity. Unlike the other great eschatological events of the cross (Lk 23:45), Pentecost (Acts 2:17-21), and the destruction of Jerusalem (Lk 21:25-26), this eschatological event will not be manifested as a sign. Instead, it *is* the end.

If we look at Lk 21:25-28 we see that, after Luke finished his graphic description of earthly events surrounding the destruction of Jerusalem (Lk 21:(12)20-24), he reverts to a description of "heavenly signs" (Lk 21:25a, cf. Lk 21:11). Lk 21:25a follows Mt 24:29b as his source. Apparently, Luke connects this with some additional prophetic material of his own on "the trauma of the end" (Lk 21:25b-26). The use of the genitive absolute, ἀποψυχόντων ἀνθρώπων, indicates a Lukan literary preference.[59]

Luke omits part of Mt 24:30 for reasons we have already indicated. Luke omits Mt 24:31 because his writings indicate that he is not interested in the widespread early Christian motif of believers being snatched into the heavens and the descriptions of cosmic judgment. Instead, he is interested in the redemption of believers at the end (Acts 3:22). This exhortation "to watch" for the coming of the Son of Man is an important part of Luke's eschatological discourse. It is reinforced by the fulfillment of preliminary signs (Lk 21:8-11), persecution (Lk 21:12-19), and the fall of Jerusalem (Lk 21:20-26, 28a).

The parable of the fig tree (Lk 21:29-31/Mt 24:32-33) is the first of two concluding exhortations on the theme of "watchfulness" within the final Lukan eschatological discourse. A glance at the synopsis indicates that Luke follows his source (Mt 24:32-36) fairly closely.

In Lk 21:29 Luke has one of his five uses of the construction, εἶπεν δέ/καί + παραβολή.[60] This appears to be a Lukan reformulation of his source (Mt 24:32). Luke's addition, πάντα τὰ δένδρα, is apparently made in the interest of his non-Palestinian audience.[61]

---

[59] Collison, *Usages in Luke*, 77-78.
[60] Collison, *Usages in Luke*, 223.
[61] Joachim Jeremias, *The Parables of Jesus*, 2nd revised edition translated by S.H. Hooke from the 6th German ed., 1962 with revisions which take into account the 8th

Βλέποντες ἀφ᾽ ἑαυτῶν (Lk 21:30) is Lukan redaction to reinforce the imperative γινώσκετε. The use of ἑαυτοῦ rather than σεαυτοῦ occurs 11 times in Luke and constitutes one of his linguistic usages.[62] In Lk 21:31, ἡ βασιλεία τοῦ θεοῦ is a Lukan linguistic preference occurring almost forty times in Luke-Acts.[63]

Lk 21:32-33 reveals very close dependence on his source, Mt 24:34-35. Here, as in Lk 21:23, a Matthean linguistic feature λέγω ὑμῖν + οὐ μή subjunctive verb + ἕως + subjunctive verb (Mt 5:26; 16:28; 23:39; *24:34*; 26:29 [cf. Mk 13:30; Lk 21:32]) appears. Again, this evidence is consistent with the view that Luke was dependent upon Matthew. Luke was probably as puzzled about the context of Mt 24:36 as are modern commentators. Probably because he did not want to create an unnecessary tension with what he had said about the nearness of the end throughout the discourse, Luke decides to omit Mt 24:36.

Luke has nearly finished welding all of the material he intended to use from Matthew 24 and which he had not used earlier in Lk 12:35-48 and Lk 17:20-37 into his discourse (Lk 21:5-33). Apparently, on the basis of the Two-Gospel Hypothesis, Luke has in his own store of source material some further material on urgent watchfulness (Lk 21:34-36). This pericope has close affinities with 1 Thess. 5:3. There Paul utilized it in a paraenetic context — which is similar to its function in Lk 21:34-36. Perhaps Luke conflates this material with Mt 24:42 to serve as his second warning to watch for the coming of the Son of Man.

In 21:34, προσέχετε ἑαυτοῖς is a favorite Lukan phrase (Lk 12:1, 17:3, cf. Lk 20:46). κραιπάλη is a *hapax legomenon* for the whole of the NT. Lk 21:35 reflects the language of Isa 24:17 (LXX). This is an indication of the traditional nature of this material. The use of δέομαι in Lk 21:36 is worthy of notice. δέομαι occurs 8 times in Luke and only 1 time in Matthew. It is a certain linguistic usage of Luke.[64]

With this final use of paraenetic material, Luke concludes his composition on the basis of his foundational source, Mt 24:1-51. Luke will never again use Matthew 24 as a source for the composition of his Gospel.

We have seen how Luke utilized Matthew 24 three times for compositional purposes. He first used Mt 24 in Lk 12:35-48 (on the need for appropriate readiness for the coming of the Son of Man). Second, when

---

German ed., 1970, (New York: Charles Scribner and Sons, paperback ed. of 1972) 29, 119-120.
   [62] Collison, *Usages in Luke*, 200-201.
   [63] Collison, *Usages in Luke*, 169-170.
   [64] Collison, *Usages in Luke*, 44.

Luke presents Jesus' "observations on the coming of the kingdom and the Son of Man" he returns to Matthew 24. Third and finally, when he gives Jesus' last eschatological discourse on the destruction of Jerusalem and the end of the temple in connection with the final eschatological scenario, again he uses material which is found in Matthew 24 as well as *Sondergut*.

II. MARK'S USE OF MATTHEW 24-25 AND LUKE 21
AS MAJOR SOURCES IN THE COMPOSITION OF MARK 13

Mark's Compositional Method

Given the pre-supposition of the Two-Gospel Hypothesis, when Mark is about to compose chapter 13, he has in front of him two major sources for Jesus' eschatological discourse, Mt 24:1-25:46 and Lk 21:5-36. Mark composes his single account of Jesus' last eschatological discourse, Mk 13:1-37, using these two basic sources.

Our synopsis illustrates how Mark followed procedures in the composition of Mk 13 that seem to be characteristic of the compositional method he used throughout his Gospel. That is to say, Mark should not be understood as an author who went through his two major sources mechanically and included material from them only when both sources agreed or where Mark considered it necessary to harmonize them. Rather Mark was a composer of a Gospel (Mk 1:1). His principle of composition was not just a mechanical re-presentation of the words and deeds of Jesus which he found in his two sources. His gospel was, rather, a theological reflection on Jesus' life. The suggestion made by many, and recently endorsed by Stuhlmacher, that Mark's outline of Jesus' life conforms with the outline provided in the Hellenistic-Jewish kerygmatic speeches of Peter in Acts may be endorsed.[65]

Mark usually preferred narrative to discourses in his composition. The lengthy eschatological discourse of Jesus is, therefore, an unusual literary unit in Mark's gospel. Apparently he included it in his account because it binds together his passion narrative, which starts with the denunciation of the temple in Chapters 11-12, with the charges of false prophecy against the temple (14:58; 15:29) which surface in Mark's account of the passion.[66] Mark's procedure is to follow the order and

---

[65] Peter Stuhlmacher, "The Gospel of Reconciliation in Christ - Basic Features and Issues of a Biblical Theology of the New Testament," *Horizons in Biblical Theology* 1 (1979) 175.

[66] Donald Juel, *Messiah and Temple* SBLDS 31 (Missoula, Montana: Scholars Press, 1977) 204-205.

wording of Matthew's eschatological discourse, conflating it with wording or parallels from Luke which, of course, have the same order as Matthew. But even here Mark adheres to a principle of brevity. He omits nearly all of the logia in Matthew 24:37-25:46, much of Mt 24:1-36 which is not found in Lk 21, *all* of Lk 21:5-36 which is not found in Matthew 24, and nearly all of Lk 17:20-37 and 12:35-48 which Luke took, in part, from Mt 24.

Moreover, especially in Mk 13:33-37, Mark strives for brevity in his composition. Mark (13:1-37) overwhelmingly limits himself to source material common to Matthew 24 and Luke 21. Indeed, whenever Mark finds material unique to Matthew 24, he usually omits it. Similarly, whenever Mark finds material unique to Luke 21 he always omits it (cf. Mt 24:10-12, 26-28, 30a, Lk 21:12a, 14a, 16b, 18, 21b-22, 23b-24, 25b-26a, 28, 29b-30a). By the use of such compositonal techniques as omissions, redaction, conflation, et al., Mark composed primarily by using those materials which Matthew and Luke shared — in this case their shared accounts of Jesus' last eschatological discourse.

One further point. Mark tends to follow the wording of his Matthean source closely. With the exception of Mt 24:10-12, 26-28, 30a (no parallels in Luke) Mark has everything in the Matthean version of the last eschatological discourse from Mt 24:1 to 24:36. Aside from an occasional word or phrase he may introduce from Luke into Matthew, Mark does not include material from Luke 21 which has no parallel in Matthew. But on several occasions Mark will copy material from Matthew which is not in Luke. For example, see Mk 13:19b-23, 27, 32.

What this seems to indicate is that Mark has great respect for Matthew (the original repository of the Palestinian material?) and wished to combine the texts of Matthew 24 and Luke 21, while closely following the wording of Matthew. At the same time, he avoided contradicting the meaning and sense of Luke. These are Mark's two basic compositional principles throughout his Gospel. They are particularly evident in the composition of Mark 13.

Mark's composition of 13:1-37 is placed within a very carefully planned structure. This is reflected by Mark's use of a major *inclusio*. This *inclusio* opens with the disciples' request that Jesus tell them about the last days, εἶπον ἡμῖν (13:4), and closes with Jesus' response, ὁ δὲ ὑμῖν λέγω πᾶσιν λέγω (13:37). Within this major *inclusio* (Mk 13:4-37) are two other minor ones (Mk 13:9-23 and Mk 13:33-37). The first of these opens with the words, βλέπετε δὲ ὑμεῖς ἑαυτούς (13:9), and closes similarly with, ὑμεῖς δὲ βλέπετε (13:23a). This *inclusio* circumscribes the persecutions which are the beginning of the birth-pangs of the end

(13:8c). These things must take place first (13:10). Afterward will come the Son of Man (13:24-27). This is followed by some sayings exhorting the hearers to recognize the urgency of the times (13:28-31).

This leads to the second short *inclusio*. Mark opens this *inclusio* with the imperatives, βλέπετε, ἀγρυπνεῖτε (13:33), and closes it with the synonymous imperative, γρηγορεῖτε (13:37). In this way he emphasizes the need for faithful watching. Indeed this emphasis on watching which is stressed in the last short *inclusio* recurs repeatedly throughout the discourse (13:5, 9, 18, 23, 33, 35, 37). By combining the materials shared by Matthew and Luke, Mark composed a timely warning for his readers. He advises them not to be led away by false teachers. After Jesus' death, the world must go through terrible times, including the destruction of the temple. Only after these hardships will the Son of Man come. The important thing is to be ready for his coming. It is the duty of Mark's readers "to watch!"

The literary evidence — the shared order of pericopes, the evidence of conflation in Mark, common omissions in the Synoptic eschatological discourses, shared literary details such as characteristic words, phrases, and literary structure — indicates that Mark most probably utilized two major sources in the composition of Mk 13:1-37, namely Mt 24 and Lk 21.

The shared order of pericopes on the presupposition of the Two-Gospel Hypothesis indicates that Mark followed the common order of pericopes in Matthew 24 and Luke 21 through Mk 13:1-37 without exception.

On a number of occasions Mark has conflated Matthew and Luke. Examples are noted in the analysis. Mark's omissions from Mt 24 are particularly striking. Mark omits from Matthew only Mt 24:10-12, 26-28, 30a. None of these has a Lukan parallel. In accord with his general principle, Mark has preferred Matthew in these instances. When he does not follow Matthew it is because there is no text shared by Matthew and Luke. He, therefore, omits.

Similarly, the verses that Mark omits from Lk 21 are also striking. These are limited to verses which have no parallel in Matthew 24 (Lk 21:12, 14a, 16b, 18, 21b-22, 23b-24, 25b-26a, 28, 30a). This is strong literary evidence in favor of our fundamental hypothesis concerning Mark's general compositional method and its particular application in chapter 13. Mark is attempting to establish a common text based on his sources, Matthew and Luke, but greater respect is shown to the wording of Matthew.

Finally, the linguistic evidence supports our thesis. As will be shown in the analysis, most of the words and phrases in Mark which differ from Matthew and Luke can be explained as Markan linguistic characteristics.

In summary, we conclude that the phenomena of order, omissions, conflation, and linguistic details provide different yet complementary types of literary evidence that Mark utilized two major sources in composing Mk 13, namely, Mt 24 and Lk 21.

THE COMPOSITION OF MARK 13:1-37 FROM MATTHEW AND LUKE

Mark 13:1-8/Mt 24:1-8/Lk 21:5-11

Mark opens his composition in 13:1 with the genitive absolute construction, καὶ ἐκπορευομένου αὐτοῦ ἐκ τοῦ ἱεροῦ (cf. Mk 10:17 and 10:46). The compound verb followed by the use of the same preposition is a frequently recurrent literary feature of Mark's text.[67] Mark's choice of the genitive absolute rather than the nominative participle, ἐξελθών, (Mt 24:1) is an example of his frequent use of the genitive absolute construction to open a literary unit. Mark's singular, εἷς τῶν μαθητῶν, is curious in light of the fact that both Matthew and Luke have more than one disciple around Jesus on this occasion. The riddle is solved, however, when we note that "τις or εἷς + the partitive genitive" is another Markan linguistic characteristic.[68] Mark also introduces διδάσκαλε into his 13:1. Mark has διδάσκαλε as an address to Jesus 10 times. On this occasion he may have taken it from Lk 21:7. The use of ἴδε, particularly used as a verb in a clause, is also a Markan linguistic characteristic.[69] Finally, in 13:1, Mark has ποταποὶ λίθοι καὶ ποταπαὶ οἰκοδομαί. At this point Mark appears to have conflated Matthew (τὰς οἰκοδομάς) and Luke (λίθοις). In so doing, Mark utilizes a favorite literary device. Namely, he uses the adjective ποταπός in a duplicate or synonymous expression.[70]

In Mk 13:2 the construction, καὶ + εἶπεν with ὁ Ἰησοῦς as the subject + a personal pronoun, is used 4 times by Mark (1:17; 2:19; 10:49; 13:2). He probably uses this construction to mediate between the different wording of Matthew and Luke. Mark makes it emphatically clear that Jesus spoke the prophecy about the destruction of the temple by

[67] F. Neirynck, *Duality in Mark: Contributions to the Study of the Markan Redaction* BETL 31 (Leuven: Leuven University Press, 1972) 75.

[68] David B. Peabody, *Mark as Composer* (Macon GA: Mercer University Press, 1987) Table 74 on 58 and Table 136 on 82.

[69] Peabody, *Mark as Composer*, Table 125 on 78 and Table 88 on 63.

[70] Neirynck, *Duality in Mark*, 105.

including the name of Jesus.[71] In the same way, Mark makes it clear that the references of Mt 24:2, ταῦτα πάντα, and Lk 21:6, ταῦτα ἅ, refer to the temple (τὰς μεγάλας οἰκοδομάς). This is another instance where Mark has introduced repetition in wording (Mk 13:1, οἰκοδομαί; Mk 13:2, οἰκοδομάς).[72] In 13:2b Mark follows Matthew closely with one double negative and adds another double negative as a duplicate expression (οὐ μή bis).[73]

Mark has one source, Matthew, to open Mk 13:3 and he follows it closely. In his other two references to the Mount of Olives, Mark uses τὸ ὄρος in a prepositional phrase (11:1, πρός; 14:26, εἰς, as in 13:3).[74] The phrase, κατέναντι τοῦ ἱεροῦ, is Markan redaction (cf. Mk 12:41).[75] It is interesting to note that Mark has καθίσας κατέναντι τοῦ γαζοφυλακίου in 12:41. Both of these phrases are unique to Mark and may be considered an example of Mark's repetition of formulae.[76]

Mk 13:3b appears to reveal conflation (cf. ἐπηρώτησαν in Lk 21:7/ ἐπηρώτα in Mk 13:3, no parallel in Mt; and κατ᾽ ἰδίαν in Mt 24:3/ Mk 13:3, no parallel in Lk). Mk 13:3 ends with a Markan expression, "Peter, James, John and Andrew."[77] In Mark, Andrew appears 4 times. Mk 1:16/ Mt 4:18, 1:29, 3:18/Mt 10:2/Lk 6:14, 13:3. These are the only times Andrew appears in the synoptics. Andrew always appears in contexts in Mark where Peter, James, and John are also mentioned (1:16; 1:29; 3:17; 13:3). This appears to be a Markan term for an inner group of disciples (cf. τινων of Lk 21:5).[78]

Mark 13:4 is a vital verse in the Markan account. It seems to function as the beginning of an *inclusio* for the total Markan discourse (cf. εἶπον ὑμῖν of Mk 13:4 and ὁ δὲ ὑμῖν λέγω, πᾶσιν λέγω at the end of the discourse at 13:37).

For the first question, "When shall these things be?" Mark follows his sources with insignificant variations. In the composition of the second question, "What is the sign when all these things are about to be accomplished?" Mark follows καὶ τί τὸ σημεῖον in both of his sources. Like Luke, Mark does not use Matthew's παρουσία in his gospel.

---

[71] E. P. Sanders [*The Tendencies of the Synoptic Tradition*, SNTSMS 9 (Cambridge: Cambridge University Press, 1969) 275] argues that the addition of proper names is "strong" evidence for an editorial tendency of a later gospel writer.

[72] Neirynck, *Duality in Mark*, 129.

[73] Neirynck, *Duality in Mark*, 105.

[74] Peabody, *Mark as Composer*, Table 228 on 105.

[75] Peabody, *Mark as Composer*, Table 239 on 110.

[76] Neirynck, *Duality in Mark*, 95.

[77] cf. Neirynck, *Duality in Mark*, 110; Peabody, *Mark as Composer*, Table 21 on 41.

[78] The account both represents a demonstrated tendency to use a grouping characteristic of Mark and also adds more vivid detail to the Markan account.

Rather, Mark copies the Lukan clause. But Mark uses συντελεῖσθαι like Matthew (συντελείας) rather than Luke's γίνεσθαι and thus conflates. The creation of ταῦτα... πάντα (Mk 13:4) is important for Markan redaction in Mk 13 (cf. Mk 13:29, 30).

In 13:5a, Mark resolves a slight difference between his sources by resorting to his characteristic construction, ἄρχομαι (always in the aorist tense) + the infinitive (26 times in Mark) to open the long discourse.[79] For his 13:5, Mark follows βλέπετε in both his sources which is in keeping with his redactional style and emphasis.[80]

In 13:6, Mark comes back to follow his sources closely. He drops ὁ χριστός from Mt 24:5 because, for his non-Palestinian audience, it is a proper name for Jesus rather than a general term for the Messiah. He also drops γάρ where Mt 24:5 and Lk 21:8c agree. Mark is conscious of the repetitive use of πλανᾶν in his Matthean source (Mt 24:4, 5). Mark prefers to repeat wording so he chooses to follow Matthew for his 13:6b rather than Luke who varies his wording (Lk 21:8a, μὴ πλανηθῆτε; Lk 21:8c, μὴ πορευθῆτε ὀπίσω αὐτῶν).

Mark opens his 13:7 by using the Lukan ὅταν δὲ ἀκούσητε (13:7/ Lk 21:9). This conforms with Mark's earlier procedure at 13:3 where he adopted Luke's wording (Lk 21:7, cf. Mt 24:3). However, he quickly reverts back to his usual procedure of following Matthew closely for the rest of his 13:7 (Mt 24:6; cf. Lk 21:9).

Mk 13:8a follows Mt 24:7a word for word. There is almost complete agreement with Luke (Lk 21:10) at this point also. In his 13:8b Mark has mainly retained the wording of Mt 24:7b, but he prefers to conflate Lk 21:11a and Mt 24:7c to form a duality, ἔσονται... ἔσονται (The first verb is from Matthew; the second, from Luke).[81] Mark essentially maintains the wording of Mt 24:8 with his ἀρχὴ ὠδίνων ταῦτα because Lk 21:12 has altered Mt 24:8 so radically that Mark finds himself unable to conflate Matthew and Luke at this point.

A synopsis of Mark 13:1-8 reveals several important minor agreements which occur between Matthew and Luke against Mark. These are: the omissions of εἷς, διδάσκαλε, ἴδε and Mark's dualism with οἰκοδομάς from Mk 13:1-2 (cf. Mt 24:1-2 and Lk 21:5-6); the omission of Mark's dualistic use of a double negative (Mk 13:2-3; cf. Mt 24:2 and Lk 21:6); καταλυθήσεται (Mt 24:2/Lk 21:6; cf. Mk 13:2, καταλυθῇ); the omission of κατέναντι τοῦ ἱεροῦ (Mk 13:3 cf. Mt 24:3 and Lk 21:6); the omission of the proper names, "Peter, James and John

[79] Peabody, *Mark as Composer*, Table 67 on 54.
[80] Peabody, *Mark as Composer*, Table 121 on 75.
[81] Neirynck, *Duality in Mark*, 80.

and Andrew" (Mk 13:3; cf. Mt 24:3 and Lk 21:7); λέγοντες (Mt 24:3/Lk 21:7; cf. Mk 13:3, omit); εἶπεν (Mt 24:4/Lk 21:8; cf. Mk 13:5, ἤρξατο λέγειν); γάρ (Mt 24:5/ Lk 21:8c; cf. Mk 13:6); the omission of ὅτι (Mk13:6 cf. Mt 24:5/Lk 21:8c); the omission of γάρ (Mt 24:6/Lk 21:9; cf. Mk 13:7).

These so-called "minor agreements" constitute strong evidence in favor of the Two-Gospel Hypothesis which accepts the direct literary dependence of Luke upon Matthew. This same evidence is anomolous for the Two-Document Hypothesis which maintains that these agreements of Matthew and Luke against Mark are the result of accidental coincidence in their independent editing of their Markan source.

Mk 13:9-13/Mt 10:17-22/Mt 24:9-14/Lk 21:12-19/Lk 12:11-12

At this place (Mk 13:9) Mark faces a very thorny compositional problem. On the basis of the Two-Gospel Hypothesis, Mark has in front of him 3 or 4 accounts of the persecution of the disciples that have close literary affinities (Mt 24:9-14/Lk 21:12-19; Mt 10:17-22; and Lk 12:11-12). First, he had Mt 24:9-14/Lk 21:12-19. Since Mark found the account of the eschatological discourse in the same literary context in his two sources (Matthew-Luke), and Mark had followed the same order in his composition, one would expect that Mark would conflate his two sources in this literary context (Mt 24/Lk 21) and move on with his composition. But Mark observes that Lk 21:12-19 is actually closer to Mt 10:17-22 than it is to Mt 24:9-14. Mark has to deal with a Matthean doublet (Mt 24:9-14/Mt 10:17-22). Mark also may have observed that Lk 12:11-12 has close literary affinities with Mt 10:19-20. Mark would then have to take two Lukan units (Lk 21:12-19 and Lk 12:11-12) into consideration in his composition as well as two Matthean units (Mt 10:17-22/Mt 24:9-14). In order to make his own composition Mark must conflate more than Mt 24:9-14 and Lk 21:12-19. Mark has at least three variants of the same tradition before him and possibly a fourth. In these situations, Mark appears to follow the text of the two closest parallels. This Markan compositional procedure causes him to follow Mt 10:17-22/Lk 21:12-19 fairly closely, rather than Mt 24:9-14. With this in mind, we may now comment on Mark's compositional method, verse by verse.

Mk 13:9a opens with a redactional use of βλέπετε, imperative, to mean "watch" or "beware" (cf. Mk 13:5). The fundamental idea of "heeding" or "watching" undergirds the whole Markan composition of the eschatological discourse. (See βλέπετε at Mk 13:5, 9, 23; βλέπετε, ἀγρυπνεῖτε, Mk 13:33; see also γρηγορῇ, Mk 13:34; and γρηγορεῖτε,

Mk 13:35, 37 with similar meanings.)[82] Furthermore, there appears to be some evidence that Mark uses a longer phrase which includes this use of βλέπετε to construct an *inclusio* around his discussion of persecution. The words which enclose this *inclusio* are related to one another chiastically. See Mk 13:9, βλέπετε δὲ ὑμεῖς ἑαυτούς and Mk 13:23a, ὑμεῖς δὲ βλέπετε. Such a structure almost certainly indicates redaction by the author of Mark. It is precisely these features of Mark's text which find no place in either Matthew or Luke.

Mark (13:9) now comes to Lk 21:12/Mt 10:17/Mt 24:9 which all include the use of the verb, παραδίδωμι. Following the principle of accepting the text of the majority of witnesses, Mark uses παραδώσουσιν from Mt 10:17/Mt 24:9 rather than παραδιδόντες from Lk 21:12. Because Mt 10:17-22 and Lk 21:12-19 are similar in wording, Mark immediately turns from Mt 24:9 and elects to follow the wording of Mt 10:17-18 as the basis for his composition in Mk 13:9-13. This accounts for the Markan omissions at Mk 13:9, (10)11-12 from Mt 24:9-13. In keeping with his procedure earlier in the chapter, Mark occasionally conflates material from Luke with Matthew. (See, for instance, εἰς συναγωγάς, Lk 21:12 / Mk13:9; cf. Mt 10:17, ἐν ταῖς συναγωγαῖς αὐτῶν.) Mark apparently noted the discrepancy in his sources between μαστιγώσουσιν (Mt 10:17) and ἀπαγομένους (Lk 21:12). Mark, therefore, goes his own way with a neutral δαρήσεσθε (cf. Lk 12:47).

Toward the end of his 13:9 Mark finds himself copying Mt 10:18b. At this point Mark's close observation of the text of Matthew causes him to note the repeated language of Matthew.

Mt 10:17	Mt 24:9
παραδώσουσιν γὰρ ὑμᾶς εἰς συνέδρια καὶ ἐν ταῖς συναγωγαῖς αὐτῶν	τότε παραδώσουσιν ὑμᾶς εἰς θλῖψιν
Mt 10:18b	Mt 24:14b
εἰς μαρτύριον αὐτοῖς καὶ τοῖς ἔθνεσιν	εἰς μαρτύριον πᾶσιν τοῖς ἔθνεσιν
Mt 10:21b-22b	Mt 24:9, 10a
καὶ θανατώσουσιν αὐτούς	καὶ ἀποκτενοῦσιν ὑμᾶς

---

[82] Cf. R. Pesch, *Naherwartungen: Tradition und Redaktion in Mark 13* (Düsseldorf: Patmos Verlag, 1968) 15-18, does an excellent job of highlighting this point.

καὶ ἔσεσθε μισούμενοι   καὶ ἔσεσθε μισούμενοι
ὑπὸ πάντων   ὑπὸ πάντων τῶν ἐθνῶν
διὰ τὸ ὄνομά μου   διὰ τὸ ὄνομά μου
and Mt 10:22b   Mt 24:13
ὁ δὲ ὑπομείνας   ὁ δὲ ὑπομείνας
εἰς τέλος   εἰς τέλος
οὗτος σωθήσεται...   οὗτος σωθήσεται...
ὅταν δέ...   ὅταν οὖν...

Mark takes these into consideration while composing his own literary unit at Mk 13:9-13. Mark conflates the first doublet (Mk 13:9b-10/Mt 10:17-18/Mt 24:9,14) and reproduces the fourth (Mk 13:13b). Then Mark makes these doublets serve as boundaries (beginning and ending) of his additional copying from Matthew 10:18b-22.

Since Mark perceived a doublet in Mt 24:14b and 10:18b, he conflated these texts from Matthew in composing Mk 13:9.

With the prominent addition of πρῶτον (cf. Lk 21:9), Mark then condenses Mt 24:14a to form Mk 13:10. Jeremias argued that just as Mk 7:27, which includes πρῶτον, is secondary to Mt 15:26, so also Mt 24:14a is the older form of the logion paralleled by Mk 13:10.[83] This allows Mark to say what he perceives to be the essential message of the unit in his sources: Before the end, there will be persecutions. It also allows him to make a connection between κηρύσσειν and εὐαγγέλιον at Mk 13:10 which occurs frequently in Mark (Mk 1:14; 13:10; 14:9; 16:15)."[84] Furthermore, this enables Mark to pick up ὅταν (Mt 10:19 / Mt 24:15 / Lk 12:11) for his 13:11 and later, after this unit, ὅταν δέ (Lk 21:20a and Mt 10:23a) to introduce Mk 13:11-14 and Mk 13:14f. respectively.

The synopsis indicates that Mk 13:11-13 seems to follow the text of Mt 10:19-22 closely. There is a beautiful example of Mark following the majority of the witnesses to a text when he composes Mk 13:12b-13 (cf. Mt 10:21b-22/24:9-10a/Lk 21:16c-17). With the completion of Mk 13:13 Mark has finished his conflation of material outside of Mt 24/ Lk 21. He is now ready to revert back to his main source (at Mt 24:15) to commence another unit of the eschatological discourse in the

---

[83] Joachim Jeremias, *Jesus' Promise to the Nations* (Philadelphia: Fortress Press, reprint edition, 1982) 23. Perhaps our analysis is confirmed by the interesting argument of G. D. Kilpatrick, ["The Gentile Mission in Mark and Mark 13:9-11,"*Studies in the Gospels: Essays in Memory of R.H. Lightfoot* (Oxford: Oxford University Press, 1955) 145-158] which unites Mk 13:9-10 and thus changes the punctuation of the Nestle text by deleting the period in Mk 13:9b.

[84] Peabody, *Mark as Composer*, Table 11 on 38.

Matthean-Lukan sequence on the general theme of persécution. The omission of Mt 24:9-13 in Mk 13:9(10)-13 is, therefore, explained by Mark's use of Mt 10:17-19 in this context.

The composition of this unit within the eschatological discourse has always posed major difficulties for the advocate of the Two-Source Hypothesis. First, if Mark is the earlier gospel used by the others, why do both Matthew and Luke diverge in sequence and in content at Mark 13:8 and come back together at the same place (Mk 13:15)? Yet they do not diverge in sequence anywhere else throughout the entire eschatological discourse. Second, how can one account for the composition of Mt 24:9-14 and Lk 21:12-19 given the presupposition that Matthew and Luke both used Mk 13:9-13 as their major source?

In order to explain this phenomenon, advocates of the Two-Source Theory have at their disposal two basic alternatives. Either they can attempt to explain how first Matthew and then Luke made use of Mk 13:9-13 alone (Matthew and Luke both have material similar to Mark 13 elsewhere in their gospels) or they may bring "Q" into the picture to help explain the synoptic phenomena. Both of these positions taken by advocates of Markan priority fail when followed consistently.

First, if we presume that Matthew is using only Mk 13:9-13 as a source, one must say that he did so to form Mt 10:17-22.[85] Mt 10:17-22 is part of the Matthean commission of the twelve. Because Matthew uses this material in ways similar to Mark (a similar audience, a similarity of persecution themes) such a move would be understandable. However, grave difficulties arise when we examine the compositional procedure of Matthew in 24:9-14 on the basis of Markan priority. For his 24:9b he creates a doublet with Mt 10:21b-22a if he is using Mk 13:12b-13a as a source! For Mt 24:10-12 Matthew paraphrases Mark or uses some other source material on persecution of the disciples.[86] Mt 24:13 would come from Mk 13:13b and Matthew would have created a second doublet with his 10:22b. Finally, Mt 24:14 would be taken from Mk 13:10 and another partial doublet would be created with Mt 10:18b. Matthew would have brought 24:9-14 into agreement with Mk 13:9-13, but only at the price of an extremely clumsy redactional procedure with a trail of doublets left behind in his wake. Such a compositional procedure is possible but hardly likely.[87]

[85] Bultmann, *History*, 122.

[86] *Ibid.*

[87] Bo Reicke, "A Test of Synoptic Relationships Matthew 10:17-23 and 24:9-14 with Parallels," *New Synoptic Studies: The Cambridge Gospel Conference and Beyond* (ed William R. Farmer; Macon GA: Mercer University Press, 1983) 213-214.

Even more difficult, on the basis of the priority of Mark, would be the composition of Lk 21:12-19. According to this theory, before Luke came to chapter 21 he had already copied Mk 13:11 fairly closely to form Lk 12:11-12. When Luke constructs 21:12-19, he paraphrases not only Mk 13:11, but also all of Mk 13:9 and 12a (cf. Lk 21:12b and 16). He drops Mk 13:10 and 12b. He copies Mk 13:13a (Lk 21:17), adds 21:18 from his own sources, and forms 21:19 from Mk 13:13b to create what would be an amazing redactional amalgamation of paraphrasing, copying, omitting, and providing additional unique material all within seven verses![88] As Bo Reicke says with reference to Luke's supposed activity at this point according to Markan priority:

> No author would have treated a document in such a perverse way that in one case [12:11-12] he preserved some of the phrases but radically changed the place of the unit, and in the other case exactly preserved the place but radically changed the phrases.[89]

Mt 24:9-14 and Lk 21:12-19 appear to be the products of very awkward and clumsy compositional procedures, on the presupposition of Markan priority. Perhaps it is credible that one of these authors would do such a thing. That both did so, appears to be an impossibility.[90]

If we bring "Q" into the picture it helps if we continue to remember that we are talking about literary relationships among five and not just three synoptic passages. In this case, Lk 12:11-12 (in the context of Jesus' mission discourse to the twelve in Galilee) stands in a literary relationship with Mt 10:19 (Jesus' mission discourse to the twelve in Galilee). Ordinarily on the Two-Source Theory, this would mean Lk 12:11-12/Mt 10:19 is "Q".[91] But this view involves one in a fundamental methodological problem because Mt 10:19 has some literary relationship with Mk 13:11. Is "Q" the source of Mark? This is impossible because "Q", by definition, is material common to Matthew and Luke which is not in Mark. *Logically, "Q" cannot be defined expressly as non-Markan material and, at the same time, be the source of Mark.*[92] This is just as true if one suggests that Mark may not have

---

[88] *Ibid.*

[89] *Ibid.*

[90] *Ibid.*

[91] cf. Schulz, *Q: Die Spruchquelle*, 442-444.

[92] Reicke, "A Test of Synoptic Relations," 214; C.F. Burney, *The Poetry of Our Lord*, (Oxford: Clarendon Press, 1925) 9, forgot this point when he supposed that Q was the common source of Mk 13:9(10)-13, Mt 10:17-22, and Lk 12:11-12, and that Matthew, for his entire 24:9-13, paraphrased Q to give it an eschatological flavor in keeping with the context.

used the "Q" which Luke and Matthew used (Lambrecht's "Q^Mt" and "Q^Mk").[93] The logical fallacy in this type of argumentation remains. The difficulties are only increased by the multiplication of hypothetical sources.

Moreover, even if it be granted that "Q" exists and that we have here an overlap between Mark and "Q", on what compositional basis did Mark choose to use "Q" in his composition of Mk 13:9-13, but fastidiously choose to omit from "Q" in other places? (i. e. Mt 24:26-28/Lk 17:23-24, 37b; Mt 24:37-41/Lk 17:26-27; 34b-36; Mt 24:43-51/Lk 12:39-46).

The Two-Source Theory cannot explain the compositional history of Mk 13:9-13 and its parallels as adequately as the Two-Gospel Hypothesis.

Mk 13:14-23/Mt 24:15-25/Lk 21:20-24

Mark, having finished his copying from Mt 10:17-22, follows ὅταν δέ as a *Stichwort* to bring him back to his main source, Mt 24:15 (Mt 10:23/Mt 24:15/Mk 13:14/Lk 21:20). Mark copies Mt 10:23a/Lk 21:20 (rather than Mt 24:15a) to form his 13:14a and moves through this next unit (Mk 13:14-23) according to his well established procedure of closely following the wording of Matthew and conflating with Luke when he is able (Mt 24:15-25/Lk 21:20-24).

In Mark 13:14, Mark drops τὸ ῥηθὲν διὰ Δανιὴλ τοῦ προφήτου from Matthew as Luke did. This is a clear case of Mark omitting where Luke omits because Mark no longer has two sources to unite. The "weakening" of Mk 13:14a vis-à-vis Mt 24:15b may represent Mark's attempt to bring the content of Mt 24:15 and Lk 21:20 closer together, or may be a reflection of Mark's eschatological agenda (cf. 2 Thess. 2:3f.). The imperatives, μὴ καταβάτω and μηδὲ εἰσελθάτω of Mk 13:15 constitute another Markan duality and probably represent conflation of his sources (Mt 24:17, μὴ καταβάτω; Lk 21:21, μὴ εἰσερχέσθωσαν; Mk 13:15, μὴ καταβάτω μηδὲ εἰσελθάτω; cf. Lk 17:31, μὴ καταβάτω).[94]

Mk 13:15-16 has no parallels with Luke 21. Luke has already used Mt 24:17-18 at Lk 17:31. So Luke paraphrased Mt 24:17-18 or used Sondergut (at Lk 21:21b-22). Since Lk 17:31 could be read by Mark as confirmation that Mt 24:17-18 was more original than Lk 21:21b-22, Mark could freely copy Mt 24:17-18 and omit the secondary form of

---

[93] J. Lambrecht, *Die Redaktion der Markus-Apokalypse; Literarische Analyse und Strukturuntersuchung* AB 28 (Rome: Päpstliches Bibelinstitut, 1967) 144.

[94] Neirynck, *Duality in Mark*, 105.

this same tradition at Lk 21:21b-22. Mk 13:15-16 thus follows Mt 24:17-18.

Mk 13:17 copies the common wording of Mt 24:19 and Lk 21:23.

Mk 13:18 is a case where Mark follows Matthew where there is no text present in Luke.[95] Mark maintains the χειμῶνος of Matthew but he drops μηδὲ σαββάτῳ. The latter would have had little interest for Mark's wider audience beyond Palestine.

Mk 13:19-20 follows the text of Matthew (Mt 24:21-22) closely. Apparently, Mark could not conflate Lk 21:23b-24 with Mt 24:21-22, so, following the basic principle we noted earlier, Mark follows the text of Matthew closely. Note the minor agreement of Matthew and Luke against Mark in the use of ἔσται in contrast to Mark's ἔσονται (Mt 24:21/Lk 21:23b; cf. Mk 13:19).

In 13:19 Mark adds αἱ ἡμέραι ἐκεῖναι. It is interesting to note that Matthew has ἡμέραι ἐκεῖναι twice in his 24:22 and Mark changes it both times to τὰς ἡμέρας (Mt 24:22/Mk 13:20)! Again Matthew and Luke agree against Mark in the use of μεγάλη (Mt 24:21/Lk 21:23b; cf. Mk 13:19). τοιοῦτος (which Matthew and Luke both omit on the Two-Document Hypothesis) is probably Markan. It is used 6 times by Mark without parallels in either Matthew or Luke. It is used twice in Luke and 3 times in Matthew.[96] The expression ἀπ᾽ ἀρχῆς κτίσεως and the expression κτίσεως ἣν ἔκτισεν (13:19) are Markan.[97] In the latter expression we have the combination of two Markan linguistic characteristics, (1) the use of a verb + a relative pronoun + a cognate accusative and (2) the use of a synonymous expression.[98] Mark is the only gospel writer who uses κτίσις.

In 13:20 Mark inserts κύριος which interprets ὁ θεός in Mk 13:19. Mark changes the διὰ δέ of Mt 24:22 to ἀλλὰ διά to form another characteristic Markan dualistic negative-positive construction, οὐκ ἄν... ἀλλά.[99] Again Mark uses (1) a verb + a relative pronoun + a cognate accusative and (2) a synonymous expression when he modifies Matthew's τοὺς ἐκλεκτούς to τοὺς ἐκλεκτοὺς οὓς ἐξελέξατο.[100]

[95] ἡ φυγὴ ὑμῶν in Mark has good attestation in Alexandrian and Koine texts. Thus it is accepted.

[96] Mt 9:8; Mt 18:5/Mk 9:37; Mt 19:14/Mk 10:14/Lk 18:16; Lk 9:9; Mk 4:33; 6:2; 7:13; 13:19.

[97] Peabody, *Mark as Composer*, Table 169 on 91, and Table 216 on 104.

[98] Neirynck, *Duality in Mark*, 76, 105. Furthermore, the construction of a noun (κτίσις) + relative pronoun + a verb which is a cognate of the noun used before the relative pronoun is found in Mk 3:28; 7:13; 10:38; 13:19, 20. Cf. Peabody, *Mark as Composer*, Table 169 on 91.

[99] Neirynck, *Duality in Mark*, 90.

[100] Neirynck, *Duality in Mark*, 105.

There is no parallel in Luke 21 to Mk 13:20-23. However, as we said earlier, an *inclusio* begins with Mk 13:9a and ends with Mk 13:23a. Apparently Mark saw Mt 24:22-24, with its strong statements on persecution, as appropriate material to conclude this *inclusio*.

The inclusio is as follows:

Mk 13: 9 βλέπετε δὲ ὑμεῖς ἑαυτούς
Mk 13:23   ὑμεῖς δὲ βλέπετε

Mark's use of ἴδε as a verb in Mk 13:21bis in contrast to Matthew's ἰδού (Mt 24:23) conforms with Markan literary style. Mk (13:23b) copies Mt 24:25. With this verse, the pericope concludes. The second major omission of Matthew 24 by Mark occurs when Mark does not copy Mt 24:26-28. But, since Luke (21) had omitted Mt 24:26-28, so did Mark in this case. This second great omission from Matthew 24 by Mark is thereby explained.

Mk 13:25-27/Mt 24:26-31/Lk 21:25-28

The reversal of the order of the phrases in Mt 24:29a by Mark (13:24a) conforms to Markan literary style. Mark here provides a duplicate expression featuring the word, ἐκεῖνος.[101] It also indicates that, for Mark, the appearance of the Son of Man will definitely come after the crisis in the holy city (Mk 13:14-23). In Mk 13:24b Mark remains close to the text of Matthew but the ἔσονται of Lk 21:25a (Mk 13:25) has been conflated with a form of πίπτω from Matthew by Mark in Mk 13:25a (ἔσονται... πίπτοντες).[102] As is his usual practice, Mark does not follow the Lukan addition of 21:25b-26a. At Mk 13:25, Mark changes the concurrent testimony of Matthew and Luke, αἱ δυνάμεις τῶν οὐρανῶν, to αἱ δυνάμεις αἱ ἐν τοῖς οὐρανοῖς. Apparently, for Mark, there may be powers which are in the heavens, but these are different from the "powers of the heavens."

Mark omits Mt 24:30a, perhaps because it deals with the Jewish idea of the "tribes" (φυλαί) of the earth. Again, since Mark follows the principle of producing a text which tends to have the mutual support of both Matthew and Luke and since there is no parallel in Luke here (Mt 24:30a; cf. Lk 21:26), Mark (13:25) simply omits Mt 24:30a. Mark may also see a tension between Lk 21:25, σημεῖα ἐν ἡλίῳ, and the reference to the σημεῖον of the Son of Man in heaven in Mt 24:30 and

[101] Neirynck, *Duality in Mark*, 95.

[102] Mk 13:25b has a use of the article which is not in Matthew or Luke. Neirynck, *The Minor Agreements of Matthew and Luke against Mark with a cumulative list* BETL 37 (Leuven: Leuven University Press, 1974) 286, has identified eleven of these instances in Mark.

this may explain his omission of both passages with their references to signs.

After seeing that Mt 24:30b and Lk 21:27 both agree that the coming of the Son of Man is connected with the clouds Mark conflates Mt 24:30b and Lk 21:27. Mark 13:26 has the mediatory ἐν νεφέλαις (Luke, ἐν νεφέλῃ, ἐν + the dative but singular; Matthew, ἐπὶ τῶν νεφελῶν, plural but genitive). Mark alters the common testimony of Matthew and Luke that the Son of Man will come "with power and much glory" to say that the coming will be with "much power and glory."

Mk 13:27 generally follows Mt 24:31, but he omits the Jewish "apocalyptic" detail of the trumpet sound, μετὰ σάλπιγγος μεγάλης (cf. 1 Thess 4:16, ἐν σάλπιγγι θεοῦ). Mark also rearranges Matthew's Semitic statement about the heavens to make better sense for his non-Palestinian audience.

Mark drops Lk 21:28 because there is no parallel in Matthew.

Mk 13:28-32/Mt 24:32-36/Lk 21:29-33

Mark goes into the unit on the fig tree following his usual procedure. He disregards the Lukan framework (21:29) and follows the word order of Matthew closely (Mk 13:28/Mt 24:32; cf. Lk 21:29). Neirynck has noted that Mark has piled up several cognate verbs in rapid succession here.[103]

Mt 24:32/Mk13:28	⟶	γένηται		
		γινόμενα	⟵	Mk 13:29/Lk 21:31
Mt 24:34/Mk 13:30	⟶	γένηται	⟵	Mk 13:30/Lk 21:32
cf. Mt 5:19				

This evidence suggests that Mark has conflated at this point. He takes one form of the word from Matthew, another form of the word from Luke and a third form of the word derives from the concurrent testimony of both Matthew and Luke. Also, in Mk 13:29, after Mark uses γινόμενα from Lk 21:31, he uses ἐπὶ θύραις from Mt 24:33 rather than ἡ βασιλεία τοῦ θεοῦ from Lk 21:31. This appears to be another conflation. Mt 24:33 and Lk 21:31 agree against Mark (13:29) on the use of ὅτι. At Mk 13:30 there is another minor agreement between Matthew and Luke. Both use ἕως ἄν, rather than the μέχρις οὗ in Mark. This difference is not substantial, however. Daniel 11:36 in the LXX has ἕως ἂν συντελεσθῇ. ἡ ὀργή... γίνεται while Daniel 11:36 Theodotian has μέχρις οὗ συντελεσθῇ. ἡ ὀργή... γίνεται.[104] The two readings appear to be interchangeable.

---

[103] Neirynck, *Duality in Mark*, 80.

[104] For a thorough analysis of μέχρις οὗ in Mark 13:30 see David Peabody, "A Pre-Markan Prophetic Sayings Tradition and the Synoptic Problem," *JBL* 97 (1978) 391-409.

In Mk 13:31, Mark follows Matthew and Luke closely. Mark who prefers dualisms follows Luke here with his double use of παρελεύσον-ται.

At 13:32, Mark turns again to follow Mt 24:36. There is no parallel in Luke.

Mk 13:33-37 (a summary of Lk 21:34-36 and Mt 24:37-25:30)

With 13:32 Mark has paved the way for his final exhortations on watchfulness. On the Two-Gospel Hypothesis Mark now has in front of him Lk 21:34-36 and Mt 24:37-25:46; one literary unit and a "block" of eschatological material. This material is very difficult to conflate. As was the case in several other places in his gospel at the end of a segment of source material, Mark decides to conclude his version of Jesus' last eschatological discourse with a summary of his sources.[105] In this instance, Mark juxtaposes these sources, using conflation to splice them together. The synopsis indicates Mark's procedure.

Mark gives a summary of Lk 21:34-36 at Mk 13:33 and then a summary of Mt 24:37-25:46 for Mk 13:34-37. All of this is done within the perameters of the total compositional plan of Mark which focuses on the need of his readers to watch for the unexpected coming of the Son of Man.

Mk 13:33-37 can be broken down into two pericopes: 13:33-34 and 13:35-37. Both begin and end with an imperative which issues a call to watch.

Mark condenses Lk 21:34-36 to form his 13:33a. In keeping with his tendency throughout chapter 13, Mark tends to omit or "reduce" material that only comes to him from Luke. Mk 13:33a is a conflated Markan version of the watchwords, προσέχετε ἑαυτοῖς (Lk 21:34) and ἀγρυπνεῖτε (Lk 21:36).[106] The added statement of the call to pray in Mk 13:33, if it is genuine, may reflect Lk 21:36 (ἀγρυπνεῖτε... δεόμε-νοι). Wording similar to Mk 13:33a is found in Mk 14:38 where it is well attested. The UBS committee believed that καὶ προσεύξεσθε in Mk 13:33a was added by copyists as a "natural addition" under the influence of Mk 14:38.[107] There is good textual support from each of the major text types for the longer reading at Mk 13:33a. Thus, we believe it should be retained.

In 13:33b, Mark has made his transition over to the Matthean source by means of his method of conflation. Mark's text, οὐκ οἴδατε...

---

[105] Orchard, *Matthew, Luke and Mark*, 86.
[106] Farmer, *Synoptic Problem*, 278.
[107] Metzger, *Textual Commentary*, 112.

καιρός appears to be a conflation of Lk 21:36 (καιρῷ) with Mt 25:13 (οὐκ οἴδατε).

Before we look at Mk 13:34, the structure of 13:33-37 should be recalled. The whole of 13:33-37 seems to be structured by a dualism of imperatives which form the beginning and the ending for two pericopes. See βλέπετε, ἀγρυπνεῖτε... γρηγορῇ at 13:33-34 and γρηγορεῖτε... γρηγορεῖτε at 13:35-37. The content of Mk 13:34-37 is supplied by a paraphrase of the common theme of the unit in Mt 24:37-25:30, namely, the departure of a prominent man and his sudden return (24:43-44, 45-51; 25:1-13, 14-30). Of course, Matthew is referring to the expectation of the parousia of Jesus. Mark has the same presupposition.

Mark (13:34) adds the detail of the man "leaving his house" (ἀφεὶς τὴν οἰκίαν αὐτοῦ) to his text of Mt 25:14 to emphasize that the man who will return is the lord "of the house" (τῆς οἰκίας) which he also adds to his text of Mt 24:42/Lk 12:37.

Mark condenses Mt 25:14-15 to form his 13:34. He substitutes ἐξουσίαν for Matthew's τάλαντα to make his text more applicable to the later church's need to exercise authority in the face of the delay of the parousia. The Markan addition of θυρωρός is a *hapax legomenon* in the NT. It is probably meant to highlight the demand to watch. With the further addition of γρηγορῇ, Mark completes his literary unit at 13:33-34.

For his 13:35-37 Mark uses the *Stichwort*, γρηγορεῖν, to take him from Mk 13:34 to Mt 24:42-43. He both copies and paraphrases Mt 24:42 to form his 13:35. Perhaps Lk 12:37a or some *Sondergut* with similar wording is also in Mark's mind. The same applies at Mk 13:35-36/Lk 12:37-38. At 13:36, Mark brings to a climax his summary. ἐξαίφνης may reflect Mark's use of αἰφνίδιος in Lk 21:34 to highlight the need for patient waiting for the parousia. καθεύδοντας in Mk 13:36 appears to reflect Mt 25:5, ἐκάθευδον.

Finally, Mk 13:37 functions to conclude the major *inclusio* of the discourse (13:4, 37)[108] This may not be Markan redaction alone. It may also reflect Mark's use of *Sondergut* which is also reflected in Lk 12:41, 44 as well as Mt 25:13. In Lk 12:41 Peter poses the question to Jesus, "Lord, do you say this parable to us or also to everyone?" In Mk 13:37 Jesus answers, "What I say to you, I say to all, 'Watch.'"

Our explanation of the composition of Mk 13:33-37 is simple and straightforward. By contrast, this pericope presents obvious difficulties

---

[108] J. Lambrecht, *Markus-Apokalypse*, 272.

for those who claim Markan priority. For instance, why do Matthew and Luke diverge so widely if they copied Mark closely throughout the eschatological discourse? To counteract this difficulty it is generally conceded by partisans of the Two-Source Hypothesis that Mark is secondary here: "Mark's account is secondary, and this is frequently noted in the commentaries".[109]

The response of those who advocate the priority of Mark to this dilemma is to appeal again to "Q". Put more specifically, it is said that Mark has combined his own redaction (usually 13:33, 37) with source material which is supposed to have come from "Q". A more sophistica-ted version of this approach is that of Lambrecht. He believes that Mark has created his 13:33-37 from fragments of four parables (Lk 12:35-38 The Watchful Servants, Lk 12:39-40/Mt 24:42-44, The Thief; Lk 12:42-46/Mt 24:45-51, The Faithful Householder and Lk 19:12-27/Mt 25:14-30, The Pounds/Talents) which were in a "Q" tradition of parables from which Matthew and Luke at different times drew Matthew 24-25 and Luke 12 respectively.[110] Tuckett says some-thing similar, arguing that the source which was available to Mark was definitely pre-Lukan. However, as in our previous discussion, such an explanation is problematic. If Mark is thought to have drawn upon a "pure "Q" source", the question remains, "How can a hypothetical source ("Q"), which is defined expressly as non-Markan material, at the same time, be the source of Mark?" Second, if it is argued that Mark uses "Q" as a basis for his compositon of Mk 13:34-36, why did he omit from "Q" in those passages where "Q" is supposed to be the source of Matthew 24 and Luke 17? Third, the need to hypothesize a multiple "Q" provides another reason why the Two-Source Theory is untenable. Multiplying hypothetical sources is not necessary because a simpler explanation is available.

In brief, that simpler explanation may be summarized as follows: In Mk 13:33-37, Mark set out to give a summary of the eschatological material in his sources, Mt 24:37-25:30 and Lk 21:34-36. Mark accom-plishes this through the literary technique of juxtaposition.

First, he condensed Lk 21:34-36 into 13:33a. Then Mark conflated Mt 24:13 and Lk 21:36 to make his transition into Matthew with his 13:33b. Now in Matthew, Mark condenses Mt 24:14-15 to form Mk

---

[109] C. M. Tuckett, *Griesbach Hypothesis*, 108, gives an extensive list of recent commentators who take this position.
[110] Lambrecht, *Markus-Apokalypse*, 250-251.

13:34, and Mt 24:42-43 to form 13:35. Finally, Mt 25:5, 12 was condensed and supplemented with some additional material to form Mk13:36-37.

CONCLUSION

The Two-Gospel Hypothesis rests upon two foundational pillars: the external testimony of the earliest Church Fathers that Matthew was the first of the canonical gospels to be written and the internal evidence of order of pericopes which suggests that Mark is a conflation of Matthew and Luke.

This paper complements these two major arguments. Our analysis of the compositional history of Jesus' eschatological discourses within the Synoptic gospels provides linguistic and stylistic evidence which confirms the conclusion that the order of composition of these eschato-logical discourses was first, Mt 24:1-51; second, Lk 12:35-48; third, Lk 17:20-37; fourth, Lk 21:5-36 and finally, Mk 13:1-37. Those who reverse the order of compositon and suggest that Mk 13:1-37 was the source for Matthew 24, Lk 12, Lk 17, and Lk 21 cannot explain the compositional history of these units — especially the composition of Mk 13:9-13, 33-37, and parallels — as satisfactorily as those who advocate the Two-Gospel Hypothesis.[111]

Allan J. McNICOL

---

[111] Cf. below, Appendix: "Synopsis. The Eschatological Discourse" (615-628).

RESPONSE TO THE TWO-SOURCE HYPOTHESIS

RESPONSE TO THE STATEMENT OF THE HYPOTHESIS

1. History of the debate.

Neirynck's statement that the debate over the synoptic problem began in the 18th century is a common misperception. A number of important events that shaped the entire Enlightenment (i.e., current) form of the debate took place long before the 18th century. However, an adequate treatment of this issue cannot be attempted here. D. Peabody will discuss certain aspects of the 19th century debate at a special *ad hoc* session later on in the program.

2. The problem of which synopsis to use.

Neirynck's position paper leaves a confusing impression with respect to this issue. In his "Note on the Questionnaire", Neirynck begins by denying that the question regarding which synopsis he uses is "helpful" only to then go on and specify three synopses that he thinks should be used, without indicating how he would reconcile their considerable differences of arrangement. But then he adds that even these three are faulty and should be fundamentally altered. Later in his Position Paper, he devotes many pages of discussion to the issues involved in synopsis construction because one major result of his Textual Discussion is his belief that all existing synopses should be "corrected". Hence, while it is clear that the question which synoptic arrangement Neirynck uses is in fact of major importance to him, he does not treat the issue in a straightforward manner.

3. The role and importance of patristic testimony.

Neirynck basically rejects the patristic testimony as being of little value for source-critical research. We disagree with this conclusion, but will reserve the discussion of this issue until we come to the segment of the program devoted to the patristic evidence.

4. The relation between of source theories and theology.

Neirynck says that the value of source theories for theology/preaching "are irrelevant. The practicability of [a] theory for the preacher should not become a critical principle in gospel criticism". We view Neirynck's opinion here as rather naive, insofar as he seems to be unaware of the built-in theological agendas already present in all gospel criticism including source theories.

5. The arguments for the priority of Mark.

(a) Neirynck's main reason for asserting the priority of Mark.

Since 1973, Neirynck has been proposing a major alteration of the usual (Streeterian) statement of the argument from order of pericopes to support the priority of the Gospel of Mark (see his references in note 6 on p. 7; see also his article on the "Synoptic Problem" for the *Interpreter's Bible Dictionary Supplement Volume,* Abingdon 1976). He repeats it here. His central contention is that "a more concrete approach" focuses on the *agreement* in order of pericopes Matthew//Mark and Luke// Mark. The differences in order for Matthew//Mark are restricted to the early section of Mark 1:21-6:13, and Luke's "transpositions" are relatively few in number compared to the widespread agreement in order of pericopes throughout Luke//Mark. "The basic statement remains the common order Mark-Matthew and Mark-Luke". Neirynck's complaint is that the usual statement: "Matthew and Luke almost never agree against Mark in order of pericopes; and where Luke differs, Matthew is similar to Mark's order, and where Matthew differs, Luke is similar" — is "too abstract". By this he means that since these divergences are relatively infrequent, to focus on them instead of the great preponderance of agreement in order of pericopes is a procedure that is not "concrete" enough. Or, as Neirynck puts it in another place, "the *basic phenomenon* to be reckoned with is the common order between Matthew and Mark and Mark and Luke" (*Interpreter's Dictionary of the Bible Supplement*, p. 846 col.a).

This methodological starting point proposed by Neirynck is based on Lachmann, who noted "that the variation [among the relative orders of the Gospels] appears greatest if all three writers are compared together... It is less if Mark is compared with the others one by one. That shows what I must do: first compare Mark with Matthew and afterwards consider the order of Luke and Mark." (see N. H. Palmer, "Lachmann's Argument," *NTS* 13 (1966-67) 370; quoting K. Lachmann, *De ordine narrationum,* p. 574; cf. Neirynck, "The Argument from Order and St. Luke's Transpositions," *EphTheolLov* 49 (1973) 792: "In this question we have to go back to the original statement of Lachmann."). Our response is simple: if one splits up the evidence into two halves at the outset, there is no possibility of ever seeing (or having to explain) the literary evidence regarding the phenomena of order that the Two-Gospel Hypothesis considers central for understanding and solving the Synoptic Problem.

We agree with Neirynck that the argument from order of pericopes is the fundamental starting point. However, it is precisely here that the Two-Gospel Hypothesis decisively parts company with the approach proposed by Neirynck. He has asked: "Is there any scientific basis for the assumption that all three Gospels should be 'viewed together at once'?" ("The Griesbach Hypothesis: the Phenomenon of Order," *EphTheolLov* 58 (1982) 115 n.19). We reply: of course there is. It is an elementary error in methodology to *begin* by splitting the evidence up into disconnected fragments before any critical analysis has had an opportunity to examine the data in an undisturbed condition.

(b) Doublets and the Q Hypothesis.

Having based his chief argument for the priority of Mark upon Lachmann's dichotomy of the synoptic evidence, Neirynck then establishes the existence of Q upon Weisse's long-since discarded argument from doublets. "These doublets offer decisive evidence for a second common source besides Mark [for Matthew and Luke]". We can see nothing "decisive" about these doublets for proving the existence of an independent written source Q for Matthew and/or Luke. Some are simply redactional repetitions for specific theological or apologetic purposes, others are two versions of a similar event.

(c) The main objections against the priority of Mark.

Neirynck apparently believes that the two main objections against the priority of Mark are "the so-called primitivity of Matthew and the Mt/ Lk agreements against Mark in the triple tradition". We note that these are not our main objections against the priority of Mark. Our three fundamental objections to the priority of Mark are: (i) certain repeated linguistic characteristics of Markan redaction do not show up in either Matthew or Luke, (ii) while linguistic characteristics of Matthew and Luke do show up in parallel passages of Mark (see D. Peabody, *Mark as Composer* 1986). These two sets of evidence are important microstructural "one-way indicators" of literary dependence.

A third set of data has to do with the phenomena of order: (iii) the order of *pericopes* in Mark is similar to both Matthew and Luke where their order is similar, and in between these pericopes Mark's order is almost always similar to the one or the other, i.e., Mark's order of pericopes is rarely different from both simultaneously. Moreover, in the order of *details within pericopes*, there is precisely the same concatenation of alternating agreement and disagreement as seen on the macroscopic or pericope level. Taken together, these three (or four) sets of data are in our judgment fatal to any theory that Matthew and Luke independently copied Mark. In addition, we also consider the historical evidence from the patristic testimony unfavorable to the theory of Markan priority (see comments of Dom Bernard Orchard in response to the paper by Prof. Merkel, pp. 591-604).

(d) What is the central problem to be explained?

Neirynck says "the central problem of our discussion is that of Matthean originality versus Markan priority". We do not view this as an adequate description of "the central problem." For one thing, Neirynck's formulation consists of an arbitrary restriction of our attention to only two of the Gospels. All four Gospels must be investigated together within the context of contemporaneous Jewish and Hellenistic culture, with full attention paid to the patristic testimony. However, as far as the Synoptic Gospels specifically are concerned, this is "the central problem" to be explained, viz., *the total concatenation of alternating agreement and disagreement in order, with respect to whole pericopes among all three Gospels, and of the various details within the pericopes.*

(e) Verification of hypotheses.

Finally, we agree with the concluding statement of Neirynck that a source hypothesis must be verified (or falsified) by "an examination of language, style and content", i.e., that the only way in which the relatively greater "plausibility" of one hypothesis can be demonstrated compared to other hypotheses is by numerous detailed, redaction-critical studies.

RESPONSE TO THE TEXTUAL DISCUSSION

At the Cambridge Griesbach Colloquium held in 1979, it was unanimously voted that there should be another Gospel Conference which would conduct a full-scale review of the three major source theories currently in use. It was additionally recommended unanimously that this proposed conference should give special attention to a number of fundamental methodological disputes, specifically naming: the argument from order, criteria for determining primary and secondary Jesus tradition, the question of the minor agreements against Mark, the compositional methods of the evangelists, and the question of the relation between the Gospel of John and the Jesus tradition. Consequently, at subsequent meetings of the Planning Committee, it was decided by the leaders of the three Research Groups that each would present an analysis of a triple-tradition passage of the Gospels, and, in addition, would include a discussion of one of the methodological issues listed above. Accordingly, Frans Neirynck chose Matt. 4:23-5:2 because he said it would throw light the methodological issue of the argument from order of pericopes. Regarding his discussion of Matt. 4:23-5:2 and parallels, we wish to make the following observations:

(a) Matthaean "anticipations."

Neirynck's elaborate theory of "Matthean anticipations" seems as far-fetched today as it did in 1967, when he published a study on this same passage in an attempt to deal with what was perceived to be the major liability of the Two-Document Hypothesis in the eyes of French Multiple-Stage Theorists (such as Xavier Léon-Dufour, Lucien Cerfaux and Jacques Dupont), namely, the confusing jumble of parallel texts corresponding to Matthew 4:23-11:1. See "La rédaction matthéenne et la structure du premier évangile," in *De Jésus aux Évangiles. Tradition et rédaction dans les Évangiles synoptiques,* ed. I. de la Potterie, *BETL* 25 (1967) 41-73. We find little, either in that discussion or this one, in the way of evidence from literary precedents or of the church's historical setting or of the author's theological motivations, to balance or justify the complicated manipulation of words and phrases Neirynck alleges the author of Matthew to have carried out. As a result, this textual discussion is perceived by us, at least, as an arid mechanical *tour de force* having little human feeling, historical validity or persuasive power.

(b) The phenomenon of order of pericopes.

Neirynck does use this passage to provide a discussion of the phenomenon of order, according to his analysis of Matthew//Mark. In doing so, he has fulfilled that part of the assignment, namely to deal with a particular methodological issue in light of the text he has chosen.

(c) Proposed revision in synopsis arrangement.

At the end of his discussion, Neirynck proposed that all existing synopses should be altered to fit his theory of the proper place to locate the Sermon on the Mount relative to Mark's order. We find this an appropriate recommendation, given Neirynck's source-critical approach, i.e., it illustrates our contention that all synoptic arrangements are theory-based rather than "theory neutral" (see Dungan, "Synopses of the Future" p. 317-47). Of course this also means that other hypothetical reconstructions of the synoptic interrelationships will find other alternative synoptic arrangements preferable.

(d) Our alternative synoptic arrangement.

The Jerusalem Symposium Planning Committee requested that each Hypothesis Group include in its critique of the other two Groups' Textual Discussions *its own synoptic arrangement of the others' passages.* The reason for this request was to ascertain whether different synoptic theories actually did require radically dissimilar synoptic arrangements, so that the very synoptic evidence itself shifted depending on which synoptic theory one adopted, or whether there was actually very little change in the deployment of the synoptic parallels, regardless of which theory was being used.

Accordingly, the Two-Gospel Hypothesis Group hereby offers an alternative synoptic arrangement of the same material that Neirynck has discussed. In doing so, it will become immediately obvious that we have taken into consideration all *three* synoptic Gospels (as our hypothesis requires) instead of just discussing Matthew//Mark (as Neirynck's hypothesis requires). Secondly, we have carried through a very brief redactional/theological analysis to indicate Mark's motivation for including or excluding material from his sources at each step along the way. Our assignment is merely to show that an alternative analysis to Neirynck's is *just as plausible* as his.

Chart Showing Mark's Use of Matthew and Luke

Procedure

Since our Hypothesis asserts that Matthew did not make any use of Mark, we cannot reply directly to Neirynck's discussion of Matt. 4:23-5:2. However, we can show how this material would be understood from a Two Gospel Hypothesis perspective and deal with all of the same passages Neirynck does (with the addition of the parallels in Luke which he does not discuss). For this reason, we have had to prepare a synoptic chart radically dissimilar to Neirynck's, and, for that matter, any currently in print.

We prepared this chart in the following steps: using the text of Nestle-Aland 26th ed. (but adopting a number of variant readings suggested by McNicol and Peabody), we first divided the text of Mark up into meaning units using repeated linguistic phrases in the text of Mark as our guide (see charts in Peabody, *Mark as Composer* pp. 35-130). Next, we ascertained the divisions between larger or smaller collocations of stories, what we call "part one," "part two," etc., by attempting to discern the author's theological/narrative concerns, according to which he originally divided up or arranged his narrative into parts. Only then did we, thirdly, look at the parallel narratives of Matthew and Luke in an effort to discover the relationship between the accounts in Mark's narrative and the parallel accounts in Matthew and Luke. As we worked through Mark in this way, we repeatedly confirmed what was originally said by Griesbach, namely, that it was not at all difficult to see when Mark is following one or another of his sources, and, when he switches from one to the other, why he does so at that precise point, and finally, when he comes back to the former, he always resumes following the former Gospel at precisely the point where he had left off. *N.B. In order to see this purposeful utilization by Mark of one source and then the other, we had to rely on* Griesbach's Synoptic Chart — *not any modern synopsis currently in use. If one uses any of them, it is impossible to see what we see using this chart.*

Our study revealed that Mark used each and every story that came up in the same relative order in his sources. We have indicated this triple sequential order of pericopes by means of the hyphens. However, painstaking analysis showed further that these triple tradition pericopes in Mark are always closer in form and wording to one or the other of his sources. We have indicated this closer content relationship by the means of the single solid line and arrow.

These solid lines plus arrow are significant for another reason. By following the arrows down the chart, it is possible to see Mark moving purposefully back and forth between his sources. At this point, one is granted a remarkable glimpse of an orderly creative process guided by Mark's theological agenda. We will comment on these as occasion warrants.

In the observations which follow, the first observation will focus on the theological and narrative concerns evident in that pericope while the comments in brackets will focus on redactional data.

1. *The Appearance of Jesus Christ, the Son of God. Mk 1:1-20*

Introduction. Mk 1:1-3

Mk's famous opening verse contains the reference to "the Gospel of Jesus Christ" thereby indicating the title of this writing. [Mk conflates Mal 3:1 with the Isa 40:3 quote in his sources, creating a minor agreement against him.]

Mt 3:4-6,11 ←——— Ministry of John. Mk 1:4-8 — Lk 3:3b, 3a

John the Baptist functions as the alter-ego, Christ's counterpart in the early rising action of Mk. [In general, Mk is closer to Mt but he omits considerable material present in both sources.]

Mt 3:13-17 — Appearance of Jesus; Baptism. Mk 1:9-11 ——→ Lk 3:21f.

Moving to the momentous baptism scene, Mk, with Lk, avoids Mt's embarrassing dialogue, also using Lk's version of the Voice from Heaven.

Mt 4:1-11 — Temptation. Mk 1:12-13 — Lk 4:1-13

Mark alters the story of the tempting of God's Son, focusing instead on contending with wild beasts. [The ending "angels ministered unto him" Mk gets from Mt not Lk, and he follows Mt for the next two stories.]

Mt 4:12-17 ←——— Jesus Begins Ministry. Mk 1:14-15 — Lk 4:14-15

The opening contrapuntal theme continues; John is imprisoned, Jesus picks up the proclamation and carries on. [Mk adopts Lk's briefer form but follows Mt's wording, except for the quote from Isaiah.]

Mt 4:18-22 ←——— Call of Four Disciples. Mk 1:16-20 (cf. Lk 5:1-11)

Jesus authoritatively calls four disciples who "immediately" follow him. [This story brings Mk to the introitus to Mt's Sermon on the Mount 4:23ff. which Mk desires not to repeat in his narrative, preferring Lk's dramatic healings as a way of continuing the thread of Jesus' early activities.]

(Mt 4:24-7:29 Sermon on the Mount)

2. *Jesus the Great Healer. Mk 1:21-45*

(Lk 4:16-30 Sermon & rejection at Nazareth)

(Mt 7:28f.) Jesus Goes to Capernaum. Mk 1:21-28 ——→ Lk 4:31-37

Jesus preaches with authority in the synagogue and "immediately" is confronted by a demoniac who openly attacks him. Jesus casts out the demon; his fame begins. [Mk's additions to Lk's account heighten the dramatic effect.]

(Mt 8:14f.) Goes to House of Simon. Mk 1:29-31 ———→ Lk 4:38-39

The fast-paced narrative continues. Jesus "immediately" enters Peter and Andrew's house "with James and John" [a Markan addition] and heals Peter's mother-in-law.

(Mt 8:16f.) Heals Many Sick (a summary). Mk 1:32-34 ———→ Lk 4:40f.

Jesus' fame is astonishing; "the whole town gathers at his door" [a Mkan additional detail] and he heals many sick. [A famous "duplicate expression" composed of halves from Mt and Lk is found in vs. 32; vs. 34 is another example of weaving together words from Mt and Lk.]

(Mt 4:23) Preaching/Healing Tour. Mk 1:35-39 ———→ Lk 4:42-44

Jesus leaves Capernaum on a preaching-healing tour of "all Galilee." [Mk joins Mt 4:23 with Lk 4:44. Then, since Lk next has the call of the first three disciples 5:1-11, Mk skips to Lk 5:12-16, the Cleansing of the Leper, which Mt also has immediately after the Sermon on the Mount at 8:1-4. Thus Mk can return to Mt's order once again having passed over the Sermon.]

(Lk 5:1-11 Call of Three)

Mt 8:1-4 --- Healing of the Leper. Mk 1:40-45 ———→ Lk 5:12-16

The first healing of his tour. [This is a classic example of Mk's procedure in conflating two accounts in Mt and Lk. Words and phrases are interlaced into "duplicate expressions" and in the process Mk adds or omits tiny details this creating the familiar pattern of "minor agreements" (both positive and negative). Basically, he follows Lk's form and works in Mt's details.]

(Mt 8:5-34 Various stories located elsewhere in Lk//Mk)

3. Jesus' Conflicts with the Scribes and Pharisees. Mk 2:1-3:6

Transition Passage. Mk 2:1-2

Jesus returns "again" to Capernaum to "his home;" the "crowds gather" and he speaks "the Word" to them. [This is one of the

important παλιν retrospective passages (Peabody 1987, 128-130) forming a major, unique redactional feature of Mk. Mk continues with a
block of six conflict stories in Lk's order.]

Mt 9:1-8 — Heals Paralytic. Mk 2:3-12 ⟶ Lk 5:17-26

These stories depict a series of clashes between Jesus and Pharisees
which gradually intensify until they begin to plot to kill him. [Mk is
carefully following Lk but he works in details from Mt, with expansions, which cause the cluster of minor agreements we can see, particularly in vss. 6, 8 and 9.]

Mt 9:9 — Call of Levi. Mk 2:13-14 ⟶ Lk 5:27-28

The opening verse is replete with Mkan redactional characteristics that
are completely missing in the two parallel accounts: Jesus goes out
"again" "by the sea" where "the crowd" comes "and he teaches them."
On the way he sees and calls Levi to be his disciple. [The additional "son
of Alphaeus" is missing from Mt and Lk.]

Mt 9:10-13 — Eating with Publicans. Mk 2:15-17 ⟶ Lk 5:29-32

The series of conflict stories continue. [Minor agreements occur in vss
15,16.]

Mt 9:14-17 — Controversy over Fasting. Mk 2:18-22 ⟶ Lk 5:33-39

A fourth dispute erupts because Jesus and his disciples do not fast.
Jesus' answer is an ominous "dark saying." [Mk's additions to his
sources causes an important minor agreement (omission) in vs. 19.]

(Mt 9:18-11:30 Various stories located elsewhere in Lk.)

Mt 12:1-8 — Working on the Sabbath. Mk 2:23-28 ⟶ Lk 6:1-5

In this and the next conflict story, the theme is Jesus' superior grasp of
the true meaning of Sabbath observance. Mk's additions to the accounts
in both sources are negligible until we come to the major added
comment in vs. 27, which is Mk's attempt to clarify the ambiguous Son
of Man saying in his sources. The effect heightens Jesus' status as one
who is above petty Jewish/Gentile demarcations, showing him to be the
universal savior. [Mk basically accepts Lk's abbreviation of Mt, but
note the common agreements caused by the additions in vs. 26 and the
change in word order in vs. 28.]

Mt 12:9-14 — Healing on the Sabbath. Mk 3:1-6 ⟶ Lk 6:6-11

Jesus goes out "again" into a "synagogue" (Mkan redactional characteristic) and heals a man. [Mk basically follows Lk's alterations of Mt although his additions in vss. 4-5 increase the dramatic tension. The addition of "immediately with the Herodians" in vs. 6 is Mkan (cp. 12:13). At the very end, Mk shifts back to Mt's conclusion of the account: "and they took counsel how they might kill him" (cp. Lk 6:11). With this, Mk next fashions a complex transition passage, bringing the rising action in Chapter 3 to a peak.]

Mt 12:15-16 (cp. 4:23-25) ←——— Transition. Mk 3:7-12 (Lk 6:17-19)

Jesus goes back "to the sea" and "great crowds" gather from all directions. Mk creates an impressive list of regions and cities that conflates Mt and Lk. Although Mk has moved to Mt 12:15, the same account comes up a few verses later in Lk 6:17ff. To these Mk adds details from Mt 4:23-24 and a new location "by the sea" "in the boat" (cp. Mk 4:1) "on account of the crowds" (cp. Mk 2:4). Then he combines the list of cities in Lk 6:17 with a similar list in Mt 4:25 to produce an even more powerful impression of the extent of Jesus' fame than either source had at this point. Finally, Mk omits (with Lk) the continuation of Mt's version (the lengthy O.T. quote). The whole scene has been carefully composed to prepare the way for the momentous next story: the repeated hostility of the Jewish leadership leads Jesus to choose twelve closest disciples to constitute the "true Israel" of the New Age.

(Mt 12:17-21 O.T. quotation)

4. Jesus Creates a Brotherhood of Twelve Closest Disciples. Mk 3:13-35

(Mt 10:1-4)   Choice of Twelve. Mk 3:13-19 ———→ Lk 6:12-16

Using carefully chosen words (cp. both sources), Mk emphasizes that Jesus personally chose twelve disciples "to be with him" (vs. 14). From this point on, Mk will portray Jesus regularly giving this inner circle of brothers secret instruction — a feature Mk stresses unlike either of his sources (see Peabody 1987, chart 120 p. 181; chart 204 p. 271; chart M p. 393; and discussion on pp. 365-369). [The list of names in vss. 14-19 is slightly different from both sources, with the famous minor agreement in vs. 17. At this point in Lk's order comes Lk's Sermon on the Plain (6:17-49) which Mk wishes to avoid, so he moves back to Mt and rejoins his narrative at precisely the point where he left it, i.e., 12:16.

Skipping the lengthy O.T. quote (Mt 12:17-21) he resumes his story with Mt 12:22ff, the Beelzebul Controversy.]

(Lk 6:17-49 Sermon on the Plain)

(Lk 7:1-8:3 Various stories located elsewhere in Mt.)

Transition. Mk 3:20

Opening this section is another Mkan παλιν retrospective phrase that describes Jesus' return to Capernaum, and "again" the crowds gather "so that no one can eat." These Mkan redactional additions are missing in Mt and Lk.

Jesus' Kinsmen Come to Take Him Away. Mk 3:21

Interpreting 'οι παρ αυτου to mean "Jesus' relatives," Mk immediately sets up a violent contrast over against the thrilling scene of the Choice of the Twelve while Jesus' own family think he is possessed. Although this theme is in his sources, Mk has emphasized the contrast by creating this scene, which is not in either source, to form the pendant to vs. 31f.

Mt 12:22-37 ←——— Beelzebul Controversy. Mk 3:22-30 (Lk 11:15-23)

Mk abruptly goes on to add that Pharisees "coming down from Jerusalem" (a Mkan addition) have come to attack Jesus along the same line as his family, only their conclusion is far more ominous: Jesus casts out demons with the aid of Satan. Then Mk says, in a detail missing in both sources, that Jesus answered them "in parables" (vs. 23), i.e., using mystical language the opponents could not possibly understand. [Mk's version of the Beelzebul controversy has always given Two Document Theorists considerable difficulty because of several massive "minor agreements" against Mk, causing some to postulate a "Mark - Q" overlap. When viewed as a unit (Mk 3:20-35), it is not difficult to see Mk's striking theological and narrative purpose; coming to a head in the next section.]

Mt 12:46-50 ←——— Jesus' True Mother, Brothers. Mk 3:31-35 (Lk 8:19-21)

The gripping scenes in Chapter Four come to a climax as Mk (skipping over Mt 12:38-45) explicitly describes Jesus' mother and brothers standing outside calling him to come out. Perceiving their ominous intentions, Mk says Jesus looks around at "the crowd seated around him" (Mkan addition) and asks "Who are my mother and brothers and sisters?..." Thus Mk rounds out the stories begun in 3:13 with an extraordinary ironic ending. The theme of the entire section is the contrast between Jesus' true and his false family.

5. The Crowds Get Parables, Jesus' Brotherhood Gets Secret Explanations. Mk 4:1-34

Mt 13:1-9 ←————Jesus Teaches in Riddles. Mk 4:1-9 — Lk 8:4-8

Following a typical Mkan πάλιν scene change: "again he began to teach them beside the sea" (cp. Mt 13:1), Mk portrays Jesus as intentionally concealing the message of salvation from "those outside" by speaking to them only "in parables." Thus Mk continues to develop the theme of mysterious election, viz., the hardening of "those outside" while "you" are given the true meaning plainly.

Mt 13:10-23 ←————— Jesus Explains to His Disciples. Mk 4:10-20
                                                                    — Lk 8:9-15

Mk's familiar scene-change in vs. 10 is a typical redactional addition to his sources: public teaching in parables followed by secret interpretation to his disciples. We may be certain that the other parables in this collection also had secret (oral) interpretations not included here. [Mk follows Mt's order but he adopts Lk's abbreviation of the story, especially omitting the lengthy O.T. quote. He adds details causing minor agreements in omission, e.g., vs. 13. Mk notes that Mt next has the redundant Parable of the Tares, so he moves across to the collection of mystic sayings in Lk 8:16.]

(Mt 13:12) Mystic Sayings on Light/Seeing. Mk 4:21-25 ————→ Lk 8:16-18
Mk's principal theme linking these parables is the mystery of election.

(Mt 13:24-30 Parable of Tares)

The Seed Growing Secretly. Mk 4:26-29

Mk adds a parable not in either of his sources, continuing the theme of the mystery of God's ways.

Mt 13:31-32 ←——— Mustard Seed. Mk 4:30-32 (Lk 13:18-19)

Mk turns back to Mt for one more "seed" parable, making some minor additions in vss. 31,32.

(Mt 13:33 Parable of Leaven)

Mt 13:34-35 ←——— Conclusion. Mk 4:33-34

Skipping Mt's Parable of the Leaven, Mk finds a summary passage in Mt 13:34f., and converts it into a conclusion that looks back to the opening lines in 4:1. This concludes Mk's description of Jesus teaching parables to the crowd followed by private explanation to his disciples. [Mk omits the rest of Mt's parables (Tares Explanation, Treasure, Pearl, Dragnet), and switches to Lk, going to the exact point where he left him, namely at 8:18, and resumes there. However, the next story in Lk is about Jesus' True Mother, etc. (8:19-21) and he has already told that, so he moves forward to the next story, Stilling the Storm (Lk 8:22-25).

(Lk 8:19-21 Jesus' True Mother/Brothers)
(Mt 13:36-52 Various parables)

6. Christ's Divine Power Demonstrated. Mk 4:35-6:6

(Mt 8:23-27)   *Stilling the Storm. Mk 4:35-41* ———→ Lk 8:22-25

Mk resumes the narrative of Jesus' mighty deeds, except that each new miracles increases in divine power and magnitude. [Mk has added numerous details to the story in his sources so that this story abounds in minor agreements (both positive and negative), as Mk retells the story with the vivid eyewitness verisimilitude of Peter's memory.

(Mt 8:28-34)   Gerasene Demoniac. Mk 5:1-20 ———→ Lk 8:26-39

The Christ can heal a whole "herd" of demons, utterly beyond the power of mortal healers. [Continuing on with Luke (using his change in place name) Mk works in a few words from Mt and adds numerous details (creating many minor agreements) which heighten the dramatic vividness of the whole story.]

(Mt 9:18-26) Jairus' Daughter, Bleeding Woman. Mk 5:21-43 ———→
Lk 8:40-56

Two amazing healings in quick succession. [Mk begins this story with another παλιν phrase. The two stories were already combined in Mt whence Lk got them, but Mk adds numerous details (creating a whole pattern of minor agreements).]

Mt 13:53-58 ←——— Jesus' Rejection at Nazareth. Mk 6:1-6   (Lk 4:16-30)

Despite the miraculous events just described telling of Jesus' incredible powers, his own home town rejects him with contempt and unbelief. [At this point in Lk's outline, Mk comes to the story of the Sending Out of the Twelve. Mk/Peter sees this event as the beginning of the most glorious period in Jesus' Galilee ministry. In his ironic, contrapuntal style, however, he will first interpose Mt's account of the contempt and unbelief still prevailing, despite everything, in Jesus' home town. Interrupting his use of Lk, Mk moves over to Mt to the end of the Parable Discourse (13:52) and relates the sad story of the hardness of heart in Jesus' own hometown.]

7. The Climax of Jesus' Ministry in Galilee. Mk 6:7-8:10

(Mt 9:35; 10:1-14) Sending Out of the Twelve. Mk 6:7-13 ⟶ Lk 9:1-6

Mk now begins describing the glorious final days in the region of Galilee and beyond, leading up to the Confession of Peter followed by the first warnings about Jesus' imminent death. [Mk moves back to Lk for this (and the next) story, working in details from Mt and adding features of his own (e.g., vs. 8). Noteworthy is Mk's version's exclusive mention of the activity of the Twelve, omitting any mention of Jesus' instructions to proclaim the Kingdom of God mentioned in both sources. Mk/Peter may have considered it a misleading concept to his Roman patrons.

Mt 14:1-2 — Herod's View of John. Mk 6:14-16 ⟶ Lk 9:7-9

Mk's contrapuntal style continues as he now harks back to the grim ending of John the Baptist, the "precursor" to Jesus. Mk dramatically relates the details of this brutal, decadent court, foreshadowing Jesus' own eventual doom. [Mk relies mostly on Lk's account, but continues on without the slightest pause to give Mt's version of the story of John's death, which Lk omitted. Like the Beelzebul Controversy, this is a vivid illustration of Mk's "zig zag" *within* a single story.]

Mt 14:3-12 ⟵ Death of John the Baptist. Mk 6:17-29

[Mt's spare account is vividly amplified by Peter/Mk.]

Mt 14:13-21 ⟵ Return of the Twelve, Feeding of the 5000
— Lk 9:10-17

In the sharpest possible contrast to the foregoing story, Mk next portrays Jesus gloriously reaching the high point of his ministry in Galilee, prior to the dramatic finale of the Passion Narrative itself. The disciples return with joyous tidings and then there is a miraculous feast for more than 5000 people on a hill looking out over the Sea of Galilee, hearkening forward to the Great Messianic Banquet in the Age to Come, forecasting the great Ingathering under Christ's banner. The story ends with a short summary (Mk 6:53-56) of the way in which droves of people came to Jesus for healing, and "all who touched him were cured." In Mk's outline, Jesus has advanced from triumph to triumph, despite the increasingly loud rumblings of thunder on the horizon. But now the whole key changes. The very next story in Mk 7 points toward the end by relating the first of a series of clashes with "the Pharisees." [Although Mk relies on Mt for the story of the 5000, he is also back in step with Lk's order again, and his account is a skillful blend of details from both narratives, with numerous additional "eye-witness" details.]

[From this point on, Mk is mostly in step with Mt's order.]

David L. DUNGAN

RESPONSE TO MULTI-STAGE HYPOTHESIS

I. The "Fundamental Principle"

The advocates of the Multi-Stage theory affirm that the Synoptic problem is complex and, therefore, requires a complex explanation. One may agree with the advocates of the Multi-Stage theories in saying that the Synoptic problem is complex and that it may, in fact, require a complex explanation. But (1) that explanation should be no more and no less complex than the literary data require and (2) simpler solutions to the problem should be tried first, as a matter of principle, and then, if necessary, excluded, before more complex solutions should be tried.

The advocates of the Multi-Stage theories contrast their position with that of the advocates of the Two-Gospel theory by noting that the Multi-Stage theories explain the relationships among the gospels as the result of some indirect literary dependence among the gospels whereas the other two theories (Two-Gospel and Two-Document) explain the relationships among the gospels as the result either of direct literary dependence among the canonical gospels (Two-Gospel) or the combination of direct literary dependence (Mt and Lk depend on Mk directly) and indirect literary dependence (Mt and Lk independently depend on "Q") (Two-Document theory).

The two fundamentally different presuppositions about the nature of the relationships among the gospels — that the relationships are direct or that the relationships are indirect — produce quite different results when the gospel texts are analyzed and have very different implications for how the whole discussion of the gospels may proceed.

For instance, the advocates of the Multi-Stage hypothesis make considerable use of arguments based upon shared language among the Synoptic evangelists for indicating the direction of literary dependence between any two of the three gospels. But, as Hans Herbert Stoldt has demonstrated with reference to the work of Holtzmann[1] who, like Boismard and his team, presupposed that the relationships among the gospels were indirect (1863) rather than direct (but cf. 1880)[2], it is

---

[1] Hans Herbert Stoldt, *Geschichte und Kritik der Markus-Hypothese* (Göttingen: Vandenhoeck & Ruprecht, 1977). ET: Donald L. Niewyk, *History and Criticism of the Marcan Hypothesis* (Macon, GA: Mercer University Press, 1980).

[2] Edward Simons, *Hat der dritte Evangelist den kanonischen Matthäus benutzt?* (Bonn,

impossible to isolate the linguistic characteristics of a document which is not extant. Therefore, if one cannot isolate the linguistic characteristics of nonexistent documents, one certainly cannot use such linguistic characteristics to indicate anything about the sequence and inter-relationships of extant documents which are only presupposed to include parts of such hypothetical sources. If an argument for solving the Synoptic problem which makes use of shared language is to have probative value, it must be an argument which presupposes a direct literary relationship among the Synoptic gospels from the outset.

For this reason, the members of this Two-Gospel research team would not want to be identified with one aspect of the work of Malcolm Lowe and David Flusser.[3] While there is much in their work which the Two-Gospel team could affirm, the presupposition that the gospels are indirectly related to one another is not one of the areas where such affirmation is possible.

As the paper by the advocates of the Multi-Stage hypothesis may suggest, the Two-Gospel hypothesis is, in this respect, closer to the Two-Document hypothesis than it is to the Multi-Stage hypothesis. In this way, it is the Two-Document hypothesis rather than the Multi-Stage theory which represents "the bridge" between the other two hypotheses. The Two-Gospel hypothesis presupposes no hypothetical sources to explain any of the agreements among the Synoptics which could be explained by direct literary dependence. The Two-Document Hypothesis presupposes one hypothetical source to explain some of the agreements among the Synoptics which could be explained by direct literary dependence (the so called "Q" material). But the Multi-Stage hypotheses presuppose many hypothetical sources to explain all of the agreements among the Synoptic Gospels which could be explained by direct literary dependence.

Like the advocates of the Multi-Stage hypothesis, however, the advocates of the Two-Gospel hypothesis believe it is important to consider all of the literary facts which present themselves for observation within the Synoptic gospels. For this reason, the authors of three doctoral dissertations produced at S.M.U. have attempted to make significant, even if not comprehensive, contributions to scholarly understanding of those literary features of the texts of the Synoptic

1880). Following his reading of this work H.J. Holtzmann gave up his previous belief in the independence of Matthew and Luke, as Farmer has noted *The Synoptic Problem: A Critical Analysis* (New York: Macmillan, 1964) 40.

[3] Malcolm Lowe and David Flusser, "Evidence Corroborating a Modified Proto-Matthean Synoptic Theory," *NTS* 29 (1983) 25-47.

gospels which may be said, in some ways, to be "characteristic" of one or more of these gospels. The dissertations produced by Dennis Tevis on the gospel of Matthew and by David Peabody on the gospel of Mark make use of methods for isolating some of the linguistic characteristics of those gospels (especially some "favorite or habitual expressions") which methods make no presuppositions about the sequence or inter-relationships of the Synoptic gospels. [4] The dissertation produced by F.J.G. Collison on Luke does, in fact, presuppose that Luke made use of Matthew as part of its method for isolating the linguistic characteristics of Luke. [5] However, whenever this presupposition would produce different results if Luke had used Mark as a source rather than Matthew these are duly noted. Collison's work, therefore, can be used with confidence both by advocates of Matthean priority and by advocates of Markan priority. Even those who advocate Lukan priority will find most of Collison's conclusions about the linguistic characteristics of Luke sustainable since his judgements about characteristic usages of Luke are made, in the first instance, on the basis of recurrent usage in passages which function compositionally within Luke's gospel, and these passages remain more or less constant regardless of one's source hypothesis.

With these three dissertations in hand, to be supplemented perhaps by comparative vocabulary studies and other studies which tend to focus on grammatical and syntactical features of these three gospels, New Testament scholars are now in a better position than in any previous time in the history of the discussion of the Synoptic problem to evaluate how the evidence based upon shared linguistic features weighs when the great bulk, if not all, of that type of evidence is taken into account.

It may be repeated here that a linguistic argument for solving the Synoptic problem has validity if, and only if, one presupposes that the relationships among the gospels were (1) literary and (2) direct, one extant gospel being directly dependent upon another. The advocates of the Multi-Stage hypotheses cannot legitimately appeal to such an argument since it is impossible to isolate the linguistic characteristics of any document which is not extant.

---

[4] Dennis Gordon Tevis, *An Analysis of Words and Phrases Characteristic of the Gospel of Matthew* (Ann Arbor, MI: University Microfilms International, 1983), David Barrett Peabody, *The Redactional Features of the Author of Mark: A Method Focusing on Recurrent Phraseology and Its Application* (Ann Arbor, MI: University Microfilms International, 1983); *Mark as Composer* (New Gospel Studies, 1; Macon, GA: Mercer University Press, 1987).

[5] Franklyn J.G. Collison, *The Linguistic Usages in the Gospel of Luke* (Ann Arbor, MI: University Microfilms International, 1979).

The history of the discussion of the Synoptic problem in the nine-teenth century will reveal that other procedures such as reconstructing a source for the Synoptic gospels from materials which they share and then attempting to isolate the linguistic characteristics of that source and then utilizing those characterics to prove both the existence of that source and the sequence and interrelationships among the Synoptic gospels result in what one might expect from such a procedure, hopelessly circular argumentation which proves nothing.

II. Justification of the fundamental principle

1. The advocates of the Two-Gospel hypothesis have no need to debate with the advocates of the Multi-Stage theory about the inade-quacies of the Two-Document hypothesis. We agree with the following:

a) The so-called "minor agreements" of Matthew and Luke against Mark within the material shared by all three Evangelists (especially when those agreements are taken together as a set within any given pericope and include both positive and negative agreements) remain the most important literary evidence against the view that Mt and Lk independently made use of Mark. We would add that if these "minor agreements" demonstrate that Mt and Lk were not independent of one another, then the need for "Q" is also obviated. If Mt and Lk stand in a relationship of direct literary dependence, this relationship would account not only for all of the "Markan" material but also for all of the so-called "Q" material as well.

b) The second weakness in the Two-Document theory cited by the advocates of the Multi-Stage theory is the difficulty in explaining the "minor doublets" in Mk. Professor Neirynck prefers the term "duality" to refer to this same characteristic of Mark's text, but his own research demonstrates that the term which would include all of the evidence he discusses should be "multiplicity." [6] There are, at times, more than two repetitions of language within a relatively short literary context in Mark. To label the phenomenon "duality" is misleading. "Duality" may have been chosen, perhaps like the term "Doublets" discussed below, by advocates of Markan priority simply for its rhetorical value in discounting arguments like the one marshalled by the advocates of the Multi-Stage theory on the basis of literary data like Mark 1:32/Matthew 8:16/Luke

---

[6] Frans Neirynck, *Duality in Mark: Contributions to the Study of Markan Redaction*, BETL 31 (Leuven: Leuven University Press, 1972, ²1988). See also Peabody's discussion of this work in *Redactional Features of Mark*, 26-29.

4:40. The advocates of the Two-Gospel hypothesis, however, as represented by this research team (unlike De Wette, Bleek,[7] and, now, the advocates of the Multi-Stage theories) would not marshall such evidence as proof of the validity of the Two-Gospel hypothesis. Such evidence is merely consistent with that hypothesis. We may grant Professor Neirynck the point that various types of repetitions of language are, in fact, characteristic of the literary style of the entire text of Mark, but it is not clear, at this stage of research, what import that fact may have for suggesting the direction of literary dependence between any two of the three Synoptic gospels.

It is clear, however, the Matthew and Luke were capable of utilizing similar "dualities" in contexts apart from a Markan parallel. Therefore, if Mt and Lk made use of Mark, there is no reason why they would have attempted to avoid these dualities in Mark when they were capable of using them elsewhere in their gospels apart from a Markan parallel. On the other hand, if such "dualisms" are characteristic of the text of Mark, and there can be little doubt of that in the light of Professor Neirynck's thorough analysis of the phenomenon, then it would be quite natural for the redactor of Mark's gospel who was responsible for these dualities, if he made use of Mt and Lk, to have combined two distinct but similar expressions from his two sources into a dualistic expression. But, again, such evidence in no way may be said to prove the validity of the Two-Gospel hypothesis. It is merely literary evidence which is consistent with that hypothesis.

c) The third weakness in the Two-Document hypothesis which is pointed out by the advocates of the Multi-Stage theories is the problem of the common omissions by Mt and Lk of certain pericopes from Mark (Mk 4:26-29; 7:32-36; and 8:22-26). Of course, the problem of omissions, if it is a problem, must be faced by advocates of all source hypotheses which accept some direct literary relationship among the gospels. This problem is minimized when Mark is placed first in the sequence of composition (Two-Document theory) and maximized when Mark is placed last in that sequence (Two-Gospel theory).

But the problem of omissions actually may be more of a problem for the piety of the literary critics approaching the texts of the Synoptic gospels than a problem to be explained by literary criticism.

[7] Wilhelm Martin Leberecht De Wette, *An Historico-Critical Introduction to the Canonical Books of the New Testament*, ET of the 5th improved and enlarged German edition by Frederick Frothingham (Boston: Crosby, Nichols, 1858); Friedrich Bleek, *Einleitung in das Neue Testament*, published posthumously in 1862; 2nd ed., revised by his son Johannes Friedrich Bleek, and ET by William Urwick (Edinburgh, 1869; 3rd ed., 1875, and 4th ed., 1886 revised by W. Mangold).

Since the texts which are under consideration are not only documents from the Hellenistic world but also sacred texts for a believing community, it is difficult for some critics approaching these texts to understand why this or that passage in Gospel A, being perceived as very valuable by the critic examining the texts of the gospels, could possibly have been omitted by Evangelist B, if that passage had appeared in his source.

But we know that making omissions from earlier sources was a standard practice of authors writing in a period roughly contemporary with that of the Synoptic evangelists. For instance, Plutarch says, regarding his comparison of the lives of Alexander and Julius Caesar:

> ...because of the number of their deeds to be treated I shall make no other preliminary statement than to beg my readers not to criticize me if I do not describe everything or narrate fully any of their celebrated exploits in each case, and if instead I curtail most of these. For I am writing biography, not history...[8]

A section from Aelius Aristides' preface to his *Panathenaic Oration* is also revealing.

> Then if the speech were about some other city, it would not be possible to omit the deeds which will have to be omitted, but it would have been enough to mention these alone. For they are the sort for which one would have searched; and many, if it were possible, would pay much to buy them as their own. But since it is equally difficult to choose what must be omitted and to discuss properly the best material, and since no one even in a simple narrative has ever recounted everything, but all speakers have had very much to say on behalf of this single city, moreover nearly more on behalf of it alone than on behalf of all the others together, a detailed account of each individual act is impossible, but it is necessary to omit most things, so that we may employ what is the greatest.[9]

Perhaps one will say that these authors from the Hellenistic period were not writing sacred texts and the Evangelists were. Therefore, one could claim that the literary procedures of the Evangelists would be different. Of course, it is impossible to know just how the Synoptic evangelists perceived their literary tasks, but, even assuming that they intended to write "Scripture," and intended to preserve "Tradition" fully, there is some evidence from an anonymous author from the Hellenistic period that he was quite willing to omit material from his sources even when he was writing a sacred text.

---

[8] As cited and translated by Roland Mushat Frye, "The Synoptic Problems and Analogies in Other Literatures," in *The Relationships among the Gospels: An Interdisciplinary Dialogue* (William O. Walker, ed.; San Antonio, TX: Trinity University Press, 1978) 274.

[9] Publius Aelius Aristides, "The Panathenaic Oration," § 90 (194D), ET by C.A. Behr, *Aristides I* (LCL 458; Cambridge: Harvard University Press, 1973) 72-73.

However, as soon as Thou recognized, O Master, that I was neglecting Thy divine book (*theia biblos*), I invoked Thy providence and, being filled by Thy divinity (*theiotes*) I eagerly hastened to the Heaven-sent prize of Thy narrative (*historia*). For I hope to make Thy intention widely known through my prophecy. In fact I have already written a plausible explanation of the story (*mythos*) of the creation of the world [by turning it into] natural concepts (*physiko logo*) closer to the truth.

Throughout the writing I added what was lacking and removed what was superfluous so that I wrote briefly an overly wordy narrative (*diegema*) and told once a repetitive story (*allattologos mythos*). Accordingly, O Master, I deem the book to have been finally completed according to Thy kindness and not according to my intention. A writing (*graphe*) such as this suits Thy divinity, O Asklepios, for Thou has disclosed it! Thou, greatest of Gods and Teacher, shalt be made known by the thanks of all people. For every gift of a votive offering or a sacrifice lasts only for the moment, and immediately perishes, while scripture (*graphe*) is an undying thanks (*athanatos charis*) since it rejuvenates the memory [of God's kindness] again and again. And every Greek tongue shall tell of Thy story (*historia*) and every Greek man shall worship Imouthes of Ptah. [10]

Of course one could also cite John 20:30 and/or John 21:25 as examples of Christian author(s) who omitted material from their sources.

Now Jesus did many other signs in the presence of the disciples which are not written in this book, but these are written that you may believe that Jesus is the Christ, the Son of God, and that believing you may have life in his name.

But there are also many other things which Jesus did; were every one of them to be written, I suppose that the world itself could not contain the books that would be written.

It would also appear that Papias was aware of some critics of Mark's gospel who apparently had accused him of making omissions and of making false statements, but Papias defended Mark's literary procedure: "...Mark did nothing wrong in thus writing down single points as he remembered them. For to one thing he gave attention, to leave out nothing of what he had heard and to make no false statements in them." [11]

It may be noted here that the problem of omissions implicit in the criticisms of Mark to which Papias responds requires some standard of comparison, some document(s?) which records what Mark allegedly has omitted. Since we know that Papias knew the gospel of Matthew, that

---

[10] As cited and translated by David R. Cartlidge and David L. Dungan, *Documents for the Study of the Gospels* (Philadelphia: Fortress, 1980) 124.

[11] Eusebius of Caesarea, *Ecclesiastical History* 3.39.15, ET by Kirsopp Lake (LCL 153; Cambridge: Harvard University Press, 1965) 296-297.

gospel may have been the standard which these critics of Mark had in mind. Eusebius' silence on Papias' statements about Luke, if he made any, makes a judgement about Mark's relationship to Luke, as perceived in this period, something which cannot be known.

Perhaps most to the point for advocates of the Two-Gospel hypothesis are the comments by Arrian in his preface to his life of Alexander. This text gives testimony to a literary procedure in antiquity not unlike that imagined for Mark on the Two-Gospel theory.

> Wherever Ptolemy the son of Lagos (cf. Matthew) and Aristoboulos the son of Aristoboulos (cf. Luke) have both written the same things concerning Alexander the son of Philip (cf. Jesus), these I (cf. Mark) have written as being completely true. But those things [they wrote] that are not the same, I chose [from the one or the other] those things which seemed to me more believable and, at the same time, more interesting.
> Many other writers have written things about Alexander, nor is there anyone about whom more discordant things are written. But to me Ptolemy and Aristoboulos seem more credible to use in my own account because Aristoboulos fought beside King Alexander [cf. Matthew, a disciple of Jesus] while Ptolemy besides fighting with him, was king later on, and for him to lie were even more shameful than for Aristoboulos... There are still other writings I have used, which contain things that seemed to me to be worth telling, and are not completely incredible [cf. Mark 4:26-29; 7:32-36 and 8:22-26].[12]

With respect to the problem (?) of Luke's omission of Matthew 14:22-16:12/Mark 6:45-8:26, one could imagine that Luke found this material either "less believable" or "less interesting" than the material he did choose to include (cf. Luke 9:51-18:14). Perhaps Luke recognized, as modern students of the gospels do, that Matthew 14:13-21, the Feeding of the Five Thousand, and Matthew 15:32-39, the Feeding of the Four Thousand, are variants of a single story. If this story took place once one could legitimately jump from one to the other and, presumably, not sacrifice anything of any historical value which fell in between (cf. Luke 1:1-4). And if one is going to omit one of the two feeding stories, then the passage which looks back upon the two feedings retrospectively can also be omitted (Mt 16:7-12). And, if the material which falls between the Feeding of the Four Thousand (Mt 15:32-39) and this retrospective passage (Mt 16:7-12) is to be recorded elsewhere in Luke (Mt 16:1-6; cf. Lk 11:16, 29; 12:1) then, when Luke begins to use Matthew again at the Confession at Caesarea Philippi (Mt 16:13-20/Lk 9:18-22) everything of historical value within Mt 14:22-16:12 would be preserved in Luke's gospel.

<hr>

[12] As cited and translated by David R. Cartlidge and David L. Dungan, *Documents*, 126.

But in principle, "omissions" need not be a problem requiring explanations at all. Perhaps advocates of the Multi-Stage theories perceive the fact that they can explain the growth of the Synoptic tradition in a way which constantly allows for incremental gain, i.e. such that omissions from the tradition were never made, to be a strength of their position. But, given what is known about actual literary procedures in antiquity it is unnecessary to imagine or to prefer any such procedure. As E.P. Sanders has demonstrated from some of the earliest Christian documents[13] and as Roland Mushat Frye has demonstrated from the known literary history of later documents, there is no canon of literary composition which would lead one to think that the gospel traditions would have grown unilaterally by means of incremental gain. In fact, Frye has shown that

> In terms of length, the argument that the greater length of an account evidences a later development holds true for stages in the work of a single author but not for redaction, by different authors. Digests typically and even by definition follow the prior establishment of the importance of longer works.
> 3. In terms of conflation, the procedure postulated for Mark in the Griesbach Hypothesis conforms closely to what can be seen wherever I have found a literary work in which conflation is demonstrable beyond a shadow of doubt. There are probably exceptions of which I am unaware, but the following characteristics are widespread enough to be regarded as highly typical: alternation between or among Vorlagen, condensation of overall or total length of the Vorlagen, frequent expansion within pericopes, and addition of lively details to provide a fresher and more circumstantial narrative. Here the conformity to general literary patterns that we find in the Griesbach explanation of Synoptic order is not only very impressive, but telling evidence in its favor.[14]

2. Alleged difficulties with the Two-Gospel Hypothesis have also been pointed out by the advocates of the Multi-Stage theory. Of course, the advocates of the Two-Gospel theory must debate with these.

"Major Doublets" in Matthew and Luke are avoided by Mark. It is difficult to understand just why for the advocates of the Multi-Stage theory (or the Two-Document Hypothesis for that matter, since precisely the same argument from doublets now appears in Neirynck's Position Paper!) the presence of doublets in the gospels of Matthew and Luke can be an argument in favor of the Two-Document hypothesis.

Advocates of the Two-Gospel hypothesis affirm some of the insights

---

[13] E.P. Sanders, *The Tendencies of the Synoptic Tradition* (SNTSMS 9; Cambridge University Press, 1969).

[14] Frye, "Synoptic Problems", 285.

of the form critics. For instance, members of this team do not doubt that traditions about Jesus probably circulated independently in many of the forms known from other Hellenistic literature, i.e. parables, chreiai, miracle stories, wisdom sayings, hymns, etc. And whatever use some of the canonical evangelists may have made of earlier gospels now also included in the canon we recognize that every one of these evangelists also had access to other traditional material (written and/or oral).

It is intrinsically probable that some traditions about Jesus were remembered, preserved and passed on with somewhat different word-ings by individuals or smaller groups within the larger fellowship of the early church. Doublets within any of the Synoptic gospels need represent nothing more and nothing less than two or more variants of a tradition going back to a single original. Again, once piety is overcome, it is unnecesary to imagine two actual feedings of the multitudes. These are easily explained as tradition variants. It may be noted here that this is one doublet that Mark's gospel contains and which calls into question the claims of the advocates of the Multi-Stage theory that Mark "carefully avoided major doublets which he found in Mt and in Lk." And what of the "triplets," the Passion Prediction passages which, in Luke, becomes a quadruplet (Lk 9:22; 9:43-45; 17:24-25; 18:31-34).

Like the "dualities" of Frans Neirynck, the term "doublet" may have more rhetorical value than descriptive value. The logion, "Let him hear who has ears to hear," also recurs in more than two contexts within the Synoptic gospels (Mt 11:15; Mt 13:9/Mk 4:9/Lk 8:8; Mk 4:23; Mt 13:43 and Lk 14:35).

The question of "doublets" within the Synoptic gospels clearly requires further research and that research needs to begin with a definition of the term.

The advocates of the Multi-Stage hypothesis have said that it is necessary to account for all of the literary facts which present them-selves for observation within the Synoptic gospels. Presumably this means that it is necessary to consider all of the relevant evidence within any particular category. If one does this for the "Doublets," laying aside for the moment the issue of defining the term, what does this evidence actually suggest?

Let us take the list of doublets within the Synoptic gospels as compiled by Sir John Hawkins in his classic work, *Horae Synopticae,* as normative.[15] And let us assume, with the advocates of the Multi-Stage

---

[15] John C. Hawkins, *Horae Synopticae: Contributions to the Study of the Synoptic Problem* (Oxford: Clarendon Press, [2]1909, reprint 1968) esp. 80-107.

theories, that the maximum amount of relevant evidence should be taken as supporting the Two-Document hypothesis. That is one should consider not only those cases where one instance of a doublet appears in Mt/Mk/Lk and the other appears in Mt/Lk but also those cases where one member appears in Mt/Mk and the other in Mt/Lk or where one member appears in Lk/Mk and the other in Lk/Mt as evidence in favor of the Two-Document hypothesis.

Hawkins lists a total of 32 different doublets within the Synoptic gospels, 22 in Matthew, 1 in Mark, 11 in Luke (but 3 of these also appear as doublets in Matthew and therefore were numbered in his 22) plus the logion, "He who has ears [to hear], let him hear" [22 + 1 + (11-3) + 1 = 32]. Among these 32 there are 12 instances which meet the criteria outlined above and which, therefore, potentially provide evidence in support of the Two-Document hypothesis.

Of course, this means that there are another 20 doublets [32-12 = 20] which do not meet these criteria and therefore do not support the Two-Document hypothesis and must, therefore, be explained by an appeal to some other hypothesis. In balance then, when all of the evidence from "Doublets" is taken into consideration, as the advocates of the Multi-Stage theory require, there is almost twice as much evidence [20/12] in support of some other hypothesis as there is in support of the Two-Document hypothesis, assuming, of course that there is a valid argument for Markan priority from the appearance of Doublets and the advocates of the Two-Gospel hypothesis are doubtful about that.

3. The advocates of the Multi-Stage hypotheses claim that, since neither the Two-Document nor the Two-Gospel hypothesis is adequate, it is necessary to appeal to hypothetical documents to explain the literary data within the Synoptics. They say this is necessary because no one of the Synoptics always is the most primitive when compared to the two others. Rather, each one of the three Synoptics is sometimes primitive and sometimes secondary when compared with the other two.

The advocates of the Multi-Stage theories claim that the account of the Healing of the Leper, at least when the canonical texts are compared, leaving aside Egerton 2, demonstrates the validity of the Two-Gospel hypothesis. The textual analysis of this passage (below, 254-258) confirms this claim. The advocates of the Two-Gospel hypothesis are glad to accept this evidence in support of their hypothesis and leave it to the advocates of the Two-Document hypothesis to rebut the claims made about this text by the advocates of the Multi-Stage theories.

III. Extra-Synoptic Testimony

1. The Patristic Quotations. In their work with the Patristic quotations, the advocates of the Multi-Stage theories have demonstrated the existence of variants within the gospel manuscript tradition. But no one challenges that fact. What they have not demonstrated is that such data require the existence of earlier gospel redactions not now extant to explain the evidence.

2. The non-canonical gospels. The advocates of the Multi-Stage theories claim that texts other than that of Egerton 2 relating to the Healing of the Leper could be used to reconstitute the history of the gospel redactions. If so, let it be done. Until it is, this must be considered an empty claim.

3. The ancient testimonies. We reserve our comments on the Patristic evidence for the program segment of the conference relating to it.

IV. The First Account of the Multiplication of the Loaves

In order to understand the literary history of this section of the Synoptic gospels from the perspective of the Two-Gospel hypothesis, it is necessary first to reconstruct Luke's redaction of Matthew and then to consider Mark's use of both Matthew and Luke.

Luke has introduced his own redactional concerns into the introduction to the Feeding of the Five Thousand in a number of ways.

First, Luke introduces the return of the apostles in Luke 9:10 whom he had depicted as being sent out at 9:1-6. Only the story of Herod's response to what he had heard about Jesus and the comparison of Jesus with John the Baptist, or Elijah or "one of the prophets of old" [Lk 9:7-9; cf. Lk 9:18] intervenes between the sending of the twelve [Lk 9:6] and their return [Lk 9:10]. This literary structure of the sending and return of disciples is repeated in Luke 10:1, 17 and represents Lukan redaction.

The uses of ὑποστρέφω and ἀπόστολος in the statement of the return of the apostles in the introduction of the Feeding of the Five Thousand can be traced to Luke's hand [see Collison 67, 168]. Διηγεῖσθαι may also be Lukan [Mk 5:16; Mk 9:9; Lk 8:39; 9:10; Acts 8:33; 9:27; 12:17, and Hebrews 11:32 are all the NT occurrences of this word. There are no usages shared by Luke and Mark.]

In addition to providing this general setting, Luke, on the Two-Gospel hypothesis, has altered Matthew's locale for the feeding from "a desert place" [Mt 14:14] which Jesus reaches "in a boat" to "a city called Bethsaida." The phrasing of this change also reflects Luke's style [Collison 179].

Once this change of locale was made by Luke, other omissions from the text of Matthew were necessitated. Since the locale is now "in a city called Bethsaida," it is not appropriate to have crowds follow Jesus "on foot, from the cities." Thus, Luke omits these words from Matthew [14:13; cf. Lk 9:11].

The detail of "pity upon the crowd" was probably part of the earliest tradition since this detail is found both in the Feeding of the Five Thousand [Mt 14:14/Mk 6:34] and in the tradition variant, the Feeding of the Four Thousand [Mt 15:32/Mk 8:2]. But this detail might also reflect Matthean redaction which is borrowed by Mark two of the three times it occurs in Matthew [Mt 9:36; Mt 14:14/Mk 6:34; Mt 15:32/Mk 8:2]. In fact the language of Mark 6:34 seems to reflect a conflation of Matthew 9:36 with the parallel in Matthew 14:14.

While both Matthew and Mark, perhaps in dependence upon Matthew, have Jesus express compassion upon the crowd(s) on more than one occasion, Luke seems to reserve this compassion as an expression for individuals [the widow at Nain (Lk 7:13), the man who was robbed, stripped, and beaten on the road to Jericho (Lk 10:33, cf. v. 30) and the Prodigal Son (Lk 15:20)]. This may explain Luke's omission of this general expression of compassion in his version of the one Feeding he records [Lk 9:10-17].

When Mark came to this story in his sources, Matthew [14:13-21] and Luke [9:13-17], since he had followed Luke's redactional procedure in sending out the twelve [Mk 6:7-13/Lk 9:1-6 cf. Mt 10:1,5] and Luke's procedure of using Herod's response to Jesus to allow for time to intervene between the sending of the twelve and their return [Mk 6:14-16/Lk 9:7-9 cf. Mt 14:1-2], he continues to follow Luke's redaction in then recording the return of the apostles [Mk 6:30/Lk 9:10] but only after inserting the story of John's death from Matthew [Mt 14:3-12/Mk 6:17-29] which he found in the parallel to the Lukan material which he had taken as his basic guide in this section of his gospel [Lk 9:1-6/Mk 6:7-13; Lk 9:7-9/Mk 6:14-16/Mt 14:1-2; Mt 14:3-12/Mk 6:17-29; Lk 9:10-17/Mk 6:30-44/Mt 14:13-21]. The insertion of this material from Matthew at this point would allow the reader of Mark's gospel to imagine a longer passage of time between the sending out and the return of the disciples than that provided by Luke's very brief interlude [Lk 9:7-9].

When Mark next comes to the actual setting for the Feeding of the

Five Thousand, he is confronted by the discrepancy between Matthew's "desert place" and Luke's "city called Bethsaida." Since Luke's setting is less appropriate for the feeding since food would be readily available in a city, Mark follows Matthew, including the detail of the journey "in the boat into the desert place." The detail of the crowds following "on foot from the cities," which was inappropriate for Luke, is also adopted by Mark since he has chosen Matthew's setting for the Feeding in contrast to Luke.

As noted above, the detail of "pity upon the crowd" could be part of the earliest tradition. Or this evidence could actually suggest Mark's literary dependence upon Matthew.

There is, in summary, nothing in this section of the Synoptic gospels which cannot be easily explained on the basis of the Two-Gospel hypothesis and some of the evidence actually helps to demonstrate the validity of that hypothesis.

David B. PEABODY

THÉORIE DES NIVEAUX MULTIPLES

I. Son principe fondamental

Contrairement aux deux groupes concurrents qui rassemblent, d'une part les défenseurs de la théorie des Deux Sources, d'autre part les défenseurs de la théorie des Deux Évangiles (Griesbach *redivivus*), le groupe C n'est pas homogène; il englobe des théories qui ne se rejoignent qu'en partie. Ces théories, certes, sont unies par un principe fondamental, mais qui peut être appliqué selon des modalités différentes. Il vaudrait donc mieux parler de "théories (au pluriel) des Niveaux Multiples". Pour mieux préciser leur principe fondamental commun et ce qu'il a d'original, rappelons brièvement les principes sur lesquels se fondent la théorie des Deux Évangiles et celle des Deux Sources.

La théorie des Deux Évangiles est celle qui se présente sous la forme la plus simple: Matthieu est l'évangile premier, fondamental; Luc dépend de Matthieu; Marc dépend à la fois de Matthieu et de Luc. Si Mc est plus court que ses sources, c'est qu'il les a abrégées. Notons un point essentiel: les rapports de dépendance entre les trois Synoptiques sont envisagés exclusivement au niveau de leur rédaction *actuelle*; ces rapports peuvent et doivent s'expliquer sans faire appel à quelque source hypothétique, dont par ailleurs nous ne posséderions plus aucune attestation directe. La théorie des Deux Sources est plus complexe puisqu'elle admet l'existence d'une source hypothétique, Q, dont proviendraient les matériaux communs à Mt et à Lc, ignorés de Mc. Mais lorsqu'il s'agit des matériaux communs aux trois Synoptiques, elle rejoint la théorie des Deux Évangiles pour admettre que les rapports entre Mt, Mc et Lc peuvent et doivent s'expliquer au niveau de leur rédaction *actuelle*. Elle s'en sépare toutefois radicalement en affirmant la priorité de Mc, dont dépendraient Mt et Lc. Ces deux derniers évangiles seraient indépendants l'un de l'autre.

Les diverses théories des Niveaux Multiples ont en commun le principe fondamental suivant, par lequel elles se distinguent de la théorie des Deux Évangiles et de la théorie des Deux Sources: même lorsqu'il s'agit des matériaux communs aux trois Synoptiques, les rapports entre ces évangiles doivent s'expliquer, non par dépendance directe, mais en faisant appel à des sources hypothétiques plus anciennes dont ils dépendent. Par exemple, les contacts littéraires entre Mt et Mc devraient s'expliquer, non par dépendance directe de Mt par rapport à Mc (Deux Sources) ni de Mc par rapport à Mt (Deux Évangiles), mais par dépendance envers une ou plusieurs sources hypothétiques qui pourraient être, soit un proto-Matthieu, soit un proto-Marc, soit des documents plus anonymes. Le problème synoptique est complexe; il ne peut être résolu que par une solution complexe. La théorie des Deux Sources comme celle des Deux Évangiles sont trop simples pour rendre compte de *tous* les faits littéraires qui se présentent à l'observation. Il est trop simple d'affirmer la priorité absolue de Mc par rapport à Mt et à Lc; il est trop simple d'affirmer la priorité absolue de Mt par rapport à Lc et à Mc. La priorité devra être donnée tantôt à Mt, tantôt à Mc, voire même à Lc, selon que l'un ou l'autre de ces évangiles sera resté plus fidèle que les autres à leurs sources communes.

Remarquons d'ailleurs que certains partisans, soit de la théorie des Deux Sources, soit de la théorie de Griesbach, ont amorcé un mouvement dans le sens que nous préconisons. Pour rendre compte des accords Mt/Lc contre Mc, dans les sections qu'ils ont en commun, nombre d'adeptes de la théorie des Deux Sources, dont Bultmann, ont été contraints d'admettre que Mt et Lc dépendraient, non du Mc actuel, mais d'une forme plus ancienne: proto-Marc ou Ur-Markus. Ils ont donc reconnu que, sous sa forme radicale, la théorie des Deux Sources était trop simple pour rendre compte de tous les faits littéraires présentés par les Synoptiques; ils ont dû faire appel à une source hypothétique dont nous n'avons plus aucune attestation directe. De même, le professeur Flusser,[1] favorable à une solution qui donne la priorité à l'évangile de Matthieu (théorie de Griesbach), admet que Mc et Lc dépendraient, non du Mt actuel, mais d'une forme plus archaïque, en fait un Mt écrit en hébreu puis traduit en grec.[2] En schématisant ces deux tendances, on obtiendrait les relations suivantes, à ne considérer que les matériaux communs aux trois Synoptiques:

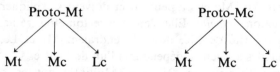

Ces deux schémas ne sont pas inconciliables. Ils pourraient se compléter en se juxtaposant, ce qui donnerait une des formes possibles des théories des Niveaux Multiples:

---

[1] M. Lowe and D. Flusser, "Evidence Corroborating a Modified Proto-Matthean Synoptic Theory", *NTS* 29 (1983) 25-47.

[2] Flusser admet aussi une influence de Marc et de Luc sur la rédaction actuelle de Matthieu.

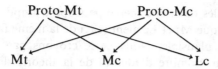

Ce schéma n'est que théorique. On pourra le simplifier si l'on juge superflue l'une ou l'autre des relations entre les Synoptiques et leurs sources. On pourra en revanche le compléter si d'autres relations s'avèrent nécessaires: existence éventuelle d'un Proto-Luc, possibilité de remonter à des documents plus anciens que le proto-Mt ou le Proto-Mc. Certains enfin pourront prendre leurs distances à l'égard des dénominations "Proto-Mc" et "Proto-Mt".

II. Justification du principe fondamental

Il se trouve que les théories des Niveaux Multiples ont la possibilité de concilier, dans une certaine mesure, les exigences contradictoires de la théorie des Deux Sources et de la théorie des Deux Évangiles. Cela tient au fait qu'elles sont beaucoup plus souples et que, en raison même de leur souplesse, elles peuvent rendre compte de faits littéraires en apparence contradictoires. Mais il ne faudrait pas en conclure qu'elles ont été élaborées *afin de* concilier deux théories concurrentes. La nécessité de recourir à des sources hypothétiques dont dépendraient nos trois Synoptiques découle d'une observation attentive des textes et d'une volonté de tenir compte de *tous* les faits littéraires qu'ils présentent. C'est ce qu'il nous faut expliquer maintenant. Nous le ferons en indiquant les faits littéraires que, à notre avis, la théorie des Deux Sources et la théorie des Deux Évangiles sont incapables de justifier; en évoquant aussi les faits littéraires positifs qui invitent à remonter plus haut que les Synoptiques sous leur forme actuelle.

1. Parlons d'abord de la théorie des Deux Sources. Une de ses principales faiblesses consiste dans son incapacité à rendre compte de façon plausible des accords mineurs Mt/Lc contre Mc.[3] Puisque Mt et Lc dépendent de Mc, puisque Mt et Lc sont indépendants l'un de l'autre, il faut expliquer comment ils ont pu se mettre d'accord contre Mc. Les arguments que l'on invoque doivent avoir valeur probante, dans chaque cas, à la fois pour Mt *et* pour Lc. Par ailleurs, ils doivent avoir une telle valeur contraignante que, si les accords Mt/Lc contre

---

[3] F. Neirynck, *The Minor Agreements of Matthew and Luke against Mark* (BETL 37; Leuven, 1974).

Mc sont accumulés dans une même péricope d'amplitude restreinte, la probabilité pour que Mt et Lc aient réagi de la même façon, à x reprises différentes, reste plausible. Nous ne le croyons pas. Rappelons que, pour cette raison, nombre d'adeptes de la théorie des Deux Sources ont été contraints de recourir à l'hypothèse d'un Ur-Markus dont dépendraient Mt et Lc, et que le Mc actuel aurait quelque peu modifié. Notons qu'il n'y a pas de problème, ici, pour la théorie des Deux Évangiles puisqu'elle admet une dépendance directe de Lc par rapport à Mt. Pour les partisans des théories des Niveaux Multiples, les accords Mt/Lc contre Mc pourront s'expliquer par référence à une source commune qui pourrait être, soit un Proto-Mt, soit un Proto-Mc, soit un document plus anonyme.

Une autre faiblesse de la théorie des Deux Sources est la difficulté qu'elle a de justifier les doublets mineurs de Mc. Par "doublet mineur" nous entendons la convergence chez Mc d'expressions plus ou moins analogues qui sont attestées à l'état simple, d'une part chez Mt, d'autre part chez Lc.[4] L'un des cas les plus connus est celui de Mc 1:32 où se lit la formule *opsias de genomenēs hote edysen ho hēlios*, tandis que l'on a simplement *opsias de genomenēs* dans Mt et *dynontos de tou hēliou* dans Lc. De tels doublets mineurs sont très fréquents chez Mc. Dira-t-on, avec la théorie des Deux Sources, que Mc avait un style naturellement redondant et que Mt et Lc l'ont simplifié en choisissant, comme par hasard, chacun la formule que l'autre laissait tomber? Il est beaucoup plus normal de supposer, soit que Mc fusionne les textes de Mt et de Lc (Deux Évangiles), soit que Mc fusionne les textes de deux sources différentes, l'une utilisée par Mt/Mc, l'autre par Lc/Mc. Dans le cas que nous avons cité plus haut, un indice stylistique rend spécialement difficile la solution proposée par la théorie des Deux Sources: aussi bien Mt que Mc ont une liaison par *de*, ce qui correspond au style de Mt (14:15,23; 20:8; 26:20; 27:57) et non à celui de Mc qui préfère la liaison par *kai* (6:47; 14:17; 27:57; cf. 4:35).

Une autre faiblesse de la théorie des Deux Sources est la difficulté qu'elle a d'expliquer pourquoi Mt et Lc, d'un commun accord, auraient éliminé certaines péricopes qu'ils lisaient dans Mc, comme la parabole de la semence qui croît toute seule (Mc 4:26-29), la guérison du sourd-bègue (7:32-36) et celle de l'aveugle de Bethsaïde (8:22-26). Difficulté encore d'expliquer pourquoi Lc aurait omis la longue section marcienne qui va de la marche sur les eaux à l'épisode des pains oubliés (Mc 6:45

---

[4] F. Neirynck, *Duality in Mark. Contributions to the Study of the Markan Redaction* (BETL 31; Leuven, 1972, ²1988). – P. Rolland, "Marc, première harmonie évangélique?", *RB* 90 (1983) 23-79.

à 8:21). Lc aura pu vouloir éviter le doublet des deux récits de multiplication des pains; mais pourquoi aurait-il omis tous les autres épisodes? Cette seconde difficulté doit embarrasser aussi la théorie des Deux Évangiles puisque Mt offre la même séquence que Mc:

Nous pensons donc que les théories des Niveaux Multiples peuvent rendre compte de certains faits littéraires que la théorie des Deux Sources est incapable de justifier. Sur ces points, elles se sentent mieux en harmonie avec la théorie des Deux Évangiles.

2. Mais la théorie des Deux Évangiles souffre elle aussi de faiblesses congénitales. Signalons d'abord le problème de l'existence de doublets majeurs dans les Synoptiques, c'est-à-dire de sections, le plus souvent des paroles du Christ, qui sont attestées sous deux formes plus ou moins différentes. Le doublet est parfait lorsque l'une des formes est attestée par Mt, Mc et Lc; l'autre forme par Mt et Lc seulement. Mais il faut tenir compte aussi des cas où l'une des formes du doublet fut supprimée soit par Lc, soit par Mt, ce qui donne comme témoins des deux formes du doublet: tantôt Mt/Mc et Mt/Lc, tantôt Lc/Mc et Lc/Mt. Dans tous ces cas, Mc n'atteste qu'une des formes du doublet tandis que l'autre est connue de Mt et de Lc. La théorie des Deux Évangiles n'explique pas cette présence de doublets dans les Synoptiques. Bien plus, elle se trouve en contradiction avec elle-même. D'une part, en effet, elle nous montre Mc accumulant les doublets mineurs, fusionnant les expressions analogues qu'il lisait soit dans Mt soit dans Lc (cf. *supra*, à propos de la théorie des Deux Sources), et d'autre part elle pense que Mc aurait soigneusement évité les doublets majeurs qu'il trouvait dans Mt et dans Lc. Avouons que ce n'est pas très logique! Ici, la théorie des Deux Sources est mieux inspirée en admettant que les doublets proviennent de deux sources différentes dont l'une (Q) était ignorée de Mc. Tout en admettant cette position de principe, les théories des Niveaux Multiples diront que la première source n'était pas Mc lui-même, mais un document plus ancien connu des trois Synoptiques. Il restera d'ailleurs à préciser la nature et l'homogénéité de la fameuse source Q. Sur ce point, les théories des Niveaux Multiples restent ouvertes. Notons en passant que les matériaux communs à Mt/Lc et ignorés de Mc, attribués couramment à la source Q, se présentent sous deux formes très différentes. Tantôt, les textes sont quasi identiques dans Mt et dans Lc; tantôt ils revêtent une forme très différenciée. La même source Q aurait-elle été utilisée de façon si peu homogène par Mt et par Lc? Il est probablement trop simple d'attribuer à la même source Q *tous* les matériaux de la double tradition (Mt/Lc).

Une autre faiblesse de la théorie des Deux Évangiles est la difficulté qu'elle a d'expliquer pourquoi Mc aurait volontairement omis tant de matériaux qu'il lisait dans ses deux sources: Mt et Lc. Prétendre que Mc l'aurait fait parce qu'il voulait s'attacher aux récits plus qu'aux paroles de Jésus est une solution boiteuse. D'une part, en effet, Mc retient un certain nombre de paroles de Jésus; pourquoi alors aurait-il volontairement omis le discours inaugural du Christ, ou n'en aurait-il pas retenu au moins l'essentiel? Par ailleurs, dans la perspective de la théorie des Deux Évangiles, il aurait omis aussi un certain nombre de récits attestés par Mt et par Lc. Encore une fois, pourquoi toutes ces omissions? Il est beaucoup plus plausible d'admettre, avec la théorie des Deux Sources, que Mc n'a pas connu ces matériaux communs à Mt/Lc. On pourra dire aussi que, même si Mc les a connus, ils ne se trouvaient pas dans sa source principale, le Proto-Mc, et qu'il n'a pas jugé opportun de modifier par trop la structure fondamentale de sa source. Sur ce point précis, les théories des Niveaux Multiples pourront proposer des hypothèses différentes.

Citons, à titre d'exemple, un autre cas où il semble difficile de faire dépendre les autres Synoptiques de Mt. Lorsqu'il raconte les événements qui tournent autour de la résurrection de Jésus, Mt met en œuvre une série de thèmes qui étaient courants dans la littérature hellénistique à propos des délivrances miraculeuses: précautions prises par les opposants pour garder la prison (cf. Mt 27:66), la porte de la prison s'ouvre d'elle-même, ou sur l'intervention d'un messager divin, le tout étant accompagné d'un tremblement de terre et d'une grande lumière (cf. Mt 28:1-4), conséquence du miracle pour les opposants (Mt 28:11-15).[5] Lc connaît parfaitement ce schéma et le met en œuvre dans les Actes, surtout en 12:1-23 à propos de Pierre. Par ailleurs, toujours dans les Actes, Lc s'attache à mettre en parallèle le destin des apôtres et celui de Jésus. Dans ces conditions, est-il vraisemblable que dans son propre récit de résurrection de Jésus, il ait systématiquement éliminé à peu près tous les détails matthéens qui évoquent le schéma hellénistique traditionnel? On pourrait apporter bien d'autres exemples analogues.

La théorie des Deux Évangiles, en donnant la priorité absolue à l'évangile de Mt, ferme les yeux sur les très nombreux cas où cet évangile apparaît secondaire par rapport aux deux autres Synoptiques; nous allons revenir sur ce point dans la section suivante.

3. Nous venons de voir que, pour certaines options essentielles, les

---

[5] R. Kratz, *Auferweckung als Befreiung. Eine Studie zur Passions- und Auferstehungs- theologie des Matthäus* (Stuttgart, KBW, 1973).

théories des Niveaux Multiples se rapprochaient: tantôt de la théorie des Deux Évangiles contre celle des Deux Sources, tantôt de la théorie des Deux Sources contre celle des Deux Évangiles. D'une façon plus positive, disons pour quelles raisons il nous semble *nécessaire* de recourir à l'existence de documents hypothétiques dont dépendraient les trois Synoptiques, même lorsqu'il s'agit des sections communes à Mt, Mc et Lc.

a) Une première raison est que chacun des trois Synoptiques offre, par rapport aux deux autres, des traits tantôt primitifs, tantôt secondaires. On ne peut donc donner une priorité absolue ni à Mt, ni à Mc, ni bien entendu à Lc. Pour déterminer quels sont les traits primitifs et les traits secondaires, les théories des Niveaux Multiples n'ont pas de recette spéciale; elles demandent simplement que l'on ne cherche pas à les minimiser, à les ignorer ou à les nier lorsqu'ils ne s'accordent pas avec telle théorie adoptée. A ce point de vue, les théories des Niveaux Multiples sont bien placées puisqu'elles sont prêtes à reconnaître ces notes primitives ou secondaires dans tous les Synoptiques, même dans Lc. Pour illustrer ce principe, nous nous bornerons à donner quelques exemples tirés de l'évangile de Mt.

Une tradition très ancienne, et sur laquelle nous aurons à revenir plus loin, affirme que l'évangile de Mt est le premier en date et qu'il fut écrit en hébreu. Or l'évangile grec de Mt est celui qui, dans bien des cas, permet les meilleurs rétroversions en hébreu parce que la structure de ses phrases est de forme plus hébraïque que grecque. Ce point fut récemment mis en évidence par le professeur Flusser et par Philippe Rolland pour les épisodes: guérison du fils du centurion (Mt 8:5-10, 13), guérison de l'homme à la main desséchée (Mt 12:9-13), opinion d'Hérode sur Jésus (Mt 14:1-2), Jésus dit pourquoi il parle en paraboles (Mt 13:10-11a, 13),[6] discussion sur le jeûne (Mt 9:14-17).[7] Dans tous ces récits, il est impossible de faire dépendre Mt de Mc; s'il y a dépendance, c'est de Mc par rapport à Mt, ou plus probablement par rapport à une forme plus ancienne de Mt.

Voyons de plus près l'épisode où Hérode donne son opinion sur Jésus. Le récit matthéen, de facture très hébraïque (sauf pour la fin du v. 2) comme l'a fait remarquer le professeur Flusser, est des plus simples: Hérode pense que Jésus est Jean-Baptiste ressuscité. Le récit de Mc au contraire est complexe: il contient le même thème que celui de

---

[6] D. Flusser, article cité note 1.

[7] P. Rolland, "Les prédécesseurs de Marc. Les sources présynoptiques de Mc, II, 18-22 et parallèles", *RB* 89 (1982) 370-405.

Mt (Mc 6:16), mais aussi tout un développement sur l'opinion que les gens ont de Jésus (6:14b-15) qui a son équivalent dans le récit de la confession de Pierre à Césarée. Mais il est clair que Mc fusionne deux récits d'origine différente, comme l'indique la *Wiederaufnahme: kai ekousen ... akousas de.* Ici encore, le récit de Mt est certainement plus primitif que celui de Mc.[8]

Mais prenons le passage dans lequel Jésus explique pourquoi il parle en paraboles (Mt 13:10-15). Il est clair que le v. 12, contenant le logion de Jésus "Car quiconque a, il lui sera donné", est une addition matthéenne tardive; ce logion se lit dans un autre contexte en Mc/Lc et Mt l'a inséré ici en raison du verbe commun "donner". Par ailleurs, dans les trois Synoptiques, la suite du texte contient une citation *approximative* de Is 6:9-10. Mt, et lui seul, continue en redonnant une citation du même texte d'Isaïe, *littérale* cette fois et faite d'après la Septante, citation qu'il introduit par la formule "Et est accomplie pour eux la prophétie d'Isaïe disant..." Dans ce cas encore, il est clair que cette citation littérale d'Isaïe ne peut pas être primitive. Pour les deux points que nous venons de signaler, le texte de Mt est plus tardif que ceux de Mc et de Lc; il ne peut pas être la source de Lc et de Mc.

J.A.T. Robinson, reprenant une réflexion de Harnack, a donc raison d'écrire: "Matthew could therefore in a real sense turn out to be both the earliest and the latest of the synoptists". Mais ce phénomène est impossible à justifier si l'on se refuse à faire appel à des documents plus anciens pour expliquer les rapports entre les Synoptiques; leurs rapports mutuels ne peuvent s'expliquer au niveau des rédactions actuelles.

b) Prenons le problème par un autre biais, celui des caractéristiques stylistiques et théologiques. De ce point de vue encore les rapports entre les Synoptiques ne sont pas constants. On constatera tantôt une influence de Mt sur Mc/Lc, tantôt une influence de Mc ou même de Lc sur Mt. Prenons par exemple le récit de la guérison du lépreux (Mt 8:1-4 et par.).[9] Dans les trois Synoptiques, Jésus guérit le lépreux en le touchant, après avoir étendu la main; mais ce geste et ce mode de guérison sont typiquement matthéens. Jésus donne ensuite une consigne de silence qui, dans Mc comme dans Mt, est exprimée sous une forme matthéenne et non marcienne. On devrait donc admettre que les récits de Mc et de Lc dépendent de celui de Mt, en accord avec la théorie des Deux Évangiles.

---

[8] P. Benoit et M.-É. Boismard, *Synopse des quatre évangiles en français*, Tome II: *Commentaire*, par M.-É. Boismard avec la collaboration de A. Lamouille et P. Sandevoir (Paris, Cerf, 1972) 216-218. C'est aussi la position de D. Flusser, dans l'article cité note 1.

[9] Voir en Appendice la discussion de ce texte.

Mais reportons-nous au contraire à la formule qui, en Mt 11:16, introduit la parabole des enfants qui jouent sur une place: *tini de homoiôsô ... homoia estin*. Elle a son équivalent exact dans le parallèle de Lc 7:31: *tini oun homoiôsô ... homoioi eisin*. Or une telle formule ne se lit nulle part ailleurs chez Mt, malgré le grand nombre de paraboles qu'il nous a transmises. Elle est au contraire bien attestée en Lc 13:18-21, au début des paraboles jumelles du grain de sénevé et du levain, tandis que Mt n'a conservé que la seconde partie de la formule: *homoia estin*. On est en droit de conclure que, dans tous ces textes, Lc est plus primitif que Mt. Il est probable que tous deux dépendent d'une source commune, comme l'admet la théorie des Deux Sources.

Prenons un autre exemple qui met en cause Mc et Mt. Dans Mc, un avertissement solennel donné par Jésus est introduit régulièrement par l'impératif *blepete* (4:24; 8:15; 12:38; 13:5,9,23,33) tandis que Mt préfère *prosechete* (6:1; 7:15; 10:17; 16:6,11; opposer Mt à Mc pour les trois derniers textes). On est alors en droit de conclure que si, en 24:4, Mt emploie *blepete*, c'est par influence marcienne.

Nos conclusions précédentes sont encore confirmées: pour expliquer les rapports entre les Synoptiques, il est nécessaire de faire appel à des documents plus anciens, sous peine de se heurter à des difficultés insurmontables.

III. Témoignages extra-Synoptiques

Voyons maintenant dans quelle mesure les témoignages extra-Synoptiques peuvent favoriser les théories des Niveaux Multiples. Nous allons examiner successivement: les citations patristiques anciennes, les évangiles non canoniques, enfin les témoignages anciens concernant la composition des évangiles.

1. *Les citations patristiques.*

Nous ne donnerons que deux exemples pour illustrer comment se pose le problème. La parole du Christ rapportée en Mt 5:37 nous a été transmise sous deux formes différentes:
— ἔστω δὲ ὁ λόγος ὑμῶν ναὶ ναί, οὒ οὔ
— ἔστω δὲ ὑμῶν τὸ ναὶ ναὶ καὶ τὸ οὒ οὔ
La première forme est celle qui se lit en Mt 5:37 au témoignage de presque tous les manuscrits; seul le Koridethi donne quelques échos de la seconde forme. La seconde forme est attestée par Justin, Clément

d'Alexandrie, les Homélies Clémentines et encore Épiphane, qui tous se réfèrent à l'évangile; mais elle était connue de l'auteur de l'épître de Jacques (5:12) et même de Paul en 2 Cor 1:17. On est en droit de conclure que Justin et les autres ont connu une forme de l'évangile de Matthieu différente de celle que nous avons maintenant.

Reportons-nous alors à la citation de Mt 5:16 que Justin donne dans le même passage de sa première Apologie. Voici à la suite le texte de Mt et celui de Justin:

— οὕτως λαμψάτω τὸ φῶς ὑμῶν ἔμπροσθεν τῶν ἀνθρώπων ὅπως ἴδωσιν ὑμῶν τὰ καλὰ ἔργα καὶ δοξάσωσιν τὸν πατέρα ὑμῶν τὸν ἐν τοῖς οὐρανοῖς

— λαμψάτω δὲ ὑμῶν τὰ καλὰ ἔργα ἔμπροσθεν τῶν ἀνθρώπων ἵνα βλέποντες θαυμάζωσιν τὸν πατέρα ὑμῶν τὸν ἐν τοῖς οὐρανοῖς

Au moins pour la première partie de la citation, cette forme de texte est connue aussi de Clément d'Alexandrie et d'Origène. Ne proviendrait-elle pas d'un état plus ancien de l'évangile de Mt dans lequel le v. 16 suivait immédiatement le v. 14a, sans le logion du v. 15 que Mc et Lc citent dans un tout autre contexte?

Les citations patristiques nous permettraient donc de constater que l'évangile de Mt a existé sous plusieurs formes grecques. Il serait intéressant de pouvoir faire la même expérience à propos des citations de l'évangile de Mc; mais ce n'est guère possible étant donné la rareté de ces citations chez les auteurs anciens.

2. *Les évangiles non canoniques.*

Certains auteurs ecclésiastiques anciens, comme Clément d'Alexandrie, Origène, Eusèbe de Césarée, Épiphane, Jérôme, attestent qu'il a existé de nombreux évangiles aujourd'hui perdus: l'évangile des Hébreux, celui des Nazaréens, celui des Ébionites, dont ils nous ont conservé de rares citations. Le papyrus Egerton 2, écrit vers 125, contient des passages évangéliques qui recoupent les récits synoptiques ou sont propres à ce document. Mentionnons encore l'évangile de Thomas, dont nous n'avons plus qu'une traduction copte et quelques fragments grecs. Tous ces textes attestent que la tradition évangélique est une chose complexe et confirment qu'il a pu exister des formes évangéliques plus anciennes que celles que nous possédons maintenant sous les noms de Matthieu, de Marc et de Luc. En Appendice, nous donnons la discussion du récit de la guérison d'un lépreux, d'après Mc 1:40-45 et par., dans laquelle nous croyons pouvoir montrer que le papyrus Egerton 2 a connu ce récit sous une forme plus simple, dégagée de toute influence matthéenne, et qui pourrait remonter à un proto-Luc. Nous sommes persuadés que d'autres textes des évangiles non canoniques pourraient être utilisés pour reconstituer l'histoire des rédactions évangéliques.

3. *Les témoignages anciens.*

Voyons enfin les témoignages des auteurs anciens concernant la composition des quatre évangiles; ils ont été rassemblés dans les Synopses de Aland (531-548) et de Huck-Greeven (viii-x). Dans quelle mesure peut-on s'appuyer sur eux pour déterminer la priorité relative des évangiles canoniques sous leur forme actuelle? Favorisent-ils une théorie synoptique plutôt que telle autre?

Le premier témoignage complet sur la chronologie relative des quatre évangiles est celui d'Irénée de Lyon, vers 185: Matthieu écrivit le premier, chez les Hébreux et dans leur langue, tandis que Pierre et Paul prêchaient l'évangile à Rome; après la mort des deux apôtres, Marc, disciple et interprète (*hermēneutēs*) de Pierre, mit par écrit la prédication de celui-ci; vient ensuite l'évangile de Luc, disciple de Paul; enfin celui de Jean. Presque tous ces renseignements se retrouvent plus tard chez Origène, qui se réfère à la "tradition", et dans les prologues évangéliques dont il est difficile de dater la composition.

Ce témoignage d'Irénée doit être confronté avec celui de Papias (vers 135) et avec celui de Clément d'Alexandrie, qui tous deux se réfèrent au témoignage des "Anciens", probablement des gens de la deuxième génération chrétienne. Les données les plus homogènes concernent Marc, interprète de Pierre, dont il aurait mis par écrit la prédication. Mais tandis que Clément d'Alexandrie dit que Marc écrivit du vivant de Pierre, Papias (suivi par Irénée), sans le dire explicitement, suppose plutôt une rédaction un peu plus tardive. Les données concernant Matthieu sont plus vagues. Papias affirme que son évangile aurait été écrit en hébreu. Clément d'Alexandrie nous dit simplement que les évangiles écrits les premiers furent ceux qui donnent la généalogie de Jésus (Mt et Lc); il ne s'oppose donc pas, bien au contraire, à une priorité matthéenne. Quant à Luc, nous ignorons ce qu'en disait Papias. Clément d'Alexandrie place la rédaction de son évangile avant celle de Mc; mais Irénée tient une position inverse.

De ces divers témoignages, on peut conclure avec quelque vraisemblance: la première rédaction évangélique fut celle de Matthieu; il aurait composé son évangile pour les Hébreux habitant la Palestine et dans leur langue (hébreu ou araméen, les deux interprétations sont possibles). L'évangile de Marc aurait été composé à Rome pour transmettre aux chrétiens l'essentiel de la prédication de Pierre; il serait postérieur à celui de Matthieu. La tradition reste divisée quant à la chronologie relative des évangiles de Marc et de Luc.

En référence à ces données traditionnelles (dans la mesure où l'on peut se fier à elles), la théorie des Deux Évangiles (Griesbach *redivivus*) souffre de deux faiblesses majeures. La première concerne la composition de l'évangile de Marc. Même en admettant que Marc ait écrit après Luc, si l'on préfère le témoignage de Clément d'Alexandrie à celui d'Irénée, peut-on dire qu'il s'est contenté de fusionner en les raccourcissant les évangiles de Matthieu et de Luc (sous leur forme actuelle) alors que les témoignages les plus anciens font de lui un disciple de Pierre qui aurait mis par écrit la prédication de l'apôtre dans la mesure où il pouvait s'en souvenir? La théorie des Deux Sources est mieux inspirée en faisant de Mc un évangile de base, indépendant de ceux de Mt et de Lc. Il resterait toutefois à prouver que notre Mc actuel est identique à celui dont parlaient les Anciens; qui oserait s'en porter garant?

Par ailleurs, la théorie des Deux Évangiles a probablement raison, contre la théorie des Deux Sources, lorsqu'elle veut revaloriser l'évangile de Matthieu. Mais elle abuse de son avantage lorsqu'elle prétend que l'évangile *grec* de Mt, tel que nous l'avons maintenant, est l'évangile primordial dont dépendraient Lc et Mc; la tradition parle d'un évangile *en hébreu*, ce qui n'est pas pareil. Même si certains auteurs ont souligné, encore récemment, la facture hébraïque d'un certain nombre de phrases matthéennes, ce qui confirmerait la donnée traditionnelle d'un Matthieu-hébreu primitif, nous ne savons strictement rien quant au rapport exact qui a existé entre ce Matthieu-hébreu primitif et notre Matthieu-grec actuel. Il est donc abusif de s'appuyer sur la tradition pour affirmer que l'évangile grec de Matthieu, sous sa forme actuelle, serait la source utilisée par Luc et par Marc.

En fait, les données traditionnelles, si on les tient pour authentiques (et pourquoi ne le seraient-elles pas?), nous orientent vers une solution complexe du problème synoptique. Elles supposent à l'origine des rédactions synoptiques au moins deux évangiles indépendants l'un de l'autre: celui de Matthieu, écrit en Palestine, et celui de Mc, écrit à Rome et écho des traditions pétriniennes. Elles affirment également que l'évangile de Matthieu fut écrit primitivement en hébreu; puisque nous le possédons maintenant en grec, il y eut au moins deux états différents de cet évangile. Rappelons enfin que, au témoignage de Luc lui-même, "beaucoup ont entrepris de composer un récit des événements qui se sont déroulés parmi nous, d'après ce que nous ont transmis ceux qui furent dès le début témoins oculaires et serviteurs de la Parole" (Lc 1:1-2); Luc savait donc qu'il était loin d'être le premier à écrire, même si son "beaucoup" doit être compris au sens de "plusieurs".

Marie-Émile BOISMARD

INTRODUCTION AU PREMIER RÉCIT DE LA MULTIPLICATION DES PAINS
(Mt 14:13-14; Mc 6:30-34; Lc 9:10-11)

Note: le texte adopté est celui de la Synopse de Kurt Aland; celui de la Synopse de H. Greeven ne s'en distingue que par la variante εἰς ἔρημον τόπον τῷ πλοίῳ en Mc 6:32.

Dans ce récit, on compte 89 mots chez Mc, 36 chez Mt et 39 chez Lc. Or, fait remarquable, les trois Synoptiques n'ont en commun que la préposition *eis*, la locution adverbiale *kat'idian* et, à la dernière phrase, la conjonction *kai*. Cela donne comme proportion: chez Mc, 3 mots sur 89, soit 3,37%; chez Mt, 3 mots sur 36, soit 8,33%; enfin chez Lc 3 mots sur 39, soit 7,69%. C'est infime, d'autant que l'accord sur la conjonction *kai* est dépourvu de toute signification. Dès le départ, la théorie des Deux Sources aussi bien que celle de Griesbach sont en difficulté: comment expliquer que les trois récits, qui par hypothèse dépendent les uns des autres (quel que soit l'ordre de dépendance) n'aient en commun qu'un nombre infime de mots? La difficulté disparaît si l'on admet, derrière les Synoptiques, au moins deux Documents différents dont ils dépendraient: c'est ce que nous proposerons au terme de ces analyses.

Nous allons procéder de façon très "sémitique", en forme de chiasme: aperçu rapide sur Mc, puis sur Mt; analyse approfondie de Lc; retour au texte de Mt, puis à celui de Mc.

1. *Le récit de Mc.* — Le récit de Mc se rattache à celui de la mission des Douze (6:6b-13) par delà les récits de l'opinion d'Hérode sur Jésus (vv. 14-16) et de la mise à mort de Jean par Hérode (vv. 17-29). Le v. 30 en effet met en scène les disciples au retour de leur mission. Ce récit de Mc est nettement plus développé que ceux de Mt et de Lc. Rien qu'aux vv. 32-34, il contient 48 mots, contre 36 dans le parallèle de Mt et 31 dans le parallèle de Lc. De plus, le v. 31 de Mc, soit 25 mots, ne trouve aucun écho dans Mt ni dans Lc. Quant à son v. 30, qui contient 16 mots, il a son parallèle dans le v. 10a de Lc, qui n'en a que 8.

Comme corollaire de cette évaluation statistique, il faut noter le dédoublement des thèmes dans Mc. La séquence κατ'ἰδίαν εἰς ἔρημον τόπον du v. 31 se retrouve, inversée, au v. 32. Par ailleurs, au v. 33, il y a interférence de deux groupes différents (sans parler des apôtres): les *polloi* mentionnés au v. 31 autour de Jésus et des apôtres, qui les voient partir en bateau (v. 33a) et qui, à pied, les devancent (fin du v. 33); les *polloi* qui apprennent par ouï-dire que Jésus s'est retiré en un lieu désert et qui accourent de toutes les villes (v. 33bc).

Nous aurons à revenir plus loin sur cette complexité du récit de Mc, opposée à la simplicité des récits de Mt et de Lc.

2. *Le récit de Mt.* — Contrairement à celui de Mc, le récit de Mt se rattache étroitement au contexte précédent: les disciples de Jean annoncent à Jésus le meurtre de leur Maître par Hérode (v. 12); à cette nouvelle, Jésus se retire en un lieu désert (v. 13). Le lien est analogue à celui que l'on a entre 12:14: les Pharisiens décident la mort de Jésus, et 12:15: en l'apprenant, celui-ci se retire.

Le récit de Mt contient un grand nombre de traits de facture typiquement matthéenne, surtout au v. 13 et dans la seconde moitié du v. 14.

Au début du v. 13, le verbe *anachōrein* est très matthéen (10/1/0/1/2) (= ordre: Mt, Mc, Lc, Jn, Ac). Il est enchâssé dans un début de phrase dont on a l'équivalent en 12:15:

14:13: ἀκούσας δὲ ὁ Ἰησοῦς ἀνεχώρησεν ἐκεῖθεν

12:15: ὁ δὲ Ἰησοῦς γνοὺς ἀνεχώρησεν ἐκεῖθεν

Typique du style de Mt est le thème des foules qui suivent Jésus; chez lui, c'est à 7 reprises que le verbe *akolouthein* a comme sujet le substantif *ochlos*, le plus souvent au pluriel.

Voici les textes:

14:13 καὶ ἀκούσαντες οἱ ὄχλοι ἠκολούθησαν αὐτῷ

 4:25 καὶ ἠκολούθησαν αὐτῷ ὄχλοι πολλοί

 8:1   ... ἠκολούθησαν αὐτῷ ὄχλοι πολλοί

12:15 καὶ ἠκολούθησαν αὐτῷ (ὄχλοι) πολλοί

19:2 καὶ ἠκολούθησαν αὐτῷ ὄχλοι πολλοί

20:29 ... ἠκολούθησαν αὐτῷ ὄχλος πολύς

        (ἠκολούθησαν αὐτῷ ὄχλοι πολλοί: dans P[45] D et les latins)

21:9 οἱ δὲ ὄχλοι οἱ προάγοντες καὶ ἀκολουθοῦντες

En 12:15, le sujet *ochloi* est tombé par haplographie dans le texte Alexandrin. En 20:29, il est difficile de décider si c'est le texte Occidental qui a harmonisé sur la formule habituelle en Mt, ou si c'est le texte Alexandrin qui a abandonné la formule habituelle pour adopter le singulier. En 21:9, on notera que le parallèle de Mc a une formule analogue, mais sans le mot *ochloi*, ce qui confirme le caractère matthéen de la formule que nous analysons ici.

Si, en 14:13, le substantif précède le verbe, contrairement à l'habitude, c'est en raison du participe qui l'affecte (comparer 9:8; 22:33 d'une part, 7:28; 9:33; 12:23 d'autre part). Une comparaison avec 22:33 est spécialement intéressante:

14:13 καὶ ἀκούσαντες οἱ ὄχλοι ἠκολούθησαν

22:33 καὶ ἀκούσαντες οἱ ὄχλοι ἐξεπλήσσοντο

Chez Mc, en revanche, nous ne trouvons qu'une seule fois *ochlos* comme sujet de *akolouthein*:

5:24: καὶ ἀπῆλθεν μετ᾽ αὐτοῦ καὶ ἠκολούθει αὐτῷ ὄχλος πολύς

La phrase est au singulier et le verbe à l'imparfait, ce qui donne un ensemble assez différent de la phrase matthéenne stéréotypée.

Notons enfin le thème des guérisons, en finale du récit. Il se lit après celui des foules qui suivent Jésus en 12:15 et en 19:1-2 (cf. *supra*); nous reviendrons plus loin sur la structure semblable des Sommaires de 12:15; 14:13-14 et 19:1-2.

En conclusion, on peut donc affirmer que les vv. 13 et 14b du récit de Mt ont une tonalité typiquement matthéenne.

3. *Le récit de Lc.* — a) Quand on compare le récit de Lc à ceux de Mt et de Mc, on observe le fait littéraire suivant.

— Le début du récit de Lc (v. 10a) et le début du récit de Mc (v. 30) n'ont pas de parallèle chez Mt. Or ici, les textes de Lc et de Mc sont étroitement apparentés. Sur les 8 mots de Lc, 6 se retrouvent absolument identiques chez Mc, soit une proportion de 75%. Quant aux 2 autres, ils présentent le même changement qu'en un autre passage où Lc et Mc sont en parallèle (Mt étant absent):

Mc 6:30 καὶ *συνάγονται* ... καὶ *ἀπήγγειλαν* αὐτῷ πάντα ὅσα ἐποίησαν

Lc 9:10 καὶ *ὑποστρέψαντες* ... *διηγήσαντο* αὐτῷ ὅσα ἐποίησαν

Mc 5:19 ὕπαγε ... καὶ ἀπάγγειλον αὐτοῖς ὅσα ὁ κύριός σοι πεποίηκεν

Lc 8:39 ὑπόστρεφε ... καὶ διηγοῦ ὅσα σοι ἐποίησεν ὁ θεός

Nous reviendrons plus loin sur le problème de savoir qui ici est premier, de Mc ou de Lc. Constatons seulement que les textes de Mc et de Lc ne diffèrent que par des retouches stylistiques mais qu'ils sont fondamentalement identiques.

— Mais *dès que* Mt entre en parallèle avec Mc et Lc, c'est-à-dire à partir du v. 10b de Lc, ce dernier n'offre plus de contacts significatifs avec Mc mais en offre au contraire de nombreux et significatifs avec Mt. Qu'on en juge.

Les accords Lc/Mc contre Mt se réduisent à un *kai* initial, sans grande signification, un *gnontes* de Lc apparenté au *epegnōsan* de Mc, enfin au thème commun de la prédication aux foules, en finale, mais exprimé chez Mc et Lc en termes *totalement* différents, si bien qu'il est difficile de parler d'un emprunt de l'un à l'autre.

Voici en revanche quels sont les contacts de Lc/Mt contre Mc:

Mc	Mt	Lc
ἀπῆλθον	ἀνεχώρησεν	ὑπεχώρησεν
καὶ ἐπέγνωσαν πολλοί	καὶ ἀκούσαντες οἱ ὄχλοι	οἱ δὲ ὄχλοι γνόντες
συνέδραμον ἐκεῖ	ἠκολούθησαν αὐτῷ	ἠκολούθησαν αὐτῷ
	καὶ	καὶ τοὺς χρείαν ἔχοντας
	ἐθεράπευσεν	θεραπείας
	τοὺς ἀρρώστους αὐτῶν	ἰᾶτο

A ces contacts positifs Lc/Mt contre Mc, il faudrait ajouter les contacts négatifs suivants: tous deux ignorent le v. 31 de Mc (25 mots!), tous deux omettent le thème des gens qui voient partir Jésus et les disciples (v. 33a de Mc), tous deux omettent le thème des gens qui devancent Jésus et ses disciples (v. 33e de Mc).

Nous avons vu tout à l'heure que tous les mots du texte de Mt qui se retrouvent chez Lc, soit identiques, soit analogues, étaient typiquement matthéens. Il est clair alors que, aux vv. 10b-11, Lc ne dépend plus de Mc (pour rester dans la perspective de la théorie des Deux Sources), mais de Mt.

b) Mais poussons un peu plus loin le problème. Selon la théorie des Deux Sources, Mt et Lc dépendraient tous deux de Mc, qu'ils auraient remanié l'un et l'autre *sans se connaître*. Il est vrai que, *dato non concesso*, Mt pourrait s'expliquer comme un remaniement du texte de Mc: son texte est parfaitement matthéen. Mais qu'en est-il de Lc? Pourrait-il s'expliquer, malgré tout, comme un remaniement du texte de Mc, ces remaniements provenant de la façon habituelle d'écrire de Lc? Reprenons en détail quelques-uns des accords Lc/Mt contre Mc.

— Nous n'insisterons pas sur le contact entre les verbes de même racine *anachōrein* et *hypochōrein*, bien que le second ne soit pas tellement lucanien puisqu'on ne le retrouve qu'une fois ailleurs dans le NT, en Lc 5:16 (il est vrai en contexte analogue, cf. *infra*). Mais notons le changement du pluriel (Mc) en singulier (Mt/Lc). Ce changement s'imposait chez Mt, qui ne mentionne pas le retour des apôtres et laisse Jésus seul en scène. Mais il ne s'imposait pas du tout chez Lc qui, comme Mc, parle de Jésus et des apôtres au v. 10a. Le changement du pluriel en singulier était même si peu normal pour lui qu'il l'a obligé à ajouter les mots *paralabōn autous* afin d'indiquer que les apôtres étaient aussi du "voyage". Le verbe au singulier, chez Lc, ne peut donc s'expliquer qu'en fonction du texte de Mt.

— Selon la théorie des Deux Sources, Lc et Mt auraient changé le *polloi* de Mc en *hoi ochloi*. Notons d'abord que Lc n'avait aucune raison contraignante de changer l'adjectif substantivé de Mc. Si Mt l'évite d'ordinaire, il n'en va pas de même de Lc qui l'utilise 3 fois seul (1:1; 7:21; 14:16), et qui même une fois transforme l'adjectif *polla* de Mc 1:34 en adjectif substantivé *apo pollōn* (Lc 4:41). Mais même en admettant qu'il ait voulu changer le terme de Mc, il avait bien d'autres possibilités que d'adopter l'expression *hoi ochloi* (= Mt); mettre par exemple *ochloi polloi* (Lc 5:15; 14:25), ou *ochlos polys* (7:11), ou encore *poly plēthos* (23:27), etc. Il serait donc étonnant que Lc ait choisi ici juste l'expression que Mt avait adoptée!

— Enfin, que penser de la formule *ēkolouthēsan autō*, si typiquement matthéenne comme on l'a noté plus haut? Chez Lc, nous avons une seule fois ailleurs le rapprochement du verbe *akolouthein* et du substantif *ochlos*, en Lc 7:9, mais dans une formulation littéraire qui n'a rien à voir avec celle que nous avons ici: καὶ στραφεὶς τῷ ἀκολουθοῦντι αὐτῷ ὄχλῳ εἶπεν. Mais pour se persuader que nous ne sommes pas ici devant une formule lucanienne, il n'est que de nous reporter aux divers textes où Lc veut exprimer la même idée, parfois en même contexte; les voici:

4:42 ... ἐπορεύθη εἰς ἔρημον τόπον καὶ οἱ ὄχλοι ἐπεζήτουν αὐτὸν
      καὶ ἦλθον ἕως αὐτοῦ

5:15 καὶ συνήρχοντο ὄχλοι πολλοὶ ἀκούειν καὶ θεραπεύεσθαι ἀπὸ
      τῶν ἀσθενειῶν αὐτῶν· 16 αὐτὸς δὲ ἦν ὑποχωρῶν ἐν ταῖς ἐρήμοις

14:25 συνεπορεύοντο δὲ αὐτῷ ὄχλοι πολλοί

7:11 καὶ συνεπορεύοντο αὐτῷ οἱ μαθηταὶ αὐτοῦ καὶ ὄχλος πολύς

23:27 ἠκολούθει δὲ αὐτῷ πολὺ πλῆθος τοῦ λαοῦ

Ac 21:36 ἠκολούθει γὰρ τὸ πλῆθος τοῦ λαοῦ

D'après tous ces textes, on voit que si Lc avait remanié ici le texte de Mc, il aurait eu relativement peu de chances d'utiliser la formule *hoi ochloi*; il aurait eu peu de chances d'utiliser le verbe *akolouthein*; et enfin, il aurait certainement mis le verbe à l'imparfait, et non à l'aoriste. Les chances pour que, en retravaillant le texte de Mc, il ait obtenu un texte si proche de celui de Mt sont pratiquement nulles.

En conclusion de toutes ces analyses, nous pouvons affirmer que, aux vv. 10b-11, Lc ne peut pas dépendre de Mc, avec lequel il n'offre à peu près aucun contact (contrairement à ce qui se passait au v. 10a), mais qu'il dépend certainement du texte matthéen.

c) Reste le problème posé par les vv. 10a de Lc et 30 de Mc: lequel des deux textes est antérieur à l'autre? Est-ce Lc qui dépend de Mc, en accord avec la théorie des Deux Sources, ou Mc qui dépend de Lc, en accord avec la théorie de Griesbach? Il est impossible de répondre à cette question en raisonnant à partir d'un texte aussi court. Le thème, on l'a vu, se lit aussi en Mc 5:19-20 et Lc 8:39; mais cela ne fait pas avancer le problème. On trouve une formulation littéraire analogue en

Mc 3:8, mais aussi en Ac 14:27; 15:4; 15:12. Du point de vue du vocabulaire, le verbe *hypostrephein* chez Lc est une note secondaire, car ce verbe est exclusivement lucanien (0/0/21/0/12). En revanche, le titre de "apôtres", qui se lit dans Mc et dans Lc, n'est pas en faveur d'une priorité de Mc puisqu'il est également lucanien (6 fois dans Lc et 28 fois dans Ac). On ne le lit qu'ici dans Mc, le texte de 3:14 étant douteux. On aurait donc ici une influence de Lc sur Mc. Par ailleurs, il est plus facile d'imaginer Mc amplifiant et glosant le texte de Lc que Lc abrégeant celui de Mc.

Les deux textes offrant des notes secondaires, on peut se demander s'ils ne dépendraient pas tous deux d'un Document plus ancien, qui pourrait être un Mc plus primitif que celui que nous avons maintenant. Mais il est nécessaire d'analyser d'autres textes pour pouvoir se faire une opinion sur ce point. Laissons donc ici la question ouverte.

4. *Retour au récit de Mt.* — Les analyses que nous avons faites à propos de Lc nous ont amené à rejeter la théorie des Deux Sources qui nie tout rapport direct entre Mt et Lc. Celles que nous allons faire à propos de Mt vont nous inciter à prendre nos distances à l'égard de la théorie de Griesbach: nous admettrons en effet qu'il faut distinguer deux états de la tradition matthéenne, un proto-Matthieu et une ultime rédaction matthéenne, Lc dépendant du proto-Matthieu et non du Matthieu tel que nous l'avons actuellement.

Reprenons la comparaison entre les textes de Mt et de Lc, mais cette fois d'un point de vue matthéen. Nous avons vu tout à l'heure que Lc dépendait fondamentalement du texte matthéen (aux vv. 10b-11). Mais il existe un problème du fait que toute une section de ce texte matthéen ne trouve aucun écho chez Lc: il s'agit de la fin du v. 13 et du v. 14 de Mt. On ajoutera à ce passage les mots *en ploiō* du v. 13a, sans équivalent chez Lc et qui font opposition au *pezē* de la fin du v. 13 (en revanche, on peut penser que Lc a changé la formule *eis erēmon topon* de sa source matthéenne en *eis kaloumenēn Bēths.*, fortement marqué de son style). Cela fait donc 15 mots du texte de Mt qui n'ont aucun écho en Lc.

Or, en comparant maintenant Mt à Mc, on constate le fait littéraire suivant. Lorsque Lc fait écho aux textes de Mt et de Mc, les contacts de vocabulaire entre Mt et Mc sont faibles: 6 mots (dont 2 *kai*) sur 21 (chez Mt), soit une proportion de 28,57%. En revanche, lorsque Lc cesse de faire écho aux textes de Mt et de Mc, ceux-ci deviennent quasi identiques, la seule variante étant constituée par un changement de cas pour le pronom personnel final. On a donc une proportion de 14,5 sur 15 mots, soit 96,67%! Comment expliquer ce fait littéraire? Notons en passant que la théorie des Deux Sources se trouve encore ici dans une impasse; elle doit admettre que Mt, suivant Mc de façon très libre, se met à adopter son texte à 100% précisément là où Lc l'abandonne, et cela sans connaître Lc, et pour un total de 15 mots! La théorie de Griesbach serait elle aussi en difficulté. Selon elle, Lc aurait abrégé le texte de Mt, et Mc aurait complété le texte de Lc en reprenant *ad litteram* au texte de Mt tout ce que Lc en avait laissé tomber. Mais pourquoi cette différence de traitement entre les textes? Pourquoi Mc se mettrait-il soudain à suivre Mt mot à mot? Ceci serait d'autant plus étrange que son v. 33 est plus proche de Mt que de Lc, avec la précision que Jésus se rend "vers un lieu désert", et non "vers une ville appelée Bethsaïde", comme le dit Lc.

Pour résoudre cette difficulté, nous proposons l'hypothèse suivante, que nous appuierons ensuite par quelques arguments supplémentaires. Il faut distinguer deux niveaux rédactionnels dans Mt: un proto-Matthieu et une ultime rédaction matthéenne. Le proto-Matthieu ne contenait pas la section où les textes de Mt et de Mc sont identiques; elle aurait été ajoutée par l'ultime Rédacteur matthéen qui aurait copié Mc (ou un proto-Marc, cf. les analyses ultérieures portant sur d'autres textes) mot à mot. Quant à Lc, il dépendrait du proto-Matthieu, d'où son silence concernant la section où Mt et Mc sont identiques.

Pour vérifier la justesse de cette hypothèse, mettons en regard le texte de Mt 14:13, celui de Lc 9:10b-11, le texte enfin des Sommaires de Mt 12:15 et de Mt 19:1-2. Pour Mt 14:13-14, nous disposerons légèrement en retrait toute la section qui, absente de Lc, est à près de 100% identique à Mc:

Mt 14:13s	Lc 9:10b-11	Mt 12:15	Mt 19:1s
ἀκούσας δὲ ὁ Ἰησοῦς	καὶ...	ὁ δὲ Ἰησοῦς γνοὺς	καὶ
ἀνεχώρησεν ἐκεῖθεν	ὑπεχώρησεν	ἀνεχώρησεν ἐκεῖθεν	ἦλθεν
ἐν πλοίῳ			
εἰς ἔρημον τόπον			εἰς τὰ ὅρια τῆς Ἰ.
κατ' ἰδίαν	κατ' ἰδίαν		πέραν τοῦ Ἰορδάνου
	εἰς πόλιν καλ. Β.		
καὶ		καὶ	καὶ
ἀκούσαντες οἱ ὄχλοι	οἱ δὲ ὄχλοι γνόντες		
ἠκολούθησαν αὐτῷ	ἠκολούθησαν αὐτῷ	ἠκολούθησαν αὐτῷ	ἠκολούθησαν αὐτῷ
		ὄχλοι πολλοί	ὄχλοι πολλοί
πεζῇ ἀπὸ τῶν πόλεων καὶ ἐξελθὼν εἶδεν πολὺν ὄχλον καὶ ἐσπλαγχνίσθη ἐπ' αὐτοῖς			
καὶ ἐθεράπευσεν	καὶ τοὺς χρείαν	καὶ ἐθεράπευσεν	καὶ ἐθεράπευσεν
τοὺς ἀρρώστους	ἔχοντας θεραπείας		
αὐτῶν	ἰᾶτο	αὐτοὺς πάντας	αὐτοὺς ἐκεῖ

Il est facile de voir que, en Mt 14:13s, toute la section identique à Mc vient en surcharge dans une structure typiquement matthéenne attestée par Mt 12:15 et 19:1-2. En revanche, le texte de Lc reste conforme à cette structure matthéenne et est donc plus "matthéen" que le parallèle de Mt 14:13s. Une conclusion s'impose: Lc dépend d'un proto-Matthieu que l'ultime Rédacteur matthéen a surchargé au moyen d'éléments repris à 100% de Mc.

Ajoutons encore quelques remarques qui vont appuyer cette conclusion. En Mt 14:14, les mots identiques au texte de Mc (placés en retrait) forment en partie doublet avec Mt 9:36: ἰδὼν δὲ τοὺς ὄχλους ἐπλαγχνίσθη περὶ αὐτῶν. Pourquoi ce doublet dans Mt, sinon parce que le thème, au chapitre 14, est repris de Mc? On notera d'ailleurs que, en 9:36 comme en 14:13b (dans la section authentiquement matthéenne) le mot "foule" est au pluriel, ce qui correspond au style de Mt; en revanche, dans la section identique à Mc, le mot "foule" est au singulier, ce qui correspond au style de Mc. Dans le premier récit de multiplication des pains, Mt a toujours le mot "foule" au pluriel (vv. 13, 15, 19, 22, 23) sauf au v. 14! L'emprunt à Mc devient tout à fait évident.

Enfin, le texte actuel de Mt n'est pas très cohérent. Tout d'abord il est étrange que Mt ait employé le mot "accompagner" pour décrire le mouvement des foules: Jésus part en bateau tandis que les foules vont à pied! Par ailleurs, au v. 13b, les foules sont déterminées (présence de l'article défini) tandis qu'au v. 14a Jésus voit "une foule", indéterminée, alors qu'il s'agit des mêmes gens. Toutes ces difficultés disparaissent si l'on enlève du texte de Mt toute la section identique à Mc.

L'hypothèse initiale est donc maintenant largement confirmée; il faut distinguer chez Mt deux états différents: un proto-Matthieu, dont Lc dépend, et une ultime Rédaction matthéenne qui a complété le texte du proto-Matthieu au moyen d'éléments repris littéralement (à 100%) de Mc (ou tout au moins de la tradition marcienne).

Note: au terme de ces analyses sur le texte de Mt, on pourra se reporter à l'introduction du récit de la multiplication des pains en Jn 6:1-2: on y retrouve la séquence du proto-Matthieu, plus proche d'ailleurs de 19:1-2 que de 14:13-14: μετὰ ταῦτα ἀπῆλθεν ὁ Ἰησοῦς πέραν τῆς θαλάσσης ... ἠκολούθει δὲ αὐτῷ ὄχλος πολὺς ὅτι ἐθεώρουν τὰ σημεῖα ἃ ἐποίει ἐπὶ τῶν ἀσθενούντων.

5. *Retour au récit de Mc.* —

En donnant au début de cette discussion un bref aperçu sur le récit de Mc, nous avons dit qu'il décrivait deux mouvements de foules, très différenciés: d'une part, des gens se trouvant autour de Jésus et des apôtres les voient partir en bateau et, à pied, les devancent; d'autre part des gens apprennent (par ouï-dire) que Jésus s'est déplacé et, de toutes les villes environnantes, ils accourent auprès de lui. Voici le texte grec disposé de façon à faire ressortir ces deux mouvements différents:

ἦσαν γὰρ οἱ ἐρχόμενοι	
καὶ οἱ ὑπάγοντες *πολλοί*...	
καὶ ἀπῆλθον ἐν τῷ πλοίῳ...	(καὶ ἀπῆλθεν)
καὶ εἶδον αὐτοὺς ὑπάγοντας	καὶ ἐπέγνωσαν *πολλοὶ*
καὶ πεζῇ...	καὶ ἀπὸ πασῶν τῶν πόλεων
προῆλθον αὐτούς	συνέδραμον ἐκεῖ

Voyons d'abord le texte placé dans la colonne de droite. Complété par le thème de l'enseignement de Jésus (fin du v. 34 de Mc), il constitue un Sommaire qui se suffit à lui-même et qui forme l'équivalent exact du Sommaire du proto-Matthieu. Pour s'en convaincre, il suffit de se reporter au Sommaire attesté par Mt 19:1-2 et Mc 10:1:

Mt 14	Mc 6	Mt 19:1s	Mc 10:1
ἀκούσας δὲ ὁ Ἰησοῦς	καὶ	καὶ...	καὶ ἐκεῖθεν ἀναστὰς
ἀνεχώρησεν ἐκεῖθεν ()	(ἀπῆλθεν)	ἦλθεν	ἔρχεται
εἰς ἔρημον τόπον	εἰς ἔρημον τόπον	εἰς τὰ ὅρια τῆς Ἰ.	εἰς τὰ ὅρια τῆς Ἰ.
κατ' ἰδίαν	κατ' ἰδίαν	πέραν τοῦ Ἰορδάνου	πέραν τοῦ Ἰορδάνου
καὶ ἀκούσαντες	καὶ ἐπέγνωσαν		
οἱ ὄχλοι	πολλοὶ		
	καὶ () ἀπὸ πασῶν		
	τῶν πόλεων		
ἠκολούθησαν αὐτῷ ()	συνέδραμον ἐκεῖ ()	ἠκολούθησαν αὐτῷ	συμπορεύονται πάλιν
		ὄχλοι πολλοὶ	ὄχλοι πρὸς αὐτὸν
καὶ ἐθεράπευσεν	καὶ ἤρξατο διδάσκειν	καὶ ἐθεράπευσεν	καὶ ... ἐδίδασκεν
τοὺς ἀρρώστους αὐτῶν	αὐτοὺς πολλά	αὐτοὺς ἐκεῖ	αὐτούς

Il est remarquable que, dans les deux séquences, les divergences entre Mc et Mt sont en partie identiques. Tout d'abord, tandis que Mt utilise uniformément le verbe *akolouthein*, Mc emploie aux deux passages un verbe de mouvement avec le suffixe *syn*. Par ailleurs, dans l'une et l'autre séquence, Mt a en finale le thème des guérisons tandis que Mc a celui de l'enseignement des foules par Jésus.

Il serait vain, ici, de se demander si c'est le proto-Matthieu qui dépend de la tradition marcienne ou au contraire le (proto-)Marc qui dépendrait de la tradition matthéenne. Ce passage, à lui seul, ne donne aucun élément de solution. On peut faire remarquer toutefois que, surtout pour la première séquence (Mt 14 et Mc 6), les contacts de vocabulaire entre Mc et Mt sont si pauvres que l'on serait tenté de conclure à deux traditions plus ou moins indépendantes, ou tout au moins à deux traditions déjà très différenciées.

Revenons maintenant au second mouvement de foule noté plus haut et que Mc a fusionné avec celui que nous venons d'analyser. Il ne trouve aucun écho dans les textes de Mt et de Lc, et donc dans le texte du proto-Matthieu. D'où peut-il provenir? Voici une hypothèse que nous proposons (car il faut bien proposer une hypothèse, mais il serait possible d'en imaginer d'autres).

Reportons-nous au second récit de multiplication des pains, en Mt 15 et Mc 8. Chez Mt, ce récit est introduit par un Sommaire analogue à ceux que nous avons étudiés plus haut: Jésus se déplace, il monte sur une montagne, les foules viennent avec leurs malades, Jésus les guérit (15:29-31). Il n'en va pas de même chez Mc où le second récit de multiplication des pains est complétement coupé du contexte qui précède et commence par une formule rédactionnelle: "En ces jours-là de nouveau tandis qu'il y avait une grande foule et qu'ils n'avaient pas de quoi manger..." Pour une raison qui nous échappe, Mc n'aurait-il pas déplacé l'introduction au deuxième récit de multiplication des pains pour la fusionner avec l'introduction au premier récit? Un indice pourrait étayer cette hypothèse. Dans le *premier* récit de multiplication des pains, Mc a voulu introduire le détail des 200 deniers de pain en utilisant comme cheville rédactionnelle une phrase en provenance du *second* récit: "Mais lui leur dit: Combien avez-vous de pains?" (Mc 6:37-38). Ce remaniement est absent des parallèles de Mt et de Lc. Ainsi, Mc aurait fusionné les deux introductions aux récits de multiplication des pains, comme, à propos d'un détail, il fusionne aussi les deux récits eux-mêmes.

Quoi qu'il en soit de cette hypothèse, il reste que le texte de Mc apparaît au moins aussi complexe que celui de Mt; il faut parler d'une tradition marcienne qui a connu des étapes différentes; notons-le, dans le cas présent, c'est le texte *complexe* de Mc qui a influencé l'ultime rédaction matthéenne.

Au terme de ces analyses, il est possible de proposer les conclusions suivantes. Il faut distinguer deux états successifs de Mt: un proto-Matthieu (grec) et le Matthieu actuel; ce dernier fut complété d'après l'évangile de Marc, repris *ad litteram*. L'évangile de Luc dépend du proto-Matthieu pour les vv. 10b-11. L'évangile de Marc ne dépend pas du proto-Matthieu: ils ont trop peu de mots en commun pour que cette hypothèse puisse être retenue (ce qui exclut aussi une dépendance du proto-Matthieu par rapport à Mc); il représente une tradition plus ou moins indépendante, mais de forme complexe. Les rapports entre Lc et Mc sont difficiles à préciser, à ne tenir compte que de ce texte; tous deux semblent dépendre d'un texte plus ancien (un proto-Marc?).

Bien entendu, il n'est pas question de formuler une théorie synoptique à partir de l'analyse d'un seul texte. Les conclusions précédentes devraient être nuancées grâce à l'analyse de nombreux autres textes.

APPENDICE: LA GUÉRISON DU LÉPREUX

Mc 1:40-44; Mt 8:1-4; Lc 5:12-14;
papyrus Egerton 2; cf. Mt 9:27-30; Lc 17:11-19

1. *Affinités des récits synoptiques.* — Nous ne tiendrons pas compte des introductions du récit propres à Mt (v. 1) et à Lc (v. 12a).

Au début du récit (vv. 2a de Mt, 40a de Mc, 12b de Lc, jusqu'à la ligne pointillée portée sur la Synopse), chaque évangéliste suit sa voie propre, très marquée par son style. Le v. 2a de Mt a son équivalent exact en 9:18; le v. 40a de Mc est analogue à 5:22, avec son présent historique typique du style de Mc; le v. 12b de Lc est aussi très lucanien. Il est impossible de rien tirer de ce début de récit, la priorité pouvant être donnée aussi bien à l'un qu'à l'autre.

En revanche, pour l'essentiel de la péricope, les trois Synoptiques offrent des récits très apparentés, comme le prouve la proportion des mots qu'ils ont en commun. Aux vv. 40b-44, Mc a 62 mots; aux vv. 2b-4, Mt en a 46; aux vv. 12c-14, Lc en a 47. Le nombre de mots communs aux trois Synoptiques, identiques ou quasi identiques, est de 36. Cela donne comme proportions: 58,06% pour Mc; 78,26% pour Mt; 76,59% pour Lc. C'est excellent.

2. *Tonalité matthéenne des trois récits.* — Les trois récits se déroulent de façon strictement parallèle. Or, tous les trois sont marqués par la façon d'écrire de Mt.

a) Dans les trois récits, Jésus guérit au moyen d'un geste et d'une parole. Analysons ce geste.

— ἐκτείνας τὴν χεῖρα. Cette formule, au participe, ne se lit ailleurs qu'en Mt 12:49; 14:31; 26:51. Elle est donc matthéenne. De plus, ailleurs, c'est seulement dans Mt que l'on voit Jésus "étendre la main" (12:49; 14:31). Ce geste attribué à Jésus est donc de coloration matthéenne.

— ἥψατο αὐτοῦ. Pour guérir le lépreux, Jésus le toucha. Ailleurs chez Mc, ce verbe n'est utilisé à propos de guérison qu'en 7:33, dans le cas du sourd-bègue. Jésus "touche" d'abord la langue du malade avec sa salive, puis il donne un ordre et le sourd-bègue se trouve guéri. Mais, si Jésus "touche" la langue du malade, c'est seulement pour y déposer de la salive; le fait de "toucher" n'a pas, de soi, valeur curative. Il en va différemment dans les récits matthéens. Comparons les récits de Mt et de Mc concernant la guérison de la belle-mère de Pierre:

Mc 1:31 ἤγειρεν αὐτὴν κρατήσας τῆς χειρὸς καὶ ἀφῆκεν αὐτὴν ὁ πυρετός.

Mt 8:15 ἥψατο τῆς χειρὸς αὐτῆς καὶ ἀφῆκεν αὐτὴν ὁ πυρετός.

Dans Mc, le fait de prendre la main de la malade a simplement pour but de l'aider à se lever. Dans Mt au contraire, c'est le fait de "toucher" la main de la malade qui effectue la guérison: il a bien une vertu curative par lui-même.

Dans Mc, pour guérir l'aveugle de Jéricho, Jésus dit simplement une parole "Va, ta foi t'a sauvé", et il recouvre aussitôt la vue (Mc 10:52). Dans Mt au contraire, Jésus "touche" les yeux des aveugles et ils recouvrent aussitôt la vue:

Mt 20:34 ἥψατο τῶν ὀμμάτων αὐτῶν καὶ εὐθέως ἀνέβλεψαν.

Même geste, en termes identiques, dans le récit de la guérison des deux aveugles, en Mt 9:29.

Ainsi, que ce soit par la formule "ayant étendu la main", surtout dite de Jésus, ou par l'importance essentielle donnée au fait de "toucher" le malade pour le guérir, le récit de la guérison du lépreux, dans les trois Synoptiques, est de tonalité matthéenne.

b) Après avoir guéri le lépreux, Jésus lui impose une consigne de silence, exprimée en termes presque identiques dans Mc et dans Mt. De telles consignes de silence sont fréquentes chez Mc; mais celle-ci offre des traits qui la distinguent des autres et lui donnent une tonalité matthéenne. Dans Mc, si l'on met à part les cas où Jésus impose silence à un esprit mauvais (1:25; cf. 4:39), une consigne de silence concernant la foule ou les disciples est toujours introduite par un verbe signifiant "commander" (soit *epitiman*, en 3:12; 8:30; soit *diastellesthai*, en 5:43; 7:36; 9:9); de plus, elle est toujours formulée en style indirect. Chez Mt au contraire, on constate une tendance à remplacer le style indirect par le style direct, introduit par le verbe "dire". Comparons par exemple Mc 9:9 et Mt 17:9, qui sont parallèles, textes auxquels nous ajouterons Mt 9:30:

Mc 9:9   διεστέλλατο αὐτοῖς ἵνα μηδενὶ ἃ εἶδον διηγήσωνται.

Mt 17:9   ἐνετείλατο αὐτοῖς λέγων· μηδενὶ εἴπητε...

Mt 9:30   ἐνεβριμήθη αὐτοῖς ὁ Ἰ. λέγων· ὁρᾶτε, μηδεὶς γινωσκέτω.

Or, dans l'épisode de la guérison du lépreux, la formule de Mc aussi bien que celle de Mt correspond à la formule matthéenne:

Mc 1:44: καὶ λέγει αὐτῷ · ὅρα μηδενὶ μηδὲν εἴπῃς.

Mt 8:4: καὶ λέγει αὐτῷ · ὅρα μηδενὶ εἴπῃς.

Un autre détail doit être noté: l'impératif *hora* suivi de la négation *mē* (ici, sous forme composée). Ici seulement chez Mc, elle revient trois fois ailleurs chez Mt: 9:30; 18:10; 24:6. La tonalité matthéenne de la formule apparaît quand on compare ces deux textes parallèles:

Mc 13:7 () μὴ θροεῖσθε.

Mt 24:6 ὁρᾶτε μὴ θροεῖσθε.

On peut donc affirmer que, dans Mc comme dans Mt, la consigne de silence est exprimée en termes matthéens et non marciens.

c) Après la consigne de silence, Jésus ordonne au lépreux d'aller se montrer au prêtre afin de faire constater sa guérison (Lv 13:49). Il devra également *offrir* un don. Ce verbe, *prospherein*, n'est pas inconnu de Mc (2:4; 10:13); mais il est utilisé surtout par Mt (15 fois en tout) qui, contrairement à Mc, l'emploie volontiers à propos de "choses" que l'on offre (2:11; 5:23, 24; 22:19; 25:20). Ce n'est qu'un détail, mais qui prend sa valeur après les remarques précédentes.

d) Ajoutons un dernier détail. Le lépreux s'approche de Jésus en lui disant: ἐὰν θέλῃς, δύνασαί με καθαρίσαι. Comparons cette phrase, attestée par les trois Synoptiques, à deux autres passages analogues, l'un propre à Mc et l'autre propre à Mt:
Mc 9:22: ἀλλ' εἴ τι δύνῃ, βοήθησον ἡμῖν...
Mt 9:28: πιστεύετε ὅτι δύναμαι τοῦτο ποιῆσαι
Ce dernier texte, on le voit, est très proche de celui qui se lit dans les trois Synoptiques pour la demande du lépreux à Jésus; ce détail prendra toute son importance au paragraphe suivant.

3.   *Le récit du papyrus Egerton 2.* — Le papyrus Egerton 2 (vers 125) contient un récit de guérison d'un lépreux de même facture que celui des Synoptiques, mais sans les traits matthéens que nous venons de relever: au lieu de "Si tu veux, tu peux me guérir", le lépreux dit simplement: "Si tu veux, je suis guéri"; Jésus le guérit par la vertu de sa parole et sans le toucher; il ne lui donne aucune consigne de silence. On ne peut rien dire du dernier détail matthéen car le papyrus est lacuneux et n'a pas la finale du récit. Même si le papyrus offre des notes secondaires, en particulier tous les détails par lesquels le lépreux raconte comment il a contracté la lèpre, ces détails ont été ajoutés à un récit archaïque *de caractère non matthéen*. Étudions de plus près ce problème.

a) La forme de récit donnée par Egert. 2 est sans aucun doute plus primitive que la forme matthéenne.
— La guérison est effectuée de façon simple, par un ordre de Jésus, et non de façon complexe comme dans Mt.
— La formule de Egert. 2 "si tu veux, je suis guéri" est plus primitive que celle de Mt "si tu veux, tu peux me guérir".
— Egert. 2 n'a pas la consigne de silence. Or cette consigne se concilie difficilement avec l'ordre d'aller faire constater officiellement la guérison par les autorités religieuses; c'est un élément ajouté dans la tradition matthéenne.

— L'ordre d'offrir ce qu'a prescrit Moïse, de tonalité matthéenne on l'a vu, est aussi un élément ajouté: il est inséré maladroitement entre l'ordre d'aller se montrer au prêtre et la formule "en attestation pour eux"; d'après Lv 24:2ss, en effet, il appartenait aux prêtres de constater officiellement la guérison d'un lépreux; la formule "en attestation pour eux" se rapporte donc à l'ordre de se montrer aux prêtres, et non au fait d'offrir un présent.

Le récit matthéen, passé dans Mc et dans Lc, n'est donc que la réinterprétation par Mt (ou un ancêtre du Mt actuel) d'un récit plus archaïque attesté par Egert. 2.

b) Egert. 2 dépend d'un récit *de forme lucanienne.*

— Le lépreux s'adresse à Jésus en lui disant *didaskale Iēsou* de même que les dix lépreux dont parle Lc 17:13 lui disent *Iesou epistata*; il n'existe pas d'autre exemple dans tout le NT de cette double appellation. De plus, dans ce même récit de la guérison des dix lépreux (17:14) Jésus dit aux lépreux: πορευθέντες ἐπιδείξατε ἑαυτοὺς τοῖς ἱερεῦσιν; c'est, transposée au pluriel, la formule que l'on trouve dans le récit du papyrus. On notera en passant que, dans Mt/Mc, cet ordre est introduit par l'impératif *hypage*, que Lc évite toujours. Dira-t-on que Egert. 2 a fusionné les textes de la guérison du lépreux et de la guérison des dix lépreux? Ce ne serait guère vraisemblable. D'ailleurs, pour exprimer la guérison du malade, Egert. 2 a une formule très lucanienne qui ne se retrouve, ni dans le présent récit des Synoptiques, ni dans le récit des dix lépreux; elle a son équivalent exact en Ac 12:10, dans un contexte totalement différent:

Ac 12:10   καὶ εὐθέως ἀπέστη ὁ ἄγγελος ἀπ᾽ αὐτοῦ
Egert. 2   καὶ εὐθέως ἀπέστη ἀπ᾽ αὐτοῦ ἡ λέπρα

Le verbe utilisé dans ces deux textes se lit 4 fois dans Lc, 6 fois dans Ac, 4 fois seulement dans les épîtres pauliniennes, jamais dans Mt, Mc ou Jn.

Nous sommes donc amenés à distinguer deux états dans la tradition lucanienne: un proto-Luc, dont dépendrait Egert. 2, dont le récit de la guérison du lépreux offrirait beaucoup d'affinités littéraires avec celui de la guérison des dix lépreux raconté en Lc 17:12-19; une ultime rédaction lucanienne qui aurait révisé le récit du proto-Luc en fonction du récit matthéen.

c) Sur au moins un point le récit du proto-Luc semble secondaire par rapport à celui de Mt: la façon dont est formulée la guérison. On vient de voir que la formule par laquelle il l'exprime était typiquement lucanienne; or celle de Mt "et fut purifiée sa lèpre" est certainement plus primitive (cf. Lv 14).

4. *Le récit de Mc.* — Une fois que l'on a reconnu le caractère secondaire du récit de Mc, on admettra sans trop de peine que la façon dont il exprime la guérison du lépreux est un compromis entre la formule de Mt et celle de Lc: "aussitôt s'éloigna de lui la lèpre et il fut purifié". On notera toutefois que l'ordre des mots dans Mc est plus conforme à l'ordre lucanien que dans Lc! On s'en rendra compte en comparant tous ces textes:

Ac 12:10   καὶ εὐθέως ἀπέστη ὁ ἄγγελος ἀπ᾿ αὐτοῦ
Egert. 2   καὶ εὐθέως ἀπέστη ἀπ᾿ αὐτοῦ ἡ λέπρα
Mc 1:42   καὶ εὐθὺς ἀπῆλθεν ἀπ᾿ αὐτοῦ ἡ λέπρα
Lc 1:38   καὶ   ἀπῆλθεν ἀπ᾿ αὐτῆς ὁ ἄγγελος
Lc 2:15   ὡς   ἀπῆλθον ἀπ᾿ αὐτῶν ... οἱ ἄγγελοι
Lc 5:13   καὶ εὐθέως ἡ λέπρα ἀπῆλθεν ἀπ᾿ αὐτοῦ

Ces analyses nous font adopter, pour ce texte, des conclusions proches de celles de la théorie des Deux Evangiles (Griesbach): Luc et Marc dépendent en grande partie de Matthieu, et Marc pourrait avoir fusionné Matthieu et Luc. Bien entendu, on pourrait supposer que Luc et Marc dépendent d'un proto-Matthieu, mais ici, aucun argument n'oblige à l'admettre. Le texte du papyrus Egerton 2 montre que le problème est en fait plus complexe: il permet d'atteindre un récit qui n'avait pas été influencé par la tradition matthéenne, et qui pourrait remonter à un proto-Luc.

M.-É. BOISMARD

RÉPONSE AUX DEUX AUTRES HYPOTHÈSES

I. LA THÉORIE DES DEUX SOURCES

Notre dialogue avec les partisans de la *Théorie des Deux Sources* se limitera à une discussion de la première partie du texte qu'ils ont choisi pour illustrer leur position: le sommaire de Mc 3:7-12, avec ses parallèles de Mt 4:25; 12:15-16; Lc 6:12-19; 4:41a. Nous allons montrer que, dans ce cas particulier, Marc apparaît secondaire; son texte, bien loin d'être la source utilisée par Matthieu et Luc, apparaît comme la fusion des sommaires attestés par Matthieu et par Luc. Pour ce texte précis, nous donnerions donc raison à la *Two-Gospel Hypothesis* contre la *Théorie des Deux Sources*, avec toutefois des précisions qui seront notées en leur temps.

Mc 3:7-12 et parallèles

I. *Statistiques.*

Les statistiques que nous allons donner portent sur les textes de Mc 3:7-12; Mt 4:25 et 12:15-16; Lc 6:12-19 et 4:41a (voir les textes disposés en synopse). En Mt 12:15, nous avons maintenu le mot *ochloi*, toujours présent dans Matthieu pour ce genre de phrase; le texte Alexandrin l'a omis par haplographie. La présence ou l'absence de ce mot ne changerait d'ailleurs rien aux analyses qui vont suivre.

Les deux passages de Matthieu comptent ensemble 36 mots; Marc en a 103; les deux passages de Luc totalisent 80 mots.

Il n'y a que 9 mots communs aux trois textes: *kai, polys, apo, kai, Jerusalem, ioudaia, therapeuein, kai, epitiman.* Cela donne une proportion de 25% pour Matthieu, de 8,74% pour Marc, de 11% pour Luc, ce qui est relativement peu.

On notera que, sur ces 9 mots communs aux trois Synoptiques, il y a 3 *kai*, qui n'ont à peu près aucune signification lorsqu'il s'agit de noter la parenté entre ces textes. Si l'on ne tenait pas compte de ces 3 *kai*, la proportion des mots communs aux trois Synoptiques serait ramenée à 16,66% pour Matthieu, 5,82% pour Marc et 7,5% pour Luc. Des proportions aussi faibles sont difficiles à justifier pour des théories qui voudraient faire dépendre tous les textes, soit du seul Marc (*Deux Sources*), soit du seul Matthieu (*Two-Gospel*). Elles s'expliquent beau-

	Mt 12: 15 ὁ δὲ Ἰησοῦς γνοὺς	Mc 3: 7 καὶ ὁ Ἰησοῦς	Lc 6: 17 καὶ καταβὰς μετ᾽ αὐτῶν
Mt 4:25	ἀνεχώρησεν ἐκεῖθεν	μετὰ τῶν μαθητῶν αὐτοῦ	ἔστη ἐπὶ τόπου πεδινοῦ
25 καὶ ἠκολούθησαν αὐτῷ	καὶ ἠκολούθησαν αὐτῷ	ἀνεχώρησεν πρὸς τὴν θάλασσαν	
ὄχλοι πολλοὶ	ὄχλοι πολλοὶ		καὶ ὄχλος πολὺς μαθητῶν αὐτοῦ
		καὶ πολὺ πλῆθος	καὶ πλῆθος πολὺ τοῦ λαοῦ
ἀπὸ τῆς Γαλιλαίας		ἀπὸ τῆς Γαλιλαίας	
		ἠκολούθησεν	
καὶ Δεκαπόλεως			ἀπὸ πασῆς τῆς Ἰουδαίας
		8 καὶ ἀπὸ Ἰεροσολύμων	καὶ Ἰερουσαλὴμ
καὶ Ἰεροσολύμων			
καὶ Ἰουδαίας		καὶ ἀπὸ τῆς Ἰδουμαίας	
		καὶ πέραν τοῦ Ἰορδάνου	καὶ τῆς παραλίου Τύρου καὶ Σιδῶνος
καὶ πέραν τοῦ Ἰορδάνου		καὶ περὶ Τύρον καὶ Σιδῶνα	
		πολὺ πλῆθος	18 οἳ ἦλθον ἀκοῦσαι αὐτοῦ
		ἀκούοντες ὅσα ἐποίει ἦλθον	καὶ ἰαθῆναι ἀπὸ τῶν νόσων αὐτῶν
		πρὸς αὐτόν.	
		9 καὶ εἶπεν τοῖς μαθηταῖς αὐτοῦ	
		ἵνα πλοιάριον προσκαρτερῇ αὐτῷ	καὶ οἱ ἐνοχλούμενοι
		διὰ τὸν ὄχλον ἵνα μὴ θλίβωσιν αὐτόν.	ἀπὸ πνευμάτων ἀκαθάρτων
			ἐθεραπεύοντο
		10 πολλοὺς γὰρ ἐθεράπευσεν	19 καὶ πᾶς ὁ ὄχλος
		ὥστε ἐπιπίπτειν αὐτῷ	ἐζήτουν ἅπτεσθαι αὐτοῦ
		ἵνα αὐτοῦ ἅψωνται	ὅτι δύναμις παρ᾽ αὐτοῦ ἐξήρχετο
			καὶ ἰᾶτο πάντας.
		ὅσοι εἶχον μάστιγας.	
		11 καὶ τὰ πνεύματα τὰ ἀκάθαρτα	4,41 ἐξήρχοντο δὲ καὶ δαιμόνια ἀπὸ
		ὅταν αὐτὸν ἐθεώρουν	πολλῶν
	καὶ ἐθεράπευσεν αὐτοὺς πάντας	προσέπιπτον αὐτῷ καὶ ἔκραζον	
		λέγοντα ὅτι σὺ εἶ ὁ υἱὸς τοῦ θεοῦ.	κραυγάζοντα καὶ
		12 καὶ πολλὰ ἐπετίμα αὐτοῖς	λέγοντα ὅτι σὺ εἶ ὁ υἱὸς τοῦ θεοῦ.
	16 καὶ ἐπετίμησεν αὐτοῖς	ἵνα μὴ φανερὸν αὐτὸν ποιήσωσιν.	καὶ ἐπιτιμῶν ...
	ἵνα μὴ φανερὸν αὐτὸν ποιήσωσιν		

coup mieux dans le cas d'hypothèses plus complexes qui, dans ce cas particulier, supposeraient deux documents différents dont dépendraient nos évangiles actuels.

Matthieu et Marc ont en commun 26 mots, ce qui donne une proportion de 72,22% pour Matthieu et de 25,24% pour Marc. Du point de vue matthéen, la proportion est très bonne, mais elle reste médiocre pour Marc.

Marc et Luc ont 35 mots communs, ce qui donne une proportion de 33,98% pour Marc et de 43,75% pour Luc. Du point de vue lucanien, la proportion est moyenne; elle reste assez faible pour Marc.

Il n'y a que 10 mots communs entre Matthieu et Luc, soit une proportion de 27% pour Matthieu et de 12,5% pour Luc. En plus des 9 mots communs aux trois Synoptiques (dont 3 *kai*; cf. supra), ils ne s'accordent contre Marc que sur le mot *ochlos*, contact peu significatif étant donné la fréquence de ce substantif chez l'un et chez l'autre.

De cet ensemble de statistiques, on constate qu'il n'existe aucun lien spécial entre Matthieu et Luc, mais en revanche des rapports plus particuliers entre Matthieu et Marc d'une part, Luc et Marc d'autre part. On a l'impression de se trouver devant deux traditions parallèles, relativement indépendantes: l'une serait connue de Matthieu, l'autre de Luc, et Marc les aurait fusionnées. La suite des analyses va confirmer ce que les données statistiques permettent de pressentir.

II. *Les foules et Jésus* (Mc 3:7-11 et par.).

1. *Le récit de Matthieu.* Mt 12:15 offre une structure typiquement matthéenne. La phrase *kai ēkolouthēsan autō ochloi polloi* est comme un refrain qui revient à plusieurs reprises dans Matthieu: 4:25; 8:1; 19:2; 20:29; voir aussi 14:13, sous une forme un peu différente. En 14:13 et surtout 19:2, le thème se complète par celui des guérisons effectuées par Jésus, avec la formule *kai etherapeusen autous*, comme ici. Le parallèle le plus proche de 12:15 est 19:2.

Étant donné l'identité des formules *kai ēkolouthēsan autō ochloi polloi*, on serait tenté de considérer 4:25 et 12:15 comme le dédoublement d'un même texte. Mais cette hypothèse ne s'impose pas puisque la formule, on vient de le voir, était relativement fréquente chez Matthieu.

Donc, 4:25 et 12:15 sont des textes de facture parfaitement matthéenne, sans aucune fausse note. Bien entendu, à ce point de nos analyses, il est impossible de dire si cette systématisation des formules est le fait de Matthieu lui-même ou pourrait remonter, au moins en partie, à une "tradition" matthéenne plus ancienne.

2. *Le récit de Luc*. Le récit de Lc 6:17-19, beaucoup plus original par rapport à Matthieu que celui de Marc, est également de facture très lucanienne, qu'il s'agisse du vocabulaire ou de la structure des phrases:

vocabulaire:
ὄχλος + génitif: Lc 5:29; 7:12; Ac 1:15; 6:7 seulement
πλῆθος: 0/2/8/2/17/3 (πλῆθος πολύ: 0/2/3/0/2/0)
                    (πλῆθος τοῦ λαοῦ: Lc 1:10; 6:17; 23:27; Ac 21:35)
Ἱερουσαλήμ: 2/0/27/0/39/11
ἰάομαι (bis): 3/1/11/2/4/3
ζητεῖν + infinitif: 2/1/8/11/5/4
θεραπεύεσθαι (passif): 0/0/4/1/4/2

phrases analogues:
Lc 6:18 οἳ ἦλθον ἀκοῦσαι αὐτοῦ καὶ ἰαθῆναι ἀπό ...
Lc 5:15 καὶ συνήρχοντο ὄχλοι πολλοὶ ἀκούειν καὶ θεραπεύεσθαι
                    ἀπό ... (venir écouter: cf. Lc 15:1; 21:38)
Lc 6:18 οἱ ἐνοχλούμενοι ἀπὸ πνευμάτων ἀκαθάρτων ἐθεραπεύοντο
Ac 5:16 καὶ ὀχλουμένους ὑπὸ πνευμάτων ἀκαθάρτων οἵτινες ἐθερα-
                    πεύοντο ἅπαντες
Lc 6:19 ἐζήτουν ἅπτεσθαι αὐτοῦ ὅτι δύναμις παρ' αὐτοῦ ἐξήρχετο
Lc 8:46 ἥψατό μου τις, ἐγὼ γὰρ ἔγνων δύναμιν ἐξεληλυθυῖαν ἀπ'
                    ἐμοῦ

Dans son ensemble, le récit de Luc est donc de tonalité nettement lucanienne.

3. *Le récit de Marc*. Le récit de Marc se caractérise, et par sa complexité, et par ses notes stylistiques non marciennes.

Il décrit deux mouvements de foule par rapport à Jésus: au verset 7, une grande foule *suivit* Jésus; au verset 8, une grande foule *vint* vers lui. Le premier mouvement de foule correspond à celui que décrit Matthieu, avec le même verbe; le second mouvement correspond à celui que décrit Luc, avec le même verbe. Par ailleurs, la nomenclature des régions d'où viennent les foules combine celles de Matthieu et de Luc, en partie différentes.

Selon la *Théorie des Deux Sources*, Matthieu et Luc auraient simplifié le texte de Marc, choisissant, comme par hasard, chacun ce que l'autre rejetait. Selon la *Two-Gospel Hypothesis*, Marc aurait fusionné les textes de Matthieu et de Luc. Cette seconde hypothèse nous semble la seule valable, en la formulant d'une façon plus générale: Marc aurait fusionné les textes *attestés* par Matthieu et par Luc. La raison en est que Marc utilise ici un vocabulaire qui lui est étranger et qui, au contraire, est tout à fait normal chez Matthieu et chez Luc.

— Le verbe *anachōrein* (Matthieu/Marc) ne se lit qu'ici chez Marc mais 9 fois ailleurs chez Matthieu.

— Le substantif *plēthos* (Luc/Marc) ne se lit qu'ici chez Marc (et 2 fois!) mais 7 fois ailleurs chez Luc et 17 fois dans les Actes. Le terme marcien habituel est *ochlos*.

— Pour décrire les mouvements de foule, Marc a d'abord l'aoriste *ēkolouthēsen*, avec Matthieu (au pluriel), puis l'aoriste *ēlthon*, avec Luc. Or, dans ce genre de description, il utilise presque partout ailleurs l'imparfait ou le présent. Voici les textes, en tenant compte du vocabulaire utilisé ici :

— *akolouthein*, dit d'un groupe ou d'une foule :

    2:15 ἦσαν γὰρ πολλοὶ καὶ ἠκολούθουν αὐτῷ

    5:24 καὶ ἠκολούθει αὐτῷ ὄχλος πολύς

    15:41 αἳ ... ἠκολούθουν αὐτῷ καὶ διηκόνουν αὐτῷ (Matthieu a l'aoriste)

    6:1 καὶ ἀκολουθοῦσιν αὐτῷ οἱ μαθηταὶ αὐτοῦ

— *ochlos* :

    2:13 πᾶς ὁ ὄχλος ἤρχετο πρὸς αὐτόν

    3:20 συνέρχεται πάλιν ὁ ὄχλος

    4:1 συνάγεται πρὸς αὐτὸν ὄχλος πλεῖστος

    9:25 ἰδὼν ὅτι ἐπισυντρέχει ὄχλος

    10:1 συνπορεύονται πάλιν ὄχλοι πρὸς αὐτόν (Matthieu a l'aoriste)

    5:21 συνήχθη ὄχλος πολὺς ἐπ' αὐτόν

    (seul exemple avec l'aoriste)

— *erchesthai* :

    1:45 καὶ ἤρχοντο πρὸς αὐτὸν πάντοθεν

    2:13 πᾶς ὁ ὄχλος ἤρχετο πρὸς αὐτόν

Les *deux* aoristes utilisés par Marc aux versets 7 et 8, qui correspondent à des aoristes chez Matthieu et chez Luc, sont donc tout à fait exceptionnels.

Complétons ces analyses stylistiques en jetant un regard sur le verset qui précède ce sommaire dans Matthieu et dans Marc (Mt 12:14 et Mc 3:6). La formulation en est très proche l'une de l'autre :

Mt: ἐξελθόντες δὲ οἱ Φ. συμβούλιον ἔλαβον κατ' αὐτοῦ ὅπως αὐτὸν ἀπολέσωσιν

Mc: καὶ ἐξελθόντες οἱ Φ.; ... συμβούλιον ἐδίδουν κατ' αὐτοῦ ὅπως αὐτὸν ἀπολέσωσιν

Ce genre de phrase avec *symboulion* ne se lit ailleurs chez Marc qu'en

15:1 tandis qu'il est relativement fréquent chez Matthieu: 22:15; 27:1
(= Mc 15:1); 27:7; 28:12. On pourrait faire l'hypothèse selon laquelle
Matthieu aurait systématisé une formule qu'il lisait ici chez Marc. Mais
il faudrait alors expliquer dans le texte de Marc la présence de la
conjonction *hōste* (= Matthieu), qu'il n'utilise nulle part ailleurs tandis
qu'elle est fréquente chez Matthieu: 17/1/7/1/15/42; comparer spécialement Mc 14:55 et Mt 26:59. Ce cas s'ajoute à ceux que nous avons
constatés dans le sommaire qui suit; il permet de conclure que Marc
dépend, ici comme aux versets 7 et 8, d'un texte matthéen.

La seule solution logique, pour justifier *l'ensemble* de ces faits littéraires,
est de conclure que Marc fusionne les textes attestés par Matthieu et
par Luc. Sur ce point précis, nous sommes proches de la *Two-Gospel
Hypothesis*.

III.   *La consigne de silence* (versets 16 de Matthieu et 12 de Marc).

Elle est exprimée en termes quasi identiques dans Matthieu et dans
Marc. Mais, contrairement à ce que nous avons constaté dans le
sommaire précédent, elle a une tonalité plutôt marcienne et elle se
comprend mieux dans Marc que dans Matthieu.

Le mot *phaneron* ne se lit qu'ici chez Matthieu, alors qu'on le
retrouve encore en Mc 4:22 et surtout Mc 6:14, à propos de Jésus et
avec une idée analogue à celle qui est exprimée ici: *phaneron gar egeneto
to onoma autou*. Ajoutons que le verbe *phaneroun* se lit en Mc 4:22
tandis qu'il est ignoré de Matthieu et de Luc, et que l'adverbe *phanerōs*,
inconnu également de Matthieu et de Luc, se lit en Mc 1:45; Jn 7:10 et
Ac 10:3. La formulation du thème, dans Matthieu comme dans Marc,
serait donc plus marcienne que matthéenne.

D'autre part, le contexte est bien meilleur dans Marc que dans
Matthieu. Pour le comprendre, reportons-nous aux autres consignes de
silence communes à Matthieu et à Marc. En Mc 8:20 et Mt 16:20, elle
fait suite à une confession de foi de Pierre; en Mc 9:9 et Mt 17:9,
elle vient après la déclaration de Dieu sur Jésus: "Celui-ci est mon
Fils bien-aimé". Celle de Mc 3:12 se situe exactement dans la même
perspective: après la confession de foi des esprits impurs: "Tu es le Fils
de Dieu".

Les autres consignes de silence suivent toujours un fait précis: la
guérison d'un individu particulier: Mc 1:44 et Mt 8:4; cf. Mc 5:43;
7:36. Ailleurs, on ne trouve donc jamais de consigne de silence après un
sommaire aussi général que celui de Mt 12:15.

Il faut donc admettre que la consigne de silence, ici d'origine
marcienne, est passée de Marc dans Matthieu.

L'ensemble des textes que nous venons d'analyser fait toucher du doigt la complexité du problème synoptique. Aux versets 15 de Matthieu et 7-8 de Marc (cf. aussi les versets 14 de Matthieu et 6 de Marc), il faut admettre un emprunt de Marc à la tradition matthéenne et à la tradition lucanienne. En revanche, aux versets 16 de Matthieu et 12 de Marc, c'est Matthieu qui subit l'influence de la tradition marcienne. Pour justifier ce double phénomène, il est nécessaire de remonter plus haut que nos évangiles actuels, en admettant, par exemple, l'existence d'un proto-Matthieu et d'un proto-Marc.

II. LA «TWO-GOSPEL HYPOTHESIS»

Réservant à la session plénière la discussion de l'exposé général, nous allons concentrer nos remarques sur la discussion de la composition du discours eschatologique. Nous avons d'ailleurs la conviction que le problème synoptique doit être résolu à partir d'une discussion serrée des textes synoptiques beaucoup mieux que par des considérations générales.

Le discours eschatologique de Matthieu 24 et parallèles

Une discussion sur la composition du discours eschatologique de Matthieu 24 et parallèles, texte long et difficile, demanderait tout un volume! Nos remarques ne pourront être que fragmentaires, mais porteront sur le fond même du problème.

Selon les partisans de la *Two-Gospel Hypothesis*, le discours eschatologique aurait été composé par Matthieu, sous la forme qu'il revêt maintenant dans cet évangile. Luc dépendrait entièrement de Matthieu. Il aurait gardé l'essentiel du discours matthéen en 21:5-36, mais en aurait réutilisé certaines sections pour composer d'autres discours du Christ: en 12:11-12; 12:35-48; 17:20-37. Quant à Marc, il n'aurait conservé en son chapitre 13 que certaines sections de Matthieu, spécialement celles qu'il lisait aussi en Lc 21; il aurait purement et simplement éliminé tout le reste.

Dans les pages suivantes, nous allons examiner successivement les problèmes posés par: l'activité rédactionnelle de Marc; les sections communes à Matthieu-Luc mais absentes de Marc; les sections attestées par les trois Synoptiques; les sections propres à Luc 21.

I. *L'activité rédactionnelle de Marc*

Elle est décrite aux pages 32-34 du rapport. Les principes sont simples. 1. Marc s'est donné comme but premier de composer un texte unifié à partir des sections communes à Matthieu et à Luc. Ce principe vaut pour tout l'évangile; il se vérifie ici en ce que: d'une part Marc se limite massivement aux textes communs à Matthieu/Luc; d'autre part il omet en général les textes propres à Matthieu ou à Luc. En agissant ainsi, il évite les contradictions qui pourraient exister entre les textes de Matthieu et de Luc. 2. Mais la source principale de Marc reste Matthieu; c'est pourquoi Marc omet toutes les sections propres à Luc tandis qu'il garde quelques sections matthéennes omises par Luc.

Ces deux principes sont quelque peu contradictoires; si Marc, en effet, veut réduire Matthieu et Luc à leur plus petit commun dénominateur, pourquoi garde-t-il des sections matthéennes omises par Luc? Quels critères le poussent à renoncer à son principe général pour conserver, malgré le silence de Luc, telle ou telle section de Matthieu? On aimerait que les partisans de la *Two-Gospel Hypothesis* nous le disent. Nous allons voir d'ailleurs que, à pousser un peu plus loin l'enquête, on arrive à de curieux résultats. Faisons l'inventaire des textes matthéens qui, selon la *Two-Gospel Hypothesis*, auraient été, soit complètement omis par Luc, soit placés dans un autre contexte (ses chapitres 12 et 17), et voyons comment Marc se comporte vis-à-vis d'eux (les chiffres renvoient aux versets de Matthieu 24):

— Versets *omis* par Luc et Marc: 10-12; 30a
— Versets *omis* par Luc, gardés par Marc: 8, 20, 21b-25, 31, 36
— Versets *déplacés* par Luc, omis par Marc: 26-28; 37-41; 43-51
— Versets *déplacés* par Luc, gardés par Marc: 17-18

Nous arrivons à ce résultat curieux: Marc aurait conservé à peu près les 3/4 des versets complètement omis par Luc; en revanche, il aurait éliminé presque tous les versets que Luc avait simplement déplacés (en ses chapitres 12 et 17). Si le but premier de Marc était *the formation of a common unified account out of Matthew and Luke* (p. 32), c'était une curieuse façon de procéder! A sa place, n'aurait-on pas essayé plutôt de conserver les textes matthéens que Luc avait simplement déplacés, surtout lorsque les textes de Matthieu et de Luc étaient de formulation quasi identique.

Le comportement de Marc serait d'autant moins compréhensible que, de l'aveu même des partisans de la *Two-Gospel Hypothesis* (p. 51), il se serait inspiré de Lc 12:37-38.41 pour composer sa parabole sur la vigilance, en 13:35-37. On en arrive à cette situation invraisemblable:

— Marc garde les vv. 8, 20, 21b-25, 31, 36 de Matthieu, complètement omis par Luc.
— Marc omet les vv. 43-51 de Matthieu, qu'il lisait en termes quasi identiques en Lc 12:39-40 et 42-46
— Mais Marc s'inspire de Lc 12:37-38.41 pour composer sa para-

bole sur la vigilance, bien que ces versets de Luc soient absents de Matthieu.

Où sont les deux "principes" qui auraient guidé l'activité littéraire de Marc?

II. *Les sections communes à Mt/Lc*

Des sections communes à Matthieu et à Luc, mais absentes de Marc, nous n'analyserons que Mt 24:37-41 = Lc 17:26-35, textes dans lesquels Matthieu et Luc offrent assez de divergences pour donner prise à la critique littéraire. Nous allons voir que aussi bien Matthieu que Luc offrent l'un par rapport à l'autre des notes secondaires, ce qui oblige à remonter à une source commune dont ils dépendent; par ailleurs, l'analyse du vocabulaire commun aux deux textes fait penser que cette source est de tradition lucanienne (proto-Luc).

1.   Une première approche des textes semble donner raison à la *Two-Gospel Hypothesis*, au moins en ce qui concerne la priorité matthéenne du discours. Voici comment on pourrait expliquer l'évolution des textes dans cette perspective. Dans Matthieu, le discours apparaît assez homogène, centré sur le thème du déluge: aux versets 37-39, le déluge est donné comme type de ce qui arrivera lors de la Parousie du Fils de l'homme; allusion au déluge est faite au moyen d'une citation de Gn 7:13 (cf 7:7), complétée par Gn 7:17 (cf. 7:6). Les vv. 40-41 annoncent ce qu'il en sera des humains lors de la Parousie: les uns seront pris, les autres laissés; ce thème s'inspire de Gn 7:23, où il est dit que, lors du déluge, tous les êtres vivants "furent effacés (*exēleiphthēsan*) de la terre et ne fut laissé (*kateleiphthē*) que Noé et ceux qui étaient avec lui dans l'arche".

En reprenant ce texte pour former son discours eschatologique du chapitre 17, Luc l'aurait complété en ajoutant le thème de la destruction de Sodome, à laquelle échappa Lot. Cette addition lucanienne était d'autant plus spontanée que les deux thèmes du déluge et de la destruction de Sodome étaient souvent unis dans la tradition juive. Il aurait donc composé ses versets 28-30 à l'analogie des versets 26-27, en citant Gn 19,24 pour évoquer la catastrophe qui s'était abattue sur Sodome. Sur sa lancée, il aurait encore ajouté les versets 31-33 en s'inspirant de Gn 19,17, texte dans lequel l'ange dit à Lot: σῷζων σῷζε τὴν σεαυτοῦ ψυχήν· μὴ περιβλέψῃς εἰς τὰ ὀπίσω μηδὲ στῇς ἐν πάσῃ τῇ περιχώρῳ· εἰς τὸ ὄρος σῷζου μήποτε συμπαραλημφθῇς. En 17:31, Luc aurait repris le texte de Mt 24:17-18 qui lui permettait d'évoquer Gn 19,17, comme il le dit explicitement au verset 32, en complétant *opisō* en *eis ta opisō*. Par ailleurs, le logion du v. 33 allait également très bien dans le sens de Gn 19:17, avec le thème de "sauver son âme". On notera que ce logion devait se trouver dans le *Sondergut* de Luc; si Luc en effet avait composé lui-même le texte, il aurait écrit *tēn psychēn autou sōsai*, comme en Lc 9:24 et parallèles, en accord avec la Septante de Gn 19:17. Ajoutons enfin que le double *paralemphthēsetai* des versets 34-35 correspond au *symparalemphthēs* de Gn 19:17; mais ce verbe est attesté aussi dans le parallèle matthéen, ce qui pose un problème sur lequel nous reviendrons plus loin.

Tout ceci semble très cohérent; mais cette solution tient-elle compte de toutes les données du problème?

2. Revenons au texte de Matthieu. Contrairement à Luc, nous l'avons noté, il ne donne qu'un seul exemple de cataclysme pour préfigurer la Parousie du Fils de l'homme: le déluge. Mais la formule qui exprime la comparaison entre les deux événements est dédoublée! On la trouve d'abord au verset 37, où elle reste en l'air; puis elle est reprise aux versets 38a et 39b, où elle encadre la mention du déluge. Ce dédoublement de la formule de comparaison est la preuve irréfutable que Matthieu dépend d'une source qui contenait, comme l'atteste Luc, les deux exemples du déluge et de la destruction de Sodome; on a noté plus haut (avec les partisans de la *Two-Gospel Hypothesis*) que ces deux événements étaient souvent unis dans la tradition juive. Ce n'est donc pas Luc qui aurait ajouté l'exemple de la destruction de Sodome; c'est Matthieu qui l'a supprimé, tout en conservant la formule de comparaison entre cette destruction de Sodome et ce qui arrivera aux Jours du Fils de l'homme.

Un indice stylistique confirme que, dans Matthieu, le texte primitif a subi des remaniements. Au v. 38a, au lieu de l'expression habituelle *hōsper gar* (Mt 24:27.37; 12:40; cf. 13:40) on lit *hōs gar*. Pourquoi cette anomalie? Elle trahit la main d'un rédacteur. Nous pensons que Matthieu dépend d'un texte qui avait même structure que celui de Luc:

— première formule de comparaison: Mt 37 et Lc 26
— exemple du déluge: Mt 38b-39a et Lc 27
— début de la deuxième formule de comparaison: Mt 38a et Lc 28
— exemple de la destruction de Sodome: Lc 29
— fin de la deuxième formule de comparaison: Mt 39b et Lc 30

En supprimant l'exemple de la destruction de Sodome, Matthieu aurait transféré le début de la deuxième formule de comparaison avant l'exemple du déluge, changeant le *hōsper gar* en *hōs gar*.

Il existe encore une raison de penser que Matthieu dépend d'une source qui avait les deux exemples du déluge et de la destruction de Sodome. On a vu plus haut que les versets 40-41 de Matthieu, comme les versets 34-35 de Luc, dépendent de Gn 7:23 où il est dit que tous les êtres vivants "furent effacés" (*exēleiphthēsan*) de la terre tandis que Noé seul "fut laissé" (*kateleiphthē*). Mais dans Matthieu et Luc, au lieu du verbe "furent effacés" on a le verbe *paralambanesthai* qui s'explique par influence de Gn 19:17, où il est prescrit à Lot de fuir au plus vite "de peur que tu ne sois pris-avec" (*mēpote symparalemphthēs*). Matthieu dépend donc d'une source qui avait les deux exemples du déluge et de la destruction de Sodome.

3. Revenons au texte de Luc; nous allons montrer que lui non plus n'est pas primitif. Si l'on analyse l'ensemble formé par les versets 23-35, on constate le phénomène suivant. Lorsque Luc est en parallèle *avec le seul Matthieu*, il offre un texte homogène: la venue eschatologique du Fils de l'homme sera aussi soudaine que l'éclair (Lc 23-24 = Mt 26-27); elle provoquera une catastrophe cosmique analogue au déluge (Lc 26-27 = Mt 37-39) ou à la destruction de Sodome (Lc 28-30; cf Mt 38a et 39b); lors de cette catastrophe, il s'effectuera une séparation entre les hommes: les uns seront pris et les autres laissés (Lc 34-35 = Mt 40-41), comme cela s'était produit lors du déluge (Gn 7:23) et lors de la destruction de Sodome (Gn 19:17). Tout est donc centré sur la destruction du monde ancien lors de la venue eschatologique du Fils de l'homme.

Au verset 31, Luc n'est plus en parallèle avec le seul Matthieu, mais aussi avec Mc 13:15-16; or ce verset détonne dans ce contexte de fin du monde. En effet, lors de la catastrophe eschatologique, peu importe que l'on se trouve ici ou là, que l'on se hâte de fuir ou que l'on reste sur place: le monde entier sera emporté par le cataclysme! L'invitation à fuir sans entrer dans sa maison pour y prendre ses affaires et sans regarder en arrière ne se comprend que dans un contexte de catastrophe politique telle que la destruction de Jérusalem, contexte qui est précisément celui de Mc 13:1-4 (plutôt que Mt 24:1-3; cf. *infra*). Il faut en conclure que Luc a déplacé de son contexte primitif (ruine de Jérusalem) le thème de la fuite rapide (Lc 17:31) pour l'insérer dans un discours de fin du monde qu'il tenait d'une source connue aussi de Matthieu. Nous avons déjà dit plus haut le motif de ce déplacement: Luc a pris l'expression *mē epistrepsatō (eis ta) opisō* pour une allusion à Gn 19:17, et donc à l'épisode de la destruction de Sodome, comme il le dit explicitement au verset 32. C'est aussi sous l'influence de Gn 19:17 que Luc a ajouté le logion du verset 33; inconnu de Matthieu et de Marc dans ce contexte.

Dans le discours de Lc 17:23-35, il faut donc distinguer: des matériaux connus seulement de Luc et de Matthieu qui concernent la venue du Fils de l'homme à la fin des temps et la destruction du monde ancien; des matériaux connus des trois Synoptiques et qui concernent la ruine de Jérusalem (ou du Temple). Les premiers proviennent d'une source connue de Matthieu et de Luc; les seconds d'une source qu'il restera à préciser. Nos analyses nous orientent vers une solution de type "Théorie des Deux Sources", et non de type *Two-Gospel Hypothesis*.

4. Est-il possible de préciser la nature de cette source qui contenait le discours eschatologique et dont dépendent Matthieu et Luc? Pour le tenter, il faut analyser le vocabulaire *commun* à Matthieu et à Luc, le seul dont on soit sûr qu'il remonte à leur source commune, en le comparant au vocabulaire habituel de Matthieu, à celui de Luc, enfin à celui des autres textes de la double tradition (Matthieu/Luc).

a) La première expression typique que nous rencontrons est la formule de comparaison ὥσπερ γὰρ ... οὕτως ἔσται (Mt 24:27 = Lc 17:24). Voici les autres occurrences de cette formule ou de formules très voisines:

Mt 24:27 ὥσπερ γὰρ ... οὕτως ἔσται ἡ παρουσία τοῦ υἱοῦ τοῦ ἀνθρώπου
Lc 17:24 ὥσπερ γὰρ ... οὕτως ἔσται ὁ υἱὸς τοῦ ἀνθρώπου ἐν τῇ ἡμέρᾳ αὐτοῦ

Mt 24:37 ὥσπερ γὰρ ... οὕτως ἔσται ἡ παρουσία τοῦ υἱοῦ τοῦ ἀνθρώπου
Lc 17:26 καὶ καθὼς ἐγένετο ... οὕτως ἔσται ἐν ταῖς ἡμέραις τοῦ υἱοῦ τοῦ ἀνθρώπου

Mt 24:38s ὡς γὰρ ... οὕτως ἔσται ἡ παρουσία τοῦ υἱοῦ τοῦ ἀνθρώπου
Lc 17:28s ὁμ. καθὼς ἐγένετο ... κατὰ τὰ αὐτὰ ἔσται ᾗ ἡμέρᾳ ὁ υἱὸς τοῦ ἀνθρώπου ἀποκαλύπτεται

Mt 12:40 ὥσπερ γὰρ ... οὕτως ἔσται ὁ υἱὸς τοῦ ἀνθρώπου ἐν τῇ κοιλίᾳ.
Lc 11:30 καθὼς γὰρ ἐγένετο ... οὕτως ἔσται καὶ ὁ υἱὸς τοῦ ἀνθρώπου τῇ γενεᾷ...

Mt 13:40 ὥσπερ οὖν ... οὕτως ἔσται ἐν τῇ συντελείᾳ τοῦ αἰῶνος.
ἀποστελεῖ ὁ υἱὸς τοῦ ἀνθρώπου ...

Les formules sont beaucoup plus unifiées dans Matthieu que dans Luc. Par ailleurs, la dernière se lit dans un texte propre à Matthieu. On serait donc tenté de déclarer la formule matthéenne. Mais il faut être prudent car on sait que Matthieu a tendance à systématiser ses formules et à unifier ses textes parallèles. D'autre part, on a déjà vu que, en 24:38, Matthieu avait légèrement modifié la formule stéréotypée. De même, dans le texte propre à Matthieu, au lieu de *hosper gar* habituel on a *hosper oun*, et la référence au Fils de l'homme n'est pas immédiatement dépendante de la formule *houtos estai*, comme partout ailleurs. Ces divergences pourraient indiquer un style imitatif. Il faut donc garder la possibilité d'une formule remontant à la source de Matthieu et de Luc, que Matthieu aurait quelque peu systématisée et réutilisée en 13:40, que Luc aurait adaptée à son propre style.

Le double thème "manger/boire" (versets 38 de Matthieu; 27-28 de Luc) ne se lit ailleurs que dans des textes communs à Matthieu/Luc (Mt 6:31 = Lc 12:29; Mt 11:18s = Lc 7:33s; Mt 24:49 = Lc 12:45) et dans des textes propres à Luc, où il est spécialement fréquent: 5:30,33; 10:7; 12:19; 13:26; 17:8 (bis); 22:30; Ac 9:9; 23:12,21. On notera qu'ici, pour dire "manger", Matthieu a le verbe *trôgein* tandis que partout ailleurs dans cette expression double on a le verbe *esthiein*. Matthieu serait donc secondaire par rapport à Luc.

Quant à l'expression ἄχρι ἧς ἡμέρας, de Mt 24:38 = Lc 17:27, elle est nettement lucanienne. Matthieu n'utilise nulle part ailleurs la préposition *achri*, ignorée de Marc et de Jean; elle se lit en revanche encore 3 fois dans Luc et 16 fois dans les Actes. La formule en question se retrouve en Lc 1:20 et Ac 1:2; *achri* liée à *hēmera* en Ac 2:29; 20:6; 23:1; 26:22 et 27:33.

S'il faut choisir en faveur d'une source matthéenne, d'une source lucanienne ou d'une source hypothétique Q, la balance penche assez nettement en faveur d'une source lucanienne. Mais les arguments en ce sens ne sont pas assez forts pour emporter la conviction; il faut donc élargir quelque peu notre enquête.

b) Étudions le vocabulaire commun à Matthieu/Luc dans la section concernant le témoignage de Jésus sur le Baptiste (Mt 11:2-11.16-19; Lc 7:18-35); selon la *Two-Gospel Hypothesis*, cette péricope serait de Matthieu; selon la *Théorie des Deux Sources*, elle proviendrait de la source Q. Dans les développements qui vont suivre, les chiffres donnent la fréquence de l'expression en question successivement dans Mt/Mc/Lc/Jn/Ac/Reste du NT; les chiffres concernant Luc et Actes seront soulignés.

— *prosdokan* (Mt 11:3; Lc 7:19): 2/0/6/0/5/3. Les deux occurences en Matthieu sont ici et Mt 24:50 = Lc 12:46. Dans le reste du NT, les 3 occurences sont concentrées en 2 Pierre 3:12-14. La coloration lucanienne est confirmée par le substantif *prosdokia*: Lc 21:26 et Ac 12:11 pour tout le NT.

— Couple "entendre/voir" ou "voir/entendre" (Mt 11:4; Lc 7:22), avec des verbes différents pour signifier "voir": 1/0/1/1/5/0 (Jn 3:22; Ac 2:33; 4:20; 8:6; 19:26; 22:15).

— *makarios ... hos* (Mt 11:6; Lc 7:23). Les "macarismes" sont fréquents dans Matthieu et Luc; mais on ne trouve ailleurs la construction avec un relatif qu'en Lc 14:15 (*hostis*).

— *exerchesthai idein* (Mt 11:8; Lc 7:25); ailleurs seulement en Lc 8:35; cf. 14:18.

— *nai legō hymin* (Mt 11:9; Lc 7:26); c'est le cas le plus significatif. Luc n'aime pas la formule sémitique *amēn legō hymin*, si fréquente dans les autres évangiles: 31/13/6/25/0/0. Il remplace donc *amēn* soit par *alethōs* (Lc 9:27; 12:44; 21:3), soit par *nai* (ici avec Matthieu et Lc 11:51; 12:5). L'expression ne peut absolument pas être d'origine matthéenne.

— Les formules qui introduisent une parabole sont fréquentes dans les évangiles, surtout dans Matthieu. Voici celles que l'on trouve en Mt 11:11 et Lc 7:31, avec les autres cas de formules analogues:

Lc 7:31s   τίνι οὖν ὁμοιώσω ... καὶ τίνι εἰσὶν ὅμοιοι; ὅμοιοί εἰσιν ...

Mt 11:11   τίνι δὲ   ὁμοιώσω ...   ὁμοία ἐστίν ...

Lc 13:20s τίνι ὁμοίωσω ...   ὁμοία ἐστίν ...

Mt 13:33   ὁμοία ἐστίν ...

Lc 13:18s τίνι ὁμοία ἐστίν ... καὶ τίνι ὁμοιώσω αὐτήν; ὁμοία ἐστίν ...

Mt 13:31   ὁμοία ἐστιν ...

Mc 4:30s   πῶς ὁμοιώσωμεν ... ἢ ἐν τίνι αὐτὴν παραβολῇ θῶμεν; ὡς ...

Lc 6:47s   ὑποδείξω ὑμῖν τίνι ἐστιν ὅμοιος.   ὅμοιός ἐστιν ...

Mt 7:24   ὁμοιωθήσεται ...

Pour introduire une parabole, le simple *homoia estin* se lit encore en Mt 13:44.45.47; 20:1; cf. 13:52: c'est incontestablement la formule matthéenne. Les formules complexes sont au contraire typiquement lucaniennes. Le texte de Mt 11:11 ne peut donc absolument pas être matthéen; selon toute vraisemblance, Matthieu le reprend à une source lucanienne.

— *prosphōnein* (Mt 11:16; Lc 7:32): 1/0/4/0/2/0

— "manger/boire" (Mt 11:19; Lc 7:34); à propos du texte précédent, nous avons noté que ce couple ne se lisait ailleurs que dans des textes de la double tradition (Matthieu/Luc) et dans des textes propres à Luc (8 fois) ou en Actes (3 fois).

— *philos* (Mt 11:19; Lc 7:34): 1/0/15/6/3/4

Bien qu'elles ne soient pas aussi caractéristiques, citons encore les formules suivantes:

— *ērxato legein* (Mt 11:7; Lc 7:24): 3/6/9/0/0. Notons qu'en Lc 11:29 cette formule est précédée d'un génitif absolu, comme ici dans Matthieu et dans Luc.

edikaiōthē hē sophia (Mt 11:19; Lc 7:35). Verbe *dikaioun*: 2/0/5/0/2 (très fréquent chez Paul); *sophia*: 3/1/6/0/4 (très fréquent chez Paul). L'association de ces deux mots est plus normale chez Luc que chez Matthieu.

La coloration lucanienne de toutes ces expressions est indéniable; une origine matthéenne de ces textes est impossible (contre la *Two-Gospel Hypothesis*).

c) L'analyse des textes quasi identiques de Mt 3:7b-10 et de Lc 3:7b-9 va confirmer le résultat de l'enquête précédente, tout en permettant de préciser les procédés littéraires de Matthieu.

— ποιήσατε οὖν καρπὸν ἄξιον (καρποὺς ἀξίους) τῆς μετανοίας
axios et génitif de la chose: 2/0/5/0/6/6; l'autre cas matthéen est en Mt 10:10 = Lc 10:7.
axios construit sur les verbes *poiein* ou *prassein*: 1/0/4/0/4/1.
metanoia: 2/1/5/0/6/8; l'autre cas matthéen est en 3:11, donc en même contexte.

Pour l'ensemble de la phrase, comparer avec Ac 26:20: ἄξια τῆς μετανοίας ἔργα πράσσοντας.

— πατέρα ἔχομεν τὸν ᾽Αβραάμ ... ἐγεῖραι τέκνα τῷ ᾽Αβραάμ
Ce double thème est inconnu de Matthieu et de Marc, mais fréquent chez Luc: 1:73; 13:7; 16:24.30; 19:9; Ac 7:2; 13:26. Il se lit encore chez Jn 8:33-40 (par influence paulinienne) et chez Paul: Rom 4:1.12; 9:7; 11:1; 2 Cor 11:22; Gal 3:7.29 (cf. Jac 2:21).

De ce thème, on rapprochera celui de l'Alliance conclue avec Abraham, en Lc 1:72-73; Ac 3:25 et Gal 3:14-17.

On notera en passant l'expression de Mt 3:9 *mē doxēte legein* (Lc: *mē arxēte legein*), conforme au style de Luc; *dokein* + infinitif: 1/1/5/2/3/17; ne proviendrait-elle pas d'un proto-Luc?

— Venons-en maintenant aux vv. 7b de Matthieu et de Luc. L'expression *gennēmata echidnōn* ne se lit ailleurs qu'en Mt 12:34 et 23:33. Elle semble très matthéenne! Mais Matthieu n'aurait-il pas systématisé une expression qu'il lisait ici dans sa source? Pour répondre à cette question, comparons les divers textes où revient cette expression:

Mt/Lc, ici : γεννήματα ἐχιδνῶν, τίς ὑπέδειξεν ὑμῖν φυγεῖν ἀπὸ τῆς μελλούσης ὀργῆς;
Mt 23:33   γεννήματα ἐχιδνῶν,   πῶς   φύγητε ἀπὸ τῆς κρίσεως τῆς γεέννης
Mt 12:34   γεννήματα ἐχιδνῶν,   πῶς δύνασθε ἀγαθὰ λαλεῖν πονηροὶ ὄντες.

La phrase de Mt 23:33 est très matthéenne: *krisis* au sens eschatologique: 9/0/3/10/0; et surtout *geenna*: 7/3/1/0/0/0 (les 3 occurrences dans Marc sont 9:43.45.47 = Mt 5:29.30). En revanche, la phrase commune à Matthieu (3:7b) et à Luc (3:7b) est de tonalité lucanienne: *hypodeiknymi*: 1/0/3/0/2/0; thème de la colère eschatologique: Lc 21:23 (cf. Jn. 3:36 et Paul); comparer la structure de la phrase avec celle de Lc 21:36: ἐκφυγεῖν ταῦτα πάντα τὰ μέλλοντα γίνεσθαι. Malgré l'expression *gennēmata echidnōn*, les versets 7b de Matthieu et de Luc sont de tonalité lucanienne, comme les versets suivants. On peut donc conclure

que Matthieu a systématisé l'expression *gennēmata echidnōn* qu'il lisait
dans sa source. De même, en 7:19 il reprendra *ad litteram* le texte de
3:10b.

L'analyse du vocabulaire des sections parallèles de Mt 11:2-11,15-19
= Lc 7:18-35 d'une part, de Mt 3:7b-10 = Lc 3:7b-9 d'autre part, a
prouvé que l'origine de ces textes était lucanienne, mais que Matthieu
avait tendance à systématiser certaines expressions qu'il lisait dans ses
sources. Nous pouvons maintenant revenir au discours eschatologique
de Lc 17 et à ses parallèles qui se trouvent dans Mt 24. Le tout remonte
à un proto-Luc, comme le prouvent les expressions lucaniennes *achri tēs
hēmeras* et "manger/boire", qui se lisent aussi bien dans Matthieu que
dans Luc; mais Matthieu a systématisé la formule *hōsper gar ... houtōs
estai*, d'où sa présence dans un texte propre à Matthieu (13:40), qui
contient d'ailleurs quelques variantes par rapport à la formulation
habituelle.

III. *Les sections communes aux trois Synoptiques*

Ce sont les textes les plus difficiles à analyser et les plus complexes.
Notre intention n'est pas d'offrir une solution complète qui expliquerait
la genèse de ces textes; en accord avec le principe fondamental des
théories des *Niveaux Multiples*, nous allons montrer que cette genèse ne
peut s'expliquer, ni à partir du texte actuel de Matthieu (contre la *Two-
Gospel Hypothesis*), ni à partir du texte actuel de Marc (contre la
Théorie des Deux Sources).

1. *Les introductions* (Mt 24:1-3; Mc 13:1-4).

Tandis que dans le discours de Jésus les textes de Matthieu et de
Marc sont très proches l'un de l'autre, souvent même identiques, il n'en
va pas de même dans l'introduction à ce discours. Dans l'ensemble,
Matthieu et Marc suivent leur propre style comme on peut le constater
en comparant par exemple Mt 24:3a avec Mt 14:15; 21:23 et surtout
27:19, ou Mc 13:1 avec Mc 10:17, ou encore Mc 13:3 avec Mc 9:28.
On ne peut évidemment rien tirer de cette constatation. Mais voyons de
plus près le problème en élargissant les perspectives.

Prenons d'abord les versets 1-3 de Matthieu; on y relève quelques
expressions exclusivement ou quasi exclusivement matthéennes:

— *proserchesthai* à l'indicatif (vv. 1 et 3): 22/0/2/1/3; noter que les
deux occurrences lucaniennes (1:17 et 13:31) ne recoupent pas celles de
Matthieu. D'une façon plus précise, la construction de phrase que l'on
a au v. 3: *proserchesthai* à l'indicatif + *autōi* + sujet + participe (le
plus souvent *legontes*) se lit encore en Mt 9:1; 13:36; 14:15; 15:30;

19:3; 21:23; 22:23; 26:69. Si Luc et Marc dépendaient de Matthieu, pourquoi auraient-ils systématiquement évité *tous les deux* ces 22 emplois de *proserchesthai* à l'indicatif?

— *parousia* (v. 3): 4/0/0/0/0/13 (Mt 24:3.27.37.39). Pourquoi Marc et Luc évitent-ils ce mot matthéen si fréquent dans le reste du Nouveau Testament?

— *synteleia tou aiōnos* (v. 3), expression propre à Matthieu dans tout le Nouveau Testament (13:39.40.49; 24:3; 28:20). Matthieu l'a probablement formée en s'inspirant des chapitres 11 et 12 du livre de Daniel, où le mot *synteleia*, au sens eschatologique, revient 13 fois, dont 6 fois avec un déterminatif temporel (11:6.13.35; 12:4.7.13). Mais Marc ne dépendrait-il pas de cette expression matthéenne en son verset 4? Selon les partisans de la *Two-Gospel Hypothesis*, la formule de Marc *tauta syntelesthai panta* serait un compromis entre le *synteleias* de Matthieu et l'expression *tauta ginesthai* de Luc; mais selon toute vraisemblance la formule de Marc reprend celle de Dan 12:7 *kai syntelesthēsethai panta tauta*, sans dépendre ni de Matthieu ni de Luc. La formule matthéenne est donc inconnue de Marc aussi bien que de Luc.

En définitive, le texte de Matthieu contient trop d'expressions exclusivement matthéennes pour pouvoir être considéré comme la source de Luc et de Marc.

Qu'en est-il de celui de Marc? On note d'abord au v. 3 la mention de Pierre, Jacques, Jean et André, absente des parallèles de Matthieu et de Luc. Le même phénomène s'était produit dans le récit de la guérison de la belle-mère de Pierre (Mc 1:29 et par.). Par ailleurs, en 3:16-18, Marc nomme les disciples dans cet ordre tandis que les parallèles de Matthieu et de Luc placent André aussitôt après son frère Pierre. Nous nous trouvons donc devant des textes nettement marciens. Si Matthieu et Luc dépendaient de Marc, pourquoi auraient-ils omis la mention des quatre disciples aussi bien ici que dans le récit de la guérison de la belle-mère de Pierre?

Au même verset 3, la précision *katenanti tou hierou* est absente des parallèles de Matthieu et de Luc; or on trouve une expression analogue en Mc 12:41, absente du parallèle de Luc. Si Matthieu et Luc dépendaient de Marc, pourquoi cet accord dans l'omission d'une précision qui n'offre aucune difficulté?

Notons enfin, toujours au v. 3, l'imparfait *epērōta*, assez typique du style de Marc: 0/15/5/0/0 (noter que les cinq occurrences dans Luc ne recouvrent pas celles de Marc). Si Matthieu et Luc dépendaient de Marc, pourquoi auraient-ils systématiquement évité ces 15 imparfaits de

Marc? Ce serait d'autant plus étrange pour Luc qu'il utilise lui aussi, à
l'occasion, cet imparfait, mais indépendamment de Marc.

Un autre problème est posé, à la fin du verset 1, par les deux
expressions de Marc *lithoi* et *oikodomai*, dont la première est attestée
par Luc et la seconde par Matthieu. Comme on peut le constater
souvent ailleurs, il semble bien que Marc combine les textes de Matthieu
et de Luc.

Quoi qu'il en soit de ce dernier point, le texte de Marc contient lui
aussi, trop d'expressions exclusivement marciennes, ou quasi exclusivement marciennes, pour pouvoir être considéré comme la source de
Matthieu et de Luc.

Puisque ni Matthieu, ni Marc, ne peuvent être la source des deux
autres évangiles, il faut remonter plus haut qu'eux pour expliquer le
problème synoptique.

2. *Se garder des faux christs.*

Dans le discours eschatologique, l'avertissement qu'il faut se garder
des faux christs revient à trois reprises, sous forme de triplet:

    a) Mt 24:4b-5 = Mc 13:5b-6 = Lc 21:8
    b) Mt 24:23-25 = Mc 13:21-23
    c) Mt 24:26 = Lc 17:23

En étudiant les sections propres à Matthieu/Luc et ignorées de Marc,
nous avons vu que la dernière forme du triplet provenait du proto-Luc.
Peut-on préciser d'où proviennent les deux autres? Une origine lucanienne est exclue; le problème se circonscrit donc à Matthieu et à Marc.

Dans le premier texte, commun aux trois Synoptiques, on lit l'impératif *blepete* dans Matthieu, Marc et Luc. C'est le seul cas dans Matthieu,
alors que cet impératif est fréquent dans Marc: 1/7/2/0/1. Matthieu
préfère *prosechete*, comme Luc: 5/0/4/0/2. Pour se rendre compte des
préférences, on comparera Mt 10:17; 16:6 avec Mc 13:9 et 8:15. Par
ailleurs, dans les trois Synoptiques on a la construction *eleusontai …
legontes*. Matthieu n'ignore pas l'emploi de *erchesthai* suivi d'un participe; il l'a en 11:18.19 = Lc 7:33.34, mais on a vu plus haut que ce
texte provenait d'un proto-Luc; il l'a aussi en 14:25, mais en même
temps que Marc. La construction paraît alors plus marcienne que
matthéenne puisqu'elle se lit encore en Mc 1:39; 1:40 et surtout 5:35:
erchontai … legontes. Grâce à ces deux particularités stylistiques, on
peut dire que le premier texte sur les faux christs est de tonalité
marcienne et non matthéenne. On notera que Matthieu a explicité un
texte trop concis en ajoutant le prédicat *ho christos*.

Dans le second texte, commun à Matthieu et à Marc, le thème des faux prophètes est ajouté à celui des faux christs; or ce thème ne se lit ailleurs qu'en Mt 7:15 et 24:11. Par ailleurs, la formule matthéenne "ils donneront de grands signes" est plus primitive que celle de Marc "ils feront de grands signes", d'après Deut 13:2 dont ce texte s'inspire. Selon toute vraisemblance, ce second texte sur les faux christs est d'origine matthéenne.

Il y aurait donc eu: influence de la tradition marcienne sur Matthieu (premier texte) et influence de la tradition matthéenne sur Marc (deuxième texte). Ceci suppose que l'on admette l'existence d'un proto-Matthieu et d'un proto-Marc, les influences réciproques s'étant exercées au niveau des ultimes rédactions matthéenne et marcienne.

Résumons la situation. Dans le discours eschatologique de Mt 24, nous trouvons un triplet concernant la venue des faux christs. Le premier texte de ce triplet est attesté par Mt/Mc/Lc, le deuxième par Mt/Mc, le troisième par Mt/Lc. Selon la *Two-Gospel Hypothesis*, les trois variantes du triplet remontent à l'évangile de Matthieu tel que nous l'avons maintenant (mais comment expliquer ce triplet sinon en recourant à des sources indéterminées?). Selon la *Théorie des Deux Sources*, la première variante du triplet remonterait à Marc (sous sa forme actuelle), comme aussi la deuxième; la troisième proviendrait de la source Q. Les théories des *Niveaux Multiples*, beaucoup plus souples, permettent de proposer une hypothèse qui ne sort pas du cadre de la tradition synoptique: la première variante du triplet provient d'un proto-Marc, la deuxième d'un proto-Matthieu, la troisième d'un proto-Luc. C'est au niveau des ultimes rédactions matthéenne, marcienne et lucanienne que ces diverses traditions se seraient influencées les unes les autres.

3. *Persécutions à venir.*

C'est la section la plus embrouillée! Mais elle va confirmer les résultats des analyses de la section précédente: il faut admettre aux ultimes niveaux rédactionnels des influences réciproques des traditions matthéenne et marcienne.

La situation se présente ainsi. Nous avons trois textes quasi intégrale-ment parallèles: Mt 10:17-22 = Mc 13:9-13 = Lc 21:12-19. Seuls, ceux de Marc et de Luc sont intégrés au discours sur la ruine du Temple; celui de Matthieu est intégré dans un discours missionnaire que Jésus aurait prononcé beaucoup plus tôt. Par ailleurs, dans le discours matthéen sur la ruine du Temple, on retrouve le début et la fin de ces trois textes parallèles, qui forment donc doublet dans Matthieu: il s'agit de Mt 24:9.13, avec les vv. 10-12 qui sont propres à Matthieu et le v. 14 qui est plus ou moins parallèle à Mc 13:9c-10. Enfin, Lc 12:11-12 contient le thème de l'assistance de l'Esprit lorsque les prédicateurs de l'évangile seront traînés devant les tribunaux; il y a donc également un doublet dans Luc, son texte de 12:11-12 étant littérairement plus proche de Mt 10:19 que de Mc 13:11.

Que tirer de cet imbroglio? Essayons de nous laisser guider par les textes, sans idée préconçue.

a) Analysons d'abord les trois textes parallèles de Mt 10, Mc 13 et Lc 21, en donnant toute notre attention aux textes de Matthieu et de Marc.

Un premier fait s'impose à nous: les textes de Matthieu et de Marc ne sont pas homogènes. Le discours de Jésus s'y déroule d'abord à la deuxième personne du pluriel (vv. 17-20 de Matthieu et 9-11 de Marc), puis on passe brusquement à la troisième personne (vv. 21 de Matthieu et 12 de Marc), pour revenir à la deuxième (vv. 22a de Matthieu et 13a de Marc) et finir à la troisième (vv. 22b de Matthieu et 13b de Marc). Luc a bien vu la difficulté et il s'est arrangé pour tout mettre à la deuxième personne du pluriel, quitte à remanier assez profondément la rédaction primitive (voir ses versets 16 et 19).

aa) Voyons d'abord les textes à la deuxième personne du pluriel. Il y est question avant tout de la prédication de l'évangile et des difficultés, voire des persécutions, que rencontreront les missionnaires. Ces textes sont beaucoup mieux en situation dans le discours missionnaire de Mt 10 que dans le discours sur la ruine du Temple de Mc 13. Le vocabulaire commun à Matthieu et à Marc permet d'ailleurs d'assigner une origine matthéenne à ces textes:

— *en ekeinē tē hōra* (Mt 10:19 = Mc 13:11); ailleurs en Mt 8:13; 18:1; 26:55; cf. *apo tēs hōras ekeinēs* en Mt 9:22; 15:28; 17:18; nulle part ailleurs chez Marc.

— *eneken emou* (Mt 10:18 = Mc 13:9), comme en Mt 5:11; 10:39; 16:25; ailleurs, Marc a la formule plus complète *eneken emou kai tou euaggeliou* (ou même simplement *eneken tou euaggeliou*, si l'on tient compte de la critique textuelle): Mc 8:35; 10:29.

— *hēgemon*: 9/1/2/0/6; contrairement à Matthieu, Marc ne donne jamais ce titre à Pilate.

— être frappé dans les synagogues (Mt 10:17; cf. Mc 13:9), comme en Mt 23:34.

On notera plus spécialement que la mention des sanhédrins et des synagogues se comprend mieux dans un contexte palestinien. On est tout à fait dans la perspective que suppose Mt 10:6 et 23: "Allez plutôt vers les brebis perdues de la maison d'Israël ... Vous n'aurez pas achevé de faire le tour des villes d'Israël que sera venu le Fils de l'homme".

On peut conclure: les consignes aux missionnaires, rédigées à la deuxième personne du pluriel, ont leur origine dans le discours missionnaire de Mt 10; c'est de là qu'elles sont passées dans le discours sur la ruine du Temple de Marc et de Luc.

ab) Voyons maintenant les textes à la troisième personne.

— Les versets 21 de Matthieu et 12 de Marc sont quasi identiques, mais leur vocabulaire n'offre rien de spécifique. Un indice toutefois permet de penser qu'ils sont mieux en situation dans le discours de Marc que dans celui de Matthieu. Dans Marc, les versets 8 et 12 se complètent pour exprimer des thèmes repris de Is 19:2:

Mc 13	Is 19:2
8 ἐγερθήσεται ἔθνος ἐπὶ ἔθνος καὶ βασιλεία ἐπὶ βασιλείαν	καὶ πολεμήσει
12 καὶ παραδώσει ἀδελφὸς ἀδελφὸν εἰς θάνατον	ἄνθρωπος τὸν ἀδελφὸν αὐτοῦ καὶ ἄνθρωπος τὸν πλησίον αὐτοῦ πόλις ἐπὶ πόλιν (καὶ βασιλεία ἐπὶ βασιλείαν) TM: ממלכה בממלכה

Ces deux thèmes complémentaires sont séparés dans Matthieu: une partie en 24:7 et une partie en 10:21, preuve que ce verset 21 n'est plus dans son contexte primitif mais fut transféré du discours sur la ruine du Temple dans le discours missionnaire. Dans Marc, les deux thèmes complémentaires sont séparés par les versets 9-11, ce qui confirme les conclusions précédentes: ces versets 9-11 proviennent du discours de mission et ils ont été transférés ici de façon malencontreuse par le rédacteur marcien.

— Le logion sur la nécessité de "tenir" jusqu'à la fin se lit en termes identiques en Mt 10:22b, Mt 24:13 et Mc 13:13b. Il a certainement son origine dans le discours sur la ruine du Temple et semble être de rédaction matthéenne. Il s'inspire en effet de Daniel 12:12 et l'on sait que le discours eschatologique comporte de nombreuses citations de ce prophète. La rédaction matthéenne apparaît lorsque l'on rapproche Mt 24:3,13 de Dan 12:12-13.

Mt 24	Dan 12 (Theodotion)
3 καὶ τί τὸ σημεῖον τῆς σῆς παρουσίας καὶ συντελείας τοῦ αἰῶνος;	12 μακάριος ὁ ὑπομένων καὶ φθάσας εἰς ἡμέρας χιλίας τριακοσίας τριάκοντα πέντε
13 ὁ δὲ ὑπομείνας εἰς τέλος οὗτος σωθήσεται.	13 ... ἔτι γὰρ ἡμέραι εἰς ἀναπλήρωσιν συντελείας καὶ ἀναστήσῃ εἰς τὸν κλῆρόν σου εἰς συντέλειαν ἡμερῶν.

Il apparaît donc qu'il y eut une harmonisation du discours de mission de Mt 10 sur le discours eschatologique de Mc 13 et une harmonisation du discours sur la ruine du Temple de Mc 13 sur le discours de mission de Mt 10. Les sections formulées à la deuxième personne du pluriel sont passées du discours de mission dans le discours sur la ruine du Temple; les sections formulées à la troisième personne sont passées du discours sur la ruine du Temple dans le discours de mission.

b) La section de Mt 24:9-14 est difficile à analyser. Elle n'est pas homogène de plusieurs points de vue. D'une part, la formulation passe brusquement de la deuxième personne du pluriel (v. 9) à la troisième personne du pluriel (vv. 10-12). D'autre part, tandis que les vv. 9 et 13 sont en étroit parallèle avec Mc 13:9a.13, les versets 10-12 sont propres à Matthieu (malgré les contacts thématiques du v. 10 de Matthieu avec le verset 12 de Marc), et le verset 14 a son parallèle dans les versets 9c-10 de Marc. On notera que ce verset 14 est incompatible avec Mt 10:23: "Vous n'aurez pas achevé de faire le tour des villes d'Israël que sera venu le Fils de l'homme". Il semble que ces versets 9-14 soient une composition du Rédacteur matthéen.

c) Il y a peu de choses à dire du texte de Lc 21:12-19. Sa rédaction est assez libre et il est difficile de dire s'il se rapproche littérairement du texte de Mc 13 ou de celui de Mt 10. On a vu qu'il avait amélioré le discours en mettant tout à la deuxième personne du pluriel (vv. 16 et 19). Aux versets 14-15, il a retravaillé sa source en fonction de son propre vocabulaire et des thèmes qui lui sont chers.

En 12:11-12, Luc est plus proche de Mt 10:19-20 de Mc 13:11; il a donc connu le discours missionnaire tel qu'il est en Matthieu.

De toutes ces analyses, on peut conclure qu'il est impossible de tenir Mt 10:17-22 pour la source de Mc 13:9-13, comme le voudrait la *Two-Gospel Hypothesis*, ni Mc 13:9-13 pour la source de Mt 10:17-22, comme le voudrait la *Théorie des Deux Sources*. Le problème est beaucoup plus complexe et ne peut être résolu qu'en faisant appel à des états des discours antérieurs aux rédactions actuelles de Matthieu et de Marc.

4. *La venue du Fils de l'homme* (Mt 24:29-31; Mc 13:24-27).

Le thème de la fin du monde et de la venue du Fils de l'homme se lit en termes souvent identiques dans Matthieu et dans Marc, le texte de Matthieu contenant simplement quelques détails absents de celui de Marc (verset 30a de Matthieu, et mention du son de la trompette au v. 31). Il existe de bonnes raisons de penser que ce thème est d'origine matthéenne, d'où il est passé chez Marc.

a) Dans l'introduction du discours, nous l'avons vu, Marc et Luc ne mentionnent que la ruine du Temple dans la question que posent à Jésus ses interlocuteurs. Matthieu au contraire a joint au thème de la ruine du Temple celui de la Parousie et de la fin du monde. Qu'implique pour lui ce double thème? Pour le savoir, reportons-nous à la parabole de l'ivraie (13:24-30), à son explication (13:36-43), à la parabole du filet jeté dans la mer (13:47-50), textes qui sont tous propres à Matthieu. Lors de la "fin du monde" (*synteleia tou aiōnos*: vv. 39.40.49), le Fils de l'homme enverra ses anges (13:41.49) afin de séparer justes et impies; les impies seront exterminés tandis que les justes seront rassemblés dans le royaume (13:30.43.48).

C'est le scénario qui est décrit en Mt 24:29-31 comme en Mc 13:24-27: le monde chancelle, le Fils de l'homme arrive sur les nuées du ciel, il envoie ses anges rassembler tous les élus. Rapprochons quelques textes significatifs, tirés de Matthieu:

24:3   τί τὸ σημεῖον τῆς σῆς παρουσίας καὶ συντελείας τοῦ αἰῶνος
24:31   καὶ ὄψονται τὸν υἱὸν τοῦ ἀνθρώπου ἐρχόμενον ... (= Marc/Luc)
         καὶ ἀποστελεῖ τοὺς ἀγγέλους αὐτοῦ καὶ ἐπισυνάξουσιν τοὺς ἐκλέκτους (= Marc)
13:40   οὕτως ἔσται ἐν τῇ συντελείᾳ τοῦ αἰῶνος
13:41   ἀποστελεῖ ὁ υἱὸς τοῦ ἀνθρώπου τοὺς ἀγγέλους αὐτοῦ καὶ συλλέξουσιν ...
13:30   τὸν δὲ σῖτον συναγάγετε εἰς τὴν ἀποθήκην μου

Pour contester l'origine matthéenne de ce double scénario de la fin du monde et de la Parousie du Fils de l'homme, on pourrait objecter que, pour compenser ses paraboles du chapitre 13, Matthieu se serait inspiré du scénario qu'il lisait en Mc 13:24-27 de même qu'il se serait inspiré des textes donnant la prédication de Jean Baptiste en Mt 3:12 et Lc 3:17. Mais il resterait à expliquer pourquoi, dans l'introduction du discours, Matthieu est le seul à parler de Parousie et de fin du monde tandis que Marc et Luc ne parlent que de la ruine du Temple.

b) Il existe d'ailleurs un autre indice qui prouve l'origine matthéenne du thème de la venue du Fils de l'homme dans ce discours eschatologique; c'est le logion sur l'ignorance du jour et de l'heure exprimée en Mt 24:36 et Mc 13:32. D'après les paraboles sur la vigilance qui se lisent aussi bien dans Marc que dans Matthieu, ce logion concerne certainement le retour du Christ à la fin des temps. Or il est exprimé en termes dont on ne trouve pas d'équivalent ailleurs chez Marc tandis qu'ils sont bien attestés chez Matthieu. Notons d'abord la formule *peri de tas hēmeras ekeinas ē tēs hōras*, on comparera avec Mt 24:50 = Lc 12:46: *hēxei ho kyrios tou doulou ekeinou en hēmera hē ou prosdoka kai en hōra hē ou ginōskei*, et avec Mt 25:13: *gregoreite oun hoti ouk oidate tēn hēmeran oude tēn hōran*. Sur le thème de "l'heure" à laquelle le Fils de l'homme doit revenir, voir encore Mt 24:44 = Lc 12:40.

Quant à la formule *oudeis oiden ... oude ho hyios ei mē ho pater*, il faut la comparer à Mt 11:27 (cf. Lc 10:22): *kai oudeis epiginōskei ton hyion ei mē ho pater*; ce sont les seuls textes des Synoptiques où l'on ait la juxtaposition des termes absolus "le Fils", "le Père" (de ton si johannique), et la formule *oudeis ... ei mē ho pater*.

Même si Matthieu tient tous ces textes, soit de la source Q, soit d'un proto-Luc, il les connaît tandis que Marc les ignore. Ils ne peuvent absolument pas être de tradition marcienne. Ceci confirme que c'est dans la tradition matthéenne et non dans la tradition marcienne que provient, dans le discours eschatologique, le thème du retour du Fils de l'homme.

c) Considérons enfin le logion attesté en termes quasi identiques par Mt 24:34, Mc 13:30 et Lc 21:32. Il y est dit que tous les événements dont il vient d'être question dans le discours eschatologique arriveront avant que "cette génération ne passe". Il faut donc situer du vivant, même de cette génération, le retour du Fils de l'homme. Or cette perspective temporelle est celle de Matthieu. Elle est explicitement mentionnée en Mt 10:23, texte dans lequel Jésus dit aux prédicateurs de l'évangile: "Vous n'achèverez pas le tour des villes d'Israël avant que ne vienne le Fils de l'homme". De même, le texte de Mt 16:27-28 dit explicitement que le retour du Fils de l'homme dans sa gloire, pour le grand jugement, se fera du vivant même de beaucoup de ceux qui sont là à écouter le Christ. Voyons au contraire le parallèle de Mc 9:1. D'une part, il ne parle pas de la venue du Fils de l'homme mais seulement de la venue en puissance du royaume de Dieu. Par ailleurs, il est introduit par la formule rédactionnelle "et il leur disait", ce qui indique un logion indépendant du texte qui précède (texte sans aucun doute eschatologique). Or la provenance de ce logion pourrait bien être matthéenne. On notera en effet la formule *heōs an*, attestée dans les trois Synoptiques, que Matthieu utilise encore ailleurs en 2:13; 5:18 (bis); 5:26; 10:11; 23:39 et 24:34, tandis que Mc ne l'a ailleurs qu'en 6:10, texte qui recoupe celui de Mt 10:11. En Mc 13:30, on a *mechris hou* tandis que les parallèles de Matthieu et de Luc ont *heōs an*.

En définitive, on peut conclure que le thème de la venue du Fils de l'homme dans le discours eschatologique est de tradition matthéenne. La tradition marcienne primitive ne devait comporter que les sections qui concernent directement la destruction du Temple (et donc de Jérusalem), et c'est pourquoi l'introduction du discours ne mentionne que la destruction du Temple.

L'analyse des textes communs à Matthieu, Marc et Luc a montré une forte influence matthéenne sur les rédactions marcienne et lucanienne ce qui, dans une certaine mesure, donnerait raison à la *Two Gospel Hypothesis* contre la *Théorie des Deux Sources*. Mais il est impossible de justifier tous les faits littéraires présentés par ces textes en recourant au seul texte de Matthieu. Il y eut influences réciproques des traditions matthéenne et marcienne qui se font sentir au niveau des rédactions actuelles.

IV. *Les sections propres à Luc*

Les analyses de Lc 17:23-35 et des parallèles matthéens avaient permis de déceler l'existence d'un discours apocalyptique remontant à un proto-Luc dont dépendraient les rédactions actuelles de Luc 17 et de Matthieu 24. L'analyse des petites sections propres à Luc dans le discours eschatologique de Lc 21 va permettre de retrouver un discours de Jésus, remontant lui aussi au proto-Luc, qui concernait la ruine de Jérusalem sans qu'il y soit question de la venue du Fils de l'homme à la fin des temps.

1. Le texte de Lc 21:20-28 se compose de deux éléments bien différenciés: une rédaction originale, sans parallèle dans Matthieu et dans Marc (sinon un mot commun par-ci par-là), entrecoupée de courts sections qui, elles, sont identiques ou quasi identiques aux textes de Matthieu et de Marc. Les versets originaux sont: 20, 21b-22, 23b-25, 28; les versets identiques à ceux des deux autres Synoptiques sont: 21a, 23a, 26-27. Selon une hypothèse déjà présentée par V. Taylor, T.W. Manson, P. Winter et surtout A. Salas, Luc dépendrait d'une source plus ancienne qu'il aurait complétée en y insérant des fragments repris *ad litteram* de Matthieu ou de Marc. Selon les partisans de la *Two-Gospel Hypothesis*, Luc se serait contenté de compléter le texte de Matthieu en y insérant des compositions de son crû (on verra plus loin qu'effectivement le langage est lucanien). Mais cette solution simpliste ne rend pas compte de certaines difficultés du texte actuel de Luc. Par exemple, au verset 20, Jésus indique le signe permettant de reconnaître que la ruine de *Jérusalem* est proche. Le verset 21b précise: "Que ceux qui seront *en elle* s'en éloignent et que ceux qui seront à la campagne n'entrent pas *en elle*". Mais le verset 21a, absolument identique aux parallèles de Matthieu et de Marc, rompt cette séquence harmonieuse en introduisant la mention de la Judée qu'il faut fuir sans retard. Avec ce verset 21a, les pronoms *autēs* et *autēn* du verset 21b se rapportent à la Judée nommée au verset 21a, et non plus à Jérusalem mentionnée au verset 20. Le verset 21a apparaît donc comme un corps étranger dans un ensemble cohérent dont il détruit l'harmonie. Il faut dire que le

verset 21 a (identique à Matthieu et à Marc) a été inséré entre les versets 20 et 21 b (propres à Luc), et non que les versets 20 et 21 b auraient été ajoutés pour encadrer le verset 21 a. La difficulté du texte lucanien, sous sa forme actuelle, vient de ce que l'évangéliste veut fusionner des textes primitivement indépendants.

De même, le verset 28 se comprend mal après le verset 27. Au verset 27, en effet, nous avons une description de la venue du Fils de l'homme "avec grande puissance et gloire" quasi identique à ce qu'elle est dans Matthieu et surtout dans Marc; ce retour du Christ marque évidemment l'arrivée des temps eschatologiques. Alors, comment Luc peut-il écrire au verset 28: "Levez vos têtes parce que votre délivrance *est proche*"? La délivrance n'aurait-elle pas été effectuée par la venue du Fils de l'homme? Si Luc avait composé de son crû ce verset 28, il aurait écrit "parce que votre délivrance *est arrivée*". Ici encore, la difficulté du texte lucanien provient de ce que l'évangéliste veut fusionner deux textes primitivement indépendants.

2.   Pour A. Salas, cette source distincte de Matthieu et de Marc, que l'on peut reconstituer par delà la rédaction actuelle de Luc, serait un proto-Luc. Nous le croyons aussi, car le vocabulaire et le style sont lucaniens.

— *kykloun*: ici et Ac 14:20; Jn 10:24; Heb 11:30
— *hierousalēm* (bis): 2/0/26/0/39/11
— *ekchōrein*: hapax du NT; mais cf. *hypochōrein*: Lc 5:16; 9:10.
                           anachōrein: Ac 23:19; 26:31 et Matthieu
— *chōra*: 2/4/9/3/8/1
— *ekdikēsis*: Lc 18:7.8; 21:22; Ac 7:24 et Paul
— *pimplēmi*: 2/0/13/0/9/0
— *plēsthēnai panta ta gegrammena*: cf. Lc 18:31; 22:37; 24:44;
                               Ac 13:29
— *ēchos*: Lc 4:37; 21:25; Ac 2:2; Heb 12:19
— *prosdokia*: Lc 21:26; Ac 12:11; cf. *prosdokan*: 2/0/6/0/5/3
— *eperchesthai*: 0/0/3/0/4/2
— *oikoumenē*: 1/0/3/0/5/5
— *anakyptein*: Lc 13:11; 21:28 (Jn 8:7.10)
— *epairein*: 1/0/6/3/5/3

3.   Quelle était l'introduction du discours dans le proto-Luc? L'hypothèse la plus simple serait de proposer l'introduction du discours actuel, en Lc 21:5-7, ce qui expliquerait qu'elle soit si différente de celles qui se lisent dans Matthieu et dans Marc. Les gens avec lesquels Jésus dialogue ne sont, ni ses disciples (Matthieu), ni un de ses disciples

(Marc), mais des personnes anonymes (*tinōn legontōn*) qui se trouvàient sur l'esplanade du Temple; pourquoi Luc aurait-il "dépersonnalisé" le récit qu'il aurait repris de Matthieu ou de Marc? Par ailleurs, le début du dialogue se tient tandis que Jésus se trouve encore dans le Temple, tandis que Matthieu et Marc disent explicitement qu'il en est sorti. Enfin, c'est toujours dans le Temple que Jésus prononce son discours devant les mêmes gens anonymes, tandis que dans Matthieu et dans Marc il se trouve sur le mont des Oliviers, assis avec ses disciples. Toutes ces particularités du texte lucanien ne seraient-elles pas plus faciles à justifier si Luc dépendait d'un proto-Luc? L'argument n'est toutefois pas très convaincant, car l'insistance à placer Jésus dans le Temple pourrait provenir, chez Luc, d'un motif théologique.

Il est possible de proposer une meilleure solution. Dans Matthieu et Marc, le discours de Jésus concerne la ruine *du Temple*, annoncée en Mt 24:2 et Mc 13:2 (cf. Lc 21:6). Mais dans les sections propres à Luc, il s'agit d'une façon plus générale de la ruine *de Jérusalem*, annoncée explicitement dès le verset 20. Le glissement de perspective est évident si l'on compare Mt 24:25 et Lc 21:20; dans le texte de Matthieu, le "signe" de la fin sera la profanation du Lieu Saint (= le Temple) par l'abomination de la désolation (*bdelygma tēs erēmōseōs*); mais le texte lucanien porte: "Lorsque vous verrez Jérusalem encerclée par les armées, alors sachez que sa désolation (*erēmōsis*) est proche". Cette destruction de Jérusalem sera encore rappelée au verset 24 au moyen d'une citation de Zacharie 12:3: Jérusalem sera foulée aux pieds par les Nations. Les sections propres à Luc ne mentionnent jamais le Temple. Reportons-nous alors à Lc 19:41-44, texte propre à Luc dans lequel Jésus annonce précisément la ruine de Jérusalem. Ce passage est en partie parallèle à Mt 24:1-3 et à Mc 13:1-4 puisque la destruction de Jérusalem est annoncée dans les mêmes termes que la destruction du Temple: "Ils ne laisseront pas pierre sur pierre en toi" (19:44). Selon toute probabilité, nous avons là l'introduction au discours de Jésus sur la ruine de Jérusalem dans le proto-Luc. Ainsi, dans Matthieu et Marc, nous avons une annonce de la ruine *du Temple* suivie d'un discours de Jésus donnant les signes avant-coureurs de cette ruine; dans le proto-Luc, on avait une annonce par Jésus de la ruine *de Jérusalem* (19:41-44) suivie par un discours donnant les signes avant-coureurs de cette ruine de Jérusalem (21:7 ou un texte analogue, puis 21:20,21b etc.).

Le style lucanien de 19:41-44 est très marqué:
— *hōs* conjonction: 0/2/26/20/34/13; *hōs ēggisen*, comme en 19:29
— *klaō epi*: Lc 23:28 (bis)
— *ta pros eirēnēn*: Lc 14:32

— *nyn de*: dans les Synoptiques, ailleurs seulement en Lc 16:25; mais fréquent chez Jean et Paul.

— *hēxousin hēmerai*; cf. *eleusontai hēmerai*: Lc 17:22; 21:6

— *synechein*: 1/0/<u>6</u>/0/<u>3</u>/2

— *anth'hōn*: Lc 1:20; 12:3; Ac 12:23. Dans Lc 1,20 et Ac 12:23, les thèmes sont analogues: un châtiment est annoncé, puis Luc donne la raison de ce châtiment en une phrase construite sur *anth'hōn*.

c) Quelle était la conclusion du discours sur la ruine de Jérusalem dans le proto-Luc? Les versets 29-33 du chapitre 21 de Luc reprennent *ad litteram* les textes de Matthieu et de Marc, et sont donc du Rédacteur lucanien. Nous avons ensuite les consignes de sobriété et de vigilance des versets 34-36 qui, de nouveau, offrent un texte propre à Luc (sauf deux contacts avec Mc 13:33: *agrypneite/kairos*). Selon toute vraisemblance, il s'agit là d'un texte du proto-Luc. Il serait tentant de voir là la conclusion du discours sur la destruction de Jérusalem selon ce document, et c'est la position adoptée par A. Salas et que nous avions nous-mêmes proposée dans le rapport préliminaire. Cette solution toutefois ne va pas sans difficulté. Dans le discours du proto-Luc sur la ruine de Jérusalem, en effet, il n'est pas question de la venue du Fils de l'homme, mentionnée explicitement dans notre texte (21:36); cette mention serait-elle alors une addition du Rédacteur lucanien? Ce ne serait pas impossible, mais il se présente une autre alternative: Lc 21:34-36 serait la finale du discours eschatologique que nous avons analysé à propos de Lc 17 et de ses parallèles de Mt 24. Le double thème de rester sobre et de veiller convient beaucoup mieux à un discours sur le retour du Fils de l'homme (Lc 17:22-30) qu'à un discours sur la destruction de Jérusalem (Lc 21). Par ailleurs, Salas a bien montré que l'expression de 21:35 *epi prosōpon pasēs tēs gēs* provenait de Gn 7:23, texte qui, nous l'avons vu, avait commandé la rédaction de Lc 17:34-35 et de Mt 24:40-41. Le texte de Lc 21:34-36 se situerait donc parfaitement dans la ligne du discours de Lc 17 sur la venue soudaine du Fils de l'homme.

Nous laissons ouvert le problème des rapports entre Lc 21:34-36 et 1 Thess 5:1-6.

d) Il reste un dernier problème à étudier. Nous avons vu que le Rédacteur lucanien avait rédigé le discours du chapitre 21 en insérant, dans un texte du proto-Luc, des sections reprises du discours sur la ruine du Temple tel qu'il se lit dans Matthieu et dans Marc. En le faisant, Luc dépend-il de Matthieu, ou de Marc, ou de l'un et de l'autre?

On ne peut rien tirer des versets 21a et 23a de Luc puisque les trois Synoptiques ont le même texte. Il est possible que le verset 23b de Luc ait subi l'influence de l'autre tradition; en ce cas, son *estai gar anagchē megalē* dépendrait en partie du texte de Matthieu *estai gar tote thlipsis megalē*, et ne devrait rien à celui de Marc. De même au verset 26b, Luc a *tōn ouranōn* avec Matthieu, au lieu de *en tois ouranois* (Marc). Au verset 27, Luc suit au contraire le texte court de Marc, sauf pour la position de l'adjectif *pollēs* en finale. Il ne faut pas oublier enfin le texte de Lc 17:31 qui provient de Mt 24:17-18 ou de Mc 13:15-16. La rédaction lucanienne, ici assez indépendante, se rapproche plutôt de celle de Matthieu, sauf pour l'expression *eis ta opisō*; mais on a vu que celle-ci pouvait avoir été influencée par Gn 19:17.

En résumé, Luc semble plutôt dépendre du texte matthéen, sauf pour son verset 27. Dans ce dernier cas, dépend-il de Marc, ou d'un proto-Matthieu qui aurait été surchargé au niveau de la Rédaction matthéenne? Il est impossible de répondre à partir des seuls textes que nous venons d'étudier.

Conclusions générales

Selon la *Two-Gospel Hypothesis*, il faudrait expliquer ainsi les relations entre les trois Synoptiques pour le discours eschatologique qui suit l'annonce de la ruine du Temple. Le texte fondamental serait celui de Mt 24-25, qui donnerait de ce discours la forme la plus primitive qui nous soit parvenue. Luc ne dépendrait que de Matthieu, mais qu'il aurait profondément remanié: il aurait déplacé un certain nombre de sections pour former ses discours eschatologiques des chapitres 12 et 17; il aurait supprimé quelques sections; il aurait amplifié plusieurs passages en introduisant des gloses de son crû. Quant à Marc, il aurait composé son discours du chapitre 13 en ne gardant que les sections communes à Mt 24 et à Lc 21, mais en donnant toutefois une préférence au texte de Matthieu.

Cette façon de voir les choses se heurte à plusieurs objections. D'une part, la façon de procéder de Marc apparaît incohérente et ne correspondrait que très imparfaitement aux principes qu'il aurait voulu suivre selon la *Two-Gospel Hypothesis*. Par ailleurs, les sections matthéennes qui sont ignorées de Marc et qui se lisent dans d'autres contextes chez Luc (aux chapitres 12 et surtout 17) ont un vocabulaire qui n'est absolument pas matthéen; elles ne peuvent donc pas être d'origine matthéenne et doivent provenir d'une source particulière, comme l'affirme la *Théorie des Deux Sources*; mais nous pensons que cette source n'est autre qu'un proto-Luc. Notons que, si l'on refuse le recours à des sources différentes, il est impossible d'expliquer les doublets qui se lisent dans nos évangiles actuels, et spécialement dans le discours eschatologique. Enfin, même si l'on peut reconnaître une influence matthéenne assez marquée dans les sections du discours communes aux trois Synoptiques, certaines de ces sections sont beaucoup trop complexes pour pouvoir s'expliquer sans recourir à des rédactions antérieures à nos rédactions actuelles.

M.-É. BOISMARD

PART TWO

INVITED PAPERS ON RELATED ISSUES

THE HISTORY OF THE SYNOPTIC DISCUSSION

The three Gospels according to Matthew, Mark, and Luke are called "synoptic" because their texts can be studied in parallel columns in a so-called Synopsis (in Greek σύνοψις, "survey"), which discloses their similarities and differences. Any adequate synopsis must present the units of each Gospel in their own sequence. The first Greek synopsis of this kind was published in 1774 by Johann Jakob Griesbach in Halle,[1] and the expression "synoptic" was used thereafter for the Gospels in question.

Reading the Gospels in a synopsis facilitates the study of the "synoptic problem." This expression implies discussion of the historical, literary, and theological relationships between Matthew, Mark, and Luke.

I

Several attempts to compare and harmonize the Gospels were already made in antiquity. One notes especially the lists of analogous passages constructed by Eusebius which received general attention.[2] But a more detailed analysis of synoptic analogies or differences was only possible after the publication of Griesbach's Synopsis and its successors. During the decades before and after A.D. 1800, Protestant theologians in Germany developed four theories to answer the synoptic question with regard to the genealogy of traditions: (1) the utilization hypothesis; (2) the proto-gospel theory; (3) the tradition hypothesis; (4) the multiple source theory. With some variations, and sometimes in combination with each other, these four theories are still of importance for the scholarly discussion, which has now become international and inter-confessional.

---

[1] Originally the presentation of Matthew, Mark, and Luke in parallel columns was part of Griesbach's general New Testament text edition: J.J. Griesbach, *Libri historici Novi Testamenti graece, 1* (Halle, 1774). Two years later Griesbach printed the text of the first three Gospels in separate form: *Synopsis evangeliorum Matthaei, Marci et Lucae* (Halle, 1776). Numerous new editions and revisions have later appeared in various languages.

[2] Reprinted in K. & B. Aland, *Novum Testamentum graece*, 26th ed. (Stuttgart: Deutsche Bibelstiftung, 1979), 73-78.

1. The Utilization Hypothesis

Implying that one evangelist was dependent upon another, the utilization theory is a theory which has mostly been regarded as the least complicated. The order in which the utilization took place, however, could always be pictured in different manners.

(a) In the old church and later, Matthew was granted priority because his Gospel introduces the Canon and because he is mentioned among the Apostles. Thus the sequence Matthew — Mark — Luke was represented by Origen and Ammonius in the 3rd century and by Augustine around the year 400.[3] In later centuries this order was accepted for instance by the Dutch scholar Hugo Grotius in 1641.[4]

(b) In publications of the years 1783 and 1789-90, Griesbach suggested the sequence Matthew — Luke — Mark.[5] On the basis of his Synopsis he saw the possibility of regarding the Second Gospel as a short recapitulation of the two others. Just because he presented the synoptic Gospels in parallel columns without changing the order of each text, Mark's consistently intermediate position became evident to him.

---

[3] Origen quoted by Eusebius in his *History* VI.25.3,6. Ammonius Alexandrinus quoted by Eusebius in his *Epistula ad Carpianum*, reprinted in Aland (n. 2), 73-74: a synopsis beginning with Matthew. Augustine, *De consensu evangelistarum* I. 23, reprinted in *Corpus scriptorum ecclesiasticorum latinorum 43* (Vienna: F. Tempsky, 1904), 3-6: "Mark the successor and abbreviator of Matthew." In IV. 10-11, however, Mark was also said partly to follow Luke: see D. Peabody, "Augustine and the Augustinian Hypothesis," in W.R. Farmer (ed), *New Synoptic Studies* (Macon GA: Mercer University Press, 1983), 37-64.

[4] H. Grotius, *Annotationes in libros evangeliorum* (Amsterdam, 1641), 5-8: Hebrew Matthew → Greek Mark; p. 594: Matthew → Mark → Luke.

[5] J.J. Griesbach, *Fontes unde evangelistae suas de resurrectione Domini narrationes hauserint*, Osterprogramm der Universitaet Jena, 1783; reprinted in Griesbach, *Opuscula academica*, 2 (Jena: Fromann, 1825), 241-256; idem, *Commentatio qua Marci evangelium totum e Matthaei et Lucae commentariis decerptum esse monstratur, scripta nomine Academiae Jenensis 1789-1790 jam recognita multisque argumentis locupletata*, printed in J.C. Velthusen e.a. (ed.), *Commentationes theologicae*, 1 (Leipzig, 1794): 360ff.; reprinted in Griesbach, *Opuscula academica*, 2:358-425. Reprint and English translation in J.B. Orchard & T.R.W. Longstaff (eds.), *J.J. Griesbach. Synoptic and Textcritical studies 1776-1976*, SNTSMS 34 (Cambridge: University Press, 1978), 74-102.

Earlier suggestions to place Mark historically after Matthew and Luke are known (1) from the patristic time and (2) from the 18th century, though Griesbach did not mention this. Re (1): Around the year 200, Clement of Alexandria said in his *Hypotyposeis* that Matthew and Luke had preceded Mark (see Eusebius, *History* VI. 14.5-7). Two hundred years later, Augustine declared a similar view to be a possible alternative, partly correcting the position taken earlier in his *de consensu evangelistarum* (see above, note 3). Re (2): Shortly before Griesbach's time, the order Matthew → Luke → Mark had been proposed by Henry Owen, *Observations on the Four Gospels, Tending Chiefly to Ascertain the Times of their Publication, and to Illustrate the Form and Manner of their Composition*

Mark's arrangement of the material is sometimes in simultaneous correspondence with that of Matthew and Luke, at other times in alternating correspondence with that of Matthew or that of Luke.

Griesbach's important student Professor Wilhelm Martin Leberecht de Wette of Basel supported his theory by analyzing numerous passages which could further demonstrate the alternating dependence of Mark upon the two other evangelists.[6]

During the second third of the 19th century, Griesbach's theory was also represented by Ferdinand Christian Baur in Tübingen and the members of his school. But since they applied Hegel's dialectic process of thesis, antithesis, and synthesis to the synoptic material, their expositions became rigorously schematic and brought the historical views of Griesbach and de Wette into discredit.[7]

(c) In the year 1786, exactly between the two studies of Griesbach quoted above, the priority of Mark in relation to Matthew and Luke was suggested by Gottlob Christian Storr.[8] At that time Storr was a professor in Tübingen, and later became a chaplain of the court in Stuttgart. In spite of his great renown, the priority of Mark suggested by Storr did not find many adherents in his lifetime, because his contemporaries were still partial either to Matthew or to the oral tradition.

After the political revolution of the year 1830, however, German protestants began to develop a predilection for Mark. The homely reports of Mark pleased a generation stamped by bourgeois liberalism

(London, 1764), p. 32; and the order Luke → Matthew → Mark by Anton Friedrich Büsching, *Die vier Evangelisten mit ihren eigenen Worten zusammengesetzt und mit Erklaerungen versehen* (Hamburg, 1766), 99, 108, 118-120. Circumstances which indicate that Griesbach knew of Owen's and Büsching's studies have been pointed out by Frans Neirynck, "The Griesbach Hypothesis: The Phenomenon of Order," *EphTheolLov.* 58 (1982) 111-122, esp. 116-117 (in note 24, a reference to observations of H. Marsh made in A.D. 1789); and D. Dungan, "The Purpose and Provenance of the Gospel of Mark according to the Two-Gospel (Owen-Griesbach) Hypothesis," in *New Synoptic Studies* (1983; see above, n. 3), 411-440, esp. 412-414. Yet even if Griesbach knew of Owen's and Büsching's studies, he did not quote them.

[6] W.M.L. de Wette, *Lehrbuch der historisch kritischen Einleitung in die kanonischen Buecher des Neuen Testaments* (Berlin: Reimer, 1826), 128-171; 5th enlarged ed. (1848), 131-179.

[7] On the synoptic theory of Griesbach and its later development: W.R. Farmer, *The Synoptic Problem. A Critical Analysis* (New York: Macmillan, 1964; 3rd edition, Macon, GA: Mercer Univ. Press, 1976) 5-9. B. Reicke, "Griesbach's Answer to the Synoptic Question," and "Introduction" (to his Commentatio), in *J.J. Griesbach ... 1976* (above, note 5), pp. 50-73.

[8] G.C. Storr, *Über den Zweck der evangelischen Geschichte und der Briefe des Johannes* (Tübingen; Osiander, 1786); 2nd ed. (1810), 274-307.

and realism, and which insisted upon empirical immanence and historical reliability in written documents. Matthew and Luke were regarded as more encumbered with speculative theology. Thus the philologist Karl Lachmann in Berlin declared in a famous paper of 1835 that early traditions on the life of Jesus had included five "corpuscles" of a report already structured, which the synoptic evangelists had been able to use. Lachmann claimed that Mark had preserved the pre-established order in a more pure form than either Matthew or Luke.[9] He did not regard Mark as the source of Matthew and Luke, for he based his thinking on the tradition hypothesis that will be treated below as number (3); but just because Lachmann found the Second Gospel most in harmony with pre-literary traditions, he claimed respect for Mark and caution against Matthew.

(d) The Two-Document Theory. It was the same bourgeois realism, implying an inclination to seek the foundations of the Gospel literature in historical documents unencumbered by advanced theology, that led Karl August Credner of Giessen in 1836 to go one step further than Lachmann and assume that (a) Mark was a source used by Matthew and Luke.[10] Storr had made the same suggestion fifty years earlier (above, p. 293) but, independently of him, Credner gave the priority of Mark a new support that was soon amplified by others. At the same time Credner supposed that Matthew and Luke had used a second written source, containing (b) sayings of Jesus. He believed like Friedrich Schleiermacher that Bishop Papias of Hierapolis (ca. A.D. 110), when treating the compilation of the λόγια in Hebrew by Matthew, used this Greek word to signify only "sayings" of Jesus — although Papias evidently meant the λόγια of Matthew and especially Mark in the broader sense of "reports": on the Lord (cf. below, p. 299). Credner thus became the father of the rapidly growing two-source theory, according to which Matthew and Luke had been using Mark and what has later been called "Q" in the sense of an unknown document containing sayings of Jesus.

In the year 1838 the philosopher Christian Hermann Weisse of Leipzig delivered further inducement to regard the presumed sayings or Logia of Matthew and the Gospel of Mark as the two sources of Matthew and Luke, which he did with extensive references to Schleier-

---

[9] C. Lachmann, "De ordine narrationum in evangeliis synopticis," *Theologische Studien und Kritiken* 8 (Hamburg, 1835), 570-590.
[10] K.A. Credner, *Einleitung in das Neue Testament* (Halle: Waisenhaus, 1836), pp. 201-205.

macher and Lachmann.[11] Like several contemporaries Weisse was eager to use written documents as sources for his picture of Jesus, and since he felt bound to see the Son of Man merely under human aspects, Mark and the Logia suited his purpose best. In particular, Weisse was afraid that David Friedrich Strauss, whose radical protrait of Jesus had just appeared in a second edition, would lead people to replace history with mythology.[12] He therefore alluded to Strauss in the title of his book ("kritisch ... bearbeitet") and started his discussion by rejecting the hypothesis of an oral tradition which Strauss represented.[13]

A second proclamation of Mark's priority happened to appear simultaneously with Weisse's book of 1838. Its author was a pastor in Dresden by the name of Christian Gottlob Wilke, and without knowing Lachmann's and Weisse's works in favour of Markan priority, he published his rather polemic book after ten years of struggle with the synoptic problem.[14] While he was occupied with this book, numerous and important theologians still preferred to derive the synoptic material either from Matthew or from an oral tradition. In sharp opposition to his contemporaries, Wilke alleged that a written report on the life of Jesus must have existed from the very beginning and that Mark must be identified with this document because of its historical orientation. It followed that Luke was based on Mark and Matthew on Luke.[15] Wilke's purely literary analysis yielded an extreme form of the utilization hypothesis, implying the sequence Mark — Luke — Matthew.

It took some time until Weisse's and Wilke's preferences for Mark became influential; but the triumph of liberal theology after the revolution of 1848 concentrated the interest on Mark again.

The first scholar of importance who took up the two-document theory in this period was the orientalist Heinrich Georg August Ewald in Göttingen, a forceful representative of liberal protestantism. In his papers on the subject printed in 1848-51, Ewald went one step further

[11] C.H. Weisse, *Die evangelische Geschichte kritisch und philosophisch bearbeitet*, 1-2 (Leipzig: Breitkopf & Haertel, 1838). Vol. 1 refers to Schleiermacher on pp. 34-38, Lachmann on pp. 38-40, Mark on pp. 56-83, and the Logia on pp. 83-87.

[12] D.F. Strauss, *Das Leben Jesu kritisch bearbeitet*, 2 vols. (Tübingen: Osiander, 1835-36; 2nd ed. 1837). ET George Eliot, *The Life of Jesus Critically Examined*, ed. with introduction by Peter C. Hodgson, "Lives of Jesus Series" (Philadelphia: Fortress Press, 1972; London: SCM Press, 1973).

[13] Weisse (n. 11), vol. 1, 3-16.

[14] C.G. Wilke, *Der Urevangelist oder exegetisch kritische Untersuchung über das Verwandtschaftsverhältnis der drei ersten Evangelien* (Dresden & Leipzig: G. Fleischer, 1838).

[15] Wilke (n. 14), 4-17 (a synopsis proceeding from Mark to Luke and further to Matthew); 656-685 (Mark used by Luke and Matthew); 685-692 (Luke used by Matthew).

and introduced the distinction of a proto-Mark from Mark.[16] In a commentary on the synoptic Gospels of the year 1850 Ewald was so confident of his scheme that he distributed the pretended sources on different script types, and in the preface expressed a conviction that his literary analysis would both enable the public to realize the value of true religion demonstrated by him in this way, and bring about the unity of all Germans.[17] Afterwards a unification of the Germans may at least be said to have been established in the field of synoptic criticism, for the successes of liberal theologians made the two-document hypothesis a generally accepted principle.

A book published in 1863 by Heinrich Julius Holtzmann in Heidelberg, called *Die synoptischen Evangelien,* secured the final victory of this hypothesis in protestant Germany. Referring to Weisse, Wilke, and Ewald, Holtzmann stated the priority of a proto-Mark named Alpha and of a proto-Matthew symbolized by the letter Lambda.[18] The symbol Lambda was used for the presumed collection of sayings called Logia, which Schleiermacher had ascribed to Matthew by means of a peculiar interpretation of Papias (cf. p. 299), and it corresponds to what has later been standardized with the letter Q.

Holtzmann's theory and similar presentations of the utilization hypothesis were accepted by a growing number of scholars in Germany and other countries, either with various simplifications or further complications. From the Protestant quarter it was also spread to Catholic scholars. Thus generations of students were told by their professors that Mark and the Logia, or some predecessors of them, were the literary sources of the synoptic material.

As to other countries, this German theory was especially cultivated in England at the university of Oxford, where members of a seminar on the synoptic problem held regular meetings since 1894. Some of their studies were published in A.D. 1911 by William Sanday of Christ Church, Oxford, and he introduced his article by this declaration: "We assume what is commonly known as the 'Two-Document Hypothesis.'"[19]

---

[16] H.G.A. Ewald, "Ursprung und Wesen der Evangelien," *Jahrbücher der biblischen Wissenschaft,* 1 (Göttingen, 1848): 113-154, 138-147; 2 (1849): 180-224, 191-195; 3 (1851): 140-174.

[17] H. Ewald, *Die drei ersten Evangelien uebersetzt und erklaert* (Göttingen: Dietrich, 1850), pp. XVIII-XIX.

[18] H.J. Holtzmann, *Die synoptischen Evangelien. Ihr Ursprung und geschichtlicher Charakter* (Leipzig: Engelmann, 1863), on predecessors: 29-33, 36-38; on Alpha: 56-111; on Lambda: 126-157; summary: 162-168.

[19] W. Sanday, ed., *Studies in the Synoptic Problem, by Members of the University of Oxford* (Oxford: Clarendon Press, 1911), 3.

Among the contributors were several renowned scholars, such as Willoughby Charles Allen, Sir John Hawkins, and Burnett Hillman Streeter.

In the year 1924 the last-mentioned contributor to Sanday's collection, B.H. Streeter, published an impressive volume that was to receive decisive importance for the whole English-speaking world. Rejecting any suggestion of a proto-Mark, he called the use of Mark's present Gospel by Matthew and Luke "a fundamental discovery."[20] He also found the Logia source, now called Q, an indispensable assumption, but since he also combined Q with a proto-Luke called L and a proto-Matthew called M, the result was a four document hypothesis.[21] At any rate the self-confident exposition of Streeter has led many scholars in England and America to regard the two-document theory as indispensable.

Today the dependence of Matthew and Luke upon Mark and the unknown document called Q is accepted by innumerable theologians and laymen of every nationality and confession. It is generally taken for granted without any discussion. Although detailed investigations of the literary relationships between Matthew, Mark, and Luke have inspired several experts of higher criticism to more complicated stemmata, including a proto-Matthew, a proto-Mark, or a proto-Luke as well as different levels of a Q, most theologians are satisfied with the simple pattern Mark + Q = the substance of Matthew and Luke. This common opinion does also provide the basis for numerous theological expositions, in which Matthew and Luke are treated as secondary in comparison with Mark and Q. Matthew and Luke are thus supposed to have changed given documents in a very subjective way, but the adherents of the two-source hypothesis have normally avoided the inconvenience of explaining this circumstance.

2. The Proto-Gospel Theory

From the attempts to reconstruct a proto-Matthew and the like, there is but a step to the second form of the classical synoptic theories presented in Protestant Germany toward the end of the eighteenth century, that is, the so-called proto-gospel-theory. It was developed by Gottfried Ephraim Lessing at Wolfenbüttel in 1779, and implies that

---

[20] B.H. Streeter, *The Four Gospels. A Study of Origins Treating of the Manuscript Tradition, Sources, Authorship, & Dates* (London: Macmillan, 1924; 2nd ed. 1926), on the synoptic problem: 149-360, on Mark's basic function: 157-201.

[21] Streeter (n. 20), 199-270.

an unknown document is regarded as the common source of the four Gospels or at least of three or two of them.

Lessing started from information offered by patristic writers about the original language of the First Gospel. Papias of Hierapolis in Phrygia had found out around A.D. 110 that Matthew had collected in Hebrew what Papias called the λόγια (Eusebius, *History* III.39.16). In antiquity this statement was not referred to any collection of sayings like the hypothetic Q, but to a Gospel report written by Matthew in Hebrew or perhaps in Aramaic. Further comments by Epiphanius and Jerome from the end of the fourth century led to an identification of this Hebrew Matthew with the so-called Gospel of the Hebrews, or that of the Nazareans used by Jewish-Christians in Syria.[22] In the year 1689 Richard Simon of Normandy, the pioneer of biblical criticism, took these patristic indications into account when he stated that the Aramaic proto-Matthew of the Nazareans had been the source of the first Gospel in the Canon.[23] Lessing, who was then a librarian in Wolfenbüttel, used these patristic traditions as a point of departure while endeavoring to bridge over the chronological distance between the life of Jesus and the redaction of the canonical Gospels. With great elan he wrote some theses on the subject in 1779 which, after his death, were published by his brother in 1784. According to Lessing, the Aramaic Matthew of the Nazareans was the original document from which all canonical and apocryphal Gospels had emerged.[24]

Some scholars found this explanation much too simple. One reaction was that of the Göttingen polyhistor Johann Gottfried Eichhorn, who endeavored to improve the proto-gospel hypothesis in 1794 by inserting several intermediate stages.[25] He took over his theory of auxiliary sources from a colleague of his in Göttingen by the name of J.B. Koppe, who had suggested a plurality of shorter and longer sources now lost, thus inaugurating the multiple-source theory mentioned below (p. 304). Eichhorn's eclecticism resulted in an extraordinarily complicated pic-

---

[22] Quotations of Epiphanius and Jerome in W. Schneemelcher, *Neutestamentliche Apokryphen*, 1 (Tübingen: Mohr & Siebeck, 1959), 90-100, 104-108.

[23] R. Simon, *Histoire critique du texte du Nouveau Testament* (Rotterdam, 1689), 71-100.

[24] G.E. Lessing, "Neue Hypothesen über die Evangelisten als bloss menschliche Geschichtsschreiber betrachtet," *Theologischer Nachlass* (Berlin, 1784), 45-72, esp. 68; "Theses aus der Kirchengeschichte," ibid., 73-82, esp. 80.

[25] J.G. Eichhorn, "Über die drei ersten Evangelien," *Allgemeine Bibliothek der biblischen Litteratur*, 5 (Leipzig, 1794), pp. 759-996.

ture of a development on several levels, and few of his contemporaries found it convincing.

In the year 1832 a limited form of the proto-gospel theory, also based on Papias' declaration concerning Matthew, was introduced by Friedrich Schleiermacher in Berlin. His suggestion gradually brought about the wide-spread conception of a specific Logia source or Q.[26] Schleiermacher's innovation consisted in a particular interpretation of Papias' information that Matthew had put together the λόγια in Hebrew (Eusebius, *History*, III.39.16). He explained λόγια in this passage as "sayings" and believed Papias had referred to a document containing sayings of Jesus, which should be understood as the source of the material common to Matthew and Luke but not found in Mark.

Schleiermacher's translation of λόγια "sayings" was conventional and influenced by New Testament passages (for instance, Rom. 3:2). But it was not in accordance with the technical meaning in which Papias used the word λόγια, judging from the fragments of his book available in patristic quotations. The word is found three times in the extant fragments of Papias, and the context makes it obvious that Papias used λόγια in the technical sense of "reports" or "traditions," including quotational elements as well as narrative units. He called his book "Investigations of the λόγια" (Eusebius, *History* III,39.1), and by this Greek expression meant the canonical Gospels whether they contain sayings or narratives. Papias then used the same expression, λόγια, with reference to all units of tradition contained in the Gospel of Mark (ibid. 39.15). By defining these units as dealing with "things either said or done by Christ" (ibid.), Papias made it evident that for him the λόγια written down by Mark included both types of tradition: quotations as well as narratives. There is every reason to give those λόγια which Papias mentioned as collected by Matthew the same technical meaning of tradition units, including both sayings and narratives. According to what Papias declared, the Hebrew composition of Matthew was not a collection of quotations, but a Gospel like Mark, and he added that it had been translated into Greek by others (Eusebius, *History*, III.39.16). Papias was also understood to have spoken of a whole Gospel by those patristic authors, who referred to the Gospel of the Hebrews or that of the Nazarenes (above, p. 298).

On this account Schleiermacher must be said to have misinterpreted

---

[26] F. Schleiermacher, "Über die Zeugnisse des Papias von unseren beiden ersten Evangelien," *Theologische Studien und Kritiken* 5 (Hamburg, 1832), 735-768, esp. 738-758.

the words of Papias about Matthew. In the same arbitrary way he did not understand the notice of Papias on Mark as referring to the Second Gospel, which ought to have been natural, but to a proto-Mark supposed to have been a preliminary report containing narratives.[27]

In spite of these deficiencies Schleiermacher's suggestions of 1832 were, soon after his death in 1834, taken over by Credner in 1836 and then used in the powerful two-document hypothesis. Only the assumption of a proto-Mark has not generally been preserved by later advocates of the Logia source. In fact most scholars or laymen, who have regarded a Logia document or what is called Q as the one source, have acquiesced in the extant text of Mark as being the other source. An influential representative of this position, partly inspired by William Wrede in Breslau, was Rudolf Bultmann in his wide-spread *History of the Synoptic Tradition* (discussed below in connection with form criticism, pp. 306-307). Without permitting any questioning of the sources, Bultmann treated Mark and Q as two source documents absolutely established and universally accepted, and emphatically denied the existence of any Gospel before Mark.[28]

Actually the powerful two-source theory implies a combination of (1) the utilization hypothesis in the Markan form with (2) the proto-gospel theory in a limited form. A background is found in two of the classical theories inaugurated before 1800, as mentioned above. For when the assumption of Mark's priority was prepared by Lachmann in 1835, further proposed by Credner in 1836 and firmly contended by Weisse and Wilke in 1838, it meant a reincarnation of (1) the utilization hypothesis according to that Markan alternative which had been presented by Storr in 1786 (above, p. 293). And when Schleiermacher suggested the existence of a Logia source in 1832, he created a limited analogy to (2) the unknown proto-gospel which had been presupposed by Lessing in 1784 (above, p. 298).

3. The Tradition Hypothesis

A third attempt to answer the synoptic question was the tradition hypothesis, by which the similarities and deviations of the synoptic reports were ascribed to an oral tradition represented by the apostles

---

[27] Ibid., 758-767.

[28] R. Bultmann, *Die Geschichte der synoptischen Tradition*, FRLANT, N.F. 12 (Göttingen: Vandenhoeck & Ruprecht, 1921; 2nd ed., 1931; 3rd ed., 1957; Ergänzungsheft, 1958). Bultmann declared about Mark and Q (1st ed. p. 194, 2nd and 3rd ed. p. 347): "Ich setze nur die sog. Zwei-Quellen-Theorie voraus;" and concerning Mark (1st ed. p. 226, 2nd and 3rd ed. p. 394): "Auf keinen Fall ist eine seiner Quellen als Evangelium zu bezeichnen... Denn beide (Mt und Luk) legen den Mk-Aufriss zugrunde." In this regard the impact of the scribal tradition in question was strong enough to entail leaving out any motivation.

and evangelists. This theory was developed in Weimar by Johann Gottfried Herder and made public in 1796-97.[29]

Herder rejected both theories mentioned above, that is, the utilization hypothesis and the proto-gospel theory. Instead he conjectured that a proto-Mark in Aramaic had been the "protoplasm" of a living "Gospel Saga," by which expression he meant the common oral tradition of the early church. Based on the preaching of the apostles and the expositions of evangelists like Philip and others (Acts 21:8; Eph. 4:11), this proto-Mark had been developed in oral form between A.D. 34 and 40. Later it had also been written down, but not officially disseminated. Some thirty years later a messianic elaboration of proto-Mark had been written and published, and this was the Aramaic proto-Matthew or the Gospel of the Nazareans. When the Christian message was spread among the nations and translated into Greek, these two Palestinian sources gave rise to our Gospels: Mark in the sixties on the basis of proto-Mark; Luke in the same years on the basis of proto-Matthew.

Herder's reference to a proto-Mark and proto-Matthew partly anticipated the later two-document hypothesis. But since he referred to a living oral tradition, Herder's theory was basically different, and he rejected all ideas of redactional activity on literary terms such as would be done in a chancellery. His observations are still noteworthy, because an oral tradition was absolutely the first stage and has certainly influenced the literary products. This is also realized in our days since the inauguration of the form-critical approach, that will be mentioned below.

More specifically the judgment of Herder on the Gospel traditions was based on the following principles: Each of the first apostles and their assistants, the evangelists, transmitted the oral message in his own way. They offered a living report, not dead letters written by hand (Rom. 10:8-18; 2 Cor. 3:7).[30] A fundamental unity was guaranteed by their common task, which consisted of historical information about Jesus as the Messiah. Paul also emphasized that nobody can lay another ground for belief than what had been done by Jesus Christ (1 Cor. 3:11).[31] However, the report on the events was always given form in a personal way. It is anachronistic to find the extant plurality disturbing and to attempt to reconstruct homogeneous sources.

[29] J.G. Herder, *Christliche Schriften*, 2 (Riga, 1796): 149-233; 3 (1797): 301-416; reprinted in *Sämtliche Werke*, ed. by B. Suphan, 19 (Berlin: Weidmann, 1880): 194-225, 380-424.
[30] Herder (n. 29), 2, 190, 196; 3, 306.
[31] Ibid., 2: 185-188.

Herder rejected current methods of literary criticism by these frank declarations:

> Considering the manner in which Gospels were understood at the time in question, namely that Gospels contain oral records in written form, there was no objection to adding new oral communications, thus supplementing extant Gospels...[32] It was only natural that several Gospels were composed...[33] The whole idea that our Evangelists had been like scribes (*scribae*) who collected treatises and supplemented, improved, collated and compared each with the other, is ... extraordinarily inconsistent and unnatural with regard to their situation and intention, also to the purpose of their respective Gospels ... Assumptions of this kind lead to such a confusion that all points of contradiction between the Evangelists become even more conspicuous. Ultimately, one does not know which Evangelist would have copied the other, or supplemented, abbreviated, disrupted, improved, corrupted him or even stolen from him ... In fact, not one of them endeavored to surpass and subdue the other, but each simply presented his report. Perhaps none of them had seen the Gospel of another, and even if this had been possible for one author, he did not make use of it when he wrote his own Gospel.[34]

While the synoptic problem continued to be discussed, however, Herder's ironical observations were suppressed by eager representatives of literary criticism. In modern synoptic research a picture may still be found of the muddle deplored by him.

Herder's accentuation of the oral tradition was in any case clarified and substantiated in 1818 by the young grammar schoolmaster Johann Carl Ludwig Gieseler, a mediating theologian who became a well-known church historian in Bonn and Göttingen.[35] Gieseler suggested a more distinct separation of the oral and written stages than Herder had indicated.[36] He wanted to explain similarities and differences between the Gospels under practical and psychological aspects. Even if this approach was generally neglected in the 19th century, it proved valuable again in the 20th century when form criticism began to pay attention to the life-setting and the structures of the oral traditions (below, pp. 305-306). A statement of Gieseler, which is especially instructive, may be quoted here:[37]

---

[32] Ibid., 180 note 1.
[33] Ibid., 186-187.
[34] Ibid., 191-193.
[35] J.C.L. Gieseler, *Historisch-kritischer Versuch über die Entstehung und die frühesten Schicksale der schriftlichen Evangelien* (Leipzig: Engelmann, 1818).
[36] Ibid., 55, 83.
[37] Ibid., 90.

Assuming a common oral source is the most convenient means to explain how the following state of things has emerged: The more the stories appeared important to the disciples, the more they were told in a congruous way. It was these units that were most often presented, and being frequently repeated they preserved their original form in a more pure way than did other stories. Concerning the latter it was the matter and not so much the form that was recalled by the individuals. But here, too, the noticeable expressions are more or less identical, while before and after those expressions there is variation in the form of synonyms. This exactly had to be the natural consequence of an oral prototype.

Gieseler did not exclude a theoretical possibility that some traditions were recorded in written form rather early, although no evidence for this is available.[38] But he emphasized that oral teaching remained an essential practice for a considerable length of time, after written documents had appeared.[39] Gieseler pointed out three general characteristics of this oral teaching. (1) Memorizing was a living reality in antiquity. It was cultivated successfully and was often regarded as more reliable than fixed documents. (2) An oral paradosis is close in harmony with the intellectual standard of the Palestinian believers and the Hebraizing diction of the synoptic Gospels.[40] (3) For a long time the Canon was fluctuating, and this also confirms the relative indifference of the early church to written documents as long as living traditions existed.[41]

Among the examples quoted by Gieseler, the reference to a letter of Ignatius written in A.D. 114 is especially instructive (Ignatius, *Letter to the Philadelphians* VIII.2)[42] Opposing contemporary literalists who required written documents (ἀρχεῖα) in order to believe the preaching of the church, Ignatius remarked that documents were easy to falsify (Ignatius, *Philadelphians* VIII,2). In his eyes the only authentic testimonies were Christ's cross, death, and resurrection as well as the belief in these facts. Thus, like Paul, Ignatius referred to items of the orally transmitted kerygma (1 Cor.15:1-8).

When these observations were published by Gieseler in 1818, romanticism was dominating in literature, and German scholars were still inclined to prefer oral traditions. In the bourgeois period after A.D. 1830, however, literary documents were required again, and twenty years after Gieseler's book a new reasoning in terms of records and offices

---

[38] Ibid., 91.
[39] Ibid., 116-118.
[40] Ibid., 88, 93-111.
[41] Ibid., 142-203.
[42] Ibid., 160-164.

broke through when Weisse and Wilke ascribed priority to Mark and inaugurated the triumph of the two-document theory.

4. The Multiple-Source Theory

The fourth synoptic theory to be considered here implies the assumption of multiple sources. Its pioneer was a professor in Göttingen by the name of Johann Benjamin Koppe, later a chaplain at the court of Hannover.

Koppe thought of the "numerous" writers to whom Luke has alluded in 1:1, and suggested in an essay of 1782 that a plurality of shorter and longer units should be sought behind the extant Gospels.[43] These multiple sources were supposed to have been spread among the Christians in oral and written form, and moulded into narratives, speeches, parables, sayings of Jesus and other form categories. By his reference to such units, Koppe anticipated two important theories of later date: the fragment theory of F. Schleiermacher and the form criticism of M. Dibelius (below, pp. 305-306).

As mentioned above, Koppe's productive colleague J.G. Eichhorn in Göttingen combined Lessing's proto-gospel theory with this multiple-source theory in a paper of 1794, but his contemporaries found the pedigree designed by Eichhorn too complicated (above, p. 298).

Yet the hypothesis of multiple sources was taken up again in a book on Luke published by Friedrich Schleiermacher in 1817, that is, several years before the above-mentioned Logia source was averred in his article of 1832 (p. 299). Unlike what he was going to do when dealing with the Logia source, Schleiermacher rejected in that earlier work the anachronisms of the utilization and proto-gospel theories. He characterized his reactions in this way: "I find myself in a German book factory of the eighteenth or nineteenth centuries, not in the very beginnings of Christianity."[44] Schleiermacher preferred to assume there was a number of written sources, which he called notes or reports, and in principle his version of the multiple-source theory was a multiple-fragment hypothesis. More precisely, Schleiermacher suggested that after the dispersion of the disciples in Jerusalem their oral reports had been written down by auditors. This material developed into smaller and greater collections of topical reports, such as speeches, stories, and the narrative of Christ's passion and resurrection. Independently

---

[43] J.B. Koppe, *Marcus non epitomator Matthaei* (Programm der Universität Göttingen, 1783); reprinted in D.J. Pott & G.A. Ruperti (ed.), *Sylloge commentationum theologicarum*, 1 (Göttingen: Vandenhoeck & Ruprecht, 1800): 35-69, esp. 66.

[44] F. Schleiermacher, *Über die Schriften des Lukas. Ein kritischer Versuch* (Berlin: Reimer, 1817), 6.

of each other the synoptic redactors then used such collections.[45] Although this reconstruction of the process involved a background in the oral traditions, Schleiermacher did not pay much attention to the activity of the apostles, but concentrated his interest on circumstances in the diaspora. On the whole he did not find the oral reports of the early disciples as important as the written notes of the auditors, which he postulated. This centrifugal and pluralising tendency, as well as the assumption of fragmentary notes, involved several uncertain factors, and so Schleiermacher's multiple-source theory of 1817 did not convince his contemporaries who preferred more documentary evidence.

A hundred years later, however, Schleiermacher's fragment hypothesis of 1817 was partly called to new life by the pioneers of form criticism, who championed a multiple-source theory. To be sure, form criticism is not only a modern counterpart to Schleiermacher's fragment hypothesis in so far as it represents a modified version of the multiple-source theory, for the new approach is also related to Herder's tradition hypothesis. Similar to what has been observed about the two-document theory — that it represents a combination of (1) the utilization hypothesis in its Markan form with (2) the proto-gospel theory in a limited form —, thus form criticism has adjusted (3) Herder's tradition hypothesis to (4) Schleiermacher's fragment theory. This compromise implies restrictions on both sides. On the one hand, form criticism wants to study preliterary traditions like Herder, but is only concerned with short elements and not with comprehensive structures; on the other hand, the material collected by the evangelists is supposed to have consisted of numerous isolated fragments like those of Schleiermacher, but they are conceived as oral units and not as written notes.

It was the later Heidelberg professor Martin Dibelius who presented the program of form criticism in the year 1919, elaborating impressions received during his studies in Leipzig and Berlin. Among his teachers in Leipzig was Georg Heinrici, who published a book on New Testament literature in 1908 and traced its roots back to early Christian mission and oral form-categories like teaching, prophecy, hymnology, and prayer.[46] Three esteemed teachers of Dibelius in Berlin were the theologians Hermann Gunkel and Adolf Deissmann, who emphasized folklore aspects of the Old and New Testament traditions, and the

---

[45] Ibid., 7-14; cf. his *Einleitung ins Neue Testament*, ed. by G. Wolde (Berlin: Reimer, 1845), 315. On his exegesis in general: H. Weisweiler, "Schleiermachers Arbeiten zum Neuen Testament" (Diss. Bonn, 1972).

[46] G. Heinrici, *Der literarische Charakter der neutestamentlichen Schriften* (Leipzig: Dürr, 1908), 23-48, 100-127.

philologist Eduard Norden, who published a classical work on the "Formgeschichte," which means form history although the current English term has become form criticism.[47]

Dibelius wanted to discontinue regarding the synoptic Gospels as compositions of authors displaying literary material, and instead to regard them as compilations of popular micro-literature elements. The practical basis or "life-setting" (*Sitz im Leben*) of the elements called pericopes was defined as early Christian "preaching," which Dibelius understood to include both sermons and teaching. He distributed the pericopes in different categories, and the most important of those suggested by Dibelius were "paradigm" (short narrative ending in a point); "novel story" (longer narrative with several details); "parenesis" (admonition based on words of Jesus); and "myth" (revelation of his messianic sovereignty).

Just after the first World War this new approach to the Synoptics was embraced as a refreshing renewal among German scholars. In the year 1919 already, Dibelius was followed by his former student Karl Ludwig Schmidt who declared the individual pericopes of the Gospels as the original material and the general itinerary as redactional arrangement.[48] Other young scholars in Germany, in turn, applied the form-critical program to the disputation pericopes and the passion narrative.[49]

In 1921 Rudolf Bultmann submitted the whole synoptic material to a similar criticism in a book which became a standard work for generations. He adopted two principles of Dibelius' form criticism, first by starting with smaller units of the synoptic tradition and then by asking for their life-setting in the church.[50] In practice, however, Bultmann degraded the form-critical method to an instrument which he used in order to carry out certain ideas about the development of the original message into a Hellenistic cult-myth. The analysis of the forms was thus used for several alterations or transpositions of the material which he needed.

Bultmann actually started with the result to which he wanted to come, and summarized the process assumed in the following words:[51]

---

[47] M. Dibelius, *Die Formgeschichte des Evangeliums* (Tübingen: Mohr & Siebeck, 1919), 2-15; enlarged 2nd ed. (ibid., 1933), 1-34.

[48] K.L. Schmidt, *Der Rahmen der Geschichte Jesu. Literarkritische Untersuchungen zur ältesten Jesusüberlieferung* (Berlin: Trowitzsch & Sohn, 1919), v, 317.

[49] M. Albertz, *Die synoptischen Streitgespräche. Ein Beitrag zur Formgeschichte des Urchristentums* (Berlin: Trowitzsch & Sohn 1921); G. Bertram, *Die Leidensgeschichte Jesu und der Christuskult. Eine formgeschichtliche Untersuchung*, FRLANT, N.F. 15 (Göttingen: Vandenhoeck & Ruprecht, 1922).

[50] R. Bultmann, *Geschichte der synoptischen Tradition* (n. 28).

[51] Ibid., 1st ed. 226-227.

The type of a Gospel meets us first in Mark, and one may say that Mark has created it. By no means is any of his sources to be called a Gospel... For neither Matthew nor Luke have used such a product: both are based on Mark's outline. In any case, the Gospel is a creation of Hellenistic Christianity... There was need of a cult-legend for the Kyrios of the Christian cult. Since the pattern of the Christ-myth had to be illustrated, it needed to be combined with traditions about the history of Jesus... Thus the Gospels are cult-legends. Mark has created this type. The myth of Christ gives his book ... a unity which is not biographical, but simply based on the myth. Matthew and Luke have ... enforced the other aspect by taking up historical traditions not found in Mark, yet available to them. [52]

The goal determined in this quotation was reached in three steps: (1) Form-critical principles were used to show that Mark had only isolated pericopes at his disposal, no coherent information on the life of Jesus. (2) Literary criticism was added on the basis of the two-document hypothesis in order to illustrate changes of the pericopes supposed to have taken place in connection with a centrifugal movement from Jerusalem to Hellenism, which Bultmann found essential. (3) From religio-historical points of view, this dislocation of the material from the center to the periphery implied that Bultmann dispossessed the Palestinian church described in Acts of any productive importance. Instead he associated the material collected by Mark with the so-called Hellenistic community. By the latter he meant pre-Pauline churches in Syria and elsewhere which he, under the influence of Wilhelm Bousset, had promoted to a decisive historical factor and equipped with a cult-legend and Christ-myth, although no such complexes are described in relevant texts. At last Matthew and Luke were assumed to have supplemented Mark by particular material in order to give the reports a more historical appearance, and in this case Bultmann alluded to the source called Q.

For a long time Bultmann's monumental work has deeply affected form criticism and synoptic discussion in Germany along with other countries. His quick jump from a form-critical analysis to manipulations with the two sources and his violent move of the data to the Hellenistic periphery did not disturb the experts, but was eagerly imitated.

A similar use of form criticism in combination with the two-source theory has dominated synoptic research since 1921, and the primary form-critical impulses have therefore gone off the rails. In principle,

---

[52] In the 2nd and 3rd editions Bultmann gave this summary an expanded form, see pp. 394-397. He also replaced the radical term "Christ-myth" by the milder expression "kerygma of Christ," p. 396, but the religio-historical pattern remained the same.

the analysis of micro-structural forms and the determination of their categories were meant to illustrate oral traditions but, in analogy to Bultmann, numerous scholars have presented form-critical preliminaries merely in order to sort out written texts of supposed earlier or later origin, and to confirm their conceptions of doctrinal evolution within early Christianity. In reality the deductions have moved backwards from the literary results desired, so that form criticism has not been practised for its own sake. Until and even after the second World War the synoptic discussion has been waning, because the pattern of form criticism and the two-source theory have been widely understood as representing final truth. Certainly, new outlines have also been drawn up after the war, as will be indicated below, but leading textbooks and commentaries are still dominated by faithfulness to this mixture of two approaches that represent widely differing levels of the material contained in the synoptic Gospels. [53]

II

Modern Attitudes and Recent Contributions

After the second World War new attitudes to the synoptic material and new discussions of the synoptic problem may be observed. The perspectives have developed in two opposite directions.

(a) On the one hand inherited synoptic questions have sometimes been relinquished by modern expositors. Some believe that all historical factors of interest have already been explained by the two-source theory; others feel that such background circumstances are of no hermeneutical relevance. Two new synoptic programs have thus appeared on the stage, and their representatives are in both cases occupied with analysis of the extant texts without discussing the sources. One of the schools presents itself as "redaction criticism," since it wants to establish what the Gospel redactors had intended to make of their material. The other movement is known as "structural linguistics," which means that a so-called linguistic analysis is used to display logical structures within given textual units. In the present treatment, it will be enough to recall a few details concerning the origins and the principles of these two attempts, which seek to interpret the synoptic Gospels on levels above the genealogy of their traditions.

---

[53] Examples of textbooks in German representing form criticism together with the two-source theory: W.G. Kümmel, *Einleitung in das Neue Testament* (Heidelberg: Quelle & Meyer, 1963, and later editions), 20-44; J. Schmid, *Einleitung in das Neue Testament* (Freiburg: Herder, 1973), 279-296; Ph. Vielhauer, *Geschichte der urchristlichen Literatur* (Berlin: de Gruyter, 1975), 268-280.

Redactional criticism, or what German scholars call "Redaktions-geschichte," has become an important approach in connection with the revival of theological studies in Germany after the last war. Among its pioneers were Günther Bornkamm, Hans Conzelmann and Willy Marxsen — former students of Bultmann's, who also based their conceptions on the two-source theory but desired to find out more about the contents and the structure of each synoptic Gospel in its present form.[54] Younger scholars of different nationalities have followed them with a multitude of dissertations and monographs. In spite of the general enthusiasm, redaction criticism does not represent a new method, but the resumption of an old endeavour in biblical theology to search for peculiarities within each of the Gospels.[55] No doubt the new contributions of redactional criticism have also clarified the message of the synoptic evangelists. But on the other hand a serious restraint is placed on several monographs and commentaries practising redaction criticism, because some form of the two-document hypothesis is forced upon the individual witness of each Gospel in a mechanical way. The outcome is that what Matthew and Luke have written is relativized and deprived of its own life and value. Primary attention is not drawn to the actual message of each one in objective comparison with that of the other evangelists, but to his presumed manipulations of Mark and Q. Right or wrong, the two-source theory has thus become an obstacle to a consistent development of redactional criticism, because it does not always permit Matthew and Luke to speak for themselves.

Adherents of the approach called structural linguistics avoid this dependence on a literary source theory. They follow an international and interdisciplinary program developed by philologists for the inter-pretation of texts in general, and its application to biblical documents is only secondary. Inspiration to the program called "linguistics" came from a book, published in 1916 and based on lectures delivered in Geneva by the comparative philologist Ferdinand de Saussure. He drew up methodological differences between "diachronical" and "syn-chronical" investigations of language and literature, emphasising that philology does not only have to illustrate the historical development of given units, but also to analyse their logical composition independently

---

[54] G. Bornkamm, "Die Sturmstillung im Matthäusevangelium," in *Wort und Dienst*, N.F. 1 (Bielefeld, 1948): 49-54; H. Conzelmann, *Die Mitte der Zeit. Studien zur Theologie des Lukas* (Tübingen: Mohr & Siebeck, 1954); W. Marxsen, "Redaktionsgeschichtliche Erklärung der sogenannten Parabeltheorie des Markus," *ZThK* 52 (1952) 255-271.

[55] The title of J. Rohde, *Die redaktionsgeschichtliche Methode. Einführung und Sich-tung des Forschungsstandes* (Hamburg: Furche, 1966), gives the impression of a special method. But on p. 13 the author has observed that redactional criticism is rather an expansion of form-critical perspectives.

of historical circumstances.[56] The linguistic method of de Saussure has later been called "structural semantics" because of a textbook, which is representative of the method's current form and was published in 1964 by the Russian scholar Algirdas Greimas in Paris.[57] Avoiding so-called diachronical questions, the structuralists analyse given texts in a synchronical framework with the aid of a rather complicated philosophical or sociological terminology.

Structuralistic liberation from the preoccupation with historical problems has also inspired New Testament scholars to apply linguistic hermeneutics to the synoptic material. A need was felt to get beyond the stereotyped combination of form criticism with the two-source theory which had been dominating for several decades.[58] Thus linguistic schedules were rapidly spread from Paris over the entire theological world, and presently the movement is popular in France, North America, and South Africa. It is also possible that some of the linguistic experiments with technical conceptions and distinctions will yield permanent results in biblical studies.[59] Of course the synoptic problem itself has not been promoted by the structuralists, because their methodology prescribes that historical questions are left aside. Nevertheless this movement is also of interest within the history of the synoptic discussion, since it represents dissatisfaction with the routine subjection of synoptic exegesis to an established pattern of Gospel sources.

Redactional criticism and structural linguistics are thus connected with different inclinations to let the inherited discussion of synoptic problems rest in peace.

(b) In other contexts a forceful revival of the synoptic discussion is noticeable after the second World War. Essentially the new drives are modifications and modernizations of the four alternatives that were elaborated in the eighteenth and nineteenth centuries, although the perspectives have also been widened. Some distinguished scholars will thus be mentioned below as examples of modern analogies to the

[56] F. de Saussure, *Cours de linguistique générale, publié par Ch. Bally & A. Riedlinger* (Lausanne: Payot, 1916), 139-144. Several later editions; with introduction and notes by T. de Mauro (Paris: Payot, 1972).

[57] A.J. Greimas, *Sémantique structurale. Recherche de méthode* (Paris: Larousse, 1964).

[58] A general stagnation of form criticism was observed by E. Güttgemanns, *Offene Fragen zur Formgeschichte des Evangeliums. Eine methodologische Skizze der Grundproblematik der Form- und Redaktionsgeschichte* (München: Kaiser, 1970), 35-39.

[59] Summary and support of linguistic hermeneutics in biblical contexts: R. Kieffer, "Die Bedeutung der modernen Linguistik für die Auslegung biblischer Texte," *Theologische Zeitschrift* 30 (1974) 223-233.

classical theories. Among them are representatives (1) of a utilization hypothesis, who plead either for the priority of Matthew in analogy to Griesbach or for that of Mark in analogy to Storr; (2) of a proto-gospel theory in essential analogy to that of Lessing; (3) of a multiple source theory comparable to suggestions by Koppe and Eichhorn; and (4) of an oral tradition hypothesis reminiscent of Herder's view. Evidence for the permanent impact of the four alternatives is offered by the fact that eminent proponents of each view have been invited to defend their options at this international and interconfessional symposium on the synoptic problem, which is meeting here in Jerusalem during two weeks before Easter.

Only a few names and data connected with the renewal of the four approaches in question can be recalled here.

(1) After the last war the dominating Markan form of the utilization hypothesis was first criticized by Basil Christopher Butler in London, who took up the Augustinian theory in 1951 and defended the sequence Matthew — Mark — Luke.[60] This thrust did not find great support.

More successful was the campaign against the established consensus which William Reuben Farmer of Dallas began in a book of 1964, stating that Griesbach's subordination of Mark to Matthew and Luke is the simplest answer to the synoptic question.[61] Several scholars have welcomed this form of the utilization theory, which avoids the assumption of unknown sources, and have supported it by informative publications and conferences.[62]

Certainly most adherents of Markan priority and the source called Q have not been willing to give up their convictions. In the main, they do not even find it necessary to discuss the synoptic problem any more. A laudable exception is Frans Neirynck of Leuven, who has deeply felt the challenge of theories based on Matthew's priority and developed an immense erudition in order to secure the leading position of Mark. He did it first in a monograph of 1972 on dual phrases in Mark, and then in numerous later studies.[63]

[60] B.C. Butler, *The Originality of St. Matthew. A Critique of the Two-Document Hypothesis* (Cambridge: University Press, 1951), 170.

[61] W.R. Farmer, *The Synoptic Problem. A Critical Analysis* (New York: Macmillan, 1964; 3rd ed., Macon: Mercer University Press, 1976), 211.

[62] Of special importance was the symposium held at the University of Münster in 1976 to celebrate the bicentenary of Griesbach's Synopsis; see J.B. Orchard & T.R.W. Longstaff, eds., *J.J. Griesbach. Synoptic and Textcritical Studies, 1776-1976*, SNTS Monog. Ser. 34 (Cambridge: University Press, 1978).

[63] F. Neirynck, *Duality in Mark. Contributions to the Study of the Markan Redaction*, Bib. Eph. theol. lov. 21 (Leuven: University Press, 1972); see further, in collaboration with Th. Hansen & F. van Segbroeck, *The Minor Agreements of Matthew and Luke against Mark, with a Cumulative List*, Bib. Eph. theol. lov. 37 (1974).

(2) It was nevertheless in Leuven, where Neirynck had studied, that a revival of Lessing's proto-gospel theory had been developed by leading Roman-Catholic professors. In a lecture given there in 1952, Léon Vaganay of Lyon suggested that one should begin with Papias' indication of the Aramaic Matthew, a source which he supposed to have been a collection of speeches, and in addition think of another source behind Luke.[64] At the same time Lucien Cerfaux of Louvain supported Vaganay but also characterized Greek versions of this Aramaic Matthew as intermediary sources of the canonical Matthew, whereas Mark and Luke were regarded as later compositions.[65] Somewhat later Xavier Léon-Dufour, then active in Lyon, expressed fundamental agreement with Cerfaux in a well-known textbook, although he added the assumption that preliterary traditions have determined the form of the Aramaic Matthew as well as of intermediary Greek predecessors to Matthew, Mark, and Luke.[66]

(3) Since the last-mentioned Roman-Catholic scholars did not see the canonical Gospels as derivating immediately from the proto-Gospel of Matthew, but added several intermediary sources, their synoptic genealogies were not only reincarnations of Lessing's proto-gospel theory, but also of the multiple-source theory inaugurated by Koppe. They combined two of the classical alternatives, corresponding to what Eichhorn had done in 1794 (above, p. 298).

A further step toward an elaborate multiple-source theory was taken in 1972 by Marie-Émile Boismard at the École Biblique of the Dominicans in Jerusalem. Without the aid of a hypothetical proto-gospel, Boismard started with preliminary stages of the canonical Gospels corresponding to those presumed by the scholars mentioned at the end of the foregoing paragraph.[67] He first called them A, B, C, and Q, but later simplified his terminology by only referring to a pre-Matthew, a pre-Mark, and a pre-Luke.[68] These three sources were treated as earlier redactions of the extant Gospels, and were supposed to have been edited independently of each other except that pre-Matthew had inspired

[64] L. Vaganay, *La question synoptique*, Anal. lov. biblica et orientalia II, 31 (Louvain: Publications universitaires, 1952) 7.
[65] L. Cerfaux, *La mission de Galilée dans la tradition synoptique*, Analecta ... II, 36 (ibid., 1952), 5, 42. Cf. idem, "Luc," in *Dictionnaire de la Bible*, Supplément 5 (Paris: Letouzey, 1957), col. 565.
[66] X. Léon-Dufour, "Les évangiles synoptiques," in A. Robert & A. Feuillet (ed), *Introduction à la Bible*, 2 (Tournai: Desclée, 1959): 143-320, esp. 293-295 and 319-320.
[67] M.-É. Boismard, "Introduction," in Pierre Benoit & M.-É. Boismard, *Synopse des quatre Évangiles en français avec parallèles des Apocryphes et des Pères*, 2 (Paris: Cerf, 1972): 15-59.
[68] Boismard's position paper; see in this volume, pp. 231-233.

pre-Luke. What is called pre-Matthew and pre-Mark would therefore have been two independent sources behind three of the extant Gospels, whereas pre-Luke would only have contributed to Mark and Luke.

Recently, a former student of the same Jerusalem school has developed a similar multiple-source theory. This is Philippe Rolland who teaches at a Sulpician seminary in France. Starting with a "Gospel of the Twelve" in Jerusalem he advances three intermediary sources treated as documents and localized to Caesarea, Antioch, and to later Pauline centers as well. By combining two of these intermediary documents in different ways he constructs sources of each synoptic Gospel.[69] His theory is based on studies of double phrases in Mark, which correspond to single phrases either in Matthew or Luke. These double phrases have been observed and discussed in the past, especially by Neirynck (above, p. 311), but Rolland has set their number at no less than 174. In contrast to Neirynck, he understands them as evidence for a Markan conflation of sources behind Matthew and Luke, thus approaching Griesbach's theory without subscribing to it.[70]

(4) Beside the modernizations of different utilization and source theories, mentioned above in paragraphs 1-3, a renascence of Herder's and Gieseler's oral tradition hypothesis is also discernible in contemporary synoptic discussions. To support this view analogies have been collected from contexts outside the New Testament, partly from Judaism and partly from folklore.

Oral traditions found in Judaism have been emphasized by Swedish scholars who have studied in Uppsala. Their inspiration came from the orientalist Henrik Samuel Nyberg, who analysed the prophecies of Hosea in 1935.[71] Drawing attention to the dominating function of living traditions in oriental literature, Nyberg rejected the mechanical dissection of texts which has often been practiced in biblical criticism. Similar principles were applied to the Gospels in 1957 by the Uppsala theologian Harald Riesenfeld in a lecture by which he inaugurated a congress at Oxford.[72] According to him the oral teaching of Jesus was

---

[69] Ph. Rolland, "Les évangiles des premières communautés chrétiennes," *RB* 90 (1983) 161-201.

[70] Idem, "Les prédécesseurs de Marc. Les sources présynoptiques de Mc II, 18-22 et parallèles," *RB* 89 (1982) 370-405; "Marc, première harmonie évangélique?," ibid. 90 (1983) 23-79.

[71] H.S. Nyberg, *Studien zum Hoseabuch. Zugleich ein Beitrag zur Klärung des Problems der alttestamentlichen Textkritik*, Uppsala universitets årsskrift 1935: 6 (Uppsala: Lundequistska, 1935).

[72] H. Riesenfeld, *The Gospel Tradition and Its Beginnings. A Study in the Limits of "Formgeschichte"* (London: Mowbray, 1957); reprinted in Texte und Untersuchungen ... 73 (Berlin: Akademie-Verlag, 1959) 43-65; also in *The Gospel Tradition* (Philadelphia: Fortress Press, 1970), 1-29.

the direct source of the Gospel tradition. To illustrate such dependence of the Gospels on Christ's oral teaching, the Uppsala theologian Birger Gerhardsson, later professor in Lund, wrote a dissertation in which he ascribed the oral traditions of the rabbis to an elaborate memorization practice, and then presumed a corresponding practice behind the Jesus traditions of the apostles,[73] though he admitted that private notes were sometimes a support to memorization. In subsequent publications Gerhardsson has defended his comparison of the rabbinic and the apostolic traditions.[74]

The use of folklore to illustrate oral traditions behind the written Gospels was a starting-point for pioneers of form-critical studies, but remained in the background and was actually neglected in favour of the two-source theory (above, p. 305). In recent years some American theologians have found it valuable again to apply folkloristic observations to the synoptic problem. Research work done by scholars of Harvard University have made New Testament scholars acquainted with the way in which great epics have been orally transmitted from generation to generation in regions now belonging to Yugoslavia. Impressive material was recorded as early as 1913-1919 by Mathias Murko in Vienna[75] and has been supplemented in campaigns undertaken since 1930 by Milham Parry[76] and Albert Bates Lord[77] of Harvard. Village reciters studied by these scholars proved to have the capacity of memorizing an immense amount of traditional material and, in one case, a minstrel was able to quote around 80,000 verses by heart.[78] Most interesting was this observation: Whereas the structure of the story told in the epic was preserved without changes by different

[73] B. Gerhardsson, *Memory and Manuscript. Oral Tradition and Written Transmission in Rabbinic Judaism and Early Christianity*, Acta Seminarii neotestamentici upsaliensis 20 (Lund: Gleerup, 1961); conclusions: 328-335.

[74] Idem, *Tradition and Transmission in Early Christianity*, Coniectanea neotestamentica 20 (Lund: Gleerup, 1964); *Die Anfänge der Evangelientradition* (Wuppertal: R. Brockhaus, 1977); ET *The Origins of the Gospel Traditions* (Philadelphia: Fortress Press, 1979).

[75] M. Murko, "Bericht über eine Bereisung von Nordwestbosnien ... behufs Erforschung der Volksepik der bosnischen Mohammedaner," Sitzungsberichte der Kaiserlichen Akademie der Wissenschaften in Wien, Philosophisch-historische Classe 173 (Wien, 1913); other reports in Sitzungsberichte 176 (1915), and 179 (1915); furthermore "Neues über südslawische Volksepik," *Neue Jahrbücher für das klassische Altertum* 43 (1919) 273-296.

[76] M. Parry, "Studies in the Epic Technique of Oral Verse-Making," *Harvard Studies in Classical Philology* 41 (1930) 73-149; 43 (1932) 1-50. On the application of M. Parry's ideas to Plato by J.A. Notopoulos, see "Mnemosyne in Oral Literature," *Transactions of the American Philological Association* 69 (1938) 465-495.

[77] A.B. Lord, "Homer and Huso," *Transactions...* (see note 76) 67 (1936) 106-113; 69 (1938) 439-445; and numerous later studies on ancient Greek and southern Slav literature.

[78] Murko (n. 75), *Neue Jahrbücher* 284-285.

traditionists from generation to generation, the expressions used by them were varied with considerable freedom.

Confrontation with the flexibility of such oral traditions has also impressed historians of ancient Greek literature.[79] Although most New Testament scholars are used to thinking in terms of fixed sources, some have also been willing to learn from experiences made by students of folklore and oral traditions. This is evident from the interdisciplinary dialogue arranged in 1977 by William O. Walker at Trinity University of San Antonio, Texas. Here the above-mentioned folklore specialist, A.B. Lord of Harvard, gave the first main lecture and illustrated possibilities to explain the similarities and differences between the Gospels by paying attention to such unity of stability and flexibility as is found in oral traditional literature.[80]

At the same colloquium a professor of Judaic studies, Lou H. Silberman of Vanderbilt University in Tennessee, illustrated the remarkable wandering of fixed themes in Jewish literature and found similar cases in the Gospels.[81] He explained this wandering of text units as evidence for their earlier participation in oral traditions, of which flexibility was characteristic.

Silberman's instructive conclusion may be rendered here:[82] "A century ago, scholars assumed unquestioningly that a literary work had its sources in literary works (for, after all, were not these scholars themselves ransacking literary works to fabricate new literary works?). And even now, when we have come to affirm that behind some or many of the literary works we deal with there is an oral tradition, we still manipulate such traditions as though they too were 'literary' works."

This is reminiscent of a passage quoted above from J.C.L. Gieseler's support of Herder's theory (above, pp. 302-303). It was as early as 1818 that Gieseler made these reservations against the anachronistic view of the evangelists as working in their studies with manuscripts, which they sometimes copied and sometimes changed.

---

[79] H. Fränkel, *Dichtung und Philosophie des frühen Griechentums*, 2nd ed. (München: Beck, 1962) 9-27; A. Lesky, *Geschichte der griechischen Literatur*, 2nd ed. (Bern: Franke, 1963), 32-58; C.A. Trypanis, *Greek Poetry from Homer to Sefiris* (London: Faber & Faber, 1981), 32. Further titles in E.R. Haynes, *A Bibliography of Studies Relating to Parry's and Lord's Oral Theory*, Documentation and Planning Series 1 (Cambridge/Mass.: Harvard University Press, 1973).

[80] A.B. Lord, "The Gospels as Oral Traditional Literature," in W.O. Walker (ed.), *The Relationships Among the Gospels. An Interdisciplinary Dialogue* (San Antonio: Trinity University Press, 1978), 33-91.

[81] L.H. Silberman, "Habent sua fata libelli. The Role of Wandering Themes in Some Hellenistic Jewish and Rabbinic Literature," in Walker, *The Relationships* (n. 80) 195-218.

[82] Silberman (n. 81), 215.

In recent years the synoptic problem has thus been taken up again by several open-minded theologians and historians. Many scholars not mentioned here have also taken part in the discussion. Unfortunately no agreement can be observed. In fact, the four leading theories which German Protestants, like Storr and Griesbach, Lessing, Koppe, and Herder, elaborated shortly before 1800 are still competing with each other in the modernized forms which are found in the contemporary discussion. As far as the synoptic question is concerned, scholars are still divided into the four camps at issue. Each group seeks illumination from a different span of the horizon.

Whichever of the four options is preferred, the present author wants to emphasize that it ought to be supplemented by considerations about the empirical circumstances under which the oral traditions were developed in the early church and then adopted by the evangelists. It is a question of the concrete historical relationships between tradition and redaction as well as between the oral and the written gospel.

Representatives of redactional criticism have been occupied with this problem. But their dependence on the two-source theory implies that reflections of the oral traditions are only seen in Mark and Q, not in what Matthew, Mark, and Luke show together or when they are compared with each other.

Similar limitations are found in recent attempts to reconstruct the development from Jesus to the oral traditions and the written documents. Werner H. Kelber's book of 1983, *The Oral and Written Gospel*, takes the Mark and Q hypothesis for an established truth and uses hermeneutical rules for a categorical separation of the oral traditions and the written documents.[83] Two impressive volumes of papers delivered at Cambridge in 1979 and Tübingen in 1982, both published in 1983, certainly open more possibilities to follow the lines from Jesus to the apostles and the evangelists.[84] But several of the articles still reduce such possibilities by not taking sufficiently into account that oral traditions must have been a link between Jesus and the written material in all its parts, and not only with regard to one Gospel or some other document elected to be a source.[85]

Bo Reicke

---

[83] W.H. Kelber, *The Oral and the Written Gospel. The Hermeneutics of Speaking and Writing in the Synoptic Tradition, Mark, Paul, and Q* (Philadelphia: Fortress Press, 1983).

[84] W.R. Farmer (ed.), *New Synoptic Studies. The Cambridge Gospel Conference and Beyond* (Macon, GA: Mercer University Press, 1983). P. Stuhlmacher (ed.), *Das Evangelium und die Evangelien. Vorträge vom Tübinger Symposium 1982* (Tübingen: Mohr & Siebeck, 1983).

[85] B. Reicke, "A Test of Synoptic Relationships: Matthew 10:17-23 and 24:9-14 with Parallels," *New Synoptic Studies* (n. 84), 209-229.

SYNOPSES OF THE FUTURE

The purpose of this report is to extend the discussion in synopsis criticism begun in my earlier paper.[1] The focal question remains the same: what is the relationship between synopsis construction and the Synoptic Problem?[2] Taking recently published research into account, this report will consider the question: Can there be a neutral synopsis? In the second part of the report, I make a few proposals regarding synopses of the future. The new synopses will be designed to facilitate the three basic tasks of Gospel research, namely, text criticism, analysis of the pre-composition oral tradition period (form criticism), and research on the different Evangelists' techniques of composition (redaction criticism).

A. CAN THERE BE A NEUTRAL SYNOPSIS?

As Huck had before him, H. Greeven insisted in the preface to his revision of Huck-Lietzmann's *Synopse* that his arrangement sought to "maintain a strict neutrality before the various solutions of the Synoptic Problem."[3] Similarly, F. Neirynck recently insisted that "a gospel synopsis cannot be bound to one particular theory."[4] It is my impression that most scholars agree with this view. Nevertheless, I must ask: how is it possible for a synopsis to be strictly neutral with respect to a solution to the Synptic Problem? No one has yet demonstrated whether this is even possible. On the contrary, the evidence seems to indicate that it is quite impossible. It comes from both levels which make up any and all synopses: (1) the text, and (2) the arrangement of the text, which depends on (3) the division into pericopes. We will consider each of these in turn.

---

[1] "Theory of Synopsis Construction," *Biblica* 61 (1980) 305-329.

[2] Dom Bernard Orchard initially drew the attention of the scholarly world to the little-realized correlation between synopsis construction and the Synoptic Problem in his article, "Are All Gospel Synopses Biassed?" in *Theolog. Zeitschr.* 34 (1978).

[3] H. Greeven, A. Huck, *Synopse der drei ersten Evangelien*; 13. Aufl., völlig neu bearbeitet; J.C.B. Mohr (Paul Siebeck) Tübingen 1981; p. v.

[4] F. Neirynck, "The Sermon on the Mount in the Gospel Synopsis," *Eph. Theol. Lov.* 52 (1976) 350-357; see p. 356 [rpr. in *Analecta Lovaniensia Biblica et Orientalia*, ser. v fasc. 21; in *Evangelica*, BETL 60, Leuven 1982, 729-736; see p. 735].

1. The text of any synopsis cannot be neutral.

At the second Ampleforth Conference on the Gospels (April 1983) hosted by Dom Henry Wansbrough of Ampleforth Abbey, G.D. Kilpatrick observed that modern text criticism of the Gospels tended to rely on the Two-Document Hypothesis. This was of course news to no one. In his *Textual Commentary on the United Bible Societies' New Testament* (the third edition), B. Metzger had listed among the "internal evidence" used by the UBS editorial committee, "The priority of the Gospel According to Mark," saying that this theory functioned to help them decide "what the author [of Luke or Matthew or Mark] was more likely to have written."[5] For example, it would have been presupposed in the committee's decisions to adopt readings reflecting what they thought were the original author's style and vocabulary.[6] This is because most existing discussions of the evangelists' linguistic usage do presuppose the Two-Document Hypothesis.[7] An exception is M.-É. Boismard and others, who simply count the occurrences of a word using their concordances, thinking that the resulting ratios are evidence of "vocabulary preference" — a singularly ill-considered kind of approach.[8]

The treatment of "harmonizations" is another kind of "internal evidence" mentioned by Metzger that required the assumption of the Two-Document Hypothesis.[9] For example, if one assumes that Matthew and Luke independently copied material from Mark (as the Two-Document Hypothesis stipulates), and, in a passage where both have one reading that is different from the parallel in Mark but the same as the other's, and other readings where they differ from Mark and also from each other, the UBS committee usually chose the latter readings on the grounds that Matthew and Luke could not have independently changed the text of Mark in precisely the same way.[10] But if one

---

[5] See B. Metzger, *A Textual Commentary on the Greek New Testament. A Companion Volume to the United Bible Societies' Greek New Testament (third edition)*. United Bible Societies, London-New York, 1971; pp. xxviif.

[6] Loc. cit.

[7] See however, the forthcoming trio of monographs on the style of Matthew, Mark, and Luke, respectively, to be published by Mercer University Press: David Peabody on Mark, Frank Collison on Luke, and Dennis Tevis on Matthew. These will be the first studies of the style of the evangelists that consciously strive to be independent of any source theory in the way they analyze the texts.

[8] See, for a typical example, Boismard's list of "caractéristiques lucaniennes du rédacteur matthéen," *Synopse*, II p. 38.

[9] Op. cit. above, note 4, p. xxvii.

[10] See the comments of K. Elliott, "Textual Criticism, Assimilation and the Synoptic Gospels," in *New Test. Stud.* 26 (1979/80) 231-242. For the work of K. Aland and B. Aland, see most recently: *Der Text des Neuen Testaments. Einführung in die wissenschaft-*

hypothecates the opposite situation, i.e., that Luke copied directly from the Gospel of Matthew (as is stipulated in the Two-Gospel and so-called Augustinian Hypotheses)[11], then a reading where both diverged from the text of Mark in precisely the same way would be chosen as the more original reading. So it is obvious that which theory one chooses will make a considerable difference. Here is a concrete illustration of the close relationship between source criticism and text criticism. In A. Lindemann's recently published survey of research on the Synoptic Gospels,[12] he makes this observation on Greeven's decision to print the longer reading in Mark 10:21f ἄρας τὸν σταυρόν (supported by אΑΓΦsy[p,s]λWbo[pt]sa, etc.). If Greeven is right, it would add another case of a negative "minor agreement" of Matthew and Luke against Mark. The shorter reading in Mark (found in B א C DΔΘΨ etc.) is, in Greeven's opinion, a case of later assimilation of Mark to the shorter text of Matthew and Luke. A. Lindemann notes:

> Die Gegenfrage (Warum haben Mt und/oder Lk den Hinweis auf das Kreuztragen von Mk nicht übernommen?) setzt die Hypothese der Mk-Priorität voraus und enthält insofern kein im eigentlichen Sinn text-kritisches Argument.[13]

But this strict dichotomy is actually rather misleading as Lindemann concedes in a telling parenthesis added immediately:

> (Wenn freilich, wovon ich allerdings überzeugt bin, aus vielerlei anderen Gründen die Mk-Priorität außer Frage steht, dann ist der Kurztext bei Mt und Lk wohl doch ein Indiz dafür, daß beide in ihrer Vorlage den Langtext nicht lasen — und dafür spricht ja schließlich auch die Qualität des Handschriftenbefundes bei Mk.)[14]

Here we clearly see the interplay between text criticism and source criticism. Although some scholars are a little uneasy with Metzger's forthright admission that the UBS editorial committee used the Two-Document Hypothesis as part of their "internal evidence," I would argue that he did the right thing in identifying which one they used,

---

lichen Ausgaben sowie in Theorie und Praxis der modernen Textkritik, Deutsche Bibelgesell-schaft 1982, Stuttgart; p. 292f.

[11] I use the term so-called since what is universally believed to have been Augustine's view of the sequence of composition is erroneous; the actual Augustinian view has only recently been rediscovered; see David B. Peabody, "Augustine and the Augustinian Hypothesis: A Reexamination of...de consensu evangelistarum," in W. R. Farmer, ed., *New Synoptic Studies*, Mercer University Press (Macon, GA 1983) pp. 37-64.

[12] "Literaturbericht zu den Synoptischen Evangelien 1978-1983," *Theol. Rund.* 49 (1984) 223-276.

[13] Ibid., p. 249.

[14] Loc. cit.

since text critics cannot avoid using some sort of source theory in any case.[15]

In fact, there are some indications that the source theory is more important, in one sense, than the manuscript evidence. Consider the view of the text critics who deny that there is any real distinction between "internal" and "external" criteria. They assert that the process of constructing a critical text is not a neat, logical procedure at all. For one thing, the manuscript evidence is often ambiguous and contradictory, defying neat categorization. In a famous reversal of Westcott and Hort's maxim: "Knowledge of documents should precede final judgements upon readings," C.H. Turner prefaced his exhaustive study of Marcan style by saying, "Knowledge of an author's usage should precede final judgement upon readings."[16] E. Epp comments: Turner "indicated in a striking fashion the need to take internal evidence most seriously, particularly stylistic and philological features, and that these are crucial if not conclusive in text-critical decisions."[17] G. D. Kilpatrick agreed, saying:

> ... the decision [as to the best reading] rests ultimately with the criteria [concerning harmonization, style, language and theology] as distinct from the manuscripts, and our evaluation of the manuscripts must be determined by [these] criteria.[18]

In striking contrast to all this, particularly in view of the explicit testimony of two of his fellow committee members (Metzger and Kilpatrick) on the UBS editorial committee, Kurt Aland has not indicated one way or the other what his own views are of the relationship between text criticism and source criticism.[19] One would have thought that in his latest and most comprehensive statement of the theory and practice of text criticism, there would be some sort of discussion of this fundamental question, but this does not seem to be the

---

[15] See, on this whole subject, the excellent article by G.D. Fee, "Modern Text Criticism and the Synoptic Problem," in J. B. Orchard and T.R.W. Longstaff, eds; *J.J. Griesbach: Synoptic and Text-critical Studies 1776-1976;* Cambridge University Press 1978; pp. 154-169. See further, idem, "A Text-critical Look at the Synoptic Problem," in *Nov. Test.* 22 (1980) 12-28.

[16] C.H. Turner, "Marcan Usage," in *Journ. Theol. Stud.* 25 (1923-24) p. 377. Cited in E. Epp, "The Eclectic Method in New Testament Textual Criticism: Solution or Symptom?" *Harv. Theol. Rev.* 69 (1976) 211-257; reference on p. 250.

[17] Epp, op. cit., p. 250.

[18] G. D. Kilpatrick, "Western Text and Original Text in the Gospels and Act," in *Journ. Theol. Stud.* 44 (1943) 25-26; cited in Epp, op. cit., p. 251.

[19] This curious lacuna is true of all his writings on text criticism, but see especially his most recent, definitive work: *Einführung in ...der Textkritik*, cited in note 9.

case.[20] This gaping lacuna in his definitive statement of text critical methodology is all the more regrettable, because it appears that he played a major role in shaping the text used by the United Bible Societies. H. Greeven shows that he is fully cognizant of the dimensions of the interplay of text criticism and source criticism. In the preface to his new synopsis he writes:

> [Harmonistic readings have been excluded from the text, but fully included in the apparatus. In this way, scholars can clearly see that] the Synoptic Problem is mirrored precisely in the history of the text, namely in an unremitting tendency to harmonization. We must always keep before our eyes this trend and especially the significant tendency to assimilate to Matthew, if we wish appropriately to investigate textual questions in the Synoptic Gospels.[21]

In conclusion, with the possible exception of Kurt Aland (for whom we have no explicit statement one way or the other), all scholars seem to agree that the process of establishing a critical text of the Gospels can not be "neutral" with regard to a consistent and rigorous use of one particular source hypothesis (eclectic use of a number of different hypotheses must be avoided). Hopefully, it will be the correct hypothesis!

Of course, this means that all text critics are involved in a *circulus in probando*:

1. Young scholars are taught to use a critical text (e.g., Nestle-Aland 26th or UBS 3rd) which has been prepared by a committee consistently assuming the Two-Document Hypothesis.

2. Using this text, they form their own impressions of the likelihood of the priority of the composition of Mark and the secondary or derivative character of Matthew and Luke.

3. Then they complete their doctorates and perhaps are fortunate enough to find employment in a famous institute for text criticism where

---

[20] In this respect, the "Zwölf Grundregeln für die textkritische Arbeit," are at once curiously vague and old-fashioned. Although his research institute has performed a magnificent service in collecting and comparing manuscripts and critical editions, as a theoretician, K. Aland leaves much to be desired. Although he uses commonly accepted principles, his central tendency seems to recommend what one might call trained intuition. As proof of this, consider Grundregel 12:

"Die ständig erneuerte Erfahrung im Umgang mit der handschriftlichen Überlieferung ist die beste Lehrmeisterin der Textkritik. Wer produktiv an ihr teilnehmen will, sollte vorher mindestens eine großen frühen Papyrus, eine bedeutende Majuskel und eine wichtige Minuskel vollständig kollationiert haben, die reinen Theoretiker haben in der Textkritik oft genug mehr Schaden als Nutzen angerichtet." (p. 283)

Note how this 'rule' does not prescribe any methodological or scientific procedure at all. It merely recommends to all would-be text critics that they get plenty of exercise with the texts. Is this supposed to magically train the text-critic's nose to find the right reading?

[21] Op. cit. above note 2, p. vi.

— under the guidance of the master — they continue to shape the text of the Gospels using this hypothesis...

4. ...so that future generations of young scholars will read their critical text and see how true the Two-Document Hypothesis is according to the evidence in their critical texts — perhaps by now labeled "the new Standard Text."

5. And so the cycle repeats itself.

Two observations. First, we must not be under the illusion that this circular process is avoidable.

Second, the only defense against the dangers obviously inherent in such a circular situation is to produce a variety of critical texts relying upon different source hypotheses, so that, by comparing critical texts, we will at least have some idea how much difference each source theory makes. In this respect, the new text and apparatus of H. Greeven is a major contribution. Similarly, the *Greek New Testament According to the Majority Text,* edited by Z.C. Hodges and A. L. Farstad (Nashville, Camden, New York; Thos. Nelson & Sons 1982), is also important to have — if only for purposes of comparison. Likewise, the new Greek synopsis of Orchard is another example of what must be done. Confronted by a critical text based upon the priority of Mark, Orchard had no choice but to work out his own text. His hypothesis (the Two-Gospel Hypothesis) said that Luke had directly copied Matthew, and so readings in Luke and Mark that had been discarded by Nestle and Aland as secondary assimilations, were restored by Orchard as more original.[22] In a few reviews, Orchard was chided for creating a "biased text" — as if the reviewers themselves were somehow in possession of an unbiased text.

2. The arrangement of any synopsis cannot be neutral.

The most widely used synopses in the world today each claim to be "objective" arrangements of the Gospel texts, "neutral" with regard to the Synoptic Problem in the way the texts are paralleled to each other. If these claims are correct, it would seem appropriate to expect these

---

[22] See his Table in *A Synopsis of the Four Gospels in Greek* (T & T Clark, Edinburgh 1983), pp. 307-340. In general, Orchard preferred to leave dubious longer readings in the text, marked off by half-brackets (more than 60 times, including the Longer Ending of Mark). However, it is clear that Orchard (working with G. Kilpatrick) only dealt with some of the more important cases. A thorough reconstruction of the text of the Gospels on the basis of the Two-Gospel Hypothesis still remains to be done.

synopses to be nearly identical in (a) the number of pericopes, and (b) the arrangement of pericopes. What is in fact the situation?

Huck has a total of 259 pericopes while Aland has 304 (excluding the strictly Johannine passages). Out of these totals, approximately 190 are similar — which is to be expected. Around 110 (roughly 33%) are different — which is too many if these are "neutral" synopses. The differences are of three kinds: in approximately 30 pericopes Huck has material in one pericope which Aland has divided into two pericopes; second, there are 4 cases where Huck has one pericope which Aland has divided into three pericopes; and third, about 40 pericopes have been divided differently.[23] Is either of them the "neutral" synopsis?

In practice, the synopsis editor divides up the Gospel narratives with one eye constantly on divisions he has already made in the parallel Gospels. The process of dividing up the material and the process of arranging the primary parallels take place simultaneously and influence each other continuously as the synopsis editor moves back and forth, shaping and arranging the parallels in his synopsis. Once the primary parallels are lined up, the secondary and tertiary parallels are inserted into the outline. Faced with the complex and subjective judgements all this calls for, any pretence of "neutrality" or "objectivity" on the part of the synopsis editor must vanish into thin air. There is, unfortunately, no Ariadne's thread to guide the synopsis editor through the labyrinth of Synoptic interrelationships.

I am aware that this is not the conventional wisdom on the matter. F. Neirynck's comment reflects the consensus:

> Modern synopses [have as] their basic principle ... to present the text of each gospel in its consecutive order and to repeat gospel sections out of order as often as the parallelization with the other gospels may require. This principle is clear enough and it should normally result in an objective tool for the comparative study of the gospels.[24]

We have all heard this oft-repeated principle. It is ironic to see it quoted again on the rare occasion when Neirynck himself will bring forward absolutley devastating evidence against it. Nevertheless, in

---

[23] Although the text has been completely recast, Greeven did not to my knowledge change Huck's pericope divisions except in a few minor cases.

[24] "The Sermon on the Mount in the Gospel Synopsis," *Eph.Theol.Lov.* 52 (1976) p. 350. K. Aland's version of this "basic principle" is quite similar:

"This Synopsis can be used apart from all theories of source criticism, for the text of each of the four Gospels has been reproduced in its continuity... For every section of the Synopsis all the relevant passages of the other Gospels are given again in full, and in this way the user has each time the entire material placed before his eyes in what I hope is a perspicuous form."

(Preface, *Synopsis Quattuor Evangeliorum*, editio tertia 1965, p. xi)

doing so Neirynck has performed the valuable service of focusing attention precisely upon the fatal flaw in this "basic principle": it says nothing whatever about the synoptic editor's repeated experience of having arbitrarily to choose between equally valid alternative configurations of primary parallel pericopes. Consider this question: where should the synopsis-maker put the Sermon on the Mount vis-a-vis the order of Mark?

(Table I)

WHERE SHOULD THE SERMON ON THE MOUNT BE PARALLELED TO MARK?[25]

1. The arrangement of Tischendorf, Lagrange, Larfeld, Burton-Goodspeed, Benoit, Aland, Orchard.

MATTHEW	MARK	LUKE
	1,21-28 Heal in synagogue	4,31-37 Heal in synagogue
	1,29-31 Peter's mother-in-law	4,38-39 Peter's mother-in-law
	1,32-34 Healing in evening	4,40-41 Healing in evening
	1,35-38 Jesus leaves Capharnaum	4,42-43 Jesus leaves Capharnaum
4,23 Preaching in Galilee	1,39 Preaching in Galilee	4,44 Preaching in Galilee
		5,1-11 Catch of fish
	1,40-45 Heal leper	5,17-26 Heal paralytic
	2,1-12 Heal paralytic	5,17-26Heal paralytic
	2,13-17 Call of Levi	5,27-32 Call of Levi
	2,18-22 Question of John	5,33-39 Question of John
	2,23-28 Grain on sabbath	6,1-5 Grain on sabbath
	3,1-6 Heals hand	6,6-11 Heals hand
	3,7-12 Heal multitudes	
	3,13-19 Call of Twelve	6,12-16 Call of Twelve
4,24-5,2 Great crowds gather from all directions		6,17-20a Heals multitudes
5,3-7,29 Sermon on the Mount		6,20b-49 Sermon on the Plain
8,1-4 Heal leper		
8,5-13 Centurion's servant		7,1-10 Centurion's servant

---

[25] These tables are based on the article by F. Neirynck just cited; see note 4 above. Besides tthe location of the Sermon on the Mount, Neirynck proposes several other alternative arrangements (see pp. 351f.). These will no doubt be seen in the forthcoming Dutch synopsis by A. Denaux and M. Vervenne.

(Table II)

2. The arrangement of Huck (incl. translations) Schmid, Sparks, *et al.*

MATTHEW	MARK	LUKE
	1,21-28 Heal in synagogue	4,31-37 Heal in synagogue
	1,29-31 Peter's mother-in-law	4,38-39 Peter's mother-in-law
	1,32-34 Healing in evening	4,40-41 Healing in evening
	1,35-38 Jesus leaves Capharnaum	4,42-43 Jesus leaves Capharnaum
4,23 Preaching in Galilee	1,39 Preaching in Galilee	4,44 Preaching in Galilee
		5,1-11 Catch of fish
5,1-7,29 Sermon on Mount		
8,1-4 Heal leper	1,40-45 Heal leper	5,12-16 Heal leper
8,5-13 Centurion's servant		
8,14-15 Peter's mother-in-law		
8,16-17 Discipleship		
8,18-22 Saying about discipleship		
8,23-27 Calming of storm		
8,28-34 Gadarene demoniac		
9,1-8 Heal paralytic	2,1-12 Heal paralytic	5,17-26 Heal paralytic
9,9-13 Call of Levi	2,13-17 Call of Levi	5,27-32 Call of Levi
9,14-17 Fasting	2,18-22 Fasting	5,33-39 Fasting
9,18-26 Jairus' daughter		
9,27-31 Two blind men		
9,32-34 Heal two demoniacs		
9,35-10,16 Send out Twelve		
10,17-11,1 Mission sermon		
11,2-6 Baptist's question		
11,7-19 Jesus' words on John the Baptist		
11,20-24 Woe to Galilean cities		
11,25-27 Jesus thanks the Father		
11,28-30 Comfort for heavy-laden		
12,1-8 Plucking grain on sabbath	2,23-28 Grain on sabbath	6,1-5 Grain on sabbath
12,9-14 Heals man's hand	3,1-6 Heals man's hand	6,6-11 Heals man's hand
12,15-21 Heals multitudes	3,7-12 Heals multitudes	6,17-19 Heals multitudes
	3,13-19 Call of Twelve	6,12-16 (sic) Call of Twelve
		6,20-49 Sermon on Plain

(Table I)

Comments:

a. These editors do not seem to be primarily intent on locating the Sermons at the most appropriate point in Mark's order. Instead, they appear to have been primarily concerned to bring together two sets of redactional passages in Matthew and Luke, namely, the preaching and healing summary in Matthew 4:23//Mark 1:39//Luke 4:44, and the preaching and healing summary in Matt. 4:24- 5:2//Luke 6:17-20a.

b. This arrangement has the additional attraction of bringing the two Sermons of Matthew and Luke opposite to each other.

c. The result is that the Sermon on the Mount comes after Mark 3:13-19, which is not about a sermon at all, but the Call of the Twelve. To be sure, Mark opens the scene by saying Jesus "went up on a mountain." But even so, locating the Sermons at this point in Mark's order seems more like an unavoidable necessity than an appropriate parallel location.

(Table II)

Comments:

1. Judging from Huck's placement of the Sermon on the Mount directly after Mark's summary in 1:39, rather than Mark 3:19, it would seem that Huck arranged Matthew's material with an eye on the Markan outline rather than Luke's (in contrast to the synopses listed above).

2. An even clearer sign that Mark's order is still guiding Huck is the placement of Luke 6:17-19 (Healing of the Multitudes) next to Mark 3:7-12. He then puts Luke 6:12-16 (Call of the Twelve) beside Mark 3:13-19, and prints it in regular type (with bold for the heading), despite the fact that it is out of order. This is conclusive proof that Huck is still allowing his belief in the priority of Mark to guide his arrangement of the primary order of parallel pericopes, despite what he said in the preface about his synopsis being "neutral." Strangely, Schmid does exactly the same thing.

(Table III)

Comments:

a. Neirynck writes "Huck's arrangement of the gospel parallels needs further correction in this section"[26], by which he means his arrangement. "All agree," he adds, that "Matt. 4:23(-25) is parallel to Mark 1:16-20... and that the conclusion of the Sermon in Matt. 7:28b-29

---

[26] Ibid., p. 355.

(Table III)

3. Neirynck's proposal (the same arrangement as Griesbach's chart).

MATTHEW	MARK	LUKE
4,23-5,2 Summary passage 5,3-7,27 Sermon on Mount	1,21 Preach in Capharnaum	4,31 Preach in Capharnaum
7,28-29; 8,1 Conclusion	1,22 "Astonished at his teaching"	4,32 "Astonished at his teaching"
	1,23-28 Heal in synagogue	4,33-37 Heal in synagogue
8,2-4 Heal leper 8,5-13 Centurion's servant		
8,14-17 Peter's mother-in-law	1,29-34 Peter's mother-in-law	4,38-41 Peter's mother-in-law
	1,35-39 Simon follows Jesus	4,42-44 Simon follows Jesus 5,1-11 Catch of fish
	1,40-45 Heal leper	5,12-16 Heal leper
		—
		—
		—
		6,20-49 Sermon on Plain

clearly corresponds with Mark 1:22."[27] Hence, concludes Neirynck, Huck's arrangement, as well as the older one, is to be rejected.

b. Neirynck goes on to note that his arrangement is congenial to the redactional programmes of both the Two-Document Hypothesis as well as the Two-Gospel Hypothesis, and therefore his arrangement should be adopted by the adherents of each school of thought.[28]

General observations on Tables I, II and III.

1. There does not seem to be any formal justification or necessary reason for choosing one of these arrangements over against the other two. Neirynck tries to make a case for his arrangement, but his literary evidence is very slight, and by no means universally accepted. Table I shows that other considerations lead to different arrangements. Neirynck points these out, noting that the arrangement in Table I is

[27] Loc. cit.

[28] Ibid., p. 357. F. Neirynck's position paper at the Jerusalem Symposium on the Gospels dealt with this same cluster of pericopes at great length. However, readers may find his earlier article helpful; see "La rédaction matthéenne et la structure du premier évangile," in I. de la Potterie, ed., De Jésus aux Évangiles. Tradition et Rédaction dans les Évangiles synoptiques, BETL 25 (1967), pp. 41-73.

preferred by those who hold the Proto-Mark Hypothesis, as well as the so-called "Primitive Oral-Gospel" Hypothesis. He thinks his arrangement will be more useful to adherents of the Two-Document Hypothesis and the Two-Gospel Hypothesis.[29] In other words, Neirynck makes it clear that, in the absence of any formal or necessary reason, one's source theory should influence one's choice of alternative configurations.

2. Depending on which is chosen, the synopsis editor must place a large number of pericopes in a particular configuration of the primary parallel order, covering material extending through approximately eight chapters in Matthew, three in Mark and three in Luke. This is clearly one of the most far-reaching of all "judgement calls" involved in setting up a synopsis.

3. The historian's understanding of the redactional activity of each Evangelist will vary drastically, depending on which synoptic arrangement he uses. Let us ask this question: How much of the confusion and disagreement in our current scholarship regarding the theological programmes of each of the Evangelists is due, at least in part, to a naive and uncritical reliance upon differently configured synopses (each claiming to be "objective")?

The first point is worthy of being repeated, since it bears most directly on the theme of our discussion: In the placement of the Sermon on the Mount vis-a-vis the order of Mark, there does not appear to be any necessary or intrinsic principle to guide the synopsis editor as he considers the alternatives and selects one way to display the primary order of parallel pericopes among the Synoptic Gospels. All he has is intuition, educated guessing and a pragmatic preference based on his favorite source theory.

In the Second Ampleforth Gospel Conference (1983), C. Tuckett addressed himself to the question of whether there was an "objective" method for identifying the common primary order of pericopes, and reached essentially the same conclusion that we have, but by a different route. He suggested that while one might be able to say objectively that certain pericopes were "in order," one could never find an objective way to say in what way certain pericopes were "out of order." The reason for this curious fact is because the original order must be known, in order to say which pericopes are "out of order" in the disarranged series. I propose that we call this "Tuckett's Dilemma" in honor of its discoverer.

---

[29] Op. cit. above, note 4, p. 356f.

"How does one define a disagreement in order? An agreement in order is relatively easy to define: if two writers X and Y have two units of tradition, a and b, then if a precedes b in X and Y, there is agreement in order.

A disagreement is, at one level, a failure to agree, i.e., if one writer has ab and the other has ba. But can one be more precise beyond making the negative statement that there is a failure to agree? Suppose X and Y have four pericopes abcd in the order X: a b c d, Y: a c b d. Clearly there is failure to agree in order. Further, most would assume that a and d are in the same order in the two texts. But which element, or elements, is, or are, out of order? There are at least three ways of illustrating the parallels diagramatically:

(i)	X	Y		(ii)	X	Y		(iii)	X	Y
	a	a			a	a			a	a
	b					c			b	c
	c	c			b	b			c	b
		b			c					
	d	d			d	d			d	d

According to (i) b is out of order; according to (ii) c is out of order; according to (iii) both b and c are out of order. At the purely formal level, there appears to be no way of claiming in absolute terms which of these three is the most preferable way of describing the pattern of agreement and disagreement in order between X and Y. Furthermore, the way in which the parallels are initially set up inevitably affects in a significant way the description of the differences of order. A different scheme of parallelisation produces a quite different set of non-parallels."[30]

If we turn to the Gospels, we can find numerous examples of Tuckett's Dilemma.

Dozens of examples of conflicting arrangements (clearly relying upon numerous unexplained "judgement calls") like the foregoing could be given from synopses now in print. It is quite beyond me why, despite our at least marginal awareness of this diversity, there is so little discussion about it. On the contrary, we seem to be in the grip of this smug but absolutely groundless conviction that our synopses are "objective."

---

[30] See "Arguments from Order: Definition and Evaluation," in *Synoptic Studies. The Ampleforth Conferences of 1982 and 1983*; ed. C. M. Tuckett (JSOT Press, Sheffield, England 1984), pp. 198-199.

(Table IV)

Which is the "objective" arrangement?

BENOIT

Matt 5-7	Sermon on Mount	Sermon on Plain Luke 6,20-49
Matt 10-11	Mission Discourse	
Matt 13	Parables	Parables Luke 8,5-16
		Mission Discourse Luke 9,1-6
Matt 18	Community Regulations	Community Regulations Luke 9,46-48
Matt 23	Woe to Pharisees	Woe to Pharisees Luke 20,45-47
Matt 24-25	Last Judgement	Last Judgement Luke 21

HUCK

Matt 5-7	Sermon on Mount	
Matt 10-11	Mission Instructions	
		Sermon on Plain Luke 6,20-49
Matt 13	Parables	Parables Luke 8,5-16
		Mission Discourse Luke 9,1-6
Matt 18	Community regulations	Community regulations Luke 9,46-48
Matt 23	Woe to Pharisees	Woe to Pharisees Luke 20,45-47
Matt 24-25	Last Judgement	Last Judgement Luke 21

ORCHARD

Matt 5-7	Sermon on Mount	Sermon on the Plain Luke 6,20-49
		Parables Luke 8,5-16
Matt 10-11	Mission Discourse	Mission Discourse Luke 9,1-6
Matt 13	Parables	
Matt 18	Community regulations	Community regulations Luke 9,46-48
Matt 23	Woe to Pharisees	Woe to Pharisees Luke 20,45-47
Matt 24-25	Last Judgement	Last Judgement Luke 21

I suggest that it is not possible to decide a single one of these choices without explicit or implicit appeal to some kind of synoptic source hypothesis. What is the synopsis editor doing, if not seeking to recapitulate the original, historical web of multiple relationships among the Gospel pericopes? — in other words, arrive at some sort of source hypothesis? It is almost the same task as someone writing a redactional analysis of the evangelists' compositional activity.

The great problem is: which *chain of pericopes* will he create, running throughout the length of the Gospels? What *series* of pericopes will he match up, in the full knowledge that if he puts them one way, he will have to forego other possible points of common linkage? This is no longer the elementary question of keeping each Gospel's order intact throughout the synopsis. This is a very different question: what common *order* or chain of pericopes among all three (or four) Gospels will he decide upon? A lot hangs on this decision. For example, someone may use his common order as evidence for the existence of the pre-redactional Ur-Gospel. Someone else will use the common order he composes as evidence for the stages of composition of the Gospels. A third person will look at his common order of pericopes and see evidence of dynamic theological trends in the early Church. There are a number of ultra-sensitive questions which hang in the balance as the Synopsis editor works his way through the Gospel narratives, arbitrarily deciding which pericopes to put next to each other in some sort of continuous chain. At the very least, he will be laying down what is widely regarded as the fundamental evidence for any source hypothesis.

These considerations prompt me to make the following observation: all of the major synopses published so far — and certainly the three or four most popular today — were constructed by text critics and philologians, not historians much less theologians. Could this be one of our great flaws in methodology? This task is too theological to leave to text critics and philologians. They treat the Gospels like a giant puzzle, cutting up the narratives into tiny bits and pieces and putting them here and there, with a deaf ear to the theological harmonies they are destroying. Perhaps the way to proceed would be to prepare a pre-liminary redactional analysis of each Gospel independently *before* beginning the task of dividing up the narratives. Then these redactional studies could be used as a guide to determine which paragraphs to place next to each other. They could eventually become mini-commentaries explaining the "judgement calls" made along the way, and published as a companion to the finished synopsis.

Of course, no one would then dare to claim that any of it represented neutral, objective, absolute Truth. Each synopsis so constructed would have printed pericopes next to each other on the basis of an *assumed* original common order of parallel pericopes. The grounds for this assumption would be stated in the Preface, and they would, of course, be multiple: theological, literary, historical, intuitive.[31]

---

[31] In this respect, Reuben J. Swanson, *The Horizontal Line Synopsis of the Gospels* (Dillsboro, Western North Carolina Press 1975), avoids the whole problem by the expedient of printing each Gospel successively as the "lead Gospel" in separate parts of the Synopsis (or now in separate volumes). In this arrangement, the text of the "lead Gospel" is printed in order at the top of each cluster of parallel lines, and the other Gospels are disarranged to fit it. The same applies to the forthcoming synopsis edited by Robert Funk.

Of course, these problems have long been recognized. Up until recently, it has been customary simply to rearrange the texts according to some preconceived order (Gospel harmonies). Griesbach's own synopsis, which is the first attempt to avoid rearranging each Gospel while at the same time parallelizing as many pericopes as possible, did not succeed in attracting many adherents. His own student De Wette abandoned his master's

It appears that we must contend with something akin to Heisenberg's "principle of indeterminancy" here. As everyone knows, Werner Heisenberg (and others) proved that in the realm of sub-atomic phenomena, it is impossible to study such infinitesimally small phenomena without disturbing them by the very act of observation. Every experiment produces the evidence which is examined by that experiment; the resulting hypotheses are therefore simply the arbitrary constructs produced by those experiments. Fully aware of this circularity in its methods, modern physics avoids terms like "laws of nature," and speaks instead of "quanta" that are known to be "statistically probable." Similarly, it is impossible to study the Synoptic phenomena without making synoptic charts and columns — arranged according to one's source theory — which deploy the evidence in such a way that one can see the evidence for one's synoptic theory. Then one proceeds to make better, newer synopses (based on one's source theory), etc. etc. etc. It is like the *circulus in probando* described above with regard to text criticism. In short, all of our scholarship is essentially an exercise in circular reasoning, and "the objective facts" are forever indeterminable in any direct sense. Hence, the analogy with Heisenberg's "principle of indeterminacy."

In summary, the best policy would be for synopsis editors to state explicitly what assumptions have guided them as they constructed their synopses. "Judgment calls" should be identified as such and discussed, whether in the preface or in a separate publication. Since a source theory is as indispensible for constructing the text as it is for constructing the synopsis, the best policy would be to openly use a single theory

---

synoptic arrangement, and published a revision that was a poor compromise. It keeps to a unified, Griesbachian order for the early pericopes (John the Baptist, the Baptism of Jesus, and the Temptation) and then adopts a serial presentation for the "Galilean Ministry". When the Passion narrative commences, it resumes a common primary order. See the *Tabula Argumentorum in Synopsis evangeliorum... ex recensione Griesbachii;* 2nd ed. 1818, Berlin, pp. vi-x.

This complex tangle of parallels in the early part of the Gospels may have prompted Lagrange to cut the Gordian knot by assimilating the texts of Matthew and Mark to the order of Luke, offering nothing more to justify this astonishing procedure than the patently flimsy excuse that Luke was the one Evangelist who explicitly claimed to have composed his narrative ἀκριβῶς καθεξῆς (see M.J.Lagrange and C. Lavergne, *Synopsis Evangelica,* Paris, 1926; p. x).

There is manifold evidence that the ancient fathers also struggled with this part of the Gospels. The common solution then seems to have been to use Matthew (or Matthew plus John as being the two apostles among the Evangelists) as the "bedrock" order of pericopes and assimilate the other Gospels to it (e.g., the Ammonian Canons, the Eusebian Canons, Tatian's Diatessaron, and the detailed harmony in Books II and III of Augustine's *de consensu evangelistarum*).

rigorously and consistently throughout, rather than to muddle along in a random and confused manner pretending not to use any (which is one of the many reasons why I say Aland and Huck are at present among the least serviceable of synopses).

3. The division into pericopes cannot be "neutral."

I mentioned above that our two most widely used "neutral" synopses differed about 30% from each other with respect to the total number and size of pericopes. Although scholars tend to be irritated by Aland's excessive atomization of the text, they simply turn to Huck-Lietzmann (or now Greeven) for a slightly different arrangement — or they just use the Nestle-Aland text and make up their own pericopes.

Few realize that the question of the division into pericopes is a third area fraught with complications and paradoxes so far-reaching that it is my impression that both Huck/Greeven and Aland are really useful for little more than text critical study.

Touching on this in my previous essay[32], I did not bring out sufficiently there the specific way in which a task as seemingly innocent as dividing the text into pericopes has an enormous impact on how one visually perceives the Synoptic Problem. Perhaps I may give an illustration.

At the present time, there is confusion as to whether pericopes should represent divisions the evangelists themselves made in their narratives and sources[33], or whether the pericopes should be the tiny fragments

---

[32] See op. cit. above note 1, p. 321ff.

[33] An unusually clear statement of this approach is to be found in the *Harmony* of Stevens and Burton. In an Appendix entitled "Principles and Methods with Which the Harmony is Constructed" they say:

> [We have followed] the general principle of preserving as far as possible the structure of each gospel [because] it is important that the gospel history should be read by paragraphs, not by verses... [This] has led us to abandon the plan adopted by those harmonies which make it a matter of chief importance that similar sentences or even phrases stand opposite one another on the page. This plan involves infinite *dissection* in the gospel narratives... [Thus we have] contented ourselves with placing parallel *paragraphs* opposite one another, leaving it to the student to make the more detailed comparison himself. This method is the more necessary because there are so many different kinds of parallelism... This arises from the fact that the various writers differ widely in style and in their method of narration. *No printed page can adequately exhibit the exact character of the parallelism between paragraphs of dissimilar scope and structure"*

See W. A. Stevens and E. D. Burton, *A Harmony of the Gospels for Historical Study. An Analytical Synopsis of the Four Gospels;* 5th ed. 1905; New York, Charles Scribner's Sons; p. 252 (italics added in last sentence only); see further pp. 249ff. Cp. the statements of J. B. Orchard, *A Synopsis of the Four Gospels in Greek* (1983), p. xv.

they received from oral tradition, according to the assumptions of Form Criticism. The best example of the latter is the synopsis published by W.E. Bundy in 1932. He commented on this important problem in his introduction:

> "...There will also be a difference of opinion with regard to the division into paragraphs. [My divisions] are much briefer and more than twice as numerous as is usual in [other synopses]... In general, each paragraph represents a piece of tradition concerning Jesus that came down to the Synoptic writers in oral or written form...The division into paragraphs, then, is an attempt to get back as near as possible to the primitive pieces of tradition concerning Jesus from which our first three Gospels were derived and composed...We now recognize the fact that our Gospel accounts of Jesus are at best fragmentary and chaotic [he then lists types of tradition: conflicts, wonder works, sayings, parables, etc. and concludes:] This most recent line of quest in the life-of-Jesus research (*Formgeschichte*) is yielding desirable results relative to the pre-Gospel state of the earliest Christian story of Jesus, and it is fundamental in synopsis-making."[34]

Bundy accordingly came up with no less than 465 pericopes (saying that he could have subdivided some of them still further). This is the highest number for any Two-Document Hypothesis synopsis ever published (he also explicitly oriented his arrangement of pericopes according to that theory). It is not the most atomistically divided synopsis ever published, however. A. Wright's complex oral theory led him to publish a synopsis (1896, 1st ed.) in which the Gospels are grouped and regrouped in more than 800 pericopes.

However, scholars have long known about these variations in pericope size among the various synopses without taking them very seriously. The first sign that there might be more than met the eye here was the publication of W. R. Farmer's *Synopticon* (Cambridge, 1969), in which he sought to display parallelism of wording without divisions into pericopes typical of synopses. The only divisions he used were the paragraphs of the Nestle 25th text.[35] The intention was to focus strictly upon the phenomena of parallelism without getting entangled in the

---

[34] W.E. Bundy, *A Syllabus and Synopsis of the First Three Gospels*, Bobbs-Merrill, Indianapolis 1932; pp. 13-14.

[35] See W.R. Farmer, *Synopticon. The Verbal Agreement between the Greek Texts of Matthew, Mark and Luke Contextually Exhibited;* Cambridge Univ. Press 1969; second page of the Introduction. In some ways, it would make sense to use Swanson's *Horizontal Line Synopsis* in tandem with Farmer's Synopticon, to verify the use of colors in the latter with the actual parallel texts printed in the former. Swanson's Greek synopsis also has an excellent, new apparatus with the unusual feature of full citation of the variants in horizontal parallelism with the text, so that the eye can easily perceive the important variant readings. In this way, one is able to pursue the Synoptic Problem on down into the history of the texts of the Gospels.

confusing phenomena of differing pericope sizes among the several Gospels. Few have grasped the value of this instrument, however, and it is still rarely used.

Then in 1978 E. P. Sanders drew attention to a curious and little-noticed fact: the way one perceived the evidence bearing on the Synoptic Problem, in particular the traditional argument from order of pericopes, varied according to whether one used a synopsis having large or one having small pericopes.

> "The [traditional] argument from order deals only with full pericopes, and further, with full pericopes as they are presented in Tischendorf's synopsis. The restriction of the question to *full pericopes* was quite reasonable when the goal of research was to find a biographical outline of Jesus' life to substitute for the Johannine outline, confidence in which had been destroyed by Strauss. Naturally, only the *main events* were significant. Whenever two gospels agreed in the placement of a pericope, their agreement was attributed to faithful copying of the Ur-gospel...But once the question becomes the *strictly literary* one of whether there was some contact between Matthew and Luke, it is clear that the limitation [of the argument] to full [event-oriented] pericopes is unwarranted...Tischendorf's pericopes are longer than those in Huck, his successor... Instances in which neither Matthew nor Luke supports Mark's order were overlooked [by Woods, Hawkins, et al.] because they were not [set out as] independent pericopes in Tischendorf's synopsis, as they had been in Huck's."[36]

The distinction Sanders is drawing here needs to be clearly grasped. In the 19th century and before, he says, the goal was to construct harmonies of the Gospels whose divisions documented successive episodes in the life and ministry of Jesus. Thus, they tended to have large, "anecdote-sized," or event-sized pericopes. Furthermore, it was thought that these anecdotes were handed down in the oral tradition to the Evangelists (who, in the case of Matthew and John, were eye-witnesses of the same events themselves), and they more or less smoothly combined these anecdotes into full-length narratives. Huck's synopsis was different in that it had its origin as the display mechanism for a complicated literary hypothesis involving two stages of Mark's composition, a Logia source, and so on. The result was that Huck broke the narratives and anecdotes up into numerous tiny elements, and displayed their agreement and disagreement, in a way that had never been done before.

How did Huck's *Synopse* affect the debate over the Synoptic Problem? The answer is as strange as it is simple. In fact, we are dealing

---

[36] E.P. Sanders, "The Argument from Order and the Relationship between Matthew and Luke," in *New Test. Stud.* 15 (1969) p. 252f.

with something so elementary that no one, with the single exception of
E. P. Sanders, has even noticed it. He saw how it drastically affected one
of the pillar arguments of the whole debate: the argument from order of
pericopes. Let me explain.

The observation regarding the alternating support in order of pericopes
between Matthew, Mark and Luke, was the keystone of the theory of J.
J. Griesbach. He probably did not invent this argument himself, but
found it in the work of such contemporaries as the English scholar,
Henry Owen[37], or Anton Friedrich Büsching[38]. Shortly after his
publication of his hypothesis, however, this observation became the
object of intense debate. Eventually, after extensive reformulation by a
number of French, German and English scholars[39], it emerged upside
down, as it were, due to a serious procedural error that was mainly
caused by Christian Hermann Weisse[40]. This procedural error then
passed on undetected into the scholarly discussion on both sides of the
channel, appearing most notably in the definitive treatment of the
Synoptic Problem by B. H. Streeter (1924), where it can be found as the
third "reason" for accepting the *priority* of Mark[41] — which is the exact
opposite of Griesbach's conclusion!

How could this strange reversal take place? Although a number of
explanations have been put forward which take into account the climate
of opinion prevailing at the time, which for various theological and
political reasons *wanted* Mark to have been written first rather than
Matthew, there is another feature of the post-Griesbach discussion that
was at least as devastating as the theological war against David
Friedrich Strauss and the Tübingen school, and much more subtle. This
is the phenomenon which has been drawn to our attention by E. P.
Sanders: the customary statement of the argument from order of
pericopes made sense to him if he used Tischendorf's synopsis to

---

[37] See Henry Owen, *Observations on the Four Gospels;* London 1764.

[38] See Anton Friedrich Büsching, *Die vier Evangelisten mit ihren eigenen Worten
zusammengesetzt und mit Erklarungen versehen;* Hamburg 1766.

[39] For the history of this period, see especially H.-H. Stoldt, *Geschichte und Kritik der
Markushypothese;* Vandenhoeck & Ruprecht 1977; Engl. transl. by Donald L. Niewyk,
History and Criticism of the Marcan Hypothesis; Mercer University Press 1980. The E.T.
has an additional foreword by W. R. Farmer and a very informative Appendix by Charles
E. Wolfe listing 180 "minor agreements against Mark" together with text-critical notes.

[40] This procedural error was first noted by B. C. Butler in *The Originality of St
Matthew. A Critique of the Two-Document Hypothesis;* Cambridge 1951; in a chapter
entitled "The Lachmann Fallacy." For a more full discussion, see Stoldt, op. cit. above,
pp. 47-68.

[41] B. H. Streeter, *The Four Gospels;* Macmillan 1924; p. 151, see also pp. 161f.

examine the evidence for it, but that it didn't if he used Huck. What a strange situation! Which synopsis should he use?

What if Griesbach's statement regarding the order of pericopes, namely, the alternating support he observed between Mark and the other two Synoptic Gospels, what if Griesbach's statement became meaningless because scholars began to use other synopses in which (a) the Gospel narratives were divided differently, and (b) the common order of parallel pericopes was differently arranged? Wouldn't it be inevitable that the phenomenon Griesbach thought he saw would simply disappear? Of course! In point of fact, his "discovery" was literally buried beneath an avalanche of alternative synoptic charts, diagrams and synopses. Holtzmann's encouragement of Albert Huck to produce a synopsis that fit *his* theory was not only prudent, it was absolutely necessary, if he wanted others to see what he saw in the texts.

What was Griesbach's statement regarding the alternating support in order of pericopes among the Synoptic Gospels? Perhaps it won't hurt to repeat his original statement of it:

> "Mark compiled his whole work (apart from about twenty-four verses which he added from his own sources...) from the works of Matthew and Luke in such a manner that
> (A) it can be easily shown what he took from the one and what he took from the other;
> (B) he retained the order observed by Matthew in such a way, that wherever he forsakes it he sticks to the path of Luke and follows him and the order of his narrative step by step, to such an extent that
> (C) the verses and words where he passes from Matthew to Luke or returns from Luke to Matthew can not only be pointed out, but also
> (D) the probable reason can generally be given why at a given time he deserted Matthew (though he had set himself to use him as his chief guide) and attached himself to Luke and why putting Luke away he once more attached himself to Matthew; and further
> (E) it can also be understood why, precisely in this passage of Mattw and not in another, he again connects up the thread which he had previously broken by passing over to Luke."[42]

Then Griesbach added a table, saying

> "You can see with your own eyes [in the following chart] Mark having the volumes of Matthew and Luke at hand, continually consulting each, extracting from each whatever he thought would most benefit his readers, now laying aside Matthew, now Luke for a little while, but always returning to the very same place of either one where he had begun to diverge from him."[43]

[42] See J. B. Orchard and T.R.W. Longstaff eds, *J.J.Griesbach: Synoptic and Text-Critical Studies 1776-1976*; Cambridge Univ. Press 1978; p. 108.
[43] Loc. cit.

GRIESBACH'S CHART

Matt	Mark	Luke
[Cap. 1 et 2.]	−	
3,1 – 4,22.	← 1,1-20.	
	1,21-39.	→ 4,31-44.
	−	[5,1-11.]
	1,40 – 3,6.	5,12 – 6,11.
12,15.16.	← 3,7-12.	
[12,17-21]	−	
	3,13-19.	→ 6,12-16.
12,22.23.	← 3,20.21.	
12,24-32.	3,22-30.	
[12,33-37.]	−	
[12,38-45.]	−	
12,46-50.	3,31-35.	
13,1-23.	4,1-20.	
	4,21-25.	→ 8,16-18.
[13,24-30.]	← 4,26-29.	
13,31.32.	4,30-32.	
13,34.35.	4,33.34.	
	−	[8,19-21.]
	4,35-41.	→ 8,22-25.
	5,1-43.	8,26-56.
13,53-58.	← 6,1-6.	
	6,7-13.	→ 9,1-6.
14,1-2.	6,14-16.	9,7-9.
14,3-12.	← 6,17-29.	
	6,30.31.	→ 9,10.
14,13-21.	← 6,32-44.	→ 9,11-17.
14,22 – 16,12.	← 6,45 – 8,21.	
−	8,22-26.	
16,13 – 18,9.	← 8,27 – 9,50.	→ 9,18-51.
[18,10-35.]	−	
	−	[9,51 – 18,14.]
19,1-12.	← 10,1-12.	
19,13 – 23,1.	← 10,13 – 12,38.	→ 18,15 – 20,45.
[23,1-39.]	−	
	12,38-44.	→ 20,45 – 21,4.
24,1-36.	← 13,1-32.	→ 21,5. sqq.
[24,37 – 25,46.]	← 13,33-36.	
26,1 – 28,8.	14,1 – 16,8.	
	16,9.	
[28,9-15.]	−	
[28,16.17.]	−	
	16,10-13.	→ 24,10-35.
	16,14.	24,36-43.
28,18-20.	← 16,15-18.	
	16,19.	→ 24,50.51.
	16,20.	

This is Griesbach's chart (omitting the explanatory notes). Note how large the pericope divisions are in this chart — whole stories, or even chains of stories in each division. I have added the arrows to indicate when Mark moved from one text to the other, taking what he wanted there, and then always coming back and resuming the narrative in the first Gospel at the very spot he left when he went across to the other. It is quite remarkable, once one has actually seen this simple and purposeful pattern.

Now look at the *Parallelenregister* in any edition of Huck and see if this pattern can be seen. Virtually impossible. The whole visual impact of Huck's *Parallelenregister* is too complicated and filled with minutiae. But the real reason why it is impossible to use Huck's synopsis to verify Griesbach's observation is because he sliced up the anecdotes and then set up the common order of parallel pericopes in a radically different arrangement than Griesbach used in his Chart (see Tables II and III above, pp. 325, 327). Huck's arrangement makes it virtually impossible to understand Mark's use of his two *Vorlagen* if one assumes Griesbach's theory of the order of composition. But equally as important, Huck's much smaller pericope divisions completely obscure the methodical process Griesbach thought he detected in Mark's artful combination of his two source documents, destroying completely all traces of Mark's simple, step-wise procedure. Instead, looking at Huck[44] one is compelled to envision Mark darting rapidly back and forth between the texts of Matthew and Luke, "like a fly in a bottle" (as one scholar derisively put it), picking up certain words and phrases and skipping over others, for no apparent reason. It's no wonder. Huck's synopsis was never designed to lay out the evidence that Mark was written *last*. It was designed to exhibit the evidence for Holtzmann's theory of the independent use of Mark (and a Logia source) by Matthew and Luke. Huck explains this in the very first sentences of the Preface to his first edition (1892):

> "Vorliegende 'Synopse der 3 ersten Evangelien' erhebt keinen Anspruch auf selbständige, wissenschaftliche Bedeutung. Sie will in erster Linie nur eine Ergänzung zu dem betreffenden Kommentar von Holtzmann ... bilden

---

[44] Huck's layout in the *Parallelenregister* (pp. vi-x) of his first edition is identical to the one given by Holtzmann in his *Handkommentar zum Neuen Testament*, 1. Aufl. 1889; Freiburg i. B., J.C.B. Mohr; Bd. 1 *Synoptiker*; pp. 10-12. In an appended statement at the end of Huck's Vorwort, Holtzmann said that he, in turn, had found the synopses of Schulze (1861 and 1886 [2te Aufl.]) and Sevin (1866) exceptionally useful. He does not explain why he used them instead of Tischendorf.

und das Studium dieses Buches erleichtern. Dem entsprechend ist die ganze Einrichtung getroffen... auch bezüglich der Eintheilung der Perikopen weicht die Synopse nur an 3 Stellen etwas vom HC. ab."[45]

So the pericope divisions in Huck's first edition are strictly based upon Holtzmann's first edition of his *Handkommentar zum Neuen Testament* (vol. I, 1889, 2nd ed., 1892). What that means is that the narratives of both Matthew and Luke were divided up strictly according to (a) the parallel in Mark, or (b) according to a presumed Logia source, or (c) according to other presumed sources. Furthermore, the orders of pericopes in Matthew and Luke were *disarranged* so that they conformed to Mark's order.

But then, in one of those ironic twists of academic fate, not long after Huck had published his companion synopsis, Holtzmann changed his mind. Immediately, Huck's first (and second) editions were obsolete. Tiring of this unpredictable situation, Huck struck out on his own, and in his 3rd edition, claimed that his synopsis was "neutral" with regard to any source theory. But it is obvious that he did not create his third edition *ab initio*. He merely moved Mark into the middle column, kept the very small pericope divisions he had inherited from Holtzmann, and instituted a sort of wobbling primary order of pericopes, alternating between having Matthew's and Luke's pericopes follow the order of Mark's (one blatant case of disarrangement left over from his Holtzmann days we noted above). Otherwise, he matched up the Q pericopes.

The stark deficiencies of Huck's synopsis would have been felt sooner, if it had not been for the fact that all these things came to pass precisely during the heyday of the theory of Markan priority. For numerous theological and political reasons already discussed elsewhere, this hypothesis was swiftly gaining in popularity, both in England and Germany; naturally America followed suit. Huck's synopsis came to be preferred to Tischendorf's because it fit right into this movement — even lending the hypothesis of Markan priority an aura of "scientific objectivity" with its claim of "neutrality" regarding its arrangement. Indeed, Huck's tiny pericope divisions even fit in perfectly with that subsequent German pasttime, "Form Criticism." All things considered, "Huck" has been a phenomenally successful synopsis.

I beg the reader's forgiveness for such a lengthy digression into past history, but it seemed necessary in order to grasp the significance of E. P. Sanders' observation regarding the relationship between the synopsis one uses, and one's perception of the argument from order.

[45] Albert Huck, *Synopse der drei ersten Evangelien;* Freiburg, J.C.B.Mohr 1892; p. v.

What is the moral of our story? Simply this: we must get in the habit of citing the synopsis we are using whenever we make any claims with respect to the evidence regarding the order of pericopes — or any other aspect of the Synoptic Problem. Different synopses exhibit different evidence.

Conclusion to Part A.

These three lines of argument, dealing with the text, with arrangement of pericopes in primary common order, and with division into pericopes, all point to one and the same conclusion: a synopsis that is "neutral" with respect to the Synoptic Problem is impossible. We have not realized this heretofore, and as a result, the scholarly community has been caught, literally for centuries, in a "war of the synopses" which has been extraordinarily confusing. The deleterious impact on Gospel scholarship has been enormous: a stunted and distorted conception of the earliest Gospel tradition[46]; universal use of a single critical text of the New Testament that a disturbing number of text-critics find quite unsatisfactory[47]; and a conception of the literary methods of the evangelists that is strikingly out of touch with the realities of the early Church and the world it inhabited[48].

Instead of "general purpose" synopses, wouldn't it be better to have synopses that were specifically designed to help us with the problems we are working on, synopses that were especially created to assist our

---

[46] B. Gerhardsson, *Memory and Manuscript* (Lund 1966) remains the most important research in this problem area, although Bo Reicke has also recently published a major contribution: *The Roots of the Synoptic Gospels* (Philadelphia, Fortress Press 1896). Furthermore, the participants at the Jerusalem Symposium on the Interrelationship of the Gospels unanimously called for a follow-up international conference on this whole subject: "The Gospel Tradition Before, In, and Beside the Gospels." It will take place in two parts: Dublin 1989, Milan 1990.

[47] See for example the observations of E. Epp, "The Eclectic Method in New Testament Textual Criticism: Solution or Symptom?" in *Harv. Theol. Rev.* 69 (1976) 211 -257; and idem, "A Continuing Interlude in New Testament Textual Criticism?" *Harv. Theol. Rev.* 73 (1980) 131-151.

[48] A striking feature of the scholarly situation with respect to the whole question of the compositional methods employed by the Evangelists is the comparatively immobilized German and French discussion (the former apparently still mesmerized by the utterly outdated monograph by K.L.Schmidt, *Der Rahmen der Geschichte Jesu*, Berlin 1919), as compared with the Anglo-Saxon. In the latter case, out of a vigorous discussion, the following studies might be mentioned: H. Cadbury, *The Making of Luke-Acts* (Macmillian 1927, repr. SPCK 1961); M. Hadas and M. Smith, *Heroes and Gods. Spiritual Biographies in Antiquity* (Harper & Row 1965); C.H.Talbert, *Literary Patterns, Theological Themes and the Genre of Luke-Acts* (Scholars Press 1977); and P. Shuler, *A Genre for the Gospels. The Biographical Character of Matthew* (Fortress Press 1982).

research in the three major areas in Gospel research? Perhaps I may give some examples of the new designs we need.

B. Synopses of the Future

In view of the foregoing argument, it seems best to give up the illusion that our synopses can be neutral with respect to the Synoptic Problem. Better to recognize that inevitable fact and instead to design synopses that will assume *different* synoptic theories in order to compare the results. In order to accomplish this, it seems wise, to begin with, to stop trying to construct "multi-purpose" synopses, such as we have at present. Precisely by trying to do all tasks, they succeed in doing none very well.

Perhaps we could adopt as the fundamental principle of our new generation of synopses: "form must follow function." This approach has the virtue of focusing our attention at the outset on the primary task for which we intend to use each synopsis. With this clearly in mind, we can design and redesign the synopsis in any way we wish until we have one that will do exactly what we want it to.

I see three basic functions or purposes for which synopses are needed. There may be more than three, but, if so, I am not aware of them. They are the following (these are not arranged in any particular order): (A) study of the text, (B) study of the pre-Gospel tradition, (C) study of the final written composition. For convenience' sake, let us call these Type A, Type B, and Type C synopses, respectively.

Type A Synopses — for use in text-criticism

Function: The function of these synopses will be to assist in reconstructing the *autograph* version(s) of each Gospel. This endeavor, however, will proceed in full awareness of the probability that there may never have been *one* original autograph copy, that instead a number of slightly different "original" copies may have been composed orally or in writing by the same author (or his school) over a period of time. By recognizing at the outset that "publishing" in the modern sense of the term, whereby we refer to the production of a fixed, printed text, is almost totally inappropriate as a model for understanding the "publishing" of the Gospels in the much more fluid conditions of the oral-culture of that day, these synopses would strive to reproduce visually the "dynamic text" situation of the original version(s) of the Gospels.

Form: To be fully useful, such a synopsis must be arranged in a meticulous word by word, space for space, line by line correlation. Whether they are arranged in verticle or horizontal columns is a matter of preference. R. Swanson's *Horizontal Line Synopsis* is remarkably easier to use for this sort of detailed comparison, it seems to me. On the other hand, since the vertical column synopses are so familiar, many will continue to prefer them. Of course, these synopses will require a full apparatus and extensive partristic citations, quotations from apocryphal sources, and so on.

Best examples at present: Aland and Greeven are already close to the ideal in all of the above respects. Swanson is particularly easy for minute comparison.

Relations to the Synoptic Problem: It would be interesting to use different source theories to establish different critical texts, in order to see how much difference there would actually be between them, as to the text itself. It might turn out that, after such an experiment, the difference between several such "alternative texts" would be negligible (viz., slightly more than the margin of error of any reconstructed text). Then we really would be in a position to speak of a verified *text* of the Gospels that was "neutral" with respect to the Synoptic Problem!

Type B Synopses — for use in the study of the pre-Gospel oral tradition.

Function: The chief purpose for these synopses will be to help us focus on the pre-redactional period of the Gospel tradition. At present, there are no synopses strictly dedicated to that task. However, one scholar in particular has pioneered in this area. M.-É. Boismard's analyses, in volumes II and III of the *Synopse des quatre Évangiles*, contains, for each pericope, a detailed history of its tradition, from earliest form to latest, accompanied by synoptic charts and diagrams — drawing on a wide range of patristic citations, apocryphal writings, and manuscript readings. Each of these "mini- synopses" reveals his understanding of the historical sequence of the pre (or post-)- redactional Gospel tradition.

The difficulty of such an endeavor must not be underestimated. It is clear, for example, that Boismard has consistently sought to reconstruct the oral (or written) history of each sayings tradition or narrative pericope, many times down into the third or fourth century, solely on the basis of the evidence. That is, he has been wise enough to avoid the Nestle text. How many Gospel scholars have the training to undertake this sort of fundamental reconstruction of the history of the tradition?

Instead, the rest of us think we can deal with the pre-redactional, oral period using the Nestle-Aland text. But this procedure is obviously doomed to failure, since so much important evidence has long since been thrown away by generations of text critics, or it is there in the cryptic footnotes, tiny shards and slivers of alternative readings. Never do we look up the full text of the alternative traditions, so that we might be in a position to perceive any complete alternative *patterns*, within which the variant word or punctuation might take on real meaning. The result is that we publish a lot of nonsense about the oral tradition.

We must look at the actual ancient traditions in their wholeness, if we really want to examine scientifically the pre-compositional Gospel tradition. We must read the actual text of Vaticanus or Sinaiticus, the Syriac versions, actual quotations of Epiphanius or Irenaeus in their contexts, if we hope to reconstruct the earliest stages of the Gospel tradition. In fact, this new focus on the oral tradition may throw some light on the problems plaguing text critics today, floundering as they are in a morass of confusion (baptized as a method and called "eclecticism") following the collapse of the Westcott-Hort text-type theories. If we can discern early tendencies in the oral- tradition period, we may find that they link up with similar tendencies in the post- redactional period, when the Gospels were being copied or cited in different ways, presumably in the same centers that produced them.

Form: Taking Boismard's work as a guide, we need a new synopsis format. As a "Synopsis of the Oral Tradition," it would be divided up according to specific pericopes or stories in their pre-redactional form, as they were presumably handed down in the oral tradition. Each Gospel pericope would be displayed in isolation, using vertical columns for purposes of minute comparison. The earliest version would be printed in the far left column, then the next oldest and the next, proceeding across the page to the most recent. Included with the charts (at the bottom of the page) would be comments on the successive versions, so that discussion and evidence would be seen together.

The material might be arranged in divisions according to Form Critical rubrics, such as: parables, healing stories, apophthegmata, apocalypses, laws, etc., etc., and each case with numerous parallels from Jewish, Greek, and Roman traditions.

Best examples at present: With the exception of Boismard, there are no adequate examples of this type of synopsis in print at present. Even the case of Boismard is confusing, since his "mini-synopses" bear no noticeable relation to the same pericopes in the Synopsis in Vol. I, which was independently prepared by P. Benoit.

There is one earlier example of an oral- tradition synopsis. The *Synopsis* of Arthur Wright (1903) is a superb creation exhibiting remarkable attention to minute variations in textual detail. Since he assumed the Oral Hypothesis, he made full use of textual variants, displaying these in a very sophisticated page layout.

Relation to the Synoptic Problem: The central function of this synopsis would be to facilitate Form Critical study of the Gospel tradition dduring its oral period. In particular, it would help scholars deal with the problem of dating different versions of a story or saying. To this end, it would seek to identify reliable indicators of early or late tradition. The indicators commonly used now are: the presence of semitisms, longer or shorter version of the story or saying, clear or broken form, poor or good Greek, etc. These have each come under heavy attack[49] and at present there is little agreement as to whether there are any reliable indicators of the earliness or lateness of a tradition. For this reason, a research tool such as this would be especially useful to scholars working on the Synoptic Problem, since judgments respecting early and late forms of traditions are unavoidable.

Type C Synopses — for use in studying the literary cmposition of the Gospels.

Function: These synopses will be specifically designed to aid in analysis of the literary composition of the Gospels. However, they will be so constructed as to highlight the likelihood that the Evangelists did not each use the same methods when composing their narratives. This feature would set these synopses apart from all existing or previously published synopses. These would be the first to emphasize rather than conceal the different habits and strategies of composition adopted by each Evangelist.

As such, these synopses will also be intended to reveal each Evangelist's major, distinctive theological concerns, precisely as revealed by the way he arranges and augments his source material. This might be considered a synopsis specifically designed for the theologian or historian use, i.e., for those who want a more nuanced and concrete historical theology of the New Testament. A synopsis of this type would facilitate understanding of the distinctive ways each Evangelist made use of the Jesus tradition, as compared with Paul, the authors of the Pastorals, 1 Peter, Hebrews, etc.

---

[49] See on this whole subject, E. P. Sanders, *Tendencies of the Synoptic Tradition* [S.N.T.S. Monograph Series 9]; Cambridge University Press 1969.

Form: The pericope divisions would be according to the "stories" (individual units) and "chapters" (groups of units) as understood or intended by the Gospel authors themselves. N.B. The common order of parallel pericopes would be set up explicitly using a particular source theory, and would take one "lead Gospel" at a time as the focus of study in successive parts of the synopsis.

In addition, there would be some sort of commentary explaining the Evangelist's supposed compositional activity, located at the bottom of each page. As part of this, comparative notes or references to similar compositional procedures from the Greco-Roman and Jewish world would be helpful (cp. Wettstein). There would also be a minimal textual apparatus that mentioned only the most important variant readings. The introduction would spell out the source theory guiding the construction and arrangement of the whole synopsis.

These detailed synopses need to be supplemented by large wall charts of the type published by J. Barr, *Chart of Synoptic Relationships*. These large multi-columned, multi-color charts enable one to see the whole pattern of the interrelations among the Evangelists, providing a valuable "bird's eye view" of the whole "forest." Sometimes this is lost sight of as one labors down among the individual "trees" in the Synoptic Problem.

Relation to the Synoptic Problem: these synopses would in fact represent full-scale demonstrations of one particular solution to the Synoptic Problem. That is, each synopsis of this sort would be a complete redactional, theological analysis of the Gospel-creating activity of each Evangelist, according to one particular source hypothesis... the ultimate test of its *Brauchbarkeit*. Naturally, one would expect the number of such synopses to equal the number of competing hypotheses that there are in the field today.[50] Best examples at present: As noted, there are no really good examples of this sort of synopsis available at the moment. There are good examples of aspects of one, however. For example, I might mention P. Vannutelli's usually overlooked writings which contain superb comparative charts for elucidating the Gospel compositional activity. F.W. Beare's *Companion* has the sort of brief compositional-theological glosses that I have in mind. Orchard has an excellent Introduction (to the Greek synopsis) that spells out the source theory that guided his synopsis construction; see also the introductions of W.A. Stevens-E.D. Burton, and Sparks.[51]

[50] It was unanimously agreed by the participants at the Jerusalem Symposium on the Interrelations among the Gospels, that this "holistic" treatment was the only really decisive test of any hypothesis.

[51] See, among many useful works by P. Vannutelli, *Gli Evangeli in Sinossi. Nuovo Studio del Problema Sinottico*; Torino-Roma, Casa Editrice Marietti 1931. Further, F.W. Beare,

Conclusion

It may be that others will envision still other types of synopses that would be useful for studying major problem-areas of the Gospels, but until we break free from the prison of our existing synopses, we will continue to stumble painfully down the road, hobbled by poorly designed instruments, and making very little progress in these three great areas of research: text criticism, form criticism and redaction criticism.

David L. Dungan

Supplementary Note

«Synopsis of the Future» was first published in *Biblica* 66 (1985) 457-492.

Page 324, note 25 has been corrected here (465: «his [sic] forthcoming Dutch synopsis»). Cf. A. Denaux and M. Vervenne, *Synopsis van de eerste drie evangeliën*, Leuven-Turnhout, 1986. See the review, «The VBS Synopsis», in *ETL* 62 (1986) 145-154, esp. p. 151.

Page 326: «All agree that Matt. 4,23(-25) is parallel to Mark 1,16-20». For this quotation (= 469), compare the text in *ETL* 52 (1976), p. 355 (= *Evangelica*, p. 734): «All agree on Mt 4,18-22 // Mk 1,16-20, ...». Cf. *ETL* 62 (1986), p. 151, n. 11.

Page 327 (= 470), note 28: cf. in this volume, pp. 23-46.

The Earliest Records of Jesus. A Companion to the Synopsis of the First Three Gospels by Albert Huck; Nashville, Abingdon Press 1962. Further, for the English version, see *A Synopsis of the Four Gospels in a New Translation Arranged According to the Two-Gospel Hypothesis,* Mercer University Press 1982; the Greek text was subsequently published by T.& T. Clark, Ltd., Edinburgh, 1983. As the Greek edition was intended for scholars, it is the Preface to this synopsis in which Orchard most fully spelled out his thinking on synopsis construction. Finally, Wm. Arnold Stevens and Ernest DeWitt Burton, *A Harmony of the Gospels for Historical Study. An Analytical Synopsis of the Four Gospels;* New York, Charles Scribner's Sons, 5th ed. 1905.

THE RELEVANCE OF TEXTUAL CRITICISM
TO THE SYNOPTIC PROBLEM

Detailed study of the Synoptic Problem involves the careful comparison of the Greek text of the Gospels. Insofar as printed editions of the Gospels vary, it is not surprising that in some respects the conclusions drawn from one text may differ from conclusions drawn from a different text.[1]

The suspicion is however sometimes voiced, especially by those arguing against the Two-Document Hypothesis, that the principles on which the printed editions of the Greek New Testament produced in the last one hundred years or so are established are biased towards the theory of Markan priority. This suspicion is reinforced by Metzger's advice in the introduction to his commentary on the United Bible Societies text[2] that a textual critic needs to take into account the priority of Mark when assessing textual variation. This remark may be taken to imply that the editors of the United Bible Societies text (= UBS³) and by extension Nestle-Aland (= N-A²⁶) and Aland's Synopsis (= Syn¹³) were influenced by such a consideration. I have not in fact detected such a bias in this so-called standard text: if there was any bias influencing the editors it was that of Westcott and Hort and the dominance of ℵ B. In any case Metzger himself seldom appeals to the Two-Document Hypothesis or to Markan priority when assessing the variants included in the *Commentary*.

Three recent Gospel synopses are in regular use by those working on the Synoptic Problem. These are (i) Aland *Synopsis Quattuor Evangeliorum* now in its 13th edition. This text favours the readings of the so-called great uncials; (ii) Greeven's revision of Huck's Synopsis (= H-G¹³) which tends to print readings that make the Gospel parallels dissimilar on the principle that scribes were responsible for many of the harmonizing variants found in the ms. tradition; and (iii) J. B. Orchard's *A Synopsis of the Four Gospels,* the text in which veers towards the Textus Receptus insofar as he favours the longer variants. In a recent article[3] I have examined the text of these three editions and

---

[1] See my "Textual Criticism, Assimilation and the Synoptic Gospels," in *NTS* 26 (1980) 231-242.

[2] B.M. Metzger, *A Textual Commentary on the Greek New Testament* (United Bible Societies, 1971), xxviii.

[3] "An Examination of the Text and Apparatus of the Three Recent Greek Synopses," in *NTS* 32 (1986) 557-582.

although each has a different way of displaying the parallels and of dividing the pericopes, both of which features may legitimately be said to favour one or other solution to the Synoptic Problem, the text itself does not favour one solution by design of the editor and to that extent the text may be described as neutral. Those who base their studies only on the printed text credit the editor with an omniscience that is misplaced. In critical editions the printed text is not to be considered as representing at each point of variation the editor's confident judgement on the originality of the text he prints: often editors are faced with a dilemma in selecting which of several competing variants to print and some readings inevitably relegated to the margin are sometimes of equal importance to them. Such readings are classified by the letter B in the apparatus to the UBS edition. But regardless of editorial decisions as to what is placed in the margin the reader who ignores the textual apparatus does so at his peril.

For those who wisely keep a close eye on the apparatus two tasks are demanded. One is to assess which reading is original whenever textual variation occurs; the other task, equally important yet often neglected, is to try to explain how the variant(s) arose. In many cases, as is shown in the apparatus to H-G[13], harmonization to a Synoptic parallel is a frequent cause of scribal activity.

Nevertheless a too rigid application of the rule of dissidence can be misleading and other factors need to be taken into account, as I indicated in my 1980 *NTS* article (cf. n. 1) from which the following four examples are taken.

1. It is particularly important when evaluating the likeliest direction of change and assimilation to take all the variants in the parallels into account. It is all too easy to be dogmatic about the direction in which assimilation is likeliest to have gone when *only* one Gospel's variants are discussed. For instance at Mark 2:16 Metzger's *Commentary* tells us that the longer text εσθιει και πινει is due to assimilation to Luke and that the shorter text εσθιει was followed by Matt. 9:11 who added ο διδασκαλος υμων, an expression which in turn was adopted by C L at Mark 2:16. Why could we not equally assume Luke copied Mark's longer text and that some scribes at Mark 2:16 assimilated this to Matt. 9:11?

2. At Mark 12:36 υποκατω is printed in UBS[3] on the grounds that υποποδιον has been introduced from the parallel in Luke 20:43 (= Acts 2:35). But υποκατω, which is found in some of the mss. of Matthew, may have been responsible for scribes' altering an original υποποδιον in Mark to υποκατω. υποποδιον in Luke is not firm in the tradition either. υποκατω may in fact be original throughout the Synoptics, and scribes

may have been responsible for correcting all Synoptic Gospels to the LXX form.

3. Matthew 23:38 is another instance of this need to resolve variants in all the parallels independently of, yet alongside, the need to be alert to the phenomenon of harmonization. Here Syn¹³ includes ερημος in the text making Matthew and Luke dissimilar, whereas Syn⁸ (= N-A²⁵) omits ερημος, with B L making Matthew and Luke parallel. Yet some mss. of Luke add ερημος. The issue here is further complicated by the fact that the variants occur in a quotation from Jeremiah, and scribal assimilation to the LXX may again be responsible for the variants in both Gospels.

4. Another typical textual problem involving assimilation is at Luke 8:8. The mss. are divided here between επι την γην and εις την γην. επι agrees with Matt. 13:8 and εις with Mark 4:8. In both of these parallels the preposition is firm in the tradition so a decision has to be made which variant in Luke is original and which preposition has been introduced by scribes through assimilation to one or other of the parallels. Do Matthew and Luke agree against Mark here (a 'minor agreement') or is Luke dependent on Mark (to use the language of the Two-Document Theory)?

Even though we ought not to apply the rule of dissimilation mechanically, nonetheless the assumption that scribes often harmonized parallel texts is likely to be generally valid and is a useful rule of thumb when considering variants in the Synoptic Gospels. However, if one wished to argue that, say, the author of Luke copied large quanitites of the Gospel of Matthew into his narrative and that as a consequence many of the allegedly harmonistic readings were *original to Luke* then one would have contrary difficulty in explaining how and why scribes created variants that had the effect of making the parallels more dissimilar.

Let us grant the general validity of the principle that many harmonizing readings are the result of scribes' assimilating parallels either deliberately to remove apparent inconsistencies or unconsciously through their familiarity with the parallel version. Let us further grant that those who rewrote a written source, either as an author adapting the work of predecessors or as a scribe slavishly copying a document, tended to improve on the language they were using. With these principles let us see what this means when one examines (a) the printed text and (b) the apparatus to the printed text.

As an example let us take Matt. 19:24 parallel Mark 10:25 parallel Luke 18:25. Here Syn¹² reads:

Matt.: δια ... διελθειν/εισελθειν εις

Mark: δια ... διελθειν/εις ... εισελθειν
Luke: δια ... εισελθειν/εις ... εισελθειν
H-G¹³ has:
Matt.: δια ... εισελθειν/εις
Mark: δια ... διελθειν/εις ... εισελθειν
Luke: δια ... εισελθειν/εις ... εισελθειν
Orchard has:
Matt.: δια ... εισελθειν/εις
Mark: δια ... εισελθειν/εις ... εισελθειν
Luke: δια ... διελθειν/εις ... εισελθειν

If one looked at the text of these three editions on the basis of the principle that later authors improved the style of earlier writings then in H-G¹³ one would deduce that Mark is more primitive, that the inelegant διελθειν δια and εισελθειν εις are avoided by the later and dependent Gospels of Matthew and Luke albeit in different ways. In Aland's text one could not argue in that direction as both Matthew and Mark display this poor style in which a verb is compounded with and followed by the same preposition: only Luke has attempted to modify the form. In Orchard it is Luke whose text seems to be the more primitive: Mark has improved Luke, and Matthew has further improved the text. The reason why these editions differ is of course because the mss. vary and each editor has selected different variants as the original because of the ms. support. But I am convinced that none of the editors has selected readings (either here or elsewhere) with a 'solution' to the Synoptic Problem in mind. We can but deduce the editors' motives: Aland seems to be printing the reading of B in this example (and I do not think even the most suspicious critic of editorial bias in favour of the Two-Document Hypothesis would claim that the scribe of B was a Markan priorist!); Greeven has to a certain extent kept his guiding principle of dissidence in mind; Orchard's motive is unclear.

The textual apparatus for the above example shows the following variants from Aland's text:

Matt. 19:24	διελθειν	v.l. εισελθειν
	εισελθειν	v.l. omit
Mark 10:25	διελθειν	v.l. εισελθειν
	εισελθειν	v.l. omit
Luke 18:25	εισελθειν¹	v.l. διελθειν
	εισελθειν²	v.l. omit

On the basis of this information and given freedom to select among the variants one could create a biased text and thus print:
either all three gospels in agreement:

as (i)   δια ... διελθειν/εισελθειν ... εις
or (ii)   δια ... εισελθειν/εισελθειν ... εις
or (iii) δια ... διελθειν/omit εισελθειν
or (iv)   δια ... εισελθειν/omit εισελθειν²,

or all three gospels in disagreement [here we assume δια διελθειν and εις ... εισελθειν (or εισελθειν εις) is the most primitive combination (= A); that δια ... εισελθειν and εισελθειν εις is an improvement on this (= B); that δια ... διελθειν and omit εισελθειν² is a similar improvement (= C); and that δια ... εισελθειν and omit εισελθειν² a further improvement (= D); we also assume the direction of change is from A forwards]:

A   B   C
A   C   D
A   B   D

where in turn we can make Mark read A, Matthew A, Luke A and so on in various permutations and combinations,
or only two of the gospels in agreement so that for example reading A is found in both Matthew and Mark but not in Luke and so on:

A (in two gospels) → B (in one gospel)
A (in two gospels) → C (in one gospel)
A (in two gospels) → D (in one gospel)
A (in one gospel) → B (in two gospels)
A (in one gospel) → C (in two gospels)
A (in one gospel) → D (in two gospels).

All these permutations and combinations seem to be possible. But what check can we have on such apparent liberty? Can we select freely among the ms. tradition in this way? Can we do as E. J. Epp implies[4] and intuitively select from the mss.? The answer to the last two questions is 'No' and to the first 'Yes, there are checks'. The example set out above is rare in that the apparent freedom demonstrated there is not allowed to us throughout the apparatus. In many cases the textual tradition is not so fluid. A popular saying such as that concerning the rich, and present in all three Synoptic Gospels, inevitably lent itself to harmonizing one way or another.

To create a biased text therefore is possible only to a very limited extent and the result would be a maverick text unscientifically established. On text-critical criteria whether one adopts eclectic principles or the cult of the 'best' ms. or indeed the majority Byzantine text it would appear

---

[4] In "A Continuing Interlude in New Testament Textual Criticism," in *HTR* 73 (1980) 142-143.

to be impossible to create a text designed to accord with one specific solution to the Synoptic Problem. I shall now try to prove this by means of an examination of the lists in the introduction to Allen's commentary on Matthew.[5] Even though the commentary itself is out-of-date the arguments based on the lists on pp. XIX-XXXI are typical of many favouring Markan priority. The evidence he presents is intended to prove that Matthew has improved on Mark's language and style, and that Mark is therefore prior to Matthew. If it could be proved that the text used by Allen was biased in favour of Markan priority then the evidence drawn from these lists would be invalid. For the purpose of this experiment I worked through Allen's lists checking on the firmness of the text. For instance on p. XXV Allen deals with a topic we have already considered above, namely the verbs prefixed with and followed by the same preposition. Here occasionally the apparatus to both Matthew and to Mark allows us to reverse Allen's list thanks to harmonizing variants in both directions. Thus at Matt. 4:18 one could in theory print παραγων παρα with D and in the parallel at Mark 1:16 print περιπατων. (cf. also at Matt. 24:1 where εκ can be read with B and the parallel at Mark 13:1 where απο can be read with ψ). But, in general, the variants are not available for one to be wildly selective in taking from the apparatus readings designed to reverse Allen's lists and arguments.

Similarly, on p. XX in Allen's list of changes from imperfect to aorist, although one can occasionally find harmonizing variants that allow one to have Matthew read the imperfect and Mark the aorist (e.g. Matt. 19:13 *v.l.* επετιμων parallelling Mark 10:13 *v.l.* επετιμησαν), the majority of instances included by Allen are firmly established in the mss.

One finds slightly more manoeuvrability, as one might expect, where the inclusion or omission of particles is concerned. C. H. Turner[6] arguing in favour of Markan priority in view of the asyndetic nature of his Greek shows how either Matthew or Luke or both tend to eliminate this feature of Markan style by adding a particle. Here, as Turner's own list betrays, several mss. of Mark also include a particle thereby preventing one from accepting all of his examples as firm occurrences of asyndeton in Mark (e.g. Mark 1:8 *v.l.* + μεν; 1:22 *v.l.* + και[2]; 2:21 *v.l.* + δε; 3:27 *v.l.* + αλλα; 9:38 *v.l.* + και or + δε) but, as with the examples above concerning compounded verbs and tense changes, not all the examples are questionable.

---

[5] W.C. Allen, *International Critical Commentary on Matthew* (Edinburgh 1907).
[6] "Marcan Usage," in *JTS* 28 (1927) 5f.

Even when harmonizing variants allow one the liberty of reversing Allen's (and Turner's) lists, it is improper to accept such readings without checking if they agree with the author's established style and usage elsewhere.

Whether or not Allen's lists are complete or capable of improvement does not affect our judgement based on the experiment. The same is true of C. H. Turner. It may well be that both lists can be extended or adjusted but I can find in neither Allen nor Turner that uncomfortable parallels have been neglected or bypassed. This judgement means that we cannot avoid dealing with the fact that Mark seems to prefer the historic present and imperfect to the aorist; that he prefers to prefix verbs with a preposition that occurs elsewhere in the same sentence; and that asyndeton is a feature of his style. These and the other features isolated by Allen and Turner encourage them to deduce that Mark's Gospel was prior to Matthew and Luke who frequently altered these features of Markan style when using Mark in the composition of their own Gospels. Those who take a different view of the Synoptic Problem from Allen, Turner and other Markan priorists cannot ignore the features of Markan style that they illuminate but they must explain the differences between Mark's style and that of Matthew and/or of Luke in other ways. As scholars cannot substantially alter the text used by Allen then they must explain the phenomena listed by him in accordance with their chosen solution to the Synoptic Problem.

Given the fact that the textual tradition is not as fluid as the earlier example taken from Matt. 19:24 and parallels might have led the uninitiated to presuppose, and that in many places our text is firmly based and without textual variation, we may now specify clearly what has already been apparent from the above experiment taken from Allen (and Turner), namely, that the style of the individual authors in the New Testament in general, and in the Gospels in particular, can be established and it is this that is one of the strongest checks on our ability to select readings at random from the apparatus. Markan usage can be established and classified; similarly, distinctive features of both Matthaean and Lukan style can be drawn up from the firm instances in their writings. Such instances allow us to assess the originality of the text when variation occurs. The resultant text arising from the principle that a variant in accord with the author's style elsewhere is likely to be original (other things being equal) will present itself irrespective of and independent of any theory of Gospel priority. A broader principle is sometimes applicable, namely that New Testament usage as a whole can be established and, as with the principle of the individual author's usage, this can be used when assessing variants. Let us demonstrate these principles by taking some examples.

1. In our printed editions οχλοι occurs at Mark 10:1. This is the only occurrence of the plural of this noun in Mark compared with nearly forty occurrences of the singular. Matthew uses both the singular and the plural; the parallel to Mark 10:1 in Matt. 19:2 has the plural. A variant in Mark reads the singular (συνερχεται παλιν ο οχλος a formula that is consistent with Markan usage elsewhere (3:20)) but even Greeven's edition prints the plural in both these parallels here. Advocates of the Two-Gospel Hypothesis could presumably defend the originality of the plural by arguing that here Mark took it over from Matthew; advocates of the Two-Document Hypothesis could allow Mark this exceptional plural and argue that Matthew took it from Mark. But, unless it can be convincingly explained why Mark on this one occasion chose to use the plural, there are strong reasons to reject the arguments attributed to the advocates of both these positions and instead to argue in favour of the consistency of Markan style. The reading οχλοι can easily be explained as a harmonizing variant to the Matthaean parallel; if οχλοι were original then one would be obliged to argue, somewhat speciously, that at least one scribe, although lacking modern conveniences like concordances, recognised that the plural was alien to Mark's normal practice and substituted the plural for the more characteristic singular during his copying.

2. If the criterion of author's style takes precedence over the rule of dissimilarity as I believe it should, then ην at Mark 1:39 should be printed as original — not ηλθεν. Greeven here makes the parallels between Mark-Luke dissimilar, but Mark's characteristic use of the periphrastic construction (cf. Allen, p. XXII and Turner (*JTS* xxvɪ 1924 pp. 14ff.)) makes it likely that ην κηρυσσων is original to Mark and that ηλθεν was introduced both because of the proximity of this verb in the preceding verse and because of the need to justify the use of εις in 1:39 (cf. Turner, *JTS* xxvɪɪɪ 1927 p. 349). The use of εις is characteristic of Mark. On the basis of the Two-Document Hypothesis one would argue that Luke copied Mark's periphrastic construction but Matthew, like scribes of Mark later, avoided this construction by providing εις with a suitable verb of motion. On the basis of the Two Gospel Hypothesis these features would have to be explained on other grounds. In any case ην ought to appear in Mark on text critical grounds and without regard to any one solution to the Synoptic Problem.

3. At Luke 17:24 it can be argued on the basis of the usual printed text that ωσπερ has been introduced from the apocalyptic discourse in Matt.

24:27 even though Luke does not like this characteristically Matthaean word. The proponents of the Two-Gospel Hypothesis do indeed argue along these lines in their discussion of the apocalyptic discourse included in this collection of symposium papers. This use of ωσπερ is then said to be indicative of the provenance of Luke's material in this part of Luke 17: thus stands the argument, but if one examines the apparatus to Luke 17:24 it will be seen that there is a variant ως. The only other occurrence of ωσπερ in Luke at 18:11 is similarly not firm. If ως is original at 17:24 then this tells us nothing about Luke's alleged use of Matthew and this part of the argument cannot apply.

4. Another argument used in the discussion of the apocalyptic discourse paraded at the symposium is based on μεχρις ου at Mark 13:30 compared with the parallel in Matt. 24:34 and Luke 21:32 both of which read εως αν. On the basis of the printed editions one could note the 'minor agreement' of Matthew and Luke against Mark, or one could point to Luke's apparent use of Matthew and to Markan posteriority. But if one reads as original the *v.l.* εως ου or the *v.l.* εως αν in Mark then these arguments are invalid.[7] The moral once again is that the firmness of the text needs to be established before firm pronouncements can be made.

5. An instance of New Testament usage as a whole being applied to textual variation may now be given as a concluding example. The NT authors tended to qualify μαθητης, usually by a possessive pronoun. This was necessary when the Gospels were first being written in so far as leaders other than Jesus had disciples. We read in the New Testament of the disciples of John and the disciples of the Pharisees, for example. Later in the life of the church 'his disciples' came more frequently to mean Jesus' disciples and hence scribes of NT mss. often felt free to omit the possessive pronoun with reference to Jesus' disciples and to speak of them only as the disciples. Hence there are many *v.ll.* adding or omitting the possessive after μαθηται. Wherever such variation occurs we should add the possessive (usually αυτου). Adjusting our printed editions of Mark in this way would mean that only at 4:34 is μαθητης unqualified by αυτου — and there ιδιος makes the possessive unnecessary. In Matthew too any exceptions to μαθηται αυτου are explicable on

---

[7] If one were to adjust the text of Mark in this way then one would need to explain how μεχρις ου came to be included in the text of Mark by scribes. εως was a preposition only in Hellenistic times: μεχρι or αχρι was considered to be the Attic preference, hence scribes influenced by neo-Atticism would have substituted εως ου or εως αν in their text of Mark. On Atticism see further below (cf. Blass-Debrunner *Grammar* § 216 and note Dan 11:3 LXX εως αν; Theodotion μεχρις ου).

similar grounds. The general rule can be made to apply to Luke and John. To accept the possessive wherever possible has implications for the parallels.[8] As far as the Synoptic Gospels are concerned, accepting the originality of αυτου throughout the Gospels even when it is not textually certain means that the resultant synopsis so printed gives us more similarities between the Gospels. Where Matthew, Mark and Luke are in parallel μαθηται αυτου would occur in all three gospels as follows:

    (a)   Matt. 12:1 = Mark 2:23 = Luke 6:1
    (b)   Matt. 14:19 = Mark 6:41 = Luke 9:16
    (c)   Matt. 19:13 = Mark 10:13 = Luke 18:15
    (d)   Matt. 21:1 = Mark 11:1 = Luke 19:29.

For (b) Syn[13] prints the shorter text in Matthew and Luke, and brackets αυτου in Mark thus showing apparent agreement of Matthew and Luke against Mark. For (c) in Syn[13] all three gospels have the text without the possessive and for (d) Syn[13] has only Mark with αυτου.

Where two Gospels only are in parallel our acceptance of αυτου makes 12 further agreements between these Gospels:

Mark 8:27 (pr.)	= Luke 9:18	Matt. 15:12	= Mark 7:17
Matt. 13:10	= Luke 8:9	Matt. 15:32	= Mark 8:1
Matt. 23: 1	= Luke 20:45	Matt. 15:33	= Mark 8:4
Matt. 26:40	= Luke 22:45	Matt. 15:36	= Mark 8:6
Matt. 14:15	= Mark 6:35	Matt. 26:19	= Mark 14:16
Matt. 14:22	= Mark 6:45	Matt. 26:36	= Mark 14:32

Again, these arguments are the result of and secondary to the discussions based on style. Work on the Synoptic question needs to take account of these consequences: the Synoptic Problem has not determined the text.

Those who wish to establish an author's style need to take into account variants to the printed texts as C.H. Turner did, albeit in a limited way, in the 1920s and as Nigel Turner did in Vol IV of Moulton's *Grammar*.[9] To draw up statistics on an author's style, or make conclusions on New Testament usage based only on the evidence of one printed text ignoring the apparatus is liable to create distortions and to imbue one particular printed edition with having the monopoly of original readings, a claim denied by even the most confident editors of a New Testament text!

We have referred above on several occasions to the principle of

    [8] I have discussed this issue fully in 'Mathētēs with a Possessive in the New Testament," in *ThZ* 35 (1979) 300-304.
    [9] J.H. Moulton, *A Grammar of New Testament Greek* vol. IV, by Nigel Turner (Edinburgh 1976).

dissimilarity and also to the generally more convincing rules concerning author's style. There are other principles that can be and should be appealed to both to guide one through the plethora of variants to be found in a good apparatus and also to prevent one's text from being based entirely on subjective criteria, thus allowing this text to be charged with being only 'intuitively' edited.[10] One further principle that may be mentioned here is that of first century Koine Greek. Grammarians whose works have come down to us like Moeris and Phrynichus pronounced on what was and what was not good Greek. Many of their statements are relevant for explaining how several variants occurred in the New Testament ms. tradition.[11] If we acknowledge that scribes, who were often the educated men of their day, influenced by the pronouncements of the Atticist grammarians, would occasionally try to impose Attic readings on the mss. they were copying, then a criterion for dealing with variation would be that Atticizing variants should be eliminated.[12] Conversely, *v.ll.* that betray less good Greek or Semitisms are likely to be original, other things being equal. If one recognises and applies criteria such as these to decide on variations in the mss. then the resultant text is likely to represent the words of the original New Testament authors more closely than the text found in current printed editions, but these principles in no way depend on or presuppose any one Synoptic theory. It is for those who formulate solutions to the Synoptic Problem to decide if such a resultant text supports their solution or not.

Conjectural emendation

The only way in which one could adjust the evidence shown by Allen, C.H. Turner, *et al.* in order to draw up lists that seemed to prove that Mark's language was always superior to, or later than, or dependent on, that of Matthew (and Luke) would be to resort to conjecture. Although some have advocated conjectural emendation as a legitimate way of

[10] In "Can We Recover the Original New Testament?" in *Theology* 77 (1974) 338-353, I have set out criteria that can be used to establish a text on thorough-going eclectic lines.

[11] Cf. my "Phrynicus' Influence on the Textual Tradition of the New Testament," in *ZNW* 63 (1972) 133-138, and "Moeris and the Textual Tradition of the Greek New Testament," in J. K. Elliott, ed. *Studies in New Testament Language and Text* [*Novum Test Supp* 44], (Leiden 1976) 144-152.

[12] See G.D. Kilpatrick, "Atticism and the Text of the Greek New Testament," in J. Blinzler, O. Kuss, F. Mussner, eds., *Neutestamentliche Aufsätze:* Festschrift für Prof. J. Schmid (Regensburg 1963) 125-137. Cf. also Id., "Atticism and the Future of *ZHN*," in *NovT* 25 (1983) 146-151; further, "Eclecticism and Atticism," in *ETL* 53 (1977) 107-112.

tackling the text,[13] to do so would be dangerous and unnecessary. Conjectural emendations of the text of the New Testament have generally not found favour in scholarly circles and may legitimately be called a rewriting of the New Testament. The apparatus to both N-A[25] and N-A[26] bears eloquent testimony to many ingenious conjectures proposed in the recent past, but few of these conjectures have convinced editors of a Greek New Testament. G. D. Kilpatrick in the Metzger *Festschrift* has provided a powerful attack on the suggestion that one may resort to conjectural readings.[14] One would indeed be on a slippery slope if one advocated a solution to the Synoptic Problem on the basis of a conjectural text designed specifically to support such a theory.

Conclusion

No one edition of the Greek New Testament nor any one synopsis is likely to be one hundred percent correct in printing the original text. As far as the Synoptic Gospels are concerned it can be argued that in many ways Greeven's text probably comes closest to the ideal when compared with Aland and Orchard but this does not mean that there is no room for improvement. Far from it. The carefully selective apparatus in his edition and indeed in that of Aland enables the careful scholar to exercise his own editorial freedom. It is vital that those who work on the Synoptic Problem utilize the apparatus. Without it, statistics and arguments about parallels may be incorrect, distorted and create biased conclusions. However, the apparatus to these synopses is selective and the wise scholar should also check the fuller apparatus available in the texts of von Soden, and Legg (for Matthew and Mark), despite the faults in these editions, as well as in Tischendorf[8] and in the International Greek New Testament Project's edition of Luke. Only when one is armed with the information available from such tools can one confidently assert which text is textually uncertain and which text firm.

J. K. ELLIOTT

---

[13] J. Strugnell, "A Plea for Conjectural Emendation in the New Testament," in *CBQ* 36 (1974) 543-558.

[14] G. D. Kilpatrick, "Conjectural Emendation in the New Testament," in E. J. Epp and G. D. Fee, eds., *New Testament Textual Criticism: Its Significance for Exegesis* (Oxford 1981) 349-360.

ZUKUNFTSMUSIK

Some Desirable Lines of Exploration
in the New Testament Field

To Geza and Pamela Vermes

Never before have I been officially encouraged to indulge in this pastime and I appreciate the privilege.[1]

1. A dictionary like Kittel's,[2] specialising in theological themes, needs constant updating — even if we leave aside certain pervasive simplifications in the area of semantics which have lately come under attack.[3] The scant article on the Land, γῆ, for example,[4] must be completely redone in view of W.D. Davies's pioneering work.[5] A more general desideratum is the inclusion of quite a few concepts at first sight not qualifying. In fact, just because the theology is in these cases implied, part of an overall attitude, rather than explicit, ad hoc, we may come here upon clues to deeper strata. Φιμόω, "to muzzle", to be adverted to below (under 5) has no entry. I published both a lecture and a little book on the Scriptural use of "sudden" and a number of particles denoting "at once".[6] Since, as quite often, I did not spell out my major intent, I was apparently misunderstood as being interested in nothing but philological exactitude. But I meant more. "Sudden" is apt to reflect an inner experience clearly reaching into the numinous: "and suddenly there was a multitude of the heavenly host"(Lk. 2:13). But even the innocuous-seeming "at once" can be far from religiously neutral.

---

[1] I am grateful to William David Davies for his criticism and encouragement in the preparation of this essay.

[2] G. Kittel set it up, editing *Theologisches Wörterbuch zum Neuen Testament*, vol. 1, in 1933.

[3] Spearheaded by J. Barr, *The Semantics of Biblical Language*, 1961.

[4] Sasse, in vol. 1, pp. 676ff.

[5] It will suffice to name *The Gospel and the Land*, 1974.

[6] *Suddenness and Awe in Scripture*, 1963, and *The Sudden in the Scriptures*, 1964.

Two examples:

(i) Mark employs εὐθύς 40 to 50 times against 15 to 20 in Matthew, 17 in Luke cum Acts, 6 in John. Even though the literal sense "at once" is not seldom present, the sense "duly" — OED: "in due manner, order, form or season" — is never absent and at times the only one. Jesus at Capernaum taught as one having authority "and εὐθύς there was in their synagogue a man with an unclean spirit" (Mk. 1:23). "Duly" and nothing else. It is Mark's way of conveying his fundamental estimate of these events: they take place one after another in a planful (*planmäßig*), inevitable unfolding. Three stretches are lacking the significant connective: the day of questions, the apocalypse and the passion. These he took over from elsewhere without bringing them into line. To the first I shall return below (under 4).

It may be worth adding that the shading-off of εὐθύς into "duly" does not originate with Mark; it is met with, e.g., in Aristotle.[7] The root meaning of the word is "straight", and English "straight" or "straightways" also occasionally veers towards "duly".

(ii) Παραχρῆμα, which we may translate "forthwith" in order to keep it apart from εὐθύς, occurs in one Matthean pericope, never in Mark, 16 times in Luke *cum* Acts, never in John. Luke's predilection for the word is explicable by its frequence in medical literature. However, in the New Testament it invariably refers to the immediate, miraculous actualisation of a decision from on high, mostly of Jesus. He takes Jairus's daughter by the hand and tells her to arise "and her spirit came again and she arose forthwith" (Lk 8:55). Peter, in his name, commands a lame man to walk and takes him by the hand "and forthwith his feet received strength" (Acts 3:7). Again, Peter tells Sapphira that she is doomed to instant death "and she fell down forthwith" (Acts 5:10). The quick success of a wonder-worker's intervention is, of course, a widespread phenomenon: in Lucian, a magician assembles all reptiles of a farm and blows on them "and they were instantly — αὐτίκα — burned".[8] On a vulgar level, the illusionist's "*presto*" belongs here. Yet there are also those in touch with powers that will cure or destroy over time. I guess this delayed-action prodigy is a later growth; for one thing, the evidence is so much less evident.

---

[7] Aristotle, *Metaphysics*, 4.2.6.10.1004a.
[8] Lucian, *The Lover of Lies*, 13 i.f.

But it, too, goes back to long before New Testament times.[9] At any rate, Luke's παραχρῆμα does tell us something about his thoughts concerning the effect of a divine or divinely-sanctioned verdict. In the one Matthean pericope with παραχρῆμα, incidentally, the fig-tree cursed by Jesus withers "forthwith" while Mark has the disciples find it withered a day later (Matt. 21:19f.; Mk. 11:13f.).

2. It so happens that a passage containing εὐθύς furnishes what I regard as conclusive proof that Matthew draws on Mark, our written Mark (Matt. 3:16; Mk. 1:10). Let me at the outset reassure upholders of the former's priority that I shall eventually meet them a quarter of the way (under 5).

To start with Matthew: "Having been baptized, Jesus at once came up out of the water; and behold, the heavens were rent and he saw the Spirit of God descending." "He at once came up out of the water" — this is passing strange. Why ever should he have stayed down? Now look at Mark. Jesus was baptized "and at once, having come up out of the water, he saw the heavens rent and the Spirit descending". To put "at once" in front, next to a participle not linked to it, and only then the verb which it does qualify is a favourite Marcan device: Jesus is sending two disciples to a certain village "and at once, having entered into it, you will find a colt tied" (Mk. 11:2). The statement "and at once, having come up out of the water, he saw" etc. is tremendously meaningful. Εὐθύς here signifies "and directly" as well as "and duly". It is at the moment of his emerging from baptism that a proselyte to Judaism's transmutation takes place: "He immerses and comes up, behold, he is like an Israelite in all respects".[10] Matthew makes two sentences of Mark's one, changing the participle into a finite mood. The result ought to be: "Jesus came up and at once the heavens were rent". But he mispunctuates his source, joins the adverb to the participle and reads "and at once having come up, he saw the heavens rent". Hence the absurd ring to his presentation. It is readily explained in this way and I do not think it can be in any other. Luke, not surprisingly, cuts out the coming up altogether; it is on Jesus's praying that the heavens open.

3. My inference from this episode would hold even without the Jewish pattern behind Mark. Even without it, that is, he would make sense while Matthew would be intelligible only as proceeding from his

---

[9] The two kinds of miracles represent a dichotomy met in practically all areas of life. In a forthcoming paper, "The Moment and the Flow of Time", I give other examples.

account. At this juncture, however, I confess that time and again I find
Mark preserving more accurately the conditions of Jesus's ministry,
both as to basic, popularly-shared Jewish life and beliefs and as to
peculiar traits of the protagonist's circle. Such an impression, of course
is not reached without close attention to extra-Biblical material shed-
ding light on the contemporary situation, Midrash and Talmud *inter
alia*.

Take the battle between precept and example as man's guide. I shall
be brief about it, since I have said enough elsewhere.[11] The main trend
of the period, spreading from Sadducees to other groups, was to confine
fully-binding force to precept alone. The Zadokite Fragments,[12]
combating polygamy and probably also divorce, adduce three verses
from the Pentateuch: "Male and female created he them", at the time
understood to describe the ideal, androgynous Ur-Adam,[13] "The ani-
mals went in two by two" (Gen. 7:9) and "The king shall not multiply
wives to himself" (Deut. 17:17). The first two offer examples, the third
is a precept. It is safe to assume that the third — not really a good text
for general consumption — was appended in response to the movement
just mentioned. Similarly, both Matthew (19:3f.) and Mark (10:2f.), in
the controversy about divorce, begin with "Male and female created he
them" and then add "And the twain shall be one flesh" (Gen. 2:24).
No doubt in this case, too, the example once stood by itself but was
gradually found inadequate in debate with opponents.

When we go on from here to the Sabbath dispute caused by the
disciples plucking corn, Mark (2:23ff.) — followed by Luke (6:1ff.) —
is content with the example of David and his band who, as they were
hungry, ate of the shewbread reserved for the priests (1 Sam. 21:3ff.).
Matthew provides supplementary defence based on precept (Matt. 12:1ff.);
according to the Book of Numbers the Temple service overrides the
Sabbath restrictions (Num. 28:9f.) — *a fortiori* (yes, the text needs
a highly-refined extensive interpretation by the method "light and
weighty" to be applicable) the present, greater task will do so. The
reverse development is out of the question: had Mark had the more

[10] *Babylonian Talmud* Yebamoth 47b.

[11] *The New Testament and Rabbinic Judaism* (1956, repr. 1973), pp. 71ff., "Responsi-
bilities of Master and Disciples", in *NTS* 19 (1972) 4ff., and *The Old Testament in the
New: a Jewish Perspective*, section III. Of the last-mentioned piece, only the German
translation by W. Schuller has so far appeared, *Das Alte Testament im Neuen aus jüdischer
Sicht*. It forms vol. 10, 1984, of the series *Xenia*, and section III is found on pp. 10f.

[12] *Zadokite Fragments* 7.1ff.

[13] Genesis 1.27, 5.2, Genesis Rabba on 1.26f., *Mekhilta* on Exodus 12.40; Philo,
Creation, 24.76, *Allegorical Interpretation*, 2.4.13, *Who is the Heir*, 33.164.

cogent argument available, he would not have dropped it. It should be remembered that at Rome also, by the 1st century, example no longer sufficed in matters of licit or illicit. [14]

Another problem I need not enlarge on is denial of one's faith under duress. [15] The Marcan account of Peter's conduct (Mk. 14:66ff.), when suspected of association with Jesus, precisely reflects the position of the sages, in essence going back to the Old Testament era. His first reply is to one person only, the High Priest's maid, and the formulation is evasive, "I do not understand". According to majority doctrine, a renunciation in private was less terrible than outright disavowal. [16] The second reply is to the maid amidst bystanders: in public, though still oblique. Then the bystanders press him and he swears: "I know not the man". In public and direct: the extreme betrayal. None of the parallels in the other three gospels is equally pristine (Mt. 26:69ff.; Lk. 22:55ff.; Jn. 18:16ff.).

It may be worth pointing out that there is nothing academic about the distinctions here operative. Any member of an embattled minority would be familiar with them. They are indeed a sort of natural law, apt to recur wherever certain conditions exist. In Europe, in the 1930s and 1940s, I suppose there was hardly a state or group that did not at some stage or other arrive at the norm — often felt rather than spelled out — that, while to save your neck by a concession in private and/or ambiguous might be venial, a public, unqualified abandonment of your cause would not: its effect would be so much more devastating.

4. About my next item I discover one or two new facets each time I return to it. [17] It is in any case particularly relevant to this conference's endeavor. It may be observed at once that it, too, involves a matter which, though most present-day students will find it recondite, was anything but that for the nuclear Christian sect: the Passover-eve recital, the Haggadah.

This time I begin with Mark. Four questions are considered in succession: Is it lawful to pay tribute to Caesar? Asked by Pharisees

---

[14] A related illustration may be found in my "The Three Quotations from Homer in *Digest*, 18.1.1.1", in *Cambridge Law Journal*, 10 (1949), 215.

[15] See "Limitations on Self-Sacrifice in Jewish Law and Tradition", in *Theology*, 72 (1969) 291 ff.

[16] E.g. Genesis Rabba on 35.17 referring to the disguise of students of Joshua ben Hananiah in a persecution around A.D.100; *Tanhuma* on Numbers 20.12 for the publicity of Moses's disbelief; Esther Rabba on 2.20 for the queen's tacit concealment of her religion.

[17] Matthew 22.15ff., Mark 12.13ff., Luke 10.25ff., 20.20ff. See my *New Testament and Rabbinic Judaism*, pp. 158ff.,"The Earliest Structure of the Gospels", in *NTS* 5 (1959) 180ff., and *He That Cometh* (1966), pp. 8ff.

and Herodians. If a woman goes through a number of levirate marriages, whose wife will she be on resurrection? Asked by Sadducees. Which is the foremost commandment? Asked by a scribe admiring Jesus' stand. How can the Messiah be David's son (in accordance with numerous texts — at least as understood at the time)[18] seeing that David (in Ps. 110:1) calls him as Lord? Asked by Jesus. As there is no logical or historical link between these matters, their compilation has been looked on as relatively late and artificial. In reality, what we have before us is the earliest composite chapter in the gospels.

There is first-century evidence in the Talmud[19] of a division of questions into four types: "of wisdom", about points of law; "of vulgar mockery", such as whether the child Elisha brought back to life (2 Kg. 4:18f.) conveyed uncleanness, as a corpse; "of the proper way of the land", about practical piety; and "of interpretation", about inconsistencies in the Bible, as when one verse speaks of God's choice of Zion, another of his rejection (Ps. 132:13; cf. Jer. 32:31). The New Testament questions manifestly fall under this schema: the inquiry concerning the permissibility of tribute, the gibe at resurrection, the wish for an overall direction, the puzzle of contradiction. It can be shown, however, that they are put together, not from any scholastic bent, but in analogy to a section of the Haggadah.[20] In it, the four Pentateuchic admonitions to instruct the youth in the subject of the exodus are taken to represent the categories under notice. The passage mentioning "the testimonies, statutes and judgements which the Lord has commanded us" (Deut. 6:20f.) represent legal exploration. That where the youth asks "What mean you by this service?" (Exod. 12:26) — "you" instead of "we" — represents contemptuous disavowal of communion. That with the general "What is this?" (Exod. 13:14) represents honest, open search. That where the instruction refers to "what the Lord did unto me when I came forth from Egypt" (Exod. 13:8) is at variance with other statements according to which the Lord rescued not "me" but "us", "your fathers", etc. (Deut. 26:8; Josh. 24:6).

The dependence of the Marcan piece on the Seder is beyond doubt. The four classes appear in the same sequence, different from the Talmudic one. The answer to the juridical problem is cryptic in both cases. (When those out to inflame the Romans against Jesus speak of an absolute prohibition of tribute (Lk. 23:2), they are misrepresenting

---

[18] II Samuel 7.12f., Isaiah 11.1, 10, Jeremiah 23.5, Psalms 89.4f., 132.11 etc.

[19] *Babylonian Talmud* Niddah 69bff.

[20] In the first, pre-meal half, beginning: "With regard to four sons, disciples, speaks the Torah".

him.) While these and other, similar data might be held inconclusive, what clinches the argument is that both in the Haggadah and in Mark — and not in the Talmudic paradigms — the final question is put by the instructor. Moreover, as if to underline its singularity, in both — and not in the Talmud — it is left unanswered. Why? The authors of the Passover liturgy noticed that the first three of their quotes respecting instruction employ some phrasing like "and when your son asks you in time to come, you shall say"; whereas the fourth one, omitting the son's initiative, starts right off "and you shall show your son in that day, saying". Whence they inferred that Scripture distinguishes between the following four characters among sons or disciples: the wise one, asking about law, the wicked one, asking in order to jeer, the simply pious one, asking for plain guidance — these three are pretty obvious — and far less obvious, the one who refrains from asking. He is to be stimulated by father or master, who will cite him a text controverted elsewhere. To add the solution would defeat the aim, which is the encouragement of participation. Jesus' closing riddle is intelligible only — but also fully — against the background of the Passover Haggadah.

Indeed, it is more faithful to its model than most current editions and translations make it look. In the Haggadah, the fourth category is introduced thus: "And he who does not know how to ask, you [father or master] open for him [i.e. open the discourse for him by posing a text to be elucidated]".[21] In precise conformity, Mark introduces it "And no one any further dared to ask him, and commending the discourse Jesus said". Ordinarily, the section "And no man any further dared to ask him" is treated, not as leading up to the fourth question, by Jesus, but as depicting the effect of his reaction to the third. But that reaction is the opposite of intimidating; his concluding words are "You are not far from the kingdom". Besides, my paragraphing is supported by excellent medieval authority.[22] The New English Bible accepts it.[23] But it still omits the initial "and"; and it substitutes the elegant "and Jesus went on to say" for the heavy "and commencing the discourse Jesus said". Yet, while "to commence and say"[24] is often rather eroded,

---

[21] On the sense of פטה, "to open", see W. Bacher, *Die bibelexegetische Terminologie der Tannaiten* (1899), pp. 162f.

[22] See J. Weiss, *Die drei älteren Evangelien*, 3rd ed., 1917.

[23] *New Testament and Rabbinic Judaism* (1961), p. 81.

[24] Ἀποκρίνομαι καὶ λέγω, in Hebrew אנא ואמר; e.g. Deuteronomy 21.7, Job 3.2. In old-fashioned German Bibles, one often finds *anheben und sagen*, more satisfactory than the scrupulous "to answer and say" or *antworten und sagen*. Though, come to think of it, it does obscure the ultimate provenance of the phrase. So does *das Wort nehmen und sagen*,

denoting little more than "to speak", in the present instance it has its full value: emphatically, the master makes the beginning. I am not saying that, had I been on the Dodd committee, I might not, in deference to the less pedantic reader — the "simply pious" — have voted for the smoother expression.

The day of questions allows us a moving glimpse of the kind of Seder celebrated by the believers in the very first decades after the crucifixion: in the main traditional, with the customary elaborations of the Mosaic exodus supplemented and slowly replaced by parallels from the more recent one. They had not so far developed their own literary structures, the new wine was as yet poured into old bottles. One result, by the way, is that (except for minor adjustments) the material of the supplements must be extremely near in date to the events; in other words, there is the strongest presumption in favour of the historicity (on the whole) of the four incidents here assembled. However, to pursue this line would take me too far from the central topic.

Very likely the chapter is one of those reported by Eusebius[25] — who quotes Papias, who quotes yet prior testimony — to have reached Mark from Peter. Let us go again through the four portions. The problem of tribute to Caesar is closely related to that of temple tax, brought up in Matthew, with Peter a prominent figure. I have suggested elsewhere that the episode is more significant than commonly thought.[26] An intriguing feature may be added: Jesus does not wait for Peter to ask — he might never have done so — but "anticipates" him[27] and himself raises the question, about law this time. As for Jesus's rebuttal of the denial of resurrection, in a lecture just published I remark on Peter, in Acts, distinctly harking back to it.[28] Brotherly love appears in I Peter 3:9 but, admittedly, no extensive apostolic communication would be without some such maxim and in any case the authorship of the Epistle is uncertain. What is striking, however, is Peter's intense

---

to which E. Klostermann resorts: *Das Markusevangelium* (4th ed., 1950), p. 128. But it gets the meaning absolutely.

[25] *Ecclesiastical History*, 3.39.15.

[26] Matthew 17.24ff.; see *NTS* 19 (1972-73) 13ff.

[27] A concept worth studying. It recurs, e.g., in Jonah 4.2, I Thessalonians 4.15, Josephus, *Jewish Antiquities*, I Proem 3.12; *Life*, 315; Jerusalemite Megilla 74a. See my *Typologie im Werk des Flavius Josephus*, vol. 6 of *Sitzungsberichte der Bayerischen Akademie der Wissenschaften*, Phil.-Hist. Klasse, 1977, pp. 4f. (repr. in *Freiburger Rundbrief*, 31 (1979), 60; English translation in *Journal of Jewish Studies* 31 (1980) 19f.), and "Jonah: a Reminiscence" in *Journal of Jewish Studies*, 35 (1984) p. 39.

[28] Acts 3.13ff., 5.30; see *The Old Testament in the New*, section II, German translation by W. Schuller, vol. 10 of *Xenia* pp. 14ff.

engagement in question 4, the son of David — Lord of David discrepancy, in his Pentecostal address (Acts 2:25ff.), with echoes later on
(Acts 5:31). It was taken for granted, of course, that, as Scripture
cannot err, every conflict between two (or more) passages must, on
careful probing, turn out to be merely apparent: the passages, it will
emerge, cover different ground, each of them having its own range of
validity. In the Talmudic paradigm adduced above, the line "God has
chosen Zion" — from the Psalter, i.e. David — is regarded as applying
to the time before Solomon married the daughter of Pharaoh (1 Kg.
11:1), the line "the city has been a provocation of my anger" — from
Jeremiah — to the time after. From the answer to the wicked questioner
in the Passover Haggadah, it can be seen that one way of reconciling
the statement "the Lord freed me from Egypt" with references to the
freeing of "us", "your fathers" or the like, was to assign to the former
the message that deliverance took place only for the sake of him who
trusts in God and not for his scoffing adversary. Peter (if I may give a
deplorably rough summary) explains that, while David cherished the
promise that the Messiah would be a descendant of his, he also foresaw
that that personage would be far superior to him, in being raised from
Hades to a seat at the right hand of God without experiencing
corruption.

Quite apart from these details — if Mark received this Passover
Seder collage from Peter, it would chime in exactly with what we find in
Eusebius: Peter "shaped his teachings in accordance with the demands
of any occasion, instead of purporting to make an orderly presentation
of the Lord's sayings; so that Mark did nothing wrong in thus writing
down some pieces as he remembered them". An explicit apology,
required at a time when it was still feasible directly to compare, or
contrast, the actual sequence, etc. of the incidents with that adjusted to
novel requirements — to the revised Passover-eve recital, for instance.
Suppose, as an example, that the clash with the Sadducees, question 2,
in reality took place before that with the Pharisees and Herodians,
question 1. Peter, we are given to understand, switched them around so
as to fit into the customary Seder; and Mark, in adopting his order,
acted only as a loyal transmitter whom it would be unfair to censure.
Let us recall at this juncture the conspicuous absence of the Marcan
εὐθύς. No "and duly there were the Sadducees" or the like. This chapter
is not part of the *planmäßige* course of events: it is structured so as to
satisfy a χρεια, a particular want.

When I appealed to ancient Church tradition about thirty years ago, the reaction was so cool that in the first draft of this paper I still felt I had to defend myself. To judge by the present symposium, however, respect for that witness is increasing. At any rate, a major reason for spurning it is surely that it has not seemed possible to make sense, real, concrete sense, of Eusebius's text (except by doing violence to it, one way or another). Well, it is possible: the shaping of the material with a view to the demands of the Seder worship is a case — there may be others — perfectly according with what we are told. Here may be the place to stress that there would scarcely be a greater communal need around, say, A.D. 40, than for guidance on just those issues (the sequence being determined by the Haggadah model): (1) What did the group owe to the foreign government and the native priesthood, an unholy alliance between which had just contrived the horrid death of its head? (2) What about resurrection, linchpin of the group's hope? (3) What, beyond all minutiae, did the group's head expect of members and would-be members big or small, near or far? (4) What about the strangely miraculous Messiahship of the group's head? Peter, or whoever amplified the recital expounding the old redemption with parallels from the new, chose well.

In passing — the Haggadah introduces one "who does not know how to ask" whereas Mark has "no one dare to ask". The character under review is met in Philo, as "not daring."[29] (Generally, this root is quite rare in his work.) The perfect man, we are told, ought to teach "those of the young who are willing; and if a less daring one hesitates through awe — or shame — and is slow to come forward to learn, he himself ought to go and pour out guidance". "Not to know how to" and "not to dare to" are near enough; psychology will find countless ties; either, for example, may cause or result from the other. Still, they are not identical. My hunch is that "not to dare to" would be more readily used of a disciple's position vis-à-vis the master, a Socrates, an Apollonius, a Hillel, "not to know how to" of an as yet untrained son's vis-à-vis his father. The former has more of an aura of formal distance about it. Even while the Temple stood, only a fraction of Jewry made the Passover pilgrimage. Since A.D. 70, the Jewish Seder has become largely confined to the family. Largely, never absolutely; and especially in the immediate post-destruction phase, approximations to the past were sought — witness an illustrious gathering at Lydda, under Gamaliel II, mentioned in the Tosephta,[30] and one at Bene-Berak, under

[29] Philo, *Special Laws*, 4.26.140.

[30] *Tosephta* Pesahim 10.12. 31. C.K. Barrett points out to me that the disciple who does not ask yet receives the appropriate instruction may be in John's mind in several

Eliezer ben Hyrcanus, Joshua ben Hananiah, Eleazar ben Azariah, Akiba and Tarphon, which actually came to be commemorated in the Haggadah itself. But with no more groups of devotees going up to Jerusalem under a revered leader, the dice were loaded in favour of a family affair. It is not surprising, therefore, that "not to know how to" alone survives in the liturgy.

When we now proceed to Matthew and Luke, their versions are plainly due to incomprehension of the original scheme. The straightforward, pious seeker has become a decoy — though an inquiry concerning the most basic commandment is hardly a promising trap. Luke, in addition, transfers this section to a totally different context which, it has been noticed, it does not fit; while the questioner, despite his bad faith, still earns Jesus's approval. As for the lack of daring, Matthew gives it what seems to him a more plausible place at the end of the entire chapter: nobody could answer Jesus's question and that stopped people asking him. In Luke, the clause still precedes Jesus's question. But from forming the introduction — "and no one dared and Jesus commenced" — it is turned into the reason some scribes admire his refutation of the Sadducees: they admire it, that is, "because [γάρ] no one any further dared to ask him anything". The Midrash of the four sons or disciples is shattered and scattered. Far be it from me to deny that, in the process, valuable new perspectives have been introduced.

How, one may wonder, could somebody as close to Jewish practice as Matthew deal with the material in this insensitive fashion? The answer is that, once the chapter was transmitted by itself, no longer embedded in the regular Passover service, it was easy to miss the connection. After all, it has taken till the mid-twentieth century to rediscover it. We must bear in mind that the exchanges presented, though they were no longer of such acute concern in his day as in Peter's, were still important enough. Right to the present their weight has seemed to scholars adequate ground for their being placed together

---

verses of ch. 16. Perhaps 4.33f. is a further instance: much as in 16.19f., Jesus replies to a question the disciples put, not to him, but to each other. Complex problems are raised by 21.12: none of the disciples "dares to examine Jesus" as, risen, he shows himself a third time. Whoever authored this pericope just conceivably preferred "to examine" to "to ask" in order to indicate that what still puzzles the disciples, by now clear as to the identity of their visitor, is his precise nature in this state, no longer with the dead but not yet ascended. Nor shall I inspect an occasion when the disciples "fear to ask Jesus" about a particularly frightening matter, Mark 9.32, Luke 9.45.

[32] Luke 10.25ff. See J.M. Creed, *The Gospel According to St Luke* (1930), p. 151.

by evangelical redaction.[33] It is only natural, therefore, that, unschooled in higher criticism, he did not go behind the compendium at hand: strong corroboration, once again, of his coming in the wake of Mark, removed from the original setting by a decisive step.

It may be worth noting that divergencies independent of the overall scheme confirm Mark's antiquity. In the debate about resurrection, in Mark, Jesus appeals to "the Book of Moses, at the Bush". "The Bush" is the Rabbinic appellation of the relevant portion. Matthew — though not Luke — drops this detail. In my lecture just adverted to, I attach importance also to Mark's mention of "the power of God" — dropped by Luke though not by Matthew — as well as to his use, once, of "to be waked" instead of "to be raised" or "to rise" — met in neither of the other two. In the summary advice, Mark alone quotes "Hear, O Israel, the Lord our God is the only Lord". Moreover, the scrupulous repetition of Jesus's advice to the qustioner, culminating in an expansion, is consonant with a method of study then prevailing: but I cannot here dwell on it.[34] Neither Matthew nor Luke reproduces it (understandably: it sounds *de trop*) except that the latter, under its influence, assigns the whole answer to the questioner — which renders the *mala fide* motivation all the more incongruous.

Two objections to the foregoing exposé have been communicated to me. One is that the Pharisaic-Herodian question about tax concerns political controversy, and hence falls outside the law. This presupposes a fairyland where the two provinces are kept apart. It does not exist anywhere today — think, in the U.S.A., of conscription, desegregation, restrictions on trade with Cuba — and it did not then. Rabbinic decisions on fiercely debated public issues are legion. Quite a few are alluded to in the New Testament: e.g. re the Samaritans[33] and re litigation against a fellow-Jew before a heathen court.[35] As for tax to the Romans, Judas of Galilee condemned it as recognition of their sovereignty in the place of God's.[36] The evolution culminating in the slogan "The law of the State is the law"[37] is beset by difficulties with tax; and Paul, preaching submission, singles out this item (Rom. 13:1f.). While a Mishnaic provision treats murderers, robbers and tax-collectors as equally deserving to be misled, the part regarding tax-collectors is

[33] See K.H. Rengstorf, *Das Evangelium nach Lukas* (9th ed.), pp. 225ff., seeing in the first three sections Jesus' separation from the various religious parties and in the fourth a counter-attack on the scribes.

[34] Matthew 10.5, Luke 10.29ff., John 4.7ff.

[35] I Corinthians 6.1.

[36] Acts 5.37, Josephus, *Jewish War*, 2.8.1.118, 2.17.8.433; *Jewish Antiquities,* 18.1.1.4f.

[37] *Babylonian Talmud* Baba Qamma 113a.

toned down in the Gemara: a political change.[38] That already Old
Testament laws often deal with topics involving acute political tensions
is well known: the position of slaves,[39] naturalization,[40] limitations on
the monarchy,[41] mixed marriage.[42] Nor should it be thought that this
class has come to an end. It never will. The period of terror 1933-1946
and again the building up of Israel have produced a large number of
opinions having to do with politics, affected by it and trying to affect
it.[43] Note: "Permissible", ἔξεστιν, occurs six more times in Mark,
invariably respecting a legal, halakhic point.[44]

The other objection is that, contrary to my assumption, the Ur-
Christians may not have had a Passover service at all. I shall not submit
detailed evidence. It is so unlikely: an abandonment, at one blow,
nation-wide, of the cherished institution. It may, however, be useful to
expand slightly on the scenario. To begin with the sizable part of the
population not journeying to the capital but spending the festival
at home. Some families would consist entirely of unbelievers, some
entirely of believers, and some of both. (A simplification, since it leaves
out degrees of belief or unbelief.) In the third — no doubt fairly
numerous — group, an abrupt, concerted opting out of the believers
would have meant forgoing a unique opportunity for propagating the
good news. As for the pilgrims — more engaged theologically, on the
whole, than those staying behind — believers would tend to join
together. Thus a growing proportion of Passover-eve companies at
Jerusalem was fervently dedicated to the new faith. It was here, above
all, that reports and reflections about the recent, ultimate salvation
were appended to those about the preparatory one, gradually linked
together and in the end given decisive prominence. Certainly, before
long, as other occasions for formulating end-time history developed —
the daily sacred meal assemblies, for example[45] — and as Gentile

---

[38] *Mishnah* Nedarim 3.4, *Babylonian* Nedarim 28a.

[39] E.g. Exodus 21.2ff., 20f., 26f.

[40] E.g. Deuteronomy 23.4ff

[41] E.g. Deuteronomy 17.14ff.

[42] E.g. Ezra 9, Nehemiah 13.23ff.

[43] It would be interesting to search the Rabbinic sources for rulings the political
component of which is submerged. W.G. Braude, *Jewish Proselyting* (1940), p. 52, rightly
affixes the attribute "aristocratic" to the circles opposing the abolition of the Biblical anti-
Ammonite and anti-Moabite paragraphs. Again, one could imagine that when Akiba, an
admirer of Bar-Kochba's, had the Shophar blown after the New Year's benedictions
acknowledging God as King, this Halakhah was expressing defiance of Roman domina-
tion; see my "Johanan ben Beroqa and Women's Rights", *Zeitschrift der Savigny-
Stiftung*, vol. 99, 1982, Roman. Abt., p. 23.

[44] Mark 2.24, 26 (twice), 3.4, 6.18, 10.2.

[45] See J. Jeremias, *Die Abendmahlsworte Jesu* (3rd ed., 1960), pp. 60f.

converts played an increasing role, this Christian Seder lost in importance. Still, it ought to be granted ten to fifteen years, ten to fifteen
most intense, most productive years.

5. A reservation is none the less called for. In Mark and Luke, Jesus
"answers well" or "says well" when challenged by the Sadducees, in
Matthew he "muzzles" them, φιμόω. It is not unthinkable that
Matthew, independently of any other source, wants a more forceful
expression. But I wonder. It is a most uncommon one. Elsewhere in the
gospels it is confined to the defeat of a subhuman aggressor: an unclean
spirit in one Marcan pericope — where Luke follows suit[46] — a raging
storm in another — with neither Matthew nor Luke conforming.[47] In
the Epistles (if we disregard references to the Old Testament prohibition of muzzling an ox while threshing)[48] it occurs once only, in
I Peter. Here, indeed, it is employed much as in the dispute with the
Sadducees: the apostle — or his amaneuensis — writes that Christians
should by their goodness "muzzle the ignorance of foolish men".[49]
What chiefly deserves attention is the Haggadah's use of a comparable
term: the reply to the scoffer is "to blunt his teeth". (A fairly literal
application is met, for example, in the comment that Esau kissed Jacob
in order to bite him but the latter's neck turned into marble, so the
former's teeth became blunt;[50] the transferred one in the prediction
that Shiloh, the Messianic king, will blunt the teeth of the nations.)[51]
Maybe — but this is not essential to my argument — a variant of the
liturgy once contained the very term "to muzzle", הסם, quite fitting:
the Targum to the Psalter has every liar's mouth "muzzled".[52] We
should bear in mind the fluidity, even within literal muzzling, between
different shades. Thus Paul, in quoting the law about the ox, puts the
cruder κιμόω, to which quite a few copyists prefer the Septuagintal
φιμόω.[53] Anyhow, I suspect that Matthew in this passage enshrines a
Haggadah tradition equal in antiquity with Mark's and, who knows?,
supplied by the proto-Matthew in Hebrew we hear of from Eusebius.
By the way, Hebrew rather than Aramaic (which is regularly substituted
nowadays) would be the natural choice for an evangelist in direct touch
with the primitive Christian Seder celebrations, dominated by Hebrew.

[46] Mark 1.25, Luke 4.35.
[47] Mark 4.39, Matthew 8.26, Luke 8.24.
[48] Deuteronomy 25.4; I Corinthians 9.9 (see below; I Timothy 5.18.
[49] I Peter 2.15. See E.G. Selwyn, *The First Epistle of St Peter* (1946), p. 173.
[50] Genesis Rabba on 33.4.
[51] Genesis Rabba on 49.10.
[52] Psalms 107.42. On the other hand, in Psalms 39.2, the sufferer puts a muzzle on his
own mouth when irked by the wicked.
[53] See H. Lietzmann, *An die Korinther* I/II (4th ed. by W.G. Kümmel 1949), p. 41.

Am I making too much of a single phrase? It does not, however, stand alone. I have already furnished grounds for deriving the Massacre of the Innocents from the Seder. In this case, Matthew passes on a fully-fledged Ur-Christian parallel to the Passover-eve exegesis of a kind of Credo from Deuteronomy. The first story Matthew tells of Jesus, that is, corresponds to the first story in the Haggadah. [54]

I find nothing of the sort in Luke.

6. The Third Gospel, in fact, not unexpectedly offers a contrast to the first two, being far less closely tied to the traditional Judaism of the time. Its author's dissociation from it becomes manifest when we look, say, at his report in Acts of the installation of seven servers of tables. [55] Throughout his writings, he attaches particular relevance to the concept of Jesus as the new Moses, the final prophet predicted by Deuteronomy, mighty in deed and word, and delivering his people despite their rejection of him [56] — perhaps partly because, for him, Jesus, like Moses, is "the founder of a religion". [57] In this report, then, he makes the Mosaic pattern continue in the Church, the new holy community which, he realizes, must be prepared for a long march. With outstanding artistry he alludes to the appointment of Joshua as well as three other Old Testament chapters where Moses delegates some of his burdens: the creation of judges for routine disputes, the promotion of seventy elders to assist him and the creation of officers of the tribes. In none of all this, however, can he be shown to draw on Rabbinic interpretations of or legends built up around those texts.

We may obtain help from here for assessing certain passages in his Gospel: reflections rooted in Rabbinic teaching do not presumably originate with him. Take the Parable of the Unjust Steward. [58] Its basic

[54] Matthew 2. See *The New Testament and Rabbinic Judaism*, pp. 189ff., and *NTS* 5 (date) 194ff.

[55] Acts 6.1ff. See my "Neglected Nuances of Exposition in Luke-Acts," pt. 2, A Reform in Acts and its Models, in *Aufstieg und Niedergang der Römischen Welt*, ed. H. Temporini and W. Haase Vol. 25.3 (1985), pp. 2346ff.

[56] Deuteronomy 18.15ff.; 34.12; Luke 7.16, 39; 13.33; 24.19; Acts 3.22f.; 7.20ff. See my review of G. Vermes, *Jesus the Jew*, 1973, in *Journal of Jewish Studies*, 25 (1974) 333.

[57] See C.K. Barrett, *Luke the Historian in Recent Study* (1961), p. 58.

[58] Luke 16.1ff. See my "Shame Culture in Luke," in *Paul and Paulinism, Essays in honour of C.K. Barrett*, ed. by M.D. Hooker and S.G. Wilson, 1982, pp. 360f.; "Neglected Nuances", pt. 1, Encomium Prudentiae pp. 2234ff.; and "The Old Testament in the New," section VI, German translation by W. Schuller, vol. 10 of *Xenia*, pp. 24ff. For me, Luke 16.8 has become something of an advertisement of the rule of thumb in favour of the troublesome sense (allied to *lectio difficilior*). When, about forty years ago, — see "Concerning the Reconstruction of the Aramaic Gospels", in *Bulletin*, 29 (1945-46) 71 — I differed from C.C. Torrey and expressed preference for the text as it stands "just because it is so inconvenient", I had no inkling that some day I might hit on an explanation.

message is to emulate, in the ultimate crisis that has arrived, the tycoon's henchman who in the nick of time undoes some of his cruel work by lightening the load of the debtors. An excursus represents him as dubiously motivated — afraid of shameful poverty, intent on providing himself with grateful supporters — and emphasizes that even so he receives praise from Jesus.[59] This expresses the pragmatic standpoint versus the perfectionist in a debate dividing the Rabbis. It is worth noting that the pragmatists took the description in Genesis of Noah as virtuous "in his generation" in the sense of "compared with others in that inferior epoch" such relative superiority, we hear from Philo and Judah ben Ilai, sufficed for his salvation though he would not have passed in a godly age.[60] Just so, Jesus explains that those belonging to the pre-redemption aeon, when they behave like the steward, rank as wiser "for their generation", "considering their surroundings", than would the sons of the light, the redeemed ones. It is safe to regard the whole of this as a pre-Lucan elaboration: a conclusion corroborated by the attempt in the following verses to mitigate the effect and veer towards perfectionism.

On the other hand, when the original ending of the episode of the young Jesus abandoning his parents for a debate in the Temple is toned down, *entschärft*, by the assurance that he "subjected himself to them",[61] quite possibly we have to do with an amendment by Luke. By this time, the sect was consolidated; and whereas, earlier on, the young were to break away from their stubborn elders for a radically fresh start, what was now needed for an orderly development was respectful submission.

7. My inclination is obviously against speculative, absolutist theories and in favour of flexible ones, re-tested again and again. The proof of the pudding is in the eating thereof. No case, no line, no particle is so trivial that it may not require modification or even scrapping of the most logically argued, magnificent general proposition. Which leaning does not prevent me from seeing the value of the opposite.

No doubt the progress of mathematical machinery will be of colossal help to synoptic research. I regret that I am too set in my ways to take the big step from disputation to computation. Let me end up, then, by indicating an inadequately tapped potential of a different kind.

A hope, however faint, I am prey to is that more earnest attention will be paid in future to the Jewish material. With some notable

---

[59] "The lord" with the definite article must refer to him.
[60] Genesis 6.9, Philo, *On Abraham*, 7.36ff., Genesis Rabba on 6.9.
[61] Luke 2.41ff. See my *Civil Disobedience in Antiquity* (1972), pp. 47ff.

exceptions such as G. Vermes's *Jesus the Jew*,[62] New Testament research is satisfied with scratching the surface, i.e., a dutiful acknowledgment of Strack-Billerbeck or the like. Few texts omitted there are ever inspected. As if — I am exaggerating, though not overmuch and in a good cause — as if classical specialists in Socrates were content to analyze Dr. Adam's *Religious Teachers of Greece* supplemented by the *Oxford Companion*, but never went into the writings of his age and in his language. Whereas, naturally, they are expected to talk and write in fifth-century B.C. Greek better than those who lived then: Ionic, Doric, Laconian, lapidary, tragic, colloquial. Hardly any probers into Christian origins are fluent — really fluent — in the tongue Jesus spoke. Recently, working in a splendid academic theological library, I needed a Passover Haggadah. They had one poor old copy in a remote corner amidst low-ranking fringe liturgy. I asked around a little among the students present — admittedly no scientific poll — and not one of them had ever thought of looking up the little volume, be it even for a glance at the vernacular. Yet that is where it all started. How are we to account for this amazing situation?

Before trying an answer, I ought to clarify my approach in two respects. firstly, I do not subscribe to the rigid doctrine that the insider alone understands, that only a Jew, a Christian, a black, an Aryan, a woman, a man, can appreciate the experience and thinking of the group.[63] No doubt part of it is inaccessible. But a great deal is not, and part is actually easier for non-members to be aware of, as proved by Shakespeare on Othello and Shylock, de Toqueville on the Americans, Ruth Fulton Benedict on the Japanese. Nor, indeed, are such ectogenous insights confined to sympathizers. As love may make blind, hate may make seeing. Just remember the grains, or lumps, of truth about the enemy unearthed in sectarian polemics. Folk wisdom agrees with me, applying to the individual what I am here saying about groups. A seeker for advice is told, on one occasion, that there is nothing for it but to look into his own heart, on another, that he should make an effort to stand outside himself. Often the latter position has its advantages.

As for the capacity of a literary product to be comprehended beyond its original circle, it is futile to deny it in the face of Aesop's fables, the Thousand-and-One-Nights, the stories of Helen of Troy or Heracles or Parsifal, the teachings of Confucius or Buddha, the Bible itself. Granted

---

[62] 1973, repr. 1981.

[63] Cf. the penetrating and wide-ranging discussion by W.D. Davies in "Reflections in Retrospect, 1950-1980", *Bulletin of Duke Divinity School*, October 1982, pp. 33ff.

that some points will be missed in the transition, a large number will come through and, once again, the foreign recipient may make contributions enriching the native interpretation. Simple, basic features may be discovered or re-discovered — the "parallelism of members" in Hebrew poetry, for instance, described by Bishop Lowth of the eighteenth century. (A little like the disclosure to M. Jourdain in *Le Bourgeois Gentilhomme* that he has talked prose all his life.) Or profound implications: the Oedipus complex, the Hebrew monarchy as the exemplar of institutions flawed yet divinely sanctioned in order to prevent worse, "for the hardness of your heart".

Secondly, I do not believe in scholarship as the sole key to a great work. A reader or listener genuinely attuned needs none of the philologist's equipment to enter into the author's world. He may find treasures old and new in a translation of a translation of a translation. Schopenhauer became acquainted with the Upanishads through a Latin rendering of a Persian rendering; Philo relied chiefly on the Septuagint. In fact, many an intuition arrived at outside academia has proved valuable inside. (Which does not mean that others must be of lesser worth.) Hunches of long ago, such as that the tale of Noah and Ham alludes to castration, or that there is a point in Esther not revealing her lineage rather than telling a falsehood about it,[64] tend to be taken up by modern exegesis. To be sure, a wealth of information of a certain kind is open only to the savant: how Israelite prophecy relates to Canaanite, or Pauline oratory to Hellenistic. But certain other kinds are probably rendered harder of attainment by his very mindset. An analphabet in a "backward" region may hear more than a professor in "the stars in their courses fought with Sisera" or "not what I will but what thou wilt".

My observations, then, have regard only to our peculiar fraternity, pledged by the meticulous application of agreed methods over time to build up a, by and large, dependable body of knowledge, ever growing in breadth, depth and refinement — despite its intrinsic, never quite eradicable, shortcomings. It is within this context only that the neglect of a cluster of sources manifestly of first-rate importance calls for an explanation.

Two reasons one occasionally comes across — I say, occasionally, because in the main the phenomenon is not faced — do certainly play a role. One is the inordinate difficulty of the documents in question. Much of the discussion baffles even a student with perfect Hebrew and

---

[64] See above, n. 16.

Aramaic, so idiosyncratic are its logic and formulation; in fact, the majority of present-day Rabbis leave huge chunks alone. Moreover, the dating of utterances and of what they are about not seldom raises problems. And so on. To brush aside something one cannot cope with as irrelevant is a common and, up to a point, sound defence mechanism. I have elsewhere confessed to my shelving away a textbook on Roman law in Bulgarian sent me from Sofia, persuading myself that it was unlikely to prove of substantial aid. Still, there must be more to the general, persistent shelving away under notice. After all, in other provinces — say, cuneiform or Homeric studies — similar obstacles have acted as a worthwhile challenge rather than a keep-off sign.[65] Hittite fragments are exploited to the full though the language is beset with riddles. In my own lifetime, the Babylonian and Assyrian laws and Hammurabi himself, as well as the *Iliad* and *Odyssey* and their constituent parts, have been assigned to considerably varying epochs; yet the experts soldier on, conscious of the price of letting go.

The other reason given here and there is anti-semitism. Since this emotion, like its counterpart anti-gentilism, operates in untold guises, from the most direct and brutal to the most oblique and rarefied, far be it from me to make light of it. None the less, I wonder whether a third factor is not at work, in addition to these two: a reluctance unreservedly to humanize Jesus — his human side, that is — to place him right in, not above, his historical and social milieu. For the safeguarding of reverential distance, it is better not to know too much. In an entirely different connection, several decades ago, I commented on the cosmetic apparatus of theologians to Father Corbishley. "O yes", he replied, "they are all monophysites". It is an instinctive attitude, avowed neither to the world nor to the self, hence the more compulsive. Being brought up in that stern, orthodox branch of Judaism where God is the wholly other, I have every sympathy with it.

In the 'fifties and 'sixties, as the Dead Sea Scrolls became a popular sensation, there was a moment of suspense. That a valid, scholarly appraisal of the New Testament presupposes familiarity with the surrounding evidence — familiarity as easy as that of the Socrates scholar with Plato, Aristophanes, Thucydides — loomed as an inescapable

---

[65] Here is a relatively simple shot at sorting out different strata in the Haggadah — admitting that the result may be proved wrong by superior reconsideration or fresh evidence. Twice a series of divine benefactions is enumerated, once in verse and once in prose. It is only the latter version which characterizes the Temple as built "to atone for all our transgressions". Which suggests a date for it from before A.D. 70 and a later one for the poetic list. A turning of prose into poetry is in any case more likely than the reverse. See *NTS* 5 (1958/59) 176.

conclusion; and a few enthusiasts indeed believed that henceforth thorough immersion in the Jewish sources would be *de rigeur* in the pertinent Departments. Significantly, too, I heard of two learned Jewish converts to Christianity who were so bowled over as to consider going back on their conversion. They had, plainly, been unrealistic before — otherwise the finds would have made no difference one way or the other. (It may not be accidental that they were Protestants, less comfortable, it would seem, with the divinity of Jesus than Catholics and in consequence keener on eliminating the other side. Corbishley is a Catholic. True, J.A.T. Robinson, who, in *The Human Face of God*, (1973) movingly pleads against monophysitism, is an Anglican, while C.K. Barrett, who in *Jesus and the Gospel Tradition* (1967) can write that "the suffering was more acute than the human Jesus had foreseen",[66] is a Methodist.) By now, however, the flurry is over and things are pretty much back to normal.

Support for my guess may be gleaned from many other spheres of Western culture, but I shall restrict myself to one illustration. When I came to England before World War II, under the Lord Chamberlain's rules — since dropped — it was permissible to bring God on the stage, but not Jesus. Whatever the official argumentation, the true aim of this at first sight, to a Jew at least, staggering arrangement was protection of Jesus's divinity. God is in no need of such a measure. It matters not what you do to him: he may break into a guffaw, sneeze, show sexual interest, perform a handstand — he remains God. Jesus' divine side, the rules imply, is too precarious, so the safer course is to suppress the human one altogether.[67]

To expand the quest in the direction I am advocating would require not only tremendous, confident openness but also much bureaucratic, unselfish labour. For, if serious, lasting gains are desired, to begin with, a considerable number of young graduands or graduates must be sent out for long, intensive training; not, that is, to get a smattering, but to become masters. The reward of their seniors would consist in watching

---

[66] P. 108.

[67] A little comparable to the blockage in the New Testament field is that in medieval Roman and Canon Law, whose exponents are not at home, by proper standards, in Islamic (or, for that matter, medieval Jewish) Law. The next fundamental breakthrough will come through a generation seriously exploring the mutual influence between West and East. In this case, too, the difficulty of the task is not the only obstacle. Among the others are a time-hallowed feeling of superiority and the fear of what may emerge. *Experto crede!* While a Director of the Robbins Library at the U.C. Berkeley School of Law, I had ample opportunity of watching the feeding and starving of different interests — the starving often from non-remembrance or, if memory was jolted, relieved by the expression of unspecified good intentions for the future.

the new, ampler inquiries take root and bear fruit. Who can say it will not happen? *"Omnam lo' ka'asher yir'e ha'adham 'abhal lakkol zeman we'eth lekhol hephes tahath hashshamayim.* "Indeed, not as man sees; but for everything there is a moment, and a time for all business under heaven". Thus, Wessely, in 1782, calling on the Austrian Jews to respond to Joseph II's Edict of Tolerance and add a broad education in German to the traditional, exclusive concern with Torah.

David DAUBE

NOTE: This paper was first published in *BJRL* 68 (1985-86) 53-75.

THE SYNOPTIC GOSPEL DEBATE

A Re-Examination from an African Point of View

The Synoptic Problem is posed not only because of the fact that the first three Gospels obviously have extensive similarities in the outline of Jesus' ministry, but also for the considerable differences which they contain. The first three Gospels were apparently written in some particular chronological order because there is also considerable agreement in their order of arrangement. In addition, there exists a remarkable relationship within the individual pericopes where there is verbatim agreement in phrases and sentences. Multitudes of examples can be cited to demonstrate that the relationship cannot be due to mere coincidence but must be the result of literary dependence. The major problem is how to determine which Gospel was written first and which of the remaining two was written second. It is the task of the Synoptic Problem to discover that sequential order.

Prior to the period of Enlightenment, the opinion of Augustine prevailed, that Mark was an epitomizer of Matthew's Gospel, which was thought to be the oldest and most important of the Gospels. Mark is the least quoted Gospel by the Church Fathers and Matthew is the most quoted. This is partly because Matthew, in addition to his peculiar material, contains almost everything that is in Mark and it is regarded as the work of an Apostle. During the Middle Ages and the Reformation period, the Synoptic accounts were generally harmonized as much as possible. Post-Reformation Protestant Orthodoxy spent most of its energy in trying to find solutions to apparent contradictions within the Synoptic Gospels. But the smoothing out of the contradictions between the Evangelists could no longer answer most of the questions raised by Enlightenment. The Synoptic Problem which was first recognized by Augustine now became very real. The last two centuries, therefore, have witnessed numerous and varied proposed solutions. But radical scholars, over the years, have through the multiplication of hypothetical sources made the problem more difficult to solve.

I. MODERN SYNOPTIC STUDIES

The Gospel parallels published by J.J. Griesbach[1] (1774-1776) marked the end of the period of Gospel harmonization and the smoothing out of contradictions between the Evangelists and the beginning of scientific investigation of the nature of the Synoptic Problem. Griesbach raised doubts on the possibility of satisfactorily harmonizing the closely related but conflicting chronologies of the three Gospels. W.R. Farmer correctly remarks that Griesbach's harmony was in fact "a harmony to end all harmonization" because "henceforth those who followed in his footsteps would no longer seek to reconcile the conflicting chronologies of the Gospels but rather would seek to understand the relations between the Gospels in terms of their direct literary dependence or in terms of their indirect literary dependence through the mutual use of earlier hypothetical sources."[2]

Lessing had earlier on in his work composed in 1778 but published in 1784 proposed the existence of a Gospel of the Nazarenes or the Gospel of the Hebrews written in Aramaic soon after the death of Jesus. Although the Gospel is now lost, it was known to the Church Fathers.[3] Griesbach in 1783 accepted the Augustine view that none of the Evangelists wrote in ignorance of the work of his predecessors but he rejected the idea that Mark had only abbreviated Matthew. He was of the view that Mark wrote after Matthew and Luke and was dependent on both of them. While Griesbach's hypothesis provides a basis for explaining the Synoptic phenomenon, it could not explain why the order of events of the two earliest Evangelists' remain hopelessly irreconcilable. But J.G. Eichhorn proposed a plurality of sources and postulated that the three Synoptic Gospels were based on four revised editions of an original Aramaic Gospel, with each Evangelist making use of a different edition of it.[4] Eichhorn's idea was later slightly modified by Marsh who thought that the Ur-gospel must have been an Ur-Marcus.[5] Furthermore, Schleiermacher in his own contribution said

---

[1] J.J. Griesbach published his synopsis as a part of first edition of his Greek New Testament in 1744 but later republished the Synopsis separately in 1776. Four editions of the Synopsis were published under different titles; see E. Lohse, *The Formation of the New Testament*, tr. M.E. Boring (Nashville: Abingdon Press 1972) 121-131.

[2] W.R. Farmer, *The Synoptic Problem; A Critical Analysis* (New York: Macmillan 1964) 5f.

[3] Ibid. p. 4

[4] Ibid. pp. 9-11.

[5] Ibid pp. 11-15.

that Papias' Mark was different from our canonical Mark and that the Logia of Matthew was not a Gospel. According to him, both Papias' Mark and Matthew's Logia were collections of Jesus' sayings. Consequently the common material between Matthew and Luke was said to be due to the Matthean saying source. He concluded that Mark's Gospel was a later Gospel with close affinities with the apocryphal Gospels and that Matthew drew on the Logia of Papias and that Luke drew upon canonical Matthew.[6] However, Weisse made what he called a constructive attempt to enable Christianity to lay claim to the eyewitness account through Mark and the Logia. He objected to Matthew being the earliest and most reliable record of Christian beginnings. He claimed that Matthew was dependent on Mark and the Logia, the two primitive and apostolic sources which belonged to the eyewitness period. He also said that Luke was also dependent on these two eyewitness documents. Thus we have the famous Two Document Hypothesis.[7]

In 1818 J.K.L. Gieseler produced what might be called a prototype of oral theory stating that the apostolic preaching must have taken some concrete forms which would make them a kind of basic oral Gospel. He thought that this primitive oral tradition was structured into an Aramaic oral Gospel in Palestine between AD 35 and 40. He claimed further that the Apostles orally communicated this oral Gospel to their disciples, who later committed the oral Gospel to writing. This oral Gospel survived later on in a modified form in the Gospel of the Nazarenes, which was preserved in the original Aramaic, but the needs of the Gentile mission made a translation necessary. It is the Aramaic and the Greek versions of this Gospel that later became the main sources of the three Evangelists, which each of them used differently according to his special purpose. Thus Matthew produced a Palestinian Gospel, Mark a modified Palestinian Gospel and Luke a Pauline Gospel. The literary differences between them are due to the respective author's training and ability. However, it was in Westcott's presentation that we have the classical formulation of the oral theory. He claimed that since the Jews would not commit their oral traditions to writing, the primitive Christian leaders probably accepted that practice.

---

[6] F. Schleiermacher, *A Critical Essay On the Gospel of St. Luke*, ET 1825; cited in D. Guthrie, *New Testament Introduction*, 3rd ed. rev., (London: Tyndale Press 1970) 123f.

[7] W.R. Farmer, op. cit. pp. 22-25.

He said further that since the Apostles were preachers and not writers, literary enterprise would not at all occur to them. They gave most of their attention to those narratives which they often needed for preaching. The written Gospels later came into being in consequence of the needs of the early Christian Community. Westcott quoted Papias to support his position. According to him, the simplicity of Mark shows that it was the most direct representation of the Evangelic tradition and that Matthew and Luke were recensions of the simple narratives.[8]

The Mutual Dependence theory which prepared the ground for the Two-Document Hypothesis was propounded by C. Lachmann, claiming that Mark was basic, followed by Matthew and Luke. H.J. Jameson accepted the theory but claimed that Matthew was basic to Mark and that Luke made use of Matthew and Mark. Simon expressed a different opinion based on the Mutual Dependence theory, claiming that Luke used Matthew.[9] The Documentary Hypothesis itself proposed two written sources — the canonical Mark or an Ur-Marcus and another source used by Matthew and Luke in different ways. The later source was named Q. Since the Q source theory could not explain the divergences between Matthew and Luke, Q became not just a single source but a multiplicity of sources. B. H. Streeter modified this by proposing a four-source theory. He limited Q to material common to Matthew and Luke and proposed M for material peculiar to Matthew and L for material peculiar to Luke. This means Matthew = Mark + Q + M and Luke = Mark + Q + L.[10]

The Priority of Mark

The Hypothesis of the priority of Mark has many limitations. The first is the many agreements between Matthew and Luke against Mark. These were at first explained on the basis of an Ur-Marcus that was later copied by Matthew and Luke. But Streeter argued that these

---

[8] B.F. Westcott, *An Introduction to the Study of the Gospels*, (1888, first published in 1851) pp. 167ff.

[9] H.G. Jameson, *The Origins of the Synoptic Gospels*, 1922; V.H. Stanton, *The Gospels as Historical Documents*, vol. II p. 30; cf. A. Farrer, in *Studies in the Gospels. Essays in Memory of R. H. Lightfoot*, ed. D.E. Nineham, (Oxford: Blackwell 1955) 55ff. W. Lockton, in *Church Quarterly Review* July 1922.

[10] B.H. Streeter, *The Four Gospels. A Study of Origins* (London: Macmillan 1924); V. Taylor, *The Life and Ministry of Jesus* (1954) p. 14; F.C. Grant, *The Gospels, their Origin and Growth*, (1957) pp. 50, 51; A.H. McNeile, *New Testament Introduction* 2nd ed. rev. by C.S.C. Williams, (Oxford: Univ. Press 1953) 59ff.

agreements against Mark were due to scribal corruptions. According to him, Matthew and Luke made use of Mark independently and that the agreements between them were due to simple, natural editorial corrections. He also suggested that Mark and Q might have overlapped at these points and that Matthew and Luke preferred the Q versions to Mark.

Another limitation of Marcan priority is the so-called "Great Omission" (Luke completely omits Mark 6:45-8:26). This important omission demands some satisfactory explanation. One explanation is that an editor added this section to the Original Mark after Luke had made use of it. This theory requires the acceptance of the Ur-Marcus hypothesis. But there would be no justifiable reason to add this section later on if it was not there originally. The language and style of the section do not support this thesis. For this hypothesis to be viable it has to be proved conclusively that Matthew did not know Mark until the supposed editor had added the section to Mark. Another theory is that Luke omitted a similar incident in 8:19-21 and he probably omitted this section because it did not suit his purpose or for the reason of economy of space or for the reason of accident. Another guess of Streeter's is that Luke used a mutilated copy of Mark which did not contain this section.[11] As a result of these challenges to the established concept of Marcan priority, it is fast becoming clearer that the theory may not be as assured as it once seemed to be. So much rethinking and reasoning is going on.

African Christianity and Synoptic Studies

It is an irony of history that Africa, which was a leading centre for Old Testament Studies before the time of Christ and the cradle of New Testament Studies, is today still relatively young in the field of Biblical Studies. Although the critical study of the Bible had begun in the West

---

[11] E.A. Abbott, *The Corrections of Mark Adopted by Matthew and Luke*, (London: Black 1901); F.C. Burkitt, *The Gospel History and Its Transmission*, (Edinburgh: T & T Clark 1911) 42-58; J.C. Hawkins, *Horae Synopticae. Contributions to the Study of the Synoptic Problem*, (Oxford: Clarendon Press) 174ff.; W. Sanday ed., *Studies in the Synoptic Problem*, (Oxford: Clarendon Press 1911) 20ff; B.H. Streeter, op. cit. pp. 293-331; K. & S. Lake, *An Introduction to the New Testament* (1938) pp. 6ff.; C.C. Torrey, *The Four Gospels, A New Translation*, (1933); T. Nieklin, *Gospel Gleanings* (1950) 3ff.; W. Bussmann, *Synoptische Studien* I, (1925) 1-66; N. B. Stonehouse, *Origins of the Synoptic Gospels, Some Basic Questions*, (London: Tyndale 1964) 63ff.; C.H. Turner, "Historical Introduction to the Textual Criticism of the New Testament. Part 2, *JThSt* 10 (1908-09) 175ff.; J.P. Brown, "An early revision of the Gospel of Luke" in *JBL* 78 (1959) 215-227; J. Martin, *The Reliability of The Gospels* (Hodder & Stoughton 1959).

before the beginning of the last century missionary enterprise in Africa, the missionaries did not import into Africa along with the Gospel the radical approach to the study of the Bible. Today, there must be well over a thousand various types of Theological Colleges in Africa which sprang up within the last 150 years. In spite of the high level of training obtaining in some of them, more than 90% of the schools are still unwilling to expose their students to the critical study of the Bible. In the University Departments of Religious Studies where students are exposed to the critical study of the Bible, sometimes students are not kept up-to-date in their studies. The present vogue in post-indepen-dence Africa is the study of African Indigenous Religion and Culture and Phenomenology of Religion. This has to be done in order to get the support of the various Governments. Consequently, the number of Biblical Scholars are still very few. Another problem is that the current concern of the majority of Biblicists and theologians in Africa is the contextualization of the Christian message, the indigenization of the Church and Christian theology in Africa. Hence it is difficult to point to any distinctive major contribution coming from Africa on the Synoptic Studies as of now.

But as for Christianity in Africa, the concern for the truth is still whole and unfragmented. The liberal scholars' approach to the ques-tion of Gospel history has not been the best or the right way to understand the milieu out of which the Gospels emerged. Consequently, this has affected the scholars' understanding of the Gospels, their nature, origins and interpretation. One of the major causes is that there is a wide gap between the thought-world of the Bible and that of the Western critics today. Today the majority of African Christians still regard the Bible as the word of God and sometimes interpret it literally. This uncritical approach is not because Africans have not developed sufficient scientific minds in order to be able to look at the Bible critically. Apparently, the reason is that the thought-world of Africa and that of the Bible are very similar. [12]

This obviously leads to the following pertinent questions: Of what value to African Christianity is the current debate on the Synoptic Gospels? What can African Christianity benefit from the critical study of the Gospels which has dominated the West for more than two centuries? Is it possible to pursue the question of the sequential order and literature of the Gospels purely from academic point of view, quite

---

[12] S.O. Abogunrin, "The Modern Search of the Historical Jesus and Christianity in Africa," *Africa Theological Journal* 9 (1980) 26.

unrelated to the attested primitive traditions of the immediate generations after the Apostolic age? Can African Christian Scholars brush aside the age-long accepted traditions and convictions of the Church from the beginning, in our endeavour to sound modern, before we can explain the phenomenon of the Gospels? In the light of the African experience is the multiplication of hypothetical sources the best solution to the Synoptic Problem? It is not possible to address ourselves fully to these important questions in an essay of this nature. Certainly African Christianity has benefited tremendously from the results of the cumulative labour of the Gospel researchers. It has kept African Christians aware of the questions being raised about the Gospels, which to them are perhaps the most important part of the New Testament.

The majority of African Christians still live in the world of the New Testament, where the belief in demons and a host of unseen supernatural powers was potent and real. A Jesus emptied of all the supernaturalism contained in the Gospels would be meaningless in the African context. Today, Africa has the largest number of prophets and miracle workers working after the example and promise of Jesus Christ. For African Christians, the Gospels themselves are more important than their putative sources. Ancient traditions are still much cherished in Africa. As of today, the history of most African peoples are still unwritten but their history still lives on in the form of oral traditions, songs, family eulogies and genealogies, most of which had taken definite forms centuries or many generations ago. Therefore, the concern for the truth and objectivity by serious scholars should not mean the rejection of the age-long traditions and beliefs. Instead it should be a commitment to thorough investigations of those traditions without preconceived notions.

The multiplication of hypothetical sources such as the Ur-Gospel, the Greek and Aramaic versions of the Gospel of the Nazarenes, the Oral Gospel, Ur-Marcus, Ur-Matthew, the Proto-Luke, the Logia, Q, Q a, Q b, Q c, Q d, M, L, the priority of Mark, the Recensions of the various Gospels, mutilated Gospels, etc. have failed to provide satisfactory solution to the Synoptic Problem. The modern approach to history is quite alien to the approach of the ancients. It is unacademic and unscientific to impose our present Western understanding and interpretation of history on the ancient people. The Gospels are essentially a product of faith and the experiences of committed individuals and the community of believers. The Gospels therefore require some kind of special treatment and understanding. Since both written and unwritten historical traditions are still cherished in Africa and oral traditions still remain the main sources of African history, it is necessary at this stage to critically examine what the ancient patristic traditions say about the sequential order of the Gospels before taking a position on the issue.

II. Patristic Traditions of the Sequential Order of the Gospels

a) Clement of Alexandria

The first most explicit statement on the sequential order of the Gospel comes from Clement of Alexandria, who was born around A.D. 155. Alexandria was the metropolis of Egypt throughout the Hellenistic and Roman period. In pre-Christian times, it had become preeminently the home of philosophy and theosophy. Judaism also flourished there at the turn of the century. The Alexandrian Greek translation of the Old Testament provided the early Church with a Greek Bible. Most of the quotations of the Hebrew Scriptures by the New Testament writers are based on this Greek translation. By the end of the second century Alexandria had become the leading centre of Christian theology and Biblical interpretation. The Alexandrian Christian School achieved its deserved fame and reached its highest peak of influence under the leadership of Titus Flavius Clemens and Origen his successor. During its heyday, the School greatly influenced the leaders of the Palestinian Church, notably Julius Africanus and Alexander of Jerusalem.[13] Clement, who lived in this important centre, travelled very widely. He visited important places like Palestine, Syria, Greece, Italy and Egypt. In his search for higher instruction and distinguished teachers, after his conversion, he made personal contacts with many Elders of the Mediterranean world. He finally met Pantaenus of Egypt of whom he says, "Like the Sicilian bee, he plucked flowers from the apostolic and prophetic meadow and filled the souls of his disciples with genuine, pure knowledge."[14]

Clement, the first Christian scholar, was a man of wide reading. He was versed in all branches of Greek literature and in all the systems of philosophy, as well as the Old and the New Testament Scriptures and the Apocryphal books. He was well familiar with the writings of the Gnostics and other heretics. He later suceeded Pantaenus as head of the Catechetical School in A.D. 190. Clement's charming literary temper, his attractive candour and unassailable courage made him the

---

[13] E.S. Moyer, *The Great Leaders of The Church*, Vol. I, (Chicago: Moody Bible Institute 1951) 67-69.
[14] Ibid. p. 67.

Christian giant of the end of the second century and a pioneer in Christian theology and Gospel Studies.

It was this well informed Christian Scholar whom Eusebius reported to have made the first important statement about the origin and sequential order of the canonical Gospels. In his sixth book of *Ecclesiastical History*, Eusebius reports as follows:

"And again in the same books Clement has inserted a tradition of the primitive elders with regard to the order of the Gospels as follows. He used to say that those Gospels were written first which include the genealogies and the Gospel according to Mark came into being in this manner: When Peter had publicly preached the word at Rome and by the Spirit had proclaimed the Gospel, that those present ... exhorted Mark (as one who had followed him, i.e. Peter) for a long time, ... to make a record of what was said: and that he did this and distributed ... the Gospel among those that asked him.... But that John, last of all, conscious that the outward facts had been set forth in the Gospels (i.e. those with geneaologies and Mark) was urged by his disciples ... and moved by the Spirit composed a spiritual Gospel."[15]

Clement's statement is perhaps the strongest and oldest external evidence for the Two Gospel Hypothesis, which means, in the first instance, that the Gospels of Matthew and Luke were written first and that Mark and John followed in that order. It is clear that Clement's statement has to do with the sequential order of the four Gospels (περὶ τῆς τάξεως τῶν εὐαγγελίων) — "concerning the order of the Gospels." As mentioned earlier on, Clement travelled extensively. This means that he must have established contacts with various Christian teachers before he met Pantaenus in the eighties of the second century. Of course, Clement apparently was not referring to his teachers here but to the traditions "of the primitive elders" (τῶν ἀνέκαθεν πρεσβυτέρων). Most probably some of the primitive elders might be those who knew the Gospel writers or at least those who knew their followers. Clement was a responsible Christian scholar, reputable for his academic excellence and competence. Clement, a man with such a disciplined critical mind, would not have uncritically accepted the traditions of the primitive elders if it was not well founded. He lived at a period when a few of the disciples of the Apostles and many who knew these disciples would still be alive. Besides, Clement made the statement in a city reputable for its high standard of scholarship, where a baseless thesis could not go unchallenged. Clement was therefore most likely citing an authentic tradition. The network of the sources of information available to

[15] Eusebius, *E. H.* 6.14:5-7; Clem. *Hypotyposeis* 6.

Clement was widespread and obviously covered the whole of the Mediterranean, the Near East, North Africa and parts of Europe.

However, W.R. Farmer raised an important issue on this point. According to him, it is difficult to know how closely Eusebius was citing Clement and to what extent he has paraphrased him. Moreover, it is not clear how much of the Clementine tradition came from "the primitive elders."[16] However, Eusebius is one of the most reliable ancient sources of information with regard to the early traditions of the Church. Eusebius, bishop and founder of the theological school at Caesarea, was the ecclesiastical and spiritual voice of the Constantinian age and the heir and master of the Origenist tradition, who, by his best known work *Ecclesiastical History,* liberated Christian chronology from the bonds of apocalypticism, basing it on purely chronological foundations. This work is the most important Church history of ancient times, invaluable not only for its wealth of material but for the preservation of the most ancient traditions of the Church. This man, born only about a generation after Clement, was well informed and most likely could not have misunderstood Clement. The fact that he preserved other apparent contradictory views on the sequential order of the Gospels suggests that he was an objective historian.

But Clement did not categorically state which of the Gospels with geneaologies was written first. Moreover, can the assertion "and that the Gospel according to Mark came into being in this manner" really refer to the sequential order of Mark? Clement obviously was referring to the Gospel order. Of course, "In this manner" is a brief information on how the Gospel was composed. But the fact that Clement was concerned with the sequential order is brought out clearly in the statement: "But that John, last of all, conscious that the outward facts had been set forth in the Gospels (i.e., with geneaologies and Mark) was urged by his disciples ... and divinely moved by the Spirit, composed a spiritual Gospel." If we accept that Clement is right with regard to the order of the Gospel of John, he is apparently pronouncing on the order of the first three Gospels also. The statement is clear enough and any muddling up cannot be convincingly proved. According to tradition, Mark was the acclaimed founder and first bishop of Alexandria.[17] If this tradition is authentic, there must be some well-founded historial reasons for placing the Gospel written by Mark third.

---

[16] W.R. Farmer, "The Patristic Evidence Re-examined: A Response to George Kennedy," in *New Synoptic Studies, The Cambridge Gospel Conference and Beyond,* ed. W.R. Farmer, (Macon: Mercer University Press 1983) 7-8.

[17] Eusebius *E. H.* 2.16.1.

At the time of Clement, the Church at Alexandria must be well-familiar with the traditions relating to the origin of the Gospel of its founder and first spiritual leader. But the pronouncements of some other early Church Fathers on the Gospels raise some problems about the validity of Clement's statement.

b) Papias

Irenaeus described Papias as the hearer of John and a companion of Polycarp, but Papias never made such claims in his five volumes titled: *Expositions of the Oracles of the Lord.* Eusebius quoting Papias says:

> "But I will not hesitate to set down for thy benefit, along with the interpretations, all that ever I carefully learnt and carefully recalled from the elders, guaranteeing its truth. For I did not delight, as most men do, in those who have much to say, but in those who teach what is true; not in those who recall foreign commandments, but in those who recall the commandments given by the Lord to faith and reaching us from the truth itself. And if anyone chanced to come who had actually been a follower of the elders, I would inquire as to the discourses of the elders, what Andrew or what Peter said or what Philip or what Thomas or James or John or Matthew or another of the Lord's disciples, and the things which Ariston and John the elder, disciples of the Lord, say. For I suppose that things out of books did not profit so much as the utterances, of a voice which liveth and abideth."[18]

This citation is intended to clarify the position of Papias in the history of the transmission of the apostolic tradition. Eusebius was concerned that Irenaeus claimed for Papias the honours which Papias never claimed for himself. He felt that Papias might have not known John and any of the apostles but agreed that he received the contents of the Faith from those who were the pupils of the Apostles. But inspite of Eusebius' criticism of Irenaeus, Papias is a figure who is eminently worthy of our close attention.[19] Papias' statement has nothing to do with the sequential order of the Gospels, but the names of the two Evangelic-Apostles are included among the list of the seven Apostles mentioned. Strangely enough, Andrew was listed before Peter and John before Matthew, though John is generally believed to be the last Gospel. Papias' comment is also important because it shows that during the first half of the second century there still existed the living voices of the disciples of the Apostles and that the oral testimonies of

---

[18] Eusebius *E.H.* 3.39; Irenaeus *adv. haer.* 5.33-4; quoted from *A New Eusebius, Documents Illustrative of the History of the Church to AD 337*, ed. J. Stephenson, London: S.P.C.K. 1970) 50f.

[19] N.B. Stonehouse, op. cit. p. 11

those who knew the Apostles were more cherished than books and also that the living voices of the Apostles were the yardsticks for testing the authenticity of any written or oral traditions. This means that the immediate post-apostolic age made every effort to see that the purest apostolic traditions were preserved.

On Mark, Papias says:

> "The Elder used to say this also: 'Mark became an interpreter of Peter and he wrote down accurately but not in order, as much as he remembered of the sayings and doings of Christ. For he was not a hearer or a follower of the Lord ... but of Peter who adapted his teachings to the needs of the moment and did not make an ordered expositions of sayings of the Lord. And so Mark made no mistake when he thus wrote down some things as he remembered them; for he made it his especial care to omit nothing of what he heard and to include no false statement therein.'"[20]

On Matthew, Papias says: "So then Matthew recorded the oracles (τὰ λόγια) in the Hebrew tongue and each interpreted them to the best of his ability."[21]

By the statement "the Elder used to say" Papias refers to what he heard constantly from the Elder. Although Mark was not a disciple of Jesus, he was a follower of Peter. Mark's chronology is certainly faulty, but this is primarily due to Mark's purpose and the fact that he based his account on the preaching of Peter and recorded things as he remembered them. Peter in his citations of the events of the Lord's life in his preaching was not concerned with chronology but with the needs of his Church and immediate environment. Obviously, Mark was criticised for its faulty chronology after its publication, but the usual explanation offered by Ariston and John the Elder whenever Mark's Gospel was criticised was that Mark's principal concern was the accurate reporting of events and not chronology. But was the criticism of Mark based on the chronologies of Matthew and Luke, which probably had been published earlier, or on the living voices of the Apostles and their followers? Or is it an indirect reference to the existence of other written documents then regarded as authentic but which are no longer extant today?

What Papias says on Matthew is not helpful. It is not clear whether the Logia of Matthew is the same as the canonical Matthew or whether it refers to an Ur-Gospel or to Ur-Matthew or to the Aramaic Gospel

---

[20] Eusebius, *E. H.* 3.39:3-4.
[21] Eusebius 2.39:16.

of the Nazarenes or to Q etc. Papias' statement on Matthew is not useful in relation to the Gospel order. Of course the fact that he mentioned Mark first does not mean that Mark wrote first. Papias has neither approved nor disproved Clement's position.

c) Irenaeus

Irenaeus, bishop of Lyons at the end of the second century stated that Matthew published his Gospel among the Hebrews in their tongue while Peter and Paul were preaching the Gospel and founding the Church in Rome. After their death, Mark, Peter's interpreter and disciple handed down to us in writing the substance of Peter's preaching. Luke, the follower of Paul, set down in a book the Gospel preached by his teacher. He concludes that John the disciple of the Lord produced his Gospel while he was living in Ephesus.[22] Irenaeus stature as a Churchman and theologian was distinguished. His early life being in Asia Minor, he must have had personal contacts with Polycarp and the Elders of Asia. He therefore was not just a spokesman for an isolated and remote section of the Church. Irenaeus was in a position of being better informed with regard to earlier traditions than many of his contemporaries.

The Gospel which Matthew published in the Hebrew tongue while Peter and Paul were still active in Rome might be Matthew, if the word "tongue" refers to the style or manner of writing rather than the spoken language. Of course there is no reason why the original Matthew could not have been written in Aramaic.[23] With regard to Mark and Luke, it does appear that Irenaeus was not particularly concerned with the sequential order but with the fact that they were rather composed after the death of the two Apostles. Irenaeus probably mentioned Mark first because it is concerned with Peter, the Prince of the Apostles. Nevertheless, Irenaeus believed Matthew to be first since he claimed that it was written while Peter and Paul were still active in Rome and that Mark

---

[22] Eusebius 5.5:1-4.

[23] The fact that almost all the Church Fathers who commented on the origin of the Gospels spoke of an Aramaic Gospel or a Gospel by Matthew published in the Hebrew tongue might mean that a kind of Gospel existed originally in Aramaic. Although it is generally accepted among scholars that the present Matthew was first written in Greek, it has not been proved conclusively that canonical Matthew could not have been a Greek translation of the original Aramaic Gospel. The fact that no such Gospel exists in Aramaic today does not invalidate the possibility. Some of the Gospels and letters mentioned by some of the Church Fathers are no longer extant and we cannot on that basis conclude that such documents never once existed though they may now be lost beyond redemption. The Aramaic Gospel of Matthew might have suffered the same fate through the vicissitudes of history.

and Luke were written after the death of the two Apostles. The word "afterwards" which introduces the statement on John's Gospel suggests that Irenaeus believed that it was the last Gospel. Irenaeus' main purpose was to combat the heretics and to connect the composition of the canonical Gospels with the Apostles and apostolic personalities.

The Muratorian Canon, which probably dates from the end of the second century, speaks clearly on Luke and John. It refers to the third Gospel as one composed by Luke, the physician and companion of Paul. Although he did not see the Lord in the flesh, he set down the events as far as he could then ascertain and began the story from the birth of John the Baptist. The Muratorian Canon says that St. John is the fourth Gospel. Origen and Augustine[24] also have the order — Matthew, Mark, Luke and John. According to Augustine, Mark closely followed Matthew and looked like his attendant and epitomizer.[25] Tertullian simply said: "Of the Apostles, therefore, John and Matthew instil faith into us. Of the apostolic men, Luke and Mark renew it."[26] In addition, the Latin manuscripts which contain the four canonical Gospels in the text previous to the revision of Jerome, the order which one commonly find is Matthew, John, Luke and Mark. This arrangement apparently reveals simultaneously the order of dignity and the sequential order of Clement, that is of the Apostles, Matthew, then John and of apostolic men, Luke, then Mark.

All the ancient traditions cited above unanimously agree on the fact that Matthew was the first Gospel and that John was last. They apparently differ only on which of Mark and Luke should be placed second and third. It is significant that the confusion borders on the Gospels written by the apostolic men. Eusebius reported these apparently contradictory views on the sequential order of the Gospels without any personal comment. He was aware of the Clementine tradition which places Luke before Mark. Moreover Origen, a pupil of Clement, must be aware of Clement's testimony. If Origen had thought that his own order rather than that of Clement was the historical order, would Origen, that giant scholar and theologian, not have stated that categorically? The placing of Mark before Luke was most likely due to the influence of the Church at Rome, probably reflecting the priority of Peter over Paul (the two Apostles associated with the two Evangelists), rather than the order of composition. The order of Matthew, John,

[24] W.R. Farmer, *New Synoptic Studies*, 25.

[25] It is true that on a few occasions Mark gives the impression of epitomizing the Matthean material. But on the whole, Mark was rather amplifying Matthew.

[26] N.B. Stonehouse, op. cit. p. 7.

Luke and Mark is aimed at introducing the readers first to the Gospels written by the Apostles so that such readers may assess the Gospels by the apostolic men in the light of those written by the Apostles. Similarly the order of Matthew, Mark, Luke and John is to help the readers to read the Gospels by the Apostles first and last so that such readers may view the Gospels written by the followers of the Apostles in the light of the first and last Gospels.

The so-called Monarchian Prologue to St. Mark's Gospel which has been dated at the end of the fourth century, practically at the time of Jerome, shares the opinion of Clement with regard to the chronological order of the four canonical Gospels.[27] But the Monarchican Prologue to Luke's Gospel by contrast maintains that Luke is the third Gospel written under the impulse of the Holy Spirit in Achaia; after Matthew and Mark had been composed in Judea and Italy respectively. But the statement is made without any documentary evidence or historical explanation and authority. The Monarchian Prologue to Mark is based on Clement's two century old evidence, which he too based on the general opinion of the primitive Elders.

However, it is not possible to settle categorically the question of the extent to which we should really trust the unanimous testimony of the Church Fathers, that Matthew was written before all the other canonical Gospels and that John was written last. Although the evidence of the Church Fathers are quite late and dated between the third and fourth centuries, nevertheless they are about sixteen hundred years closer to the actual events than us today. Therefore, the patristic evidence cannot be dismissed as totally irrelevant. Matthew and Luke belong to the two mainline church traditions — Jewish and Gentile. Matthew retains features which were peculiarly Jewish and reflects the interest of the earlier Jewish mission while Luke retains features reflecting the Gentile interest and was more suited for use in the Gentile Churches. Since most of these traditions came from the Church Fathers in the Gentile Churches, one would have expected them to give priority and pride of place to Luke and not to Matthew. The attribution of priority and pride of place to a predominantly Jewish Gospel obviously reveals the reliable historical candour of the Gentile Churches with regard to the sequential order of the four Gospels.[29]

---

[27] J. Regul, *Die antimarcionistischen Evangelienprologe* p. 263; W.R. Farmer, *New Synoptic Studies* pp. 23f.

[28] Ibid. p. 23.

[29] W.R. Farmer, *The Synoptic Problem* p. 225.

III. WHICH WAY FORWARD?

The four Gospels are the most important Christian basic books. Their supreme importance lies in the fact that they are our major sources of the Lord's life and teaching. Without them our information about the nature of Jesus' life, person and character would be very scanty. Therefore the question of the sequential order of the Gospels is as important as their sources. In the light of the above, the Two Gospel Hypothesis appears to be the most viable, having the strong support of both the external and internal evidence. We shall, therefore, pitch our tent with Clement of Alexandria by postulating that Matthew is the earliest Gospel and that Luke is apparently the next in order. Luke obviously made use of Matthew but in addition had access to some other written and oral sources. Luke was dependent on Matthew for the general order and form of his Gospel. The third Gospel was Mark, who closely worked with the texts of Matthew and Luke which were then available to him. Surely, one cannot deny the fact that both Matthew and Luke must have had some written and unwritten sources in common. Nevertheless, appeals to such hypothetical sources may not be the best way of explaining the puzzle of similarities, extensive verbal agreement and order of arrangement, as well as the dissimilarities, in the Synoptic Gospels.[30] While the existence of hypothetical documents should be accepted as a probability, this does not necessarily have to be the starting point for an impartial investigator of the Synoptic Problem. It does appear that it is still possible to solve the Synoptic Problem without appealing to an unreasonably high number of hypothetical documents.

The puzzle of the Synoptic Gospels becomes less complicated when Mark is placed third, because Mark tends to agree more closely with Matthew when they follow an order different from Luke, but more closely with Luke when they follow an order different from Matthew.[31] The fact that Matthew and Luke hardly agree in order against Mark is rather a strong point against the priority of Mark. It is easier to explain that Mark was writing third with no chronological information of his own apart from those contained in Matthew and Luke. Moreover, many of the reasons still being advanced for the priority of Mark are due to Mark's literary ability and the fact that he had the advantage of knowing both Matthew and Luke. A striking example of Matthew —

---

[30] Ibid. pp. 200-201.
[31] Ibid. p. 211.

Luke agreement against Mark is the dating of the cleansing of the Temple which Matthew and Luke dated Sunday, the Triumphal Entry day, but which Mark dated Monday, the following day. It is easier for the Evangelist writing third to shift position always and follow one Evangelist. Whenever Matthew's and Luke's orders vary, scholars who advocate the priority of Mark have not been able to explain satisfactorily how Matthew and Luke would sometimes independently reproduce the Marcan order and content for their Gospels.

On the issue of Patristic traditions, there are two current extreme views on this. These are: 1) that the external evidence does not contain sufficient data for scientific criticism because the witnesses cannot be relied upon to preserve authentic traditions since their approach was unscientific; and 2) that the testimony of the ancient witnesses is inviolable and therefore unquestionably true. While it is true that some of the ancient traditions have been found to be inaccurate, it is wrong to assume that only statements which can be analysed in accordance with modern scientific formulae can be valid. Although the Church Fathers lived in an age which was largly non-critical and "unscientific," most of their testimonies have been able to survive the rigorous scientific analysis of our age. Minor apparent contradictions and faults in the tradition cited by some Church Fathers should not lead to a wholesale rejection of these traditions.

In Africa today, the primary source of history is still largely oral tradition. The fact that investigators are often confronted with apparently conflicting traditions may not necessarily impugn the validity of such historical facts. It is often left to such investigators to scientifically analyse their collections and determine whether the contradictions are real or only apparent. It is significant that all of the ancient evidence is generally unanimous on the first and last Gospels; the problem lies with Mark and Luke. It is important to note that our imagination about what could have happened about two thousand years ago may not actually reflect the true position of things then.[32] Furthermore, it is a very dangerous procedure to brush aside external evidence which is basic to any serious scientific historical evidence. To discuss the Synoptic Problem on the basis of internal evidence to the exclusion of external evidence will amount to discussing the whole problem in an historical vacuum, which consequently must lead to wrong conclusions. It is equally unscientific to base one's findings in a matter of this nature on external evidence to the total neglect of the internal testimony.

[32] D. Guthrie, op. cit. p. 221.

Similarly, perhaps if the place of oral tradition in the composition of the Gospels could be satisfactorily determined, the Synoptic Problem would be half-solved. According to E.J. Goodspeed:

> The earliest Gospel was unwritten. It arose in that Jewish atmosphere in which the pious course was not to write and read but to compose and memorise. Jewish ways of treating the interpretation of the Law affected their first treatment of their memories of Jesus, whose sayings early Jewish Christians naturally preserved as they did those of their great rabbis in memorized form. [33]

Goodspeed correctly pointed out that there was a period of the oral transmission of the Gospel before the written Gospels came into existence. But the exact period of the oral transmission is difficult to fix.

The oral transmission of the Gospel is related to the Form Criticism of the Gospels, which, though it is not an alternative to the Source Criticism of the Gospels, arose in consequence of the weakness of source criticism. Source criticism confines itself to existing documents. All that the source criticism of the Gospels has been able to show over the centuries is the multiplication of hypothetical sources. Form criticism seeks to fill the gap of between thirty to forty years before the first written Gospel appeared. But form criticism failed to achieve its laudable objectives of discovering how the traditions now contained in the Gospels first took concrete forms before being committed to writing. This was so because it was a challenge to the historicity of Mark which had been assigned priority and on which the other two Evangelists were said to have depended. Form Criticism was therefore a challenge to the historicity of the three Synoptic Gospels. Secondly it was an attempt to modernize the Gospels. The form critics assumed that the Gospel traditions at the oral stage were conditioned by missionary needs. They argued that the stories were created by professional story tellers and that such stories existed in isolated units. The form critics were of the view that Mark later on imposed his own framework on what were previously independently circulating units. The negative approach of the form critics has not allowed them to propose positive solutions to the problem. [34]

Undoubtedly, before the written Gospels appeared, many of the Gospel traditions had taken definite forms. This would mean that

[33] E.J. Goodspeed, *The Formation of The New Testament*, (Chicago: University of Chicago Press 1927) 33.

[34] S.O. Abogunrin, *Africa Theological Journal*, p. 22; R. Bultmann, *Jesus Christ and Mythology* (London: S.C.M. Press 1958); "The New Approach to the Synoptic Problem" (1926) in *Existence and Faith*, trans. S. Ogden, (Cleveland and New York: World/ Collins, 1960) 39ff.

correspondence among the Synoptic Gospels must not be traced to hypothetical written sources alone but also to the forms of oral tradition before the first written Gospel appeared. The stories of Jesus' sayings, parables, healings, miracles, etc. must have been told and retold in the early Church. Within this period of thirty to forty years of oral transmission, those traditions must have assumed concrete forms. Many forms of Jesus' sayings must have been memorized and some translated into Church hymns. The constant appeal to hypothetical sources by modern scholars gives the impression that they believe that the Evangelists were so ignorant and uninformed about the traditions of Jesus before they began to write that they had to depend on existing written documents for the composition of their Gospels. But the Evangelists were prominent members of the early church where those traditions took definite forms and they were certainly familiar with those traditions and their formation.

Today in Africa, many languages are yet to be reduced to writing and many of those that have been reduced to writing either have only parts of the Scriptures in their own languages or nothing at all. Moreover, a large percentage of African Christians are still illiterate. In such places, the Bible Stories still circulate in the form of oral tradition. Like the Apostles who were eyewitnesses, the Gospel stories are told by those who can read the Bible either in English or French. Most of these illiterate Christians know many stories of the Bible and know a large portion of the Scriptures by heart. Obviously a situation similar to this must have occured in the primitive Church, especially with regard to some of the early writings during the oral stage that were used for catechical purposes.

Another example is the *Ifa*[35] system among the Yoruba[36] of West Africa. The *Ifa Corpus* is the Yoruba unwritten sacred scriptures. The *Ifa Corpus* contains sixteen major chapters and 256 sub-chapters. It takes at least seven years of full-time apprenticeship to begin to learn the scriptures by heart and to know the various myths which fully explain the meaning of each sub-chapter. However, there are so many of these subsidiary myths that it is not possible for any Ifa priest or expert to memorize all of the myths and their interpretations. That is

[35] *Ifa* refers to the divination instruments and the belief system which Orunmila, the Oracular divinity, introduced into the world. Orunmila was present when God created everything else and he is therefore called Elerin Ipin (the Witness of Destiny), i.e. one who knows the essential nature of every creature. His name represents the divine wisdom.

[36] The Yoruba people are the largest single ethnic group in West Africa, found mainly in Nigeria and the Republic of Benin.

why, after the seven-year training, graduates still go from one teacher to another to learn even more. A sub-chapter, which may be about ten to forty verses of a Psalm, may have more than ten different myths that explain the meanings, purpose and application of the passage to physical, moral and spiritual life. It is in the *Ifa corpus* that we find the most ancient and purest traditions about the Yoruba people and the related groups, God, divinities, the myths of the Creation — the universe, man, the other living beings on earth, and finally the here-after. The Yoruba ancient scriptures are memorized and recited in poetical forms like Quranic students. In spite of the fact that many of the experts today are literate and well-informed, the old system of memorization and recitation is the only way of learning and practicing.

Earlier on, we related the testimony of Irenaeus, that as late as the third decade of the second century, people still preferred the living voice of those who knew the Apostles to anything written. Therefore, similar-ities and divergencies in details may, to some extent, be due to the forms of oral traditions at different important centres from which the Gospels originated. Sometimes, in Africa what is important is not the variants but the central truth. For example the Yoruba have at least two versions of the Creation story but the central truth in the myths is that God is the Source-Being who gave origin to all else. Similarly, there are at least five myths about the Fall, but the central point stressed by all the myths is the fact that a woman was responsible for the strained relationship between Heaven and Earth.[37] The period of the oral transmission of the Gospel, therefore, needs a critical look. A positive open-minded approach, rather than the negative approach of the form critics, may yield fruitful results.

On the Marcan priority, serious doubts have been raised about John Mark's authorship of our canonical Mark. The most scholarly objec-tion so far raised is the one by Pierson Parker.[38] He claims that our second Gospel is secondary in character and cannot be the work of any Jew or Jewish Christian; and of course, it is certainly neither that of Peter nor that of his follower. In support of his argument for the secondary quality of Mark, Parker pointed to the author's ignorance of the geography of Palestine. Furthermore, Parker said that the author of Mark was ignorant of the politics of Palestine when he referred to

---

[37] S.O. Abogunrin, "St Paul's Idea of the Pre-Gospel Man according to Romans" in *Kiabara* Port Harcourt University Journal of Humanities 31 (1980) 5-31.

[38] P. Parker, "The Posteriority of Mark" in *New Synoptic Studies*, ed. W. R. Farmer, pp. 67-142.

Herod Antipas as king, in contrast to Matthew and Luke who called him tetrarch. Parker quoted about nine instances of the Mark's use of alleged Aramaic words and phrases and ably demonstrated that the author knew little Hebrew or Aramaic (Mk.3:17; 5:41; 7:11, 34; 8:10; 9:50; 10:46; 14:36; 15:34). Parker also claimed that Mark was ignorant of Judaism and made mistakes in quoting the Old Testament Scriptures. He raised question about Mark's knowledge of history, his chronology of Jesus' ministry and Jesus' relationship with the Twelve. Parker argued further that if this Gospel indeed stemmed from Peter, the Prince of the Apostles, it should have been the most prized book in the early church. Instead it was almost studiedly ignored until after A.D. 150 and was even less used than the other Gospels until the 19th Century radicalism. Although the modern scholars do not always agree on the sources used by Mark, there is the general agreement that he drew on prior written documents. Yet of all the conceivable Evangelists, the two least in need of written sources would have been Peter or his adopted "son" John Mark. He concluded that the author was partisan of the Gentile faction of the Church, one who was highly impatient with the leadership of Peter and the Twelve. The vividness and theological finesse of the Gospel of Mark, concluded Parker, was due to his skill as a writer and his Roman theological point of view.

While some of the points raised by Parker about Mark's knowledge of the geography of Palestine, his chronology, his citation of the Old Testament texts and his wrong use of Aramaic words are valid, such problems are not necessarily peculiar to Mark. It is possible for scholars to find points in favour of the priority of Mark here, concluding that Matthew and Luke wrote later in order to correct these weaknesses of Mark. However, there may be other equally plausible explanations. The problems may have been caused by Mark's low level of education and literary ability. The fact that Mark came from Jerusalem might mean that he did not knew Palestine well. Perhaps the first time he travelled outside of Jerusalem as a young man was when he accompanied Paul and Barnabas on their first missionary journey. Parker's thesis has no support of any external evidence and the internal evidence on which he based his hypothesis lacks sufficient strength needed to add credence to his idea of a Gentile Italian theologian other than Mark as the author of Mark.

Clement had claimed that the Gospels with genealogies were written first. Many critical scholars agree that the genealogies were old and of Palestinian origin. Both Hebraic and Qumran influences may be uncovered from Lucan and Matthean infancy narratives. Both infancy narratives appear to belong to older sources of tradition and perhaps to the early fragments of writings used for both missionary and apologetic purposes. Generally speaking, genealogies in the Bible and Africa are more than a mere listing of the names of the ancestors or families, communities and individuals or simply a registration of people, as in modern census. Paul in his letters gives the indication of the importance of genealogy. Genealogies as given in the Bible have their various uses in unfolding the history of redemption. By means of geneaological records, Matthew has summarised the history of redemption from the call of Abraham to the coming of Christ, and Luke from Adam, the father of the whole human race, to advent of the Redeemer.

But what about the problem of discrepancies between Matthew and Luke? The agreement between the two lists is only from Abraham to David. In Africa, and especially among the Yoruba and the related groups, family tables as contained in various family eulogies, always include a long list of the ancestors and the achievements of each of them are summarized in a few sentences. In fact each of the Yoruba names is a full sentence. The family eulogies always contain the purest and most reliable history of a family or people. For example, among the Yoruba, in the naming ceremony of a child the grandparents name the child first, then the parents, and then other close relatives give names to the child. At birth I was given the following names by parents and close relations: Kolade, Oyinloye, Aransiola, Ajibade, Olabanji, Olatunji, Jimoh, Aina, Ajirinnibi, Ajide and later on, the baptismal name Samuel. Any of those who gave me names at birth and is still alive calls me by the name he or she gave me at birth. Therefore, if you ask for my name among the members of my family, the name you are given sometimes may depend on the person from whom you ask. Moreover several names in a family eulogy may refer to one individual rather than several ancestors. For example my family eulogy goes thus: (1) the Son of Aramuduye (2) the Son of Onileowo (3) the Son of Olaluwoye (4) the son of Akangbe, Jaiyeola (5) the Son of Omolewa, Emeso (6) the Son of Petu, Fatunke (7) the Son of Abolarin (8) the Son of Olayode (9) and the Son of Isola, Abogunrin. The list of the thirteen names in 1-9 refers to four ancestors only. Numbers 1-2 is the grandfather of 2-4. The name of the father of 2-4 has not survived in the family eulogy, probably because he died too young or for some other reason; 5-6 refer to the father of the mother of 7-9 who belonged to a different family but his names are included in our family genealogical tree because Owolewa Emeso Petu Fatunke was a great historical figure; and 7-9 refer to my father. Could it be that something similar to this has happened to Luke's genealogical tree and that some of the names on his list properly belong to Mary's family? This could easily happen if Mary was Luke's informant here. The list therefore may be a mixture of Joseph's and Mary's family genealogical tables.

But if Mark was copying Matthew and Luke why would he have left out the birth narratives? The same question may be asked as to why Mark ended at the middle of the resurrection story. One obvious reason is that Mark is third and that he felt that this was unnecessary since Matthew and Luke had already dealt adequately with this. Again, the birth narratives were included by the first two Evangelists for apologetic reasons to answer the Jewish charges of unchastity against Mary and the assigning of divinity to Christ by the early Church. But the major reason for the Marcan omission of the birth narratives might be due to his own limitations when he was confronted with two apparently contradictory accounts and he was not in a position to decide which of the accounts to adopt. Furthermore, some scholars have suspected a great omission between Mark 1:1: Ἀρχὴ τοῦ εὐαγγελίου Ἰησοῦ Χριστοῦ [υἱοῦ θεοῦ] and 1:2: καθὼς γέγραπται ἐν τῷ Ἡσαίᾳ προφήτῃ ... Could it be that Mark intends to go ahead to give the account of the birth of Jesus after the statement: "The beginning of the Gospel of Jesus Christ (the Son of God)". If this assumption be true, this may well explain the reason why Mark breaks off in the middle of the resurrection story (16:8) and that the various reasons advanced so far for the break at that point may not be accurate.[41] After the accounts of the empty tomb in Matthew and Luke, Mark was confronted with the Matthean account of the resurrection appearance in Galilee and the Lucan account of the resurrection apperances in Judea. Mark was probably forced to a halt here, apparently because he did not know which of the traditions to follow since they appeared to him to be irreconcilable. He probably was not able to conclude the Gospel either before his death or before the Gospel went into circulation.

Similarly the so-called Great Omission of Mark by Luke can best be explained by assuming that the section was never part of Luke and that Mark writing third had taken over the material from Matthew. The fact that most of Mark is paralleled in Matthew and Luke suggests that

[39] J.G. Machen, *The Virgin Birth of Christ*, (Grand Rapids: Baker Book House 1980); R. E. Brown, *The Virginal Conception and Bodily Resurrection of Jesus*, (London: G. Chapman 1974); R.E. Brown, S.S. *The Birth of The Messiah. A Commentary On the Infancy Narratives of Matthew and Luke* (New York: Image Books 1979).

[40] C.F.D. Cranfield, *The Gospel According to St. Mark* (Cambridge 1959).

[41] S.O. Abogunrin, "The Four Current Endings of St. Mark, A Problem of Authenticity" in *ORITA Ibadan Journal of Religious Studies*, 13 (1981) 29-38.

Mark must have had the advantage of making use of the two earlier Gospels. As for chronology, the person writing third has the advantage of deciding which order he prefers whenever the two Gospels do not agree or even to break with the two of them where they both have a common order. An example of this is the cleansing of the Temple.

CONCLUSION

It is clear from the above that the less controversial solution to the Synoptic Problem, which can boast of both internal and external support, is the Two-Gospel Hypothesis. This position assigns priority to Matthew and claims that Matthew is the major source of Luke, who wrote second, while Mark the third Gospel drew on Matthew and Luke. This is not to suggest that the less controversial hypothesis is necessarily the correct solution. But all the earliest and most reliable witnesses of the Church Fathers affirmed the priority of Matthew and according to Clement, the Gospels with genealogies, Matthew and Luke, were written before Mark and John. The Two-Gospel Hypothesis is therefore based on the second century witness of Clement. The onus of proof lie on those who in the 18th and 19th centuries deny the testimony of those who lived closer to the events they described.

The Two-Gospel Hypothesis does not deny the use of sources by the Evangelists, but it denies an extensive appeal to a ridiculously unlimited number of hypothetical sources to explain the phenomena of the Synoptic Problem. Augustine is correct when he asserts that no one of the Evangelists wrote in ignorance of the work of his predecessor. Thus according to the Two-Gospel Hypothesis, Matthew write first, Luke wrote next making use of Matthew and Mark wrote third drawing on Matthew and Luke. Scholars who advocate the priority of Mark require us to accept numerous and confusing hypothetical sources and this has made a satisfactory solution to the Synoptic Problem more difficult. The Two-Gospel Hypothesis does not base its arguments on the internal evidence alone but assumes the existence of some written forms of the Gospel traditions. This is made plain in the preface to the Gospel of Luke. But none of these early writings in Aramaic and Greek could be described as a Gospel. Undoubtedly the three Evangelists benefitted from such documents circulating in isolated units. Nevertheless, such fragmentary documents apparently did not constitute the major sources of the Evangelists. All hypotheses which fail to take cognisance of the significant role and contribution of the eye-witnesses and their followers in the formulation of the Gospel traditions do not rest on a sure foundation since the apostolic witness to the events of Christ is really the foundation of the Gospel stories.

But how did Mark, which had been neglected for about 1700 years, suddenly come into prominence during the last two centuries? The Reformation and the Enlightenment stimulated a renewed interest in the study of the Bible. Ecclesiastical pronouncements and Church tradition could no longer shield the Scriptures from impartial investigations. Since the rejection of tradition was now the vogue, it was logical for radical Biblical Scholars to reject the traditional view on the sequential order of the Gospels and to think of alternatives. Apparently, they felt that the solution to the Synoptic Problem might be found in the neglected Gospel of Mark. Greater interest in the Gospel of Mark therefore developed to the neglect of ancient traditions, the role of the eye-witnesses and their disciples and the formative oral period. Consequently, this led to the raising of the third Gospel to the position of the first Gospel. And in spite of the many difficulties created by this conclusion, the majority of Protestant scholars have slavishly accepted this as solution for over a century.

The supreme task of New Testament Scholarship in Africa is not in further complicating the already confused and confusing situation, by making its own addition to the number of hypothetical sources of the Gospels, but to make Christ crucified a living reality in the thought of our time and to renew in it once again the awe and wonder of the Christian faith and the courage the risen Lord Jesus Christ inspired in the Evangelists.[42] This is not to say that African Christianity is not interested in the current critical probings and debates. If African Christianity should neglect this aspect, how can it be well-equipped to face the challenge of today and the future? Of course, if Christian faith is to be rational, it cannot avoid philosophical probings and the evidence it uses to support its biblical interpretations must be convincing.[43] The appeal for faith and commitment cannot ultimately be separated from historical and literary investigations. The reality of the situation is that all the conclusions which reject tradition in favour of the priority of Mark have succeeded in further complicating the Synoptic Problem. It is now difficult for a scholar to remember all the proposed hypothetical sources. The sharp disagreements among scholars on the nature of and which material belong to the various hypothetical sources further complicate the issue. The solution to the

---

[42] S.O. Abogunrin, *Africa Theological Journal* 9 (1980) 28.

[43] S.O. Abogunrin, "The Language and Nature of the Resurrection in the New Testament," in *Journal of the Evangelical Theological Society* 24 (1981) 55-65.

Synotic Problem, therefore, may never be found in the multiplication of hypothetical sources but in tradition and an objective and closer study of the texts of the Gospels, upon which no preconceived frame-work has been imposed, before the scholarly study begins.

In the New Testament, the Gospel was first preached by Jesus and subsequently by his disciples. Jesus came not only to preach the Gospel but in order that there might be a Gospel to preach. The four Gospels form the main source of our knowledge of the Lord's life. This is why scholars have given so much attention to them. It is customary to regard the Gospels as the chronological accounts of the Lord's life, but they are not strictly speaking biographies. Each of them concentrates only on a small part of Jesus' life; their main purpose was to record facts as well as their theological implications. It is in fact not by accident that they were called Gospels. The Evangelists were not literary men and they did not pretend to be so. They had no interest in conforming to the traditional pattern which modern scholars often look for or impose on them. Their sole aim was to relate the events of the life of a Man who had radically changed their lives. The four Evangelists, though each of them writing from his distinctive point of view, all agree in presenting us with a heart-compelling picture of Jesus as the Messiah of Israel, the saviour of the World, the Servant of the Lord and the Friend of sinners, the Son of God and the Son of Man. The Gospels were written in the Church and for the Church. They all agree on the purpose and mission of the Church on earth.

It is important to realize that the Gospels themselves are more important than their putative sources. While it is good to consider their hypothetical sources, it is better still to consider the use of those hypothetical sources by the Evangelists. What is important for Christian theology and preaching in Africa is not the multiplication of hypothetical sources, such as the the so-called Original Gospel, Ur-Marcus, Ur-Matthew, the Logia, the priority of Mark, Proto-Luke, various Qs etc., or the academic theories aimed at proving the reality of those hypothetical sources, but the contents of the Gospels themselves and their interpretation in the light of the situations which gave birth to them.

The Two-Gospel Hypothesis is historically and literarily sound. In Africa, the Jesus whose message can be meaningful in the African local situation is the Jesus whose history is contained in the Gospels. It is this Jesus, the Eternal World of God, that can indeed become flesh and dwell within the local environments of Africa. Metaphorically speaking, it is He who can become incarnate, as it were, in the totality of the lives and situation of the people to whom He is preached in Africa. A Yoruba adage says: "If one no longer knows where he is going, the best thing is to return home." If the two centuries-old effort to find a solution to the Synoptic Problem has produced no more satisfactory or acceptable solution that the multiplication of hypothetical sources, there may be some wisdom in the serious academic re-examination of the Patristic traditions and the Two-Gospel Hypothesis. The solution may ultimately be found there.

Samuel Oyinloye ABOGUNRIN

NOTE: This paper was first published in *African Journal of Biblical Studies* 2 (1987) 25-51: "The Synoptic Gospel Debate: A Re-Examination in the African Context."

JOHN AND THE SYNOPTICS

I. An Independent Oral and/or Written Tradition?

The relationship of John to the Synoptic Gospels is a problem yet to be solved in New Testament research. Until World War II the predominant view was that John used one, two or all Synoptic Gospels. After the research done on this material by P. Gardner-Smith shortly before the outbreak of the War, a trend away from that position gained momentum. A new consensus seemed to emerge: John was independent of the synoptics.[1]

Many scholars who followed this trend assume that John utilizes an ancient oral tradition independent of the other gospels. A major work along this avenue of research was C.H. Dodd's book *Historical Tradition in the Fourth Gospel* (Cambridge 1963, reprint 1965). Dodd attempted to uncover the traditional material in John by comparing it with what is most obviously related to the Synoptic Gospels, namely, the passion narratives. He then proceeds with the analysis to the materials where there are fewer and fewer apparent synoptic contacts: the narratives of Jesus' ministry, those regarding John the Baptist and the first disciples, and, finally, the discourse materials.

Among the scholars who more or less accept the theory that John builds on oral tradition which is wholly, or mainly, independent of the Synoptics are: R. Bultmann (1955, etc.); P. Borgen (1959); D.M. Smith (1963, etc.); R. Schnackenburg (1965); C.H. Dodd (1965); A. Dauer (1972).[2]

---

[1] Cf. D. Moody Smith, Jr., "John and the Synoptics: Some Dimensions of the Problems," *NTS* 26 (1980), 425-26; F. Neirynck, "John and the Synoptics," in M. de Jonge (ed.), *L'évangile de Jean*, BETL 44 (Leuven, 1977), 73ff.

[2] R. Bultmann, "Zur johanneischen Tradition," *ThLZ* 60 (1955) 524; P. Borgen, "John and the Synoptics," *NTS* 5 (1959), 246-259, reprinted in id., *'Logos was the True Light' and other Essays on the Gospel of John* (Trondheim, 1983) 67-80; D. Moody Smith, Jr., "The Source of the Gospel of John: An Assessment of the Present State of the Problem," *NTS* 10 (1963/64) 336-51; E. Haenchen, "Johanneische Probleme," *ZTK* 56 (1959), 19-54; R.E. Brown, *The Gospel according to John* I: I-XII; II: XIII-XXI (Garden City, N.Y., 1966 and 1970); see also id., "Incidents that are Units in the Synoptic Gospels but Dispersed in St. John," *CBQ* 23 (1961) 143-60; B. Lindars, "Two Parables in John," *NTS* 16 (1969/70) 318-29; id., *The Gospel of John* (London 1972); R. Schnackenburg, *Das Johannesevangelium: I. Einleitung und Kommentar zu Kap. 1-4; II. Kommentar zu Kap. 5-12; III. Kommentar zu Kap. 13-21* (Freiburg, 1965, 1971 and 1975); C.H. Dodd, *Historical*

In his survey of the writings of Dodd and others, R. Kysar makes the following observations: "...Dodd's proposal along with others like it raises anew the persistent questions about the nature of the early Christian traditions — questions which must be answered before proposals such as Dodd's can prove very helpful. For example, exactly how rich and creative was the pre-literary history of the gospel materials?... What is needed, it seems to me, is a more highly developed method of johannine form criticism; and until such methodology can be developed, our efforts in this regard may satisfy little more than the fancy. Dodd began our effort toward the development of a johannine form critical method but that method still remains essentially primitive and crude years after his initial endeavours."[3]

In recent years the view that John is dependent upon the Synoptic Gospels has gained new impetus. For example, F. Neirynck and M. Sabbe reject theories of "unknown" and "hypothetical" sources behind John, whether they are supposed to be written or oral.[4] Neirynck writes that "...not traditions lying behind the Synoptic Gospels but the Synoptic Gospels themselves are the sources of the Fourth Evangelist."[5] Similarly M. Sabbe concludes his study of John 18:1-11 in this way: "For better understanding of the relation between John and the Synoptic Gospels and for a more homogeneous explanation of John's text as a whole, the awareness of the redactional creativeness of John combined with a direct dependence upon the Synoptics, is more promising."[6]

A more complex hypothesis has been suggested by M.-É. Boismard.[7] In agreement with Neirynck, he believes that the author of the Fourth Gospel knew all three Synoptic Gospels. While Neirynck explains the differences between John and the Synoptics as the work of the Evangelist himself, Boismard attributes these differences, as well as the similarities, to various types of sources. According to Boismard, the author of

---

Tradition in the Fourth Gospel (Cambridge, 1965); A. Dauer, *Die Passionsgeschichte im Johannesevangelium* (München, 1972).

[3] R. Kysar, *The Fourth Evangelist and His Gospel* (Minneapolis, Minn., 1975) 66-67.

[4] F. Neirynck, "John and the Synoptics" (1977), 103-106; id., *Jean et les Synoptiques. Examen critique de l'exégèse de M.-É. Boismard* (Leuven, 1979); M. Sabbe, "The Arrest of Jesus in Jn 18,1-11 and its Relation to the Synoptic Gospels," in M. de Jonge (ed.), *L'Évangile de Jean* (Leuven, 1977), 205-234.

[5] F. Neirynck, "John and the Synoptics" (1977), 106.

[6] M. Sabbe, "The Arrest of Jesus,"233.

[7] M.É. Boismard, *L'évangile de Jean.* In *Synopse de quatre évangiles en français,* ed. P. Benoit and M.-É. Boismard (Paris, 1977). For surveys, cf. F. Neirynck, "John and the Synoptics," 82-93; D. Moody Smith, "John and the Synoptics," *Biblica,* 63 (1982) 106-111.

the Gospel of John, whom he calls Jn II-B (ca. 90-100 A.D.), revised his own first recension of the Gospel which Boismard calls Jn II-A. The primary source behind Jn II-A is Document C (Jn I, ca. 50 A.D.), which is also one of the sources behind the Synoptic Gospels. Finally, a later redactor (Jn III) worked over the finished Gospel, making some changes and additions.[8]

Against this background it seems pertinent to look afresh on Paul's letters in order to gain insight into pre-synoptic usage of gospel materials. In this way we may find evidence as to the form and the method employed in the transmission of tradition and thus make the hypothesis of oral tradition less hypothetical.

Among the passages containing traditional gospel material in Paul's letter, the passages on the Lord's supper in 1 Cor 10:3-4.16.17.21 and 11:23-29 (34) stand out. Only here does Paul use a unit of gospel tradition of some length.[9] What can we learn from these passages about agreements with the Synoptics and about the nature of the pre-synoptic use of gospel materials?

1. A comparison between I Cor 10:3-4.16.17.21; 11.23-29 and Mark 14:22-25 makes possible the following generalizations: Between mutually independent versions (units of oral/written tradition) there may be close verbal agreement in the form of sentences, word pairs and set-phrases, single words and/or corresponding variant terms.

The agreement between John 2:13-22; 6:51-58 and the Synoptics are not closer, nor more striking, than those between the above mentioned Pauline passages and Mark, and, in the case of John 5:1-18, the agreements with the Synoptics are even fewer.

Thus, our analysis of these three Johannine passages supports the hypothesis that John and the Synoptics are mutually independent.

2. What is the nature of the tradition behind the gospels? The passages examined in I Cor 10 and 11 show that units of tradition were received and handed on and that they were used and activated in the Christian communities (I Cor 11:23-25(26)). Some modifications took place in the process, but the formulations were quite stable even during decades of transmission (cf. I Cor 11:23-26 with Mk 14:22-25).

---

[8] Cf. F. Neirynck, *Jean et les Synoptiques*, 9-16.

[9] Concerning Paul and the gospel tradition in general, see the recent works by D.L. Dungan, *The Sayings of Jesus in the Churches of Paul* (Philadelphia, 1971); B. Fjärstedt, *Synoptic Tradition in I Corinthians* (Uppsala, 1974); Dale C. Allison, Jr., "The Pauline Epistles and the Synoptic Gospels: The Pattern of Parallels," *NTS*, 28 (1982) 1-32; P. Stuhlmacher, "Jesus Tradition im Römerbrief," *TheolBeiträge* 14 (1983) 240-250; id. (ed.), *Das Evangelium und die Evangelien*, WUNT 28 (Tübingen, 1983), 16-20; 157-182.

Interpretative activity is also evident. The expositions can have the form of a commentary attached to a cited unit of tradition. In this way I Cor 11: (26)27-34 is attached to the quoted institution of the Lord's Supper in vv 23-25 (26), and Jn 5:10-18 is attached to the story in vv 1-9. In the same manner Jn 2:17-22 is attached as an exposition of the cleansing of the temple in vv 13-16. The unit of tradition may also be presupposed, and not quoted, as is the case in the discussion of the Lord's Supper in I Cor 10:3-4.16-17.21 and Jn 6:51-58.

3. The expositions have largely the form of paraphrases of sentences, phrases, word sets, and words from the given tradition. Synonyms may be used, and expressions may be rephrased. In the expository paraphrase, words and fragments from the tradition may be moulded into traditional form.

4. The transmission and exposition of tradition can take both a written and oral form. The written form is found in written documents, as I Cor, Jn and the Synoptics. The oral form seems primary, however, for the following reasons: a) Paul states explicitly that I Cor 11:23ff was brought orally to the church in Corinth. Thus, there is a basis for assuming that the tradition as recorded in the Gospels was also primarily transmitted orally. b) Paul gives his expositions of the gospel tradition in written form because he is not present himself and thus cannot interpret the tradition in person (i.e. orally). This evidence suggests that similar kinds of exposition in the four gospels primarily originated in oral settings. c) The material discussed in I Cor 10 and 11 and in the Gospels belong to identifiable pericopes. Among the passages discussed in John, Jn 2:13-22 and 5:1-18 are easily delimited from their contexts, while 6:51-58 is part of the more complex entity of Jn 6 understood as a whole. Both in I Cor 10 and 11 and in Jn 2:13-22; 5:1-18 and 6:51-58 the tradition is interpreted in order to meet the concerns and needs of the Christian communities. This observation also speaks in favour of the view that the oral form is primary, although written form also may be used.

Paul and Mark

Paul, in I Cor 11:23ff, and Luke 22:15-20 represent a version of the institution different from the one in Mk 14:22-25 and Mt 26:26-28.[10] A comparison between Paul and Mk-Mt is of importance, nevertheless,

---

[10] G. Bornkamm, *Studien zu Antike und Christentum, Gesammelte Aufsätze, II*, (München, 1963), 152; H. Schürmann, *Der Einsetzungsbericht* (Münster 1955), p. 1 (Lk 22:19-20 is halfway between Mk/Mt and Paul).

since we can see in this way what kind of agreement might exist between two mutually independent versions of the same unit of tradition.[11] Since there is hardly any specific agreement between Paul's eucharistic passages and Mt, the comparison will be limited to Mk.

The correspondences between eucharistic traditions in I Cor and Mk 14:22-25 are:

Sentences (almost verbatim agreement):

I Cor 11:24: τοῦτό μού ἐστιν τὸ   Mk 14:22 τοῦτό ἐστιν τὸ σῶμά μου
σῶμα...

Scattered parts of sentences (phrases):

I Cor 11:25 τοῦτο... ἡ... διαθήκη... ἐν Mk 14:24 τοῦτο... τὸ αἷμά μου τῆς
τῷ ἐμῷ αἵματι   διαθήκης
I Cor 11:23 ἔλαβεν ἄρτον   Mk 14:22 λαβὼν ἄρτον
I Cor 11:24 ἔκλασεν καὶ εἶπεν   Mk 14:22 ἔκλασεν... καὶ εἶπεν

Word sets:

I Cor 11:26 ἐσθίητε τὸν ἄρτον ... τὸ ποτήριον πίνητε
I Cor 11:27 ἐσθίῃ τόν ἄρτον... πίνῃ τὸ ποτήριον
            τοῦ σώματος... τοῦ αἵματος...
I Cor 11:28 ... τοῦ ἄρτου ἐσθιέτω... τοῦ ποτηρίου πινέτω
I Cor 11:29 ... ἐσθίων... πίνων... ἐσθίει... πίνει...
            τὸ σῶμα
I Cor 11:25 ... τὸ ποτήριον ... πίνητε Mk 14:22-24 ... ἐσθιόντων... ἄρτον...
                                                              τὸ σῶμα
I Cor 10:3-4 ... ἔφαγον ... ἔπιον   ... ποτήριον ... ἔπιον ...
                                                              τὸ αἷμα
I Cor 10:16 τὸ ποτήριον ... τοῦ αἵματος ... τὸν ἄρτον ...
            κλῶμεν ... τοῦ σώματος ...
            I Cor 10:17 ἄρτος ... σῶμα ... ἄρτου
            I Cor 10:21 ... ποτήριον ... πίνειν ... ποτήριον ...

Single words

I Cor 11:24 εὐχαριστήσας   Mk 14:23 εὐχαριστήσας
I Cor 11:24 ὑπέρ   Mk 14:24 ὑπέρ
I Cor 11:23 παρεδίδετο   Mk 14:21 παραδίδοται
I Cor 10:16 εὐλογίας ὃ εὐλογοῦμεν   Mk 14:22 εὐλογήσας
I Cor 10:17 οἱ πολλοί ... πάντες   Mk 14:23-24 πάντες ... πολλῶν

Variant words (corresponding in meaning):

I Cor 11:24 εὐχαριστήσας   Mk 14:22 εὐλογήσας
I Cor 11:25 ἐμῷ   Mk 14:24 μου
I Cor 11:23 ἐν τῇ νυκτί   Mk 14:17 ὀψίας
I Cor 11:26 ἄχρι οὗ   Mk 14:25 ἕως τῆς ἡμέρας ἐκείνης ὅταν

---

[11] About Mk's independence of Paul, see H. Schürmann, *Einsetzungsbericht*, 8.

There are 68 words in I Cor 11:23b-26. Of those, 25 words are also used in Mk 14:22-25. Out of 49 words in I Cor 11:23b-25, 21 are found in Mk 14:22-25. Thus, 1/3 to almost 1/2 of the number of words used here are the same coming from two mutually independent versions of this unit of tradition.

This comparison makes possible the following generalization: Between mutually independent versions of units of oral and/or written traditions there may be close verbal agreements in the form of sentences, word pairs and sets, single words, and corresponding variant terms. At the same time there are differences which give each version its distinctive character. There are no specific agreements found in the contexts of the passages in Paul and the passage in Mk, apart from the fact that Paul seems to presuppose a passion narrative, corresponding to the passion narratives in the Gospels.

After having examined the agreements between the eucharistic traditions in I Cor and Mk, our analysis also raises the question: What insights can these passages in I Cor 10 and 11 give us into the nature of the pre-synoptic traditions?

Tradition Received and Handed On. I Cor. 11:23-25(26)

It is commonly recognized that Paul in I Cor 11:23ff cites the institution of the Lord's supper as a unit of tradition. This is made clear by Paul's introductory sentence: "I have received (παρέλαβον) from the Lord that which I have given (παρέδωκα) to you." The two verbs are equivalents of two rabbinical technical terms for the transmitting of tradition, קִבֵּל מִן and מָסַר לְ.[12] I Cor 11:23 then indicates that the chain of tradition goes back to the words of Jesus, and that as the Lord, his institution of the Supper had juridical (binding) authority for the congregation in Corinth.[13]

Although Paul cites this given unit of tradition about the Lord's Supper, he at the same time brings interpretative elements into his rendering. This interpretative element is especially evident in v. 26. Paul here formulates a sentence parallel to v. 25b, so that at first Jesus seems to be still speaking:

[12] Cf. J. Jeremias, *The Eucharistic Words of Jesus* (New York, 1955), 128f.; H. Riesenfeld, *The Gospel Tradition* (Philadelphia, 1970), 15-18; B. Gerhardsson, *Memory and Manuscript* (Uppsala 1961), 288ff.; 305; 321f; id., *Die Anfänge der Evangelientradition* (Wuppertal, 1977), 27.

[13] Cf. H. Conzelmann, *Der erste Brief an die Korinther* (Meyer; Göttingen, 1969), 230-31; B. Gerhardsson, *Memory*, 322; P. Stuhlmacher, *Das Evangelium und die Evangelien*, 19; G. Bornkamm, *Studien*, 146-148; E. Käsemann, *Essays on New Testament Themes* (Naperville, Ill., 1964), 120-132.

25, ὁσάκις ἐὰν πίνητε ...
26, ὁσάκις γὰρ ἐὰν ἐσθίητε ... καὶ ... πίνητε,

In spite of this similarity, v. 26 is Paul's own formulation of the traditional phrase, since in this sentence he refers to Jesus in the third person as the Lord: "For as often as you eat this bread and drink this cup, you proclaim the Lord's death until he comes." In this formulation Paul moreover draws on words about eschaton (ἄχρι οὗ ἔλθῃ), which in varied formulation also occur in the synoptic accounts.[14]

An Attached Paraphrasing Commentary

By this interpretative formulation in v. 26 Paul sets the theme, "to eat the bread and drink the cup," within the perspective of eschaton. This perspective dominates the subsequent verses.[15]

Before analysing I Cor 11:27-34, we will first present the text:[16]

I Cor 11.23-34:
"The text"
23 Ἐγὼ γὰρ παρέλαβον ἀπὸ τοῦ κυρίου, ὃ καὶ παρέδωκα ὑμῖν, ὅτι ὁ κύριος Ἰησοῦς ἐν τῇ νυκτὶ ᾗ παρεδίδοτο ἔλαβεν ἄρτον
24 καὶ εὐχαριστήσας ἔκλασεν καὶ εἶπεν, τοῦτό μού ἐστιν τὸ σῶμα τὸ ὑπὲρ ὑμῶν. τοῦτο ποιεῖτε εἰς τὴν ἐμὴν ἀνάμνησιν.
25 ὡσαύτως καὶ τὸ ποτήριον μετὰ τὸ δειπνῆσαι, λέγων, τοῦτο τὸ ποτήριον ἡ καινὴ διαθήκη ἐστὶν ἐν τῷ ἐμῷ αἵματι, τοῦτο ποιεῖτε, ὁσάκις ἐὰν πίνητε, εἰς τὴν ἐμὴν ἀνάμνησιν.

Theme:
26 ὁσάκις γὰρ ἐὰν ἐσθίητε τὸν ἄρτον τοῦτον καὶ τὸ ποτήριον πίνητε, τὸν θάνατον τοῦ κυρίου καταγγέλλετε, ἄχρι οὗ ἔλθῃ.

Commentary:
27 Ὥστε ὃς ἂν ἐσθίῃ τὸν ἄρτον ἢ πίνῃ τὸ ποτήριον τοῦ κυρίου ἀναξίως, ἔνοχος ἔσται τοῦ σώματος καὶ τοῦ αἵματος τοῦ κυρίου.
28 δοκιμαζέτω δὲ ἄνθρωπος ἑαυτόν, καὶ οὕτως ἐκ τοῦ ἄρτου ἐσθιέτω καὶ ἐκ τοῦ ποτηρίου πινέτω.
29 ὁ γὰρ ἐσθίων καὶ πίνων κρίμα ἑαυτῷ ἐσθίει καὶ πίνει μὴ διακρίνων τὸ σῶμα.
30 διὰ τοῦτο ἐν ὑμῖν πολλοὶ ἀσθενεῖς καὶ ἄρρωστοι καὶ κοιμῶνται ἱκανοί.
31 εἰ δὲ ἑαυτοὺς διεκρίνομεν, οὐκ ἂν ἐκρινόμεθα.
32 κρινόμενοι δὲ ὑπὸ τοῦ κυρίου παιδευόμεθα, ἵνα μὴ σὺν τῷ κόσμῳ κατακριθῶμεν.
33 Ὥστε, ἀδελφοί μου, συνερχόμενοι εἰς τὸ φαγεῖν ἀλλήλους ἐκδέχεσθε.
34 εἴ τις πεινᾷ, ἐν οἴκῳ ἐσθιέτω, ἵνα μὴ εἰς κρίμα συνέρχησθε.

[14] H. Conzelmann, *An die Korinther* 237; cf. J. Jeremias, *The Eucharistic Words*, 115; E. Käsemann, *Essays*, 121; G. Bornkamm, *Studien*, 148.
[15] Cf. E. Käsemann, *Essays*, 121-132.
[16] See especially E. Käsemann, "Sätze heiligen Rechtes im Neuen Testament," *NTS* I (1954/55) 248ff., id., *Essays* 122ff.; G. Bornkamm, *Studien* 168.

1 Cor 10:16-17.21:

16 τὸ <u>ποτήριον</u> τῆς εὐλογίας, ὃ εὐλογοῦμεν, οὐχὶ κοινωνία ἐστὶν τοῦ <u>αἴματος</u> τοῦ χριστοῦ; τὸν <u>ἄρτον</u>, ὃν κλῶμεν, οὐχὶ κοινωνία τοῦ <u>σώματος</u> τοῦ χριστοῦ ἐστιν;

17 ὅτι εἷς <u>ἄρτος</u>, ἓν <u>σῶμα</u> οἱ πολλοί ἐσμεν, οἱ γὰρ πάντες ἐκ τοῦ ἑνὸς ἄρτου μετέχομεν.

21 οὐ δύνασθε <u>ποτήριον</u> κυρίου πίνειν καὶ <u>ποτήριον</u> δαιμονίων.

By using technical terms for the transmission of tradition (παρέλαβον-παρέδωκα) Paul introduces in I Cor 11:23 a quote of the Institution of the Lord's Supper (11:23b-25).

In vv. 27ff. Paul gives a paraphrasing commentary on the quoted unit of tradition. From this fact we see that (already) in the middle of the fifties the Jesus-tradition was so fixed that it was quoted and used as basis for an added exposition. As can be seen from the words underscored with a single line in vv. 27ff., Paul utilizes fragments — words and phrases — from the quoted tradition and builds them into a paraphrasing exposition which applies it to a case-situation. In Paul's exposition the genitive τοῦ κυρίου (v. 27) serves as a clarifying addition to the fragments from the quoted tradition, ...τὸ ποτήριον and ...τοῦ σώματος... As can be seen from the words underscored by a double line, legal terms are woven together with these fragments from the tradition of the Lord's Supper. Such legal terms are: ἀναξίως, ἔνοχος ἔσται (v. 27); and κρίμα ... διακρίνων ... in v. 29. In vv. 30-2 Paul elaborates upon these legal terms, without drawing on fragments from the eucharistic tradition. Finally, in vv. 33-4 he returns to the explicit discussion of the eucharistic meal. Here he refers back to the institution of the Lord's Supper, vv. 23ff., and even back to the situation in Corinth, pictured in vv. 17ff. In these concluding verses, 33-4, we again, as in vv. 27-9, find terminology from (the eucharistic) meal (τὸ φαγεῖν-ἐσθιέτω) woven together with a legal term (κρίμα).

Although Paul writes the exposition himself and applies the eucharistic tradition to a specific case, he nevertheless uses traditional ethical/legal forms. The form of casuistic legal clauses is especially evident:[17]

27 ὃς ἂν ἐσθίῃ ... ἔνοχος ἔσται...
29 ὁ γὰρ ἐσθίων ... κρίμα ἑαυτῷ ἐσθίει...

For such casuistic statements see Mt. 5:21, 22, etc. See examples from the Old Testament and from the Qumran writings in W. Nauck, *Die Tradition und der Charakter des ersten Johannesbriefes*, WUNT 3 (Tübingen, 1957), pp. 29ff. Examples from rabbinic writings and Philo are given by P. Borgen, *Bread from Heaven* (Leiden, 1965, reprint

1981), esp. pp. 88f.; see further P. Fiebig, *Der Erzählungsstil der Evangelien* (Leipzig, 1925), pp. 3-20.

The following sentences give rules for avoiding judgment:

31 εἰ δὲ ἑαυτοὺς διεκρίνομεν, οὐκ ἂν ἐκρινόμεθα
32 κρινόμενοι ... παιδευόμεθα, ἵνα μὴ ...
34 εἴ τις πεινᾷ, ἐν οἴκῳ ἐσθιέτω, ἵνα μὴ ...

The form of v. 31 is similar to that of John 3.18 and Matt. 6.14. All these sentences give the condition (in conditional clauses, I Cor 11.31 and Matt 6.14, or by a participle, John 3.18) for avoiding (I Cor 11:31 and John 3.18) or gaining (Matt 6.14) what is stated in the main verb. To the sentences in I Cor 11.32 and 34 where the main verb is followed by ἵνα μή, to show what is to be avoided, there are parallel forms in Matt. 5.25; John 5.14; Luke 12.58 and Matt 7.1. The common parenetic imperative is used in I Cor 11.28 (δοκιμαζέτω) (cf. v.34), and in v. 33 (ἐκδέχεσθε). Finally, v. 30 has a descriptive sentence by which Paul explains phenomena which exist in the Corinthian Church.

The exposition is in argumentative form. The case of eating unworthily is stated in v. 27, an exhortation then follows in v. 28, followed by the rationale in v. 29 (γάρ). The negative effect which this has (διὰ τοῦτο) on the Corinthian church is narrated in v. 30. In vv. 31-32 the opposite alternative is presented, and then in v. 33 ff. the conclusion is drawn.

This analysis shows that Paul uses a variety of forms in his elaboration and that he changes style from third person singular to first and second person plural, and from indicative to imperative, etc. Paul's style is, moreover, argumentative. He draws logical conclusions.

This analysis indicates that the help to be gained from an author's own particular style and other individual characteristics is limited. On the basis of such criteria one can hardly draw the conclusion that I Cor 11:27-29 is produced by Paul himself, since traditional style and terminology are used here. The section is, nevertheless, composed by Paul, and the following guide rule can be formulated: In the expository paraphrasing of gospel traditions, both words and phrases are fused together into traditional forms.[18]

---

[18] Cf. A.G. Wright, "The Literary Genre Midrash," *CBQ* 28, (1966), 110-111: "What the ancient writer was aware of was that he wrote within a particular tradition: it was this that largely decided the literary form to which we have given a name. He was a Deuteronomist, a priestly writer, a follower of the sages, an anthologist of the prophets, or the like." (Quotation from B. Vawter, "Apocalyptic: Its Relation to Prophecy," *CBQ* 22 (1960), 33); R. Le Déaut, "A propos a Definition of Midrash," *Interpretation*, 25 (1971) 270: "The authors were conscious of writing in a tradition rather than in a certain literary form." Cf. also P. Borgen, *Bread from Heaven*, NTSup 10 (Leiden, 1965) 59.

Moreover, Paul does not indicate that he uses a novel approach when he comments on a given unit of tradition. From this one can assume that there were two activities running parallel in the church communities: a) gospel tradition was being received, preserved and handed on, exemplified by I Cor 11:23ff. and b) it was commented upon, paraphrased and applied to relevant concerns and situations, as exemplified by I Cor 11:27ff.

Fragments. Eucharist and Manna.

After we have analysed I Cor 11:23-34, some remarks should be added on I Cor 10:3,4,16,17 and 21. It is significant that Paul here uses an expository paraphrase of fragments from the eucharistic tradition without first quoting the tradition itself.[19]

16 τὸ ποτήριον τῆς εὐλογίας, ὃ εὐλογοῦμεν, οὐχὶ κοινωνία ἐστὶν τοῦ αἵματος τοῦ χριστοῦ; τὸν ἄρτον, ὃν κλῶμεν, οὐχὶ κοινωνία τοῦ σώματος τοῦ χριστοῦ ἐστιν;
17 ὅτι εἷς ἄρτος, ἓν σῶμα οἱ πολλοί ἐσμεν, οἱ γὰρ πάντες ἐκ τοῦ ἑνὸς ἄρτου μετέχομεν.
21 οὐ δύνασθε ποτήριον κυρίου πίνειν καὶ ποτήριον δαιμονίων.

The words underscored by a single line are taken from the eucharistic tradition, as quoted in I Cor 11:23ff. The terms underscored with a dotted line, ... τῆς εὐλογίας, ὃ εὐλογοῦμεν, raise the question whether Paul also draws on other versions of the tradition,[20] since the corresponding term in I Cor 11:24 is εὐχαριστήσας, just as in Luke 22:17,19. On the other hand, Matt 26:26 and Mark 14:22 have εὐλογήσας.

In I Cor 16-17,21 the fragments from the eucharistic tradition occur within the context of I Cor 10:14-22. The heading of the passage is Paul's paraenetic imperative in v. 14: φεύγετε ἀπὸ τῆς εἰδωλολατρίας, "Flee from idolatry." The reference to the Lord's Supper (vv 16-17.21) and to the Law of Moses (Lev 7:6.15; Deut 18:1-4) in v. 18 serves as argumentative basis for the warning against idolatry. The conclusion in v. 21-22 has the form of a rule for mutually exclusive alternatives:

---

[19] Cf. H. Schürmann, *Ursprung und Gestalt* (Düsseldorf, 1970), 86. H. Conzelmann, *An die Korinther* 201f. J. Héring, *Le Royaume de Dieu et sa venue* (Neuchâtel, 1959); J. Jeremias, *The Eucharistic Words* 131.

[20] Such a version of the eucharistic tradition would draw on the Jewish technical terms for the cup of wine over which the thanksgiving after the meal has been said; cf. Strack-Billerbeck IV, 72; 628; 630f.; H. Conzelmann, *An die Korinther* 202; C.K. Barrett, *The First Epistle to the Corinthians* (New York, 1968) 231.

v. 21 οὐ δύνασθε ποτήριον κυρίου πίνειν καὶ ποτήριον δαιμονίων
οὐ δύνασθε τραπέζης κυρίου μετέχειν καὶ τραπέζης δαιμονίων.
("You cannot drink the cup of the Lord and the cup of demons.
You cannot partake of the table of the Lord and the table of demons").

The same form is found in Mt 6:24 (Lk 16:13):

v. 24 οὐ δύνασθε θεῷ δουλεύειν καὶ μαμωνᾷ.
("You cannot serve God and Mammon").

Thus, in I Cor 10:21a Paul's paraphrase of a fragment from the eucharistic tradition has been given a traditional form, a form which also occurs in the Gospels in Mt 6:24 par.[21]

The passage from I Cor 10:14-22 reflects its oral nature. Paul exhorts the Corinthian church by means of a letter in lieu of appearing in person. The oral style is especially evident when Paul in v. 15 addresses the church as if he was speaking to them: "I speak (λέγω) as to sensible men; judge for yourselves what I say (ὅ φημι)."

Formulations from the eucharistic tradition are also reflected in the haggadic reference to the manna and the well in the desert, I Cor 10:3-4, when it is said: "...they all ate the same spiritual food, and they all drank the same spiritual drink." In this passage Israel typifies the Christian people of God. In this way the events of the journey through sea and desert are applied to baptism (v.2) and the Lord's Supper (vv 3-4). The formulation in I Cor 10:3-4 seems even to reflect eucharistic phrases, as can be seen from the similarity to the wording in I Cor 11:26.

I Cor. 10:3: ...τὸ αὐτὸ πνευματικὸν βρῶμα ἔφαγον ...
        4: ...τὸ αὐτὸ πνευματικὸν ἔπιον πόμα ...

I Cor. 11:26 ...ἐσθίητε τὸν ἄρτον ...
        ...τὸ ποτήριον πίνητε ...

As can be seen from these observations, already in the mid-fifties the biblical stories about the manna and the well are being applied to the Lord's Supper.[22]

By comparing the eucharistic traditions recorded in I Cor 10 and 11 with Mk 14:22-25, we thus have shown that close agreement may exist between two mutually independent versions of the same unit of tradition. Furthermore, the analysis of I Cor 10 and 11 has given us insight

---

[21] Cf. A. Resch, *Der Paulinismus und die Logia Jesu*, Texte und Untersuchungen, N.F. 12 (Leipzig, 1904), 53.
[22] Cf. E. Käsemann, *Essays* 114; H. Schürmann, *Ursprung und Gestalt* (Dusseldorf, 1970), 173.

both into the tradition received and handed on, and into the expository use of the tradition. Although the passages are part of a written document, its oral form seems to be primary.

Eucharistic Traditions in John, Paul and the Synoptics

Paul's usage of eucharistic gospel traditions in I Cor 10:3-4, 16-17, 21 and 11:23-34 can further our understanding of John's use of tradition. It can strengthen the hypothesis that John draws on oral traditions and is independent of the Synoptic Gospels. Such a theory does more than just allude to unknown and hypothetical sources behind John. Paul makes it possible to provide dated evidence for analogous use of gospel tradition independent of the Synoptics.

The best starting point for the examination of the hypothesis is found in John 6:51b-58, since John here draws on eucharistic tradition in a way which comes very close to Paul's handling of it. John has closer agreements with Paul than with the Synoptics.

The agreements between Jn and Paul are:

Jn 6:51-58 and I Cor 10:3-4, 16-17, 21; 11:23-29.

Word sets.

Jn 6:53	φάγητε τὴν σάρκα πίητε αὐτοῦ τὸ αἷμα	I Cor. 11:24-25	τὸ σῶμα ... ἐν τῷ ἐμῷ αἵματι
6:54	ὁ τρώγων μου τὴν σάρκα καὶ πίνων μου τὸ αἷμα	11:27	τοῦ σώματος καὶ τοῦ αἵματος
6:55	ἡ ... σάρξ μου καὶ τὸ αἷμά μου	10:16	τοῦ αἵματος ... τοῦ σώματος
6:56	ὁ τρώγων μου τὴν σάρκα καὶ πίνων μου τὸ αἷμα	11:26	ἐσθίητε ... πίνητε
6:57	ὁ τρώγων με	11:27	ἐσθίῃ ... πίνῃ
	52 τὴν σάρκα ... φαγεῖν	11:28	ἐσθιέτω ... πινέτω
6:58	ὁ τρώγων τοῦτον τὸν ἄρτον	11:29	ὁ ... ἐσθίων ... πίνων ... ἐσθίει καὶ πίνει
6:55	βρῶσις ... πόσις	10:3-4	ἔφαγον ... ἔπιον
		10:3-4	βρῶμα ... πόμα

Sentences (in parts)

Jn 6:51b	ὁ ἄρτος ... ὃν ἐγὼ δώσω ἡ σάρξ μού ἐστιν ὑπέρ ...	I Cor. 11:23-4	... ἄρτον ... τοῦτό μού ἐστιν τὸ σῶμα τὸ ὑπέρ ...
		Lk 22:19	... ἄρτον ... ἔδωκεν ... τοῦτό ἐστιν τὸ σῶμά μου τὸ ὑπέρ ...

Subject matter, not words

Jn 6:53 ... οὐκ ἔχετε ζωὴν ἐν ἑαυ-	I Cor. 11:29	... κρίμα ...
τοῖς	11:34	... μὴ εἰς κρίμα ...
6:54 ... ἔχει ζωὴν αἰώνιον	11:32	... μὴ σὺν τῷ κόσμῳ
κἀγὼ ἀναστήσω αὐτὸν		κατακριθῶμεν
τῇ ἐσχάτῃ ἡμέρᾳ		

M.-É. Boismard[23] emphasizes the agreements between John 6:51b and I Cor 11:24: John reflects a liturgical tradition here which is represented by Paul's version of the institution of the Lord's Supper. (Boismard thinks that Luke 22:19b is probably an addition by a scribe.) Moreover, Boismard suggests that John's term "my flesh" instead of "my body" in the synoptic and Pauline versions of the institution, translates Jesus' own words in Aramaic. Thus, John here renders a tradition which is independent of the Synoptics, in spite of the verbal similarities which exist. Boismard's view that John has stronger kinship with Paul than with the Synoptics, should be more thoroughly investigated.

1. John presupposes the institution of the Lord's Supper and paraphrases parts from it, without quoting the story of the institution itself. Similarly, Paul in I Cor 10:16-17, 21 selects words from the eucharistic tradition without quoting it. The story of the institution is presupposed as known, so that the commentary in I Cor 11:(26)27ff is also a close parallel, although the institution is quoted in 11:23-25(26).

2. John and Paul use tradition in the same way. They make expository paraphrases of fragments. The fragments consist of word sets. The sets in John 6:51b-58 are ὁ ἄρτος/βρῶσις – ἡ σάρξ, πόσις – τὸ αἷμα, and φαγεῖν (τρώγειν) – πίνειν. Correspondingly, the Pauline word sets in I Cor 10:3-4, 16-17, 21 and 11:27-29 are: ὁ ἄρτος/βρῶμα – τὸ σῶμα, ποτήριον/πόμα – τὸ αἷμα, and ἐσθίειν/φαγεῖν – πίνειν.

3. There are similarities between John and Paul with regard to the form given to the expository paraphrases. In John 6:53 the eucharistic fragments are built into a sentence where a conditional clause (ἐάν) is followed by the main clause. Correspondingly, in I Cor 11:27 Paul paraphrases words from the tradition to a sentence where a conditional relative clause (ὃς ἄν) is followed by a main clause. In John 6:54,56,57,58 a participial phrase tied to the subject takes the place of the subordinate clause, as also is the case in I Cor 11:29 (ὁ ... ἐσθίων καὶ πίνων). In both places there is variation of style between second and third person.

Moreover, both Jn and Paul use argumentative style. For example,

---

[23] M.-É. Boismard, *L'évangile de Jean*, 204-205.

negative and positive alternatives are presented to the readers (Jn 6:53-54; I Cor 11:27-28), and the rationale (γάρ) is given (Jn 6:55; I Cor 11:29). Then a conclusion is drawn (Jn 6:58; I Cor 11:33).

4. Both John and Paul apply the biblical story of the manna and the well to the eating and drinking in the Lord's Supper. In John 6:(31)51b-58 words from the eucharistic tradition are made part of the midrashic exposition of the Old Testament text on the manna, cited in v. 31. In I Cor 10:3-4 the Israelites' eating and drinking in the desert typify the Lord's Supper. Against this background, it is probable that John 6:55 ("For my flesh is food (βρῶσις) indeed, and my blood is drink (πόσις) indeed") refers to the manna and the well, just as do the corresponding terms (βρῶμα-πόμα) in I Cor 10:3-4.[24]

5. Moreover, both John 6:41,43 and I Cor 10:10 refer to murmurs by the Israelites in the desert.

6. The formulation in Jn 6:51b ὁ ἄρτος δὲ ὃν ἐγὼ δώσω ἡ σάρξ μού ἐστιν ὑπὲρ τῆς τοῦ κόσμου ζωῆς, is similar to I Cor 11:24 τοῦτό μού ἐστιν τὸ σῶμα τὸ ὑπὲρ ὑμῶν and Lk 22:19 τοῦτό ἐστιν τὸ σῶμά μου τὸ ὑπὲρ ὑμῶν διδόμενον, and reflects wording in the presupposed insti- tution story in the Johannine community.

The fact that the verb δίδωμι is used in Jn 6:51b-52 and Lk 22:19, but not in I Cor 11:23ff, cannot undermine the view that Jn 6:51b-58 is in closest agreement with I Cor 10:3-4,16-17. 21; 11:23-34, especially since the term in Jn 6:51-52 is a repetition of the word ἔδωκεν from the Old Testament quotation in Jn 6:31.[25]

Finally the form of the larger passage from Jn 6:31-58 should be sketched out, and the discussion of oral tradition pursued further.

In my book "Bread from Heaven" I examined material exemplifying the midrashic character of John 6:31-58. The quotation from the Old Testament, "Bread from heaven he gave them to eat" (v.31), is para- phrased throughout vv.32-58. The systematic structure of this para- phrasing method becomes evident from the fact that the quotation's final word "to eat" (φαγεῖν) does not occur in vv. 32-48. In verse 49, however, this word from the Old Testament quotation is introduced into the exposition, and in the remaining part of the discourse this term (and its synonym τρώγειν) has a central position.[26]

In each part of the exposition the interpretation presented is questioned by "the Jews." In the first part, vv 32-48, objection is raised against the

[24] Cf. P. Borgen, *Bread*, 91-92, where reasons are given for the preference of the reading ἀληθῶς instead of ἀληθής.

[25] P. Borgen, *Bread*, 86-90.

[26] P. Borgen, *Bread*, 33-35.

identification of Jesus with the "bread from heaven" (v.31). The basis
for this objection is the gospel tradition about Jesus as son of Joseph:
"Is not this Jesus, the son of Joseph whose father and mother we
know? How does he now say 'I have come down from heaven'?" (John
6:42).[27]

Correspondingly, in the second part, vv 49-58, the use of the term "to
eat" (v 31) in connection with Jesus is questioned. This time gospel
traditions about the eucharist are utilized: "How can this man give us
his flesh to eat?" (v 52-58).[28]

What in our analysis indicates that Jn draws on oral tradition? First,
the close agreement between Jn 6:51-58 and Paul in parts of I Cor 10
and 11, make it probable that Jn is not dependent upon the Synoptics.
Neither can it be maintained that Jn is dependent upon Paul's letter in I
Cor. Thus, Paul and Jn most probably draw on oral eucharistic
traditions, combined with the biblical/haggadic stories about the
manna and the well. Second, the common celebration of the eucharist
supports the view that not only Paul, but also Jn, utilizes liturgical
traditions. Third, I Cor 10:17, 21 shows that the story of the institution
was already known in the mid-fifties to readers in the Corinthian
church, and expository elaboration could therefore presuppose this
story of institution. Jn 6:51-58 has the same usage of word sets, etc.
from the institution of the Lord's Supper, the same form, argumentative style, etc. There are, therefore, strong arguments in favour of
drawing the conclusion that Jn 6:51-58, just as I Cor 10:16-17, 21,
presupposes the oral tradition about the Lord's Supper and develops
expository paraphrase on parts of it.

John's use of the term ἡ σάρξ, and not τὸ σῶμα which is found in
the synoptic and Pauline versions, is consistent with this conclusion.
The Johannine version of the institution is also documented by Ignatius' use of the term ἡ σάρξ in Rom 7:3; Philad 4:1; Smyr 7:1, and also
by Justin in Apol I:66:2.29.[29]

This understanding agrees generally with Boismard's, when he suggests
that John here reflects a liturgical and oral tradition which is also
represented by Paul. Boismard fails to connect this conclusions to his
analysis of other parts of the Gospel of John, where he rather employs
literary source criticism. With reference to the background supplied by
Jn 6:51-58 the following question is pertinent: Are there other passages

---

[27] P. Borgen, *Bread*, 80-83.
[28] P. Borgen, *Bread*, 87ff.
[29] R.E. Brown, *John I*, 285. In *Apol. I* 66:3 Justin has τὸ σῶμα.

in Jn which have a connection with the life of the Johannine community, its transmission and exposition of tradition?

II. "TEXT" AND COMMENTARY

In the preceding sections we discussed the expository use of fragments of the tradition in Jn 6:51b-58 where the unit of tradition was presupposed and not stated. Using I Cor 11:23-34 as a model we shall now examine some of the passages in John where a unit of tradition is followed by an expository commentary. Passages such as Jn 2:13-22; 5:1-18; 9:1-41 and 12:44-50 fall into this category. In this paper, Jn 5:1-18, and 2:13-22 will be in the center of discussion. Jn 9:1-41 cannot be included since the analysis would then expand beyond limit of this paper. The author has, however, analysed Jn 12:44-50 in a recent publication.[30]

This kind of commentary is identified on the basis of the following criteria: 1. Words and phrases from the quoted tradition are repeated and paraphrased in the commentary. (This criterion is central for delimiting the commentary in Jn 5:1-18.) 2. The commentary may elaborate upon a theme not only by using words and phrases, but also by employing varied forms of repetition, such as the use of synonyms, metaphorical expressions, biblical phrases and quotations, etc. to comment upon the theme and words concerned. Jn 2:13-22 and 12:44-50 follow to some degree this more complex method in addition to repeating words and phrases in a direct way.

Various gospel traditions may be worked into such commentaries.[31]

John 5:1-18

In John 5:1-18, vv 1-9 quote a story about healing from the tradition, and the commentary then follows in vv 10-18.

Dodd, and other scholars, have shown that the story about healing, vv 1-9, has the same form as several stories about healing in the Synoptics. Dodd deals only with John 5:10-18 in a summary fashion

---

[30] P. Borgen, "The Use of Tradition in John 12:44-50," in P. Borgen, *Logos*, 1983, 49-66; first published in *NTS* 26 (1979), 18-35.

[31] Such commentaries are also found in the Synoptics, as shown by J. Wanke in his study "Kommentarworte. Älteste Kommentierungen von Herrenworten," *BibZeit* N.F. 24 (1980) 208-233; cf. G.N. Stanton, "Matthew as a Creative Interpreter of the Sayings of Jesus," in P. Stuhlmacher (ed.), *Das Evangelium und die Evangelien* (Tübingen, 1983) 273-287.

without examining it.[32] In these verses phrases from the quoted unit of tradition (vv 1-9) are repeated and paraphrased. This commentary has a systematic outline: In vv 10-13 the sentence ἆρον τὸν κράβατόν σου καὶ περιπάτει from v 8 (also in v 9) is repeated and paraphrased.

In vv 14-16 the phrase ὑγιὴς γενέσθαι/ἐγένετο ὑγιής (vv 6 and 9) is repeated and paraphrased. Finally in vv 17-18, the speaking and acting person in the story of healing, Jesus himself becomes the explicit focal point of the commentary.

The term σάββατον in v 9 is repeated in each of the three parts of the commentary — in v 10, v 16 and v 18 respectively. These repetitions of words and phrases from the quoted story of healing end in v 18, which thus marks the close of the combined quotation and commentary in 5:1-18. The Evangelist elaborated upon the christological theme of 5:1-18 in the discourse of 5:19ff. Up to this point Jn 5:1-18 is in accord with the model form of quoted tradition and attached commentary found in I Cor 11:23-34. Is the paraphrastic commentary in Jn 5:10-18, like the one in I Cor 11:27ff, put into traditional form?

There is little in common formally between Jn 5:10-18 and I Cor 11:27ff, apart from the expository paraphrase. In both cases, however, narrative stories are interpreted, viz. the act of healing (Jn) and the story of a meal (I Cor). While the exposition in I Cor 11:27ff is a didactic monologue, the exposition in Jn 5:10-18 has the form of a dialogue, more precisely of a legal debate on a controversial action (miracle) performed on the sabbath.

The differences between Jn and Paul should not be exaggerated, however. In I Cor 10:14-22 questions are also formulated, (vv 16.18) as well as questions and answers (vv 19-20). Similarly, the exposition of the eucharist in Jn 6:51-58 includes the schema of question and answer (v 52ff).

Nevertheless, concerning traditional forms there are closer agreements between Jn 5:1-18 and passages which state a case followed by a judicial exchange. Consequently, with regard to form, Mt 12:1-8 (plucking grain on the sabbath), and Lk 13:10-17 (the healing of a crippled woman on the sabbath), parallel in an interesting way Jn 5:1-18.[33] A

---

[32] C.H. Dodd, *The Interpretation of the Gospel of John* 320, characterizes briefly vv. 10-18 as the transition from the narrative of the healing at Bethesda to the discourse which follows.

[33] Rabbinic parallels might also have been included, e.g. Mishna Terumot 8:1:
Case:
"(If a priest) was standing and offering sacrifices at the altar, and it became known that he is the son of a divorcee or of a ḥaluṣah...
Debate:
R. Eliezer says, 'All sacrifices that he had (ever) offered on the altar are invalid.'

synoptic presentation of these three passages makes the agreement of form evident. Since a comparison between Mt 12:1-8 and Mk 2:23-28 is also of interest for our discussion, the Markan version is included in the presentation. The agreement of form raises the question of Jn's dependence on (or independence of) the Synoptic Gospels, and therefore agreements of content are included in this survey.

John 5:1-18
The case, vv. 1-9

Μετὰ ταῦτα ἦν ἑορτὴ τῶν Ἰουδαίων, καὶ ἀνέβη Ἰησοῦς εἰς Ἱεροσόλυμα. 2 ἔστιν δὲ ἐν τοῖς Ἱεροσολύμοις ἐπὶ τῇ προβατικῇ κολυμβήθρᾳ ἡ ἐπιλεγομένη Ἑβραϊστὶ Βηθζαθά, πέντε στοὰς ἔχουσα. 3 ἐν ταύταις κατέκειτο πλῆθος τῶν ἀσθε-νούντων, τυφλῶν, χωλῶν, ξηρῶν. 5 ἦν δέ τις ἄνθρωπος ἐκεῖ τριάκοντα [καὶ] ὀκτὼ ἔτη ἔχων ἐν τῇ ἀσθενείᾳ αὐτοῦ· 6 τοῦτον ἰδὼν ὁ Ἰησοῦς κατακείμενον, καὶ γνοὺς ὅτι πολὺν ἤδη χρόνον ἔχει, λέγει αὐτῷ, Θέλεις ὑγιὴς γενέσθαι; 7 ἀπεκρίθη αὐτῷ ὁ ἀσθενῶν, Κύριε, ἄνθρωπον οὐκ ἔχω, ἵνα ὅταν ταραχθῇ τὸ ὕδωρ βάλῃ με εἰς τὴν κολυμβήθραν· ἐν ᾧ δὲ ἔρχομαι ἐγώ, ἄλλος πρὸ ἐμοῦ καταβαίνει. 8 λέγει αὐτῷ ὁ Ἰησοῦς, Ἔγειρε ἆρον τὸν κράβαττόν σου καὶ περιπάτει. 9 καὶ εὐθέως ἐγένετο ὑγιὴς ὁ ἄνθρωπος, καὶ ἦρεν τὸν κράβατ-τον αὐτοῦ καὶ περιεπάτει. Ἦν δὲ σάββα-τον ἐν ἐκείνῃ τῇ ἡμέρᾳ.

Matth 12:1-8
The case, v. 1

Ἐν ἐκείνῳ τῷ καιρῷ ἐπορεύθη ὁ Ἰη-σοῦς τοῖς σάββασιν διὰ τῶν σπορίμων· οἱ δὲ μαθηταὶ αὐτοῦ ἐπείνασαν, καὶ ἤρξαντο τίλλειν στάχυας καὶ ἐσθίειν.

Expository dialogue, vv. 10-18,

10 ἔλεγον οὖν οἱ Ἰουδαῖοι τῷ τεθεραπευ-μένῳ, Σάββατόν ἐστιν, καὶ οὐκ ἔξεστίν σοι ἆραι τὸν κράβαττον. 11 ὁ δὲ ἀπεκ-ρίθη αὐτοῖς, Ὁ ποιήσας με ὑγιῆ ἐκεῖνός μοι εἶπεν, Ἆρον τὸν κράβαττόν σου καὶ περιπάτει. 12 ἠρώτησαν αὐτόν, Τίς ἐστιν

Expository dialogue, vv. 2-8,

2 οἱ δὲ Φαρισαῖοι ἰδόντες εἶπαν αὐτῷ, Ἰδοὺ οἱ μαθηταί σου ποιοῦσιν ὃ οὐκ ἔξεστιν ποιεῖν ἐν σαββάτῳ. 3 ὁ δὲ εἶπεν αὐτοῖς, Οὐκ ἀνέγνωτε τί ἐποίησεν Δαυὶδ ὅτε ἐπείνασεν καὶ οἱ μετ' αὐτοῦ; 4 πῶς εἰσῆλθεν εἰς τὸν οἶκον τοῦ θεοῦ καὶ τοὺς

But R. Joshua declares them valid. If it became known that he is blemished... his service is invalid."

Cf. also A. Peck, "Cases and Principles in Mishna: A Study of Terumot Chapter Eight," in W.S. Green (ed.), *Approaches to Ancient Judaism* 3 (Chico, California, 1981), 35-46.

ὁ ἄνθρωπος ὁ εἰπών σοι, Ἆρον καὶ περιπάτει; 13 ὁ δὲ ἰαθεὶς οὐκ ᾔδει τίς ἐστιν, ὁ γὰρ Ἰησοῦς ἐξένευσεν ὄχλου ὄντος ἐν τῷ τόπῳ. 14 μετὰ ταῦτα εὑρίσκει αὐτὸν ὁ Ἰησοῦς ἐν τῷ ἱερῷ καὶ εἶπεν αὐτῷ, Ἴδε ὑγιὴς γέγονας· μηκέτι ἁμάρτανε, ἵνα μὴ χεῖρόν σοί τι γένηται. 15 ἀπῆλθεν ὁ ἄνθρωπος καὶ ἀνήγγειλεν τοῖς Ἰουδαίοις ὅτι Ἰησοῦς ἐστιν ὁ ποιήσας αὐτὸν ὑγιῆ. 16 καὶ διὰ τοῦτο ἐδίωκον οἱ Ἰουδαῖοι τὸν Ἰησοῦν, ὅτι ταῦτα ἐποίει ἐν σαββάτῳ. 17 ὁ δὲ Ἰησοῦς ἀπεκρίνατο αὐτοῖς, Ὁ πατήρ μου ἕως ἄρτι ἐργάζεται, κἀγὼ ἐργάζομαι. 18 διὰ τοῦτο οὖν μᾶλλον ἐζήτουν αὐτὸν οἱ Ἰουδαῖοι ἀποκτεῖναι, ὅτι οὐ μόνον ἔλυεν τὸ σάββατον, ἀλλὰ καὶ πατέρα ἴδιον ἔλεγεν τὸν θεόν, ἴσον ἑαυτὸν ποιῶν τῷ θεῷ.

ἄρτους τῆς προθέσεως ἔφαγον, ὃ οὐκ ἐξὸν ἦν αὐτῷ φαγεῖν οὐδὲ τοῖς μετ᾽ αὐτοῦ, εἰ μὴ τοῖς ἱερεῦσιν μόνοις; 5 ἢ οὐκ ἀνέγνωτε ἐν τῷ νόμῳ ὅτι τοῖς σάββασιν οἱ ἱερεῖς ἐν τῷ ἱερῷ τὸ σάββατον βεβηλοῦσιν καὶ ἀναίτιοί εἰσιν; 6 λέγω δὲ ὑμῖν ὅτι τοῦ ἱεροῦ μεῖζόν ἐστιν ὧδε. 7 εἰ δὲ ἐγνώκειτε τί ἐστιν, Ἔλεος θέλω καὶ οὐ θυσίαν, οὐκ ἂν κατεδικάσατε τοὺς ἀναιτίους. 8 κύριος γάρ ἐστιν τοῦ σαββάτου ὁ υἱὸς τοῦ ἀνθρώπου.

Mark 2:23-28 *The case, v. 23*	Luke 13:10-17 *The case, vv. 10-13*

23 Καὶ ἐγένετο αὐτὸν ἐν τοῖς σάββασιν παραπορεύεσθαι διὰ τῶν σπορίμων, καὶ οἱ μαθηταὶ αὐτοῦ ἤρξαντο ὁδὸν ποιεῖν τίλλοντες τοὺς στάχυας.

10 Ἦν δὲ διδάσκων ἐν μιᾷ τῶν συναγωγῶν ἐν τοῖς σάββασιν. 11 καὶ ἰδοὺ γυνὴ πνεῦμα ἔχουσα ἀσθενείας ἔτη δέκα ὀκτώ, καὶ ἦν συγκύπτουσα καὶ μὴ δυναμένη ἀνακύψαι εἰς τὸ παντελές. 12 ἰδὼν δὲ αὐτὴν ὁ Ἰησοῦς προσεφώνησεν καὶ εἶπεν αὐτῇ, Γύναι, ἀπολέλυσαι τῆς ἀσθενείας σου, 13 καὶ ἐπέθηκεν αὐτῇ τὰς χεῖρας· καὶ παραχρῆμα ἀνωρθώθη, καὶ ἐδόξαζεν τὸν θεόν.

Expository dialogue, vv. 24-28	*Expository dialogue, vv. 14-17*

24 καὶ οἱ Φαρισαῖοι ἔλεγον αὐτῷ, Ἴδε τί ποιοῦσιν τοῖς σάββασιν ὃ οὐκ ἔξεστιν; 25 καὶ λέγει αὐτοῖς, Οὐδέποτε ἀνέγνωτε τί ἐποίησεν Δαυίδ, ὅτε χρείαν ἔσχεν καὶ ἐπείνασεν αὐτὸς καὶ οἱ μετ᾽ αὐτοῦ; 26 πῶς εἰσῆλθεν εἰς τὸν οἶκον τοῦ θεοῦ ἐπὶ Ἀβιαθὰρ ἀρχιερέως καὶ τοὺς ἄρτους τῆς προθέσεως ἔφαγεν, οὓς οὐκ ἔξεστιν φαγεῖν εἰ μὴ τοὺς ἱερεῖς, καὶ ἔδωκεν καὶ τοῖς σὺν αὐτῷ οὖσιν; 27 καὶ ἔλεγεν αὐτοῖς, Τὸ σάββατον διὰ τὸν ἄνθρωπον ἐγένετο, καὶ οὐχ ὁ ἄνθρωπος διὰ τὸ σάββα-

14 ἀποκριθεὶς δὲ ὁ ἀρχισυνάγωγος, ἀγανακτῶν ὅτι τῷ σαββάτῳ ἐθεράπευσεν ὁ Ἰησοῦς, ἔλεγεν τῷ ὄχλῳ ὅτι Ἓξ ἡμέραι εἰσὶν ἐν αἷς δεῖ ἐργάζεσθαι· ἐν αὐταῖς οὖν ἐρχόμενοι θεραπεύεσθε καὶ μὴ τῇ ἡμέρᾳ τοῦ σαββάτου. 15 ἀπεκρίθη δὲ αὐτῷ ὁ κύριος καὶ εἶπεν, Ὑποκριταί, ἕκαστος ὑμῶν τῷ σαββάτῳ οὐ λύει τὸν βοῦν αὐτοῦ ἢ τὸν ὄνον ἀπὸ τῆς φάτνης καὶ ἀπαγαγὼν ποτίζει; 16 ταύτην δὲ θυγατέρα Ἀβραὰμ οὖσαν, ἣν ἔδησεν ὁ Σατανᾶς ἰδοὺ δέκα καὶ ὀκτὼ ἔτη, οὐκ ἔδει λυθῆναι ἀπὸ τοῦ

τον· **28** ὥστε κύριός ἐστιν ὁ υἱὸς τοῦ
ἀνθρώπου καὶ τοῦ σαββάτου.

δεσμοῦ τούτου τῇ ἡμέρᾳ τοῦ σαββάτου;
17 καὶ ταῦτα λέγοντος αὐτοῦ κατησ-
χύνοντο πάντες οἱ ἀντικείμενοι αὐτῷ καὶ
πᾶς ὁ ὄχλος ἔχαιρεν ἐπὶ πᾶσιν τοῖς
ἐνδόξοις τοῖς γινομένοις ὑπ' αὐτοῦ.

John 5:1-18 and Synoptics

Sentences (almost verbatim agreement)
Jn 5:8   ἔγειρε ἆρον τὸν κράβατόν σου
   καὶ περιπάτει

Jn 5:9   ... εὐθέως ... ἦρεν τὸν κράβατον αὐτοῦ καὶ περιπάτει

Mk 2:9   ἔγειρε καὶ ἆρον τὸν κράβατόν σου καὶ περιπάτει

Jn 5:10 ἆραι τὸν κράβατον

Mk 2:11 ἔγειρε ἆρον τὸν κράβατόν
   σου καὶ

Jn 5:11 ἆρον τὸν κράβατόν σου καὶ
   περιπάτει

Mk 2:12 ἠγέρθη καὶ εὐθὺς ἄρας τὸν
   κράβατον

Jn 5:12 ἆρον καὶ περιπάτει

(Jn 8:11 μηκέτι ἁμάρτανε)

Jn 5:14 μηκέτι ἁμάρτανε

Part of Sentences
Jn 5:10 σάββατόν ... οὐκ ἔξεστίν σοι
   (ἆραι)

Mt 12:2 (cf. Mk 2:24) ὃ οὐκ ἔξεστιν
   (ποιεῖν) ἐν σαββάτῳ

Words
Jn 5:6   ... ἰδὼν ὁ Ἰησοῦς ... λέγει
Jn 5:10 ... ἔλεγον ... οἱ (Ἰουδαῖοι)...
(Jn 5:3D παραλυτικῶν)

Mk 2:5   ἰδὼν ὁ Ἰησοῦς ... λέγει
Mk 2:24 οἱ (Φαρισαῖοι) ἔλεγον
Mk 2:3   παραλυτικόν

Subject Matter, not Words
Jn 5:18 making himself equal with God ⎫
Jn 5:14 Sin no more   ⎬

Mt 2:7 It is blasphemy. Who can
forgive sins but God alone?

Jn 5:16 The Jews persecuted Jesus ⎫
                                  ⎪
                                  ⎬
Jn 5:18 the Jews sought all the more ⎪
   to kill him.   ⎭

Mk 3:6 The Pharisees went out, and
immediately held council with the
Herodians against him, how to destroy him.

Jn 5:17 My Father is working still,
   and I am working

Mt 12:8 (cf Mk 2:27; Lk 6:5) For the
Son of Man is lord of the sabbath.

As the basis for our analysis of these points of agreement between Jn
and the Synoptics, the views of Boismard, Sabbe, Neirynck, Lindars
and Brown should be given in outline.

Boismard finds three levels in John 5:1-18. The original part of John
5:1-18 ran like this: "After this there was a feast and Jesus went up to
Jerusalem. And a certain man was there who had been ill. When Jesus
saw him, he said to him: "Rise, and take your pallet and walk." And at
once the man (rose) and took up his pallet and walked." This story was
part of the first stage (John II-A) of the Gospel written by the

Evangelist. In his final version (John II-B) he added all the rest of John 5:1-18, except for parts of v 16 and all of v 17-18 which were added by the later Redactor (John III). Boismard therefore thinks that John II-B changed the original story of healing into a controversy on the sabbath.[34]

M. Sabbe is right when he objects to Boismard's reconstruction of the original story of healing, that it (John II-A as a whole) has no theological significance. This in itself makes one want to question just that very probability.[35]

In his comments on Boismard's analysis. Neirynck maintains that there is no need for distinguishing between stages Jn II-A and II-B. Since, according to Boismard, an expansion and reworking of the material have taken place in Jn II-B, why would not then Jn II-B also have extensively reworked the story of healing itself on the basis of Mk 2:1-12 (the healing of the paralytic) illuminated by the sabbath controversy in Mk 3:1-6?[36]

An alternative hypothesis is suggested by Lindars.[37] According to him, the verbal similarities between Jn 5:8-9a and Mk 2:9,11-12a are so close that it can scarcely be doubted that an almost identical source lies behind them both. It is also possible that Jn has taken the reference to the sabbath (Jn 5:9b), from background material to Mk 2:1-3:6, since the sabbath is discussed in Mk 2:23-28 and 3:1-6.

The agreements listed above should be discussed against this background. Do the agreements between Jn 5:1-18 on the one hand and Mt 12:1-8 and Lk 13:10-17 on the other hand indicate that Jn is dependent upon the Synoptic Gospels? An argument in favour of dependency must take cognizance of the fact that all three pericopes have the same structure: A case of sabbath violation is followed by a legal dispute. In addition, it might be argued that Mt's interpretative expansion in Mt 12:1-8 of Mk 2:23-28, could suggest that Jn 5:1-18 is a product based on Markan material. G. Stanton's analysis of Mt 12:5-8 can be quoted here.[38] "While it is possible that verses 5-7 may all stem

---

[34] M.-É. Boismard, *L'évangile de Jean*, 156-165.

[35] M. Sabbe, "John and the Synoptists: Neirynck vs. Boismard," *ETL* 56 (1980) 125-130, 130.

[36] F. Neirynck, *Jean et les Synoptiques* 177-180.

[37] B. Lindars, *John* 209.

[38] G. Stanton, "Matthew as a Creative Interpreter of the Sayings of Jesus," in P. Stuhlmacher (ed.), *Das Evangelium und die Evangelien* (Tübingen, 1983) 275. It should be added here that in the judicial debates in John and Mt, Jesus refers to scriptural passages. Mt 12:3-7 refers to 1 Sam 21:1-6; Lev 24:5-9; Num 28:9-10 and Hos 6:6. The words of Jesus in Jn 5:17 draw on Jewish exegetical traditions tied to Gen 2:2f. and Ex 20:11. Cf. R.E. Brown, *John I*, 216-217; P. Borgen, *'Paul Preaches Circumcision and Pleases Men' and other Essays on Christian Origins* (Trondheim, 1983) 180; 184-185 and id., "Creation, Logos and the Son: Observations on John 1:1-15 and 5:17-18," *Ex Auditu*, 3 (1987) 88-92.

from the evangelist, verse 7 is almost certainly part of the evangelist's own addition to and interpretation of Mark 2:23-28. Matthew is stressing that God is merciful and that Sabbath commandment should be considered in the light of his kindness. The Sabbath commandment is not abolished; it is subordinated to the kindness and mercy of God. In this way the conduct of the disciples is defended."

Mt understood the exposition as enhancing the meaning of the received word of Jesus, and therefore as also having the form of a saying of Jesus. Jn has the same understanding of the expository elaborations of the Gospel tradition in the dialogue in Jn 5:10-18.

Finally, the strongest argument in favour of Jn's dependence is the verbatim agreement between Jn 5:8 etc. (ἔγειρε ἆρον τὸν κράβατόν σου καὶ περιπάτει, etc.) and Mk 2:9 (ἔγειρε καὶ ἆρον τὸν κράβατόν σου καὶ περιπάτει, etc.).

As for this phrase, "take up your mat and walk," etc. (Jn 5:8, etc. and Mk 2:9, etc.) it should be noted that another stereotyped phrase from the gospel tradition has also been worked into the paraphrase of the commentary, namely μηκέτι ἁμάρτανε (v 14) which also occurs in the non-Johannine pericope of Jn 7:53-8:11.[39] By analogy, the use of this stereotyped phrase in these two mutually independent stories also supports the view that the expression "take up your pallet and walk" (Jn 5:8, etc., Mk 2:9, etc.) is a stereotyped phrase as well and could occur in various contexts in stories which are independent of each other.[40] Apart from this phrase the two stories of healing, Jn 5:1-9 and Mk 2:1-12, are very different with hardly any further verbal agreement. Thus, the stories are much more different than are the Pauline (I Cor 11:23-26) and Markan (Mk 14:22-25) stories of the Lord's Supper, where there is close agreement between sentences, phrases and words, although they are mutually independent.

The other agreements listed in the survey also call for comment.

The agreement between Jn 5:10 ...οὐκ ἔξεστιν... and Mt 12:2 is due to the fact that a traditional form corresponding to Paul's use of traditional (gospel) forms in I Cor 10:21 and 11:27ff is used in Jn's paraphrase.

The references to the persecution of Jesus (Jn 5:16), and the seeking to kill him (v 18), are all features which have a basis in the gospel

[39] B. Lindars, *John* 312, seems to think that the phrase in Jn 8:11 is taken from 5:14. If so, it shows how a stereotyped phrase may be extracted from a story, leaving the rest of the story intact. Against Lindars it may be said that the phrase has a more natural place in the context of 8:11, while it is used rather abruptly in 5:14.

[40] Cf. E. Haenchen, *Johannesevangelium* 269: "'wandernde' Einzelzüge."

tradition. The persecution of Jesus and the search to kill Jesus are elements which are central in Jn, as can be seen from 5:16.18; 15:20; 7:19-20.25; 8:37.40; 11:53. They are also central to the Johannine community since a direct correlation is made between the persecution of Jesus and attempts to kill him, and the persecution of the disciples the Christians and attempts to kill them, Jn 15:20; 16:2.[41] The passion narratives and the killing of Jesus show that these elements have a firm basis in the gospel tradition and in history.

Jn 5:16.18 and Mk 3:6 par, connect this motif in the gospel tradition with Jesus' apparent violation of the sabbath in different ways. There is no verbal agreement between Mk 3:6 and Jn 5:16.18, and thus it seems arbitrary to draw the conclusion that Jn here is dependent on Mk as indicated by Neirynck. Jn's independence is supported by the observation that the expository commentary in Jn 5:10-18 is attached to the story (the case) just as in Mt 12:1-8 and Lk 13:10-17, while the corresponding discussion in Mk 3:1-6 precedes the story of healing.

The motif of blasphemy in Jn 5:18 ("making himself equal with God") has a distinctive use that is different from the corresponding use of this motif in Mk 2:7 par and 14:64 par. Thus, these parallels do not prove that Jn is dependent upon the Synoptics. Arguments based on form can also be advanced against Jn's dependency on the Synoptics. In spite of the similarity of form between, on the one hand Jn 5:1-18 and on the other Mt 12:1-8 and Lk 13:10-17, Jn has a distinctive use of this common form. The form can hardly be said to be taken from the synoptic passages: Only in Jn 5:10-18 does the legal debate have the function of changing the stage (vv 10-13 the Jews and the person healed; vv 14 Jesus and the healed person; vv 15-18 the healed person, the Jews and Jesus). Moreover, only in Jn 5:10-18 are phrases from the story (the case) repeated quite mechanically in the subsequent legal debate. Only Jn has, therefore, an extensive paraphrase of parts of the case-story used as a "text."

The question still remains as to whether the passage comes from an oral tradition or whether it is based on a written document. Three points suggest that Jn 5:1-18 not only draws on oral tradition, but is itself an oral unit which has been written down.

1.) The story of healing, (Jn 5:1-9), has the same form as have the stories of healing in the Synoptics. Consequently, Jn here seems to reproduce transmitted tradition corresponding to Paul's rendering of the eucharistic tradition in I Cor 11:23-25(26). The expository

---

[41] Cf. Pancaro, *The Law in the Fourth Gospel* (Leiden, 1975), 45f.

commentary in Jn 5:10-18 corresponds to Paul's commentary in I Cor 11:(26)27ff. Jn 5:1-18, as a whole, is therefore a unit parallel to I Cor 11:23-34, and results from a corresponding expository activity in the Johannine community.

2.) This hypothesis is supported by a consideration of the Sitz im Leben of Jn 5:1-18. The life setting of the passage concerns the controversy between the church and the synagogue, in which Christology, the sabbath and the Law of Moses were central issues. The importance of these questions for understanding the actual situation of the Johannine community is evident from Jn 9:1-41. The studies of J.L. Martyn and S. Pancaro have shown that the history of the Johannine community is reflected in these two passages.[42]

3.) The evangelist has more interest in the Christological aspect as such than in the sabbath question. Accordingly, in the discourse which follows in Jn 5:19ff phrases and terms about the sabbath and the sabbath controversy are not repeated any more, whereas the Christological idea in Jn 5:17, ("My Father is at work even till now, and so I am at work too,") is developed.[43]

Our analysis has shown that Jn 5:1-18 follows a traditional structure in which a controversial state of affairs concerning the sabbath is followed by judicial dialogue. Paul in I Cor 11:23-34 uses the same basic form of a story from the gospel tradition followed by an exposi-

---

[42] J.L. Martyn, *History and Theology in the Fourth Gospel* (New York, 1968; 2nd rev. ed., Nashville, Tenn., 1979); S. Pancaro, *The Law*, 497-512.

[43] Additional note on Jn 5:9: Did the point about the sabbath belong to the story of the healing in the oral transmission, or was it added to form a basis for the expository dialogue found in Jn 5:10-18? This question has been much debated, since the reference to the sabbath in v 9b seems to be an addition to the story about healing. R.E. Brown, in discussing E. Haenchen's view that the reference to the sabbath and the sabbath controversy in vv 9b-13 constitutes a secondary addition to the healing narrative, says: "One almost needs the Sabbath motif to give this story significance." (R.E. Brown, *John I*, 210).

Two further observations support the view of Brown. The story of healing, (Jn 5:1-9), is a tradition with legal authority (cf. I Cor 11:23-25/6) which legitimates the attitude of the Johannine community towards the Sabbath (the Law of Moses). Consequently the commentary given in vv 10-18 presupposes that the story of the healing already was known to be connected with the sabbath. The expositor therefore does not need to prove to his readers that the healing story raises the problem of sabbath observance.

Furthermore, the reference to the sabbath in v 9b at the end of the story of the healing corresponds to Paul's formulation of I Cor 11:26, where he extracts from the quoted tradition the theme to be dealt with in the commentary. Thus, the sabbath motif is placed in Jn 5:9b as a topical heading for the succeeding commentary and it is based on the meaning of the healing story.

This use of the sabbath reference in v 9b as a topical heading is in accordance with the scholarly form of commentary found in vv 10-18, using repetition of phrases and alluding to midrashic exegesis.

tory commentary of legal nature. Since the similarities between the two mutually independent traditions of I Cor 11:23-25(26) and Mk 14:22-25 are much more extensive and clearer than they are between Jn 5:1-18 and the Synoptics, the Johannine passage is certainly independent of the Synoptic Gospels.

Jn 5:1-18 is probably an oral unit transmitted and exposed through activity of the Johannine community. This view is supported by the parallel structure of "text" and "commentary" in I Cor 11:23-34 and by the life setting of Jn 5:1-18 where we find conflicts bet\ween church and synagogue about the sabbath and the Law of Moses in relation to Christology. By adding Jn 5:19ff to the sabbath controversy, the evangelist seems to want to develop the Christological aspect more independently of the sabbath controversy.[44]

John 2:13-22

Before we analyse the way in which gospel material has been used in John 2:13-22, the similarities to the Synoptic Gospels and Acts should be noted and discussed. The similarities are:

John 2:13-22 and the Synoptics

I. 2:13-17

A) Agreements with all the Synoptics:

Parts of sentences.

Jn 2:14 ἐν τῷ ἱερῷ τοὺς πωλοῦντας	Mt 21:12/Mk 11:15/Lk 19:45 εἰς τὸ ἱερόν ... τοὺς πωλοῦντας

Words

Jn 2:16 (μὴ) ποιεῖτε	Mt 21:13 ποιεῖτε Mk 11:17 πεποιήκατε Lk 19:46 ἐποιήσατε
Jn 2:16 τὸν οἶκον ... οἶκον 17 τοῦ οἴκου	Mt 21:13/Mk 11:17/Lk 19:46 ὁ οἶκος...

B) Agreements with Mt and Mk

Parts of sentences

Jn 2:15 τὰς τραπέζας ἀνέστρεψεν	Mt 21:12/Mk 11:15 τὰς τραπέζας ... κατέστρεψεν
Jn 2:16 τοῖς τὰς περιστερὰς πωλοῦσιν	Mt 21:12/Mk 11:15 τῶν πωλούντων τὰς περιστεράς

Words

Jn 2:14 ἐν τῷ ἱερῷ	Mt 21:12/Mk 11:15 ἐν τῷ ἱερῷ
Jn 2:14 περιστεράς	Mt 21:12/Mk 11:15 τὰς περιστεράς
Jn 2:15 τῶν κολλυβιστῶν	Mt 21:12/Mk 11:15 τῶν κολλυβιστῶν

[44] Cf. C.K. Barrett, *The Gospel according to St. John* 2nd ed. (London, 1978), 257ff.

C) Agreement with Mt
Part of sentences
Jn 2:15 πάντας ἐξέβαλεν

Mt 21:12 ἐξέβαλεν πάντας

II. 2:18, etc

Parts of sentences
Jn 2:18 ταῦτα ποιεῖς

Mt 21:23/Mk 11:28/Lk 20:2 ταῦτα ποιεῖς

Words
Jn 2:13 εἰς Ἰεροσόλυμα

Mk 11:27 εἰς Ἰεροσόλυμα

Jn 2:14 ἐν τῷ ἱερῷ

Mk 11:27/Lk 20:1 ἐν τῷ ἱερῷ (Mt 21:23 εἰς τὸ ἱερόν)

Jn 2:18 σημεῖον (question)

Mt 12:38-39/Mk 8:12; 16:2/Lk 11:29 σημεῖον (question)

Subject matter, not words
Jn 2:18 τί σημεῖον δεικνύεις ἡμῖν

Mt 21:23/Mk 11:28/Lk 20:2 ἐν ποίᾳ ἐξουσίᾳ

III. 2:19-20

Parts of sentences
Jn 2:19 λύσατε τὸν ναὸν τοῦτον

Mk 14:58 καταλύσω τὸν ναὸν τοῦτον (Mt 26:61 καταλῦσαι τὸν ναόν).

Jn 2:19-20 ἐν τρισὶν ἡμέραις

Mt 26:61/Mk 14:58 διὰ τριῶν ἡμερῶν

Jn 2:19 λύσατε τὸν ναὸν τοῦτον

Mt 27:40/Mk 15:29 ὁ καταλύων τὸν ναόν

Jn 2:19 ἐν τρισὶν ἡμέραις

Mt 27:40/Mk 15:29 ἐν τρισὶν ἡμέραις

Jn 2:19 λύσατε τὸν ναὸν τοῦτον

Acts 6:14 καταλύσει τὸν τόπον τοῦτον

Words
Jn 2:20 οἰκοδομήθη

Mt 26:61 οἰκοδομῆσαι
Mk 14:58 οἰκοδομήσω

Jn 2:20 ὁ ναὸς οὗτος

Mk 14:58 τὸν ναὸν τοῦτον

Jn 2:21 τοῦ ναοῦ

Mk 14:58/15:29/Mt 26:61/27:40 τὸν ναόν

Variant words
Jn 2:19 ἐγερῶ 20 ἐγερεῖς

Mt 26:61 οἰκοδομῆσαι
Mk 14:58 οἰκοδομήσω

Boismard[45] distinguishes between three stages: C, Jn II-A and II-B. The first stage, C reads: (14) "and he found in the temple those who were selling oxen and sheep and pigeons, and the moneychangers (15) and...he drove all out of the temple (16b) and he said (:) ...'Take these things away. Do not make my Father's house a house of trade'".

Then Jn II-A adds verse 18: "The Jews then said to him, 'What sign have you to show us for doing this?'" Finally, the remaining parts of

[45] M.-É. Boismard, *L'évangile de Jean*, 107ff.

Jn 2:13-22 are expansions attributed to Jn II-B. In Jn II-B much comes from the Synoptics and at this stage the story of cleansing finds its present place in the Gospel.

Neirynck[46] agrees with Boismard about the dependence on the Synoptics but disagrees with him when a distinction is made between Jn II-A and II-B. Neirynck objects against the classification of the request for a sign (v 18) to Jn II-A. He rightly refers to the parallel request for a sign in Jn 6:30 which Boismard refers to Jn II-B, not to Jn II-A.

Neirynck also points to weaknesses and inconsistencies in Boismard's distinction between different levels in II-B and II-A: Since Boismard thinks that 2:13-15 (parts) 16a.17.18.19-22 resulted from the redactional activity of the Evangelist (Jn II-B), a very strong justification must be given by him for separating vv 14.15 (parts) and 16b into a source of its own. Neirynck does not find that Boismard has proven the case sufficiently. For example, Boismard states that the expression "my Father's house" (v 16b) is typical for level C. The phrase, however, only occurs once elsewhere in the Gospel of John, (in Jn 14:2), and there "house" is the rendering of οἰκία, whereas the form οἶκος is used in 2:16b. Two occurrences of a phrase, even in variant forms, are not sufficient basis for calling the phrase "typical." Furthermore, it is hardly defensible to refer the words πρόβατον, βοῦς (sheep, oxen) to Jn II-B in v. 15, while the same words are referred to source C in v 14.

Neirynck points to the fact that the cleansing of the temple in Mk 11:15-19 is followed by the controversy concerning the authority of Jesus in Mk 11:28. He maintains that the similarity here with Jn 2:13-18 (the cleansing and the request for a sign) cannot be denied. This observation is important, and we have also noted some verbal agreements between Jn 2:13-18 and Mk 11:27-28 par. Thus it seems that Neirynck's view finds good support here. In addition to verbal agreement between Jn's account of the cleansing of the temple and the account in Mk, there is significant agreement in the sequence of the cleansing, the request for a sign (Jn), and the question about authority (Mk).

Nevertheless, these similarities speak rather in favour of the views of Dodd, Brown, and others that the material in Jn 2:13-22 is not taken from the Synoptic Gospels, but represent an independent tradition running parallel to the synoptic tradition:

1. With regard to the verbal agreements between Jn 2:13-22 and one

---

[46] F. Neirynck, *Jean et les Synoptiques*, 86-90.

or more of the Synoptic Gospels, it must be said that they are not stronger than between the Pauline version of the institution of the Lord's supper, I Cor. 11:23-26, and the Markan version in Mk 14:22-25. (There are, for example, 60 words in Jn 2:14-16. Of these, 19 words are also used in Mk and Mt together. The corresponding figures for I Cor. 11:23b-26 and Mk 14:22-25 are 68/25. Moreover, besides phrases and words, there is agreement between one complete sentence in I Cor. 11:23-26 and Mk 14:22-25, while only agreements of phrase and word are present between Jn 2:13-16 and the Synoptic parallels).

2. There is similarity of sequence. The challenge to Jesus in Mk 11:27-28 is separated from the cleansing in Mk 11:15-17; yet the challenge seems to refer to the cleansing of the temple. As suggested by Dodd, Brown and others, it is probable that Mk has split up what belonged together in the pre-Markan stage of the tradition, a tradition testified to by John's independent witness.[47]

3. The employment of the word of Jesus about the destruction and rebuilding of the temple in Jn 2:19ff., does not weaken the theory of mutual independence between Jn and the Synoptics in Jn 2:13-22, although the saying found in Jn 2:19ff has close verbal agreements with the Synoptics. One important difference, however, is that Jn is the only one to use ἐγείρειν (to raise up) (syn: οἰκοδομεῖν).

Jn's term is a proper word for construction, but may also refer to the resurrection of the body. Another difference is Jn's use of the imperative, λύσατε, which puts the burden of the destruction on "the Jews" (Jn 2:17).

These distinctive features fit well with the theological tendencies in Jn. They might seem, therefore, to be due to modifications of the Markan or Matthean texts. This is hardly the case, however. Jn 2:19ff does not reflect any specific points from the contexts of the saying in Mt and Mk. The forms of the saying in Mk and Mt themselves show that interpretative adaptations also have been at work in those Gospels. This is most clearly seen in Mk 14:58 where there is a contrast found between the temple that is made with hands and another that is not made with hands. The saying functions here as prophecy of a new temple, being of an entirely different nature than that in connection with the Jerusalem temple. Moreover, the use of this saying in the story on Stephen in Acts 6:14[48] indicates that it was used in the debates and

[47] C.H. Dodd, *Interpretation*, 300-303; 450-451; id., *Historical Tradition*, 89-91; Brown, *John I*, 118-121.

[48] The saying does not occur in Lk, although it is used in Acts, the second volume of the same work.

controversies between the early church and the Jewish authorities. This was also probably the Sitz im Leben of Jn 2:13-22. The passage reflects a situation where the church, from a christological basis, was attempting to emancipate herself from the Jerusalem temple and its worship.

Although there is not extensive use of words from the story of the cleansing (2:13-16) in the subsequent section of vv 17-22, several features suggest that Jn 2:17-22 is an expository commentary on the temple incident in vv 13-16:

1. The terms τὸ ἱερόν (vv 14-15) and ὁ οἶκος (v 16) are interpreted in vv 17-22. In the Old Testament quotation from Ps 69:9 in Jn 2:17 the term ὁ οἶκος from v 16 is repeated, and in vv 18-21 the synonym ὁ ναός is used in the word of Jesus about the destruction of the temple and in the elaboration which follows.

2. The concluding remark in v 22 "..and they believed the Scripture and the word which Jesus had spoken," ties the quotation of Ps 69:9 in v 17 and the subsequent word of Jesus together.[49] They indicate the meaning of the cleansing of the temple.

3. It is clear that verse 17 introduces the interpretation of the cleansing, since it is said that the disciples, against the background of the temple incident, remembered the Old Testament word from Ps 69:9.

4. The request for a sign in v 18 refers back to the cleansing with the words "these things" (ταῦτα).

From this analysis it is seen that in Jn 2:13-22 the Evangelist has brought into his Gospel a unit from the expository activity of the Johannine community, a unit corresponding to Paul's expository interpretation of the institution of the Lord's Supper in I Cor 11:23-34 and the exposition of the healing story in Jn 5:1-18. Already in the Johannine community the story of the cleansing of the temple had been used separately from the Passion narrative to throw light upon the community's attitude towards the temple.[50]

---

[49] See B. Lindars, *John*, 144: Scripture in v 22 refers back to Ps 69:9 cited in v 17: "... it is a fragment of a whole psalm which is known to be a Passion proof text in the primitive Church"; cf. R. Schnackenburg, *Johannesevangelium I*, 367; E. Haenchen, *Johannesevangelium*, 203. C.K. Barrett, *St. John* 201, thinks that v 22 probably means that the Old Testament predicts in a general way the vindication of the Messiah.

[50] Cf. C.H. Dodd, *Historical Tradition* 91; id., *Interpretation* 300-302; E. Haenchen, *Johannesevangelium* 201-203; P. Borgen, *Essays on Christian Origin* 136-138; R.E. Brown, *The Community of the Beloved Disciple* (New York, 1979) 49.

Conclusion

The aim of this paper has been twofold:

1. to discuss the agreements between Jn 2:13-22; 5:1-18; 6:51-58 and the Synoptics against the background of the two mutually independent traditions recorded in I Cor 10:3-4,16,17,21; 11:23-34 and Mark 14:22-25.

The conclusion of the study is that the agreements between Jn 2:13-22; 6:51-58 and the Synoptics are neither closer, nor more striking, than those between the above mentioned Pauline passages and Mark, and in the case of Jn 5:1-18 there are less agreements with the Synoptics. To this extent the analysis of these three Johannine passages supports the hypothesis that Jn and the Synoptics are mutually independent.

2. to throw light upon the transmission of tradition and expository and paraphrasal usage of it in the Gospel. Here the transmission and expository use of the eucharistic tradition in I Cor 10 and 11 have proved to be relevantly parallel.

Although written documents have been examined, the oral tradition seems to be the primary source behind the documents. Also here the parallels between the passages discussed in Jn and those in I Cor 10 and 11 give support to this interpretation. Both in I Cor 10 and 11 and in Jn 2:13-22; 5:1-18 and 6:51-58 the traditions are interpreted to meet the challenges which existed in the Christian communities.

Peder BORGEN

JOHN AND THE SYNOPTICS

Response to P. Borgen

In *Bread from Heaven* (1965) Peder Borgen compares Jn 6:51b-58 with 1 Cor 11:23-26,27-29: "Paul shows the way a tradition about the eucharist can be reduced to fragments and used in a paraphrasing exposition. Paul's eucharistic comments suggest that fragments from the eucharistic traditions may have been paraphrased in a similar way in John 6,51-58". "The corresponding points between John and the haggadah of I Cor. 10,1-4 indicate that fragments from a haggadic story about the manna and the well are also used in this section of John".[1]

In a more recent contribution on "The Use of Tradition in John 12.44-50" (1979) the hypothesis is reformulated and further developed in an application to other discourse material. The Pauline passages of 1 Cor 10 and 11 are presented as an exemple of the use of a tradition in the form of a quote followed by an exposition, in 1 Cor 11:23b-25(26) and 27-34, and in the form of an expository paraphrase of fragments from the eucharistic tradition itself, in 1 Cor 10:16-17,21, comp. Jn 6:51-58. In Jn 12:44-45 a traditional Jesus-logion is quoted in a way which corresponds to Paul's quotation of the eucharistic tradition in 1 Cor 11:23ff., and Jn 12:46-50 is an expository elaboration of the Jesus-logion corresponding to Paul's paraphrase of eucharistic words in 1 Cor 11:27ff. and 10:16-17,21.[2]

In his paper on "John and the Synoptics" (1984) P. Borgen takes a new step by extending this approach to the "narrative" material in Jn 2:13-22 and 5:1-18. The initial hypothesis concerning Jn 6:51-58 tends to become now a general method for the study of tradition in John. In Jn 2 and 5 a unit of tradition is followed by an expository commentary and this larger structure of "text" and commentary has its background in oral tradition, in the expository activity of the Johan-

---

[1] *Bread from Heaven. An Exegetical Study of the Concept of Manna in the Gospel of John and the Writings of Philo* (SupplNT, 10), Leiden, 1965, 91, 92.

[2] "The Use of Tradition in John 12.44-50," *NTS* 26 (1979-80) 18-35; reprinted in *Logos Was the True Light and Other Essays on the Gospel of John*, Trondheim, 1983, 49-66 (esp. 49-54).

nine community. Borgen's conclusion is quite clear: "the analysis of these three Johannine passages (Jn 2:13-22; 5:1-18; 6:51-58) supports the hypothesis of Jn and the Synoptics being mutually independent".[3]

I. THE BORGEN-DAUER THESIS

The name of Peder Borgen has been connected with the study of John and the Synoptics for more than thirty years. I found the first reference to his name in *NTS*, September 1955.[4] His dissertation, mentioned there by his teacher N.A. Dahl, was published, at least in part, four years later in an article entitled "John and the Synoptics in the Passion Narrative", in *NTS* 1959.[5] He proposes the following thesis: "A direct literary relationship between John and the Synoptics cannot be considered, but, on the other hand, units of synoptic material have been added to the Johannine tradition".[6] This last conclusion is repeated in 1983: "at points influence from the Synoptics is probable", with a reference to his earlier article and to A. Dauer's monograph on the passion narrative in John (1972) where "the same hypothesis (is) developed".[7]

The Borgen-Dauer thesis accepts a mediate contact of John with the Synoptics, some elements of the written synoptic Gospels being fused together with the pre-Johannine oral tradition.[8] However, some significant variations can be observed in Dauer's defence of the common thesis. Dauer does not avoid calling it a pre-Johannine *source* and he reckons with the possibility of a *written* source: "ein zusammen-

---

[3] A slightly revised version of P. Borgen's 1984 paper (without the section on Jn 2:13-22) has appeared in 1987 under the title, "John and the Synoptics: Can Paul Offer Help?," in G.F. HAWTHORNE & O. BETZ (eds.), *Tradition and Interpretation in the New Testament*, FS E.E. Ellis, Grand Rapids, MI - Tübingen, 1987, 80-94 (cf. 87: "In this paper, John 5:1-18 will be in the center of the discussion"). In the introduction he refers to my "John and the Synoptics" (1977) to illustrate the "new impetus" given to the view of John's dependence. In the quotation of my conclusion ("not traditions ... but the Synoptic Gospels themselves") the words "regarding Jn 20" are omitted and a generalizing comment is added: "F. Neirynck rejects theories of 'unknown' and 'hypothetical' sources behind John, whether they are supposed to be written or oral" (80).

[4] N.A. DAHL, "Die Passionsgeschichte bei Matthäus," *NTS* 2 (1955-56) 17-32 (32).

[5] *NTS* 5 (1958-59) 246-259; reprinted in *Logos*, 67-80.

[6] *Ibid.*, 80.

[7] *Logos*, 87 (cf. 91, n. 27). Another reference to Dauer is found in the Preface to *Logos*: "A. Dauer uses this thesis and builds further on my studies" (6).

[8] See my survey "John and the Synoptics" (1977), 93-95; = *Evangelica*, 1982, 385-387.

hängende — schriftliche(?) — Quelle".[9] Both Borgen and Dauer take notice of the specific agreements between John and the individual synoptic Gospels. I quote one of Dauer's partial conclusions: "Die Erzählung der joh Quelle [Jn 18:12-27] ist wieder nur verständlich, wenn die Synoptiker als existent und bekannt angenommen werden; nur so lassen sich die Parallelen zu den von Matthäus und Lukas am Mk-Stoff vorgenommenen Änderungen verstehen".[10] In Borgen's article the emphasis is much more on "parallel tendency", "common tradition" and "mutually independent traditions".[11] Yet, the presence of synoptic material "added to the Johannine tradition" was noted in Jn 18:10-11,26; 19:1-3 and 19:31,38,40-42, and he has reprinted this article in 1983 without withdrawing that conclusion: "John is based essentially on independent tradition, even though it had been influenced by the synoptic accounts".[12]

II. 1 COR 11:23-25(26) AND 27-34

The point of departure of Borgen's paper is a comparison between 1 Cor 11:23-25(26) and Mk 14:22-25, the two versions of the eucharistic tradition. This comparison should show what kind of agreements may exist between two mutually independent versions of the same unit of tradition. And in view of the fact that the agreements between John and the Synoptics are not closer, nor more striking, and, in the case of Jn 5:1-18, even fewer, he concludes that in the passages considered John and the Synoptics are mutually independent.

Borgen proceeds to this "generalization" without even asking the question whether the example of the eucharistic tradition is indeed generalizable. The case of 1 Cor 11:23-25 is in some sense unique. More than in any other portion of the gospels liturgical practice is involved here, and it is far from evident that the degree of agreement that exists between 1 Cor 11:23b-25 and Mk 14:22-25 can be used as a

---

[9] A. DAUER, *Die Passionsgeschichte im Johannesevangelium* (SANT, 30), München, 1972, 335 (see also 227). On Dauer's later study, *Johannes und Lukas. Untersuchungen zu den johanneisch-lukanischen Parallelperikopen Joh 4,46/Lk 7,1-10 — Joh 12,1-8/Lk 7,36-50; 10,38-42 — Joh 20,19-29/Lk 24,36-49* (FzB, 50), Würzburg, 1984, compare F. NEIRYNCK, "John 4,46-54: Signs Source and/or Synoptic Gospels," *ETL* 65 (1984 376-381; "Lc 24,36-43. Un récit lucanien," in *À cause de l'évangile. FS J. Dupont* (Lectio Divina, 123), Paris, 1985, 655-680 (esp. 657-665: "Jn 20,19-20").

[10] *Die Passionsgeschichte*, 99.

[11] Cf. Dauer's critical remarks: 131, n. 200; 170, n. 33; 171, n. 38.

[12] *Logos*, 6.

criterion in the study of John and the Synoptics. In this connection the counting of the words in 1 Cor 11:23b-25 is quite irrelevant.

A comparative study of 1 Cor 11:23b-25 and Mk 14:22-25 raises much more critical problems than Borgen seems to suggest in his paper. The possibility of Markan redaction and of Pauline interpretation within the traditional unit of verses 23b-25 is not even mentioned, although it is not at all improbable that the two traditions in their pre-Pauline and pre-Markan form would show an even higher degree of similarity.

Many scholars will agree, I think, with Borgen's description of 1 Cor 11:23-24 as "tradition received and handed on" and "paraphrasing commentary attached". "He (Paul) utilizes fragments — words and phrases — from the quote and builds them into a paraphrasing exposition together with legal terms, etc.". "Paul writes the exposition himself and applies the eucharistic tradition to a specific case".

Borgen is much less convincing in the commentary he adds to his own analysis. Paul uses traditional ethical/legal forms, but what is meant by "fused into traditional forms" (see "the guiding rule")? The tradition of 1 Cor 11:23b-25 "was brought orally to the church in Corinth", but Borgen tends to disregard the distinction between tradition and exposition when he maintains that "the oral form is primary", although the written form of the exposition in 1 Cor 11:27ff. is evident.

In fact, Borgen's use of 1 Cor 11:23-34 as a model in his analysis of Jn 2:13-22 and 5:1-18 is almost contradictory. In 1 Cor 11 the quote of a pre-Pauline tradition is followed by Paul's own exposition. A comparable situation in the Gospel seems to be the transmission of a traditional story (2:13-16; 5:1-9) followed by the evangelist's own expository commentary (2:17-22; 5:10-20).

III. "Text" and "Commentary"

In the section on Jn 6 Borgen reformulates his position regarding Jn 6:51b-58, with a few observations on the midrashic character of Jn 6:31-58 (cf. *Bread*). More innovating is the section on *"Text" and Commentary* where he uses the "model" of 1 Cor 11:23-34 in an analysis of Jn 5:1-18 and 2:13-22.

Of course, the notions of repetition, paraphrase and commentary are not new in the interpretation of John. In Borgen's hypothesis, however, the paraphrasing commentary is rather pre-Johannine: "text" and

"commentary" (5:1-9, 10-18; 2,13-16, 17-22) form a traditional unit
from the transmitting and expository activity of the Johannine community.[13]

Jn 5:1-18

Borgen compares Jn 5:1-18 with the sabbath controversies in
Mt 12:1-8 and Lk 13:10-17 and concludes that the three passages
follow a traditional structure for a controversial case being discussed by
means of a subsequent judicial dialogue. Although Mt 12:5-7 is probably Matthew's interpretative expansion of Mk 2:23-28,[14] he rejects
such an interpretative use of Markan material in Jn 5:1-18 because of
some distinctive features in Jn 5:10-18. The verbatim agreement between Jn 5:8 and Mk 2:9 is waved aside as a stereotyped phrase,[15] and
with regard to possible connections of Jn 5:18 with Mk 2:7 (blasphemy) and of Jn 5:16,18 with Mk 3:6 (the persecution and the
attempt to kill Jesus) he uses the word "arbitrary":[16] there are no
verbal agreements and, contrary to the expository commentary in
Jn 5:10-18, the corresponding discussion in Mk 3:1-6 precedes the
healing.

My first observation concerns the synoptic passages of Mt 12:1-8
and Lk 13:10-17. Unfortunately, the presentation of the "text" (with
the separation of "the case" and the "expository dialogue": Mt 12:1,2-
8 and Lk 13:10-13,14-17) is not followed by a real "commentary". The
brief remark that the pericope of Lk 13:10-17 "is peculiar to Lk, and
does not come from the other gospels" seems to suggest, although not
unambiguously, that "at least the pericope as such" is traditional.[17] It
could be mentioned that the style of the story is Lukan and that some
commentators have "the impression that we have here to do with a
more sophisticated type of writing than we find in Mark" and therefore
"suppose the evangelist himself to be responsible for the actual compo-

---

[13] My response will concentrate on his analysis of Jn 5:1-18 and 2:13-22, of direct
relevance to the theme of our discussion, "John and the Synoptics." On the problem of
Paul and the Synoptics, see F. NEIRYNCK, "Paul and the Sayings of Jesus," in A. VANHOYE
(ed.), L'Apôtre Paul. Personnalité, style et conception du ministère (BETL, 73), Leuven,
1986, 265-321.

[14] Cf. supra, 428.

[15] Cf. 429.

[16] Cf. 430.

[17] In the 1984 paper: "a pericope which is peculiar to Luke, and does not come from
the other gospels (at least not the pericope as such)" (34).

sition".[18] In his monograph on the miracle stories in Luke (1977), U. Busse has made the suggestion that "Die Auseinandersetzung mit dem Synagogenvorsteher sei kompositionell nachträglich in eine vorge-gebene Wundererzählung aus dem Sondergut eingefügt, die Lukas dementsprechend überarbeitet habe".[19] Anyway the problem of John and the Synoptics cannot be discussed without a more thoroughgoing examination of the synoptic parallels. The repetition of phrases, a "distinctive feature" in Jn 5:1-18,[20] is not wholly absent in Lk 13:10-17:

11 ἰδοὺ ... πνεῦμα ἔχουσα ἀσθενείας ἔτη δεκαοκτώ

   16 ἣν ἔδησεν ὁ σατανᾶς ἰδοὺ δέκα καὶ ὀκτὼ ἔτη

16b ἔδησεν   16c ἀπὸ τοῦ δεσμοῦ τούτου

12 ἀπολέλυσαι   15 λύει   16 λυθῆναι

10 ἐν τοῖς σάββασιν   14 τῷ σαββάτῳ   14b τῇ ἡμέρᾳ τοῦ σαββάτου

   15 τῷ σαββάτῳ   16c τῇ ἡμέρᾳ τοῦ σαββάτου

14 τῷ ὄχλῳ   17 πᾶς ὁ ὄχλος

Another "distinctive feature" and one of the "stronger arguments against John's dependence on the Synoptics" is the elaborate form of changing the stage in Jn 5:10-18.[21] In fact, this feature is "distinctively Johannine", and not "distinctively traditional". It has been described by C.H. Dodd as "a kind of dramatic technique", "the device of two stages upon which the action is exhibited".[22] In Jn 5, the healed person is with:

1-9   Jesus (at the Sheep Pool)

    10-13 the Jews

14   Jesus (in the temple)

    15-18 the Jews and Jesus

---

[18] J.M. CREED, Luke, 1930, p. 182.

[19] U. BUSSE, Die Wunder des Propheten Jesus (FzB, 24), Stuttgaart, 1977, ²1979, 293. For a tentative reconstruction of the traditional healing story in vv. 11-13, cf. 297. The debate in vv. 14-16 is secondarily added, "eine luk. Komposition, wobei er offensichtlich nur ein freies Wanderlogion zur Auffüllung der Argumentation benutzt hat" (ibid). Vv. 10 and 17 are attributed to Lukan redaction (294, 297). Compare also M. TRAUTMANN, Zeichenhafte Handlungen Jesu. Ein Beitrag zur Frage nach dem geschichtlichen Jesus (FrB, 37), Würzburg, 1980, 191-192; E. SCHÜSSLER FIORENZA, In Memory of Her. A Feminist Reconstruction of Christian Origins, New York, 1983, 125: "it is possible that the healing story Luke 13:10-13 was originally independent and was expanded to a dialogue at a later stage".

[20] The phrase on "distinctive features" (1984, 33) has been revised in the published text (1987, 89: "a distinctive use of this common form").

[21] Cf. supra, 430.

[22] The Interpretation of the Fourth Gospel, 315 (Jn 4); 347-348 (Jn 7-8); Historical Tradition in the Fourth Gospel, 96-97 (Jn 18,28-19,16). See also A. DAUER, Die Passions-geschichte, 102-103; et al.

Compare the healing of the blind man on the sabbath (9:14, cf. 5:9b)
in Jn 9:1-7 | the people: 8-12 | the Pharisees: 13-17 (the man), 18-23
(the parents), 24-34 (the man) | Jesus: 35-41. There is nothing similar in
Mt 12:1-8. But no attention is given to the parallel text of Mk 2:23-28.
This is most curious since it is normally not Mt 12:1-8 but Mk 2:1-3:6,
and especially 2:1-12 and 2:23-28; 3:1-6, which is cited as the synoptic
parallel. In Mark the two sabbath pericopes are closely connected.
Together they form the conclusion of the section of controversies (2:1-
3:6). In Matthew they are separated from Mt 9:1-17 = Mk 2:1-22 and,
as a result of the Matthean expansions in 12:5-7 and 11-12a and the
transitional formula μεταβὰς ἐκεῖθεν in 12:9a, the two pericopes are
more clearly distinguished than they are in Mark. I can agree with
R. Pesch's form-critical description of the connection of 3:1-6 with
2:23-28, at least with this reservation: the connection is not necessarily
pre-Markan. I quote:[23]
"a) in V 2 sind die Pharisäer von 2,24 (vgl. V 6) als Subjekt vorausgesetzt, d.h., die vorangehende Erzählung ist vorausgesetzt, und durch sie
sind Auflauern und Anklageabsicht motiviert;
b) Jesus Frage von V 4 (hier keine Gegenfrage) ist auf die Pharisäer-
frage 2,24 polemisch bezogen: Stichwortverbindungen: ἔξεστιν, τοῖς
σάββασιν;
c) in V 1 (wie in den Formulierungen von VV 2.4) ist die Angabe von
2,23, daß das erzählte Geschehen *am Sabbat* spielt, vorausgesetzt; in
einer selbständigen Erzählung wäre eine ausführlichere Exposition not-
wendig;
d) auch der Vergleich mit anderen Perikopenanfängen (z.B. 2,13; 6,1;
8,27; 11,11) kann den nicht-selbständigen Charakter unserer Erzählung
bestätigen"
    When we take Mk 2:23-3:6 as one section in Mark there is no
ground for the objection that the discussion precedes the healing since
the second pericope is a continuation of the debate following the
plucking of grain on the sabbath. And the Johannine change of the
stage has a synoptic analogy in Mk 3:1.

    A most typical sentence in Borgen's paper is found on p. 34:[24] "The
agreement between Jn 5:10 ... οὐκ ἔξεστιν ... and Mt 12:2 is due to the
circumstances that a traditional form is used in Jn's paraphrase,
corresponding to Paul's use of traditional (gospel) forms in 1 Cor 10:21

---

[23] *Das Markusevangelium*, vol. I, 188.
[24] 1984, 34. Cf. *supra*, 429.

and 11:27ff" (sic). Οὐκ ἔξεστιν is treated as an isolated phrase and the striking parallelism between the structure of Jn 5:1-18 and Mk 2:1-12; 2:23-3:6 receives no consideration:[25]

John	Mark
5:1-9a the healing	2:1-12 the healing
8 ... ἆρον τὸν κράβαττόν σου	11 ... ἆρον τὸν κράβαττόν σου
9 ... ἦρεν τὸν κράβαττον αὐτοῦ	12 ... ἄρας τὸν κράβαττον
9 ἦν δὲ σάββατον ἐν ...	2:23 ἐν τοῖς σάββασιν
10 ἔλεγον οὖν οἱ Ἰουδαῖοι ...·	24 καὶ οἱ Φαρισαῖοι ἔλεγον ...·
σάββατόν ἐστιν,	... ποιοῦσιν τοῖς σάββασιν
καὶ οὐκ ἔξεστίν σοι	ὃ οὐκ ἔξεστιν.
ἆραι τὸν κράβαττόν σου.	
the *man* carrying his bed	the *disciples* plucking grain
11-16 *Jesus* ὁ ποιήσας αὐτὸν ὑγιῆ	3:1-6 *Jesus* εἰ ... θεραπεύσει αὐτόν
... ἐν σαββάτῳ (cf. 7:23)	2 τοῖς σάββασιν
	4 ἔξεστιν τοῖς σάββασιν
17 ... ἐργάζομαι.	ἀγαθὸν ποιῆσαι ... ἢ ἀποκτεῖναι;
18 ἐζήτουν	6 συμβούλιον ἐδίδουν κατ' αὐτοῦ
αὐτὸν ... ἀποκτεῖναι	ὅπως αὐτὸν ἀπολέσωσιν.

Compare Mk 3:6 (and Jn 5:18) with:

Mk 11:18 ἐζήτουν   πῶς αὐτὸν   ἀπολέσωσιν
    12:12 ἐζήτουν   αὐτὸν   κρατῆσαι
    14:1 ἐζήτουν ... πῶς αὐτὸν ... κρατήσαντες ἀποκτείνωσιν.

The seeking to kill Jesus is indeed "central in Jn" (5:18; 7:1,19,20,25; 8:37,40; 11:53; cf. persecution: 5:16; 15:20), but in John and Mark the motif appears here for the first time (Jn 5:18; Mk 3:6) and in both gospels it is connected with the violation of the sabbath and in both gospels too it is found at the conclusion of the same pattern: first the healing, then a controversial sabbath case in the action of people who are related to Jesus: the healed man and the disciples, and finally Jesus' healing activity as a violation of the sabbath. No modern interpreter of the gospel of Mark can blame the Fourth Evangelist for having made the connection between Mk 2:1-12 and Mk (2:23-28) 3:1-6.

Three other features in Jn 5:10-18 can be explained in the light of Mk 2:1-12.
1. In the healing stories of Jn 5 and Mk 2 special emphasis is given to the order of Jesus: "rise, take up your bed, and walk" (Jn 5:8;

[25] My suggestion is, of course, not that "John has changed the term 'disciples' into the term 'man' ", or that the man became a disciple, but the contrast Jews – Jesus (and the healed man) in John can be compared with that of the Pharisees – Jesus (and the disciples, the healed man) and its role in the narrative of Mk 2:23-28; 3:1-6.

Mk 2:11). In both gospels the phrase is repeated in the description of the healing as an immediate execution of Jesus' order (Jn 5:9; Mk 2:12) and, more significantly, the phrase is also used in the debate, in Jn 5:12 (cf. 11) in the sabbath discussion (τίς ἐστιν ... ὁ εἰπών σοι·), and in Mk 2:9 in the debate about forgiveness of sin (τί ἐστιν εὐκοπώτερον ... ἢ εἰπεῖν·).

Jn 5	Mk 2
	11 σοὶ λέγω,
8 ἔγειρε ἆρον τὸν κράβαττόν σου καὶ περιπάτει	ἔγειρε ἆρον τὸν κράβαττόν σου καὶ ὕπαγε ...
9 καὶ εὐθέως ἐγένετο ὑγιὴς ...	12 καὶ ἠγέρθη
καὶ ἦρεν τὸν κράβαττον αὐτοῦ καὶ περιε-	καὶ εὐθὺς ἄρας τὸν κράβαττον ἐξῆλθεν ...
πάτει	
(10) ἆραι τὸν κράβαττόν σου	
(11) ... μοι εἶπεν·	
ἆρον τὸν κράβαττόν σου καὶ περιπάτει	
12 τίς ἐστιν ὁ ἄνθρωπος ὁ εἰπών σοι·	9 τί ἐστιν ... ἢ εἰπεῖν·
	ἔγειρε
ἆρον καὶ περιπάτει.	καὶ ἆρον τὸν κράβαττόν σου καὶ περιπάτει;

2. Jn 5:14 ἴδε ὑγιὴς γέγονας, μηκέτι ἁμάρτανε ... The healing and the forgiveness of sin are closely connected in the story of Mk 2:1-12. Compare 2:9 and 5b,10b-11. In light of the parallel in Mark, the healed paralytic is a man to whom Jesus has said: your sins are forgiven. As far as I see, this distinctive feature, the association of forgiveness and healing, is wholly absent in the case of the *adultera*!

3. The motif for the Jews seeking to kill Jesus is not only the violation of the sabbath (Jn 5:18). One can compare once more with Mk 3:6: "Die Tötungsabsicht der Gegner erscheint am Ende der Perikope nicht besonders angemessen, wohl nach 2,1-3,5!", and: "Der Vorwurf der Lästerung [2:7] muß ... mit 3,6 in Verbindung gesehen werden".[27]

Jn 5:18: ὅτι οὐ μόνον ἔλυεν τὸ σάββατον, ἀλλὰ καὶ πατέρα ἴδιον ἔλεγεν τὸν θεὸν ἴσον ἑαυτὸν ποιῶν τῷ θεῷ. Cf. v. 17, "My Father is working still and I am working," and Schnackenburg's commentary: "Dem Mann ist mit der Heilung zugleich seine Sünde von Gott vergeben worden; das ist es, was Jesus mit dem Satz meint: 'Mein Vater arbeitet bis jetzt' (V 17)".[27] Compare Mk 2:7 βλασφημεῖ· τίς δύναται ἀφιέναι ἁμαρτίας εἰ μὴ εἷς ὁ θεός; In this connection Jn 10,33 should

[26] J. GNILKA, *Das Evangelium nach Markus*, vol. I, 126, 102 (see also 100).
[27] R. SCHNACKENBURG, *Das Johannesevangelium*, vol. II, 123.

be quoted: ... περὶ βλασφημίας, καὶ ὅτι σὺ ἄνθρωπος ὢν ποιεῖς σεαυτὸν θεόν (cf. v. 36).

In a final objection, Borgen opposes to the (traditional) sabbath question in Jn 5:10-18 the evangelist's own discourse in 5:19ff. in which "the Christological idea in Jn 5:17 is developed more independently".[28] The evangelist's interest in the christological aspect is rightly emphasized, but it is precisely the weakness of Borgen's analysis, it seems to me, that he has not been able to grasp the christological (!) orientation in the progression from the healing in 5:1-9 to 5:18.

Jn 2:13-22

Borgen's reaction to the hypothesis of John's dependence on the Synoptics is less negative with regard to Jn 2:13-22. He also recognizes that in this case "there is not extensive use of words from the story of the cleansing (2:13-16) in the subsequent section of vv. 17-22".[29] Nevertheless his conclusion will be that "in Jn 2:13-22 the Evangelist has brought into his Gospel a unit from the expository activity of the Johannine community".[30]

---

[28] Borgen departs from almost all commentators by withdrawing 5,17-18 from the evangelist's redaction. Cf. H. KOTILA, Umstrittener Zeuge. Studien zur Stellung des Gesetzes in der johanneischen Theologiegeschichte (AASF Diss., 48), Helsinki, 1988, 19: "die communis opinio der Exegeten, dass die V. 17-18 in ihrer heutigen Fassung von E stammen. (n. 1:) Dies bestreitet heutzutage kaum jemand."
Borgen's distinction between the "case" in vv. 1-9 and the "expository dialogue" in vv. 10-18, both pre-Johannine, can be compared with the separation of tradition (vv. 2-9b) and redaction (vv. 9c-16) in J. Becker's (and Bultmann's) pre-Johannine SQ. The communis opinio is well represented in Fortna's new reconstruction of the Source: 5:2-9b (with a tacit correction of his earlier hypothesis: v. 14 is no longer mentioned).
But this scholarly consensus is not without fail. The miraculous knowledge of Jesus in v. 6b may be due to the evangelist, "der einzige Einschub des Evangelisten" for R. Schnackenburg and more recently for U. Schnelle. M.-É. Boismard attributes to the evangelist not only v. 6b but also v. 7 and finally the entire vv. 6b,c,7, and he reduces the traditional healing story to vv. 5-6a,8-9b. My objections to this understanding of vv. 6b-7 as an insertion into a preexistent story have received a positive response in L.T. Witkamp's study. Starting from B. Lindars's description of 5:2b-9 as a fusion of two distinct stories, an amalgamation possibly due to John himself, Witkamp reckons with "intentional composition" of the evangelist redacting his traditional material. He accepts "a tradition-historical connection" between the formulation of Jesus' words in Jn 5:8 and Mk 2:9,11. Cf. L.T. WITKAMP, The Use of Traditions in John 5,1-18, in JSNT 25 (1985) 19-47; E.T. of Chapter V in his dissertation: Jesus van Nazareth in de gemeente van Johannes. Over de interaktie van traditie en ervaring, Kampen, 1986, 114-138.
[29] Cf. supra, 436.
[30] Ibid.

Borgen presents three observations in favour of the theory of mutual independence between John and the Synoptics in Jn 2:13-22.

1. The verbal agreements are not stronger than between 1 Cor 11:23-26 and Mk 14:22-25. — As I noted above, this liturgical tradition is not an acceptable standard in the study of the gospels. The "agreement of one complete sentence in 1 Cor 11:23-26 and Mk 14:22-25" is that of τοῦτό μου ἐστιν τὸ σῶμα / τοῦτό ἐστιν τὸ σῶμά μου!

2. The agreement of sequence: Mk 11:15-17 and 11:27-28 probably "belonged together in a pre-Markan stage of the tradition, a tradition for which Jn testifies as an independent witness".

It can be noted that Borgen fully recognizes the agreement between Jn 2:18 (τί σημεῖον δεικνύεις ἡμῖν ὅτι) ταῦτα ποιεῖς and Mk 11:28a (ἐν ποίᾳ ἐξουσίᾳ) ταῦτα ποιεῖς; (cf. 28b ἢ τίς σοι ἔδωκεν τὴν ἐξουσίαν ταύτην ἵνα ταῦτα ποιῇς). The possibility of a pre-Markan sequence can be considered (e.g., Mk 11:15, 28a, 29a, 30)[32] and John's immediate association of the cleansing and the question can be based on a pre-Johannine tradition. But, at a closer examination, this appears to be an unnecessary hypothesis.

In Mark the account of the cleansing is "sandwiched" between the two parts of the story about the fig tree, but there can be no doubt that ταῦτα ποιεῖς in 11:28 refers back to the temple cleansing. In both Matthew and Luke the complexity of the Markan composition (and its chronology of three days: cf. 11:11a, 15a, 27a) has been reduced by putting together the two parts of the story about the fig tree (Matthew) or by eliminating it (Luke):

Mt	Mk	Lk
(I) 21:(1-9),10-11	(I) 11:(1-10),11	19:(29-40),(41-44)
21:12-13		
21:14-17		
(II) 21:18-19	(II) 11:12-14	——
	11:15-15	—— 19:45-46
	11:18-19	—— 19:47-48 Summary
21:20-22	(III) 11:20-25	——
21:23-27	*11:27-33*	—— 20:1-7

[31] "As suggested by Dodd, Brown and others it is *probable* that Mk has split up ..." (Borgen). Cf. R.E. BROWN, *John*, vol. I, 119: "As Buse and Dodd suggest, it is quite *possible* that the intervening material has split up what was originally one scene" (italics mine).

[32] See, e.g., P.J. FARLA, *Jesus' oordeel over Israël*, Kampen, 1978, 142.

A more radical simplification of the story is found in Jn 2:13ff. But, much better than Matthew and Luke, John has preserved the Markan meaning of the question about authority (ταῦτα ποιεῖς). John shows here a correct understanding of the Markan intercalation (or alternation):

Mk 11:	1-11	——
	——	12-14
	15-19	——
	——	20-25
	27-33	——

As noted above, the sequence (and combination) of the healing and the sabbath debate in Jn 5:1-18 is another example of John's understanding of the Markan composition (the concentric structure of Mk 2:1-3:6).

3. Although the saying about the destruction and rebuilding of the temple in Jn 2:19 "has close verbal agreement with the Synoptics", there is "one important difference" (Jn uses ἐγείρειν). Another difference is John's use of the imperative, λύσατε. The answer is given by Borgen: "These distinctive features fit well into the theological tendencies in Jn."

Two more specific observations are added. First, Jn 2:19 does not reflect "any specific points" from the saying in Matthew and Mark. — Borgen correctly notes that the imperative λύσατε "puts the burden of the destruction on 'the Jews'", but he does not say more about his interpretation of λύσατε. Is it a conditional sentence (Dodd: "If you destroy this temple, I will raise it up"), or rather a prophetic imperative (cf. Bultmann, et al.)? In this last solution λύσατε (and ἐγερῶ) refer to the future and John's form of the saying comes close to Mk 14:58 καταλύσω – οἰκοδομήσω (ctr. Mt 26:61 δύναμαι καταλῦσαι – οἰκοδομῆσαι).

Secondly, "Acts 6:14 indicates that the saying was used in debates and controversies between the early church and the Jewish authorities". — Before drawing any conclusion about "the Sitz im Leben of Jn 2:13-22" a correct understanding of the saying in Acts 6:14 should be given. I quote G. Schneider's commentary on Acts: "Mit Sicherheit verwendet hier Lukas das Tempelwort Jesu aus der markinischen Prozeßszene (Mk 14,57f) und ändert es zu diesem Zweck um".[33]

Borgen's final observation concerning Jn 2:17 (ὁ οἶκος), 18 (ταῦτα),

---

[33] G. SCHNEIDER, Die Apostelgeschichte, vol. I, 438.

19-21 (ὁ ναός), 22 (Scripture and the word of Jesus) are, of course, quite acceptable in the hypothesis of John's dependence on the Synoptics.

V. CONCLUSION

The "form" of expository interpretation and paraphrasing commentary can be employed in the interpretation of the Fourth Gospel, although the vague description of this "form" will have to be specified in each peculiar section of the Gospel. But it has no relevance in a discussion about John's dependence on the Synoptics. And if any conclusion can be drawn from the "model" of 1 Cor 11:23-25,(26) and 27-34, it would be that a "tradition" (saying or narrative) can be used by John as a starting point for a further elaboration. However, the presence of this structure, "text" and "commentary", allows of no conclusion about pre-Johannine or synoptic origin of this tradition.[34]

F. NEIRYNCK

---

[34] This text was delivered at the Jerusalem meeting, April 16, 1984. Only a few updating notes were added to the original Response (notes 3, 9, 13, 25, 28).

JOHN AND THE SYNOPTICS

Tradition Received and Handed on.
A Paraphrasing Commentary Attached

Let me start with Neirynck's conclusion which indicates some common ground between us:
"And if any conclusion can be drawn from the "model" of I Cor 11:23-25 (26) and 27-34, it would be that a "tradition" (saying or narrative) can be used by John as a starting point for a further elaboration" (p. 450). In like manner Neirynck states: "Many scholars will agree, I think, with Borgen's description of I Cor 11:23-34 as 'tradition received and handed on' and 'paraphrasing commentary attached'. 'He (Paul) utilizes fragments — words and phrases — from the quote and builds them into a paraphrasing exposition together with legal terms, etc.' 'Paul writes the exposition himself and applies the eucharistic tradition to a specific case'" (p. 441).

Some point should be presented here already at the outset:

1. Paul gives evidence for the existence of this model already in the fifties, that is, in the pre-synoptic and pre-Johannine period.

2. Paul shows that such paraphrasing commentary could have a unit of oral tradition as "text". Since the commentary addresses itself to a specific issue in the Corinthian Church and is part of a letter to that Church, it replaces the orally delivered instruction which Paul would have given if he had been present in person.

3. Paul gives evidence for the fact that a unit of tradition and the subsequent commentary could be presented together, separate from a comprehensive Gospel Document.

In this way we receive a glimpse into pre-synoptic and pre-Johannine handling of tradition.

Neirynck and I seem to be in general agreement that this use of tradition is not limited to the pre-synoptic and pre-Johannine stage. There are three main possibilities:

a) The quotation of a tradition followed by a subsequent paraphrazing commentary may belong to the pre-synoptic and pre-Johannine stages;

b) it may result from an evangelist's own interpretation of oral tradition or

c) it may take place when a section of a Gospel was used as the text to be commented upon and paraphrased.

One difference between Neirynck and myself seems to be that he is more hesitant to consider possibilities 1. and 2. I must add here that when I discuss possibilities 1. and 2., I base the discussion on analysis of documents. The question asked is: how far can such settings (1. pre-synoptic and pre-Johannine and 2. the evangelist's own interpretation of oral tradition) explain, in a plausible way, the features of the document concerned?

The Eucharistic Tradition

Neirynck writes: "The case of 1 Cor. 11:23-25 is in some sense unique. More than in any other portion of the gospels liturgical practice is involved here and it is far from evident that the degree of agreement that exists between 1 Cor. 11:23b-25 and Mk 14:22-25 can be used as a criterion in the study of John and the synoptics" (pp. 440-1). A reference to this occurs later in his response: "As I noted above, this liturgical tradition is not an acceptable standard in the story of the gospels" (p. 448).

Neirynck seems to hold the view that the wording of the eucharistic tradition was more stable and fixed in its versions than was the wording in other gospel traditions.

Neirynck relies here on a view which seem to have become a kind of stereotype. He does not present documentation in support of this interpretation. There is a remark in his response, however, which seems to imply that the eucharistic traditions in 1 Cor 11:23b-25 and Mk 14:22-25 are not so unique, as thought to be the case, since Neirynck maintains that here, just at other places, one should question whether or not possible editorial modifications of the tradition are probable.

Several observations show that the eucharistic tradition should be discussed together with the gospel material in general.

a) In Mt, Mk and Lk the eucharistic tradition is part of the Gospels. It is placed together with the other traditions about Jesus' words and actions. Consequently, the story of the institution of the eucharist is an integral part of the general run of each one of these gospels.

b) As Neirynck seems to indicate, if one holds the view that the wording of the eucharistic tradition is stable and fixed in a unique way, does it mean that the text of the gospel traditions had no stability at all at the oral stage?

c) The existence of different versions of the eucharistic tradition shows that it was not unique, but functioned in a way similar to that of the rest of the gospel tradition. The most obvious documentation of this is the Markan version, the longer and shorter version of Luke, and I Cor 11:23-25 (26) seen within this context.

d) The eucharistic tradition can be used as basis for paraphrasing commentary, just as the other gospel traditions can, for example in applying the tradition to a specific issue.

e) Paul says explicitly in I Cor 11:23 that he has received the eucharistic text as tradition, and that he has transmitted it to the church in Corinth. The usual technical terms for the transmission of tradition is used by him (παρέλαβον, παρέδωκα).

Conclusion: Evidence from the texts does not support the view that the eucharistic tradition is unique. (See now further: P. Borgen, "Natt-verdstradisjonen i 1 Kor 10 og 11 som evangelietradisjon," *Svensk Exegetisk Årsbok*, 51, (1986) 32-9). It can be seen as other tradition can. As for the different versions, and Mk's independence of Paul, I refer to G. Bornkamm and H. Schürmann. An extensive list of scholars could here be added.

It may also be added that I compare texts of Paul and Mark in their present form because these are the texts we know. They also have their place in the transmission process of the tradition: They therefore illustrate what kind of agreement can exist between two independent versions of the same unit of tradition.

John 6:51b-58

As for Jn 6:51b-58 the conclusion of my analysis is that the agreement in wording, style and content between John 6:51-58 and I Cor 10:3-4, 10,16-17,21 and 11:23-29 show that John draws on eucharistic and manna traditions in a way similar to Paul: These similarities show that John is here closer to Paul than to the Synoptics. Since John elsewhere is not dependent upon I Cor., however, he is not dependent on Paul in John 6:51b-58 either. Thus, John utilizes an independent tradition on the institution of the Lord's Supper, and presupposes that the eucharistic tradition already was associated with the biblical stories on the manna and the well. It is in accordance with this conclusion of John's independence that he uses the term η σάρξ and not τὸ σῶμα which is found in the synoptic and Pauline version. The Johannine version of the institution is also documented by Ignatius' use of the term ἡ σάρξ in Rom 7:3; Philad. 4:1; Smyr 7:1 and also by Justin in Apol I:66:2,29.

Our conclusion puts us in general agreement with Boismard's interpretation, when he suggests that John here reflects a liturgical tradition which is also represented by Paul. Boismard fails to draw the line from this conclusion to his analysis of other parts of the Gospel of John, where he rather employs literary source criticism. Against the background of Jn 6:51-58 this question is pertinent: Are there other passages in Jn which have their setting in the life of the Johannine community and its transmission and exposition of tradition?

In his response, Neirynck mentions my discussion of Jn 6:51b-58 in passing, without thereby making any comments on it. Since I here find myself in general agreement with Boismard, I expected to find Neirynck's treatment of this passage in his extensive discussion of Boismard's view in his book *Jean et les Synoptiques. Examen critique de l'exégèse de M.-E. Boismard.* He refers to verses in 6:51ff in his discussion of Boismard's analysis on textual criticism (pp. 25,32-34,37) and stylistic characteristics (pp. 46,55,68,69,210,211,214,225,228,229, 232, 260,295).

There is no discussion, however, of Boismard's treatment of Jn 6:51b-58 as a whole. Boismard (pp. 204-205) stressed the agreement between Jn 6:51b and I Cor. 11:24, while in Neirynck's book I Cor 11:24 does not appear in the index. Thus, in both cases Neirynck has neither analysed nor made any comments on Jn 6:51b-58. I regret this, since in Jn 6:51b-58 and in I Cor 10 and 11 both eucharistic traditions and manna traditions are used. Consequently, Jn 6:51b-58 is a good starting point for our discussion of John.

John 5:1-18

Neirynck discusses at some length my analysis of Jn 5:1-18. As I read his response, he does not object to my understanding of the form of the passage, viz. that it follows a traditional structure for a controversial case being discussed by means of a subsequent halakhic dialogue.

I do not see any need for presupposing either Mk, Mt, or Lk as a source for this passage. The features of the passage, both in form and content, can be satisfactorily explained in the following two partly alternative ways:

1. The Evangelist utilized an instance of healing on the sabbath as case story on the basis of which he developed a halakhic debate thereby relating christology to the sabbath question.

This understanding parallels nicely the combined Busse-Neirynck interpretation of Lk 13:10-17 where Lk utilizes a story of sabbath healing as a case story. He then repeats phrases from the story in a subsequent halakhic dialogue. Neirynck is not precise in his citation cf me when he states my view in this was: "The repetition of phrases, a 'distinctive feature' in Jn 5:1-18 ..." (p. 443). My point is that only in Jn 5:10-18 phrases from the story (the case) are repeated quite *mechanically* (p. 430).

2. The Evangelist records a sabbath healing which had already served in the Johannine community as a case story together with a subsequent halakhic debate.

Since the application of christology to the sabbath question does not seem to be of central importance in the Evangelist's own situation, I am inclined to find this alternative to be the more probable one. There are scholars, however, who hold the view that the sabbath question and the question of the temple, etc. are central issues also at the time when the Gospel was written.

The choice between these two alternatives does not affect my thesis as such that Jn here is independent of the Synoptics and that the features of the passage receive a plausible and sufficient explanation in this way.

Moreover, several observations speak against the theory that Jn uses elements from Mk 2:1-3:6. Some of these are:

a) the healing in Mk 2:1-12 takes place in Capernaum, whereas in Jn 5:1ff it takes place in Jerusalem at the Beth-zatha pool. This difference cannot be explained by Jn's interest in Jerusalem, since the healing in Jn 4:46 is located in Capernaum and the feeding of the five thousand in Jn 6 took place at the lake of Galilee.

b) Nothing is said in Mk 2:1-3:6 about "the carrying of the mat" being a violation of the sabbath. The reason is, of course, that the healing in 2:1-12 did not take place on the sabbath. Moreover, it seems improbable that such an interpretation in Jn 5:1-18 is based upon the healing of the man with a withered hand in Mk 3:1-6. In addition, the story in Mk 3:1-6 is located in Galilee.

c) In Mk 2:1-3:6 only Mk 2:23-28 has the same form as the one found in Jn 5:1-18: a controversial case is discussed by means of a subsequent judicial dialogue. In Mk 2:23-28 there is also an appeal to Scripture corresponding to the allusion to Gen 2:1ff in Jn 5:1-18. The Scripture references are so different, however, that there can be no question of dependence. Mk 2:23-28 is not a story of healing and can therefore not be the basis for Jn 5:1-18.

3. Neirynck lists the word "man", Jn 5:9, and the word "disciples" Mk 2:24, among the agreements which to him show that Jn is dependent on Mk. His view that Jn has a literary dependence on Mk then

means that Jn has changed the term "disciples" in Mk into the term "man". This point seems to lack plausibility.

4. Neirynck suggests that Jn's change of the scene in Jn 5:10-18 derives from Mk 3:1ff. This cannot be the case, since Mk 3:1ff introduces a new case study (Mk 2:23ff, the plucking of the grain; 3:1ff, the healing of a person with a withered hand). Moreover, Jn changes the stage three times (vv 10-13; the Jews and the person healed; v. 14: Jesus and the healed person; vv 15-18: the healed person, the Jews and Jesus).

5. Neirynck stresses that in Jn 5:18 and Mk 3:6 the motif "of the seeking to kill Jesus" appears for the first time in both gospels. The motif occurs, however, in two different healing stories, the healing of the person with withered hand (Mk 3:1ff) and the healing of the paralytic, (Jn 5:1ff). And if Jn was dependent on Mk for this common motif, he should than have already mentioned it in Jn 2:13-18 as part of the cleansing of the temple, from its use in Mk's story on the cleansing of the temple in Mk 11:15-18.

6. The interpretation of Jn 5:1-18 suggested in my paper explains the form of the passage and the method used in the expository dialogue. It also explains why this elaboration of the healing story would be acceptable to the readers. The person who developed the paraphrasing dialogue in Jn 5:10-18 had as point of departure the givenness of the healing story, just as Paul has, as point of departure for his paraphrasing exposition (1 Cor 11:27ff), the givenness of the tradition in I Cor. 11:23-25(26). Accordingly, Jn 5:1-9 renders a unit of tradition which has been handed down and received, and which for that reason has authority and served as basis for paraphrasing exposition.

As far as I can see, Neirynck has not clarified the Fourth Evangelist's method, the form used in his treatment of Mk, his understanding of Mk (and tradition), or how and why his readers would find his treatment of Mk acceptable and authoritative.

Conclusion: A plausible explanation of the features found in the text (Jn 5:1-18) is that a healing story (5:1-9) is taken up from oral tradition, and used as an authoritative case study for the halakhic debate (vv 10-19). It is consistent with this view that the healing story (5:1-9) has the same form as some of the other healing stories in the gospels.

In the above analysis several objections have been raised against the view that Jn 5:1-18 is dependent upon Mk 2:1-3:6. It should be added that if Jn's readers knew Mk, and the Evangelist had treated Mk 2:1-3:6 in a violent manner, it would be hard to understand how they could accept both the method used and the outcome as authoritative.

Agreement, disagreement, desiderata

From the deliberations at the symposium some points of agreements and disagreements emerged:

There was broad agreement that Jn 6:51b-58 draws on a tradition that was abroad in the community. This tradition shows closer agreements with 1 Cor 10 and 11 than with the Synoptics. Similarly, there was broad agreement that a traditional healing story lies behind Jn 5:1-18.

Generally, one agreed that the Gospel of John should not be studied in isolation from the study of the Synoptic Gospels. Studies along these lines will not only throw light upon the Gospel of John, but will also prove fruitful for the study of the Synoptic Gospels.

Among the points of disagreement the following might be listed.

Borgen regards the sentence "take up your mat and walk" (Jn 5:8, etc. and Mk 2:9 etc.) as a stereotype phrase which would occur in various contexts, with no dependence among the stories. Neirynck and others think that the phrase comes from Mk 2:9 and cannot be isolated from its context. Borgen evaluates other similarities between Jn 5:1-18 and Mk 2:1-3:6 to be too distant and vague to indicate Jn's dependence of Mk. Moreover, the differences also speak against such dependence.

Neirynck and others think that the verbatim agreement between Jn 5:8 and Mk 2:9, the similarity of sequence between Jn 5:1-18 and Mk 2:1-3:6 (first the healing and then a controversial sabbath case in the action of people who are together with Jesus) prove, as part of a larger theory of Johannine dependence, that Jn is dependent on Mk.

These different views reflect different evaluations of what kinds of similarities prove dependence and what kinds of agreements are normal in mutually independent written or oral stories. Correspondingly, dissimilarities are also evaluated in different ways.

Another type of disagreement was also voiced at the symposium. Some (as did Neirynck and Borgen) look primarily to the Synoptic Gospels, the rest of the New Testament and the Jewish surroundings (not excluding Hellenistic influence) for analogies to the transmission and interpretation of the Johannine tradition and/or written gospel.

Others (such as David Dungan) raised the question whether one should look for analogies elsewhere, as for example in some of the Nag Hammadi documents.

In order not to make the "Desiderata" too comprehensive, the list is limited to three points:

1. Further studies should be undertaken on the agreements between Jn and each other gospels, Mt, Mk and Luke respectively.

2. The gospel material elsewhere, especially in the Pauline corpus, should be studied with regard to content, transmission and interpretative methods used, to see if more light might be thrown on Jn's use of oral and/or written sources.

3. In general the question of method and form used by the Johannine Community/the Evangelist in the handling of the gospel material should receive more emphasis. Analogous phenomena, not only in Paul but also elsewhere, should be examined and be brought more fully into the discussion.

P. BORGEN

THE GENRE(S) OF THE GOSPELS

There is little need to present a detailed review of earlier discussions of the question of gospel genre(s). Such reviews have been ably presented and are readily available, the most recent of which appears in the Tübingen volume made available to participants of the present 1984 Jerusalem Symposium on the Gospels.[1] One would do well, however, to note several points of convergance among those "histories of the question" written in recent years.

First, in each case the question of the genre(s) of the gospels is a subject thought worthy of examination and discussion. Twenty years ago, this would not have been the case; for Karl Ludwig Schmidt's work was considered definitive.[2] The canonical gospels were *sui generis* as literature, and the form critics primarily concerned themselves with the individual pericopes apart from the literary whole. By contrast, today one is not surprised to see another approach to the question of the "Genre of the Gospels" as the subject of an article in a scholarly journal, title or subtitle of a forthcoming publication, or as a task commissioned by one of the major scholarly series, such as *Hermeneia*.[3] It is now apparent that the question of gospel genre is important, not only because of its introductory character but because of its crucial importance to the interpreter (hermeneutics). Conclusions regarding the nature of any piece of writing affect one's assessments of the information contained therein. In the case of the gospels, the information from which historical-critical conclusions are to be drawn directly pertains to Jesus and indirectly, the early Christian community(ies).

Second, the solutions offered by critics to the problem of the genre(s) of the gospels are directly related to the extent to which the evangelists

---

[1] Robert Guelich, "The Gospel Genre," *Das Evangelium und die Evangelien: Vorträge von Tübinger Symposium 1982,* ed. Peter Stuhlmacher, Wissenschaftliche Untersuchungen zum Neuen Testament, Vol. 28, ed. Martin Hengel und Otfried Hofius (Tübingen: J.C.B. Mohr, 1983), pp. 183-201.

[2] K.L. Schmidt, "Die Stellung der Evangelien in der allgemeinen Literaturgeschichte," *EUCHARISTERION: Studien zur Religion und Literatur des Alten und Neuen Testaments; Hermann Gunkel zum 60 Geburtstag,* ed. Hans Schmidt (Göttingen: Vandenhoeck & Ruprecht, 1923), pp. 50-134.

[3] *Hermeneia,* a scholarly series published by Fortress Press, recently commissioned M. Eugene Boring of Texas Christian University, to author the forthcoming edition on the genre of the gospels.

are perceived as having been motivated by external and/or internal factors. Prof. Guelich prefers the terms "analogical" and "derivational" while making the same point.[4] More recent discussions have largely mirrored the dichotomy evident in a comparison of the works of Votaw and Schmidt.[5] The former argued that "popular biography" of the ancient world (external factor) best provides the literary context for understanding the gospels, whereas the latter argued that since the gospels more properly fall into the *Kleinliteratur* classification, their present form and character are best explained as having emerged from within (internal factor) the church's proclamation (i.e., *sui generis*). Arguments similar in principal to Votaw's position have been offered by scholars including Hadas and Smith,[6] Talbert,[7] Shuler,[8] and more recently by Hengel.[9] Scholars closer to Schmidt's views include Dibelius,[10] Bultmann,[11] Kümmel,[12] Robinson,[13] Via,[14] Gundry,[15] and Guelich.[16]

The works of Koester, Stanton and Aune, though very different in their respective approaches to the question, are nevertheless more representative of positions which include both external and internal motivational factors. Koester identifies several external literary types

[4] Guelich, "The Gospel Genre," pp. 185ff. and 196ff.

[5] C.W. Votaw's work was the author of "The Gospels and Contemporary Biographies," *American Journal of Theology* 19 (1915): 47-73, 217-249; later published under the title, *The Gospels and Contemporary Biographies in the Graeco-Roman World* (Philadelphia: Fortress Press, Facet Books, 1970).

[6] Moses Hadas and Morton Smith, *Heroes and Gods* (New York: Harper & Row, 1966).

[7] Charles Talbert, *What Is a Gospel?* (Philadelphia: Fortress Press, 1977).

[8] Philip L. Shuler, *A Genre for the Gospels: The Biographical Character of Matthew* (Philadelphia: Fortress Press, 1982).

[9] Martin Hengel, "Probleme des Markusevangeliums," *Das Evangelium und die Evangelien* (cf. above, n. 1), pp. 223-224.

[10] Martin Dibelius, *From Tradition to Gospel* (New York: Charles Scribner's Sons, 1934), p. 2.

[11] Rudolf Bultmann, *History of the Synoptic Tradition* (New York: Harper & Row, 1963), pp. 371-373.

[12] Werner Georg Kümmel, *Introduction to the New Testament* (Nashville: Abingdon Press, 1975), pp. 35ff.

[13] James M. Robinson, *A New Quest of the Historical Jesus* (London: SCM Press, 1963), p. 55.

[14] Dan O. Via, *Kerygma and Comedy in the New Testament: A Structuralist Approach to Hermeneutic* (Philadelphia: Fortress Press, 1975).

[15] Robert H. Gundry, "Recent investigations into the Literary Genre 'Gospel'," *New Dimensions in New Testament Study*, ed. R.N. Longenecker and M.C. Tenney (Grand Rapids: Zondervan Publishing Company, 1974), pp. 97-114.

[16] See n. 1.

with which smaller literary units of the gospels may be associated (e.g., sayings, aretalogies, revelation discourses, and creedal affirmations), but the final products are distinctively Christian creations (i.e., *sui generis*).[17] Stanton, on the other hand, admits that the gospels are best understood when read against the backdrop of ancient biographical literature, but then retreats by stating that they are not biographies, strictly speaking, and do not belong to a genre of biography.[18] Aune explains the gospels as having emerged from within the church's faith but seems to admit the role of external factors as the gospels after Mark reflect a process of "literaturization" or movement in the direction of literature.[19] One may conclude, therefore, that assessing the impact of external and internal factors on canonical gospel formation, whether by affirming the one and denying the other or by mediating in such a way as to affirm both, has been a major task dominating the gospel genre question of both past and present discussions.

Third, it is clear that presuppositions which specify a certain sequence in which the gospels were written significantly impact upon the conclusions of gospel genre critics. What one carries into combat certainly affects the outcome of the battle. It is important to be reminded that all of the discussions mentioned above have taken place within a scholarly environment dominated by the Marcan priority solution to the question of sequence. For example, Aune's view of "literaturization," which has received favourable comments from both Gundry and Guelich,[20] would not appear so convincing were it not clearly evident to Aune and those who share a similar view that Mark, having written first, originated the gospel form. The case for literaturization is logically set forth by positing a line of natural development from the less complete Mark through the refining efforts of Matthew, Luke and John, even though models for such a process are as difficult to document in the ancient world as are precise biographical parallels. The reasonableness of Aune's argument turns on a specific understanding of gospel sequence. One can only guess how compelling such an explanation would have

[17] Helmut H. Koester, "One Jesus and Four Primitive Gospels," *Harvard Theological Review* 2 (1968), later reprinted in James M. Robinson and Helmut H. Koester, *Trajectories through Early Christianity* (Philadelphia: Fortress Press, 1971), pp. 158-204.

[18] G.N. Stanton, *Jesus of Nazareth in New Testament Preaching* (Cambridge: The University Press, 1974), pp. 67-136, esp. p. 117.

[19] D.E. Aune, "The Problem of the Genre of the Gospels: A Critique of C.H. Talbert's What is a Gospel?," *Gospel Perspectives: Studies of History and Tradition in the Four Gospels*, Vol. 2, ed. R.T. France and David Wenham (Sheffield, England: JSOT Press, 1980), p. 45.

[20] Guelich, "The Gospel Genre," p. 203.

been if at the time of Aune's writing the predominant view had been either of the other two hypotheses currently under discussion by this Symposium. While it is true, therefore, that questions of genre are important to discussions of the sequence of gospel composition, the major thrust resulting from the Jerusalem Conference may be just the reverse: that is, the real impact may be that of the conclusions of this conference upon the future discussions of the genre(s) of the gospels.

The present work shares the view that the question of the genre(s) of the gospels is an important question worthy of the gospel critics' efforts. With regard to the impact of external and/or internal factors on gospel literary formation, the present work is to be more closely associated with that of Stanton. The difference is that the present writer argues for the identification of the gospels with a specific type of ancient biographical literature, and yet admits to the significant role of faith (kerygma) in determining the final form and character of these cult narratives. Finally, with respect to presuppositions of sequence, the present work attempts neutrality; however, the reader will soon recognize that this attempt grows out of a genuine respect for the view that the question of the sequence of the gospels is truly an open one.

The format for this presentation consists of the enumeration of four theses for consideration followed by a brief discussion of each. The first three theses are directly related to the question of genre. Whereas these three theses are equally valid for understanding the formation of any *bios* narrative, they are being presented here with specific reference to issues of gospel literature formation. The fourth thesis identifies the gospels with a type of Hellenistic biography known as encomium biography.

Thesis I: *The shift from individual sources, whether circulating as individual or collected traditions, to the form of a "story" about Jesus constituted a literary, genre decision of the redactors/authors/evangelists.*

That traditions related to Jesus circulated prior to their incorporation into a "gospel" is not a point of contention. Indeed, the consensus of gospel research confirms the presence of such traditions, and attributes to them the character of orally transmitted material. It is clear, however, that what we find in the canonical gospels is more than collections of material or random duplication of individual Jesus traditions. New Testament studies currently employ references to "structure," "outline," "purpose," "milieu," "redactor" and even "theology" with regard to each of the four evangelists' works. Consequently, one can no longer speak of the gospels as accidental products of random selection. Rather are they works reflecting redactional and authorial intent. Based on a discussion by Norman Petersen, such recognition of authorial intent raises the question of genre. He writes:

> The bridge between collection and another genre is crossed, descriptively and normatively, at the moment when an intent beyond the explicit claims of the component material is given either formal (structural, compositional) or material (simple editorial) expression in a text. That is to say, a collection becomes something else at that moment when mere concatenation is replaced by composition at whatever level of sophistication.[21]

One can conclude that current gospel research is based on a view of the gospels as more than literary accidents. The question of the genre(s) of the gospels, therefore, is the problem of identifying the literary pattern behind the evangelists' use and arrangement of those sources which comprise their present narratives.

Thesis II: *It cannot be documented that such a literary decision could have resulted in the creation/choice of a totally non-existent and therefore completely unique literary form.*

At the heart of the second thesis is the presupposition that behind the present form of the gospels is the evangelist's desire to communicate. It is reasonable to expect that the evangelist would utilize whatever native abilities and literary resources available to him in order to be understood by his readers. Paul did not invent the personal letter form. He adopted a familiar form, modified it according to personal, theological purposes, and thereby effectively communicated with his readers. It is doubtful that the evangelists would have been any less motivated by a desire to communicate.

Given the author's desire to communicate, a desire that urges him to the proper choice of the medium of communication, it is highly unlikely that a genre would emerge from a literary vacuum. Thus Wellek and Warren write: "The totally familiar and repetitive pattern is boring; the totally novel form will be unintelligible — is indeed unthinkable."[22] Further, "the genre represents, so to speak, a sum of aesthetic devices at

---

[21] Norman Petersen, "So-called Gnostic Type Gospels and the Question of the Genre 'Gospel'" (The Task Force on Gospel Genre, 1970 SBL Gospels Seminar), p. 25.

[22] Rene Wellek and Austin Warren, *Theory of Literature* (New York: Harcourt, Brace, Jovanovich, 1949), p. 226.

hand, available to the writer and already intelligible to the reader."[23] It is generally thought that new genres are formed by creative use of and variations from existing forms.

The relationship of communicator to recipient no doubt offers at least partial explanation for why the question of the genre of the gospels continues to surface. What is the common denominator by which communication is made possible? Shouldn't an interpreter of a piece of writing expect to be able to identify a common link or form by which and through which a writer delivers his material? This is one reason why Schmidt's postulation of the *sui generis* origin of the gospel form continues to gnaw at this gospel critic. The common denominator between communicator and recipient remains elusive. The same is true with those theoretical explanations which seek to explain how the gospels could be *sui generis* and still display form through some process of expanding the kerygma. For what reason would such a process of expansion have been undertaken if not to focus upon the *bios* of Jesus? One would have an answer to a very important question were that person to recognize that the evangelists were communicating information about Jesus, whether to persuade or enlighten, and have accomplished their tasks in a way that resembles the *bios* narratives of the ancient world. In this case, the examination of *bios* genre relationships would focus upon precisely that point of contact between writer and reader. This would be true even if it were concluded with Dodd and Guelich that Mark, as an example, did in fact accomplish his task with Acts 10:36-43 as his criteria.[24]

The identification of ancient *bios* literature as the link between communicator and recipient would greatly facilitate our understanding the written form of the gospels. The forms employed in the gospels would then be understood as having been meaningful not only to those sending the message but also to the audience. Hirsch's comments truly deserve further attention of gospel critics:

> This is one of the many penetrating observations that E.H. Gombrich makes in his book, *Art and Illusion*. He quotes approvingly Quintilian's remark, "Which craftsman has not made a vessel of a shape he has never seen." This tendency of the mind to use old types as the foundation for new ones is, of course, even more pronounced when communication or representation is involved. Not every convention could be changed all at once, even if the craftsman were capable of such divine creativity, because then his creation would be totally incommunicable, radically ambiguous.[25]

---

[23] Ibid., emphasis added.

[24] Guelich, "The Gospel Genre," pp. 204-216.

[25] E.D. Hirsch, *Validity in Interpretation* (New Haven: Yale University Press, 1967), p. 104.

Thesis III: *The gospels were no doubt received as popular "lives" of Jesus, and the Jesus Tradition by being so incorporated became more powerful in authenticating the person of Jesus within the life of the community.*

Even a cursory reading of any one of the gospels confirms the conclusion that traditions attributed to Jesus have been presented so as to give emphasis not merely to the traditions concerning Jesus but also to his person. There is emphasis upon the function, character, and nature of the glorified Christ, an emphasis upon the total event that bears testimony to God's soteriological activity. This emphasis upon the person of Jesus, which is developed by the use of traditions associated with Jesus, constitutes the *bios* character of the evangelists' work.

The recognition of this *bios* factor produces the impression, even among contemporary readers, that the gospels are biographies,[26] and genre discussions have correctly focused upon ancient biographical works.[27] Such investigations, however, have been complicated by the fact that biography, as we moderns understand it, did not exist in antiquity. This does not mean that the ancients did not celebrate the lives of esteemed personages in their literature. Indeed, the opposite was the case, and further work in the area of ancient *bios* narratives makes clearer the exact relation of the gospels to ancient *bios* literature.

References in Polybius (*Histories* X 21.8), Cicero (*Epistulae ad Familiares* V. xii. 3), Lucian (*History* 7), Cornelius Nepos (*Pelopidas* XVI. 1.1) and Plutarch (*Alexander* I. 1-3) give evidence for a popular form of *bios* literature where the purpose was primarily that of praise. In these references, this literature is consistently contrasted with history. Several of these references employ the term encomium as a designation, and a reading of the rules for this rhetorical device helps one to understand more clearly this ubiquitous literary type, genre.[28] Encomium biographies included the topics one expects to find in biographies: family

[26] See Hengel, above n. 9.

[27] See, for example, Moses Hadas and Morton Smith, *Heroes and Gods;* Charles H. Talbert, *What Is a Gospel?;* and Philip L. Shuler, *A Genre for the Gospels.*

[28] The Polybius and Lucian treatises specifically refer to "encomium" in contrast to "history." Representative of the rhetorical rules for writing encomia are Aristotle, *Rhetorica* I.6.9; *Rhetorica ad Alexandrum* III-IV; Cicero, *Rhetorica ad Herennium* and *De Partitione oratoria* XXI; and Quintilian, *Institutio oratoria* III.7. 10-18. Classical examples of encomia are *Helen, Busiris,* and *Evagoras* by Isocrates and *Agesilaus* by Zenophon. For relevant discusssions, see D.R. Stuart, *Epochs of Greek and Roman Biography* (Berkeley: University of California Press, 1928); Arnaldo Momigliano, *The Development of Greek Biography* (Cambridge: Harvard University Press, 1971); and Shuler, *A Genre for the Gospels,* pp. 36-87.

background, birth (and events surrounding birth), accounts of child-hood and youth, the career, manner of death, and events following death. It is to be noted, however, that the primary focus was upon the "adult," and all topics tended to be used to serve the author's portrayal of the adult. In addition, two literary techniques were employed: amplification and comparison. Amplification is the process by which the author "amplifies" those points he is trying to make either by a process of selection, an emphasis upon a few aspects of the character at the expense of a complete account, and/or the omission of material that does not fit in with the author's literary purposes. Comparison demonstrates how the chosen subject excels those with whom he comes into contact or with whom he may be compared.

Authors who wrote in this medium display various, though closely related, purposes. Some are exercises in literary models, others attempt to defend, while still others are very close to funeral eulogies. The common thread is that of praise, intended to enlist a praise response that could range anywhere from mere pleasure to emulation. All of the topics and literary techniques were employed in the author's accepted task; i.e., the favorable portrayal of persons whose significance was clearly demonstrable in his adult life and death.

Into this literary milieu the gospels make their appearance in the first century CE. With this kind of backdrop, it is not difficult to understand how Jewish religious traditions and concepts could have been enjoyed by Gentile readers (a recognition that none of the gospels pre-date the Gentile mission made official in Acts 15). A unique proclamation has been transmitted in a relatively common praise form. No doubt, the gospels were received by their original readers as biographies containing the summons of faith in the Messiah, Jesus of Nazareth.

Thesis IV: *The best way of viewing the emergence of the synoptic gospels from the perspective of genre is that they belong to the hellenistic biography classification; more specifically, encomium biography.*

According to H.I. Marrou, the encomium was an elementary exercise in the educational systems throughout the Greco-Roman world. As such, its rules for composition were rigidly set forth and rigorously applied at the beginning of a student's exposure to compositional skills. Whereas encomia written as "models" in the ancient world reflect this literary rigor, most of the works which fall within the encomium biography classification are less restricted by strict adherence to the rhetorical rules of composition. *Bios* works from the period roughly contemporary with Jesus tend to reflect, on the one hand, evidence of the impact of encomium writing, while, on the other hand, considerable variety when authorial intent rather than rhetorical rules shape the narrative. Such examples as Suetonius' *Deified Julius*, Tacitus' *Agricola*, Lucian's *Demonax*, Philo's *Life of Moses*, and several of Plutarch's *Lives* come to mind.

It is important to emphasize the less restrictive view of writing *bios* narratives in antiquity because many gospel scholars presuppose that the impact of *bios* literature upon gospel formation and that of the kerygma upon gospel formation are mutually exclusive factors (i.e., external vs. internal factors).[29] Except perhaps for the "models" and works of the rhetoricians,[30] there is insufficient evidence for one to conclude that a genre dominates an author. It seems rather to serve an author's purpose.[31] What an author wants to communicate affects the genre he chooses, the selection of the material or traditions he utilizes, the specific content of the form (including order) by which he will present his portrait, and the various techniques he will employ in order to strengthen his case. Why would such a procedure be different for the evangelists? The case they are making integrally involves the kerygma, and the kerygma as they perceive it most certainly affects the manner, form,[32] and content. Consequently, to argue that the evangelists utilize a recognizable *bios* narrative genre in order to communicate to an audience in no way minimizes the influence of the kerygma upon their

[29] Though not explicity stated, the positions of both Gundry (n. 15 above) and Guelich (n. 1 above) do not admit to the impact of external factors when discussing the genre of the gospels as literary wholes.

[30] The rhetorical works listed in n. 27 above are restrictive in their proscriptions, and relatively strict adherence to these rules are evident in the works of Isocrates and Zenophon. Later biographical works of an encomium type, however, are not as bound by the conventions of these rhetoricians.

[31] As circumstances surrounding the subject vary, so do the topoi and conventions utilized by the writers. The controlling factor in these compositions seems to have been the purposes behind the narratives, the type of information with which the author worked, and his use of the narrative for communication.

[32] "Form" here refers to the order and use of those topoi considered important for the development of the pattern. For example, in a *bios* pattern, one would normally expect to find a birth account followed by early childhood and youth accounts. On the other hand, such topoi are not absolute requirements. The works of Diogenes Laertius do not include these topoi in every instance, but one does not remove his works from the classification of bios literature. Why should it be different with the gospels? If Mark, for example, is making use of a kerygmatic formula as Dodd and Guelich have suggested (above, n. 24), one which does not include the inherent requirement for the inclusion of such material for faithful proclamation, then one would readily expect to see a variation in the bios pattern being developed by a Christian writer such as Mark.

works. On the contrary, the observation that the evangelists have chosen to adhere to their sources as closely as they apparently have, both in terms of content and order, argues for the crucial role of the kerygma in gospel formation.[33]

For gospel critics, the greatest task is associating the gospels with any existing genre of antiquity. This is true for two reasons. First, in the past the methodology of genre identification has usually involved one-to-one comparisons. Such comparisons, however tended to accent the differences at the expense of genre affinities.[34] Furthermore, the variety within *bios* literature complicated the recognition of gospel genre identity. Second, one must again be reminded of the problem of beginning with the presupposition that Mark is the earliest gospel. Reinforced by Mark's perceived incompleteness, Mark has been seen as the original preserver of Jesus tradition. Under such a view, Matthew and Luke become secondary productions which carry on Mark's initial activities out of loyalty to the tradition more than any genre motive.[35] Without denying loyalty to tradition, the picture for gospel genre changes significantly if the synoptic gospels are recognized as Hellenistic biographies and if Mark is not viewed *de facto* as the earliest of the three. With the task in mind, attention now will be given to associating the gospels with encomium biography. This will be attempted not by one-to-one comparisons but through examples of topoi, literary techniqes, and authorial intent.

The relationship of Matthew's gospel to encomium biographical literature has been discussed in an earlier book previously cited.[36] For the present, a summary of the research will suffice.

Clearly, many of the topoi common to encomium biographies are present in Matthew. Further, Matthew uses the topoi in the same manner and for the same reasons that they were incorporated by writers of encomium biographies. There is, for example, Matthew's emphasis on Jesus' illustrious family background — illustrious, that is, from the view of Jewish messianic expectations. This occurs in the genealogy (Mt.

---

[33] In other words, one need not argue for mutual exclusiveness of external and internal factors. To this writer, it appears that both were instrumental in the production of our present gospels.

[34] See, for example, Karl Ludwig Schmidt's (above, n. 2) response to C.W. Votaw (above, n. 5). The failure of such one-to-one comparisons has led to the general view that there are simply no examples with which the gospels may be compared. The view of the present paper is that the problem is with the methodology of comparison and not with the absence of literary examples.

[35] Helmut Koester's article "One Jesus and Four Primitive Gospels" is representative (see n. 17).

[36] Shuler, *A Genre*, pp. 36 ff.

1:1-17) in which the emphasis is both upon God as creator (four women
and a multiple of seven in the number of generations separating the
three periods) and upon David (DVD: $4+6+4=14$). The designation
of Joseph as δίκαιος represents an encomium-type emphasis upon the
character of Joseph's role as Jesus' "earthly" father (1:19). In chapter 2,
Matthew identifies the place of Jesus' birth. At the same time, he
reconciles those Old Testament traditions that would point to the birth
place of "the one who is to come" as Bethlehem, with reference to his
being from Nazareth. Also, the subject, "king of the Jews," is raised
with reference to Jesus in contrast to Herod, and there is the soteriological
allusion to Moses. In addition, one notes the reference to dreams and
the role of the "star" for the Magi, again common features of encomium
biographies. In Chapter 4, Matthew presents the temptation of Jesus
which happens at the transition point between his youth and his
ministry. Jesus is here displayed as a young man of obvious moral
perseverance who is fully prepared for the task ahead.

The combination of these common topoi in the first four chapters of
Matthew is also instructive, because the result is Matthew's way of
convincingly preparing for his presentation of Jesus' career as an adult.
Such a purpose is the main function of these topoi in encomium
biographies. Presupposed in all ancient biographical works is the adult
portrait. Preliminary events such as birth, childhood, and youth
accounts prepare the reader for the adult career. In Matthew's gospel,
the identity is the crucial point, and it is developed in an ascending
manner. Chapter one points to Jesus as "son of David." Chapter two
points to his kingly and soteriological nature. Chapter three builds to
his identification after baptism as "son" and the first eleven verses of
chapter four specifically include his title "son of God." Matthew's
procedures here are exemplary of encomium biography.

For the most part, the career is presented in a manner consistent with
the nature of Jesus as Messiah. Words and deeds (the forms of
proclamation and miracle stories) are the proper subjects just as oration
is to the orator, laws and actions to the statesman, or battles are to the
soldier. The material is well structured and the emphases carefully
presented. Still, there does not seem to be a forcing of rhetorical device.
It is the nature of the subject and the evangelical purposes of Matthew
that guide his hand. There are no rhetoric vs. theology motifs in
Matthew's work; rather, a devout Christian writer is conveying his
account of Jesus in the most compelling manner of which he is capable.

Two additional topoi are utilized by Matthew worthy of note: death,
and resurrection. The manner of Jesus' death would not have been the

easiest death for a writer of encomium biography to treat. In fact, had it
not been for the crucial role it played in early Christian proclamation
(e.g., Phil. 2:6-11 and speeches of Acts), Matthew might have omitted
an account of Jesus' death altogether (as would have been legitimate in
such ancient writings). As Matthew's story unfolds, however, it is clear
that he has chosen not to avoid the account; but, instead, to turn it into
an account worthy of praise. Jesus is the victim of the opponents' plot
(e.g., 26:3-5; 27:1). Supernatural events surround his death just as in the
case of his birth. The wife of his judge, Pilate, warns him to have
nothing to do with this "righteous" man following a dream (27:19). His
betrayer hangs himself; his judge washes his hands of what is taking
place (27:24-26); and the centurion acknowledges Jesus as "son of God"
(27:54).

Proof of the resurrection comes from those hired to guard the
sepulcher: i.e., having been made fully aware of the resurrection rumor,
this event could not be stopped. Of course, testimony of the resurrection
also comes from the disciples who witnessed it. Thus, in his treatment of
death and resurrection, Matthew transforms the lowliest of deaths into a
victorious glorification of Jesus. This kind of testimony and literary
procedure is fundamental to the apologetic motive often found in
encomium biography. Literary topoi, and Matthew's use thereof, point
to the encomium biography genre.

The two most common literary techniques employed in this genre are
amplification and comparison. Both are utilized by Matthew in his
gospel. Previously discussed was Matthew's "amplification" of the
preliminary episodes by which the identity of Jesus is developed. Also, a
process of selection is surely evident in the manner by which Matthew
presents Jesus' death in strictly positive and praise worthy terms. The
length of the passion account alone demonstrates Matthew's use of
amplification of this most important event in Jesus' career. Finally, the
decisions involved in the presentation of Jesus' ministry reflect Matthew's amplification of these teachings and actions which instruct the
reader in the nature and significance of this soteriological event. It is
evident that Matthew has chosen his sources and utilized his traditions
in such a way as to create his portrait for the purpose of enlisting the
response of faith.

Comparison is also important to Matthew. It is functional in his
clarification of the relationship between John the Baptist and Jesus.
After identifying the message of John with that of Jesus (3:2 and 4:17)
and after the reader notes that John's opponents are those of Jesus (3:7),
it is John himself who declares his unworthiness to participate in the

baptism. If John is one deserving of the reader's attention, how much more so is Jesus! Elsewhere, comparison is evident in Matthew's portrayal of Jesus and his opponents. From Chapter 12 on, the conflicts produce no victories for Jesus' opponents. In fact, in chapter 22, Jesus' generally passive and controlled character becomes aggressive. The opponents are unable to respond to Jesus' question, a fact that reduces them to sinister silence. Jesus far surpasses his opponents. What has been noted of John the Baptist and the opponents is equally true of all the personages with whom Jesus may be compared. Such comparisons as developed by Matthew lead only to Jesus' far superior qualities when viewed along side of the other characters in Matthew's gospel.

The primary purpose of encomium biographies is praise. At times this purpose incorporated apologetic concerns while at other times emulation seems to have been important to the writer. The religious character of Matthew's gospel causes Matthew to desire both praise and emulation of Jesus as his reader's response, and then some. Matthew is really writing for faith. To believe is to become a part of the church's mission of baptism and making disciples (16:20). Matthew's purpose, therefore, is to work not only toward the recognized goals of encomium biography, but to move beyond them for faith, edification and training. Indeed, analysis of Matthew's overall structure reflects not only the desire for a faith response, but also yields the purpose of instructing the believers in the exacting demands of discipleship (1-11) with Jesus' own ministry providing the true discipleship paradigm even unto death and beyond (12-28).[37] In view of our considersation of topoi, literary techniques, and authorial intent, one can understand Matthew's appeal within the Christian community of the first century A.D., both Jew and Gentile. "Gospel" has been transmitted in a recognized and easily received, ubiquitous literary pattern.

It is more difficult to see Mark as a part of the encomium biography genre when one considers the topoi common to the genre. Mark says nothing about the birth and genealogical history of Jesus. He omits references to childhood and youthful excellence. The popular association of such topoi with "biography" in general and with ancient biography in particular has led scholars to declare Mark incapable of being classified as a biographical genre. Such arbitrariness does not do justice to ancient writing for several reasons. First, such topoi comprise the preliminary portion of the narrative and, because of the preoccupation with the "adult career," are not integral to biographical literature

---

[37] Ibid., pp. 103-106.

of the ancient world. They appear only to serve the author's purpose in
his portrait of the adult. Consequently, ancient authors are granted
considerable freedom in the use of such topoi.[38] Second, to deny Mark
biographical genre classification, one would have to argue that function-
ally Mark has no alternative preliminary section which contributes to an
adult literary portrait consistent with Marcan intentions. Otherwise, one
may argue as will be the case in this paper, that Mark has chosen an
alternative literary route. Such a decision would not automatically deny
Mark's gospel encomium biographical status. Third, the total structure
along with Mark's use of other topoi common to the encomium
biography actually argues for his inclusion therein. Items two and three
deserve further comment.

To the modern reader, the manner by which Mark opens his narrative
is both abrupt and unusual when viewed alongside the other canonical
gospels and other ancient biographical works. Close examination
reveals that his procedure is not without precedent[39] or intent. Mark's
work in the first chapter is carefully structured. After setting the thesis in
Mk. 1:1, he moves directly into his narrative. His starting point is at the
"beginning" (1:1); namely, John the Baptist and Isaiah's passage
fulfilled by John's ministry (1:2). John truly "prepares" for the ministry
of Jesus, and his references here to John and the baptism of Jesus serve
simultaneously as a preliminary account pointing ahead to Jesus'
ministry. To this preliminary material Mark adds a mere reference to
Jesus' temptation designed by the omission of details not to call
attention to the account itself while yet calling attention to Jesus'
significant qualifications more in evidence during his ministry and death.
The introductory section (1:1-13), therefore, functions as a preliminary
section which prepares the reader for Jesus' ministry. Though avoiding
more common topoi and moving quickly and concisely through his task,
Mark's work here reflects encomium biography motifs.

Mark moves to the ministry without delay. What Jesus preached is
summarized in 1:15 followed quickly by the selection for four disciples
(vv. 16ff.). An unclean spirit recognizes Jesus' authority (v. 24) and his
fame spreads (vv. 28 and 45). In the brief span of chapter one, Mark sets
the stage for his work in a preliminary section and then reveals several
important themes: Jesus' identity, his call to discipleship, the content of
his preaching and view of his deeds, and testimony to his success

[38] Ibid., pp. 34-67
[39] Plutarch, for example, does not record the events of birth and/or youth excellences
of Camillus.

thoughout Galilee. Such a procedure does not seem foreign to encomium biography.

One further notes that, contrary to more commonly held opinion, this
chapter of Mark is far more than a collection of random, unrelated
traditions simply allowed to fall accidently into place. An examination
of Mark's use of ευθυς reveals that Mark intends to present a simple,
rapidly moving narrative, one designed to confront the reader with the
urgency of Jesus' messianic mission. The use of ευθυς is characteristic of
Mark. This term is found seven times in Matthew, two times in Luke-
Acts and three times in John, while Mark uses it some forty-two times.
In the first two chapters alone, Mark uses the term seventeen times,
eleven of which occur in chapter one. Thus, Mark's intention is to create
a rapidly moving narrative depicting Jesus' intense activities. In fact,
Lightfoot sees 1:1-32 as Mark's presentation of the first day (v. 32) of
Jesus' manifestation.[40]

It is this view of Mark's redactional activity that accounts for his
omission of more commonly found topoi such as those noted in
Matthew. Furthermore, given his intention, his use of birth or youth
accounts would only interfere with the very effect Mark is clearly
attempting to achieve. Rather than moving Mark out of the encomium
biography, the effect he creates may now be seen as complying with the
broader goals of encomiastic literature.

Other common topoi are to be noted in Mark's presentation of a
ministry of deeds and words. This portion is designed to bring the
reader to the point of Jesus' death which is viewed by Mark as that of
the suffering Messiah locked in a cosmic struggle against evil[41]. In
addition to the topos of death, his gospel concludes in a manner which
leaves the reader with the inference and anticipation of things that
happen after Jesus' death.

Mark too employs literary techniques found in encomium biography.
One notices, for example, the way by which through an apparent
process of selection Mark has emphasized or amplified Jesus' deeds
thereby presenting more of the "miracle worker" than the preacher/
teacher. Also, his decision to begin with John the Baptist and end with

---

[40] R.H. Lightfoot, taking note of the impression Mark creates in chapter 1, suggests
that "St. Mark desires to give at the outset a picture of typical activities of Jesus Christ
under the form of events loosely represented as occurring more or less within twenty-four
hours; ...it is the day of the manifestation, or epiphany, of our Saviour Jesus Christ;... It
is one of intense activity and unceasing strain for the Lord." R.H. Lightfoot, *The Gospel
Message of St. Mark* (Oxford: Clarendon Press, 1950), pp. 24ff.

[41] See James M. Robinson, *The Problem of History in Mark* (London: SCM Press,
1962).

death also reflects Mark's amplification of this portion of God's soteriological event. One final example may be noted in Theodore Weeden's discussion of Marcan characterization.[42] In his discussion of Mark's use of "crowds," it is clear that Mark amplifies the response to Jesus' ministry. Weeden writes:

> That role [scil., the role played by the crowd] is to dramatize, by contrast with the religious leaders, the positive response to Jesus. The crowds flock to him with eagerness (1:32ff., 37; 3:7-12; 4:1; 6:53-56; 9:15; 11:8ff.) listen to his teaching enthusiastically (1:22, 27; 12:37b) and respond to his healing powers with anticipation (1:32ff.; 3:7ff.; 6:53ff.).[43]

One cannot fail but note the manner in which Mark depicts Jesus as far superior to all the personages in his work. John the Baptist comes closest to a position of comparison, but the two are kept far apart and John receives less attention than in the other texts. Also long noted among New Testament scholars is the superiority of Jesus over all his disciples. Of all of the gospels, Mark is the hardest on the disciples, and Jesus, by comparison, towers over them. Finally, Jesus' control over demons and spirits signifies his power over evil.

Consideration of Mark's authorial intent reveals literary purpose similar to that of Matthew. Mark portrays the Messiah whose identity cannot be suppressed and who is locked in a cosmic struggle against evil. Faith is the response intended by Mark, for to the believer belongs final victory anticipated at the time of the suffering Messiah's return (Parousia). Mark tells his story persuasively and, as a result, Mark's gospel has been characterized as one sermon (Marxsen).[44] Such evangelistic purpose is truly compatable with encomium biography, and Mark's use of topoi and literary technique warrants the inclusion of his "gospel" therein.

Of the four evangelists, Luke is the one whose relationship to Hellenistic literature is more readily acknowledged by New Testament scholars. His use of the prologue (Lk 1:1-4) and travel narrative (9:51ff.), coupled with his composition of the development of the early church in Acts, are examples of Luke's affinities with literature of the period.[45] The present analysis further confirms Luke's relationship to ancient literature, and, in particular, points to chacteristics commonly found in encomium biographical literature.

---

[42] Theodore Weeden, *Mark: Traditions in Conflict* (Philadelphia: Fortress Press, 1971), pp. 13ff.

[43] Ibid., p. 22.

[44] W. Marxsen, *Introduction to the New Testament* (Philadelphia: Fortress Press, 1968), p. 144.

[45] Kümmel, *Introduction*, pp. 98-100.

As with Matthew and Mark, Luke uses topoi common to ancient *bios* narratives. His use of topoi surrounding birth is now expanded to include that of John the Baptist as well as Jesus. Clearly, John's birth is meant to be viewed as forerunner to Messiah, and the angelic visitation, summaries of nurture (1:80; 2:40; 52) and prophetic statements of Zechariah and Simeon accent God's soteriological actions throughout the narrative. Luke also includes an account of the youthful Jesus going to the temple as a twelve year old (2:41-51). This event, which features Jesus in meaningful dialogue with teachers (2:46), impresses one with Jesus' exceptional insight and understanding while preparing (the reader in a special way) for Jesus' divine mission ("...I must be in my Father's house," 2:49). Other topoi in the preliminary section include place of birth (2:1ff) and familial relationships (genealogy, 3:23ff). In each instance, these "preliminary" events prepare the reader for Luke's portrait of the adult career of Jesus.

The presentation of Jesus' ministry employs topoi identical with that of Matthew and Mark; namely, words and deeds Luke tends to keep these two topoi in balance. The call to discipleship is a call to the balanced totality of Jeus' ministry (cf. Luke 24:19). This balance/ emphasis is made especially clear at two crucial points: 1) the call of Peter who responded to the miraculous catch in the context of the proclaimed word (5:1-11) and 2) the beginning of the church at which time 3,000 people responded to Peter's proclamation preceded by the miracle of language (Acts 2:1-21).

The topoi surrounding death focus upon Jesus' innocence. The charges are false and yet designed to incur a sentence of death from civil authorities (23:1-2). The contrast of Jesus' innocence (Lk. 23:4, 14, 22) with Barabbas's guilt aptly characterizes Jesus as upright victim. A similar contrast occurs in the crucifixion of Jesus with two other criminals (23:39ff). Also, illustrations of Jesus' character in death are the prayer for the forgiveness of those crucifying him (23:34) and his committal into the Father's hands (23:46). The topoi surrounding what happens after Jesus' death consist of an empty tomb, the road to Emmaus story and appearances in Jerusalem, divine commentaries on the vindication of Jesus and his ministry. Luke's gospel, too, may be classified as encomium biography when the topoi utilized are considered.

Luke also includes literary techniques common to encomium biography. Previously mentioned in Luke's amplification of John's birth in God's soteriological plan (evidenced by the obvious association with Abraham and Sarah). The clearest example of amplification is Luke's technique of creating a special, final journey to Jerusalem between 9:51-

18:27 with an emphasis upon Jesus' rendezvous with death (cf. esp. 9:51; 13:22, 33; 17:11; 19:28). This amplified journey serves as the vehicle for material unique to Luke. One also notices the correspondence between this view of Jesus' journey in Luke's gospel and the journeys of Paul in Acts.

Luke uses comparison initially in order to keep the persons of John the Baptist and Jesus distinct while, at the same time, acknowledging the significant contribution both ministries make to God's soteriological design. One notices the close parallelism of the stories of conception (1:5-25//1:26-28) and birth (1:57-79//2:1-39). Also to be noted are the two parallel statements of nurture (1:80//2:40). Throughout, however, Luke is careful to keep the two distinct thereby avoiding possible confusion. John has his function: so does Jesus. John's is a ministry of expectation, pointing ahead to one who is to come. Jesus is the expected one as indicated by the third nurture summary (2:52) and the traditions of chapter 3 (see also 4:17-21). John's secondary character and that of his ministry in Luke (cf. also Acts 18:24f.; 19:1f.) serves to enhance the central importance of Jesus. Additional comparative work could be done with other persons included in Luke's gospel; however, such endeavors are not necessary. For Luke, Jesus is one whose identity, accomplishments, and faith are second to none.

Considerations of the authorial intent behind Luke's gospel are complicated by recent discussions of Acts. The present work shares the views of scholars including Talbert and, more recently, Marshall, who argue that Luke's purposes in writing his gospel are related to his reasons for writing Acts.[46] Talbert, for example, argues that Acts was part of Luke's original scheme: consequently, Luke-Acts together belong to that genre which includes the biographical accounts of philosophers and their schools (e.g., the works of Diogenes Laertius). Clearly, Marshall draws his conclusions regarding Luke's purposes from a consideration of Luke and Acts together. Our own views of Luke's purposes as an author, therefore, are being deferred to a point following a brief consideration of Acts.

The assessment of Luke as "historian" is derived primarily from

---

[46] Charles H. Talbert, *Literary Patterns, Theological Themes, and the Genre of Luke-Acts* (Missoula: Society of Biblical Literature and Scholars Press, 1974) and I. Howard Marshall, "Luke and his 'Gospel'," *Das Evangelium und die Evangelien* (cf. above, n. 1), pp. 289-308.

Acts.[47] Acts contains Luke's presentation of the development of the believing community following the Ascension, the transition account between the two works. It is soon clear that Luke's view of sacred history produces certain observable contrasts between his gospel and Acts. For example, Jesus is the main character and guiding hand for the unfolding of Luke's gospel: whereas in Acts, there are several main characters (most especially, Peter and Paul), all of whom function and act under the guidance of the Holy Spirit. In Luke's gospel, disciples are those who follow Jesus; whereas in Acts "following Jesus" is no longer a viable option and discipleship is now understood in terms of being a part of the believing community (2:44; 4:4, 32; 5:14; 9:42; 11:21; et al.) or, in other words, the church (5:11; 7:38; 8:1, 3; 9:31; et al.).

Contrast, however important, is not the focal point of Luke's presentation. Rather, Luke gives emphasis to the continuity which exists between gospel and church. The delicate balance between word and deed, which constitutes a point of continuity between the faith response to Jesus' ministry and that of the early Christian church, has already been mentioned (above, p. 475). Along with this balance of word and deed, one notes that the continued emphasis upon the sermons in Acts along with evidences of signs and wonders brings the ministry of those in the church into continuity with the words and deeds of Jesus. For Luke, the ministry of Jesus, in all its fullness, continues in the ministry of the church. And the opposition that confronted Jesus may be expected by those who carry on his ministry.[48] Further, the special journey of Jesus (Luke 9:51ff.) which provides the vehicle for preaching finds a corresponding theme in Acts in the preaching journeys of Peter and especially Paul.[49]

Within Acts itself, the emphasis upon harmony and continuity continues. There is harmony in the development of the church through the guidance of the Holy Spirit. Peter carries the mission forward among the Jews up to chapter 15; Paul, among the Gentiles thereafter. The Gentile mission, which must have been a point of contention within the infant

[47] See, for example, Martin Dibelius, *Studies in the Acts of the Apostles* (London: SCM Press, 1956), pp. 123ff.; C.K. Barrett, *Luke the Historian in Recent Study* (London: Epworth Press, 1961); Hans Conzelmann, *The Theology of St. Luke*, E.T. by Geoffrey Buswell (New York: Harper and Brothers, 1960), pp. 12ff.; idem., *Die Apostelgeschichte*, Handbuch zum Neuen Testament (Tübingen: J.C.B. Mohr, 1963), pp. 6-8; and Ernst Haenchen, *Die Apostelgeschichte, Kritisch-exegetischer Kommentar über das Neue Testament* (Göttingen: Vandenhoeck und Ruprecht, 1956), pp. 40-41.

[48] Marshall, "Luke and his 'Gospel'," p. 302.

[49] Marshall shares a similar, though not identical, view. In addition, he further identifies a continuity of Christology and eschatology; ibid., p. 301.

church, is not of Pauline origin even though effectively carried out by Paul. The real source is God. The mission to the Gentiles was originally initiated through the conversion of the Ethiopian eunuch with the assistance of Philip (Acts 8:26ff.), insured through the conversion of Saul (Acts 9), and validated convincingly by means of Peter's visions prompting him to assist in the conversion of Cornelius and his household (Acts 10. Cf. also 11:1-18). When the decision to accept the Gentile mission is made in Acts 15, one observes continuity among the leadership. It is certainly no accident that Luke records the words of Peter and James as carrying the day while merely referring to the fact that Paul and Barnabas also addressed the council. Not only is there harmony among the leaders at this conference (with such a broad scope, there is little need to share the conflict between Paul and Peter in Gal. 2), the transition of leadership from Peter to "James and the elders" reflected in chapter 15 is smooth and harmonious.[50] There is indeed continuity between the old and new guard: a continuity provided by the common faith in the"gospel." The same continuity is evident in the transfer of the center of the church from Jerusalem to Rome as evident in the abrupt and obviously incomplete manner by which Luke brings Acts to a stopping point. Acts has no conclusion; for the reader is a part of the church about which Luke writes, and he continues to share the continuity and unity of the believing community.

It is clear that Luke had a purpose when he wrote, and it was his desire to present it as persuasively as possible. The prologue does serve as an introduction to both his gospel and Acts. When taken separately, Luke's gospel shares many of the characteristics of encomium biographical literature and would qualify for classification therein. Luke presents his case for God's soteriological act in and through Jesus, the glorified Messiah. It is equally clear, however, that Luke intends even more when his gospel is examined alongside Acts. The origin of the believing community is traced to the proclamation of the word (gospel as retold in Peter's initial sermon and in those which follow) and the performance of the deed. The church is the community that believes,[51] and the ministry of the church truly participates in the ministry of Jesus in the presence and under the direction of the Holy Spirit. As the "portrait" of the believing community unfolds, the reader's faith response desired by Luke includes not only belief in Jesus Christ but

[50] See Haenchen, above, n. 46.

[51] It is instructive to note here that encomia were written about many topics including gods, people, and cities to mention only a few. Given Lucian's "How to Write History," one observes how encomiastic purposes find their way into writing history.

also participation in the life and ministry of the church. One concludes, therefore, that Luke-Acts confronts the reader with an encomiastically charged account of Jesus-church to which the proper response is faith-participation.[52]

One hardly need be reminded that the gospel attributed to John is very different from the three synoptics. The problem of whether or not there is a relationship between John and Matthew, Mark and Luke, has been a much discussed issue among Johannine scholars.[53] In addition, considerable attention has been devoted to source criticism in John's work to the extent that questions of whether or not one may refer to an "author" or "redactor" could affect one's understanding of this gospel's genre classification. With Dunn, the present analysis will focus on the final form of our present gospel.[54]

The initial problem previously confronted in Mark's gospel also presents itself in John's. In a consideration of topoi, John's gospel avoids references to birth, early childhood, and youth accounts. Here again, as with Mark, one observes that John has indeed chosen another route to accomplish in his narrative what such topoi do in other preliminary accounts. There can be no mistake as to the identity or the importance of the subject of John's narrative by the time the reader reaches the beginning of the adult Jesus in chapter 2. The prologue uniquely sets forth the source and nature of Jesus Christ, and includes a preview of themes which appear elsewhere in John's gospel (e.g., light and life, grace and truth, spiritual birth, faith). Like Mark, John then moves directly to the testimony of John the Baptist which does not, however, include reference to the baptism of Jesus. It is through the use of titles that John prepares his readers for the ministry of the Messiah (Jesus' adult career). This is first accomplished in the prologue ("Word was God," John 1:1; "true light," 1:9; "Son from the Father," 1:14, 18; and "Christ," 1:17). It is indirectly presented in John the Baptist's reply to the direct question, "Who are you?" (1:19). The Baptist responds negatively: "I am not the Christ" (1:2), neither is he Elihah nor a

---

[52] To say that an account is "encomiastically charged" is not to question the historicity or historical value of the information utilized therein. It does mean, on the other hand, that the author exercises control consistent with his purposes over how that information is interpreted.

[53] For a more recent review of the discussion, see Raymond E. Brown, *The Gospel According to John (i-xii)*, The Anchor Bible (New York: Doubleday and Company, 1980), pp. XLIV-LI.

[54] James D.G. Dunn, "Let John be John: A Gospel for Its Time," *Das Evangelium und die Evangelien* (cf. above, n. 1), pp. 309-310.

prophet (1:21). Such negative responses by the Baptist serve to accent
the titles to be given Jesus: "Lord" (1:23), "Lamb of God" (1:29, 36),
"Rabbi" (1:38), "Son of God" (anticipated in 1:34 and identified in
1:49), and "Son of man" (1:51). Therefore, John's preliminary section,
by specifically identifying the narrative's subject, sets the stage for the
adult career in a manner consistent with encomium biographical procedures.

John also employs words and deeds as his major topoi for the
ministry section proper. By comparison with Matthew, Mark, and
Luke, John has highlighted these topoi by emphasizing seven major
events and referring to these miracle accounts as "signs."[55] The
"words" receive special emphasis by John's presentation of extensive
discourses which are attributed to Jesus.[56]

John treats the death of Jesus in a manner which commends him to
the reader. At the arrest, Jesus' acceptance of his role is first indicated by
twice identifying himself to those in authority; then responding when
Peter offers resistance, "Put your sword into its sheath; shall I not drink
the cup which the Father has given me?" (18:11). The trial clearly
emphasizes his innocence. Pilate, his judge, three times affirms his
innocence (18:38; 19:6, 12), and further implies it by refusing to change
the title on the cross from "Jesus of Nazareth, the King of the Jews" to
the title requested by the chief priest, "This man said, I am King of the
Jews" (19:19, 21). Jesus' physical resurrection is supported by an
account of the empty tomb (20:1-10), an appearance to Mary (20:11ff.),
and Thomas' demand and act of touching the nail marks and placing his
hand in Jesus' side (20:19ff.). Thus, John too, in a manner consistent
with encomium biography, has depicted the vindication and glorification
of the crucified Christ.

John also incorporates the literary techniques of amplification and
comparison. One first observes how the many deeds of Jesus are now
reduced to a select number traditionally recognized as seven. One may
argue that this stems from John's sources, however, the choice to accept
and transmit them as "signs" denotes John's adherence to this amplification technique. Also, it has been convincingly argued that John
presents his traditions and sayings in thematically organized units.[57]
Davies, for example, identifies eight episodes, each one followed by an

[55] R. E. Brown, *The Gospel According to John*, pp. CXXXVIII-CXLIV; W.D. Davies,
Invitation to the New Testament, Anchor Books (New York: Doubleday and Company,
1969), pp. 440-465; and C.H. Dodd, *The Interpretation of the Fourth Gospel* (Cambridge:
The University Press, 1965), pp. 297-389.

[56] Ibid.

[57] Ibid.

appropriate discourse.[58] Brown makes a similar argument.[59] Regardless of whether one is convinced by either of these views or adopts another, John's narrative of the adult career is thematically structured and this is one of the ways recommended for encomium writing by the rhetoricians.[60] Two examples will suffice. The organization of chapters 2-4 may be explained thematically. Sign one (2:1-11) depicts the new order which replaces the old in the symbolism of the new wine that is even better than the old.[61] The cleansing of the Temple episode (2:13ff.) serves to confirm the impact of the newly initiated order. The story of Jesus' encounter with Nicodemus (3:1ff) affirms that one's access to the new order is through a "new birth" (v. 3) brought about through faith (vv. 12, 15.; cf. 1:12-13). The inclusiveness of this new order is of such a nature that it is available to even those of Samaria who believe (4:39-42). In three of these episodal units, water is important: water into wine (2:1ff.), new birth in terms of "born of water and the Spirit" (3:5), and the reference to "living water" (4:7-15; esp. v. 11). By organizing this section thematically, the new order brought about by Jesus is amplified for the reader's consideration and the reader is brought to the point of the second sign. The second example is John's presentation of Jesus' feeding of the five thousand (6:1-14) followed by a discourse on Jesus as the "bread of life" (especially vv. 15ff.). Finally, one clearly sees amplifications in the words of the officer: "No man ever spoke like this man" (7:46).

Comparison also is important to John's portrait. One notes, for example, now the superiority of Jesus to John the Baptist is specifically stated by the Baptist ("He who comes after me ranks before me, for he was before me." 1:15) and receives additional emphasis later ("He who comes after me, the thong of whose sandal I am not worthy to untie." 1:27). That the stature of Jesus is second to none is clear in the comparison between Jesus and those who oppose him. Those who would seek to stop him, dare not out of fear (e.g., 7:13). Jesus impresses even these men with his teaching (7:14ff.). In John's gospel, therefore, literary techniques do encourage encomium biographical classification.

John's purposes for writing his gospel have been discussed most recently by Dunn.[62] John's own statement appears in chapter 20 and

---

[58] Davies, *Invitation*, pp. 443-444.

[59] Brown, *The Gospel According to John*, pp. CXLVIIIff.

[60] For example, see Quintilian, *Institutio oratoria*, III. 7. 10-18.

[61] Brown, *The Gospel According to John*, pp. 103-105. See also, C.K. Barrett, *The Gospel According to St. John* (London: SPCK, 1960), pp. 156-158, and Dodd, *Interpretation*, pp. 223ff., esp. p. 226.

[62] Dunn, "Let John be John," pp. 317ff.

specifically states the response he desires: "but these are written that you may believe that Jesus is the Christ, the Son of God, and that believing you may have life in his name." (20:31). While this is similar to what has been concluded of the other three canonical gospels, only Luke makes a similar statement of authorial intent. One notes that in accomplishing his purpose, John gives emphasis to Jesus having come from the Father[63] and to Jesus as the glorified Messiah (e.g., 12:16). He not only writes for faith response, but also instructs his readers in the consequences in store for those who respond in faith (e.g., 15:18ff.; 16:1ff.; 17:6ff).[64] John, therefore, has carefully selected and presented his case for Jesus with the specific intentions of enlisting a positive response and of preparing those who respond for what they may expect to encounter. Even though he has chosen to do so in a manner distinct from the other gospels, his purposes and his choice of the *bios* form qualifies him for identification as a "gospel" in the canonical sense, and points to classification within the encomium biography genre.

The primary goal of the present work has been to address the question of the "genre(s) of the gospels." I have taken the personal liberty of further limiting the question to "genre" instead of "genres." This was not done because of the conviction that the four canonical gospels are identical, or that variations and modifications do not raise the question of different genre classifications. There are differences, and such questions are valid ones. It is the argument of this work, however, that where the totality of the texts are concerned, the canonical gospels are best understood in terms of the encomium biographical pattern. Where there are such variations or expansions, as are evident in the case with Mark's gospel and in Luke's more inclusive purposes by his addition of Acts, the creation of sub-genres in the former case and the impact of one genre upon another, in the latter, best account for the phenomena. Conclusions of this nature, however, must, for the present, defer to further research and another agenda.

To undertake even the task of discussing the genre of the gospels for any reason other than denying there is one is much too ambitious a task for a Symposium upon the relationships among the gospels as traditionally understood. While our tentative investigations can only serve to point ahead to more research, conclusions based upon our progress thus far are worthy of being clearly set forth. First, the

---

[63] As Son, both pre-existent (1:1, 8:25) and united with the Father (e.g., 10:30).

[64] One sure consequence was expulsion from the synagogue (chapter 9). See J.L. Martyn, *History and Theology in the Fourth Gospel* (Nashville: Abingdon, 1979), esp. chapter 2.

question of the genre(s) of the gospels is by no means closed because New Testament scholarship cannot agree on a satisfactory solution. Second, that the evangelists were trying to communicate with their hearers/readers is a fact integral to their narratives. Third, the ancient world did celebrate the lives of persons with narratives of praise and persuasion. Fourth, encomium biography provides a literary context within which the four canonical gospels, conveying the kerygmatic concerns of their authors, may be fruitfully read and interpreted.

Philip L. SHULER

THE GENRE(S) OF THE GOSPELS

RESPONSE TO P. L. SHULER

I

The determination of the genre of the Gospels is of great significance for their historical understanding and interpretation. Philip L. Shuler's contribution to the determination of this genre is helpful in its clarity: "...the canonical gospels are best understood in terms of the encomium biographical pattern" (p. 482). Instead of following form criticism by continuing to view the Gospels as a literary Gattung *sui generis*, it would be more appropriate, according to Shuler, to characterize them as popular, Hellenistic biographies of Jesus. In their composition, the four Gospels follow "a specific type of ancient biographical literature" (p. 462), which he finds attested in Polybius, Cicero, Lucian, Cornelius Nepos, Plutarch and other Greek and Latin authors of the Hellenistic period, namely, the encomian or laudatory biography (p. 465). The concern of such a biography, above all, is to portray a certain personality and his/her work as praiseworthy; historical viewpoints play only a subsidiary role (or none at all) in the presentation. The authors of this type of biography limit themselves in their writing to a few, standardized biographical forms of topoi concerning family extraction, the circumstances surrounding the person's birth and death, and the career of the hero. Their work only consists of a few crucial points. Finally, the literary technique used in the popular biography followed, above all, the two rules of comparison and amplification. The composition of such biographies was practiced in the Greek schools of rhetoric (p. 466).

According to Shuler, the biblical evangelists made use of this literary genre in order to present the Gospel-tradition in a form which was especially understandable to the readers and hearers of their time; precisely as encomian biographies of Jesus, the Gospels were to serve in the strengthening of faith, edification and instruction of the church members in the Greek-speaking mission communities. Shuler thus shares this literary-critical judgment of the Gospels as vitae with Charles

Talbert[1] and also refers to Martin Hengel[2] for support. Robert Guelich's[3] disagreement with his assesssment and the devastating critique of Talbert's position by David E. Aune[4] have not hindered him from extending the view he first developed in regard to Matthew in his monograph, *A Genre for the Gospels — The Biographical Character of Matthew* (Philadelphia, Fortress Press 1982), to all of the biblical Gospels in the lecture now before us. In doing so, he hopes to gain a significant degree of flexibility regarding the question being debated in our symposium as well, namely, the mutual relationship of the Gospels.

II

Whoever must examine the historical credibility and hermeneutical productivity of Shuler's thesis can hardly overlook, right from the beginning, one fact: the classical philologists Albrecht Dihle[5] and Hubert Cancik[6], who recently have also taken up the question of the genre of the Gospels, are significantly more cautious in their answers than Shuler. Indeed, both also emphasize that the biblical Gospels are in some accord with the polymorphic, Hellenistic biographies in terms of structure and content. At the same time, however they also call attention to the considerable differences between those biographies and the Gospels: for Dihle, the main difference lies in the anthropological and historiographical presuppositions with which the writers of the *vitae* and evangelists approach their respective works.[7] For Cancik, the degree to which the material in the Gospel of Mark is historicized is so advanced over against a popular *vita*, such as Lucian's *Demonax*, that he advises against an identification of the Gospels with a (popular) *vita* in Shuler's sense.[8] In addition, Aune's reference to the difference between the *vitae* and the Gospels, being well grounded both philologi-

---

[1] Charles Talbert, *What is a Gospel?* Philadelphia 1977.

[2] Martin Hengel, *Zur urchristlichen Geschichtsschreibung*, Stuttgart 1979, 20ff. Cf. his *Probleme des Markusevangeliums*, in *Das Evangelium und die Evangelien*, ed. P. Stuhlmacher, Tübingen 1983, 221-271, esp. 223ff.

[3] Robert Guelich, *The Gospel Genre*, in *Das Evangelium* (see n. 2) 183-219, esp. 190ff.

[4] D.E. Aune, "The Problem of the Genre of the Gospels: A Critique of C.H. Talbert's *What is a Gospel?*" in *Gospel Perspectives*, Vol. II, ed. R.T. France and David Wenham, Sheffield 1981, 9-60.

[5] Albrecht Dihle, "Die Evangelien und die griechische Biographie," in *Das Evangelium* (see n. 2), 383-411.

[6] Hubert Cancik, "Bios und Logos, Formengeschichtliche Untersuchungen zu Lukians 'Demonax'," in *Markus Philologie*, ed. H. Cancik, Tübingen 1984, 115-130.

[7] Cf. Dihle, above n. 5, 406f.

[8] Cf. Cancik, above n. 6, 92ff.

cally and historically, merits attention: while the Gospels have a distinct function in and for the Christian communities to which they were written, no comparable function has yet to be discovered for the vitae; at the outset the Gospels were anonymous books, the *vitae*, in contrast, bear in most cases an exact indication of authorship; the Greek of the Gospels is non-literary, while the *vitae* correspond stylistically to the taste of the literary upperclass of the Hellenistic world.[9] If one takes these arguments together, it appears advisable not to ratify Shuler's identification of the Gospels with popular, Hellenistic biography without examination. For the comparison of the *vitae*-literature from antiquity with the Gospels from the perspective of the history of literature leads to certain facts which cannot be sufficiently understood with Shuler's identification.

III

If one turns to the biblical texts themselves and considers the history of their early Christian reception and effect, certain perspectives also arise which recommend caution in regard to Shuler's suggested solution.

1. The biblical Gospels, their literary formation and their communities.

The literary and rhetorical ability needed for the composition of *vitae* in the Hellenistic period could be acquired only in the highest levels of the Greek educational system.[10] Is it probable that the biblical evangelists went through this expensive, "academic" education in one of the schools of rhetoric or academies in Alexandria, Antioch or Athens?[11] Even when one takes into account the "literary" prologue of the Gospel of Luke (Lk 1:1-4), the possibility hardly exists, on the basis of the New Testament and the witness of the Church Fathers, for answering this question positively. Moreover, the sociological composition of the early Christian communities makes it quite improbable that the evangelists consciously formed their Gospels as *vitae*: the *bioi* known to us are directed toward the literarily-educated upper-class, while the presenta-

---

[9] Cf. Aune, above n. 4, 44ff.

[10] Martin P. Nilsson, *Die hellenistische Schule*, München 1955, 16.

[11] Note Nilsson's statement, ibid, 51: "Die hellenistische Schule hat den Grund gelegt für die ausgedehnte literarische Tätigkeit des hellenistischen Zeitalters; die wenigsten hatten Geld und Gelegenheit, sich an irgendeinen der grossen Brennpunkte der Gelehrsamkeit und der Philosophie zu begeben, nach Athen, Rhodos, Alexandria. Wer das wollte, musste es auf eigene Faust machen."

tion and language of the Gospels had to be understood, above all, by the "small people", who, up until the third century A.D., made up the majority of the Church.[12]

2. The self-designation of the biblical Gospels.

The titles and signatures of the Gospels present a special problem for both textual and literary criticism. We will come back to this later (see below, pp. 492ff.). But if we disregard the inscriptions and subscriptions for a moment, the following facts emerge:

a) *The Gospel of Matthew* begins in 1:1 with the definition: βίβλος γενέσεως Ἰησοῦ Χριστοῦ = the book of the genealogy (or better: history)[13] of Jesus Christ. According to Matthew 28:19-20 the Gospel is intended to aid the disciples in their mission by helping them to fulfill their commission "to teach" others "to observe everything" that Jesus commanded and taught. It is difficult to conceive how these conceptions of "history" and "doctrine/teaching" can be brought together with the genre of the βίος.

b) The Gospel of Mark is placed under the catch-word "the Gospel of Jesus Christ" as indicated in 1:1. According to 1:15, the Gospel is Jesus' own message. Hence, the Gospel of Mark is to be understood as that book which reports the preaching of Jesus, his deeds and his fate. As such, it is intended to support the preaching of the Gospel to all the nations of the Gentiles which precedes the Parousia of the Son of Man (cf. 13:10). The fact that it should be taken literally to be a (popular) *vita Jesu* is not indicated by the notions εὐαγγέλιον and κηρύσσειν. history of the concept "Gospel" points much more toward the conception of eschatological proclamation, teaching and tradition (see below, pp. 489ff.).

c) The Gospel of Luke intends to offer a historically accurate διηγησις = an account/narrative of the history of Jesus. This narrative is based on the investigation of various reports from eyewitnesses of the work of Jesus and is intended to assist Theophilus in recognizing that the words and facts concerning which he has been instructed (from a Christian perspective) are historically reliable. In Acts 1:1, "Luke" refers back to the Gospel. He refers to it here simply as a λόγος and designates the

---

[12] According to Origen, *Contra Celsum* III 44, Celsus also accused the Christian missionaries of showing "that they want and are able to convince only the foolish, dishonourable and stupid, and only slaves, women, and little children." Trans. H. Chadwick: *Origen: Contra Celsum,* Cambridge 1965, 158.

[13] Concerning this translation, cf. Theodor Zahn, *Das Evangelium des Matthäus,* Erlangen 1922[4], 41f.

Acts of the Apostles in the same way as well. Thus, Lk 1:1-4 and Acts 1:1ff. once again point to the Gospel as a (reliable) historical narrative, not, however, to a Hellenistic βίος, for which, by definition, history plays only a subordinate role, or even no role at all.

d) The Gospel of John, according to 20:30f., intends to be a book in which the signs of Jesus are reported; the written account of these signs is intended to assist one's faith. In 21:24f. the so-called "beloved disciple" (John), around whom a Christian group is gathered, is designated as the chief witness for the tradition and design of the Gospel. Moreover, on the basis of 21:25 it becomes clear that the Gospel of John contains only a collected selection of the traditions which were known to this "Johannine circle". Thus, 20:30f. and 21:24f. give the reader no hint of an encomian biography. In fact, the claim to truth which stands behind the Gospel (cf. 1:17; 14:6; 16:13) even excludes the conscious choice of this genre. For according to the definitions of Cicero, Lucian, Plutarch and others cited by Shuler, the βιος is a genre that consciously deals with historical truth in broad outline; the Gospel of John raises a contrary claim.

The question which emerges as a result of this overview is how Shuler's definition of the Gospels as *vitae* relates to the fact that none of the gospels, from their own perspective, can be recognized to have been composed as laudatory biographies of Jesus, or to express the desire to be read as such.

3. *The witness of the Church Fathers*

The witness of the Church Fathers leads to a similar state of affairs. Whenever the so-called "Apostolic Fathers" or the later "Church Fathers" come to speak of the Gospels, there is no indication that they themselves or the Christians in their communities ever perceived the Gospels as *vitae* in Shuler's sense! Even Celsus and Porphyry show no trace off such a literary evaluation of the Gospels in their critique of Christianity and the Gospels. The question is whether this state of affairs is coincidental. On the basis of Justin's designation of the Gospels as ἀπομνημονεύματα τῶν ἀποστόλων = memoirs of the apostles[14], the opposite seems to be the case: the designation"*vitae*" for the Gospels was unknown to the Fathers and also contradicts their esteem for these books as revelatory writings which were read in the

---

[14] This designation has been analyzed most recently by Luise Abramowski: "Die 'Erinnerungen der Apostel' bei Justin," in *Das Evangelium* (see above n. 2) 341-353, esp. 346ff.

early Christian worship service next to, and with the same authority as the prophets (cf. *Apology* I 67).

Therefore, inasmuch as the literary evaluation of the Gospels as laudatory *vitae* cannot be verified either from the compositional presuppositions of the evangelists and early Christian communities, or from the New Testament texts, or from the witness of the Church Fathers, it is advisable to be cautious in regard to Shuler's definition. His sentence: "No doubt, the gospels were received by their original readers as biographies containing the summons of faith in the Messiah, Jesus of Nazareth"(13),[15] cannot be confirmed by the biblical texts and the history of their reception in early Christianity. The Gospels are not concerned with encomian *vitae*, but with a biographically accented narrative of Jesus' work, word and fate, i.e. of his history. The Gospels served in the gatherings of the community and in the early Christian services of worship as writings to be read publicly (cf. Mk 13:14; Rev 1:3 and Justin, *Apology* I 67).

IV

Shuler consciously formulated his definition of the Gospels independent of any specific theory concerning the mutual relationship of the Gospels. In the same way, the arguments which we have brought into the discussion up until now against Shuler's explanation are also independent of any such theory. The situation changes, however, as soon as one asks how the Gospels came to be called "Gospels" at all. Shuler does not raise this question, although he remarks concerning the Gospel of Matthew: "'Gospel' has been transmitted in a recognized and

---

[15] Martin Hengel also writes: "Die Hörer des Markusevangeliums und der nachfolgenden Evangelien haben diese nie anders als im Sinne von einzigartigen 'Biographien' verstanden, die den Weg und die Lehre des einzigartigen Messias und Gottessohnes Jesus von Nazareth bezeugen. Daß die Evangelien eine literarische 'Gattung' von ganz neuer und besonderer Art seien, hat in der Antike niemand gedacht. Nicht die literarische 'Gattung', sondern die darin dargestellte Person und ihr Heilswerk waren 'einzigartig'." *Probleme des Markusevangelium* (see n. 2), 224. This sentence also needs to be made more precise. It must be taken into consideration, of course, that when Hengel characterizes the Gospels as biographies he understands them differently than Shuler, i.e. he does not place them in contrast to historical writing (which in regard to the Jewish material is an entirely inappropriate contrast), but understands them as a presentation of the history of Jesus. In addition, Hengel does not leave the "Sitz im Leben" of the Gospels open. On pages 255ff he works out in a precise manner that the Gospel of Mark was written as a teaching or doctrinal discourse for the worship service. Moreover, according to Hengel, what applies for the Gospel of Mark is also applicable, at least, for the Gospel of Matthew.

easily received, ubiquitous literary pattern" (471). The possibility for explaining this process which is most enlightening historically comes about, however, if one takes the Gospel of Mark as the starting point.

In early Christianity, in the period before the writing of the Gospels, "Gospel" meant (1) the message of the mission, which was preached by the apostles and missionaries (cf. Rom 1:16; Gal 1:11; I Peter 4:17 etc.). At the Apostolic Council in Jerusalem the "Gospel for the uncircumcized (= the Gentiles)" entrusted to Paul and the "Gospel for the circumcized (= the Jews)" entrusted to Peter were distinguished, without maintaining a dogmatic difference between the two. The term can also be used in conjunction (2) with the fundamental catechetical tradition concerning Jesus' death of atonement, burial, resurrection on the third day and his first appearances before Peter and the Twelve, etc. (cf. I Cor 15:1-11). Finally, it is striking that (3) in Acts 10:36-43 a paradigm for preaching is presented in which the ῥῆμα = the history of the work of Jesus "beginning from Galilee after the baptism which John preached" is understood as a development of the "Gospel" of peace (= salvation) preached by God himself through Jesus Christ.[16] Graham N. Stanton,[17] Robert Guelich[18] and others have shown that this pattern for preaching most probably represents a kerygmatic tradition which has been assimilated by Luke. In it a midrashlike wickerwork of Ps 107:20; Is 52:7 (Nah 2:1); Is 61:1; Deut 21:22 and Hos 6:2 comprises the string of motifs needed in order to narrate the history of the work of Jesus for the purpose of proclamation.

If one comes to the Gospel of Mark from this background, he/she is struck by two things: The word is used repeatedly by Mark and with a particular emphasis (cf. 1:1,14f.; 8:35; 10:29; 13:10; 14:9 and 16:15). At the same time, the entire book is presented thematically in the light of this expression as indicated by 1:1. Mark thus narrates the history of the work of Jesus "beginning from Galilee after the baptism which John preached" (Acts 10:37) and allows the Gospel of God to be preached by Jesus himself (compare 1:14f. with Acts 10:36). The structural relationship between Acts 10:36ff. and the Gospel of Mark has already been recognized for a long time. This kinship caused Martin Dibelius[19] and

---

[16] For the use of the word "Gospel", cf. Peter Stuhlmacher, "Zum Thema: Das Evangelium und die Evangelien," in Das Evangelium (see n. 2), 1-26, 20ff., and his "Das paulinische Evangelium," in Das Evangelium (see n. 2), 157-182.

[17] Graham N. Stanton, Jesus of Nazareth in New Testament Preaching, Cambridge 1974, 67-85.

[18] Robert Guelich, "The Gospel Genre" (see n. 3), 209ff.

[19] Martin Dibelius, Die Formgeschichte des Evangeliums, Tübingen 1959³, 232f.

Charles H. Dodd,[20] above all, to understand the Gospel of Mark to be a literary development of the kerygmatic scheme of Acts 10. I continue to consider this, as I have in the past, together with Robert Guelich and many others, to be correct.

For that kerygmatic "pattern", interestingly enough, can be brought together equally well with the Gospel of Mark both grammatically and from the perspective of the history of tradition. For that scheme and the Gospel of Mark already belong together in that both are brought into association with Peter. If one follows the Papias-tradition (which is historically credible throughout)[21] that (John) Mark worked as Peter's ἑρμηνευτής and that after Peter's martyrdom he recorded the preaching of his master (in its main features) an entirely organic continuity of tradition results from Acts 10:36ff. to the Gospel of Mark. One can cast doubt on this continuity critically, but it is difficult to replace it with a better explanation. For the introduction of the Gospel of Mark confirms it, even to the point of the grammatical details.

A comparison of Mk 1:1 with Hosea 1:2(LXX) makes it probable that verse 1 is to be understood as the title of the book. Recently, Robert Guelich[22] has called attention to the fact that the expression καθὼς γέγραπται never begins a new thought in the New Testament, but always connects a preceding text with a subsequent quotation from Scripture; it is improbable that Mk 1:2 constitutes an exception to this rule. Rather, Mk 1:1 and 1:2-3 form one integrated sentence. It reads: "The beginning of the Gospel of Jesus Christ, the Son of God, as written in Isaiah the prophet: Behold ...". As is well known, the mixed quotation in Mk 1:2f. from Mal 3:1 and Ex 23:20 and Is 40:3, presents an exegetical problem of long standing; in the so-called Majority-text this problem has even led to a change in the description of the citation. But if one reads Mk 1:1-3 from the perspective of the tradition in Acts 10:36ff., the sentence construction becomes apparent: the evangelist begins with a narration of that divine Gospel, which was promised in Is

---

[20] Charles Harold Dodd, *The Apostolic Preaching and its Developments*, New York 1962, 46ff.

[21] The debate concerning the credibility of the Papias witnesses has been opened anew by M. Hengel and L. Abramowski in the Tübingen symposium. Cf. *Das Evangelium* (see n. 2), 244ff. and 349f. The fact that Peter made us of John Mark as a ἑρμηνευτής (= interpreter, translator, stylist and reduplicator), in spite of his own knowledge of Greek, is very probable. Even Josephus, according to *Contra Apionem* I 50, employed several co-workers in the composition of his works πρὸς τὴν Ἑλληνίδα φωνήν.

[22] "The Gospel Genre" (see n. 3), 204ff. Cf. also his essay "'The Beginning of the Gospel' — Mark 1:1-15," in *Biblical Research* 27, 1982, 5-15.

52:7; 61:1f. and fulfilled historically in the appearance of the Messiah, Jesus Christ. This Gospel finds its beginning in the fact that God sent the baptizer John to be the prophetic preparer of the way for his son as announced in Mal 3:1 and Ex 23:20. The baptizer is the "voice of one crying in the wilderness" from Is 40:3. The promise of Is 61:1f. is realized in the baptism of Jesus: he is endowed with the Spirit and called to the office of the messianic Son of God (1:10f.). As the son of God he endures the temptation. Following the temptation he takes up the work of the messianic "good tidings" according to Is. 52:7 (Nah. 2:1): he proclaims the Gospel of the inauguration of the reign of God and summons his listeners to faith in this message (1:14f.). Unless everything is misleading, in Mk 1:1-15 the evangelist links together the Peter-tradition from Acts 10:36ff. standing before his eyes with his own literary presentation. His application of Scripture matches the use of Scripture in Acts 10:36ff. Thus, the presentation of Mark follows the trail which the "pattern" from Acts 10 has laid.

The pattern from Acts 10:36ff. understands the Gospel of God to be the history of the work of Jesus since his baptism by John the Baptist. This is also exactly what we find in Mark. His literary Gospel is not an encomian biography of Jesus, but the narrative of the history of Jesus as the realization of the Gospel. Thus, if one understands the genre of the Gospels from the outline of Mark, the fact that Matthew chooses the title βίβλος γενέσεως for his Gospel, Luke the simple designation διήγησις or λόγος and John the name βίβλος explains itself without great difficulty: the evangelists beside and after Mark understand their presentations, even more decisively than he does, in the sense of narratives of the history of Jesus. The Apostolic Fathers and the Church Fathers follow them and see in the Gospels, as a logical consequence, the "memoirs of the apostles" (Justin),[23] "records of the teaching discourses of the Lord" (Eusebius),[24] or even simply "Gospels". The opponents of the Christians, Celsus and Porphyry, do not contradict this understanding of the Gospels, but rather attempt to demonstrate that the evangelists have engaged in falsifying history.[25]

---

[23] Apologie I 33,5; 66,3; 67,3 etc.
[24] Kirchengeschichte III 24,5. Cf. Helmut Merkel, *Die Pluralität der Evangelien*, Bern, 19f.
[25] Especially characteristic is the introductory sentence of the fragment from Porphyry identified by Adolf von Harnack in Makarius Magnes II 12: τοὺς εὐαγγελιστὰς ἐφευρετὰς οὐχ ἱστορίας τῶν περὶ τὸν Ἰησοῦν γεγενῆσθαι πράξεων. Cf. A. v. Harnack, *Porphyrius – "Gegen die Christen"*, 15 Bücher, Berlin 1916.

V

Finally, the fact that the Gospel of Mark occupies a key position for the determination of the genre of the Gospels is also indicated by the titles of the Gospels. In the last years, Hans Frhr. von Campenhausen[26], David Aune[27] and Martin Hengel[28] have called attention to the fact that these superscriptions are substantially older than one has assumed up until now. They probably go back to the period before the demarcation of the four-Gospel-canon. Papias already seems to presuppose them, since only from them does it become clear who composed the individual Gospels.

The significance of these superscriptions to the Gospels is twofold: the superscriptions and inscriptions are intended to make the individual documents used for public reading distinguishable from one another in the libraries of the churches. And, when the Gospels are read aloud in the worship service these titles and signatures enable the community to recognize which book is being read to them.

Before the four Gospels were unifed in one single codex, the superscription ran, ευαγγελιον κατα Μαρκον / Μαθθαιον / Λουκαν / Ιωαννην = "The (one) Gospel in the draft of ...". Within the four-Gospel-canon and in the large manuscripts of the bible, however, it was then sufficient simply to write κατα Μαρκον / Μαθθαιον ... instead of the complete title.

How the titles to the books came into existence can still be recognized in the beginning of the Gospel of Luke: the Gospel itself, like all four Gospels, is anonymous; only the prologue dedicated to the distinguished "Theophilus" (Lk 1:1-4) allows us to recognize the individual signature of the author. Moreover, "Luke" appears to combine with his dedication the expectation that Theophilus will be able to "publish" the work dedicated to him. In this case, however, documents had to bear an inscription and subscription in order to be of use in the libraries (see above). Hence, we must take into account that the superscriptions over the Gospels (just like the signatures) go back to the period of the "publication" of these books for the use of the Church.

[26] Hans Freiherr von Campenhausen, *Die Entstehung der christlichen Bibel*, Tübingen 1968, 203n.121.

[27] "The Problem of the Genre" (see n. 4), 44. In contrast to v. Campenhausen, Aune still proceeds from the supposition that the superscriptions, which were handed down in such astounding unanimity, "were affixed to each of the gospels only after they had been assembled into a fourfold collection (ca. A.D. 125)."

[28] Cf. his Akademieabhandlung, *Die Evangelienüberschriften*. A summary has appeared in the Jahrbuch der Heidelberger Akademie der Wissenschaften, 1981, 104f. In the following text I am summarizing Hengel's arguments.

The wording of the superscriptions and signatures is striking. For a simple designation of authorship it would have corresponded to literary convention and have been sufficient simply to write Μαρκου / Ματθαιου ... ευαγγελιον (Ιησου Χριστου). The choice fell, however, to ευαγγελιον κατα ..., and was so transmitted in the manuscripts without exception. The significance of this is clear: the title itself is intended to express the fact that the Gospel is the one message of salvation (from God) which the different evangelists repeat, each in their own manner.

If we attempt to ascertain the reasons for the choice of this special type of superscript and signature, once again we are compelled by the nature of the material itself to direct our attention to the Gospel of Mark. For the superscript corresponds exactly to the attempt which Mark engages in, namely, to report the Gospel (of Peter) in the form of a book. The Gospel of Mark was displaced in the practice of public reading within the worship service with varying degrees of rapidity in the various provinces of the Church by the Gospels of Matthew and John. Nevertheless, it maintained itself as the "tradition of Peter", and the authority of the "Rock" (Mt 16:18) gave to its superscription an authority which extended beyond the authority of Mark's Gospel as such. In contrast, the existence of the titles to the Gospels can only be explained on the basis of Mattthew with great difficulty, while not at all from Luke and John, since they avoid the term εὐαγγέλιον (Luke first uses it in Acts 15:7 and 20:24). But if one begins with Mark, all of the problems fall into place and it becomes clear, once again, why the Gospels are called "Gospel".

VI

Philip L. Shuler's definition of the Gospels as popular, Hellenistic *vitae* is not verified by the texts. The biographical accentuation of the presentation of the evangelists is entirely undeniable, but it is better taken into consideration when we call the Gospels presentations of the history of Jesus as "salvation event" (*Heilsgeschehen*). The Gospels cannot be incorporated into the genre of the *vita* or βιος. Their subject matter, purpose and use all indicate that they are to be considered independent books. They summarize the Jesus-tradition according to the pattern established in the narrative preaching about Jesus (cf. Acts 10:36ff.) and are intended to be read in the gatherings of the community for the purpose of instruction and edification.

Peter STUHLMACHER

NACHTRAG

Ever true to the assigned task, Peter Stuhlmacher has not been timid in his response to Shuler's "The Genre(s) of the Gospels." It is not possible in this *Nachtrag* to respond to all of Stuhlmacher's objections, but perhaps a few observations would be helpful.

First, Stuhlmacher, citing works by Aune, Dihle, and Cancik, is impressed with their conclusion that the gospels are products of the uneducated and are non-literary productions (two references). Although this is not really a point of disagreement, such a conclusion is based upon the examination of those *vitae* texts that have survived the centuries, all of which are literary examples. It is doubtful that the gospels would have survived independently apart from the community that preserved and revered them. What Stuhlmacher fails to acknowledge is that Shuler nowhere argues that the gospels were written to be literary encomia. Shuler's argument is: the encomium was such a ubiquitous rhetorical device that its influence was a dominant factor in gospel formation as evidenced form-critically by the authors' obvious shift from the presentation of collected traditions to that of a *bios* portrait.

Second, Stuhlmacher rightly credits the role of the community in the formation and use of the gospels. As Stuhlmacher himself observes, both agree on the primary functions as being teaching and edification. Stuhlmacher's argument is that such functions are not associated with encomium *bios* narratives. Ancient *bios* narratives do reflect similar functions, however. Tacitus' *Agricola*, for example, contains functions related both to apology and emulation, functions which relate quite well with the gospel narratives. These functions are also closely related to those of instruction and edification. The objects of the teaching and edifying are illustrated in Jesus who, in a real sense, serves as model.

Third, there is an implied assertion in Stuhlmacher's response: namely, that understanding the gospels as *bios* narratives tends to minimize their credibility. This assertion surfaces in his discussion of the gospels as historical narratives. The real problem separating Shuler and Stuhlmacher on this point is precisely what kind of "history" was intended by the evangelists. One gains much historical insight into the character of Agricola from Tacitus' apologetic work, but very little insight into the geography of England. Surely the same is true with the evangelists. For example, the Lucan travel narrative is a literary creation in that it creates a setting within the story, but does not reconstruct the journey with any degree of historical accuracy. There is, however, a more serious objection to Stuhlmacher's argument. On the one hand, he wants to take at face value the claims of these documents and relates their claims to historical and truth narrations: on the other hand, he adopts the views of Dodd and Guelich with respect to the shaping of the gospel narratives in accordance with the early Christian preaching evidenced in Acts and the prophetic utterances of II Isaiah. For this writer, it is a contradiction to reject the persuasive styles of the ancient rhetoricians based on the absence of historical emphasis while, at the same time, accepting the narrative preaching at face value as maintaining historical integrity. Shuler's point is that the narrative preaching evident in the gospels incorporated the persuasive style present in the rhetorical educational system, a procedure which does not automatically imply historical irresponsibility.

Fourth, Stuhlmacher has much to say about the title of the gospel narratives. If they are encomium *bioi*, then why were they not called such? To this question, there is no definitive answer. Although this argument from omission appears to be persuasive on the surface, David Balch has convincingly identified a similar situation in his discussion of Josephus' *Contra Apionem* in comparison with Dionysius of Halicarnassus' apologetic encomium of Rome in *Antiquities* I.9-11.29.[1] One concludes that even though epideictic literature was very important within the first century C.E. milieu, there were writers who preferred not to use epideictic designations in their titles. Precisely how much weight one places on the absence of such a designation on the gospel texts will have to be determined by the individual exegete. Obviously, Shuler and Stuhlmacher disagree on this point.

In conclusion, Stuhlmacher's careful work has to be carefully considered and evaluated. I continue to stand by the paper as originally presented.

P.L. SHULER

---

[1] David Balch, "Two Apologetic Encomia: Dionysius on Rome and Josephus on the Jews," *Journal for the Study of Judaism*, Vol. XII, N° 1-2 (1982), pp. 102-122.

THE GOSPEL TRADITION

In preparation for this symposium our three research teams have analysed a number of synoptic texts. The material from these teams demonstrates how complicated the problems are and how penetrating the analysis becomes when it is done thoroughly. Analyses of this kind are necessary and important; what we have for sure from Early Christianity is the writings preserved in the New Testament. On the other hand, Early Christianity was something more than texts and text production. We must also try to reconstruct the historical contexts in which these documents originated and from which they took their material, not in the least the tradition that these books presuppose. Therefore, our program includes a study of the gospel tradition as well.

PROLEGOMENA

Our inclusive word "tradition" covers a complicated reality, a phenomenon so basic and omnipresent in human existence that a rational fluoroscopy is difficult to make. The complex and partly elusive phenomenon of tradition is studied in many disciplines. Yet, it seems to be a fact that we still look in vain for works which collect and combine insights from all the different disciplines and try to make an all-comprehensive and synthetic description of the phenomenology of tradition: what tradition is and how it functions as an integrated totality and in all its aspects.[1]

Historically, Christianity may be characterized as a new tradition which originates within a well developed mother-tradition and gradually liberates itself from this; at the same time it also receives influences from other traditions in the milieu. This paper will deal with the gospel tradition, seen as part of the Early Christian tradition. Let me indicate the way I delimit my subject. Certainly I am going to

---

[1] Cf., however, P.-G. Müller, *Der Traditionsprozess im Neuen Testament. Kommunikationsanalytische Studien zur Versprachlichung des Jesusphänomens* (Freiburg, Basel, Wien: Herder, 1982) 11-111, and E. Shils, *Tradition* (London: Faber & Faber, 1981). For literature on the gospel tradition, see R. Riesner, *Jesus als Lehrer. Eine Untersuchung zum Ursprung der Evangelien-Überlieferung* (WUNT 2.R., 7; 2nd ed.; Tübingen: Mohr, 1984) 503-68, 615.

mobilize insights from many areas and many disciplines but the historical sphere we shall directly deal with in this paper is Early Christianity
in the New Testament period against its background in the Judaism of
the centuries around the beginning of our time-reckoning and in its so-
called "Hellenistic" surroundings. Within this area we shall study
tradition in its most important aspects, especially "the gospel tradition." With the last designation — as well as with the name "the
concrete Jesus-tradition" — I mean the tradition about the teaching,
works and fate of Jesus during his life on earth (including the signs of
his resurrection), in concreto, mainly tradition of the sort which has
been compiled in the synoptic Gospels (and in a more decked-out form
in the Gospel of John).

It seems to be possible to analyse and discuss the Early Christian
(and the Jewish) tradition with the aid of a rather simple model of
investigation which I will soon present. But let me first say that I
am aware of the fact that further distinctions and classifications are
possible and desirable; however, such specifications belong to more
penetrating analysis and specialized debate. I am also aware of the fact
that my terminology is somewhat rough. It is, however, handy, and that
is important even in scholarly discussions. Finally, I also know that my
distinctions sometimes appear artificial, since tradition in its best stages
is a rather well integrated, organically coherent entity. Yet, I intend my
distinctions to be realistic; very commonly the different aspects of
tradition are disjoined and the different elements exist separately. We
do need a convenient term for each one of them.

One of the purposes of our symposium is to emphasize questions
where further research and discussion are desirable. I shall mention
here a very great number of such questions, old and new, and put a
special stress on some of them. The "answers" I sketch very briefly are
primarily meant as illustrations of the model of investigation and of the
problems; as solutions of complicated problems they are rather
approximate and preliminary.

I am a Christian, brought up in the Lutheran tradition. Certain
proclivities and accents will presumably reveal that. And in no way do I
reject different attempts to clarify the Early Christian tradition from
confessional points of departure. In his book *Der Traditionsprozess im
Neuen Testament* (1981), Paul-Gerhard Müller has made an insightful
and many-sided analysis of the verbal New Testament tradition from a
Catholic standpoint. Similar works ought to be done from non-Catho-
lic positions as well. However, the approach I present here is not
founded on any specific theological basis. Apart from certain outlooks

and by-the-way comments, I here tackle the problem of tradition by means of secular scholarship. While this facilitates discussion with non-theological disciplines, I want to point out, on the other hand, that my approach leads to bad theology if naively developed into a New Testament theology. In an historical study of the origin and first development of Christianity, one must consider the earth-bound human reality with its whole mixture of conflicting elements, shortcomings, compromises and the like. If, on the other hand, a *New Testament theology* shall be able to give a fresh picture of Early Christianity's message and content of faith, it cannot begin in the outer, earthly dimensions but must take the eruptive center of the message itself, as its starting point, i.e. those views and perspectives that filled Jesus and his followers and created Early Christianity: "The Reign of Heaven," Christ, the gospel — as preached and believed.

I. A MODEL OF INVESTIGATION

It is my conviction that historical research must try to make very concrete reconstructions of the past, preferably in the form of vivid, visual pictures of the complex realities. The sources do not always allow that. But we can often advance rather far in the right direction if we apply, on the one hand, general ("phenomenological") insights about the way in which human beings function both individually and communally, and, on the other hand, special insights from that historical sphere in which the object of research is situated and from the analogies closest to it.

For the study of the Early Christian tradition we need a model of investigation. I have used one such model (with increasing discursiveness) in my works on the problem of tradition.[2] This model makes it possible to dissect the complicated phenomenon of Early Christian tradition, to elucidate its different aspects in congruent ways, to keep in

---

[2] *Memory and Manuscript. Oral Tradition and Written Transmission in Rabbinic Judaism and Early Christianity* (ASNU 22; Lund: Gleerup, Copenhagen: Munksgaard, 1961; 2nd ed. 1964), *Tradition and Transmission in Early Christianity* (ConNT 20; Lund: Gleerup, Copenhagen: Munksgaard, 1964), *The Origins of the Gospel Traditions* (Philadelphia: Fortress, 1979; also published in German, Swedish, Danish, French, Spanish and Italian); "Der Weg der Evangelientradition," in *Das Evangelium und die Evangelien. Vorträge vom Tübinger Symposium 1982* (WUNT 28; ed. P. Stuhlmacher, Tübingen: Mohr, 1983) 79-102. In the following I will make frequent reference to these writings in order to indicate the continuity and development of my work on the problem of tradition in the hopes of eliminating any existing misunderstandings of my position.

mind the most important of them in the analyses of the texts, and to discuss the problems involved in a handy language.

The model is based on general "phenomenological" insights gained in many areas, times and disciplines, but it is specifically constructed for a study of the Early Christian tradition connected with its historical milieus, especially its Jewish mother-tradition. I shall here present it briefly but yet in a more developed and explicated way that I have done before.[3] The model is simple: a basic distinction is made between "inner" and "outer" tradition, and, within the outer tradition four separate aspects are to be noted: verbal, behavioural, institutional and material tradition.

In the following I shall first present the model of investigation in general, phenomenological terms and then more concretely show what it means when applied to the mother-tradition of Christianity and to Early Christianity itself. Then I shall discuss the different aspects in somewhat more detail in relation to Early Christianity. The main stress will be laid upon the gospel tradition.

1. Survey

a) Inner tradition

When tradition functions ideally, it is animated, it "lives." It is carried and kept together by an inner engagement, by belief, convictions, values, views. An ideal traditionist is like a torch that lights other torches, some rabbis used to say.

A vital content of mind cannot remain locked up in the individual. It expresses itself in the fellowship, it becomes a "message" which is communicated to other people, it spreads to the environment and to next generation, if it is strong. It generates tradition. The decisive, "living" part of this, however, is difficult to analyse and describe. The words we use to indicate that one human being influences others are rather vague. We say that he "inspires" others, "convinces" others, "dominates" others, is "contagious" and so on. This is a kind of communication — a handing over and a receiving; therefore the word tradition is appropriate: "inner tradition." It is of course necessary to study the inner tradition but it is not easy. As an object of research it is elusive and difficult to grasp as is "life" itself: it is mobile, includes changes and variations, some parts grow, other parts decline, renewal

---

[3] Cf. *Memory* 71-78, 290-94, *Tradition* 7, *Origins* 11-14, 31-32.

occurs and "death." An analysis — which I am not going to do here — must include many aspects; cognitive, emotive, and volitional aspects, maybe more.

What is easier to come to grips with is the outward forms the inner tradition assumes. It not only expresses itself in a mental way, it also *externalizes* itself in visible and audible outward forms. These I call "outer tradition."

b) Outer tradition

The outward forms of a tradition can be of many kinds. For our purpose it seems to be enough that we specify four such forms or "dimensions":

(1) Verbal tradition (word-tradition). Non-verbally inner tradition finds expression in inarticulate sounds, glances, mimicry, movements of head, gestures with the hands, pointing and signing with the fingers and other forms of "body-language." But the communication acquires quite another precision when language is used, when verbal communication and verbal transmission occurs. By verbal tradition I mean words, utterances, texts, writings etc., which articulate the content of the inner tradition (both its old and its new elements). I do not only mean firm formulas and texts but also the free, flexible elements that are used in order to express the content of tradition. Basically the verbal tradition is oral. In cultures where writing has had an influencial position, for a long time, the oral language is, however, often more or less clearly structured according to patterns of the written language; here the interaction between the written and the spoken word is a very interesting problem.

Language plays an immensely vital role for almost all efficient transmission of tradition.[4] Certainly human beings can hand over much to each other and to future generations without words, but normally language plays a key role in most kinds of transmission of tradition. With language we can fix a content of mind, take care of it in an effective way and spread it through a communication which is more distinct and explicit than other forms of outer tradition. As a rule the different forms of outer tradition interplay but the verbal tradition is without doubt the most influential of them all. With the aid of language we can steer the course of tradition, indicate the programmatic center of it, make distinctions and specifications, revise or alter it, and so on.

---

[4] Müller writes: "Keine Tradition funktioniert nämlich ohne Sprache"; *Traditionsprozess* 15. For my part I would not go that far.

(2) Behavioural tradition (practical tradition). The inner life of humans expresses itself in different behaviours as well. A prominent, influential human being transmits consciously and unconsciously his way of appearing and acting to others. A basic mechanism is the fact that spontaneously we imitate those humans we look up to, venerate, admire and love. The authoritative, admired human being is a "message" per se. Parents, teachers, masters and other "impressive" men or women become pattern-forming. We speak of "the force of the example" and, with the awareness thereof, demand that persons in official position be irreproachable and "set good examples." Presumably this mechanism of imitation often corresponds to the proclivity of the influential individual to externalize himself forcefully in the fellowship, come forward from obscurity and silence, assert his influence, get his own way, "set the tone" or whatever we may call it. In this way the programmatic part of the behavioural tradition tends to concentrate on that which the influential individuals want to pass on.

(3) Institutional tradition. Vital inner tradition creates — in any case if it is of a religious nature — engagement and fellowship. And every human community organizes itself and institutionalizes itself. The process starts immediately. A fellowship is formed and a gulf begins growing between insiders and outsiders; and furthermore, within the former role-division, hierarchy and organization develop. If this did not happen, the members would be nothing but isolated individuals, only loosely connected to each other, and the group would soon be dissolved. To create coherent community these mechanisms are necessary: social fellowship, order, organization, structures, establishments.[5] A long experience tells us also that such phenomena are hard to destroy once they have developed, and difficult to change or abolish. — This I call "institutional tradition."

(4) Material tradition ("thing"-tradition). It is reasonable that we also discern a fourth form of outer tradition. The inner tradition often needs to use inanimate objects as means: specific localities, special clothes, tools or other outward equipment, vital for the efficient function of tradition. This we may designate as "material tradition."[6]

---

[5] See B. Holmberg, *Paul and Power. The Structure of Authority in the Primitive Church as Reflected in the Pauline Epistles* (Philadelphia: Fortress, 1980).

[6] In my earlier writings I have not isolated "material tradition" as a specific aspect but included it in the "institutional tradition."

2. Commentary

In the ideal case these different aspects function in interaction. The carriers, filled by the inner tradition, effectively make use of the different parts of the outer tradition. New members are won and socialized into this multi-dimensional tradition. When this process is successful, the new tradition is *internalized* in the new member so that he becomes a genuine and "living" traditionist himself. In such cases the differentiation of aspects may appear somewhat artificial.

But the situation is not often an ideal one. The different aspects of a rich tradition do not belong together by necessity; they must be kept together by an inner engagement. And they are different even in regard to mobility and flexibility. The inner tradition may be very mobile — develop, change, be renewed — without the outward forms being able to keep pace with it. The outer forms have a stiffness and firmness, which the inner tradition does not have. Intra muros some people may accept parts of the outer tradition but not all of it, and they may even adopt most of the outer tradition without acquiring the living inner engagement. Extra muros an outsider can come across single, isolated elements from this tradition: get an inanimate object in his hand without knowing how to use it, meet forms of organization that he can do nothing but wonder about, see behaviour that appears meaningless to him, hear words that he cannot understand. This shows that it is meaningful in an investigation to separate the different aspects so that we can speak about them one by one when necessary (often it is not at all necessary).

I should perhaps mention two more observations of a general kind. The outward forms of tradition are — when they emerge — motivated and more or less necessary. Otherwise they would not arise so regularly. But they are also problematic. First, they are as a rule convention- alizing elements as such. Few people can verbalize their inward ex- periences in totally adequate words, least of all their deepest and most overwhelming experiences. Few people can create new words, expres- sions, texts. We must more or less all make use of linguistic means which already exist, when we shall verbalize our experiences and communicate them to others. Already at the first verbalization the original content of mind becomes domesticated and conventionalized to some extent.

The same applies to our behaviour. Few people are radically creative in their behaviour and actions. Already existing patterns are taken into use as models, with minor or major alterations. Even as to organization and institutional forms human imagination is limited; in addition we are dominated by certain general mechanisms of a socio-psychological character. Social organization and institutionalized forms are seldom radically new. A new movement must as a rule content itself with existing forms in its first phase. This fact reduces its possibility of being original. In all dimensions we see that the outer forms of tradition are intrinsically more or less domesticating and conventionalizing factors.

Second, outer tradition has a general tendency to exist on its own and run idly. These firm forms can be in use even when there is no inward engagement behind them. And once they are well established they generally are very difficult to reform or exchange. Therefore, they usually keep their form a long time even when the inner tradition has developed and changed so as to require altered or new outward forms. The history of religion is full of pious words and texts, which many people take to their lips but only few follow in life and action; rites, habits and customs which long ago lost their original rationale but are still practiced; institutional forms which go on in their beaten tracks in spite of the fact that they hinder rather than serve their original aims; things out-dated and unfit which should have been discarded centuries ago but are still in use. Summa: inner tradition needs outer tradition but the later is always problematic; it must be under permanent supervision if it shall continue to be an adequate tool for the inner tradition.

3. Programmatic tradition and de facto tradition

No new tradition makes all things new. Emotionally it can be felt so, the mottos can run so, but in real life a new tradition initially changes nothing but a small, illuminated circle within the existing realities.[7] If, however, the new tradition is strong and vital, it widens its area successively: ever more of the inherited realities are taken up in the light of new awareness and made the object of consideration and decision, with or without alterations.

In order to keep this in mind one must, I think, make a distinction between programmatic tradition and de facto tradition. The former designation stands for that which is new or penetrated by the new

---

[7] Cf. *Tradition* 22-23.

tradition, the latter for the immense older tradition which is still there without having been consciously accepted or consciously rejected.

The de facto tradition is of interest from many angles, not only as the mother-womb which has given birth to the new tradition and as the mother-breast on which it can live for a long time. An important problem is the fact that even leading representatives of the new tradition may spread much older, uncontrolled de facto tradition: they practice old values and behaviour which they have not contemplated and spread them without being aware of it.

In the sources, de facto tradition is difficult to come to grips with. That which is common and self-evident is only mentioned by accident in the sources. In contrast the sources provide an effective witness about the programmatic tradition: one is occupied with this, one speaks about this. This fact is especially evident when the traditionists expressly indicate that this shall be observed and maintained as tradition: φυλάσσειν, τηρεῖν, ἱστάναι, κατέχειν, κρατεῖν, etc.[8] Even summons to take heed, listen, "see and hear," and the like, are telling, as are exhortations to receive and accept.

II. CHRISTIANITY'S JEWISH MOTHER-TRADITION

In its first formative period, Early Christianity received influences from many corners. It would, however, be a serious historical mistake to put these influences on the same level. One of them must be placed in a class by itself and called the mother-tradition of Christianity. Jesus, the twelve and almost every man in a leading position in the first decades of Early Christianity were Jews by birth and upbringing, being socialized in the Jewish tradition.

Jesus confined himself almost exclusively to the Jewish population of Palestine, and the Early Christian mission was primarily directed to Jews or proselytes and other people who were already attracted by Judaism. Christianity was born within Judaism. Neither Jesus nor the Church in its first decades ever wanted to be anything else than Israel: they looked upon themselves as the *true* Israel. Their message presented news from Israel's God: what he now wanted to do and what he now had to say to his people — in a new time. In one way we could say that the original Christian message can be regarded as a concentration and

---

[8] Cf. O. Cullmann, *Die Tradition als exegetisches, historisches und theologisches Problem* (Zürich: Zwingli, 1954) 12-16, *Memory* 288-91, *Origins* 25-28.

radicalization of the ancient belief within the covenant between Israel
and its God.

Early Christianity initially felt at home in Judaism and from it
inherited considerable inhibitions and reservations to other cults and
everything which was connected with them: paganism, heathenism!
Therefore we have all reason to call the Judaism of antiquity Early
Christianity's "mother-tradition." This must not prevent a full consideration of the fact that the Jews were "Hellenized" to a considerable
degree at this time, even the Jews in Palestine. Nor must it prevent us
from seeing the influences from different "Hellenistic" traditions that
had their impact nonetheless upon Christian communities during the
decades — and centuries — which followed.

Let us now apply our model to ancient Judaism, let us say from
200 BC to AD 200.

a) Inner tradition

The Jews in Palestine at the beginning of our Christian era constituted
a relatively pluralistic society. Yet, it does not seem far-fetched to speak
of "Judaism" at that time — they even had themselves the designation
Ἰουδαισμός[9] — and to take the pious, religiously active Jews as the
most representative Jews, in any case when we are looking for the
mother-tradition of Christianity. To these Jews Jewish identity and
inherited tradition in its totality was a programmatic concern, the
Torah-tradition in all its aspects.

This Jewish tradition was immensely rich and multifarious. Yet, it
had a vital inner life: the Torah-centric relation to "the only true God"
with its different elements: faith, love, obedience, loyalty in emotions,
thought, word, action towards God and a corresponding attitude to
fellow human beings. To the pious representatives of the Torah-tradition this was a conscious program. They wanted to stand in covenant
with God, and tradition showed what this covenant meant in its
different aspects. As to Israel as a people, the Temple, the synagogues,
the schools and other institutions were devoted to God and revealed his
gifts and his demands.[10] As to the individual pious man, the centre of
the covenant and the Torah-tradition is made clear to him, when twice
a day he actualizes to himself the covenant by reading the Shema. First
he "takes the yoke of the Reign of Heaven" upon himself by affirming

---

[9] E.g. 2 Macc 2:21, 8:1, 14:38. Cf. Gal 1:13, 14. Note that the term is used in the
singular; "Judaisms" is a modern manner of speaking.

[10] Cf. *Memory* 71-78; see also Riesner, *Jesus* 97-245.

God's sovereign position as the only true God with the words: "The Lord our God, the Lord is one Lord." Then he takes upon himself "the yoke of the commandments," all of them in condensed form, by accepting the claim that he shall love the Lord his God with his whole heart, his whole soul and all his resources. Before Him who is One, God's people and every member of it shall be one. Here, as in many other ways, we see the program that everything shall be put under the grace and will of God and that the individual as well as the people shall accept all of it. Thus, a strong tendency toward unity is characteristic for the leading representatives of the Torah-tradition.[11]

Of course we must consider the de facto pluralism in Israel when trying to make a careful detailed description of the situation. How much of the rich heritage had at this time been consciously taken into the enlightened spot, invented and regulated? How many of the Jews did in fact accept this program whole-heartedly and in all its breadth? Where shall we put the tepid Jews? Uneducated Jews? People in isolated areas? And so forth. But these are common problems irrespective of what model we choose.

b) Outer tradition

(1) Verbal tradition. In the ancient Jewish tradition language plays an accentuated role; seeing and "visions" are not so much in the forefront as are words, speaking, and hearing. The Torah-tradition was passed on with the aid of a rich treasure of authoritative terms, expressions, formulas, motifs, texts and writings, preserved in an oral and written tradition with both firm and flexible elements: Torah as words. (I do not take "Torah" in the narrow sense "law" but in its wider sense "teaching": all that which was classified as God's authoritative teaching to his people, directly or indirectly.[12] And I repeat once more that this word-tradition had a large flexible sector.[13])

[11] For literature on the role of the Shema in early Judaism and early Christianity, see *Origins* 93-94.

[12] Even in *Memory* I did not take the word "Torah" in the narrow meaning "law," nor "Oral Torah" in the narrow meaning "the halacha-rules." This seems to have escaped the notice of J. Neusner, in spite of the fact that it is stated and explained rather clearly in the first chapter of *Memory*, 19-32; it is even printed in italics: *"In this investigation we shall use the term Torah, without qualification, as a collective designation for the Jew's sacred authoritative tradition (doctrine) in its entirety;"* 21. I also tried to clear away misunderstanding about this in *Tradition* 7: "Torah does not contain texts alone, nor are all texts legal rules." Again, my designation "verbal tradition" not only covers texts but all other authoritative teaching expressed in words as well, even flexible words; "verbal" means here "articulated" (see *Tradition* 7). In addition, when I say that the written Torah must always have had oral Torah at its side, I do not mean that Moses received the Rabbinic halacha-rules on Sinai, but simply that no law-maker can express *everything* in

(2) Behavioural tradition. "The life in the Torah" (ἡ ἔννομος βίωσις, Sir prol) was eminently an inherited, characteristic way of life, conscious patterns for the way in which the people and different groups and individuals should live: rites, customes, ethos, halacha. Here we meet Torah as practice.[14]

(3) Institutional tradition. The faithful Jews also maintained a rich inheritance of institutions and establishments, social structures, hierarchy, official divisions of role and more of the same. Even this was accepted as ordered by God; this was Torah as institution.

(4) Material tradition. The Torah-tradition finally included sacred localities, clothes, tools and other outward things: the Temple, the synagogues, scrolls, phylacteries, tassels on cloaks etc., things of importance for life in the Torah. If the expression can be allowed, I would like to call it "Torah as things."

III. The Early Christian Tradition

We will now see in what way our model separates different aspects within the Early Christian tradition. Let me start with a brief survey.

1. Survey

a) Inner tradition

The heart of Early Christianity was a Jesus Christ-centered relation to God: faith, love, obedience, loyalty, etc., and a corresponding attitude toward fellow human beings.

b) Outer tradition

(1) Verbal tradition. The programmatic speaking of Early Christianity has a centre: Jesus Christ, interpreted as the decisive, final Savior

---

his brief written rules. From the very beginning the text needs oral complements, exposition, and additional teaching. I regret that Neusner, who has clarified important aspects of the Rabbinic halacha-tradition so brilliantly (cf. below n. 70), has presented *my* position as if I was an old Jewish fundamentalist, believing that the halacha-rules of the tannaitic and amoraic Rabbis were received by Moses on Sinai in their present form; see e.g., Neusner, *The Rabbinic Traditions about the Pharisees before 70* (3 vols; Leiden: Brill, 1971) vol. 3. 146-48, 163-77; further, "The Rabbinic Traditions about the Pharisees before 70 A.D.: The Problem of Oral Tradition," *Kairos* 14 (1972) 57-70.

[13] See above n. 12 and below nn. 44 and 57.

[14] For an illustration, see *Memory* 181-89.

and Lord. One speaks about him, preaches about him, teaches about him, quotes sayings from him and tells narratives about him. Texts arise, some very firm, some more or less flexible. Gradually, smaller or larger written records are made, and letters are written about his mysteries. As time goes on more comprehensive writings are composed. In a living interaction we meet here firm and flexible elements with all kinds of intermediate forms: the Christ-tradition as words.

(2) Behavioural tradition. Linked up with inherited Jewish behavioural tradition and in its centre dominated by the practice and teaching of Jesus, Early Christianity develops a characteristic way of life. It is rich and variegated but it is very revealing that the program for the adherents of Jesus is called "the life in Christ," "following Jesus" or "imitation of Christ." Here we meet the Christ-tradition as practice. [15]

(3) Institutional tradition. Jesus attracts a central group of adherents, binds them to his person and becomes their exclusive leader and inspirer. A delimited group is formed around him and an elementary organization starts developing. After the departure of the exclusive master this group must be reconstructed and reorganized. This hastens the process of institutionalization; division of roles, hierarchy and organization develops. The Christ-tradition gets institutional forms.

(4) Material tradition. When it goes about outward things the Jesus-movement and the young Church do not need any specifically new things at the beginning. They take what they need from the mother-tradition. Not until later does the specifically Christian material tradition become interesting.

2. Inner tradition

Looking backward historically, we see that Jesus initiates a new tradition in the bosom of the Jewish mother-tradition. It is not difficult to understand that this historical volcanic eruption begins as an inner tradition; a strong conviction of faith and a firm consciousness of vocation makes Jesus turn to the community — "to appear publicly before Israel" — in order to influence his people with words and deeds. Within the mother-tradition — "the convenant" — he concentrates on the basic statements about God and his mighty deeds and proclaims to his people that God soon will take power in a new way. It will soon be

---

[15] Note the expression ἔννομος Χριστοῦ in 1 Cor. 9:21. Cf. E. Larsson, *Christus als Vorbild. Eine Untersuchung zu den paulinischen Tauf- und Eikontexten* (ASNU 23; Lund: Gleerup, Copenhagen: Munksgaard, 1962), E. Cothenet, Imitation du Christ, *Dsp* fasc. 48-49 (1970) 1536-82.

seen what it means that God is God: the Lord is One and only One is the Lord. In this perspective he calls his people to repentance and inculcates the other side of the matter: God's people shall love God with their whole heart and their whole soul and all their resources.[16]

The demand that the community and the individual shall be "perfect" in their inner life (their "heart") and thus undivided, whole and without blemishes and defects before God was a basic ideal in the mother-tradition but Jesus accentuated it with a new radicalism. We then notice that the dominant men in the young Church share this engagement with its total demands. Certainly, Luke's notice in Acts 4:32 paints a very idealized picture of the Christian mother-community in Jerusalem, but the words are telling: "the whole company of those who believed were of one heart and one soul, and no one said that any of the things which he possessed was hiw own, but they had everything in common."[17] Many passages in the New Testament documents stress the demands for unity and consistency: one shall be a Christ-centered worshipper of God in everything. And the communities shall be united and unanimous in spite of a legitimate variety, inspired by one and the same Spirit, have one mind, "think the same" and so-forth.[18]

If one is aware of the complexity of the problems and the potential complications, it is thus possible to regard Early Christianity as a new tradition with an eruptive centre of inner tradition which expresses itself in words and behavior, forms a new fellowship with an inceptive institution very early and which in the long run also has its consequences as to outward things.

Of course, the most important question concerns the character and content of the inner tradition, but I cannot stop to discuss this matter now.[19]

3. Outer tradition

As we shall deal at length with "the gospel tradition" I shall comment on the verbal tradition last, despite the fact that in so doing the four aspects of outer tradition come in reverse order.

---

[16] For literature on these themes in the gospel tradition, see *Origins* 93-94.

[17] See my article "Einige Bemerkungen zu Apg 4, 32," *ST* 24 (1970) 142-49.

[18] See e.g. Acts 2:44-47, 4:32, Rom 12:3-13, 15:5-6, 1 Cor 1:10-13, 12:4-31, Eph 4:1-16, Phil 1:27, 2:1-4, 3:14-16, 3:15-16 Col 3:14-15 — not to speak of ethical texts like Matt 5:17-48. See further my book *The Ethos of the Bible* (Philadelphia: Fortress, 1981).

[19] I have tried to do so in other connections; see the literature mentioned in *Origins* 93-94.

1. Material tradition

The theme "Early Christianity and Material Tradition" is a fascinating subject, still not very well clarified: what role did the Temple, the synagogues, Torah-scrolls, phylacteries and the like play for Jesus and Early Christianity; how did the development go, and how did Early Christianity's own material tradition evolve? We must of course consider the various components separately and also distinguish between different persons, groups, geographic areas and phases in the development of Early Christianity. The attitudes varied. Those who had pronouncedly spiritualized views and regarded Christianity as a "worship in spirit and truth" and those who remained faithful attenders at the Temple and synagogue with sustained respect for phylacteries etc., cannot all be treated alike. Pauline and Johannine areas were not totally similar, nor do the oldest Pauline letters and the Pastoral letters reflect the same situation.

Telling is the strong difference between the Christians' attitude to the religious material tradition among the Jews and their attitude to things connected with pagan cults and pagan sacred practices.

In general I think we can say that the attitude to Jewish material tradition is a combination of familiarity, freedom and incipient liberation. The crux of the matter is the fact that the inner tradition generated great freedom towards all outward things, even the most religious ones. One could do equally well with them or without them. Certainly the Christian Jews mourned when the Temple fell, but their own divine service was not interrupted. Certainly it was extremely distressing for them to leave the synagogue fellowship when this became necessary, but their own worship could continue just the same; the choice of some other room was no matter of principle. How the Christian Jews stopped using phylacteries, tassles and the like we do not even know. The development was obviously so undramatic that no source has noticed it.

Of course, a development in the direction towards a specifically Christian material tradition started quite early. Certain things gradually became sacred; localities with certain furnishings, clothes, eucharistic vessels etc. But we do not see much of this in the New Testament.

Of special interest is the question of the attitude to holy books, both as holy writ and as sacred things. Jesus and the leading men in Early Christianity probably ascribed to the opinion that the ancient holy scriptures should be treated with veneration, even as scrolls. Nothing indicates, however, that the writings and books produced by Early

Christianity itself were immediately regarded as holy scriptures, even less as sacred things. Possibly the Book of Revelation is an exception (see 1:1-3, 22:18-19). If notebooks were used, they were simply private means, not holy scriptures. They are not even mentioned in the New Testament. The books of which we catch a glimpse are the ancient holy scriptures. The written Gospels — presumably written in codex form — were not initially regarded as holy scriptures or sacred books. This did not come until later.

I shall not linger on this. However, I will stress once more that this aspect — material tradition — is also of importance for a realistic historical picture of the gospel tradition during the first century.

2. Institutional tradition

Jesus and Early Christianity lived in a world which was well institutionalized: politically, economically, socially and religiously; from the greatest structures of the Roman Empire down to the individual families, Jewish and non-Jewish alike. Jesus and the Christians were dependent upon this and accepted very much of it.[20] To the extent that these different institutions were of any importance to Early Christianity's programmatic tradition, we must take them into consideration. The attitudes to these different institutions, in principle and in practice, and the degree of radicalism and conservatism in relation to them need to be studied in order to gain an adequate picture of the Early Christian tradition.

More important for our investigation of the gospel tradition, however, is the process of institutionalization within Early Christianity itself. Two things are especially interesting:

(1) Jesus not only attracts throngs of people who listen to him accidentally or for some short period, and sympathizers at various places in Palestine. He gathers around himself a number of persons who become his "primary group": they "are with" him (εἶναι μετά), they "follow" him (ἀκολουθεῖν), they are his "disciples" (μαθηταί), they are his "brother and sister and mother."[21] This information in our

---

[20] From a theological point of view one thing is especially interesting in this connection: the fact that Jesus and his followers consciously refrained from making political responsibility their own specific cause. They presupposed that the different political rulers had a mission from God, which Jesus did not want to take from them: God's "secular realm" (Luther).

[21] Examples: εἶναι μετά, Mark 3:14, 5:18, 14:67, Matt 26:69, 71, Luke 22:59; εἶναι σύν, Luke 8:38, 22:56; ἀκολουθεῖν, Mark 1:18, 2:14, 8:34, 10:21, 28, Matt 4:20, 22, 8:19 22, 9:9, 10:38, 16:24, 19:21, 27, 28, Luke 5:11, 27, 28, 9:23, 57, 59, 61, 18:22, 28, John

sources is extremely important from a "phenomenological" point of
view. We recognize the pattern: the strong and exclusive gathering
around Jesus creates an incipient gulf between insiders and outsiders, a
gulf which becomes even more pronounced when the Jesus-movement is
reconstructed after Easter.

(2) Within this primary group emerges an embryonic organization: a
certain ranking order becomes natural, a certain distribution of roles
etc. Twelve disciples have a special position as a kind of symbolical
collegium around the master; three of them constitute an inner circle
and one of these is the primus. It seems to me very likely that Jesus
himself took the initiative to organize in this elementary fashion his
closest adherents. Even if he did not, it is easy to explain that this
organization originated very soon in the most permanent fellowship
around him; that is the way fellowship generally behaves!

If we consider this fact — institutional tradition in Early Christianity
— we can be rather sure as to one thing. The followers of Jesus —
before and after his departure — did not think that the truth about
their master was to be found among the outsiders. Of course, rumors
were spread about Jesus. Even if our sources did not say a word to that
effect, we should be rather sure that rumors went out (διαφημίζειν)
and that many people heard about the fame of Jesus (ἡ ἀκοὴ 'Ιησοῦ).[22]
But our knowledge about the way institutionalization functions teaches
us that an engaged and structured religious community does not think
much of outsider rumors and talk. What has authority is that which is
cultivated intra muros: here the true insights are to be found. And here,
inside the walls, all do not enjoy the same authority. Some have a
reputation of being especially well informed, and a preference for
"those in the know" is general in a fellowship.[23] Simple phenomenological insights tell us that those in the best position to spread recollec-
tions and traditions about Jesus within Early Christianity were those
who had the reputation of being well informed, especially those who
could say that they had seen with their own eyes and heard with their
own ears. (A curious fact in contemporary New Testament scholarship
is that the synoptic tradition cries out for actual originators but most

---

1:43, 8:12, 12:26, 21:19, 22, ἔρχεσθαι ὀπίσω, Mark 1:17, Matt 4:19. "My brother, sister
and mother," Mark 3:31-35, Matt 12:46-50, Luke 8:19-21.

[22] Cf. e.g. Mark 1:45, Matt 9:31, 28:15 (διαφημίζειν); Mark 1:28, Matt 4:24, 14:1
(ἀκοή).

[23] Some revealing New Testament texts: John 15:26-27, 19:35, 21:24, Luke 1:1-4, 24:
44-49, Acts 1:1-3, 8, 21-26, 2:32, 4:19-20, 5:15-16, 29-32, etc., 1 Cor 15:5-8, 11, 2 Cor 11:5,
12:11, Gal 1:18-20, 2:1-10 etc.

leading scholars show very little proclivity for suspecting the twelve or other people with first-hand knowledge of Jesus.)[24]

3. Behavioural tradition

I am very much in doubt that any nation in the world can compete with the Jewish people in awareness and sophistication of their own way of life in every detail. The development in that direction had reached very far even in New Testament times. A strong political threat from different forces of occupation and a powerful spiritual and cultural threat from the flourishing Hellenistic culture had made the Jews observant and sensitive and evoked a remarkable zeal to defend Jewish identity and tradition — ὁ Ἰουδαισμός — in all its aspects, and not least the Jews' characteristic way of life with its many rules for religion and morality: rites, customs, ethos, halacha.

Certainly the degree of awareness, enlightenment and actual observance shifted very much within pluralistic Judaism: from individual to individual, group to group, stratum to stratum, area to area. From this point of view the disciples of Jesus presumably had rather different backgrounds. The diversity was even greater later on when the Church included people from many different parts of the Roman empire and not only Jews.

For a study of the gospel tradition an investigation of Jesus' and Early Christianity's relations to the Jewish behavioural tradition is extremely important, especially in light of Jesus' admonition to put one's confession and insights into practice: "do" the word.[25] Very roughly speaking, the pattern of Jesus' own attitude to the behavioural aspect of the Jewish mother-tradition is that he shows very little interest in halachic minutiae but a very strong interest in the central ethos of the mother-tradition, which may be summarized in formulas such as "the great and first commandment" (Matt 22:38), "the weightiest matters of the law" (Matt 23:23) or in some other way. His own "new

---

[24] In his article "*Episkopē* and *episkopos*: the New Testament Evidence," *TS* 41 (1980) 322-38, R. Brown concludes concerning the twelve: "The image of them as carrying on missionary endeavors all over the world has no support in the NT or in other reliable historical sources. The archeological and later documentary evidence that Peter died at Rome is credible, but the rest of the Twelve could have died in Jerusalem so far as we have trustworthy information", 325. I think it is very proper indeed to ask the question: What did this highly reputed collegium actually do during its many years in Jerusalem?

[25] I am thinking of all texts where the *motif* is present, not only of passages containing the verb ποιεῖν.

teaching" is a radicalization of the central core within the verbal Torah.[26]

The fact that the ethical teaching of Jesus was strongly centered around the basic norms indicates that he focused the interest of his adherents upon these. This also means — and it is important to observe this — that he even made their practical imitation of him rather specific. When in love, admiration and veneration they emulated their master, it was natural to pay the greatest attention to that which was a central concern for the master himself and imitate him in such matters, not in various outward details. Thus the imitation of Jesus assumed a profile different from the imitation of rabbis with different specializations, in spite of the fact that the same socio-psychological mechanisms were at work in both cases.[27]

This we see very clearly in Paul. When he suggests Christ as a model, he never mentions concrete details in Jesus' conduct but always the central principle in his attitude: his self-sacrificing love demonstrated in action. We can certainly say that all of Paul's direct references to Jesus as an ethical model are concrete examples of ἀγάπη. We also see that Paul sometimes puts forward himself and even other prominent representatives of Jesus' ethos as secondary models for imitation. It should be noted that he aims at the true reception of the message from and about Jesus Christ, thus as words and as a practical life accordingly.[28]

So much for the general (primarily ethical) behavioural tradition. But some *specific* parts of Early Christianity's behavioural tradition also deserve attention if we want to put the gospel tradition in a realistic historical framework: a. rites in the context of worship; b. practices in teaching and other specific forms of verbal transmission; and c. therapeutic activity.

    a. It goes without saying that the forms of Early Christian worship were borrowed from Jewish practice: liturgical praying, recitation and singing, sacred meals and so on. We can call this the "liturgical tradition of behaviour."

    b. Most interesting for the study of the gospel tradition is of course the specific behavior of verbal communication and transmission,

---

[26] See e.g. my book *Ethos* 33-62, 124-26, and cf. H. Braun, *Spätjüdisch-häretischer und frühchristlicher Radikalismus* (BHT 24; 2 vols.; Tübingen: Mohr, 1957).

[27] This is my answer to M. Hengel, *Nachfolge und Charisma* (BZNW 34; Berlin: Töpelmann, 1968) 46-79, who paints a sharp contrast between Jesus and the rabbis. In my opinion Hengel overlooks the general socio-psychological mechanisms which operate in both contexts, in spite of all differences.

[28] On the imitation motif among the rabbis, see *Memory* 181-89; on the motif in the Pauline material, see 292-94 and *Ethos* 72-76, 89-90, 124-26.

the forms for reading, teaching, exhortation, discussions and so
forth, both the genuine Jewish models with their different degrees
of "Hellenization" and the subsequent side-influences from different traditions in the Early Christian milieus. This I shall discuss
at length shortly.

c. A third area requiring special attention concerns the therapeutic
practices in Early Christianity: healings and exorcisms, carried out
in accordance with the example and, perhaps, instructions of
Jesus. This seems to have taken different forms: a more charisma-
tic one, handled by individuals with a specific χάρισμα ἰαμάτων
(cf. 1 Cor 12:9), and one of a more institutionalized character,
handled by specific men in office (cf. Mark 6:7-13, Jak 5:14-15),
with possible combinations and intermediate forms. This aspect of
the behavioural tradition is of interest because it was programmatic
for Jesus and Early Christianity: to the central task belonged not
only preaching and teaching but also healing and exorcism.[29]
Therefore we must investigate this part of the behavioural tradition
and its relation to the gospel tradition.[30] Which older models did
Jesus himself link up with, totally or in part? To what extent was
his own practice an object of imitation? To what extent did he give
direct instructions? What role did concrete traditions about Jesus'
teaching and therapeutic practice — the gospel tradition — play
for Early Christianity's practice in this respect? And can we
reckon with the possibility that therapeutic practices in the Church
after Easter have influenced the gospel tradition?

4. Verbal tradition

I have not written the foregoing pages without my reasons. In order
to emphasize the need for concreteness in our historical reconstruction
and interpretation of the transmission of the gospel tradition, I have
tried to draw the reader's attention to pertinent mechanisms in Early
Christian tradition which must be taken into consideration when working with the concrete Jesus-tradition.

We are now prepared to enter the central area of our subject, Early
Christianity's verbal tradition. I will group my observations and reflections under 10 headings.

[29] See e.g. Mark 1:39, Matt 4:23, 9:35, Luke 4:16-24, 31-37, 40-41, and Mark 3:13-15,
Matt 10:1-8, Luke 9:1-2, Acts 3:6, 4:29-30, 5:12-16.
[30] For literature on the miracles of Jesus, see my book *The Mighty Acts of Jesus
According to Matthew* (Scripta minora Reg. Soc. Hum. Lit. Lundensis 1978-1979:9;
Lund: Gleerup, 1979). On healing as a vital part of Jesus' activity, see pp. 20-51.

1. The information of the Lukan prologue

Let me start with some general comments on the prologue to Luke-Acts (Luk 1:1-4). This is the most important item of information which is preserved from the first Christian centuries about the pre-history of the Gospels. The fragments of information in Papias, Irenaeus, Clement, the prologues etc.,[31] certainly deserve all the interest they have received. But these notices are not as old as the Lukan prologue and they seem to give a somewhat anachronistic picture of the origin of the Gospels. They hardly reveal any awareness of two important facts: that the Gospels build upon a common oral tradition and that there must also be some kind of *literary* connection between them, in any case between the synoptics. In this material from the Ancient Church we get the picture of an individual teacher who had preached and taught with great authority and then written down his material himself (Matthew, John) or had some follower who committed his teaching to writing (Mark, Luke). I do not think these items of information are freely made up, but they seem to give us a somewhat anachronistic picture. Let me quote the ancient prologue to Luke's two-volume work (Luke 1:1-4):

> Since many writers have undertaken to compile an orderly account of the events that have come to fulfilment among us, just as the original eyewitnesses and ministers of the word passed them on to us, I too have decided, after tracing everything carefully from the beginning, to put them systematically in writing for you, Theophilus, so that Your Excellency may realize what assurance you have for the instruction you have received.[32]

Seven points should be observed in this brief text.

(1) "Luke" wants to present an orderly account (διήγησις) of the Jesus-event, but he indicates that this attempt is innovative. Like a number of predecessors, he has felt the need and made the attempt to put together the material about Jesus into an organized, synthetic presentation, but the material did not have this form from the beginning.

(2) Luke classifies his material as tradition and indicates that it is insider-tradition, which is there intra muros ecclesiae. It is all about

---

[31] The most important material from the fathers is conveniently brought together in K. Aland, *Synopsis quattuor evangeliorum* (Stuttgart: Würt. Bibelanstalt, 1964) 531-48. See also W. Rordorf, A. Schneider, *Die Entwicklung des Traditionsbegriffs in der Alten Kirche* (Traditio Christiana 5; Bern & Frankfurt a.M.: Lang, 1983).

[32] Fitzmyer's translation. On the exegetical problems in Luke 1:1-4, see J. A. Fitzmyer, *The Gospel According to Luke I-IX* (AB 28; New York: Doubleday, 1981) 287-302, and H. Schürmann, *Das Lukasevangelium* (HTKNT 3:1; Freiburg, Basel, Wien: Herder, 1969) 1-17.

"events that have come to fulfilment among us"; the information has "been passed on to us" (παρέδωσαν ἡμῖν). This means that the material has been preserved and exists within the Church.

(3) Luke also mentions the originators of the material. The tradition stems from "the original eyewitnesses (αὐτόπται) and ministers of the word." In the Lukan usage this means the closest followers and disciples of Jesus, first of all the twelve but hardly exclusively.

(4) The originators are not only called "eyewitnesses" but also "ministers of the word" (ὑπηρέται τοῦ λόγου). Thus, they have not only quoted and reported what they had heard and seen but have also been active as ministers of the word as well, which must mean that they have preached, taught and expounded the scriptures and so on. In Acts 6:4 their main activity is called "ministry of the Word" (διακονία τοῦ λόγου).

(5) Luke knows about earlier attempts to compile an orderly account of the Jesus-event. "Many" (πολλοί) is certainly a conventional exaggeration, but Luke would hardly use this phrase if he was just thinking of one or two specific predecessors.

(6) For his own part Luke had a special purpose when he wrote his Gospel. It is a matter of dispute whether his words about his own carefulness imply criticism of his predecessors. If so, he expresses himself so discreetly that the reader does not notice it without being suspicious. One thing, however, Luke expresses clearly. He has a special purpose which obviously his predecessors did not have: his ambition is to write history (cf. also 1:5, 2:1-2, 3:1-2). This aim makes him combine two subjects which usually were kept apart: on the one hand the teaching, work and fate of Jesus, and on the other hand the fate of the Christian message during the first decades of the Church.[33] Luke's way of dedicating his work to the illustrious Theophilus gives us reason for believing that his opus is not written for the communities but for cultivated individuals within the Church and presumably also outside it; for the public market.[34] This confers on the Gospel of Luke a *specific* nature which must be kept in mind both in the discussion about Luke's way of handling the oral tradition and in the analysis of the relations between the three synoptic Gospels.[35]

[33] Cf. I. H. Marshall, Luke and his "Gospel," *Das Evangelium und die Evangelien* (WUNT 28; ed. P. Stuhlmacher, Tübingen: Mohr, 1983) 289-308.
[34] Cf. M. Dibelius, *Aufsätze zur Apostelgeschichte* (FRLANT 60; 5th ed.; Göttingen: Vandenhoeck & Ruprecht, 1968) 79 and 118.
[35] Cf. W. C. van Unnik, "Remarks on the Purpose of Luke's Historical Writing (Luke 1:1-4)," *Sparsa collecta* (3 vols.; NovTSup 29-31, Leiden: Brill, 1973) 1. 6-15.

(7) Luke reveals here — as he does in the main text of his work as well — that he has a general respect for reliable tradition and faithful traditionists. I do not think it is correct to interpret this respect as nothing but a secondary feature, due to the point of time, the individuality of the author or his special purpose. This seems to be typical insider-evaluations: respect for "our own" tradition and a preference for "those in the know."

2. Oral and written transmission

Language is a vocal means of communication; it is spoken, it sounds, it is heard. As we are presently dealing with antiquity — thus not the time of the printed word or the time of silent reading — it is important to keep in mind that even the written word is a vocal word. It is very misleading if, in our discussions about conditions in antiquity, we put oral and written delivery side by side on the same level as two entirely comparable entities and proclaim that the one is made for the eye, the other for the ear, the one is visual, the other auditive, and so on.[36] In antiquity, words were written down in order to be read out. Even the written word was formulated for the ear. One read aloud when reading for oneself or asked a slave or a friend to read aloud. (Public reading was also common.) There is much evidence for this in the sources, both from the Greek-Roman and from the Jewish worlds. The author speaks, and the reader speaks as well; the reader hears what the text says, even when reading alone, and so on.[37] Even the copyists used to read vocally when they copied.

This also means that it is misleading to say that the written word is visual. Before the eye nothing but a picture stands: letters, lines, columns. The illiterate can see no more than this visual picture. To be able to read is to be able to change letters and lines into functioning language; otherwise one cannot understand the text. This was especially obvious in the youth of the art of writing, during the millennia when

---

[36] Thus W. H. Kelber, *The Oral and the Written Gospel. The Hermeneutics of Speaking and Writing in the Synoptic Tradition, Mark, Paul, and Q* (Philadelphia: Fortress, 1983) passim.

[37] See above all J. Balogh, "Voces Paginarum," *Philologus* 82 (1926-27) 84-109, 202-40, and further G.L. Hendrickson, "Ancient Reading," *The Classical Journal* 25 (1929-30) 182-96. E. S. McCartney, "Notes on Reading and Praying Audibly," *Classical Philogy* 43 (1948) 184-87. On the conditions in the ancient near east, see O. Roller, *Das Formular der paulinischen Briefe. Ein Beitrag zur Lehre vom antiken Briefe* (BWANT 58; Stuttgart: Kohlhammer, 1933) 220-23; rabbinic material in S. Krauss, *Talmudische Archäologie* ed. by Ges. zur Förd. der Wiss. des Judent. (*Schriften;* 3 vols; Leipzig: Fock, 1912) 3.227-29. See also *Memory* 163-68 and cf. n. 82 below.

one read aloud. The writing down means that the spoken word is frozen in order to be thawed and revived as language, as a spoken word. Therefore, oral devices are very self-evident even in written texts: rhythm, metre, euphony, paronomasia, alliterations and the like. It is a great mistake to believe that the written word was something totally different from the spoken word in antiquity. This applies both to the Greek-Roman and to the Near Eastern cultures.

During recent generations some very interesting research has been devoted to "orality" in societies where writing has not yet influenced language. Attempts have been made not least by English and American scholars to clarify in what way the purely spoken word functions and how a purely oral tradition is handed on.[38] It is very clear that writing influences the thinking and speaking in the direction of discursiveness and linearity; it may even influence the experience itself. But pure "orality" can only be found in a few societies. In "civilized" societies untouched orality is dead almost everywhere. In societies where writings have been in use for a long time it is very hard to find source material that is completely uninfluenced by writing. On the other hand, it is of course important to remember that even in our own "developed" societies the oral language has preserved certain parts of its distinctiveness and has succeeded in doing so in the face of the written language in a surprisingly tough way.

In his very interesting book *The Oral and the Written Gospel* (1983), Werner Kelber has made a broad attempt to interpret the Early Christian process of tradition with the help of the modern folk-loristic model of "orality." His point of departure is that there is a decisive and consistent difference of principle between orality (oral delivery, always flexible) and textuality (written delivery). In his view proper texts are to be found solely within written tradition. From here they may enter the realm of oral tradition as memorized texts, but that causes no change: now they are borrowed, and if they have a firm wording they are a foreign body in the oral context. Orality is always characterized by flexibility: the speaker adapts his words to his listeners; in one way these influence his speaking so strongly that sender, message and receivers form a synthetic unity: "the oral synthesis."[39] In orality the narrator takes his raw material from an inherited stock-in-trade of words, formulas, motifs, themes, plots, devices etc., but he never formulates his presentation of the "tradition" in exactly the same way

[38] For literature, see Kelber, *Oral* 227-39.
[39] Kelber 19, 40 (n. 179), 147, 168-77.

twice. Every delivery ("performance") is a new variation; the model is "composition in transmission."[40] Now Kelber tries to demonstrate that the Jesus-tradition started as orality and went through its most decisive alteration when the written word could take full control, i.e., when the oral gospel tradition had become written Gospels. The first written Gospel — Mark — was a revolutionary phenomenon, a radical shift of medium: orality had become textuality, flexibility had become a fixed entity, the audible word had become a visible word, the living speech had become a book.

There are many good observations and stimulating points of view in Kelber's book, and some of them could be illustrated with material from the theological discussions in the Ancient Church and at the Reformation about "the living voice of the gospel" (*viva vox evangelii*). Yet, Kelber's approach seems to me to be basically inadequate.

The society where Jesus appeared — even the small towns in the Galilean countryside — was no pre-literary society. Nothing indicates that the formative milieu of Jesus was not at all or only to a small degree influenced by the written word. It seems to be quite clear that the holy scriptures were in high regard in the family and synagogue community in which Jesus grew up, and that influences from these writings strongly affected thinking and speaking in this milieu and with Jesus himself. Nor is there any doubt that Jesus had obtained a considerable education in reading the holy scriptures — including memorizing of the texts — and was strongly affected by this extensive text material. All the scriptural words, formulas, motifs and patterns as well as allusions and quotations we meet in the recorded sayings of Jesus cannot possibly be secondary altogether.

The verbal Jesus-tradition was at no stage pure "orality" in the meaning theorists of orality give the term. Already in the mind of Jesus the incipient parts of the gospel tradition were influenced by an older tradition which was partly oral partly written, and the gospel tradition retained in many ways this contact the whole time until the final redaction of the synoptic Gospels, and afterwards as well.

3. The interaction between written and oral tradition

Occasionally, in certain places in his book, Kelber is aware of many complications[41], but his main reasoning is always based on a view which makes a very clear contrast between the spoken and the written

---

[40] Kelber 30 and passim.
[41] Kelber e.g. 17, 23, 29-30, 73-74, 93.

words: "Contemporary theorists of orality appear virtually unanimous in emphasizing the linguistic integrity of the difference between spoken versus written words."[42] When in an "oral society" one version of the ongoing oral narrating is committed to writing, a radical shift of media occurs, and this shift has far-reaching consequences. It seems to me, however, that this model cannot give us much help in trying to understand the relation between oral and written Torah-tradition and gospel tradition in antiquity. The complicated situation can be illustrated with an example.[43] Let us imagine how a text from the written tradition, e.g., from the Book of Isaiah, could function in a synagogue in Galilee in the New Testament period. The inherited message from Isaiah appeared in many different forms:

(1) It appeared in the scroll in the form of letters, lines and columns as *ketāb*, "the writing," before the eyes, in other words as an orthographic tradition in Hebrew;

(2) It was read aloud in an inherited audible wording, as *miqrā'*, "the reading", a traditional, vocal reading in the old original language;

(3) It was also mediated in a translated form, transposed to the living language of the people (Aramaic) as *targūm*, a tradition of translation. This could be of different kinds but the most common choice was a middle way between a too literal and a too free translation. In order to make the ancient text comprehensible, the targumist adapted it (a) to the new language, (b) to a new situation (more or less);

(4) If the reading and the targum was followed by a didactic speech (*midrāsh, derāshāh*), the content of the text could be clarified in more detail in a fourth form of delivery, as midrashic tradition: exposition and application.

To the extent that the old Isaiah scroll was in the hands of learned men at a synagogue service, it may have happened that the people in the synagogue in New Testament time had the text presented to themselves in a more clear and "living" way than those who listened to it when it was read the first time. This is the case in spite of the fact that the written text had hardly been altered at all during the centuries since the book was written. Radical shift of medium or not — the question is not very simple!

In the synagogue service the problem of oral and written transmission was solved brilliantly; what solution could be more ingenious? The

---

[42] P. 14. Kelber's book contains numerous untenable generalizations of the differences between the oral and the written word.

[43] Cf. *Memory* 67-60, and 33-42; R. Riesner, *Jesus* 137-51.

two media stood in very intimate interaction, the advantages of both were exploited and the disadvantages were reduced to a minimum.

I am not saying that the gospel tradition was handed on this way. My example from the Jewish milieu was chosen to show how complicated the relation between oral and written transmission can be; a simple model from oral cultures does not take us very far.

4. Firm and flexible elements

There are very clear differences between spontaneous oral talking and a markedly written presentation, and it is very interesting to study them. But a simple distinction between orality and textuality does not solve many problems. Both oral and written delivery and transmission can appear in a thousand forms. Both can be flexible — not only the oral tradition; both can be firm — not only the written tradition. And two of the most fascinating problems here are (1) what role the firm elements play, and (2) the very interaction between these firm elements and the great flexible, "living" part of the verbal tradition.

In spite of forceful criticism of principle, Kelber offers a sympathetic and partly very good picture of my own approach (pp. 8-14), but curiously enough he fails to see the role of the flexible part of tradition and of the interplay between firmness and flexibility in my approach.[44] My starting point was the observation that the ancient Jewish *tradition* was so rich, living, flexible, and creative, in most contexts, and yet many *texts* were transmitted with extreme care for the exact wording. Therefore my question was: where and how were texts reproduced without significant change? In other words, I indicated a total picture but concentrated my actual attention on a specific part of the whole.[45]

It is not true that "texts" only appear in written tradition or in traditions which are influenced by the written word. It is not true that all oral presentation is adapted to the listener and therefore constantly influenced by the situations of use. As for the ideal linguistic communication, it is of course a fact that the speaker's words are perfectly adapted to the listener and his situation, but this only happens when the speaker has an unlimited freedom of choosing his words himself. As soon as he tries to render what somebody else has said — reproduce the real utterance of this person — his possibilities of adapting his language to the listener are reduced. And the more he has reasons for giving a

---

[44] See especially *Memory* 19-21, 41-42, 71-78, 79-84.
[45] *Memory* 19-32, 33-42, 71-78.

direct quotation, the less he can decide what wording his communication shall have. The one who will programmatically hand on verbal
tradition has only limited freedom.

It is quite clear that the phenomenon we call a "text" — a self-
contained, rounded utterance, shorter or longer, with a more or less
fixed wording — has arisen in the oral stage of language. We may take
the proverb as an example. It is a text which has a very firm wording
indeed; even a very slight alteration brings about protests from the
audience! And the proverb is clearly an *oral* text. There are written
collections, but they are secondary. There are proverbs formulated by
some writer, but they are imitations. We also know of other oral texts
with a very firm wording: certain types of songs and poems, certain
sacred texts, legal texts, genealogies and so forth. Not least interesting
are those texts that are often handed on in spite of the fact that the
transmitter himself does not understand the words he is reciting from
memory.[46]

Therefore it seems to me that we cannot possibly accept the simplified view that oral communication is always a flexible communication,
the firmest elements of which are certain standardized expressions and
formulas and other clichés, motifs, plots, certain linguistic devices and
the like. And it is quite clear that we do not get very helpful models
from this type of orality for our study of Early Christianity and its
mother-tradition in antiquity.

On the other hand, it is extremely important to investigate the
interaction between the fixed and the flexible elements in tradition,
especially the model "text and commentary." This applies to different
types of oral tradition and different individual texts with an oral pre-
history. But it also applies to written tradition. Written texts were often
changed in antiquity, a little in any case, but more important is the fact
that they were transformed into an oral presentation when they were
read and thereby usually got support from additional, flexible oral
language. As long as written documents were hardly more than an aid
to the oral presentation, the declamations and readings were connected
with clarifying oral elements. When anyone in antiquity read a book
aloud for others, the reader or some other expert had to be prepared
for questions: the obscurities of the text were to be mastered by re-
reading, clarifications, comments and perhaps exposition.[47] Our own

---

[46] *Memory* 123-36.

[47] Even the classical procedure of the grammarian, who taught children to read texts,
is revealing. It included four elements: criticism of the text (διόρθωσις), reading (ἀνάγνω-
σις), explication (ἐξήγησις) and judgement (κρίσις); *Memory* 124-25.

perfectly printed book-pages cause us to miss historical realities of this kind.

Kelber's main interest is not history but rather language and literary phenomena.[48] I do not find much about the behavioural, institutional and material dimensions of tradition in his approach. In fact his model "orality contra textuality" does not seem to harmonize very well with the historical realities we get a glimpse of in our sources. In the New Testament Jesus from Nazareth is nowhere presented as a popular "performer" who entertains crowds with oral narratives or oral poetry of the type folk-lorists often speak of. He has original traits but he is classified as a teacher and a prophet (διδάσκαλος, προφητής) — and more than a teacher and a prophet (cf. below 534-38).[49] It is said that he preaches and teaches (κηρύσσειν, διδάσκειν) — and that he heals sick people and expels demons. It seems very odd to me to put Jesus in the category where the folk-lorists place their oral narrators and oral poets.

Our sources also tell us that Jesus used to teach with the aid of παραβολαί (meshālim).[50] In the ancient Jewish texts we see that mashal is a very broad designation which can be used for a long series of different linguistic creations. But these have three things in common: (1) they are texts (oral texts primarily, but also written ones) — not free streams of words, (2) they are brief — not whole books, and (3) they have an artistic design — they differ from careless everyday speech.

Related to Jesus' custom of teaching with the aid of parabolai (let me call them meshalim, in the plural) is the fact that all items of the proper sayings-tradition from Jesus extant in the synoptic Gospels, have the form of meshalim: the items are texts, they are brief, and they are artistically designed. This applies to the extremely short items (let me call them logia) and to the somewhat longer but still very short narrative parables. One can always discuss how to divide the "speeches" of Jesus in the synoptic Gospels, but let us disregard differences in detail for the moment. In his book Jesus als Lehrer (1981), Rainer Riesner divides the synoptic collections of sayings into 247 independent units. About 65% of these are not more than two verses long. Only 12% are longer than four verses.[51]

The possibility that this picture only reflects a late stage of transmission, when literacy and textuality had got control over a tradition

[48] Oral 18; cf. 8 and 70-77.
[49] See further Riesner, Jesus, and cf. now E. P. Sanders, Jesus and Judaism (London: SCM, 1985).
[50] Esp. Mark 4:2, 33-34, Matt 13:3, 34-35.
[51] Riesner, Jesus 392-93.

which was oral and flexible in its first stage, seems to be quite unrealistic. There were firm elements within the synoptic word-tradition even from the beginning; a mashal is a mashal.

On the other hand, there was of course also a living, flexible exchange of words. The sources show not only that Jesus communicated meshalim but also that he was talking to people, answering questions, discussing, preaching, teaching, exhorting, etc. All this was, of course, not done exclusively in the form of meshalim.

We have observed the fact that the firm text often needs commentary. This applies to texts of the mashal-type to a special degree. When in the Gospels we see that Jesus must explain what he has said in a mashal, this must not be a secondary feature in the tradition. Nobody can express puzzling proverbs and amazing parables without being questioned or feeling himself that something needs explanation. Meshalim — most types of this complex category — evoke curiousity, wonder, pondering, questions, discussions.[52]

As for the narratives about Jesus, a few exceptions may lead one to think of oral narration of the common popular type (flexible "composition in transmission"). Martin Dibelius called these narratives *Novellen* (Tales) and regarded them as more "secular" (*weltlich*) than the other material and more secondary as well. He also thought that these narratives had not been in use in Early Christian preaching as had the other narratives but that they stemmed from special "narrators."[53] On this point Dibelius has received very little following. Kelber now puts forward the thesis that the pre-Markan narrative material in its entirety comes from oral narration of the common popular type.

A thorough analysis of the entire narrative material in the synoptic tradition will reveal to what extent a thesis of this kind can stand the test. But I do not think this model is very adequate as to narrative tradition either. Our sources from Early Christianity do not say a word about narrators of this type. And what we meet in the bulk of the synoptic narrative tradition is texts which very briefly and schematically present single episodes from the activity of Jesus. The presentation is usually so concentrated and terse that the wording does not allow much scope for variations. We read a brief description of the situation leading up to a saying of Jesus, a recording of a conversation with one or two rejoinders, or a brief account of a case of healing or exorcism. The

[52] From this point of view note e.g. Mark 4:10, 34, 7:17, 8:16-17, 9:32, 10:10, 24, 26, 13:14.

[53] *Die Formgeschichte des Evangeliums* (2nd ed.; Tübingen: Mohr, 1933) 66-100, esp. 66-67, 94-100.

superfluous words in a pericope of this kind are few, the margin for variations very small. It is difficult to see it otherwise than that these condensed narratives have been *texts* even at their oral stage, notwithstanding that the demand for unaltered wording has not been as strong in the narrative elements as in the sayings of Jesus in these texts. It is also easy to imagine that the *narrative* texts have been more readily influenced by the narrator's overall picture of Jesus and of his actual aim than are the sayings of Jesus.[54]

In his book, Werner Kelber stresses the importance of considering the social involvement of the gospel tradition (pp. 14-43 et passim). To him, however, the social factors occur primarily in the form of social pressure from the audience on the narrator. The presence and character of the audience, and the social surroundings of it, influence rather strongly the way the narrator formulates his presentation. Kelber characterizes *my* approach as "a model of passive transmission" and notes in my description "a virtual exemption of the oral Torah from active social engagement" (pp. 8-14). This is a misunderstanding. My view is that the Torah was a very "living" factor in the Jewish milieu and that the gospel tradition belonged to the concrete existence of the Jesus-movement and the Early Church, and was transmitted within the frame of the Early Christian "work with the word."[55] In *Memory and Manuscript* I attempted to give a concrete picture of some aspects of this "word with the word," which, of course, was influenced by the social conditions of the teachers involved. Their way of collecting, selecting, formulating and re-formulating, interpreting and expounding, grouping and re-grouping the traditional texts does not go on without influence from their present situation: they are affected themselves, they take positions themselves, they get questions from others and so on. Not even the most "academic" halachists among the Rabbis were completely uninfluenced by the social life around them; such is the case even more so far as the "haggadic" teachers are concerned!

5. The origin and character of the gospel tradition

If Jesus was a child prodigy and if he was remarkable when growing up, it is possible that his family spread a sort of tradition about him already at that time, in free wording. But we can only speculate about this; in the Gospels the material from the time before Jesus began his public ministry is both scanty and fragile. The proper, specific Early

---

[54] Cf. my article *Weg* 96-101.
[55] *Memory* 324-35, *Tradition* 37-47, *Origins* 67-91, *Weg* passim.

Christian tradition does not start until Jesus "appears publicly before Israel."

A. How can we imagine the beginning of that gospel tradition which records Jesus' preaching and teaching in *words*?

It starts when Jesus "opens his mouth and teaches" and gains sympathizers, adherents, and disciples, who accept his message.

We have already underlined two basic facts: that our sources tell us that Jesus taught with the aid of short, artistically formulated texts, and that the extant material in the synoptic sayings tradition is a series of such texts. It is important to notice that the synoptics use the same word for parables and logia: both are παραβολαί (*meshālim*).[56] We must of course analyze the material more closely and categorize it more precisely for our aims, but it is interesting that the Early Christian transmitters and evangelists did not see any difference in principle between logia and parables. Evidently they were transmitted in the same way, even if it was easier to make adjustments in the wordings of a longer parable than in a brief proverbial logion.

These texts were presumably transmitted as memorized texts in roughly the same way as the Jewish mashal-tradition, with roughly the same technique as Jewish material of similar types (note that the haggadic material had normally freer wording than the halacha-rules). I have tried to illustrate this in my previous writings on the subject[57], and need not repeat myself here.

I have also stressed the fact that all verbal tradition has a very wide sector of flexible words. This phenomenon is not, however, as interesting as are the firm elements, since it is so general, so common, and so difficult to separate from everyday talking. But it is important to be aware of the fact that the verbal tradition does include this phenomenon and that it is a vital part of it: texts must very often be interpreted

---

[56] Note how the word παραβολή is used in most cases in the parable chapter (Mark 4:1-34, Matt 13:1-52, Luke 8:4-18), and cf. Mark 7:17, Matt 15:15, Luke 6:39. In Luke 4:23 the word means "proverb."

[57] In *Memory* I worked on the base of a very broad conception of the word "Torah." I did not take it in the narrow sense "law" but in its broadest meaning, as a collective designation for the Jew's sacred authoritative tradition in its entirety (cf. above n. 12). I also stressed the well-known fact that, within this circle, the haggadic material had normally a freer wording than the halacha-rules, and the fact that "most of the gospel material is haggadic material," 335 (with reference to 96-97 and 146-48); see also 136-45, 177-81 and further *Tradition* 33-37, *Origins* 67-77, *Weg* 93-96. Yet many critics have ascribed to me the view that Jesus was a Torah-teacher in the meaning a "teacher of the law." When I say that Jesus was a "parabolist" (*mōshēl*) I only specify more precisely the designation "haggadist;" cf. *Origins* 70. Kelber (*Oral* 38, n. 131) is mistaken when he takes this as a revocation of my earlier position (that Jesus was a "teacher of the law"!).

or expounded, especially if they have the form of puzzling logia or thought-provoking parables.[58]

I do not think I shall linger on this for the moment. But let me illustrate the phenomenon that the verbal tradition includes an interaction between elements of different character with an example I drew attention to in *Memory and Manuscript* (p. 145). In the parable chapter of Matthew (13:1-52) we find Jesus teaching with the aid of parables. In order to illuminate the different ways of receiving the message of the Rule of Heaven Jesus relates to the people (1) the parable of the sower (vv. 3-9). This is a text with a firm wording; the small margin of alteration can be measured by way of a comparison between the parallels. The content of the parable is also clarified (2) in the form of an interpretative exposition presented as complementary teaching for the disciples (vv. 10-23). The vocabulary is of another type in this exposition than in the parable itself, and many signs give us reason to think that these wordings were less fixed at the beginning than were the wordings of the parable itself. In the long run, however, they have become fixed as well. The parable is finally (3) treated as a well-known text with a name: ἡ παραβολὴ τοῦ σπείραντος (v. 18). For the stranger this name is an empty designation. But within the circle where this parable is a well-known text from Jesus, this name is a terse actualization of the parable and its message.[59]

Here we get a concrete example of the inner secrets of the verbal tradition. Explicit and implicit forms, exhaustive and concise versions may lie side by side. A wealth of different forms is natural in a millieu where a certain verbal tradition is cultivated. One can quote a text verbally, or almost verbally, one can render it more freely, paraphrase it or hand on its message in the form of an interpretation; one can condense it into a brief formula, even a name.[60] If we come across one of these forms we cannot conclude that the other forms did not exist for this author. To ask how much Paul knew of the concrete Jesus-tradition — or in what forms he knew it — is not the same as studying direct quotations in the letters he occasionally wrote to particular communities.[61]

---

[58] See above, nn. 12 and 44.

[59] Another example is the parable of the tares in Matt 13: mashal (vv. 24-30), exposition (vv. 37-43), name (v. 36); *Memory* 145. We must also remember that pupils in the Hellenistic schools learned both to present a theme briefly and to develop it broadly (*brevitas, amplificatio*).

[60] See further *Memory* 130-36, 171-81.

[61] *Memory* 290-302, *Origins* 33-41. Cf. T. Holtz, Jesus-Überlieferung und Briefliteratur, *Wiss. Z. Univ. Halle* 34'85G, H. 1 (1984) 103-12.

B. As for the *mighty deeds* of Jesus, the rumors certainly spread as soon as somebody was impressed by Jesus. But the inner circle within the Jesus-movement and the Church afterwards claimed to have more definite knowledge. During the time of Jesus there perhaps was no urgent reason for creating firm texts about the mighty acts of the master. Possibly, however, some such texts were needed when Jesus sent out his disciples in order to spread his message during his activity in Galilea; the traditions about this commissioning do not seem to be post-Easter fictions.[62] In Matt 11:4-6 par., we get an interesting picture of a situation in which some of John the Baptist's disciples are made transmitters of Jesus-tradition to the Baptist. What occasional "Jesus-propagandists" said about the master (cf. e.g., Mark 1:45, 5:19-20) is not easy to know; their narration was hardly of the concise synoptic type.[63]

On the whole, I think we must conclude that the real need for brief, pointed narratives about the characteristic deeds of Jesus did not arise until after the departure of the master, when the leadership shifted over from Jesus himself to others, above all the twelve. When they preached and taught about Jesus as the Messiah, the Son of God, and discussed his secrets with each other and with opponents and critics, it certainly was not natural to confine themselves to the sayings of Jesus. And when they scrutinized the holy scriptures in order to understand the Jesus-events better and find prophetical hints about him, it was maybe near at hand to formulate brief texts about his most typical deeds and about other important episodes in his life on earth. Even these brief narrative texts were probably transmitted by way of memorization; the primordial sayings-tradition set the pattern.

C. *The passion narrative* has certainly had a specific position from a very early time. In this case the events themselves were coherent; the moments came in rapid succession, not as isolated episodes, and the event as a whole cried out for another explanation than the official one that the authorities had silenced a deceiver (πλάνος). Here the adherents of Jesus needed an interpretation "from within" to set up against the official declarations of the outsiders. It is interesting to see that the passion narrative is a necklace of episodes but that these — or most of them — belong intimately together, because they narrate and interpret a common chain of events.[64]

---

[62] E. E. Ellis, "New Directions in Form Criticism," *Jesus Christus in Historie und Theologie* (Festschrift H. Conzelmann; Tübingen: Mohr, 1975) 299-315, esp. 302-04.

[63] Note, however, Riesner, *Jesus* 487-88.

[64] This ancient insight, stressed by the three pioneer form critics, has been strongly radicalized by R. Pesch in his commentary on the Gospel of Mark and in his book *Das*

As for this decisive part of the Jesus-tradition, the New Testament books are full of verbal presentations in the most different forms, from brief condensed formulas to extensive expositions in free words (the speeches in Acts, the letters).

6. The production of texts: creation, reshaping, compilation

In the New Testament discipline we must often tackle problems which initially seem to be unsolvable but which eventually turn out to be possible to handle. Let me now mention a set of such questions.

The form critics increased our sensitivity to the forms of the gospel material. Since then the achievements of redaction critics, composition critics and text theorists of various schools have sharpened our sensitivity still more and given us even better instruments for discerning the form and anatomy of the synoptic texts. At present, text pragmatic studies seem to be à la mode; one brings the intended addressees of the texts into focus and treats the texts as means of communication.

I think, however, that we can ameliorate these analyses somewhat even by working more concretely than we usually do with some elementary *historical* questions concerning the very making of the New Testament texts: How did Jesus and Early Christianity proceed, technically speaking, when they formulated and reformulated their texts? In my opinion we need rather concrete ideas of the very process of creation, both concerning the individual texts and the text collections, the final written Gospels included.

Generally speaking, I think we can isolate the creation of a text from its various uses, and fix the process of creation as an act in itself. We know that a text can arise suddenly through the prompting of the moment, in practical situations of various kind, but even then it is reasonable to ask how this came about. In most cases, however, the text is created outside the practical situations wherein it will be used, and the author is well aware of what happens in the process.[65] This applies especially to written texts.

Studies in the psychology of artistic inspiration[66] show that different authors give different answers to the question of how they create their texts. Some of them claim just to "receive" texts under strong inspir-

Evangelium der Urgemeinde. Wiederhergestellt und erläutert von Rudolf Pesch (Freiburg i. B.: Herder, 1979). See also Pesch's impressive response to his critics, "Das Evangelium in Jerusalem," *Das Evangelium und die Evangelien* 113-55.

[65] *Weg* 85-91, 96-101.

[66] T. Andrae, *Mystikens psykologi. Besatthet och inspiration* (2nd ed.; Stockholm: Verbum, 1968) 176-444.

ation; the poems "come" to them completed and perfect with metre, rhythm, rhyme and everything, and need only to be written down. Others say that their texts, even those which give the impression of being strongly "inspired," are the result of hard intellectual labor. Yet others declare that the texts certainly come to them in moments of inspiration but that they must be revised very thoroughly nevertheless in order to stand. Of course there are many possibilities between the extremes here.

Now to our material. I cannot discuss every category of text and all stages. Let me confine myself to three levels and to the main types of synoptic texts.

A. Text creation

(1) How did the genuine sayings of Jesus originate? Was Jesus a man of strong inspiration, who just "received" his logia and parables? Or was he a man who created them very consciously? In the latter case, did he normally do so in contexts of conversation, teaching, extemporaneous preaching or other communal contexts? Or did he do it in solitude? Did he repeat his texts in order to implant them firmly in his own memory? And what role did the disciples play? Were they, as it were, his note-books? Questions of this kind may seem totally impossible now, and some of them may even sound ridiculous, but they may become possible to deal with once we have tried to come to grips with the process of text creation.[67]

(2) How did the episodal narratives of Jesus originate? In this case it is hardly realistic to think of a markedly inspirational process of creation. Early Christian prophets did not present such texts. They were certainly formulated very consciously. How? Did it take place in a situation of teaching or discussion, so that someone in the session had the task of formulating the text while the others listened to his presentation and contributed with proposals of amelioration until the text was finished and accepted? Or were there always specific, skillful individuals responsible for such texts; men who created them individually outside the proper situations of teaching or study? How did that occur, to be precise? Were specific patterns consciously followed? Old Testament patterns, contemporary Jewish patterns, more decidedly Hellenistic patterns, from various schools? Was the form of the text

---

[67] I have collected some concrete material for comparison in *Memory* esp. 130-36, 171-89. I also think that the present interest in the devices of ancient rhetoric will provide us with assistance in this connection. See, e.g., V. K. Robbins, *Jesus the Teacher. A Socio-Rhetorical Interpretation of Mark* (Philadelphia: Fortress, 1984).

chosen with special regard to its primary use, that which the form critics call its proper Sitz im Leben?[68] To what extent were notebooks used in this situation (the Rabbinic material shows that such tools were not necessary)? The questions may be multiplied.

(3) Does the distinctiveness of the passion narrative motivate the supposition that it was created in some other way than the rest of the narrative traditions? In that case, how? Most of the episodes in the passion narrative are, as we know, self-contained units but at the same time natural links within the story at large: was this a result of conscious considerations on the part of those who formulated the passion narrative? Were more or different people involved in the creation of this narrative than in the other cases? Was it written down earlier than the episodal stories, maybe even from the start? (It could mainly function as a memorized text, to be recited from memory just the same.)

B. Reshaping of texts

As for the transmission of the fixed texts, the methods of the transmitter and the receiver, I think I shall not repeat here what I have written in other connections. But a cluster of questions could be formulated concerning the deliberate reformulations of the firm texts during the phase of transmission. In *Memory and Manuscript*[69] I offer some hints about the way in which transmitted texts were altered in the Rabbinic schools and sessions, but I wish I had written more about that; it would have prevented the misunderstanding that the Rabbis never changed their texts or that all types of Rabbinic texts had the same firm wording. Here, a good deal of work remains to be done if we want to understand how the variations in the firm texts have arisen.[70]

C. Text compilation

At the stage of the creation of the large written Gospels we have to ask how the Gospels were produced, technically speaking. How do we imagine that Mark, Matthew, Luke, John — let me call them so — actually proceeded, when they produced their famous books? Who were these men and how well were they versed in the Early Christian tradition in its entirety? How well were they socialized in Early Chris-

[68] For my part I do not think the text was actually formulated in the situation for which it was primarily intended to be used; *Weg* 85-91, 96-98.

[69] E.g. 77-78, 97-98, 103-12, 120-21, 152-53. Cf. also *Tradition* 37-50.

[70] J. Neusner has now summarized his illuminating studies of the specific Rabbinic methods of transmitting abbreviated halacha-rules (apodoses) in the Mishna, in a recent book, *The Memorized Torah: The Mnemonic System of the Mishnah* (Brown Judaic Studies 96; Chico: Scholars, 1985).

tianity's behavioral tradition, ethically, didactically, liturgically? What position did they have in the Church seen as a kind of institution? (Did each of them, when writing his book, have the authority of a great apostle behind himself?) And how did this influence their writing? How familiar were they with the broad verbal tradition of the Church? How much did they know of the oral textual tradition? How much did they have in the form of documents? How did they collect their material? Did they travel, search for collections, consult informants? And how did they actually proceed when compiling their books? Did they have the scrolls and codices before themselves? Did they know them more or less by heart? Did they feel a duty to copy visually from the columns in the Vorlagen or could they follow some freer model and adapt their texts in a more targumic way? Did they have in their memory oral versions of the pericopes present in their written sources, and, in such cases, did these versions have the same authority for them as the written versions? Did they use loose notes for the first phase of their attempts to combine their sources? Did they rewrite their drafts many times? Etc., etc. Such questions are not unrealistic; I think we should try to find answers, in any case for our own silent use. If we cannot form a concrete conception of the process of compiling the Gospels we have reasons to surmise that something is wrong with our solution of the synoptic question and of many other related topics.

Furthermore, if we come to grips with concrete questions of this kind, perhaps we can then also formulate criteria for deciding whether a text has been created — or reworked — as an oral text or if it has been produced in written form. I do not think we have any proper criteria for this so far.

7. The synthetization of the text material

According to Rudolf Bultmann,[71] the individual elements of the gospel tradition originated first independently of each other, but it was "in the nature of the case" that they were gathered in collections which gradually became more extensive and finally were written down. The synoptic evangelists were collectors and editors rather than authors. Yet, Mark made a pioneer achievement when writing his Gospel as the first in the series. Here the loosely conglomerated material was interpreted and organized along main lines taken from the Christology and the kerygma of the Hellenistic Church.

[71] *Die Geschichte der synoptischen Tradition* (FRLANT 29; 2nd ed; Göttingen: Vandenhoeck & Ruprecht, 1931) 393-400.

Kelber (pp. 44-89 and passim) objects that nothing in orality makes writing natural. The narration about Jesus in Early Christianity was by nature oral, pluriform and multidirectional. When Mark changed the flourishing tradition into a linear account and wrote it down, new factors were decisive, in part pronouncedly anti-traditional factors (pp. 184-226).

I do not think we can get a realistic picture of the synthesizing process if we do not consider all the dimensions of the Early Christian tradition.

This tradition was intra-ecclesiastical. The evangelists were hardly very impressed by pluriform outsider-rumors and multi-directional talk about Jesus among the people. But they were certainly very well acquainted with the insider-tradition about him. In the communities which arose around the message about Jesus Christ, there was a new, enthusiastic belief in Jesus and a living interest in his person, spirit and will. Here was an "inner tradition," a spiritual atmosphere which repelled negative interpretations of Jesus and cultivated positive ones. Certainly, opinions were divided in some questions and various conflicts were unavoidable, but all who got the floor had a positive overall picture of Jesus, his person, spirit and will, and at least a rough idea about his career and fate on earth. Already in the inner tradition there was a certain unity: an attitude towards Jesus which kept that which was said about him within a certain framework and gave it something of an organic unity.

To say this is to draw attention to the effects of "the institutional tradition" at the same time. Institutionalization had shown itself therein that a borderline had arisen between insiders and outsiders, impeding the inflow of wild, foreign or negative interpretations of Jesus. And as for the situation intra muros: those who had the highest reputation as experts concerning what Jesus had said and done — especially those who could say that they had heard and seen themselves — certainly had the best chances to set the note as traditionists (cf., e.g., Acts 1, Gal 1-2, 1 Joh 1:1-4). This reduced the pluralism of the traditions about Jesus.

Even the programmatic "behavioural tradition" which was cultivated within the Church was a synthesizing factor: a foreign body could hardly be tolerated. I am thinking of the "imitation of Christ" as a programmatic model for the Christian's lifestyle but also of the liturgical, didactic, therapeutic and exorcistic activity within the Church. Here we have another unifying factor.

Turning to "the verbal tradition" one must remember that it not only contained a number of isolated quotations from Jesus and episodal narratives about him. There were also unifying elements in this connection. Even the general usage of language in Early Christianity — the flexible, variegated way of speaking about Jesus — formed very soon a certain vocabulary, formulas, motifs, etc., which became typical. These observations remind us that the synthetization of the gospel was not something entirely secondary. Intra muros the Jesus-tradition was in *certain* respects always something of a unity, stamped by the same deeply devotional attitude to Jesus. Thus, we are moving within a frame of unity when we pose the question of how the very texts about Jesus were synthetized into orderly accounts (διηγήσεις) and became written Gospels.

The transmitted texts contained elements which were summaries and thus paved the way for a natural organization of the concrete texts. I am thinking of verbal elements which either classify and characterize the person of Jesus or briefly summarize and categorize his "works." In the former case, I aim at such designations as (Our) Teacher, the Prophet, Messiah/Christ, God's Son, the Lord, and the like. These titles characterized the person of Jesus and did so together; we know of no early Christian group which could classify Jesus with the aid of only one existing title. In this way a complex but coherent picture of Jesus' person was built up. In Early Christianity all these designations have one thing in common: they all characterize Jesus of Nazareth and do so in a positive and majestic way. Low or negative designations are not accepted. In the long run, these intra-ecclesiastical titles of Jesus become synonymous; they all function to denote the "whole" Jesus. This is a telling example of their synthesizing and unifying character. The concrete Jesus-tradition deals almost solely with the man who receives these titles.[72]

In the latter case I have in mind the fact that it was impossible already at the beginning to be content with only individual, episodal narratives about the activity of Jesus. Even from the first moment one had sometimes to be brief. Already when Jesus had preached and taught a couple of times, the disciples and others must have been able to say briefly that Jesus "preached and taught." After a while they could certainly claim that he "preached and taught about the Reign of God." In the same way they must have been able to state in general words, after having seen a couple of mighty acts, that Jesus "cured sick people and expelled demons." Such verbal elements are unavoidable in

---

[72] On Jesus as "the only teacher," see *Memory* 332-33, *Tradition* 40-43, *Origins* 47-49, *Weg* 79-82, 91-93.

every linguistically developed milieu. We may have different opinions about the factual summaries to be found in the synoptic Gospels, whether in their present form they are formulated by the evangelist or not. But it would be foolish to think that there was no need for summarizing items of this kind before the written organization of the material.

In this way we can analyze the various parts of the text tradition and observe how the different elements contain items which could help anyone who wanted to organize the material into an orderly account to find a basis for his arrangement. Let me mention a few more examples. Some traditions contained certain geographic or temporal information. Rightly or wrongly, these could offer complementary knowledge for dating or localizing other traditions lacking such information. Of great interest are retrospective or forward-pointing elements, for instance Jesus' words about his mighty deeds (Matt 11:20-24 par.) or his predictions about the passion and resurrection (Mark 8:31 with all the parallels). Elements of this kind facilitate synthesis and organization of the material. Traditions about a conflict between Jesus and his opponents included a natural relationship to the final intervention against him. And the passion narrative made it natural to look for reasons for this condemnation and for evidence for the innocence of Jesus as well in the traditions about his prior teaching and mighty deeds.[73]

I mentioned the passion narrative. It has undoubtedly played an eminent role as a first step toward a synthetic, "complete" Gospel. Here, an important part of the history of Jesus was narrated rather early in the form of an orderly account. It is easy to understand that this coherent presentation of the decisive part of Jesus' work called for a substructure, a complementary introduction. Martin Kähler's well-known description of the Gospel of Mark as a "passion narrative with an extended introduction" indicates how the evangelist got his most impressive idea for the disposition of his composition.

I break off here. My contention is that a coherent account of "all that Jesus began to do and teach" did not exist at the beginning of Early Christianity and that the first one who wrote a Gospel (I think it was Mark) certainly was a pioneer; yet, his achievement was hardly very creative. He had good text material, he did not need to reinterpret

[73] It is however very interesting to note that the opposition against Jesus' bold way of forgiving sins (Matt 9:1-8 parr.), exorcisms (Matt 9:32-34 and 12:22-24 parr.) and healings on the sabbath (e.g. Matt 12:9-14 parr.) has not been taken into account explicitly in the passion narrative in spite of the fact that all three of these points could be classified as capital crimes (a more lenient interpretation was of course also possible).

it very much nor change its form very much; even the disposition of the material was near at hand. His achievement was that he actually did what many others could also have done, but that he did it so connaturally with the material that his followers had no reason for constructing a disposition of quite another type.

8. The process of writing down

I have already pointed out that the concrete Jesus-tradition arose in a milieu strongly influenced by the holy scriptures; these "were living" through actual reading, translation, interpretation and application. During the whole time from Jesus to the evangelists, the gospel tradition had natural connections with a verbal mother-tradition within which the written word played an important role.

On the other hand, it is very striking that Jesus himself did not write. He was a man who spoke. He talked to people, he preached orally, taught orally, made mighty acts with his oral word, etc. Only in one place do our sources mention that he wrote something (John 7:53 — 8:11), but that was on the ground and nobody knows what it was. Nothing indicates that Jesus wrote down one single logion, parable or speech. Nor is it indicated anywhere that he incited cooperators or disciples to write or that he dictated to them. The verbal tradition that Jesus himself initiated, was oral.

As for the disciples, it is nowhere mentioned that they took notes or carried notebooks. They "are with" Jesus, they "follow" him, they are his "disciples," they "hear and see," they remember, and they sometimes question Jesus about something he had said or done. Thus the disciples have seen and heard, they remember, ponder and discuss Jesus and his words and deeds.

When the exclusive master suddenly has departed, the Jesus-movement must be reconstructed and consolidated, a process the sociological consequences of which we can guess only to a certain degree. Nothing indicates, however, that the adherents of Jesus immediately change the medium of communication. They do not sit down in order to write a monograph about Jesus, a book to be duplicated and distributed. They do what we may expect disciples in this milieu to do: they continue in the footsteps of their master, they follow his aims, his behavior and teaching and perhaps even direct instructions given; they carry on his work along his characteristic lines. What Acts and other New Testament writings say or reflect seems to be very probably true, namely, that the disciples of Jesus preach and teach "in the name of Jesus" and about Jesus, they heal sick people and expel demons "in the name of Jesus" etc.[74] This is not strange at all, especially if earlier they had had the task of helping the master in his work. That the new situation forces them to ponder and discuss more seriously than before the person and work of Jesus, especially his death, goes without saying; that they have much stronger reasons now than before for scrutinizing the holy scriptures in order to gain clarity, is easy to imagine. Of course nothing hampers them from taking various new steps as well; not least their strong conviction that the crucified Jesus is risen and that the Spirit is with them inspires them to new initiatives.

We do not get many indications about the role of writing in this connection. It is possible that notes and notebooks were taken into use early at this time; our sources are, alas, completely silent about it. Even less do we find anywhere an exhortation to use such means. We might, however, imagine that some such writing was done quite informally, for practical reasons; in such case it is no mystery that our sources do not mention it. But it is not at all self-evident. Even less is it true that Early Christianity relied upon the written word.[75] If we look at the words and expressions used to characterize the verbal activity of Jesus and Early Christianity, they do not exclude written means but neither do any of them give a clear or even natural hint at the use of written notes which were read aloud. Such words as κηρύσσειν, διδάσκειν, ὁμιλεῖν, διαλέγεσθαι, παρακαλεῖν, νουθετεῖν, etc., aim primarily at an oral activity, not at a written one.

However, it can hardly be doubted that notebooks began to be used when the collections became more extensive than in the earliest period. But suddenly, and within a short period of time, from late sixties onwards, written Gospels appeared within the Church. We do not know how many they were, only that four of them very easily forced out the other ones. It is rather difficult to explain this transition to written Gospels. Probably many factors were intertwined and none of them alone was decisive.

We have to do with two questions: Why was the text material gathered into extensive collections? And why were these collections now properly written down?

The first question is not difficult to answer. What we call "collecting

---

[74] See e.g. Acts 4:17, 18, 5:28, 40, 9:27, 28, and 3:6, 4:7, 10, 30, 16:18.

[75] Thus J. Neusner, *Rabbinic Traditions* 3. 154. The gospel tradition was after all not written down immediately, and Paul could not possibly regard his oral teaching less important or less reliable than his letters. He only wrote letters when he could not come in person.

mania" is a hypertrophy of a general human proclivity: what we find interesting and important we save and gather, be it stamps, anecdotes, knowledge or whatever. It is not difficult to understand that those in Early Christianity who had to use the concrete Jesus-traditions more than others, "collected" such texts; both interest and necessity forced them to do so. It was natural as well that structured collections of this kind emerged and expanded. Even the will to remember leads us to a conscious gathering and grouping of memory material. It is a precaution against forgetfulness. Other factors contributed as well, not least, the needs of the communities. It is easy to imagine that notebooks were more and more taken into use in this work with the texts. Great synthetical collections of the same type as the Q-collection or the Gospel of Mark are thus "in the nature of the case." And proper books had to come, sooner or later.

The Q-collection hardly had as well a structured disposition as did the Gospel of Mark. This Gospel is not merely an extensive notebook (ὑπόμνημα). The author shows a desire to write for others, and his desire has taken him a step further than to the collection of material in a big notebook; he has arranged his texts in accordance with an overall view of Jesus and his work. On the other hand, the Gospel of Mark may not be a proper book (ἔκδοσις) in all respects, written for common use.[76] The Gospel of Matthew, for its part, is a book in the more strict sense of the word, even if it was not written for the public market. It was presumably intended for a Church province, maybe for the Church everywhere. The Lukan writings seem to be written primarily for individual, cultivated Christians but probably for cultural outsiders as well. The Gospel of John gives the impression of having been designed for communities in the Johannine Church province.

Why this remarkable writing? To some extent it may have happened by accident: local conditions in the community where the first of the evangelists wrote or the personal qualities of the evangelist may have occasioned the writing of the first Gospel. With the model given and the first literary attempt made, the undertaking was copied by more men in Early Christianity. It is also a striking fact that the synoptics belong together. They are not three independent eruptions of creativity; they have some cause in common.

[76] On the difference between properly published books and written notes, see V. Burr, "Editionstechnik," *RAC* 4 (1959) 597-610. For Jewish material, cf. S. Lieberman, *Hellenism in Jewish Palestine* (New York: Jew. Theol. Sem. of Amer., 1950) 83-99. See also the discussion in *The Relationships Among the Gospels. An Interdisciplinary Dialogue* (ed. W.O. Walker, Jr.; San Antonio: Trinity University Press, 1978) 123-92.

The fact that time went on was also a factor, in itself. "The beginning: and the first "fathers" thereby got their patina. It is always difficult for the present and the authorities of the present to gain the acknowledgement, prestige and authority of "the fathers" and "the good old days." In this case the personal disciples of Jesus — especially the twelve — had furthermore an immense authority as "eyewitnesses," and because they had the reputation of having been authorized by Jesus himself, the Risen One, and because they had such a position within the Church. It is easy to understand that the death of these pillars and other eyewitnesses sharpened the demand for the legacy to be preserved carefully and committed to writing.

Neither is it impossible that some of these "fathers," Peter for instance, had something to do themselves with the matter. Peter may have given Mark occasion to write, or even urged him to do so, before his own death.

Another "natural" guess is that the progressive institutionalization and consolidation of the Church made it desirable to have better books than before for the different needs of the communities.

Concrete events outside the Church might have played their role as well, especially the fall of Jerusalem and the destruction of the temple in the year 70 A.D.[77] We know what a catastrophe this was to the Jews and what strivings for consolidation it evoked. The Christian sources do not give us reason for believing that the fate of Jerusalem in the year 70 shook Early Christianity as much as Judaism, but it is reasonable to presume (1) that even those Jews who had become Christians were influenced by this catastrophe and its immediate consequences: the holy city and the Temple could no longer be what they had been; (2) that the Palestinian authorities of Early Christianity could no longer have the same influence as before in the Church while other Christian centres gained greater influence; (3) that the fact that Judaism after the fall of the Temple consolidated itself hastened Early Christianity's consolidation with defence and contra-attacks against the mother-religion. In these ways the fate of Jerusalem and the Temple may have effected the work with the Jesus-tradition in Christian centres and contributed to the origin of solid, written Gospels.

9. The polyphonic character of the written Gospel

The Early Church was not only a number of independent congregations; there was also a common sense of unity: we are the Church of

[77] Cf. Kelber, *Oral* 210-11.

Christ. A sign of this is the fact that the Gospels were so quickly distributed to other communities. They were commune bonum for the Christians.

A classical point in the discussion about the Fourth Gospel is the question of whether this Gospel was written to complete the other Gospels or to replace them. This question is, however, pertinent for each one of the synoptic Gospels as well. And it is important: Was this book written in order to be *the* Gospel in a community or was it written in order to function as one of many voices in a choir? Only if we know for sure that an evangelist intends his book to be the exclusive Gospel for his community can we take his book as a full presentation of his own total view. If he was writing in order to enrich existing collections and/or Gospels, it is not unlikely that he could presuppose very much and allow himself a one-sidedness in his selection of material and in his accentuations which he might otherwise have avoided.

Let me just hint at a few points. In the Gospel of John we easily see which disciple is the ideal one in the Johannine Church: "the Beloved Disciple." But Peter and the twelve are not rejected. We may suspect criticism against them, but their authority is respected. We get a similar impression in the notices in 20:30-31, and 21:24-25, the words about the selection the evangelist has made from the Jesus-tradition. Nothing here indicates that the Gospel of John is intended to be the only acceptable Gospel. The spirit in these notices is not exclusive. The Gospel of John has not come to displace but to complete the others.

In the Lukan prologue we cannot read for sure any criticism against Luke's predecessors. If Luke reproaches them, he does so in an almost indiscernible way. He reveals no wish to displace other Gospels. What he says clearly is that his book will fulfil a special function which obviously the other "orderly accounts" he knows cannot fulfil. The Lukan writings are intended to be used as a complement to other Gospels. Therefore, we cannot presume that Luke presents everything he accepts concerning Jesus in his Gospel.

The author of the Matthean Gospel does not say one explicit word about himself and his informants. In the finale of the book (28:16-20) we read, however, that Jesus gives his disciples the command to teach all nations "to observe all that I have commanded you." Certainly this has in view not only sayings of Jesus of a commanding character but the authoritative Jesus-tradition in its entirety. We get the impression that the Gospel of Matthew is intended to be as complete as possible when it goes about the concrete Jesus-tradition. It shall be an all-comprehensive instrument for all tasks which the Risen One has given his Church. On the other hand, it is not likely that Matthew thinks he has collected "everything" in his book and that, therefore, this Gospel shall replace the other collections of Jesus-tradition. We can see how Matthew uses the Gospel of Mark (I think he does). The latter is almost totally swallowed up; the *material* in the book of Mark becomes almost superfluous now. The same applies to the Q-collection. But, even though Matthew reworks his two main sources in this way, he treats the material in them with a striking respect. Nowhere does he reveal suspicion or negativism against his sources or their authors. Therefore he certainly has not wanted to silence the oral tradition, refute the older collections or dispatch the Gospel of Mark to the geniza. The Gospel of Matthew is not written in an exclusive spirit. The evangelist stood in a tradition, in which Kings and Chronicles could stand side by side and a scriptural verse could be interpreted in many ways by one and the same teacher. Matthew certainly would not mind that the vivid Gospel of Mark was used even in the future.[78]

It is not easy to know, how Mark thought of earlier materials concerning the words and deeds of Jesus. Like Matthew, he finds no need to say a word about himself or his work. For my part I think that Mark has no intention to write a complete account of Jesus' words and deeds — "all about Jesus" — or to replace other attempts. Nor do I believe the many new hypotheses about his severe polemics against the family of Jesus, the twelve, Early Christian prophets and whatever.[79] To me it seems probable that Mark knows about the Q-collection and respects it. Nothing indicates that Mark was so abnormal that he held the sayings of Jesus in contempt. He simply makes a narrow selection. The limited space he gives the sayings material in his book (some 27% of the total text) might very well have the explanation that there already existed a good and respectable collection which Mark neither wanted to integrate into his own presentation nor to replace. If the abrupt ending of Mark's Gospel is not due to some external, accidental fact — that one or two leaves are missing or that the evangelist's work was interrupted or that he wanted to write one more volume like Luke without being able to do so — it might have the explanation that the resurrection narratives were very well known texts, which perhaps even had a prominent place in the eucharistic liturgy. This is a hypothetical guess but hardly more far-fetched than a lot of other arguments from silence concerning the Gospel of Mark.

[78] The fact that the Gospel of Mark actually did come in the shadow of Matthew's Gospel, is another matter.

[79] Thus Kelber, *Oral* esp. 90-105 with references.

The synoptic Gospels have a very simple canon history. This is easy to explain. They were rooted in the same tradition; they stemmed from circles whose members obviously knew each other rather well; as literary works they originated in connection with each other and were not written in order to displace each other. It was only natural that in many congregations they were added to one another immediately in the beginning. The fact that they seem to have got a "flying start" in the Church and an uncontested authority from the very beginning, presumably means that they came from leading Christian authorities and centres. In the competition with other "orderly accounts" they were victorious; the fight was scarcely hard. It was a matter of "the survival of the fittest" but also dependent on certain privileges; these three did not have to fight each for himself; they belonged together and had a common authority.

The written gospel of the Church is a polyphonic gospel — or tetraphonic gospel. This is not an entirely secondary fact, simply due to the recording of the gospel tradition and the inclusion of four records in a canon. To some extent it is even founded in the fact that the oral gospel tradition intra muros ecclesiae was a plurality with a consider-able homogeneity, and the fact that the evangelists did not intend to silence each other. It soon became difficult in the Church to keep the witnesses of the different evangelists apart.[80] This is irritating to us New Testament scholars today, when we work hard in order to see the distinctive profile of the different books as clearly as possible. But the four evangelists could certainly have written as Paul did: "Whether then it is I or they, so we preach and so you believed"(1 Cor 15:11).[81]

10. Holy writ and *viva vox*

The spoken and the written word both have their advantages and their disadvantages. This subject is very fascinating. From before the era of perfectly printed books and rapid, silent reading, we have many utterances on this problem. Well known are Plato's words about the stupid written book, which can do nothing but repeat the same words, and the early Christian fathers' appreciative testimonies about the living voice in contrast to books.[82] Martin Luther took up this theme

---

[80] Cf. H. Merkel, *Die Pluralität der Evangelien als theologisches und exegetisches Problem in der Alten Kirche* (Traditio christiana 3; Bern & Frankfurt a. M.: Lang, 1978).

[81] Cf. the attitude expressed in Phil 1:18.

[82] Plato, *Phaedros* 274b-78a; cf. Epist. II (314) and VII (340-42). On different aspects of the problem oral and written delivery in antiquity and in the Ancient Church, see H. Frhr. von Campenhausen, *Kirchliches Amt und geistliche Vollmacht in den ersten drei Jahrhunderten* (BHT 14; Tübingen: Mohr, 1942) 221-33, L. Vischer, "Die Rechtfertigung

in a remarkable way, insisting on the principle that the gospel (das Evangelium) is not holy scriptures but a living, sounding word: *viva vox*.[83]

In this paper I have rejected much in Werner Kelber's book, *The Oral and the Written Gospel*. His approach is based on all too simple contrast between the spoken and the written word, between orality and written delivery (textuality). Nonetheless, I think his mobilizing of observations from Anglo-American studies of "orality" — particularly if this category is taken in a more pluralistic form[84] — is valuable: from here the New Testament debate can be vitalized in questions concerning the gospel tradition and hermeneutics. In fact, Kelber's ambition is not only to elucidate the relation between the oral and the written gospel, but also, at the same time, to clarify the "oral psychodynamics" and to work out an "oral hermeneutic" as a complement to the usual hermeneutic which he calls a textual one.

I cannot follow Kelber very far in these points either. Yet, I think his subjects are important. Jesus and Early Christianity presented their own, new, specific message — from the eruptive centre of their "inner tradition" — in oral forms first of all, and did so in a cultural setting where writings were never far away. This means that the transition to a stage where the oral gospel had basically become one or many books was not a superficial, technical triviality. Granted this significant change did not occur immediately when the Gospels were written (the oral tradition and the oral activity in other forms continued); something had started which in the long run would have important consequences. One hundred years later or so the written Gospels had attained the position as holy scriptures and as primary sources for the Christian message. This process is a captivating object for historical study. But it also has deep theological and existential implications. It concerns themes that are among the greatest realities of the Church: law and gospel, holy writ and *viva vox evangelii*.

Birger GERHARDSSON

NOTE: *The Gospel Tradition* has appeared in 1986 as no. 15 in *Coniectanea Biblica: New Testament Series*.

der Schriftstellerei in der Alten Kirche," *TZ* 12 (1956) 320-36, E. F. Osborn, "Teaching and Writing in the First Chapter of the Stromateis of Clement of Alexandria," *JTS* NS 10 (1959) 335-43, H. Karpp, "Viva vox," *Mullus* (Festschrift T. Klauser, JAC Erg.-bd 1; Münster i. W.: Aschendorff, 1964) 190-98. Cf. also n. 37 above.

[83] See R. Prenter, *Spiritus creator. Studier i Luthers theologi* (2nd ed.; Copenhagen: Samlerens Forlag, 1946) 127-37.

[84] A good example is R. Finnegan, *Oral Poetry. Its Nature, Significance and Social Context* (Cambridge: Cambridge University Press; London, New York, Melbourne, 1977) and idem, *Oral Literature in Africa* (Oxford: Clarendon Press, 1970).

OBJECTIVITY AND SUBJECTIVITY
IN HISTORICAL CRITICISM OF THE GOSPELS

Over the past decade or so there has been no lack of publications treating the criteria for historicity judgments on gospel traditions.[1] This is not to say that a solid consensus has begun to heave into view. The present situation is characterized rather by confusion and disagreement. Confusion has been the legacy of the night battle, now petering out, between biblicists and methodical sceptics. Disagreement bears partly on which criteria are most cogent and which most regularly apposite,[2] partly on whether any of the criteria are in fact up to the task for which they have been devised.[3]

The purpose of this study is, first, to offer an account of the bases on which judgments of historicity and non-historicity are properly made; second, to consider an objection, namely, that in the light of the subjectivity with which indices to historicity are applied, it seems to

---

[1] A selection of discussions since 1971: C.F.D. Moule, "The Techniques of New Testament Research: A Critical Survey" in *Jesus and Man's Hope II*, edited by D.G. Miller and D.Y. Hadidian; Pittsburgh: Pittsburgh Theological Seminary, 1971, pp. 29-45. D.G.A. Calvert, "An Examination of the Criteria for Distinguishing the Authentic Words of Jesus," *New Testament Studies 18* (1971-71) pp. 209-218. R.S. Barbour, *Traditio-Historical Criticism of the Gospels*, London, SPCK, 1971. D. Lührmann, "Die Frage nach Kriterien für ursprüngliche Jesusworte — eine Problemskizze" in *Jésus aux origines de la christologie*, edited by J. Dupont; Gembloux: Duculot, 1975, pp. 59-72. Robert H. Stein, "The 'Criteria' for Authenticity" in *Gospel Perspectives. Studies of History and Tradition in the Four Gospels*, edited by R.T. France and David Wenham; Sheffield: JSOT Press, 1980, pp. 225-263. Heinz Schürmann, "Kritische Jesuserkenntnis. Zur kritischen Handhabung des 'Unähnlichkeitskriteriums', *Bibel und Liturgie 54* (1981) pp. 17-26. E. Earle Ellis, "Gospels Criticism. A Perspective on the State of the Art" in *Das Evangelium und die Evangelien. Vorträge vom Tübinger Symposium 1982*, edited by Peter Stuhlmacher; Tübingen: Mohr, 1983, pp. 27-54.

[2] Holding the field as "most cogent" and sometimes proposed as "exclusively cogent" is the criterion of dissimilarity, formulated along the lines urged by Ernst Käsemann. The "only case," according to Käsemann, in which we have "somewhat firm ground under our feet" is when a tradition for whatever reason is unattributable either to Judaism or to Christianity; see "Das Problem des historischen Jesus," (1954) in *Exegetische Versuche und Besinnungen I*; Gottingen: Vandenhoeck & Ruprecht, 1960, pp. 187-214, p. 205. That other criteria are "more regularly apposite," however, has been proposed on occasion, e.g., "the recovery of the historical milieu" (e.g., Maria Trautmann, *Zeichenhafte Handlungen Jesu*, Würzburg: Echter Verlag, 1980, pp. 115f.) or even "multiple attestation" (e.g., Harvey K. MacArthur, "Basic Issues. A Survey of Recent Gospel Research," *Interpretation* 18 [1964] pp. 39-55, cf. pp. 47f).

[3] See especially the articles of M.D. Hooker cited below, note 19.

follow that they are ineffective; third, to offer a response to this objection, which takes account of subjectivity as component and condition of objectivity.

I

By and large, treatments of criteria for establishing the words and acts of Jesus as historical have been content to pass over in silence such questions as how exactly the criteria fit into the total process of conducting a historical investigation, whether the criteria have a limited object or are supposed to bear decisively on every act of historical judgment, and how the criteria of historicity relate to the distinction between early and late literary traditions.

Having now used the word "criteria" many times, I shall henceforward abandon it in favor of the more modest term "indices." None of the so-called criteria of historicity are in the strict sense norms or standards invariably relevant and requisite to the inference of historicity. That Jesus had disciples, that he affirmed the authority of the scriptures, that he shared in the life of synagogue and temple, that he understood God (whom he called Father) as the God of Abraham, Isaac, and Jacob, of Moses and David and Isaiah, all this is historical, though it all accords with the Judaism of the time. Again, that he proclaimed the reign of God, that he often taught in parables, that he addressed God as Abba, that he "cleansed" the temple, that he suffered crucifixion under Pontius Pilate, all this is historical, though it all accords with the faith of the earliest church. Since all these data, regardless of their accord with Judaism and Christianity, are by common consent historical, we might quietly drop the hard-line language of "criteria" as well as the doctrinaire sophistry of "methodical scepticism" (data must be taken to be unhistorical till proved otherwise by the ascertainment of their simultaneous discontinuity with Judaism and early Christianity). This is mock-rigor, which does not hold in practice. On the contrary, in the cases listed above it is historicity that holds, and is all but universally acknowledged to hold, despite the lack of discontinuity with the post-Easter church or the lack of originality vis-à-vis Judaism.

The error lay in misconceiving two distinct indices to historicity as a single acid-test failing which any given datum must be methodically branded non-historical. In other words, the question of these two indices has been thoroughly confused by their having been, first, mistakenly understood in terms of criteria in the strict sense; second, mistakenly amalgamated (by Ernst Käsemann)[4] so as to make up a single criterion; third, mistakenly represented (under the catch-phrase "methodical scepticism") as the only effective test of historicity. It is of course true that discontinuity with the post-Easter church on the part of various traditions on Jesus, or the originality of various traditions vis-à-vis Judaism, are precious indications of historicity. Indeed, discontinuity with the post-Easter church, of itself and without the need of simultaneous originality vis-à-vis Judaism, is a particularly solid index to the historicity of data. But both indices function *in sensu aiente* and not *in sensu neganti*: their presence postively tells in favor of historicity, but their absence does not positively tell against historicity. By denying that the absence of these indices positively tells against historicity, or justifies the methodical ranging of data in the non-historicity column, one breaks cleanly with the grounding of historicity judgments on mere assumption.

In the allotting of a large role to assumption the school of methodical scepticism was matched by that of methodical credulity. If the first group assumed non-historicity till proved otherwise, the second, under the banner *in dubio pro tradito*, assumed historicity unless it was ruled out by flatly contradictory data or data so contrary and unharmonizable as to infringe on the presumption of Jesus' psychological unity.

This kindly attitude toward assumption has many roots, and in the above-mentioned two schools it doubtless has some disparate roots, but we should not overlook a common root, namely, the critic's recoil from acknowledging that he does not know. All too human, the recoil is understandable but hardly justifiable. Why should assumption be allowed to dispose of residues, disguising the critic's actual state of knowledge? The naive biblicist, though readily believing that literary doublets regularly reflect repeated historical events, can hardly claim to know this. He merely believes it. Likewise, the methodical sceptic cannot fail to be aware that if authentic materials contrary to church tendencies were conserved in the gospel tradition, authentic materials in accord with church tendencies were *a fortiori* conserved. This means that there are traditions which in fact are historical but which, since they fail the acid-test of discontinuity with early Christianity, cannot be identified as historical. And though the methodical sceptic dutifully ranges in the non-historicity column all traditions that are in continuity with early Christianity (e.g., the Last Supper accounts), he knows that

---

[4] See above, note 2.

he does not know which of them are historical and which are not. In short, he knows that he does not really know whether there was a Last Supper. Why then systematically range the Last Supper accounts in the non-historicity column rather than acknowledge that in terms of his own actual knowledge the historical question remains moot? In form his negative conclusion is sham knowledge. It adds, not to real knowledge, but to the sludge of gratuitously opaque or misleading procedures.

In the context of historical investigation there is point in distinguishing between data and conclusions. Data belong to the premises, conclusions to the results, of such investigation. Both involve judgments on historicity. If judgments on data are more fundamental, those that constitute conclusions are more significant, for the point of the historical enterprise is reconstruction. New questions, especially if they are satisfactorily answered, move historical inquiry forward.

The allusion to "new questions" implies a quarrel with the assumption that legitimate historical questions are somehow to be found preformed, if not ready-made, in the sources. Intelligent men, observed R.G. Collingwood, do not ask themselves questions they do not think they can answer;[5] but granted that sensible limit, all questions are fair game. Among numerous New Testament critics, however, a certain phobia respecting such "new questions" seems to hang on, neurosis-like, from the era of positivism. Kerygma theologians, for example, winced not only at the religious significance that their Liberal predecessors attached to Jesus' "personality," but also at the very idea of posing a question (namely about the personality of Jesus) that went beyond the concerns of the sources. Consistency, happily, did not inhibit these same critics from posing their own new questions.

Historicity is one dimension of a satisfactory answer to a new historical question, but here the judgment of historicity is immediately guided, not by indices to the historicity of data, but by the argumentation that organizes data and connects an answer to a question precisely in the light of data.

Moreover, the network of relations that comes to light in the course of an investigation is likely to modify some of the inquirer's initial judgments on data, supplying new grounds for confirming or reversing them. Thus, Suetonius provided a notice to the effect that Nero at one time intended a Roman evacuation of Britain. Collingwood rejected this, not because some better authority contradicted it, but because his

---

[5] R.G. Collingwood, *The Idea of History*, Oxford: Oxford University Press, 1946, p. 281f.

reconstruction of Nero's policy, based on Tacitus, would not allow him to think that Suetonius was right.

> And if I am told that this is merely to say I prefer Tacitus to Suetonius, I confess that I do; but I do so just because I find myself able to incorporate what Tacitus tells me into a coherent and continuous picture of my own, and cannot do this for Suetonius. [6]

Let us consider a testimony from New Testament literature that, unlike Suetonius's notice, finds confirmation elsewhere in the sources. The *apo*-formula used by Paul in 1 Cor 11:23 indicates the intention to specify Jesus as the originator of the eucharistic tradition. [7] If, in addition to this, Paul can be thought to be knowledgeable on the matter and free of the suspicion of deceit, one may infer historicity. Though this direct pattern of inference is rare, owing to the rarely concrete indication that historicity is specifically comprehended within the intention of the text, it nevertheless illustrates the non-monopoly of oblique patterns of inference (indices like discontinuity and originality, which make no appeal to evidence of historical intention) on the establishing of the historicity of data.

Finally, we should fill out the account of indices that pertain to oblique patterns of inference. None of these indices are of themselves decisive, i.e., decisive in principle and so invariably decisive. Their usefulness, however, is evident; or rather, their usefulness is evident once one has satisfied oneself that the account of the gospel tradition offered by the first form critics is simply inadequate and misleading. For it should be acknowledged that, if the first Christian communities produced the gospel tradition largely with reference to their own concerns and largely without concern for the actual memory of Jesus, then discussion of these indices is superfluous. It may be well, then, to entertain at least briefly the prior question: does the gospel tradition provide us with data, and abundant data, on Jesus?

The faith-formulations of the earliest church (pre-Pauline formulas conserved by Paul, e.g., 1 Cor 11:23-25; 15:3-5, and archaic motifs such as occur in Acts 10:34-40) illuminate the structure of the earliest Christian faith as a faith that intends actual historical events. [8] Early faith-formulations accordingly offer heuristic guidance for a judgment on the hypothesis that, as penetrated by the faith of the earliest church,

    [6] Collingwood, *The Idea of History*, p. 245.

    [7] See Joachim Jeremias, *The Eucharistic Words of Jesus*, trans. N. Perrin; London: SCM 1966, pp. 202f.

    [8] See B.F. Meyer, *The Aims of Jesus*, London: SCM Press, 1979, pp. 60-69.

gospel traditions dispensed with the memory of Jesus, or freely and radically revised it to serve new communitarian purposes. Since the earliest Christian faith-formulations point in an altogether different direction, namely, to a faith that intends historical events and to the collective witness of the Jerusalem community gathered around "Cephas and ... the twelve" (1 Cor 15:5), we should positively expect gospel traditions to be filled with the memory of Jesus. This expectation hinges on a generic continuity between two liturgical and catechetical traditions: the earliest faith-formulas and their contemporary narrative counterpart, the gospel tradition. To suppose the contrary is, moreover, to overlook major data: first, that the disciples of Jesus could hardly have undertaken a mission to Israel unless they could plausibly claim to be presenting, in the light of the scriptures, an eye-witness account of Jesus;[9] second, that the reference back to Jesus — the account of the gospel tradition implicitly offered by the gospel tradition itself — is massively commended to us by the tradition-oriented character of the ancient world, specifically including the world of Palestinian Judaism.[10] In this light and only in this light can discussion of multiple and multiform attestation and of linguistic indices to historicity make positive sense.

Multiple attestation figures in the discussion insofar as "multiple" points to "early" and "early" to "historical." Both links should be understood to hold with statistical generality, neither being guaranteed in individual cases; hence, multiple attestation functions as an effective index only in conjunction with other indices. The same holds for the multiform attestation of a tradition (e.g., in narrative material and sayings material, or as parable and as saying, etc.). The operative assumptions are, first, that a datum from early tradition is more likely than one from late tradition to have found attestation in independent lines and forms of tradition; second, a datum from early tradition has a greater probability of historicity than one from late tradition. Caution is obviously in order: multiple attestation of itself cannot guarantee a given tradition as early, nor is early tradition by that mere fact guaranteed as historical. Since the most authoritative witnesses to the career of Jesus did not immediately disappear from the stage of history and the ongoing life of the church, later traditions could have arisen, and no doubt did arise, to correct or clarify earlier traditions in historically valid fashion. We cannot then exclude the possibility that a

---

[9] See Birger Gerhardsson, *Memory and Manuscript. Oral Tradition and Written Transmission in Rabbinic Judaism and Early Christianity*, Lund: Gleerup, 1961, p. 330.

[10] Gerhardsson, *Memory and Manuscript*, pp. 19-32, 324-335.

later tradition might be historically better than a more primitive tradition. Finally, there is nothing to prevent the most primitive form of a tradition from appearing in a late, even the latest, redaction.

Linguistic indices pioneered over the past century reached remarkable refinement in the gospel criticism of Joachim Jeremias and are epitomized in the first chapter of his New Testament theology.[11] They include "ways of speaking preferred by Jesus" (the use of the divine passive, antithetic parallelism, rhythmic patterns in two-beat, three-beat, four-beat, and *qînâ* metre, alliteration, assonance, paronomasia, use of hyperbole and paradox) and — of particular value as indices to historicity — irreducibly personal idiom (distinctive form and content of riddles and parables, new coinages respecting "the reign of God," a distinctive use of *'āmēn*, the use of *'abbā'* as an address of God).

Since the burden of proof falls, as Willi Marxsen argued some years ago,[12] neither on historicity nor on non-historicity, but on whoever wishes to pronounce either way, there should be three columns for judgments on historicity (historical, non-historical, and question-mark), and a full treatment of indices should include indices to non-historicity.

David Friedrich Strauss presented an early treatment of this issue. Though his criteria were partly ideological (e.g., the "impossibility" of disturbing "the chain of secondary causes"), and though ideology ultimately commanded his whole historical effort, Strauss made a beginning with his methodical observations on "plausible historical sequence" and "psychological credibility."[13] He was little interested, however, in reconstructing positive history; hence, the attempt to retrieve Jesus' horizons, perspectives, and purposes, and precisely in the light of this retrieval to raise the question of historicity respecting gospel traditions out of harmony with them, fell outside Strauss's purview. Nor did he concern himself with the history of the first Christian communities, which might have allowed him, not only to suspect (as he often did), but actually to establish, the correlation of distinctive post-Easter concerns with particular gospel traditions.

Contemporary efforts to do just these two things have so far provided the most secure way of ranging gospel traditions in the non-historicity column without methodical reliance on assumption. If, for example, it

---

[11] Joachim Jeremias, *New Testament Theology I. The Proclamation of Jesus*, trans. by John Bowden; London: SCM, 1971, pp. 1-37.

[12] Willi Marxsen, *The Beginnings of Christology*, trans. P. Achtemeier; Philadelphia: Fortress, 1969, p. 8.

[13] David Friedrich Strauss, *The Life of Jesus Critically Examined*, trans. by George Eliot; London: SCM 1972, pp. 87-91.

is possible to recover the eschatological schema supposed by the words of Jesus and if according to this schema there was a material coincidence of the day of the Son of man (resurrection, exaltation, parousia) with the last judgment and the reign of God,[14] then gospel texts, in the measure in which they reflect the expectation of an interim between, say, the glorification of Jesus and the last judgment (in accord with the whole of post-Easter Christian eschatology) are non-historical. Closely related to this is the distance between two conceptions of the entry of the gentiles into salvation: by the eschatological pilgrimage and by the world mission.[15] Gospel texts, in the measure in which they reflect the expectation of a world mission, are unhistorical. A positive reconstruction of the origins of the world mission leads correlatively to the same result. Despite multiple and multiform attestation, both the supposition of the world mission and the explicitly universalist missionary mandate of the risen Christ are unhistorical.[16]

Linguistic indices to non-historicity are available for study especially in parables research and, in particular, in Jesus' "explanations" of his parables.[17] If the hypothesis could actually be established, rather than merely posited, that early Christian prophets speaking in the name of the exalted Christ supplied the church with sayings that were finally assimilated to the synoptic tradition, this too might be made to generate some concrete indices to non-historicity.[18]

In any case, gospel criticism of immediate relevance to historical research would be immensely improved by a steep reduction in the role of assumption and a correlative insistence that the critic offer a reasoned account of all judgments on historicity, laying out the full argument for his historical conclusions, and specifying the indices that he appeals to respecting the historicity and the non-historicity of data.

---

[14] See Meyer, *Aims of Jesus* 202-209.

[15] See J. Jeremias, *Jesus' Promise to the Nations*, trans. S. H. Hooke; London: SCM, 1958.

[16] See especially Anton Vögtle, "Die ekklesiologische Auftragsworte des Auferstandenen," in *Das Evangelium und die Evangelien. Beiträge zur Evangelienforschung*, Düsseldorf: Patmos, 1971, 243-252.

[17] See, for example, J. Jeremias, *The Parables of Jesus*, trans. S.H. Hooke; London: SCM, 1963, 77-79.

[18] Thus far, however, the case has not been made. See David Hill, "On the Evidence for the Creative Role of Christian Prophets," in *NTS* 20 (1974) 262-274. See also the verdict of *non constat* in David E. Aune, *Prophecy in Early Christianity and the Ancient Mediterranean World* (Grand Rapids: Eerdmans, 1983) pp. 142-145.

II

The survey of issues offered above has been swift and schematic, but we can take time now to reflect on objections and, in view of them, to reconsider whether the indices to the historicity of gospel data are in fact up to the task for which they have been devised. In two widely noticed essays M. D. Hooker has made a series of trenchant observations on this topic.[19] The following is a summary of the first essay.

The knowledge that historical investigation of Jesus aims at is of what is characteristic of him, whereas "the traditio-historical method" (discontinuity with early Christianity and originality vis-à-vis Judaism) yields only what is unique to him. The method is effective, moreover, only on condition of "a fairly confident knowledge of both areas" (early Christianity and the Judaism contemporary with it), a condition quite imperfectly fulfilled. To say that there is no known parallel in Judaism and Christianity to some datum of the gospel tradition is an argument from silence and should be regarded as such. Further, the method dictates its own conclusions, inevitably producing a picture (e.g., an unmessianic Jesus) in keeping with the assumption of dissimilarity. The application of the method is bound to be subjective, especially when a rider is attached to dissimilarity, namely, that to be historical a datum must not only differ from Judaism and Christianity but also be "at home" in first-century Palestine.

The addition of the principle of "coherence" (data that cohere with authentic material may themselves be accepted as authentic) to that of "dissimilarity" invites a further exercise of subjectivity: it may well be that our judgments of coherence and incoherence fail to reflect accurately the mentality of first-century Palestine, which is what counts here. Again, any errors in the results obtained by the "dissimilarity" principle are liable to be magnified by the principle of "coherence." Finally, practitioners of these methods apply them selectively, so that the real criterion of judgment is the critic's particular way of construing the data in question.

Debate about "the burden of proof" is appropriate only on extremist suppositions (e.g., that the gospels give us straightforward historical reports of Jesus' words, or that Jesus himself said nothing sufficiently memorable to have come down to us). More appropriately, the burden

---

[19] M.D. Hooker, "Christology and Methodology," in *NTS* 17 (1970-71) 480-487; eadem, *"On Using the Wrong Tool,"* in *Theology* 75 (1972) 570-581.

of proof lies on each scholar who offers a judgment on any part of the material.

The conclusion of the article is a plea against "dogmatism" and an argument, first, in favor of acknowledging other principles in addition to dissimilarity and coherence (multiple attestation and what we have called above "linguistic indices"); second, in favor of applying criteria positively, not negatively (whereas the presence of an index counts in favor of historicity, its absence does not of itself count against it); third, in favor of putting a premium on convergence; fourth, in favor of insisting on a reasonable "pedigree" for gospel material (a historically plausible account of its origin), whether it be adjudged historical or not. The article ends with a word suggesting that Jesus himself used the expression "Son of man" and questioning the assumption that he made no direct messianic claims.

The second essay, though it eventually goes over the same matter and makes the same points, begins differently and especially ends differently. It begins by focusing on the failure to observe how severely limited form criticism is as a tool of inquiry into the origin and historical reliability of gospel materials; and it ends by focusing on the failure of New Testament scholars to "draw the logical conclusion" from "the inadequacy of their tools."

What is this logical conclusion? It is this: the answers that the New Testament critic gives to his historical questions about Jesus

> are very largely the result of his own presuppositions and prejudices. If he approaches the material with the belief that it is largely the creation of the early Christian communities, then he will interpret it in that way. If he assumes that the words of the Lord were faithfully remembered and passed on, then he will be able to find criteria which support him.[20]

To be sure, we need working hypotheses, but they "are only hypotheses," and as for "assured results," "there are none."

Recently, E.E. Ellis has confirmed that the indices to historicity can produce no "assured results," as "the devastating critique of M. Hooker has shown."[21] Some years earlier a more discriminating comment was made by J.B. Muddiman: "it is not clear whether [Dr. Hooker's] complaint is against the criterion of dissimilarity as such, or against its misapplication."[22] Indeed, this ambiguity pervades both

---

[20] "On Using the Wrong Tool," p. 581.

[21] E.E. Ellis, "Gospels Criticism," (see above note 1) p. 31.

[22] J.B. Muddiman, "Jesus and Fasting. Mark 2.18-22", in *Jésus aux origines* (see above, note 1), pp. 271-281, p. 271.

articles, and even if it seems to be resolved by the uncompromisingly negative conclusions of the second article (the scholar's tools are "inadequate" to his purposes and there are no "assured results"), it is not completely disposed of even here, for the wholesale theoretical repudiation of "assured results" has by no means led the writer to abandon personal assessments ("if my own assessment tends to be a more traditional one ...").[23] And there is, if not ambiguity, then simple oversight as well as rhetorical overkill in the final conclusion; for, although it is true that the critic's historical judgment is settled not by obedience to some "criterion" but by his "own understanding of the situation," and, above all, true that conclusions on the historical Jesus are bound to cohere with premises on the origin and character of the gospel tradition, it is obviously untrue that to have one's "own understanding of the situation" is inevitably to indulge in prejudice or wishful thinking, and that any set of premises on the origin and character of the gospel tradition is mere assumption, one set being no better nor worse than another. The good observations in both articles remain good, but their effect is somewhat offset by disregard of the last-mentioned home truths.

The result, then, is ambiguous. Some critical assessments are proposed as preferable to others; on the other hand, all of them are taken in the end to be "highly speculative" and hypothetical. The chaotically divergent opinions in the scholarly community "cannot all be right — though they may well all be wrong."[24]

At the root of the troubled consciousness barely disguised by this bleakly negative conclusion lies the omnipresent and unelucidated issue of "subjectivity," one of the few topics on which New Testament scholars sound almost unanimous. Everyone warns against subjectivity. The trouble with "the traditio-historical method" is that "its application is bound to be subjective,"[25] and when we turn to the principle of coherence "subjectivity is even more of a danger."[26] We should try, tentatively, to locate the most plausible *Sitz im Leben* for each text, but "always remembering the danger of subjectivity."[27] Again, "subjectivity" is the flaw in Bultmann's suggestion "that authentic teaching can be guaranteed by the presence of 'the distinctive eschatological temper which characterized the preaching of Jesus.'"[28] Though Muddi-

---

[23] "On Using the Wrong Tool," p. 580.
[24] Ibid., p. 581.
[25] "Christology and Methodology," p. 482; "Wrong Tool" p. 576.
[26] "Christology" p. 483; "Wrong Tool," p. 576.
[27] "Christology" p. 487.
[28] "Wrong Tool" p. 576.

man picked out the ambiguity that ran through the critique of dissimilarity, he nonetheless heartily commended the cautionary notes frequently sounded against "the practical danger of subjectivism."[29]

The situation, then, appears to be this: for over a hundred years New
Testament scholars, conscious of the need for objective historical
judgments, have been devising historical "criteria" and trying to make
judgments in accord with them. Some critics have acutely observed how
imperfect, if not futile, this ostensible escape from subjectivity has
turned out to be. They have concluded, at least in theory and often
against the better judgment evidenced in their practice, that the critical
enterprise is riddled to its foundations with prejudice and powerless to
produce solid results. If the tools of even the most rigorous critics fail
to eliminate subjectivity, what other conclusion can there be?

III

Another conclusion becomes not only possible but necessary as soon
as objectivity is brought into relation with its conditions. Central
among these conditions is a subject capable of cognitional self-transcendence: capable, that is, of going beyond image and symbol, supposition
and conjecture, wishful thinking and peer-group thinking, to the act of
affirming what is so. Admittedly, once truth is reached, it is intentionally
independent of the subject that reached it: that is self-transcendence
and the goal of inquiry. But the ontological home of truth is the
subject. The goal is not reached apart from a demanding process, as
the drive to truth reveals itself in wonder, converts wondering into
questioning and questioning into question-answering, solicits reflection
on the answers, and climaxes in the act of judging them to be certainly
or probably true or false. All these are activities of the subject and there
is no objectivity without all of them. Truth, in fine, ripens on the tree of
the subject, and objectivity is the fruit of subjectivity at its most intense
and persistent.

Why have we ever thought otherwise? No doubt, because objectivity
is relative to the actual process of knowing, and to the everyday world
of common sense this process is far from transparent. Still, intelligence
is not limited to the perspectives and procedures of common sense.
With help,[30] we can learn to catch ourselves in the act of knowing, and

[29] Muddiman, op. cit. p. 271.
[30] See Bernard Lonergan, *Insight. A Study of Human Understanding*, New York:
Longmans 1958; *Method in Theology* New York: Herder & Herder, 1972, pp. 3-25, 57-99.

so come to the realization that knowing is a structured manifold having
an empirical component (data), an intelligent component (questioning,
construing, defining), and a rational component (marshalling evidence,
reflecting, judging). If the process of coming to know is manifold, so
correspondingly is objectivity. Its empirical component is the givenness
of data; its intelligent component is insight, or rather the demand
expressed by a question and answered by an insight; its rational
component is the further demand for sufficient evidence that the answer
is true, met by the assembling of evidence and the reflective grasp of it
as sufficient.

If one's suppositions about knowing correspond to the views of
empiricists or positivists, objectivity will be reduced to its empirical
component. Then the big danger will be "subjectivity"; and if despite
heroic effort subjectivity cannot be eliminated, it will appear that great
projects (historical critique, for instance) must, unhappily, surrender
their claims. If one's suppositions about knowing correspond to the
views of idealists, objectivity will be reduced to its intelligent component
(e.g., the internal coherence of insight). Only if one's views tally with
those of critical realism will objectivity be acknowledged as the achievement of a full and ordered subjectivity, subjectivity that attends to data
but goes beyond data to questions, that cherishes insight but goes
beyond insight to truth.

If the conversion of "subjectivity" from a boo-word to a hurrah-
word is new to New Testament criticism, this only betrays the durable
underground attachment of New Testament studies to positivism. But
the suppositions of positivist theory and the practice of historical
criticism do not correlate. Regardless of what theoretical hunches may
be lurking in his subconscious, the practicing critic shows by his
performance how well he knows that success hinges not just on data,
but on "his own understanding of the situation." He is somehow
aware, even if he fails to bring it to thematic articulation, that everything he knows — his whole fund of experience and range of understanding and hard-won equilibrium of judgment — is quite properly at
the beck and call of all his critical endeavors.

Indices to the historicity of data do not change this; they illustrate it,
for these indices are just heuristic resources epitomizing discrete, more
or less useful, patterns of observation and inference. They function in
criticism not entirely unlike the way proverbs function in common
sense. Faced with an issue that must quickly be settled one way or
another, one might wonder which of two proverbs fits the situation:
"He who hesitates is lost"? Or "Look before you leap"? If added

insight is needed to know which piece of wisdom is relevant here and now, so in the criticism of historical data, when the indices offer mixed signals, added insight is required to know which factors tip the balance. This added insight is not a misbegotten intrusion of subjectivity; it is that without which a true judgment is simply impossible. And just as it is no defect in the indices to historicity that they sometimes offer mixed signals, so it is no defect in the critic that he should refuse to treat indices as rules to be obeyed. The defect lies rather in the theorizing that establishes this illusory dilemma: either the burden of objectivity must be borne by "criteria" expected to eliminate the bothersome business of the historian's "subjectivity," or we must stoically admit that answers are just products of presupposition and prejudice, assured results are fictitious, and all parties to the critical debate may be wrong.

The positivism of a hundred years ago called on "the sources" to turn the trick. A hankering after "objective sources," nourished on the illusion that access to history should be mediated not by the intelligence of the historian but by sources equipped to do his job for him, dominated the quest of the historical Jesus from the 1860s to the first World War. The disillusionment that followed was eventually relieved by a new faith in "method"; and though the earlier critical reaction ("blame the sources") has now given way to a new critical reaction ("blame the methods"), the fact is that the deep problem has lain neither in New Testament sources nor in historical-critical methods but in some cumbersome philosophical luggage — a medley of inadequate and misleading views of knowledge and objectivity. Bernard Lonergan has identified the core of the problem as

> an exceedingly stubborn and misleading myth concerning reality, objectivity, and human knowledge. The myth is that knowing is like seeing, that objectivity is seeing what is there to be seen and not seeing what is not there, and that the real is what is out there now to be looked at.[31]

But, as knowing is not seeing, so the criteria of objective knowing are not those of successful seeing. Objectivity is not a matter of keeping "subjectivity" from interference with seeing what is there and not seeing what is not. It is a matter, rather, of bringing subjectivity to full flower, i.e., to the point of cognitional self-transcendence. This, to be sure, is a challenge. Objectivity is the fruit not just of subjectivity but of authentic subjectivity. Owing to the heritage of human bias — unconscious motivation, individual and group egoism, the illusory omnicompetence of common sense — subjectivity is easily inauthentic. But whereas

---

[31] Lonergan, *Method* 238.

positivist theory is at a total loss here and can only urge that we all avoid dogmatism, critical realism has something both profound and useful to say.

Profound: for, the intentionality analysis at the heart of critical realism brings to light the unity of the human spirit, namely, its eros for self-transcendence. The distinct dimensions of self-transcendence — intellectual, moral, religious — are so interrelated that, when they occur within a single subject, the moral sublates the intellectual dimension, and the religious dimension sublates the moral.[32] Genetically, on the other hand, the order will often be just the opposite. The self-transcendence that is the love of God opens up the whole sphere of values; these include the value of believing religious truths; and in such belief lie impulses not only for the moral life but for the break with cognitional myth.

Useful: for, the same intentionality analysis grounds an effective hermeneutic of suspicion respecting bias, evasions, screening devices, and the ideological rationalizing of alienations — not only in others but in oneself.[33] This will not banish the perspectivism of history, but it is the beginning of a constructive response to subsurface inauthenticity in historical scholarship.

Ben F. MEYER

---

[32] Lonergan, ibid., 241-243.
[33] Lonergan, "The Ongoing Genesis of Methods," in *Studies in Religion/Sciences réligieuses* 6 (1976-77) 341-355.

RESPONSE TO B.F. MEYER

Ben Meyer's paper is a valiant attempt to cut the Gordian knot in the present impasse over the use of "criteria" in the critical reconstruction of the history of the pre-Easter Jesus. (Meyer prefers the word "indices," like R.F. Collins, whom however he does not credit for the term[1]). The present controversy concerns: (1) which criteria are most appropriate; and (2) whether the criteria are adequate at all. On topic (1) Meyer has in mind Käsemann's insistence that the index of dissimilarity is the sole viable one, and on topic (2) he has in mind the strictures of Professor Hooker in her two essays of 1970/71 and 1972.

After giving an account of the way the indices are properly employed and after considering Hooker's objection about the subjectivity with which the indices of historicity are applied, Meyer offers a way in which subjectivity may be utilized (instead of rejected) as a component and condition of objectivity. He calls it "critical realism."

The main thesis is thus epistemological. This I do not feel competent to judge though I would like to say something about the application of the various indices, and ask Dr. Meyer whether my use of them meets his requirement of critical realism.

It has been my contention for a long time, in fact since 1964 when I wrote my *Critical Introduction to the New Testament* (and I returned to the subject in an article in the Harvey McArthur Festschrift in 1982)[2] that the limitations of the various indices have to be recognized and that they have to be applied successively at particular stages of the investigation. The index of dissimilarity, as Meyer observes, and as I have myself stated, is open to the limitation occasioned by the fact that Jesus was on one hand a first century Palestinian Jew and on the other hand the founder of the Christian movement. Consequently there were obviously many topics on which Jesus agreed with his Palestinian Jewish contemporaries on the one hand and with the post-Easter Church on the other. Nevertheless it is fair to assume as the creative founder of a new movement within Judaism there were matters on

---

[1] Raymond F. Collins, *Introduction to the New Testament* (Garden City, NY: Doubleday, 1983), 181f.

[2] R.H. Fuller, "The Criterion of Dissimilarity: The Wrong Tool?" *Christological Perspectives* (ed. Robert E. Berkey and Sarah A. Edwards; New York: Pilgrim, 1982), 42-48.

which he differed from his contemporaries. Equally as the founder of a community which derived one of its major impulses from the Easter event which occurred after the founder's earthly life, there must have been matters over which Jesus differed from his followers. That justifies our use of the index of dissimilarity for the initial stages of the investigation. Without denying the historicity of other materials, but accepting the burden of proof at this initial stage, we seek first to establish a probably authentic nucleus of Jesus material. The next stage is to widen out the material by including from within the Jesus tradition all that is coherent within this central core of probably authentic material. We must of course recognize that some of the material which is not coherent with the central core may also be authentic, for presumably Jesus was capable of inconsistency on occasion. But at this stage we have no means of knowing whether such incoherent material is authentic.

The other indices — multiple attestation and the linguistic and environmental tests — do not enable us to bridge the gap between the earliest post-Easter community and Jesus. But they are helpful for the more limited task of carrying the tradition back from redaction and later tradition to the earlier post-Easter tradition. Where however this material corroborates or is consistent with what we have discovered thus far from the application of the indices of dissimilarity and of coherence, there we have additional confirmation of our reconstruction. Further, anything that is new yet coherent can be added to the reconstruction, so that at this third stage the index of coherence comes in again.

It is to be noted that although earlier Meyer uttered doubts about the index of coherence, nevertheless he applied it cautiously later on when he argued (p. 553) that Jesus material which implies an interim between resurrection, exaltation, and parousia on the one hand with the last judgment and the Kingdom of God on the other was not coherent with Jesus' eschatological stance and therefore was unauthentic. So, properly applied, the index of coherence (and note, I apply it positively) can be a useful tool. The same applies as we have seen to the indices of language and environment. By themselves they can do no more than take us back to the Palestinian Church, Jerusalem or Galilee. But when applied to the material taken into the stock of authentic Jesus material thus far they can act as supplementary confirmation.

Meyer makes the valuable point that the later tradition may be historically valid, even at times providing an authentic corrective to earlier tradition. Along the same line we might point out that multiple attestation by itself is not an excluding index. For instance the Jesus saying about a prophet not perishing outside of Jerusalem is not to be discounted as unauthentic merely because it has only single attestation (Special Luke). Earliest tradition — not only later correctives, as Meyer rightly contends — may be preserved solely in later traditions.

When our tentative reconstruction of authentic Jesus material has been made we can only claim probability, not certainty, and we must, in agreement with Meyer, avoid dogmatic self-assurance about our results. We must always be open to correction from our colleagues and must always be prepared to admit we might have been wrong. Meyer's point that we often don't know is well taken. Moreover we must never say that Jesus tradition which we have been unable to incorporate into our body of authentic material is necessarily unauthentic (even Meyer did this on one occasion when he argued that sayings implying an interim between Jesus' vindication and the final consummation are unhistorical). We can never claim more than probability, even for our negative results.

I have striven to apply the indices positively rather than negatively. But it is in the area of Christology where the indices have received mostly negative application. All christological titles are commonly eliminated from the Jesus tradition as the product of the post-Easter community. Acts 2:36 and Romans 1:3-4 provide acceptable grounds for this, but ought we not to allow for the possibility that certain titles became christological in a post-Easter sense which were already current in a different sense in the pre-Easter period? Thus there seems to be some emerging consensus that Jesus understood himself as the anointed eschatological prophet in accordance with Isaiah 61:1 during the pre-Easter period, and therefore as Messiah-Christ in this sense.[3] After Easter he was exalted to be the Christos in a kingly sense (Acts 2:36). Similarly, the term kyrios, which was certainly used as a title of majesty by the post-Easter Church, may originally, as Hahn has argued,[4] have been used as an honorific address to the pre-Easter Jesus as a Rabbi.

Perhaps the vexed question of the Son of man can be tackled along these lines. If Norman Perrin is correct in arguing that the future Son of man sayings were products of pesher development in the post-Easter community, could it be that the pre-Easter Jesus used "Son of man" as a designation of himself as eschatological prophet? In that case some of

[3] See e.g. Edward Schillebeeckx, *Jesus* (New York: Seabury, 1979), 186-87; A.E. Harvey, *Jesus and the Constraints of History* (Philadelphia: Westminster, 1982), 120-51; Rudolf Pesch, *Das Markusevangelium* (Herders Kommentar: Basel/Freiburg/Wien: Zweiter Teil, 1977), 28-47.

[4] Ferdinand Hahn, *Christologische Hoheitstitel* (Göttingen: Vandenhoeck & Ruprecht, 1963), 81-95.

the present sayings and perhaps some of the suffering sayings which
seem to be devoid of elements showing a knowledge of the detailed
passion narrative could well be authentic. Such a suffering saying
would be "The Son of man is to be delivered up into the hands of
men." Any application of the index of dissimilarity should respect the
continuity as well as the discontinuity between the pre-Easter Jesus and
the post-Easter kerygma.

Reginald H. FULLER

AFTERWORD

Dr. Fuller offers a differentiated account of the roles that diverse
indices to historicity can play in the course of an investigation. If these
roles are correlated less with genetic stages in the acquisition of
knowledge than with expository stages in a maximally cogent presentation of evidence, this strikes me as a positively helpful observation.
Actual investigation is apt to begin anywhere and to proceed by
unpredictable twists and turns, and the diverse indices are serviceable
for quite various tasks in this process. In time there supervenes on this
process a reflective grasp of the relative weight of evidence and of its
internal relationships. This impinges on the investigation and prepares
the way for an effective strategy of exposition.

I argued for "index" as distinct from "criterion" in *The Aims of Jesus*
(1979). Fr. Raymond F. Collins reviewed the book in *Louvain Studies*
(1979), particularly commending my treatment of these questions; he
also included the book in his bibliography on historical-critical methodology (*Introduction to the New Testament*, 1983). I would hazard the
guess that Fr. Collins adopted the term "indices" from me. In any case,
Dr. Fuller is quite mistaken in supposing that I adopted it from Fr.
Collins.

In the part of my paper that dealt with Dr. Hooker's work, I alluded
to a view that not uncommonly travels under the rubric "coherence":
"data that cohere with authentic material may themselves be accepted
as authentic." This "principle" strikes me as very doubtful. In practice,
however, "coherence" is sometimes used in a stronger sense: authentic
material (A) probably implies or entails some other material (B).
"Coherence" in this more rigorous usage (where the word is a mis-
nomer for implication or entailment) is very relevant indeed to historicity. Now we may take up a distinct issue. I hold that those gospel texts
are unhistorical which imply that Jesus posited an interim between

vindication (resurrection) and the final consummation when the reign of God comes ("the day of the Son of man"). The ground of this judgment is the recovery (by C.H. Dodd and Joachim Jeremias) of Jesus' own eschatological scenario, which admits of no such interim. Since I take the proposals of Dodd and Jeremias to be solidly probable, it is imposed on me with equal probability that gospel texts implying such an interim (in accord with the post-Easter church) are non-historical. Compare Collingwood's view of Neronian policy toward Britain, with his acceptance of the testimony of Tacitus and his rejection of that of Suetonius. Collingwood does not insist on "necessity" or "certainty"—just intelligibility. The same for me. There is no misuse here of "coherence."

It is quite accurate to observe that I am intent on issues of knowledge. Even when the specifics of method are analyzed and refined and seemingly agreed upon, they are differently interpreted and applied by scholars who are —though they may not be reflexively aware of it— naive realists, or positivists, or Neo-Kantians, or whatever. Despite a largely common terminology, each group consciously or unconsciously interprets every critical resource differently. New Testament scholars draw on ostensibly common methods and are bewildered by the chaos of conflicting results. This is the situation not only in historical-Jesus research and other historical research, but in efforts to resolve the Synoptic problem, in exegesis, and in biblical theology. The flight to semiotics, structuralism, and literary criticism, to social description and sociological analysis, does not relieve this chaos in the slightest. Nothing short of systematic dialectic grounded in a satisfactory account of knowledge will do.

B.F. MEYER

DIE ÜBERLIEFERUNGEN DER ALTEN KIRCHE ÜBER DAS VERHÄLTNIS DER EVANGELIEN

Im folgenden geht es darum, die altkirchlichen Zeugnisse über die Evangelien auf ihre "einleitungswissenschaftlichen" Aussagen abzuhören. Die kanonsgeschichtlichen, auslegungsgeschichtlichen und übergreifenden theologiegeschichtlichen Aspekte werden daher nur angesprochen, soweit sie zu dieser begrenzten Fragestellung etwas austragen.[1] Auch eine Forschungsgeschichte ist nicht beabsichtigt; allein die Nachzeichnung der Interpretationen des Papiasfragments könnte eine kleine Monographie ergeben. Baur und Hilgenfeld, Holtzmann, Zahn und andere haben ihre Auffassungen vom Verhältnis der Synoptiker auch in Auseinandersetzung mit Papias entfaltet.[2] Die in diesem Jahrhundert erschienenen neutestamentlichen Einleitungen zeigen ein kontinuierliches Zurückgehen des Interesses an den patristischen Überlieferungen; zum einen glaubte man sie schlecht und recht mit der vorherrschend gewordenen Zwei-Quellen-Theorie versöhnen zu können, zum anderen konnte vieles als legendarisch entlarvt und damit als historisch irrelevant beiseitegeschoben werden. Wenn W.G. Kümmel es für "geraten" hält, "die Papiasnotizen trotz ihres hohen Alters bei der Untersuchung der literarischen Beziehung der Synoptiker außer Betracht zu lassen",[3] dürfte er die im historisch-kritischen Lager verbreitete Stimmung wiedergeben.

Im Zusammenhang mit dem zerbrechenden Konsens über die Zwei-Quellen-Theorie beginnen auch die altkirchlichen Quellen eine neue

---

[1] Grundlegend: Th. Zahn, *Geschichte des neutestamentlichen Kanons*, 2 Bde (Erlangen 1888; Erlangen und Leipzig 1890); J. Leipoldt, *Geschichte des neutestamentlichen Kanons*, I, (Leipzig 1907); H.v. Campenhausen, *Die Entstehung der christlichen Bibel* (Tübingen 1968). Einiges ist in meinen Arbeiten *Die Widersprüche zwischen den Evangelien: Ihre polemische und apologetische Behandlung in der Alten Kirche bis zu Augustin* (WUNT 13; Tübingen 1971) und *Die Pluralität der Evangelien als theologisches und exegetisches Problem in der Alten Kirche* (TC 3; Bern 1978) behandelt worden, die ich im folgenden weiterführe. Eine knappen, aber instruktiven Überblick über die wichtigsten Quellen gibt jetzt W. Schmithals, *Einleitung in die drei ersten Evangelien* (Berlin, New York 1985) 30-43.

[2] Vgl. R.H. Fuller, "Baur versus Hilgenfeld: A Forgotten Chapter in the Debate on the Synoptic Problem", NTS 24 (1977/78) 355-370. Eine gute Spezialbibliographie enthält die mir erst kurz vor Abschluß des Manuskriptes zugänglich gewordene Arbeit von U.H.J. Körtner, *Papias von Hierapolis. Ein Beitrag zur Geschichte des frühen Christentums*, (FRLANT 133; Göttingen 1983) 349-357.

[3] W.G. Kümmel, *Einleitung in das Neue Testament* (20. Aufl. Heidelberg 1980) 29.

Bedeutung zu gewinnen.[4] Sie scheinen andere Lösungen der Synoptischen Frage zu begünstigen.

So ist eine erneute Prüfung angebracht. Sie muß feststellen, was eine
Quelle sagt — dabei sind alle Optionen offenzuhalten —, und warum
sie dies sagt, d.h. ob ältere Informationen bloß weitergegeben oder aus
einer aktuellen Fragestellung heraus uminterpretiert oder ob "Informationen" gar neu geschaffen werden.

I

Papias bei Euseb (H.E. 3.39. 15-16) ist das älteste außerkanonische
Zeugnis für die Evangelien des Markus und Matthäus. Vor mehr als
100 Jahren rechnete Wilh. Weiffenbach es "zu den best misshandelten
und kräftigst missverstandenen Ueberbleibseln des christlichen Alter-
tums"[5] und beobachtete, "dass Papias (genauer: der Presbyter) jedes-
mal merkwürdigerweise genau das sagt, was der betreffende Ausleger
oder Kritiker für *seine* Anschauung des synoptischen 'Räthsels' nöthig
hat".[6] Da der unmittelbare Kontext fehlt, ist schon unklar, ob Papias
hier apologetisch auf Vorwürfe gegen die Evangelien antwortet[7] oder
ob er selbst die schriftliche Überlieferung kritisieren wollte[8], um die
φωνὴ ζῶσα aufzuwerten; die Frage muß offenbleiben. Aber auch der
kirchengeschichtliche Kontext des ganzen Werkes ist unklar; Anset-
zungen zwischen 90[9] und 160[10] werden vorgeschlagen. Nun hängt die
Datierung u.a. vom Verhältnis des Papias zu den von ihm genannten
Autoritäten ab. Für die Frühdatierung müßte man votieren, wenn

---

[4] G. Kennedy, "Classical and Christian Source Criticism", *The Relationships Among
the Gospels. An Interdisciplinary Dialogue* (ed. W.O. Walker, Jr; San Antonio 1978) 125-
155, bes. 147-152; W.R. Farmer, "The Patristic Evidence Reexamined: A Response to
George Kennedy", *New Synoptic Studies. The Cambridge Gospel Conference and Beyond*
(ed. W.R. Farmer; Macon, Georgia, 1983) 3-15; G.G. Gamba, "A Further Reexamination of Evidence from the Early Tradition", *New Synoptic Studies*, 17-35; D. Peabody,
"Augustine and the Augustinian Hypothesis: A Reexamination of Augustine's Thought
in *De consensu evangelistarum*", *New Synoptic Studies*, 37-64.

[5] W. Weiffenbach, *Die Papias-Fragmente über Marcus und Matthäus eingehend exegetisch untersucht und kritisch gewürdigt* (Berlin 1878) 1.

[6] Ibid.

[7] So Th. Zahn, *Geschichte des Neutestamentlichen Kanons I*, 222; W.C. van Unnik,
Oog en oor. Criteria voor de eerste samenstelling van het Nieuwe Testament, Rede ter
gelegenheid van de 337e dies natalis der Rijksuniversiteit te Utrecht, 1973, 15.

[8] So bereits A. Hilgenfeld, "Papias von Hierapolis", ZWT 18(1875) 239-242.

[9] E. Gutwenger, "Papias – eine chronologische Studie", ZKT 69 (1947) 385-416.

[10] A. Harnack, *Geschichte der altchristlichen Literatur bis Eusebius*, T. 2/1, 2. Aufl.
(Leipzig 1897; unv. Nachdruck 1958) 356-358: zwischen 140 u. 160; H. Kraft, *Kirchen-
väterlexikon* (München 1966) 407: zwischen 130 u. 160. Weiteres bei U.H.J. Körtner,
Papias von Hierapolis, 88-94.

Papias tatsächlich ein Schüler des Evangelisten Johannes gewesen wäre. In diesem Sinne hat schon Irenäus das Papiaszeugnis verstanden. Dazu nimmt man an, daß der unter den Aposteln genannte Johannes identisch mit dem später genannten Presbyter Johannes sei, der noch am Leben gewesen sei, als Papias seine 5 Bücher schrieb, da von ihm und Aristion im Präsens (ἄτε ... λέγουσιν ...) gesprochen werde; weiterhin helfen 2. und 3. Johannesbrief zur Identifikation, da sich deren Verfasser, der natürlich der Herrenjünger sei, als ὁ πρεσβύτερος bezeichne.[11] Aber die Annahme daß der Jünger Johannes, der zusammen mit Andreas, Petrus, Philippus usw. genannt wird, derselbe sei wie der nachher mit Aristion zusammen genannte Presbyter Johannes, ist schon von Euseb zu Recht abgelehnt worden (H.E. III 39,5), neuerdings z.B. J. Munck, F.-M. Braun, G. Bornkamm, J. Regul, J. Schmid;[12] es ist nicht einzusehen, warum derselbe Mann zweimal genannt wird, beim zweiten Mal mit der zusätzlichen Bezeichnung ὁ πρεσβύτερος. Natürlich hat die dem Presbyter und Aristion beigegebene Prädikation als Jünger des Herrn (τοῦ κυρίου μαθηταί) für Verwirrung gesorgt; aber man wird damit zu rechnen haben, daß der Begriff μαθητής in der Alten Kirche gekennzeichnet ist "durch das Eindringen jenes griech[isch]-hell[enistischen] Gebrauchs von μαθητής, der die ideelle Zugehörigkeit bei dem Fehlen einer unmittelbaren Verbindung feststellt".[13] Für die Stellung des Papias ist m.E. die Reihenfolge der befragten Zeugen entscheidend: Er befragt Leute, die den Presbytern nachgefolgt waren, was diese von den Aposteln berichteten. Die Traditionskette ist also Apostel-Presbyter-Presbyterschüler-Papias.[14] Papias gehört somit an den Übergang von der 3. zur 4. christlichen Generation. Die Datierung um 110 n.Chr. dürfte am angemessensten sein. Zu diesem Zeitpunkt wird man histo-

---

[11] J. Chapman, *John the Presbyter and the Fourth Gospel* (Oxford 1911) 37-40.

[12] J. Munck, "Presbyters and disciples of the Lord in Papias", HTR 52(1959) 238; F.-M. Braun, *Jean le théologien et son évangile dans l'église ancienne* (EBib; Paris 1959) 357-362; G. Bornkamm, "πρέσβυς κτλ.", TWNT 6 (1959) 676; J. Regul, *Die antimarcionitischen Evangelienprologe* (Freiburg 1969) 117; A. Wikenhauser - J. Schmid, *Einleitung in das Neue Testament* (6. Aufl., Freiburg 1973) 211, 307-308.

[13] K.H. Rengstorf, "μανθάνω κτλ.", TWNT 4 (1942) 464. — Th. Mommsen, "Papianisches", ZNW 3 (1902) 156-159, hat diese oft emendierte Stelle durch die Athetese der Worte heilen wollen; L. Abramowski, "Die 'Erinnerungen der Apostel' bei Justin", *Das Evangelium und die Evangelien* (ed. P. Stuhlmacher; WUNT 28; Tübingen 1983) 348. Anm. 28, hat diesen Vorschlag scharfsinnig erneuert. Wahrscheinlich ist ihre Erklärung, es handle sich um eine "Irenäisierung" des Euseb-Textes, richtig. Ältere Konjekturen referiert und kritisiert U.H.J. Körtner, *Papias von Hierapolis*, 72-75.

[14] P. Corssen, "Warum ist das Vierte Evangelium für eine Werk des Apostels Johannes erklärt worden?" ZNW 2(1901) 206-207; N. Brox, *Offenbarung, Gnosis und gnostischer Mythos bei Irenäus von Lyon* (Salzburg und München 1966) 148 Anm. 107.

rische Erinnerungen noch nicht ausschließen können. Die Analyse des Papiaszitates hat schon längst zu der Annahme geführt, nur der erste Satz sei Zitat des Presbyters, das folgende dagegen Erläuterung aus der Feder des Papias.[15] Diese These ist zwar an sich einleuchtend, aber für die Gesamtauffassung nicht erheblich.

Vom Markusevangelium wird gesagt, es gehe auf die Lehrvorträge des Petrus zurück. Markus wird als Mitarbeiter, doch wohl als Dolmetscher[16] des Petrus vorgestellt, der aus dem Gedächtnis die von Petrus erwähnten Worte und Taten des Herrn aufschrieb. Damit wird die mangelnde τάξις seines Evangeliums entschuldigt.

Beide Aussagen sind schwierig zu erklären.

1) Woher kommt die Beanspruchung petrinischer Autorität für Markus? Kann sie einfach aus 1. Petr. 5,13 herausgesponnen worden sein?[17] Daß die Kritik hier vorsichtiger sein sollte, kann an Ph. Vielhauers Urteil gezeigt werden. Er fragt "Wie kaum es ... dazu, daß dieser Autor [sc. Markus] zu Petrus in Beziehung gesetzt wurde? Das Buch selbst bot dazu keinen Anlaß; denn Petrus spielt in ihm eine bedeutend weniger prominente Rolle als bei Matthäus und Lukas; ohne die Papiasnotiz käme niemand auf die Idee, im Markusevangelium persönliche Erinnerungen des Petrus zu suchen und zu finden";[18] das läßt gegen Vielhauers Intention fast so etwas wie das "Unableitbarkeitskriterium" zur Anwendung kommen: eine "unerfindbare" Nachricht wird einen geschichtlichen Kern haben!

Auch wenn die Vorstellung des Papias sicher verkürzt ist und zu

---

[15] So schon H.J. Holtzmann, *Die synoptischen Evangelien* (Leipzig 1863) 243; A. Wikenhauser-J. Schmid, *Einleitung in das NT*, 211; dagegen schon W. Weiffenbach, *Die Papias-Fragmente ...*, 12-19. H.U.J. Körtner, *Papias von Hierapolis*, 207-208, rechnet nur mit geringfügigen Ergänzungen durch Papias.

[16] Diese allgemein akzeptierte Auffassung wird schon durch die gleich folgende Aussage über Matthäus begründet; dort ist ἑρμηνεύειν das Übersetzen des hebräischen (aramäischen) Matthäusevangeliums ins Griechische. Allgemeiner, i.S. von Mittelsmann, schon Th. Zahn, *Geschichte des Neutestamentlichen Kanons I*, 878-880; neuerdings J. Kürzinger, *Papias von Hierapolis und die Evangelien des Neuen Testaments* (Eichstädter Materialien 4; Regensburg 1983) 16. In diesem Band legt Kürzinger seine früheren Aufsätze vor, ergänzt um eine Ausgabe und Übersetzung der Texte und eine Bibliographie für 1960-1981.

[17] Z.B. J. Regul, *Die antimarcionitischen Evangelienprologe*, 96; U.H.J. Körtner, *Papias von Hierapolis*, 206-215.

[18] Ph. Vielhauer, *Geschichte der urchristlichen Literatur* (de Gruyter-Lehrbuch; durchges. Nachdruck Berlin-New York 1978) 260. — Die Gegenprobe liefert gewissermaßen W. Schenk, "Das 'Matthäusevangelium' als Petrusevangelium", BZ 27(1983) 58-80, der von dem — nicht unbegründeten — Eindruck her, Matthäus habe sein Werk "als 'Petrusevangelium' auszugeben und zu legitimieren" beabsichtigt (75), das Papiaszitat recht gewaltsam auf Matthäus uminterpretiert.

unmittelbar auf Petrusmemoiren schließt[19] — Vielhauers Urteil über die Papiasnotiz "historisch wertlos" ist sicher zu kurzgeschlossen.

2) Woran orientiert sich die Kritik an der τάξις des Markusevangeliums? Da Euseb nur noch eine Äußerung des Papias über Matthäus zitiert, könnte der Vergleich zwischen Matthäus und Markus die Kritik an Markus hervorgerufen haben.[20] Das ist aber doch unwahrscheinlich, da gerade die τάξις in beiden Evangelien weitgehend dieselbe ist.[21] Da das Problem der genauen Reihenfolge im Lukasprolog (Lk 1,-14) eine gewisse Rolle spielt, dachte man an Lukas als Norm.[22] Das wäre eher denkbar, obgleich der lukanische Aufriß der Geschichte Jesu dem markinischen sehr ähnlich ist.

So bleibt die wahrscheinlichste Annahme immer noch die, daß die ganz andere τάξις des Johannesevangeliums als Maßstab genommen wurde.[23]

Die angesichts des fragmentarischen Überlieferungsbestandes mißliche Frage nach dem Vergleichsmaßstab ließe sich umgehen, wenn man mit J. Kürzinger τάξις nicht als Reihenfolge, sondern als "literarische Kunstform" verstehen dürfte; dann ließe sich die ganze Äußerung dahingehend verstehen, "daß sich Papias mit seiner betonten Rechtfertigung das Markus gegen die Kritik und Geringschätzung wendet, die aus dem stilistischen und formkritischen Anspruch seiner rhetorisch äußerst empfindlichen Umwelt kam".[24] Der Maßstab, an dem Markus

---

[19] Mit M. Hengel, "Probleme des Markusevangeliums", *Das Evangelium und die Evangelien*, kann man an einem geschichtlichen Kern der Papiasnotiz festhalten, wenn man gleichzeitig der Tatsache Rechnung trägt, daß man "den Stoffen" anmerkt, "daß sie seit über einer Generation kerygmatisch geformt worden waren" (255).

[20] So zuletzt W.G. Kümmel, *Einleitung in das NT*, 28. — U.H.J. Körtner, *Papias von Hierapolis*, 212-213, zieht dies in Erwägung, meint aber, der Presbyter und Papias hätten das Markusevangelium "an einer absoluten Leben-Jesu-Vorstellung" gemessen, "welche unter anderem auch aus dem Mt gespeist sein kann, sich aber im übrigen verselbständigt hat" (213). Diese Auskunft ist nicht gerade naheliegend.

[21] Vgl. nur W.G. Kümmel, *Einleitung in das NT*, 33.

[22] J. Munck, "Die Tradition über das Matthäusevangelium bei Papias", *Neotestamentica et Patristica. Eine Freundesgabe, Herrn Prof. Dr. O. Cullmann zu seinem 60. Geburtstag überreicht* (NovTSup 6; Leiden 1962) 249-260; vorsichtige Zustimmung bei J. Regul, *Die antimarcionitischen Evangelienprologe*, 151-152.

[23] Ältere Literatur bei H. Merkel, *Die Widersprüche zwischen den Evangelien*, 47-48; neuerdings: M. Hengel, "Probleme des Markusevangeliums", 247-248. Ein — allerdings sehr spät bezeugtes — Testimonium dafür, daß Papias das Vierte Evangelium gekannt haben dürfte, bringt F. Siegert, "Unbeachtete Papiaszitate bei armenischen Schriftstellern", NTS 27(1981) 607-609. So scheint sich die alte, verbissen geführte Diskussion darüber, ob Papias das Johannesevangelium nicht gekannt oder gar ignoriert habe, oder ob Euseb eine diesbezügliche Äußerung des Papias unterdrückt habe, zugunsten der letzgenannten Annahme zu entscheiden.

[24] J. Kürzinger, *Papias von Hierapolis und die Evangelien des NT*, 14.

gemessen wird, wäre dann die "hebräische Darstellungsweise" des Matthäus. Diese Auslegung ist oft skeptisch aufgenommen worden; so äußert B. de Solages:

> Quelle que soit l'ingéniosité de son argumentation, elle laisse sceptique. Elle suppose Papias ... très occupé(s) de problèmes de style! (lui qui n'a pas été capable d'être clair!), alors que son texte, d'un bout à l'autre, le montre préoccupé surtout de vérité. Elle suppose aussi qu'Irénée (Adversus Haereses, III, I 1) qui était de la région, et avait d'autres renseignements (et toute la tradition patristique avec lui), a fait un contresens sur l'"'Εβραῖδι διαλέκτῳ" en comprenant qu'il s'agissait de la langue des Hébreux, alors qu'il s'agirait de leur manière d'écrire (Et quelle manière, dont personne ne parle à cette époque) etc. etc.[25]

Eine neue Hypothese, die allerdings schon im 19. Jahrhundert ähnlich vertreten worden war, hat G. Kennedy eingeführt: Markus habe ursprünglich nur Notizen über die Petruspredigten gemacht, welche er später als Grundlage seines Evangeliums verwendet habe.[26] Eine solche Differenzierung zwischen zwei Stufen finde ich im Texte freilich nirgends angedeutet. Auch das Clemensfragment bei Euseb, H.E. 2.15, bringt nichts, was an einen zweistufigen Entstehungsprozeß des Markusevangeliums denken ließe: Die Hörer des Petrus fordern zwar ein ὑπόμνημα, aber Markus liefert ihnen ein Evangelium, das sofort von Petrus für die kirchliche Verwendung approbiert wird! Auch die Wiedergabe der Clementstradition in H.E. VI 14,6 läßt an keine Vorstufe zum Markusevangelium denken.

Noch weniger ergibt das Matthäusfragment des Papias. Es behauptet, Matthäus habe 'Εβραῖδι διαλέκτῳ die λόγια zusammengestellt, die jeder so übersetzte, wie er es vermochte.

Einigkeit besteht wohl heute darüber, daß die seit Schleiermacher immer wieder vertretene Deutung auf die Logienquelle unzutreffend ist; spricht doch das Markusfragment ebenfalls von λόγια κυριακά.[27] Mit dieser Äußerung scheint Papias erklären zu wollen, warum es zwei Evangelien gibt, die beide auf Matthäus als Verfasser zurückgeführt

---

[25] B. de Solages, "Le témoignage de Papias", BLE 71(1970) 11 Anm. 24. Unter den weiteren ablehnenden Stellungnahmen finden sich W.G. Kümmel, *Einleitung in das NT*, 28-29; R. Pesch, *Das Markusevangelium* I (Freiburg 1976) 5; M. Hengel, "Probleme des Markusevangeliums", 244 Anm. 54; U.H.J. Körtner, *Papias von Hierapolis*, 158.203.208.

[26] G. Kennedy, "Classical and Christian Source Criticism", 147-150; F.C. Baur, *Kritische Untersuchungen über die kanonischen Evangelien, ihr Verhältnis zu einander, ihren Charakter und Ursprung* (Tübingen, 1847) 540.571: W. Weiffenbach, *Die Papias-Fragmente ...*, 99-135.

[27] J. Kürzinger, *Papias von Hierapolis und die Evangelien des NT*, 24-25; U.H.J. Körtner, *Papias von Hierapolis*, 154-156; R. Gryson, "A propos du témoignage de Papias sur Matthieu", *ETL* 41 (1965) 530-547 (ALBO 4,27, 1965).

werden und die gewisse Ähnlichkeiten, aber auch Divergenzen aufweisen. Ich halte es für denkbar, daß Papias das judenchristliche Ebionitenevangelium kannte. Es stellt im Frg. 1 den Zöllner Matthäus besonders heraus; in Frg. 2,4 und 5 zeigt es auffällige Berührungen mit dem kanonischen Matthäus,[28] und Irenäus schreibt, die Ebioniten benützen ausschließlich das Matthäusevangelium (Adv. haer. 3.11.7), ebenso Epiphanius (Haer. 3.30.7). Sicherheit kann man leider nicht gewinnen. Im Blick auf das synoptische Problem ergibt sich:

1) Papias äußert sich nicht über das chronologische Verhältnis von Matthäus zu Markus,
2) Papias hält Matthäus und Markus für ursprünglich selbständige Werke, die auf direkter oder vermittelter Erinnerung beruhen.
3) Das Markusevangelium und die (griechische) Fassung des Matthäus sind kritisch zu betrachten, da die indirekte Zeugenschaft des einen und die späteren Übersetzungen des anderen gewisse Probleme mit sich bringen.

II

Justin der Märtyrer beruft sich öfters auf die "Erinnerungen der Apostel" (ἀπομνημονεύματα τῶν ἀποστόλων), die er einmal ausdrücklich mit den Evangelien identifiziert (1. Apol. 66,3). Diese an Xenophon erinnernde Gattungsbezeichnung hängt mit der Auffassung des Christus als Inkarnation des Logos zusammen, hat aber wohl zunächst eine antignostische Spitze gehabt.[29]

Die "Erinnerungen der Apostel" werden ausdrücklich auch auf Apostelschüler ausgedehnt (Dial. 103,8), womit im Kontext Lukas gemeint ist (es folgt ein Zitat von Lk 22,44). Später zitiert er die "Erinnerungen des Petrus", wobei er auf Mk 3,16f. hinweist (Dial. 106,3). Dies ist das einzige Zitat Justins aus dem Markusevangelium.[30]

---

[28] Vgl. die Stellenangaben bei Ph. Vielhauer "Judenchristliche Evangelien", *Neutestamentliche Apokryphen in deutscher Übersetzung I* (E. Hennecke-W. Schneemelcher; 3. Aufl., Tübingen 1959) 102-103. Schon R. Pesch, "Die Zuschreibung der Evangelien an apostolische Verfasser", ZKT 97(1975) 56-71, fragt: "Muß Papias sich bereits mit einer mehrfachen Beanspruchung des Apostels Matthäus als Evangelienautor auseinandersetzen?" (64). Ablehnend U.H.J. Körtner, *Papias von Hierapolis*, 204-2105; nach W. Schenk, "Das 'Matthäusevangelium' als Petrusevangelium", 65-66, soll Papias dagegen nur das Ebionitenevangelium gemeint haben.

[29] L. Abramowski, "Die 'Erinnerungen der Apostel' bei Justin", 341-349.

[30] Es genügt also nicht, wenn H. v. Campenhausen, *Die Entstehung der christlichen Bibel*, 198, schreibt: "Markus wird er gekannt und anerkannt haben...". Allerdings wird in *Biblia Patristica I* (hg. v. J. Allenbach, A. Benoit u.a.; Paris 1975), s.v. Markus häufig auf Justinstellen verwiesen, an denen eindeutig die Matthäus- oder Lukasparallele zitiert ist.

In der Regel zitiert er das Matthäusevangelium, öfters auch das Lukasevangelium.[31] "Justin kann das Johannesevangelium nicht fremd gebliebenen sein, aber er vermeidet, es heranzuziehen".[32] Das liegt wohl an der gnostischen Beanspruchung des 4. Evangeliums.[33]

Die wenigen Äußerungen Justins zu unserer Fragestellung zeigen, daß die hinter Papias stehenden Traditionen eine Generation später bereits in Rom bekannt sind. Die Evangelien gehen auf Apostel (Mt) oder Apostelschüler (Mk, Lk) zurück, damit wird ihre Glaubwürdigkeit begründet. An einen literarischen Zusammenhang denkt Justin nicht, auch über das zeitliche Verhältnis kann man nur indirekt Aufschluß erhalten (Apostelschüler könnten später als der Apostel geschrieben haben).

III

Irenäus von Lyon basiert sehr wahrscheinlich auf Papias,[34] ohne daß im Einzelfall Sicherheit über die Herkunft der Traditionen zu erreichen wäre. Die antignostische Frontstellung führt noch stärker als bei Justin zur Betonung der Urkundlichkeit der Überlieferung. "Dem frei und großzügig sich bewegenden mythischen Denken und der wahlweisen Begründung aus der Schrift setzt Irenäus die Verbindlichkeit der historischen Fakten und die Autorität der zuverlässigen schriftlichen Fixierung entgegen".[35]

An der Hauptstelle Adv. Haer. 3.1.2 stellt Irenäus die Evangelien in der bis heute üblichen Reihenfolge Matthäus-Markus-Lukas-Johannes vor.

Matthäus schrieb sein hebräisches (oder aramäisches) Evangelium schon, als Petrus und Paulus in Rom noch mündlich verkündigten; nach beider Tod verschriftete Markus, der Dolmetscher des Petrus, die Petruspredigt, während Lukas, der Gefolgsmann des Paulus, dessen

---

[31] *Biblia Patristica I* führt s.v. Matthäus 177 Justinstellen an. Auffällig ist, daß Justin aus der traditio triplex öfters die Lukasfassung zitiert (so 1. Apol. 15.8; 15.3; 17,2; 19.6; Dial. 81.4). — Die immer wieder geäußerte Hypothese, Justin habe aus einer Evangelienharmonie zitiert, ist unwahrscheinlich; vgl. G. Strecker, "Eine Evangelienharmonie bei Justin und Pseudoklemens?" NTS 24(1978) 297-316.

[32] H. v. Campenhausen, *Die Entstehung der christlichen Bibel*, 198. J. Regul, *Die antimarcionitischen Evangelienprologe*, 159, behauptet, Justin bringe "nirgends etwas, ein Zitat oder eine Angabe über Jesus, das nur aus Johannes stammen könnte". Die in *Biblia Patristica I*, s.v. Johannes angegebenen Justinstellen sind in der Tat meist entweder alttestamentlich gefärbt oder allgemein urchristlich; aber 1. Apol. 61.4-5 und Dial. 88.7 geben zu denken.

[33] So zu Recht J. Regul, *Die antimarcionitischen Evangelienprologe*, 159-160.

[34] Vgl. H. Merkel, *Die Widersprüche zwischen den Evangelien*, 53 Anm. 36.

[35] N. Brox, *Offenbarung, Gnosis und gnostischer Mythos bei Irenäus von Lyon*, 77.

Evangelium in einem Buch niederlegte. Zuletzt hat der in Ephesus lebende Herrenjünger Johannes das Evangelium herausgebracht. Während die Mt- und Mk-Überlieferung i.W. an Papias anschließt, bezeichnenderweise die kritischen Punkte (Übersetzungsproblematik; τάξις) aber ausläßt, wird hier Lukas, den schon Justin als Apostelschüler bezeichnet hatte, erstmals mit Paulus in Verbindung gebracht. Eine Brücke dazu könnte Kol 4,14 und 2.Tim 4,10f. gewesen sein (Adv. haer. 3.14.1 zitiert!), daneben auch der Wunsch, die beiden römischen Hauptapostel (1 Clem 5,3ff.) als wenigstens mittelbare Urheber von Evangelien zu sehen; eine Beziehung zwischen dem Verfasser der Apostelgeschichte und Paulus legen schließlich auch die "Wir-Berichte" (Apg 16, 10-17; 20, 5-21; 27, 1-28) nahe (Adv. haer. 3. 14.1 zitiert!).

Als Verfasser des Vierten Evangeliums wird bei Irenäus erstmals der mit dem Jünger von Joh 13,3 identische Johannes genannt; zugleich wird er in Ephesus lokalisiert (vgl. Adv. haer. 2.22.5). Nun beruft sich Irenäus auf Presbyter, die er ausdrücklich als Johannesschüler bezeichnet (Adv. haer. 2.22.5; 5.30.1; 5.33.3), ohne daß das sachliche Recht dieser Beziehung erkennbar wäre.[36] Somit könnte diese Tradition wohl erst in der Generation vor Irenäus entstanden sein.[37] Die späteren Ausschmückungen und Wucherungen zeigen, daß wir hier einen jungen Keim vor uns haben. Für die Situation des Irenäus ist die Betonung der Vierzahl entscheidend. Neque autem plura numero quam haec sunt neque rursus pauciora capit esse Euangelia; Natur und Heilsgeschichte belegen dies (Adv. haer. 3.11.8). In diesem Zusammenhang bringt Irenäus die Evangelisten mit den vier Tieren aus Apc 4,7 in Verbindung, wobei er die Reihenfolge Johannes-Lukas-Matthäus-Markus einschlägt; diese resultiert aus der sachlichen Entsprechung, wie Irenäus sie sieht.[38] Dasselbe gilt für die in Adv. haer. 3.9. 1-11,6 angegebene Reihenfolge Matthäus-Lukas-Markus-Johannes. Es geht um den Aufweis der Einheit des alt- und neutestamentlichen Gottes. Das Matthäusevangelium drückt sie am deutlichsten aus, auch bei Lukas läßt sie sich gut zeigen; Markus dagegen bietet wenig, Johannes schließlich ist der umstrittene und daher zuletzt behandelte Fall. So ist auch diese Anordnung nicht chronologisch gemeint. Gelegentlich finden sich diese extravaganten Anordnungen auch anderwärts wieder.[39]

[36] Vgl. J. Regul, *Die antimarcionitischen Evangelienprologe*, 134-137.
[37] Ibid. 137.
[38] Irenäus ordnet folgendermaßen zu: Löwe-Johannes; Stier-Lukas; Mensch-Matthäus; Adler-Markus. Später ändert sich dies mehrmals; vgl. Th. Zahn, *Forschungen zur Geschichte des neutestamentlichen Kanons II* (Erlangen 1883) 257-275; J. Michl, *Die Engelvorstellungen in der Apokalypse des Hl. Johannes I* (München 1937).
[39] C.R. Gregory, *Textkritik des Neuen Testaments II* (Leipzig 1902) 848-856.

1) Nach Irenäus sind die Evangelien in der Reihenfolge Matthäus-Markus-Lukas-Johannes entstanden.

2) Die vier Evangelien gehen direkt oder mittelbar auf die apostolische Verkündigung zurück; ein literarisches Verhältnis besteht nicht.

3) Die Zuordnung der Evangelisten zu den Tiersymbolen erlaubt Irenäus erstmals einen Ansatz zu einer "redaktions-theologischen Differenzierung".

IV

Das älteste Kanonsverzeichnis der Kirche ist das Muratorische Fragment, das um das Jahr 200 entstanden sein dürfte.[40] Der schlechte Zustand des Textes hat zu mancherlei Konjekturen geradezu herausgefordert; ganz ohne glättende Eingriffe wird er nicht zu verstehen sein.[41] Das Zeugnis über Lukas breitet i.W. die hinter den irenäischen Angaben stehenden Daten aus; allerdings wird die Abfassung nicht mehr nach Pauli Tod angesetzt, sondern sehr unbestimmt "nach der Himmelfahrt Christi". In Z. 4 ist die Angabe ex opinione nicht klar; nach dem Vorgang von F. Overbeck und anderen[42] dürfte zu verstehen sein "ex opinione Pauli", so daß eine Art Autorisierung durch Paulus insinuiert wäre.

Noch deutlicher ist diese Tendenz für das Johannesevangelium zu erkennen. Johannes wird durch eine Offenbarung zur Niederschrift veranlaßt, die "Mitjünger und Bischöfe" approbieren sein Evangelium. Die Augenzeugenschaft wird durch 1. Joh 1, 1-4 begründet.

> "Unverkennbar ist der Verfasser des Fragments dem Einfluß einer unkontrollierbaren frommen Legende erlegen, die schon darum nicht zuverlässig genannt werden kann, weil dann die Abfassung des Vierten Evangeliums

---

[40] Z.B. B. Altaner-A. Stuiber, *Patrologie* (7. Aufl. Freiburg 1966) 94; G. Strecker, "Muratorisches Fragment", RGG³ IV, 1191; H. v. Campenhausen, *Die Entstehung der christlichen Bibel*, 283; gegen die Spätdatierung durch A.C. Sundberg, Jr., "Canon Muratori: A Fourth Century List", HTR 66(1973) 1-41 vgl. H. Merkel, *Die Pluralität der Evangelien* ..., X Anm. 31 und jetzt auch W. Schneemelcher, *Neutestamentliche Apokryphen I* (5. Aufl. Tübingen 1987) 20 f.

[41] Wir schließen uns an die Fassung H. Lietzmanns an (KlT 1, 1933), der in Z. 3 die Konjektur Büchelers litteris anstelle von itineris übernimmt. Lietzmanns Text auch bei F.W. Grosheide, *Some early lists of the books of the New Testament* (Textus minores I; Leiden 1948), 7-11.

[42] F. Overbeck, *Zur Geschichte des Kanons* (Chemnitz 1880; unv. Nachdruck Darmstadt 1965), 135-140; zuletzt: W. Schneemelcher, "Zur Geschichte des neutestamentlichen Kanons", *Neutestamentliche Apokryphen in deutscher Übersetzung*, 19. Erwähnung verdient die Auffassung P. Corssens, *Monarchianische Prologe zu den vier Evangelien* (Leipzig 1896) 136, in Analogie zur Johannespassage solle man verstehen ex opinione [omnium].

gegen alle Tradition in die Frühzeit zu verlegen wäre, als die Apostel (Johannes und mindestens Andreas) noch beisammen waren".[43]

Das Motiv, daß Johannes von anderen gebeten und gedrängt wurde, sein Evangelium zu schreiben, findet sich später immer wieder;[44] aber schon zur gleichen Zeit ist es in den Hypotyposen des Clemens für Markus bezeugt.[45] So ist es nicht angemessen, daß J. Beumer darin einen "historischen Kern"[46] sehen will.

Die massiven göttlichen und menschen Impulse, die hinter dem Vierten Evangelium stehen sollen, sind am besten verständlich, wenn man die Ablehnung desselben durch die Aloger im Hintergrund sieht.[47] Sie gehen von einem Vergleich zwischen Johannes und den Synoptikern aus und stellen fest ὅτι οὐ συμφωνεῖ τὰ αὐτοῦ [sc. Ἰωάννου] βίβλια τοῖς λοιποῖς ἀποστόλοις.[48]

Wenden wir uns noch dem nur teilweise erhaltenen Anfangssatz zu (quibus interfuit et ita posuit), so können wir mit praktisch allen Forschern annehmen, daß er das Referat über Markus abschließt. Soll die Anwesenheit des Markus bei den Lehrvorträgen des Petrus ausgesagt werden?[49] Dann ginge das Muratorische Fragment bezüglich des Markus nicht über Irenäus hinaus. Das ist unwahrscheinlich, da es auch über Lukas und Johannes mehr sagt. So wird die alte Konjektur [ali] quibus interfuit doch wohl berechtigt sein;[50] möglicherweise wird begrenzte Augenzeugenschaft aufgrund von Mk 14, 51-52 angenommen. Später wird Markus als einer der 72 Jünger Jesu noch näher an die Ereignisse herangerückt.[51]

Durchwegs ist im Muratorischen Fragment die Tendenz zu beobachten, zwar "nicht unbedingt die apostolische, sondern vor allem die

---

[43] J. Beumer, S.J., "Das Fragmentum Muratori und seine Rätsel", TP 48(1973) 544.

[44] Euseb, H.E. 3.24.5/7/11; sog. antimarcionitischer Evangelienprolog, Fassung II (Regul 34); Prochorusakten; Hieronymus, Comm. in Matth., praef.

[45] Euseb, H.E. 6.14.6; 2.15.1.

[46] J. Beumer, "Das Fragmentum Muratori ...", 544.

[47] Th. Zahn, *Geschichte des neutestamentl. Kanons II*, 46; vorsichtiger H. v. Campenhausen, *Die Entstehung der christlichen Bibel*, 279 ("Abwehr gegnerischer Strömungen"), ähnlich J. Beumer, "Das Fragmentum Muratori ...", 544-545 und H. Burkhardt, "Motive und Maßstäbe der Kanonbildung nach dem Canon Muratori", TZ 30 (1974) 209 Anm. 20.

[48] Epiphanius, Haer. 51.4.6; vgl. zusammenfassend H. Merkel, *Die Widersprüche zwischen den Evangelien*, 34-37.

[49] So zuletzt H. v. Campenhausen, *Die Entstehung der christlichen Bibel*, 296 Anm. 246.

[50] Sie geht auf Volkmar zurück und wurde z.B. von Th. Zahn, *Geschichte des neutestamentl. Kanons II*, 17; J. Leipoldt, *Geschichte des neutestamentlichen Kanons* I, 151; W.G. Kümmel, *Einleitung in das NT*, 435, übernommen.

[51] Epiphanius, Haer. 51.6.11; Adamantiusdialog 1.5.

ursprüngliche Überlieferung festzumachen".[52] Für unsere Fragestellung ergibt sich:

1) Das Muratorische Fragment übernimmt die Reihenfolge (Matthäus-Markus-)Lukas-Johannes, rückt aber die vier Evangelien chronologisch näher zusammen.

2) An eine literarische Beziehung zwischen den Evangelien ist nicht zu denken.

3) Die höchste Anerkennung wird dem — vielleicht noch umstrittenen — Vierten Evangelium zuteil; der Ansatz zu einer sachlichen Differenzierung könnte vielleicht darin liegen, daß Johannes per ordinem geschrieben habe (= ἐν τάξει?), während ansonsten alle Glaubensinhalte in allen Evangelien gleichermaßen zu finden sind.

V

Tertullian hebt in Abwehr des einen Evangeliums Marcions stark darauf ab, daß die *vier* Evangelien von den apostolischen Gemeinden anerkannt werden, nämlich Johannes, Matthäus, Markus und Lukas; dabei sind Markus als interpres des Petrus und Lukas als discipulus des Paulus anzusehen (Adv. Marc. 4.5. 3-4). So liegt schon in der Herausstellung eines einzigen Evangeliums ein Mangel; zudem ist Lukas kein apostolus, sondern nur ein apostolicus, und schließlich ist er Gefolgsmann eines spät aufgetretene Apostels und damit selbst eine Gestalt der Spätzeit, mithin kein erstrangiger Zeuge. Diese letzlich das dritte Evangelium abwertende Verwendung der älteren Tradition ist natürlich nur aus der polemischen Abzweckung zu verstehen. "Sonst pflegt Tertullian Lukas nicht weniger zu achten als Matthäus, Paulus nicht unter die Urapostel zu drücken, und auch das traditionelle Argument von den 'apostolischen Kirchen' wird bloß ergänzend herangezogen".[53] Mit der Betonung von Lukas' später Entstehung will Tertullian dem Erzketzer Marcion eine Ohrfeige geben; Irenäus hatte das Lukasevangelium gelegentlich an die zweite Stelle gerückt, da es inhaltlich gut gegen die Gnostiker verwendbar war. Um eine rein historisch-chronologische Feststellung geht es offenbar beiden nicht.

Das sieht zunächst bei Tertullians Zeitgenossen Clemens Alexandrinus anders aus. In einem bei Euseb (H.E. VI 14) zitierten Fragment aus den Hypotyposen heißt es:

(5) "In demselben Werk bringt Clemens eine Überlieferung hinsichtlich den Reihenfolge der Evangelien, die von den vormaligen Presbytern

[52] H. v. Campenhausen, *Die Entstehung der christlichen Bibel*, 301.
[53] Ibid. 326.

stammt und folgendermaßen lautet. Er sagte, daß die Evangelien, welche Genealogien enthalten, zuerst geschrieben worden seien, (6) Beim Markusevangelium habe folgende göttliche Fügung gewaltet: Als Petrus in Rom öffentlich das Wort verkündigt und im Geist das Evangelium ausgerufen hatte, habe die große Menge seiner Zuhörer Markus gebeten, er solle doch, da er Petrus schon seit langem gefolgt sei und seine Reden im Gedächtnis habe, die Vorträge aufschreiben; der habe es getan und den Bittstellern die Evangeliumsschrift übergeben. (7) Als Petrus davon Kenntnis erhielt, habe er ihm weder einen ablehnenden noch einen aufmunternden Zuspruch gegeben. Zuletzt habe Johannes, von seinen Schülern angespornt und vom Geist inspiriert, in der Erkenntnis, daß das Leibliche in den (vorhandenen) Evangelien schon dargelegt sei, ein geistiges Evangelium verfaßt''.

Die hier anscheinend vorausgesetzte Reihenfolge Matthäus-Lukas-Markus konnte selbst A. Harnack nicht erklären, während Th. Zahn sie oberflächlich mit der sonst üblichen harmonisieren wollte. Noch jüngst wollte G. Kennedy die abweichende Reihenfolge auf eine Ungenauigkeit Eusebs zurückführen. Das ist natürlich nicht unmöglich, aber am Text nicht aufgewiesen.[54]

Zuletzt hat W.R. Farmer sich des Clemens-Zitates angenommen. Er erwägt die These, daß erst Clemens diese auf unterschiedliche Informationen zurückgehende Überlieferung zusammengestellt haben könnte. Eine erste Information (a) habe gelautet: Die Evangelien mit Genealogien wurden zuerst geschrieben. Eine zweite Information (b) habe ausgesagt: Johannes wurde später als die anderen Evangelien geschrieben, um sie in geistiger Weise zu ergänzen. Schließlich habe Clemens noch (c) eine weiterentwickelte Form der Papias-Notiz über Markus gekannt.[55] Diese Aufteilung hätte für die Anhänger der Griesbachschen Hypothese den Vorteil, daß die ihnen allein wichtige Information (a) unabhängig von der ihnen problematischen Information (c) zu sehen wäre.

Auch diese These ist natürlich nicht unmöglich, aber sie ist äußerst unwahrscheinlich. Die Information (a) ist ja eindeutig im Blick auf einen Vergleich zwischen Matthäus und Lukas mit einem oder mehreren anderen Evangelien geschrieben; isoliert gibt sie keinen rechten Sinn. Und welchen Sitz im Leben sollte eine solche rein chronologische Information gehabt haben? Ähnliches wird man für die Information (b)

---

[54] A. Harnack, *Geschichte der altchristlichen Literatur bis Eusebius*, 686; Th. Zahn, *Einleitung in das Neue Testament*, 2. Bd. (3. Aufl. Leipzig 1907) 186; G. Kennedy, "Classical and Christian Source Criticism", 150.

[55] W.R. Farmer, "The Patristic Evidence Reexamined", 6-9; Zitate S. 8.

zu bedenken haben; auch sie ist deutlich auf das Gegenüber des Johannes zu den Synoptikern formuliert. Der einzige Abschnitt, der gut für sich selbst stehen kann, ist Information (c); sie informiert über die Entstehungsverhältnisse des Markusevangeliums ohne jeden Seitenblick auf andere Schriften. Somit erscheint es unangemessen, (a) und (b) auseinanderzureißen, während die Sonderstellung der Markuspassage unbestreitbar ist.

Dieses aufgrund von kritischen Rückfragen an die Hypothese Farmers gewonnene Resultat läßt sich noch durch eine Textanalyse erhärten. Drei Gesichtspunkte erscheinen uns belangreich:

(1) Der Grundgedanke des Clemens-Zitates ist doch die Gegenüberstellung der früheren Evangelien und des Johannes. Die früheren Evangelien stellen nur die äußere Seite der Heilsbotschaft dar (τὰ σωματικά), während der späteste Evangelist das Wesentliche (πνευματικόν) bietet. Daß es den Früheren nur um die menschliche Seite des Erlösers geht, wird gleichsam in Abbreviatur durch die Nennung der Genealogien signalisiert; Johannes dagegen hat keine Genealogie und zeigt schon dadurch an, daß er die göttliche Seite des Erlösers darstellen will. Diese bei Clemens nur angedeuteten Zusammenhänge hat Origenes expliziert: Ἐπειδὴ γὰρ Ἰωάννης ἀπὸ θεοῦ ἤρξατο, οὐκ ἐγενεαλόγησεν αὐτὸν ὡς θεόν; im Unterschied zu Johannes sind die Synoptiker τὰ ἀνθρώπινα διηγούμενοι τοῦ σωτῆρος (in Lucam hom 29; p. 170f. Rauer). Das Johannesevangelium ist der Erstling der Evangelien τὸν γενεαλογούμενον εἰπὸν καὶ ἀπὸ τοῦ ἀγενεαλογήτου ἀρχόμενον (JohComm I 4,21).

Wenn das Vorhandensein oder Fehlen der Genealogie für die christologische Orientierung eines Evangeliums so wesentlich ist, dann erhebt sich allerdings die Frage: Gehört Markus nicht auf die Seite des pneumatischen Evangeliums? Das ist natürlich nicht gemeint; aber die ausführliche Darlegung über Markus gibt nicht die geringste Erklärung dafür, warum Markus auf die Seite der Evangelien mit Genealogien gehört.

(2) Über die Verfasser der "Evangelien mit Genealogien" wird keinerlei biographisches Detail gebracht; auch die Entstehungsverhältnisse ihrer Schriften werden nicht geboten. Selbst die Person der Johannes wird nicht biographisch gewürdigt, lediglich die dem letzten und pneumatischen Evangelium angemessenen Umstände werden geschildert. Die ausschließlich am biographischen Detail interessierte Markuspassage fällt hier aus dem Rahmen.

(3) Die Markuspassage ist darüber hinaus auch literarisch schlecht mit dem Kontext verbunden. Wenn das Clemens-Zitat ursprünglich über die chronologische Folge der Evangelien hätte berichten wollen, dann

müßte man irgendein sprachliches Signal erwarten, das auf diese Absicht hinwiese, beispielsweise: "Die Evangelien mit Genealogien wurden zuerst geschrieben, danach das Markusevangelium, als letzter schrieb Johannes". Oder: "Markus nimmt den dritten Platz ein".

Oder aber man müßte einen Hinweis darauf erhalten, daß Markus die beiden anderen Evangelien voraussetzt, etwa: "Markus hat die Genealogie weggelassen, da sie schon bei Matthäus und Lukas zu lesen war". Nichts dergleichen ist zu finden; die Markuspassage wird einfach mit τὸ δὲ κατὰ Μάρκον angehängt.

Diese drei Beobachtungen legen die Folgerung nahe, daß die Ausführung über Markus nicht ursprünglich in diesen Zusammenhang gehörte. Nehmen wir sie aus dem Clemens-Zitat heraus, dann ergibt sich ein klarer Gedankengang: Die Evangelien, welche Genealogien enthalten, wurden als erste geschrieben. Zuletzt hat auch Johannes, in der Erkenntnis, daß das Leibliche in den vorhandenen Evangelien schon dargelegt sei, ein geistliches Evangelium verfaßt.

Dem Clemens-Zitat läge damit eine Überlieferung zugrunde, die das Nebeneinander von drei Evangelien erklären will. Kanonsgeschichtlich ist dagegen nichts einzuwenden, da der Vier-Evangelien-Kanon erst in der Generation vor Irenäus entstanden ist und insbesondere das Markusevangelium im 2. Jahrhundert kaum eine Rolle gespielt hat. [56] Als Schüler des Irenäus hat Clemens dann die Überlieferung durch die unabhängig überlieferte Markuspassage ergänzt und damit den Vier-Evangelien-Kanon gerechtfertigt. Um aber das Überkommene möglichst schonend zu behandeln, mußte er Markus an die dritte Stelle rücken; er konnte ihn weder vor die "zuerst geschriebenen" Evangelien stellen noch nach Johannes, der ausdrücklich als letzter geschrieben haben sollte. [56a]

Die ziemlich singuläre Reihenfolge Matthäus-Lukas-Markus-Johannes geht also nicht auf alte Überlieferung, sondern auf Clemens Alexandrinus zurück.

Clemens führt die Überlieferung recht allgemein auf "die vormaligen Presbyter" zurück. W.R. Farmer zog daraus den optimistischen Schluß "that Clement did not know this as a tradition passed on by a single Elder, but that it was a tradition that was known and received in

---

[56] Vgl. H. v. Campenhausen, *Die Entstehung der christlichen Bibel*, 201 ff. und bes. 201 Anm. 110.

[56a] Damit ist der vordergründige Einwand entkräftet, den G.G. Gamba, "A Further Reexamination of Evidence ...", 21 Anm. 10, erhebt: Clemens "would have no reason at all to place Mark's Gospel after the other two..., unless it was for a definite and grounded persuasion of historical nature".

different places in the second century church". Handelt es sich jedoch um die Fusion zweier Quellen, erklärt sich der Plural einfacher.

Clemens' Schüler Origenes verteidigt wieder die irenäische Ordnung Matthäus-Markus-Lukas-Johannes, die er ausdrücklich als chronologisch bezeichnet (nach Euseb, H.E. 6.25. 4-6: πρῶτον μὲν γέγραπται τὸ κατὰ τόν ποτε τελώνην ..., δεύτερον δὲ τὸ κατὰ Μάρκον ..., καὶ τρίτον τὸ κατὰ Λουκᾶν ... ἐπὶ πᾶσιν τὸ κατὰ 'Ιωάννην. Vgl. Comm. in Joh. 1.4.22.) Daß die Termini πρῶτον, δεύτερον etc. hier nicht chronologisch zu verstehen seien, sondern nur als "a reference to the usual disposition that the canonical gospels had in the manuscripts", ist ein völlig unbegründete Behauptung.[57] Allerdings bedeutet diese chronologische Reihenfolge keine Rangfolge; denn Origenes erklärt ausdrücklich das Johannesevangelium zum "Erstling der Evangelien" (Comm. in Joh. 1.4.21/23). In der Mitte des 3. Jahrhunderts hat sich die Überlieferung in der griechischen Kirche konsolidiert; die Evangelien sind in der Reihenfolge Matthäus-Markus-Lukas-Johannes entstanden und gehen auf direkte oder indirekte Augenzeugen zurück.

Euseb von Caesarea hat die alten Überlieferungen, soweit sie erreichbar und mit dieser Grundtendenz vereinbar waren, gesammelt. Er hat der schon längst vorhandenen Tendenz nach Verstärkung der Augenzeugenschaft kräftig Raum gegeben, so in seiner Paraphrase der Markustradition, in welcher er eine ausdrückliche Approbation des Evangeliums durch Petrus berichtet (H.E. 2.15.2). Von Lukas behauptet Euseb, er habe seine Informationen nicht nur aus dem ständigen Kontakt mit Paulus, sondern auch "mit den übrigen Aposteln" gewonnen (H.E. 3.24.15).

Die Synoptiker sind nach Euseb von Johannes begutachtet und als wahrhaftig, aber unvollständig erfunden worden, da sie die Wirksamkeit Jesu vor der Verhaftung des Täufers ausgelassen hätten. Mit dieser Ergänzungstheorie konnte Euseb die Harmonistik ein gutes Stück vorantreiben (H.E. 3.24. 7-13).[58] Die Frage der Chronologie der Synoptiker wird unter diesen Voraussetzungen relativ unerheblich.

Später verbindet Epiphanius von Salamis sachliche und chronologische Gesichtspunkte, um die östliche Reihenfolge Matthäus-Markus-Lukas-Johannes zu begründen. Matthäus ist der erste Evangelist; aber Irrlehrer wie Kerinth und Ebion folgern aus seiner Darstellung der Geburt, Christus sei ein bloßer Mensch gewesen. Gleich darauf erhält

---

[57] Gegen G.G. Gamba, "A Further Reexamination of Evidence...", 34.
[58] Theodor v. Mopsuestia, Comm. in Ioh., ed. J.-M. Vosté, CSCO 116,2-5; Hieronymus, De viris ill. 9; Augustin, De cons. ev. 2.18.42 bedienen sich dieser Theorie.

Markus von Petrus die Erlaubnis zur Abfassung eines Evangeliums; er läßt die Geburtsgeschichte weg, aber sein Evangelium wird im Sinne einer adoptianischen Christologie mißverstanden. So zwingt der Hl. Geist den Lukas, ebenfalls wie Markus einer der 72 Jünger Jesu, das von den anderen Evangelisten Ausgelassene darzulegen; aber griechische Philosophen finden vermeintliche Widersprüche zwischen den Evangelien. So nötigt der Hl. Geist schließlich den neunzigjährigen Johannes, klar und deutlich die Präexistenz Christi zu lehren. Hier ist natürlich die vorgegebene Reihenfolge primär, die sachliche Begründung sekundär.

Angesichts der immer näher an die Ereignisse gerückten Evangelisten und der Beteiligung des Hl. Geistes ist die Chronologie der Synoptiker letztlich irrelevant.

VI

In der lateinischen Kirche schwankt die Reihenfolge der Evangelien noch längere Zeit. Während die altlateinischen Handschriften e,a, b,ff[2], f und q wie auch die griechischen Codices Bezae Cantabrigiensis und Freerianus die Folge Matthäus-Johannes-Lukas-Markus bieten, findet sich in k die Folge Johannes-Lukas-Markus-Matthäus.[59]

Ambrosiaster erklärt, die Anordnung der Evangelien müsse mehr in *sachlicher* als in *chronologischer* Ordnung geschehen; daher steht Matthäus als erster, weil er bei der Verheißung der Menschwerdung beginne, Lukas als zweiter, weil er die Menschwerdung beschreibe, Markus als dritter, weil er das Evangelium als im Gesetz verheißen bezeuge, Johannes als vierter, weil er den Verheißenen und Menschgewordenen als Gott erweise (vgl. App. Quaest. Novi Test. 4, ed. A. Souter, CSEL 50).

Ambrosiaster will eine sachliche Anordnung geben, die zeitliche ist lediglich eine Folge davon.

Vielen lateinischen Bibelhandschriften sind Vorreden zu den Evangelien beigegeben, die dem Leser Orientierung über Verfasser und Zweck der Schrift geben sollen.[60] Zwei Gruppen sind hier zu besprechen.

Die erste Gruppe umfaßt Prologe zu Markus, Lukas und Johannes in leicht divergierenden Fassungen;[61] sie wurden früher als antimarcioni-

---

[59] Vgl. E. v. Dobschütz, *Eberhard Nestle's Einführung in das griechische Neue Testament* (4. Aufl.; Göttingen 1923) 9.

[60] Vgl. M.E. Schild, *Abendländische Bibelvorreden bis zur Lutherbibel*, masch. theol. Diss. Heidelberg 1964; auch griechische Handschriften bieten solche Prologe, s. H. v. Soden, *Die Schriften des Neuen Testaments in ihrer ältesten erreichbaren Textgestalt I* (Berlin 1902) 301-327.

[61] Ediert von J. Regul, *Die antimarcionitischen Evangelienprologe*, 29-35.

tisch angesehen, bilden aber nach dem weithin anerkannten Nachweis von J. Regul keine ursprünglich zusammengehörige Gruppe und gehören wohl erst ins 4. Jahrhundert.[62] Der Lukasprolog setzt klar die Reihenfolge Matthäus-Markus-Lukas-Johannes voraus,[63] ist aber mehr am biographisch-erbaulichen Detail interessiert, so am asketischen Lebenswandel des Arztes Lukas, an der Abfassung des Evangeliums auf Ansporn des Hl. Geistes und an der antihäretischen Ausrichtung. Der Johannesprolog nennt Papias als Sekretär des Apostels und malt vor allem die antihäretische Zielsetzung des Evangeliums legendarisch aus; in einem Teil der Überlieferung wird auch die Ergänzungshypothese angeführt. Die kürzere Fassung des Markusprologes erklärt den vorher nur einmal (Hippolyt Refut. 7.30) erwähnten Beinamen des Markus "colobodactylus", erwähnt die Dolmetschertätigkeit bei Petrus und die Abfassung des Evangeliums in Italien; in der längeren Fassung werden noch die Approbation des Evangeliums durch Petrus, die alexandrische Wirksamkeit und der asketische Lebenswandel des Markus genannt. Die über das bisher Bekannte hinausgehenden Angaben lassen sich als Ausschmückungen im Sinne längst vorhandener Tendenzen verstehen.

Die zweite Gruppe besteht aus Vorreden zu den vier Evangelien, die meist den Vulgatahandschriften beigegeben sind.[64] Diese nach ihrer theologischen Tendenz sogenannten "monarchianischen Prologe" oder "monarchianischen Evangelienargumente" sind schon von J. Chapman mit Priscillian in Verbindung gebracht worden, und J. Regul hat dies insofern bestätigt, als er sie einem Anhänger der priscillianistischen Bewegung gegen Ende des 4. Jahrhunderts zuschreiben zu können glaubt.[65]. Darüber hinaus hat J. Regul wahrscheinlich gemacht, daß das monarchianische Lukas-Argument den sog. anti-marcionitischen Lukas-Prolog voraussetzt.[66]

Während das Argumentum Matthaei den früheren Zöllner nur kurz vorstellt, um dann seine Theologie zu charakterisieren, enthält das Argumentum Johannis mehr Biographisches. Johannes wird als der Bräutigam bei der Hochzeit zu Kana vorgestellt, den Gott gerade eben noch zur Jungfräulichkeit bekehrte; sein Tod wird im Anschluß an die

---

[62] Zustimmung zu Regul in den Rezensionen von W.G. Kümmel, TRu 35 (197-271); J. Gnilka, TRev 68(1972) 20-21; J.B. Bauer, ZKG 83 (1972) 101-103; R.M. Grant, JBL 89(1970) 381-382, aber auch von G.G. Gamba, "A Further Reexamination of Evidence...", 32.

[63] Ed. Regul 30, Z. 5-7.19-20; 31, Z. 5-6.20-21; griech. 16,7-9.20-22.

[64] Ed. J. Regul, 40-50; daneben ist J. Chapman, *Notes on the History of the Vulgate Gospels* (Oxford 1908) 217-222 zu vergleichen.

[65] J. Regul, *Die antimarcionitischen Evangelienprologe*, 242-262.

[66] Ibid. 262-265.

Johannesakten ausführlich geschildert. Daß er, der chronologisch letzte Evangelist, an zweiter Stelle im Kanon steht, wird theologisch begründet: quoniam in Domino quae novissima sunt, non velut extrema et abiecta numero sed plenitudinis opere perfecta sunt.[67]

Zwischen der Rangfolge im Kanon und der zeitlichen Reihenfolge der Entstehung wird bewußt ein Unterschied gemacht! Das monarchianische Argumentum Lucae schildert die Biographie des Lukas ähnlich wie der sog. antimarcionitische Lukasprolog. Lukas will die vor ihm geschriebenen Evangelien des Matthäus und Markus ergänzen.

Das Argumentum Marci bietet gegenüber dem sog. antimarcionitischen Markusprolog legendarische Erweiterungen, insbesondere hinsichtlich des Daumens des Evangelisten. Die Reihenfolge Markus-Lukas scheint hier aber umgekehrt zu sein, wie aus der Bemerkung hervorgeht "non laboravit nativitatem carnis quam in prioribus viderat dicere". Das hieße: Markus bemühte sich nicht, die leibliche Geburt auszusagen, welche er in den früheren Evangelien gesehen hatte. Schon P. Corssen hatte daraus gefolgert, für den Verfasser des Markusarguments seien "Matthäus und Lukas die Vorgänger des Marcus"; "Marcus tritt in ein fertiges Werk ein ('perfecti evangelii opus intrans') und seine Bedeutung liegt lediglich darin, dass er durch knappe Zusammenfassung und bedeutsame Hervorhebung des einzelnen unserem Verständnis zu Hilfe kommt".[68] Dazu würde die vorher erfolgte Erwähnung "in consonantibus" passen, die sich dann auf Matthäus und Lukas bezöge. Allerdings ist hierbei zu beachten, daß eine große Zahl von Textzeugen den Relativsatz anders liest, nämlich quod in prioribus vicerat. Als lectio difficilior haben J. Chapman und J. Regul daher diese Lesart in den Text aufgenommen. Während aber J. Regul dennoch bei der genannten Interpretation bleibt, hatte J. Chapman eine dem Kontext angemessenere Erklärung vorgeschlagen:

> The meaning of vicerat is sufficiently plain; St. Mark, entering upon the work of the perfect Gospel, and beginning with the Baptism, did not trouble to recount the birth of the flesh which in prioribus — "in his opening paragraphs" — he had conquered, viz. by declaring that the beginning of the Gospel was (not the flesh, the consonants, but) the voice, the divine soul. This is a strange expression, no doubt — nativitatem carnis in prioribus vicerat — but not too strange for our author.[69]

So gelingt Chapman eine konsistente Erklärung der ganzen Passage

---

[67] Ed. Regul 43, Z. 24-26.

[68] P. Corssen, *Monarchianische Prologe zu den vier Evangelien*, (Leipzig 1896); ebenso noch G.G. Gamba, "A Further Reexamination of Evidence...", 22-24.

[69] J. Chapman, *Notes on the History of the Vulgate Gospels*, 234.

und es erübrigt sich anzunehmen, daß hier — und nur hier — eine andere Chronologie der Evangelien vorausgesetzt würde.

Auch Augustin schließt sich zunächst ganz in dieser Überlieferung an. Mit seinem einflußreichen Werk De consensu evangelistarum aus dem Jahr 400 will er Angriffe von Porphyrianern oder Manichäern gegen die Glaubwürdigkeit der Evangelien abwehren.[70] Hauptsächlich geschieht dies durch den Perikope für Perikope erfolgenden Nachweis, daß die unterschiedlichen Fassungen derselben Geschichte keinerlei Widersprüche aufwiesen, und daß auch im ganzen der Stoff der 4 Evangelien in eine durchlaufende Erzählung gebracht werden könne. Doch ehe Augustin in mühsamer Einzelarbeit die Harmonie der Evangelisten darlegt,[71] bringt er einige grundsätzliche Erwägungen, die uns hier interessieren.

Zwei der Evangelisten, Matthäus und Johannes, waren Apostel, und damit ist die Glaubwürdigkeit ihrer Evangelien von vorneherein gesichert (1.1.1). Die göttliche Vorsehung hat aber durch den Hl. Geist auch zwei Apostelschülern die auctoritas scribendi evangelium verschafft (1.1.2). Die chronologische Folge ist Matthäus-Markus-Lukas-Johannes. Die zwei Augenzeugen flankieren gleichsam als Beschützer die beiden anderen, die den Herrn zu Lebzeiten nicht gesehen hatten, aber doch dem in ihnen redenden Christus gefolgt waren (1.2.3). Ein Grundproblem für das Verständnis Augustins sind die sehr unterschiedlichen Aussagen über göttliche und menschliche Faktoren bei der Entstehung der Evangelien. Einerseits sind die Evangelisten inspiriert: quidquid enim ille [Christus] de suis factis et dictis legere voluit, hoc scribendum illis [sc. evangelistis] tanquam suis manibus imperavit. (1.35.54). Andererseits aber geben die Evangelisten Erinnerungen wieder, die natürlich nicht wortgetreu übereinstimmen (2.12.27).

Aber schließlich ist die Erinnerung der Apostel auch von Gott gelenkt (2.21.51). Selbst für das fälschlicherweise dem Jeremia zugeschriebene Sacharjazitat in Mt 27,9 ist Gott verantwortlich (3.7.30). So kann Augustin auch einmal davon sprechen, daß die Evangelisten die Werke ihrer Vorgänger eingesehen hätten; denn zur Inspiration hat jeder auch seine eigene, persönliche Mitarbeit hinzugefügt (1.2.4).

Das Anliegen des Matthäus sieht Augustin in der Darstellung der königlichen Abstammung Christi, Lukas habe den priesterlichen Chris-

---

[70] Porphyrianer als Gegner nennt H.-J. Vogels, *St. Augustins Schrift De consensu evangelistarum, unter vornehmlicher Berücksichtigung ihrer harmonistischen Anschauungen* (Freiburg 1908), 10; dagegen habe ich im Anschluß an die ältere Auffassung Manichäer als Gegner wahrscheinlich zu machen versucht (*Die Widersprüche zwischen den Evangelien*, 224-227). Nur dazu paßt Augustins Äußerung in Retr. 2.16.

[71] Vgl. H. Merkel, *Die Widersprüche zwischen den Evangelien*, 235-250.

tus darstellen wollen. Ein derart charakteristisches Merkmal findet Augustin bei Markus nicht; da Markus den meisten Stoff mit Matthäus gemeinsam hat, mit Lukas dagegen nur recht wenig, und da er vieles fast mit denselben Worten wie Matthäus erzählt, erscheint er gleichsam als pedisequus et breviator des Matthäus (1.2.4). Aufgrund dieses Befundes könnte man das Markusevangelium fast für überflüssig halten; so trägt Augustin später noch eine Existenzberechtigung für Markus nach: weil Könige immer mit Gefolge auftreten, steht Markus neben dem Matthäus. Umgekehrt kann Lukas keinen Gefolgsmann haben, da der Hohepriester nur allein das Allerheiligste betreten darf (1.3.6). Johannes ist vor allem an die Gottheit des Herrn interessiert (1.4.7). Von dieser Charakteristik ausgehend können die Synoptiker als Anleitung für die vita activa bezeichnet werden, während Johannes der vita contemplativa habe dienen wollen (1.5.8). Zu dieser Charakteristik passen schließlich die vier Tiere der Apokalypse, die Augustin anders als Irenäus zuordnet: Matthäus = Löwe, Markus = Mensch, Lukas = Stier, Johannes = Adler.

An einer Stelle des letzten Buches (4.10.11) sieht es nun allerdings so aus, als ob Augustin trotz der ausdrücklichen Ablehnung eines Gefolgsmannes für Lukas doch die Griesbachsche Reihenfolge Matthäus-Lukas-Markus verträte. Diese meist übergangene Stelle hat D. Peabody einer minutiösen Analyse unterzogen.[72]

Der Einfachheit halber sei das Ergebnis in der von Peabody selbst gegebenen Form mitgeteilt:[73]

THE BIPARTITE STATEMENT ABOUT SYNOPTIC RELATIONSHIPS IN AUGUSTINE'S *DE CONSENSU EVANGELISTARUM* 4.10.11

The Subject:	Et ideo Marcus,	And in this way, Mark,
1. The Symbolic Relationship	qui in illo mysterio quattuor animalium hominis videtur demonstrare personam,	who seems to indicate the figure of the man in that mystical symbol of the four living creatures,
Option A	vel	either
2. The Personal Relationship	Matthaei magis comes videtur	appears to be the companion of Matthew to a greater extent
	quia	as
3. The Textual Relationship	cum illo plura dicit	he narrates many things in common with him
	propter	because of

[72] D. Peabody, "Augustine and the Augustinian Hypothesis".
[73] D. Peabody, aaO, 56-57.

4. The Thematic Relationship	regiam personam quae incomitata esse non solet,	the kingly figure who is not accustomed to be without attendants,
Aside 1: Reflective Reference	quod in primo libro commemoravi;	as I said in the first book,
Option B	vel	or else,
Aside 2: Critical Judgment and Personal Preference	quod probabilius intelligitur,	in accordance with the more probable account of the matter,
2. The Personal Relationship	cum ambobus *incedit*.	he walks with both [Matthew and Luke].
	Nam	For,
3. The Textual Relationship	quamvis Matthaeo in pluribus tamen in aliis nonnullis Lucae magis congruit:	although he agrees with Matthew in many things, he neverthelesss agrees with Luke to a greater extent in several others
	Ut hoc ipso demonstretur	*And* by this very fact it may be demonstrated that he stands related
1. The Symbolic Relationship	ad leonem et ad vitulum,	to the lion and to the calf
4. The Thematic Relationship	hoc est, et ad regalem quam Matthaeus, et ad sacerdotalem quam Lucas insinuat personam, id quod Christus homo est, pertinere,	that is to say, both to the kingly figure which Matthew emphasizes and to the sacerdotal figure which Luke emphasizes wherein Christ also appears as man,
1. The Symbolic Relationship	quam figuram Marcus gerit pertinens ad utrumque.	as the figure which Mark bears relates to both.

Peabody erkennt, daß Augustin in ganz paralleler Weise von zwei Möglichkeiten spricht, das Verhältnis der drei Synoptiker zu verstehen, wobei er vier Ebenen unterscheidet: die symbolische, persönliche, textliche und thematische Beziehung: Entweder steht Markus nur zu Matthäus in Beziehung, wie in Buch 1 behauptet worden war, oder aber — und das erscheint Augustin hier als wahrscheinlicher — Markus steht in einer Beziehung zu Matthäus und Lukas. Auch wenn man die Parallelität beider Aussagen nicht ganz so streng wie Peabody wird sehen können,[74] so ist doch diese Aussage zu Recht hervorgehoben.

---

[74] Während bei der ersten Möglichkeit die persönliche Beziehung Folge der literarischen und thematischen Beziehung ist, ist bei der zweiten Möglichkeit die persönliche und die thematische Beziehung Folge der literarischen Beziehung.

Aber Peabody geht u.E. etwas zu schnell über den Kontext dieses einen
analysierten Satzes hinweg. Er stellt richtig fest:

> Within the somewhat broader context of Augustine's statement in 4.10.11
> this statement about Mark and his relationship(s) to the other Synoptics
> should be understood as an elaboration of the basic distinction which
> Augustine whishes to draw between the Synoptics and John. This distinc-
> tion is made by Augustine both at the thematic and at the symbolic
> levels.[75]

Wenn wir dieser Fährte folgen, ergibt sich als Struktur des ganzen
Abschnittes:

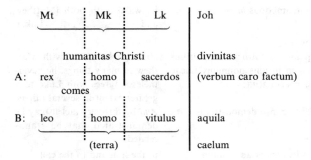

Nachdem der analysierte Satz als Einleitung zur Besprechung des
johanneischen Sondergutes steht, soll er zusammenfassend die "Synoptiker" von Johannes abheben. Das geschieht durch die Opposition
humanitas-divinitas. Aber unter dem Stichwort humanitas sind die Drei
durchaus keine Einheit; denn sie stellen die humanitas ja unter den drei
Aspekten rex-homo-sacerdos dar, wobei rex und homo zusammengehören,
aber der sacerdos noch etwas Eigenständiges daneben bleibt. Und nun
führt Augustin die in Option A noch fehlenden Tiersymbole ein; damit
werden die drei erdgebundenen Gestalten des Löwen, Menschen und
Stieres zu einer Einheit gegenüber der am Himmel fliegenden Gestalt
des Adlers. Die Opposition Erde-Himmel, die die Synoptiker zur Einheit zusammenschweißt, wird zwar in unserem Abschnitt nur angedeutet
(... sicut aquila in his, quae Christus sublimius locutus est inmoratur
nec in terram quodammodo nisi raro descendit), ist aber dem Leser
bereits aus 1.6.9 bekannt: haec autem animalia tria, sive leo sive homo
sive vitulus, in terra gradiuntur, unde isti tres evangelistae in his
maxime occupati sunt, quae Christus in carne operatus est ... at vero
Johannes supra nubila infirmitatis humanae velut aquila volat ... (vgl.
auch Tract. in Joannis evang. 36.5).

---

[75] D. Peabody, "Augustine and the Augustinian Hypothesis", 57.

So kommt Augustin zu der neuen, "wahrscheinlicheren" Auffassung aus dogmatischen Gründen, weil sie den consensus trium evangelistarum besser hervortreten läßt. Inwieweit er damit — i.S. der modernen Forschung — an ein literarisches Verhältnis denkt, ist nicht leicht zu entscheiden, da die Inspiration ja den übergreifenden Horizont darstellt. Die Einzelerklärung des consensus evangelistarum ist jedenfalls ohne diese "neue" Auffassung ausgekommen. Es liegt nahe, an das im Blick auf einen ähnlichen Fall formulierte Wort H.-J. Vogels zu denken: Augustin "bot die Lösungen, wie der Augenblick sie eingab".[76]

VII

Die Einzelergebnisse müssen hier nicht wiederholt werden; es sollen einige allgemeine Folgerungen gezogen werden.

1) Die einzige Nachricht, die sich nicht einfach aus späteren Tendenzen ableiten läßt, dürfte die Papiasnotiz über das Markusevangelium sein. Um 110 n.Chr. wußte man noch, daß das Markusevangelium auf Petrus zurückgehende Stoffe enthält und daß diese Stoffe vor der Verschriftung der mündlichen Verkündigung gedient hatten. Jede Quellentheorie sollte m.E. dieses Faktum in Anschlag bringen.

2) Bereits die Angabe des Papias über einen hebräischen (aramäischen) Urmatthäus dürfte als Interpretation des Faktums zweier ähnlicher Evangelien unter dem Namen des Matthäus anzusehen sein. Auch die Spätdatierung des Vierten Evangeliums könnte aufgrund eines Rückschlusses aus seiner entwickelten Christologie erfolgt sein. Trotz des Vorherrschens erbaulicher Interessen gab es auch scharfsinnige Denker in der Alten Kirche. Daß Lukas weder eine chronologisch frühe Stellung noch Augenzeugenschaft zukommt, ist aus seinem Prolog zu entnehmen (Lk 1,1-4).

3) Die "kanonische" Reihenfolge war primär chronologisch gedacht; Umstellungen dienten der Hierarchisierung. Doch findet man hier keine historisch verwertbaren Aufschlüsse.

4) Bei den Kirchenvätern herrscht die Auffassung vor, die Evangelien gingen unmittelbar oder mittelbar auf Augenzeugen zurück. An eine literarische Beziehung zwischen den Evangelien dachte man in der Alten Kirche nur in Ausnahmefällen, und dann stehen dogmatische Erwägungen im Hintergrund. So sollte sich keine moderne "Benutzungshypothese" auf die Kirchenväter berufen.

---

[76] H.-J. Vogels, *St. Augustins Schrift De consensu evangelistarum*, 110 Anm. 1.

5) Die Kirchenväter haben sich aus Liebe zum Evangelium mit Leidenschaft von ihren Denkvoraussetzungen aus um das Verständnis der Evangelien bemüht. Recht verstandene Kontinuität fordert, daß wir mit den uns gegebenen Möglichkeiten das Unsere tun.

Helmut MERKEL

RESPONSE TO H. MERKEL

In this response to the report of Prof. Merkel, I shall begin with some general observations regarding modern scholarly attitudes toward the Fathers, which Prof. Merkel seems to entertain as well, and then I shall concentrate on the main problem, namely, the composition of the Gospel of Mark in the light of the patristic testimony, especially that of Clement of Alexandria (cf. *EH* VI, 14, 5-7). For a more extensive discussion, the reader is referred to Orchard & Riley, *The Order of the Synoptics* (Peeters/Mercer 1987).

Professor Merkel has provided us with a comprehensive survey of the patristic evidence regarding the origins of the Gospels, but in the time allotted to me it is impossible to respond to all the issues raised by him. As regards the attitude of scholars toward the Fathers, the following should be noted. In the first place, it is clear from the tone of Prof. Merkel's lecture that, in company with the majority of modern scholars, he has in general a rather poor opinion of the historical value of the Church Fathers. There is a tendency to patronize them and at times there is even a suspicion that their religious fervor prevents them from telling the truth. I find it noteworthy that this sceptical attitude is not shared by secular colleagues in classical studies. To them, such ancient scholars as Justin Martyr, Irenaeus, Clement of Alexandria, but above all such eminent philosophers and theologians as Origen and Augustine, have been rightly venerated for their outstanding knowledge, scholarship, intelligence, culture and piety. I suggest that the devotion to truth and capacity to embrace it of such intellects as these is hardly less than that of the modern scholars who today feel qualified to question their competence and integrity.

In the second place, the principal concern of the ancient Fathers was first to verify and then to proclaim the accurate transmission of the tradition received from the Apostles; the question of the order and mutual dependence of the Gospels was seldom envisaged and was in any case regarded as of secondary importance.

Thirdly, the integrity of Eusebius of Caesarea, whose *Ecclesiastical History* is the main source of our information about its earliest period, has on the whole survived the onslaughts of critics of his accuracy. He had a first-hand knowledge of the Church's history and access to documents that can never be rivalled again since they have mostly now perished or vanished. Research now indicates that when Eusebius both gives a quotation and also mentions the source of this quotation, he tends to report it accurately.

Fourth, the widely shared assumption, that Papias is the source of the only historically certain piece of evidence regarding apostolic authorship of the Gospels, is completely false. We can clearly surmise that the depth and quality of the orthodox Church's tradition, which first began to surface in massive fashion in response to the one-sided assertions of Marcion (c. 130-150), was originally immensely greater than the small amount of written evidence that has survived. As a result, uncritical modern scholars regularly undervalue the depth and breadth of the continuous line of tradition of the 12 Bishops of Rome from Peter to Eleutherius listed by Irenaeus (*Adv. Haer.* III, 3, 3.), who adds that if it were not too tiresome he could have added other names to the independent inquiry of Clement into the long list of ancient authorities he quotes in *EH* V.11.

Fifth, modern critics continue to ignore the evidence before their eyes. What prevents them from perceiving that the oldest and the universal designation of Mark is 'the recorder (GR hermeneutes) and disciple of Peter', which means that the earliest tradition indicates that Mark is *not* the author of the Gospel, nor even the editor, but only the *agent*, the mouth-piece of the words of the Apostle Peter? Yet Markan Priorists continue to speak and to write of Mark as if he were truly the author/editor of the Gospel, in plain contradiction.

EUSEBIUS AS HISTORIAN OF THE GOSPELS

First, a brief word about the qualifications of Eusebius as a historian. Eusebius Pamphili (c. 260-340), Bishop of Caesarea in Palestine, was not only very interested in the establishment of the N.T. Canon, but essayed to play a part in fixing it. This is clear from his treatment of the Apocalypse and the Letter to the Hebrews. We also know that he had read and digested all the sources of information on the origins of the Gospels available to him in the great library at Caesarea, which had been painstakingly collected by Origen and Pamphilus. Most of these sources were subsequently lost or destroyed, so that his quotations form our only access to such important works as, for instance, Papias' *Five Books of Exegesis of the Lord's Sayings*. In fact he came as close to any of his contemporaries to knowing all that was then to be known about the origins of the canonical writings, and was widely recognised as a specialist in this field with unique qualifications, for instance by the Emperor Constantine. Like all the Ancients, however, he was chiefly concerned with the verification of the apostolic tradition, namely the authentic handing on of eye-witness accounts derived from the original Twelve. He also knew of at least two traditions about the order of composition of the Gospels, viz, the order Mt-Mk-Lk, and the order Mt-Lk-Mk. And because he follows a strictly chronological order in his *EH*, he also spaces out the information about the origins of the gospels according to the chronological order of his sources. Thus he gives Peter's side of the composition of Mark in Bk II, 15, then a general survey of the composition of all four Gospels in Bk III, 24-25, about the time of the death of the Apostle John; he gives the witness of Papias's Presbyter in Bk III, 39, 15; he gives testimony of Irenaeus in Bk V, 8, and the testimony of Clement Alex, in Bk VI, 14, 5-7; he gives the witness of Origin in Bk VI, 25, 4.

It is often asserted that these texts are mutually inconsistent, cannot therefore be trusted and should consequently be ignored. But we have already seen that there has never been any authority on the Gospels the equal of Eusebius in his closeness to apostolic times and places, in his knowledge, in his careful handling of his sources, and in the meticulous accuracy of his quotations from the authorities he recognizes. My intention now is to show that there is, surprisingly, no real inconsistency whatever in the various items of tradition that Eusebius has gathered, and that, on the contrary, they together offer a clear and consistent picture of the history of the composition of Mark. It is also clear that he has no special interest in any particular order of the appearance of the Gospels, but that he does take special interest in the problem of the composition of Mark, which seemingly was not as straightforward an affair as was the composition of Matthew, Luke and John. There is, however, one clash in particular that worries many students, namely Origen (*EH* VI, 25, 3-6), writing about the Canon of Old and New Testament, declares that Matthew was the first written of the four Gospels, that Mark was the second, Luke third, and John the fourth and last. Eusebius nowhere queries this order despite Clement's statement that Matthew and Luke were written before Mark, nor does he try to show their compatibility. Later in this essay we shall make a suggestion as to why Eusebius thought the two different sequences compatible with each other.

It will not be scholarly to deal with the text of Bk VI, 14, 5-7 ("the Gospels with genealogies") without comparing this text with the other related texts about Mark, for they reflect light upon one another. Each of them will therefore be taken in turn and their mutual harmony explained.

THE GOSPELS WITH THE GENEALOGIES

[HE VI, 14, 5-7]

[5] αὖθις δ' ἐν τοῖς αὐτοῖς ὁ Κλήμης βιβλίοις περὶ τῆς τάξεως τῶν εὐαγγελίων παράδοσιν τῶν ἀνέκαθεν πρεσβυτέρων τέθειται, τοῦτον ἔχουσαν τὸν τρόπον. προγεγράφθαι ἔλεγεν τῶν εὐαγγελίων τὰ περιέχοντα τὰς γενεαλογίας, [6] τὸ δὲ κατὰ Μάρκον ταύτην ἐσχηκέναι τὴν οἰκο- νομίαν. τοῦ Πέτρου δημοσίᾳ ἐν Ῥώμῃ κηρύξαντος τὸν λόγον καὶ πνεύματι τὸ εὐαγγέλιον ἐξειπόντος, τοὺς παρόντας, πολλοὺς ὄντας, παρακαλέσαι τὸν Μάρκον, ὡς ἂν ἀκολουθήσαντα αὐτῷ πόρρωθεν καὶ μεμνημένον τῶν λεχθέντων, ἀναγράψαι τὰ εἰρημένα· ποιήσαντα δέ, τὸ εὐαγγέλιον μεταδοῦναι τοῖς δεομένοις αὐτοῦ· [7] ὅπερ ἐπιγνόντα τὸν Πέτρον προτρεπτικῶς μήτε κωλῦσαι μήτε προ- τρέψασθαι. τὸν μέντοι Ἰωάννην ἔσχατον, συνιδόντα ὅτι τὰ σωματικὰ ἐν τοῖς εὐαγγε- λίοις δεδήλωται, προτραπέντα ὑπὸ τῶν γνωρίμων, πνεύματι θεοφορηθέντα πνευ- ματικὸν ποιῆσαι εὐαγγέλιον. τοσαῦτα ὁ Κλήμης.

From Clem. Alex.'s Outlines as quoted by Eusebius (EH VI, 14, 5-7)

5. And again in the same books [The Outlines], Clement states a tradition of the very earliest presbyters about the order of the Gospels; and it has this form.
He used to say that the first written of the Gospels were those having the genealogies,
6. and that the Gospel of Mark had this formation. While Peter was publicly prea- ching the Word in Rome and proclaiming the Gospel by the Spirit, the audience, which was numerous, begged Mark, as one who had followed him for a long time and remembered what had been said, to write down the things he had said. And he did so, handing over the Gospel to those who had asked for it.
7. And when Peter got to know about it, he exerted no pressure either to forbid it or to promote it.

The following comments are apposite. The whole of the above extract is a quotation from Clement's *Outlines* (*Hypotyposeis*) in which he incor- porated some of his exhaustive researches over a long period to track down the witness of all the earliest surviving Presbyters from all over the East (cf. Eus. *EH* V, 11). The discriminating eye and judgement of Eusebius has selected from *The Outlines* what he regarded as essential in order to complete his record of the origins of the Gospels. The tradition then, according to Eusebius, is that both Matthew and Luke (in that order) preceded the Gospel of Mark, from which they are distinguished by having each a genealogy of Christ. There was, it seems, nothing remarkable about the process of composition of either Matthew or Luke — at any rate nothing unusual had been recorded. But there was something unusual about the composition of Mark, a fact which Eusebius had noted at Bk II, 15, where he added a reference to this chapter of Bk VI. (J.J. Griesbach was the first to argue that Mark had Matthew and Luke in front of him when he composed his Gospel.) But first let us take note of the positive statements made by Clement here in Bk VI. We are informed by Eusebius on the authority of Clement:

1. that "the Gospel of Mark" was in the first sense a spoken composition, the Holy Spirit having moved Peter to preach it.
2. that Peter's words were spoken publicly as part of his *kerygma* to a large audience in Rome before ever there was any thought of committing them to writing.
3. that the request for Peter's words to be put in writing came to Mark from some of Peter's enthusiastic hearers on this particular occasion.
4. that Mark was able to retrieve (we are not told how) the words of Peter in such a way that Peter himself was indifferent to the result.
5. that Peter "made no attempt either to forbid or to promote" the circulation of Mark's recording of what he had said. Why did Peter take such a passive stance? Two reasons spring to mind; firstly, that he had not previously considered turning his Discourses into a book, and secondly, his reluctance would be explained if there were already in existence formal presentations of the Gospel, which made a written version of Peter's words supernumerary. If there had been no other Gospel accounts in existence, he would surely have taken more care as well as more interest in promoting his own. We may possibly see here some further support for Matthew and Luke being before Mark.
6. that Mark was then able privately to hand over copies of what Peter had spoken to all who had asked for them.

An important indication of the authenticity and truth of our text will be the degree to which it dovetails with the other texts provided by Eusebius. So let us compare his Papias-citation, *EH* III, 39, 14-16.

TESTIMONY OF PAPIAS AND THE PRESBYTER TO MARK AND MATTHEW
(EH III, 39, 14-17)

[14] καὶ ἄλλας δὲ τῇ ἰδίᾳ γραφῇ παραδίδωσιν Ἀριστίωνος τοῦ πρόσθεν δεδηλωμένου τῶν τοῦ Κυρίου λόγων διηγήσεις καὶ τοῦ πρεσβυτέρου Ἰωάννου παραδόσεις· ἐφ' ἃς τοὺς φιλομαθεῖς ἀναπέμψαντες.
ἀναγκαίως νῦν προσθήσομεν ταῖς προεκτεθείσαις αὐτοῦ φωναῖς παράδοσιν ἣν περὶ Μάρκου τοῦ τὸ εὐαγγέλιον γεγραφότος ἐκτέθειται διὰ τούτων·

[14] And also in his own book he hands on other accounts of the above-mentioned Aristion of the words of the Lord and traditions of the presbyter John, to which we refer those eager for instructions.

At this point we shall, of necessity add to his utterances made above a tradition which he has expounded about Mark who wrote the Gospel, as follows:

[15] καὶ τοῦθ' ὁ πρεσβύτερος ἔλεγεν· Μάρκος μὲν ἑρμηνευτὴς Πέτρου γενόμενος, ὅσα ἐμνημόνευσεν ἀκριβῶς ἔγραψεν οὐ μέντοι τάξει τὰ ὑπὸ Κυρίου ἢ λεχθέντα ἢ πραχθέντα.
οὔτε γὰρ ἤκουσεν τοῦ Κυρίου οὔτε παρηκολούθησεν αὐτῷ,
ὕστερον δὲ ὡς ἔφην Πέτρῳ· ὃς πρὸς τὰς χρείας ἐποιεῖτο τὰς διδασκαλίας ἀλλ' οὐχ ὥσπερ σύνταξιν τῶν κυριακῶν λογίων, ὥστε οὐδὲν ἥμαρτεν Μάρκος οὕτως ἔνια γράψας ὡς ἀπεμνημόνευσεν.

ἑνὸς γὰρ ἐποιήσατο πρόνοιαν τοῦ μηδὲν ὧν ἤκουσεν παραλιπεῖν ἢ ψεύσασθαί τι ἐν αὐτοῖς. ταῦτα μὲν οὖν ἱστόρηται τῷ Παπίᾳ περὶ τοῦ Μάρκου.
[16] περὶ δὲ τοῦ Ματθαίου ταῦτ' εἴρηται·

Ματθαῖος μὲν οὖν Ἑβραΐδι διαλέκτῳ τὰ λόγια συνετάξατο, ἡρμήνευσεν δ' αὐτὰ ὡς ἦν δυνατὸς ἕκαστος.

[15] And this the presbyter used to say: Mark, being the recorder of Peter, wrote accurately but not in order whatever he [Peter] remembered of the things either said or done by the Lord.
For he had neither heard the Lord nor followed him,
but later Peter, as I said, who used to make [his] discourses according to the chreias, but not making as it were a literary composition of the Lord's sayings, so that Mark did not err at all when he wrote certain things just as he [Peter] recalled them.
For he had but one intention, not to leave out anything he had heard nor to falsify anything in them. This is what was related by Papias about the [Gospel] of Mark.
[16] But about [that] of Matthew this was said:
For Matthew composed the logia in a Hebraic style; but each recorded them as he was in a position to.

The first thing we note about this text is that it agrees with Clement that Mark is not the author but simply the agent, the recorder of Peter's words, "Mark the recorder (ἑρμηνευτής) of Peter." In this passage the Presbyter is clearly affirming that Mark in his capacity as the recorder of Peter, was absolutely faithful in reporting his words, which were Peter's "memories" or "reminiscences" of what Jesus had said and done. The Presbyter also noted that Peter's words had been recorded just as Peter had delivered them; and that Mark had done a perfect job. The Presbyter seems to indicate that some critics were unhappy with the style of Mark and that the recorded version had all the roughness of an untouched extempore oration, i.e. of a colloquial form and not the normal literary form. Nevertheless it was entirely faithful to what Peter had said.

THE IRENAEUS-CITATION (EH, V, 8)

ὁ μὲν δὴ Ματθαῖος ἐν τοῖς Ἑβραίοις τῇ ἰδίᾳ αὐτῶν διαλέκτῳ καὶ γραφὴν ἐξήνεγκεν εὐαγγελίου, τοῦ Πέτρου καὶ τοῦ Παύλου ἐν Ῥώμῃ εὐαγγελιζομένων καὶ θεμελιούντων τὴν ἐκκλησίαν. [3] μετὰ δὲ τὴν τούτων ἔξοδον Μάρκος, ὁ μαθητὴς καὶ ἑρμηνευτὴς Πέτρου, καὶ αὐτὸς τὰ ὑπὸ Πέτρου κηρυσσόμενα ἐγγράφως ἡμῖν

Now Matthew brought out a written Gospel among the Jews in their own dialect, while Peter and Paul were evangelizing in Rome and founding the Church.
[3] And after their demise Mark the disciple and recorder of Peter, he too has handed on to us in writing what Peter had preached.

παραδέδωκεν· καὶ Λουκᾶς δέ, ὁ ἀκόλου-
θος Παύλου, τὸ ὑπ' ἐκείνου κηρυσσόμε-
νον εὐαγγέλιον ἐν βίβλῳ κατέθετο.

And Luke too, Paul's follower, set down in
a book the Gospel preached by him.

[4] ἔπειτα Ἰωάννης, ὁ μαθητὴς τοῦ
κυρίου, ὁ καὶ ἐπὶ τὸ στῆθος αὐτοῦ ἀνα-
πεσών, καὶ αὐτὸς ἐξέδωκεν τὸ εὐαγγέλιον,
ἐν Ἐφέσῳ τῆς Ἀσίας διατρίβων.

[4] Then John, the disciple of the Lord, he
who also reclined on his bosom, he too
published the Gospel, while living at Ephesus in Asia.

[5] Ταῦτα μὲν οὖν ἐν τρίτῳ τῆς εἰρημένης
ὑποθέσεως τῷ προδηλωθέντι εἴρηται,

[5] These things are the ones he has related
in the third book of the aforesaid work
[Adv. Haer.].

This is the only text among all the important Fathers that seems to
pose a difficulty for accepting that Peter was himself responsible for the
text of Mark while he was preaching in Rome; this Irenaeus text of *EH*
V, 8, which is itself a quotation from *Adv. Haer.* III, 1, 1. This text
affirms the priority of Matthew, published while Peter and Paul were
preaching the Gospel and founding the Church. It means no more than
that Matthew's Gospel appeared in the course of the public life of Peter
and Paul — while they were all active missioners — with the reminder
that they became the joint founders of the Church of Rome. It makes no
other claim for Matthew, except that it can be presumed that his Gospel
was also known to both Peter and Paul.

In Section 3 it is to be noted that Irenaeus refers to Mark in the same
way as Papias' Presbyter does, as "the disciple and *recorder* of Peter." It
is sometimes said that Irenaeus was only repeating what Papias'
Presbyter had been saying. This is undoubtedly true, but all are agreed
that the Presbyter was a contemporary of John and had independent
authentic knowledge. In any case, what one knows to be the truth one
can only go on repeating without addition or adulteration. So Irenaeus
is here assuming that, as the recorder and interpreter of Peter, Mark
knew him and worked with him on his Gospel. This Section is
unfortunately nearly always misinterpreted: "But after their demise,
Mark himself ... has also handed on to us in writing what had been
proclaimed by Peter." These words have widely been taken to mean that
Mark wrote his Gospel *after Peter's death*. This is erroneous, for it
ignores a number of factors:

1) Irenaeus in this passage is only concerned with the continuance of
   one and the same Gospel proclamation, first during Peter's lifetime
   and then after his death by his Gospel, the Gospel of Mark.
2) There is no indication that Irenaeus is here concerned with the
   chronological order of Mark, but only with its authenticity.
3) The true meaning is that the message which Mark recorded for Peter

and which Peter proclaimed throughout his life continued to be proclaimed after his death by means of his Gospel, which had been composed during his lifetime.

4) This is the force of the perfect tense παραδέδωκεν, "has handed on" — *scil.*, after his death, in his writing. This interpretation of our text, though first proposed by Dom John Chapman in 1904 and supported by A. Harnack in 1911, has been totally and most unfortunately overlooked by most scholars. (See J. Chapman, 'St Irenaeus and the Dates of the Gospels,' *JTS* 6 (1904-05), 563-69; A. Harnack, *The Date of Acts,* ET, London 1911; G.G. Gamba, 'La Testimonianza di S. Ireneo in *Adv. Haer.* III, 1, 1, e la Data di Composizione dei Quattri Vangeli Canonici,' *Salesianum*, 39 (1977), 545-585). Thus there is no inconsistency between it and the other passages.

PETER'S PREACHING IN ROME (EH II, 15)

Eusebius (EH II, 15,1-16,1)

15 [1] οὕτω δὴ οὖν ἐπιδημήσαντος αὐτοῖς τοῦ θείου λόγου, ἡ μὲν τοῦ Σίμωνος ἀπέσβη καὶ παραχρῆμα σὺν καὶ τῷ ἀνδρὶ καταλέλυτο δύναμις· τοσοῦτον δ' ἐπέλαμψεν ταῖς τῶν ἀκροατῶν τοῦ Πέτρου διανοίαις εὐσεβείας φέγγος, ὡς μὴ τῇ εἰς ἅπαξ ἱκανῶς ἔχειν ἀρκεῖσθαι ἀκοῇ μηδὲ τῇ ἀγράφῳ τοῦ θείου κηρύγματος διδασκαλίᾳ, παρακλήσεσιν δὲ παντοίαις Μάρκον, οὗ τὸ εὐαγγέλιον φέρεται ἀκόλουθον ὄντα Πέτρου, λιπαρῆσαι, ὡς ἂν καὶ διὰ γραφῆς ὑπόμνημα τῆς διὰ λόγου παραδοθείσης αὐτοῖς καταλείψοι διδασκαλίας, μὴ πρότερόν τε ἀνεῖναι ἢ κατεργάσασθαι τὸν ἄνδρα, καὶ ταύτῃ αἰτίους γενέσθαι τῆς τοῦ λεγομένου κατὰ Μάρκον εὐαγγελίου γραφῆς.

[2] γνόντα δὲ τὸ πραχθέν φασι τὸν ἀπόστολον ἀποκαλύψαντος αὐτῷ τοῦ πνεύματος, ἡσθῆναι τῇ τῶν ἀνδρῶν προθυμίᾳ κυρῶσαί τε τὴν γραφὴν εἰς ἔντευξιν ταῖς ἐκκλησίαις. Κλήμης ἐν ἕκτῳ τῶν Ὑποτυπώσεων παρατέθειται τὴν ἱστορίαν, συνεπιμαρτυρεῖ δὲ αὐτῷ καὶ ὁ Ἱεραπολίτης ἐπίσκοπος ὀνόματι Παπίας. τοῦτον δὲ Μάρκου μνημονεύειν

1. So then, when the divine word made its home among them [the Romans], the power of Simon [Magus] was extinguished and straightway destroyed with the man himself. So greatly then did the brightness of true religion light up the minds of Peter's hearers that they were not satisfied to have a once-for-all hearing nor with the unwritten teaching of the divine proclamation, but with appeals of every kind begged Mark, the follower of Peter, whose gospel we have, to leave them too a memorial in writing of the teaching given them by word of mouth. Nor did they cease until they had persuaded the man, and in this way became the cause of the written gospel according to Mark.

2. And it is said that the apostle, when the fact became known to him through the revelation of the Spirit, was pleased with the eagerness of the men and approved the writing for use in the churches. Clement relates the anecdote in the sixth book of the *Outlines*, and Papias, bishop of Hierapolis, also bears witness to it and Peter mentions Mark in his first letter.

τὸν Πέτρον ἐν τῇ προτέρᾳ ἐπιστολῇ· ἣν καὶ συντάξαι φασὶν ἐπ᾽ αὐτῆς Ῥώμης, σημαίνειν τε τοῦτ᾽ αὐτόν, τὴν πόλιν τροπικώτερον Βαβυλῶνα προσειπόντα διὰ τούτων· ἀσπάζεται ὑμᾶς ἡ ἐν Βαβυλῶνι συνεκλεκτὴ καὶ Μάρκος ὁ υἱός μου.

16 [1] Τοῦτον δε᾽ Μάρκον πρῶτόν φασιν ἐπὶ τῆς Αἰγύπτου στειλάμενον, τὸ εὐαγγέλιον, ὃ δὴ καὶ συνεγράψατο, κηρῦξαι, ἐκκλησίας τε πρῶτον ἐπ᾽ αὐτῆς Ἀλεξανδρείας συστήσασθαι.

Indeed they say that he composed it at Rome itself, and that he indicates this when referring figuratively to the city as Babylon in these words: 'The elect [church] that is in Babylon greets you and so does my son Mark' [1 Pet 5:13].

16,1. They also say that this Mark set out for Egypt and was the first to proclaim the gospel which he had written, and the first to set up churches in Alexandria itself.

Our next comparison is with the passage in Bk II, 15, where Eusebius gives in his own words a colourful and somewhat bombastic account of what Clement soberly describes as "Peter's audience begging him (παρακαλέσαι) to write down the things Peter had said." Furthermore, whilst in the Clement quotation above Peter is said to have been preaching in the Holy Spirit, Eusebius now adds two comments: that Peter learnt of Mark's capitulation to the demands of the audience through the same Spirit and gave the resulting Gospel his approval; and that "Peter approved the writing for use in the Churches" — a statement possibly based on hindsight. Note also that Eusebius quotes Papias as identifying our Mark with "Peter's son Mark" in 1 Pet 5:13.

PETER AND THE PRAETORIAN *EQUITES* ("KNIGHTS") — cf. 1 Pet 5:13

Clem, Alex., Adumbr. in Ep. can,
in 1 Pet 5:13

Clem, Alex., Adumbr. in Ep. can,
in 1 Pet 5:13

Marcus Petri sector praedicante Petro evangelium palam Romae coram quibusdam Caesareanis equitibus et multa Christi testimonia proferente, petitus ab eis, ut possent quae dicebantur memoriae commendare, scripsit ex his quae a Petro dicta sunt evangelium quod secundum Marcum vocitatur; sicut Lucas quoque Actus Apostolorum stilo exsecutus agnoscitur et Pauli ad Hebraeos interpretatus epistolam.

[The Greek text of the above has been lost.

Mark, the follower of Peter, while Peter was publicly preaching the Gospel at Rome before some of Caesar's knights and producing many testimonies about Christ, on their asking him to let them have the written record of the things that had been said, wrote the gospel which is called the Gospel of Mark from the things said by Peter — just as Luke is recognized as the pen that wrote the Acts of the Apostles and as the translator of the Letter of Paul to the Hebrews.

There is a note in Migne, Patr. Graeca,
IX.729-30 suggesting that the above Latin
text was translated by Cassiodorus from a
part of Clement's *Outlines* that is no longer
extant.].

Anonymous early Christian scribes have rescued this additional information about the circumstances in which the Gospel of Mark was composed and it agrees very well with the data of our other texts. It happened while Peter was in Rome and while he was preaching. What is additional is that on one or more occasions there were present higher officials of the Praetorium (the centre of government in Rome), belonging to the class of *equites*, or "knights." This reveals that these occasions must have been special and that these "knights" were influential enough to be able to persuade Mark to obtain copies of what Peter had preached. And this argues that for this series of Discourses Mark had arranged for Greek shorthand writers to take down Peter's words; in fact it was a regular habit for important speakers, e.g. senators, to have their orations recorded as they spoke them. Consequently, the author of this anecdote is able to compare Mark's action as being similar to Luke acting as the "pen" that wrote the Acts, and as the "translator" of the letter of Paul to the Hebrews; for him Mark was no more than the "interpreter" (*hermēneutēs*).

The combination of all these texts gives us a consistent and thoroughly realistic picture of the composition of the Gospel of Mark. It may be re-stated as follows.

During Peter's period of evangelisation in Rome the Gospel of Matthew was already in existence (*EH* VI, 14, 6), and so was the Gospel of Luke, the "other Gospel with the genealogy" (*EH* VI, 14, 5). His disciple Mark was with him, acting as his secretary and as his "son" and support in his old age (1 Pet 5:13). And then for some reason not disclosed to us, Peter decided to give a series of discourses (*didaskalias*, *EH* III, 39, 15) that was attended by members of the corps of *equites*, high-ranking officials of the Praetorium (cf. *Adumbr. in ep. can.* at 1 Pet 5:13), who received his discourses with great enthusiasm. The occasion was sufficiently important for Mark (Peter's agent or *hermēneutēs*) to secure the services of Greek stenographers, of whom there were many in imperial Rome at that time (see Marrou, "History of Education," *Encyclopedia Britannica,* 1967 ed., vol. 6:328a). Peter's numerous personal testimonies about Christ were the topic of these Discourses (cf. *Adumbr.* at 1 Pet 5:13). The *equites* were so impressed by Peter's witness that they begged Mark to let them have the text of what Peter had said.

The narrative that emerged was written in Greek and was nothing other than our present Gospel of Mark, absent the last twelve verses (Mk 16:9-20). Peter himself seems to have been surprised at all the fuss and gave permission to Mark to circulate the transcript to those who asked for it, although he did nothing either to promote or to hinder its circulation (*EH* VI 14,7). All this must have happened about AD 62, since Peter was martyred at some date between 64 and 67, and at about the time when Mark was in intimate contact with him (1 Pet 5:13), Paul and Luke being there as well (cf. Col 4:10, 14; Philem 23).

But the contrast in literary style between this unedited colloquial record of Peter's Discourses on the one hand and the standard book-form and style of both Matthew and Luke on the other (though Matthew wrote in a Hebrew style and Luke in the Greek style) - this contrast was so great as to cause not a little adverse comment among Christians in the years that followed. It must have led some of them publicly to disparage Mark. The Papias-Citation in *EH* III 39, 15-16 reveals how "The Presbyter" (whom many believe to be John the Apostle and Evangelist) took up the defence of Mark at some date between AD 62 and 90. Mark himself, said the Presbyter, had neither heard the Lord nor followed Him, but in Papias' account the Presbyter was emphatic that Mark's record of Peter's memories of the things said or done by the Lord were accurate and word for word. This record made by Mark was not "in order" (*taxei*), nor was it a literary composition (*syntaxis*), but it was a collection of stories (*chreiai*) about the Lord. Any defects in the text were not to be blamed on Mark, for "he had but one intention, not to leave out anything he had heard and not to alter (falsify) anything." Here then we have a clear description of the lack of literary style in Mark and this is adequately explained if Mark was simply an accurate verbatim transcript of Peter's Discourses.

To complete our picture of the composition of Mark we have now to find out why Peter undertook to deliver what was a very special set of Discourses (as the presence of the *equites* seems to show). Eusebius records in *EH* III, 24, that Matthew and John were the only members of the Twelve to bequeath us their memoirs of the Lord's doings and that there is a firm tradition that they only took to writing out of necessity. There is also the opinion of Augustine that each of the evangelists knew of the work of his predecessor(s), i.e., hence the second evangelist knew the work of first, the third knew the other two, and that the fourth knew the other three. Since Clement states that the Gospels with genealogies were written before Mark, it will be legitimate to ask if Mark shows any signs of knowledge of Matthew and Luke. The answer is definitely in the affirmative. From the time of J. J. Griesbach it has been noted that:

> "Mark retained the order observed by Matthew in such a way, that whenever he forsakes it he sticks to the path of Luke and follows him and the order of his narrative step by step, to such an extent that the verses and words where he passes from Matthew to Luke or returns from Luke to Matthew ...
> Briefly you can see, as with your own eyes, Mark having the volumes of Matthew and Luke at hand, continually consulting each ... now laying aside Matthew, now Luke, for a little, but always returning to the very same place of either one where he had begun to diverge from him"
> (J.B. Orchard, et al., eds., *J.J. Griesbach: Synoptic and Text-critical Studies, 1776-1976*, Cambridge, 1978, p. 108).

In other words, Mark's text reveals to us that Peter was blending together the traditions of Matthew and Luke, i.e. the tradition of Peter and the Church of Jerusalem with the tradition of Paul and the Church of the Gentiles. And here we have an adequate reason for surmising that Peter was responding to a request from Paul to lend his authority to the Gospel of his disciple Luke, which he wished to disseminate as a manifesto among his Gentile Churches, as a counterbalance to Matthew which was possibly viewed as the Manifesto of the Church of Jerusalem.

Clement of Alexandria was right then in claiming that the Gospel of Mark was subsequent to Matthew and Luke, the two Gospels with genealogies. Thus the order of composition was truly Matthew - Luke - Mark; but the Roman Church was right to place Mark between Matthew and Luke in order to signal the part played by Peter in linking Luke to Matthew.

Thus, the historical data are completely satisfied by recognising the dependence of Mark on Matthew and Luke, the order of composition being Mt-Lk-Mk; whilst the order Mt-Mk-Lk indicates the Roman Church's recognition of the mediating role of Peter in the process. The above represents merely a hypothesis, but it is strengthened by its many points of agreement with historical data.

On the other hand, it is obvious that the Hypothesis of Markan Priority is incompatible with the recorded statements of the Fathers. Indeed, to my mind the Patristic Evidence and the Markan Priority Hypothesis are mutually exclusive. If the one is right, the other has to be wrong; *tertium non datur*. Therefore those who are totally convinced of the priority of Mark are also sure that the Fathers were wrong. Hence Markan Priorists have logically concentrated on searching for discrepancies to invalidate elements of the patristic witness. Naturally, in recent years, and particularly since the revival of the Griesbach or Two-

Gospel Hypothesis, special attempts have been made to negate the Clement of Alexandria passage.

For instance, F. Neirynck has noted six alternative interpretations of *EH* VI 14, 5-7 in an "Additional Note on Patristic Testimonies," in his refutation of the Two-Gospel Hypothesis (see below p. 605). They are far from compelling, i.e.: that we cannot be sure that the quotation is either correct or authoritative; that τάξις (order) might also mean simply 'a list'; that δέ in this context is not adversative; that Eusebius' judgement was at fault in offering this quotation; that the 'Gospels' mentioned may not have been our Matthew and Luke, but some unknown apocryphal gospels; that the Presbyter has simply made a mistake (*apud* T. Zahn); etc. Naturally, such attempts must be fairly taken into account by any serious historian.

Professor Merkel, however, has offered a rather unusual, not to say novel, explanation of Clement's meaning. He has suggested that the controlling theme of this passage is the contrast between σωματικά and πνευματικά, so that the contrast intended is between *the three Synoptics and John*. My reply is: the passage indeed goes on to contrast the Synoptics with John in this way, but the controlling theme is clearly announced at the beginning, *viz.*, it is a question of the τάξις of the Gospels, *i.e., their sequence or order*. The point of Sect. 6 is precisely to illustrate that Mark has an unusual origin, different in character from that of the two Gospels with the genealogies. Thus Merkel's argument is beside the point. His theory also involves suggestions that Sect. 6 is an interpolation and he further argues that if Eusebius really intended to say that Mark was third in order, he should have made it clearer, which is a rather odd suggestion. This was not Eusebius' problem! He goes on finally to suggest that Clement has himself interpolated this Mark passage from an earlier tradition and he further insists that the mid-2nd century presbyters whom Clement consulted "only knew three Gospels (Mt, Lk, Jn)." This is why, Merkel concludes, Clement felt it necessary to insert Mk here to line up with the tradition of Irenaeus.

These suggestions though ingenious are hardly convincing. We know that Papias knew of Luke and John as well as Matthew and Mark because he wrote commentaries on the former two. It is moreover incredible that the learned men whom Clement sought out, from whom he learned the apostolic tradition from "the ancient elders" regarding the fact that "the Gospels with geneaologies were written before those without," would not themselves have known of the four canonical Gospels. All four had long since been circulating widely in Asia, as well as elsewhere. Such arguments are little more than grasping at straws.

Our conclusion must be that the patristic evidence has been for too long underrated and neglected, and that, properly understood, it can prove to be of the greatest value in helping us to understand the circumstances surrounding the original composition of the Gospel of Mark, as well as pointing us toward the proper solution of the Synoptic Question.

Bernard ORCHARD

Note on Patristic Testimonies

The so-called external evidence of Patristic witnesses played an important role in the history of the synoptic problem. In recent studies, however, there is a growing skepticism about the value of Patristic statements regarding the Gospels.

The theory of Matthean priority has its connections with the Patristic tradition of the Hebrew Matthew which ultimately relies on Papias' testimony, and Schleiermacher's interpretation of τὰ λόγια, in the same sentence of Papias, prepared for the Q hypothesis. Today very few defenders of Q will maintain (with H. Koester, II, 172) that "we might understand Papias' remark as a reference to the Synoptic Sayings Source." A justification for the meaning τὰ λόγια = Sayings can be found neither in Papias' text on Mark (τὰ ὑπὸ τοῦ κυρίου ἢ λεχθέντα ἢ πραχθέντα = τὰ κυριακὰ λόγια) nor in the use of the word λόγιον in the Patristic writings of the second century (R. Gryson, 1965). And those who reject J. Kürzinger's understanding of Ἑβραΐδι διαλέκτῳ ("in a Jewish style") have to confess that Papias' Hebrew (or Aramaic) Matthew can be quite different from our canonical Greek Matthew (Boismard): "Diese Papiasnotiz ist für den Ursprung des Mt historisch wertlos" (P. Vielhauer, 262).

Much emphasis is laid now by the neo-Griesbachians on the testimony of Clement of Alexandria: προγεγράφθαι ... τῶν εὐαγγελίων τὰ περιέχοντα τὰς γενεαλογίας (in Eusebius, *HE* VI,14,5). The text was quoted alread by de Wette and understood in the light of the Griesbach hypothesis: "er hält das erste und dritte Evangelium für die früher geschriebenen, was richtig zum Charakter dieses Evangeliums [Mk] stimmt" (§ 100 *b*). For T. Zahn this is not the only way of interpreting "the tradition of the early elders" and he suggests the possibility that "jene Presbyter nur sagen wollten, Mt habe früher als Mr. und Lc früher als Jo geschrieben" ([3]1907, II, 186, n. 9), but he also adds: "wenn man seine sehr kurze Angabe genau nehmen darf" (182). Recently, a more satisfactory interpretation has been proposed by George Kennedy ("Classical and Christian Source Criticism," 1978): "The passage could also be understood as a tradition that the two gospels with genealogies ... and also Mark ... were *progegraphtai*, 'written before.' Before what? The Greek particle *de* in 6.14.6 can perfectly well associate Mark with the other two gospels rather than with John, which is specially said to be the last in order; thus we have a contrast of the Synoptics with John" (150).

But even if the statement would be that Mt and Lk (the gospels with genealogy) were written before Mk, can we agree with Farmer's thesis: "That Mark was written after both Matthew and Luke is in accord with the earliest and best external evidence on the question" (*The Synoptic Problem*, 225)? J.A.T. Robinson has rightly observed (*Redating the New Testament*, 107) that "this tradition can scarcely be used, as it is by Farmer, in support of his hypothesis that Mark represents a literary conflation of Matthew and Luke, since the same tradition went on to say of the origin of the gospel of Mark:

> When Peter had publicly preached the word at Rome, and by the Spirit had proclaimed the Gospel, that those present, who were many, exhorted Mark, as one who had followed him for a long time and remembered what had been spoken, to make a record of what was said; and that he did this, and distributed the Gospel among those that asked him. And that when the matter came to Peter's knowledge he neither strongly forbade it nor urged it forward."

This implies clearly that Peter was still alive at the time of the composition of Mark. It looks like a legendary development of what is told by Papias[1]. And Farmer seems to agree since in his opinion "there is no external evidence" that the gospel of Mark has been written earlier than "between A.D. 100 and A.D. 125" (226)[2].

F. NEIRYNCK

---

[1] P. Vielhauer, *Geschichte der urchristlichen Literatur*, 260, n. 4: "Irenäus läßt Mk nach dem Tode Petri, Clemens Alex. dagegen schon bei seinen Lebzeiten und Origenes auf Diktat des Petrus abgefaßt sein, und nach Euseb hat der Apostelfürst das Buch für den kirchlichen Gebrauch approbiert: je später die Nachrichten, desto patriarchalischer das Evangelium. Sie gehen alle auf die Papiasnotiz zurück und sind historisch wertlos."

[2] This Additional Note on Patristic Testimonies (1984) was an addendum to my earlier "Note on the Questionnaire" (1983).

PART THREE

CONCLUSION

AGENDA FOR FUTURE RESEARCH

[The very last session of the Symposium was devoted to the production of two lists: one list containing those points concerning which we found ourselves in agreement, and another list containing items about which we still found ourselves in disagreement or wanted further study. These two lists are here reproduced, as requested by the Participants, without explanatory comment. If anyone has questions about any of these items, he or she may contact one of the Participants for a fuller explanation. Ed. note.]

The following items represent areas of unanimous agreement:
1. the existence of direct literary relationship involving the Synoptic Gospels.
2. the existence and use of earlier traditions in the Synoptic Gospels.
3. that a literary, historical and theological explanation of the evangelists' compositional activity, giving a coherent and reasonable picture of the whole of each Gospel, is the most important method of argumentation in defense of a source hypothesis.
4. that the Gospel of John must always be included in study of the Synoptic Gospels.

The following items were identified as areas of disagreement; i.e., as desiderata for future research:
1. The phenomenon of order among pericopes.
2. The patterns of agreement in order within pericopes.
3. Whether one may identify redactional features in a Gospel independently of a source-hypothesis.
4. Whether doublets have significance in solving the Synoptic Problem.
5. Evaluation of the minor agreements of Matthew and Luke against Mark by means of probability analysis.
6. Whether the compositional activity of the evangelists was influenced by the genre(s) of the Gospels.
7. The Jesus tradition outside the Gospels with reference to the Synoptic Problem/all four Gospels.
8. Principles of synopsis construction.

9. Old Testament quotations or allusions in the Gospels with reference to the Synoptic Problem.
10. The process of handing on tradition.
11. Potential approaches to the Synoptic Problem in Asian and African contexts.
12. The socio-historical setting of each Gospel.
13. Theological implications of each research paradigm.
14. A more satisfactory way of stating the synoptic phenomenon and of posing the synoptic problem.
15. Computer-aided statistical analysis of the synoptic phenomena.

SERMON
IN THE NOTRE DAME OF JERUSALEM CHAPEL
AT THE CONCLUSION OF THE SYMPOSIUM

Easter Day, April 22, 1984

"Lord, speak to us on this day of your resurrection from death
and let us share your glorious and victorious life."

.The holy word of God, addressed to us at our eucharistic service here in
this chapel on the evening of this Easter Sunday, tells us about a
meeting of the Risen Lord with his apostles in the evening just after the
discovery of the empty tomb on a Sunday some 1,950 years ago. It is the
evangelist John who has witnessed to this meeting in the Fourth Gospel,
chapter 20, verses 19 to 23:

> *"Peace be with you", he said.*
> *And when he had said this, he showed them his hands and his side.*
> *At the sight of the Lord the disciples rejoiced.*
> *"Peace be with you", he said again.*
> *"As the father has sent me, so I send you."*
> *Then he breathed on them and said: "Receive Holy Spirit.*
> *If you forgive men's sins, they are forgiven them.*
> *If you hold them bound, they are held bound."*

It is a special message that God conveys to us on the evening of this
Easter Sunday here in Jerusalem, after our serious and fruitful work on
the "interrelatio evangeliorum."

We have no reason to fear the Jews as the apostles did after they had
seen their master and Lord exposed to hatred, torture, and execution.
But in other regards our situation is a similar one. Like the apostles, we
are sitting together in a room not very remote from the place where
Jesus Christ was buried and where Mary Magdalene and other eye-
witnesses had found his tomb empty on the first day of the week. And
like the apostles in the room where they were assembled, we receive an
opportunity to be confronted with the Risen Lord who comes to give us
peace and courage, strength and guidance. He brings these gifts in the
form of bread and wine, the elements by which he chose to convey his
body and blood to us, thus delivering us from sin and death.

It is not only for his first readers, but also *for us* that John has
described how the disciples at their assembly found Jesus standing

before them. Whenever two or three disciples are gathered in the name of Jesus, he is himself in their midst.

For us the evangelist has also witnessed that Jesus greeted his disciples with these cordial words: "Peace be with you." There should be no reason for them, and shall be no reason for us, to fear other men. Jesus proved it by showing the apostles his wounds, for just by his suffering and death he overcame the powers of corruption and mortality and since then he lets all believers share his victory. No wonder that his appearance then permitted the disciples to rejoice, and we rejoice with them in the present moment.

A second greeting including the same words, "Peace be with you," leads on to a solemn proclamation. In this case Jesus declares: The sending of the Son by the Father is to be continued in the sending of the disciples by the Son. Here again the words of Christ are meant to be of importance for all of us. We are sent to preach and teach, to live and work, as witnesses to Christ's wonderful victory over sin and death. All men on earth shall be reached by the good message about Jesus, his sacrifice and victory, and the members of this Symposium have a particular responsibility to obey the words of Christ when he spoke about sending his disciples out into the world.

Those who are sent out, however, will not be lost in the world. Jesus says to them: Receive Holy Spirit, and he also confers this spirit upon them. In the context of the Fourth Gospel, the communication of the Holy Spirit to the apostles on the evening of Easter Sunday is the fulfillment of a promise given earlier in his farewell speech when he spoke of the Paraclete, the spirit of truth by which the disciples will be strengthened in this world. John has reported how the apostles received this spirit on Easter Day, and Luke how all believers then received it at Pentecost. Do we consider that we have also received this Holy Spirit by our baptism in the name of Jesus Christ? It seems that sometimes we forget or suppress this fact. May the confrontation with John's report on the experience of the apostles just after Christ's resurrection help us to realize what precious gift we have received in the Holy Spirit conferred upon all of us by Christ himself.

Being together in this moment to celebrate the holy communion, let us also remember what Christ finally said to his apostles in the room where they were assembled. He said: "If you forgive men's sins, they are forgiven. If you hold them bound, they are held bound." Christ died for our sins and his death implied victory over sin and death. Therefore he also expects us to forgive every sin committed against us by other men. After our theological discussions during the last weeks, this admonition of Jesus Christ to forgive the sins of our neighbours is very important, even quite essential for us. Let us pray with the apostle Paul that God's peace, which surpasses our scholarly rationality, will preserve our hearts and thoughts in Christ Jesus. Amen.

Praise be to God, the Father, the Son and the Holy Ghost, for what he shows us in his holy Gospels. Amen.

BO REICKE

APPENDIX

SYNOPSIS
THE ESCHATOLOGICAL DISCOURSE

SYNOPSIS A

Matthew 24:42-44   Luke 12:35-40

35 Ἔστωσαν ὑμῶν αἱ ὀσφύες περι-
εζωσμέναι καὶ οἱ λύχνοι καιόμενοι·
36 καὶ ὑμεῖς ὅμοιοι ἀνθρώποις
προσδεχομένοις τὸν κύριον ἑαυτῶν
πότε ἀναλύσῃ ἐκ τῶν γάμων,
ἵνα
ἐλθόντος καὶ κρούσαντος
εὐθέως ἀνοίξωσιν αὐτῷ.
37 μακάριοι οἱ δοῦλοι ἐκεῖνοι,

42 Γρηγορεῖτε οὖν, ὅτι οὐκ οἴδατε   οὓς ἐλθὼν
ποίᾳ ἡμέρᾳ ὁ κύριος ὑμῶν ἔρχεται.   ὁ κύριος εὑρήσει γρηγοροῦντας·
ἀμὴν λέγω ὑμῖν ὅτι περιζώσεται
καὶ ἀνακλινεῖ αὐτοὺς καὶ παρελθὼν
διακονήσει αὐτοῖς.
38 κἂν ἐν τῇ δευτέρᾳ κἂν ἐν τῇ τρίτῃ
φυλακῇ
ἔλθῃ καὶ εὕρῃ οὕτως, μακάριοί εἰσιν
ἐκεῖνοι.

43 Ἐκεῖνο δὲ γινώσκετε   39 τοῦτο δὲ γινώσκετε,
ὅτι εἰ ᾔδει ὁ οἰκοδεσπότης ποίᾳ   ὅτι εἰ ᾔδει ὁ οἰκοδεσπότης ποίᾳ
φυλακῇ ὁ κλέπτης ἔρχεται,   ὥρᾳ ὁ κλέπτης ἔρχεται,
ἐγρηγόρησεν ἂν καὶ   [ἐγρηγόρησεν ἂν καὶ]
οὐκ ἂν εἴασεν διορυχθῆναι   οὐκ ἂν ἀφῆκεν διορυχθῆναι
τὴν οἰκίαν αὐτοῦ.   τὸν οἶκον αὐτοῦ.
44 διὰ τοῦτο καὶ ὑμεῖς γίνεσθε ἕτοιμοι,   40 καὶ ὑμεῖς γίνεσθε ἕτοιμοι,
ὅτι ᾗ οὐ δοκεῖτε ὥρᾳ   ὅτι ᾗ ὥρᾳ οὐ δοκεῖτε
ὁ υἱὸς τοῦ ἀνθρώπου ἔρχεται.   ὁ υἱὸς τοῦ ἀνθρώπου ἔρχεται.

Matthew 24:45-51	Luke 12:41-48
	41 Εἶπεν δὲ ὁ Πέτρος·
	κύριε, πρὸς ἡμᾶς τὴν παραβολὴν
	ταύτην λέγεις ἢ καὶ πρὸς πάντας;
	42 καὶ εἶπεν ὁ κύριος·
45 Τίς ἄρα ἐστὶν ὁ πιστὸς δοῦλος	Τίς ἄρα ἐστὶν ὁ πιστὸς οἰκονόμος
καὶ φρόνιμος	ὁ φρόνιμος,
ὃν κατέστησεν ὁ κύριος	ὃν καταστήσει ὁ κύριος
ἐπὶ τῆς οἰκετείας αὐτοῦ	ἐπὶ τῆς θεραπείας αὐτοῦ
τοῦ δοῦναι αὐτοῖς	τοῦ διδόναι
τὴν τροφὴν ἐν καιρῷ;	ἐν καιρῷ [τὸ] σιτομέτριον;
46 μακάριος ὁ δοῦλος ἐκεῖνος	43 μακάριος ὁ δοῦλος ἐκεῖνος
ὃν ἐλθὼν ὁ κύριος αὐτοῦ	ὃν ἐλθὼν ὁ κύριος αὐτοῦ
εὑρήσει οὕτως ποιοῦντα·	εὑρήσει ποιοῦντα οὕτως.
47 ἀμὴν λέγω ὑμῖν ὅτι	44 ἀληθῶς λέγω ὑμῖν ὅτι
ἐπὶ πᾶσιν τοῖς ὑπάρχουσιν αὐτοῦ	ἐπὶ πᾶσιν τοῖς ὑπάρχουσιν αὐτοῦ
καταστήσει αὐτόν.	καταστήσει αὐτόν.
48 ἐὰν δὲ εἴπῃ ὁ κακὸς δοῦλος ἐκεῖνος	45 ἐὰν δὲ εἴπῃ ὁ δοῦλος ἐκεῖνος
ἐν τῇ καρδίᾳ αὐτοῦ·	ἐν τῇ καρδίᾳ αὐτοῦ·
χρονίζει μου ὁ κύριος,	χρονίζει ὁ κύριός μου ἔρχεσθαι,
49 καὶ ἄρξηται τύπτειν	καὶ ἄρξηται τύπτειν
τοὺς συνδούλους αὐτοῦ,	τοὺς παῖδας καὶ τὰς παιδίσκας,
ἐσθίῃ δὲ καὶ πίνῃ μετὰ τῶν μεθυόντων,	ἐσθίειν τε καὶ πίνειν καὶ μεθύσκεσθαι,
50 ἥξει ὁ κύριος τοῦ δούλου ἐκείνου	46 ἥξει ὁ κύριος τοῦ δούλου ἐκείνου
ἐν ἡμέρᾳ ᾗ οὐ προσδοκᾷ	ἐν ἡμέρᾳ ᾗ οὐ προσδοκᾷ
καὶ ἐν ὥρᾳ ᾗ οὐ γινώσκει	καὶ ἐν ὥρᾳ ᾗ οὐ γινώσκει
51 καὶ διχοτομήσει αὐτὸν	καὶ διχοτομήσει αὐτὸν
καὶ τὸ μέρος αὐτοῦ	καὶ τὸ μέρος αὐτοῦ
μετὰ τῶν ὑποκριτῶν θήσει·	μετὰ τῶν ἀπίστων θήσει.
	47 Ἐκεῖνος δὲ ὁ δοῦλος ὁ γνοὺς
	τὸ θέλημα τοῦ κυρίου αὐτοῦ
	καὶ μὴ ἑτοιμάσας ἢ ποιήσας
	πρὸς τὸ θέλημα αὐτοῦ
	δαρήσεται πολλάς·
	48 ὁ δὲ μὴ γνούς,
	ποιήσας δὲ ἄξια πληγῶν
	δαρήσεται ὀλίγας.
	παντὶ δὲ ᾧ ἐδόθη πολύ,
	πολὺ ζητηθήσεται παρ' αὐτοῦ,
	καὶ ᾧ παρέθεντο πολύ,
	περισσότερον αἰτήσουσιν αὐτόν.

SYNOPSIS B

Matthew 24:23, 26-27	Luke 17:20-25
	20 Ἐπερωτηθεὶς δὲ ὑπὸ τῶν Φαρισαίων πότε ἔρχεται ἡ βασιλεία τοῦ θεοῦ ἀπεκρίθη αὐτοῖς καὶ εἶπεν·
23 Τότε ἐάν τις ὑμῖν εἴπῃ·	οὐκ ἔρχεται ἡ βασιλεία τοῦ θεοῦ μετὰ παρατηρήσεως,
ἰδοὺ ὧδε ὁ χριστός, ἤ· ὧδε, μὴ πιστεύσητε·	21 οὐδὲ ἐροῦσιν· ἰδοὺ ὧδε ἤ· ἐκεῖ,
	ἰδοὺ γὰρ ἡ βασιλεία τοῦ θεοῦ ἐντὸς ὑμῶν ἐστιν.
	22 Εἶπεν δὲ πρὸς τοὺς μαθητάς· ἐλεύσονται ἡμέραι ὅτε ἐπιθυμήσετε μίαν τῶν ἡμερῶν τοῦ υἱοῦ τοῦ ἀνθρώπου ἰδεῖν καὶ οὐκ ὄψεσθε.
26 ἐὰν οὖν εἴπωσιν ὑμῖν· ἰδοὺ ἐν τῇ ἐρήμῳ ἐστίν, μὴ ἐξέλθητε· ἰδοὺ ἐν τοῖς ταμείοις, μὴ πιστεύσητε·	23 καὶ ἐροῦσιν ὑμῖν· ἰδοὺ ἐκεῖ, [ἤ] ἰδοὺ ὧδε· μὴ ἀπέλθητε μηδὲ διώξητε.
27 ὥσπερ γὰρ ἡ ἀστραπὴ ἐξέρχεται ἀπὸ ἀνατολῶν καὶ φαίνεται ἕως δυσμῶν, οὕτως ἔσται ἡ παρουσία τοῦ υἱοῦ τοῦ ἀνθρώπου·	24 ὥσπερ γὰρ ἡ ἀστραπὴ ἀστράπτουσα ἐκ τῆς ὑπὸ τὸν οὐρανὸν εἰς τὴν ὑπ' οὐρανὸν λάμπει, οὕτως ἔσται ὁ υἱὸς τοῦ ἀνθρώπου [ἐν τῇ ἡμέρᾳ αὐτοῦ].
	25 πρῶτον δὲ δεῖ αὐτὸν πολλὰ παθεῖν καὶ ἀποδοκιμασθῆναι ἀπὸ τῆς γενεᾶς ταύτης.

Matthew 24:37-39, 17-18	Luke 17:26-32
37 Ὥσπερ γὰρ αἱ ἡμέραι τοῦ Νῶε, οὕτως ἔσται ἡ παρουσία τοῦ υἱοῦ τοῦ ἀνθρώπου.	26 καὶ καθὼς ἐγένετο ἐν ταῖς ἡμέραις Νῶε, οὕτως ἔσται καὶ ἐν ταῖς ἡμέραις τοῦ υἱοῦ τοῦ ἀνθρώπου.
38 ὡς γὰρ ἦσαν ἐν ταῖς ἡμέραις [ἐκείναις] ταῖς πρὸ τοῦ κατακλυσμοῦ τρώγοντες καὶ πίνοντες, γαμοῦντες καὶ γαμίζοντες,	27 ἤσθιον, ἔπινον, ἐγάμουν, ἐγαμίζοντο,

618 A.J. McNICOL

ἄχρι ἧς ἡμέρας εἰσῆλθεν
Νῶε εἰς τὴν κιβωτόν,
39 καὶ οὐκ ἔγνωσαν ἕως
ἦλθεν ὁ κατακλυσμὸς
καὶ ἦρεν ἅπαντας,

οὕτως ἔσται [καὶ] ἡ παρουσία
τοῦ υἱοῦ τοῦ ἀνθρώπου.

17 ὁ ἐπὶ τοῦ δώματος

μὴ καταβάτω
ἆραι τὰ ἐκ τῆς οἰκίας αὐτοῦ,
18 καὶ ὁ ἐν τῷ ἀγρῷ
μὴ ἐπιστρεψάτω ὀπίσω
ἆραι τὸ ἱμάτιον αὐτοῦ.

ἄχρι ἧς ἡμέρας εἰσῆλθεν
Νῶε εἰς τὴν κιβωτὸν
καὶ
ἦλθεν ὁ κατακλυσμὸς
καὶ ἀπώλεσεν πάντας.
28 ὁμοίως καθὼς ἐγένετο ἐν ταῖς ἡμέραις
Λώτ·
ἤσθιον, ἔπινον, ἠγόραζον, ἐπώλουν,
ἐφύτευον, ᾠκοδόμουν·
29 ᾗ δὲ ἡμέρᾳ ἐξῆλθεν Λὼτ ἀπὸ Σοδόμων,
ἔβρεξεν πῦρ καὶ θεῖον ἀπ' οὐρανοῦ
καὶ ἀπώλεσεν πάντας.
30 κατὰ τὰ αὐτὰ ἔσται ᾗ ἡμέρᾳ
ὁ υἱὸς τοῦ ἀνθρώπου ἀποκαλύπτεται.
31 ἐν ἐκείνῃ τῇ ἡμέρᾳ
ὃς ἔσται ἐπὶ τοῦ δώματος
καὶ τὰ σκεύη αὐτοῦ ἐν τῇ οἰκίᾳ,
μὴ καταβάτω
ἆραι αὐτά,
καὶ ὁ ἐν ἀγρῷ ὁμοίως
μὴ ἐπιστρεψάτω εἰς τὰ ὀπίσω.

32 μνημονεύετε τῆς γυναικὸς Λώτ.

Matthew 10:39; 24:40-41, 28

10:39 ὁ εὑρὼν τὴν ψυχὴν αὐτοῦ

ἀπολέσει αὐτήν,
καὶ ὁ ἀπολέσας τὴν ψυχὴν αὐτοῦ
ἕνεκεν ἐμοῦ
εὑρήσει αὐτήν.

24:40 τότε δύο ἔσονται ἐν τῷ ἀγρῷ,
εἷς παραλαμβάνεται
καὶ εἷς ἀφίεται·
41 δύο ἀλήθουσαι ἐν τῷ μύλῳ,
μία παραλαμβάνεται
καὶ μία ἀφίεται.
24:40

24:28 ὅπου ἐὰν ᾖ τὸ πτῶμα,
ἐκεῖ συναχθήσονται οἱ ἀετοί.

Luke 17:33-37

33 ὃς ἐὰν ζητήσῃ τὴν ψυχὴν αὐτοῦ
περιποιήσασθαι
ἀπολέσει αὐτήν,
ὃς δ' ἂν ἀπολέσῃ

ζῳογονήσει αὐτήν.
34 λέγω ὑμῖν,
ταύτῃ τῇ νυκτὶ
ἔσονται δύο ἐπὶ κλίνης μιᾶς,
ὁ εἷς παραλημφθήσεται
καὶ ὁ ἕτερος ἀφεθήσεται·
35 ἔσονται δύο ἀλήθουσαι ἐπὶ τὸ αὐτό,
ἡ μία παραλημφθήσεται,
ἡ δὲ ἑτέρα ἀφεθήσεται.
[36] [δύο ἔσονται ἐν τῷ ἀγρῷ
εἷς παραλημφθήσεται
καὶ ὁ ἕτερος ἀφεθήσεται.]
37 καὶ ἀποκριθέντες λέγουσιν αὐτῷ·
ποῦ, κύριε;
ὁ δὲ εἶπεν αὐτοῖς·
ὅπου τὸ σῶμα,
ἐκεῖ καὶ οἱ ἀετοὶ ἐπισυναχθήσονται.

SYNOPSIS C

Matthew 24:1-7	Luke 21:5-11
1 Καὶ ἐξελθὼν ὁ Ἰησοῦς ἀπὸ τοῦ ἱεροῦ ἐπορεύετο, καὶ προσῆλθον οἱ μαθηταὶ αὐτοῦ ἐπιδεῖξαι αὐτῷ τὰς οἰκοδομὰς τοῦ ἱεροῦ.	5 Καί τινων λεγόντων περὶ τοῦ ἱεροῦ. ὅτι λίθοις καλοῖς καὶ ἀναθήμασιν κεκόσμηται
2 ὁ δὲ ἀποκριθεὶς εἶπεν αὐτοῖς· οὐ βλέπετε ταῦτα πάντα; ἀμὴν λέγω ὑμῖν, οὐ μὴ ἀφεθῇ ὧδε λίθος ἐπὶ λίθον ὃς οὐ καταλυθήσεται.	εἶπεν· 6 ταῦτα ἃ θεωρεῖτε ἐλεύσονται ἡμέραι ἐν αἷς οὐκ ἀφεθήσεται λίθος ἐπὶ λίθῳ, ὃς οὐ καταλυθήσεται.
3 Καθημένου δὲ αὐτοῦ ἐπὶ τοῦ ὄρους τῶν ἐλαιῶν προσῆλθον αὐτῷ οἱ μαθηταὶ κατ᾽ ἰδίαν λέγοντες· εἰπὲ ἡμῖν, πότε ταῦτα ἔσται καὶ τί τὸ σημεῖον τῆς σῆς παρουσίας καὶ συντελείας τοῦ αἰῶνος;	7 Ἐπηρώτησαν δὲ αὐτὸν λέγοντες· διδάσκαλε, πότε οὖν ταῦτα ἔσται; καὶ τί τὸ σημεῖον ὅταν μέλλῃ ταῦτα γίνεσθαι;
4 Καὶ ἀποκριθεὶς ὁ Ἰησοῦς εἶπεν αὐτοῖς· βλέπετε μή τις ὑμᾶς πλανήσῃ·	8 ὁ δὲ εἶπεν· βλέπετε μὴ πλανηθῆτε·
5 πολλοὶ γὰρ ἐλεύσονται ἐπὶ τῷ ὀνόματί μου λέγοντες· ἐγώ εἰμι ὁ Χριστός, καὶ πολλοὺς πλανήσουσιν.	πολλοὶ γὰρ ἐλεύσονται ἐπὶ τῷ ὀνόματί μου λέγοντες· ἐγώ εἰμι, καί· ὁ καιρὸς ἤγγικεν· μὴ πορευθῆτε ὀπίσω αὐτῶν.
6 μελλήσετε δὲ ἀκούειν πολέμους καὶ ἀκοὰς πολέμων· ὁρᾶτε μὴ θροεῖσθε· δεῖ γὰρ γενέσθαι, ἀλλ᾽ οὔπω ἐστὶν τὸ τέλος.	9 ὅταν δὲ ἀκούσητε πολέμους καὶ ἀκαταστασίας, μὴ πτοηθῆτε· δεῖ γὰρ ταῦτα γενέσθαι πρῶτον, ἀλλ᾽ οὐκ εὐθέως τὸ τέλος.
7 ἐγερθήσεται γὰρ ἔθνος ἐπὶ ἔθνος καὶ βασιλεία ἐπὶ βασιλείαν καὶ ἔσονται λιμοὶ καὶ σεισμοὶ κατὰ τόπους·	10 Τότε ἔλεγεν αὐτοῖς· ἐγερθήσεται ἔθνος ἐπ᾽ ἔθνος καὶ βασιλεία ἐπὶ βασιλείαν, 11 σεισμοί τε μεγάλοι καὶ κατὰ τόπους λιμοὶ καὶ λοιμοὶ ἔσονται, φόβητρά τε καὶ ἀπ᾽ οὐρανοῦ σημεῖα μεγάλα ἔσται.

Matthew 10:17-22	Matthew 24:8-14	Luke 21:12-19	Luke 12:11-12
17 Προσέχετε δὲ ἀπὸ τῶν ἀνθρώπων· παραδώσουσιν γὰρ ὑμᾶς εἰς συνέδρια καὶ ἐν ταῖς συναγωγαῖς αὐτῶν μαστιγώσουσιν ὑμᾶς·	8 πάντα δὲ ταῦτα ἀρχὴ ὠδίνων. 9 Τότε παραδώσουσιν ὑμᾶς εἰς θλῖψιν	12 πρὸ δὲ τούτων πάντων ἐπιβαλοῦσιν ἐφ' ὑμᾶς τὰς χεῖρας αὐτῶν καὶ διώξουσιν, παραδιδόντες εἰς τὰς συναγωγὰς καὶ φυλακάς, ἀπαγομένους	11 Ὅταν δὲ εἰσφέρωσιν ὑμᾶς ἐπὶ τὰς συναγωγὰς καὶ τὰς ἀρχὰς καὶ τὰς ἐξουσίας, μὴ μεριμνήσητε πῶς ἢ τί εἴπητε
18 καὶ ἐπὶ ἡγεμόνας δὲ καὶ βασιλεῖς ἀχθήσεσθε ἕνεκεν ἐμοῦ εἰς μαρτύριον αὐτοῖς καὶ τοῖς ἔθνεσιν.		ἐπὶ βασιλεῖς καὶ ἡγεμόνας ἕνεκεν τοῦ ὀνόματός μου· 13 ἀποβήσεται ὑμῖν εἰς μαρτύριον.	12 τὸ γὰρ ἅγιον πνεῦμα διδάξει ὑμᾶς ἐν αὐτῇ τῇ ὥρᾳ ἃ δεῖ εἰπεῖν.
19 ὅταν δὲ παραδῶσιν ὑμᾶς,		14 θέτε οὖν ἐν ταῖς καρδίαις ὑμῶν	
μὴ μεριμνήσητε πῶς ἢ τί λαλήσητε· δοθήσεται γὰρ ὑμῖν ἐν ἐκείνῃ τῇ ὥρᾳ τί λαλήσητε· 20 οὐ γὰρ ὑμεῖς ἐστε οἱ λαλοῦντες ἀλλὰ τὸ πνεῦμα τοῦ πατρὸς ὑμῶν τὸ λαλοῦν ἐν ὑμῖν.		μὴ προμελετᾶν ἀπολογηθῆναι· 15 ἐγὼ γὰρ δώσω ὑμῖν στόμα καὶ σοφίαν ᾗ οὐ δυνήσονται ἀντιστῆναι ἢ ἀντειπεῖν ἅπαντες οἱ ἀντικείμενοι ὑμῖν.	
21 Παραδώσει δὲ ἀδελφὸς ἀδελφὸν εἰς θάνατον καὶ πατὴρ τέκνον, καὶ ἐπαναστήσονται τέκνα ἐπὶ γονεῖς καὶ θανατώσουσιν αὐτούς· 22a καὶ ἔσεσθε μισούμενοι ὑπὸ πάντων διὰ τὸ ὄνομά μου·		16 παραδοθήσεσθε δὲ καὶ ὑπὸ γονέων καὶ ἀδελφῶν καὶ συγγενῶν καὶ φίλων, καὶ θανατώσουσιν ἐξ ὑμῶν, 17 καὶ ἔσεσθε μισούμενοι ὑπὸ πάντων τῶν ἐθνῶν διὰ τὸ ὄνομά μου.	

10 καὶ τότε σκανδαλισθήσονται πολλοὶ
καὶ ἀλλήλους παραδώσουσιν
καὶ μισήσουσιν ἀλλήλους·

11 καὶ πολλοὶ ψευδοπροφῆται
ἐγερθήσονται
καὶ πλανήσουσιν πολλούς·

12 καὶ διὰ τὸ πληθυνθῆναι τὴν ἀνομίαν
ψυγήσεται ἡ ἀγάπη τῶν πολλῶν.

13 ὁ δὲ ὑπομείνας εἰς τέλος
οὗτος σωθήσεται.

14 καὶ κηρυχθήσεται τοῦτο τὸ εὐαγγέλιον
τῆς βασιλείας ἐν ὅλῃ τῇ οἰκουμένῃ
εἰς μαρτύριον πᾶσιν τοῖς ἔθνεσιν,
καὶ τότε ἥξει τὸ τέλος.

18 καὶ θρὶξ ἐκ τῆς κεφαλῆς ὑμῶν
οὐ μὴ ἀπόληται.

19 ἐν τῇ ὑπομονῇ ὑμῶν
κτήσασθε τὰς ψυχὰς ὑμῶν.

22b ὁ δὲ ὑπομείνας εἰς τέλος
οὗτος σωθήσεται.

Matthew 24:15-31	Luke 21:20-28
15 Ὅταν οὖν ἴδητε	20 Ὅταν δὲ ἴδητε κυκλουμένην ὑπὸ στρατοπέδων Ἰερου- σαλήμ, τότε γνῶτε ὅτι ἤγγικεν ἡ ἐρήμωσις αὐτῆς.
τὸ βδέλυγμα τῆς ἐρημώσεως τὸ ῥηθὲν διὰ Δανιὴλ τοῦ προφήτου ἑστὸς ἐν τόπῳ ἁγίῳ, ὁ ἀναγινώσκων νοείτω,	
16 τότε οἱ ἐν τῇ Ἰουδαίᾳ φευγέτωσαν εἰς τὰ ὄρη,	21 τότε οἱ ἐν τῇ Ἰουδαίᾳ φευγέτωσαν εἰς τὰ ὄρη καὶ οἱ ἐν μέσῳ αὐτῆς ἐκχωρείτωσαν
17 ὁ ἐπὶ τοῦ δώματος μὴ καταβάτω ἆραι τὰ ἐκ τῆς οἰκίας αὐτοῦ,	
18 καὶ ὁ ἐν τῷ ἀγρῷ μὴ ἐπιστρεψάτω ὀπίσω ἆραι τὸ ἱμάτιον αὐτοῦ.	καὶ οἱ ἐν ταῖς χώραις μὴ εἰσερχέσθωσαν εἰς αὐτήν,
	22 ὅτι ἡμέραι ἐκδικήσεως αὗταί εἰσιν τοῦ πλησθῆναι πάντα τὰ γεγραμμένα.
19 οὐαὶ δὲ ταῖς ἐν γαστρὶ ἐχούσαις καὶ ταῖς θηλαζούσαις ἐν ἐκείναις ταῖς ἡμέραις.	23 οὐαὶ [δὲ] ταῖς ἐν γαστρὶ ἐχούσαις καὶ ταῖς θηλαζούσαις ἐν ἐκείναις ταῖς ἡμέραις·
20 προσεύχεσθε δὲ ἵνα μὴ γένηται ἡ φυγὴ ὑμῶν χειμῶνος μηδὲ σαββάτῳ,	
21 ἔσται γὰρ τότε θλῖψις μεγάλη	ἔσται γὰρ ἀνάγκη μεγάλη ἐπὶ τῆς γῆς καὶ ὀργὴ τῷ λαῷ τούτῳ,
	24 καὶ πεσοῦνται στόματι μαχαίρης καὶ αἰχμαλωτισθήσονται εἰς τὰ ἔθνη πάντα, καὶ Ἰερουσαλὴμ ἔσται πατουμένη ὑπὸ ἐθνῶν, ἄχρι οὗ πληρωθῶσιν καιροὶ ἐθνῶν.
οἵα οὐ γέγονεν ἀπ᾽ ἀρχῆς κόσμου ἕως τοῦ νῦν οὐδ᾽ οὐ μὴ γένηται.	
22 καὶ εἰ μὴ ἐκολοβώθησαν αἱ ἡμέραι ἐκεῖναι, οὐκ ἂν ἐσώθη πᾶσα σάρξ· διὰ δὲ τοὺς ἐκλεκτοὺς κολοβωθήσονται αἱ ἡμέραι ἐκεῖναι.	

29 Εὐθέως δὲ μετὰ τὴν θλῖψιν
τῶν ἡμερῶν ἐκείνων,
ὁ ἥλιος σκοτισθήσεται,
καὶ ἡ σελήνη οὐ δώσει τὸ φέγγος αὐτῆς,
καὶ οἱ ἀστέρες πεσοῦνται ἀπὸ τοῦ οὐρανοῦ,

25 Καὶ ἔσονται σημεῖα ἐν ἡλίῳ
καὶ σελήνῃ
καὶ ἄστροις,

καὶ ἐπὶ τῆς γῆς συνοχὴ ἐθνῶν
ἐν ἀπορίᾳ ἤχους θαλάσσης καὶ σάλου,
26 ἀποψυχόντων ἀνθρώπων ἀπὸ φόβου
καὶ προσδοκίας τῶν ἐπερχομένων
τῇ οἰκουμένῃ,
καὶ αἱ δυνάμεις τῶν οὐρανῶν σαλευ-
θήσονται.   αἱ γὰρ δυνάμεις τῶν οὐρανῶν σαλευ-
                                               θήσονται.
30 καὶ τότε φανήσεται τὸ σημεῖον
τοῦ υἱοῦ τοῦ ἀνθρώπου ἐν οὐρανῷ,
καὶ τότε κόψονται πᾶσαι αἱ φυλαὶ τῆς
γῆς
καὶ ὄψονται τὸν υἱὸν τοῦ ἀνθρώπου   27 καὶ τότε ὄψονται τὸν υἱὸν τοῦ ἀνθρώπου
ἐρχόμενον ἐπὶ τῶν νεφελῶν   ἐρχόμενον ἐν νεφέλῃ
τοῦ οὐρανοῦ
μετὰ δυνάμεως καὶ δόξης πολλῆς·   μετὰ δυνάμεως καὶ δόξης πολλῆς.
31 καὶ ἀποστελεῖ τοὺς ἀγγέλους αὐτοῦ
μετὰ σάλπιγγος μεγάλης,
καὶ ἐπισυνάξουσιν τοὺς ἐκλεκτοὺς
αὐτοῦ
ἐκ τῶν τεσσάρων ἀνέμων
ἀπ᾽ ἄκρων οὐρανῶν ἕως [τῶν] ἄκρων
αὐτῶν.

28 ἀρχομένων δὲ τούτων γίνεσθαι
ἀνακύψατε καὶ ἐπάρατε τὰς κεφαλὰς
ὑμῶν,
διότι ἐγγίζει ἡ ἀπολύτρωσις ὑμῶν.

Matthew 5:18	Matthew 24:32-36,42	Luke 21:29-36
	32 Ἀπὸ δὲ τῆς συκῆς μάθετε τὴν παραβολήν·	29 Καὶ εἶπεν παραβολὴν αὐτοῖς· ἴδετε τὴν συκῆν καὶ πάντα τὰ δένδρα·
	ὅταν ἤδη ὁ κλάδος αὐτῆς γένηται ἁπαλὸς καὶ τὰ φύλλα ἐκφύῃ,	30 ὅταν προβάλωσιν ἤδη,
		βλέποντες ἀφ' ἑαυτῶν
	γινώσκετε ὅτι ἐγγὺς τὸ θέρος·	γινώσκετε ὅτι ἤδη ἐγγὺς τὸ θέρος ἐστίν·
	33 οὕτως καὶ ὑμεῖς ὅταν ἴδητε πάντα ταῦτα, γινώσκετε ὅτι ἐγγύς ἐστιν ἐπὶ θύραις.	31 οὕτως καὶ ὑμεῖς, ὅταν ἴδητε ταῦτα γινόμενα, γινώσκετε ὅτι ἐγγύς ἐστιν ἡ βασιλεία τοῦ θεοῦ.
18 ἀμὴν γὰρ λέγω ὑμῖν·	34 ἀμὴν λέγω ὑμῖν ὅτι οὐ μὴ παρέλθῃ ἡ γενεὰ αὕτη	32 ἀμὴν λέγω ὑμῖν ὅτι οὐ μὴ παρέλθῃ ἡ γενεὰ αὕτη
ἕως ἂν παρέλθῃ ὁ οὐρανὸς καὶ ἡ γῆ,	ἕως ἂν πάντα ταῦτα γένηται. 35 ὁ οὐρανὸς καὶ ἡ γῆ παρελεύσεται,	ἕως ἂν πάντα γένηται. 33 ὁ οὐρανὸς καὶ ἡ γῆ παρελεύσονται,
ἰῶτα ἓν ἢ μία κεραία οὐ μὴ παρέλθῃ ἀπὸ τοῦ νόμου, ἕως ἂν πάντα γένηται.	οἱ δὲ λόγοι μου οὐ μὴ παρέλθωσιν.	οἱ δὲ λόγοι μου οὐ μὴ παρελεύσονται.
	36 Περὶ δὲ τῆς ἡμέρας ἐκείνης καὶ ὥρας οὐδεὶς οἶδεν, οὐδὲ οἱ ἄγγελοι τῶν οὐρανῶν οὐδὲ ὁ υἱός, εἰ μὴ ὁ πατὴρ μόνος.	
		34 Προσέχετε δὲ ἑαυτοῖς μήποτε βαρηθῶσιν ὑμῶν αἱ καρδίαι ἐν κραιπάλῃ καὶ μέθῃ καὶ μερίμναις βιωτικαῖς καὶ ἐπιστῇ ἐφ' ὑμᾶς αἰφνίδιος ἡ ἡμέρα ἐκείνη 35 ὡς παγίς· ἐπεισελεύσεται γὰρ ἐπὶ πάντας τοὺς καθημένους ἐπὶ πρόσωπον πάσης τῆς γῆς.
	42 Γρηγορεῖτε οὖν, ὅτι οὐκ οἴδατε ποίᾳ ἡμέρᾳ ὁ κύριος ὑμῶν ἔρχεται.	36 ἀγρυπνεῖτε δὲ ἐν παντὶ καιρῷ δεόμενοι ἵνα κατισχύσητε ἐκφυγεῖν ταῦτα πάντα τὰ μέλλοντα γίνεσθαι καὶ σταθῆναι ἔμπροσθεν τοῦ υἱοῦ τοῦ ἀνθρώπου.

Mark 13:9-13 and parallels

Matthew 10:17-23a	Matthew 24:9-15a	Mark 13:9-14a	Luke 21:12-20a	Luke 12:11-12
17 προσέχετε δὲ ἀπὸ τῶν ἀνθρώπων· παραδώσουσιν γὰρ ὑμᾶς εἰς συνέδρια, καὶ ἐν ταῖς συναγωγαῖς αὐτῶν μαστιγώσουσιν ὑμᾶς·	9 τότε παραδώσουσιν ὑμᾶς εἰς θλῖψιν...	9 βλέπετε δὲ ὑμεῖς ἑαυτούς· παραδώσουσιν ὑμᾶς εἰς συνέδρια καὶ εἰς συναγωγὰς δαρήσεσθε	12 πρὸ δὲ τούτων πάντων ἐπιβαλοῦσιν ἐφ' ὑμᾶς τὰς χεῖρας αὐτῶν καὶ διώξουσιν, παραδιδόντες εἰς τὰς συναγωγὰς καὶ φυλακάς, ἀπαγομένους ἐπὶ βασιλεῖς	Luke 12:11-12
18 καὶ ἐπὶ ἡγεμόνας δὲ καὶ βασιλεῖς ἀχθήσεσθε ἕνεκεν ἐμοῦ		καὶ ἐπὶ ἡγεμόνων καὶ βασιλέων σταθήσεσθε ἕνεκεν ἐμοῦ	καὶ ἡγεμόνας ἕνεκεν τοῦ ὀνόματός μου· 13 ἀποβήσεται ὑμῖν	
εἰς μαρτύριον αὐτοῖς καὶ τοῖς ἔθνεσιν.	14β ...ἐν ὅλῃ τῇ οἰκουμένῃ εἰς μαρτύριον πᾶσιν τοῖς ἔθνεσιν,... 14a ...καὶ κηρυχθήσεται τοῦτο τὸ εὐαγγέλιον τῆς βασιλείας.	εἰς μαρτύριον αὐτοῖς. 10 καὶ εἰς πάντα τὰ ἔθνη πρῶτον δεῖ κηρυχθῆναι τὸ εὐαγγέλιον.	εἰς μαρτύριον.	
19 ὅταν δὲ παραδῶσιν ὑμᾶς,	15a ὅταν οὖν...	11 καὶ ὅταν ἄγωσιν ὑμᾶς παραδιδόντες		11 ὅταν δὲ εἰσφέρωσιν ὑμᾶς ἐπὶ τὰς συναγωγὰς καὶ τὰς ἀρχὰς καὶ τὰς ἐξουσίας,

Matthew 10	Matthew 24	Mark 13	Luke 21	Luke 12
19b μὴ μεριμνήσατε πῶς ἢ τί λαλήσητε·		**11b** μὴ προμεριμνᾶτε τί λαλήσετε,	**14** θέτε οὖν ἐν ταῖς καρδίαις ὑμῶν μὴ προμελετᾶν ἀπολογηθῆναι,	**11** μὴ μεριμνήσατε πῶς ἢ τί ἀπολογήσησθε ἢ τί εἴπητε·
19c δοθήσεται γάρ ὑμῖν		**11c** ἀλλ᾽ ὃ ἐὰν δοθῇ ὑμῖν	**15** ἐγὼ γάρ δώσω ὑμῖν στόμα καὶ σοφίαν	**12** τὸ γάρ ἅγιον πνεῦμα διδάξει ὑμᾶς
ἐν ἐκείνῃ τῇ ὥρᾳ τί λαλήσητε		ἐν ἐκείνῃ τῇ ὥρᾳ τοῦτο λαλεῖτε·	ᾗ οὐ δυνήσονται ἀντιστῆναι ἢ ἀντειπεῖν ἅπαντες οἱ ἀντικείμενοι ὑμῖν.	ἐν αὐτῇ τῇ ὥρᾳ ἃ δεῖ εἰπεῖν.
20 οὐ γάρ ὑμεῖς ἐστε οἱ λαλοῦντες ἀλλὰ τὸ πνεῦμα τοῦ πατρὸς ὑμῶν τὸ λαλοῦν ἐν ὑμῖν.		οὐ γάρ ἐστε ὑμεῖς οἱ λαλοῦντες ἀλλὰ τὸ πνεῦμα τὸ ἅγιον.		
21 παραδώσει δὲ ἀδελφὸς ἀδελφὸν εἰς θάνατον καὶ πατὴρ τέκνον, καὶ ἐπαναστήσονται τέκνα ἐπὶ γονεῖς		**12** καὶ παραδώσει ἀδελφὸς ἀδελφὸν εἰς θάνατον καὶ πατὴρ τέκνον καὶ ἐπαναστήσονται τέκνα ἐπὶ γονεῖς	**16** παραδοθήσεσθε δὲ	
			καὶ ὑπὸ γονέων καὶ ἀδελφῶν καὶ συγγενῶν καὶ φίλων, καὶ θανατώσουσιν ἐξ ὑμῶν,	
22 καὶ θανατώσουσιν αὐτούς.	**9** καὶ ἀποκτενοῦσιν ὑμᾶς,	καὶ θανατώσουσιν αὐτούς· **13**	**17**	
καὶ ἔσεσθε μισούμενοι ὑπὸ πάντων διὰ τὸ ὄνομά μου	καὶ ἔσεσθε μισούμενοι ὑπὸ πάντων τῶν ἐθνῶν διὰ τὸ ὄνομά μου.	καὶ ἔσεσθε μισούμενοι ὑπὸ πάντων διὰ τὸ ὄνομά μου.	καὶ ἔσεσθε μισούμενοι ὑπὸ πάντων διὰ τὸ ὄνομά μου.	

Matthew 10	Matthew 24	Mark 13	Luke 21
	καὶ τότε		
	σκανδαλισθήσονται πολλοί		
	καὶ ἀλλήλους παραδώσουσιν		
	καὶ μισήσουσιν ἀλλήλους·		
	11		
	καὶ πολλοὶ ψευδοπροφῆται		
	ἐγερθήσονται		
	καὶ πλανήσουσιν πολλούς·		
	12		
	καὶ διὰ τὸ πληθυνθῆναι τὴν ἀνομίαν		
	ψυγήσεται ἡ ἀγάπη τῶν πολλῶν.		
			18
			καὶ θρὶξ ἐκ τῆς κεφαλῆς ὑμῶν
			οὐ μὴ ἀπόληται.
			19
22	13	13b	ἐν τῇ ὑπομονῇ ὑμῶν
ὁ δὲ ὑπομείνας εἰς τέλος	ὁ δὲ ὑπομείνας εἰς τέλος	ὁ δὲ ὑπομείνας εἰς τέλος	κτήσασθε τὰς ψυχὰς ὑμῶν.
οὗτος σωθήσεται.	οὗτος σωθήσεται.	οὗτος σωθήσεται.	
	14		
	καὶ κηρυχθήσεται		
	τοῦτο τὸ εὐαγγέλιον		
	τῆς βασιλείας		
	ἐν ὅλῃ τῇ οἰκουμένῃ		
	εἰς μαρτύριον		
	πᾶσιν τοῖς ἔθνεσιν,		
	καὶ τότε ἥξει τὸ τέλος.		
23	15	14	20
ὅταν δέ...	ὅταν οὖν...	ὅταν δέ...	ὅταν δέ...

Mark 13:33-37 and parallels

Matthew 25:13-15	Mark 13:33-34	Luke 21:34-36, 12:37a
	33 βλέπετε ἀγρυπνεῖτε [καὶ προσεύχεσθε]	34 προσέχετε δὲ ἑαυτοῖς μήποτε βαρηθῶσιν ὑμῶν αἱ καρδίαι ἐν κραιπάλῃ καὶ μέθῃ καὶ μερίμναις βιωτικαῖς, καὶ ἐπιστῇ ἐφ᾽ ὑμᾶς αἰφνίδιος ἡ ἡμέρα ἐκείνη, 35 ὡς παγίς. ἐπεισελεύσεται γὰρ ἐπὶ πάντας τοὺς καθημένους ἐπὶ πρόσωπον πάσης τῆς γῆς.
13 γρηγορεῖτε οὖν ὅτι οὐκ οἴδατε τὴν ἡμέραν οὐδὲ τὴν ὥραν	οὐκ οἴδατε γὰρ πότε ὁ καιρός ἐστιν.	36 ἀγρυπνεῖτε δὲ ἐν παντὶ καιρῷ. δεόμενοι ἵνα κατισχύσητε ἐκφυγεῖν ταῦτα πάντα τὰ μέλλοντα γίνεσθαι, καὶ σταθῆναι ἔμπροσθεν
14 Ὥσπερ γὰρ ἄνθρωπος ἀποδημῶν ἐκάλεσεν τοὺς ἰδίους δούλους καὶ παρέδωκεν αὐτοῖς τὰ ὑπάρχοντα αὐτοῦ, 15 καὶ ᾧ μὲν ἔδωκεν πέντε τάλαντα, ᾧ δὲ δύο, ᾧ δὲ ἕν, ἑκάστῳ κατὰ τὴν ἰδίαν δύναμιν, καὶ ἀπεδήμησεν.	34 ὡς ἄνθρωπος ἀπόδημος ἀφεὶς τὴν οἰκίαν αὐτοῦ καὶ δοὺς τοῖς δούλοις αὐτοῦ τὴν ἐξουσίαν ἑκάστῳ τὸ ἔργον αὐτοῦ καὶ τῷ θυρωρῷ ἐνετείλατο ἵνα γρηγορῇ.	τοῦ υἱοῦ τοῦ ἀνθρώπου. 12:37 μακάριοι οἱ δοῦλοι ἐκεῖνοι,

Matthew 24:42-43 25:5, 12-13	Mark 13:35-37	Luke 12:37b, 38a, 41, 44
24:42 γρηγορεῖτε οὖν ὅτι οὐκ οἴδατε ποίᾳ ἡμέρᾳ ὁ κύριος ὑμῶν ἔρχεται 43 ἐκεῖνο δὲ γινώσκετε ὅτι εἰ ᾔδει ὁ οἰκοδεσπότης ποίᾳ φυλακῇ...	35 γρηγορεῖτε οὖν οὐκ οἴδατε γὰρ πότε ὁ κύριος τῆς οἰκίας ἔρχεται. ἢ ὀψὲ ἢ μεσονύκτιον ἢ ἀλεκτοροφωνίας ἢ πρωΐ,	37 οὓς ἐλθὼν ὁ κύριος εὑρήσ γρηγοροῦντας· ... 38 κἂν ἐν τῇ δευτέρᾳ κἂν ἐν τῇ τρίτῃ φυλακῇ
25:5 ...καὶ ἐκάθευδον. 25:12 λέγω ὑμῖν, οὐκ οἶδα ὑμᾶς. 25:13 γρηγορεῖτε	36 μὴ ἐλθὼν ἐξαίφνης εὕρῃ ὑμᾶς καθεύδοντας. 37 ὃ δὲ ὑμῖν λέγω πᾶσιν λέγω, γρηγορεῖτε.	ἔλθῃ καὶ εὕρῃ οὕτως, ... 41 Εἶπεν δὲ ὁ Πέτρος, Κύριε, πρὸς ἡμᾶς τὴν παραβολὴν ταύτην λέγεις ἢ καὶ πρὸς πάντα 44 ἀληθῶς λέγω ὑμῖν ὅτι ἐπὶ πᾶσιν τοῖς ὑπάρχουσιν αὐτο αὐτοῦ

INDEXES

INDEX OF BIBLICAL REFERENCES
INDEX OF ANCIENT WRITERS
INDEX OF AUTHORS
LIST OF CONTRIBUTORS
CONTENT ANALYSIS

The indexes are compiled by Rita Corstjens

INDEX OF BIBLICAL REFERENCES

OLD TESTAMENT

GENESIS

1:27	363
2:1ff	455
2:2-3	428
2:24	363
5:2	363
6:9	375
7:6	267
7:7	267
7:9	363
7:13	267
7:17	267
7:23	113, 114, 267, 269, 286
19:17	114, 267, 268, 269, 287
19:24	267
22:10	96
24:34	110
24:54	110
26:30	110
27:25	110
31:46	110
31:54	110

EXODUS

12:26	365
13:8	365
13:14	365
20:11	428
21:2ff	372
21:20-21	372
21:26-27	372
23:20	491
24:10	110
25:13	96
30:25	96
32:6	110
34:28	110

LEVITICUS

7:6	417
7:15	417
13–14	104, 106
13:1	104
13:49	104, 256
13:58	105
14	257
14:1	104
14:4	104
14:5	104
14:20	104
14:23	104
14:32	104
14:36	104
14:40	104
22:4	96
24:2ff	257
24:5-9	428

NUMBERS

12:10	96
20:12	364
28:9-10	363, 428

DEUTERONOMY

6:20-21	365
7:15	29
8:15ff	374
13:2	120, 277
17:14ff	372
17:17	363
18:1-4	417
21:7	366
21:22	490
23:4ff	372
25:4	373
26:8	365
28:61	29
34:12	374

JOSHUA
24:6 365

RUTH
3:18 101

JUDGES
3:21 96
15:15 96

1 SAMUEL
21:1-6 428
21:3ff 363

2 SAMUEL
7:12-13 365

1 KINGS
11:1 368

2 KINGS
4:1–8:6 137
4:18-19 365
5:1 96
5:10 106
5:12 106
5:13 106
5:14 106
5:27 96
15:5 96

EZRA
9 372

NEHEMIAH
13:23ff 372

1 MACCABEES
1:54 150

2 MACCABEES
2:21 506
8:1 506
14:38 506

JOB
3:2 366

PSALMS
39:2 373

69:9 436
77:2 35
89:4-5 365
107:20 490
107:42 373
110:1 365
132:13 365
132:11 365

ISAIAH
6:9-10 238
7:14 77
9:1-2 141
11:1 365
11:10 365
19:2 279
24:17 181
29:13 40
40:3 208, 491
52:7 490, 491
53:4 29
55:10 101
55:11 101
61:1-2 491
61:1 490, 563
65:6 101

JEREMIAH
32:31 365
23:5 365

DANIEL
8:13 150
8:18 100
9:21 100
9:27 150
9:26 179
10:1 101
10:10 100
10:16 100
10:18 100
11 120
11:3 356
11:6 275
11:13 275
11:35 275
11:36 75, 196
12 120, 124
12:4 275
12:7 124, 275

12:11	150
12:12-13	279
12:12	279
12:13	124, 275

HOSEA
1:2	490
6:2	490
6:6	428

JOEL
| 2:28-32 | 175 |

JONAH
| 4:2 | 367 |

NAHUM
| 4:1 | 490, 491 |

ZECHARIAH
| 12:13 | 285 |

MALACHI
| 3:1 | 208, 491 |

NEW TESTAMENT

MATTHEW
1	339, 469
1:1-17	469
1	487
18	77, 179
19	469
23	77, 179
25	101
2	339, 374, 469
2:6	123
7	427
8	45
11	32, 104, 256
12	45, 91
13	45, 91, 121, 282
14	45, 91
22	45, 91
23	45
3	469
3:1–4:22	339
3:1-12	23
2	101, 470
3:4–6:11	208
3:5	33, 44
7-12	43
7-10	9, 43, 111, 112, 273, 274
7	111, 273, 470
8-9	112
9-10	43
9	112, 273
10-12	43
10	111, 274

11-12	43
11	273
12	120, 281
13-17	23, 208
16	102, 362
4–13	40
4	469
4:1-11	23, 208
1	102
4:12–13:58	40
4:12-17	23, 24, 208
12	45, 46, 91
13	28
14-16	28
17	470
18-22	23, 24, 27, 30, 208
18	186, 353
19	513
20	512
22	23, 512
4:23ff	208
4:23–13:58	14
4:23–11:1	14, 20, 22, **23-46**, **40-42**, 205
4:23–9:34	46
4:23–8:17	34, **38-39**
4:23–5:2	14, 21, **23-46**, **26-36**, 205, 206, 327
23-25	23, 211, 326
23-24	**26-30**, 32, 38, 46, 211
23	22-24, 26-31, 35, 38, 42, 46, 106, 209, 324-326, 516
4:24–7:29	208

4:24–5:2	23, 324, 326	6:1-18	45
4:24-25	29, **30-33**, 38, 46	1	239
24	23-25, 28-33, 35, 38, 39, 44, 46, 513	2	45
		4	45
4:25–5:2	35, 45	5	45
4:25–5:1	23	14	416
4:25	23-25, **32-33**, 34, 36, 38, **42-46**, 211, 245, 259-261	16	45
		18	45
5–7	39, 41, 141, 330	19-23	163
5:1–7:29	160, 325	21	163
5:1–7:28	163	22-23	163
5:1-2	23, **33-36**, 37, 46	24	418
1	23-25, 33-38, 46	25	112, 166
2-12	23	26	112
2	24, 35, 46	30	112
5:3–7:29	324	31	110, 271
5:3–7:27	36, 327	7:1	416
5:3-12	25	11	121
4	148	12	148
5	149	13-14	39
6	58	15	120, 239, 277
5:7–7:29	16	16	112
5:7	149	19	111, 274
10-12	148	22-23	39
11	123, 124, 148, 278	24-27	148
12	121	24	112, 272
13-20	148	7:28–8:1	35
14	240	7:28-29	25, 35, 37, 46, 208, 326, 327
15	240	28	24, 34-36, 38, 246
16	45, 240	29	24, 25
17-48	510	8–9	22, 38, 39
18	59, 121, **174-182**, 282, 624	8:1–9:34	160
19	196	8:1-17	38, 39
21-26	149	1-4	209, 238, **254-258**, 324, 325
21	415	1	33-36, 245, 254, 261, 327
22	415	2-4	21, 39, **94-107**, 254, 327
23	32, 104, 256	2	34, 96, 105, 254
24	32, 104, 256	3	94, **96-97**, **98-100**, 105, 106
25	101, 416	4	32, 94-96, **100-104**, 255, 264
26	78, 101, 121, 181, 282	5-34	209
29-30	40, 148	5-13	39, 324, 325, 327
29	273	5-10	39, 41, 237
30	273	5	39
31-32	40	6	31, 39
37	239	7	29
43-48	149	8	122
45	45	11-12	39
46	112	12	165
47	112, 122	13	29, 39, 41, 124, 237, 278

14-17	327		27-30	**254-258**
14-16	39		28	99, 104, 256
14-15	8, 38, 100, 209, 325		29-30	98
14	39, 102		29	98, 99, 255
15	98, 99, 100, 254		30	98, 99, 102, 103, 255
16-17	38, 46, 209, 325		31	99, 103, 513
16	8, 24, 29, 31, 32, 38, 39, 42,		32-34	27, 325, 537
	220		32-33	28
17	29, 38, 45, 58		32	27 31
8:18–13:58	40		33	27, 31, 246
8:18-34	21		9:35–11:1	46
18-27	46		9:35–10:16	325
18-22	325		9:35	21, 24, **26**, 27, 29, 41, 42, 46,
18	8, 35, 39, 41, 102			102, 215, 516
19-22	38, 41, 46		36	35, 229, 251
19	512		37ff	39
22	512		37-38	41
23-27	214, 325		38	45
23-34	41		10–11	330
23	35		10	70, 74, 80, 278-280
25	34		10:1-14	21, 41, 215
26	101, 373		1-8	516
28-34	214, 325		1-4	211
28	31		1	26, 29, 34, 46, 229
32	101		2-4	20, 37
33	31		2	186
34	45		5-42	16, 160
9:1-17	22, 38, 41, 444		5	26, 102, 229, 371
1-8	210, 325, 537		6	278
1	274		7-14	41
2	31		8	106
8	194, 246		9-10	101
9-13	325		10	273
9	102, 210, 512		11	27, 121, 282
10-13	210		14	149
11	349		15	149
13	149		16	148
14-17	210, 237, 325		10:17–11:1	325
9:18–11:30	210		10:17-23	79, 191, 625-627
9:18-26	21, 41, 103, 214, 325		17-22	40, 70, 71, 74, 78, 80, 118,
18	254			**122-124**, 158, **174-182**, **188-**
19	102			**193**, 277, 280, 620, 621
21	122		17-20	79 118 **122-123** 278
22	124, 278		17-19	191
23	102		17-18	177, 189, 190
24	45		17	70, 123, 189, 239, 276, 278
25	99, 100, 101		18-22	190
26	30, 101, 103		18	123, 177, 189-191, 278
27-31	98, 99, 103, 104, 325		19-22	190

19-20	70, 79, 177, 188, 280
19	79, 190, 192, 278
21-22	124, 189-191
21	79, 124, 148, 177, 278, 279
22	79, 118, 124, 148, 178, 190, 191, 278, 279
23	80, 123, 190, 193, 278, 280, 282
28	109, 112, 148
32	124, 148
33	148
34-36	148
38	512
39	123, 148, 172, 278, 618
40-42	149
42	122
11:1	26, 42, 46
2ff	111
2-19	41
2-11	271, 274
2-6	325
2	42
3	271
4-6	38, 530
4	111, 271
5	106
6	271
7-19	325
7-9	110, 111
7	110, 112, 272
8	272
9	109, 272
11	272
13	58
15-19	274
15	226
16-19	271
16	110, 239, 272
18-19	271
18	110, 276
19	59, 110, 111, 272, 276
20-24	41, 325, 537
25-27	325
27	122, 282
28-30	325
12	42, 471
12:1ff	363
12:1-16	41
12:1-14	22

1-8	210, 325, 424, 425, 428, 430, 442, 444
1	42, 102, 357, 425, 442
2-8	425, 442
2	427, 429, 444
3-7	428
4	121
5-8	428
5-7	428, 442, 444
7	149, 429
8	427
9-14	210, 325, 537
9-13	237
9	444
10	101, 102
11-12	444
11	58 100
13	97
14	22, 45, 245, 263, 265
15-21	325
15-16	24, 29, 33, **42-46**, 211, 259
15	23, 33, 42, 44, 45, 46, 91, 92, 211, 245, 246, 250, 251, 259-261, 264, 265, 339
16	32, 33, 42, 44, 101, 211, 260, **264-265**, 339
17-21	29, 58, 211, 212, 339
20	121
22-37	212
22-24	537
22	28, 31, 339
23	246, 339
24-32	41, 339
31	166
33-37	339
34	111, 273
35-38	65
38-45	212, 339
38-39	433
40	268 270
46-50	41, 212, 339, 513
48	166
49	26, 96, 97, 254
13	22, 42, 330, 529
13:1-52	529
1-35	41
1-23	339
1-9	213
1	35, 102, 213

2	35		14	252
3-50	16, 160		14:1-2	215, 229, 237, 339
3-9	529		1	40, 42, 513
3	525		2	237
8	350		3-12	215, 229, 339
9	226		12	93, 245
10-23	213, 529		13-21	215, 224, 229, 339
10-15	238		13-14	**81-93, 81-82**, 92, **244-253**
10-11	237		13	33, 45, 46, 81, 82, 91-93, 102,
10	34, 101, 357			245, 246, 249-251, 261
11	124		14	29, 35, 82, 93, 229, 249, 251
12	213, 238		15	8, 26, 34, 234, 251, 274, 357
13	111, 229, 237		16	102
14-15	40		19	251, 357
16	111		14:22–16:12	224, 339
17	111		14:22	101, 251, 357
18	529		23	8, 234, 251
19	27		25	276
24-30	120, 213, 281, 339, 529		27	102
30	120, 281		28-31	97
31	272, 339		31	96, 97, 254
31-33	110		33	102
31-32	213		35	32
32	339		36	122
33	101, 214, 272		15	253
34-35	214, 525		15:1	34
34	102, 339		3-6	40
35	35, 45, 339		7-9	40
36-52	214		12	34, 357
36-43	120, 149, 281		15	101, 528
36	34, 274, 529		21	23, 45, 91, 102
37-43	529		22	29, 31, 101
39	275, 281		23	34
40-43	120		25	101
40	120, 268, 270, 271, 274, 275,		28	29, 102, 124, 278
	281		29-31	92, 253
41	120, 281		29	23, 32, 45, 102
42	165		30	23, 33, 274
43	226, 281		32-39	224
44	272		32	102, 229, 357
45	272		33	357
47-50	120, 281		34	102
47	272		36	357
48	281		16:1-6	224
49-50	120		2	8
49	275 281		2-3	67
50	165		6	102, 103, 239, 276
52	215, 272		7-12	224
53-58	41, 214, 339		7	101, 102

8	102, 103
11	239
16:13–18:9	339
16:13-20	224
18	493
20	101, 102, 264, 471
21	101, 102, 124
22	102
24	102, 148, 512
25-27	148
25	123, 172, 278
27-28	282
28	78, 121, 181
17:6-7	100
7	100
9	101, 102, 255, 264
15	31
16	28, 32
17	102, 166
18	28, 102, 124, 278
19	28, 34
22	102
23	101, 148
24ff	367
24	124
25	34, 124
18	330
18:1	34, 101, 102, 124, 278
1-35	16, 160
5	194
6	102, 103
8-9	40
10-35	339
10	102, 255
14	103, 121
21	34, 112
23-35	149
24	32
34	101
19:1-12	339
1-2	43, 92, 246, 250-252
1	44, 102
2	29, 33, 43, 245, 261, 355
3-9	40
3-4	363
3	101, 102, 275
4-6	40
7-8	40
8-9	40

19:13–23:1	339
19:13	32, 353, 357
14	194
21	121, 512
24	350, 351, 354
27	512
28	512
29	123, 124
20:1	272
8	8, 234
18	123
19	101
29-34	98, 103
29	33, 245, 261
33-34	98
33	98
34	98, 255
21:1-9	448
1	102, 357
4-5	58
9	245
10-17	117
10-14	117
10-11	448
12-13	40, 448
12	102, 432, 433
13	432
14-17	40, 448
14	29
17	117
18-22	40
18-19	40, 448
19-20	362
19	122
20-22	448
23-27	448
23	34, 274, 275, 433
33	101
41	166
43	166
22	471
22:13	165
15ff	364
15-16	44
15	44, 45, 264
16-32	133
18	102
19	32, 104, 256
23	34, 275

33	246
38	514
44	121
23	56, 141, 330
23:1-39	16, 160, 339
1	35, 102, 119, 357
2	35
15	27
23	59, 514
27-39	149
33	111, 273
34	59, 123, 278
35	45
36	109
38	350
39	78, 101, 121, 181, 282
24–25	16, 64, 157, 160, **182-200**, 287, 330
24	16, 17, 64, 69-72, 77, 78, 80, 108, 118, 157-159, 162, 165, **168-173** 171, 174, 178, 181-183, 188, 190, 195, 199, 200, **265-288**
24:1-42	77, **174-182**
1-36	64, 183, 339
1-8	**185-188**
1-7	619
1-3	118, **119**, 269, **274-276**, 285
1-2	187
1	34, 102, 119, 183, 185, 353
2	119, 149, 186, 187, 285
3	34, 35, 119, 120, 171, 175, 186-188, 274, 275, 279, 281
4-51	**163-167**
4-5	73, 118, 120, 176, 276
4	73, 187, 188, 239
5	122, 187, 188
6-7	176
6	102, 187, 188, 255
7	118, 176, 187, 279
8-14	620, 621
8	72 187, 266
9-15	625-627
9-14	40, 69, 118, **122-124**, 176, 178, **188-193**, **280**
9-13	70, 148, 158, 177, 189, 191, 192
9-12	177
9-10	190
9	70, 78, 79, 122, 177, 178, 189-191, 277, 280
10-14	120
10-12	70, 74, 78, 122, 157, 176, 178, 183, 184, 191, 266, 277, 280
10	65, 122, 189
11	120, 122, 277
13	79, 118, 122, 124, 178, 190, 191, 277, 279, 280
14-15	198, 199
14	27, 70, 79, 122, 150, 157, 177, 178, 189-191, 198, 277, 280
15-31	622
15-25	**193-195**
15-22	178
15-20	178
15-16	72
15	150, 169, 178, 190, 193
17-18	69, 72, 79, 116, 171, 173, 178, 193, 194, 266, 267, 287, 617
17	193
18	65, 71, 171, 172
19-22	149
19	77, 179, 194
20-22	157
20-21	169
20	179, 266
21-25	266
21-22	118, 179, 194
21	118, 169, 194
22-24	195
22	169, 179, 194
23-25	65, 71, 72, 118, **120**, 276
23	71, 72, 168, 169, 179, 195, 617
24-25	72, 157, 179
24	120, 122
25	195, 285
26-40	169
26-31	**195-196**
26-28	65, 70, 71, 78, 173, 179, 183, 184, 193, 195, 266
26-27	108, 169, 269, 617
26	169, 170, 276
27	65, 114, 170, 171, 268, 270, 275, 356
28	170, 173, 618
29-36	65
29-31	118, **120-121**, **280-283**
29	65, 169, 179, 180, 195

30	70, 71, 78, 157, 165, 180, 183, 184, 195, 196, 266, 280	10-13	163
		10	163
31	71, 121, 157, 170, 180, 196, 266, 280, 281	11	163
		12-13	628
32-36	180, **195-196**, 624	12	200
32-33	64, 180	13-15	628
32	180, 196	13	75, 122, 163, 198, 281
33	196	14-30	65, 165, 198, 199
34-35	181	14-15	75
34	78, 118, **121**, 181, 196, 282, 356	20	32, 104, 256
		26	190
24:36–25:13	163	31-46	148, 149
24:36	71, 118, **121**, 157, 163, 181, 183, 197, 266, 281	30	149, 165
		32	122
24:37–25:46	183, 197, 339	46	149
24:37–25:30	75, **197-200**	26:1–28:8	339
24:37–41	65, 108, 173, 193, 266, 267	26:1-2	101
37-39	16, 267, 269	2	123
37-38	171	3-5	470
37	65, 113, 163, 169-171, 268, 270, 275, 617	4	45
		6	102
38-39	268, 270, 617	13	26
38	110, 112-114, 171, 268-271	15	101
39	101, 113, 114, 163, 169-171, 268, 269, 275	17	34
		19	102, 357
40-41	114, 172, 267, 269, 286, 618	20	8 234
40	171, 172	26-28	411
41	172	26	102, 417
42-51	60, 79, 164, 172	27	101
42-44	199, 615	29	78, 181
42-43	198, 200, 628	36	101, 102, 357
42	64, 67, 69, 76, 79, 163, 164, 181, 198, 624	38	163
		40	163, 357
43ff	64, 76	41	163
43-51	64, 66, 71, 165-167, 193, 266	51	96, 97, 254
43-44	78, 164, 198	52	97, 124
43	67, 79, 163, 164, 166	55	35, 124, 278
44	66, 122, 163, 166, 281	59	45, 264
45-51	78, 165, 198, 199, 616	61	433, 449
45	91	63	102
46	166	66	101
48-51	149	68	11
48	166	69ff	364
49	110, 165, 271	69	275, 512
50	122, 163, 165, 271, 281	27:1	45, 264, 470
51	65, 67, 165, 166	2ff	123
25:1-30	157	3-10	44
1-13	65, 163, 165, 198	5	45
5	198, 200, 628	7	44, 264

9	585
11	102, 123
14	123
15	123
19	274, 470
21	123
24-26	470
27	123, 170
33	166
40	433
54	470
55	43
57	8, 234
58	34
66	236
28:1-4	236
9-15	339
11-15	44, 236
12	44, 264
14	123
15	513
16-20	542
16	339
17-20	149
17	339
18-20	339
18	100
19-20	487
19	122
20	275

MARK

1	39 42
1:1-32	473
1-20	**208**, 339
1-15	491
1-13	472
1-9	23
1-3	155, 208, 491
1	155, 182, 403, 472, 487, 490, 491
2-3	491
2	472 491
4-8	208
5	44
7-8	46
8	353
9-11	208
10-11	23 491

10	362
11	102
12-13	23, 208
14-15	23, 24, 27, 41, 208, 490, 491
14	24, 28, 45, 46, 190
15	24, 46, 155, 472, 487
16ff	472
16-20	21, 23, 24, 27, 30, 41, 208, 326
16	186, 353
17	185, 513
18	512
1:21–6:13	14, 21, 22, 40, 202
1:21–3:6	22
1:21-45	38, **208-209**
21-39	21, 30, 41, 339
21-38	27
21-34	8
21-29	8
21-28	30, 208, 324, 325
21-22	27, 30, 37
21	24, 25, 27, 30, 35, 39, 42, 46, 84, 90, 327
22	24, 34-36, 46, 327, 353
23-28	327
23-27	24, 27, 28, 30
23	30, 361
24	472
25	100, 101, 102, 255, 373
28	24, 25, 28, 30, 35, 44, 46, 103, 115, 472, 513
29-34	8, 39, 327
29-31	30, 38, 100, 209, 324, 325
29	8, 39, 83, 84, 186, 275
30	8, 99
31	98-100, 106, 254
32ff	474
32-34	24, 29, 30, 32, 38, 39, 209, 324, 325
32	8, 9, 24, 25, 29, 30-32, 38, 39, 46, 107, 209, 220, 234, 473
33	8, 29, 30
34	24, 25, 27, 29-33, 38, 42, 46, 86, 101, 107, 209, 248
35-39	209, 327
35-38	324, 325
35	8, 9, 84
37	474
39	23, 24, 26-28, 30, 46, 276, 324-326, 355, 516

1:40–3:6	41, 339
1:40-45	39, 94, 99, 100, 103, 105, 106, 209, 240, 324, 325, 327
40-44	**94-107, 254-258**
40	99, 104, 106, 254, 276
41	**96-100**, 101, 105, 106
42	94, 99, **104-107**, 258
43-44	103
43	99, 103, 105
44	99, **100-104**, 255, 264
45	30, 42, 43, 84-89, 99, 103, 115, 263, 264, 472, 513, 530
2:1–3:6	22, **209-211**, 428, 444, 449, 455, 456
2:1–3:5	446
1-22	39, 41, 444
1-12	39, 324, 325, 428, 429, 444-446, 455
1-2	209
1	39
2	43, 86, 87, 89, 90, 115
3-12	210
3	31, 427
4	31, 87, 211, 256
5	427, 446
6	110, 210
7	430, 442, 446
8	210
9	210, 427-429, 442, 446, 447, 457
10-11	446
11-12	428
11	427, 445-447
12	106, 108, 427, 445, 446
13-17	324, 325
13-14	210
13	43, 87, 263, 444
14	108, 512
15-17	210
15	43, 86, 210, 263
16	110, 210, 349
17	91
18-22	210, 237, 324, 325, 555
18	101, 110, 112
19	185, 210
21	353
23ff	363
2:23–3:12	41
2:23–3:6	444, 445

2:23-28	210, 324, 325, 425, 426, 428, 429, 442, 444, 445, 455, 456
23	89, 108, 357, 426, 444, 445
24-28	426
24	372, 427, 444, 445
26	121, 210, 372
27	210, 427
28	210
3:1-6	210, 324, 325, 428, 430, 442, 444, 445, 455-457
1	444
2	102, 444, 445
4-5	211
4	372, 444, 445
5	97, 107
6	9, 44, 45, 211, 263, 265, 427, 430, 442, 444-446, 456
7ff	9
7-19	37, 38
7-12	20, 21, 24, 25, 29, 32, 33, 37, 41, 211, **259-265**, 324-326, 339, 474
7-11	**261-264**
7-10	44, 92
7-8	23, 32-34, 38, **42-46**, 265
7	9, 24, 25, 33, 34, 43, 45, 46, 86, 109, 260, 262-264
8	24, 25, 32, 33, 43, 87, 90, 109, 115, 249, 260, 262-264
9	24, 34, 87, 260
10	24, 29, 32-34, 86, 87, 260
11-12	29, 32, 86, 90
11	42, 86, 101, 260
12	33, 42, 44, 89, 101, 255, 260, **264-265**
13-35	**211-213**
13-19	20, 21, 41, 46, 211, 324-326, 339
13-15	516
13	24, 25, 28, 34, 37, 38, 42, 46, 213
14-19	211
14-15	90
14	34, 211, 249, 512
15	29
17	186, 211, 401
16-19	41
16-18	275
16-17	572

18	186	4:35–5:20	39, 41
20-35	212	4:35ff	39
20-30	41	35-41	214, 339
20	43, 87, 88, 212, 263, 339, 355	35	8, 9, 39, 234
21	212, 339	36	35, 83
22-30	41, 212, 339	38	101, 112
22	115	39	100, 101, 107, 255, 373
23	212	41	101
27	353	5:1-43	339
28	194	1-20	214
31-35	21, 41, 212, 339, 513	1	83
31-32	212	2	31
34-35	97	7	101, 109
34	26 97	9	119
4:1-34	41 **213-214** 528	10	89
1-25	21	14	108, 110
1-20	339	15	31, 110
1-9	213	16	228
1-2	89	17	89
1	43, 86, 87, 89, 211, 214, 263, 474	18	512
		19-20	248, 530
2	89, 101, 525	19	246
4	109	20	32, 89
8	350	21-43	41, 85, 214
9	226	21	43, 85-87, 263
10-20	213	22	254
10	213, 526	23	89
12	111	24	42, 43, 85, 86, 246, 263
13	112, 213	26	89
15	107	27	85
21-25	213, 339	28	122
21	112	29	107, 109
22	42, 264	30	85, 90
23	226	31	85
24	44, 239	34	109, 124
25	44	35	112, 276
26-34	13	37	83
26-29	13, 213, 221, 224, 234, 339	38	83, 89
26	101	39	112
30-32	213, 339	40	83
30-31	272	41-42	100
30	110	41	99, 100, 401
31	101, 213	42	99, 100, 107
32	213	43	30, 89, 101, 103, 255, 264
33-34	214, 525	6	252
33	89, 194, 339	6:1-6	21, 30, 41, 214, 339
34	85, 339, 526	1	43, 263, 444
4:35–6:6	**214-215**	2	90, 110, 194
4:35–5:43	41	6-13	244

6	24, 26, 27, 41, 42, 46	7:1	87
6:7–8:10	**215-216**	5	101
6:7-13	41, 215, 229, 339, 516	6-8	40
7-11	41	6	101
7	26, 29, 89, 90	9-13	40
10	282	11	401
12-13	90	13	85, 194
13	29, 90	17	85, 357, 526, 528
14-16	15, 215, 229, 244, 339	25	31
14-15	238	26	101
14	40, 42, 264	27	190
16	238	29	28
17-29	215, 229, 244, 339	30	28, 124
18	372	31-37	13, 98
30-44	229	31	32
30-34	**81-93, 244-253**	32-36	221, 224, 234
30	81, 83, 87, 93, 108, 229, 244, 246, 248, 339	32	33, 98
		33	85, 98, 254
31-34	**92-93**	34	401
31	82, 83, 85, 86, 91-93, 244, 245, 247, 339	35	107
		36	101, 103, 255, 264
32-34	244, 339	8	253
32-33	88	8:1	86, 357
32	45, 82-84, 92, 93, 115, 244	2	229
33	33, 43, 83, 85, 87, 92, 93, 244, 245, 247, 250	4	357
		5	92
34	29, 35, 83, 85-89, 92, 93, 229, 252	6	357
		10	401
35	85, 101, 357	11	89
36	26, 85	12	433
37-38	92, 112, 253	15	103, 239, 276
37	84	16-17	526
41	85 357	16	102
42	107	18	111
6:45–8:26	13, 85, 224, 385	19-21	385
6:45–8:21	234, 339	20	264
6:45	357	22-26	13, 98, 221, 224, 234, 339
46	88	22	83, 88, 98
47	9, 234	23	85, 98
50	97, 101	25	98, 107
51	97	8:27–9:50	339
52	102	8:27	85, 119, 357, 444
53-56	92, 216, 474	29	119
53-54	83	30	101, 102, 255
54	92	31	89, 124, 537
55-56	92	32	102
55	32 92	34	512
56	122	35	123, 131, 155, 278, 490
7	216	38	123

9:1	78, 282	38-39	155	
2	83, 85	38	194	
7	102	41	89	
9	101-103, 228, 255, 264	46-52	98, 103	
14	83, 86	46	33, 84, 86, 87, 185, 401	
15	474	47	89, 101, 110	
17	32, 101	48	86, 87, 102	
18	28, 32	49	185	
22	256	51-52	98	
25	43, 87, 92, 263	51	98	
26	87	52	98, 99, 107, 255	
27	28, 99, 124	11–12	182	
28	85, 274	11:1-11	449	
30	83	1-10	117, 448	
32	109, 370, 526	1	84, 107, 115, 186, 357	
33	83, 124	2	101, 362	
34	102	8ff	474	
37	194	8	86	
38	353	9	102	
41	122	11	40, 117, 444, 448	
43	40, 273	12-19	40	
45	40, 273	12-14	20, 40, 117, 448, 449	
47	40, 273	12	83	
50	401	13-14	362	
10:1-12	339	13	121	
1	29, 33, 43, 44, 86, 87, 252, 263, 355	15-19	117, 434, 449	
		15-18	456	
2-9	40	15-17	40, 117, 435, 448	
2-3	363	15	83, 89, 432, 448	
2	102, 372	17	29, 112, 432	
3-5	40	18-19	40, 117, 448	
4-6	40	18	445	
6-9	40	19-20	83	
10-12	40	20-25	20, 40, 448, 449	
10	526	21	101	
10:13–12:38	339	27-33	448, 449	
10:13	256, 353, 357	27-28	434, 435 448	
14	194	27	83, 433, 448	
17	119, 185, 274	28	101, 433, 434, 448	
19	124	29	448	
21	512	30	448	
24	526	12:1	89 110	
25	350, 351	12	109, 445	
26	526	13ff	364	
28	89, 110, 512	13-27	133	
29-30	131	13	45, 211	
29	123, 124, 155, 278, 490	14	95, 101, 107	
32	83, 89, 110	15	104, 112	
33	115	16	104	

18	101, 119
24	112
26	112
28-31	21
35	101
36	101, 349
37	86
38-44	339
38	101, 239
41-44	119
41	186, 275
13	64, 69, 70, 74, 77, 78, **79-80**, **118-124**, 157-159, **182-200**, 278, 280, 287
13:1-32	339
1-8	78, **185-188**
1-4	269, **274-276**, 285
1-2	187
1	78, 80, 119, 185, 186, 274, 276, 353
2-3	187
2	112, 116, 117, 119, 185-187, 285
3	80, 85, 101, 119, 186-188, 274, 275
4-37	183
4	80, 120, 121, 124, 183, 186, 187, 198, 275
5-23	73
5-7	73
5-6	118, 120, 276
5	73, 89, 110, 184, 187, 188, 239
6	73, 122, 187, 188
7	118, 187, 188, 255
8	75, 80, 118, 123, 124, 184, 187, 191, 279
9-23	73, 183
9-14	625-627
9-13	40, **73-75**, 78-80, **122-124**, 158, **188-193**, 200, 277, 280
9-11	79, 118, **123-124**, 278, 279
9-10	118, 123, 190, 280
9	73, 79, 80, 118, 122, 123, 184, 188-190, 192, 195, 239, 276, 278, 280
10	27, 78, 79, 122, 123, 155, 156, 158, 184, 190-192, 487, 490
11-14	190
11-13	190
11-12	189
11	71, 78, 79, 118, 122, 190, 192, 278, 280
12-13	118, 124, 190, 191
12	78, 79, 118, 122-124, 192, 278-280
13	78, 79, 118, 122, 124, 155, 190-192, 278-280
14-32	75
14-23	**193-195**
14-15	190
14	80, 114, 116, 117, 193, 489, 526
15-16	116, 193, 194, 269, 287
15	80, 116, 117, 191, 193
16	80, 116
17	77, 179, 194
18	184, 194
19-23	183
19-20	118, 194
19	194
20-23	195
20	194
21-23	73, 118, 120, 158, 276
21	195
22	120, 122
23	73, 183, 184, 188, 189, 195, 239
24-27	118, 120, 184, **280-283**
24	195
25-27	**195-196**
25	80, 195
26	80, 114, 121, 196
27	158, 183, 196
28-32	**196-197**
28-31	184
28	80, 196
29	80, 187, 196
30	75, 78, 118, 120, 181, 187, 196, 282, 356
31	73, 197
32-37	155
32	118, 120, 122, 183, 197, 281
33-37	60, **75-76**, 118, 158, 166, 167, 183, **197-200**
33-36	339
33-34	197, 198, 628
33	75, 80, 184, 188, 197, 199, 239, 286

34-37	197, 198		65	11, 89, 101, 110
34-36	199		66ff	364
34	75, 188, 198, 200		67	101, 512
35-37	71, 76, 197, 198, 266, 628		69	89, 110
35-36	198		71	89
35	122, 184, 189, 198, 200		72	109
36-37	200		15:1	45 264
36	158, 198		2	102
37	76, 119, 155, 183, 184, 189, 198, 199		3	89
			4	119
14:1–16:8	339		12	112
14:1	445		14	102
2	109		18	102
3-9	21		21	109
4	102		27	182
9	26, 155, 190, 490		28	182
11	109		29	433
12	84, 101		33	108
16	357		34	102, 401
17	9, 234, 412		39	101
18	83, 84		41	43, 87, 263
19	89, 110		42	9
20	412		43	109
21	412		16:2	433
22-25	410-413, 418, 429, 432, 435, 437, 441, 448, 452		3	112
			9-20	601
22-24	412		9	339
22	83 412, 417		10-13	339
23-24	412		14	339
23	412		15-18	339
24	101, 412		15	155, 190, 490
25	78, 412		19	339
26	84, 186		20	339
32	83, 84, 357			
33	83, 89		**LUKE**	
36	401		1:1-14	570
38	197		1-4	224, 474, 486, 488, 493, 513, 517, 589
43	109			
47	96		1-2	243
48	124		1	86, 248, 304
49	109		3	151
51-52	576		4	151
55	264		5ff	151
57-58	449		1:5–9:51	161
58	182, 433, 435, 449		1:5-25	476
61	119		5	518
62	121		10	262
63	91, 101		17	274
64	430		20	112, 179, 271, 286

24	513	27	106
26-28	476	31-44	21, 30, 41, 339
38	105 258	31-37	208, 324, 325, 516
44-49	513	31	84 327
57-79	476	32	327
72-73	273	33-37	327
73	273	35	373
80	475, 476	37	30, 115, 284
2:1ff	475	38-41	327
1-39	476	38-39	209, 324, 325
1-2	518	38	84
1	115, 151	40-41	209, 324, 325, 516
13	360	40	9, 29, 221
15	105, 258	41	32, 86, 90, 248, 259, 260
17	89	42-44	209, 327
33	89	42-43	324, 325
38	89	42	9, 84, 248
40	475, 476	43	89
41ff	375	44	117, 209, 324-326
41-51	475	5:1-11	21, 23, 41, 208, 209, 324, 325,
46	475		327, 339, 475
49	475	1-3	89
52	475, 476	1	86, 89
3	476	3	86, 89
3:1-2	518	11	512
1	151	5:12–6:16	23
3	208	5:12–6:11	41, 339
7-9	108, **111-112**, 273, 274	5:12-16	209, 324, 325, 327
7	111, 112, 273	12-14	**94-107, 254-258**
8	110, 112	12	254
9	111	13	84, 96, 105, 258
10-14	112	14	96
17	281	15	30, 85-87, 89-91, 248, 262
21-22	208	16	84, 115, 247, 284
23	151, 475	17-39	84
4:1-13	208	17-26	210, 324, 325
5	115	17-20	153
12	105	17	86, 90, 91, 115
13	105, 112	21	110
14-15	29, 30, 41, 208	26	108
14	30	27-32	324, 325
15	30	27-28	210
16-30	21, 30, 41, 208, 214	27	512
16-24	516	28	108, 512
16	30	29-32	210
17-21	476	29	86 262
21	110	30	110, 271
23	30, 91, 528	31	91
25-27	153	32	91

33-39	210, 324, 325	12	86 88, 262
33	110, 271	13	229
6:1ff	363	16	374
1-5	210, 324, 325	17	30
1	89, 108, 165, 357	18ff	111
3	165	18-35	39, 41, 42, 108, **109-111**, 271,
5	427		274
6-11	210, 324, 325	18-23	90
6	90	19	271
8	165	21	29, 86, 90, 248
10	97	22-23	38
11	211	22	106, 111, 271
12-20	37	23	271
12-19	259	24-26	110, 111
12-16	20, 21, 37, 41, 211, 324-326,	24	110, 112, 272
	339	25	272
12-13	37	26	109, 110, 272
12	37	31-32	272
13-16	37	31	110, 239
14	186	32	272
16	23	33-34	271
17-49	211, 212	33	110, 112, 276
17-20	37, 324, 326	34	110-112, 272, 276
17-19	20, 21, 41, 42, 90, 211, 262,	35	59 272
	325, 326	36-50	21
17	37, 42, 43, 86, 109, 115, 117,	39	374
	211, 260, 262	49	110
18-19	90	8:1-3	21
18	29, 38, 42, 86, 90, 91, 260, 262	1	27, 89
19	42, 90, 260, 262	4-18	21, 41, 528
20-49	37, 39, 41, 90, 324, 325, 327,	4-8	213
	330	4	86, 87
20-23	152	5-16	330
20	37	5	109
22	124	8	226, 350
24-26	152	9-15	213
33	122	9	357
39	528	16-18	213, 339
42	67	16	213
47-48	272	18	214
47	112	19-21	21, 41, 212, 214, 339, 513
7:1–8:3	212	22-56	41
7:1-10	39, 41, 42, 90, 324	22-25	214, 339
1	36, 37, 39	24	373
7	122	26-56	339
9	88, 248	26-39	214
10	124	26	83
11-17	90	28	109
11	85-88, 248	34	108

35	110, 272
37	84
38	84, 512
39	228, 246, 248
40-56	85, 214
40	85
42	85
43	90, 91
44	85
45	85
46	85, 90, 262
47	90, 109
48	109
51	83
55	361
9:1-10	85
1-6	41, 215, 228, 229, 330, 339
1-2	90, 516
1	29, 90, 152
2	90
6	90, 228
7-9	215, 228, 229, 339
9-10	11, **82-93**
9	194
10-17	85, 215, 229
10-11	11, **81-93, 244-253**
10	13, 81-85, 88, 91, 93, 108, 115, 228, 229, 246-248, 284, 339
11-17	339
11	81, 82, 85, 88-91, 93, 165, 229
12	84, 85
13-17	229
13	84
16	85, 357
18-51	339
18-22	224
18	13, 85, 228, 357
22	89, 170, 226
23	512
24	69, 172, 268
27	78, 109, 165, 272
28	83, 85
29	170
37	85, 86
41	166
43-45	226
45	109, 370
46-48	330
51ff	474, 477
9:51-18:27	475
9:51-18:14	16, 18, 152, 158, 161, 224, 339
9:51	87, 476
9:53	87
57ff	39
57-60	41, 46
57	512
59	512
61	512
10:1-16	154
1-12	41
1	228
7	110, 271, 273
8	27
10	27
12	152
13-15	41
13-14	44
17	228
21	110
22	282
23	85
24	111
25ff	364, 370
25-28	21
29ff	371
33	95, 229
34	95
35	95
11:14	28, 31
15-23	212
16	13, 89, 224
19	66
29	110, 224, 272, 433
30	270
38	13
42	59
49	59, 66
51	110, 109, 272
12	64, 70, 71, 74, 76, 199, 200, 266, 287
12:1	110, 181, 224
3	286
4-12	152
4-5	109
4	109
5	109, 110, 112, 272
8	124
11-12	70, 71, 78, 79, 158, 177, **188-**

	193, 265, 277, 278, 280, 620, 621, 625-627	14	443
		15	67, 443
11	190	16	443
12	71	17	443
19	110, 271	18-21	110, 239
20	172	18-19	213, 272
22	66	18	110
29	110, 271	20-21	272
31	152	20	110
34	163	22	87, 476
35-48	157, 159, 162, **163-167**, 174, 181, 183, 200, 265	23-27	39
		26	110, 271
35-40	615	28-29	39
35-38	64, 71, 76, 163-165, 199	28	65, 165
35-37	76	31	274
35	163 164	33-35	178
36-37	164	33	374, 476
36	163	35	78, 174
37-38	79, 164, 198, 266	14:3-4	90
37	67, 163, 198, 628	5	100
38	628	15	90, 271
39-46	60, 66, 71, 165, 172, 193	16	86, 90, 248
39-40	163-167, 199, 266	18	110, 272
39	163, 164, 166	20	66
40	66, 166, 281	25	86, 87, 248
41-48	163, 616	31	90
41	155, 164, 198, 266, 628	32	285
42-46	165-167, 199, 266	35	226
42	91, 165	15:1	262
43	166	2	95
44	109, 165, 198, 272, 628	7	91
45	110, 165, 166, 271	11-32	153
46	67, 165, 166, 271, 281	20	229
47-48	165	16:1ff	374
47	189	8	374
56	67	9	111
58	416	13	418
59	78	17	59, 121
13:1-5	152, 153	24	273
7	273	25	166, 286
10-17	424, 426, 428, 430, 442, 443, 454	30	273
		17	17, 64, 68, 70, 71, **108-117**, 199, 200, 266, 274, 283, 286, 287
10-13	426, 442		
10	90, 443		
11-13	443	17:3	181
11	284 443	8	110, 176, 271
12	443	11-19	95, **254-258**
14-17	426, 442	11	87, 476
14-16	443	12-19	257

13	95 257	34	172
14	95, 106, 257	35	172
17	106	36	171, 172
20-37	157, 159, **168-173**, 174, 179, 181, 183, 200, 265	37	170, 172, 173, 193
		18:7	153, 284
20-26	617	8	153 284
20-23	176	11	356
20-21	168, 169	18:15–24:53	161
20	168, 169	18:15–20:45	339
21	168	18:15	357
22-37	162, 168	16	194
22-30	286	18	175
22	68, 168-170, 172, 173, 286	22	512
23-37	16	25	350, 351
23-35	269, 270, 283	28-30	152
23-24	68, 70, 108, 112, 169, 173, 193, 239, 269	28	512
		31-34	226
23	168-170, 276	31	83, 115, 152, 179, 284
24-25	226	35	84
24	114, 168-172, 270, 355, 356	36	86
25-37	170	39	86
25-34	172	19	75
25-32	170	19:9	273
25	89, 108, 170, 171	11-27	65, 165
26-35	267	11	115
26-30	16, 112	12-27	199
26-29	68	12	75
26-27	69, 108, 171, 173, 193, 267, 269	28	476
		29-40	117, 448
26	113, 170, 171, 268, 270	29	84, 285, 357
27-32	617	32	84
27-28	271	36	86
27	108, 110, **112-114**, 170, 171, 268, 271	39-40	117
		41-44	108, 114, 115, **117**, 152, 285, 448
28-30	108, 267, 269		
28-29	68, 69, 113, 171, 270	41-42	115
28	110, 112-114, 268	41	115, 117
29	113, 171, 268	42-44	174, 178
30-31	69, 171	42	115
30	113, 114, 170, 171, 173, 268	43-44	115, 116
31-33	267	43	115
31	79, 116, 171, 172, 178, 193, 267, 269, 287	44	115-117, 176, 285
		45-48	117
32-33	172	45-46	117, 448
32	267, 269	45	89, 432
33-37	618	46	432
33	69, 268, 269	47-48	117, 448
34-36	193	47	175
34-35	108, 112, 114, 172, 173, 268, 269, 286	20:1-7	448
		1	433

2	433		14-15	79, 114, 177, 280
9-16	153		14	78, 183, 184
9	89, 110		16-17	190
19	109		16	177, 183, 184, 192, 278, 280
20ff	364		17	78, 192
20-38	133		18	74, 114, 178, 183, 184, 192
20-24	117		19	178, 179, 192, 278, 280
21-22	114		20-28	174, 178, 283, 622
21	114 175		20-27	174
23-24	114		20-26	180
25-26	114		20-24	15, 174, 178, 180, **193-195**
26	114		20	78, 108, 114, 115, **116**, 117,
27	114			176, 178, 179, 190, 193, 283-
28	114			285
43	349		21-28	159
20:45–21:4	339		21-22	79, 108, 114, 178, 183, 184,
20:45-47	330			194, 283
45	357		21	78, 79, 115, **116**, 117, 178,
46	181			193, 283-285, 287
21	64, 70-72, 74, 80, **108-117**,		22	115, 179, 193, 284
	157, 158, 178, **182-200**, 265,		23-25	283
	278, 283, 286, 287, 330		23-24	108, 114, 178, 179, 183, 184,
21:2	175			194
3	109, 165, 272		23	77, 78, 179, 181, 194, 273,
5-11	**185-188**, 619			283, 287
5-36	64, **77-79**, 157-159, 162, **174-**		24	112, 115, 179, 285
	182, 183, 200, 265		25-28	180, **195-196**
5-33	181		25-26	108, 114, 180, 183, 184, 195
5-7	114, 174, 284		25	78, 115, 179, 180, 195, 284
5-6	153, 174, 187		26-27	283
5	78, 175, 186, 339		26	78, 115, 195, 271, 284, 287
6	78, 175, 186, 187, 285, 286		27	78, 113, 170, 174, 180, 196,
7	78, 85, 119, 120, 171, 175,			284, 287
	178, 185-188, 285		28	108, 114, 115, 174, 176, 180,
8-11	174, 180			183, 184, 196, 283, 284
8	78, 174, 176, 179, 187, 188,		29-33	174, **196-197**, 286, 624
	276		29-31	64, 180
9-10	176		29-30	114, 183
9	78, 178, 187, 188, 190		29	180, 196
10-11	114		30	78, 181, 184
10	176, 187		31	78, 181, 196
11	78, 176, 180, 187		32-33	181
12-20	625-627		32	78, 181, 196, 282, 356
12-19	69, 74, 78, 152, 158, 174, 176,		33	73, 194
	178, 180, **188-193**, 277, 280,		34-36	75, 80, 108, 113, 114, 174,
	620, 621			181, **197-200**, 286, 624, 628
12-13	177		34	80, 181, 197, 198
12	78, 114, 176, 180, 183, 184,		35	113, 181, 286
	187, 189, 192, 193			

36	75, 80, 113, 174, 181, 197, 198, 273, 286		28	285
			29-31	116
38	262		30	110
22:2	109		34	475
4	84		39ff	475
5	109		44	108
8	84		45	180
14	84		46	475
15-20	411		51	109
15-18	21		55	87
16	78		24:4	170
17	417		6	89
18	78		10-35	339
19	417, 420, 421		12	176
21-23	21		13	87
23	89		15	87
24-27	21		19	374, 475
30	110, 271		28	87
33-34	21		36-43	339
37	115, 284		44-49	115
39	84		44	89, 115, 179, 284
40	84		47	78
44	572		50	339
45	357		51	339
52	109			
53	109		**JOHN**	
54	88		1:1	479 482
55ff	364		2	479
56-62	21		9	479
56	512		12-13	481
59	512		14	479
61	109		15	481
63-65	21		17	479
63	89		18	479
64	11		19	479
66-71	21		21	480
66	9		23	480
71	91		27	481
23:1-2	475		29	480
2	365		34	480
4	475		36	480
5	30, 117		38	480
9	119		43	513
14	475		49	480
22	166, 475		51	480
26-49	21		2	479
26	109		2:1-11	481
27-31	117		13ff	481
27	88, 248, 262			

13-22	410, 411, 423, **432-436**, 437-439, 441, 442, **447-450**	9-16	447
		9-13	431
13-18	434, 456	9	424, 427, 428, 431, 444-446, 455
13-17	432, 433		
13-16	411, 435, 436, 441, 442, 447	10-20	441
13-15	434	10-19	456
13	433	10-18	411, 423-426, 429-431, 442, 443, 445, 447, 455, 456
14-16	435		
14-15	436	10-13	424, 430, 456, 443
14	432-434	10	424, 427, 429, 444-446
15	432-434	11-16	445
16	432, 434, 435	11	427, 446
17-22	411, 436, 441, 442, 447	12	427, 446
17	432, 434, 449	14-16	424
18-21	436	14	94, 416, 427, 429, 430, 443, 446, 447, 456
18	433, 434, 436, 448, 449		
19-22	434, 435	15-18	430, 443, 456
19-21	450	16	424, 427-429, 442, 445
19-20	433	17-18	424, 428, 447
19	433, 449	17	427, 428, 431, 445-447
20	433	18	424, 427, 429, 430, 442, 444, 446, 447, 456
21	433		
22	436, 450	19ff	424, 431, 432, 447
3:1ff	481	6:1-14	481
2	95	1-2	251
3	481	15ff	481
5	481	30	434
15	481	31-58	421, 441
18	416	31	421, 422
22	271	32-58	421
36	273	32-48	421
4:7ff	371	41	421
7-15	481	42	422
11	481	43	421
33-34	370	49-58	422
39-42	481	49	421
46	455	51-58	410, 411, 419-424, 437-439, 441, **453-454**, 457
5:1-18	410, 411, **423-432**, 436-441, **442-447**, 449, **454-456**, 457		
		51-52	421
1-9	411, 423-425, 430, 431, 441-443, 445, 447, 456	51	420, 421, 454
		52-58	422
2-9	447	53-54	421
3	427	53	420
5-6	447	54	420
6-7	447	55	421
6	424, 427, 447	56	420
7	447	57	420
8-9	428, 447	58	420, 421
8	424, 427, 429, 442, 445-447, 457	7:1	445
		10	264

13	481
14ff	481
19-20	430
19	445
20	445
23	445
25	430, 445
46	481
7:53–8:11	429, 538
8:7	284
10	284
11	427
12	513
25	482
33-40	273
37	430, 445
40	430, 445
9	482
9:1-41	423, 431
1-7	444
8-12	444
13-17	444
14	444
18-23	444
24-34	444
35-41	444
10:24	284
30	482
33	446
36	446
11:53	430, 445
12:16	482
26	513
44-50	423, 438
46-50	438
13:3	574
14:2	434
15:18ff	482
20	430, 445
26-27	513
16:1ff	482
2	430
19-20	370
17:6ff	482
18:1-11	409
10-11	440
11	480
12-27	440
16ff	364

26	177, 440
38	480
19:1-3	440
6	480
12	480
19	480
21	480
31	440
35	513
38	440
40-42	440
20	481
20:1-10	480
11ff	480
19ff	480
30-31	488, 542
30	223
31	482
21:12	370
19	513
22	513
24-25	488, 542
24	513
25	223, 488

ACTS OF THE APOSTLES

1	535
1:1ff	488
1-3	513
1	487
2	112, 271
3	89
7	176
8	513
15	262
17	488
21-26	513
2:1-21	475
2	284
17-21	175, 180
25ff	368
26	563
29	112, 271
32	513
33	271
35	349
44-47	510
44	477
3:6	516, 539

7	100, 361		35	35
13ff	367		9	478
20	176		9:9	110, 271
22-23	374		16	112
22	180		27	228, 539
25	273		28	539
4:1-4	177		31	30, 477
4	477		42	30, 477
7	539		10	478, 490, 491
10	539		10:3	264
17	539		34-40	550
18	539		34	35
19-20	513		36ff	490, 491, 494
20	271		36-43	464, 490
29-30	516		36	490
30	539		37	30, 490
32	477, 510		41	95
5:8	110		11:1-18	478
10	361		3	95
11	477		21	477
12-16	516		12:1-23	236
5:14–6:1	177		1	271
5:14	477		6	172
15-16	13, 513		10	95, 105, 257, 258
16	262		11	271, 284
28	539		17	228
29-32	513		18	9
30	367		23	286
31	368		13:11	112
36	176		12	110
37	371		21	110
40	539		26	273
6:1ff	374		29	115, 284
4	518		45-51	153
7-15	177		14:6	488
7	262		20	284
14	433, 435, 449		27	249
7:2	273		15	466, 477, 478
18	112		15:4	249
19	172		7	493
20ff	374		12	249
24	284		16:10-17	574
38	477		13	488
8:1	477		18	539
3	477		35	9
6	271		18:14	35
12	89		24-25	476
26ff	478		19:1-2	476
33	228		8	89

12	29
26	271
20:5-21	574
6	112, 271
24	493
28	172
35	112
21:8	301
35	262
36	88, 248
38	176
22:10	89
15	271
27	110
23:1	112, 271
12	9, 271
19	84, 85, 284
21	271
24:1-17	177
25:16–26:32	177
26:8	166
20	112, 273
22	112, 271
31	84, 284
27:1-28	574
33	9, 112, 271
34	178
39	9
28:19	177

ROMANS

1:3-4	563
1:16	489
3:2	299
4:1	273
4:12	273
9:7	273
10:8-18	301
11:1	273
12:3-13	510
13:1-2	371
15:5-6	510

1 CORINTHIANS

1:10-13	510
3:11	301
6:1	371
9:9	373
9:21	509

10	413, 418, 422, 437, 438, 457
10:1-4	438
2	418
3-4	410-412, 418-421, 437, 453
3	417
4	417
10	421, 453
14-22	417, 418, 424
14	417
16-17	411, 415, 417, 419-422, 438, 453
16	410, 412, 417, 424, 437
17	410, 412, 417, 422, 437
18	417, 424
19-20	424
21-22	417
21	410, 411, 415, 417-422, 429, 437, 438, 444, 453
11	413, 418, 422, 437, 438, 457
11:23-34	414, 417, 419, 421, 423, 431, 432, 436, 437, 441, 451
23-29	410, 453
23-26	411, **413-414**, 415, 417, 420, 429-432, 434, 438, **440-441**, 448 450-453, 456, 550
23-24	441
23	412, 413, 415, 453, 550
24	412, 417, 420, 421, 454
25	412-414
26-34	411, 420, 424
26	412-414, 418, 431
27-34	411, 414, 415, 417, 420, 424, 429, 431, 438, 441, 445, 450, 451, 456
27-29	415, 416, 420, 438
27-28	421
27	412, 415, 416, 420
28	412, 416
29	412, 415, 416, 420, 421
30-32	415
30	416
31-32	416
31	416
32	416, 420
33-34	415
33	416, 421
34	416, 420
12:4-31	510
9	516

15:1-11	490
1-8	303
3-5	550
5-8	513
5	551
11	513, 544

2 CORINTHIANS

1:17	240
3:7	301
11:5	513
22	273
23	57
12:11	513

GALATIANS

1–2	154, 535
1:11	489
1:13	506
1:14	506
1:18-20	513
1:22	149
2	478
2:1-10	513
2:9	138
3:7	273
3:14-17	273
3:29	273

EPHESIANS

4:1-16	510
4:11	301

PHILIPPIANS

1:18	544
1:27	510
2:1-4	510
2:6-11	470
3:14-16	510
3:15-16	510

COLOSSIANS

3:14-15	510
4:10	601
4:14	574, 601

1 THESSALONIANS

4:15	367

4:16	196
5:1-6	286
5:3	181

2 THESSALONIANS

2:3-4	193

1 TIMOTHY

5:18	373

2 TIMOTHY

4:10-11	574

PHILEMON

23	601

HEBREWS

11:30	284
11:32	228
12:19	284

JAMES

2:21	273
5:12	240
5:14-15	516

1 PETER

2:12	45
2:15	373
2:17	137
3:9	367
4:17	489
5:9	137
5:13	569, 599-601

2 PETER

3:12-14	271

1 JOHN

1:1-4	535, 575

REVELATION

1:1-3	512
1:3	489
4:7	574
22:18-19	512

INDEX OF ANCIENT WRITERS

AMMONIUS 129, 292
ARISTIDES
The Panathenaic Oration 222
ARISTION 567
ARISTOPHANES 378
ARISTOTLE
Metaphysics 4.1004a 361
Rhetorica I.6.9 465
Rhetorica ad Alexandrum III-IV 465
ARRIAN 224
AUGUSTINE 48, **50-51**, 53, 132, 145, 292, 381, 382, 394, 404, 586, 587, 589, 591, 601
De consensu Evangelistarum 129
2.18.42 581
4.10.11 50, 130, 588
1.2.4 51
Retr. 2.16 585

CELSUS 488, 492
CICERO 484, 488
Epistulae ad Familiares V.12.3 465
Rhetorica ad Herennium 465
De Partitione oratoria XXI 465
CLEMENT OF ALEXANDRIA 47, **48-49**, 50, 53, 94, 125-130, 133, 144-146, 239-242, **388-391**, 393-396, 401, 404, 517, 578, 580, 581, 591-596, 601-603, 605, 606
Hypotyposeis 49, 129, 145, 292, 576, 577
Hypotyposeis 6, 125, 389
Outlines 600
Adumbr. in Ep. can. 599, 600
CLEMENT OF ROME
I Clem 5,3ff 574
CORNELIUS NEPOS 484
Pelopidas XVI.1.1 465

DIOGENES LAERTIUS 467, 476
DIONYSIUS OF HALICARNASSUS
Antiquities I.9-11.29 496

EPIPHANIUS 240, 298, 344, 581
Haer.
3.30.7 572

6.10ff. 53
51.4.6 576
51.6.11 576
EUSEBIUS xv 47-49, 125-129, 145, 146, 224, 240, 291, 368, 369, 394, 492, 570, 577, 578, **592-594**, 606
Ecclesiastical History
II.15 571, 593, 594, 598, 599
II.15.1—15.1 598
II.15.1 576
II.15.2 581
II.16.1 390
III.23 53
III.24 601
III.24-25 593
III.24.5 576
III.24.7-13 581
III.24.7 576
III.24.11 576
III.24.15 581
III.39 391
III.39.14-17 595
III.39.14-16 595
III.39.15-16 601
III.39.15 223, 593, 600
III.39.1 299
III.39.3-4 392
III.39.5 568
III.39.15-16 567
III.39.15 223, 367
III.39.16 298, 392
V.5.1-4 393
V.8 593, 596, 597
V.11 592, 594
VI 595
VI.14.5-7 47, 125, 292, 389, 591, 593, 594, 603
VI.14.5 126, 600, 605
VI.14.6 571, 576, 600
VI.14.7 601
VI.25.3-6 52, 593
VI.25.3 292
VI.25.4-6 581
VI.25.4 593
VI.25.6 292

IGNATIUS 128
  Rom 7,3 422, 453
  Phild
  4,1 422, 453
  8,2 303
  Smyrn 7,1 422, 453
IRENAEUS 144-146, 241, 242, 344, **393-395**, 517, 568, 575-577, 580, 586, 591, 593, 596, 603, 606
  Adversus Haereses
  II.22.5 574
  III.1.1 52, 571, 597
  III.1.2 573
  III.3.3 592
  III.9.1-11 574
  III.9.6 574
  III.11.7 572
  III.11.8 574
  III.14.1 574
  V.30.1 574
  V.33-34 391
  V.33.3 574
ISOCRATES 467
  Helen 465
  Busiris 465
  Evagoras 465

JEROME 240, 298, 394
  Comm. in Matth., praef. 576
  De viris ill. 9 581
  Prol. Quatt. Evang. 53
JOSEPHUS 491
  Contra Apionem 496
  Jewish Antiquities
  1.12 367
  18.4-5 371
  18.261-309 149
  20.182-196 150
  Jewish War
  2.118 371
  2.184-187 149
  2.192-203 149
  2.271 150
  2.433 371
  Life 315 367
JUSTIN xv 45, 239, 240, 488, 492, 591
  Apol.
  I.15.3 573
  I.15.8 573

I.17.2 573
I.19.6 573
I.31 57
I.61.4-5 573
I.66.2 422, 453
I.66.3 572
I.66.29 422, 453
I.67 489
Dial.
81.4 573
88.7 573
103.8 572
106.3 572

LUCIAN 484, 488
  Demonax 467, 485
  History 7 465
  How to Write History 478
  The Lover of Lies 13 i.f. 361

MARCION 52, 127, 131, 577, 592
  Evangelion 147

ORIGEN 129, 146, 240, 241, 292, 388, 394, 591-593, 606
  Commentary on Matthew 52
  Commentary on John
  I.4.21 579 581
  I.4.22 581
  I.4.23 581
  Contra Celsum III.44 487
  In Lucam hom 29 579

P. EGERTON 2 **94-96**, 254, **256-257**
PAMPHILUS 129, 592
PANTAENUS 388
PAPIAS xv 128, 223, 224, 241, 294, 298-300, 312, 367, 383, 384, **391-393**, 517, 566-574, 583, 589, 592, 593, 597, 601, 603, 605, 606
  Exposition of the Lord's Oracles 129
PHILO 377, 415
  Life of Moses 137, 467
  On Abraham 375
  Creation 24.76 363
  Allegorical Interpretation 2.4.13 363
  Who is the Heir 33.164 363
  Special Laws, 4.26.140 369

PHILOSTRATUS
    Life of Apollonius of Tyana   137
PHOTIUS   49
PLATO   378
    Phaedros 274b-78a   544
    Epist. II.314   544
    Epist. VII.340-342   544
PLUTARCH   222, 472, 484, 488
    Alexander I.1-3   465
    Lives of Famous Men   137, 467
POLYBIUS   484
    Histories X.21.8   465
POLYCARP   128, 145, 146, 391, 393
PORPHYRY   488, 492

QUINTILIAN   464
    Institutio oratoria III.7.10-18   465, 481

RABBINICA
Mishna
    Nedarim 3.4   372
Tosephta
    Pesahim 10   369
Babylonian Talmud
    Baba Qamma 113a   371
    Nedarim 28a   372
    Niddah 69b   365
    Yebamot 47b   363
Jerusalem Talmud
    Megilla 74a   367
Genesis Rabbah
    1,26-27   363
    6,9   375

33,4   373
35,17   364
49,10   373
Mekhilta on Ex
    12,40   363
Esther Rabbah
    2,20   364
Tanhuma
    Num 20.12   364

SEDULIUS SCOTUS   47, **49-50**, 53, 126
SOCRATES   378
SUETONIUS   549, 550, 565
    Deified Julius   467

TACITUS   496, 550, 565
    Agricola   137, 467
TATIAN   94
    Diatessaron   147
TERTULLIAN   394
    Adv. Marc.
    IV.2.1-5   52
    IV.2.1   52
    IV.2.2   52
    IV.2.4   52
    IV.5.3-4   577
    IV.5.3   52
THEODORE OF MOPSUESTIA
    Comm. in Ioh.   581
THUCYDIDES   378

XENOPHON   467, 572
    Agesilaos   465

INDEX OF AUTHORS

The asterisk denotes full bibliographical information.
For the list of the contributors, see page 668.

ABOGUNRIN, S.O. 386* 398 400* 403* 405
ABBOTT, E.A. 385*
ABRAMOWSKI, L. 488* 491 568* 572
ADAM, J. 376
ALAND, B. 291* 292 318
ALAND, K. 23 82 241 244 291* 292 318 320
   321 323 324 333 343 348 351 517
ALBERTZ, M. 306*
ALLEN, W.C. 106 297 353*-355 358
ALLISON, D.C., Jr. 410*
ALTANER, B. 575*
ANDRAE, T. 531*
AUNE, D.E. 460 461* 462 485* 486 492 495
   553*

BAARLINK, H. 117*
BACHER, W. 366*
BALCH, D. 496*
BALOGH, J. 519*
BARBOUR, R.S. 546*
BARR, J. 346 360*
BARRETT, C.K. 369 374* 379 417* 432*
   436 477* 481
BAUER, J.B. 583
BAUR, F.C. 133 293 566 571*
BEARE, F.W. 114* 346*
BECKER, J. 447
BELL, H.I. 95
BENOIT, P. 117 238* 324 330 344
BEUMER, J. 576*
BEYER, K. 101*
BILLERBECK, P. 376 417
BLASS, F. 356
BLEEK, F. 21 107* 133 139 221*
BOISMARD, M.-É. 6 9 13-17 23 25 42-45 79
   81-85 87-91 94* 95 97 100 102 104 105-
   109 111 113-118 122 124 173* 217 238*
   312* 318 343 344 409* 410 420 422 427
   428 433 434 447 454 605
BORGEN, P. 408* 415 416* 421-423* 428*
   436 438*-441 444 447-449 451-453 457
BORING, M.E. 459

BORNKAMM, G. 309* 411* 413 414 453
   568*
BRANDENBURGER, E. 121*
BRAUDE, W.G. 372*
BRAUN, F.-M. 568*
BRAUN, H. 515*
BROWN, J.P. 385*
BROWN, R.E. 403* 408* 422 427 428 431
   436 448 479* 480 481 514
BROX, N. 568* 573
BUCHANAN, G.W. 63* 69
BÜSCHING, A.F. 293* 336*
BULTMANN, R. 168* 169 191 300* 306 307
   309 398* 408* 447 449 460* 534* 556
BUNDY, W.E. 334*
BURKHARDT, H. 576*
BURKITT, F.C. 385*
BURNEY, C.F. 192*
BURR, V. 540*
BURTON, E.D. 324 333* 346 347*
BUSE, I. 448
BUSSE, U. 105* 443* 454
BUSSMANN, W. 385*
BUTLER, B.C. 4* 7 54 55* 311* 336*

CADBURY, H. 341*
CALVERT, D.G.A. 546*
CAMPENHAUSEN, H. VON 48* 52 145 492
   544* 566* 572 573 575-577 580
CANCIK, H. 485* 495
CARTLIDGE, D.R. 223* 224
CATCHPOLE, D.R. 68*
CERFAUX, L. 4 205 312*
CHADWICK, H. 487*
CHAPMAN, J. 4 49* 50 568* 583* 584 598
COLLINGWOOD, R.G. 549* 550 565
COLLINS, R.F. 561* 564
COLLISON, F.J.G. 164* 165 168-172 175-
   181 219* 228 229 318
CONZELMANN, H. 309* 413* 414 417 477*
CORSSEN, P. 568* 575* 584
COTHENET, É. 509*

CRANFIELD, C.F.D. 403*
CREDNER, K.A. 294* 300
CREED, J.M. 370* 443
CULLMANN, O. 505*

DAHL, N.A. 439*
DAUBE, D. 360* 363* 364* 374* 375
DAUER, A. 408 409* 439 440* 443
DAVIES, W.D. 360 376* 480* 481
DEBRUNNER, A. 356
DEISSMANN, A. 305
DELOBEL, J. 29
DENAUX, A. 25 324 347
DE SAUSSURE, F. 309 310*
DE SOLAGES, B. 571*
DE WETTE, W.M.L. 107 133 139 221* 293*
    331 605
DIBELIUS, M. 304-306* 460* 477* 490 518*
    526
DIHLE, A. 485* 495
DOBSCHÜTZ, E. VON 582*
DODD, C.H. 408* 423 424* 434-436 443
    448 449 464 467 480* 481 490 496 565
DONALDSON, T.L. 37* 38
DUNGAN, D.L. 20 47 54* 159* 206 223*
    224 293* 410* 457
DUNN, J.D.G. 479* 481
DUPONT, J. 79* 115 116* 205

EGGER, W. 43*
EICHHORN, J.G. 298* 304 311 312 382
ELLIOTT, J.K. 318* 348* 357* 358*
ELLIS, E.E. 530* 546* 555
EPP, E.J. 320* 341* 352*
EWALD, H.G.A. 295 296*

FARLA, P.J. 448*
FARMER, W.R. 4 6 14-16 20* 47 48* 52 53*
    54* 57 63* 69 160* 161 164* 177 197
    218 293* 311* 316* 334* 382 383 390*
    394 395 567* 578 580 606
FARRER, A. 18 384*
FARSTAD, A.L. 322
FEE, G.D. 320*
FIEBIG, P. 416*
FINNEGAN, R. 545*
FITZMYER, J.A. 84 89 90 164* 169 517*
FJÄRSTEDT, B. 410*

FLUSSER, D. 218* 232* 237 238
FORTNA, R.T. 447
FRÄNKEL, H. 315*
FRIEDRICHSEN, T.A. 11*
FRYE, R.M. 222* 225
FUCHS, A. 10 79
FULLER, R.H. 561* 564 566*
FUNK, R. 331

GABLER, J.B. 22
GABOURY, A. 40
GAMBA, G. 48* 50 567* 580 581 583 584
    598
GARDNER-SMITH, P. 408
GERHARDSSON, B. 314* 341* 413* 499* 500
    502 510 515 516 527 551*
GIESELER, J.C.L. 302* 303 313 383
GNILKA, J. 25 28 36 40 446 583
GOMBRICH, E.H. 464
GOODSPEED, E.J. 324 398
GOULDER, M.D. 11* 18 62*
GRANT, F.C. 384*
GRANT, R.M. 583
GREEVEN, H. 82 117 241 244 317* 319 322
    323 333 343 348 355
GREGORY, C.R. 574*
GREIMAS, A.J. 310*
GRIESBACH, J.J. 23 53 133 134 291* 292*
    293 316 331 336-338 382 595 602
GRONEWALD, M. 94
GROSHEIDE, F.W. 575*
GROTIUS, H. 292*
GRYSON, R. 571* 605
GUELICH, R. 37* 38 459* 460 461 464 467
    485* 490 491 496
GÜTTGEMANNS, E. 310*
GUNDRY, R.H. 25 32 40 159* 460* 467
GUNKEL, H. 305
GUTHRIE, D. 383* 397
GUTWENGER, E. 567*

HADAS, M. 341* 460* 465
HAENCHEN, E. 408* 429 431 436 477* 478
HAHN, F. 563*
HANSEN, T. 11* 311*
HARE, D.R.A. 74*
HARNACK, A. 36 109 110 143 238 492 567*
    578 598
HARTMAN, L. 124

HAWKINS, J.C. 12* 108 160* 226* 227 297 335 385*
HAYNES, E.R. 315*
HEINRICI, G. 305*
HEISENBERG, W. 332
HELD, H.J. 106*
HENDRICKSON, G.L. 519*
HENGEL, M. 460* 465 485* 489 491 492 515* 570* 571
HERDER, J.G. 301* 302 305 311 313 316
HÉRING, J. 417*
HILGENFELD, A. 566 567*
HILL, D. 553*
HIRSCH, E.D. 464*
HODGES, Z.C. 322
HOLMBERG, B. 502*
HOLTZ, T. 529*
HOLTZMANN, H.J. 135 217 218 296* 337 338* 340 566 569*
HOOKER, M.D. 546 554* 555 561 564
HORT, F.J.A. 320 344 348
HUCK, A. 23 117 241 317* 323 325-327 330 333 335 337 338 340* 348

JAMESON, H.G. 384*
JASCHKE, H. 89*
JEREMIAS, J. 109 110* 111 180* 190* 372* 413* 417 550* 552* 553* 565
JUEL, D. 182*

KÄHLER, M. 537
KÄSEMANN, E. 413* 414* 418 546* 548
KARPP, H. 545*
KELBER, W.H. 316* 519*-523 525-528 535 541 543 545
KENNEDY, G. 48* 567* 571 578 605
KIEFFER, R. 310*
KILPATRICK, G.D. 36 37 190* 318 320* 322 358* 359*
KINGSBURY, J.D. 160*
KITTEL, G. 360
KLOPPENBORG, J.S. 36* 37
KLOSTERMANN, E. 106 367*
KÖRTNER, U.H.J. 566*-572
KOESTER, H. 146 460 461* 468 605
KOPPE, J.B. 298 304* 311 312 316
KOTILA, H. 447*
KRAFT, H. 567*

KRATZ, R. 236*
KRAUSS, S. 519*
KRIEGER, K.-S. 25*
KÜMMEL, W.G. 12 134 308* 460* 474 566* 570 571 576 583
KÜRZINGER, J. 569* 570 571 605
KYSAR, R. 409*

LACHMANN, K. 21 22 134 202 294* 295 300 384
LAGRANGE, M.-J. 324 332*
LAKE, K. 385*
LAKE, S. 385*
LAMBRECHT, J. 193* 198 199
LAMOUILLE, A. 25 82 117 238
LANGE, J. 25* 28 46 122*
LARFELD, W. 324
LARSSON, E. 509*
LAVERGNE, C. 332*
LE DÉAUT, R. 416
LÉGASSE, S. 109
LEIPOLDT, J. 566* 576
LÉON-DUFOUR, X. 205 312*
LESKY, A. 315*
LESSING, G.E. 298* 300 304 311 312 316 382
LIEBERMAN, S. 540*
LIETZMANN, H. 333 373* 575
LIGHTFOOT, R.H. 473*
LINDARS, B. 408* 427-429 436 447
LINDEMANN, A. 319*
LOCKTON, W. 384
LOHFINK, G. 25* 32 38
LOHSE, E. 382*
LOISY, A. 116
LONERGAN, B. 557* 559 560
LONGSTAFF, T.R.W. 3* 311* 337*
LORD, A.B. 314* 315*
LOWE, M. 218 232*
LÜHRMANN, D. 68* 546*
LUZ, U. 25 36 40

MACHEN, J.G. 403
MAIER, A. 7
MANSON, T.W. 35 283
MARROU, H.I. 466 600
MARSH, H. 293 382

MARSHALL, I.H. 109 116 163* 174 476* 477 518*
MARTIN, J. 385*
MARTYN, J.L. 431* 482*
MARXSEN, W. 309* 474* 552*
MASSAUX, É. 146
MCARTHUR, H.K. 546*
MCCARTNEY, E.S. 519*
MCKNIGHT, E.V. 63*
MCLOUGHLIN, S. 10*
MCNEILE, A.H. 384*
MCNICOL, A.J. 16 47 63 77* 79 207
MERKEL, H. 48* 204 492 544* 570 573 575 576 585 591 603
METZGER, B.M. 67* 170* 176 197 318* 319 320 348* 349 359
MEYER, B.F. 550* 553 561-563
MEYER, H.A.W. 88
MICHL, J. 574*
MIGNE, J.P. 49 126 600
MILLIGAN, G. 91
MOMIGLIANO, A. 465*
MOMMSEN, T. 568*
MOULE, C.F.D. 546*
MOULTON, J.H. 91 357*
MOYER, E.S. 388*
MUDDIMAN, J.B. 555*-557
MÜLLER, P.-G. 497* 498 501
MUNCK, J. 568* 570*
MURKO, M. 314*

NAUCK, W. 415
NEIRYNCK, F. 3* 6* 7* 9* 10* 11* 14 15* 20 22* 25* 40 46* 48 54* 55 60* 63 71 73 81* 82* 94* 97 107 134 185*-187 193-196 201-207 220* 221 225 226 233* 234* 293* 311*-313 317* 323 324 326 327 347 408* 409* 410 427 428 430 434 439* 440* 442* 451 452 454 456 457 603
NEUSNER, J. 17* 507 508* 533* 539
NIEKLIN, T. 385*
NILSSON, M.P. 486*
NORDEN, E. 306
NYBERG, H.S. 313*

ORCHARD, J.B. 3* 47 136 161* 197 204 311* 317 322 324 330 333 337* 346-348 91 602*

OSBORN, E.F. 545*
OVERBECK, F. 575*
OWEN, H. 133 134 156 292* 293 336*

PALMER, N.H. 202
PANCARO, S. 430* 431
PARKER, P. 400* 401
PARRY, M. 314*
PASQUIER, H. 3
PEABODY, D.B. 47 48* 51 75* 80 185*-187 190 194 196* 201 203 207 211 219* 220 292* 318 319* 567* 586-588
PECK, A. 425*
PERRIN, N. 563
PESCH, R. 105* 121 124 189* 444 530* 531 563* 571* 572
PETERSEN, N. 463*
POLAG, A. 36 37 109 112 113
PRENTER, R. 545*

QUASTEN, J. 49*

REGUL, J. 49* 50 52 395* 568* 569 570 573 574 582-584
REICKE, B. 3 22 79 191* 192 293* 316* 341*
RENGSTORF, K.H. 371* 568*
RESCH, A. 418*
RIESENFELD, H. 313* 413*
RIESNER, R. 497* 506 525 530
RILEY, H. 591
ROBBINS, V.K. 532*
ROBINSON, J.A.T. 238 379 460* 606
ROBINSON, J.M. 473*
ROHDE, J. 309*
ROLLAND, P. 9* 13 15* 16 80 234* 237* 313*
ROLLER, O. 519*
RORDORF, W. 517*
ROTHFUCHS, W. 29*
RUSHBROOKE, W.G. 89

SABBE, M. 409* 427 428*
SALAS, A. 283 284 286
SANDAY, W. 296 297* 385*
SANDERS, E.P. 20 54* 101 186* 225* 335* 336 340 345* 525*
SANDEVOIR, P. 238

SASSE, H. 360
SCHENK, W. 36 37 109 569* 572
SCHILD, M.E. 582*
SCHILLEBEECKX, E. 563*
SCHLEIERMACHER, F. 133 146 295 299* 300 304* 305 383* 605
SCHMID, J. 91 109 116 308* 325 326 568* 569
SCHMIDT, K.L. 306* 341* 459* 460 464 468
SCHMITHALS, W. 88 121 566*
SCHNACKENBURG, R. 408* 436 446 447
SCHNEEMELCHER, W. 298* 575*
SCHNEIDER, A. 517*
SCHNEIDER, G. 449
SCHNELLE, U. 447
SCHÜRMANN, H. 37 113 411* 412 417* 418 453 517* 546*
SCHÜSSLER FIORENZA, E. 443*
SCHULZ, S. 109 110 113 172* 192
SCHULZE, M.H. 338
SCHWARZ, F.J. 7 14
SELWYN, E.G. 373*
SENIOR, D.P. 97*
SEVIN, H. 338
SHILS, E. 497*
SHULER, P.L. 341* 460* 465 468 484-486 488 489 494-496
SIEGERT, F. 570*
SILBERMAN, L.H. 315*
SIMON, R. 298*
SIMONS, E. 217*
SKEAT, T.C. 95
SMITH, D.M., Jr. 408* 409*
SMITH, M. 341* 460* 465
SPARKS, H.F.D. 325 346
STANTON, G.N. 423* 428 460 461* 490*
STANTON, V.H. 384*
STECK, O.H. 109
STEIN, R.H. 546*
STEPHENSON, T. 12
STEVENS, W.A. 333* 346 347*
STOLDT, H.H. 54* 217* 336*
STONEHOUSE, N.B. 385* 391 394
STORR, G.C. 293* 294 300 311 316
STRACK, H.L. 376 417
STRAUSS, D.F. 133 295* 336 552*
STRECKER, G. 58* 573* 575
STREETER, B.H. 297* 336* 384* 385

STRUGNELL, J. 359*
STUART, D.R. 465*
STUHLMACHER, P. 182* 316* 410* 413 490 495 496
STUIBER, A. 575*
SUNDBERG, A.C., Jr. 575*
SWANSON, R.J. 331* 334 343
SYREENY, K. 37 38*

TALBERT, C.H. 63* 341* 460* 465 476* 485*
TAYLOR, V. 283 384*
TEVIS, D.G. 66 78 160* 166 219* 318
THEISSEN, G. 32*
THOMPSON, W. 160*
TISCHENDORF, C. 324 335 336 338 340 359
TORREY, C.C. 374 385*
TRAUTMANN, M. 443* 546*
TRYPANIS, C.A. 315*
TUCKETT, C.M. 4* 7* 11* 15 20 53* 54* 55 57 58 59* 61 63* 65 67 74 76 135 166* 199 328 329*
TURNER, C.H. 83 320* 353*-355 357 358 385*
TURNER, N. 357

UNTERGASSMAIER, F.G. 116*

VAGANAY, L. 4* 6 12 18 20* 22 91 312*
VANNUTELLI, P. 346*
VAN SEGBROECK, F. 3* 11* 311*
VAN UNNIK, W.C. 518* 567*
VERHEYDEN, J. 117*
VERMES, G. 374* 376
VERVENNE, M. 25 324 347
VIA, D.O. 460*
VIELHAUER, P. 68* 308* 569* 572* 605 606
VISCHER, L. 544*
VÖGTLE, A. 553*
VOGELS, H.-J. 585* 589
VOLKMAR, G. 576
VOTAW, C.W. 460* 468

WALKER, R. 58*
WALKER, W.O., Jr. 160* 315 540*
WANKE, J. 423*
WANSBROUGH, H. 318
WARREN, A. 463*

WEEDEN, T. 474*
WEGNER, U. 36*
WEIFFENBACH, W. 567* 569 571
WEISS, B. 106 107
WEISS, J. 366*
WEISSE, C.H. 6 203 294 295* 296 300 304 336 383
WEISWEILER, H. 305*
WELLEK, R. 463*
WENHAM, D. 79
WESTCOTT, B.F. 320 344 348 383 384*
WETTSTEIN, J.J. 346
WIKENHAUSER, A. 568* 569

WILKE, C.G. 18 295* 296 300 304
WINTER, P. 283
WITKAMP, L.T. 447*
WOJCIECHOWSKI, W. 106*
WOODS, F.H. 335
WREDE, W. 146 300
WRIGHT, A.G. 334 345 416

ZAHN, T. 48 49* 487* 566* 567 569 574* 576 578* 603 605
ZELLER, E. 133 135
ZMIJEWSKI, J. 114* 116 117

LIST OF CONTRIBUTORS

This list also includes the names of the Participants to the 1984 Symposium (p. XXIV) and of other persons who are mentioned in the Introduction.

ABOGUNRIN, S.O. **381-407** XXIV XXV XXVII
ALAND, K. X
BENOIT, P. XXV XXVI XXX
BOISMARD, M.-É. **231-288** XVII XVIII XXII XXIV-XXVI
BORGEN, P. **408-437 451-458** XXIV XXVI XXVII XXIX
BUTLER, B.C. XXI
CIVU, A. XXIV XXIX XXXI
COLLISON, F.J.G. XII XVII XXIX
DALTON, W. XVII XXIV
DAUBE, D. **360-380** XXIV XXVII XXX
DUNGAN, D.L. IX-XXX **201-216 317-347** XVII XVIII XXII-XXVI XXIX
ELLIOTT, J.K. **348-359** XXII XXIV XXVI XXVIII XXIX
FARMER, W.R. **125-156** IX* X XII* XIII* XVII XXII XXIV XXV XXVIII
FITZMYER, J.A. XIII
FULLER, R.H. **561-564** XXIV XXVII
GERHARDSSON, B. **497-545** XVII XXIV XXV XXVII
GRÄSSER, E. X
GREEVEN, H. X
GUELICH, R. XXIV XXVIII XXIX
HANSEN, T. XI*
HASHIMOTO, S. XXIV XXV XXVII
LEE, J.Y. XXIV XXV XXVII

LOHSE, E. X
LONGSTAFF, T.R.W. X* XI* XII*
LUZ, U. XVII XVIII XXIV
MATHES, R. XXIII-XXV XXIX XXXI
MCNICOL, A.J. **157-200** XXII XXIV XXIX
MEJÍA, J. XVII XXIII XXIV XXVII
MERKEL, H. **566-590** XXII XXIV XXVIII
MEYER, B.F. **546-560 564-565** XXIV XXIX XXVII-XXIX
MILLER, D.G. IX
NEIRYNCK, F. **3-46 77-124 438-450 605-606** XI* XII* XVII XVIII XXII XXIV-XXVII XXXI
ORCHARD, J.B. **591-604** X* XII* XIII* XVII XXII XXIV XXV XXVIII
OUTLER, A. XI
PEABODY, D.B. **217-230** XII* XXII XXIV XXVI XXIX
REICKE, B. **291-316 611-613** X XVII XVIII XXII XXIV XXV XXVIII XXIX
RENGSTORF, K.H. X
RIESNER, R. XXII XXIV XXVI XXIX
ROLLAND, P. XXII XXIV XXIX
SHULER, P.L. **459-483 495-496** XXIV XXVII
STUHLMACHER, P. **484-494** XV* XVII XVIII XXII XXIV XXVI-XXIX
TEVIS, D.G. XII
THOMAS, P.A. XII*
TUCKETT, C.M. **47-76** XIII* XV* XXII XXIV XXVII XXIX
TYSON, J.B. XI*
VAN SEGBROECK, F. XI* XII* XXII XXIV XXVI XXIX
WALKER, W.O., Jr. XI*
WANSBROUGH, H. XIV XV XVII XVIII XXIII-XXV XXVIII XXIX

CONTENT ANALYSIS OF PART ONE

THE THREE MAJOR POSITION PAPERS

THE TWO-SOURCE HYPOTHESIS 3-124

INTRODUCTION 3-22
1. The Phenomenon of Order (7-8). — 2. Duality in Mark (8-10). — 3.
The Minor Agreements of Matthew and Luke against Mark (10-11). —
4. The Source Doublets in Matthew and Luke (12-13).
Preliminaries: I. The Assumptions of the Two-Source Theory Compared
with the Other Hypotheses (14-18). — II. The Phenomenon of Order: 1.
The Absence of Matthew-Luke Agreements (19-20). 2. The Argument
from Order for Markan Priority (20-22). Note: The Markan Order in
the Proto-Gospel (22).

MATTHEW 4:23 - 5:2 AND THE MATTHEAN COMPOSITION OF 4:23 - 11:1
23-46
1. Analysis of Mt 4:23 - 5:2 (26-36). — 2. The Setting of the Sermon in
Q (36-38). — 3. The Composition of Mt 4:23 - 8:17 (38-39). — 4. Mt
4:23 - 11:1 and the Relative Order of Mark (40-42). — 5. The Doublets
of Mt 4:25 and 12:15(-16) (42-46). — 6. Conclusion (46).

RESPONSE TO THE TWO-GOSPEL HYPOTHESIS 47-80
I. The Position Paper: 1. External Evidence (27-53). — 2. Order (54-56).
— 3. The Gospels in Their Historical Context (56-57). — 4. Criteria
(57-58). — 5. Q (59-61). — 6. The "Economy" of the 2GH (61-62).
II. The Eschatological Discourse: 1. Luke (64-70). — 2. Mark (70-73);
Mark 13:9-13 and Parallels (73-75); Mk 13:33-37 and Parallels (75-76).
— Note on the Eschatological Discourse: Luke 21:5-36 (77-79); Mark
13:1-37 (79-80).

RESPONSE TO THE MULTIPLE-STAGE HYPOTHESIS 81-124
I. The Introduction to the Feeding Story: 1. Matthew 14:13-14 (81-82).
— 2. Luke 9:9-10 (82-92). — 3. Mark 6:31-34 (92-93).
II. The Healing of the Leper: 1. P. Egerton 2 (94-96). — 2. How
"Matthean" Are the Three Synoptic Stories? (96-104). — 3. Mark 1:42
(104-107).
III. The Eschatological Discourse: A. Luke 17 and 21, Two Proto-
Lukan Discourses?: 1. A New Debate: Q or Proto-Luke (108-114). 2.

Proto-Luke in Lk 21 (114-117). — B. Mark 13 and Proto-Matthew: 1. The Introduction (Mt 24:1-3) (119-120). 2. The False Prophets (Mt 24:23-25) (120). 3. The Coming of the Son of Man (Mt 24:29-31) (120-121). 4. The Sayings in Mt 24:34,36 (121-122). 5. Mk 13:9-13 and the Doublet in Mt 10:17-22; 24:9-14 (122-124).

THE TWO-GOSPEL HYPOTHESIS 125-130

THE STATEMENT OF THE HYPOTHESIS 125-156
I. The Tradition of the Church (125-130). — II. The Purpose of Mark on the Two-Gospel Hypothesis (130-132). — III. Literary Evidence (132-136). — IV. Answers to Planning Committee's Questions: Presuppositions (136-138); Overview of the Theory (138-147); The Value for Theology/Preaching (147). — V. An Historical Account of the Composition of the Gospels: The Gospel of Matthew (147-151); The Gospel of Luke (151-154); The Gospel of Mark (154-156).

THE COMPOSITION OF THE SYNOPTIC ESCHATOLOGICAL DISCOURSE 157-200
Preface (157-159). — I. Luke's Use of Matthew 24 as a Major Source in the Composition of his Eschatological Discourses: Matthew (159-160); Luke (160-162).
A. Lk 12:35-48 / Mt 24:42-51 (163-167); B. Lk 17:20-37 / Mt 24:1-51 (168-173); C. Lk 21:5-36 / Mt 24:1-42/10:17-22/5:18 (174-182). — II. Mark's Use of Matthew 24-25 and Luke 21 as Major Sources in the Composition of Mark 13 (182-200); The Composition of Mark 13:1-37 from Matthew and Luke (185-200). Conclusion (200).

RESPONSE TO THE TWO-SOURCE HYPOTHESIS 201-216
The Statement of the Hypothesis: 1. History of the Debate (201). — 2. Which Synopsis to Use (201). — 3. Patristic Testimony (201). — 4. Source Theories and Theology (202). — 5. The Arguments for the Priority of Mark (202-204). — The Textual Discussion (204-206). Chart Showing Mark's Use of Matthew and Luke (206-216).

RESPONSE TO THE MULTI-STAGE HYPOTHESIS 217-230
1. The "Fundamental Principle" (217-220). — 2. Justification of the Fundamental Principle (220-227). — 3. Extra-Synoptic Testimony (228). — 4. The First Account of the Multiplication of the Loaves (228-230).

THE MULTIPLE-STAGE HYPOTHESIS 231-288

THÉORIE DES NIVEAUX MULTIPLES 231-243
I. Son principe fondamental (231-233). — II. Justification du principe
fondamental (233-239). — III. Témoignages extra-synoptiques: Les
citations patristiques (239-240); Les évangiles non canoniques (240-
241); Les témoignages anciens (241-243).

INTRODUCTION AU PREMIER RÉCIT DE LA MULTIPLICATION DES PAINS 244-258
1. Le récit de Mc (244-245). — 2. Le récit de Mt (245-246). — 3. Le
récit de Lc (246-249). — 4. Retour au récit de Mt (249-251). — 5.
Retour au récit de Mc (251-253). — Appendice: La guérison du lépreux
(254-258).

RÉPONSE AUX DEUX AUTRES HYPOTHÈSES 259-288
I. La théorie des deux sources. Mc 3:7-12 et parallèles (259-265): 1.
Statistiques (259-261). 2. Les foules et Jésus (261-264). 3. La consigne
de silence (264-265).
II. La "Two-Gospel Hypothesis". Le discours eschatologique de Matthieu 24 et parallèles (265-288): 1. L'activité rédactionnelle de Marc
(265-267). 2. Les sections communes à Mt/Lc (267-274). 3. Les sections
communes aux trois Synoptiques (274-283). 4. Les sections propres à
Luc (283-287). — Conclusions générales (287-288).

BIBLIOTHECA EPHEMERIDUM THEOLOGICARUM LOVANIENSIUM

LEUVEN UNIVERSITY PRESS / UITGEVERIJ PEETERS LEUVEN

Series I

* = Out of print

1. *Miscellanea dogmatica in honorem Eximii Domini J. Bittremieux*, 1947.
*2-3. *Miscellanea moralia in honorem Eximii Domini A. Janssen*, 1948.
*4. G. Philips, *La grâce des justes de l'Ancien Testament*, 1948.
*5. G. Philips, *De ratione instituendi tractatum de gratia nostrae sanctificationis*, 1953.
6-7. *Recueil Lucien Cerfaux*, 1954. 504 et 577 p. FB 1000 par tome. Cf. *infra*, nos 18 et 71.
8. G. Thils, *Histoire doctrinale du mouvement œcuménique*, 1955. Nouvelle édition, 1963. 338 p. FB 135.
*9. J. Coppens et al., *Études sur l'Immaculée Conception*, 1955.
*10. J.A. O'Donohoe, *Tridentine Seminary Legislation. Its Sources and its Formation*, 1957.
*11. G. Thils, *Orientations de la théologie*, 1958.
*12-13. J. Coppens, A. Descamps, É. Massaux (éd.), *Sacra Pagina. Miscellanea Biblica Congressus Internationalis Catholici de Re Biblica*, 1959.
*14. *Adrien VI, le premier Pape de la contre-réforme*, 1959.
*15. F. Claeys Bouuaert, *Les déclarations et serments imposés par la loi civile aux membres du clergé belge sous le Directoire (1795-1801)*, 1960.
*16. G. Thils, *La «Théologie Œcuménique». Notion-Formes-Démarches*, 1960.
17. G. Thils, *Primauté pontificale et prérogatives épiscopales. «Potestas ordinaria» au Concile du Vatican*, 1961. 103 p. FB 50.
*18. *Recueil Lucien Cerfaux*, t. III, 1962. Cf. *infra*, n° 71.
*19. *Foi et réflexion philosophique. Mélanges F. Grégoire*, 1961.
*20. *Mélanges G. Ryckmans*, 1963.
21. G. Thils, *L'infaillibilité du peuple chrétien «in credendo»*, 1963. 67 p. FB 50.
*22. J. Férin & L. Janssens, *Progestogènes et morale conjugale*, 1963.
*23. *Collectanea Moralia in honorem Eximii Domini A. Janssen*, 1964.
24. H. Cazelles (éd.), *De Mari à Qumrân. L'Ancien Testament. Son milieu. Ses Écrits. Ses relectures juives* (Hommage J. Coppens, I), 1969. 158*-370 p. FB 900.
25. I. de la Potterie (éd.), *De Jésus aux évangiles. Tradition et rédaction dans les évangiles synoptiques* (Hommage J. Coppens, II), 1967. 272 p. FB 700.
26. G. Thils & R.E. Brown (éd.), *Exégèse et théologie* (Hommage J. Coppens, III), 1968. 328 p. FB 700.
27. J. Coppens (éd.), *Ecclesia a Spiritu sancto edocta. Hommage à Mgr G. Philips*, 1970. 640 p. FB 1000.

28. J. COPPENS (éd.), *Sacerdoce et célibat. Études historiques et théologiques*, 1971. 740 p. FB 700.
29. M. DIDIER (éd.), *L'évangile selon Matthieu. Rédaction et théologie*, 1971. 432 p. FB 1000.
*30. J. KEMPENEERS, *Le Cardinal van Roey en son temps*, 1971.

SERIES II

31. F. NEIRYNCK, *Duality in Mark. Contributions to the Study of the Markan Redaction*, 1972. Revised edition with Supplementary Notes, 1988. 252 p. FB 1200.
32. F. NEIRYNCK (éd.), *L'évangile de Luc. Problèmes littéraires et théologiques*, 1973. *L'évangile de Luc – The Gospel of Luke.* Revised and enlarged edition, 1989. x-590 p. FB 2200.
33. C. BREKELMANS (éd.), *Questions disputées d'Ancien Testament. Méthode et théologie*, 1974. *Continuing Questions in Old Testament Method and Theology.* Revised and enlarged edition by M. VERVENNE, 1989. 245 p. FB 1200.
34. M. SABBE (éd.), *L'évangile selon Marc. Tradition et rédaction*, 1974. Nouvelle édition augmentée, 1988. 601 p. FB 2400.
35. B. WILLAERT (éd.), *Philosophie de la religion – Godsdienstfilosofie. Miscellanea Albert Dondeyne*, 1974. Nouvelle édition, 1987. 458 p. FB 1600.
36. G. PHILIPS, *L'union personnelle avec le Dieu vivant. Essai sur l'origine et le sens de la grâce créée*, 1974. Édition révisée, 1989. 299 p. FB 1000.
37. F. NEIRYNCK, in collaboration with T. HANSEN and F. VAN SEGBROECK, *The Minor Agreements of Matthew and Luke against Mark with a Cumulative List*, 1974. 330 p. FB 900.
38. J. COPPENS, *Le Messianisme et sa relève prophétique. Les anticipations vétérotestamentaires. Leur accomplissement en Jésus*, 1974. Édition révisée, 1989. XIII-265 p. FB 1000.
39. D. SENIOR, *The Passion Narrative according to Matthew. A Redactional Study*, 1975. New impression, 1982. 440 p. FB 1000.
40. J. DUPONT (éd.), *Jésus aux origines de la christologie*, 1975. Nouvelle édition augmentée, 1989. 458 p. FB 1500.
41. J. COPPENS (éd.), *La notion biblique de Dieu*, 1976. Réimpression, 1985. 519 p. FB 1600.
42. J. LINDEMANS & H. DEMEESTER (éd.), *Liber Amicorum Monseigneur W. Onclin*, 1976. XXII-396 p. FB 1000.
43. R.E. HOECKMAN (éd.), *Pluralisme et œcuménisme en recherches théologiques. Mélanges offerts au R.P. Dockx, O.P.*, 1976. 316 p. FB 1000.
44. M. DE JONGE (éd.), *L'Évangile de Jean. Sources, rédaction, théologie*, 1977. Réimpression, 1987. 416 p. FB 1500.
45. E.J.M. VAN EIJL (éd.), *Facultas S. Theologiae Lovaniensis 1432-1797. Bijdragen tot haar geschiedenis. Contributions to its History. Contributions à son histoire*, 1977. 570 p. FB 1700.
46. M. DELCOR (éd.), *Qumrân. Sa piété, sa théologie et son milieu*, 1978. 432 p. FB 1700.
47. M. CAUDRON (éd.), *Faith and Society. Foi et Société. Geloof en maatschappij. Acta Congressus Internationalis Theologici Lovaniensis 1976*, 1978. 304 p. FB 1150.

48. J. KREMER (éd.), *Les Actes des Apôtres. Traditions, rédaction, théologie*, 1979. 590 p. FB 1700.
49. F. NEIRYNCK, avec la collaboration de J. DELOBEL, T. SNOY, G. VAN BELLE, F. VAN SEGBROECK, *Jean et les Synoptiques. Examen critique de l'exégèse de M.-É. Boismard*, 1979. XII-428 p. FB 1400.
50. J. COPPENS, *La relève apocalyptique du messianisme royal*. I. *La royauté – Le règne – Le royaume de Dieu. Cadre de la relève apocalyptique*, 1979. 325 p. FB 1000.
51. M. GILBERT (éd.), *La Sagesse de l'Ancien Testament*, 1979. Nouvelle édition mise à jour, 1990. 455 p. FB 1500.
52. B. DEHANDSCHUTTER, *Martyrium Polycarpi. Een literair-kritische studie*, 1979. 296 p. FB 1000.
53. J. LAMBRECHT (éd.), *L'Apocalypse johannique et l'Apocalyptique dans le Nouveau Testament*, 1980. 458 p. FB 1400.
54. P.-M. BOGAERT (éd.), *Le Livre de Jérémie. Le prophète et son milieu. Les oracles et leur transmission*, 1981. 408 p. FB 1500.
55. J. COPPENS, *La relève apocalyptique du messianisme royal*. III. *Le Fils de l'homme néotestamentaire*, 1981. XIV-192 p. FB 800.
56. J. VAN BAVEL & M. SCHRAMA (éd.), *Jansénius et le Jansénisme dans les Pays-Bas. Mélanges Lucien Ceyssens*, 1982. 247 p. FB 1000.
57. J.H. WALGRAVE, *Selected Writings – Thematische geschriften. Thomas Aquinas, J.H. Newman, Theologia Fundamentalis*. Edited by G. DE SCHRIJVER & J.J. KELLY, 1982. XLIII-425 p. FB 1400.
58. F. NEIRYNCK & F. VAN SEGBROECK, avec la collaboration de E. MANNING, *Ephemerides Theologicae Lovanienses 1924-1981. Tables générales. (Bibliotheca Ephemeridum Theologicarum Lovaniensium 1947-1981)*, 1982. 400 p. FB 1600.
59. J. DELOBEL (éd.), *Logia. Les paroles de Jésus – The Sayings of Jesus. Mémorial Joseph Coppens*, 1982. 647 p. FB 2000.
60. F. NEIRYNCK, *Evangelica. Gospel Studies – Études d'évangile. Collected Essays*. Edited by F. VAN SEGBROECK, 1982. XIX-1036 p. FB 2000.
61. J. COPPENS, *La relève apocalyptique du messianisme royal*. II. *Le Fils d'homme vétéro- et intertestamentaire*. Édition posthume par J. LUST, 1983. XVII-272 p. FB 1000.
62. J.J. KELLY, *Baron Friedrich von Hügel's Philosophy of Religion*, 1983. 232 p. FB 1500.
63. G. DE SCHRIJVER, *Le merveilleux accord de l'homme et de Dieu. Étude de l'analogie de l'être chez Hans Urs von Balthasar*, 1983. 344 p. FB 1500.
64. J. GROOTAERS & J.A. SELLING, *The 1980 Synod of Bishops: «On the Role of the Family». An Exposition of the Event and an Analysis of Its Texts*. Preface by Prof. emeritus L. JANSSENS, 1983. 375 p. FB 1500.
65. F. NEIRYNCK & F. VAN SEGBROECK, *New Testament Vocabulary. A Companion Volume to the Concordance*, 1984. XVI-494 p. FB 2000.
66. R.F. COLLINS, *Studies on the First Letter to the Thessalonians*, 1984. XI-415 p. FB 1500.
67. A. PLUMMER, *Conversations with Dr. Döllinger 1870-1890*. Edited with Introduction and Notes by R. BOUDENS, with the collaboration of L. KENIS, 1985. LIV-360 p. FB 1800.
68. N. LOHFINK (éd.), *Das Deuteronomium. Entstehung, Gestalt und Botschaft / Deuteronomy: Origin, Form and Message*, 1985. XI-382 p. FB 2000.

69. P.F. FRANSEN, *Hermeneutics of the Councils and Other Studies*. Collected by H.E. MERTENS & F. DE GRAEVE, 1985. 543 p. FB 1800.

70. J. DUPONT, *Études sur les Évangiles synoptiques*. Présentées par F. NEIRYNCK, 1985. 2 tomes, XXI-IX-1210 p. FB 2800.

71. *Recueil Lucien Cerfaux*, t. III, 1962. Nouvelle édition revue et complétée, 1985. LXXX-458 p. FB 1600.

72. J. GROOTAERS, *Primauté et collégialité. Le dossier de Gérard Philips sur la Nota Explicativa Praevia (Lumen gentium, Chap. III)*. Présenté avec introduction historique, annotations et annexes. Préface de G. THILS, 1986. 222 p. FB 1000.

73. A. VANHOYE (ed.), *L'apôtre Paul. Personnalité, style et conception du ministère*, 1986. XIII-470 p. FB 2600.

74. J. LUST (ed.), *Ezekiel and His Book. Textual and Literary Criticism and their Interrelation*, 1986. X-387 p. FB 2700.

75. É. MASSAUX, *Influence de l'Évangile de saint Matthieu sur la littérature chrétienne avant saint Irénée*. Réimpression anastatique présentée par F. NEIRYNCK. Supplément: *Bibliographie 1950-1985*, par B. DEHANDSCHUTTER, 1986. XXVII-850 p. FB 2500.

76. L. CEYSSENS & J.A.G. TANS, *Autour de l'Unigenitus. Recherches sur la genèse de la Constitution*, 1987. XXVI-845 p. FB 2500.

77. A. DESCAMPS, *Jésus et l'Église. Études d'exégèse et de théologie*. Préface de Mgr A. HOUSSIAU, 1987. XLV-641 p. FB 2500.

78. J. DUPLACY, *Études de critique textuelle du Nouveau Testament*. Présentées par J. DELOBEL, 1987. XXVII-431 p. FB 1800.

79. E.J.M. VAN EIJL (ed.), *L'image de C. Jansénius jusqu'à la fin du XVIIIe siècle*, 1987. 258 p. FB 1250.

80. E. BRITO, *La Création selon Schelling. Universum*, 1987. XXXV-646 p. FB 2980.

81. J. VERMEYLEN (ed.), *The Book of Isaiah – Le Livre d'Isaïe. Les oracles et leurs relectures. Unité et complexité de l'ouvrage*, 1989. X-472 p. FB 2700.

82. G. VAN BELLE, *Johannine Bibliography 1966-1985. A Cumulative Bibliography on the Fourth Gospel*, 1988. XVII-563 p. FB 2700.

83. J.A. SELLING (ed.), *Personalist Morals. Essays in Honor of Professor Louis Janssens*, 1988. VIII-344 p. FB 1200.

84. M.-É. BOISMARD, *Moïse ou Jésus. Essai de christologie johannique*, 1988. XVI-241 p. FB 1000.

85. J.A. DICK, *The Malines Conversations Revisited*, 1989. 278 p. FB 1500.

86. J.-M. SEVRIN (ed.), *The New Testament in Early Christianity – La réception des écrits néotestamentaires dans le christianisme primitif*, 1989. XVI-406 p. FB 2500.

87. R.F. COLLINS (ed.), *The Thessalonian Correspondence*, 1990. XV-546 p. FB 3000.

88. F. VAN SEGBROECK, *The Gospel of Luke. A Cumulative Bibliography 1973-1988*, 1989. 241 p. FB 1200.

89. G. THILS, *Primauté et Infaillibilité du Pontife Romain à Vatican I et autres études d'ecclésiologie*, 1989. XI-422 p. FB 1850.

90. A. VERGOTE, *Explorations de l'espace théologique. Études de théologie et de philosophie de la religion*, 1990. XVI-709 p. FB 2000.

91. J.C. DE MOOR, *The Rise of Yahwism: The Roots of Israelite Monotheism*, 1990. XII-315 p. FB 1250.
92. B. BRUNING, M. LAMBERIGTS & J. VAN HOUTEM (eds.), *Collectanea Augustiniana. Mélanges T.J. van Bavel*, 1990. 2 tomes, XXXVIII-VIII-1074 p. FB 3000.
93. A. DE HALLEUX, *Patrologie et œcuménisme. Recueil d'études*, 1990. XVI-887 p. FB 3000.
94. C. BREKELMANS & J. LUST (eds.), *Pentateuchal and Deuteronomistic Studies: Papers Read at the XIIIth IOSOT Congress Leuven 1989*, 1990.
95. D.L. DUNGAN (ed.), *The Interrelations of the Gospels. A Symposium Led by M.-É. Boismard – W.R. Farmer – F. Neirynck, Jerusalem 1984*, 1990. XXXI-672 p. FB 3000.
96. G.D. KILPATRICK, *The Principles and Practice of New Testament Textual Criticism. Collected Essays*. Edited by J.K. ELLIOTT, 1990. XXXVIII-489 p. FB 3000.

ORIENTALISTE, P.B. 41, B-3000 Leuven